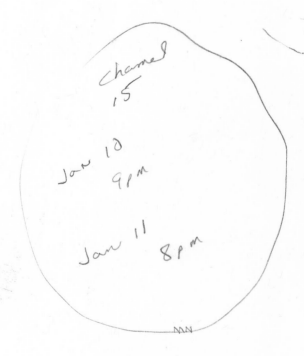

THE WESTERN HERITAGE

[FRONTISPIECE] This splendid late-medieval tapestry is one of
a series called The Hunt of the Unicorn. The mythical white
unicorn, horselike, goat-bearded, and with a single long horn
from its forehead, was famous in antiquity and the Middle
Ages as wild, swift, and difficult to capture. By the late
fifteenth century, the probable date of this French or Flemish
tapestry, a widespread belief held that only a virgin could
entice the animal to sleep in her presence and thus be brought
to captivity. Even then, as shown here, the unicorn would
attempt to escape. Beliefs such as these were the bases for
numerous allegorical interpretations, some amorous, some
religious, of the unicorn's story, and the story's rendition
in art has revealed a colorful gallery of medieval types,
society, costumes, and botany, as well as popular mythology.
The uncertainty of the meaning of the repeated monogram of
an A and a backwards E points up how little is known of the
origin and ownership of the tapestry series. Possibly the
letters, appearing at least seven times in this one scene,
are the first and last of Anne (of Brittany), and the work
may have celebrated her 1499 marriage to King Louis XII of
France; the centered FR monogram is a later addition and
perhaps refers to a subsequent owner or to King Francis I
of France. [Metropolitan Museum of Art, New York; gift of
John D. Rockefeller, Jr., 1937.]

THE WESTERN HERITAGE

DONALD KAGAN
STEVEN OZMENT
FRANK M. TURNER

Yale University

MACMILLAN PUBLISHING CO., INC.

New York

NOTE
The dates cited for monarchs and popes are generally the years of their reigns rather than of their births and deaths.

COPYRIGHT © 1979, MACMILLAN PUBLISHING CO., INC.

PRINTED IN THE UNITED STATES OF AMERICA

MACMILLAN PUBLISHING CO., INC.
866 Third Avenue, New York, New York 10022
COLLIER MACMILLAN CANADA, LTD.

Library of Congress Cataloging in Publication Data

Kagan, Donald.
    The Western heritage.

    Includes bibliographies and index.
    1. Civilization, Occidental. I. Ozment, Steven E.,
joint author. II. Turner, Frank Miller, joint author.
III. Title.
CB245.K28   909'.09'821   78-18450
    ISBN 0-02-361840-X
    ISBN 0-02-361930-9 pbk.

Printing: 3 4 5 6 7 8   Year: 9 0 1 2 3 4 5

Preface

The Western Heritage recounts the experience of the peoples—primarily European—who shaped and in turn were formed by the civilization of the West. Although it owes much to earlier cultures, particularly those of the Near East, Western civilization proper began in ancient Greece and Rome. It received an infusion of new religious values and institutions from Christianity, and it devised new political and social systems during the European Middle Ages. The years of the Reformation witnessed a profound religious revolution and counterrevolution that has divided Western culture to the present day. Yet in the same era Western peoples settled the lands of North and South America and established commercial routes across the globe. The forces that made for an intellectual and artistic Renaissance brought further confidence to the West and paved the path for the Scientific Revolution and the Enlightenment. Since the seventeenth century the nations of the West have transformed their own societies and governments through industrialization, liberal democracy, and various models of socialism. Technological and military power allowed the nations of the West to dominate major portions of the rest of the world with immense consequences for both themselves and for the peoples they dominated. Even when societies outside the West have rejected the Western pattern, they have often used Western values, political ideologies, and technology to do so. Consequently, for better or worse the civilization of the West has become the most influential culture of the world.

For most people who live in the West, its society, values, and institutions seem normal, and those of other cultures appear peculiar. The opposite may in fact be true. Compared to other modes of life, the civilization that developed in Europe and spread abroad is unusual and even unique. In these pages, and within a fairly traditionally chronological framework, we describe some of that civilization's most important features and show how they evolved and molded the distinctive character of the West and in turn the nature of its impact on the rest of the world. We examine, for example, the special and complicated relationship between religion and the state. We trace the related theme of the growth of constitutional government and democracy, both of which stand as rare achievements in the human experience. The distinctive cultivation of rational thought is our third major concern. Through its influence on philosophy, natural science, and applied technology, such thought has produced unique ways of understanding and controlling physical nature. Finally, perhaps the most unusual feature of Western civilization, which, like the others mentioned here, should emerge from this account, is its cultivation of the faculty of criticism and the intensity with which the West has applied such criticism to its own experience. No other culture has committed itself so thoroughly to the Socratic proposition that the unexamined life is not worth living.

Because of these distinctive characteristics of its culture, Western civilization, unlike other civilizations, most notably that of ancient Egypt, did not reach a stable form early in its history and then stand still. On the contrary, religious turmoil, political conflict, a continuing struggle to master physical nature, the shifting balances of economic affairs, and the inclination toward self criticism produced in the West perhaps the most changeable and changing civilization in history. Another factor encouraging this cultural restlessness has been the habit of Western people to look to the past for guidance. Repeatedly when they have sought a better future, they have consulted their history and have found in it the source of diverse and often competitive ideals and models. In general, the people of the West have understood themselves to be heirs of a useful and instructive past. We hope to aid the reader in understanding the character and meaning of that heritage.

We do not write about Western civilization and its contacts with the rest of the world merely because it is our own. We think it impossible in the length of this work, a length determined by the time usually allotted for an introductory history survey, to do justice to all the world's civilizations and cultures. To render even incomplete justice to a single civilization is challenge enough. But we also believe that in recent years the study of the West has become relatively neglected in the worthy but perhaps vain attempt to provide within one work a comprehensive, balanced global outlook. The result has too frequently been an inadequate grasp not only of other cultures but of our own as well. Furthermore, in our time, the Western proclivity to self-criticism has led in some cases to a decline in the study of history itself. Some people apparently believe that the social and technological developments of this century—and the manifold problems in their wake—have forever separated the present from the past. We reject such an attitude. Men and women living in the West today are what they are, bearing their particular anxieties and holding their special hopes, because they possess a distinctive cultural and political heritage. We shall consider our task accomplished if the curious and serious reader leaves this work with a fuller appreciation of what it means to be such a Western person.

D. K.
S. O.
F. M. T.

New Haven, Connecticut

Contents

13
THE LATE MIDDLE AGES AND THE RENAISSANCE: DECLINE AND RENEWAL (1300–1527)

Contents   **xi**

Contents **xiii**

Documents

Illustrations in Color

Maps

by THEODORE R. MILLER

An Album of Illustrations in Color

[1] The mythical struggle between ancient heros and the warrior women, the Amazons, was a popular theme in Greek sculpture and painting. For example, the famous Mausoleum at Halicarnassus had a frieze illustrating the theme. Here is a much earlier Attic black-figure storage jar of about 540 B.C. depicting the hand-to-hand combat of Achilles with the Amazon queen. It is now in the British Museum, London. [The Granger Collection.]

[2 BELOW] The first battle between Alexander the Great (on the fragmentary horse at the left) and Darius III of Persia (center). This mosaic copy of a late fourth-century B.C. Greek painting was made in Alexandria in Egypt and was found at Pompeii in Italy in 1831. It is now in the museum at Naples. The battle is identified as that of Issus (333 B.C.) where Alexander made his way from Asia Minor into Syria, an important step on his circuitous route toward the heart of the Persian Empire. [SCALA/Editorial Photocolor Archives.]

[3 LEFT] Among the few surviving Roman paintings are the first-century frescoes found at Pompeii, where they were protected for about 1800 years by their burial under volcanic ash from the eruption of Vesuvius in A.D. 79. From Pompeii (and now in Naples) is this realistic painting of the wounded Aeneas who, according to some legends, was the founder of Rome and thus a popular epic literary subject. Here the hero seems to maintain his bravery while under a surgeon's treatment. [Editorial Photocolor Archives.]

[4 BELOW] Also from Pompeii is this painting of an architectural perspective with its center occupied by Dionysus, god of wine, supported by two friends in his revelry. The wall has been moved to the Naples museum. [SCALA/Editorial Photocolor Archives.]

[5 OPPOSITE TOP] The comfort in which a substantial Roman citizen of the mid-first century could live is shown by the excavated and restored House of the Vetii in Pompeii. [SCALA/Editorial Photocolor Archives.]

[6 OPPOSITE BELOW] Dura Europos was founded in the fourth century B.C. as a Hellenistic caravan-fortress city on the Euphrates River (in modern eastern Syria) and for the next six centuries its position on the east-west trade route and its many masters made it a cultural crossroads. Excavations in the last fifty years have revealed surprising remains, such as this Roman-like wall painting in a synagogue of Hellenized Jews of about A.D. 250 of the Biblical scene of Samuel anointing the young David, future king of Israel. It is now at Damascus. [Photo by Fred Anderegg. Plate VII from *Symbolism in the Dura Synagogue* by Erwin Goodenough. Bollingen Series XXXVII, vol. 11. Copyright © 1964 by Princeton University Press. Reproduced by permission.]

[7] The story of the preparation for and the
outcome of the Norman invasion of England in 1066
is told in graphic detail on the Bayeux tapestry—
a 230-foot length of linen 18 inches wide on which
scene after scene was embroidered and labeled not
long after the events themselves. The work is
still displayed in the Town Hall of Bayeux, France.
Here is an episode in the successful Norman charge
against the English at the Battle of Hastings.
[The Granger Collection.]

[8 OPPOSITE] Saint Mark's in Venice is a vast
depository of Byzantine-style architecture and
decoration. Mosaics dating from the Middle Ages
and into modern times cover almost all available
space. Here are the familiar incidents of Noah
and the flood as presented by thirteenth-century
artists. [SCALA/Editorial Photocolor Archives.]

C4 *Color Album*

[9] Scenes from the life of Saint Francis of Assisi
were painted by Giotto in a chapel of the Franciscan
convent church of Santa Croce in Florence about 1317–
1320—less than a century after Francis's death. The
death is shown here in far more human and appealing
terms than those of earlier more rigid and formal
religious art. The condition of the work is explained
by its being whitewashed over for more than a century
before its rediscovery and poor repainting in the
mid-nineteenth century; it was cleaned and restored
in 1958–1959. [SCALA/Editorial Photocolor Archives.]

VINDICTEMOLES DOMVS EGRA 7 MORTVA PROLES

[10] A stained glass window in a fourteenth-century chapel of Canterbury Cathedral in England reflects the profound concern with the plague that swept Europe at the time. Note the victim, probably dead, lying toward the bottom of the scene; his distraught relatives have been grouped into stylized but affecting postures of grief. [The Granger Collection.]

[12] The south side and the rear of the cathedral at Bourges, France, as seen from the adjacent bishop's garden. Much of the characteristic Gothic exterior "skeleton" of the thirteenth-century structure is immediately noticeable. The building is unusual in its lack of transepts. [The Granger Collection.]

[11 OPPOSITE] For many, one of the heights of medieval architecture is achieved in the cathedral group at Florence—the Cathedral itself (mostly fourteenth century) with its great dome by Filippo Brunelleschi; the Bell Tower (mid-fourteenth century), built to the original Gothic design by Giotto; and the Baptistry (mostly eleventh century, with much detail added later), with its three sets of bronze doors by Lorenzo Ghiberti and Andrea Pisano. Seen here are the profiles of the Baptistry and the Bell Tower. [The Granger Collection.]

[13 OPPOSITE] Illuminating, the decorating and illustrating of handwritten books for wealthy patrons, was a specialized and refined art in the later Middle Ages. One of the most extraordinary of such books is *Les très riches heures du duc de Berry*, illuminated by the Flemish painter Pol de Limbourg and his two brothers early in the fifteenth century. This serial illustration from it makes the story of Adam and Eve a sort of Gothic dance; from the left: Eve tempted by the serpent, Adam tempted by Eve, God admonishing the couple, and, finally, the expulsion from Paradise. The book is now in the Musée Condé, Chantilly, France. [Editorial Photocolor Archives.]

[14 RIGHT] A miniature from the *Vigiles de Charles VII* by Martial d'Auvergne (late fifteenth century) shows the English siege of Orleans in 1429, the low point for the French in the Hundred Years' War. It is in the Bibliothèque Nationale, Paris. [The Granger Collection.]

[15 BELOW] The Ca' d'Oro ("Golden House," from its formerly gilt façade, *ca.* 1440) on the Grand Canal in Venice uses the locally modified Gothic style for domestic architecture. [Editorial Photocolor Archives.]

[16] The Dutch painter Hieronymus Bosch (*ca.* 1450–1516) has given art historians a field day in their attempts to analyze his fantastic work. The sample reproduced here is the "Hell" panel of his so-called *Garden of Delights* triptych. Ostensibly a religious work, it is full of highly uncertain symbolism that apparently derives from medieval literature, theology, folklore, and eroticism. Part of the interest for the amateur observer is in the hundreds of curious details that repay a search through this remarkable hell; a magnifying glass is helpful. It is now in the Museo del Prado, Madrid. [SCALA/Editorial Photocolor Archives.]

[17 OPPOSITE] A portrait of Pope Julius II (1503–1513) by Raphael. Julius was perhaps the strongest of the Renaissance popes between the mid-fifteenth and mid-sixteenth centuries. Extremely vigorous and opinionated, he actually led his troops in battle in defense of the papal lands. Too, he was an important international politician of the period, he patronized artists, and he pushed forward the plan to demolish Emperor Constantine's fourth-century basilica of Saint Peter in Rome, which was tottering, to make way for what was to become the present structure. His portrait is now in the Uffizi Gallery in Florence. [The Granger Collection.]

Color Album CI3

IHS

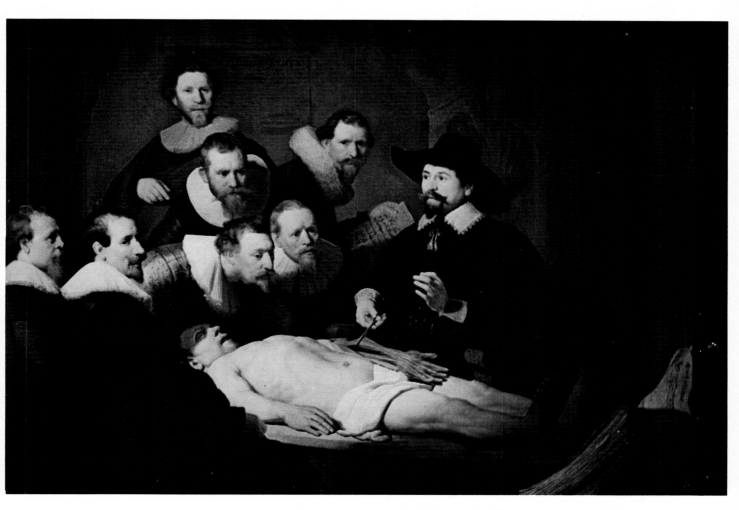

[18 OPPOSITE] Among the most distinctive paintings of the sixteenth and seventeenth centuries are those by El Greco ("The Greek," 1541–1614). Born Domenikos Theotocopulos on Crete, he learned to paint at home, at Venice, and at Rome and then spent most of his mature life in Spain. His color, religious yearning, mysticism, drama, complexity, and use of the fantastic can be sampled in the allegory reproduced here. The picture is sometimes called The Dream of Philip II and was painted about 1579 for the Escorial, where it remains. The central group seems to celebrate the joint efforts of the papacy, Venice, and Spain that led to the defeat of the Turks at the naval battle of Lepanto in 1571. Pope Pius V faces us from the center of the group. Kneeling before him are El Greco's patron, King Philip (in black), and the Doge of Venice (in a gold robe). To the left of the pope is Philip's illegitimate half brother Don John (who was the hero of Lepanto), his eyes turned toward heaven. Infidels find their doom in the maw of a sea monster (right) representing hell, and the characteristic angelic hosts hover over all. [SCALA/ Editorial Photocolor Archives.]

[19] Often called The Anatomy Lesson, this painting by Rembrandt is of a public anatomy demonstration in Amsterdam conducted by Dr. Nicolaas Tulp, leader of the city's surgeons' guild, in January 1632. The broken-necked corpse is that of a persistent thief and would-be murderer known as Aris Kindt, who had been hanged the preceding day. The work reflects early modern success in gaining respectable approval for scientific study of the human body; in addition, it has been a continuously popular piece of art by one of the greatest masters. It is in the Mauritshuis in The Hague. [The Granger Collection.]

[20] Philip IV was king (1621–1665) of a fading Spain that was being superseded in European primacy by France. But in Diego Velázquez (1599–1660) Spain produced one of the seventeenth century's master painters. This is one of his portraits of the king. It is in the National Gallery in London. [The Granger Collection.]

[21] William Hogarth (1697–1764) did immensely popular paintings and etchings of scenes from the rich variety of English life in the eighteenth century. He was frequently satirical and witty, and his works make up a realistic survey of society from top to bottom. The dissolute party shown here is The Orgy, third in a series called The Rake's Progress. It dates from approximately 1734 and is in the Sir John Soane's Museum, London. [The Granger Collection.]

[22] Even when past the height of its medieval commercial power, Venice in the eighteenth century was a wealthy and unusually picturesque city. One of the numerous painters of its canals, festivals, and buildings was Giovanni Antonio Canaletto (1697–1768), represented here by his Stonemason's Yard, a behind-the-scenes picture of a humbler, seamier side of the city than that usually painted. Painted near 1740, it is in the National Gallery, London. [The Granger Collection.]

[23] La Fontaine, by Jean Baptiste Siméon Chardin (1699–1779). Chardin was an important painter much admired by contemporaries such as Diderot for his pictures of quite ordinary people and situations in pre-Revolutionary France—a schoolmistress at work, a housewife returning from the market, and, shown here, the domestic scene of a woman drawing water and, probably, preparing to cook the meat hanging above her. The picture is in the National Gallery, London. [The Granger Collection.]

[24] In a painting attributed to Pietro Longhi (1702–1785), The Banquet at the Palazzo Nani, we see a self-conscious party of aristocratic Venetian ladies and gentlemen posing at a large formal dinner. The picture is in the Ca' Rezzonico in Venice. [SCALA/ Editorial Photocolor Archives.]

[25] A portion of the vast mid-eighteenth-century fresco that decorates the dining room of the bishop's residence, Würzburg, West Germany. The artist was Giambattista Tiepolo (1696–1770), and the building itself was designed by his contemporary, Balthasar Neumann (1687–1753). (See the illustration, page 575.) The scene is of the medieval ceremony of the royal investiture of a bishop (kneeling)—but with the principals portrayed in sixteenth-century dress. The overall fresco is one of the high points of Baroque decoration. [Adelmann/Editorial Photocolor Archives.]

[26] George Stubbs (1724–1806) was an artist with a special—even scientific—interest in animals, a concern that led him to dissect horses in order to get the creatures' anatomy just right. His works have been eagerly collected in this century. Lady and Gentleman in a Carriage (1787), seen here, is in the National Gallery, London. [The Granger Collection.]

[28 RIGHT] This handsome portrait (1788) of the eighteenth-century French chemist Antoine Lavoisier and his wife is by Jacques Louis David (1748–1825). Long owned by Rockefeller University, the picture was recently purchased by the Metropolitan Museum of Art, New York. Unlike Lavoisier, guillotined by the ungrateful French Revolutionists, the artist David lived to portray many events of the Revolution and the Napoleonic period. [The Granger Collection.]

[29 BELOW] The crucial naval battle of Trafalgar in 1805 between the English and the French fleets quickly caught the imagination of the English artist Joseph Mallard William Turner (1775–1851). He visited Nelson's ship immediately on its return to England with the admiral's body and in 1806 exhibited his first painting of the battle. The picture here (from the National Maritime Museum, London) is a later one (1820). Nelson's flagship, *Victory*, is in the center at the height of the battle. [The Granger Collection.]

[27 OPPOSITE, BELOW] Venice may have declined as a commercial power, but as a subject for its own artists and for those of other countries it was ever fascinating. In the generation following Canaletto, Francesco Guardi (1712–1793), as in this view of the Piazza San Marco, carried on the tradition of recording the city that was itself rapidly becoming a museum. The painting hangs in the National Gallery, London. [The Granger Collection.]

[30] The work of the Spanish artist Francisco Goya (1746–1828), like David's, spanned Old Regime, Revolution, Napoleon, and Restoration. In 1814 he painted The Third of May 1808 in continuing revulsion and protest over the gunning down of Spanish hostages by French troops during the Napoleonic invasion of Spain. It remains a powerful indictment of human brutality and the horror of war. The painting is in the Prado, Madrid. [SCALA/Editorial Photocolor Archives.]

[31 OPPOSITE, TOP] The painter John Constable (1776–1837) failed to find wide popularity in his lifetime. He kept his attention on the peaceful English countryside that was destined to become the victim of industry, railways, and mines, and today we find his work an important record of a different world. This is his Haywain, painted in 1821. It hangs now in the National Gallery, London. [The Granger Collection.]

[32 OPPOSITE, BOTTOM] The hard, never-ending physical labor of the agricultural poor is the subject of The Gleaners by the Frenchman Jean François Millet (1814–1875). Millet is often thought over-sentimental, but this 1857 picture is a strong record of the necessary way of life of millions in the nineteenth century. It is in the Louvre, Paris. [The Granger Collection.]

[33–34] Edouard Manet (1832–1883) created something of a scandal with his 1861 Luncheon on the Grass. The woman's undress was a shock to bourgeois attitudes, and official exhibition of the work was refused. Ironically, the arrangement of figures was almost identical with that of three undressed people in a famous Raphael drawing, and a similar grouping of clothed men and nude women by the Renaissance artist Giorgione (*ca.* 1476–1510), called Country Concert, had long hung quietly in the Louvre. Both the Giorgione [TOP] and the Manet [BOTTOM] are shown here, for they are both finally and happily displayed today in the Louvre. [SCALA/Editorial Photocolor Archives; The Granger Collection.]

[35 OPPOSITE] Nineteenth-century Romanticism reached, literally, a reckless height in the castle of Neuschwanstein, ordered by the unstable King Ludwig II of the south German state of Bavaria. When the castle was built between 1858 and 1886, art and literature had taken on a character of realism; but architecture tended to remain elaborate and ornate—although Neuschwanstein in its spectacular setting was, of course, too extreme to be typical. [The Granger Collection.]

C24 *Color Album*

[36] The Third-Class Carriage (*ca.* 1860) is an example of the realism of the French artist Honoré Daumier (1808–1879). In addition to pictures with sharp political and social messages, Daumier produced such gentle, sympathetic works as this one of poor, almost defeated folk. It is in the Metropolitan Museum of Art, New York. [The Granger Collection.]

[37] The railway figures also in The Station at Penge (1871) by Camille Pissarro (1831–1903). Railroads caused a transportation revolution in the nineteenth century comparable to that of air travel in our own day, and artists were not long in creating a new kind of landscape that incorporated the new technological development. The machine, artists found, had esthetics of its own. This picture is in the Courtauld Institute, London. [The Granger Collection.]

[38] The Moulin de la Galette (1876) is by Pierre Auguste Renoir (1841–1919). One aspect of Parisian bourgeois leisure activity is illustrated in this painting of everyday friends of the artist enjoying the wine and the dancing at an outdoor café. The work is in the Louvre, Paris. [The Granger Collection.]

[39] This 1889 painting, The Starry Night by the Dutchman Vincent van Gogh (1853–1890), breaks out of earlier, more staid views of nature and the landscape. To van Gogh the heavens themselves are an exciting theater of colorful and continuing movement. [The Museum of Modern Art, New York.]

[40] Paul Cézanne (1839–1906) painted several pictures called The Card Players. Like the others, this one from about 1890 captures the personalities of its (probably) working-class subjects and is a realistic, unromanticized view of ordinary life. The painting is in the Jeu de Paume, Paris. [The Granger Collection.]

[41 BELOW, LEFT] Although the subject is too broad for such a narrow definition, "modern art" for many means abstract, nonrepresentational painting and sculpture. This aspect of modern painting is illustrated by the colorful Panel (3) by the Russian-French artist Wassily Kandinsky (1866–1944). Note that "modern" antedates World War I, for this work was painted in 1914. [The Museum of Modern Art, New York.]

[42 BELOW, RIGHT] Another popular Spanish artist—although he is taken less seriously by many critics—is Salvador Dali (born 1904). The odd, bleak landscape of his Persistence of Memory (1931) reminds some viewers of dreams and probably derives in part from the spread of Freud's ideas and general twentieth-century interest in the unconscious. [The Museum of Modern Art, New York.]

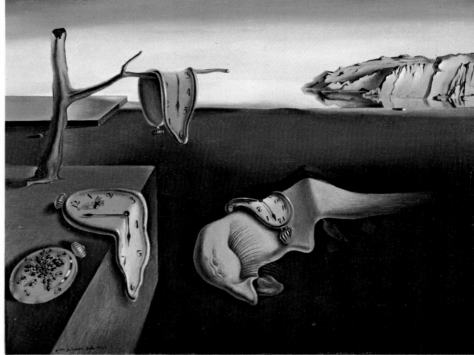

[43] Perhaps the best known painter of recent years is the Spaniard Pablo Picasso (1881–1973). His art went through a number of phases. The picture shown here, Three Musicians, comes from 1921 when he was interested in breaking his subjects down into planes, lines, and geometric bodies. [The Museum of Modern Art, New York.]

(Another Picasso painting in his later style is on page 898.)

[46–47] The Georges Pompidou National Center of Art and Culture in Paris, named for a recent president of France, was built in the 1970s to designs by an Italian-English team of architects, Renzo Piano and Richard Rogers. We spoke earlier of a Gothic structure's "skeleton" being, in a sense, external and visible. Here the designers have managed to make the building appear to be almost all skeleton and in the meantime have achieved a colorful display of its engineering and functional elements. [French Government Tourist Office, New York.]

THE WESTERN HERITAGE

2

I
The World Before the West

Early Humans and Their Culture

SCIENTISTS estimate that the earth may be as many as six billion years old, that manlike creatures may have appeared three to five million years ago, and that our own species of human being goes back about fifty thousand years. Humans are different from other animals in that they are capable of producing and passing on a culture. Culture may be defined as the ways of living built up by a group and passed on from one generation to another. It may include behavior, material things, ideas, institutions, and beliefs. The source of humanity's creation of material culture is the hands. We can touch the balls of our fingers with the ball of our thumb, something no other creature can do, and so we can hold and make tools. The source of our ability to create ideas and institutions is in our capacity to speak, and this is what allows us to transmit our culture to future generations. Whether man's ability to make a material culture is more important than the ability to speak, and therefore to think abstractly, is an interesting question, but clearly both are needed for the development of human culture.

Anthropologists designate early human cultures by their tools. The earliest period is the Paleolithic (from Greek, "old stone") Age. In this immensely long period people were hunters, fishermen, and gatherers, but not producers, of food. They learned to make and use tools of stone and of perishable materials like wood, to make and control fire, and to pass on what they learned in understandable language. In the regions where civilization ultimately was born, people depended on nature for their

food and were very vulnerable to attacks from wild beasts and to natural disasters. Since their lives were often "solitary, poor, nasty, brutish, and short," their responses to troubles and dangers were filled with fear. Their minds endowed all the objects they met with life or spirit, and they tried their best to put themselves in the right relationship to all these forces. They trusted magic, incantations, and ritual. Evidence of this Paleolithic culture have been excavated or found in caves in widely scattered areas of Europe, Asia, and Africa.

Human life in the Paleolithic Age easily lent itself to division of labor by sex. The men engaged in hunting, fishing, making tools and weapons, and fighting against other families, clans, and tribes. The women, less mobile because of frequent child bearing, smaller in stature, and less strong and swift than the men, gathered nuts, berries, and wild grains; wove baskets; and made clothing. Women gathering food must have discovered how to plant and care for seeds. This knowledge eventually made possible the Age of Agriculture—the Neolithic Revolution—but anthropologists disagree on why that revolution occurred. In many areas, right into our own time, some isolated portions of humankind have been content to continue to live in the "Stone Age" unless compelled by more advanced cultures to change; why toil in fields, on a South Sea island, if fruit, vegetables, and fish are plentiful and free, the weather is wonderful, and there's a party on the beach? Some scientists suggest that the shift to agriculture by late Paleolithic groups was the result of increasing population, others that unfavorable climate changes made the shift necessary. Perhaps men became farmers merely because stronger men ordered them to do so—hunter-gatherers continued, but as hunters and gatherers of farmers' taxes. However it happened, some ten thousand years ago parts of what we now call the Middle East began to shift from a hunter-gatherer culture to a settled agricultural one. People began to use precisely carved stone tools, so we call it the Neolithic (in Greek, "new stone") Age. Animals were domesticated as well as food crops. The important invention of pottery made it

The Sphinx. The great Sphinx is located at Giza, near modern Cairo. It seems to have been associated with the pyramid of Khafre, a king who ruled Egypt some time after 2600 B.C. The origin of the colossal lion with the head of a man is unknown, but the face is thought to be a likeness of the pharaoh himself. [Hirmer Fotoarchiv München.]

possible to store surplus liquids, just as the invention of baskets had earlier made it possible to store dry foods. Cloth came to be made from flax and wool. Crops required constant care from planting to harvest, so Neolithic man built permanent buildings, usually in clusters near the best fields.

It is not at all clear that the agricultural revolution produced a Neolithic population explosion. Anthropologists suggest that village living produced a much greater incidence of disease, there being no provision for the disposal of human and animal waste. The Neolithic villages also provided attractive targets for raiders. These hazards kept population growth modest while greatly increasing the status of warriors and of priests, who not only conducted rituals connected with planting, rainmaking, and harvest but were thought to be able to ward off misfortunes caused by witchcraft, sorcery, and evil spirits. Village headmen increased in prestige because of the multiplication of legal disputes and of decisions to be made on behalf of the entire community.

Neolithic villages and their culture, gradually growing from and replacing Paleolithic culture, could be located in almost any kind of terrain. But about four thousand years before the Christian era—evidently because of a drying trend in climate—people began to move in large numbers into the river-watered lowlands of Mesopotamia and Egypt. This shift evolved into a new style of life—an urban society and civilization. The shift was accompanied by the gradual introduction of new technologies, including metal weapons and other implements in place of stone ones, and by the invention of writing.

Again, we do not know why men first chose to live in cities, with their inherent disadvantages: overcrowding, epidemics, wide separation from sources of food and raw materials, and the concentration of wealth that permitted organized warfare. Perhaps cities were created because, to quote the Greek philosopher Aristotle, "Man is by nature a social animal"; perhaps they arose merely because they offered more possibilities for amusement, occupational choice, and enrichment than had the Neolithic villages. In any event, by about 3000 B.C., when the invention of writing gave birth to history, urban life was established in the valleys of the Tigris and Euphrates rivers in Mesopotamia (modern Iraq) and of the Nile in Egypt. Somewhat later, urban life arose in the Indus valley of India and the Yellow River basin of China. The development of urban centers by no means meant the disappearance of numerous outlying peasant agricultural

Paleolithic and Neolithic works.

OPPOSITE: Paleolithic cave painting from Dordogne in France. Deep in caves in southern France and northern Spain are wall paintings of hundreds of animals—bison, deer, horses, and oxen. They are shown in remarkable realism. Often they are shown as hunted by men, sometimes with a spear sticking in them. [Bettmann Archive.]

LEFT: Paleolithic hand axe. This prehistoric flint tool was found along the Thames River in England. [The University Museum, University of Pennsylvania, Philadelphia.]

CENTER: Paleolithic "Venus" figure. This is one of the many female figurines found in widely scattered sites of the late Paleolithic period; it is from Willendorf in modern Austria and is in a Vienna museum. The figurines are made of stone, ivory, or clay. The emphasis on sexual characteristics and the absence of facial features suggest that they may have had a magical or religious significance as part of fertility rites. [Courtesy of the American Museum of Natural History, New York.]

RIGHT: Neolithic pottery. These three pots from Bohemia give evidence of the age of agriculture. Their invention made it possible to store food for future use. [The University Museum, University of Pennsylvania, Philadelphia.]

villages. Nevertheless, with the coming of cities, writing, and metals, humankind had attained civilization.

Early Civilizations to About 1000 B.C.

Civilization, then, is a form of human culture in which many people live in urban centers, have mastered the art of smelting metals, and have developed a method of writing. The rich alluvial plains where civilization began made possible the production of unprecedented surpluses of food—but only if there was an intelligent management of the water supply. Proper flood control and irrigation called for the control of the river by some strong authority capable of managing the distribution of water. This control and management required careful observation and record keeping. The first use of writing may have been to record the behavior of the river and the astronomical events that gave clues about it. It was used by the power-

Cuneiform writing. Writing with a stylus that left wedge-shaped (cuneiform) impressions in wet clay seems to have been invented by the Sumerians and to have developed from a kind of picture writing.

The clay tablet, RIGHT, is Sumerian from the city of Nippur in Mesopotamia. It is the record of a mortgage. [The University Museum, University of Pennsylvania, Philadelphia.]

BELOW is a very late example of cuneiform carved into stone in an inscription at Persepolis in modern Iran; here the script is used for the Old Persian language of the time of King Xerxes in the fifth century B.C. [AHM.]

ful individuals (the kings) who dominated the life of the river valleys to record their possessions, by priests to record omens, by merchants and craftsmen to record business transactions, and by others to record acts of the government, laws, and different kinds of literature.

This widely varied use of writing reflects the complex culture of the urban centers in the river valleys. Commerce was important enough to support a merchant class. Someone discovered how to smelt tin and copper to make a stronger and more useful material—bronze—that replaced stone in the making of tools and weapons; the importance of this technological development is reflected in the term "Bronze Age." The great need for record keeping created a class of scribes, because the picture writing and complicated scripts of these cultures took many years to learn and could not be mastered by many. To deal with the gods great temples were built, and many priests worked in them. The collection of all these people into cities gave the settlements an entirely new character. Unlike Neolithic villages, they were communities estab-

lished for purposes other than agriculture. The city was an administrative, religious, manufacturing, entertainment, and commercial center.

The logic of nature pointed in the direction of the unification of an entire river valley. Central control would put the river's water to the most efficient use, and its absence would lead to warfare, chaos, and destruction. As a result, these civilizations produced unified kingdoms under powerful monarchs who came to be identified with divinity. The typical king in a river valley civilization was regarded either as a god or as the delegate of a god. Around him developed a rigid class structure. Beneath the monarch was a class of hereditary military aristocrats and a powerful priesthood. Below them were several kinds of freemen, mostly peasants, and at the bottom were many slaves. Most of the land was owned or controlled by the king, the nobility, and the priests. These were traditional, conservative cultures of numerous peasant villages and urban centers of administration, commerce, and religious and military activity. Culture pat-

Gudea of Lagash. Among the most remarkable works of sculpture from the Sumerian period in Mesopotamia are the twenty or so statues of Gudea, ruler of the city of Lagash about 2100 B.C. This is the head of one of them. [Courtesy of the Museum of Fine Arts, Boston; Francis Bartlett Donation.]

Stele of victory of Naramsin. Naramsin was the successor of Sargon of Akkad, the Semitic king who conquered the Sumerians. He lived some time before 2200 B.C. The topmost figure is the king, armed with bow and arrows, climbing a mountain. The stele commemorates a military victory. [Musée du Louvre, Paris. Maurice Chuzeville.]

terns took form early and then changed only slowly and grudgingly.

Mesopotamian Civilization

The first civilization appears to have arisen in the valley of the Tigris and Euphrates rivers, Mesopotamia ("the land between the rivers" in Greek). Its founders seem to have been a people called Sumerians who came down from the mountains and hills to the northeast and controlled the southern part of the valley (Sumer), close to the head of the Persian Gulf, by the dawn of history, around 3000 B.C. At first, city-states about one hundred square miles in size dotted the landscape. Ur, Erech, Lagash, and Eridu are examples of such cities that archaeologists have revealed to us. Quarrels over water rights and frontiers led to incessant fighting, and in time, stronger towns conquered weaker ones and expanded to form larger units, usually kingdoms. While the Sumerians were fighting their neighbors and among themselves for supremacy in the south, a people from the Arabian Desert on the west called Semites had been moving into Mesopotamia north of Sumer. Their language and society were different from those of the Sumerians, but they soon absorbed Sumerian culture and established their own kingdom, with its capital at Akkad, near a later city known to us as Babylon. The most famous Akkadian king was Sargon, who conquered Sumer and extended his empire in every direction. Legends grew up around his name, and he is said to have conquered the "cedar forests" of Lebanon, far to the west near the coast of the Mediterranean Sea. He ruled about 2340 B.C. and established a family, or dynasty, of Semitic kings that ruled Sumer and Akkad for two centuries.

External attack and internal weakness destroyed Akkad. About 2125 B.C. the city of Ur in Sumer revolted and became the dominant power, and this Third Dynasty of Ur established a large empire of its own. About 2000 B.C., however, it was swept aside by another Semitic invasion, which ended Sumerian rule forever. Thereafter

Early Civilizations to About 1000 B.C. 7

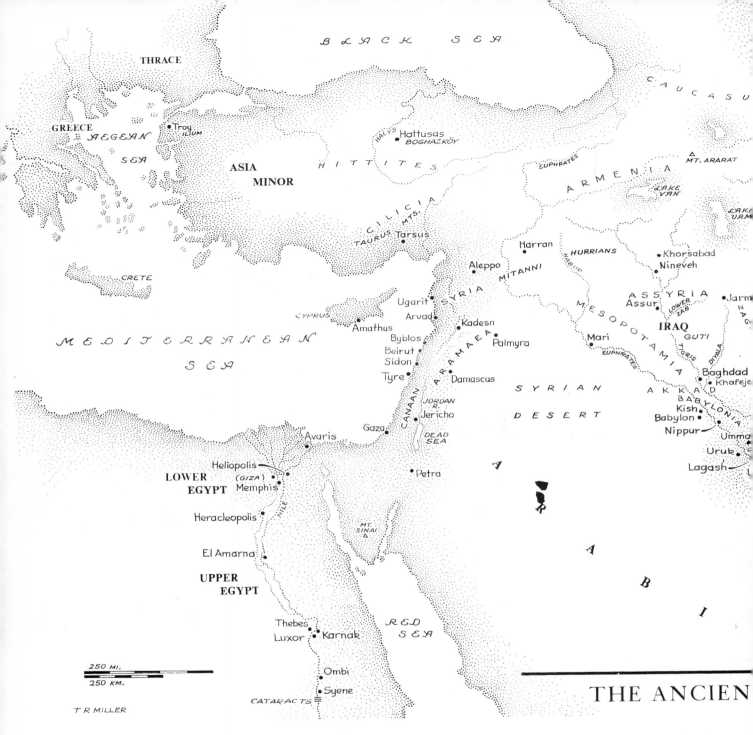

THRACE

BLACK SEA

CAUCASUS

GREECE
AEGEAN
SEA

Troy
ILIUM

ASIA
MINOR

HITTITES

Hattusas
BOGHAZKÖY

HALYS

EUPHRATES

ARMENIA

MT. ARARAT

LAKE
VAN

LAKE
URM

CRETE

CILICIA
TAURUS MTS.
Tarsus

Harran

HURRIANS

Khorsabad
Nineveh

ASSYRIA

Jarm

MEDITERRANEAN
SEA

CYPRUS

Amathus

Ugarit
Arvad

Aleppo

SYRIA

MITANNI

Assur

LOWER
ZAB

MESOPOTAMIA

ZAG

Kadesn

Byblos
Beirut
Sidon
Tyre

ARAMAEA

Palmyra

Mari

IRAQ

GUTI

TIGRIS

EUPHRATES

Baghdad
Khafeje

DIYALA

CANAAN

Damascus

SYRIAN

AKKAD

BABYLONIA

Kish

JORDAN
R.
Jericho

DESERT

Babylon

Nippur

Umma

Gaza

DEAD
SEA

Uruk

Avaris

Lagash

Heliopolis
(GIZA)
Memphis

Petra

A

LOWER
EGYPT

R

Heracleopolis

NILE

MT.
SINAI

A

El Amarna

B

UPPER
EGYPT

I

Thebes
Luxor

Karnak

RED
SEA

250 MI.
250 KM.

Ombi

Syene

T R MILLER

CATARACTS

THE ANCIEN

Semites ruled Mesopotamia, but the foundations of their culture were Sumerian. The Semites changed much of what they inherited; but in law, government, religion, art, science, and all other areas of culture, their debt to the Sumerians was enormous.

The fall of the Third Dynasty of Ur put an end to the Sumerians as an identifiable group. The Sumerian language survived only in writing, as a kind of sacred lan-

guage known only to priests and scribes, preserving the cultural heritage of Sumer. For about a century after the fall of Ur, dynastic chaos reigned, but about 1900 B.C. a Semitic people called the Amorites gained control of the region, establishing their capital at Babylon. The high point of this Amorite, or Old Babylonian dynasty came more than a hundred years later under its most famous king, Hammurabi. He is best known for the law code

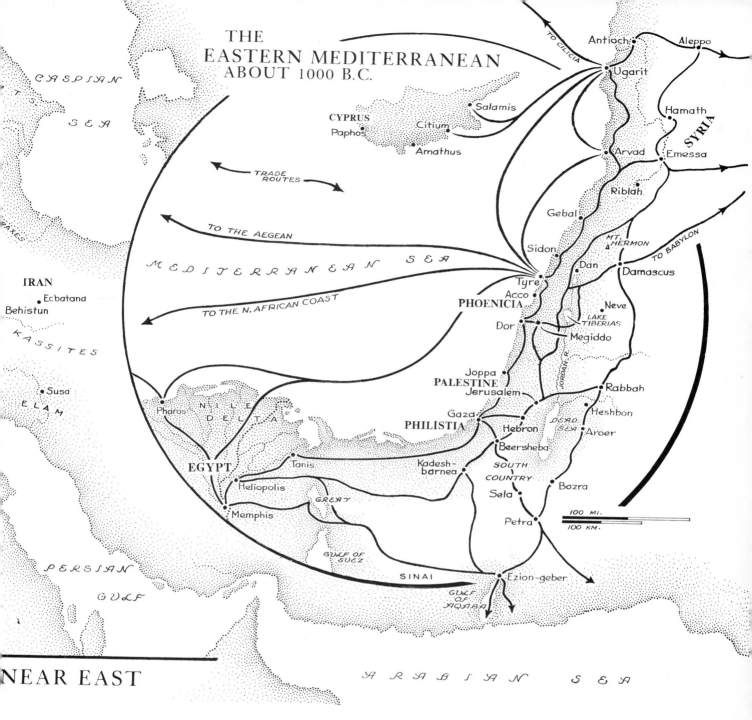

THE EASTERN MEDITERRANEAN ABOUT 1000 B.C.

CASPIAN SEA

CYPRUS
Paphos
Citium
Amathus
Salamis

TRADE ROUTES

TO THE AEGEAN

MEDITERRANEAN SEA

TO THE N. AFRICAN COAST

IRAN
Ecbatana
Behistun

KASSITES

Susa

ELAM

Antioch
Aleppo
Ugarit
TO CILICIA

Hamath
SYRIA
Arvad
Emessa
Riblah
Gebal
MT. HERMON
TO BABYLON
Sidon
Dan
Damascus
Tyre
Acco
PHOENICIA
Neve
Dor
LAKE TIBERIAS
Megiddo
JORDAN R.
Joppa
PALESTINE
Jerusalem
Rabbah
Heshbon
Gaza
PHILISTIA
Hebron
DEAD SEA
Aroer
Beersheba
Kadesh-barnea
SOUTH COUNTRY
Bozra
Sela
Petra

Pharos
NILE DELTA
Tanis
EGYPT
Heliopolis
GREAT
Memphis

GULF OF SUEZ

PERSIAN GULF

SINAI

Ezion-geber
GULF OF AQABA

100 MI.
100 KM.

ARABIAN SEA

NEAR EAST

connected with his name. Codes of law existed as early as the Sumerian period and Hammurabi's plainly owes much to earlier models, but it is the fullest and best-preserved legal code we have from ancient Mesopotamia. The code reveals a society strictly divided in class; there were nobles, commoners, and slaves, and the law did not treat them equally. In general, punishments were harsh, literally applying the principle "an eye for an eye, a tooth

for a tooth." The prologue to the code makes it clear that law and justice come from the gods through the king.

About 1600 B.C. the Babylonian kingdom fell apart under the impact of invasions from the north and east by the Hittites and the Kassites. The Hittites were only a raiding party who plundered what they could and then withdrew to their home in Asia Minor. The Kassites stayed and ruled Mesopotamia for five centuries.

GOVERNMENT. From the earliest historical records it is clear that the Sumerians were ruled by monarchs in some form. The first historical city-states had kings or priest-kings who led the army, administered the economy, and served as judges and as intermediaries between their people and the gods. At first the kings were thought of as favorites and representatives of the gods; later they instituted cults that worshiped them as divine. This union of church and state (to use modern terminology) in the person of the king reflected the centralization of power typical of Mesopotamian life. The economy was managed from the center by priests and king and was planned very carefully. Each year the land was surveyed, fields were assigned to specific farmers, and the amount of seed to be used was designated. The government estimated the size of the crop and planned its distribution even before it was planted.

This process required a large and competent staff, the ability to observe and record natural phenomena, a good knowledge of mathematics, and, for all of this, a system of writing. The Sumerians invented the writing system known as cuneiform (from the Latin *cuneus*, "wedge") because of the wedge-shaped stylus with which they wrote on clay tablets; the writing also came to be used in beautifully cut characters in stone. Sumerians also began the development of a sophisticated system of mathematics that reached a peak after 2000 B.C. in the "Old Babylonian" period. The calendar they invented had twelve lunar months. To make it agree with the solar year and make possible accurate designation of the seasons, they introduced a thirteenth month about every three years.

RELIGION. The Sumerians and their Semitic successors believed in gods in the shape of humans who were usually identified with some natural phenomenon. They were pictured as frivolous, quarrelsome, selfish, and often childish, differing from humans only in their greater power and their immortality. They each appear to have begun as local deities. The people of Mesopotamia had a vague and gloomy picture of the afterworld. Their religion dealt with problems of this world, and they em-

Hammurabi Creates a Code of Law in Mesopotamia

Hammurabi's Babylonian empire stretched from the Persian Gulf to the Mediterranean Sea. Building on earlier laws, he compiled one of the great ancient codes. It was discovered about seventy-five years ago in what is now Iran. Hammurabi, like other rulers before and after, represents himself and his laws as under the protection and sponsorship of all the right gods. Property is at least as sacred as persons, and the eye-for-an-eye approach characterizes the code. Here are a few examples from it.

LAWS

IF A SON *has struck his father, they shall cut off his hand.*

If a seignior has destroyed the eye of a member of the aristocracy, they shall destroy his eye.

If he has broken another seignior's bone, they shall break his bone.

If he has destroyed the eye of a commoner or broken the bone of a commoner, he shall pay one mina of silver.

If he has destroyed the eye of a seignior's slave or broken the bone of a seignior's slave, he shall pay one-half his value.

If a seignior has knocked out a tooth of a seignior of his own rank, they shall knock out his tooth.

If he has knocked out a commoner's tooth, he shall pay one-third mina of silver. . . .

EPILOGUE

I, Hammurabi, the perfect king,
was not careless (or) neglectful of the black-headed (people),
whom Enlil had presented to me,
(and) whose shepherding Marduk had committed to me;
I sought out peaceful regions for them;
I overcame grievous difficulties; . . .
With the mighty weapon which Zababa and Inanna entrusted to me,
with the insight that Enki allotted to me,
with the ability that Marduk gave me,
I rooted out the enemy above and below;
I made an end of war;
I promoted the welfare of the land;
I made the peoples rest in friendly habitations; . . .
The great gods called me,
so I became the beneficent shepherd whose scepter is righteous. . . .

James B. Pritchard, *Ancient Near Eastern Texts,* 2nd ed. (Princeton: Princeton University Press, 1955), pp. 164–180.

The code of Hammurabi. This is a cast of the stele on which is inscribed in cuneiform characters the law code issued by the Babylonian king Hammurabi (*ca.* 1792–1750 B.C.). In the relief at the top the king stands before the sun god and receives the law from him. The original stele is in the Louvre in Paris. [Courtesy of the Oriental Institute, University of Chicago.]

ployed prayer, sacrifice, and magic to achieve their ends. Expert knowledge was required to reach the perfection in wisdom and ritual needed to influence the gods, so the priesthood flourished. A high percentage of the cuneiform writing we now have is devoted to religious texts: prayers, incantations, curses, omens. It was important to discover the will and intentions of the gods, and the Sumerians sought hints in several places. The movements of the heavenly bodies were an obvious evidence of divine action, so astrology was born. They also sought to discover the divine will by examining the entrails of sacrificial animals for abnormalities. All of this required armies of scribes to keep great quantities of records and learned priests to interpret them.

Religion, in the form of myth, played a large part in the literature and art of Mesopotamia. In poetic language, the Sumerians and their successors told tales of the creation of the world, of a great flood that almost destroyed mankind, of an island paradise from which the god Enki was expelled for eating forbidden plants, of a hero named Gilgamesh who performed many great feats in his travels, and many more.

Religion was also the inspiration for the most interesting architectural achievement in Mesopotamia—the ziggurat. The ziggurat was an artificial stepped mound surmounted by a temple. It perhaps recalled the mountain origins of the Sumerians. Neighbors and successors of the Sumerians adopted the style, and the eroded remains of many of these monumental structures, some partly restored, still dot the Mesopotamian landscape.

Egyptian Civilization

While a great civilization arose in the valley of the Tigris and Euphrates, another, no less important, emerged in Egypt. The center of Egyptian civilization was the Nile River. From its source in central Africa the Nile runs north some 4000 miles to the Mediterranean, with long navigable stretches broken by several cataracts. Ancient Egypt included the 750 miles of the valley from the First Cataract to the sea and was shaped like a funnel

Sumerian statuettes from Tell Asmar. The tallest
figure in this collection of gods, priests, and
worshipers is the god Abu, the "lord of vegetation."
The group was found buried beside the altar of a
temple at a site near modern Baghdad dating from
3000–2500 B.C. [Courtesy of the Oriental Institute,
University of Chicago.]

with two distinct parts. Upper (southern) Egypt was the
stem, consisting of the narrow valley of the Nile. The
broad, triangular Delta, which branches out about 150
miles from the sea, was Lower Egypt. The Nile alone
made life possible in the almost rainless desert that surrounded it. Each year the river flooded and covered the
land, and when it receded, it left a fertile mud that could
produce two crops a year. The construction and maintenance of irrigation ditches to preserve the river's water,
with careful planning and organization of planting and
harvesting, produced agricultural prosperity unmatched
in the ancient world.

The Nile also served as a highway connecting the long,
narrow country and encouraging its unification. Upper
and Lower Egypt were, in fact, already united into a
single kingdom at the beginning of our historical record,
about 3100 B.C. Nature helped protect and isolate the
ancient Egyptians from outsiders. The cataracts, the sea,
and the desert made it difficult for foreigners to reach
Egypt for friendly or hostile purposes. Egypt knew far
more peace and security than Mesopotamia. This security, along with the sunny, predictable climate, gave

Egyptian civilization a more optimistic outlook than the
civilizations of the Tigris–Euphrates, which were always
in fear of assault from storm, flood, earthquake, and
hostile neighbors.

The more than three-thousand-year span of ancient
Egyptian history is traditionally divided into thirty-one
royal dynasties, from the first, founded by Menes (so-
called later by the Greeks; he may have been the Egyptian Narmer), the unifier of Upper and Lower Egypt, to
the last, established by Alexander the Great, who conquered Egypt, as we shall see, in 332 B.C. The dynasties
are conventionally arranged into periods. (See table.) The
unification of Egypt was vital, for even more than in
Mesopotamia, the entire river valley required central
control of irrigation. By the time of the Third Dynasty,
the king had achieved full supremacy, had imposed inter-

The ziggurat at Ur. This structure, originally crowned with a temple, at the ancient Sumerian city of Ur (in modern Iraq) dates back to the twenty-first century B.C. and has been partially restored. [AHM.]

mud Brick Temple

Dynasties (Roman Numerals)

EARLY DYNASTIC PERIOD (I–II)	ca. 3100–2700 B.C.
OLD KINGDOM (III–VI)	2700–2200 B.C.
FIRST INTERMEDIATE PERIOD (VII–X)	2200–2052 B.C.
MIDDLE KINGDOM (XI–XII)	2052–1786 B.C.
SECOND INTERMEDIATE PERIOD (XII–XVII)	1786–1575 B.C.
NEW KINGDOM (OR EMPIRE) (XVIII–XX)	1575–1087 B.C.
POST-EMPIRE (XXI–XXXI)	1087–30 B.C.

Reconstruction of the temple oval at Khafaje. The remains of this temple complex (not far from Baghdad in modern Iraq) have made a probable reconstruction possible. It reveals an elaborate religious establishment of the early third millenium B.C. that was even earlier than the ziggurat at Ur and the major pyramids of Egypt. [H. D. Darby. Courtesy of the Oriental Institute, University of Chicago.]

nal peace and order, and his kingdom enjoyed great prosperity. The capital was at Memphis in Upper Egypt, just above the Delta. The king was no mere representative of the gods but a god himself. The land was his own personal possession and the people his servants.

Nothing better illustrates the extent of royal power than the three great pyramids built as tombs by the kings of the Fourth Dynasty. The largest, that of Khufu (or Cheops), was originally 481 feet high and 756 feet on each side; it was made up of 2,300,000 stone blocks averaging 2.5 tons each. It is said by the much later Greek historian Herodotus to have taken 100,000 men twenty years to build. The pyramids are remarkable not only for the technical skill needed to build them but even more for what they tell us of the royal power. They give evidence that the Egyptian kings had enormous wealth, the power to concentrate so much effort on a personal project, and the confidence to undertake one of such a long duration. There were earlier pyramids and many were built later, but those of the Fourth Dynasty were never surpassed.

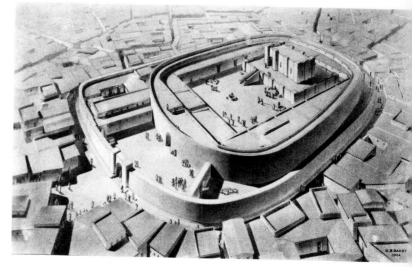

Early Civilizations to About 1000 B.C. 13

THE OLD KINGDOM. In the Old Kingdom royal power was absolute. The pharaoh, as he was later called, governed his kingdom through his family and appointed officials removable at his pleasure. The peasants were carefully regulated, their movement was limited, and they were taxed heavily, perhaps as much as one fifth of what they produced. Luxury accompanied the king in life and death, and he was raised to a remote and exalted level by his people. Such power and eminence cannot be sustained long by force alone. The Egyptians worked for the king and obeyed him because he was a living god on whom life, safety, and prosperity depended. He was the direct source of law and justice, so no law codes were needed.

In such a world, government is merely one aspect of religion, and religion dominated Egyptian life. The gods of Egypt had many forms: animals, humans, and natural forces. In time, Re, the sun god, came to have a special dominant place, but for centuries there seems to have been little clarity or order in the Egyptian pantheon. Unlike the Mesopotamians, the Egyptians had a rather clear idea of an afterlife. They took great care to bury their dead properly and supplied the grave with things that the departed would need for a pleasant life after death. The king and some nobles had their bodies preserved as mummies. Their tombs were beautifully decorated with paintings; food was provided at burial and even after. Some royal tombs were provided with full-sized ships for the voyage to heaven. At first, only kings were thought to achieve eternal life; then nobles were included; finally all Egyptians could hope for immortality. The dead must be properly embalmed and the proper spells written and spoken. Later on a moral test was added.

The Egyptians developed a system of writing not much later than the Sumerians. Though the idea may have come from Mesopotamia, the script was independent. It began as picture writing and later combined pictographs with sound signs to produce a difficult and complicated script that the Greeks called *hieroglyphics*

The Gilgamesh Epic Recounts the Great Flood in Mesopotamia

The best preserved version of the Mesopotamian story of the Great Flood is preserved in the Gilgamesh Epic, composed about 2000 B.C. The story told here resembles the Biblical tale in many ways.

FOR *six days and [seven] nights the wind blew, and the flood and the storm swept the land. But the seventh day arriving did the rainstorm subside and the flood which had heaved like a woman in travail; there quieted the sea, and the storm-wind stood still, the flood stayed her flowing. I opened a vent and the fresh air moved over my cheek-bones. And I looked at the sea; there was silence, the tide-way lay flat as a roof-top—but the whole of mankind had returned unto clay. I bowed low: I sat and I wept: o'er my cheek-bones my tears kept on running.*

When I looked out again in the directions, across the expanse of the sea, mountain ranges had emerged in twelve places and on Mount Nisir the vessel had grounded. Mount Nisir held the vessel fast nor allowed any movement. For a first day and a second, fast Mount Nisir held the vessel nor allowed of any movement. For a third day and a fourth day, fast Mount Nisir held the vessel nor allowed of any movement. For a fifth day and a sixth day, held Mount Nisir fast the vessel nor allowed of any movement.

On the seventh day's arriving, I freed a dove and did release him. Forth went the dove but came back to me: there was not yet a resting-place and he came returning. Then I set free a swallow and did release him. Forth went the swallow but came back to me: there was not yet a resting-place and he came returning. So I set free a raven and did release him. Forth went the raven—and he saw again the natural flowing of the waters, and he ate and he flew about and he croaked, and came not returninng.

D. Winton Thomas (Ed.), *Documents from Old Testament Times* (London: Thomas Nelson and Sons, Ltd., 1958; New York: Harper Torchbooks, 1961), pp. 22.

("sacred carvings"). Though much of what we have is preserved on wall paintings and carvings, most of Egyptian writing was done with pen and ink on a fine paper made from the papyrus reed found in the Delta. Egyptian literature was more limited in depth and imagination than the Mesopotamian writings. There are hymns, myths, magical formulas, tales of travel, and "wisdom literature," bits of advice to help one get on well in the world. But there was nothing as serious and probing as the story of Gilgamesh in the happier and simpler world of Egypt.

THE NEAR EAST AND GREECE ABOUT 1400 B.C.

About 1400 B.C. the Near East was divided among four empires. Egypt went south to Nubia and north through Palestine and Phoenicia. Kassites ruled in Mesopotamia, Hittites in Asia Minor, and Mitanni in Assyrian lands. In the Aegean the Mycenaean kingdoms were at their height.

THE MIDDLE KINGDOM. The power of the kings of the Old Kingdom waned as priests and nobles gained more independence and influence. The governors of the regions of Egypt called *nomes* gained hereditary claim to their offices, and their families acquired large estates. About 2200 B.C. the Old Kingdom collapsed and gave way to decentralization and disorder. Finally, the nomarchs (governors) of Thebes in Upper Egypt gained control of the country and established the Middle Kingdom, about 2000 B.C. The rulers of the Twelfth Dynasty restored the pharaoh's power over the whole of Egypt, though they could not completely control the nobles who ruled the nomes. Still, they brought order, peace, and prosperity to a troubled land. They encouraged trade and extended Egyptian power and influence northward toward Palestine and southward toward Ethiopia. Though

they moved the capital back to the more defensible site at Memphis, they gave great prominence to Amon, a god especially connected with Thebes. He became identified with Re, emerging as Amon-Re, the main god of Egypt. The kings of this period seem to have emphasized their role in doing justice. In their statues they are often shown as burdened with care, presumably concern for their people. Tales of the period place great emphasis on the king as interested in right and in the welfare of his people. Much later, in the New Kingdom, ethical concerns appeared, as they had in the law codes of Mesopotamia, but the divine status of the king gave them a novel place in religion as well.

THE NEW KINGDOM (THE EMPIRE). The Middle Kingdom disintegrated in the Thirteenth Dynasty with the resurgence of power of the local nobility. About 1700 B.C. Egypt suffered an invasion. Tradition speaks of a people called the Hyksos who came from the east and conquered the Nile Delta. They seem to have been a collection of Semitic peoples from the area of Palestine and Syria at the eastern end of the Mediterranean. Egyptian nationalism reasserted itself about 1575 B.C., when a dynasty from Thebes drove out the

Early Civilizations to About 1000 B.C. 15

Hyksos and reunited the kingdom. In reaction to the humiliation of the Second Intermediate Period, the pharaohs of the Eighteenth Dynasty, the most prominent of whom was Thutmose III, created an absolute government based on a powerful army and an Egyptian empire extending far beyond the Nile valley.

From the Hyksos the Egyptians learned new military techniques and obtained new weapons. To these they added determination, a fighting spirit, and an increasingly military society. They pushed the southern frontier back a long way and extended Egyptian power farther into Palestine and Syria and beyond to the upper Euphrates River. They were not checked until they came into conflict with the powerful Hittite empire of Asia Minor. Both powers were weakened by the struggle, and though Egypt survived, it again became the victim of foreign invasion and rule, as one foreign empire after another took possession of the ancient kingdom.

The Eighteenth Dynasty, however, witnessed an interesting religious revolution. One of the results of the successful imperial ventures of the Egyptian pharaohs was the growth in power of the priests of Amon and the threat it posed to the position of the king. When young Amenhotep IV came to the throne before the middle of the fourteenth century B.C., he determined to resist the priesthood of Amon. He was supported by his family and advisers and ultimately made a clean break with the worship of Amon-Re. He moved his capital from Thebes, the center of Amon worship, and built an entirely new city about three hundred miles to the north at a place now called El Amarna. The new god was Aton, the physical disk of the sun, and the new city was called Akhtaton. The king changed his own name to Akhnaton, "It pleases Aton." The new god was different from any that came before him, for he was believed to be universal, not merely Egyptian. Unlike the other gods, he had no cult statue but was represented in painting and relief sculpture as the sun disk. Hymns to him suggest that this religion had an unusual ethical content, emphasizing truth and love.

The great pyramids of Egypt.
ABOVE: These colossal tombs of three of the pharaohs of the Fourth Dynasty (*ca.* 2620–2480 B.C.) are at Giza near Cairo. From left to right, they are the tombs of Menkaure, Khafre, and Khufu—the last being the oldest and largest. The smaller tombs nearby may belong to the pharaohs' wives and noble retainers. [Library of the Egyptian Museum, Cairo.]
OPPOSITE: Cross section of the pyramid of Khufu showing the arrangement of the interior chambers and passages in the largest of the pyramids. The base of the structure covers an area of more than thirteen acres. [Banister Fletcher, *A History of Architecture on the Comparative Method,* 18th edition (London: Athlone Press, 1969), p. 32.]

The universal claims for Aton led to religious intolerance unknown to the worshipers of the other gods. Their temples were shut down and the name of Amon-Re was chiseled from monuments on which it was carved. The old priests, of course, were deprived of their posts and privileges, and the people who served the pharaoh and his god were new, sometimes even foreign. The new religion, moreover, was more remote than the old. Only the pharaoh and his family worshiped Aton directly, while the people worshiped the pharaoh. Akhnaton's interest in religious reform led him to ignore foreign affairs, which proved disastrous. The Asian possessions of Egypt fell away, and this imperial decline and its economic consequences must have caused further hostility to the new religion. When the king died, a strong counterrevolution swept away the work of his lifetime. The new pharaohs restored the old religion and wiped out as much as they could of the memory of the worship of Aton. Amon returned to the center of the pantheon at Thebes, the restored capital, and his priests regained their power. A general named Horemhab became king, restored order, and recovered much of the lost empire. He referred to Akhnaton as "the criminal of Akhtaton" and erased his name from the records. Akhnaton's city and memory

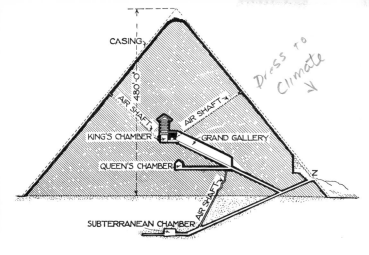

disappeared for over three thousand years, to be rediscovered only by chance about a century ago.

For the rest of its independent history, Egypt returned to its traditional culture, but its mood was more gloomy. The Book of the Dead, a product of this late period, was a collection of spells whereby the dead could get safely to the next world without being destroyed by a hideous monster. Egypt itself would soon be devoured by powerful empires no less menacing.

Ancient Near Eastern Empires

In the time of the Eighteenth Dynasty in Egypt, new groups of peoples had established themselves in the Near East: the Kassites in Babylonia, the Hittites in Asia Minor, and the Mitannians in northern Mesopotamia. They all spoke languages in the Indo-European group, which includes Greek, Latin, Sanskrit, Persian, Celtic, and the Germanic languages and is thought to have originated in the Ukraine (now the southwestern Soviet Union) or to the east of it. The Kassites and Mitannians were warrior peoples who ruled as a minority over more civilized folk and absorbed their culture without changing it. The Hittites arrived in Asia Minor about 2000 B.C., and by about 1500 B.C. they had established a strong, centralized government with a capital at Hattusas (near Ankara, the capital of modern Turkey). Between 1400 and 1200 B.C. they contested Egypt's control of Palestine and Syria and were strong enough to achieve a dynastic marriage with the daughter of the powerful Nineteenth-Dynasty pharaoh, Ramses II, about 1265 B.C. By 1200 B.C. the Hittite kingdom was gone, swept away by

Pharaoh Menkaure and his queen. This Fourth Dynasty monarch built the third and smallest of the great pyramids at Giza. The frontality of the two figures and the extension of the left foot of each in this slate sculpture from Giza are typical of Egyptian statues. (About 2550 B.C.) [Courtesy of the Museum of Fine Arts, Boston; MFA Expedition Fund.]

the arrival of new, mysterious Indo-Europeans. However, Neo-Hittite centers flourished in Asia Minor and Mesopotamia for a few centuries longer.

In most respects the Hittites reflected the influence of the dominant Mesopotamian culture of the region, but their government resembled more closely what we know of other Indo-European cultures. Their kings did not claim to be divine or even to be the chosen representatives of the gods. In the early period the king's power was checked by a council of nobles, and the assembled army had to ratify his succession to the throne. The Hittites appear to have been responsible for a great technological advance, the smelting of iron. They were unable to benefit much from its use for weapons, leaving that advance to others. The Hittites also played an important role in transmitting the ancient cultures of Mesopotamia and Egypt to the Greeks, who lived on their frontiers.

The fall of the Hittites was followed shortly by the formation of empires that dominated the Near East's ancient civilizations and even extended them to new areas. The first of these empires was established by the Assyrians, whose homeland was in the valleys and hills of northern Mesopotamia on and to the east of the Tigris

Some examples of Egyptian wall decorations.
ABOVE: Painting in the tomb of a nobleman at Thebes from the Eighteenth Dynasty (fourteenth century B.C.). It is typical of the many wall paintings in which hieroglyphic writing is included. In this picture grieving women are approached by servants carrying necessities for the afterlife of the deceased, including a bed, chests of clothes, and other comforts. [AHM.]
OPPOSITE ABOVE: Another tomb decoration, this one in low relief. These are relatives of the deceased courtier Ramose from his tomb at Thebes. (Fourteenth century B.C.) [AHM.]
OPPOSITE BELOW: Painting and sculptured reliefs covered nearly every available foot of space in Egyptian temples as well as in tombs. Here Pharaoh Seti of the Nineteenth Dynasty (fourteenth century B.C.) is refreshed by the breath of life administered by a god on his left in Seti's temple at Abydos. [AHM.]

[Text continued on page 22]

Egyptian spearmen. These warriors, carved of wood and painted, belong to the Middle Kingdom period of Egypt—to the Eleventh Dynasty (ca. 2134-1991 B.C.). Also existing is a companion group of archers. [Library of the Egyptian Museum, Cairo.]

I8 *The World Before the West*

Akhnaton worshipping Aton. The scene carved into this stone stele shows Eighteenth-Dynasty Pharaoh Akhnaton (1367–1350 B.C.) paying homage to the newly enthroned god, Aton, the disk of the sun. [Library of the Egyptian Museum, Cairo.]

(handwritten margin notes: "ratical", "wrote hymes", "considered a no-no", "very elegant", "Childhood disease? for rounded hips.")

Akhnaton Intones New Hymns to Aton, the One God

These hymns were composed in the reign of Amenhotep IV (1367–1350 B.C.)—Akhnaton, as he called himself after instituting a religious revolution in Egypt.

THOU *makest the Nile in the Nether World,*
Thou bringest it as thou desirest,
To preserve alive the people of Egypt
For thou hast made them for thyself,
Thou lord of them all, who weariest thyself for them;
Thou lord of every land, who risest for them.
Thou Sun of day, great in glory,
All the distant highland countries,
Thou makest also their life,
Thou didst set a Nile in the sky.
When it falleth for them,
It maketh waves upon the mountains,
Like the great green sea,
Watering their fields in their towns.

How benevolent are thy designs, O lord of eternity!
There is a Nile in the sky for the strangers
And for the antelopes of all the highlands that go about
    upon their feet.
But the Nile, it cometh from the Nether World for
    Egypt.

Thou didst make the distant sky in order to rise therein,
In order to behold all that thou hast made,
While thou wast yet alone
Shining in thy form as living Aton,
Dawning, glittering, going afar and returning.
Thou makest millions of forms
Through thyself alone;
Cities, villages, and fields, highways and rivers.
All eyes see thee before them,
For thou art Aton of the day over the earth,
When thou hast gone away,
And all men, whose faces thou hast fashioned
In order that thou mightest no longer see thyself alone,
[Have fallen asleep, so that not] one [seeth] that which
    thou hast made,
Yet art thou still in my heart.

REVELATION TO THE KING

There is no other that knoweth thee
Save thy son Akhnaton.
Thou hast made him wise
In thy designs and in thy might.

(old horse nose.!)

UNIVERSAL MAINTENANCE

The world subsists in thy hand,
Even as thou hast made them.
When thou hast risen they live,
When thou settest they die;
For thou art length of life of thyself,
Men live through thee.

The eyes of men see beauty
Until thou settest.
All labour is put away
When thou settest in the west.
When thou risest again
[Thou] makest [every hand] to flourish for the king
And [prosperity] is in every foot,
Since thou didst establish the world,
And raise them up for thy son,
Who came forth from thy flesh,
The king of Upper and Lower Egypt,
Living in Truth, Lord of the Two Lands,
Nefer-khepru-Re, Wan-Re (Akhnaton),
Son of Re, living in Truth, lord of diadems,
Ikhnaton, whose life is long;
(And for) the chief royal wife, his beloved,
Mistress of the Two Lands, Nefer-nefru-Aton,
    Nofretete,
Living and flourishing for ever and ever.

James H. Breasted, *The Dawn of Conscience* (New York: Charles Scribners' Sons, 1933, 1961), p. 137.

Statue of Akhnaton. This portrayal of the revolutionary pharaoh, unflattering in its realism, is characteristic of the unusual art of his reign with its emphasis on truth. [Library of the Egyptian Museum, Cairo.]

River. They had a series of capitals, of which the great city of Nineveh is perhaps best known (modern Mosul, Iraq). They spoke a Semitic language and, from early times, were a part of the culture of Mesopotamia. Akkadians, Sumerians, Amorites, and Mitannians had dominated Assyria in turn. The Hittites' defeat of Mitanni liberated the Assyrians and prepared the way for their greatness from earlier than 1000 B.C. By 665 B.C. they had come to control everything from the southern frontier of Egypt, through Palestine, Syria, and much of Asia Minor, down to the Persian Gulf in the southeast. They succeeded in part because they made use of iron weapons. Since iron is more common than copper and tin, it was possible for them to arm more men more cheaply. The Assyrians were also fierce, well disciplined, and cruel. Their cruelty was calculated, at least in part, to terrorize real and potential enemies, for the Assyrians boasted of their brutality.

Unlike earlier empires, the Assyrian Empire systematically and profitably exploited the area it held. The Assyrians employed different methods of control, ranging from the mere collection of tribute, to the stationing of garrisons in conquered territory, to removing entire populations from their homelands and scattering them elsewhere, as they did to the people of the kingdom of Israel. Because of their military and administrative skills, they were able to hold vast areas even as they absorbed the teachings of the older cultures under their sway.

In addition to maintaining their own empire, the Assyrians had to serve as a buffer of the civilized Middle East against the barbarians on its frontiers. In the seventh century B.C. the task of fighting off the barbarians so drained the over-extended Assyrians that the empire fell because of internal revolution. A new dynasty in Babylon joined with the rising kingdom of Media to the east (in modern Iran) to defeat the Assyrians and destroy Nineveh in 612 B.C. The successor kingdoms, the Chaldean or Neo-Babylonian and the Median, did not last long but were swallowed by 539 B.C., by yet another great eastern empire, that of the Persians. We shall return to the Persians in Chapter 3.

Israel

None of the powerful kingdoms we have described has had as much influence on the future of Western civilization as the small stretch of land on the eastern shore of the Mediterranean between Syria and Egypt. The three great religions of the modern world outside the Far East—Judaism, Christianity, and Islam—trace their origins, at least in part, to the people who arrived there a little before 1200 B.C. and the book that recounts their experiences, the Old Testament of the Bible.

Before the Israelites arrived in their promised land, it was inhabited by groups of people speaking a Semitic language called Canaanite. The Canaanites lived in walled cities and carried on a version of Mesopotamian

The Hittites. Remains of the Lion Gate at Boghazköy, which is a Turkish town in north-central Asia Minor believed to be at or near the ancient Hittite capital of Hattusas. These gates are part of a vast complex of walls, temples, archives, and a palace at this site. The Hittites played a great part in Near Eastern history between 1500 and 1200 B.C. [Editorial Photocolor Archives.]

culture that included the worship of many gods. The arrival of the Israelites probably forced them northward to settle among similar people who inhabited the coastal land of Phoenicia. The Phoenicians were an important commercial people from a very early time. They seem to have developed a simplified system of writing that lacked only vowel signs to be a true alphabet. They founded colonies as far west as Spain, though their most famous was Carthage, near modern Tunis in north Africa. Sitting astride all trade routes, the Phoenician cities were important sites for the transmission of culture and knowledge from east to west.

The history of the Israelites must be pieced together from various sources. They are mentioned only rarely in the records of their neighbors, so we must rely chiefly on their own account, the Old Testament. It is not intended as a history in our sense but is a complicated collection of historical narrative, wisdom literature, poetry, law, and religious witness. Scholars of an earlier time tended to discard it as a source for historians, but the most recent trend is to take it seriously while using it with caution.

We need not reject the tradition that the patriarch Abraham came from Ur in Mesopotamia about 1900 B.C. and wandered west to tend his flocks in the land of the Canaanites. Some of his people settled there and others wandered into Egypt, perhaps with the Hyksos. By the thirteenth century B.C., led by Moses, they had left Egypt and wandered in the desert until they reached Canaan. They established a united kingdom that reached its peak under David and Solomon in the tenth century B.C. The sons of Solomon could not maintain the unity of the kingdom, and it split into two parts: Israel in the north and Judah, with its capital at Jerusalem, in the south. The rise of the great empires brought disaster to the Israelites. The northern kingdom fell to the Assyrians in 722 B.C., and its people were scattered and lost forever. These were the ten lost tribes. Only the kingdom of Judah remained, and hereafter we may call the Israelites Jews.

In 586 B.C. Judah was defeated by the Babylonian king Nebuchadnezzar II. He destroyed the great temple built

A late Hittite war chariot. The Hittites were probably the earliest major users of iron implements and of the horse. This relief, now in the Ankara museum, shows a pair of horse-drawn Hittite fighters oblivious to the defeated enemy below. It is from the eighth century B.C., by which time the formerly unified empire had been succeeded by several scattered Hittite groups. [AHM.]

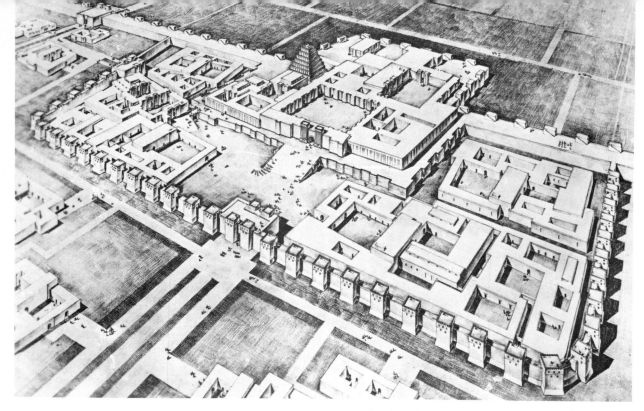

An Assyrian palace. This is a reconstruction drawing of the palace complex of King Sargon II (722–705 B.C.) at Khorsabad (in modern Iraq). [Charles Altman. Courtesy of the Oriental Institute, University of Chicago.]

by Solomon and took thousands of hostages off to Baby-lon. When the Persians defeated Babylonia, they ended this Babylonian Captivity of the Jews and allowed them to return to their homeland. After that the area of the old kingdom of the Jews in Palestine was dominated by foreign peoples for some twenty-five hundred years until the establishment of the State of Israel in A.D. 1948.

Religion

The fate of this small nation would be of little interest were it not for its unique religious achievement. The great contribution of the Jews is the idea of monotheism, the existence of one universal God, the creator and ruler of the universe. This idea may be as old as Moses, as the Jewish tradition asserts, but it certainly dates as far back as the prophets of the eighth century B.C. The Jewish God is neither a natural force nor like man or any other creature; he is so elevated that those who believe in him may not picture him in any form. The faith of the Jews is

A winged bull-man monument from Khorsabad. Like other Assyrian capitals, Khorsabad in the late eighth century B.C. was decorated to awe the visitor and display the Assyrians' might. This formidable but rather complacent creature had many relatives in all major Assyrian centers. He is over fifteen feet tall. [Courtesy of the Oriental Institute, University of Chicago.]

Assyrians plundering. This low relief depicts king Ashurbanipal (688–after 633 B.C.) sacking a city taken from an enemy. Under this king the Assyrian Empire controlled more territory than any state before that time. [Courtesy of the Trustees of the British Museum, London.]

given special strength by their belief that God made a covenant with Abraham that his progeny would be a chosen people who would be rewarded for following his commandments and the law he revealed to Moses.

A novelty of Jewish religious thought is the powerful ethical element it introduces. God is a severe but just judge. Ritual and sacrifice are not enough to achieve his approval. Man must be righteous, and God himself appears to be bound to act righteously. The Jewish prophetic tradition was a powerful ethical force. The prophets constantly criticized any falling away from the law and the path of righteousness. The prophets placed God in history, blaming the misfortunes of the Jews on God's righteous and necessary intervention to punish them for their misdeeds, but the prophets also promised the redemption of the Jews if they repented. The prophetic tradition expected the redemption to come in the form of a Messiah who would restore the house of David. The Christians eventually seized on this tradition and believed that Jesus of Nazareth was that Messiah.

It is impossible in a short space to recount all the ways in which the Jewish religious ideas influenced the future development of the West, both directly and indirectly. It is clear, however, that belief in an all-powerful creator, righteous himself and demanding righteousness and obedience from mankind, a universal God who is the father and ruler of all humans, is a critical part of the Western heritage.

Assyrian King Tiglath-Pileser III. This is an eighth-century B.C. relief from one of the Assyrian capitals, Nimrud (in modern Iraq). [AHM.]

General Outlook of Near Eastern Cultures

Our very brief account of the history of the ancient Near East so far reveals that the various peoples and cultures were different in many ways, yet the distance between all of them and the emerging culture of the Greeks, to whom we shall be turning our attention, is striking. We can see this best by comparing the approach of the other cultures to several fundamental human problems with the way some Greeks treated the same problems. The great questions are these: What is the relationship of man to nature? to the gods? to other men? These questions involve attitudes toward religion, philosophy, science, law, justice, politics, and government in general.

For the peoples of the Near East there was no simple separation between man and nature or even between animate creatures and inanimate objects. Humanity was part of a natural continuum, and all things partook of life and spirit. They imagined the universe to be dominated by gods more or less in the shape of humans, and the world they ruled was irregular and unpredictable, subject to divine whims. The gods were capricious because nature seemed equally capricious.

One Egyptian text speaks of man as "the cattle of god." The Babylonian story of creation makes it clear that man's function is merely to serve the gods. The creator Marduk says,

I will create Lullu "man" be his name,
I will form Lullu, man.
Let him be burdened with the toil of the gods,
   that they may freely breathe.[1]

In a world ruled by powerful deities of this kind human existence was precarious. Even disasters that we would think human in origin they saw as the product of divine

1 H. Frankfort et al., *Before Philosophy* (Baltimore: Penguin Books, 1949), p. 197.

The Second Isaiah Defines Hebrew Monotheism

The strongest statement of Hebrew monotheism is found in these words of the anonymous prophet whom we call the Second Isaiah. He wrote during the Hebrew exile in Babylonia, 597–539 B.C.

42

⁵ Thus *says God, the* Lord,
  who created the heavens and stretched them out,
  who spread forth the earth and what comes from it,
  who gives breath to the people upon it and spirit
    to those who walk in it:
⁶ *"I am the* Lord, *I have called you in righteousness,*
  I have taken you by the hand and kept you;
I have given you as a covenant to the people,
  a light to the nations,
⁷   *to open the eyes that are blind,*
to bring out the prisoners from the dungeon,
  from the prison those who sit in darkness.
⁸ *I am the* Lord, *that is my name;*
  my glory I give to no other,
  nor my praise to graven images.
⁹ *Behold, the former things have come to pass, and*
  new things I now declare;
before they spring forth I tell you of them."

.   .   .   .   .   .

44

⁶ *Thus says the* Lord, *the King of Israel and his Redeemer, the* Lord *of hosts:*
"I am the first and I am the last; besides me there is no god.
⁷ *Who is like me? Let him proclaim it,*
  let him declare and set it forth before me.
Who has announced from of old the things to come?
  Let them tell us what is yet to be.
⁸ *Fear not, nor be afraid;*
  have I not told you from of old and declared it?
  And you are my witnesses!
Is there a God besides me?
  There is no Rock; I know not any."

.   .   .   .   .   .

49

²² *Thus says the Lord* God:
"Behold, I will lift up my hand to the nations,
  and raise my signal to the peoples;
  and they shall bring your sons in their bosom,
  and your daughters shall be carried on their shoulders.
²³ *Kings shall be your foster fathers,*
  and their queens your nursing mothers.
With their faces to the ground they shall bow down to you,

The Hebrews established a unified kingdom in Palestine under Kings David and Solomon in the tenth century B.C. After the death of Solomon, however, the kingdom was divided into two parts—Israel in the north and Judah, with its capital Jerusalem, in the south. North of Israel were the great commercial cities of Phoenicia.

and lick the dust of your feet.
Then you will know that I am the LORD;
those who wait for me shall not be put to shame."

²⁴ *Can the prey be taken from the mighty, or the captives*
of a tyrant be rescued?
²⁵ *Surely, thus says the* LORD:
"Even the captives of the mighty shall be taken,
and the prey of the tyrant be rescued,
for I will contend with those who contend with you
and I will save your children.
²⁶ *I will make your oppressors eat their own flesh,*
and they shall be drunk with their own blood as
with wine.
Then all flesh shall know
that I am the LORD *your Savior,*
and your Redeemer, the Mighty One of Jacob."

Revised Standard Version of the Bible (New York: Division of Christian Education, National Council of Churches, 1952).

will. So a Babylonian text depicts the destruction of the city of Ur by invading Elamites as the work of the gods, carried out by the storm god Enlil:

Enlil called the storm.
　The people mourn.
Exhilirating winds he took from the land.
　The people mourn.
Good winds he took away from Sumer.
　The people mourn.
He summoned evil winds.
　The people mourn.
Entrusted them to Kingaluda, tender of storms.
He called the storm that will annihilate the land.
　The people mourn.
He called disastrous winds.
　The people mourn.

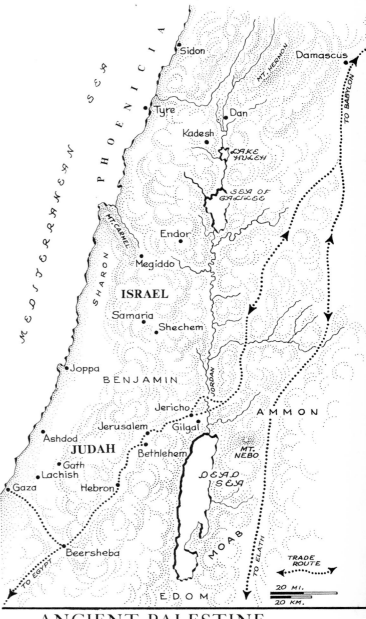

ANCIENT PALESTINE

General Outlook of Near Eastern Cultures **27**

Enlil—choosing Gibil as his helper—
Called the (great) hurricane of heaven.
   The people mourn.[2]

The helpless position of mankind in the face of irra-tional divine powers is clearly shown in both the Egyp-tian and the Babylonian versions of the story of the flood. In one Egyptian tale, Re, the god who had created man, decided to destroy him because of some unnamed evil the god had suffered. He sent the goddess Sekhmet to ac-complish the deed, and she was in the midst of her task, enjoying the work and wading in a sea of blood, when Re changed his mind. Instead of ordering a halt, he poured seven thousand barrels of blood-colored beer in Sekhmet's path. She quickly became drunk, stopped the slaughter, and preserved mankind. In the Babylonian story the motive for the destruction of humanity is more obvious: "In those days the world teemed, the people multiplied, the world bellowed like a wild bull, and the great god was aroused by the clamour. Enlil heard the clamour and he said to the gods in council, 'The uproar of mankind is intolerable and sleep is no longer possible by reason of the babel.' So the gods in their hearts were moved to let loose the deluge."[3] The gods repented to a degree and decided to save one family, Utnapishtim and his wife, but they seem to have chosen him whimsically, for no particular reason.

In such a universe man could not hope to understand nature, much less control it. At best he could try by magic to use some mysterious forces against others. An example of this device is provided by a Mesopotamian incantation to break a sorcerer's spell. The sufferer tries to use the magical powers inherent in ordinary salt to fight the witchcraft, addressing the salt as follows:

O Salt, created in a clean place,
For food of gods did Enlil destine thee.

2 Frankfort et al., p. 154.
3 *The Epic of Gilgamesh*, translated by N. K. Sandars (Baltimore: Penguin Books, 1960), p. 105.

Without thee no meal is set out in Ekur,
Without thee god, king, lord, and prince do not smell
   incense.
I am so-and-so, the son of so-and-so,
Held captive by enchantment,
Held in fever by bewitchment.
O Salt, break my enchantment! Loose my spell!
Take from me the bewitchment!—and as my Creator
I shall extol thee.[4]

Man's relationship to the gods is equally humble. He has no doubt that they can destroy mankind and may do so at any time for no good reason. He may, and indeed must, try to win them over by prayers and sacrifices, but there is no guarantee of success. The gods are bound by no laws and no morality. The best behavior and the greatest devotion to the cult of the gods are no defense against the divine and cosmic irrationality.

In these earliest civilizations man's relations with his fellowman were guided by laws, often set down in writ-ten codes. The basic question about law concerns its legitimacy: Why, apart from the lawgiver's power to coerce obedience, should anyone obey the law? For the Egyptians the answer was simple: the law came from the king and the king was a god. For the Mesopotamians the answer was almost the same. They believed that the king was a representative of god, so that the laws he set forth were equally divine. The prologue to the most famous legal document in antiquity, the Code of Hammurabi, makes this plain:

I am the king who is preeminent among kings;
my words are choice; my ability has no equal.
By the order of Shamash, the great judge of heaven
   and earth,
may my justice prevail in the land;
by the word of Marduk, my lord,
may my statutes have no one to rescind them. . . .

4 Frankfort et al., p. 143.

The Hebrews introduced some important new ideas. Their unique God was capable of great anger and destruction, but he was open to persuasion and subject to morality. He was therefore more predictable and comforting, for all the terror of his wrath. The biblical version of the flood story, for instance, reveals the great difference between the Hebrew God and the Babylonian deities. The Hebrew God is powerful and wrathful, but he is not arbitrary. He chose to destroy his creatures, mankind, for their moral failures, because "the wickedness of man was great in the earth, and that every imagination of the thought of his heart was evil continually . . . the earth was corrupt in God's sight and the earth was filled with violence."[5] When he repented and wanted to save someone, he chose Noah because "Noah was a righteous man, blameless in his generation."[6]

That God is bound by his own definition of righteousness is neatly shown in the biblical story of Sodom and Gomorrah. He has chosen to destroy these wicked cities but feels obliged first to inform Abraham because of his covenant with him.[7] In this passage Abraham calls on his Lord to abide by his own moral principles and the Lord sees his point. In such a world there is the possibility of order in the universe and on this earth. There is also the possibility of justice among men, for the Hebrew God provides his people with law. Through his prophet Moses he provides men with regulations that will enable them to live in peace and justice. If they will abide by the law and live upright lives, they and their descendants can expect happy and prosperous lives. This idea is quite different from the uncertainty of the Babylonian view, but like it and its Egyptian partner it leaves no doubt of the centrality of the divine. Cosmic order, human survival, and justice among men are all dependent on God.

Toward the Greeks and Western Thought

Different approaches and answers to many of the same concerns will be offered by ancient Greek thought. Calling attention, even this early, to some of those differences will help to point up the distinctive outlook of the Greeks and of the later cultures of Western civilization that have drawn heavily on them.

The Greeks had much in common with the ideas of earlier peoples. Their gods had most of the characteristics of the Mesopotamian deities; magic and incantations played a part in their lives; and law was usually connected with divinity. Many, if not most, Greeks in the ancient world must have lived their lives with notions not very different from those held by other peoples. But the surprising thing is that some Greeks developed ideas that were strikingly different and in so doing set a part of mankind on an entirely new path. As early as the sixth century B.C. some Greeks living in the Ionian cities of Asia Minor raised some questions and suggested some answers about nature that produced an intellectual revolution. In speculating about the nature of the world and its origin, they made guesses that were completely naturalistic and made no reference to supernatural powers. One historian of Greek thought has put the case particularly well:

> In one of the Babylonian legends it says: "All the lands were sea. . . . Marduk bound a rush mat upon the face of the waters, he made dirt and piled it beside the rush mat." What Thales did was to leave Marduk out. He, too, said that everything was once water. But he thought that earth and everything else had been formed out of water by a natural process, like the silting up of the Delta of the Nile. . . . It is an admirable beginning, the whole point of which is that it gathers together into a coherent picture a number of observed facts without letting Marduk in.[8]

Thales was the first Greek philosopher. His putting of the question in a naturalistic form as early as the sixth century B.C. may have been the beginning of the unre-

5 *Genesis* 6:5-11.   6 *Genesis* 6:9.   7 *Genesis* 18:20-33.   8 Benjamin Farrington, *Greek Science* (London: 1953), p. 37.

servedly rational investigation of the universe, and so the beginning of both philosophy and science.

The same relentlessly rational approach was used even in regard to the gods themselves. In the same century as Thales, Xenophanes of Colophon expressed the opinion that men think that the gods are born and have clothes, voices, and bodies like themselves. If oxen, horses, and lions had hands and could paint like men, they would paint gods in their own image; the oxen would draw gods like oxen and the horses like horses. Black people believed in flat-nosed, black-faced gods, and the Thracians in gods with blue eyes and red hair.[9] In the fifth century B.C. Protagoras of Abdera went so far in the direction of agnosticism as to say, "About the gods I can have no knowledge either that they are or that they are not or what is their nature."[10] This rationalistic, skeptical way of thinking carried over into practical matters as well. The school of medicine led by Hippocrates of Cos (about 400 B.C.) attempted to understand, diagnose, and cure disease without any attention to supernatural forces or beings. One of the Hippocratics wrote of the mysterious disease epilepsy: "It seems to me that the disease is no more divine than any other. It has a natural cause, just as other diseases have. Men think it divine merely because they do not understand it. But if they called everything divine which they do not understand, why, there would be no end of divine things."[11] By the fifth century B.C., too, it was possible for the historian Thucydides to analyze and explain the behavior of men in society completely in terms of human nature and chance, leaving no place for the gods or supernatural forces.

The same absence of divine or supernatural forces characterized Greek views of law and justice. Most Greeks, of course, liked to think in a vague way that law came ultimately from the gods. In practice, however, and especially in the democratic states, they knew very well that laws were made by men and should be obeyed because they represented the expressed consent of the citizens. Law, according to the fourth century B.C. statesman Demosthenes, is "a general covenant of the whole State, in accordance with which all men in that State ought to regulate their lives."[12]

The statement of these ideas, so different from what came before the Greeks, opens the discussion of most of the issues that appear in the long history of Western civilization and that remain major concerns in the modern world: What is the nature of the universe and how can it be controlled? Are there divine powers, and if so, what is man's relationship to them? Are law and justice human, divine, or both? What is the place in human society for freedom, obedience, reverence? These and many other problems were either invented or intensified by the Greeks. We now need to see whether there was something special in the Greek experience that made them raise these questions in the way that they did.

SUGGESTED READINGS

W. F. ALBRIGHT, *From the Stone Age to Christianity* (New York, 1957). An original and interesting interpretive study.

W. F. ALBRIGHT, *Archaeology of Palestine* (Harmondsworth, 1960). A study of the physical remains by a great scholar.

J. H. BREASTED, *Ancient Egyptian Religion* (New York, 1961). An illuminating study by one of the great Egyptologists.

V. GORDON CHILDE, *What Happened in History* (Baltimore, 1946). A pioneering study of human prehistory and history before the Greeks from an anthropological point of view.

HENRI FRANKFORT, *Birth of Civilization in the Near East* (New York, 1968). A good brief study of the transition to civilization.

HENRI FRANKFORT et al., *Before Philosophy* (Harmondsworth, 1949). A brilliant examination of the mind of ancient man from the Stone Age to the Greeks.

9 Frankfort et al., pp. 14–16.

10 Diels, *Fragmente der Vorsokratiker*, Fifth ed., Ed. by Walther Kranz, (Berlin, 1934–1938) Frg. 4.

11 Diels-Kranz Frgs. 14–16.

12 Against Aristogeiton, 16.

ALAN GARDINER, *Egypt of the Pharaohs* (Oxford, 1961). A sound narrative history.

O. R. GURNEY, *The Hittites* (Harmondsworth, 1954). A good general survey.

W. W. HALLO and W. K. SIMPSON, *The Ancient Near East: A History* (New York, 1971). A fine survey of Egyptian and Mesopotamian history.

JACQUETTA HAWKES, *Prehistory and the Beginning of Civilization* (London, 1963).

SAMUEL N. KRAMER, *The Sumerians: Their History, Culture and Character* (Chicago, 1963). A readable general account of Sumerian history.

S. MOSCATI, *Ancient Semitic Civilizations* (New York, 1960). A general survey of the ancient Semites.

A. T. OLMSTEAD, *History of Assyria* (New York, 1923). A good narrative account.

H. M. ORLINSKY, *Ancient Israel* (Ithaca, N.Y., 1960). Chiefly a political survey.

JAMES B. PRITCHARD (ed.), *Ancient Near Eastern Texts Relating to the Old Testament* (Princeton, 1969). A good collection of documents in translation with useful introductory material.

G. ROUX, *Ancient Iraq* (New York, 1964). A good recent account of ancient Mesopotamia.

SAMUEL SANDMEL, *The Hebrew Scriptures* (New York, 1963). An examination of the Bible's value as history and literature.

K. C. SEELE, *When Egypt Ruled the East* (Chicago, 1965). A study of Egypt in its imperial period.

ROLAND DE VAUX, *Ancient Israel: Its Life and Institutions* (New York, 1961). A fine account of social institutions.

JOHN A. WILSON, *Culture of Ancient Egypt* (Chicago, 1956). A fascinating interpretation of the civilization of ancient Egypt.

2
The Rise of Greece

WESTERN civilization began with the Greeks. In the years after Greek-speaking peoples settled the lands surrounding the Aegean Sea in the second millennium B.C., a style of life was established and ideas, values, and institutions were formed that spread far beyond the Aegean corner of the Mediterranean Sea. They later influenced and shaped Roman society. Preserved and adapted by the Romans, Greek culture powerfully influenced the society of western Europe in the Middle Ages and dominated the Byzantine Empire in the same period. The civilization emerging from this experience spread across Europe and in time crossed the Atlantic to the Western Hemisphere. The passage of time and the shrinking of distances between peoples in the modern world have helped obscure the difference between this civilization and the typical organization of man in society. It is worth noticing that this uniqueness was present from the origin of Western civilization with the Greeks.

At some time in their history the Greeks of the ancient world founded cities on every shore of the Mediterranean Sea, and pushing on through the Dardanelles, they placed many settlements on the coasts of the Black Sea in southern Russia and as far east as the approaches to the Caucasus Mountains. The center of Greek life, however, has always been the Aegean Sea and the lands in and around it. This location at the eastern end of the Mediterranean

very early put the Greeks in touch with the more advanced or earlier civilizations of the Near East: Egypt, Asia Minor, Syria–Palestine, and, through it, the rich culture of Mesopotamia. A character in one of Plato's dialogues says "Whatever the Greeks have acquired from foreigners they have, in the end, turned into something finer." [1] This proud statement indicates at least that the Greeks were aware of how much they learned from other civilizations.

The Bronze Age on Crete and on the Mainland to About 1200 B.C.
The Minoans

One source of Greek civilization is found in the culture of the large island of Crete in the Mediterranean. With Greece to the north, Egypt to the south, and Asia to the east, Crete could be the cultural bridge between the older civilizations and the new one of the Greeks. The Bronze Age came to Crete not long after 3000 B.C., and in the third and second millennia B.C. a civilization arose that powerfully influenced the islands of the Aegean and the mainland of Greece. This civilization has been given the name *Minoan*, after Minos, the legendary king of Crete.

On the basis of pottery styles and the excavated levels where the pottery and other artifacts are found, scholars have divided the Bronze Age on Crete into three major divisions and these, in turn, into three subdivisions each. Dates for Bronze Age settlements on the Greek mainland, where the term "Helladic" is used, are derived from the same chronological scheme (see table overleaf).

During the Middle and Late Minoan periods in the cities of eastern and central Crete, a civilization developed that was new and unique in its character and its beauty. Its most striking feature is presented by the palaces uncovered at such sites as Phaestus, Haghia Triada, and, most important, Cnossus. These palaces were built around a central court with a labyrinth of rooms sur-

The funeral games of Patroclus. According to the story in Homer's *Iliad*, Patroclus was the close friend of Achilles, a hero of the Greeks in their ten-year war with the Trojans. Patroclus was killed in battle. After his death was mourned, he was then celebrated in a rousing series of games among the Greeks camped before Troy. On this fragment of a painted vase, the enthusiastic crowd of Greek soldiers is enjoying the races. The vase was painted by Sophilus, who worked between 590 and 570 B.C. [TAP–National Archaeological Museum, Athens.]

1 Plato, *Epinomis*, 987 d.

33

Minoan pottery. This vase is a good example of the fine Minoan pottery that has been found on Crete. It shows an octopus amid seaweed and cuttlefish. It belongs to the late Minoan period (1400–1150 B.C.) and comes from Gournia; it is now in the museum at Heraklion, Crete. [TAP–Art Reference Bureau.]

snake has symbolism

Snakes had religious

They shed
Gave life
Took life

(Cobra)

Minoan snake goddess. This gold and ivory statuette, dated to the sixteenth century B.C., gives evidence of the remarkable grace of Minoan art and of the wealth that was a part of Minoan society. [Courtesy of the Museum of Fine Arts, Boston; gift of Mrs. W. Scott Fitz.]

EARLY MINOAN, 2900–2100 B.C.	EARLY HELLADIC, 2900–1900 B.C.
MIDDLE MINOAN, 2000–1575 B.C.	MIDDLE HELLADIC, 1900–1580 B.C.
LATE MINOAN, 1575–1050 B.C.	LATE HELLADIC, 1580–1150 B.C.
LATE MINOAN I, 1757–1500 B.C.	LATE HELLADIC I, 1580–1500 B.C.
LATE MINOAN II, 1500–1400 B.C.	LATE HELLADIC II, 1500–1425 B.C.
LATE MINOAN III, 1400–1150 B.C.	LATE HELLADIC III, 1425–1150 B.C.

rounding it. Some sections of the palace at Cnossus were as much as four stories high. The basement contained many storage rooms for oil and grain, apparently paid as taxes to the king. The main and upper floors contained living quarters as well as workshops for making pottery and jewelry. There were sitting rooms and even bathrooms, to which water was piped through excellent plumbing. The ceilings were supported by lovely columns, which tapered downward, and many of the walls carried murals showing landscapes and seascapes, festivals, and sports. The palace design and the paintings show the influence of Syria, Asia Minor, and Egypt, but the style and quality are unique to Crete.

Along with palaces, paintings, pottery, jewelry, and other valuable objects, writing of three distinct kinds was found. The first was pictographic, called hieroglyphic, though the script is not Egyptian and is still unreadable. The other two are linear scripts simply called A and B. Linear A is clearly the older of the two, from which

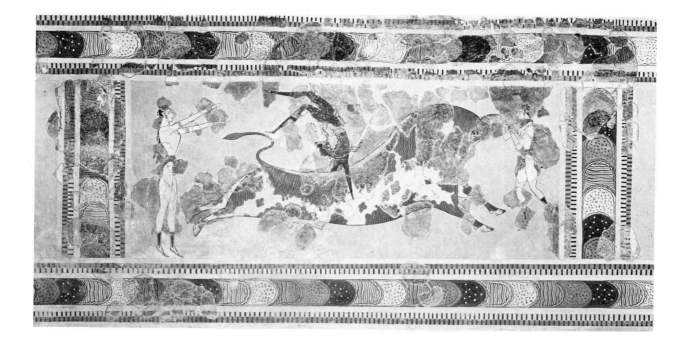

Linear B developed. It is found at various sites on Crete, but nowhere else. On the island, Linear B is found only at Cnossus, but it appears at many places on the mainland. We cannot read Linear A, but in 1953 Linear B was deciphered to the satisfaction of most scholars and proved to be an early form of Greek. The script is written on clay tablets like those found in Mesopotamia. They were preserved accidentally, being hardened in a great fire that destroyed the palace. They reveal an organization centered on the palace in which the king ruled and was served by an extensive bureaucracy who kept remarkably detailed records. We learn how much individual citizens owed the king in agricultural products and livestock. A certain Dunios, for instance, owed the palace 2,200 liters of barley, 526 of olives, 568 of wine, 15 rams, 8 yearlings, 1 ewe, 13 he-goats, 12 pigs, 1 fat hog, 1 cow, and 2 bulls. This sort of organization is typical of what we find in the Near East but nothing like what we will see among the Greeks, yet the inventories are written in a form of Greek. Why should Minoans, who were not Greek, write in a language not their own? This question raises the larger one of what the relationship was between Crete and the Greek mainland in the Bronze Age and leads us to an examination of mainland, or Helladic, culture.

The Mycenaeans

In the third millennium B.C. most of the Greek mainland, including many of the sites of later Greek cities, was settled by people who used metal, built some impressive houses, and traded with Crete and the islands of the Aegean. The names they gave to places, which were

The palace of Minos at Cnossus, Crete. This is a labyrinthine complex of rooms and courts dating from around the middle of the second millenium B.C. ABOVE: The bull fresco; this mural shows youths leaping over a charging bull as part of what is thought to have been a religious ritual. [SCALA/ Editorial Photocolor Archives.] BELOW: A portal (partially reconstructed); notice the characteristic and unusual downward-tapering columns. [Bettmann Archive.]

Solid hammering Gold wore on face

reflecting warfare

sometimes preserved by later invaders, make it clear that they were not Greeks and spoke a language that was not Indo-European. These may have been the people the Greeks later called Pelasgians, and they probably came from Asia Minor.

Not long after the year 2000 B.C. many of the Early Helladic sites were destroyed by fire, some were abandoned, and still others appear to have yielded peacefully to an invading people. The newcomers were characterized by the use of a distinctive new pottery that we call *Minyan ware.* They were characterized by new forms of burial, different types of houses, and an increased use of bronze. Because there was no significant cultural break until the end of the Bronze Age, and because we know that the Late Helladic people spoke Greek, the likelihood is that the beginning of the Middle Helladic period signaled the arrival of the Greeks.

The invaders succeeded in establishing control of the entire mainland, and the shaft graves cut into the rock at the royal palace–fortress of Mycenae show that they prospered and sometimes became very rich. Some of these graves contained gold, jewels, ivory, and other luxuries that testify to the power and wealth accumulated by the kings buried there. At Mycenae and all over

ABOVE LEFT: Mycenaean mask. This is one of the startling masks, some of them of gold, found at excavations of sites at Mycenae that date from before the middle of the second millenium B.C. [Greek National Tourist Organization, New York.]

ABOVE: Mycenaean warriors. This fragmentary painted vase from the last phase of the Mycenaean period—probably from the thirteenth century B.C. —shows the development of well-ordered infantry with spears, shields, and armor. [TAP–National Archaeological Museum, Athens.]

BELOW: Early Helladic pottery. These early jugs come from Zigouries near the city of Corinth in Greece; they are dated to the years 2200–2000 B.C. and were used by the early inhabitants of the Greek mainland, people whom the later-arriving Greeks called Pelasgians. [Metropolitan Museum of Art, New York; gift of the Greek Government, 1927.]

storage

pouring heavy liquid

pouring light liquid

Mycenae: The lion gate. This is the entrance to the palace of the Mycenaean kings who dominated the Greek mainland in the late Helladic period (*ca.* 1580–1150 B.C.). [Bettmann Archive.]

Greece there was a smooth transition between the Middle and Late Helladic periods. At Mycenae the richest finds come from the period after 1600 B.C. and from the beginning of the Late Helladic period. The city's wealth and power reached their peak during this time, and the culture of all mainland Greece during the Late Helladic period goes by the name *Mycenaean.*

The excavation of Mycenaean sites reveals a culture influenced by, but very different from, the Minoan culture. Mycenae and Pylos were built some distance from the sea, like Cnossus. It is plain, however, that defense against attack was foremost in the minds of the founders. Both cities are built on hills in a position commanding the neighboring territory. They are surrounded by enormously powerful walls of a style called *Cyclopean,* for they seem to have required the strength of the gigantic mythological Cyclopes to lift the huge boulders into place. In troubled times cisterns were dug to hold enough

Mycenae: The "treasury of Atreus." In spite of its picturesque but inaccurate name, this is actually the entryway (*dromos*) to the *tholos,* or beehive tomb, of a Mycenaean king for whom it was built some time after 1350 B.C.

The Bronze Age on Crete and on the Mainland to About 1200 B.C. 37

A Linear B tablet. This is a clay tablet from sandy Pylos in the western Peloponnesus on the Greek mainland, dated about 1200 B.C. The language on it was deciphered only about thirty years ago by Michael Ventris, who showed it to be an early Greek dialect. The tablet is part of a palace inventory listing different kinds of vases. It survived because it was baked when the palace at Pylos was burned by invading strangers. It is now in the Athens museum. [TAP-Art Reference Bureau.]

It was hard after burned

water to withstand prolonged siege. The Mycenaean people were warriors, as their art, architecture, and weapons reveal. The success of their campaigns and the defense of their territory required strong central authority, and all our evidence shows that the kings provided it. Their palaces, in which the royal family and its retainers lived, were located within the walls; most of the population lived outside the walls. The palace walls were usually covered with paintings, like those on Crete, but instead of peaceful scenery and games, the Mycenaean murals depicted scenes of war and boar hunting.

About 1500 B.C. the already impressive shaft graves were abandoned in favor of *tholos* tombs. They were large, beehivelike chambers cut into the hillside, built of enormous, well-cut, and fitted stones, and approached by an unroofed passage (*dromos*) cut horizontally into the side of the hill. The lintel block alone of one of these tombs weighs over a hundred tons. Only a strong king whose wealth was great, whose power was unquestioned, and who commanded the labor of many men could undertake such a project. His wealth came from plundering raids, piracy, and trade. Some of this trade went westward to Italy and Sicily, but most of it was with the islands of the Aegean, the coastal towns of Asia Minor, and the cities of Syria, Egypt, and Crete. The Mycenaeans sent pottery, olive oil, and animal hides in exchange for jewels and other luxuries.

The decipherment of Linear B makes it possible for us to examine Mycenaean society and its organization more closely, for tablets containing that script are found all over the mainland from the Mycenaean period; the largest and most useful collection was found at Pylos. The tablets at Pylos reveal a world very similar to the one shown by the Linear B records at Cnossus. The king, whose title was *wanax*, held a royal domain, appointed officials, commanded servants, and kept a close record of what he owned and what was owed to him. This evidence confirms all the rest: the Mycenaean world was made up of a number of independent, powerful, and well-organized monarchies.

The Linear B tablets at Cnossus seem to belong to Late Minoan III, so that the great "palace period" at Cnossus came after an invasion by Mycenaeans in 1400 B.C. These Greek invaders inhabited a flourishing Crete until the end of the Bronze Age, and there is good reason to believe that at the height of Mycenaean power, 1400–1200 B.C., Crete was part of the Mycenaean world.

These were prosperous and active years for the Mycenaeans. Their cities were enlarged, their trade grew, and they even established commercial colonies in the east. They are mentioned in the archives of the Hittite kings of Asia Minor. They are named as marauders of the Nile Delta in the Egyptian records, and sometime about 1250 B.C. they probably sacked the city of Troy on the coast of northwestern Asia Minor, giving rise to the epic poems of Homer. Around the year 1200 B.C., however, the Mycenaean world showed signs of great trouble, and by 1100 B.C. it was gone, its palaces destroyed, many of its cities abandoned, and its art, its pattern of life, its system of writing buried and forgotten. How was the Mycenaean world destroyed?

Modern scholars have suggested theories explaining the destruction of Mycenaean civilization by means of a natural disaster. Some believe that the destruction of Cnossus and the Minoan culture was caused by the volcanic explosion of the Aegean island of Thera (modern Santorini), which blackened and poisoned the air for many miles around and sent a monstrous tidal wave to destroy the great palace civilization. Others think that the explosion took place about 1200 B.C. and explain the destruction of Bronze Age culture throughout the Aegean as a result of it. This explanation has the convenient consequence of ending Minoan and Mycenaean civilizations with one blow, but the evidence does not allow it. The Mycenaean towns were not destroyed at one time; many fell around 1200 B.C., but some flourished for another century, and the Athens of the period was never destroyed or abandoned.

No theory of natural disaster holds, and we are left to seek less dramatic explanations. The Greeks believed in a

BLACK SEA
MACEDONIA
THRACE
AXIUS
STRYMON
PINDUS MOUNTAINS
EPIRUS
THASOS
SAMOTHRACE
IMBROS
MT. ATHOS
LEMNOS
MT. OLYMPUS
TENEDOS
Troy
MYSIA
ASIA MINOR
CORCYRA
Dodona
Sesklo
Iolcus
Dimini
IONIAN SEA
AEGEAN SEA
THESSALY
ACHELOUS
LEUCAS
LESBOS
SKYROS
ITHACA
Orchomenus
Delphi
EUBOEA
CHIOS
Phocaea
LYDIA
HERMUS
CEPHALLENIA
BOEOTIA
Thebes
G. OF CORINTH
Eleusis
Colophon
ZACYNTHUS
Corinth
Athens
ATTICA
ANDROS
SAMOS
CAYSTER
Ephesus
Olympia
Mycenae
Tiryns
Asine
Lerna
CEUS
TENOS
ICARIA
MAEANDER
AEGINA
Miletus
PELOPONNESUS
MYKONOS
DELOS
CARIA
Sparta
Vaphio
Pylos
SERIPHOS
PHYLAKOPI
PAROS
NAXOS
COS
ANDROS
MELOS
THERA
CYTHERA
RHODES
CRETAN SEA
CARPATHOS
Cnossus
Gournia
CRETE
Zakro
Hagia Triada
Phaestus
MEDITERRANEAN SEA
100 MI.
100 KM.
T R MILLER

THE AEGEAN AREA IN THE BRONZE AGE

The Bronze Age in the Aegean area lasted from about 1900 to about 1100 B.C. Its culture on Crete is called Minoan and was at its height about 1900–1400 B.C. Bronze Age Helladic culture on the mainland flourished from about 1600 to 1200 B.C.

legend that told of the Dorians, a rude people from the north who spoke a different Greek dialect from that of the Mycenaean peoples. They joined with one of the tribes, the Heraclidae, in an attack on the southern Greek peninsula of Peloponnesus, which was repulsed. One hundred years later they returned and gained full control. This legend of "the return of the Heraclidae" has been identified by modern historians with the Dorian invasion, the incursion from the north into Greece by a less civilized Greek people speaking the Dorian dialect. The chances are good that the end of the Bronze Age in the Aegean came about gradually over the century between 1200 B.C. and 1100 B.C. as a result of internal conflict among the Mycenaean kings and because of continuous pressure from outsiders, who raided, infiltrated, and eventually dominated Greece and its neighboring islands. Cnossus, Mycenae, and Pylos were buried, their secrets to be kept for over three thousand years.

The Greek "Middle Ages"
to About 800 B.C.

The immediate effects of the Dorian invasion were disastrous for the inhabitants of the Mycenaean world. The palaces and the kings and bureaucrats who managed them were destroyed. The wealth and organization that had supported the artists and merchants were likewise swept away by a barbarous people who did not have the knowledge or social organization to maintain them. Many villages were abandoned and never resettled. Some of their inhabitants probably turned to a nomadic life, and many perished. The population of Greece in 1000 B.C. was surely much smaller than it had been three hundred years earlier.

Another result of the invasion was the spread of the Greek people eastward from the mainland to the Aegean islands and the coast of Asia Minor. The Dorians themselves, after occupying most of the Peloponnesus, swept across the Aegean to occupy the southern islands and the southern part of the Anatolian coast. They drove before them refugees fleeing their fury. Some of these emigrants settled in Attica, which successfully resisted Dorian attack. Most of the emigrants, however, continued eastward.

These migrations made the Aegean a Greek lake, but trade with the old civilizations of the Near East was virtually ended, nor was there much trade between different parts of Greece. The Greeks were forced to turn inward, and each community was left largely to its own devices. This happened at a time when the Near East was also in disarray, and no great power arose to impose its ways and its will on the helpless people who lived about the Aegean. These circumstances allowed the Greeks time to recover from their disaster and to create their unique style of life.

This period in Greek history is dark, for our knowledge of it rests on very limited sources. Writing disappeared after the fall of Mycenae and no new script

appeared until after 750 B.C., so we have no contemporary author to shed light on this period. Excavation reveals no architecture, sculpture, or painting until after 750 B.C.

The Age of Homer

For a picture of society in these "dark ages" the best source is Homer. His epic poems tell of the heroes who captured Troy, men of the Mycenaean age, but the world described in those poems clearly is a different one. Homer's heroes are not buried in *tholos* tombs but are cremated; they worship gods in temples whereas the Mycenaeans had no temples; they have chariots but do not know their proper use in warfare. The poems of Homer are the result of an oral tradition that went back into the Mycenaean age. Through the centuries bards sang tales of the heroes who fought at Troy, using verse arranged in rhythmic formulas to aid the memory. In this way some very old material was preserved until the poems were finally written, no sooner than the eighth century B.C., but the society these old oral poems describe seems to be that of the tenth and ninth centuries B.C.

In the Homeric poems the power of the kings is much smaller than that of the Mycenaean rulers. The ability of the kings to make important decisions was limited by the need to consult the council of nobles. The nobles felt free to discuss matters in vigorous language and in opposition

Odysseus Addresses Nobles and Commoners: Homeric Society

The *Iliad* was probably composed about 750 B.C. In this passage Odysseus is trying to stop the Greeks at Troy from fleeing to their ships and returning to their homes. The difference in his treatment of nobles and commoners is striking.

WHENEVER *he found one that was a captain and a man of mark, he stood by his side, and refrained him with gentle words: "Good sir, it is not seemly to affright thee like a coward, but do thou sit thyself and make all thy folk sit down. For thou knowest not yet clearly what is the purpose of Atreus' son; now is he but making trial, and soon he will afflict the sons of the Achaians. And heard we not all of us what he spake in the council? Beware lest in his anger he evilly entreat the sons of the Achaians. For proud is the soul of heaven-fostered kings; because their honour is of Zeus, and the god of counsel loveth them."*

But whatever man of the people he saw and found him shouting, him he drave with his sceptre and chode him with loud words: "Good sir, sit still and hearken to the words of others that are thy betters; but thou art no warrior, and a weakling, never reckoned whether in battle or in council. In no wise can we Achaians all be kings here. A multitude of masters is no good thing; let there be one master, one king, to whom the son of crooked-counselling Kronos hath granted it. . . ."

Homer, *The Iliad*, translated by A. Lang, W. Leaf, and E. Myers (New York: Random House, n.d.), pp. 24–25.

---

to the king's wishes. Achilles did not hesitate to address Agamemnon, the "most kingly" commander of the Trojan expedition, in these words: "thou with face of dog and heart of deer . . . folk devouring king." Such language may have been impolite, but it was not treasonous. The king, on the other hand, was free to ignore the council's advice, but it was risky to do so.

The right to speak in council was limited to noblemen, but the common people could not be ignored. If a king planned a war or a major change of policy during a campaign, he would not fail to call the common soldiers to an assembly, where they could listen and express their feelings by acclamation, even though they could not take part in the debate. The evidence of Homer shows that even in these early times the Greeks, unlike their predecessors and contemporaries, practiced limited constitutional government.

Homeric society, nevertheless, was sharply divided into classes, the most important division being the one between nobles and commoners. We do not know the origin of the distinction, but we cannot doubt that at this time Greek society was aristocratic. Birth determined noble status, and wealth usually accompanied it. Below the nobles were the peasants, the landless laborers, and the slaves. We cannot tell whether the peasant owned the land he worked outright and so was free to sell it or if he worked a hereditary plot that belonged to his clan and was therefore not his to dispose of as he chose. It is clear, however, that he worked hard to eke out a living.

Far worse was the condition of the laborer. The slave, at least, was attached to a family household and so was protected and fed. In a world where membership in a settled group gave the only security, the laborers were desperately vulnerable. Slaves were few in number and were mostly women, who served as maids and concubines. Some male slaves worked as shepherds. Few, if any, worked in agriculture, which depended on free labor throughout Greek history.

The Homeric poems hold up a mirror to this society, and they reflect an aristocratic code of values that powerfully influenced all future Greek thought. In classical times Homer was the schoolbook of the Greeks. They memorized his text, settled diplomatic disputes by citing passages in it, and emulated the behavior and cherished the values they found in it. Those values were physical prowess, courage, and fierce protection of one's family, friends, property, and, above all, one's personal honor and reputation. Returning home after his wanderings, Odysseus ruthlessly kills all the suitors of his wife because they have used up his wealth, wooed his wife, scorned his son, and so dishonored him. Speed of foot, strength, and most of all excellence at fighting in battle are what make a man great, yet Achilles leaves the battle and allows his fellow Greeks to be slain and almost defeated because Agamemnon has wounded his honor by taking away his battle prize. He returns not out of a sense of duty to the army but because his dear friend Patroclus has been killed. In each case the hero seeks to display the highest virtue of Homeric society, *arētē*—manliness, courage in the most general sense, and the excellence proper to a hero.

This quality was best revealed in a contest or *agon*. Homeric battles are not primarily group combats but a series of individual contests between great champions. One of the prime forms of entertainment is the athletic contest, and the funeral of Patroclus is celebrated by such a contest. The central ethical idea in Homer can be found in the instructions that the father of Achilles gives to his son when he sends him off to fight at Troy: "Always be the best and distinguished above others." Glaucus' father has given his son exactly the same orders and has added to them the injunction "do not bring shame on the family of your fathers who were by far the best in Ephyre and in wide Lycia." Here in a nutshell we have the chief values of the aristocrats of Homer's world: to vie for individual supremacy in *arētē* and to defend and increase the honor of the family. They would remain prominent aristocratic values long after Homeric society was only a memory.

The *Polis*

The characteristic Greek institution was the *polis*. The attempt to translate that word as "city-state" is misleading, for it says both too much and too little. All Greek *poleis* began as little more than agricultural villages or towns, and many stayed that way, so the word *city* is inappropriate. All of them were states, in the sense of being independent political units, but they were much more than that. The *polis* was thought of as a community of relatives; all its citizens, who were theoretically descended from a common ancestor, belonged to subgroups such as phratries, clans, and tribes, and worshiped the gods in common ceremonies.

Aristotle argued that the *polis* was a natural growth and that man was by his nature "an animal who lives in a *polis*." Man alone has the power of speech and from it derives the ability to distinguish good from bad and right from wrong, "and the sharing of these things is what

Aristotle Writes About Justice and Justifies the Polis

Aristotle (384–322 B.C.) wrote his *Politics*, from which these excerpts are drawn, about three hundred years after the rise of the *polis*, when it was beginning to lose its central position in the Greek way of life. Nonetheless, the account remains the best and fullest justification for the *polis*.

I T I S *evident, that a state is one of the works of nature, and that man is naturally a political animal, and that whosoever is naturally, and not accidentally, unfit for society, must be either inferior or superior to man; just as the person reviled in Homer,*

"No tribe, nor state, nor home hath he."

For he whose nature is such as this, must needs be a lover of strife, and as solitary as a bird of prey. It is clear, then, that man is truly a more social animal than bees, or any of the herding cattle; for nature, as we say, does nothing in vain, and man is the only animal who has reason. . . . In this particular man differs from other animals, that he alone has a perception of good and evil, of justice and injustice, and it is the interchange of these common sentiments which forms a family and a city. . . .

There is then in all persons a natural impetus to associate with each other in this manner, and he who first established civil society was the cause of the greatest benefit; for as man, thus perfected, is the most excellent of all living beings, so without law and justice he would be the worst of all; for nothing is so savage as injustice in arms; but man is born with a faculty of gaining himself arms by prudence and virtue; arms which yet he may apply to the most opposite purposes. And hence he who is devoid of virtue will be the most wicked and cruel, the most lustful and gluttonous being imaginable. Now justice is a social virtue; for it is the rule of the social state, and the very criterion of what is right.

Aristotle, *Politics and Economics*, trans. by E. Walford (London: Bell and Daldy, 1866), pp. 6–8.

makes a household and a *polis*." A man, therefore, who is incapable of sharing these things or is so self-sufficient that he has no need of them is not a man at all, but either a wild beast or a god. Without law and justice man is the worst and most dangerous of the animals. With them he can be the best, and justice exists only in the *polis*. These high claims were made in the fourth century B.C., hundreds of years after the *polis* came into existence, but they

Hoplites, or heavily armed infantrymen—the standard fighting men of the Greek city-state—donning armor. Their equipment included greaves, breastplate, helmet, and large shield. Attic cup, early fifth century B.C. [Kunsthistorisches Museum, Vienna.]

accurately reflect an attitude that was present from the first.

Development of the Polis

Originally the word *polis* referred only to a citadel, an elevated, defensible rock to which the farmers of the neighboring area could retreat in case of attack. The Acropolis in Athens and the hill called Acrocorinth in Corinth are examples. For some time such high places and the adjacent farms comprised the *polis*. The towns grew gradually and without planning, as the narrowness and winding, disorderly character of their streets show. For centuries they had no city walls. Unlike the city-states of the Near East, their sites were not chosen because of commercial convenience on rivers or the sea, nor did they grow up around a temple to serve the needs of priests and to benefit from the needs of worshipers. The availability of farmland and of a natural fortress determined their location. They were placed either well inland or far enough away from the sea to avoid piratical raids. Only later and gradually did the *agora* appear. It grew to be not only a marketplace but also a civic center and the heart of the Greeks' remarkable social life, which was distinguished by conversation and argument carried on in the open air.

Some *poleis* probably came into existence early in the eighth century B.C. The institution was certainly common by the middle of that century, for all the colonies that were established by the Greeks in the years after 750 B.C. took the form of the *polis*. Once the new institution had been fully established, true monarchy disappeared. Vestigial kings survived in some places, but they were almost always only ceremonial figures without power. The original form of the *polis* was an aristocratic republic dominated by the nobility through its council of nobles and its monopoly of the magistracies.

The Hoplite Phalanx

A new militant technique was crucial for the development of the *polis*. In earlier times the brunt of the fighting had been carried on by small troops of cavalry and individual "champions" who first threw their spears and then came to close quarters with swords. Toward the end of the eighth century B.C., however, the hoplite phalanx came into being. It remained the basis of Greek warfare thereafter.

The hoplite was a heavily armed infantryman who fought with a sword and a pike about nine feet long. These soldiers were formed into a phalanx in close order, usually at least eight ranks deep. The hoplite thrust with his pike in his right hand, protecting himself with the shield in his left. This method exposed his right side to the enemy's thrust, but the close order allowed him to find safety beneath the extended portion of the shield of the man on his right. Only the man on the extreme right was unprotected, and that position of greatest danger was

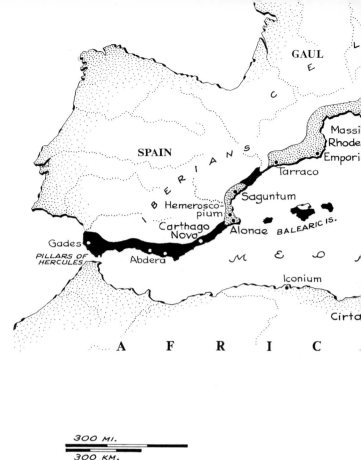

Most of the coast line of the Mediterranean and Black Seas was populated by Greek or Phoenician colonies. The Phoenicians were a commercial people who planted their colonies in North Africa, Spain, Sicily, and Sardinia, chiefly in the ninth century B.C. The height of Greek colonization came later, between about 750 and 550 B.C.

also the place of honor, reserved for an experienced and excellent warrior. So long as the hoplites fought bravely and held their ground, there would be few casualties and no defeat, but if they gave way, the result was usually a rout. The clumsy shield made running difficult, so retreating soldiers had to discard their shields. But without his shield the hoplite was vulnerable and useless. All depended on the discipline, strength, and courage of the individual soldier. At its best the phalanx could withstand cavalry charges and defeat infantries not as well protected or disciplined. Until defeated by the Roman legion, it was the dominant military force in the eastern Mediterranean.

The usual hoplite battle in Greece was between the armies of two *poleis* quarreling over a piece of land. One army invaded the territory of the other at a time when the crops were almost ready for harvest. The defending army had no choice but to protect its fields. If the army was beaten, its fields were captured or destroyed and its people might starve. In every way the phalanx was a communal effort that relied not on the extraordinary actions of the individual but on the courage of a considerable portion of the citizens. The phalanx and the *polis* arose together, and both heralded the decline of the kings. The phalanx, however, was not made up only of aristocrats. Most of the hoplites were peasants working relatively small farms. The immediate beneficiaries of the royal decline were the aristocrats, but because the existence of the *polis* depended on the small farmer, his wishes could not for long be wholly ignored. The rise of the hoplite phalanx created a bond between the aristocrats and the peasants who fought in it, and this bond helps explain why class conflicts were muted for some time. It also guaranteed, however, that the aristocrats, who dominated at first, would not always be unchallenged.

Importance of the *Polis*

The Greeks looked to the *polis* for peace, order, prosperity, and honor in their lifetime. They counted on it to preserve their memory and honor their descendants after death. Some of them came to see it not only as the ruler,

PHOENICIAN AND GREEK

but as the molder of men. It is easy to understand the pride and scorn that underlie the comparison made by the poet Phocylides between the Greek state and the capital of the great and powerful Assyrian Empire: "A little *polis* living orderly in a high place is stronger than a block-headed Nineveh."

Expansion of the Greek World

From the middle of the eighth century B.C. until well into the sixth, the Greeks vastly expanded the territory they controlled, their wealth, and their contacts with other peoples in a burst of colonizing activity that placed *poleis* from Spain to the Black Sea. A century earlier a few Greeks established trading posts in Syria. There they learned new techniques in the arts and crafts and much more from the older civilizations of the Near East. About 750 B.C. they borrowed a writing system from one of the Semitic scripts and added vowels to create the first true alphabet. The new Greek alphabet was easier to learn than any earlier writing system and made possible the widely literate society of classical Greece.

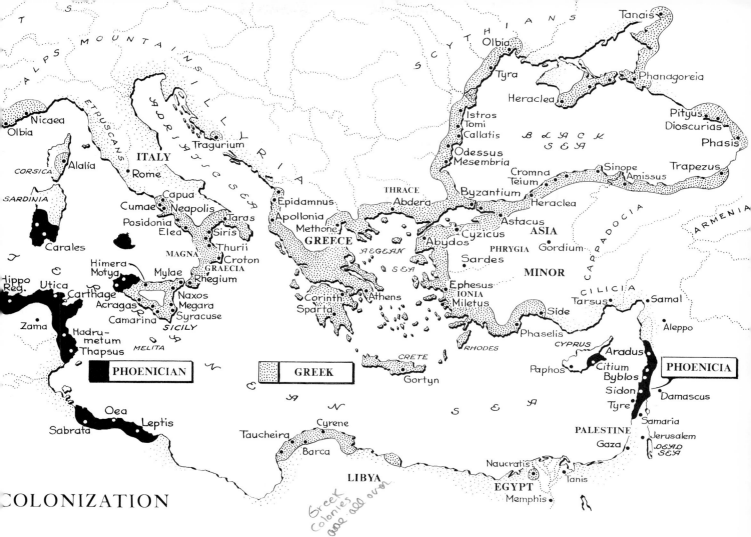

COLONIZATION

Greek Colonies all over

Syria and its neighboring territory were too strong to penetrate, so the Greeks settled the southern coast of Macedonia and the Chalcidic peninsula. These regions were sparsely settled, and the natives were not well enough organized to resist the Greek colonists. Southern Italy and eastern Sicily were even more inviting areas. Before long there were so many Greek colonies in Italy and Sicily that the Romans called the whole region *Magna Graecia* ("Great Greece"). The Greeks also put colonies in Spain and southern France. In the seventh century B.C. Greek colonists settled the coasts of the northeastern Mediterranean, the Black Sea, and the straits connecting them. About the same time they established settlements on the eastern part of the northern African coast. The Greeks now had outposts throughout the Mediterranean world.

The Greeks did not lightly leave home to join a colony. The voyage by sea was dangerous and uncomfortable, and at the end of it were uncertainty and danger. Only powerful pressures like overpopulation and land hunger drove thousands of Greeks from their homes to found new *poleis*. The Greek word for colony is *apoikia*, literally, "away home." The colony, though sponsored by the mother city, was established for the good of the colonists rather than for the benefit of those who sent it out. The colony often copied the constitution from home, worshiped the same gods at the same festivals in the same way, and carried on a busy trade with the mother city. Most colonies, though independent, were friendly with their mother cities. Each might ask the other for aid in time of trouble and expect to receive a friendly hearing, although neither was obliged to help.

Colonization had a powerful influence on Greek life. By relieving the pressure of a growing population, it was a safety valve that allowed the *poleis* to escape civil wars. By emphasizing the differences between the Greeks and the new peoples they met, colonization gave the Greeks a sense of cultural identity and fostered a Panhellenic spirit that led to the establishment of a number of common religious festivals. The most important ones were at Olympia, Delphi, Corinth, and Nemea.

Colonization also encouraged trade and industry. The

influx of new wealth from abroad and the increased demand for goods from the homeland stimulated a more intensive use of the land and an emphasis on crops for export, chiefly the olive and the wine grape. The manufacture of pottery, tools, weapons, and fine artistic metalwork as well as perfumed oil, the soap of the ancient Mediterranean world, was likewise encouraged. New opportunities allowed some men, sometimes outside the nobility, to become wealthy and important. These newly enriched men became a troublesome element in the aristocratic *poleis*, for they had an increasingly important part in the life of their states but were barred from political power, religious privileges, and social acceptance by the ruling aristocrats. These conditions soon created a crisis in many states.

The Tyrants (About 700–500 B.C.)

The crisis produced by the new economic and social conditions usually led to or intensified factional divisions within the ruling aristocracy. In the years between 700 and 550 B.C. the result was often the establishment of a tyranny.

A tyrant was a monarch who had gained power in an unorthodox but not necessarily wicked way and exercised a strong one-man rule that might well be beneficent and popular. For instance, the mythical Oedipus, in the play by Sophocles, became *tyrannos* because he took power in Thebes by solving the puzzles of the sphinx; he was an excellent ruler who was beloved by his people. The later evil reputation of tyranny was generally not earned by its founders, whose rise was usually popular and whose reign was usually successful. By the second or third generation, however, the tyrant was rarely as popular or as effective as the founder of the tyranny and therefore had to resort to harsh measures to keep power.

The founding tyrant was usually a member of the ruling aristocracy who either had a personal grievance or led an unsuccessful faction. He often rose to power because of his military ability and support from the hoplites.

Tyrtaeus Describes Excellence: Code of the Citizen Soldier

The military organization of citizen soldiers for the defense of the *polis* and the idea of the *polis* itself, which permeated Greek political thought, found echoes in Greek lyric poetry. A major example is this poem by Tyrtaeus, a Spartan lyricist who wrote about 625 B.C. It gives important evidence on the nature of warfare in the phalanx and the values taught by the *polis*.

I WOULD *not say anything for a man nor take account of him*
    for any speed of his feet or wrestling skill he might have,
not if he had the size of a Cyclops and strength to go with it,
    not if he could outrun Bóreas, the North Wind of Thrace,
not if he were more handsome and gracefully formed than Tithónos,
    or had more riches than Midas had, or Kínyras too,
not if he were more of a king than Tantalid Pelops,
    or had the power of speech and persuasion Adrastos had,
not if he had all splendors except for a fighting spirit.
    For no man ever proves himself a good man in war
unless he can endure to face the blood and the slaughter,
    go close against the enemy and fight with his hands.
Here is courage, mankind's finest possession, here is
    the noblest prize that a young man can endeavor to win,
and it is a good thing his city and all the people share with him
    when a man plants his feet and stands in the foremost spears
relentlessly, all thought of foul flight completely forgotten,
    and has well trained his heart to be steadfast and to endure,
and with words encourages the man who is stationed beside him.
    Here is a man who proves himself to be valiant in war.
With a sudden rush he turns to flight the rugged battalions
    of the enemy, and sustains the beating waves of assault.
And he who so falls among the champions and loses his sweet life,
    so blessing with honor his city, his father, and all his people,

The hoplite phalanx. This vase painting from the so-called "Chigi" vase is the earliest surviving picture of the new style of close-order, heavily armed infantry adopted by the Greeks toward the end of the eighth century B.C. Notice the large circular shields, helmets, greaves, body armor, raised spears, and the close order of the soldiers. The flute player provides music to help keep the soldiers in step.
[Hirmer Fotoarchiv München.]

with wounds in his chest, where the spear that he was facing has transfixed
    that massive guard of his shield, and gone through his breastplate as well,
why, such a man is lamented alike by the young and the elders,
    and all his city goes into mourning and grieves for his loss.
His tomb is pointed to with pride, and so are his children,
    and his children's children, and afterward all the race that is his.
His shining glory is never forgotten, his name is remembered,
    and he becomes an immortal, though he lies under the ground,
when one who was a brave man has been killed by the furious War God
    standing his ground and fighting hard for his children and land.
But if he escapes the doom of death, the destroyer of bodies,
    and wins his battle, and bright renown for the work of his spear,
all men give place to him alike, the youth and the elders,
    and much joy comes his way before he goes down to the dead.
Aging he has reputation among his citizens. No one tries to interfere with his honors or all he deserves;
all men withdraw before his presence, and yield their seats to him,
    and youth, and the men of his age, and even those older than he.
Thus a man should endeavor to reach this high place of courage
    with all his heart, and, so trying, never be backward in war.

Greek Lyrics, trans. by Richmond Lattimore (Chicago: University of Chicago Press, 1949, 1955, 1950), pp. 14–15.

He generally had the support of the politically powerless group of newly wealthy men and of the poor peasants as well. When he took power, he often expelled many of his aristocratic opponents and divided at least some of their land among his supporters. He pleased his commercial and industrial supporters by destroying the privileges of the old aristocracy and by fostering trade and colonization.

The tyrants presided over a period of population growth that saw an increase especially in the number of city dwellers. They responded with a program of public works that included improvement of the drainage systems, care for the water supply, the construction and organization of marketplaces, the building and strengthening of city walls, and the erection of temples. They introduced new local festivals and elaborated the old ones. They were active in the patronage of the arts, supporting poets and artisans with gratifying results. All this activity contributed to the tyrant's popularity, to the prosperity of his city, and to his self-esteem.

In most cases the tyrant's rule was secured by a personal bodyguard and by mercenary soldiers. An armed citizenry, necessary for an aggressive foreign policy, would have been dangerous, so the tyrants usually pursued a program of peaceful alliances with other tyrants abroad and avoided war.

End of the Tyrants

By the end of the sixth century B.C. tyranny had disappeared from the Greek states and did not return again in the same form or for the same reasons. The last tyrants were universally hated for the cruelty and repression they employed. They left bitter memories in their own states and became objects of fear and hatred everywhere. Apart from the outrages committed by individual tyrants, there was something about the very concept of tyranny that was inimical to the idea of the *polis*. The notion of the *polis* as a community to which every member must be responsible, the connection of justice with that community, and the natural aristocratic hatred of

This Athenian inscription, scratched on an Attic geometric jug dated about 725 B.C. is the earliest known
example of writing in Attica. Slightly earlier writings
in the Greek alphabet and language have been found
elsewhere, none dated before about 750 B.C. [Dr. L. H.
Jeffery, Oxford University.]

monarchy all made tyranny seem alien and offensive. The
rule of a tyrant, however beneficent, was arbitrary and
unpredictable. Tyranny came into being in defiance of
tradition and law and governed without either. Above all,
the tyrant was not answerable in any way to his fellow
citizens.

From a longer perspective, however, it is clear that the
tyrants made important contributions to the development
of Greek civilization. They put an end for a time to the
crippling civil wars that threatened the survival of the
aristocratic *poleis*. In general, they reduced the warfare
between the states. They encouraged the economic
changes that were necessary for the future prosperity of
Greece. They increased the degree of communication
with the rest of the Mediterranean world and made an
enormous contribution to the cultivation of crafts and
technology, as well as of the arts and literature. Most
important of all, they broke the grip of the aristocracy
and put the productive powers of the most active and
talented of its citizens fully at the service of the *polis*.

SUGGESTED READINGS

A. ANDREWES, *Greek Tyrants* (New York, 1963). A clear
and concise account of tyranny in early Greece.
A. ANDREWES, *The Greeks* (London, 1967). A thoughtful
general survey.
CARL W. BLEGEN, *Troy and the Trojans* (New York,
1963). A good archaeological study of Troy and its place in
Greek prehistory.
JOHN BOARDMAN, *The Greeks Overseas* (Harmondsworth,
1964). A study of the relations between the Greeks and
other peoples.
G. W. BOTSFORD and C. A. ROBINSON, JR., *Hellenic*

Herodotus Relates the Tyranny of the Cypselids of Corinth

Herodotus (*ca.* 490–425 B.C.), "the father of history," was a Greek born in the city of Halicarnassus
in Asia Minor. In this story he tells of the Cypselid
tyrants of Corinth who ruled from about 650 to
about 625 B.C.

HAVING *thus got the tyranny, he [Cypselus] showed
himself a harsh ruler—many of the Corinthians he drove
into banishment, many he deprived of their fortunes, and
a still greater number of their lives. His reign lasted
thirty years, and was prosperous to its close; insomuch
that he left the government to Periander, his son. This
prince at the beginning of his reign was of a milder
temper than his father; but after he corresponded by
means of messengers with Thrasybulus, tyrant of
Miletus, he became even more sanguinary. On one occasion he sent a herald to ask Thrasybulus what mode of
government it was safest to set up in order to rule with
honour. Thrasybulus led the messenger without the city,
and took him into a field of corn, through which he
began to walk, while he asked him again and again
concerning his coming from Corinth, ever as he went
breaking off and throwing away all such ears of corn as
over-topped the rest. In this way he went through the
whole field, and destroyed all the best and richest part of
the crop; then, without a word, he sent the messenger
back. On the return of the man to Corinth, Periander was
eager to know what Thrasybulus had counselled, but the
messenger reported that he had said nothing; and he
wondered that Periander had sent him to so strange a
man, who seemed to have lost his senses, since he did
nothing but destroy his own property. And upon this he
told how Thrasybulus had behaved at the interview.
Periander, perceiving what the action meant, and knowing that Thrasybulus advised the destruction of all the
leading citizens, treated his subjects from this time forward with the very greatest cruelty.*

Herodotus, *The Histories*, trans. by George Rawlinson (New York:
Random House, 1942), p. 414.

History, 5th ed., revised by Donald Kagan (New York,
1969). A somewhat less detailed and more general account
that carries Greek history down to the Roman conquest.
A. R. BURN, *The Lyric Age of Greece* (New York, 1960). A
discussion of early Greece that uses the evidence of poetry
and archaeology to fill out the sparse historical record.
J. B. BURY and R. MEIGGS, *A History of Greece*, 4th ed.

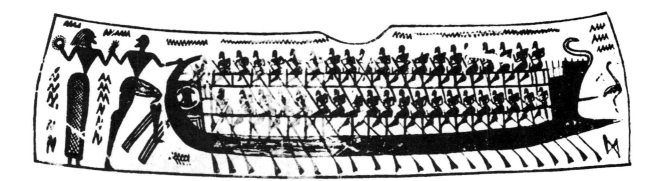

(London and New York, 1975). A thorough and detailed one-volume narrative history.

M. I. FINLEY, *World of Odysseus,* rev. ed., (New York, 1965). A fascinating attempt to reconstruct Homeric society.

M. I. FINLEY, *Early Greece* (New York, 1970). A succinct interpretive study.

S. HOOD, *The Minoans* (New York, 1971). A sketch of Bronze Age civilization on Crete.

G. S. KIRK, *The Songs of Homer* (New York, 1962). A discussion of the Homeric epics as oral poetry.

H. D. F. KITTO, *The Greeks* (Harmondsworth, 1951). A personal and illuminating interpretation of Greek culture.

H. L. LORIMER, *Homer and the Monuments* (London, 1950). A study of the relationship between the Homeric poems and the evidence of archaeology.

M. P. NILSSON, *Minoan-Mycenaean Religion and Its Survival in Greek Religion,* 2nd ed. (New York, 1968). An outstanding account of the influence of the Bronze Age on Greek history.

D. L. PAGE, *History and the Homeric Iliad,* 2nd ed. (Berkeley, 1966). A well-written and interesting, if debatable

An early large Greek ship, from a geometric Attic mixing bowl of about 775 B.C. The upper bank of rowers is not to be taken literally, as if it were a two-level ship. The artist did not know how to represent the rowers on the far side; in fact, the ship has only one bank of oars and no deck.

attempt to place the Trojan War in a historical setting.

CARL ROEBUCK, *Ionian Trade and Colonization* (New York, 1959). An introduction to the history of the Greeks in the east.

A. M. SNODGRASS, *The Dark Age of Greece* (Chicago, 1972). A good examination of the archaeological evidence.

C. G. STARR, *Origins of Greek Civilization 1100–650 B.C.* (New York, 1961). An interesting interpretation based largely on archaeology and especially on pottery styles.

EMILY VERMEULE, *Greece in the Bronze Age* (Chicago, 1972). A study of the Mycenaean period.

A. G. WOODHEAD, *Greeks in the West* (New York, 1962). An account of the Greek settlements in Italy and Sicily.

The Tyrants (About 700–500 B.C.) **49**

50

3
Archaic Greece

Sparta and Athens

GENERALIZATION about the *polis* becomes difficult not long after its appearance, for though the states had much in common, some of them developed in unique ways. Sparta and Athens, which became the two most powerful Greek states, had especially unusual histories.

Sparta

At first Sparta seems not to have been strikingly different from other *poleis,* but about 725 B.C. the pressure of population and land hunger led the Spartans to launch a war of conquest against their western neighbor, Messenia. This First Messenian War gave the Spartans as much land as they would ever need, and the reduction of the Messenians to the status of serflike helots meant that Spartans need not even work the land that supported them. The turning point in Spartan history came with the Second Messenian War, a rebellion of the helots, assisted by Argos and some of the Peloponnesian cities, about 650 B.C. The war was long and bitter and at one point threatened the existence of Sparta. After the revolt had been put down, the Spartans were forced to reconsider their way of life. They could not expect to keep down the helots, who outnumbered them perhaps ten to one, and still maintain the old free and easy habits typical of most Greeks. Faced with the choice of making drastic changes and sacrifices or abandoning their control of Messenia, the Spartans chose to introduce fundamental reforms that turned their city forever after into a military academy and camp.

A mounted archer dressed in Scythian costume rides across this Attic red-figure plate of about 515 B.C. Notice that the horse is without saddle or stirrups. The Scythians, famed for their horsemanship, lived in a large area between the Danube and the eastern Ukraine. [Ashmolean Museum, Oxford.]

The reforms are attributed to the legendary figure Lycurgus, and a man with that name may have played some part in them, but we know nothing about him. The new system that emerged late in the sixth century B.C. exerted control from birth, when officials of the state decided which infants were physically fit to survive. At the age of seven the Spartan boy was taken from his mother and turned over to young instructors who trained him in athletics and the military arts and taught him to endure privation, to bear physical pain, and to live off the country, by theft if necessary. At twenty the Spartan youth was enrolled in the army and lived in barracks with his companions until the age of thirty. Marriage was permitted, but a strange sort of marriage it was, for the Spartan male could visit his wife only infrequently and by stealth. At thirty he became a full citizen, an "equal." He took his meals at a public mess in the company of fifteen comrades. His food, a simple diet without much meat or wine, was provided by his own plot of land worked by helots. Military service was required until the age of sixty; only then could the Spartan retire to his home and family.

This educational program extended to women, too. They were not given military training, but female infants were examined for fitness to survive in the same way as males. Girls were given gymnastic training, were permitted greater freedom of movement than among other Greeks, and were equally indoctrinated with the idea of service to Sparta. The entire system was designed to transfer the natural feelings of devotion to wife, children, and family into a more powerful commitment to the *polis*. Privacy, luxury, even comfort were sacrificed to the purpose of producing soldiers whose physical powers, training, and discipline made them the best in the world. Nothing that might turn the mind away from duty was permitted. The very use of coins was forbidden lest it corrupt the desires of Spartans. Neither family nor money was allowed to interfere with the only ambition permitted to a Spartan: to win glory and the respect of his peers by bravery in war.

SPARTAN GOVERNMENT. The Spartan constitution was mixed, containing elements of monarchy, oligarchy, and democracy. There were two kings, whose power was limited by law and also by the rivalry that usually existed between the two royal houses. Their functions were chiefly religious and military. A Spartan army rarely left home without a king in command.

The oligarchic element was represented by a council of elders consisting of twenty-eight men over sixty, who were elected for life, and the kings. These elders had important judicial functions, sitting as a court in cases involving the kings. They also were consulted before any proposal was put before the assembly of Spartan citizens. In a traditional society like Sparta's, they must have had considerable influence.

The Spartan assembly consisted of all males over thirty. Theoretically they were the final authority, but because in practice debate was carried on by magistrates, elders, and kings alone, and because voting was usually by acclamation, the assembly's real function was to ratify decisions already taken or to decide between positions favored by the leading figures. In addition, Sparta had a unique institution, the board of ephors. This consisted of five men elected annually by the assembly. Originally they appear to have been intended to check the power of the kings, but gradually they acquired other important functions. They controlled foreign policy, oversaw the generalship of the kings on campaign, presided at the assembly, and guarded against rebellions by the helots. The whole system was remarkable both for the way in which it combined participation by the citizenry with significant checks on its power and for its unmatched stability. Most Greeks admired the Spartan state for this quality and also for its ability to mold its citizens into a single pattern of men who subordinated themselves to an ideal. Political philosophers from Plato to modern times have based utopian schemes on a version of the Spartan education and constitution.

By about 550 B.C. the Spartan system was well established, and its limitations were made plain. Suppression of

Plutarch Explains Lycurgus and the Spartan Constitution

Plutarch (ca. A.D. 46–120) was a Greek moralist and philosopher who wrote biographies of famous Greeks and Romans. His life of Lycurgus tells of the probably mythical figure who was thought to have founded the Spartan constitution and way of life.

To the end, therefore, that he might expel from the state arrogance and envy, luxury and crime, and those yet more inveterate diseases of want and superfluity, he obtained of them to renounce their properties, and to consent to a new division of the land, and that they should live all together on an equal footing; merit to be their only road to eminence, and the disgrace of evil, and credit of worthy acts, their one measure of difference between man and man.

Upon their consent to these proposals, proceeding at once to put them into execution, he divided the country of Laconia in general into thirty thousand equal shares, and the part attached to the city of Sparta into nine thousand. . . . A lot was so much as to yield, one year with another, about seventy bushels of grain for the master of the family, and twelve for his wife, with a suitable proportion of oil and wine. And this he thought sufficient to keep their bodies in good health and strength; superfluities they were better without. It is reported, that, as he returned from a journey shortly after the division of the lands, in harvest time, the ground being newly reaped, seeing the stacks all standing equal and alike, he smiled, and said to those about him, "Methinks all Laconia looks like one family estate just divided among a number of brothers." . . .

He commanded that all gold and silver coin should be called in, and that only a sort of money made of iron should be current, a great weight and quantity of which was very little worth; so that to lay up twenty or thirty pounds there was required a pretty large closet, and, to remove it, nothing less than a yoke of oxen. With the diffusion of this money, at once a number of vices were banished from Lacedaemon; for who would rob another of such a coin? . . .

To return to the Lacedaemonians. There discipline continued still after they were full-grown men. No one was allowed to live after his own fancy; but the city was a sort of camp, in which every man had his share of provisions and business set out, and looked upon himself not so much born to serve his own ends as the interest of his country. Therefore if they were commanded nothing else, they went to see the boys perform their exercises, to teach them something useful or to learn it themselves of

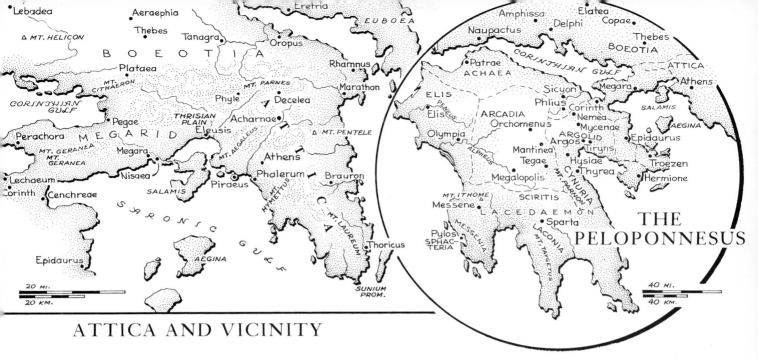

ATTICA AND VICINITY

THE PELOPONNESUS

those who knew better. And indeed one of the greatest and highest blessings Lycurgus procured his people was the abundance of leisure which proceeded from his forbidding to them the exercise of any mean and mechanical trade. Of the money-making that depends on troublesome going about and seeing people and doing business, they had no need at all in a state where wealth obtained no honour or respect. The Helots tilled their ground for them, and paid them yearly in kind the appointed quantity, without any trouble of theirs.

Plutarch, "Lycurgus," in *Lives of the Noble Grecians and Romans*, trans. by John Dryden, revised by A. H. Clough (New York: Random House, n.d.), pp. 55–56, 68.

the helots required all the effort and manpower that Sparta had. The Spartans could expand no further, but they could not allow unruly independent neighbors to cause unrest that might inflame the helots. When the Spartans defeated Tegea, their northern neighbor, they imposed an unusual peace. Instead of taking away land and subjecting the defeated state, Sparta left the Tegeans their land and their freedom. In exchange they required the Tegeans to follow the Spartan lead in foreign affairs and to supply a fixed number of soldiers to Sparta on demand. This became the model for Spartan relations with the other states in the Peloponnesus, and soon Sparta was the leader of an alliance that included every Peloponnesian state but Argos; modern scholars have given this alliance the name of the Peloponnesian League. It provided the Spartans with the security they needed, and it also made Sparta the most powerful *polis* in Hellenic

Citizens of all towns in Attica were also citizens of Athens. Sparta's region, Laconia, was in the Peloponnesus. Near-by states were members of the Peloponnesian League under Sparta's leadership.

history. By 500 B.C. Sparta and the League gave the Greeks a force capable of facing mighty threats from abroad.

Athens

Athens was slow to come into prominence and to join in the new activities that were agitating the more advanced states. In part this was because Athens was not situated on the most favored trade routes of the eighth and seventh centuries B.C., in part because its large area (about one thousand square miles) allowed population growth without great pressure, and in part because the unification of the many villages and districts into a single *polis* was not completed until the seventh century B.C.

In the seventh century B.C. Athens was a typical aristocratic *polis*. The people were divided into four tribes and into a number of clans and brotherhoods (phratries). The aristocrats held the most and best land and dominated religious and political life. There was no written law, and decisions were rendered by powerful nobles on the basis of tradition and, most likely, self-interest. The state was governed by the Areopagus, a council of nobles deriving its name from the hill where it held its sessions. Annually the council elected nine magistrates: the eponymous archon, who was the most important and who gave his name to the year; the king archon, chiefly a religious official; the polemarch or war leader; and six *thesmothetae*, legal officials. Together they made up the

Planting a crop in Attica. This scene on an Attic cup of the mid-sixth century B.C. shows a man, on the right, following a plow drawn by an ox while another sows seeds in the furrow. [Reproduced by courtesy of the Trustees of the British Museum.]

Olive harvest. This scene on an Attic jar from late in the sixth century B.C. shows how olives, one of Athens's most important crops, were harvested. [Reproduced by courtesy of the Trustees of the British Museum.]

college of archons, who joined the Areopagus after their year in office. Because the archons served for only a year, were checked by their colleagues, and looked forward to a lifetime as members of the Areopagus after their terms were ended, it is plain that the aristocratic council was the true master of the state.

In the seventh century B.C. the peaceful life of Athens experienced some disturbances, which were caused in part by quarrels within the nobility and in part by the beginnings of an agrarian crisis. In 632 B.C. a nobleman named Cylon attempted a coup to establish himself as tyrant. He was thwarted, but the unrest continued. In 621 B.C. Draco codified and published laws for the first time. Probably his work was limited to laws concerning homicide and was aimed at ending blood feuds between clans, but the precedent was important. The publication of law strengthened the hand of the state against the local power of the nobles. Further evidence of unusual activity in Attica, the region occupied by the Athenian state, toward the end of the seventh century is provided by the fruitless Athenian attempt to take Salamis and the successful colonization of Sigeum. Salamis is the island in the Saronic Gulf between Athens and its ancient enemy Megara. Its capture was vital for Athens' future as a commercial and naval state. Sigeum was located at the southern entrance to the Hellespont and was very important when Athens turned to commerce with the east. Both undertakings must have been intended to relieve economic and political pressure, but they were unsuccessful.

The root of the problem was chiefly agricultural. Many Athenians worked family farms, from which they obtained most of their living. It appears that they planted wheat, the staple crop, year after year without rotating fields or using sufficient fertilizer. In time this procedure exhausted the soil and led to bad crops. To survive, the farmer had to borrow from his wealthy neighbor to get through the year. In return he promised one sixth of the next year's crop. The arrangement was marked by the deposit of an inscribed stone on the entailed farm. Bad

Aristotle Recounts the Moderation of Solon at Athens

Aristotle wrote his history of the Athenian Constitution about 330 B.C. His account of the work of Solon (*ca.* 640–560 B.C.) is based in large measure on that statesman's own poetry.

MANY *members of the upper class had been estranged from him on account of his abolition of debts, and both parties were alienated through their disappointment at the condition of things which he had created. The mass of the people had expected him to make a complete redistribution of all property, and the upper class hoped he would restore everything to its former position, or, at any rate, make but a small change. Solon, however, had resisted both classes. He might have made himself a despot by attaching himself to whichever party he chose, but he preferred, though at the cost of incurring the enmity of both, to be the saviour of his country and the ideal lawgiver.*

The truth of this view of Solon's policy is established alike by common consent, and by the mention he has himself made of the matter in his poems. Thus:

I gave to the mass of the people such rank as befitted their need,
I took not away their honour, and I granted naught to their greed;
While those who were rich in power, who in wealth were glorious and great,
I bethought me that naught should befall them unworthy their splendour and state;
So I stood with my shield outstretched, and both were safe in its sight,
And I would not that either should triumph, when the triumph was not with right.

Aristotle, *Constitution of the Athenians*, trans. by H. G. Dakyns, in *The Greek Historians*, Vol. 2 (New York: Random House, 1942), pp. 693–694.

markable conciliatory spirit of Athens intervened. In the year 594 B.C., as tradition has it, the Athenians elected Solon as the only archon, with extraordinary powers to legislate and revise the constitution. Immediately he attacked the agrarian problem by canceling current debts and forbidding future loans secured by the person of the borrower. He helped bring back many Athenians enslaved abroad as well as freeing those in Athens enslaved for debt. This program was called the "shaking off of burdens." It did not, however, solve the fundamental economic problem, and Solon did not redistribute the land. In the short run, therefore, he did not put an end to the economic crisis, but his other economic actions had profound success in the long run. He forbade the export of wheat and encouraged that of olive oil. This policy had the effect of making wheat more available in Attica and encouraging the cultivation of olive oil and wine as cash crops. By the fifth century B.C. this form of agriculture had become so profitable that much Athenian land was diverted from grain production to the cultivation of cash crops, and Athens became dependent on imported wheat. Solon also changed the Athenian standards of weights and measures to conform with those of Corinth and Euboea and the cities of the East. This change also encouraged commerce and turned Athens in the direction that would lend her to great prosperity in the fifth century. He also encouraged industry by offering citizenship to foreign craftsmen, and his success is reflected in the development of the outstanding Attic pottery of the sixth century.

Solon also significantly changed the constitution. He divided the Athenians into four classes on the basis of wealth, measured by annual agricultural production. Men whose property produced five hundred measures were called five-hundred-measure men, and those producing three hundred measures were called cavalry; these two classes alone could hold the archonship and sit on the Areopagus. Producers of two hundred measures were called owners of a team of oxen; these were allowed to serve as hoplites. They could be elected to the council of four hundred chosen by all the citizens, one hundred

harvests persisted, and soon the debtor had to pledge his wife and children and himself as surety for the loans needed for survival. As bad times continued, many Athenians defaulted and were enslaved. Some were even sold abroad. Revolutionary pressures grew among the poor, who began to demand the abolition of debt and a redistribution of the land.

SOLON. The circumstances might easily have brought about class warfare and tyranny, but the re-from each tribe. Solon seems to have meant this council to serve as a check on the Areopagus and to prepare any business that needed to be put before the assembly. The last class, producing less than two hundred measures, were the *thetes*. They voted in the popular assembly for the archons and the council members and on any other business brought before them by the magistrates. They also sat on the new popular court established by Solon. At first it must have had little power, for most cases continued to be heard in the country by local barons and in Athens by the aristocratic Areopagus. But the new court was recognized as a court of appeal, and by the fifth century B.C. almost all cases came before the popular courts.

Solon's efforts to avoid factional strife failed. Within a few years contention reached such a degree that no archons could be chosen. Out of this turmoil emerged the first Athenian tyranny. Pisistratus, a nobleman, faction leader, and military hero, briefly seized power in 560 B.C. and again in 556 B.C., but each time his support was inadequate and he was driven out. At last, in 546 B.C. he came back at the head of a mercenary army from abroad and established a tyranny that lasted beyond his death, in 527 B.C., until the expulsion of his son Hippias in 510 B.C. In many respects Pisistratus resembled the other Greek tyrants. His rule rested on the force provided by mercenary soldiers. He engaged in great programs of public works, urban improvement, and religious piety. Temples were built and religious centers expanded and improved. New religious festivals were introduced and old ones had their public appeal increased. Poets and artists were supported to add cultural luster to the court of the tyrant.

PISISTRATUS. Pisistratus aimed at increasing the power of the central government at the expense of the nobles. The festival of Dionysus and the Great Panathenaic festival helped fix attention on the capital city, as did the new temples and the reconstruction of the Agora as the center of public life. District circuit judges were sent out into the country to hear cases, another feature that weakened the power of the local barons. All this time Pisistratus made no formal change in the Solonian constitution. Assembly, councils, and courts met; magistrates and councils were elected; Pisistratus merely saw to it that his friends were chosen. The intended effect was to blunt the sharp edge of tyranny with the appearance of constitutional government, and it worked. The rule of Pisistratus was remembered as popular and mild. The unintended effect was to give the Athenians more experience in the procedures of self-government and a growing taste for it.

INVASION BY SPARTA. Pisistratus was succeeded by his oldest son, Hippias, who followed his father's ways at first. In 514 B.C., however, his brother Hipparchus was murdered as a result of a private quarrel. Hippias became nervous, suspicious, and harsh. At last, one of the exiled noble clans, the Alcmaeonids, won favor with the Delphic oracle and used its support to persuade Sparta to attack the Athenian tyranny. Led by their ambitious king, Cleomenes I, the Spartans sent an army into Attica in 510 B.C. and deposed Hippias, who went into exile to the Persian court. The tyranny was gone.

The Spartans must have hoped to leave Athens in friendly hands, and indeed Cleomenes' friend Isagoras held the leading position in Athens after the withdrawal of the Spartan army, but he was not unopposed. Clisthenes of the restored Alcmaeonid clan was his chief rival but lost out in the political struggle among the noble factions. Isagoras seems to have tried to restore a version of the pre-Solonian aristocratic state. As part of his plan he carried through a purification of the citizen lists, removing those who had been enfranchised by Solon or Pisistratus and any others thought to have a doubtful claim. Clisthenes then took an unprecedented action by turning to the common people for political support and won it with a program of great popular appeal. In response Isagoras called in the Spartans again; Cleomenes arrived and allowed the expulsion from Athens of Clisthenes and a large number of his supporters. But the Athenian political consciousness, ignited by Solon and kept alive under Pisistratus, was fanned by the popular

Ruins of the temple of Olympian Zeus in Athens.
The construction of this enormous temple of the
Corinthian order was begun by the tyrant Pisistratus
in the second half of the sixth century B.C. as part
of his extensive program of public works and religious
celebrations. Frequently interrupted, work on the
temple was resumed in the second century B.C. and
was finally completed by order of Roman Emperor
Hadrian in the second century of the Christian era.
[Greek National Tourist Organization, New York.
Nicos Kontos.]

The so-called temple of Ceres, the Roman goddess
of agriculture, now believed actually to have been
dedicated to Athena, at the Greek colony of Paestum
in southern Italy. It was built in the sixth century
B.C. and shows many characteristic archaic features
that were much refined by the time of the classic
structures of the fifth and later centuries. [AHM.]

Ostraca found in the Athenian Agora. These inscribed potsherds date from the fifth century B.C. and bear the names of two famous Athenian statesmen, Themistocles, son of Neocles, and Aristides, son of Lysimachus. At different times each man was ostracized—*i.e.*, banished from Athens for ten years. [Agora Excavations, American School of Classical Studies at Athens.]

appeal of Clisthenes. The people would not hear of an aristocratic restoration and drove out the Spartans and Isagoras with them. Clisthenes and his friends returned, ready to put their program into effect.

CLISTHENES. A central aim of Clisthenes' reforms was to diminish the influence of traditional localities and regions in Athenian life, for these were an important source of power for the nobility and of factions in the state. He made the deme, the equivalent of a small town in the country or a ward in the city, the basic unit of civic life. It was a purely political unit that elected its own officers and replaced the phratry, where tradition and nobility dominated, as the determinant of Athenian citizenship. Henceforth the citizen rolls were kept by the deme, and Clisthenes immediately enrolled the disenfranchised who had supported him in the struggle with Isagoras. The demes, which ultimately reached about 175 in number, were divided into ten new tribes that replaced the traditional four. The demes were put together in groups of one or more to form *trittyes* or thirds. Each tribe contained one *trittys* from the inland region of Attica, one from the coast, and one from the city of Athens. The *trittyes* were carved out in such a way as to separate as much as possible the main holdings of powerful nobles from the religious shrines they controlled. The composition of each tribe guaranteed that no region would dominate any of them. Since the tribes had common religious activities and fought as regimental units, the new organization would also increase devotion to the *polis* and diminish regional divisions and personal loyalty to local barons.

Plutarch Tells of the Ostracism of Aristides

The Athenian statesman Aristides was born about 525 B.C. He was ostracized in 482.

THE *spirit of the people, now grown high, and confident with their late victory, naturally entertained feelings of dislike to all of more than common fame and reputation. Coming together, therefore, from all parts into the city, they banished Aristides by the ostracism, giving their jealousy of his reputation the name of fear of tyranny. For ostracism was not the punishment of any criminal act, but was speciously said to be the mere depression and humiliation of excessive greatness and power; and was in fact a gentle relief and mitigation of envious feeling, which was thus allowed to vent itself in inflicting no intolerable injury, only a ten years' banishment. . . . It was performed, to be short, in this manner. Every one taking an* ostracon, *a sherd, that is, or piece of earthenware, wrote upon it the citizen's name he would have banished, and carried it to a certain part of the market-place surrounded with wooden rails. First, the magistrates numbered all the sherds in gross (for if there were less than six thousand, the ostracism was imperfect); then, laying every name by itself, they pronounced him whose name was written by the larger number banished for ten years, with the enjoyment of his estate. As therefore, they were writing the names on the sherds, it is reported that an illiterate clownish fellow, giving Aristides his sherd, supposing him a common citizen, begged him to write* Aristides *upon it; and he being surprised and asking if Aristides had ever done him any injury, "None at all," said he, "neither know I the man; but I am tired of hearing him everywhere called the Just." Aristides, hearing this, is said to have made no reply, but returned the sherd with his own name inscribed.*

Plutarch, "Aristides," in *Lives of the Noble Grecians and Romans,* trans. by John Dryden, revised by A. H. Clough, (New York: Random House, n.d.), p. 396.

A new council of five hundred was invented to replace the Solonian council of four hundred. Each tribe elected fifty councilors each year, and no man could serve more than twice. The council's main responsibility was to prepare legislation for discussion by the assembly, but it also had important financial duties and received foreign emissaries. Final authority in all things rested with the assembly composed of all adult male Athenian citizens.

ABOVE, LEFT: Wrestlers. The scene is from a Greek vase of the archaic period. RIGHT: Horse-drawn chariot and charioteer. This is another archaic-period vase decoration. [Both: Antikenmuseum; Staatliche Museen Preussischer Kulturbesitz, West Berlin. Jutta Tietz-Glagow.]

Debate was free and open; any Athenian could submit legislation, offer amendments, or argue the merits of any question. In practice political leaders did most of the talking, and we may imagine that in the early days the council had more authority than it did after the Athenians became more confident in their new self-government. It is fair to call Clisthenes the father of Athenian democracy. He did not alter the property qualifications of Solon, but his enlargement of the citizen rolls, his diminution of the power of the aristocrats, and his elevation of the role of the assembly, with its effective and manageable council, all give him a firm claim to that title.

OSTRACISM. The new democracy was immediately challenged from without and within. The Athenians were able to beat off an attack by Sparta, Thebes, and Chalcis, but they needed to be constantly alert for another and also against division or even treason within their own ranks. As a response to the internal threat they invented the law on ostracism. It compelled them to vote once a year whether they wished to ostracize anyone, that is, to send him off into exile for ten years. If they voted to do so, each citizen was invited to come to the Agora on the appointed day carrying a potsherd (*ostrakon*) with the name of his candidate written on it. If there were at least six thousand votes cast, the name with the most votes was ostracized. The victim was neither accused nor convicted of any crime; his family and property were unharmed, and after a decade he could return as a citizen with full rights. The point of the law was to deter factional menaces to the new constitution by the threat of ostracizing the faction leader. It depended on a secure majority for the politician favoring the use of the device because few men would run the risk of contesting an

ostracism of which they might themselves be the victims. In future years ostracism came to be used as a vote of confidence in a democratic leader, a referendum on a policy, or a device to bring order out of a chaotic political situation. The Athenians used it sparingly, and for almost one hundred years it helped defend the democracy against subversion and factional strife.

As a result of the work of Solon, Pisistratus, and Clisthenes, Athens entered the fifth century B.C. well on the way to prosperity and democracy, much more centralized and united than it had been, and ready to take its place among the major states who would lead the defense of Greece against the dangers that lay ahead.

Aspects of Culture in Archaic Greece
Religion

Like most ancient peoples the Greeks were polytheists, and religion played an important part in their lives. A great part of Greek art and literature was closely connected with religion, as was the life of the *polis* in general. The Greek pantheon consisted of the twelve gods who lived on Mount Olympus: Zeus, the father of the gods; his wife, Hera; his brother, Poseidon; his sisters, Hestia and Demeter; and his children, Aphrodite, Apollo, Ares, Artemis, Hephaestus, and Hermes. On the one hand, these gods were seen to behave very much like mortals, with all their foibles, except that they were superhuman in these as well as in their strength and immortality. On the other hand, Zeus, at least, was seen to be a source of human justice, and even the Olympians were understood to be subordinate to the fates. Each *polis* had one of the Olympians as its tutelary deity and worshiped the god in its own special way, but all the gods were Panhellenic. In the eighth and seventh centuries B.C. common shrines were established at Olympia for the worship of Zeus, at Delphi for Apollo, at the Isthmus of Corinth for Poseidon, and at Nemea once again for Zeus. Each held athletic contests in honor of its god, to which all Greeks were invited and for which a sacred truce was declared.

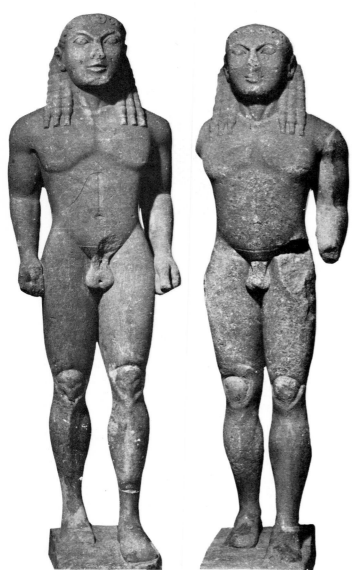

Biton and Cleobis. These marble statues from the archaic period were dedicated at the sanctuary at Delphi and are dated about 580 B.C. They picture two young Argive men who were famous examples of filial piety. They reveal the debt owed by early Greek sculptors to the Egyptians. [TAP–Delphi Museum.]

Besides the Olympians the Greeks also worshiped countless lesser deities connected with local shrines and even heroes, humans real or legendary who had accomplished great deeds and had earned immortality and divine status. The worship of these deities was not a very emotional experience. It was a matter of offering prayer, libations, and gifts in return for protection and favors from the god during the lifetime of the worshiper. There was no hope of immortality for the average man and little moral teaching. Plato, in fact, at a later date suggested that the poets be banned from the state because the tales they told of the gods were immoral and corrupting for humans. Most Greeks seem to have held to the common-sense notion that justice lay in paying one's debts; that civic virtue consisted of worshiping the state deities in the traditional way, performing required public services, and fighting in defense of the state; and that private morality meant to do good to one's friends and harm to one's enemies. In the sixth century B.C. the influence of the cult of Apollo at Delphi and of his oracle there became very great. The oracle was the most important of several that helped satisfy man's craving for a clue to the future. The priests of Apollo preached moderation; their advice was exemplified in the two famous sayings identified with Apollo: "Know thyself" and "Nothing in excess." Man needs self-control (*sophrosyne*). Its opposite is arrogance (*hybris*), which is brought on by excessive wealth or good fortune. *Hybris* leads to moral blindness and finally to divine vengeance. This theme of moderation and the dire consequences of its absence was central in Greek popular morality and appears frequently in literature.

The somewhat cold religion of the Olympian gods and of the cult of Apollo did little to attend to man's fears, hopes, and passions. For these needs the Greeks turned to other deities and rites. Of these the most popular was Dionysus, a god of nature and fertility, of the grape vine and drunkenness and sexual abandon. In some of his rites the god was followed by maenads, female devotees who cavorted by night, ate raw flesh, and were reputed to tear

The god Dionysus dancing with two maenads, who were female followers of him. The vase decoration is by a painter who worked between about 550 and 525 B.C. [Photograph Bibliothèque Nationale, Paris.]

to pieces any creature they came across. There were also mystery cults such as the one named after the legendary poet Orpheus, who sang of the murder of Dionysus by the Titans, a race of giants who had challenged Zeus. They ate Dionysus alive, but he was miraculously reborn. Man sprang from the ashes of the Titans and was partly divine and good and partly animal and evil. The Orphics interpreted the myth as a mystery and explained that man's body was impure and his soul was divine. Those initiated into the Orphic mysteries and willing to live a good life would find their souls released at death and eternal happiness. The uninitiated would dwell in Hades. Another famous mystery cult was that of Demeter and Persephone at Eleusis, an ancient fertility cult that also promised a form of immortality to its initiates. These and other miraculous cults existed for those who needed them, but they were not central to Greek religious life.

Philosophy and Science

The rational spirit characteristic of Greek geometric pottery and even of many Greek myths blossomed in the sixth century B.C. into the intellectual examination of the physical world and man's place in it that we call philosophy. It is not surprising that the first steps along this path were taken in Ionia, on the fringe of the Greek world and therefore in touch with foreign ideas and the learning of the East. These Ionians were among the first to realize that the Greek account of how the world was created and maintained itself and man's place in it was not universally accepted. Perhaps this realization helped spark the first attempts at disciplined philosophical inquiry.

Thales of Miletus, who lived early in the sixth century B.C., is the first philosopher of whom we know. He believed that the earth floated on water and that water was the primary substance. This was not a new idea; what was new was the absence of any magical or mythical elements in the explanation. Thales observed, as any man can, that water has many forms: liquid, solid, and gaseous. He saw that it could "create" land by alluvial

deposit and that it is necessary for all life. These observations he organized by reason into a single explanation that accounted for many phenomena without any need for the supernatural. The first philosopher thus set the tone for future investigations. Greek philosophers assumed that the world was knowable, rational, and simple.

The search for fundamental rational explanations of phenomena was carried forward by another Milesian, Anaximander. He imagined that the basic element was something undefined, "unlimited." The world emerged from it as the result of an interaction of opposite forces, wet and dry, hot and cold. He pictured the universe in eternal motion; all sensible things emerge from the "unlimited," then decay and return to it. He also argued that man originated in water and had evolved to his present state through several stages, including that of a fish. Anaximenes, another Milesian, believed air to be primary. It took different forms because of the purely physical processes of rarefaction and condensation. Heraclitus of Ephesus, who lived near the end of the century, carried the dialogue further. His famous saying, "All is motion," raised important problems. If all is constantly in motion it would appear that nothing ever really exists, yet Heraclitus believed that the world order was governed by a guiding principle, the Logos, and that though phenomena changed, the Logos did not. In this way speculations about the physical world, what we would call natural science, soon led the way toward even more difficult philosophical speculations about language, about the manner of human thought, and about knowledge itself.

In this climate myths, religion, and morality also came under rational investigation. Xenophanes of Colophon, who settled in Elea in southern Italy about the middle of the sixth century B.C., examined Greek myths and religious beliefs with a skeptical eye. He condemned the poets for portraying the gods as acting more shamefully than men; he also pointed out that all peoples created their gods in their own physical images and suggested that if animals could make gods, their gods would look like animals. New ideas about religion took a different form in the mind of Pythagoras, a native of Samos who settled in Croton, Italy, in the last part of the century. He did important scientific work, demonstrating the mathematical theorem that bears his name, and he pioneered in musical theory by discovering that the pitch of a string depends on its length. Behind these discoveries was the mystical belief that what was fundamental was not physical substance, but number. Number was seen also as the basis of religion, morality, and government. In all cases mathematical harmony was presumed to be the desired state. Pythagoras gathered disciples about him and organized them into a disciplined, scientific, religious, and philosophical community. The Pythagoreans believed in the transmigration of souls and that desirable eternal rest could be achieved only by the way of Pythagoras. They thought that numbers were the most real things in the universe, and they were among the first to think that the hard world we call "real"—a world we touch, taste, see, hear, and smell—was not truly real because it was always changing. They also thought that body and soul were separate, a notion foreign to Hebrew thought but one that, through Plato, would have a profound effect on the way Westerners think.

Theognis of Megara Gives Advice to a Young Aristocrat

Theognis was born about 580 B.C. and lived to see his native city Megara torn by social upheaval and civil war. His poems present the political and ethical ideas of the Greek aristocracy.

DO NOT *consort with bad men, but always hold to the good. Eat and drink with them, whose power is great, sit with them and please them. You will learn good from good men, but if you mingle with the bad you will lose such wisdom as you already have. Therefore consort with the good and one day you will say that I give good advice to my friends.*

We seek thoroughbred rams asses and horses, Cyrnus, and a man wants offspring of good breeding. But in marriage a good man does not decline to marry the bad daughter of a bad father, if he gives him much wealth. Nor does the wife of a bad man refuse to be his bedfellow if he be rich, preferring wealth to goodness. For they value possessions and a good man marries a woman of bad stock and the bad a woman of good. Wealth mixes the breed. So do not wonder, son of Polypaus, that the race of your citizens is obscured since bad things are mixed with good.

It is easier to beget and rear a man than to put good sense into him. No one has ever discovered a way to make a fool wise or a bad man good. If God had given the sons of Asclepius the knowledge to heal the evil nature and mischievous mind of man, great and frequent would be their pay. If thought could be made and put into a man, the son of a good man would never become bad, since he would obey good counsel. But you will never make the bad man good by teaching.

The best thing the gods give to men, Cyrnus, is judgment; judgment contains the ends of everything. O happy is the man who has it in his mind; it is much greater than destructive insolence and grievous satiety. There are no evils among mortals worse than these—for every evil, Cyrnus, comes out of them.

Translated by Donald Kagan in *Sources in Greek Political Thought*, ed. by D. Kagan (New York: Free Press, 1965), pp. 39–40.

Poetry

The great changes sweeping through the Greek world were also reflected in the poetry of the sixth century B.C. The lyric style, whether sung by a chorus or by one singer, predominated. Sappho of Lesbos, Anacreon of Teos, and Simonides of Cos composed personal poetry, often speaking of the pleasure and agony of love. Alcaeus

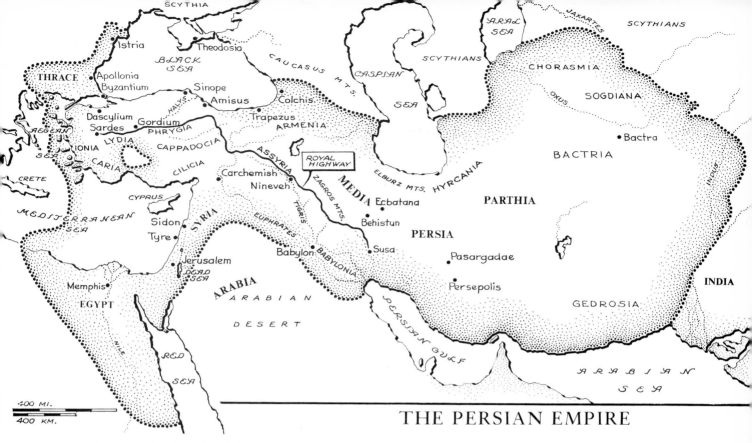

THE PERSIAN EMPIRE

The empire created by Cyrus had fullest extent under Darius when Persia attacked Greece in 490 B.C. It reached from India to the Aegean—and even into Europe—including the lands formerly ruled by Egyptians, Hittites, Babylonians, and Assyrians.

of Mytilene, an aristocrat driven from his city by a tyrant, wrote bitter invective. Perhaps the most interesting poet of the century from a political point of view was Theognis of Megara. He was an aristocrat who lived through a tyranny, an unusually chaotic and violent democracy, and an oligarchy that restored order but ended the rule of the old aristocracy. Theognis was the spokesman for the old, defeated, aristocracy of birth. He divided all men into two classes, the noble and the base; the former were good, the latter bad. A man nobly born must associate only with others like himself if he is to preserve his virtue; if he mingles with the base, he becomes base. A man born base, on the other hand, can never become noble. Only nobles can aspire to virtue, and only nobles possess the critical moral and intellectual qualities, respect or honor, and judgment. These qualities cannot be taught; they are innate. Even so they must be carefully guarded against corruption by wealth or by mingling with the base. Intermarriage between the noble and the base is especially condemned. These were the ideas of the unreconstructed nobility, whose power had been de-

stroyed or reduced in most Greek states by this time. They remained alive in aristocratic hearts throughout the next century and greatly influenced later thinkers, Plato again among them.

The Persian Wars of the Fifth Century B.C.

The Greeks' period of fortunate isolation and freedom from attack from the outside came to an end in the middle of the sixth century B.C., when the cities of Asia Minor came under the control of Lydia and its king, Croesus (ca. 560–546 B.C.). The Lydian rule seems not to have been very harsh, but the Persian conquest of Lydia in 546 B.C. brought a subjugation that was less pleasant. The Persian Empire had been created in a single generation by Cyrus the Great. In 559 B.C. he came to the throne of Persia, then a small kingdom well to the east of the lower Mesopotamian valley, unified Persia under his rule, made an alliance with Babylonia, and led a successful rebellion toward the north against the Medes, who were the overlords of Persia. In succeeding years he expanded his empire in all directions, in the process defeating Croesus and occupying Lydia. Most of the Greek cities of Asia Minor sided with Croesus and resisted the Per-

A

B

C

D

64 *Archaic Greece*

ABOVE: Royal scene of homage from the treasury at Persepolis. King Darius is seated on a throne, and his son Xerxes stands behind him. Both are carved in larger scale than the others in the relief to indicate their royal status. [Courtesy of the Oriental Institute, University of Chicago.]

OPPOSITE: The audience hall at Persepolis. Here the Persian kings of the fifth century B.C. lived in a great complex of fortresses, palaces, and other buildings. In the hall whose remains are shown here Darius and Xerxes dispensed justice and emphasized their own greatness. It is about 250 feet square and could hold about 10,000 people.

The complex also includes the palace of Darius, which appears in the background of the photograph. The complex was constructed between 518 and about 460 B.C. In 330 B.C. it was burned and buried under many feet of ashes during its occupation by the conquering Alexander the Great. Persepolis is in modern Iran. [Courtesy of the Oriental Institute, University of Chicago.]

A: Remains of King Darius's palace at Persepolis. [AHM.]

BCD: Carvings in low relief on the wall of the audience hall at Persepolis. These carvings are still in their original places and came cleanly to light after more than twenty-two centuries when they were excavated in the 1930s. [AHM.]

B: Procession of officers of the guards, alternately Medes (in round hats) and Persians (in feathered hats). Above them is the winged-disc symbol of the god Ahura Mazda.

C: Here is the frequently repeated theme of conflict between beasts at least partly mythical and their startled victims.

D: This procession is thought to record the compulsory new-year presentation of various gifts (or tribute) to the Persian king from no fewer than twenty-one subject peoples.

sians. By about 540 B.C., however, they were all subdued. The western part of Asia Minor was divided into three provinces, each under its own satrap, or governor.

The Persians required their subjects to pay tribute and to serve in the Persian army. They ruled the Greek cities through local individuals, who governed their cities as "tyrants." The Ionians had been moving in the direction of democracy and were not pleased with monarchical rule, but most of the "tyrants" were not harsh, the Persian tribute was not excessive, and there was general prosperity. Neither the death of Cyrus fighting on a distant frontier in 530 B.C. nor the suicide of his successor, Cambyses, nor the civil war that followed it in 522–521 B.C. produced any disturbance in the Greek cities. Darius found Ionia perfectly obedient when he emerged as Great King in 521 B.C.

The Ionian Rebellion

The private troubles of the ambitious tyrant of Miletus, Aristagoras, started the rebellion. He had urged a Persian expedition against the island of Naxos; when it failed, he feared the consequences and organized the Ionian rebellion of 499 B.C. To gain support, he overthrew the tyrannies and proclaimed democratic constitutions. Then he turned to the mainland states for help. As the most powerful Greek state, Sparta was naturally the first stop, but the Spartans would have none of Aristagoras' promises of easy victory and great wealth. Sparta had no close ties with the Ionians and no national interest in the region, and the thought of leaving an undefended Sparta to the helots while the army was far off for a long time was terrifying.

Aristagoras next sought help at Athens, and there the assembly agreed and voted to send a fleet of twenty ships to help the rebels. The Athenians were Ionians and had close ties of religion and tradition with the rebels. Besides, Hippias, the deposed tyrant of Athens, was an honored guest at the court of Darius, and the Great King (as the Persian rulers styled themselves) had already made it plain that he favored the tyrant's restoration. The Per-

THE PERSIAN INVASION OF GREECE

This map traces the route taken by the Persian King Xerxes in his invasion of Greece in 480 B.C. The solid lines show movements of his army, the broken lines of his fleet.

In this relief from a door jamb in his palace at Persepolis, King Darius is followed by an attendant with an umbrella. [AHM.]

sians, moreover, controlled both sides of the Hellespont, the route to the grain fields beyond the Black Sea, which were increasingly vital to Athens. Perhaps some Athenians already feared that a Persian attempt to conquer the Greek mainland was only a matter of time. The Athenian expedition was strengthened by five ships from Eretria in Euboea, which participated out of gratitude for past favors.

In 498 B.C. the Athenians and their allies made a swift march and a surprise attack on Sardis, the old capital of Lydia and now the seat of the satrap, and burned it. This caused the revolt to spread throughout the Greek cities of Asia Minor outside Ionia, but the Ionians could not follow it up. The Athenians withdrew and took no further part, and gradually the Persians imposed their will. In 495 B.C. they defeated the Ionian fleet at Lade, and in the next year they wiped out Miletus. Many of the men were killed, others were transported to the Persian Gulf, the women and children were enslaved. The Ionian rebellion was over.

In 492 B.C. Darius sent his son-in-law to restore his European possessions in Thrace to order. In spite of some resistance and the destruction of a considerable part of his fleet in a storm off Mount Athos, Mardonius was successful. Herodotus and the Greek tradition in general picture this expedition as aimed at Athens and Eretria in revenge for their part in the Ionian rebellion.

The War in Greece

In 490 B.C. the Persians launched an expedition directly across the Aegean to punish Eretria and Athens, to restore Hippias, and to gain control of the Aegean Sea. The force of infantry and cavalry under the command of Datis and Artaphernes, landed first at Naxos and destroyed it for its successful resistance in 499 B.C. Then they destroyed Eretria and deported its people deep into the interior of Persia.

The Athenians chose to risk the fate of Eretria rather than submit to Persia and restore the hated tyranny. The resistance was led by Miltiades, an outstanding soldier

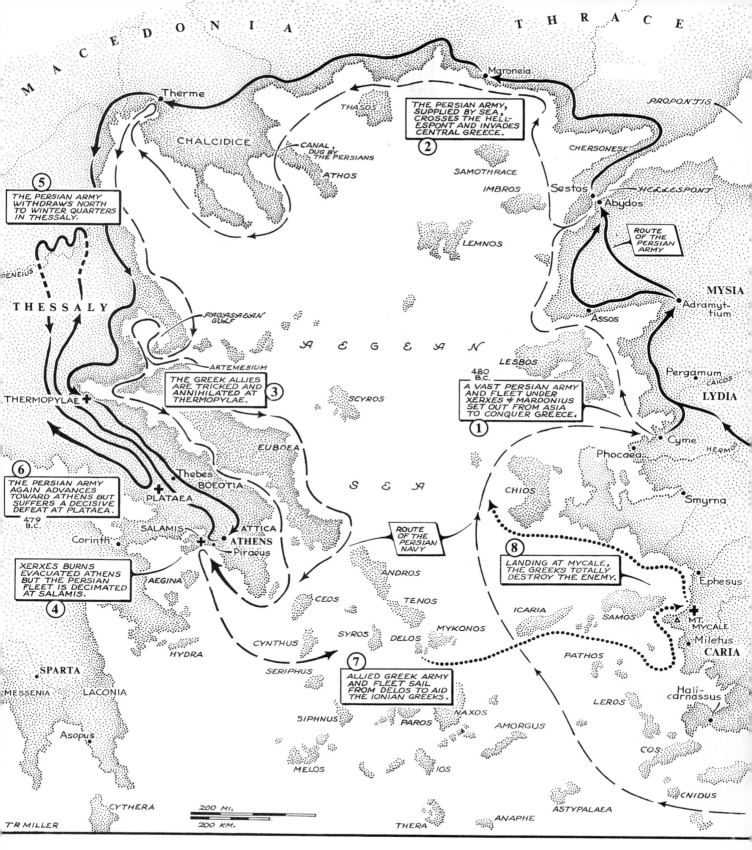

MACEDONIA

THRACE

Therme

Maroneia

THASOS

CHALCIDICE

CANAL,
DUG BY
THE PERSIANS

ATHOS

PROPONTIS

CHERSONESE

SAMOTHRACE

Sestos

HELLESPONT

IMBROS

Abydos

(2) THE PERSIAN ARMY, SUPPLIED BY SEA, CROSSES THE HELLESPONT AND INVADES CENTRAL GREECE.

ROUTE OF THE PERSIAN ARMY

(5) THE PERSIAN ARMY WITHDRAWS NORTH TO WINTER QUARTERS IN THESSALY.

PENEIUS

THESSALY

LEMNOS

MYSIA

Adramyt-tium

Assos

PAGASAEAN GULF

AEGEAN

LESBOS

Pergamum

CAICOS

Artemesium

480 B.C.

LYDIA

(3) THE GREEK ALLIES ARE TRICKED AND ANNIHILATED AT THERMOPYLAE.

SCYROS

(1) A VAST PERSIAN ARMY AND FLEET UNDER XERXES & MARDONIUS SET OUT FROM ASIA TO CONQUER GREECE.

Cyme

HERMOS

THERMOPYLAE ✝

Phocaea

EUBOEA

SEA

CHIOS

Smyrna

(6) THE PERSIAN ARMY AGAIN ADVANCES TOWARD ATHENS BUT SUFFERS A DECISIVE DEFEAT AT PLATAEA. 479 B.C.

Thebes

BOEOTIA

PLATAEA ✝

ROUTE OF THE PERSIAN NAVY

SALAMIS

ATTICA

Corinth

ATHENS

Piraeus

✝

(8) LANDING AT MYCALE, THE GREEKS TOTALLY DESTROY THE ENEMY.

Ephesus

(4) XERXES BURNS EVACUATED ATHENS BUT THE PERSIAN FLEET IS DECIMATED AT SALAMIS.

AEGINA

ANDROS

CEOS

TENOS

ICARIA

SAMOS

▲ MT. MYCALE ✝

Miletus

CARIA

CYNTHUS

SYROS

MYKONOS

DELOS

PATHOS

LEROS

SPARTA

HYDRA

SERIPHUS

(7) ALLIED GREEK ARMY AND FLEET SAIL FROM DELOS TO AID THE IONIAN GREEKS.

Hali-carnassus

MESSENIA

LACONIA

SIPHNUS

NAXOS

PAROS

AMORGUS

COS

Asopus

MELOS

IOS

ASTYPALAEA

CNIDUS

CYTHERA

200 MI.

200 KM.

THERA

ANAPHE

T.R. MILLER

The Persian Wars of the Fifth Century B.C. **67**

Bronze helmet from Marathon. It bears the inscription "Miltiades dedicated me to Zeus" and was dedicated to Zeus at his sanctuary at Olympia to commemorate the Athenian victory at Marathon in 490 B.C. [TAP–Art Reference Bureau.]

who had fled from Persian service after earning the anger of Darius. His knowledge of the Persian army and his distaste for submission to Persia made him an ideal leader. He led the army to Marathon and won a decisive victory. The battle at Marathon was of enormous importance to the future of Greek civilization. A Persian victory would have destroyed Athenian freedom, and the conquest of all the mainland Greeks would have followed. The greatest achievements of Greek culture, most of which lay in the future, would have been impossible under Persian rule. The Athenian victory, on the other hand, made a positive contribution to those achievements. It instilled in the Athenians a sense of confidence and pride in their *polis,* their unique form of government and themselves.

For the Persians Marathon was only a small and temporary defeat, but it was annoying. Internal troubles, however, prevented swift revenge. In 481 B.C. Darius' successor, Xerxes, gathered an army of at least 150,000 men and a navy of more than six hundred ships for the conquest of Greece. The Greeks did not make good use of the delay, but Athens was an exception. Themistocles had become its leading politician, and he had always wanted to turn Athens into a naval power. The first step was to build a fortified port at Piraeus during his archon-

Greek hoplite attacking a Persian soldier. The contrast between the Greek's heavy metal body armor, large shield, and long spear and the cloth and leather garments of the Persian gives some indication of the reason for the ultimate Greek victory. This Attic red-figure vase is said to be from the island of Rhodes and was made about 475 B.C. [Metropolitan Museum of Art, New York; Rogers Fund, 1906.]

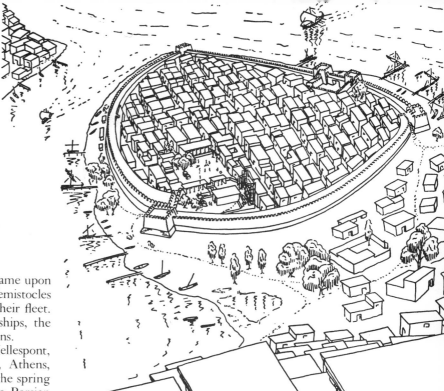

Old Smyrna. This drawing reconstructs the Ionian Greek city of Old Smyrna in Asia Minor as it appeared in the seventh century B.C. Except for the open space for the Agora, the city is packed with houses jammed within the defensive wall. [J. M. Cook: *The Greeks in Ionia and the East* (London: Thames and Hudson, 1962), p. 70. R. V. Nicholls.]

ship in 493 B.C. A decade later the Athenians came upon a rich vein of silver in the state mines, and Themistocles persuaded them to use the profits to increase their fleet. By 480 B.C. Athens had over two hundred ships, the backbone of the navy that defeated the Persians.

As the Persian army gathered south of the Hellespont, only thirty-one Greek states, led by Sparta, Athens, Corinth, and Aegina, were willing to fight. In the spring of 480 B.C. Xerxes launched his invasion. The Persian strategy was to march into Greece, destroy Athens, defeat the Greek army, and add the Greeks to the number of Persian subjects. The huge Persian army needed to keep in touch with the fleet for supplies. If the Greeks could defeat the Persian navy, the army could not remain in Greece long. Themistocles knew that the Aegean was subject to sudden devastating storms. His strategy was to delay the Persian army and then to bring on the kind of naval battle he might hope to win.

The Greek League met at Corinth as the Persians were ready to cross the Hellespont. They chose Sparta as leader on land and sea and sent a force to Tempe to try to defend Thessaly. Tempe proved to be indefensible, so the Greeks retreated and took up new positions at Thermopylae (the "hot gates") on land and off Artemisium at sea. The opening between the mountains and the sea at Thermopylae was so narrow that it might be held by a smaller army against a much larger one. The Spartans sent their king, Leonidas, with three hundred of their own citizens and enough allies to make a total of about nine thousand. The Greeks may have intended to hold only long enough to permit the Athenians to evacuate Athens, or to force a sea battle, or they may have hoped to hold Thermopylae until the Persians were discouraged enough to withdraw. Perhaps they thought of all these possibilities, for they were not mutually contradictory.

Severe storms wrecked a large number of Persian ships while the Greek fleet waited safely in their protected harbor. Then Xerxes attacked Thermopylae, and for two days the Greeks butchered his best troops without serious loss to themselves. On the third day, however, a traitor showed the Persians a mountain trail that permitted them to come on the Greeks from behind. Many allies escaped, but Leonidas and his three hundred Spartans died to the last man. At about the same time the Greek and Persian fleets fought an indecisive battle, and the fall of Thermopylae forced the Greek navy to withdraw.

If an inscription discovered in 1959 is authentic, Themistocles had foreseen this possibility, and the Athenians had begun to evacuate their homeland and move to defend Salamis. The fate of Greece was decided in the narrow waters to the east of the island. Themistocles persuaded the reluctant Peloponnesians to stay by threatening to remove all the Athenians and settle anew in Italy. The Greek ships were fewer, slower, and less maneuverable than those of the Persians, so the Greeks put soldiers on their ships and relied chiefly on hand-to-hand combat. The Persians lost more than half their ships and retreated to Asia with a good part of their army, but the danger was not over yet. Mardonius spent the winter in central Greece, and in the spring he unsuccessfully tried to win the Athenians away from the Greek League. The Spartan regent, Pausanias, then led the

The Athenian Assembly Passes Themistocles' Emergency Decree

The following is a translation of a portion of the Themistocles decree pictured on this page. See, below, the comments on the illustration.

The Gods

RESOLVED *by the Council and the People*

Themistocles, son of Neokles, of Phrearroi, made the motion:

To entrust the city to Athena the Mistress of Athens and to all the other Gods to guard and defend from the Barbarian for the sake of the land. The Athenians themselves and the foreigners who live in Athens are to send their children and women to safety in Troizen, their protector being Pittheus, the founding hero of the land. They are to send the old men and their movable possessions to safety on Salamis. The treasurers and priestesses are to remain on the acropolis guarding the property of the gods.

All the other Athenians and foreigners of military age are to embark on the 200 ships that are ready and defend against the Barbarian for the sake of their own freedom and that of the rest of the Greeks along with the Lakedaimonians, the Korinthians, the Aiginetans, and all others who wish to share the danger. . . .

When the ships have been manned, with 100 of them they are to meet the enemy at Artemision in Euboia, and with the other 100 they are to lie off Salamis and the coast of Attica and keep guard over the land. In order that all Athenians may be united in their defense against the Barbarian those who have been sent into exile for ten years are to go to Salamis and to stay there until the People come to some decision about them, while those who have been deprived of citizen rights are to have their rights restored. . . .

Translated by M. H. Jameson in "Waiting for the Barbarian," *Greece and Rome*, second series, Vol. 8 (Oxford: The Clarendon Press, 1961), pp. 5–18.

The Themistocles decree. This stone was inscribed in the third century B.C. and is thought to be a version of an Athenian decree proposed by Themistocles and passed shortly before the battle of Salamis in 480 B.C. It was discovered as recently as 1959. [Alison Frantz.]

Themistocles. This is a
late copy of a bust of the
great Athenian statesman
who was the hero of Salamis.
[Gabinetto Fotografico
Nazionale, Rome.]

largest Greek army up to that time to confront Mardonius in Boeotia. At Plataea, in the summer of 479 B.C., Mardonius died in battle and his army fled toward home.

Meanwhile the Ionian Greeks urged King Leotychidas, the Spartan commander of the fleet, to fight the Persian fleet at Samos. At Mycale, on the coast nearby, Leotychidas destroyed the Persian camp and its fleet offshore. The Persians fled the Aegean and Ionia. For the moment, at least, the Persian threat was gone.

SUGGESTED READINGS

C. M. Bowra, *Greek Elegists* (New York, 1960). This and the following book are useful literary studies of important sources for the history of the archaic period.

C. M. Bowra, *Greek Lyric Poetry from Alcman to Simonides* (Oxford, 1961).

A. R. Burn, *Persia and the Greeks* (New York, 1962). A full treatment from both sides.

R. M. Cook, *Greek Painted Pottery* (London, 1972).

E. R. Dodds, *The Greeks and the Irrational* (Boston, 1955). An excellent account of the role of the supernatural in Greek life and thought.

V. Ehrenberg, *The Greek State* (New York, 1964). A good handbook of constitutional history.

V. Ehrenberg, *From Solon to Socrates* (London, 1968). An interpretive history that makes good use of Greek literature to illuminate politics.

W. G. Forrest, *The Emergence of Greek Democracy* (London, 1966). A lively interpretation of Greek social and political developments in the archaic period.

W. G. Forrest, *A History of Sparta, 950–192 B.C.* (London, 1968). A brief but shrewd account.

P. Green, *Xerxes at Salamis* (London, 1970). A lively and stimulating history of the Persian wars.

C. Hignett, *A History of the Athenian Constitution* (Oxford, 1952). A scholarly account, somewhat too skeptical of the ancient sources.

C. Hignett, *Xerxes' Invasion of Greece* (Oxford, 1963). A valuable account, but too critical of all sources other than Herodotus.

D. Kagan, *The Great Dialogue: A History of Greek Political Thought from Homer to Polybius* (New York, 1965). A discussion of the relationship between the Greek historical experience and political theory.

G. S. Kirk and J. E. Raven, *Presocratic Philosophers* (Cambridge, 1960). A good introduction to Greek philosophy.

H. Michell, *Sparta* (Cambridge, 1952). A study of Spartan institutions.

A. T. Olmstead, *History of the Persian Empire* (Chicago, 1960). A thorough survey.

G. M. A. Richter, *Archaic Greek Art* (New York, 1949).

B. Snell, *Discovery of the Mind* (New York, 1960). An important study of Greek intellectual development.

F. Solmsen, *Hesiod and Aeschylus* (Ithaca, 1949). A fine study of the connections between the two poets.

W. J. Woodhouse, *Solon the Liberator* (New York, 1965). A discussion of the great Athenian reformer.

72

4
The Classical Period in Greece
(The Fifth Century B.C.)

The Delian League

THE UNITY of the Greeks had shown strain even in the life-and-death struggle against the Persians. Within two years of the Persian retreat it gave way almost completely and yielded to a division of the Greek world into two spheres of influence, dominated by Sparta and Athens. The need of the Ionian Greeks to obtain and defend their freedom from Persia and the desire of many Greeks to gain revenge and financial reparation for the Persian attack brought on the split.

Sparta had led the Greeks to victory, and it was natural to look to the Spartans to continue the campaign. But Sparta was ill suited to the task. It required a long-term commitment far from the Peloponnesus and continuous naval action.

The emergence of Athens as the leader of a Greek coalition against Persia was a natural development. Athens had become the leading naval power in Greece, and the same motives that led her to support the Ionian revolt moved her to try to drive the Persians from the Aegean and the Hellespont. The Ionians were at least as eager for the Athenians to take the helm as the Athenians were to accept the responsibility and opportunity.

In the winter of 478–477 B.C. the islanders, the Greeks from the coast of Asia Minor, and some other Greek cities on the Aegean met with the Athenians on the sacred island of Delos and swore oaths of alliance. As a symbol that the alliance was meant to be permanent, they dropped lumps of iron into the sea; the alliance was to hold until they rose to the surface. The aims of this new Delian League were to free those Greeks who were under Persian rule, to protect all against a Persian return, and to obtain compensation from the Persians by attacking their lands and taking booty. League policy was determined by a vote of the assembly, in which each state, including Athens, had one vote. Athens, however, was clearly designated leader.

From the first the league was remarkably successful. The Persians were driven from Europe and the Hellespont, and the Aegean was cleared of pirates. Some states were forced into the league or were prevented from leaving. The members approved the coercion because it was necessary for the common safety. In 467 B.C. a great victory over the Persians at the Eurymedon River in Asia Minor routed the Persians and added a number of cities to the league.

Cimon, son of Miltiades, the hero of Marathon, became the leading Athenian soldier and statesman soon after the Persian war. Themistocles appears to have been driven from power by a coalition of his enemies. Ironically the author of the Greek victory over Persia of 480 B.C. ended his days at the court of the Persian king. Cimon, who was to dominate Athenian politics for almost two decades, pursued a policy of aggressive attacks on Persia and friendly relations with Sparta. In domestic affairs Cimon was conservative. He accepted the democratic constitution of Clisthenes, which appears to have become somewhat more limited after the Persian war. Defending this constitution and this foreign policy, Cimon led the Athenians and the Delian League to victory after victory, and his own popularity grew with success.

The First Peloponnesian War

In 465 B.C. the island of Thasos rebelled from the league, and Cimon put it down after a siege of more than two years. The revolt of Thasos had an important influence on the development of the Delian League, on Athe-

Marble statue of the ever-youthful messenger-god Hermes holding the infant god of wine, Dionysus. It is by Praxiteles, one of the finest sculptors of antiquity, and has been dated to about 340–330 B.C. Some scholars think it is a copy of the lost original by Praxiteles. Found at Olympia in Greece in 1877, it is now in the museum at Olympia. [Bettmann Archive.]

Epidamnus

ILLYRIA

Apollonia

PAEONA

M A C E D O N I A

T H R A C E

Philippi   Abdera   Maronea

Amphipolis   Eion

Pella   Thessalonica   Stagira   Pactye

Methone   CHALCIDICE   Cardia

Pydna   Olynthus   SAMOTHRACE   Sestos   Lampsacus
             Potidaea   IMBROS   Abydos
MT.   MT.
OLYMPUS   Torone   ATHOS   Elaeus   Troy
             Scione   TROAD   PHRYGI

EPIRUS   LEMNOS   Adra-
                                                                myttium
Dodona   MYS
                                                Methymna
PENEIUS   Larisa   CAICUS
CORCYRA   MT. PELIUM   Mytilene   Atarneus
             THESSALY   LESBOS
Ambracia   Pherae   LYD
             Thysalus   PEPARETHUS   Phocaea   Cyme HERM
Anactorium   ARTEMESIUM   Magnesia
LEUCAS   THERMOPYLAE   Oreus   SKYROS   CHIOS
Sollum   Chios   Clazomenae
ACAR-   Heraclae   EUBOEA   Teos
Oenidae   NANIA   AETOLIA Elatea LOCRIS   Colophon
             Amphissa   MT. PARNASSUS Chalcis   Erythrae   Notium
Naupactus   DELPHI   Chaeronea Delium Eretria   Ephesus
             Coronea BOEOTIA   Oropus   SAMOS   Pri
CEPHALLENIA Thespiae   Thebes   Miletus
             Leuctra Plataea Decelea
ELIS ACHAEA Sicyon Megara   ATHENS   Carystus   ANDROS   ICARIA
Elis   Corinth SAL-   Piraeus   TENOS
ARCADIA   Nemea   AMIS   Thoricus AEGINA   MYKONOS Halicarnassus
Olympia   Cleonae   Laureum   KEOS   SYROS   DELOS
ZACYNTHUS   Mantinea Argos   COS
Megalopolis Tegea   MT.   Epidaurus CYNTHOS SERIPHOS PAROS
             DIDYMA Hermione   SIPHNOS NAXOS
Messene   LACONIA PELOPONNESUS   MELOS SIKINOS AMORGUS
IONIAN   MESSENIA SPARTA   IOS ASTYPALAEA CNIDUS
Pylos   MT.   PHOLEGANDROS
             Gythium TAYGETUS

SEA

CAPE   CAPE
TAENARUS   MALEA

             CYTHERA

CLASSICAL   CRETAN
GREECE   SEA   CARPATHOS

100 MI.
100 KM.

MEDITERRANEA

Tylissus Cnossus
CRETE
Gortyna

74 *The Classical Period in Greece* (*The Fifth Century* B.C.)

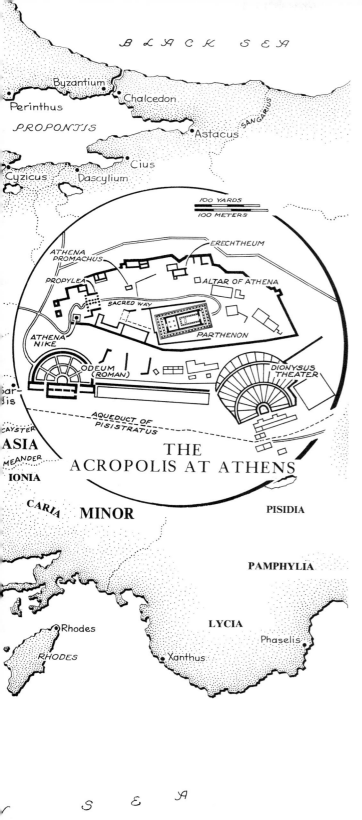

Greece in the classical period (*ca.* 480–338 B.C.) centered on the Aegean Sea. Although there were important Greek settlements in Italy, Sicily, and all around the Black Sea, the area shown in this general reference map embraced the vast majority of Greek states. The inset shows the location of the major monuments still visible on the Athenian Acropolis of the classical period.

nian politics, and on relations between Athens and Sparta. It is the first recorded instance in which Athenian interests seemed to determine league policy, a significant step in the evolution of the Delian League into the Athenian empire. When Cimon returned to Athens from Thasos, he was charged with taking bribes not to conquer Macedonia, but he was acquitted. The trial was only a device by which his political opponents tried to reduce his influence. Their program at home was to undo the gains made by the Areopagus and to bring about further changes in the direction of democracy; abroad, the enemies of Cimon wanted to break with Sparta and contest her claim to leadership over the Greeks. The head of this faction was Ephialtes. His lieutenant, and the man chosen to be the public prosecutor of Cimon, was Pericles, a member of a distinguished Athenian family. He was still a young man, and his defeat in court did not do lasting damage to his career.

When the Thasians began their rebellion, they asked Sparta to invade Athens the next spring, and the ephors agreed. An earthquake, accompanied by a rebellion of the helots that threatened the survival of Sparta, prevented the invasion. The Spartans asked their allies, the Athenians among them, for help. In Athens Ephialtes urged the Athenians "not to help or restore a city that was a rival to Athens but to let Sparta lie low and be trampled underfoot," but Cimon persuaded them to send help. The results were disastrous. The Spartans sent the Athenian troops home for fear of "the boldness and revolutionary spirit of the Athenians." While Cimon was gone, Ephialtes stripped the Areopagus of almost all its power. In the spring of 461 B.C. Cimon was ostracized, and Athens made an alliance with Argos, Sparta's traditional enemy. Almost overnight Cimon's domestic and foreign policies had been overturned.

The new regime at Athens was confident and ambitious. When Megara, getting the worst of a border dispute with Corinth, withdrew from the Peloponnesian League, the Athenians accepted the Megarians as allies. This alliance gave Athens a great strategic advantage, for

An Athenian tribute list. In 454 B.C. the Athenians moved the treasury of the Delian League to Athens and began to keep one-sixtieth of the annual contributions of the allies for themselves. On stones like this they recorded the annual assessment of each ally. The stones were set up on the Acropolis for all to see. This one records the assessment for 432–431 B.C., the first year of the Peloponnesian War. [TAP–Art Reference Bureau.]

Thucydides Recounts the Origin of the Delian League

Thucydides (*ca.* 460–400 B.C.) was an Athenian general and the historian of the Peloponnesian War. In this selection he describes the formation of the Delian League in 477 B.C.

THE *Lacedæmonians . . . sent out Dorkis and certain others with a small force; who found the allies no longer inclined to concede to them the supremacy. Perceiving this they departed, and the Lacedæmonians did not send out any to succeed them. They feared for those who went out a deterioration similar to that observable in Pausanias; besides, they desired to be rid of the Median war, and were satisfied of the competency of the Athenians for the position, and of their friendship at the time towards themselves.*

The Athenians having thus succeeded to the supremacy by the voluntary act of the allies through their hatred of Pausanias, fixed which cities were to contribute money against the barbarian, which ships; their professed object being to retaliate for their sufferings by ravaging the king's country. Now was the time that the office of 'Treasurers for Hellas' was first instituted by the Athenians. These officers received the tribute, as the money contributed was called. The tribute was first fixed at four hundred and sixty talents. The common treasury was at Delos, and the congresses were held in the temple. Their supremacy commenced with independent allies who acted on the resolutions of a common congress.

Thucydides, *The Peloponnesian War*, trans. by Richard Crawley (New York: Random House, 1951), pp. 54–56.

Megara barred the way from the Peloponnesus to Athens. It also brought on the First Peloponnesian War, for Sparta resented the defection of Megara to Athens. The early years of the war brought Athens great success. The Athenians conquered Aegina and gained control of Boeotia. At one moment Athens was supreme and invulnerable, controlling the states on her borders and dominating the sea.

In 454 B.C., however, the tide turned. In that year a disastrous defeat struck an Athenian fleet that had gone to aid an Egyptian rebellion against Persia. The great loss of men, ships, and prestige caused rebellions in the empire, forcing Athens to make a truce in Greece in order to subdue her allies in the Aegean. In 449 B.C. they ended the war against Persia. In 446 B.C. the war on the Greek mainland broke out again. Rebellions in Boeotia and Megara removed Athens' land defenses and brought a

The following labels appear on the map:

ADRIATIC SEA · Epidamnus · MAGNA GRAECIA · Apollonia · Hydrantum · CORCYRA · MACEDONIA · THRACE · BLACK SEA · Potidaea · THESSALY · Ragasae · Ambracia · Anaktorio · AETOLIA · LEUCAS · CEPHALLENIA · PHOCIS · Delphi · BOEOTIA · Thebes · EUBOEA · Eretria · ATTICA · Megara · Athens · ACHAEA · Sicyon · Corinth · Argos · Epidaurus · Elis · Olympia · ARCADIA · LACONICA · Sparta · CYTHERA · MEDITERRANEAN SEA · CRETE · THASOS · PROPONTIS · Sigeum · LEMNOS · PHRYGIA · ASIA · AEGEAN SEA · Mytilene · LESBOS · Phocaea · LYDIA · CHIOS · Colophon · Ephesus · MINOR · ANDROS · SAMOS · Magnesia · Miletus · DELOS · NAXOS · Ialysos · RHODES · CARPATHOS · 100 MI. · 100 KM.

INDEPENDENT MEMBERS
DEPENDENT MEMBERS
ALLIES

THE ATHENIAN EMPIRE ABOUT 450 B.C.

The Empire at its fullest extent shortly before 450 B.C. We see Athens and the independent states that provided manned ships for the imperial fleet but paid no tribute, dependent states who paid tribute, and states allied to but not actually in the Empire.

Spartan invasion. Rather than fight, Pericles, the commander of the Athenian army, agreed to a peace of thirty years by the terms of which he abandoned all Athenian possessions on the continent. In return, the Spartans gave formal recognition of the Athenian empire. From then on Greece was divided into two power blocs: Sparta and its alliance on the mainland and Athens ruling her empire in the Aegean.

The Athenian Empire

After the Egyptian disaster the Athenians moved the Delian League's treasury to Athens and began to keep one-sixtieth of the annual revenues for themselves. Because of the peace with Persia there seemed no further reason for the allies to pay tribute, so the Athenians were compelled to find a new justification for their empire. They called for a Panhellenic congress to meet at Athens to discuss rebuilding the temples destroyed by the Persians and to consider how to maintain freedom of the seas. When Spartan reluctance to participate prevented the congress, Athens felt free to continue to collect funds from the allies, both to maintain her navy and to rebuild the Athenian temples. Henceforth the allies would be treated as colonies and Athens as their mother city, the whole to be held together by good feeling and common religious observances.

All this could not cloak the fact that Athens was becoming the master and her allies mere subjects. By 445 B.C. only Chios, Lesbos, and Samos were autonomous and provided ships. All the other states paid tribute. The change from alliance to empire came about because of the pressure of war and rebellion and in large measure because the allies were unwilling to see to their own defense. Although the empire was not universally unpopular and had many friends among the lower classes and the democratic politicians, it came to be seen more and more as a tyranny. But the Athenians had come to depend on the empire for their prosperity and security. The Thirty Years' Peace of 445 B.C. had recognized their empire, and the Athenians were determined to defend it at any cost.

A klepsydra, or juror's water clock. The Athenians used water clocks to time speeches in their law courts. The clock shown here was found in the Athenian Agora and is now in the Royal Ontario Museum, Toronto. The mark XX shows that it holds two *choes* (about 6.5 liters); the six minutes that it would take to empty was the time allotted for rebuttal speeches in suits of a certain magnitude. [Agora Excavations, American School of Classical Studies at Athens.]

Athenian Democracy

Even as the Athenians were tightening their control over their allies at home, they were evolving the freest government the world had ever seen. This extension of the Athenian democracy took place chiefly under the guidance of Pericles, who succeeded to the leadership of the democratic faction after the assassination of Ephialtes in 462 B.C. Legislation was passed making the hoplite class eligible for the archonship, and in practice no one was thereafter prevented from serving on the basis of property class. Pericles himself proposed the law introducing pay for jury members, opening that important duty to the poor. Circuit judges were introduced, making swift impartial justice available even to the poorest residents in the countryside. Finally, Pericles himself introduced a bill limiting citizenship to those who had two citizen parents. From a modern perspective this measure might be seen as a step away from democracy, and, in fact, it would have barred Cimon and one of Pericles' ancestors. In Greek terms, however, it was quite natural. Democracy was defined in terms of those who held citizenship, and because citizenship had become a valuable commodity, the decision to limit it must have won a large majority. Participation in government in all the Greek states was also denied to slaves, resident aliens, and women.

Within the citizen body, however, the extent of the democracy was remarkable. Every decision of the state

Athens Demands Allegiance: The Oath of the Colophonians

This inscription is dated to the year 447 B.C. It shows the nature of the Athenians' control of their empire.

LET *the secretary of the boulé inscribe this decree and the oath on a stone stele in the city within the boundaries of the Colophonians; and let the colonists who have been settled in Colophon inscribe it and the oath on a stone stele in the market place within the boundaries of the Colophonians. And let the Colophonians swear the following: I will do and say and plan whatever good I can with regard to the people [demos] of the Athenians and their allies and I will not revolt from the people of the Athenians either in word or deed, either myself or in obedience to another. And I will love the people of the Athenians and I will not desert. And I will not destroy the democracy at Colophon, either myself or in obedience to another, either by going off to another city or by intriguing there. I will carry out these things according to the oath truly, without deceit and without harm, by Zeus, Apollo, and Demeter. And if I transgress may I and my descendants be destroyed for all time, but if I keep my oath may great prosperity come to me.*

Translated by Donald Kagan in *The Outbreak of the Peloponnesian War* (Ithica; N.Y.: Cornell University Press, 1969), p. 118.

had to be approved by the popular assembly, a collection of the people, not their representatives. Every judicial decision was subject to appeal to a popular court of not fewer than 51 and as many as 1,501 citizens, chosen from an annual panel of jurors widely representative of the Athenian population. Most officials were selected by lot without regard to class. The main elective officials, such as the generals and the imperial treasurers, were generally held by nobles and almost always by rich men, but the people were free to choose otherwise. All public officials were subject to scrutiny before taking office, could be called to account and removed from office during their tenure, and were held to a compulsory examination and accounting at the end of their term. There was no standing army, no police force, open or secret, and no way to coerce the people. If Pericles was elected to the generalship fifteen years in a row and thirty times in all, it was not because he was a dictator but because he was a brilliant speaker, a magnificent politician, a respected general, an acknowledged patriot, and a man patently incorruptible. When he lost the people's confidence, they

Bust of Pericles. This is a Roman copy based on a bronze original from the fifth century B.C. It is now in the Vatican. [Alinari/SCALA.]

did not hesitate to depose him from office. In 443 B.C., however, after the removal of his chief rival by ostracism, he stood at the height of his power. He had been persuaded by the defeat of the Athenian fleet in the Egyptian campaign and the failure of Athens' continental campaigns that its future lay in a conservative policy of retaining the empire in the Aegean and living at peace with the Spartans. It was in this direction that he led Athens' imperial democracy in the years after the First Peloponnesian War.

The Great Peloponnesian War and Its Aftermath

In the decade after the Thirty Years' Peace of 445 B.C. the willingness of each side to respect the new arrangements was tested and not found wanting.

About 435 B.C., however, a dispute arose in a remote and unimportant part of the Greek world, plunging the

A foundry as depicted on an Attic vase of the fifth century B.C. Greek skill in metal work reached a high level of achievement by the fifth century. The major practical use for the skill was in weapons of war, but artistic applications, especially in bronze, were also important. Here we see an artisan stoking a furnace to maintain the high but carefully controlled temperature needed in his work.

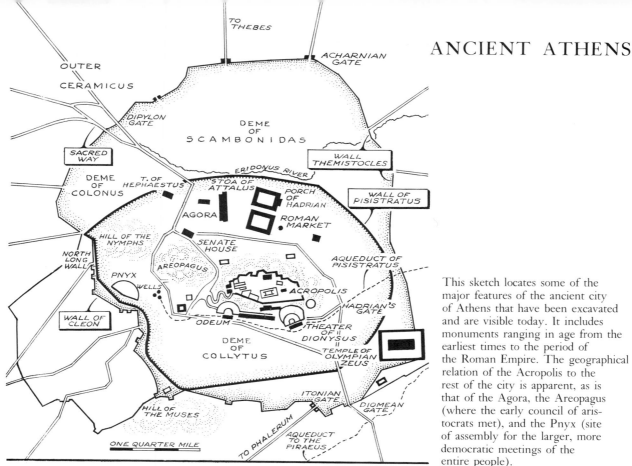

ANCIENT ATHENS

This sketch locates some of the major features of the ancient city of Athens that have been excavated and are visible today. It includes monuments ranging in age from the earliest times to the period of the Roman Empire. The geographical relation of the Acropolis to the rest of the city is apparent, as is that of the Agora, the Areopagus (where the early council of aristocrats met), and the Pnyx (site of assembly for the larger, more democratic meetings of the entire people).

Greeks into a long and disastrous war that shook the foundations of their civilization. Civil war broke out at Epidamnus, a Corcyraean colony on the Adriatic, causing a quarrel between Corcyra and her mother city and traditional enemy, Corinth. Corinth sought help from the Peloponnesian League, but Sparta stayed aloof and the Corinthians were defeated in a sea battle. Corinth, infuriated and determined to punish her upstart colonists, built a great fleet and prepared for another fight, even though the Corcyraeans had made a veiled threat to turn to Athens for help. When Corinth ignored the Spartan efforts at restraint, Corcyra asked Athens to join in an offensive and defensive alliance. For Athens to accept would almost surely mean war, at least with Corinth and probably with the whole Spartan alliance. The Athenian decision was difficult, and under the guidance of Pericles Athens tried to follow a middle path. The Athenians made a defensive alliance only and sent a very small squadron with orders to avoid battle if possible. This was an attempt to deter the Corinthians, not to defeat them, but it failed. The Corinthians attacked, and before long the Athenian ships had to intervene to save Corcyra at the battle of Sybota in the autumn of 433 B.C.

During the next winter the Corinthians urged their colony Potidaea, which was also a tribute-paying member

of the Athenian empire, to rebel. To forestall such an event, the Athenians sent troops to Potidaea to pull down its defensive walls, but the forces arrived too late and without sufficient strength. Potidaea rebelled and received an army of Corinthians to help in its defense. Now an Athenian army besieged a Corinthian army, and the chances for peace grew slimmer. During the same winter the Athenians passed a decree forbidding the Megarians access to the market and harbor of Athens and to those of the entire empire. The formal pretext was a religious infraction the Megarians had allegedly committed, but the real motive appears to have been to punish Megara for fighting, almost alone among the Peloponnesian states, alongside Corinth at Sybota. The decree was also calculated to deter other states from helping Corinth by showing that Athens could do them great economic harm without violating the terms of the Thirty Years' Peace.

The Athenian alliance with Corcyra, the siege of Potidaea, and the Megarian decree were not violations of the peace and were intended to deter war, but they caused bad feeling and alarm in Sparta. In the summer of 432 B.C. the Spartans met to consider the grievances of their allies. They were persuaded by their allies, and chiefly the Corinthians, that Athens was an insatiably aggressive power that aimed at enslaving all the Greeks,

80 *The Classical Period in Greece* (*The Fifth Century* B.C.)

and they voted for war. The treaty of 445 B.C. specifically provided that all differences be submitted to arbitration, and Athens repeatedly offered to arbitrate any question. Pericles insisted, however, that the Athenians refuse to yield to threats or commands and that they uphold the treaty and the arbitration clause. Sparta refused to arbitrate, and in the spring of 431 her army marched into Attica.

The Spartan strategy was traditional: to invade the enemy's country and threaten his crops, forcing him to defend them in a hoplite battle. Such a battle the Spartans were sure to win because they had the better army and they outnumbered the Athenians at least two to one. Any ordinary *polis* would have yielded or fought and lost, but Athens had an enormous navy, an annual income from her empire, a vast reserve fund, and long walls that connected her fortified city with the fortified port of Piraeus.

The Athenians' strategy was to allow devastation of their land to prove that Athens was invulnerable. At the same time the Athenians launched seaborne raids on the Peloponnesian coast to show that the allies of Sparta could be hurt. Pericles expected that within a year or two, three at most, the Peloponnesians would become discouraged and make peace, having learned their lesson. If the Peloponnesians held out, Athenian resources were inadequate to continue for more than four or five years without raising the tribute in the empire and running an unacceptable risk of rebellion. The plan required restraint and the leadership only a Pericles could provide.

The first year of the war went as planned, with no result. In the second year a terrible plague broke out in Athens (it eventually killed a third of the population), and the demoralized Athenians removed Pericles from office and fined him heavily. They asked for peace, but the angry Spartans refused. In 429 B.C. the Athenians returned Pericles to office, but he died before the year was over. His strategy had gone wrong and all he had worked for was in danger.

After Pericles' death there was no one in Athens with his ability to dominate the scene and hold the Athenians to a consistent policy. Two factions vied for influence: one, led by Nicias, wanted to continue the defensive policy, and the other, led by Cleon, preferred a more aggressive strategy. In 425 B.C. the aggressive faction was able to win a victory that changed the course of the war. Four hundred Spartans surrendered, and Sparta offered peace at once to get them back. The great victory and the prestige it brought Athens made it safe to raise the imperial tribute, without which Athens could not continue to fight. And the Athenians wanted to continue, for the Spartan peace offer gave no adequate guarantee of Athenian security.

In 424 B.C. the Athenians undertook a more aggressive policy: they sought to make Athens safe by conquering Megara and Boeotia. Both attempts failed, and defeat helped discredit the aggressive policy, leading to a truce in 423 B.C. Meanwhile, Sparta's ablest general, Brasidas, took a small army to Thrace and Macedonia. He captured Amphipolis, the most important Athenian colony in the region. Thucydides, the historian of the Great Peloponnesian War, was in charge of the Athenian fleet in those waters and was held responsible for the city's loss. He was exiled and was thereby given the time and opportunity to write his history. In 422 B.C. Cleon led an expedition to undo the work of Brasidas. At Amphipolis both he and Brasidas died in battle. The removal of these two leaders of the aggressive factions in their respective cities paved the way for peace. The Peace of Nicias, named for its chief negotiator, was ratified in the spring of 421 B.C.

The peace was for fifty years and guaranteed the *status quo* with a few exceptions. Neither side carried out all its commitments, and several of Sparta's allies refused to ratify the peace. Corinth urged the Argives to form a new alliance as a separate force and encouraged the war party in Sparta. In Athens Alcibiades emerged as the new leader of the aggressive faction and was able to bring about an alliance with Argos.

In 415 B.C. Alcibiades persuaded the Athenians to attack Sicily to bring it under Athenian control. The undertaking was ambitious and unnecessary, but if it had succeeded it would have deprived the Peloponnesians of all hope of western support in future wars and would have provided Athens with plenty of money for both military and domestic uses. A swift attack on Syracuse by a moderate force might have worked, but the Athenians suffered from divided counsel. Nicias opposed the expe-

The trireme was the dominant warship used by the Greeks in the fifth and fourth centuries B.C. Its superior speed, maneuverability, and tactical ability swept the seas of competition. Previous naval warfare had relied on grappling and boarding, which turned a sea fight into something very like a land battle. The trireme, however, with its metal prow, rammed the enemy at great speed, like a torpedo.

The side view drawing [OPPOSITE, TOP] shows only the top of three rows of oarsmen. The cross section drawings from the front [OPPOSITE, LEFT] show how the oars and oarsmen were arranged and how the oars struck the water and managed not to run afoul of one another. The two views of a trireme model from the front and top [OPPOSITE, RIGHT] show the positions of the three tiers of rowers. [Line drawings: J. S. Morrison and R. T. Williams: *Greek Oared Ships, 900–322 B.C.* (Cambridge: Cambridge University Press, 1968), plates 25 and 31. Photographs: J. S. Morrison, Cambridge University.]

dition, but he could not prevent it and was appointed one of its three commanders. Soon after the fleet sailed, Alcibiades was recalled to stand trial on some charges that had been trumped up by his enemies. In the end Nicias was in command of the whole expedition, and his hesitancy and lack of purpose brought disaster. In 413 B.C. the entire expedition was destroyed. The Athenians lost some two hundred ships, about forty-five hundred of their own men, and almost ten times as many allies. It was a disaster perhaps greater than the defeat of the Athenian fleet in the Egyptian campaign some forty years earlier. It shook Athenian prestige, reduced the power of Athens, provoked rebellions, and brought the wealth and power of Persia into the war on Sparta's side.

It is remarkable that the Athenians were able to continue fighting in spite of the disaster. They survived a brief oligarchic coup in 411 B.C. and won several important victories at sea as the war shifted to the Aegean. As their allies rebelled, however, and were sustained by fleets

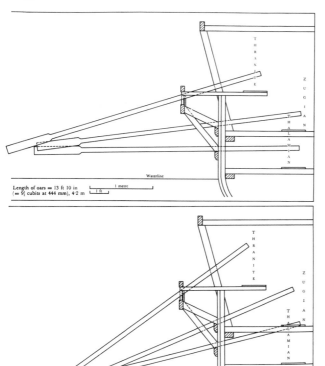

Scale 1:180
Height of deck above waterline: 8 ft
Draught: 3 ft 9 ins
Length: 115 ft
(Breadth of Hull amidships: 12 ft)
 Overall breadth including
  outriggers: 16 ft)

THRANITE

ZUGIAN

THALAMIAN

Waterline

Length of oars = 13 ft 10 in
(= 9¼ cubits at 444 mm), 4·2 m

1 metre

1 ft

THRANITE

ZUGIAN

THALAMIAN

Waterline

1 metre

1 ft

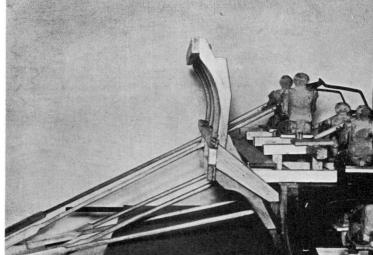

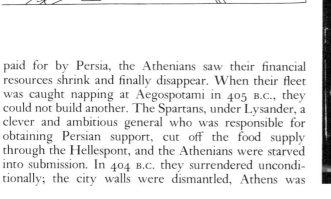

paid for by Persia, the Athenians saw their financial resources shrink and finally disappear. When their fleet was caught napping at Aegospotami in 405 B.C., they could not build another. The Spartans, under Lysander, a clever and ambitious general who was responsible for obtaining Persian support, cut off the food supply through the Hellespont, and the Athenians were starved into submission. In 404 B.C. they surrendered unconditionally; the city walls were dismantled, Athens was

The Great Peloponnesian War and Its Aftermath 83

permitted no fleet, and the empire was gone. The Great Peloponnesian War was over.

The Hegemony of Sparta

The collapse of the Athenian empire created a vacuum of power in the Aegean and opened the way for Spartan leadership, or hegemony. Fulfilling the contract that had brought them the funds to win the war, the Spartans handed the Greek cities of Asia Minor back to Persia. Under the leadership of Lysander the Spartans went on to make a complete mockery of their promise to free the Greeks by stepping into the imperial boots of Athens in the cities along the European coast and the islands of the Aegean. In most of the cities Lysander installed a board of ten local oligarchs loyal to him and supported them with a Spartan garrison. Tribute brought in an annual revenue almost as great as that the Athenians had collected.

Limited manpower, the helot problem, and traditional conservatism all made Sparta less than an ideal state to rule a maritime empire. Some of Sparta's allies, especially Thebes and Corinth, were alienated by the increasing arrogance of its policies. In 404 B.C. Lysander installed an oligarchic government in Athens whose outrageous behavior earned them the tital "Thirty Tyrants." Democratic exiles took refuge in Thebes and Corinth and created an army to challenge the oligarchy. Sparta's conservative king, Pausanias, replaced Lysander, arranging a peaceful settlement and ultimately the restoration of democracy. Thereafter Athenian foreign policy remained under Spartan control, but otherwise Athens was free.

In 405 B.C. Darius II of Persia died and was succeeded by Artaxerxes II. His younger brother, Cyrus, contested his rule and received Spartan help in recruiting a Greek mercenary army to help him win the throne. They marched inland as far as Mesopotamia, where they defeated the Persians at Cunaxa in 401 B.C., but Cyrus was killed. The Greeks were able to march back to the Black Sea and safety; their success revealed the potential weakness of the Persian Empire.

The Greeks of Asia Minor had supported Cyrus and were now afraid of Artaxerxes' revenge. The Spartans accepted their request for aid and sent an army into Asia, attracted by the prospect of prestige, power, and money. In 396 B.C. the command was given to Sparta's new king, Agesilaus. His personality and policy dominated Sparta throughout her period of hegemony and until his death in 360 B.C. Hampered by his lameness and his disputed claim to the throne, he seems to have compensated for both by always advocating aggressive policies and providing himself with opportunities to display his bravery in battle.

Agesilaus collected much booty and frightened the Persians. They sent a messenger with money and promises of further support to friendly factions in all the likely states. By 395 B.C. Thebes was able to organize an alliance that included Argos, Corinth, and a resurgent Athens. The result was the Corinthian War (395–387 B.C.), which put an end to Sparta's Asian adventure. In 394 the Persian fleet destroyed Sparta's maritime empire. Meanwhile the Athenians took advantage of events to rebuild their walls, enlarge their navy, and even to recover some of their lost empire in the Aegean. The war ended when the exhausted Greek states accepted a peace dictated by the Great King.

The Persians, frightened by the recovery of Athens, turned the management of Greece over to Sparta. Agesilaus broke up all alliances except the Peloponnesian League. He interfered with the autonomy of other *poleis* by using the Spartan army or the threat of its use to put friends in power within them. Sparta reached a new level of lawless arrogance in 382 B.C., when it seized Thebes during peacetime without warning or pretext. In 379 a Spartan army made a similar attempt upon Athens. That persuaded the Athenians to join with Thebes, which had rebelled from Sparta a few months earlier, to wage war on the Spartans. In 371 B.C. the Thebans, led by their great generals Pelopidas and Epaminondas, defeated the Spartans at Leuctra. The Thebans encouraged the Arcadian cities of the central Peloponnesus to form a federal

Xenophon Recounts How Greece Brought Itself to Chaos

Confusion in Greece in the fourth century B.C. reached a climax with the inconclusive battle of Mantinea in 361. The Theban leader Epaminondas was killed, and no other city or person emerged to provide the needed general leadership for Greece. Xenophon, a contemporary, here points out the resulting near chaos in Greek affairs—tempting ground for the soon-to-appear conquering Macedonians under their king Philip.

THE *effective result of these achievements was the very opposite of that which the world at large anticipated. Here, where well-nigh the whole of Hellas was met together in one field, and the combatants stood rank against rank confronted, there was no one who doubted that, in the event of battle, the conquerors this day would rule; and that those who lost would be their subjects. But god so ordered it that both belligerents alike set up trophies as claiming victory, and neither interfered with the other in the act. Both parties alike gave back their enemy's dead under a truce, and in right of victory; both alike, in symbol of defeat, under a truce took back their dead. And though both claimed to have won the day, neither could show that he had thereby gained any accession of territory, or state, or empire, or was better situated than before the battle. Uncertainty and confusion, indeed, had gained ground, being tenfold greater throughout the length and breadth of Hellas after the battle than before.*

Xenophon, *Hellenica*, trans. by H. G. Dakyns in *The Greek Historians*, F. R. B. Godolphin, ed., (New York: Random House, 1942), p. 221.

league, freed the helots, and helped them found a city of their own. They deprived Sparta of much of its farmland and of the men who worked it and hemmed it in with hostile neighbors. Sparta's population had shrunk so that it could put fewer than two thousand men into the field at Leuctra. Sparta's aggressive policies had led to ruin. The Theban victory brought the end of Sparta as a power of the first rank.

The Hegemony of Thebes; The Second Athenian Empire

Victorious Thebes had a democratic constitution, control over Boeotia, and two outstanding and popular generals. These were the basis for Theban power after Leuctra. Pelopidas died in a successful attempt to gain control of Thessaly. Epaminandas consolidated his work, and Thebes was soon dominant over all Greece north of Athens and the Corinthian Gulf. The Thebans challenged the reborn Athenian empire in the Aegean. All this activity provoked resistance, and by 362 B.C. Thebes faced a Peloponnesian coalition as well as Athens. Epaminondas once again led a victorious Boeotian army into the Peloponnesus, but he died in the fight, and the loss of its two great leaders ended Theban dominance.

Athens had organized the Second Athenian Confederation in 378 B.C. It was aimed at resisting Spartan aggression in the Aegean, and its constitution was careful to avoid the abuses of the Delian League. But the Athenians soon began to repeat those abuses, although this time they did not have the power to put down resistance. When the collapse of Sparta and Thebes and the restraint of Persia removed any reason for voluntary membership, Athens' allies revolted. By 355 B.C. Athens had to abandon most of the empire. After two centuries of almost continuous warfare, the Greeks returned to the chaotic disorganization of the time before the founding of the Peloponnesian League.

The Culture of Classical Greece

The repulse of the Persian invasion released a flood of creative activity in Greece rarely if ever matched anywhere at any time. The century and a half between the Persian retreat and the conquest of Greece by Philip of Macedon (479–338 B.C.) produced achievements of such quality as to justify that era's designation as the Classical Period. Ironically we often use the term *classical* to suggest calm and serenity, but the word that best describes the common element present in Greek life, thought, art, and literature in this period is *tension*. It was a time in which conflict between *poleis* continued and intensified as Athens and Sparta gathered most of them into two competing and menacing blocs. The victory over the Persians brought a sense of exultation in the capacity of man to accomplish great things and of confidence in the divine

Ruins of the theater of Dionysus in Athens. This theater, carved out of the southern slope of the Acropolis, is where the plays of Aeschylus, Sophocles, Euripides, Aristophanes, and many other tragic and comic poets were performed. It was constructed in the fourth century B.C. In the background is the modern city of Athens; note the remaining columns of the Temple of Olympian Zeus in the upper left corner. [Greek National Tourist Organization, New York. Yannis Scouroyannis.]

justice that brought arrogant pride low. But these feelings conflicted with a sense of unease as men recognized that the fate that met Xerxes awaited all men who reached too far. Another source of tension was the conflict between the soaring hopes and achievements of the individual and the claims and limits put upon him by his fellow citizens in the *polis*. These forces were at work throughout Greece, but we know them best and they had the most spectacular results in Athens in its Golden Age, the time between the Persian and the Peloponnesian wars.

Attic Tragedy

Nothing reflects these concerns better than the appearance of Attic tragedy as the major form of Greek poetry in the fifth century B.C. The tragedies were presented as part of public religious observations in honor of the god Dionysus. The whole affair was very much a civic occasion. Each poet who wished to compete submitted his work to the archon. Each offered three tragedies, which might or might not have a common subject, and a satyr play to close. The archon chose the best three competitors and awarded them each three actors and a chorus. The actors were paid by the state and the chorus by a wealthy citizen selected by the state who performed this service as *choregos* in place of paying taxes, for the Athenians had no direct taxation. Most of the tragedies were performed in the theater of Dionysus on the south side of the Acropolis, and as many as thirty thousand Athenians could attend. Prizes and honors were awarded to the author, the actor, and the *choregos* voted best by a jury of Athenians chosen by lot. On rare occasions the subject of the play might be a contemporary or historical event, but almost always it was chosen from mythology. Before Euripides it always dealt solemnly with serious

The Classical Period in Greece (The Fifth Century B.C.*)*

Sophocles. This is a Roman copy of a fourth-century B.C. Greek statue of the dramatist. [Alinari/SCALA.]

questions of religion, politics, ethics, morality, or some combination of these.

The tragedies were part of a great civic enterprise, yet the three great tragedians—the only ones whose plays have come down to us, Aeschylus (525–456 B.C.), Sophocles (497–406 B.C.), and Euripides (485–407 B.C.)—were outstanding individuals who put the stamp of their own personality and ideas on their work. In the *Oresteia* trilogy Aeschylus told of Orestes, the son of Agamemnon and Clytemnestra, who killed his mother because she and her consort had killed his father. There is conflict of a tragic quality because religion and honor require that Orestes avenge his father, but matricide is a horrible crime. The Furies, representatives of tradition and tribal religion, demand the death of Orestes. Aeschylus resolved the dilemma by deciding Orestes' fate in a trial before the Areopagus in Athens. Athena, the city's patron deity, intervenes to save Orestes and pacifies the Furies by giving them an honorable home in her city. This plot is symbolic of the tension between the religion of the tribe and the clan, with its blood feuds and vendettas, and the claim of the *polis* to the right to dispense justice. It has been said that tragedy is the conflict between right and right; the *Oresteia* presents such a conflict.

Sophocles seems not to have written connected trilogies but single plays on a theme. Compared to the powerful themes and thundering poetic language of Aeschylus, his plays may seem tamer and more serene, but even more than Aeschylus' plays the drama of Sophocles pulses with the tragic view of life characteristic of classical Greece. The *Antigone*, for instance, tells of Antigone's refusal to obey the order of her uncle Creon, king of Thebes, that forbids anyone to bury her dead brother, Polynices. One of the most basic demands of Greek religion is to bury the dead, but Polynices was a traitor, and the needs of state require such punishment. Antigone's dilemma reveals the tension between the demands of religion and the demands of secular law, between family and *polis*, between the individual and the community. Both Creon and Antigone are typical Sophoclean tragic heroes, headstrong, convinced of their rightness, determined to succeed at any cost, powerful and arrogant, and doomed to destruction by an excess of these qualities.[1]

Architecture and Sculpture

The great architectural achievements of Periclean Athens, just as much as Athenian tragedy, illustrate the magnificent results of the union and tension between religious and civic responsibilities on the one hand and the transcendant genius of the individual artist on the other. Beginning in 443 B.C. and continuing down to the outbreak of the Great Peloponnesian War, Pericles undertook a great building program on the Acropolis. The funds were provided by the income from the empire. The buildings were temples to honor the city's gods and a fitting gateway to the temples. Pericles' main purpose seems to have been to represent visually the greatness and power of Athens, but in such a way as to emphasize her intellectual and artistic achievement, her civilization rather than her military and naval power. It was as though these buildings were tangible proof of Pericles' claim that Athens was "the school of Hellas," that is, the intellectual center of all Greece.

The Parthenon is justly regarded as the acme of Greek architecture, for its subtlety and refinements, as well as its unmatched site, make it unique. The columns incline inward slightly, and lines that appear to be straight are slightly curved. The purpose of these departures in design is debated, but one distinguished historian of art provides an attractive suggestion:

1 Euripides, although almost contemporary with Sophocles, strongly reflected the intellectual currents that dominated the last third of the century; he will be discussed in that context.

The three orders of Greek architecture. These three basic orders, either in relatively pure form or as variously adapted, have enormously influenced much of the West's subsequent architecture.

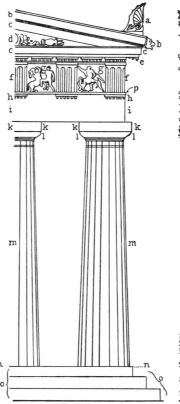
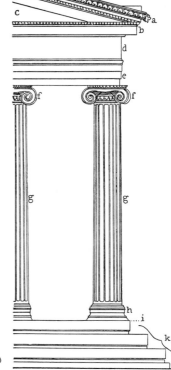

Diagram of a Doric Column and Entablature:

a Corner-Akroterion
b Sima with a lion's head as waterspout
c Geison (cornice)
d Tympanum
e Mutule with Guttae(drops)
f Triglyphs
g Metopes
h Regulae with guttae
i Architrave or Epistyle
k Abacus
l Echinus
m Shaft with 20 sharp-edged flutings
n Stylobate
o Krepis or Krepidoma
p Taenia

Diagram of an Ionic Column and Entablature

a Sima
b Geison (cornice)
c Tympanum
d Frieze
e Architrave or Epistyle (in three parts)
f Capital with Volutes
g Shaft with 24 flutings separated by fillets
h Attic Base with double Torus and a Trochilos
i Stylobate
k Krepis or Krepidoma

Corinthian Capital

The porch of the maidens on the Erechtheum. This is a uniquely designed Ionic temple built on the Athenian Acropolis near the Parthenon between about 421 and 409 B.C. It housed the shrines of three different gods and presented special architectural problems. One of its special features is the porch facing the Parthenon. In place of the usual fluted columns it uses statues of young girls taking part in a religious festival as columns. (Columns made from the draped female figure are called *caryatids*.) [Greek National Tourist Organization, New York.]

The Nike temple on the Athenian Acropolis. This small temple to the goddess of victory, of Ionic order, was built about 423 B.C. It stands modestly above and off to the right of the steps leading to the entrance gate of the Acropolis.

The Classical Period in Greece (The Fifth Century B.C.)

The Parthenon at Athens. This temple to Athena Parthenos (Athena the Maiden) was built under the direction of Pericles between 447 and 432 B.C., using funds from the treasury of the Delian League. It is generally thought to be the finest of all Greek temples. Built in the Doric order, with many subtle refinements, and crowning the Acropolis, it gave visible evidence of the greatness of Athens. [Greek National Tourist Organization, New York.]

They are intentional deviations from "regularity" for the purpose of creating a tension in the mind of the viewer between what he expects to see and what he actually does see. The mind looks for a regular geometric paradigm of a temple with true horizontals, right angles, etc., but the eye sees a complex aggregate of curves and variant dimensions. As a result, the mind struggles to reconcile what it knows with what the eye sees, and from this struggle arises a tension and fascination which makes the structure seem vibrant, alive, and continually interesting.[2]

The sculptures of the Parthenon also make artistic use of this tension. The pediments and metopes depict scenes of struggle between Greeks and Orientals, between civilization and barbarism. Olympian gods fight barbaric giants, Greeks fight Trojans and Amazons, human Lapiths fight half-beast Centaurs. The frieze on the cella is even more striking. It depicts what seems to be a Panathenaic procession, a scene of Athenians engaged in a religious rite. The sculpture of the Parthenon is a sharp departure from usual practice, which did not allow the representation of humans on temples. It is as though the Athenians, at the height of their power and confidence, were symbolically raising themselves almost to divine status even as they worshiped the gods.

Philosophy

Tragedy, architecture, and sculpture are all indications of the fifth century's extraordinary emphasis on the human being: his capacities, his limits, his nature, his place in the universe. The same concern is clear in the development of philosophy. Parmenides of Elea and his pupil Zeno, to be sure, carried on the theoretical debate about the nature of the cosmos. In opposition to Heraclitus they argued that change was only an illusion of the senses. Reason and reflection showed that reality was fixed and unchanging because it seemed evident that nothing could be created out of nothingness. Such fundamental speculations were carried forward by Empedocles

2 J. J. Pollitt, *Art and Experience in Classical Greece* (Cambridge, England: Cambridge University Press, 1972), p. 76.

[*Text continued on page 94*]

The Culture of Classical Greece 91

A metope from the Parthenon. In Doric architecture, metopes are the spaces between two triglyphs in the frieze; they were frequently decorated with carved work, and those on the Parthenon are outstanding. This sculpture is from a metope on the southern side of the Parthenon and shows a human Lapith (traditional representative of enlightenment and civilized life) fighting the half-man half-beast centaur. The scene was meant to show the struggle of Greeks and civilization against barbarians and chaos. It probably also played on proud memories of the Persian War. Parthenon sculpture was directed by Phidias, and the architect was Ictinus. [Editorial Photocolor Archives.]

OPPOSITE: Plastic model of the Athenian Agora, the civic center of classical Athens. Among the public buildings are: in front, the circular Tholos, which housed the presidents of the council and assembly; behind the Tholos, the two-story Bouleuterion, or council chamber, where the Athenian council met; to the right of the Bouleuterion, the Metroön, with many columns; and beyond the Metroön, also with many columns, the Stoa of Zeus. On the rise in the background, overlooking the Agora, is the temple of Hephaestus. [Agora Excavations, American School of Classical Studies at Athens.]

The Classical Period in Greece (The Fifth Century B.C.)

The temple of Hephaestus seen from the Athenian Agora. It was built soon after 450 B.C., about the same time as the Parthenon, and also in the Doric order. [Greek National Tourist Organization, New York.]

ABOVE: A reconstructed model of part of the sanctuary of the healing god Asclepius at Epidaurus. In the foreground is the stadium where athletic contests took place during festivals celebrating the god. In the background is the hospital area and the circular temple that covered the sacred spring. [Wellcome Institute of Medicine, London. Reproduced by courtesy of the Wellcome Trustees.]

LEFT: The theater at Epidaurus. This theater, built in the fourth century B.C., is one of the best preserved of ancient Greek theaters. Epidaurus, a city in the eastern Peloponnesus, was the site of the Sanctuary of Asclepius, the hero and god of healing. The sick and crippled came there, as to Lourdes in modern times, to be healed. The religious festivals there included theatrical performances that drew large crowds. [Greek National Tourist Organization, New York.]

of Acragas, who spoke of four basic elements: fire, water, earth, and air. Like Parmenides he thought that reality was permanent but not immobile, for the four elements were moved by two primary forces, Love and Strife, or, as we might be inclined to say more abstractly, attraction and repulsion.

This theory is clearly a step on the road to the atomic theory of Leucippus of Miletus and Democritus of Abdera. They believed that the world consisted of innumerable tiny, solid particles that could not be divided or modified and that moved about in the void. The size of the atoms and the arrangement in which they were joined with others produced the secondary qualities that the senses could perceive, such as color and shape. These qualities, unlike the atoms themselves, which were natural, were merely conventional. Anaxagoras of Clazomenae, an older contemporary and a friend of Pericles, had previously spoken of tiny fundamental particles called seeds, which were put together on a rational basis by a force called *nous* or "mind." Thus Anaxagoras suggested a distinction between matter and mind. The atomists,

Plato Reports Callicles' Views on Justice: Sophist Ethics

Plato (*ca.* 429–347 B.C.) remains, to many, the greatest of ancient philosophers. His dialogue *Gorgias* takes its name from the Sicilian sophist who lived from about 483 to 376 B.C. and was a famous teacher of rhetoric. The speaker in the following selection from the *Gorgias* dialogue is a young man named Callicles. We do not know whether he is a real or fictional character, but he represents the young Athenian nobles who challenged traditional morality in the latter part of the fifth century B.C.

THE *suffering of injustice is not the part of a man, but of a slave, who indeed had better die than live; since when he is wronged and trampled upon, he is unable to help himself, or any other about whom he cares. The reason, as I conceive, is that the makers of laws are the majority who are weak; and they make laws and distribute praises and censures with a view to themselves and to their own interests; and they terrify the stronger sort of men, and those who are able to get the better of them, in order that they may not get the better of them; and they say, that dishonesty is shameful and unjust; meaning, by the word injustice, the desire of a man to have more than his neighbours; for knowing their own inferiority, I suspect that they are too glad of equality. And therefore the endeavour to have more than the many, is conventionally said to be shameful and unjust, and is called injustice, whereas nature herself intimates that it is just for the better to have more than the worse, the more powerful than the weaker; and in many ways she shows, among men as well as among animals, and indeed among whole cities and races, that justice consists in the superior ruling over and having more than the inferior.*

Plato, *Gorgias*, trans. by Benjamin Jowett in *The Dialogues of Plato*, Vol. 1 (New York: Random House, 1937), pp. 543–544.

however, regarded "soul" or mind as material and believed that everything was guided by purely physical laws. In the arguments of Anaxagoras and the atomists we have the beginning of the philosophical debate between materialism and idealism that has continued through the ages.

These discussions interested very few, and, in fact, most Greeks were suspicious of such speculations. A far more influential debate was begun by a group of professional teachers who emerged in the mid-fifth century B.C. and whom the Greeks called *Sophists*. They traveled about and received pay for teaching practical techniques such as rhetoric, a valuable skill in democracies like Athens. Others claimed to teach wisdom and even virtue. They did not speculate about the physical universe but applied reasoned analysis to man and his beliefs and institutions. This human focus is characteristic of fifth-century thought, as is the central problem that the Sophists considered: they discovered the tension and even the contradiction between nature and custom or law. The more traditional among them argued that law itself was in accord with nature, and this view fortified the traditional beliefs of the *polis*.

Others argued, however, that laws were merely conventional and not in accord with nature. The law was not of divine origin but merely the result of an agreement among men. It could not pretend to be a positive moral force but merely had the negative function of preventing men from harming each other. The most extreme Sophists argued that law was contrary to nature, a trick whereby the weak control the strong. Critias, an Athenian oligarch and one of the more extreme Sophists, went so far as to say that the gods themselves were invented by some clever man to deter men from doing what they wished. Such ideas attacked the theoretical foundations of the *polis* and helped provoke the philosophical responses of Plato and Aristotle in the next century.

The Sophists had a profound effect on the thought and literature of the last part of the fifth century B.C. Many of the tragedies of Euripides are strikingly different from those of his predecessors. They are filled with the tricky arguments associated with Sophist rhetoric and with a skeptical view of the gods and the role they play in human lives. Many of his heroes and heroines suffer terrible fates at the hands of the gods through no apparent fault of their own. Some of his characters condemn the power of oracles, doubt the truth of legends, denounce or doubt the existence of gods, and even deny the existence of a divine order. The focus of his plays is the individual human being and the psychological forces working within him or her. Here the humanism and the tension characteristic of fifth-century thought come together as we see men and women torn by conflicting emotional needs in a world where the gods play no part or only a malevolent one.

History

The fifth century produced the first prose literature in the form of history. Herodotus, born shortly before the Persian wars, deserves his title of "the father of history," for his account of the Persian wars goes far beyond all previous chronicles, genealogies, and geographical studies and attempts to explain human actions and to draw instruction from them. Although his work was completed about 425 B.C. and shows a few traces of Sophist influence, its spirit is that of an earlier time. Herodotus accepted the evidence of legends and oracles, although not uncritically, and often explained human events in terms of divine intervention. Human arrogance and divine vengeance are key forces that help explain the defeat of Croesus by Cyrus as well as Xerxes' defeat by the Greeks. Yet the *History* is typical of its time in celebrating the crucial role of human intelligence as revealed by Miltiades at Marathon and Themistocles at Salamis. Nor was Herodotus unaware of the importance of institutions. There is no mistaking his pride in the superiority of the Greek *polis* and the discipline it inspired in its citizen soldiers and his pride in the superiority of the Greeks' voluntary obedience to law over the Persians' fear of punishment.

Thucydides, the historian of the Peloponnesian War, was born about 460 B.C. and died a few years after the end of the war he described. He was very much a product of the late fifth century, reflecting the influence of the scientific attitude of the Hippocratic school of medicine as well as the secular, man-centered skeptical rationalism of the Sophists. Hippocrates of Cos was a contemporary of Thucydides who was part of a school of medical writers and practitioners. They did important pioneer work in medicine and scientific theory, placing great emphasis on the need to combine careful and accurate observation with reason to make possible the understanding, prognosis, treatment, and cure of a disease. In the same way Thucydides took great pains to achieve factual accuracy and tried to use his evidence to discover meaningful patterns of human behavior. He believed that human nature was essentially unchanging, so that a wise man equipped with the understanding provided by history might accurately foresee events and thus help to guide them. He believed, however, that only few men had the ability to understand history and put its lessons to good use. He thought that even the wisest man could be foiled by the intervention of chance, which played a great role in human affairs. Thucydides focused his interest on politics, and in that area his assumptions about human nature do not seem unwarranted. His work has proved to be, as he hoped, "a possession forever." Its description of the terrible civil war between the two basic kinds of *polis* is a final and fitting example of the tension that was the source of both the greatness and the decline of classical Greece.

The Fourth Century B.C.

Historians often speak of the Peloponnesian War as the crisis of the *polis* and of the fourth century as the period of its decline. But the Greeks of the fourth century B.C. did not know that their traditional way of life was on the verge of destruction. Thinking men could not avoid recognizing that they lived in a time of troubles, but they responded in different ways. Some looked to the past and tried to shore up the weakened structure of the *polis*; others tended toward despair and looked for new solutions; and still others averted their gaze from the public arena altogether. All of these responses are apparent in the literature, philosophy, and art of the period.

The long Peloponnesian War and the struggles accompanying the several attempts at hegemony brought results that undermined the foundations of the *polis*. By ravaging farmland, destroying crops and houses, interfering with commerce, and using up reserve funds, the

Reconstructed model of the sacred precinct of Apollo
at Delphi on the slopes of Mount Parnassus. This
shrine of Apollo was the best known and most popular
religious center in the Greek world. Both Greeks
and foreigners came from great distances to consult
the oracle, worship the god, compete in the athletic
contests, attend festivals of drama, and bring gifts
to the god. The temple of Apollo and the theater
dominate the scene, but there are also numerous
smaller structures—treasuries, trophies, and
temples contributed by cities throughout the Greek
world and put under the protection of the god.
[Metropolitan Museum of Art, New York; Dodge Fund,
1930.]

warring armies and navies did severe and usually lasting
damage to the economic well-being that made civic life
possible. In the less favored and more badly damaged
regions many citizens were forced to leave home and hire
themselves out as mercenary soldiers to foreign kings as
well as to Greek cities. Civil strife and class conflict,
encouraged by the pressure of want and disease as well as
by the availability of help from foreign armies, were an

even more terrible legacy than poverty. Describing the
revolution at Corcyra in the Peloponnesian War, Thucydides pointed out that it was only the first of many that
convulsed the Greek cities. "War," as he said, "is a
violent teacher that brings the character of most men to a
level with their circumstances." As time passed, men
abandoned patriotism, morality, and even family to the
interests of faction.

The wars of the fourth century only intensified these
developments. Democratic revolutions, accompanied by
confiscations of property, executions, exiles, and even
greater atrocities, were answered with similar actions by
victorious oligarchs. Such upheavals left permanent scars,
and ruled out the family feeling, the sense of community,
and the commitment to the common good required for
life in the *polis*.

Drama

The tendency of some to avert their gaze from the life
of the *polis* and to turn inward to everyday life, the
family and their own individuality is apparent in the
poetry of the fourth century B.C. Tragedy proved to be a

Euripides. A Roman copy of a Greek bust of the fourth century B.C., now in the Galleria Nazionale d'Arte Antica in Rome. [Alinari/SCALA.]

form whose originality was confined to the fifth century. No tragedies written in the fourth century have been preserved, and it was common to revive the great plays of the previous century. Some of the late plays of Euripides, in fact, seem less like the tragedies of Aeschylus and Sophocles than forerunners of later forms such as the New Comedy. Plays of Euripides like *Helena, Andromeda,* and *Iphigenia in Tauris* are more like fairy tales, tales of adventure, or love stories than tragedies. Euripides was less interested in cosmic confrontations of conflicting principles than in the psychology and behavior of individual human beings. His plays, which rarely won first prize when first produced for Dionysian festival competitions, became increasingly popular in the fourth century and after.

Comedy was introduced into the Dionysian festival early in the fifth century B.C. Such poets as Cratinus, Eupolis, and the great master of the genre called Old Comedy, Aristophanes (*ca.* 450–*ca.* 385 B.C.), the only one from whom we have complete plays, wrote political comedies filled with scathing invective and satire against contemporary figures like Pericles, Cleon, Socrates, and Euripides. The fourth century, however produced what is called Middle Comedy, which turned away from political subjects and personal invective toward a comic-realistic depiction of daily life, to plots of intrigue, and to mild satire of domestic situations. Significantly the role of the chorus, which in some way represented the *polis,* was very much diminished. These trends all continued and were carried even further in New Comedy, whose leading playwright Menander (342–291 B.C.) completely abandoned mythological subjects in favor of domestic tragicomedy. His gentle satire of the foibles of ordinary people and his tales of lovers temporarily thwarted before a happy and proper ending would not be unfamiliar to viewers of modern situation comedies.

Sculpture

The same movement away from the grand, the ideal, and the general and toward the ordinary, the real, and the

individual is apparent in the development of Greek sculpture. To see these developments, one has only to compare the statue of the *Striding God of Artemisium* (*ca.* 460 B.C.), thought to be either Zeus on the point of releasing a thunderbolt or Poseidon about to throw his trident, or the *Doryphoros* of Polycleitus (*ca.* 450–440 B.C.) with the Hermes of Praxiteles (*ca.* 340–330 B.C.) or the *Apoxyomenos* attributed to Lysippus (*ca.* 330 B.C.).

Philosophy

SOCRATES. Probably the most complicated response to the crisis of the *polis* may be found in the life and teachings of Socrates (469–399 B.C.). Because he wrote nothing, our knowledge of him comes chiefly from his disciples Plato and Xenophon and from later tradition. Although as a young man he was interested in speculations about the physical world, he abandoned them and turned to the investigation of ethics and morality; as Cicero put it, he brought philosophy down from the heavens. He was committed to the search for truth and for the knowledge about human affairs that he believed could be discovered by reason. His method was to go among men, particularly those reputed to know something, like craftsmen, poets, and politicians, to question and cross-examine them. The result was always the same: men sometimes had technical information and skills but no knowledge of the fundamental principles of human behavior. It is understandable that Athenians so exposed should be angry with their examiner, and it is not surprising that they thought Socrates was undermining the beliefs and values of the *polis.* Socrates' unconcealed contempt for democracy, which seemingly relied on ignorant amateurs to make important political decisions without any certain knowledge, created further hostility. Moreover, his insistence on the primacy of his own individualism and his determination to pursue philosophy even against the wishes of his fellow citizens reinforced this hostility and the prejudice that went with it.

But Socrates, unlike the Sophists, did not accept pay

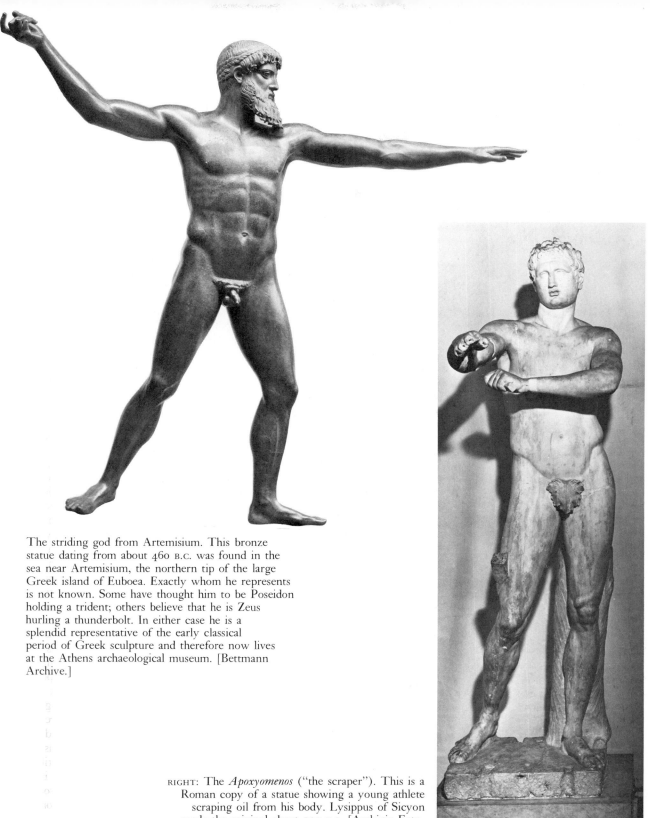

The striding god from Artemisium. This bronze statue dating from about 460 B.C. was found in the sea near Artemisium, the northern tip of the large Greek island of Euboea. Exactly whom he represents is not known. Some have thought him to be Poseidon holding a trident; others believe that he is Zeus hurling a thunderbolt. In either case he is a splendid representative of the early classical period of Greek sculpture and therefore now lives at the Athens archaeological museum. [Bettmann Archive.]

RIGHT: The *Apoxyomenos* ("the scraper"). This is a Roman copy of a statue showing a young athlete scraping oil from his body. Lysippus of Sicyon made the original about 330 B.C. [Archivio Fotografico, Musei Vaticani.]

BELOW, LEFT: The charioteer from Delphi. This is one of the few original bronze statues surviving from the fifth century B.C. and is datable to about 475 B.C. It is only one figure in what originally was a group, including a chariot, horses, and a groom, that was dedicated by a Sicilian tyrant in honor of his victory at the Pythian games at Delphi. It remains in the museum there. [Alinari/SCALA.]

BELOW, RIGHT: The *Doryphorus* ("the spear-bearer"). The young man portrayed is an athlete prepared to throw a javelin. The original, of which this is a Roman copy, was a bronze statue by the great Greek sculptor Polycleitus, who worked during the middle of the fifth century B.C. This statue was found at Pompeii and is now in the museum at Naples. [Alinari/SCALA.]

Socrates. This is a Hellenistic copy of a fourth-century B.C. statue of the great Athenian philosopher. [SCALA/Editorial Photocolor Archives.]

for his teaching; he professed ignorance and denied that he taught at all. His individualism, moreover, was unlike the worldly hedonism of some of the Sophists. It was not wealth or pleasure or power that he urged each man to seek, but "the greatest improvement of the soul." He differed also from the more radical Sophists in that he denied that the *polis* and its laws were merely conventional. He thought, on the contrary, that they had a legitimate claim on the citizen, and he proved it in the most convincing fashion. In 399 B.C. he was condemned to death by an Athenian jury on the charges of bringing new gods into the city and of corrupting the youth. His dialectical inquiries had angered many important people, and his criticism of democracy must have been viewed with suspicion, especially as Critias and Charmides, who were members of the Thirty Tyrants, and the traitor Alcibiades had been among his disciples. He was given a chance to escape, but in Plato's *Crito* we are told of his refusal because of his veneration of the laws. Socrates' career set the stage for later responses to the travail of the *polis;* he recognized its difficulties and criticized its short-comings, and he turned away from an active political life, but he did not abandon the idea of the *polis.* He fought as a soldier in its defense, obeyed its laws, and sought to put its values on a sound foundation by reason.

THE CYNICS. One branch of Socratic thought—the concern with personal morality and one's own soul, the disdain of worldly pleasure and wealth, and the withdrawal from political life—was developed and then distorted almost beyond recognition by the Cynic school. Antisthenes (*ca.* 455–*ca.* 360 B.C.), a follower of Socrates, is said to have been its founder, but its most famous exemplar was Diogenes of Sinope (*ca.* 400–*ca.* 325 B.C.). Socrates disparaged wealth and worldly comfort, so Diogenes wore rags and lived in a tub. He performed shameful acts in public and made his living by begging. Socrates questioned the theoretical basis for popular religious beliefs; the Cynics ridiculed all religious observances. As Plato said, Diogenes was Socrates gone mad. Beyond that, the way of the Cynics contradicted important Socratic beliefs. Socrates, unlike traditional aristocrats like Theognis, believed that virtue was not a matter of birth but of knowledge and that men do wrong only through ignorance of what is virtuous. The Cynics, on the contrary, believed that "Virtue is an affair of deeds and does not need a store of words and learning."[3] Wisdom and happiness come from pursuing the proper style of life, not from philosophy. They moved even further from Socrates by abandoning the concept of the *polis* entirely. When Diogenes was asked about his citizenship, he answered that he was *kosmopolites*, a citizen of the world. The Cynics plainly had turned away from the past, and their views anticipated those of the Hellenistic Age.

PLATO. Plato (429–347 B.C.) was by far the most important of Socrates' associates and is a perfect example of the pupil who becomes greater than his master. He was the first systematic philosopher and therefore the first to place political ideas in their full philosophical context. He was also a writer of genius, leaving us twenty-six philosophical discussions, almost all in the form of dialogues, which somehow make the examination of difficult and complicated philosophical problems seem dramatic and entertaining. Plato came from a noble Athenian family and looked forward to an active political career until the excesses of the Thirty Tyrants and the execution of Socrates by the restored democracy discouraged him. Twice he made trips to Sicily in the hope of producing a model state at Syracuse under the tyrants Dionysius I and II, but without success. In 386 B.C. he founded the Academy, a center of philosophical investigation and a school for training statesmen and citizens that had a powerful impact on Greek thought and lasted until it was closed by the Emperor Justinian in the sixth century A.D.

Like Socrates, Plato firmly believed in the *polis* and its values. Its virtues were order, harmony, and justice, and one of its main objects was to produce good men. Like his master, and unlike the radical Sophists, Plato thought that the *polis* was in accord with nature. He accepted Socra-

3 Diogenes Laertius, *Life of Antisthenes.*

tes' doctrine of the identity of virtue and knowledge and made it plain what that knowledge is. It is *episteme*, science, a body of true and unchanging wisdom open to only a few philosophers, whose training, character, and intellect have allowed them to see reality. Only such men are qualified to rule; they themselves will prefer the life of pure contemplation but will accept their responsibility and take their turn as philosopher kings. The training of such men requires a specialization of function and a subordination of the individual to the community even greater than that at Sparta. This specialization leads to Plato's definition of justice: that each man should do only that one thing to which his nature is best suited. Plato saw quite well that the *polis* of his day suffered from terrible internal stress, class struggle, and factional divisions. His solution, however, was not that of some Greeks, that is, conquest and resulting economic prosperity. For Plato the answer was in moral and political reform. The way to harmony was to destroy the causes of strife: private property, the family—anything, in short, that stood between the individual citizen and his devotion to the *polis*.

The concern for the redemption of the *polis* is at the heart of Plato's system of philosophy. He began by asking the traditional questions: What is a good man, and how is he made? The goodness of man belongs to moral philosophy, and when it becomes a function of the state it becomes political philosophy. Because goodness depends on knowledge of the good, it requires a theory of knowledge and an investigation of what the knowledge is that man must have in order to be good. The answer must be metaphysical and so requires a full examination of metaphysics. Even when the philosopher knows the good, however, the question remains of how the state can bring its citizens to the necessary comprehension of that knowledge. The answer requires a theory of education. Even purely logical and metaphysical questions, therefore, are subordinate to the overriding political questions. In this way Plato's need to find a satisfactory foundation for the beleaguered *polis* contributed to the birth of systematic philosophy.

Aristotle. This is a Roman copy of a Greek original. It is in the Museo delle Terme, Rome. [Alinari/SCALA.]

ARISTOTLE. Aristotle (384–322 B.C.) was a pupil of Plato's and owed much to the thought of his master, but his very different experience and cast of mind led him in some new directions. He was born at Stagirus in the Chalcidice, the son of the court doctor of neighboring Macedon. As a young man he came to study at the Academy, where he stayed until Plato's death. Then he joined a Platonic colony at Assos in Asia Minor, and from there he moved to Mytilene. In both places he carried on research in marine biology, and biological interests played a large part in all his thoughts. In 342 B.C. Philip, the king of Macedon, appointed him tutor to his son, the young Alexander (see Chapter 5). In 336 he returned to Athens, were he founded his own school, the Lyceum, or the Peripatos, as it was also called from the covered walk within it. In later years its members were called *Peripatetics.* On the death of Alexander in 323 B.C., the Athenians rebelled from Macedonian rule, and Aristotle found it wise to leave. He died at Chalcis in Euboea in the following year.

The Lyceum was a very different place from the Academy. Its members took little interest in mathematics and were concerned with gathering, ordering, and analyzing all human knowledge. Aristotle wrote dialogues on the Platonic model, but none survive. He and his students also prepared many collections of information to serve as the basis for scientific works, but of these only the *Constitution of the Athenians,* one of 158 constitutional treatises, remains. Almost all of what we possess is in the form of philosophical and scientific studies, whose loose organization and style suggest that they were lecture notes. The range of subjects treated is astonishing, including logic, physics, astronomy, biology, ethics, rhetoric, literary criticism, and politics. In each field the method is the same. Aristotle began with observation of the empirical evidence, which in some cases was physical and in others was the common opinion of men. To this body of information he applied reason and discovered inconsistencies or difficulties. To deal with these, he introduced metaphysical principles to explain the problems or to reconcile

the inconsistencies. His view in all subjects, like Plato's, was teleological; that is, both Plato and Aristotle recognized purposes apart from and greater than the will of the individual human being. Plato's purposes, however, were contained in the Ideas, or Forms, transcendental concepts outside the experience of most men, whereas for Aristotle the purposes of most things were easily inferred by observation of their behavior in the world. Aristotle's most striking characteristics are his moderation and common sense. His epistemology finds room for both reason and experience; his metaphysics gives meaning and reality to both mind and body; his ethics aims at the good life, which is the contemplative life, but recognizes the necessity for moderate wealth, comfort, and pleasure.

All these qualities are evident in Aristotle's political thought. Like Plato he opposed the Sophists' assertion that the *polis* was contrary to nature and the result of mere convention. His response was to apply the teleology he saw in all nature to politics as well. In his view matter exists to achieve an end, and it develops until it achieves its form, which is its end. There is constant development from matter to form, from potential to actual. Therefore man's primitive instincts may be seen as the matter out of which his potential as a political being can be realized. The *polis* makes man self-sufficient and allows the full realization of his potentiality. It is therefore natural. It is also the highest point in the evolution of social institutions that serve man's need to continue the species—marriage, household, village, and finally, *polis*. For Aristotle the purpose of the *polis* was neither economic nor military but moral. "The end of the state is the good life" (*Politics* 1280b), the life lived "for the sake of noble actions" (1281a), a life of virtue and morality.

Characteristically Aristotle was less interested in the best state—the utopia that required philosophers to rule it—than in the best state practically possible for men, one that would combine justice with stability. The constitution for that state he called *politeia,* not the best constitution, but the next best, the one most suited to and most possible for most states. Its quality is moderation and it naturally gives power to neither the rich nor the poor but to the middle class, which must also be the most numerous. The middle class possesses many virtues: because of its moderate wealth it is free of the arrogance of the rich and the malice of the poor. For this reason it is the most stable class. The stability of the constitution also comes from its being a mixed constitution, blending in some way the laws of democracy and of oligarchy. Aristotle's scheme was unique because of its realism and the breadth of its vision. All the political thinkers of the fourth century B.C. recognized that the *polis* was in danger and all hoped to save it. All recognized the economic and social troubles that threatened it. Isocrates, a contemporary of Plato and Aristotle, urged a program of imperial conquest as a cure for poverty and revolution. Plato saw the folly of solving a political and moral problem by purely economic means and resorted to the creation of utopias. Aristotle

combined the practical analysis of political and economic realities with the moral and political purposes of the traditional defenders of the *polis.* The result was a passionate confidence in the virtues of moderation and of the middle class and the proposal of a constitution that would give it power. It is ironical that the ablest defense of the *polis* came soon before its demise.

SUGGESTED READINGS

E. BARKER, *Political Philosophy of Plato and Aristotle* (New York, 1959). A sober and reliable account.

W. R. CONNOR, *The New Politicians of Fifth-Century Athens* (Princeton, 1971). A study on changes in political style and its significance for Athenian society.

J. DE ROMILLY, *Thucydides and Athenian Imperialism* (Oxford, 1963). A study of the historian and the great theme of his history.

G. E. M. DE STE. CROIX, *The Origins of the Peloponnesian War* (Ithaca, 1972). A rich and controversial work that places the blame for the war on Sparta.

V. EHRENBERG, *The People of Aristophanes* (New York, 1962). A study of Athenian society as revealed by the comedies of Aristophanes.

A. FRENCH, *The Growth of the Athenian Economy* (London, 1964). An interesting examination of economic developments in Athenian history.

W. K. C. GUTHRIE, *The Sophists* (Cambridge, 1971). A fine volume in an excellent history of Greek philosophy.

W. JAEGER, *Demosthenes* (Berkeley, 1938). A good biography of the Athenian statesman.

A. H. M. JONES, *Athenian Democracy* (Oxford, 1957). A collection of essay that is both scholarly and engaging.

D. KAGAN, *The Outbreak of the Peloponnesian War* (Ithaca, 1969). A study of the period from the foundation of the Delian League to the coming of the Peloponnesian War that argues that the war could have been avoided.

D. KAGAN, *The Archidamian War* (Ithaca, 1974). A history of the first ten years of the Peloponnesian War.

H. D. F. KITTO, *Greek Tragedy* (London, 1966). A good introduction.

B. M. W. KNOX, *Oedipus at Thebes* (New Haven, 1957). A

fascinating study of the relationship between drama and society in Athens.

B. M. W. KNOX, *The Heroic Temper: Studies in Sophoclean Tragedy* (Berkeley, 1964). A brilliant analysis of tragic heroism.

M. L. W. LAISTNER, *History of the Greek World from 479 to 323 B.C.* (London, 1970). A good narrative account with chapters on special subjects.

R. MEIGGS, *The Athenian Empire* (Oxford, 1972). A fine study of the rise and fall of the empire, making excellent use of inscriptions.

G. NORWOOD, *Greek Comedy* (New York, 1963). A good survey.

J. J. POLLITT, *Art and Experience in Classical Greece* (New York, 1972). A scholarly and entertaining study of the relationship between art and history in classical Greece with excellent illustrations.

A. E. TAYLOR, *Socrates* (New York, 1953). A good readable account.

A. E. ZIMMERN, *The Greek Commonwealth* (Oxford, 1961). A study of political, social, and economic conditions in fifth-century Athens.

106

5
Emergence of the Hellenistic World
(Fourth to First Century B.C.)

The Macedonian Conquest

THE QUARRELS among the Greeks brought on defeat and conquest by a new power that suddenly rose to eminence in the fourth century B.C., the kingdom of Macedon. The Macedonians inhabited the land to the north of Thessaly, and through the centuries they had unknowingly served the vital purpose of protecting the Greek states from barbarian tribes further to the north. By Greek standards Macedon was a backward, semibarbaric land. It had no *poleis* and was ruled loosely by a king in a rather Homeric fashion. He was chosen partly on the basis of descent, but the acclamation of the army gathered in assembly was required to make him legitimate. Quarrels between pretenders to the throne and even murder to achieve it were not uncommon. A council of nobles checked the royal power and could reject a weak or incompetent king. Hampered by constant wars with the barbarians, internal strife, loose organization, and lack of money, Macedon played no great part in Greek affairs up to this time. The Macedonians were of the same stock as the Greeks and spoke a Greek dialect, and the nobles, at least, thought of themselves as Greeks. The kings claimed descent from Heracles and the royal house of Argos. They tried to bring Greek culture into their court and won acceptance at the Olympic games. If a king could be found with the ability to unify his nation, it was bound to play a greater part in Greek affairs.

Philip of Macedon

That king was Philip II (359–336 B.C.), who, while still under thirty, took advantage of his appointment as regent to overthrow his infant nephew and make himself king. Like many of his predecessors he admired Greek culture. Between 367 and 364 B.C. he had been a hostage in Thebes, where he learned much about Greek politics and warfare under the tutelage of Epaminondas. His natural talents for war and diplomacy and his boundless ambition made him the ablest king in Macedonian history. Using both diplomatic and military means he was able to pacify the tribes on his frontiers and make his own hold on the throne firmer. Then he began to undermine Athenian control of the northern Aegean. He took Amphipolis for himself and gave Potidaea to Olynthus, the chief city of Chaldice, thereby guaranteeing the friendship of Olynthus to him and its hostility to Athens. Amphipolis gave him control of the Strymon valley and of the gold and silver mines of Mount Pangaeus. The income allowed him to found new cities, to bribe politicians in foreign towns, and to reorganize his army into the finest fighting force in the world.

The Macedonian Army

Philip put to good use what he had learned in Thebes and combined it with the advantages afforded by Macedonian society and tradition. His genius created a versatile and powerful army. The infantry was drawn from Macedonian farmers as well as from the hill people, who so frequently proved rebellious. In time these were integrated to form a loyal and effective national army. The infantry was armed with pikes that were thirteen feet long instead of the usual nine. They stood in a more open formation, which depended less on the weight of the charge than on the skillful use of the weapon. This tactic was effective because the phalanx was meant not to be the decisive force but merely to hold the enemy until the winning blow was struck by a massed cavalry charge on the flank or into a gap. The cavalry was made up of Macedonian nobles and clan leaders who were called Companions and who lived closely with the king and developed a special loyalty to him. In addition Philip employed mercenaries who knew the latest tactics used by mobile light-armed Greek troops as well as the most

Alexander the Great. This Hellenistic marble portrait comes from Pergamum in Asia Minor and is dated about 200 B.C. [Hirmer Fotoarchiv München.]

sophisticated siege machinery known to the Greeks. The native Macedonian army might be as large as forty thousand men and could be expanded by drafts from the allies and by mercenaries.

The Invasion of Greece

So armed, Philip turned south toward central Greece. Since 355 B.C. the Phocians had been fighting against Thebes and Thessaly. Philip gladly accepted the request of the Thessalians to be their general, defeated Phocis, and treacherously took control of Thessaly. Swiftly he turned northward again to Thrace and gained domination over the northern Aegean coast and the European side of the straits to the Black Sea. This conquest threatened the vital interests of Athens, which still had a formidable fleet of three hundred ships.

The Athens of 350 B.C. was not the Athens of Pericles. It had neither imperial revenue nor allies to share the burden of war on land or sea, and its own population was smaller than in the fifth century. The Athenians, therefore, were reluctant to go on expeditions themselves or even to send out mercenary armies under Athenian generals, for they must be paid out of taxes or contributions from Athenian citizens.

The leading spokesman against these tendencies and the cautious foreign policy that went with them was Demosthenes (384–322 B.C.), the greatest orator in Greek history. He was convinced that Philip was a dangerous enemy to Athens and the other Greeks and spent most of his career urging the Athenians to resist Philip's encroachments. When Philip attacked the Chalcidian League in 349 B.C., Olynthus, its chief city, asked Athens for an alliance. The Athenians agreed, but Philip helped stir up a rebellion in Euboea that diverted Athenian attention. The Athenian expedition to Olynthus was too small, too poorly financed, and too late. Philip took the city and destroyed it as an example to others who resisted him. The Athenians sought help in the Peloponnesus, but to no avail. In 346 B.C. they signed a treaty with Philip called the Peace of Philocrates after one of its negotiators:

Athens recognized Philip's conquests, he recognized their possessions, and the allies of each were included in the peace. But Philip was determined to attack the Phocians, deliberately omitted from the treaty. The Athenians, unwilling to protect them, preferred to believe Philip's fair words and tacitly to abandon their allies. Philip, having gained the aid of Thebes, attacked and defeated Phocis, breaking up its cities into villages. He had firmly planted Macedonian power in central Greece. The king of "barbarian" Macedon was elected president of the Pythian Games at Delphi, and the Athenians were forced to concur in the election.

Demosthenes. This is a Roman copy of a portrait bust originally made by Polyeuctus about 280 B.C. [Alinari/SCALA.]

In these difficult times it was Athens' misfortune not to have the kind of political leadership that Cimon or Pericles had offered a century earlier, which allowed for a consistent foreign policy. Many, perhaps most, Athenians accepted Demosthenes' view of Philip, but few were willing to run the risks and make the sacrifices necessary to stop his advance. Others, like Eubulus, an outstanding financial official and conservative political leader, favored a cautious policy of cooperation with Philip in the hope that his aims were limited and no real threat to Athens. Isocrates (436–338 B.C.), the head of an important rhetorical and philosophical school in Athens, looked to Philip to provide the unity and leadership needed for the pan-Hellenic campaign against Persia that he and other orators had been urging for some years. Isocrates saw the conquest of Asia Minor as the solution to the economic, social, and political problems that had brought poverty and civil war to the Greek cities ever since the Peloponnesian War. Finally, there seem to have been some Athenians who were in the pay of Philip, for he used money lavishly to win support in all of the cities.

The years between 346 B.C. and 340 B.C. were spent in diplomatic maneuvering, each side trying to win strategically useful allies. At last Philip attacked Perinthus and Byzantium, the life line of Athenian commerce, and in 340 he besieged both cities and declared war. The Athenian fleet saved both, so in the following year Philip marched into Greece. Demosthenes performed wonders in rallying the Athenians and winning Thebes over to the Athenian side, but in 338 Philip defeated the allied forces at Chaeronea in Boeotia in a great battle whose decisive blow was a cavalry charge led by the eighteen-year-old son of Philip, Alexander.

The Macedonian Government of Greece

The Macedonian settlement of Greek affairs was not as harsh as many had feared, although in some cities the friends of Macedon came to power and killed or exiled their enemies. Demosthenes continued to be free to engage in politics, and Athens was not attacked on the condition that it give up what was left of its empire and follow the lead of Macedon. The rest of Greece was arranged in such a way as to remove all dangers to Philip's rule. To guarantee his security, Philip placed garrisons at Thebes, Chalcis, and Corinth; these came to be known as the fetters of Greece. In 338 B.C. Philip called a meeting of the Greek states to form the federal League of Corinth. The constitution provided for autonomy, freedom from tribute and garrisons, and suppression of piracy and civil war. The league delegates would make foreign policy, in theory without consulting their home governments or Philip. All this was a facade; not only was Philip of Macedon president of the league, he was its ruler. Chaeronea was the end of Greek freedom and autonomy. Though its form and internal life continued for some time, the *polis* had lost control of its own affairs and the special conditions that made it unique.

Philip's choice of Corinth as the seat of his new confederacy was not out of convenience or by accident. It was at Corinth that the Greeks had gathered to resist a Persian invasion almost 150 years earlier, and it was there in 337 B.C. that Philip announced his intention to invade Persia in a war of liberation and revenge as leader of the new league. In the spring of 336 B.C., as he prepared to begin the campaign, Philip was assassinated. He was succeeded by his first son, Alexander III (356–323 B.C.), later called Alexander the Great, who came to the throne at the age of twenty.

Alexander the Great

Alexander became king of Macedon in suspicious circumstances. In the last year of his life Philip had put away Alexander's mother and married another woman, who bore him a son. This new son endangered Alexander's succession, and many suspected him and his mother of complicity in Philip's murder. Almost immediately Alexander removed all possible challengers to the throne and turned to deal with Greece, where the news of Philip's death was greeted with joy. A swift march to the south

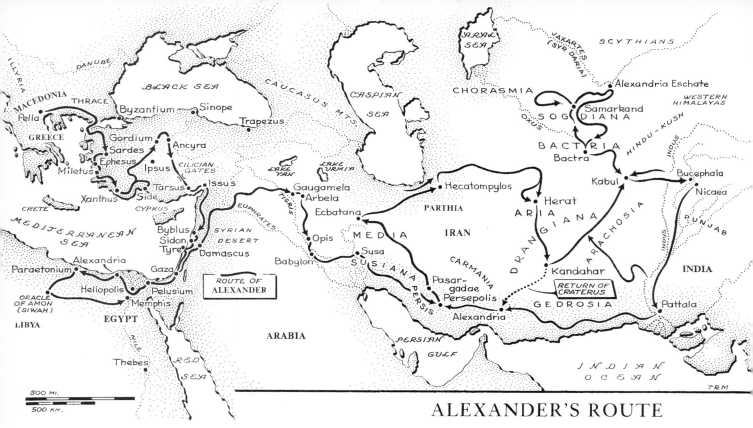

ALEXANDER'S ROUTE

The route taken by Alexander the Great in his conquest of the Persian Empire, 334–323 B.C. Starting from the Macedonian capital at Pella, he reached the Indus valley before being turned back by his own restive troops. He died of fever in Mesopotamia.

reduced Thessaly without a fight and cowed the Greek cities, who met at Corinth and elected him commander of a war of revenge against Persia. Then he moved to deal with the barbarians on Macedon's northern frontier. A rumor of his death caused a rebellion in Greece, but he returned with amazing speed and easily put it down. In spite of his Panhellenic propaganda Alexander never won the hearts of the Greeks. They gave him as little help as they could, and the constant threat of a rebellion that might be aided by the Persian fleet forced him to leave Antipater and a significant part of his army behind to keep watch on the Greeks when he left for Persia.

The Conquest of Persia and Beyond

Along with his throne, the young king inherited his father's plan to invade Persia. The idea was daring, for Persia's empire was vast and its resources enormous, but Cyrus and his Greek mercenaries had shown its vulnerability. Its size and disparate nature also made it hard to control and exploit. There were always trouble on some of its far-flung frontiers and intrigues within the royal palace. Throughout the fourth century B.C. the Persian

king called on Greek mercenaries to put down trouble. In 336 B.C. Persia was ruled by a new and inexperienced king, Darius III, but it remained formidable because of its huge army, great wealth, and a navy that ruled the sea.

In 334 B.C. Alexander crossed the Hellespont into Asia. His army consisted of about thirty thousand infantry and five thousand cavalry; he had no navy and little money. These facts determined his early strategy: he must seek quick and decisive battles to gain money and supplies from the conquered territory. He must move along the coast so as to neutralize the Persian navy by depriving it of ports. Memnon, the commander of the Persian navy, recommended the perfect strategy against this play: to retreat, scorch the earth and deprive Alexander of supplies, avoid battles, use guerrilla tactics, and stir up rebellion in Greece, but he was ignored. The Persians preferred to stand and fight; their pride and courage were greater than their wisdom.

Alexander met the Persian forces of Asia Minor at the Granicus River, where he won a smashing victory in characteristic style. He led a cavalry charge across the river into the teeth of the enemy on the opposite bank, almost losing his life in the process and winning the devotion of his soldiers. That victory left the coast of Asia Minor open, and Alexander captured the coastal cities to deny them to the Persian fleet.

In 333 B.C. Alexander marched inland to Syria, where

Arrian Describes the Banquet at Opis: Alexander's Universalism

Arrian lived in the second century, almost five hundred years after Alexander the Great, but his *Anabasis* is the best ancient source for Alexander's career. The following selection describes a banquet of reconciliation Alexander held at Opis in Mesopotamia in 324 B.C.

At length *one of them, Callines by name, a man conspicuous both for his age and because he was a captain of the Companion cavalry, spoke as follows, "O king, what grieves the Macedonians is that you have already made some of the Persians kinsmen to yourself, and that Persians are called Alexander's kinsmen, and have the honour of saluting you with a kiss; whereas none of the Macedonians have as yet enjoyed this honour." Then Alexander interrupting him, said, "But all of you without exception I consider my kinsmen, and so from this time I shall call you." When he had said this, Callines advanced and saluted him with a kiss, and so did all those who wished to salute him. Then they took up their weapons and returned to the camp, shouting and singing a song of thanksgiving. After this Alexander offered sacrifice to the gods to whom it was his custom to sacrifice, and gave a public banquet, over which he himself presided, with the Macedonians sitting around him; and next to them the Persians; after whom came the men of the other nations, preferred in honour for their personal rank or for some meritorious action. The king and his guests drew wine from the same bowl and poured out the same libations, both the Grecian prophets and the Magians commencing the ceremony. He prayed for other blessings, and especially that harmony and community of rule might exist between the Macedonians and Persians. The common account is, that those who took part in this banquet were 9,000 in number, that all of them poured out one libation, and after it sang a song of thanksgiving.*

Arrian, *The Anabasis of Alexander,* trans. by E. J. Chinnock in *The Greek Historians,* F. R. B. Godolphin, ed., (New York: Random House, 1942), Vol. 2 p. 601–602.

Zeus. At Tyre Darius sent Alexander a peace offer, yielding his entire empire west of the Euphrates River and his daughter in exchange for an alliance and an end to the invasion. But Alexander aimed at conquering the whole empire and probably whatever lay beyond that.

In the spring of 331 B.C. Alexander marched into Mesopotamia. At Gaugamela near the ancient Assyrian city of Nineveh he met Darius, ready for a last stand. Once again Alexander's tactical genius and personal leadership carried the day. The Persians were broken and Darius fled once more. Alexander entered Babylon, again hailed as liberator and king. In January of 330 B.C. he came to Persepolis, the Persian capital, which held splendid palaces and the royal treasury. This bonanza put an end to his financial troubles and put a vast sum of money into circulation, with economic consequences that lasted for centuries. After a stay of several months Alexander burned Persepolis to dramatize the completion of Hellenic revenge for the Persian invasion and the destruction of the native Persian dynasty.

The new regime could not be secure while Darius lived, so Alexander pursued him eastward. Just south of the Caspian Sea he came upon the corpse of Darius, killed by his relative Bessus. The Persian nobles around Darius had lost faith in him and joined in the plot. The murder removed Darius from Alexander's path, but now he had to catch Bessus, who proclaimed himself successor to Darius. The pursuit of Bessus, who was soon caught, and a great curiosity and longing to go as far as he could and see the most distant places took him to the Don River and the steppes of southern Russia.

Near Samarkand, in the land of the Scythians, he founded the city of Alexandria Eschate ("Furthest Alexandria"), one of the many cities bearing his name that he founded as he traveled. As part of his grand scheme of amalgamation and conquest he married the Bactrian princess Roxane and enrolled thirty thousand young Bactrians for his army. These were to be trained and sent back to the center of the empire for use later.

In 327 B.C. Alexander took his army through the

he met the main Persian army under King Darius at Issus. Alexander himself led the cavalry charge that broke the Persian line and sent Darius fleeing into central Asia Minor. He continued along the coast and captured previously impregnable Tyre after a long and ingenious siege, putting an end to the threat of the Persian navy. He took Egypt with little trouble and was greeted as liberator, pharaoh, and son of Re, whose Greek equivalent was

Nobody was prepared for Alexander's sudden death in 323 B.C., and affairs were further complicated by a weak succession—Roxane's unborn child and Alexander's weak-minded, illegitimate half-brother. His able and loyal Macedonian generals at first hoped to preserve the Empire for the Macedonian royal house, and to this end they appointed themselves governors of the various provinces of the Empire. However, the conflicting ambitions of these strong-willed men led to prolonged warfare among various combinations of them, in which three of the original were killed, and all of the direct members of the Macedonian royal house were either executed or murdered. With the murder of Roxane and her son in 310 B.C., there was no longer any focus for the enormous empire, and in 306 and 305 the surviving governors proclaimed themselves kings of their various holdings; as a sign of their right to rule they issued their own coins, with the result that we can still know approximately how some of them looked.

Three of these Macedonian generals founded dynasties of significance for the spread of Hellenistic culture:

Ptolemy I, 367?–283 B.C.; founder of the Thirty-first Dynasty in Egypt, the Ptolemies, of whom Cleopatra and her son, both of whom died in 30 B.C., were the last.

Seleucus I, 358?–280 B.C.; founder of the Seleucid dynasty in Mesopotamia.

Antigonus I, 382–301 B.C.; founder of the Antigonid dynasty in Asia Minor and Macedon.

The portraits on these coins are:

1: Seleucus I.

2 and 3: Antiochus I, 324–261 B.C.; son of Seleucus I.

4: Antiochus II, 286–247 B.C.; son of Antiochus I.

5 and 6: Ptolemy I.

7: Ptolemy II, 309–246 B.C.; son of Ptolemy I; made Alexandria the major center of Hellenistic culture.

7 and 8: Arsinoë II, the sister and second wife of Ptolemy II.

9: Demetrius I, 337?–283 B.C.; son of Antigonus I. This is the first example on the European mainland of a portrait of a living man on a coin.

10: Philetaeros. He belongs to the next generation and founded the Attalid kingdom, named after his nephew Attalus, around Pergamum in western Asia Minor.
[Courtesy of the American Numismatic Society, New York.]

Khyber Pass in an attempt to conquer India, or to be more precise, the lands around the Indus River (modern Pakistan). He reduced its king, Porus, to vassalage but pushed on in the hope of reaching the river called Ocean that the Greeks believed encircled the world. Finally, his weary men refused to go on. By the spring of 324 B.C. the army was back at the Persian Gulf and celebrated with a wild spree of drinking in the Macedonian style.

The Death of Alexander and Its Aftermath

Alexander was filled with plans for the future—for the consolidation and organization of his empire; for geographical exploration; for building new cities, roads, and harbors; perhaps even for further conquests in the west—but in June of 323 B.C. he was overcome by a fever and died in Babylon at the age of thirty-three. His memory has never faded, and he soon became the subject of myth, legend, and romance. From the beginning, estimates of him have varied. Some have seen in him a man of grand and noble vision who transcended the narrow limits of Greek and Macedonian ethnocentrism and aimed at the brotherhood of man in a great world state. Others have seen him as a calculating despot, given to drunken brawls, brutality, and murder.

The truth is probably in between. Alexander was one of the greatest generals the world has seen; he never lost a battle or failed in a siege, and with a modest army he conquered a vast empire. He had rare organizational talents, and his plan for creating a multinational empire was the only intelligent way of proceeding. He established many new cities, seventy according to tradition, mostly along trade routes. These cities had the effect of encouraging commerce and prosperity as well as introducing Hellenic civilization into new areas. It is hard to know if the vast new empire could have been held together, but Alexander's death proved that only he had a chance to succeed.

For the first seventy-five years or so after the death of Alexander the world ruled by his successors enjoyed considerable prosperity. The vast sums of money he and

they put into circulation greatly increased the level of economic activity. The opportunities for service and profit in the east attracted many Greeks and relieved their native cities of some of the pressure of the poor. The opening of vast new territories to Greek trade, the increased demand for Greek products, and the new availability of things wanted by the Greeks, as well as the conscious policies of the Hellenistic kings, all helped the growth of commerce. The new prosperity, however, was not evenly distributed. The urban Greeks, the Macedonians, and the Hellenized natives who made up the upper and middle classes lived lives of comfort and even luxury, but the rural native peasants did not. During prosperous times these distinctions were bearable, although even then there was tension between the two groups. After a while, however, the costs of continuing wars, inflation, and a gradual lessening of the positive effects of the introduction of Persian wealth all led to economic crisis. The kings bore down heavily on the middle classes, who, however, were skilled at avoiding their responsibilities. The pressure on the peasants and the city laborers became great too, and they responded by slowing down their work and even by striking. In Greece economic pressures brought clashes between rich and poor, demands for the abolition of debt and the redistribution of land, and even on occasion civil war.

These internal divisions along with the international wars weakened the capacity of the Hellenistic kingdoms to resist outside attack, and by the middle of the second century B.C. they were all gone. The two centuries between Alexander and the Roman conquest, however,

were of great and lasting importance. They saw the formation into a single political, economic, and cultural unit of the entire eastern Mediterranean coast and of Greece, Egypt, Mesopotamia, and the old Persian empire. The period also saw the creation of a new culture that took root at least in the urban portions of that vast area, one that deserves to be differentiated from the earlier one of the Greek city-states: Hellenistic culture.

Hellenistic Culture

The career of Alexander the Great marks a significant turning point in the thought of the Greeks as it is represented in literature, philosophy, religion, and art. His conquests and the establishment of the successor king-

The Mausoleum. This is a conjectural reconstruction of the tomb of King Mausolus of Caria in Asia Minor, which gave us the word "mausoleum." It was built at Halicarnassus in 353 B.C. by the widow, Queen Artemisia, and later made its way into Hellenistic lists of wonders of the world. [*World Architecture: An Illustrated History*, Trewin Copplestone, General Editor (London: Hamlyn, 1963), p. 54.]

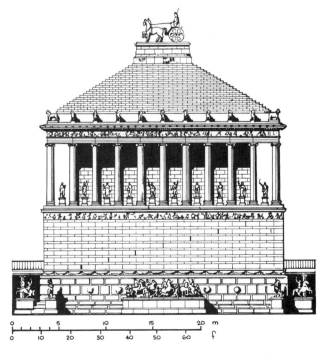

doms put an end once and for all to the central role of the *polis* in Greek life and thought. Scholars disagree about the end of the *polis*. Some deny that Philip's victory at Chaeronea put an end to its existence; they point to the continuance of *poleis* throughout the Hellenistic period and even see a continuation of them in the Roman *municipia,* but these are only a shadow of the vital reality that had been the true *polis*.

Deprived of control of foreign affairs, their important internal arrangements determined by a foreign monarch, the postclassical cities lost the kind of political freedom that was basic to the old outlook. They were cities, perhaps, in a sense, even city-states, but not *poleis*. As time passed they changed from sovereign states to municipal towns merged in military empires. Never again in antiquity would there be either a serious attack on or a defense of the *polis,* for its importance was gone. For the most part the Greeks after Alexander turned away from political solutions for their problems and sought instead personal responses to their hopes and fears, and they sought them in religion, philosophy, and magic. The confident, sometimes arrogant, humanism of the fifth century B.C. gave way to a kind of resignation of man's fate to chance, a recognition of man's helplessness before forces too great for him to manage.

Philosophy

These developments are noticeable in the changes that overtook the established schools of philosophy as well as in the emergence of two new and influential groups of philosophers, the Epicureans and the Stoics. Athens' position as the center of philosophical studies was reinforced, for the Academy and the Lyceum continued in operation, and the new schools were also located there. The Lyceum turned gradually away from the universal investigations of its founder, Aristotle, and even from his scientific interests to become a center chiefly of literary and especially historical studies.

The Academy turned even further away from its tradition. It adopted the systematic Skepticism of Pyrrho of Elis, and under the leadership of Arcesilaus and Carneades the Skeptics of the Academy became skilled at pointing out fallacies and weaknesses in the philosophies of the rival schools. They thought that nothing could be known and so consoled themselves and their followers by suggesting that nothing mattered. It was easy for them, therefore, to accept conventional morality and the world as it was. The Cynics, of course, continued to denounce convention and to advocate the crude life in accordance with nature that some of them practiced publicly to the shock and outrage of respectable citizens. Neither of these views had much appeal to the middle-class city dweller of the third century B.C., who sought some basis for choosing a way of life now that the *polis* no longer provided one ready-made.

THE EPICUREANS. Epicurus of Athens (342–271 B.C.) formulated a new teaching, which was embodied in the school he founded in his native city in 306. His philosophy conformed to the new mood in that its goal was not knowledge but human happiness, which he believed could be achieved if one followed a style of life based on reason. He took sense perception to be the basis of all human knowledge. The reality and reliability of sense perception rest on the acceptance of the physical universe described by the atomists, Democritus and Leucippus, where atoms are continually falling through the void and giving off images that are in direct contact with the senses. These falling atoms could swerve in an arbitrary, unpredictable way to produce the combinations we see in the world; Epicurus thereby removed an element of determinism that existed in the Democritean system. When a man dies, the atoms that composed him disperse so that he has no further existence or perception; therefore he has nothing to fear after death. Epicurus believed that the gods existed but that they took no interest in human affairs. This belief amounted to a practical atheism, and Epicureans were often thought to be atheists.

The purpose of Epicurean physics was to liberate man from his fear of death, the gods, and all nonmaterial or

Diogenes Laertius Lists the Principles of Stoic Philosophy

Diogenes Laertius wrote a compendium of the *Lives and Opinions of Eminent Philosophers*, probably early in the third century. Zeno (335–263 B.C.) of Citium on the island of Cyprus was the founder of the Stoic school of philosophy.

THE *end may be defined as life in accordance with nature, or, in other words, in accordance with our own human nature as well as that of the universe, a life in which we refrain from every action forbidden by the law common to all things, that is to say, the right reason which pervades all things, and is identical with this Zeus, lord and ruler of all that is. And this very thing constitutes the virtue of the happy man and the smooth current of life, when all actions promote the harmony of the spirit dwelling in the individual man with the will of him who orders the universe. . . .*

Of the three kinds of life, the contemplative, the practical, and the rational, they declare that we ought to choose the last, for that a rational being is expressly produced by nature for contemplation and for action. They tell us that the wise man will for reasonable cause make his own exit from life, on his country's behalf or for the sake of his friends, or if he suffer intolerable pain, mutilation, or incurable disease.

It is also their doctrine that amongst the wise there should be a community of wives with free choice of partners, as Zeno says in his Republic *and Chrysippus in his treatise* On Government *[and not only they, but also Diogenes the Cynic and Plato]. Under such circumstances we shall feel paternal affection for all the children alike, and there will be an end of the jealousies arising from adultery. The best form of government they hold to be a mixture of democracy, kingship, and aristocracy (or the rule of the best).*

Diogenes Laertius, *Life of Zeno*, Vol. 2, trans. by R. D. Hicks (London and New York: William Heinemann and G. P. Putnam's Sons, 1925), pp. 195, 197, 235, 237.

supernatural powers. Epicurean ethics were hedonistic, that is, based on the acceptance of pleasure as true happiness. But pleasure for Epicurus was chiefly negative, the absence of pain and trouble. The goal of the Epicureans was *ataraxia*, the condition of being undisturbed, without trouble, pain, or responsibility. Ideally a man should have

enough means to allow him to withdraw from the world and avoid business and public life; Epicurus even advised against marriage and children. He preached a life of genteel, restrained selfishness, which might appeal to intellectual men of means, but it was not calculated to be widely attractive.

THE STOICS. Soon after Epicurus began teaching in his garden in Athens, Zeno of Citium in Cyprus (335–263 B.C.) established the Stoic school, which derives its name from the *Stoa Poikile*, or Painted Portico, in the Athenian Agora, where Zeno and his disciples walked and talked beginning about 300. From then until about the middle of the second century B.C. Zeno and his successors preached a philosophy that owed a good deal to Socrates, by way of the Cynics, and was fed also by a stream of Eastern thought. Zeno, of course, came from Phoenician Cyprus; Chrysippus, one of his successors, came from Cilicia; and other early Stoics came from such places as Carthage, Tarsus, and Babylon.

Like the Epicureans, the Stoics sought the happiness of the individual. Quite unlike them, the Stoic method was a philosophy almost indistinguishable from religion. They believed that man must live in harmony within himself and in harmony with nature, and for the Stoics God and nature were the same. The guiding principle in nature is divine reason (Logos), or fire. Every man has a spark of this in him, and when he dies it returns to the eternal divine spirit. From time to time the world is destroyed by fire, from which a new world arises. The aim of man is the virtuous life, life lived in accordance with natural law, "when all actions promote the harmony of the spirit dwelling in the individual man with the will of him who orders the universe." [1] To live such a life requires knowledge possessed only by the wise man who knows what is good, what is evil, and what is neither, but "indifferent." Good and evil are dispositions of the mind or soul: prudence, justice, courage, temperance, and so on are good, whereas folly, injustice, cowardice, and the like are evil.

[1] Diogenes Laertius, *Life of Zeno* 88.

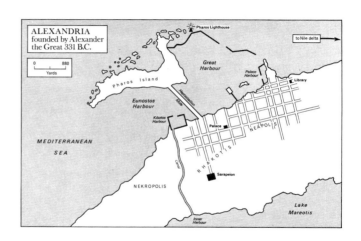

Life, health, pleasure, beauty, strength, wealth, and so on are neutral, morally indifferent, for they do not contribute either to happiness or to misery. Human misery comes from an irrational mental contraction, from passion, which is a disease of the soul. The wise man seeks freedom from passion (*apatheia*), because passion arises from things that are morally indifferent.

Politically the Stoics fit well into the new world. They thought of it as a single *polis* in which all men were brothers and children of God. Although they did not forbid political activity, and many Stoics took part in political life, withdrawal was obviously preferable because the usual subjects of political argument were indifferent. Because the Stoics aimed at inner harmony of the individual, their aim was a life lived in accordance with the divine will, their attitude fatalistic, and their goal a form of apathy, they fit in well with the reality of post-Alexandrian life. In fact, the spread of Stoicism made simpler the task of creating a new political system that relied not on the active participation of the governed, but merely on their docile submission.

Literature

The literature of the Hellenistic period reflects the new intellectual currents and, even more, the new conditions of literary life and the new institutions created in that period. The center of literary production in the third and second centuries B.C. was the new city of Alexandria in Egypt. There the Ptolemies, the kings of Egypt during that time, founded the museum, a great research institute where scientists and scholars were supported by royal funds, and the library, which contained almost half a million volumes, or papyrus scrolls. In the library were the works making up the great body of past Greek literature of every kind, a great deal of which has since been lost. The Alexandrian scholars saw to it that what they judged to be the best works were copied; they edited and criticized these works from the point of view of language, form, and content and wrote biographies of their authors. Much of their work was valuable and is

Map of Alexandria. Alexander the Great was given to founding new cities along the major trade routes in his newly conquered provinces, and several of these he allowed to be named for himself, but this one in Egypt was the only one to remain a place of consequence. His Macedonian successors, the Ptolemies, made it the capital of their Egyptian kingdom and also a center of Hellenistic culture; its library and museum were famous centers of learning and scholarship, and its lighthouse, the *Pharos*, was a marvel of construction to the ancient world. [Michael Grant, *Ancient History Atlas* (New York: Macmillan, 1971), p. 42.]

responsible for the preservation of most of ancient literature. Some of it is dry, petty, quarrelsome, and simply foolish. At its best, however, it is full of learning and perception.

The effect of this literary scholarship on Alexandrian poetry is evident in the works of Callimachus (*ca.* 305–240 B.C.) and Apollonius of Rhodes (born *ca.* 295 B.C.). Callimachus himself was a librarian and scholar, and his works—short epics called *epyllions,* epigrams, and lyric poems—are filled with learned references to obscure myths and delight in refinements of meter and phrasing whose meaning is evident only to other learned men. They appeal to the mind rather than the heart. Apollonius is best known for his long epic, the *Argonautica,* the tale of Jason's voyage in search of the Golden Fleece, which displays the same qualities. Theocritus of Syracuse (*ca.* 310–250 B.C.), the third great Alexandrian poet, is most famous for his *Idylls,* pastoral poems that sing of the virtues of the simple rural life to the sophisticated city dwellers of the Hellenistic age.

The scholarly atmosphere of Alexandria naturally gave rise to work in the field of history and its ancillary discipline, chronology. Eratosthenes (*ca.* 275–195 B.C.) established a chronology of important events dating from the Trojan War, and others undertook similar tasks. Contemporaries of Alexander, such as Ptolemy I, Aristobulus,

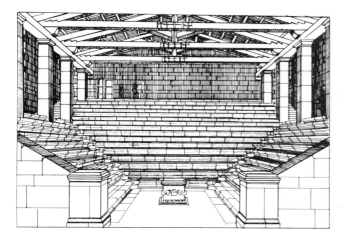

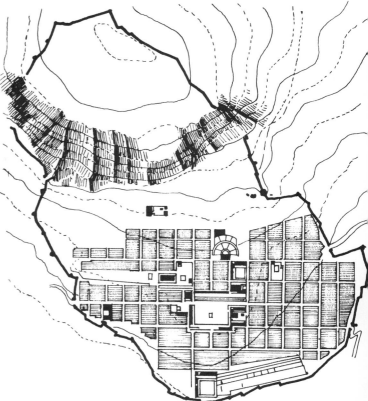

Priene was a typical small Greek city of the Hellenistic period that was located in western Asia Minor. It was moved from a former location to its present site and constructed about 350 B.C.

ABOVE RIGHT is the town plan; it is a prime example of the careful and intelligent town planning characteristic of the Hellenistic period. Despite difficulties presented by a steep hillside, the streets were laid out in a checkerboard pattern, unlike the winding streets of earlier cities. The site was chosen to give a southern exposure and a pleasant breeze from the sea. Water came down from higher land and was kept in reservoirs and piped to water fountains.

ABOVE is a reconstruction of the Bouleuterion or council hall at Priene. It was a typical center of municipal government in its period.
[Both: *World Architecture: An Illustrated History*, Trewin Copplestone, General Editor (London: Hamlyn, 1963), p. 52.]

RIGHT: The Stoa of Attalus in Athens. This is a reconstruction of a covered portico, or stoa, built in the Athenian Agora by a Hellenistic king, Attalus II (159–138 B.C.), ruler of Pergamum in Asia Minor. It was given to the Athenians by Attalus because he had studied there as a young man. [AHM.]

and Nearchus, wrote what were apparently sober and essentially factual accounts of his career. Most of the work done by Hellenistic historians is known to us only in fragments cited by later writers, but it seems in general to have emphasized sensational and biographical detail rather than the rigorous impersonal analysis of a Thucydides.

Architecture and Sculpture

The opportunities open to architects and sculptors were greatly increased by the advent of the Hellenistic

[*Text continued on page 120*]

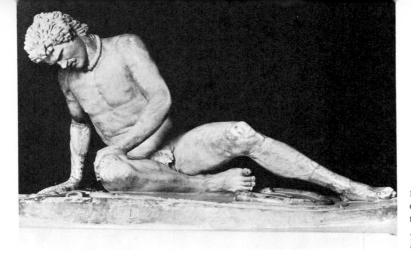

LEFT: The Dying Gaul. This is a Roman copy of one of a group originally dedicated at the temple of Athena at Pergamum by Attalus I about 230 B.C. It is now in the Museo Capitolino, Rome. [Bettmann Archive.]

LEFT: Drunken old woman, a Roman copy of a bronze original thought to be by Myron of Thebes and made in the second century B.C. Like the Dying Gaul (ABOVE) it is marked by a stark realism very different from the classical serenity of fifth-century B.C. Greek statues. [Staatliche Antikensammlungen und Glyptothek, Munich.]

BELOW: Hellenistic architectural decoration. This head of the mythological Medusa is a detail of the frieze on the temple of Apollo at Didyma in Asia Minor. The site, where earlier temples than this one had existed, was perhaps second only to Delphi in importance as a shrine to Apollo, and it, like Delphi, also housed a famous oracle through which the god could speak to petitioners. The temple was not actually completed until the reign of Roman Emperor Hadrian in the second century. [AHM.]

Emergence of the Hellenistic World (Fourth to First Century B.C.*)*

ABOVE: The great altar of Zeus at Pergamum. It was built by the Hellenistic King Eumenes II of Pergamum (died about 160 B.C.) to commemorate a victory over Gallic invaders. Present-day Bergama, Turkey is at the site of Hellenistic Pergamum. [Antikensammlung, Staatliche Museen zu Berlin (East).]

RIGHT: A detail from the frieze on the altar of Zeus at Pergamum; the sculpture shows the battle between the Olympian gods and the giants. [Antikensammlung, Staatliche Museen zu Berlin (East).]

Hero of Alexandria's devices. Hero lived late in the first century and was the author of a treatise on pneumatics. The two devices shown here have been reconstructed from his descriptions. The top one is for opening temple doors; the bottom one is a steam turbine. Both depended on the expansion of air or the vaporization of water when heated. The turbine was treated merely as a toy. The temple door appeared magically to open when a fire was lighted on the altar, illustrating one of Hero's goals for science, "producing bewilderment and awe." [H. Hodges, *Technology in the Ancient World* (Harmonsworth: Penguin Books, 1959), p. 214.]

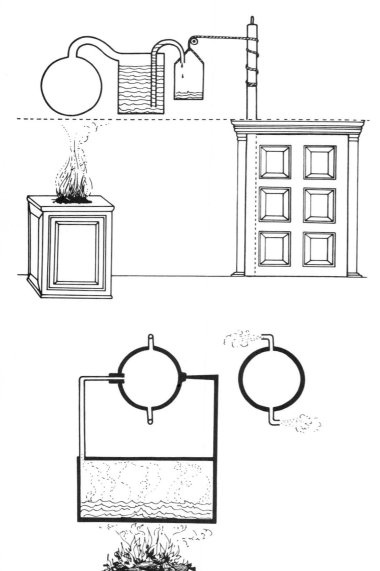

monarchies. There was plenty of money, the royal need for conspicuous display, the need to build and beautify new cities, and a growing demand for objects of art by the well-to-do *bourgeoisie*. The new cities were usually laid out on the gridiron plan introduced in the fifth century by Hippodamus of Miletus. Temples were built on the classical model, and the covered portico or *stoa* became a very popular addition to the *agoras* of the Hellenistic towns.

Sculpture reflected the cosmopolitan nature of the Hellenistic world, for leading sculptors accepted commissions wherever they were attractive, and the result was a certain uniformity of style, although Alexandria, Rhodes, and the kingdom of Pergamum in Asia Minor developed their own characteristic styles. For the most part Hellenistic sculpture carried forward the tendencies of the fourth century B.C., moving away from the balanced tension and idealism of the fifth century toward a sentimental, emotional, and realistic mode. These qualities are readily apparent in the statue of the *Dying Gaul* dedicated by Attalus I, king of Pergamum in about 225 B.C., and one of a drunken old woman in bronze cast in the second century B.C.

Mathematics and Science

Among the most spectacular and remarkable intellectual developments of the Hellenistic age were those that came in mathematics and science. The burst of activity in these subjects drew from several sources. The stimulation and organization provided by the work of Plato and Aristotle should not be ignored. To it was added the impetus provided by Alexander's interest in science, evidenced by the scientists he took with him on his expedition and the aid he gave them in collecting data. The expansion of Greek horizons geographically and the consequent contact with the knowledge of Egypt and Babylonia was also helpful. Finally, the patronage of the Ptolemies and the opportunity for many scientists to work with one another at the museum at Alexandria provided a unique opportunity for scientific work. It is not too much

Plutarch Cites Archimedes and Hellenistic Science

Archimedes (ca. 287–212 B.C.) was one of the great mathemeticians and physicists of antiquity. He was a native of Syracuse in Sicily and a friend of its king. Plutarch discusses him in the following selection and reveals much about the ancient attitude toward applied science.

Archimedes, *however, in writing to King Hiero, whose friend and near relation he was, had stated that given the force, any given weight might be moved, and even boasted, we are told, relying on the strength of demonstration, that if there were another earth, by going into it he could remove this. Hiero being struck with amazement at this, and entreating him to make good this problem by actual experiment, and show some great weight moved by a small engine, he fixed accordingly upon a ship of burden out of the king's arsenal, which could not be drawn out of the dock without great labour and many men; and, loading her with many passengers and a full freight, sitting himself the while far off, with no great endeavour, but only holding the head of the pulley in his hand and drawing the cords by degrees. . . . Yet Archimedes possessed so high a spirit, so profound a soul, and such treasures of scientific knowledge, that though these inventions had now obtained him the renown of more than human sagacity, he yet would not deign to leave behind him any commentary or writing on such subjects; but, repudiating as sordid and ignoble the whole trade of engineering, and every sort of art that lends itself to mere use and profit, he placed his whole affection and ambition in those purer speculations where there can be no reference to the vulgar needs of life. . . .*

Plutarch, "Marcellus," in *Lives of the Noble Grecians and Romans*, trans. by John Dryden, revised by A. H. Clough (New York: Random House, n.d.), pp. 376–378.

to say that the work done by the Alexandrians formed the greater part of the scientific knowledge available to men until the scientific revolution of the sixteenth and seventeenth centuries A.D.

Euclid's *Elements* (written early in the third century B.C.) remained the textbook of plane and solid geometry until just recently. Archimedes of Syracuse (*ca.* 287–212 B.C.) made further progress in geometry, as well as establishing the theory of the lever in mechanics and inventing hydrostatics. The advances in mathematics, when added to the availability of Babylonian astronomical tables, allowed great progress in the field of astronomy. As early as the fourth century Heraclides of Pontus (*ca.* 390–310 B.C.) had argued that Mercury and Venus circulate around the sun and not the earth, and he appears to have made other suggestions leading in the direction of a heliocentric theory of the universe. Most scholars, however, give credit for that theory to Aristarchus of Samos (*ca.* 310–230 B.C.), who asserted that the sun, along with the other fixed stars, did not move and that the earth revolved around the sun in a circular orbit and rotated on its axis while doing so. The heliocentric theory ran contrary not only to the traditional view codified by Aristotle but to what seemed to be common sense. Besides Hellenistic technology was not up to proving the theory, and, of course, the planetary orbits are not circular. The heliocentric theory did not, therefore, take hold. Hipparchus of Nicaea (born *ca.* 190 B.C.) constructed a model of the universe on the geocentric theory, employing an ingenious and complicated model that did a very good job of accounting for the movements of the sun, the moon, and the planets. Ptolemy of Alexandria (second century A.D.) adopted Hipparchus' system with a few improvements, and it remained dominant until Copernicus, in the sixteenth century A.D.

Hellenistic scientists made progress in mapping the earth as well as the sky. Eratosthenes of Cyrene (*ca.* 275–195 B.C.) was able to calculate the circumference of the earth within about two hundred miles and wrote a treatise on geography based on mathematical and physical reasoning and the reports of travelers. In spite of the new data that were available to later geographers, Eratosthenes' map was in many ways more accurate than the one that was constructed by Ptolemy and that became standard in the Middle Ages.

The Hellenistic Age made little contribution to the life sciences. Biology, zoology, and even medicine made little progress. Even the sciences that had such impressive achievements to show in the third century B.C. made little progress thereafter. In fact, to some extent, there was a retreat from science. Astrology and magic became the

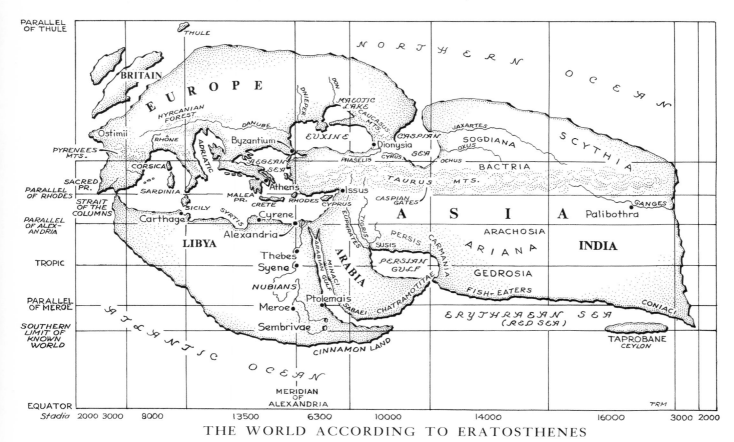

THE WORLD ACCORDING TO ERATOSTHENES

Eratosthenes of Alexandria (275–195 B.C.) was a Hellenistic geographer. His map, reconstructed here, was remarkably accurate for its time. The world was divided by lines of "latitude" and "longitude," thus anticipating our global divisions.

subjects of great interest as scientific advance lagged. The question has often been asked why science did not progress further in the ancient world: Why, for instance, was there no scientific and industrial revolution in the Hellenistic period? Many answers have been suggested, for example, the lack of an adequate base in technology and the absence of refined instruments of observation and measurement. Another explanation offered is that the deterrent effect of slavery on invention, the sharp class distinctions in ancient society, and the contemptuous attitude of gentlemen toward work separated the intellectual scientist from the practical application of his discovery. All of these conditions may have played some role, but the wrong question seems to have been asked. To ask it in the usual way is to assume that anyone understands why the scientific and industrial revolutions took place when and where they did, but that assumption is unfounded. Perhaps when historians have solved the modern problem, they may more successfully approach the ancient one.

The Achievement of the Hellenistic Age

The Hellenistic Age speaks to us less fully and vividly than that of classical Greece or of the Roman Republic and Empire, chiefly because it had no historian to compare with Herodotus and Thucydides or Livy and Tacitus. We lack the continuous, rich, lively, and meaningful narrative without which it is difficult to get a clear picture. This deficiency should not obscure the great importance of the achievements of the age. The literature, art, scholarship, and science of the period deserve attention in their own right, but beyond that the Hellenistic Age performed a vital civilizing function. It spread the Greek culture over a remarkably wide area and made a significant and lasting impression on much of it. Greek culture also adjusted to its new surroundings to a degree, unifying and simplifying its cultural cargo so as to make it more accessible to outsiders. The various Greek dialects gave way to a version of the Attic tongue, the *koinē* or common language. In the same way, the scholarship of Alexandria established canons of literary excellence and the scholarly tools with which to make the great treasures of Greek culture understandable to later generations. The syncretism of thought and belief introduced in this period also made mutual understanding and accord more

122   *Emergence of the Hellenistic World (Fourth to First Century B.C.)*

likely among peoples who were very different. When the Romans came into contact with Hellenism, they were powerfully impressed by it, and when they conquered the Hellenistic world, they became, as Horace said, captives of its culture.

To Rome and the Romans we must now turn.

SUGGESTED READINGS

C. BAILEY, *Epicurus* (Oxford, 1926). A basic account of the philosopher and his work.

E. BEVAN, *Stoics and Sceptics* (Oxford, 1913). A fundamental study of two schools of Hellenistic philosophy.

J. B. BURY (Ed.), *The Hellenistic Age* (Cambridge, 1925). A good collection of essays on various topics.

MAX CARY, *History of the Greek World from 323 to 146 B.C.* (New York, 1968). The major part is devoted to political history.

M. CLAGETT, *Greek Science in Antiquity* (London, 1957). Chiefly concerned with the Hellenistic period.

J. FERGUSON, *The Heritage of Hellenism* (New York, 1973). A good survey.

W. S. FERGUSON, *Hellenistic Athens* (New York, 1970). Reprint of an old but still valuable study.

J. R. LANE FOX, *Alexander the Great* (London, 1973). An imaginative account that does more justice to the Persian side of the problem than is usual.

PETER GREEN, *Alexander the Great* (New York, 1972). A lively biography.

G. T. GRIFFITH (Ed.), *Alexander the Great: The Main Problems* (Cambridge, 1966). A useful collection of articles.

M. HADAS, *Hellenistic Culture: Fusion and Diffusion* (New York, 1972). Uses the experience of the Jews as the chief example of interaction between Greeks and other peoples.

C. M. HAVELOCK, *Hellenistic Art* (Greenwich, Conn., 1971). A fine interpretive study.

A. H. M. JONES, *The Greek City from Alexander to Justinian* (Oxford, 1940). A fine study of the significance and spread of urban life.

J. A. O. LARSEN, *Greek Federal States* (Oxford, 1968). Emphasis on the federal movements of the Hellenistic era.

C. A. ROBINSON, JR., *Alexander the Great* (New York, 1947). A sober, level-headed assessment.

M. I. ROSTOVTZEFF, *Social and Economic History of the Hellenistic World,* 3 vols. (Oxford, 1941). A masterpiece of synthesis by a great historian.

W. W. TARN, *Alexander the Great,* 2 vols. (Cambridge, 1948). The first volume is a narrative account, the second a series of detailed studies.

W. W. TARN AND G. T. GRIFFITH, *Hellenistic Civilization* (New York, 1961). A survey of Hellenistic history and culture.

V. TCHERIKOVER, *Hellenistic Civilization and the Jews* (New York, 1970). A fine study of the impact of Hellenism on the Jews.

T. B. L. WEBSTER, *Hellenistic Poetry and Art* (London, 1964). A clear survey.

124

6

Growth of the Roman Republic to About 150 B.C.

T HE ACHIEVEMENT of the Romans was one of the most remarkable accomplishments in human history. The descendants of the inhabitants of a small village in central Italy ruled the entire Italian peninsula, then the entire Mediterranean coastline. They conquered most of the Near East and finally much of continental Europe. They ruled this vast empire under a single government that provided considerable peace and prosperity for centuries. At no time before the Romans or since has that area been united, and rarely, if ever, has it enjoyed a stable peace. But Rome's legacy was not merely military excellence and political organization. The Romans adopted and transformed the intellectual and cultural achievements of the Greeks and combined them with their own outlook and historical experience. They produced that Graeco-Roman tradition in literature, philosophy, and art that served as the core of learning for the Middle Ages and the inspiration for the new paths taken in the Renaissance. It remains at the heart of Western civilization to this day.

Prehistoric Italy

The culture of Italy developed late. Paleolithic settlements gave way to the Neolithic mode of life only about 2500 B.C. The Bronze Age came about 1500 B.C., and about 1000 B.C. Italy experienced the shock of massive migrations from the north. The invaders were warlike people who imposed their language and social organiza-

Detail of a wall painting in the Etruscan "Tomb of the Leopards" near Tarquinia in Italy. The Etruscans are exceedingly important in the background of Rome's early expansion in Italy, and much of what we know of them comes from their tombs, many of which are scattered over the countryside north of Rome. This clever musician is in a tomb of about 480 B.C. [Alinari/SCALA.]

tion on almost all of Italy. Their bronze work was better than their predecessors', and soon they made weapons, armor, and tools of iron. They cremated their dead and put the ashes in tombs stocked with weapons and armor. Before 800 B.C. people living in this style occupied the highland pastures of the Apennines. These tough mountain people—Umbrians, Sabines, Samnites, Latins, and others—spoke a set of closely related languages we call *Italic*.

They soon began to challenge the earlier settlers for control of the tempting western plains. Other peoples—Ligurians and Veneti in the north, Iapygians and Sicels in the south, among others—lived in Italy in the ninth century B.C., but the Italic speakers and three peoples who had not yet arrived—the Etruscans, the Greeks, and the Celts—would shape its future.

The Etruscans

The Etruscans exerted the most powerful external influence on the Romans. Their civilization arose in Tuscany, west of the Apennines between the Arno and Tiber rivers, about 800 B.C. Their origin is far from clear, but their tomb architecture, resembling that of Asia Minor, and their practice of divining the future by inspecting the livers of sacrificial animals point to an eastern origin.

The Etruscans brought civilization with them. Their settlements were self-governing, fortified city-states, of which twelve formed a loose religious confederation. At first these cities were ruled by kings, but they were replaced by an aristocracy of the agrarian nobles, who ruled by means of a council and elected annual magistrates. The Etruscans were a military ruling class that dominated and exploited the native Italians who worked their land and mines and served as infantry in their armies. This aristocracy accumulated considerable wealth through agriculture, industry, piracy, and a growing commerce with the Carthaginians and the Greeks.

The Etruscans' influence on the Romans was greatest

This map of the Italian peninsula and its neighbors in antiquity shows the major cities and towns, as well as a number of geographical regions and the locations of some of the Italic and non-Italic peoples of the area.

Villanovan hut urn. This burial urn of the Villanovan period in Italy (from the ninth to the seventh century B.C.) comes from a cemetary in Osteria near Rome. It is now in the Villa Giulia, Rome. [Editorial Photocolor Archives.]

ANCIENT ITALY

in religion. They imagined a world filled with gods and spirits, many of them evil. To deal with such demons, the Etruscans evolved complicated rituals and powerful priesthoods. Divination by sacrifice and omens in nature helped discover the divine will, and careful attention to precise rituals directed by priests helped please the gods. After a while the Etruscans, influenced by the Greeks, worshiped gods in the shape of humans and built temples for them.

The Etruscan aristocracy remained aggressive and skillful in the use of horses and war chariots. In the seventh and sixth centuries B.C. they expanded their power in Italy and across the sea to Corsica and Elba. They conquered Latium (a region that included the small town of Rome) and Campania, where they became neighbors of the Greeks of Naples. In the north they got as far as the Po valley. These conquests were carried out by small bands led by Etruscan chieftans who did not work in concert and would not necessarily aid one another in distress. As a result, the conquests outside Etruria were not firmly based and did not last long. Etruscan power reached its height some time before 500 B.C. By about 500 B.C. Latium had fallen away, in 474 B.C. Syracuse destroyed the Etruscan sea power, and in 438 B.C. the fall of Capua in Campania destroyed the Etruscan rule in the south. About 400 B.C. the Celts broke into the Po valley, drove out the Etruscans, and settled their

An Etruscan tumulus tomb at the ancient
city of Caere (modern Cerveteri) in Latium.
[Alinari/SCALA.]

conquered land so firmly that the Romans thereafter
called it Cisalpine Gaul. Thereafter even Etruria lost its
independence and was incorporated into Roman Italy.
The Etruscan language was forgotten and Etruscan culture gradually became only a memory, but its influence
on the Romans remained.

Royal Rome

Rome was an unimportant town in Latium until its
conquest by the Etruscans, but its location gave it several
advantages over its Latin neighbors. Its site was on the
Tiber River, fifteen miles from its mouth, at the point
where the hills on which Rome was situated made further
navigation impossible. The island in the Tiber southwest
of the Capitoline hill made the river fordable, so that
Rome was naturally a center for communication and
trade, both east–west and north–south.

Government

In the sixth century B.C. Rome came under Etruscan
control. Led by their Etruscan kings, the Roman legions,
armed and organized like the Greek phalanx, gained
control of most of Latium. They achieved this success

under an effective political and social order that gave
extraordinary power to the ruling figures in both public
and private life. To their kings the Romans gave the
awesome power of *imperium,* the right to issue commands and to enforce them by fines, arrests, and corporal
or even capital punishment. The kingship was elective
and the office appears to have tended to remain in the
same family. The Senate, however, had to approve the
candidate, and the *imperium* was formally granted by a
vote of the people in assembly. The basic character of
Roman government is already clear: great power was
granted to executive officers, but it had to be approved by
the Senate and was derived ultimately from the people.

In theory and law the king was the commander of the
army, the chief priest, and the supreme judge. He could
make decisions in foreign affairs, call out the army, lead it
in battle, and impose discipline on his troops, all by virtue
of his *imperium.* In practice the royal power was much
more limited. The second branch of the early Roman
government was the Senate. Tradition says that Romulus,
Rome's first king, chose one hundred of Rome's leading
men to advise him. Later the number rose to three hundred, where it stayed through most of the history of the
republic. Ostensibly the Senate had neither executive nor
legislative power; it met only when summoned by the
king and then only to advise him. In reality its authority

was great, for the senators, like the king, served for life. The Senate, therefore, had continuity and experience, and since it was composed of the most powerful men in the state, it could not lightly be ignored.

The Roman people were organized into the third branch of government, the curiate assembly made up of thirty groups. It met only when summoned by the king; he determined the agenda, made proposals, and recognized other speakers, if any. For the most part the assembly was called to listen and approve. Voting was not by head but by group; a majority within each group determined its vote, and the decisions were made by majority vote of the groups. Group voting was typical of all Roman assemblies in the future.

The Family

The center of Roman life was the family. At its head stood the father, whose power and authority within the family resembled those of the king within the state. Over his children he held broad powers analogous to *imperium* in the state, for he had the right to sell his children into slavery and even the power of life and death over them. Over his wife he had less power; he could not sell his wife or kill her. Her property or dowry and anything she might acquire during the marriage belonged to her husband; her legal position was very much like that of a daughter, and if her husband died she inherited a daughter's share of the estate. As the king's power was more limited in practice than in theory so it was with the father. His power to dispose of his children was limited by consultation with the family, by public opinion, and, most of all, by tradition. The wife had certain legal protections. She could not be divorced except for stated serious offenses, and even then she had to be convicted by a court made up of her male blood relatives. The Roman woman had a respected position and the main responsibility for managing the household. The father also was the chief priest of the family. Daily he led it in prayers to the dead that reflected the ancestor worship central to the Roman family and state.

ABOVE: The Tiber island at Rome. This island in the Tiber made the river fordable at its location and therefore helped determine the location of the city of Rome. Later bridges kept the crossing a popular one, as shown in this eighteenth-century etching by G. B. Piranesi.

RIGHT: Remains of the Servian wall. Roman tradition credits Servius Tullius, one of Rome's legendary kings, with building this city wall in the sixth century B.C. In fact, however, most of it was built in the fourth century B.C., but parts of it may date from the earlier period. [Alinari/SCALA.]

OPPOSITE: Clay statue of Apollo from the Etruscan city of Veii. It is dated to about 500 B.C. and gives evidence of the considerable influence of Greek culture on the Etruscans. [Deutsches Archäologisches Institut, Rome.]

Portrait of Lucius Junius Brutus. This early Brutus was the legendary founder of the Roman republic in the late sixth century B.C. This bust is in the Museo Capitolino, Rome. [Alinari/SCALA.]

Clientage

Clientage was one of Rome's most important institutions. The client was "an inferior entrusted, by custom or by himself, to the protection of a stranger more powerful than he, and rendering certain services and observances in return for this protection."[1] The Romans spoke of a client as being in the *fides* or trust of his patron, so that the relationship always had moral implications. The patron provided his client with protection, both physical and legal; he gave him economic assistance in the form of a land grant, the opportunity to work as a tenant farmer or a laborer on the patron's land, or simply handouts. In return the client would fight for his patron, work his land, and support him politically. These mutual obligations were enforced by public opinion and tradition. When early custom was codified in the mid-fifth century B.C., one of the twelve tablets of laws announced: "Let the patron who has defrauded his client by accursed." In the early history of Rome patrons were rich and powerful whereas clients were poor and weak, but as time passed it was not uncommon for rich and powerful members of the upper classes to become clients of even more powerful men, chiefly for political purposes. Because the client–patron relationship was hereditary and sanctioned by religion and custom, it was to play a very important part in the life of the Roman Republic.

Patricians and Plebeians

In the royal period Roman society was divided in two by a class distinction based on birth. The upper class was composed of the patricians, the wealthy men who held a monopoly of power and influence. They alone could conduct the religious ceremonies in the state, sit in the Senate, or hold office, and they formed a closed caste by forbidding marriage outside their own group. The plebeians must originally have been the poor and dependent men who were small farmers, laborers, and artisans, the clients of the nobility. As Rome and her population grew

1 E. Badian, *Foreign Clientelae (264–70 B.C.)* (Oxford, 1958), p. 1.

in various ways, families who were rich but outside the charmed circle gained citizenship. From very early times, therefore, there were rich plebeians, and incompetence and bad luck must have produced some poor patricians. The line between the classes and the monopoly of privileges remained firm, nevertheless, and the struggle of the plebeians to gain equality occupied more than two centuries of republican history.

The Republic and Its Constitution

Roman tradition tells us that the republic replaced the monarchy at Rome suddenly in 509 B.C. as the result of a revolution sparked by the outrageous behavior of the last kings and led by the noble families.

The Consuls

In spite of the excesses of the last kings the Romans were never willing to deprive their chief magistrates of the great powers exercised by the monarchs. They elected two patricians to the office of consul and endowed them with *imperium*. They were assisted by two financial officials called *quaestors,* whose number ultimately reached eight. Like the kings the consuls led the army, had religious duties, and served as judges. They retained the visible symbols of royalty—the purple robe, the ivory chair, and the lictors bearing rods and axe who accompanied them—but their power was limited legally and institutionally as well as by custom.

The vast power of the consulship was granted not for life but only for a year. Each consul could prevent any action by his colleague by simply saying no to his proposal, and the religious powers of the consuls were shared with others. Even the *imperium* was limited, for though the consuls had full powers of life and death while leading an army, within the sacred boundary of the city of Rome the citizens had the right to appeal to the popular assembly all cases involving capital punishment. Besides, after their one year in office, the consuls would spend the rest of their lives as members of the Senate. It was a most reckless consul who failed to ask the advice of the Senate or who failed to follow it when there was general agreement.

The many checks on consular action tended to prevent initiative, swift action, and change, but this was just what a conservative, traditional, aristocratic republic wanted. Only in the military sphere did divided counsel and a short term of office create important problems. The Romans tried to get around the difficulties by sending only one consul into the field or, when this was impossible, allowing the consuls sole command on alternate days. In really serious crises the consuls, with the advise of the Senate, could appoint a single man, the *dictator,* to the command and could retire in his favor. The *dictator's* term of office was limited to six months, but during that time he was empowered to appoint his assistant, and his own *imperium* was valid both inside and outside the city without appeal. These devices worked well enough in the early years of the republic, when Rome's battles were near home, but longer wars and more sophisticated opponents revealed the system's weaknesses and required significant changes.

Long campaigns prompted the invention of the proconsulship in 325 B.C., whereby the term of a consul serving in the field was extended. This innovation contained the seeds of many troubles for the constitution.

At first the consuls classified the citizens according to age and property, the bases of citizenship and assignment in the army. After the middle of the fifth century B.C. two censors were elected to perform this duty. They conducted a census and drew up the citizen rolls, but this was no job for clerks. The classification fixed taxation and status, so that the censors had to be men of reputation, former consuls. The censors soon acquired additional powers. By the fourth century they compiled the roll of senators and could strike senators from that roll not only for financial reasons but for moral reasons as well. The censors thus became the arbiters and defenders of Roman morality. As the prestige of the office grew, it came to be considered the ultimate prize of a Roman political career.

The Senate and the Assembly

The end of the monarchy increased the influence and power of the Senate. It became the single continuous deliberative body in the Roman state. Its members were three hundred of the leading patricians, often leaders of clans and patrons of many clients. The Senate soon gained control of finances and of foreign policy. Its formal advice was not lightly ignored either by magistrates or by popular assemblies.

The most important assembly in the early republic was the centuriate assembly. In a sense, it was the Roman army acting in a political capacity, and its basic unit was the century, theoretically one hundred fighting men classified according to their weapons, armor, and equipment. Because each man equipped himself, this meant that the organization was by classes according to wealth.

The assembly met on the Campus Martius, the drill field of the Roman army, convened by a military trumpet. Voting was by century and proceeded in order of classification from the cavalry down. The assembly elected the consuls and several other magistrates, voted on bills put before it, made decisions of war and peace, and also served as the court of appeal against decisions of the magistrates affecting the life or property of a citizen.

The Struggle of the Orders

The laws and constitution of the early republic clearly reflected the class structure of the Roman state, for they gave to the patricians almost a monopoly of power and privilege. Plebeians were barred from public office, from priesthoods, and from other public religious offices. They could not serve as judges, they could not even know the law, for there was no published legal code. The only law was traditional practice, and that existed only in the minds and actions of patrician magistrates. Plebeians were subject to the *imperium* but could not exercise its power. They were not allowed to marry patricians. When Rome acquired new land by conquest, patrician magistrates distributed it in a way that favored patricians. The patricians dominated the assemblies and the Senate. The plebeians undertook a campaign to achieve political, legal, and social equality, and this attempt, which succeeded after two centuries of intermittent effort, is called the *struggle of the orders.*

The most important source of plebeian success was the need for their military service. Rome was at war almost constantly, and the patricians were forced to call on the plebeians to defend the state. According to tradition, the plebeians, angered by patrician resistance to their demands, withdrew from the city and camped on the Sacred Mount. There they formed a plebeian tribal assembly and elected plebeian tribunes to protect them from the arbitrary power of the magistrates. They declared the tribune inviolate and sacrosanct, and any one laying violent hands on him was accursed and liable to death without trial. By extension of his right to protect the plebeians, the tribune gained the power to veto any action of a magistrate or any bill in the assembly or the Senate. By 241 B.C. thirty-one rural tribes had been added to the original four in the city to make a total of thirty-five. Thereafter no tribes were added, and new citizens took their places in the old tribes. The plebeian assembly voted by tribe, and a vote of the assembly was binding on plebeians. They tried to make their decisions binding on all Romans but could not do so until 287 B.C.

The next step was for the plebeians to obtain access to the laws, and by 450 B.C. the Twelve Tables codified early Roman custom in all its harshness and simplicity. In 445 B.C. plebeians gained the right to marry patricians. The main prize was the consulship. The patricians did not yield easily, but at last, in 367 B.C., the Licinian-Sextian Laws provided that at least one consul must be a plebeian. Before long plebeians held other offices, even the dictatorship and the censorship. In 300 B.C. they were admitted to the most important priesthoods, the last religious barrier to equality. In 287 B.C. the plebeians completed their triumph. They once again withdrew from the city and secured the passage of a law whereby deci-

Polybius Summarizes the Roman Constitution

Polybius (*ca.* 203–120 B.C.) was a Greek from the city of Megalopolis, an important member of the Achaean League. As a hostage in Rome he became a friend of influential Romans and later wrote a history of Rome's conquest of the Mediterranean lands. He praises the Roman constitution as an excellent example of a "mixed constitution" and as a major source of Roman success.

A S F O R *the Roman constitution, it had three elements, each of them possessing sovereign powers: and their respective share of power in the whole state had been regulated with such a scrupulous regard to equality and equilibrium, that no one could say for certain, not even a native, whether the constitution as a whole were an aristocracy or democracy or despotism. . . .*

⁙ ⁙ ⁙ ⁙ ⁙ ⁙ ⁙ ⁙ ⁙ ⁙ ⁙

The result of this power of the several estates for mutual help or harm is a union sufficiently firm for all emergencies, and a constitution than which it is impossible to find a better. For whenever any danger from without compels them to unite and work together, the strength which is developed by the State is so extraordinary, that everything required is unfailingly carried out by the eager rivalry shown by all classes to devote their whole minds to the need of the hour, and to secure that any determination come to should not fail for want of promptitude; while each individual works, privately and publicly alike, for the accomplishment of the business in hand. Accordingly, the peculiar constitution of the State makes it irresistible, and certain of obtaining whatever it determines to attempt. . . . For when any one of the three classes becomes puffed up, and manifests an inclination to be contentious and unduly encroaching, the mutual interdependency of all the three, and the possibility of the pretensions of any one being checked and thwarted by the others, must plainly check this tendency: and so the proper equilibrium is maintained by the impulsiveness of the one part being checked by its fear of the other. . . .

Polybius, *Histories,* Vol. 1, trans. by E. S. Shuckburgh (Bloomington: Indiana University Press, 1962), pp. 468, 473–474.

sions of the plebeian assembly bound all Romans and did not require the approval of the Senate.

It might seem that the Roman aristocracy had given way before the pressure of the lower class, but the victory of the plebeians did not bring democracy. An aristocracy based strictly on birth had given way to one more subtle, but no less restricted based on a combination of wealth

These golden Celtic drinking horns with rams' heads at the ends were made and used by Celtic peoples like the Gauls who stormed into Italy and captured Rome in 390 B.C. [Württembergisches Landesmuseum, Stuttgart.]

and birth. The significant distinction was no longer between patrician and plebeian but between the *nobiles*—a relatively small group of wealthy and powerful families, both patrician and plebeian, whose members attained the highest offices in the state—and everyone else. The absence of the secret ballot in the assemblies enabled the nobles to control most decisions and elections by a combination of intimidation and bribery. The leading families, although in constant competition with one another for office, power, and prestige, often combined in marriage and less formal alliances to keep the political plums within their own group. In the century from 233 to 133 B.C., for instance, twenty-six families provided 80 per cent of the consuls and only ten families accounted for almost 50 per cent. These same families dominated the Senate, whose power became ever greater. It remained the only continuous deliberative body in the state, and the pressure of warfare gave it experience in handling public business. Rome's success brought the Senate prestige, increased control of policy, and confidence in its capacity to rule. The end of the struggle of the orders brought domestic peace under a republican constitution dominated by a capable, if narrow, senatorial aristocracy. This outcome satisfied most Romans outside the ruling nobility because Rome conquered Italy and brought many benefits to its citizens.

The Conquest of Italy

Not long after the fall of the monarchy a coalition of Romans, Latins, and Italian Greeks defeated the Etruscans and drove them out of Latium for good. Throughout the fifth century B.C. the powerful Etruscan city of Veii, only twelve miles north of the Tiber River, raided Roman territory. After a hard struggle and a long siege, the Romans took it in 396 B.C., more than doubling the size of Rome. Roman policy toward defeated enemies used both the carrot and the stick. When they made friendly alliances with some, they gained new soldiers for their army. When they treated others more harshly by

annexing their land, they achieved a similar end, for service in the Roman army was based on property, and the distribution to poor Romans of conquered land made soldiers of previously useless men. It also gave the poor a stake in Rome and reduced the pressure against its aristocratic regime. The long siege of Veii kept soldiers from their farms during the campaign. From that time on the Romans paid their soldiers, thus giving their army greater flexibility and a more professional quality.

Gallic Invasion of Italy and Roman Reaction

At the beginning of the fourth century B.C. the Romans were the chief power in central Italy, but a disaster struck. In 390 B.C. barbaric Celtic tribes called Gauls from across the Alps defeated the Roman army and captured, looted, and burned Rome. The Gauls sought plunder, not conquest, so they extorted a ransom from the Romans and returned to their homes in the north. Rome's power appeared to have been wiped out. When the Gauls left, some of her allies and old enemies tried to take advantage of Rome's weakness, but by about 350 B.C. the Romans had recovered their leadership of central Italy and were more dominant than ever. Their success in turning back new Gallic raids added still more to their power and prestige. As the Romans tightened their grip on Latium, the Latins became resentful. In 340 B.C. they demanded independence from Rome or full equality, and when the Romans refused, they launched a war of independence that lasted until 338. The victorious Romans dissolved the Latin League, and their treatment of the defeated opponents provided a model for the settlement of Italy.

Roman Policy Toward the Conquered

The Romans did not destroy any of the Latin cities or their people, nor did they treat them all alike. Some in the vicinity of Rome received full Roman citizenship; others farther away gained municipal status, which gave them the private rights of intermarriage and commerce with Romans but not the public rights of voting and holding

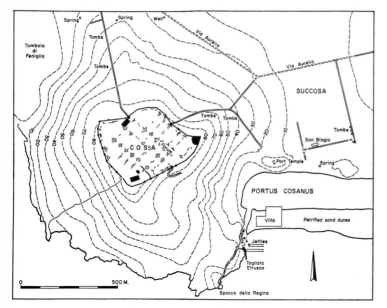

Plan of the Latin colony at Cosa on the Mediterranean coast of central Etruria, well north of Rome. It was founded in 273 B.C. on land taken from an Etruscan city that had opposed Rome. Its purpose was to punish, isolate, and keep watch over recent enemies and to guard the coast against attack. It stood atop a hill away from the beach and was surrounded by a powerful defensive wall. Later the Via Aurelia connected it with Rome. [Reprinted from E. T. Salmon, *Roman Colonization Under the Republic.* Copyright © 1970 by E. T. Salmon. Used by permission of Cornell University Press.]

office in Rome. They retained the rights of local self-government and could obtain full Roman citizenship if they moved to Rome. They followed Rome in foreign policy and provided soldiers to serve in the Roman legions.

Still other states became allies of Rome on the basis of treaties, which differed from city to city. Some were given the private rights of intermarriage and commerce with Romans and some were not; the allied states were always forbidden to exercise these rights with one another. Some, but not all, were allowed local autonomy. Land was taken from some but not from others, nor was the percentage always the same. All the allies supplied troops to the army, in which they fought in auxiliary battalions under Roman officers, but they did not pay taxes to Rome.

On some of the conquered land the Romans placed colonies, permanent settlements of veteran soldiers in the territory of recently defeated enemies. The colonists retained their Roman citizenship and enjoyed home rule, and in return for the land they had been given they served as a kind of permanent garrison to deter or sup-

press rebellion. These colonies were usually connected to Rome by a network of military roads built as straight as possible and so durable that some are used even today. They guaranteed that a Roman army could swiftly reinforce an embattled colony or put down an uprising in any weather.

The Roman settlement of Latium reveals even more clearly than before the principles by which Rome was able to conquer and dominate Italy for many centuries.

The Via Latina, here shown not far outside Rome, is one of the network of military roads that went from Rome into the Italian country. They enabled Roman legions to move swiftly to enforce their control of the peninsula—and, conversely, also served as convenient avenues of invasion. The Via Latina is thought to be the earliest of these great roads, dating to the fourth century B.C. [Fototeca Unione.]

The excellent army and the diplomatic skill that allowed Rome to separate its enemies help explain its conquests. The reputation for harsh punishment of rebels and the sure promise that such punishment would be delivered, made unmistakably clear by the presence of colonies and military roads, help account for their slowness to revolt. But the positive side, represented by Rome's organization of the defeated states, is at least as important. The Romans did not regard the status given each newly conquered city as permanent. They held out to loyal allies the prospect of improving their status, even of achieving the ultimate prize, full Roman citizenship. In so doing, the Romans gave their allies a stake in Rome's future and success and a sense of being colleagues, though subordinate ones, rather than subjects. The result, in general, was that most of Rome's allies remained loyal even when put to the severest test.

Defeat of the Samnites

The next great challenge to Roman arms came in a series of wars with a tough mountain people of the southern Appenines, the Samnites. Some of Rome's allies rebelled, and soon the Etruscans and Gauls joined in the war against Rome. But most of the allies remained loyal. In 295 B.C. the Romans defeated an Italian coalition, and by 280 they were masters of central Italy. Their power extended from the Po valley to Apulia and Lucania.

The victory over the Samnites brought the Romans into direct contact with the Greek cities of southern Italy. Roman intervention in a quarrel between Greek cities brought them face to face with Pyrrhus, king of Epirus. Pyrrhus, probably the best general of his time, commanded a well-disciplined and experienced mercenary army, which he hired out for profit, and a new weapon: twenty war elephants. He defeated the Romans twice but suffered many casualties. When one of his officers rejoiced at the victory, Pyrrhus told him, "If we win one more battle against the Romans we shall be completely ruined." This "Pyrrhic" victory led him to withdraw to Sicily. The Greek cities that hired him were forced to join the Roman confederation. By 265 B.C. Rome ruled all Italy as far north as the Po River, an area of 47,200 square miles. The year after the defeat of Pyrrhus, Ptolemy Philadelphus, king of Egypt, sent a message of congratulation to establish friendly relations with Rome. This act recognized Rome's new status as a power in the Hellenistic world.

Rome and Carthage

Rome's acquisition of coastal territory and her expansion to the toe of the Italian boot brought her face to face with the great naval power of the western Mediterranean, Carthage. Late in the ninth century B.C. the Phoenician city of Tyre planted a colony on the coast of northern Africa near modern Tunis, calling it the New City, or Carthage. In the sixth century B.C. the conquest of Phoenicia by the Assyrians and the Persians made Carthage independent and free to exploit her very advantageous situation. The city was located on a defensible site and commanded an excellent harbor that encouraged commerce. The coastal plain grew abundant grain, fruits,

and vegetables. An inland plain allowed sheep herding. The Phoenician settlers conquered the native inhabitants and used them to work the land. Beginning in the sixth century B.C. the Carthaginians expanded their domain to include the coast of northern Africa west beyond the Straits of Gibraltar and eastward into Libya. Overseas they came to control the southern part of Spain, Sardinia, Corsica, Malta, the Balearic Islands, and western Sicily. The people of these territories, though originally allies, were all reduced to subjection like the natives of the Carthaginian home territory, and they all served in the Carthaginian army or navy and paid tribute. Carthage also profited greatly from the mines of Spain and from the absolute monopoly of trade she imposed on the western Mediterranean.

Early relations between Rome and Carthage had been few but not unfriendly. Because Rome was neither a commercial nor a naval state and Carthage had no designs on central Italy, there was no reason for conflict. But an attack by Hiero, tyrant of Syracuse, on the Sicilian city of Messana just across from Italy caused trouble. Messana was held by a group of Italian mercenary soldiers who called themselves *Mamertines,* the sons of Mars. Some years earlier they had seized the city, killed the men, taken the women, and launched a career of piracy, extortion, and attacks on their neighbors. When Hiero defeated the Mamertines, some of them called on the Carthaginians to help save their city. Carthage agreed and sent a garrison, for the Carthaginians wanted to prevent Syracuse from dominating the straits. One Mamertine faction, however, fearing that Carthage might take undue advantage of the opportunity, asked Rome for help.

In 264 B.C. the request came to the Senate, where it was debated at length, and rightly so, for the issue was momentous. The Punic garrison (the Romans called the Carthaginians *Phoenicians;* in Latin the word is *Poeni* or *Puni,* hence the adjective *Punic*) was in place at Messana. The Romans knew that intervention would not be against Syracuse but against the mighty empire of Carthage, a powerful state that was getting too close to Italy.

Handwritten annotations on map: *Boundary*, *Rome*, *Ebro*, *RIVER*, *Carthag*, *feuding*

THE WESTERN MEDITERRANEAN AREA DURING THE RISE OF ROME

This map covers the theater of the conflicts between the growing Roman dominions and those of Carthage in the third century B.C. The Carthaginian empire stretched westward from the city (in modern Tunisia) along the North African coast and into southern Spain.

BELOW: The harbor of the ancient city of Carthage, near modern Tunis in North Africa, as reconstructed by an artist. [Radio Times Hulton Picture Library.]

Unless Rome intervened, Carthage would gain control of all Sicily and the straits. The assembly voted to protect the Mamertines, sent an army to Messana and expelled the Punic garrison. The Carthaginians made an alliance with Syracuse and joined in the blockade of Messana. The Romans demanded an end to the siege, and when the demand was refused, they declared war. The First Punic War was on.

The First Punic War (264–241 B.C.)

In spite of Rome's early successes Carthage would not give up, and it became clear that the Romans would need a fleet to win the war. The Romans had little naval experience and no fleet, but Roman ingenuity came to the rescue. The Romans invented the *corvus,* something like a gangplank with a spike at one end. This was held up high and suddenly lowered when the enemy ship was close enough. With the *corvus* in place the Romans could board the enemy ship and turn a sea battle into a familiar land battle. In 257 B.C. the Romans won a great naval victory and landed an army near Carthage. In this emergency Carthage rallied all its forces and called in Xanthippus, a Spartan mercenary general skilled in the latest tactics, to train and lead their forces. The Punic army defeated the overconfident Romans.

In Sicily the war settled into a stalemate. At sea the Romans continued to make great efforts but with little result. At last they built a fleet to cut off supplies to the besieged Carthaginian cities at the western end of Sicily. When Carthage sent its own fleet to raise the siege, the Romans destroyed it. In 241 B.C. Carthage signed a treaty giving up Sicily and the islands between Italy and Sicily and agreed to pay a war indemnity in ten annual installments, to keep its ships out of Italian waters, and not to recruit mercenaries in Italy. Neither side was to attack the allies of the other. Rome had earned Sicily, and Carthage could well afford the indemnity. The peace reflected reality without undue harshness. It left Carthage most of its empire and its self-respect and created no obvious grounds for future conflict. If the treaty had been carried out in good faith, it might have brought lasting peace.

The treaty did not bring peace to Carthage, even for the moment. A rebellion broke out among the mercenaries, newly recruited from Sicily and demanding their pay. In 238 B.C., while Carthage was still in danger, some of its rebellious mercenaries seized Sardinia and asked help from Rome against the natives; Rome agreed. By now the Carthaginian general Hamilcar Barca had brought victory in Africa and was preparing an expedition to regain Sardinia from the mercenary rebels. Rome trumped up the excuse that these preparations were directed against Italy and declared war on helpless Carthage. Carthage could do nothing but yield, and new terms were tacked on to the treaty of 241 B.C.: Carthage must abandon Sardinia and pay an additional indemnity of twelve hundred talents. This was a harsh and cynical action by the Romans; even the historian Polybius, a great champion of Rome, could find no justification for it. The Romans were moved, no doubt, by the fear of giving Carthage a base so near Italy, but their action was unwise. It undid the calming effects of the peace of 241 B.C. and angered the Carthaginians without preventing them from recovering their strength to seek vengeance in the future.

The Roman conquest of territory overseas presented a new problem. Instead of following the policy they had pursued in Italy, the Romans made Sicily a province and Sardinia with Corsica another. It became common to extend the term of the governors of these provinces beyond a year. The governors were unchecked by colleagues and exercised full *imperium.* New magistracies, in effect, were thus created free of the limits on the power of officials in Rome. The new populations were neither Roman citizens nor allies; they were subjects who did not serve in the army but paid tribute instead. The old practice of extending citizenship and with it loyalty to Rome stopped at the borders of Italy. Rome collected the new taxes by "farming" them out at auction to the highest bidder. The tax collectors were men below senatorial rank who became powerful and wealthy by

Livy Attributes the Second Punic War to Hannibal's Oath

In the following selection Livy tells of an oath allegedly taken by Hannibal (247–182 B.C.), the great Carthaginian general who led the fight against Rome in the Second Punic War (218–201 B.C.).

I MAY *be permitted to premise at this division of my work, what most historians have professed at the beginning of their whole undertaking; that I am about to relate the most memorable of all wars that were ever waged: the war which the Carthaginians, under the conduct of Hannibal, maintained with the Roman people. For never did any states and nations more efficient in their resources engage in contest; nor had they themselves at any other period so great a degree of power and energy. They brought into action too no arts of war unknown to each other, but those which had been tried in the first Punic war; and so various was the fortune of the conflict, and so doubtful the victory, that they who conquered were more exposed to danger. The hatred with which they fought also was almost greater than their resources; the Romans being indignant that the conquered aggressively took up arms against their victors; the Carthaginians, because they considered that in their subjection it had been lorded over them with haughtiness and avarice. There is besides a story, that Hannibal, when about nine years old, while he boyishly coaxed his father Hamilcar that he might be taken to Spain, (at the time when the African war was completed, and he was employed in sacrificing previously to transporting his army thither,) was conducted to the altar; and, having laid his hand on the offerings, was bound by an oath to prove himself, as soon as he could, an enemy to the Roman people.*

Livy, *History of Rome*, trans. by D. Spillan, et. al., (New York: American Book Company, n.d.), Vol. 2, p. 14.

---

squeezing the provincials hard. These innovations were the basis for Rome's imperial organization in the future; in time they strained the constitution and traditions of Rome to such a degree as to threaten the existence of the republic.

After the First Punic War, campaigns against the Gauls and across the Adriatic distracted Rome. Meanwhile Hamilcar Barca was leading Carthage on the road to recovery. Roman legend reports that Hamilcar, disappointed by the Punic surrender in 241 B.C. and infuriated by Rome's bad faith in 238 B.C. devoted his life to revenge. The story goes that he made his nine-year-old son,

Hannibal, swear always to be an enemy to Rome. We need not believe the story to believe that the Barca family were among many Carthaginians who did not accept defeat and aimed at vengeance. Hamilcar sought to compensate for losses elsewhere by building a Punic empire in Spain. As governor of Spain from 237 B.C. until his death in 229 B.C., he improved the ports and their commerce, exploited the mines, gained control of the hinterland, won over many of the conquered tribes, and built a strong and disciplined army.

Hamilcar's successor, his son-in-law Hasdrubal, pursued the same policies. His success alarmed the Romans, and they imposed a treaty in which he promised not to take an army north across the Ebro River in Spain, although Punic expansion in Spain was well south of that river at the time of the treaty. Even though the agreement preserved the appearance of Rome's giving orders to an inferior, the treaty gave equal benefits to both sides: if the Carthaginians agreed to accept the limit of the Ebro to their expansion in Spain, the Romans would not interfere with that expansion.

The Second Punic War (218–202 B.C.)

On Hasdrubal's assassination in 221 B.C. the army chose as his successor Hannibal, son of Hamilcar Barca, still a young man of twenty-five. He quickly consolidated and extended the Punic Empire in Spain. A few years before his accession Rome had received an offer from the people of the Spanish town of Saguntum, about one hundred miles south of the Ebro, to become the friends of Rome. The Romans accepted, thereby accepting the responsibilities of friendship with a foreign state. The Romans regarded foreign relations in terms very much like those of the personal client–patron relationship. When the Romans defeated a state or made an alliance with it, they accepted it into protection or trust (*fides*). Formal alliance legally required Rome to go to the aid of an ally threatened or attacked by another state. Friendship was less formal, but the Romans understood that to allow a state connected with Rome by friendship to suffer

Portrait of Hannibal (247–183 B.C.), the great Carthaginian general, on a coin from the Carthaginian colony of New Carthage in Spain. The reverse of the coin depicts an African elephant. [Courtesy of the American Numismatic Society, New York.]

harm would cast doubt on the value of Roman *fides*. The Roman association with Saguntum may not have violated the letter of the Ebro treaty, but it certainly was contrary to its spirit. At first Hannibal was careful to avoid interfering with the friends of Rome, but the Saguntines, confident of Rome's protection, began to interfere with some of the Spanish tribes allied with Hannibal.

Finally, the Romans sent an embassy to Hannibal warning him to let Saguntum alone and repeating the injunction not to cross the Ebro. The Romans probably expected Hannibal to yield as his predecessors had, but they misjudged their man. Hannibal ignored Rome's warning, besieged Saguntum, and took the town.

On hearing of Saguntum's fall, the Romans sent an ultimatum to Carthage demanding the surrender of Hannibal. Carthage refused, and Rome declared war in 218 B.C. Rome's policy between the wars had been the worst possible combination of approaches. She had insulted and injured Carthage by the annexation of Sardinia in 238 B.C. and had repeatedly provoked and insulted her by interventions in Spain. But for the most part Roman policy was distracted and took no measures to prevent the construction of a powerful and dangerous Punic Empire or even to build defenses against a Punic attack from Spain. Hannibal saw to it that the Romans paid the price for their blunders.

Rome had full command of the sea, for Carthage had no navy. The Roman plan was to send one army to Spain and another to Africa and to end the war quickly. Hannibal had other plans. He had a fine army of about ninety thousand infantry, twelve thousand cavalry, and thirty-seven elephants, well-trained and tested in battle and led by a great general. He needed no navy, for he would march swiftly overland into northern Italy. There he would be joined by the Gauls, eager for revenge against Rome. He would seek out the Roman army and defeat it in battle as often as necessary and thereby win over the Italian subjects of Rome. The isolated Romans would then have no choice but surrender. Between Hannibal and the Po valley stood one thousand Roman miles,

hostile tribes, and the Alps, but no other plan was possible. By September of 218 B.C. he was across the Alps. His army was weary and bedraggled and its numbers may have been reduced to as few as twenty thousand infantry, six thousand cavalry, and a few elephants, but he was in Italy and among the friendly Gauls.

Hannibal defeated the Romans at the Ticinus River and crushed the joint consular armies at the Trebbia River. In 217 B.C. he outmaneuvered and trapped another army at Lake Trasimene. Hannibal's first victory brought him reinforcements of fifty thousand Gauls, and his second confirmed that his superior generalship could defeat the Roman army. The key to success however was defection by Rome's allies. Hannibal released Italian prisoners without harm or ransom and moved his army south of Rome to encourage rebellion. But the allies remained firm, perhaps because Hannibal was accompanied by the hated Gauls, perhaps because they were not convinced yet of Rome's ultimate defeat, and perhaps even out of loyalty to Rome.

Sobered by their defeats, the Romans elected Quintus Fabius Maximus dictator. He understood that Hannibal could not be beaten by the usual tactics and that the Roman army, decimated and demoralized, needed time to recover. His strategy was to avoid battle while following and harassing Hannibal's army. When the Roman army had recovered and Fabius could fight Hannibal on favorable ground, only then would the Romans fight. Hannibal, however, was too shrewd and escaped Fabius' traps. In their anger and frustration the Romans gave Fabius the unflattering name *Cunctator*, the delayer, a name he would later bear proudly, for his strategy was sound.

In 216 B.C. Hannibal marched to Cannae in Apulia to tempt the Romans into another open fight. The Romans could not allow him to ravage the country freely, so they sent off an army of some eighty thousand men to meet him. Almost the entire Roman army was killed or captured. It was the worst defeat in Roman history; Rome's prestige was shattered, and most of her allies in southern Italy as well as Syracuse in Sicily now went over to

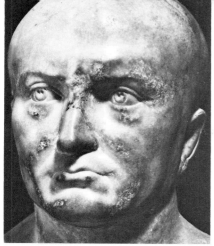

Portrait of Scipio Africanus (237–183 B.C.) [Anderson.]

The battle of Zama. This fanciful modern woodcut depicts the use of war elephants in Scipio Africanus's defeat of the Carthaginians under Hannibal at Zama in 202 B.C. [Bettmann Archive.]

Hannibal. In 215 B.C. Philip V, king of Macedon, made an alliance with Hannibal and launched a war to recover his influence on the Adriatic. For more than a decade no Roman army would dare face Hannibal in the open field, and he was free to roam over all Italy and do as he pleased.

The Romans, however, passed this sternest test of their resolve, their strength, and their alliance system. The heart of the Roman alliance in central Italy, as well as Etruria and Umbria, remained firm. Hannibal had not the numbers or supplies to besiege walled cities like Rome and the major allies, nor did he have the equipment to take them by assault. By 211 B.C. the Romans were able to recover the chief city of Campania, Capua, as well as Syracuse. To win the war in Spain, they appointed Publius Cornelius Scipio (237–183 B.C.), later called Africanus, to the command in Spain with proconsular *imperium*. This was such a breach of tradition as to be almost unconstitutional, for Scipio was not yet twenty-five and had held no high office. But he was a general almost as talented as Hannibal. In 209 B.C. he captured the main Punic base in Spain, New Carthage. His skillful and tactful treatment of the native Iberians won them away from the enemy and over to his own army. Within a few years young Scipio had conquered all Spain and deprived Hannibal of hope of help from that region.

Before that task was accomplished, however, Scipio was unable to prevent the Punic commander in Spain, Hasdrubal, Hannibal's brother, from crossing the Pyrenees with money and reinforcements for Hannibal. Hasdrubal arrived in Italy in 207 B.C., but before he could join Hannibal, he was defeated and killed at the battle of the Metaurus River. Hannibal's situation by now was desperate if not hopeless.

In 204 B.C. Scipio landed in Africa, defeated the Carthaginians, and forced them to accept a peace whose main clause was the withdrawal of Hannibal and his army from Italy. Hannibal had won every battle but lost the war, for he had not counted on the determination of Rome and the loyalty of her allies. Hannibal's return inspired Carthage to break the peace and to risk all in battle. In 202 B.C. Scipio and Hannibal faced each other at the battle of Zama. The generalship of Scipio and the desertion of Hannibal's mercenaries gave the victory to Rome. The new peace terms reduced Carthage to the status of dependent ally on Rome. The Second Punic War ended the Carthaginian command of the western Mediterranean and Carthage's term as a great power. Rome ruled the seas and the entire Mediterranean coast from Italy westward.

The Republic's Conquest of the Hellenistic World

In the East

By the middle of the third century B.C. the eastern Mediterranean had reached a condition of stability. It was based on a balance of power among the three great kingdoms, and even lesser states had an established place.

That equilibrium was threatened by the activities of two aggressive monarchs, Philip V of Macedon (221–179 B.C.) and Antiochus III of the Seleucid kingdom (223–187 B.C.). It was shattered by the death of Ptolemy IV Philopator, the king of Egypt, in 205 B.C. and the succession of the child king Ptolemy V Epiphanes. Taking advantage of the newly created vacuum, Philip and Antiochus moved swiftly, the latter against Syria and Palestine, the former against cities in the Aegean, in the Hellespontine region, and on the coast of Asia Minor. The small but important Hellenistic states of Pergamum and Rhodes, whose security had heretofore depended on the balance of power, now turned to Rome for help. The Roman Senate became convinced that Philip meant to expand his power. The threat that a more powerful Macedon might pose to Rome's friends and, perhaps, even to Italy was enough to persuade the Romans to intervene.

In 200 B.C. the Romans sent an ultimatum to Philip and brought on war. Two years later they sent out a talented young general, Flamininus, who demanded that Philip withdraw from Greece entirely. In 197 B.C., with Greek support, he defeated Philip in the hills of Cynoscephalae in Thessaly.

The peace terms reveal Rome's policy toward the Greek world at this time. Macedon was compelled to abandon all of Greece, to cease fighting the Greeks, and to pay a war indemnity that was not excessive. Macedon remained intact and independent, a useful barrier against the barbarians to the north and no longer a threat to Rome. Soon the Macedonians became allies of Rome. The Greek cities freed from Philip were made autonomous, to the chagrin of Rome's Aetolian allies, who hoped to annex some of them. The Aetolians began to stir up doubts about Roman intentions, so Flamininus made the following proclamation at the Isthmian Games of 196 B.C.: "The Roman senate and Titus Quinctius [Flamininus] their general, having conquered King Philip and the Macedonians, decree that [the Greek cities that had been ruled by Philip] shall be free, exempt from tribute, and subject to their own laws." According to Livy the audience could not believe what it had heard and required the herald to read the proclamation again: "Then they realized that the joyful news was true, and from the storm of applause and repeated cheers that arose it was perfectly evident that none of life's blessings is dearer to the people than liberty."

The Romans were quite sincere in their intention to leave the Greeks free, but the Greeks and Romans did not understand freedom in the same way. The Romans understood that their defense of the Greeks and the gift of liberty they had given them put the Greeks in the relationship of clients to the Roman patrons. They expected the Greeks to behave toward them with deference and respect. Rome favored the rule of the upper classes and oligarchic government; the Romans did not like revolution or talk of land redistribution or debt cancellation. They felt free to intervene to prevent such horrors and to prevent unwelcome quarrels between Greek states. Some Greeks understood this attitude and approved it, but many did not. The misunderstanding later proved troublesome.

Soon after the Romans withdrew from Greece, they came into conflict with Antiochus, who was expanding his power in Asia and on the European side of the Hellespont. Pursuing their own interests, the Aetolians invited Antiochus to "free the Greeks" from Roman domination. The Romans routed Antiochus at Thermopylae and quickly drove him from Greece, and in 189 B.C. they crushed his army at Magnesia in Asia Minor. The peace of Apamia in the next year deprived Antiochus of his elephants and his navy and imposed a huge indemnity on him. Once again the Romans took no territory for themselves and left a number of Greek cities in Asia free. They continued their policy of regarding Greece, and now Asia Minor, as a kind of protectorate in which they could intervene or not as they chose. They had no imperial designs and were reluctant to take on new responsibilities far from home. All they asked was that nothing should threaten Rome's tranquillity or security. Roman

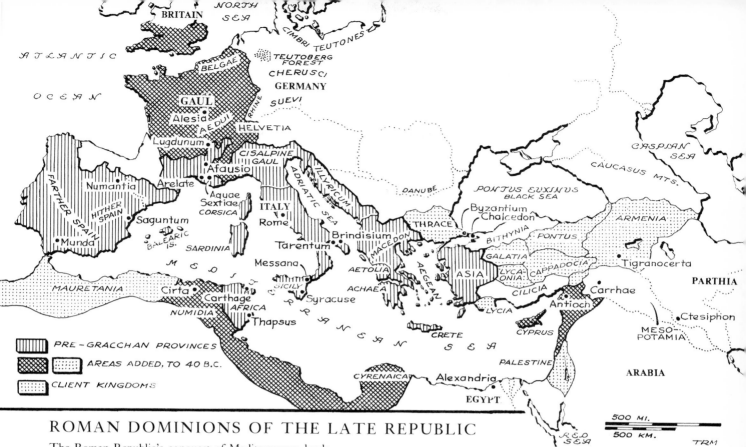

ROMAN DOMINIONS OF THE LATE REPUBLIC

The Roman Republic's conquest of Mediterranean lands
—and beyond—until about the death of Julius Caesar
is shown here. Areas conquered before Tiberius Gracchus
(*ca.* 133 B.C.) are distinguished from later ones and
from client areas owing allegiance to Rome.

intervention, however, had destroyed the previous guar-
antors of reasonable stability without providing a substitute. The Romans were soon to find that they could not
preserve the *status quo* at a distance and without effort.

In 179 B.C. Perseus succeeded Philip V as king of
Macedon. He tried to gain popularity in Greece by
favoring the democratic and revolutionary forces in the
cities. The Romans, troubled by this threat to stability,
launched the Third Macedonian War (172–168 B.C.),
and in 168 Aemilius Paullus defeated Perseus at Pydna.
The peace imposed by the Romans reveals a change in
policy and a growing harshness. It divided Macedon into
four separate republics, whose citizens were forbidden to
intermarry or even to do business across the new national
boundaries. This peace also took away the mines and
forests that provided an important source of Macedon's
wealth and imposed a small tribute.

The new policy reflected a change in Rome from the
previous relatively gentle one to the stern and businesslike
approach favored by the conservative censor Cato. The
new harshness was applied to allies and bystanders as well

as to defeated opponents. Leaders of anti-Roman factions
in the Greek cities were punished severely. The Romans,
without proof, suspected their allies in the Achaean
League of being friendly to Perseus, so they rounded up
one thousand prominent Achaeans, among them the
historian Polybius, and sent them to Rome for trial and as
hostages. The harshest treatment was accorded to the
kingdom of Epirus; seventy towns were sacked and
looted, and 150,000 people were sold into slavery.

When Aemilius Paullus returned from his victory, he
celebrated a triumph that lasted three days, during which
the spoils of war, royal prisoners, and great wealth were
paraded through the streets of Rome behind the proud
general. The public treasury benefited to such a degree
that the direct property tax on Roman citizens was abolished. Part of the booty went to the general and part to
his soldiers. New motives were thereby introduced into
Roman foreign policy, or, perhaps, old motives were
given new prominence. Foreign campaigns could bring
profit to the state, rewards to the army, and wealth, fame,
honor, and political power to the general.

Even so, the Romans made no attempt to occupy,
administer, and exploit the territory of their defeated
enemies in a systematic manner. Fearful of independent
popular commanders and afraid to give opportunities to
new men to rise, the members of the inner circle of the

The Republic's Conquest of the Hellenistic World **143**

Roman Senate were also afraid that individuals in their own group would achieve too much power and lord it over the others. As a result the Senate continued the policy of protectorates, which gave no guarantee of keeping the peace and continued to involve Rome in troubles.

In the West

Harsh as the Romans had become toward the Greeks, they were even worse in their treatment of the people of the Iberian Peninsula, whom they considered barbarians. They committed dreadful atrocities, lied, cheated, and broke treaties in their effort to exploit and pacify the natives, who fought back fiercely in guerrilla style. From 154 to 133 B.C. the fighting waxed, and it became hard to recruit Roman soldiers to fight in the increasingly ugly war. At last, in 134, Scipio Aemilianus took the key city of Numantia by siege, burned it to the ground, and put an end to the war in Spain.

Roman treatment of Carthage was no better. Although Carthage lived up to its treaty with Rome faithfully and posed no threat, some Romans refused to abandon their hatred and fear of the traditional enemy. Cato is said to have ended all his speeches in the Senate with the same sentence, "Ceterum censeo delendam esse Carthaginem" ("Besides, I think that Carthage must be destroyed"). At last the Romans took advantage of a technical breach of the peace to destroy Carthage. In 146 B.C. Scipio Aemilianus took the city, plowed up its land, and put salt in the furrows as a symbol of the permanent abandonment of the site. The Romans incorporated it as the province of Africa, one of six Roman provinces, including Sicily, Sardinia–Corsica, Macedonia, Hither Spain, and Further Spain.

The Aftermath of Conquest

War and expansion changed the economic, social, and political life of Italy. Before the Punic wars most Italians owned their own farms, which provided most of the family's needs. Some families owned larger holdings, but their lands chiefly grew grain, and they used the labor of

---

Appian Describes the Final Destruction of Carthage

Appian lived in the second century and wrote a history of Rome. In the following selection he describes the destruction of Carthage at the end of the Third Punic War (149–146 B.C.) at the hands of the Roman general Scipio Aemilianus.

THE *next day there were sacrifices and solemn processions to the gods by tribes, also games and spectacles of various kinds. The Senate sent ten of the noblest of their own number as deputies to arrange the affairs of Africa in conjunction with Scipio, to the advantage of Rome. They decreed that if anything was still left of Carthage, Scipio should obliterate it and that nobody should be allowed to live there. Direful threats were levelled against any who should disobey and chiefly against the rebuilding of Byrsa or Megara, but it was not forbidden to go upon the ground. The towns that had allied themselves with the enemy it was decided to destroy, to the last one. To those who had aided the Romans there was an allotment of lands won by the sword, and first of all to the Uticans was given the territory of Carthage itself, extending as far as Hippo. Upon all the rest a tribute was imposed, both a land tax and a personal tax, upon men and women alike. It was decreed that a prætor should be sent from Rome yearly to govern the country. After these arrangements had been carried out by the deputies, they returned to Rome. Scipio did all that they directed, and he instituted sacrifices and games to the gods for the victory. When all was finished, he sailed for home and was awarded the most glorious triumph that had ever been known, splendid with gold and gorged with statues and votive offerings that the Carthaginians had gathered from all parts of the world through all time, the fruit of their countless victories.*

Appian, *Punic Wars*, trans. by Horace White (London and New York: Macmillan, 1899), pp. 231–234.

---

clients, tenants, and hired men rather than slaves. Fourteen years of fighting in the Hannibalic war did terrible damage to much Italian farmland. Many veterans returning from the wars found it impossible or unprofitable to go back to their farms. Some moved to Rome, where they could find work as occasional laborers, but most stayed in the country to work as tenant farmers or hired hands. No longer landowners, they were no longer eligible for the army. Often the land they abandoned was gathered into large parcels by wealthy men. They converted these large units, later called *latifundia,* into large plantations for growing cash crops—grain, olives, and grapes for wine—or into cattle ranches.

The upper classes had plenty of capital to stock and operate these estates because of profits from the war and from exploiting the provinces. Land was cheap, and slaves conquered in war provided cheap labor. By fair means and foul large landholders obtained large quantities of public land and forced small farmers from it. These changes separated the people of Rome and Italy more sharply into rich and poor, landed and landless, privileged and deprived. The result was political, social, and ultimately constitutional conflict that threatened the existence of the republic.

SUGGESTED READINGS

F. E. ADCOCK, *The Roman Art of War Under the Republic* (Cambridge, Mass., 1940).

A. E. ASTIN, *Scipio Aemilianus* (Oxford, 1967). A fine biography.

E. BADIAN, *Foreign Clientelae* (Oxford, 1958). A brilliant study of the Roman idea of a client–patron relationship extended to foreign affairs.

R. BLOCH, *The Etruscans* (London, 1958). A good survey.

R. BLOCH, *Origins of Rome* (New York, 1960). A good account of the most generally accepted point of view.

G. DE BEER, *Hannibal: Challenging Rome's Supremacy* (New York, 1969). An excellent biography.

T. A. DOREY AND D. R. DUDLEY, *Rome Against Carthage* (New York, 1972). An account of the Punic wars.

R. M. ERRINGTON, *The Dawn of Empire: Rome's Rise to Power* (Ithaca, 1972). An account of Rome's conquest of the Mediterranean.

T. FRANK, *Roman Imperialism* (New York, 1914). Still a valuable work.

E. GJERSTAD, *Legends and Facts of Early Roman History* (Lund, 1962). An unorthodox but interesting account of early Rome.

L. P. HOMO, *Primitive Italy and the Beginning of Roman Imperialism* (New York, 1967). A study of early Roman relations with the peoples of Italy.

M. PALLOTTINO, *The Etruscans* (Harmondsworth, 1955). Makes especially good use of archaeological evidence.

R. E. A. PALMER, *The Archaic Community of the Romans* (Cambridge, Mass.: 1970). An interesting interpretation of early Roman customs.

E. T. SALMON, *Samnium and thg Samnites* (Cambridge, Mass.: 1967). An account of Rome's most formidable Italian opponent.

E. T. SALMON, *Roman Colonization Under the Republic* (Ithaca, 1970).

H. H. SCULLARD, *Roman Politics, 220–150 B.C.* (Oxford, 1951). A study of factions within the Roman aristocracy.

H. H. SCULLARD, *A History of the Roman World from 753 to 146 B.C.,* 3rd ed. (London, 1961). An unusually fine narrative history with useful critical notes.

H. H. SCULLARD, *Scipio Africanus: Soldier and Politician* (Ithaca, 1970).

A. N. SHERWIN-WHITE, *Roman Citizenship* (Oxford, 1939). A useful study of the Roman franchise and its extension to other peoples.

B. H. WARMINGTON, *Carthage* (London, 1960). A good survey.

146

7
Decline and Fall of the Roman Republic
(About 150–31 B.C.)

The Gracchi

BY THE middle of the second century B.C. the problems caused by Rome's rapid expansion troubled perceptive Roman nobles. The fall in status of peasant farmers made it harder to recruit soldiers and came to present a political threat as well. The patron's traditional control over his clients was weakened by their flight from their land. Even those former landowners who worked on the land of their patrons as tenants or hired hands were less reliable. The introduction of the secret ballot in the 130s made them even more independent.

In 133 B.C. Tiberius Gracchus tried to solve these problems. His mother was the daughter of Scipio Africanus; his father had the extraordinary honor of being chosen consul twice and reaching the office of censor. His sister married the great Scipio Aemilianus. He had every reason to expect a brilliant career by following the usual path within the Roman establishment. In 137 he went off to Spain as aide to the general Mancinus, and there his career suffered a reverse just as it was beginning. Tiberius negotiated a truce that allowed the Roman army to withdraw from a trap unharmed, but the Romans repudiated the treaty, putting a black mark on Tiberius' record. An attempt to compensate may partly account for his eagerness to take up a popular cause.

He became tribune for 133 B.C. on a program of land reform; some of the most powerful members of the Roman aristocracy helped him draft the bill. They meant it to be a moderate attempt at solving Rome's problems. The bill's target was public land that had been acquired and held illegally, some of it for many years. The law allowed holders of this land to retain as many as six

hundred acres in clear title as private property, but the state would reclaim anything over that. The recovered land would be redistributed in small lots to the poor, who would pay a small rent to the state and could not sell what they had received. The plan's sponsors knew that there would be senatorial opposition, and they put the bill before the assembly without the Senate's prior approval.

The bill aroused great hostility. Many senators held vast estates and would be hurt by its passage. Others thought it a bad precedent to allow any interference with property rights, even ones so dubious as those pertaining to illegally held public land. Still others feared the political gains that Tiberius and his associates would make if the beneficiaries of their law were properly grateful to its drafters.

When Tiberius put the bill before the assembly, one of the tribunes, M. Octavius, interposed his veto. Tiberius went to the Senate to discuss his proposal, but the senators continued their opposition. Tiberius now had to choose between dropping the matter and undertaking a revolutionary course. Unwilling to give up, he put his bill before the assembly again. Again Octavius vetoed, so Tiberius had him removed and deposed from office, violating the constitution. The assembly's removal of a magistrate implied a fundamental shift of power from the Senate to the people. If the assembly could pass laws opposed by the Senate and vetoed by a tribune, if they could remove magistrates, then Rome would become a democracy like Athens instead of a traditional aristocracy. At this point many of Tiberius' powerful senatorial allies deserted him.

Tiberius proposed a second bill, harsher than the first and more appealing to the people, for he had given up hope of conciliating the Senate. This bill, which passed, provided for a commission to carry it out. When King Attalus of Pergamum died and left his kingdom to Rome, Tiberius proposed to use the Pergamene revenue to finance the commission. This was a declaration of war against the rule of the Senate, if one were still needed after Octavius' deposition. It challenged the Senate's

Sculptured portrait of Sulla, the first Roman to seize control of the republic by force. [Staatliche Antikensammlungen und Glyptothek, Munich. Studio Koppermann.]

Roman aqueducts. A painting by Zeus Diemer here reconstructs the multiple intersection of several of the many aqueducts bringing water to the city of Rome from the countryside. The two or three separate channels above the arches each brought water from separate sources. The system of aqueducts was begun in the late fourth century B.C. and was enlarged until the third century of the Christian era. [Bettmann Archive.]

control both of finances and of foreign affairs. Hereafter there could be no compromise: either Tiberius or the Roman constitution must go under.

Tiberius understood the danger that he faced when he stepped down from the tribunate, so he announced his candidacy for a second successive tribunate, another blow at tradition. His opponents feared that he might go on to hold office indefinitely, to dominate Rome in what appeared to them a demagogic tyranny. They concentrated their fire on the constitutional issue, the deposition of the tribune. They appear to have had some success, for many of Tiberius' supporters did not come out to vote. At the elections a riot broke out, and a mob of senators and their clients killed Tiberius and some three hundred of his followers and threw their bodies into the Tiber River. The Senate had put down the threat to its rule, but at the price of the first bloodshed in Roman political history.

The tribunate of Tiberius Gracchus brought a permanent change to Roman politics. Heretofore Roman political struggles had generally been struggles for honor and reputation between great families or coalitions of such families. Fundamental issues were rarely at stake. The revolutionary proposals of Tiberius, however, and the senatorial resort to bloodshed created a new situation. Tiberius' use of the tribunate to challenge senatorial rule encouraged imitation in spite of his failure. From then on Romans could pursue a political career that was not based solely on influence within the aristocracy; pressure from the people might be an effective substitute. In the last century of the republic such politicians were called *populares,* where those who supported the traditional role of the Senate were called *optimates* ("the best men").

These groups were not political parties with formal programs and party discipline, but they were more than merely vehicles for the political ambitions of unorthodox politicians. Fundamental questions such as land reform, the treatment of the Italian allies, the power of the assemblies versus the power of the Senate, and other problems divided the Roman people from the Gracchi to the fall of the republic. Some popular leaders, of course, were cyni-

cal self-seekers who used the issues only for their own ambitions. Some few may have been sincere advocates of a principled position. Most, no doubt, were a mixture of the two, like most politicians most of the time.

The murder of Tiberius did not prevent the execution of his law. Between 135 and 125 B.C. the roll of Roman citizens eligible for military service increased by seventy-five thousand. But the Gracchan land law removed many Italians from public land that they had held for generations, and only Roman citizens could receive land from the commission. Italian discontent threatened the stability of the Roman Republic as well as the strength of its army, and there was popular sentiment in favor of further land legislation.

The tribunate of Gaius Gracchus was much more dangerous than Tiberius' because all the tribunes of 123 B.C. were his supporters, so there could be no veto, and a recent law permitted the reelection of tribunes. Gaius developed a program of such breadth as to appeal to a variety of groups. First he revived the agrarian commission. Because there was not enough good public land left to meet the demand, he proposed to establish new colonies, two in Italy and one on the old site of Carthage. Among other popular acts he put through a law stabilizing the price of grain in Rome, which involved building granaries to guarantee an adequate supply.

Gaius broke new ground in appealing to the equestrian order in his struggle against the Senate. The equestrians were neither peasants nor large landowners. They were businessmen who supplied goods and services to the Roman state and collected its taxes. Almost continuous warfare and the need for tax collection in the provinces had made many of them rich. Most of the time these wealthy men had the same outlook as the Senate; generally they used their profits to purchase land and to try to reach senatorial rank themselves. Still they had a special interest in Roman expansion and in the exploitation of the provinces; toward the latter part of the second century B.C. they came to have a clearer sense of group interest and to exert political influence.

In 129 B.C. Pergamum became the new province of Asia. Gaius put through a law turning over to the equestrian order the privilege of collecting its revenue. He also barred senators from serving as jurors on the courts that tried provincial governors charged with extortion. The combination was a wonderful gift for wealthy equestrian businessmen, who were now free to squeeze profits out of the rich province of Asia without much fear of interference from the governors. The results for Roman provincial administration were bad, but the immediate political consequences for Gaius were excellent. The equestrians were now given reality as a class, as a political unit that might be set against the Senate, and they might be formed into a coalition to serve Gaius' purposes.

Gaius easily won reelection as tribune for 122 B.C. He aimed at giving citizenship to the Italians, both to solve the problem they presented and to add them to his political coalition. But the common people did not want to share the advantages of Roman citizenship, and the Senate seized on this proposal as a way of driving a wedge between Gaius and his supporters. Then, making use of the tribune M. Livius Drusus, the Senate outbid Gaius for public favor. Drusus opposed Italian enfranchisement and proposed that the land distributed by the Gracchan land commission be given to the holders outright, without rent or limit on its sale. Next he proposed the settlement of not three but twelve new colonies, all in Italy, though there was not enough land in Italy to make such a program possible.

The Romans did not reelect Gaius for 121 B.C., and he stood naked before his enemies. A hostile consul provoked an incident that led to violence. The Senate invented an extreme decree ordering the consuls to see to it that no harm came to the republic; in effect this decree established martial law. Gaius was hunted down and killed. A senatorial court condemned and put to death without trial some three thousand of his followers.

Marius and Sulla

For the moment the senatorial oligarchy had fought off the challenge to its traditional position. Before long it faced more serious dangers arising from troubles abroad. The first grew out of a dispute over the succession to the throne of Numidia, a client kingdom of Rome's near Carthage. The victory of Jugurtha, who had many friends in the Roman Senate, and his massacre of Roman and Italian businessmen in Numidia gained Roman attention. Although the Senate was reluctant to become in-

Roman crane with a treadmill. This is a sketch of
a relief in the Lateran Museum in Rome. The crane
is being used in building a temple and is driven
by five men inside a great treadmill. [Josef Durm,
Die Baukunst der Römer (1885), p. 235.]

volved, pressure from the equestrians and the people
forced a declaration of war in 111 B.C.

The cleverness of Jugurtha and the difficulty of fighting on the terrain of what is modern Algeria, as well as the incompetence of the senatorial generals, prevented the Romans from winning the war quickly. As the war dragged on, the people suspected the Senate of taking bribes from Jugurtha, sometimes with good reason. They elected C. Marius (157–86 B.C.) to the consulship for 107, and the assembly, usurping the role of the Senate, assigned him to the province of Numidia. This action was significant in several ways: Marius was a *novus homo,* a "new man," that is, the first in the history of his family to reach the consulship. Although a wealthy equestrian, he was born in the town of Arpinum and was outside the closed circle of the old Roman aristocracy. His earlier career had won him a reputation as an outstanding soldier and something of a political maverick.

Marius quickly defeated Jugurtha, but Jugurtha escaped and guerrilla warfare continued. Finally Marius' subordinate, L. Cornelius Sulla (138–78 B.C.), trapped Jugurtha and brought the war to an end. Marius celebrated the victory, but Sulla, an ambitious but impoverished descendant of an old Roman family, resented being cheated of the credit he thought he deserved. Soon rumors circulated crediting Sulla with the victory and diminishing Marius' role. Thus were the seeds planted for a personal rivalry and mutual hostility that would last until the death of Marius.

While the Romans were fighting Jugurtha, a far greater danger threatened Rome from the north. In 105 B.C. two barbaric tribes, the Cimbri and the Teutones, had come down the Rhone valley and crushed a Roman army at Arausio (Orange). To meet the danger, the Romans elected Marius to his second consulship when these tribes threatened again. From 102 he served four consecutive terms until 100 B.C., when the crisis was over.

While the barbarians were occupied elsewhere, Marius used the time to make important changes in the army. He

Sallust Describes the New Model Army of Marius

Sallust (86–*ca.* 34 B.C.) wrote a number of historical monographs. In the one describing Rome's war against Jugurtha, king of Numantia in North Africa, he tells the story of the important changes in army recruitment introduced by Marius. With the aid of the new troops Marius was able to win the war against Jugurtha in the years 107–105 B.C.

M*ARIUS, who as I said before, had been made consul with great eagerness on the part of the populace, began, though he had always been hostile to the patricians, to inveigh against them, after the people gave him the province of Numidia, with great frequency and violence. . . . He also enlisted all the bravest men from Latium, most of whom were known to him by actual service, some few only by report, and induced, by earnest solicitation, even discharged veterans to accompany him. Nor did the senate, though adverse to him, dare to refuse him anything; the additions to the legions they had voted even with eagerness, because military service was thought to be unpopular with the multitude, and Marius seemed likely to lose either the means of warfare, or the favour of the people. But such expectations were entertained in vain, so ardent was the desire of going with Marius that had seized on almost all. Every one cherished the fancy that he should return home laden with spoil, crowned with victory, or attended with some similar good fortune. Marius himself, too, had excited them in no small degree by a speech. . . .*

He himself, in the mean time, proceeded to enlist soldiers, not after the ancient method, or from the classes, but taking all that were willing to join him, and the greater part from the lowest ranks.

Sallust, *Jugurtha*, trans. by J. S. Watson (London: Bohn Classical Library, 1852), pp. 171, 172, 181.

began the system of using volunteers for the army, mostly the dispossessed farmers and rural proletarians whose problems had not been solved by the Gracchi. They enlisted for a long term of service and looked upon the army not as an unwelcome duty but as an opportunity and a career. They were professionals who sought guaranteed food, clothing, shelter and the booty they hoped to get from victories. They came to expect a piece of land as a form of mustering-out pay or veteran's bonus when they retired. Volunteers were most likely to enlist with a man who was a capable soldier and influential enough to obtain what he needed for them. They looked to him rather than to the state for their rewards. He, on the other hand, had to obtain these favors from the Senate if he was to maintain his power and reputation. Marius' innovation created the opportunity for military leaders to gain enough power to challenge civilian authority.

Marius was the savior of Rome and the hero of the hour. Had he been one of the aristocracy, he could have retired in the happy expectation of future honors and respect. His origins and the pressure to take care of his veteran soldiers pointed in a different direction. To guarantee his future he needed to be consul again, and for 100 B.C. he was reelected to his sixth term with the aid of the popular leaders Saturninus and Glaucia. Their only program appears to have been to obtain land for the veterans. Marius' army reforms had integrated the Italian allies into the legions, and his land bill included them among the beneficiaries. Just as before, these benefits to the Italians alienated the Roman voters and played into the hands of the Senate, which was against the land bill. The presence of Marius' veterans cowed the assembly, however, and the bill became law.

Once his interests had been served, Marius drew back from his radical colleagues; and allowed the law to be declared invalid. He had no further program to pursue, and he seems to have wanted to achieve a respectable position in the eyes of the Senate. The elections for 99 B.C., in which Marius was not a candidate, produced disturbances. The Senate called upon Marius to save the state from his erstwhile supporters. He restored order, and once again he was the savior of Rome. The Senate, however, never trusted him and would not confer the honors he expected.

The Social War

For a decade Rome avoided serious troubles, but in that time the Senate took no action to deal with Italian discontent. The Italians were excluded from the land bill for Marius' veterans, and their discontent was serious enough

BELOW: The Roman theatre at Mérida in Spain, built in the first century B.C. It could seat 5,000 spectators and well represents the numerous such structures scattered throughout the Roman world. [Spanish National Tourist Office, New York.]

ABOVE: Model of the temple of Fortune at Palestrina. This was perhaps the largest religious sanctuary in all Italy during the republican period and was the site of a long-famous oracle. Its existing ruins date, it seems, from the first century B.C. The model suggests how impressively the architects adapted to the hilly location by using a series of terraces and ramps. [Fototeca Unione.]

to cause the Senate to expel all Italians from Rome in 95 B.C. Four years later the tribune M. Livius Drusus, the son of the tribune who had helped undermine Gaius Gracchus, put forward one bill to enfranchise the Italians, one bill to establish new colonies, and another to remove the equestrians from the extortion court juries. The younger Drusus seems to have been a sincere aristocratic reformer, but he was assassinated in 90 B.C. In frustration the Italians revolted and established a separate confederation with its own capital and its own coinage.

Employing the traditional device of divide and conquer, the Romans immediately offered citizenship to those cities who remained loyal and soon made the same offer to the rebels if they laid down their arms. Even then hard fighting was needed to put down the uprising, and by 88 B.C. the so-called Social War was over. All the Italians were Roman citizens with the protections that citizenship offered, but they retained local self-govern-

Appian Describes Sulla's Proscriptions of His Opponents

In 83 B.C. Sulla triumphed over the friends of Marius in a civil war and became dictator. In the following selection Appian describes Sulla's treatment of his defeated opponents.

SULLA *recounted Sulpicius' and Marius' insulting treatment of himself and without saying anything definite—he was unwilling to speak yet about such a move as he contemplated—warned them to be on the alert for action. They understood what he meant and, fearing they would miss the campaign, themselves made Sulla's desires explicit and urged him to take courage and lead them against Rome. He was delighted and forthwith ordered his six legions to march. . . .*

.   .   .   .

So the political struggle progressed from strife and faction to murder, and from murder to regular wars and now for the first time an army of citizens invaded their native city as if it were hostile territory. Henceforth political conflicts continued to be settled by armies, and there were constant assaults on Rome and sieges and military operations. Nothing induced any sense of shame in the authors of violence, neither the laws nor the constitution nor patriotism. Then a vote was passed that Sulpicius, who was still tribune, and Marius, who had been six times consul, and Marius' son, Publius Cethegus, Junius Brutus, Gnaeus and Quintus Granius, Publius Albinovinus and Marcus Laetorius, and about a dozen others who had fled from Rome, were enemies of the republic, having caused sedition and made war on the consuls and promised freedom to slaves to incite them to revolt. Any person was authorized to kill them without penalty or produce them before the consuls, and their property was confiscated.

Appian, *Civil Wars*, trans. by Horace White (London and New York: William Heinemann and The Macmillan Company, 1913), pp. 175–177.

ment and a dedication to their own municipalities that made Italy flourish. The passage of time blurred the distinction between Romans and Italians and forged them into a single nation.

Sulla and His Dictatorship

During the Social War Sulla had performed well, and he was elected consul for 88 B.C. and given command of the war against Mithridates, who was leading a major rebellion in Asia. At this point Marius emerged from obscurity at the age of seventy and sought the command for himself. With popular and equestrian support he got the assembly to transfer the command to him. Sulla, defending the rights of the Senate and his own interests, marched his army against Rome. This was the first time a Roman general had used his army against fellow citizens. Marius and his friends fled, and Sulla regained the command. No sooner did he leave again for Asia than Marius joined with the consul Cinna and reconquered Rome by force. He outlawed Sulla and launched a bloody massacre of the senatorial opposition. Marius died soon after his election to a seventh consulship, for 86 B.C. Cinna now was the chief man at Rome. Supported by Marius' men, he held the consulship from 87 to 84 B.C. His future depended on Sulla's fortunes in the east.

By 85 B.C. Sulla had driven Mithridates from Greece and had crossed over to Asia Minor. Eager to regain control of Rome, he negotiated a compromise peace. In 83 B.C. he returned to Italy and fought a civil war that lasted for more than a year. Sulla won and drove the Marians from Italy. He now held all power and had himself appointed dictator, not in the traditional sense, but for the express purpose of reconstituting the state.

Sulla's first step was to wipe out the opposition. The names of those proscribed were posted in public. As outlaws they could be killed by anyone, and the killer received a reward. Sulla proscribed not only political opponents but his personal enemies and men whose only crime was having wealth and property. With the proceeds from the confiscations Sulla rewarded his veterans, perhaps as many as 100,000 men, and thereby built a solid base of support.

Sulla had enough power and influence to make himself the permanent ruler of Rome, but he was traditional enough to want a restoration of senatorial government, reformed in such a way as to avoid the misfortunes of the past. To deal with the decimation of the Senate caused by the proscriptions and the civil war he enrolled three hundred new members, many of them from the eques-

LEFT: Portrait bust of Pompey the Great. This portrait, like others, illustrates the Roman preference for realistic portrayal of public figures. [Frank Brown Collection.]

RIGHT: Marcus Tullius Cicero as portrayed in a Vatican sculpture. [Alinari/SCALA.]

trian order and the upper classes of the Italian cities. Thereafter twenty quaestors, or lesser magistrates, were elected annually and automatically became senators after their term of office. Sulla's reforms enhanced senatorial power and remained in force long after his death.

Sulla retired to a life of ease and luxury in 79 B.C. He could not, however, undo the effect of his own example, of a general using the loyalty of his own troops to take power and to massacre his opponents and innocent men. His action proved to be more significant than his constitutional arrangements.

Fall of the Republic
Pompey, Crassus, Caesar, and Cicero

Within a year of Sulla's death his constitution came under assault. To deal with an armed threat to its powers, the Senate violated the very procedures meant to defend them. They gave the command of the army to Pompey (106–48 B.C.), who was only twenty-eight and had never been elected to a magistracy. Then, when Sertorius, a Marian general, resisted senatorial control, the Senate appointed Pompey proconsul in Spain in 77 B.C., once again violating the constitution by ignoring Sulla's rigid rules for office holding, which had been meant to guarantee experienced, loyal, and safe commanders. In 71 B.C. Pompey returned to Rome with new glory, his mission accomplished. In 73 B.C. the Senate made another extraordinary appointment to put down a great slave rebellion led by the gladiator Spartacus. Publius Licinius Crassus, a rich and ambitious senator, received powers that gave him command of almost all Italy and, together with the newly returned Pompey, crushed the rebellion in 71 B.C. Extraordinary commands of this sort proved to be the ruin of the republic.

Crassus and Pompey where ambitious men whom the Senate feared. Both demanded triumphs and election to the consulship for the year 70 B.C. Pompey was legally ineligible because he had never gone through the strict course of offices prescribed in Sulla's constitution, and

Crassus had a year to wait under the same law. They joined forces, though they disliked and were jealous of one another. They gained popular support by promising to restore the full powers of the tribunes, which Sulla had curtailed, and they gained equestrian backing by promising to restore equestrians to the extortion court juries. They both won election and repealed most of Sulla's constitution, opening the way for further attacks on senatorial control and for collaboration between ambitious generals and demagogic tribunes.

In 67 B.C. a special law gave Pompey *imperium* for three years over the entire Mediterranean and fifty miles in from the coast, as well as the power to raise great quantities of troops and money to rid the area of pirates. The assembly passed the law over senatorial opposition, and in three months Pompey cleared the seas of piracy. Meanwhile a new war had broken out with Mithridates, and in 66 B.C. the assembly transferred the command to Pompey, giving him unprecedented powers. He held *imperium* over all Asia, with the right to make war and peace at will, and his *imperium* was superior to that of any proconsul in the field.

Once again Pompey justified his appointment. He defeated Mithridates and drove him to suicide. By 62 B.C. he had extended Rome's frontier to the Euphrates River and had organized the territories of Asia so well that his arrangements remained the basis of Roman rule well into the imperial period. When he returned to Rome in 62 B.C., he had more power, prestige, and popular support than any Roman in history. The Senate and his personal enemies had reason to fear that he might emulate Sulla and establish his own rule.

Rome had not been quiet in Pompey's absence. Crassus was the foremost among those who had reason to fear Pompey's return. Although rich and influential he did not have the confidence of the Senate, a firm political base of his own, or the kind of military glory needed to rival Pompey. During the 60s, therefore, he allied himself with various popular leaders. The ablest of these men was Gaius Julius Caesar (102–44 B.C.), a descendant of an old

Portrait of Julius Caesar. The sculpture is in the Naples museum. [Alinari/SCALA.]

patrician family that claimed descent from the kings and even from the goddess Venus but one that was politically obscure. In spite of this noble lineage Caesar was connected to the popular party through his aunt, who was the wife of Marius, and through his own wife, Cornelia, the daughter of Cinna. Caesar was an ambitious and determined young politician whose daring and rhetorical skill made him a valuable ally in winning the discontented of every class to the cause of the *populares*. Though Crassus was very much the senior partner, each needed the other to achieve what both wanted: significant military commands whereby they might build a reputation, a political following, and a military force to compete with Pompey's.

The chief opposition to Crassus' candidates for the consulship for 63 B.C. came from Cicero (106–43 B.C.), a "new man" from Marius' home town of Arpinum. He had made a spectacular name as the leading lawyer in Rome. Cicero, though he came from outside the senatorial aristocracy, was no *popularis*. His program was to preserve the republic against demagogues and ambitious generals by making the government more liberal. He wanted to unite the stable elements of the state, the Senate and the equestrians, in a harmony of the orders. This program did not appeal to the senatorial oligarchy, but the Senate preferred him to Catiline, a dangerous popular politician thought to be linked with Crassus. Cicero and Antonius were elected consuls for 63 B.C., Catiline running third.

Cicero soon learned of a plot hatched by Catiline. Catiline had run in the previous election on a platform of cancellation of debts, which appealed to discontented elements in general but especially to the heavily indebted nobles and their many clients. Made desperate by defeat, Catiline planned to stir up rebellions around Italy, to cause confusion in the city, and to take it by force. Quick action by Cicero defeated Catiline.

Formation of the First Triumvirate

Toward the end of 62 B.C. Pompey landed at Brundisium, and, to general surprise, disbanded his army, celebrated a great triumph, and returned to private life. He had delayed his return in the hope of finding Italy in such a state as to justify his keeping the army and dominating the scene. Cicero's quick suppression of Catiline prevented his plan. Pompey, therefore, had either to act illegally or to lay down his arms. Because he had not thought of monarchy or of a revolutionary course but merely wanted to be recognized and treated as the greatest Roman, he chose the latter course. He had achieved amazing things for Rome and simply wanted the Senate to approve his excellent arrangements in the East and to make land allotments to his veterans. His demands were far from unreasonable, and a prudent Senate would have granted them and would have tried to employ his power in defense of the constitution. But the Senate was jealous and fearful of overmighty individuals and refused his requests. In this way Pompey was driven to an alliance

The Curia, or senate house of Rome. Originally built between 44 and 29 B.C., its present form was given to it by Emperor Diocletian at the end of the fourth century. It shows in its simplest form the structure known as the basilica, from which several other kinds of public buildings derived; for example, the early christian churches were based on the basilica and its elaborations. [Fototeca Unione.]

with his natural enemies, Crassus and Caesar, because all three found the Senate standing in the way of what they wanted.

In 60 B.C. Caesar returned from his governorship of Spain. He wanted the privilege of celebrating a triumph and of running for consul, but the law did not allow him to do both, requiring him to stay outside the city with his army but demanding that he canvass for votes personally within the city. He asked for a special dispensation, but the Senate refused. Caesar then performed a political miracle: he reconciled Crassus with Pompey and gained the support of both for his own ambitions. So was born the First Triumvirate, an informal agreement among three Roman politicians that further undermined the future of the republic.

Julius Caesar; His Government of Rome

Though he was forced to forego his triumph, Caesar's efforts were rewarded with election to the consulship for 59 B.C. His colleague was M. Calpurnius Bibulus, the son-in-law of Cato and a conservative hostile to Caesar and the other *populares*. He either vetoed Caesar's attempts to put through legislation desired by the Triumvirs or had tribunes do so in the assembly. When Pompey's veterans were brought in to overawe the opposition by the threat of force, Bibulus announced that he had seen evil omens and called off the assembly. Presiding magistrates had that right, but Bibulus was plainly using it for political purposes; Caesar did not hesitate to override his colleague. For the rest, Caesar did not get his triumph but won the consulship for 59 B.C. The Triumvirs' program was quickly enacted. Caesar got the extraordinary command that would give him a chance to earn the glory and power with which to rival Pompey: the governorship of Illyricum and Gaul for five years. A land bill settled Pompey's veterans comfortably, and his eastern settlement was ratified. Crassus, much of whose influence came from his position as champion of the equestrians, won for them a great windfall by having the government renegotiate a tax contract in their favor. To guarantee themselves against any reversal of these actions, the Triumvirs continued their informal but effective collaboration, arranging for the election of friendly consuls and the departure of potential opponents.

Caesar was now free to seek the military success he craved. His province included Cisalpine Gaul in the Po valley, by now occupied by many Italian settlers as well as Gauls, and Narbonese Gaul beyond the Alps, modern Provence.

Relying first on the excellent quality of his army and the experience of his officers, then on his own growing military ability, Caesar made great progress. By 56 B.C. he had conquered most of Gaul, but he had not yet consolidated his victories firmly. He therefore sought an extension of his command, but quarrels between Crassus and Pompey so weakened the Triumvirate that the Senate was prepared to order Caesar's recall. To prevent the dissolution of his base of power, Caesar persuaded Crassus and Pompey to meet with him at Luca in northern Italy to renew the coalition. They agreed that Caesar would get another five-year command in Gaul, and Crassus and Pompey would be consuls again in 55 B.C. After that they would each receive an army and a five-year command. Caesar was free to return to Gaul and finish the job. The capture of Alesia in 50 B.C. marked the end of the serious Gallic resistance and of Gallic liberty. For Caesar it brought the wealth, fame, and military power he wanted. He commanded thirteen loyal legions, a match for his enemies as well as for his allies.

By the time Caesar was ready to return to Rome, the Triumvirate had dissolved and a crisis was at hand. At Carrhae in 53 B.C. Crassus died trying to conquer the Parthians, successors to the Persian Empire. His death broke one link between Pompey and Caesar. The death of Caesar's daughter Julia, who had been Pompey's wife, dissolved another. As Caesar's star rose, Pompey became jealous and fearful. He did not leave Rome but governed his province through a subordinate. In the late 50s political rioting at Rome caused the Senate to appoint Pompey sole consul. This grant of unprecedented power and responsibility brought Pompey closer to the senatorial aristocracy in mutual fear of and hostility to Caesar. The Senate wanted to bring Caesar back to Rome as a private citizen after his proconsular command expired. He would then be open to attack for past illegalities. Caesar tried to avoid the trap by asking permission to stand for the consulship *in absentia*. The years 51–50 B.C. were spent in complicated maneuvers on both sides, but no compromise was acceptable.

Early in January of 49 B.C. the more extreme faction in the Senate had its way and ordered Pompey to defend the state and Caesar to lay down his command by a specified day. For Caesar this meant exile or death, so he ordered his legions to cross the Rubicon River, the boundary of his province. This action was the first act of the civil war. Pompey and the Senate were unprepared for his swift advance into Italy and fled to rally their forces in the east. Caesar could not prevent their escape, nor did he have a navy with which to pursue, so he turned to the west.

His subordinates gained control of Sicily and Sardinia and guaranteed the grain supply; then he crushed the Pompeian army in Spain. Although he had not hesitated to use terror and brutality against the Gauls, he spared all the captured Romans, as he did throughout the civil war. This clemency of Caesar's was new in Roman civil strife, and it won over many former enemies. He sailed to Epirus in pursuit of Pompey. In August of 48 B.C. he caught and defeated him at Pharsalus in Thessaly. Although his army was outnumbered almost two to one, Caesar's superior tactical skill as well as the discipline and loyalty of his troops brought victory. Pompey's army disintegrated, and the general fled to Egypt. The young Egyptian king, fearful of Caesar's wrath, ordered Pompey's head cut off and sent to the conqueror.

Caesar, not yet aware of the death of his rival, pursued him to Egypt. There he remained for more than a year, detained by the charms of the young queen, Cleopatra; by the need to await reinforcements to take Alexandria; and, perhaps, by dreams of a great empire in the east. From there he was forced to hurry to Pontus to deal with the rebellion of Pharnaces, son of Mithridates. He defeated him at Zela, from which he sent back his famous laconic and arrogant report: *Veni, vidi, vici* ("I came, I saw, I conquered"). In 45 B.C. he defeated the last of the enemy forces under Pompey's sons at Munda in Spain. The war was over, and Caesar, in Shakespeare's words, bestrode "the narrow world like a Colossus."

From the beginning of the civil war until his death in 44 B.C., Caesar spent less than a year and a half in Rome, and many of his actions were attempts to deal with immediate problems between campaigns. Even after his victory in the civil war, he was planning a major campaign against Parthia and eager to be off, so it is hard to be sure what organization of the state and the empire he had in mind. Suffice it to say that his innovations generally sought to make rational and orderly what was traditional and chaotic. An excellent example is Caesar's reform of the calendar. By 46 B.C. it was eighty days ahead of the proper season because the official year was lunar, containing only 355 days. Using the best scientific advice, Caesar instituted a new calendar, which, with minor changes by Pope Gregory XIII in the sixteenth century, is the one in use today. Another general tendency of his reforms in the political area was the elevation of the role of Italians and even provincials at the expense of the old Roman families, most of whom were his political enemies. He raised the number of senators to nine hundred and filled the Senate's depleted ranks with Italians and even Gauls. He was free with grants of Roman citizenship, giving the franchise to Cisalpine Gaul as a whole and to many individuals of various regions.

Caesar's plans for dealing with the immediate social and economic problems were moderate and sensible. He reduced debts to reasonable proportions and put Roman finances on a sound footing. He continued the policy of providing grain to the poor at Rome, but he cut the number of recipients from over 300,000 to half that number. He founded colonies outside of Italy to settle his veteran troops. These colonies often included the poor of Rome and so helped solve the social problem as well.

Caesar Tells What Persuaded Him to Cross the Rubicon

Julius Caesar competed with Pompey for the leading position in the Roman state. Complicated maneuvers failed to produce a compromise. In the following selection Caesar gives his side of the story of the beginning of the Roman Civil War.

THESE *things being made known to Cæsar, he harangued his soldiers; he reminded them "of the wrongs done to him at all times by his enemies, and complained that Pompey had been alienated from him and led astray by them through envy and a malicious opposition to his glory, though he had always favored and promoted Pompey's honor and dignity. He complained that an innovation had been introduced into the republic, that the intercession of the tribunes, which had been restored a few years before by Sulla, was branded as a crime, and suppressed by force of arms; that Sulla, who had stripped the tribunes of every other power, had, nevertheless, left the privilege of intercession unrestrained; that Pompey, who pretended to restore what they had lost, had taken away the privileges which they formerly had; that whenever the senate decreed, 'that the magistrates should take care that the republic sustained no injury' (by which words and decree the Roman people were obliged to repair to arms), it was only when pernicious laws were proposed; when the tribunes attempted violent measures; when the people seceded, and possessed themselves of the temples and eminences of the city; (and these instances of former times, he showed them were expiated by the fate of Saturninus and the Gracchi): that nothing of this kind was attempted now, nor even thought of: that no law was promulgated, no intrigue with the people going forward, no secession made; he exhorted them to defend from the malice of his enemies the reputation and honor of that general under whose command they had for nine years most successfully supported the state; fought many successful battles, and subdued all Gaul and Germany." The soldiers of the thirteenth legion, which was present (for in the beginning of the disturbances he had called it out, his other legions not having yet arrived), all cry out that they are ready to defend their general, and the tribunes of the commons, from all injuries.*

Having made himself acquainted with the disposition of his soldiers, Cæsar set off with that legion to Ariminum, and there met the tribunes, who had fled to him for protection.

Caesar, *Commentaries*, trans. by W. A. McDevitte and W. S. Bosh (New York: Harper and Brothers, 1887), pp. 249–250.

Suetonius Describes Caesar's Dictatorship

Suetonius (*ca.* A.D. 69–*ca.* 140) wrote a series of biographies of the emperors from Julius Caesar to Domitian. In the following selection he describes some of Caesar's actions during his dictatorship in the years 46–44 B.C.

His *other words and actions, however, so far outweigh all his good qualities, that it is thought he abused his power, and was justly cut off. For he not only obtained excessive honours, such as the consulship every year, the dictatorship for life, and the censorship, but also the title of emperor, and the surname of Father of His Country, besides having his statue amongst the kings, and a lofty couch in the theatre. He even suffered some honours to be decreed to him, which were unbefitting the most exalted of mankind; such as a gilded chair of state in the senate-house and on his tribunal, a consecrated chariot, and banners in the Circensian procession, temples, altars, statues among the gods, a bed of state in the temples, a priest, and a college of priests dedicated to himself, like those of Pan; and that one of the months should be called by his name. There were, indeed, no honours which he did not either assume himself, or grant to others, at his will and pleasure. In his third and fourth consulship, he used only the title of the office, being content with the power of dictator, which was conferred upon him with the consulship; and in both years he substituted other consuls in his room, during the three last months; so that in the intervals he held no assemblies of the people, for the election of magistrates, excepting only tribunes and ediles of the people; and appointed officers, under the name of praefects, instead of the praetors, to administer the affairs of the city during his absence. The office of consul having become vacant, by the sudden death of one of the consuls the day before the calends of January [the 1st Jan.], he conferred it on a person who requested it of him, for a few hours. Assuming the same licence, and regardless of the customs of his country, he appointed magistrates to hold their offices for terms of years. He granted the insignia of the consular dignity to ten persons of praetorian rank. He admitted into the senate some men who had been made free of the city, and even natives of Gaul, who were semi-barbarians. He likewise appointed to the management of the mint, and the public revenue of the state, some servants of his own household; and entrusted the command of three legions, which he left at Alexandria, to an old catamite of his, the son of his freed-man Rufinus.*

He was guilty of the same extravagance in the language he publicly used, as Titus Ampius informs us; according to whom he said, "The republic is nothing but a name, without substance or reality. Sylla was an ignorant fellow to abdicate the dictatorship. Men ought to consider what is becoming when they talk with me, and look upon what I say as a law."

Suetonius, *The Lives of the Twelve Caesars,* trans. by Alexander Thompson, revised by T. Forster (London: George Bell and Sons, 1903), pp. 45–47.

They also helped to bring Roman civilization to the provinces. The same process was aided by Caesar's generosity in granting citizenship to provincials, especially those in the west.

Caesar made few changes in the government of Rome. The Senate continued to play its role, in theory, but its increased size, its packing with supporters of Caesar, and his own monopoly of military power made the whole thing a sham. He treated the Senate as his creature and sometimes with disdain. His legal position rested upon a number of powers. In 46 B.C. he was appointed dictator for ten years and in the next year for life. He also held the consulship, the immunity of a tribune (although, being an aristocrat, he had never been a tribune), the chief priesthood of the state, and a new position, prefect of morals, which gave him the censorial power. He even named the magistrates for the next few years, since he expected to be away in the east, thus usurping the elective power of the assemblies.

There is considerable disagreement about Caesar's plan for the future of the Roman constitution and his own place in it. Clearly he did not mean to emulate Sulla, restore the republic, and retire into public life. Such a course might have been popular with the Senate and with traditionalists, but it would have been irresponsible, for the republican government and the class that had managed it was shattered. For some time, at least, Rome would require strong leadership. The question is whether Caesar was satisfied with his current position as dictator

Fall of the Republic 159

The Roman Forum as it might have looked by about the time of Augustus. This is a reconstructed modern rendering. [Bettmann Archive.]

The Second Triumvirate and the Emergence of Augustus

Caesar had had legions of followers, and he had a capable successor in Mark Antony. But the dictator had named his eighteen-year-old grand nephew, Gaius Octavius (63 B.C.–A.D. 14), as his heir and had left him three quarters of his vast wealth. To everyone's surprise the sickly and inexperienced young man came to Rome to claim his legacy, gathered an army, won the support of many of Caesar's veterans, and became a figure of importance—the future Augustus.

At first the Senate tried to use Octavius against Antony, but when the conservatives rejected his request for the consulship, Octavius broke with them. Following Sulla's grim precedent, he took his army and marched on Rome. There he formally assumed his adopted name, C. Julius Caesar Octavianus. Modern historians refer to him at this stage in his career as Octavian, although he insisted on being called Caesar. In August of 43 B.C. he became consul and declared the assassins of Caesar outlaws. As Brutus and Cassius had an army of their own, Octavian sought help on the Caesarean side. He made a pact with Mark Antony and M. Aemilius Lepidus, a Caesarean governor of the western provinces. They took control of Rome and had themselves appointed "Triumvirs to put the republic in order," with great powers. This was the Second Triumvirate, and unlike the first, it was legally empowered to rule almost dictatorially.

The need to pay their troops, their own greed, and the passion that always emerges in civil wars led the triumvirs to start a wave of proscriptions that outdid even those of Sulla. In 42 B.C. the triumviral army defeated Brutus and Cassius at Philippi in Macedonia, and the last hope of republican restoration died with the tyrannicides. Each of the triumvirs received a command. The junior partner, Lepidus, was given Africa, Antony took the rich and inviting east, and Octavian got the west and the many troubles that went with it. He had to fight a war against Sextus, the son of Pompey, who held Sicily. He also had

or if he aimed at the establishment of a Hellenistic monarchy, a complete departure from Roman tradition and one that would have been very unpopular. Caesar's ambition was great, and his love for rational organization may have made him want to establish a monarchy in name because one already existed in fact. On the other hand, Caesar's political shrewdness must have warned him of the danger of challenging Roman prejudices so blatantly. In any case, the enemies of Caesar were quick to seize on every pretext to accuse Caesar of aiming at monarchy. A senatorial conspiracy gathered strength under the leadership of Gaius Cassius Longinus and Marcus Junius Brutus and included some sixty senators in all. On March 15, 44 B.C., Caesar entered the Senate, characteristically without a bodyguard, and was stabbed to death. The assassins regarded themselves as heroic tyrannicides and did not have a clear plan of action after the tyrant was dead. No doubt they simply expected the republic to be restored in the old way, but things had gone too far for that. There followed instead thirteen years of civil war, at the end of which the republic received its final burial.

The Roman Forum as it looks today. The arch of
Titus is in the distance. [Bettmann Archive.]

to settle 100,000 veterans in Italy, confiscating much property and making many enemies. Helped by his friend Agrippa, he defeated Sextus Pompey in 36 B.C. Among his close associates was Maecenas, who served him as adviser and diplomatic agent. Maecenas helped manage the delicate relations with Antony and Lepidus, but perhaps equally important was his role as a patron of the arts. Among his clients were Vergil and Horace, both of whom did important work for Octavian, painting him as a restorer of traditional Roman values and as a man of ancient Roman lineage and of traditional Roman virtues and as the culmination of Roman destiny. More and more he was identified with Italy and the west as well as with order, justice, and virtue.

Meanwhile Antony was in the east, chiefly at Alexandria with Cleopatra. There, in addition to organizing affairs in the east, he had time to father a son by Cleopatra, as Caesar had done some years before. In 36 B.C. he attacked Parthia, with disastrous results. Octavian had promised to send troops to support Antony's Parthian campaign but never sent them. Antony was forced to depend on the east for support, and to some considerable degree this meant Cleopatra. Octavian clearly understood the advantage of representing himself as the champion of the west, Italy, and Rome, while representing Antony as the man of the east, the dupe of Cleopatra, her tool in establishing Alexandria as the center of an empire and herself as its ruler. Such propaganda made it easier for Caesareans to abandon their veteran leader in favor of the young heir of Caesar. It did not help Antony's cause that he agreed to a public festival at Alexandria in 34 B.C., where he and Cleopatra sat on golden thrones. She was proclaimed "Queen of Kings," her son by Caesar was named "King of Kings," and parts of the Roman Empire were doled out to her various children.

By 32 B.C. all pretence of cooperation came to an end. Octavian and Antony each tried to put the best face on what was essentially a struggle for power. Lepidus had been put aside some years earlier. Antony sought senatorial support and promised to restore the republican constitution. Octavian seized and published what was alleged to be the will of Antony, revealing his gifts of provinces to the children of Cleopatra, thereby casting the conflict in terms of east against west, Rome against Alexandria. In 31 B.C. the matter was settled at Actium in western Greece. Agrippa, Octavian's best general, cut off the enemy by land and sea, forcing and winning a naval battle. Antony and Cleopatra escaped to Egypt, but Octavian pursued them to Alexandria, where both committed suicide. The civil wars were over, and at the age of thirty-two Octavian was absolute master of the Mediterranean world. His power was enormous, but so too was the task before him. He had to restore peace, prosperity, and confidence, and all of these required the establishment of a constitution that would reflect the new realities without offending unduly the traditional republican prejudices that still had so firm a grip on Rome and Italy.

SUGGESTED READINGS

E. BADIAN, *Roman Imperialism in the Late Republic,* 2nd ed. (Oxford, 1968).

E. BADIAN, *Publicans and Sinners* (Ithaca, 1972). A study of the equestrian class at Rome.

G. P. BAKER, *Sulla the Fortunate* (Rome, 1967). A good biography.

A. H. BERNSTEIN, *Tiberius Sempronius Gracchus: Tradition and Apostacy* (Ithaca, 1978). A new interpretation of Tiberius' place in Roman politics.

H. C. BOREN, *The Gracchi* (New York, 1969). A good, brief study of the revolutionary brothers.

P. A. BRUNT, *Social Conflicts in the Roman Republic* (London, 1971).

F. R. COWELL, *Cicero and the Roman Republic* (Harmondsworth, England, 1956). A readable account of Cicero's career in the context of his times.

D. C. EARL, *The Moral and Political Tradition of Rome* (Ithaca, 1967).

M. GELZER, *Caesar: Politician and Statesman,* tr. by P. Needham (Cambridge, Mass., 1968). The best biography of Caesar.

E. S. Gruen, *The Last Generation of the Roman Republic* (Berkeley, 1973). An interesting but controversial interpretation of the fall of the republic.

T. Rice Holmes, *Caesar's Conquest of Gaul* (Oxford, 1911). The best study of the campaigns.

F. B. Marsh, *A History of the Roman World from 146 to 30 B.C.,* 3rd ed. rev. by H. H. Scullard. An excellent narrative account.

H. H. Scullard, *From the Gracchi to Nero* (London, 1963). A good narrative history with excellent critical notes.

R. E. Smith, *The Failure of the Roman Republic* (Cambridge, England, 1955). Presents an account sympathetic with the senatorial aristocracy.

R. E. Smith, *Cicero the Statesman* (Cambridge, England, 1966). A sound biography.

D. Stockton, *Cicero: A Political Biography* (Oxford, 1971). A readable and interesting study.

L. R. Taylor, *Party Politics in the Age of Caesar* (Berkeley, 1949). A fascinating analysis of Roman political practices.

L. R. Taylor, *Roman Voting Assemblies* (Ann Arbor, 1966). A study of an important constitutional problem.

H. Volkmann, *Cleopatra* (New York, 1958). A good biography.

G. Williams, *The Nature of Roman Poetry* (Oxford, 1970). An unusually graceful and perceptive literary study.

T. P. Wiseman, *New Men in the Roman Senate 139 B.C.– 14 A.D.* (Oxford, 1971). A study in family and factional politics.

8

The Early Roman Empire (31 B.C.–A.D. 180)

The Augustan Principate

IF THE problems facing Octavian after the Battle of Actium were great, so too were his resources for addressing them. He was the master of a vast military force, the only one in the Roman world, and he had loyal and capable assistants. Of enormous importance was the great, seemingly inexhaustible treasury of Egypt, which Octavian treated as his personal property. Perhaps his most valuable asset, however, was the great eagerness of the people of Italy for an end to civil war and a return to peace, order, and prosperity. In exchange for these most of them were prepared to accept a considerable abandonment of republican practices and to give significant power to an able ruler. Even the resistance of the old Roman families was greatly reduced, for a remarkable number of their members had perished in the civil wars from 49 to 31 B.C. Yet the memory of Julius Caesar's fate was still clear in Octavian's mind, and its lesson was that it was dangerous to flaunt unprecedented powers and to disregard all republican traditions.

Octavian's constitutional solution proved to be successful and lasting, subtle and effective. It was not created at a single stroke but developed gradually as Octavian tried new devices to fit his perception of changing conditions. Behind all the republican trappings and the apparent sharing of authority with the Senate, the government of Octavian, like that of his successors, was a monarchy.

Emperor Augustus (27 B.C.–A.D. 14). This statue, now in the Vatican, stood in the villa of Augustus's wife Livia. The figures on the elaborate breastplate are all of symbolic significance. At the top, for example, dawn in her chariot brings in a new day under the protective mantle of the sky god; in the center Tiberius, Augustus's future successor, accepts the return of captured Roman army standards from a barbarian prince; and at the bottom is Mother Earth with a horn of plenty. [Copyright by Leonard von Matt.]

All power, both civil and military, lay with the ruler, whether he was called by the unofficial title of "first citizen" (*princeps*), like Octavian, the founder of the regime, or "emperor" (*imperator*), like those who followed. During the civil war Octavian's powers came from his triumviral status, whose dubious legality and unrepublican character were an embarrassment. From 31 B.C. on he held the consulship each year, but this circumstance was not strictly legal or very satisfactory either. On January 13, 27 B.C., he put forward a new plan in dramatic style, coming before the Senate to give up all his powers and provinces. In what was surely a rehearsed response, the Senate begged him to reconsider, and at last he agreed to accept the provinces of Spain, Gaul, and Syria with proconsular power and to retain the consulship in Rome. The other provinces would be governed by the Senate as before. Because his were the border provinces and contained twenty of the twenty-six legions, his true power was undiminished, but the Senate responded with almost hysterical gratitude, voting him many honors. Among them was the semireligious title "Augustus," which carried implications of veneration, majesty, and holiness. From this time on, historians speak of Rome's first emperor as Augustus and of his regime as the Principate. This would have pleased him, for it helps conceal the novel, unrepublican nature of the regime and the naked power on which it rested.

In 23 B.C. Augustus resigned his consulship and held that office only rarely thereafter. Instead he was voted two powers that were to be the base of his rule thenceforth, the proconsular *imperium maius* and the tribunician power. The former made his proconsular power greater than that of any other proconsul and permitted him to exercise it even within the city of Rome. The latter gave him the right to conduct public business in the assemblies and the Senate, the power of the veto, the tribunician sacrosanctity, and a connection with the popular tradition. Thereafter there were minor changes in Augustus' position, but his powers were chiefly those conferred by the settlement of 23 B.C.

165

The Gemma Augustea. This carved onyx cameo is from the first century. The top part shows Augustus's coronation. His wife Livia, sitting next to him, is arrayed as the goddess of Rome. On the left the future emperor Tiberius is stepping from a chariot. The lower half shows prisoners of war. [Kunsthistorisches Museum, Vienna.]

Administration

Augustus made important changes in the government of Rome, Italy, and the provinces. Most of these had the effect of reducing inefficiency and corruption, eliminating the danger to peace and order from ambitious individuals, and reducing the distinction between Romans and Italians, senators and equestrians. The assemblies disappeared as a working part of the constitution, and the Senate took on most of the functions of the assemblies. Augustus purged the old Senate of undesirable members and fixed its number at six hundred. He recruited its members from wealthy men of good character, who entered after serving as lesser magistrates. Augustus controlled the elections and saw to it that promising young men, whatever their origin, served the state as administrators and provincial governors. In this way equestrians and Italians who had no connection with the Roman aristocracy entered the Senate in great numbers. For all his power Augustus was careful always to treat the Senate with respect and honor.

Among his many other talents Augustus had a genius for practical administration. He divided Rome into regions and wards with elected local officials. He gave the city, with its rickety wooden tenements, its first public fire department and rudimentary police force. Grain distribution to the poor was carefully controlled and limited, and organizations were created for providing an adequate water supply. The Augustan period was one of great prosperity, based on the wealth Augustus had brought in by the conquest of Egypt, on the great increase in commerce and industry made possible by general peace and a vast program of public works, and on a strong return to successful small farming on the part of Augustus' resettled veterans.

The union of political and military power in the hands of the *princeps* made it possible for him to install rational, efficient, and stable government for the provinces for the first time. The emperor, in effect, chose the governors, removed the incompetent or rapacious, and allowed the effective ones to keep their provinces for longer periods of time. At the same time he provided for much greater local autonomy, giving considerable responsibility to the upper classes in the provincial cities and towns and to the tribal leaders in less civilized areas.

Defense Against the Barbarians

The main external problem facing Augustus—and one that haunted all his successors—was the northern frontier. Rome needed to pacify the regions to the north and the northeast of Italy and to find defensible frontiers against the recurring waves of barbarians. Augustus' plan was to establish a frontier along the Rhine and the Danube rivers, then to join them by sturdy defenses and thereby create a solid and enduring frontier. The eastern part of the plan succeeded, and the campaign in the west started well. In A.D. 12, however, a revolt broke out led by the German tribal leader Herrmann, or Arminius, as the Romans called him. He ambushed and destroyed three Roman legions under the general Varus as they marched through the Teutoburg Forest. The aged Augustus abandoned the campaign, leaving a problem of border defense that caused great troubles for his successors.

Under Augustus the armed forces achieved true professional status. Enlistment, chiefly by Italians, was for twenty years, but the pay was relatively good and there were occasional bonuses and the promise of a pension on retirement in the form of money or a plot of land. Together with the auxiliaries from the provinces, they formed a frontier army of about 300,000 men. In normal times this was barely enough to hold the line. The Roman army permanently based in the provinces played a vital role in bringing Roman culture to the natives. The soldiers spread their language and customs, often marrying local women and settling down in the area of their service. They attracted merchants, who often became the nuclei of new towns and cities that became centers of Roman civilization. As time passed, the provincials on the frontiers became Roman citizens and helped strengthen Rome's defenses against the barbarians outside.

The Emperor Augustus Writes His Testament

Emperor Augustus wrote a record of his achievements to be read, engraved, and placed outside his mausoleum after his death. The following selections are from that document.

13. THE temple of Janus Quirinus, which our ancestors desired to be closed whenever peace with victory was secured by sea and by land throughout the entire empire of the Roman people, and which before I was born is recorded to have been closed only twice since the founding of the city, was during my principate three times ordered by the senate to be closed.

. . . .

34. In my sixth and seventh consulships, after I had put an end to the civil wars, having attained supreme power by universal consent, I transferred the state from my own power to the control of the Roman senate and people. For this service of mine I received the title of Augustus by decree of the senate, and the doorposts of my house were publicly decked with laurels, the civic crown was affixed over my doorway, and a golden shield was set up in the Julian senate house, which, as the inscription on this shield testifies, the Roman senate and people gave me in recognition of my valor, clemency, justice, and devotion. After that time I excelled all in authority, but I possessed no more power than the others who were my colleagues in each magistracy.

35. When I held my thirteenth consulship, the senate, the equestrian order, and the entire Roman people gave me the title of "father of the country" and decreed that this title should be inscribed in the vestibule of my house, in the Julian senate house, and in the Augustan Forum on the pedestal of the chariot which was set up in my honor by decree of the senate. At the time I wrote this document I was in my seventy-sixth year.

Augustus, *Res Gestae*, trans. by N. Lewis and M. Reinhold, in *Roman Civilization*, Vol. 2 (New York: Columbia University Press, 1955), pp. 13, 19.

A century of political strife and civil war had undermined many of the foundations of traditional Roman society. Augustus thought it desirable to try to repair the damage, and he undertook a program aimed at preserving and restoring the traditional values of the family and religion in Rome and Italy. He introduced laws curbing adultery and divorce and encouraging early marriage and the procreation of legitimate children. He set an example of austere behavior in his own household and even banished his daughter, Julia, whose immoral behavior had become public knowledge. He worked at restoring the dignity of formal Roman religion, building many temples, reviving old cults, and reorganizing and invigorating the priestly colleges, and he banned the worship of newly introduced foreign gods. Augustus himself occupied some of the traditional priesthoods, and writers whom he patronized, such as Vergil, pointed out his family's legendary connection with Venus. During his lifetime he did not accept divine honors, though he was deified after his death, and as with Julius Caesar, a state cult was dedicated to his worship.

Civilization of the Ciceronian and Augustan Ages

The high point of Roman culture came in the last century of the republic and during the principate of Augustus. Both periods reflected the dominant influence of Greek culture, especially in its Hellenistic mode. The education of Romans of the upper classes was in Greek rhetoric, philosophy, and literature, which also served as the models for Roman writers and artists. Yet in spirit and sometimes in form the art and writing of both periods show uniquely Roman qualities, though each in different ways.

The Late Republic

CICERO. The towering literary figure of the late republic was Cicero. He is most famous for his orations delivered in the law courts and in the Senate. Together with a considerable body of his private letters, these orations provide us with a clearer and fuller insight into his mind than into that of any other figure in antiquity. We see the political life of his period largely through his eyes. He also wrote treatises on rhetoric, ethics, and politics that put Greek philosophical ideas into Latin terminology and at the same time changed them to suit Roman conditions and values. Cicero's own views combined the teachings of the Academy, the Stoa, and other Greek schools to provide support for his moderate and conservative practicality. He believed in a world governed by divine and natural law that human reason could perceive and human institutions reflected. He looked to law, custom, and tradition to produce both stability and liberty. His literary style as well as his values and ideas was an important legacy for the Middle Ages and, reinterpreted, for the men of the Renaissance.

HISTORY. The last century of the republic produced some historical writing, much of which is lost to us. Sallust (86–35 B.C.) wrote a history of the years 78–67 B.C., but only a few fragments remain to remind us of his reputation as the greatest of republican historians. His surviving work consists of two pamphlets on the Jugurthine War and on the Catalinarian conspiracy of 63 B.C. They reveal his Caesarean and antisenatorial prejudices and the stylistic influence of Thucydides.

Julius Caesar wrote important treatises on the Gallic and civil wars. They are not fully rounded historical accounts but chiefly military narratives written from Caesar's point of view and with propagandist intent. Their objective manner (Caesar always referred to himself in the third person) and their direct, simple, and vigorous style make them persuasive even today, and they must have been most effective with their immediate audience.

Lesser prose writers engaged in scholarly research in more remote periods and on a variety of topics. Cornelius Nepos, a friend of Cicero, wrote biographies of famous men, both Roman and foreign, and M. Terentius Varro (116–27 B.C.) wrote *Portraits* of famous Greeks and Romans as well as many books of *Antiquities,* both works, unfortunately, lost. We have all of his treatises on agriculture and a considerable portion of his study of the Latin language.

LAW. The period from the Gracchi to the fall of the republic was important in the development of Roman law. Before that time Roman law was essentially national and developed chiefly by means of juridical decisions, case

---

Vergil Descants on the Destiny of Rome

Vergil (70–19 B.C.) was the leading poet of the Augustan Age. His great epic, the *Aeneid,* is full of praise for Augustus, his family, his ancestors, and the settlement of the Roman world he achieved. The *Aeneid* was written in the last decade of Vergil's life.

Now *fix your sight, and stand intent, to see*
Your Roman race, and Julian progeny.
There mighty Cæsar waits his vital hour,
Impatient for the world, and grasps his promised power.
But next behold the youth of form divine—
Cæsar himself, exalted in his line—
Augustus, promised oft, and long foretold,
Sent to the realm that Saturn ruled of old;
Born to restore a better age of gold.
Africa and India shall his power obey;
He shall extend his propagated sway
Beyond the solar year, without the starry way. . . .
. . . .
Let others better mould the running mass
Of metals, and inform the breathing brass,
And soften into flesh, a marble face;
Plead better at the bar; describe the skies,
And when the stars descend, and when they rise.
But Rome! 'tis thine alone, with awful sway,
To rule mankind, and make the world obey,
Disposing peace and war, thy own majestic way:
To tame the proud, the fettered slave to free;—
These are imperial arts, and worthy thee.

John Dryden, *The Works of Vergil* (New York: American Book Exchange, 1881), pp. 262–265.

---

by case, but contact with foreign peoples and the influence of Greek ideas forced a change. From this time on the edicts of the praetors, which interpreted and even changed and added to existing law, had increasing importance in developing the Roman legal code. Quite early the edicts of the magistrates who dealt with foreigners developed the idea of the *jus gentium* or law of peoples as opposed to that arising strictly from the experience of the Romans. In the first century B.C. the influence of Greek thought made the idea of *jus gentium* identical with that of the *jus naturale,* or natural law, taught by the Stoics. It was this view of a world ruled by divine reason that Cicero enshrined in his treatise on the laws, *De Legibus.*

POETRY. The time of Cicero was also the period of two of Rome's greatest poets, Lucretius and Catullus, each representing a different aspect of Rome's poetic

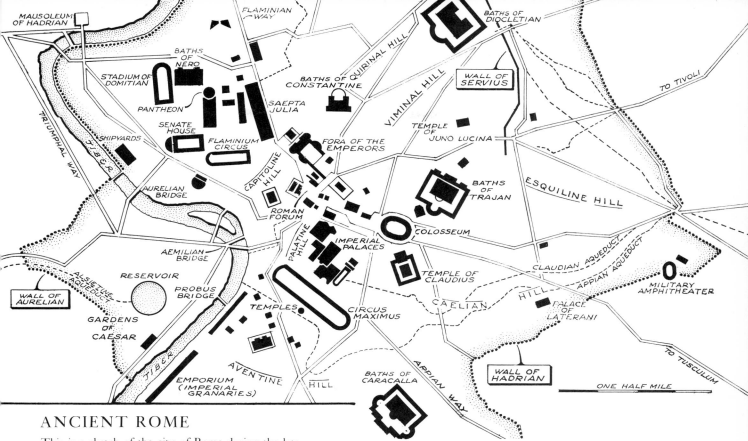

ANCIENT ROME

This is a sketch of the city of Rome during the late Empire. It indicates the seven hills on and around which the city was built, as well as the major walls, bridges, and other public sites and buildings. The Forum is between the Capitoline and Palatine hills.

tradition. The Hellenistic poets and literary theorists saw two functions for the poet, as entertainer and as teacher. They thought the best poet combined both roles, and the Romans adopted the same view. When Naevius and Ennius wrote epics on Roman history, they combined historical and moral instruction with pleasure. Lucretius (*ca.* 99–*ca.* 55 B.C.) pursued a similar path in his epic poem *De Rerum Natura* (*On the Nature of the World*). In it he set forth the scientific and philosophical ideas of Epicurus and Democritus with the missionary zeal of a man trying to save his fellowmen from fear and superstition. He knew that his doctrine might be bitter medicine to the reader: "That is why I have tried to administer it to you in the dulcet strains of poesy, coated with the sweet honey of the Muses."[1]

Catullus (*ca.* 84–*ca.* 54 B.C.) was a poet of a thoroughly different kind. He wrote poems that were personal, even autobiographical. In imitation of the Alexandrians he wrote short poems filled with learned allusions to mythology, but he far surpassed his models in intensity of

1 I, Lucretius, *De Rerum Natura*, lines 93lff.

feeling. He wrote of the joys and pains of love, he hurled invective at important contemporaries like Julius Caesar, and he amused himself in witty poetic exchanges with others. He offered no moral lessons and was not interested in Rome's glorious history or in contemporary politics. In a sense he is an example of the proud, independent, pleasure-seeking nobleman who characterized part of the aristocracy at the end of the republic.

The Age of Augustus

The spirit of the Augustan Age, the golden age of Roman literature, was quite different, reflecting the new conditions of society. The old aristocratic order with its system of independent nobles following their own particular interests was gone. So was the world of poets of the lower orders, receiving patronage from any of a number of individual aristocrats. Augustus replaced the complexity of republican patronage with a simple scheme in which all patronage flowed from the *princeps,* usually through his chief cultural adviser, Maecenas. The major poets of this time, Vergil, Horace, and Ovid, had all lost their property during the civil wars. The patronage of the *princeps* allowed them the leisure and the security to write poetry and at the same time made them dependent on him and limited their freedom of expression. They wrote on subjects that were useful for his policies and that

Aeneas at sacrifice. This is a detail of a panel on the first-century *Ara Pacis* in Rome. It shows the tall, godlike legendary Roman hero Aeneas sacrificing at a simple altar. On the left two boys also bring sacrifices. On the right of Aeneas is his faithful friend Achates. [Alinari/SCALA.]

glorified him and his family, but they were not mere propagandists. It seems evident that for the most part they were persuaded of the virtues of Augustus and his reign and sang its praises with some degree of sincerity. Because they were poets of genius, they were also able to maintain a measure of independence in their work.

VERGIL. Vergil (70–19 B.C.) was the most important of the Augustan poets. His first important works, the *Eclogues* or *Bucolics,* were pastoral idylls in a somewhat artificial mode. The subject of the *Georgics,* however, was suggested to Vergil by Maecenas. The model here was the early Greek poet Hesiod's *Works and Days,* but the mood and purpose of Vergil's poem are far different. It is, to be sure, a didactic account of the agricultural life, but it is also a paean to the beauties of nature and a hymn to the cults, traditions, and greatness of Italy. All this, of course, served the purpose of glorifying Augustus' resettlement of the veterans of the civil wars on Italian farms and his elevation of Italy to special status in the empire. Vergil's greatest work was the *Aeneid,* a long national epic that succeeded in placing the history of Rome in the great tradition of the Greeks and the Trojan War. Its hero, the Trojan warrior Aeneas, personifies the ideal Roman qualities of duty, responsibility, serious purpose, and patriotism. As the Roman's equivalent of Homer, Vergil glorified not the personal honor and excellence of the Greek epic heroes but the civic greatness represented by Augustus and the peace and prosperity he and the Julian family had given to imperial Rome.

HORACE. Horace (65–8 B.C.) was the son of a freed man and fought on the republican side until its defeat at Philippi. He was won over to the Augustan cause by the patronage of Maecenas and by the attractions of the Augustan reforms. His *Satires* are genial and humorous. His great skills as a lyric poet are best revealed in his *Odes,* which are ingenious in their adaptation of Greek meters to the requirements of Latin verse. Two of the *Odes* are directly in praise of Augustus, and many of them glorify the new Augustan order, the imperial family, and the empire.

OVID. The darker side of Augustan influence on the arts is revealed by the career of Ovid (43 B.C.–A.D. 18). He wrote light and entertaining love elegies that reveal the sophistication and the loose sexual code of a notorious sector of the Roman aristocracy. Their values and way of life were contrary to the seriousness and family-centered life Augustus was trying to foster. Ovid's *Ars Amatoria,* a poetic textbook on the art of seduction, angered Augustus, and in A.D. 8 he exiled the poet to Tomi on the Black Sea. Ovid tried to recover favor, especially with his *Fasti,* a poetic treatment of Roman religious festivals, but to no avail. His most popular work is the *Metamorphoses,* a kind of mythological epic that turns Greek myths into charming stories in a graceful and lively style. Ovid's fame did not fade with his exile and death, but his fate was an effective warning to later poets.

HISTORY. The achievements of Augustus and his emphasis on tradition and on the continuity of his regime with the glorious history of Rome encouraged both historical and antiquarian prose works. A number of Augustan writers wrote scholarly treatises on history and geography in Greek. By far the most important and influential prose writer of the time, however, was Livy (59 B.C.–A.D. 17), an Italian from Padua. His *History of Rome* was written in Latin and treated the period from the legendary origins of Rome until 9 B.C. Only a fourth of his work is extant; of the rest we have only pitifully brief summaries. He based his history on earlier accounts, chiefly the Roman annalists, and made no effort at original research. His great achievement was in telling the story of Rome in a continuous and impressive narrative. Its purpose was moral, setting up historical models as examples of good and bad behavior, and, above all, patriotic. He glorified Rome's greatness and connected it with her past, just as Augustus tried to do.

ARCHITECTURE AND SCULPTURE. The visual arts revealed the same tendencies as other aspects of Roman life under Augustus. Augustus was the great patron of the arts as he was of literature. He embarked on a building program that beautified Rome, glorified his

reign, and contributed to the general prosperity and his own popularity. Augustus boasted that he found the city in brick and left it in marble. That is an exaggeration because there were many marble buildings before his time and most of his buildings had only a marble facade. However, he filled the Campus Martius with beautiful new buildings, theaters, baths, and basilicas; The Roman Forum was rebuilt; and Augustus built a forum of his own. At its heart was the temple of Mars the Avenger to commemorate Augustus' victory and the greatness of his ancestors. On Rome's Palatine hill he built a magnificent palace for himself and a splendid temple to his patron god, Apollo. This was one of the many temples he constructed in pursuit of his religious policy.

Most of the building was influenced by the Greek classical style, which aimed at serenity and the ideal type. The same features were visible in the portrait sculpture of Augustus and his family. The greatest monument of the age is the Altar of Peace (*Ara Pacis*) dedicated in 9 B.C. Set originally in an open space in the Campus Martius, its walls still carry a relief. Part of it shows a procession in which Augustus and his family appear to move forward followed in order by the magistrates, the Senate, and the people of Rome. There is no better symbol of the new order.

Peace and Prosperity: Imperial Rome A.D. 14–180

The central problem for Augustus' successors was the position of the ruler and his relationship to the ruled. Augustus tried to cloak the monarchical nature of his government, but his successors soon abandoned all pretense. The rulers came to be called *imperator*—from which comes our word *emperor*—as well as *Caesar*. The latter title signified connection with the imperial house, and the former indicated the military power on which everything was based. Because Augustus was ostensibly only the "first citizen" of a restored republic and his powers were theoretically voted him by the Senate and

The temple of Mars the Avenger in the Forum of Augustus at Rome. This is a modern architect's model of the forum and temple built by Augustus during his years as Princeps.
The original Roman Forum of the republic, despite constant rebuilding, had been outgrown as a center of business, worship, politics, and celebration. Julius Caesar had already built a new forum nearby, and Augustus was one of several later rulers to follow suit. [Alinari/SCALA.]

The *Ara Pacis* (Altar of Peace) at Rome. This altar to the Augustan peace was dedicated in 9 B.C. as part of a broad propaganda program. Augustus responded to the widespread longing for peace after a century of strife at home and abroad, using poetry, architecture, myth, and history to enhance his image as the savior of Rome and the restorer of peace. [Alinari/SCALA.]

WALL OF ANTONINUS

WALL OF HADRIAN

N O R T H

HIBERNIA

BRITAIN

S E A

RHINE

A T L A N T I C

SEINE

Cologne

GERMANIA (INF.)

G E R M A N I A

ELBE

ODER

VISTULA

O C E A N

LUGDUNENSIS

LOIRE

GAUL

GERMANIA (SUP.)

RAETIA

DANUBE

DNIEPER

S A R M A

DNIESTER

PRUTH

AQUITANIA

CISALPINE GAUL

NOR-ICUM

(SUP.)

PANNONIA (INF.)

DACIA

DUERO

TARRACONENSIS

NARBONENSIS

EBRO

PO

DALMATIA

DANUBE

RHÔNE

(SUP.)

MOESIA (INF.)

B L A C K

LUSITANIA

CORSICA

ITALY

SPAIN

Rome

Apollonia

MACEDONIA

THRACE

Byzantium

BAETICA

BALEARIC IS.

ILLYRIA

GREECE

BITHYNIA

SARDINIA

ASIA

M

E

D

I

T

PISIDIA

MAURETANIA

Carthage

SICILY

ACHAEA

LYCIA

A F R I C A

A

F

R

I

C

A

N U M I D I A

R

R

A

N

E

A

N

CRETE

S

E

A

CYRENAICA

LIBYA

EGYP

A.D. 14 – DEATH OF AUGUSTUS

14–98 – ACQUISITIONS, AUGUSTUS TO TRAJAN

98–117 – ACQUISITIONS DURING THE REIGN OF TRAJAN

PROVINCES OF THE ROMAN EMPIRE TO A.D. 117

172 *The Early Roman Empire (31 B.C.–A.D. 180)*

MAJOR
ROADS
OF THE
ROMAN EMPIRE

The growth of the Empire to its greatest extent is here shown in three stages—at the death of Augustus in A.D. 14, at the death of Nerva in 98, and at the death of Trajan in 117. The division into provinces is also indicated. The inset outlines the main roads that tied the far-flung Empire together.

the people, he could not legally name his successor. In fact, he plainly designated his heirs by favors lavished on them and by giving them a share in the imperial power and responsibility. Tiberius (emperor A.D. 14–37),[2] his immediate successor, was at first embarrassed by the ambiguity of his new role, but soon the monarchical and hereditary nature of the regime became patent. Gaius (Caligula, A.D. 37–41), Claudius (A.D. 41–54), and Nero (A.D. 54–68) were all descended from either Augustus or his wife, Livia, and all were elevated because of that fact. In A.D. 41 the naked military basis of imperial rule was revealed when the Praetorian Guard had dragged the lame, stammering, and frightened Claudius from behind a curtain and made him emperor. In A.D. 68 the frontier legions learned what Tacitus called "the secret of Empire . . . that an emperor could be made elsewhere than at Rome." Nero's incompetence and unpopularity, and especially his inability to control his armies, led to a serious rebellion in Gaul in A.D. 68. The year 69 saw four different emperors assume power in quick succession as different Roman armies took turns placing their commanders on the throne.

Vespasian (A.D. 69–79) emerged victorious from the chaos, and his sons, Titus (A.D. 79–81) and Domitian (A.D. 81–96) carried forward his line, the Flavian dynasty. Vespasian was the first emperor who did not come from the old Roman nobility. He was a tough soldier who came from the Italian middle class. A good administrator and a hard-headed realist of rough wit, he resisted all attempts by flatterers to find noble ancestors for him. On his deathbed he is said to have ridiculed the practice of deifying emperors by saying, "Alas, I think I am becoming a god."

The assassination of Domitian put an end to the Flavian dynasty. Because Domitian had no close relative who had been designated as successor, the Senate put Nerva (A.D. 96–98) on the throne to avoid chaos. He was the first of the five "good emperors," who included Trajan (A.D. 98–117), Hadrian (A.D. 117–138), Antoni-

2 Dates for emperors give the years of each reign.

The Politicians at Pompeii Write Up Election Posters

The following are *grafitti* found on walls in the Italian city of Pompeii, which was buried by an eruption of Mount Vesuvius in A.D. 79. They give evidence of lively participation in local politics in the first century.

I

THE *fruit dealers together with Helvius Vestalis unanimously urge the election of Marcus Holconius Priscus as duovir with judicial power.*

II

The goldsmiths unanimously urge the election of Gaius Cuspius Pansa as aedile.

III

I ask you to elect Gaius Julius Polybius aedile. He gets good bread.

IV

The muleteers urge the election of Gaius Julius Polybius as duovir.

V

The worshippers of Isis unanimously urge the election of Gnaeus Helvius Sabinus as aedile.

VI

Proculus, make Sabinus aedile and he will do as much for you.

VII

His neighbors urge you to elect Lucius Statius Receptus duovir with judicial power; he is worthy. Aemilius Celer, a neighbor, wrote this. May you take sick if you maliciously erase this!

VIII

Satia and Petronia support and ask you to elect Marcus Casellius and Lucius Albucius aediles. May we always have such citizens in our colony!

IX

I ask you to elect Epidius Sabinus duovir with judicial power. He is worthy, a defender of the colony, and in the opinion of the respected judge Suedius Clemens and by agreement of the council, because of his services and uprightness, worthy of the municipality. Elect him!

X

If upright living is considered any recommendation, Lucretius Fronto is well worthy of the office.

XI

Genialis urges the election of Bruttius Balbus as duovir. He will protect the treasury.

XII

I ask you to elect Marcus Cerrinius Vatia to the aedileship. All the late drinkers support him. Florus and Fructus wrote this.

XIII

The petty thieves support Vatia for the aedileship.

XIV

I ask you to elect Aulus Vettius Firmus aedile. He is worthy of the municipality. I ask you to elect him, ballplayers. Elect him!

XV

I wonder, O wall, that you have not fallen in ruins from supporting the stupidities of so many scribblers.

N. Lewis and M. Reinhold, *Roman Civilization*, Vol. 2 (New York: Columbia University Press, 1955), pp. 326–327.

nus Pius (A.D. 138–161), and Marcus Aurelius (A.D. 161–180). Until Marcus Aurelius, each of these emperors either outlived his sons or had none and followed the example set by Nerva of adopting an able senator and establishing him as successor. The result was almost a century of peaceful succession and competent rule, which ended when Marcus Aurelius allowed his incompetent son, Commodus (A.D. 180–192), to succeed him, with unfortunate results.

The genius of the Augustan settlement lay in its capacity to enlist the active cooperation of the upper classes and their effective organ, the Senate. The election of magistrates was taken from the assemblies and given to the Senate; it became the major center for legislation; and

OPPOSITE: Aerial view of Pompeii, an Italian town on the Bay of Naples destroyed by the volcanic eruption of nearby Mt. Vesuvius which buried it in volcanic ash. This eruption was witnessed by the Younger Pliny and is described in his letters. The ruins of Pompeii were accidentally rediscovered in the 18th century and have now been largely excavated, revealing a prosperous and pleasant town of moderate size with an active local political life. (See also the pictures of Pompeii in the color album.) [Fotocielo.]

Propaganda by Emperor Domitian (A.D. 81–96). This sculpture from his reign is thought to be an attempt to justify an unpopular war in Germany in A.D. 83. Domitian, the fourth figure from the left, is depicted as reluctant to go to war but pushed into it by a divinity, perhaps the goddess Roma. [Archivio Fotographico, Musei Vaticani.]

Portrait bust of the Emperor Vespasian (A.D. 69–79). [Deutsches Archäologisches Institut, Rome.]

Emperor Trajan (A.D. 98–117). [Alinari/SCALA.]

it exercised important judicial functions. This semblance of power persuaded some contemporaries and even some modern scholars that Augustus had established a "dyarchy," a system of joint rule by *princeps* and Senate. This was never true, and the hollowness of the senatorial role became more apparent as time passed. Some emperors, like Vespasian, took pains to maintain, increase, and display the prestige and dignity of the Senate; others, like Caligula, Nero, and Domitian, degraded the Senate and paraded their own despotic power, but from the first its powers were illusory. Magisterial elections were, in fact, controlled by the emperors, and the Senate's legislative function quickly degenerated into mere assent to what was put before it by the emperor or his representatives. The true function of the Senate was to be a legislative and administrative extension of the emperor's rule.

There was, of course, some real opposition to the imperial rule. It sometimes took the form of plots against the life of the emperor. Plots and the suspicion of plots led to repression, the use of spies and paid informers, book burning, and executions. The opposition consisted chiefly of senators who looked back to republican liberty for their class and who found justification in the Greek and Roman traditions of tyrannicide as well as in the precepts of Stoicism. Plots and repression were most common under Nero and Domitian. From Nerva to Marcus Aurelius, however, the emperors, without yielding any power, again learned to enlist the cooperation of the upper class by courteous and modest deportment.

In the eastern provinces the emperor was worshiped as a god, and even in the west most emperors were deified after their death as long as the imperial cult established by Augustus continued.

The provinces flourished economically and generally accepted Roman rule easily. Imperial policy was for the most part a happy combination of an attempt to unify the empire and its various peoples with a respect for local customs and differences. Roman citizenship was spread ever more widely, and by A.D. 212 almost every inhabitant of the empire could be a citizen. Latin became the

language of the western provinces, and although the east remained essentially Greek in language and culture, even it adopted many aspects of Roman life. The spread of *Romanitas,* or Roman-ness, was more than nominal, for senators and even emperors began to be drawn from provincial families.

The army played an important role in the spread of Roman culture and the spiritual unification of the empire. The legionaries married local women and frequently settled in the province of their service when their term was over. Hadrian even began the practice of recruiting his legions from the provinces in which they would serve, and this practice became normal.

From an administrative and cultural standpoint the empire was a collection of cities and towns and had little to do with the countryside. Roman policy during the Principate was to raise urban centers to the status of Roman municipalities with the rights and privileges attached to them. A typical municipal charter left much responsibility in the hands of local councils and magistrates elected from the local aristocracy. Moreover, the holding of a magistracy, and later a seat on the council, carried Roman citizenship with it. Therefore the Romans enlisted the upper classes of the provinces in their own government, spread Roman law and culture, and won the loyalty of the influential people.

There were exceptions to this picture of success. The Jews found their religion incompatible with Roman demands and experienced savage repression of their rebellions in A.D. 66–70, 115–117, and 132–135. In Egypt the Romans exploited the Egyptian peasants ruthlessly and did not pursue a policy of urbanization.

The task of governing the vast empire required a skilled administration. Augustus kept the control of the army in his own hands but allowed senators to continue to govern some provinces. Others were run by equestrians. The emperor's own staff included an informal group of advisers, his *consilium,* and he relied on equestrians, freedmen, and even slaves to carry out details.

Claudius organized the imperial bureaucracy in a more

Tacitus Gives a Provincial View of the Imperial Peace

Tacitus (A.D. 55–*ca.* 115) was a Roman senator. He is most famous as historian of Rome for the period A.D. 14 to 68, but the following selection comes from a eulogy for his father-in-law Agricola. It gives an insight into the Roman Empire viewed critically.

THE Britons, . . . *convinced at length that a common danger must be averted by union, had, by embassies and treaties, summoned forth the whole strength of all their states. More than 30,000 armed men were now to be seen, and still there were pressing in all the youth of the country, with all whose old age was yet hale and vigorous, men renowned in war and bearing each decorations of his own. Meanwhile, among the many leaders, one superior to the rest in valour and in birth, Galgacus by name, is said to have thus harangued the multitude gathered around him and clamouring for battle:—*

"Whenever I consider the origin of this war and the necessities of our position, I have a sure confidence that this day, and this union of yours, will be the beginning of freedom to the whole of Britain. To all of us slavery is a thing unknown; there are no lands beyond us, and even the sea is not safe, menaced as we are by a Roman fleet. And thus in war and battle, in which the brave find glory, even the coward will find safety. Former contests, in which, with varying fortune, the Romans were resisted, still left in us a last hope of succour, inasmuch as being the most renowned nation of Britain, dwelling in the very heart of the country and out of sight of the shores of the conquered, we could keep even our eyes unpolluted by the contagion of slavery. To us who dwell on the uttermost confines of the earth and of freedom, this remote sanctuary of Britain's glory has up to this time been a defence. Now, however, the furthest limits of Britain are thrown open, and the unknown always passes for the marvellous. But there are no tribes beyond us, nothing indeed but waves and rocks, and the yet more terrible Romans, from whose oppression escape is vainly sought by obedience and submission. Robbers of the world, having by their universal plunder exhausted the land, they rifle the deep. If the enemy be rich, they are rapacious; if he be poor, they lust for dominion; neither the east nor the west has been able to satisfy them. Alone among men they covet with equal eagerness poverty and riches. To robbery, slaughter, plunder, they give the lying name of empire; they make a solitude and call it peace."

Tacitus, *Agricola,* in *Complete Works of Tacitus,* trans. by A. J. Church and W. Brodribb (New York: Random House, 1942), pp. 694–695.

orderly manner, putting many important posts in the hands of freedmen.

Under the "good emperors," service in the imperial bureaucracy became a career for equestrians. It became the most extensive, efficient, and honest administration the world had ever known. Its officials were educated and usually enlightened men who generally sought the welfare of those they ruled, for a successful career depended upon the approval of the emperor, and in the second century A.D. he wanted the provinces and Italy well governed.

As the efficiency of the bureaucracy grew, so did the number and scope of its functions and therefore its size. The emperors came to take a broader view of their responsibilities for the welfare of their subjects than before. Nerva conceived and Trajan introduced the *alimenta,* a program of public assistance on behalf of the children of indigent parents. More and more the emperors intervened when municipalities got into difficulties, usually financial, sending imperial troubleshooters to deal with problems. The importance and autonomy of the municipalities shrank as the central administration took a greater part in local affairs. The provincial aristocracy came to regard public service in their own cities as a burden rather than an opportunity; the price paid for the increased efficiency offered by centralized control was the loss of the vitality of the cities throughout the empire.

Augustus' successors, for the most part, accepted his conservative and defensive foreign policy. Claudius, to be sure, conquered southern Britain and annexed it as a province (A.D. 43–47), but his purpose was largely to protect Gaul against Celtic plots launched from across the channel. Vespasian and his sons pushed forward into the territory between the Rhine and the Danube to shorten the frontier and to ease communications between the armies on the two rivers.

Trajan was the first emperor to take the offensive in a sustained way. Between A.D. 101 and 106 he crossed the Danube and, after hard fighting, established the new

[*Text continued on page 180*]

OPPOSITE: Mosaic from north Africa. This floor mosaic comes from the large villa of Oudna (in modern Tunisia). This formerly Carthaginian area was part of the Roman province of Africa. The mosaic was made in the second century, and it depicts aspects of life on a large provincial estate at that time. [Musée National du Bardo, Tunis.]

LEFT: The arena and the theatre at Arles. These buildings in southern France are among the best preserved examples of Roman architecture. They date from about the beginning of the empire. The free-standing amphitheatre (or arena) appears to have been a Roman innovation; this one at Arles and the Colosseum in Rome are noteworthy examples. [French Government Tourist Office, New York.]

BELOW: The Maison Carrée at Nîmes. This lovely Roman temple, of the Corinthian order so favored by the Romans, is in southern France and was built by Augustus's friend and lieutenant, Agrippa, in A.D. 16. [French Government Tourist Office, New York.]

BELOW, LEFT: The Roman aqueduct and bridge near Nîmes in southern France, now called the Pont-du-Gard. It is one of the finest examples of its kind and was built late in the first century B.C. by order of Agrippa. [French Government Tourist Office, New York.]

Model of a Roman apartment house. This brick apartment house of the imperial period was typical of the thousands like it that housed most of the citizens of Rome. The ground floor was occupied by a row of shops, and above it were three or four stories of apartments. (For dwelling arrangements of quite a different kind, see the Pompeii residence in the color album.) [Alinari/SCALA.]

The sack of Jerusalem. This relief comes from the arch of Titus on the edge of the Roman Forum and commemorates Titus's earlier conquest of Jerusalem. It was made in A.D. 81 and shows the spoils being removed from the Temple in A.D. 70. [Alinari/SCALA.]

province of Dacia between the Danube and the Carpathian Mountains. He was tempted, no doubt, by its important gold mines, but he probably was also pursuing a new general strategy: to defend the empire more aggressively by driving wedges into the territory of threatening barbarians. The same strategy dictated the invasion of the Parthian Empire in the east (A.D. 113–117). Trajan's early success was astonishing, and he established three new provinces in Armenia, Assyria, and Mesopotamia, but his lines were overextended. Rebellions sprang up, and the campaign crumbled. Trajan was forced to retreat and died before getting back to Rome.

Hadrian returned to the traditional policy, keeping Dacia but abandoning the eastern provinces. Hadrian's reign marked an important shift in Rome's frontier policy. Heretofore, even under the successors of Augustus, Rome had been on the offensive against the barbarians. Although the Romans rarely gained new territory, they launched frequent attacks to chastise and pacify troublesome tribes. Hadrian hardened the Roman defenses, building a stone wall in the south of Scotland and a wooden one across the Rhine–Danube triangle. The Roman defense became rigid, and initiative passed to the barbarians. Marcus Aurelius was compelled to spend most of his reign resisting dangerous attacks in the east and on the Danube frontier, and these attacks put enormous pressure on the manpower and wealth of the empire.

This pressure took its toll only late in this period, which, in general, experienced considerable economic prosperity and growth. Internal peace and efficient administration benefited agriculture as well as trade and industry; farming and trade developed together as political conditions made it easier to sell farm products at a distance. This latter element encouraged the earlier tendency toward specialization of crops and the growth of large holdings. Small farms continued to exist, but the large estate, managed by an absentee owner and growing cash crops, became the dominant form of agriculture. At first these estates were worked chiefly by slaves, but in the first century this began to change. The end of wars of conquest made slaves less available and more expensive, for ancient societies never succeeded in breeding slaves. The tenant farmer or *colonus* became the mainstay of agricultural labor. Typically these sharecroppers paid rent in labor or in kind, though sometimes they made cash payments. Gradually their movement was restricted, and they were tied to the land they worked, much as were the manorial serfs of the Middle Ages. But the system was economically efficient and contributed to the general prosperity, whatever its social cost.

The Culture of the Early Empire

EDUCATION. The spread of Roman culture throughout the empire, like the spread of its political and economic institutions, produced a kind of unity that did not interfere with considerable local autonomy and variation. Urban life was its essence, and cities grew in both size and number. Each bore the signs of Roman life: baths, theaters, temples, statuary, and public buildings in the Roman style, but the most important carrier of culture, as always, was the system of education. As much as wealth, education distinguished the governing class from the lower orders, for the state provided none. Elementary learning was left to the localities and paid for by the parents who could afford it. A small number went on beyond primary school to study rhetoric and literature in preparation for a career in the law or in the imperial service. Athens continued to be the center of advanced studies, such as philosophy, medicine, law, and the higher realms of rhetorical theory, but from the first century on the emperors began the practice of patronizing higher education.

Masada. In A.D. 70, Titus, the son of Emperor
Vespasian, crushed the Jewish rebellion against
Roman occupation of Palestine that had been raging
since 66. He destroyed the Temple, plundered
Jerusalem, and killed many survivors of the siege.
The most determined resisters fled to the rocky
fortress of Masada where they held out for years.
When the Romans finally built a rampart that brought
them to the summit, the resisters committed suicide
rather than yield to them. [Israel Government
Tourist Office, New York.]

Trajan dispensing *alimenta.* This relief stands in
the Roman Forum; it shows Emperor Hadrian on the
left with a crowd in front of him. To the right,
behind the crowd facing Hadrian, is a statuary group
in which former Emperor Trajan is seated while Italia
is carrying a child to him. The monument commemorates
Trajan's institution of public support for orphan
children, and the whole scene refers to Hadrian's
continuation of that policy. [Alinari/SCALA.]

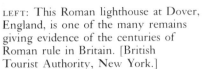

LEFT: This Roman lighthouse at Dover, England, is one of the many remains giving evidence of the centuries of Roman rule in Britain. [British Tourist Authority, New York.]

At its highest levels this system of education was bilingual and helped to preserve the tradition of Graeco-Roman culture. Below that level, on the other hand, it helped perpetuate the division between the east, where Greek was spoken, and the Latin west. Education was one vehicle of social mobility, allowing anyone who could obtain it the chance to rise, but it was also conservative. It taught the values of the ruling class, as is natural, but it provided little stimulus for criticism or innovation.

LITERATURE. In Latin literature the years between the death of Augustus and the time of Marcus Aurelius are known as the Silver Age, and as the name implies, work of high quality was produced although probably not of so high a quality as in the Augustan era. In contrast to the hopeful, positive optimism of the Augustans, the writers of the Silver Age were gloomy, negative, and pessimistic. In the works of the former period, praise of the emperor, his achievements, and the world abound; in the latter, criticism and satire lurk everywhere.

Some of the most important writers of the Silver Age came from the Stoic opposition and reflect its hostility to the growing power and personal excesses of the emperors. The most important of these was Seneca (*ca.* 5 B.C.–A.D. 65). As tutor and adviser he tried to guide the young emperor Nero along paths of Stoic virtue but failed and was driven to suicide. His satirical talents are well displayed in his travesty of the deification of Claudius, the *Apocolocyntosis,* or "pumpkinification." He also wrote many tragedies. They are based on Greek

A reconstructed Roman frontier fort in Germany. This fort *(castellum)* is called Saalburg and is near Frankfort, West Germany. It was one of about one hundred forts built to defend the triangle of land between the Rhine and Danube frontiers. Originally built by Emperor Domitian in A.D. 83, it was enlarged in the second century and held a garrison of about five hundred troops. [Saalburg-museum, Saalburg-Kastell, near Bad Homburg, West Germany.]

ABOVE: Relief from the column of Marcus Aurelius in Rome, showing Roman soldiers crossing a river on a bridge of boats. It is part of a depiction and commemoration of the Danubian campaigns of 172–175 of Emperor Marcus Aurelius (161–180). [Alinari/SCALA.]

ABOVE, RIGHT: A portion of Trajan's column. This column was erected by Trajan in his forum in Rome to commemorate his wars beyond the Danube River in Dacia from 101 to 106. It is 100 feet high, of marble, and its spiral frieze contains 2500 figures. Its intention was clearly to propagate the idea of the greatness and the achievements of the emperor by the novel device of an unrolling picture over 625 feet long. [Copyright by Leonard von Matt.]

RIGHT: Hadrian's wall. This wall, running completely across Great Britain through what is now northern England and southern Scotland, was built by Emperor Hadrian (117–138). It was probably begun in 122 to prevent communication between the northern and southern Britannic tribes. The wall was as much as twenty feet high and from six to eight feet broad. [British Tourist Authority, New York.]

models, although adapted to the tastes of Seneca's time, and had a considerable influence on the rebirth of tragedy in sixteenth-century England and seventeenth-century France. The bulk of his work, however, was in prose and was devoted to expounding Stoic philosophy, especially in its moral aspect.

Among Seneca's contemporaries were the satirical poet Persius (A.D. 34–62) and Lucan, Seneca's nephew, who was implicated in a plot against Nero and was also driven to suicide. His only surviving work is the epic poem *Pharsalia*, on the civil war between Caesar and Pompey. The hero is Pompey, and the tyrannicides Cato and Brutus are painted as men of the highest virtue. Caesar, though magnificent, is the villain whose victory means the end of Roman freedom.

The same satirical spirit was carried forward in the years of the Flavian dynasty and beyond by the poets Martial (*ca.* A.D. 40–104) and Juvenal (*ca.* A.D. 50–127). Even history and biography were written in the same mood and spirit, for Tacitus (*ca.* A.D. 55–115), whose writings are our chief source for the years A.D. 14–68, wrote history that is often hard to distinguish from satire, as are the biographies of Suetonius (*ca.* A.D. 69–140), who wrote the lives of the rulers of Rome from Julius Caesar to Domitian.

During these same years significant works were written in Greek prose as well as in Latin. History in one form or another was written by Arrian, a Greek of the second century who wrote an account of the career of Alexander the Great, and Appian of Alexandria, who lived about the same time and wrote a useful history of Rome's wars. Plutarch of Chaeroneia (*ca.* A.D. 46–*ca.* 120) wrote a set of *Parallel Lives* of great figures in Greek and Roman history, which remains a valuable source of information for modern scholars of antiquity and which powerfully helped shape the minds of educated people of the eighteenth century.

Greek was the language deemed most appropriate for philosophy and science. Epictetus (*ca.* A.D. 55–135) and the emperor Marcus Aurelius wrote important tracts on Stoic beliefs in that language. Galen (*ca.* A.D. 129–199), probably the greatest physician of antiquity, wrote his many medical works in Greek, and Ptolemy of Alexandria, whose work spanned the years A.D. 121–151 wrote on astronomy and geography. The *Almagest,* as his major work came to be known, put together the astronomical learning of the Greeks based on the geocentric theory of the universe and dominated thinking in the west until the scientific revolution of the sixteenth century.

The writers of the second century appear to have turned away from contemporary affairs and even recent history. Historical writing was about remote periods so that there was less danger of irritating imperial sensibilities. Scholarship was encouraged, but we hear little of poetry, especially any dealing with dangerous subjects.

A new genre of prose literature began to be popular in the second century A.D.: the romance. *The Golden Ass* of Apuleius may be considered the first novel ever written, and it contains many elements of romance. As a popular, easily accessible prose work, it was meant to be read privately instead of aloud in a company, and it appealed to a less cultivated audience than was required by the more aristocratic poetic genres. In the third century romances written in Greek became popular and provide further evidence of the tendency of writers of the time to seek and provide escape from contemporary realities.

ARCHITECTURE AND SCULPTURE. The prosperity and relative stability of the first two centuries of imperial Rome allowed for the full development of the Roman contribution to architecture. To the fundamental styles of buildings developed by the Greeks, the Romans added little; the great public bath and a new, free-standing kind of amphitheater were the main innovations. Nor did they depart much from the three Greek architectural orders; the Ionic, the Doric, and the Corinthian. They did add a fourth, the composite order, that lent additional strength to structures like large triumphal arches.

The main Roman contribution lay in the great size of the structures they could build and in the advances in engineering that made these large structures possible. While keeping the basic post-and-lintel construction used by the Greeks, the Romans added to it the principle of the semicircular arch, borrowed from the Etruscans. They also made good use of concrete, a building material first used by the Hellenistic Greeks but fully developed by the Romans. The new principle, sometimes combined with the new material, allowed progress over the old style. The arch combined with the post and lintel produced the great Colosseum built by the Flavians. When used internally in the form of vaults and domes, the arch permitted great buildings like the baths, of which the most famous and best preserved are those of the later emperors Caracalla and Diocletian.

One of Rome's most famous buildings, the Pantheon, begun by Agrippa and rebuilt by Hadrian, is a good

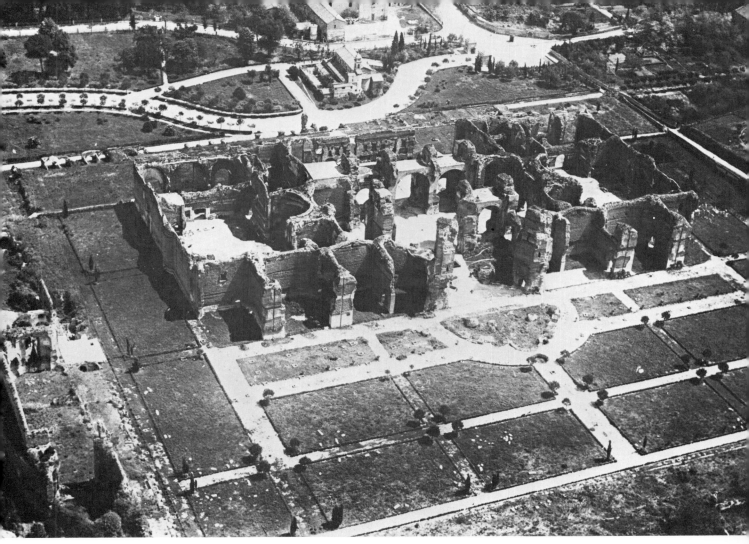

ABOVE: Ruins of the baths of Caracalla. These public baths in Rome were built by Emperor Caracalla (A.D. 211–217). In their original form they were even larger and were decorated with expensive colored marble, statues, and mosaics. This view is from the west. [Fototeca Unione.]

RIGHT: The baths of Caracalla in a cut-away partial reconstruction by C. V. Rauscher. This view is from the south; its left and front sides correspond to the back and left walls of the photograph, the front left corner of the ruin being what remains of the covered porch at the right of the drawing. [S. A. Ivanov and C. Hülsen, *Architektonische Studien*, 1898.]

example of the combination of all these elements. Its portico of Corinthian columns is of Greek origin, but its rotunda of brick-faced concrete with its domed ceiling and relieving arches is thoroughly Roman. The new engineering also made possible the construction of more

The Colosseum at Rome. The Romans called this building the Flavian Amphitheatre because it was built by three successive emperors of the Flavian family—begun by Vespasian, dedicated in A.D. 80 by his son Titus, and finished by his younger son Domitian. How it acquired its present name is uncertain; this may derive either from its enormous size or from its proximity to a colossal statue of Emperor Nero. It is said to have been built by prisoners taken in the Jewish War, and could seat 50,000 spectators for the animal hunts, gladiatorial combats, mock sea battles, and other spectacles that took place in it. [Fototeca Unione.]

OPPOSITE, ABOVE: The Pantheon at Rome. A temple, with baths and water gardens, was built on this spot by Agrippa in 27–25 B.C. Destroyed by fire, it was rebuilt in its present form by Emperor Hadrian between A.D. 117 and 125 and then repaired by Septimius Severus in about 200. [Italian Government Travel Office, New York.]

OPPOSITE, BELOW: The interior of the Pantheon, in G. B. Piranesi's eighteenth-century etching. By this time it had long been a Christian church.

mundane but more useful structures like bridges and aqueducts.

In sculpture, too, the Romans both used and departed from Greek models. There was more copying and less innovation in sculpture in the round, although portrait busts of the emperors and others show greater realism than most Greek examples. The most powerful form of Roman imperial sculpture is the relief, for whose use there were many opportunities. Triumphal arches like those of Titus, Trajan, and later emperors as well as commemorative columns like those of Trajan and Marcus Aurelius provided surfaces for the depiction of elaborate historical scenes and opportunities for developing the art of relief to a high level. In both painting and sculpture the artists of this period, except under Hadrian, turned away from the classical, aloof style of the time of Augustus to a more frontal, dramatic style that tried to involve and absorb the spectator.

SOCIETY. Seen from the harsh perspective of human history the first two centuries of the Roman Empire

The Early Roman Empire (*31 B.C.–A.D. 180*)

deserve their reputation of a "golden age," but by the second century troubles had arisen, troubles that foreshadowed the difficult times ahead. The literary efforts of the time reveal a flight from the present and from reality and the public realm to the past, to romance, to private pursuits. Some of the same aspects may be seen in the more prosaic world of everyday life, especially in the decline of vitality in local government.

In the first century members of the upper classes vied with one another for election to municipal office and for the honor of doing service to their communities. By the second century much of their zeal disappeared, and it became necessary for the emperors to intervene to correct abuses in local affairs and even to force unwilling members of the ruling classes to accept public office. The reluctance to serve was caused largely by the imperial practice of holding magistrates and councilmen personally and collectively responsible for the revenues due. There were even some instances of magistrates fleeing to avoid their office, a practice that became widespread in later centuries.

All of these difficulties reflect the presence of more basic problems. The prosperity brought by the end of civil war and the influx of wealth from the east, especially Egypt, could not sustain itself beyond the first half of the second century. There also appears to have been a decline in population for reasons that remain mysterious. The cost of government kept rising as the emperors were required to maintain a costly standing army, to keep the people in Rome happy with "bread and circuses," to pay for an increasingly numerous bureaucracy, and especially in the reign of Marcus Aurelius, to wage expensive wars to defend the frontiers against dangerous and determined barbarian enemies. The ever-increasing need for money compelled the emperors to raise taxes, to press hard on their subjects, and to bring on inflation by debasing the coinage. These were the elements that were to bring on the desperate crises that ultimately destroyed the empire, but under the able emperors, from Trajan to Marcus Aurelius, the Romans met the challenge successfully.

Matthew Reports the Sermon on the Mount

The scene of the Sermon on the Mount has always been a moving one. The precepts, including the famous Beatitudes, of Jesus' sermon have remained at the heart of Christianity's ideal ethics, however difficult they have been to put continuously into practice. Many of Christianity's early converts were from lowly classes who immediately found the Sermon on the Mount appealing. The account in the Gospel of Matthew probably dates from about A.D. 85.

SEEING *the crowds, he went up on the mountain, and when he sat down his disciples came to him. And he opened his mouth and taught them, saying:*

"Blessed are the poor in spirit, for theirs is the kingdom of heaven.

"Blessed are those who mourn, for they shall be comforted.

"Blessed are the meek, for they shall inherit the earth.

"Blessed are those who hunger and thirst for righteousness, for they shall be satisfied.

"Blessed are the merciful, for they shall obtain mercy.

"Blessed are the pure in heart, for they shall see God.

"Blessed are the peacemakers, for they shall be called sons of God.

"Blessed are those who are persecuted for righteousness' sake, for theirs is the kingdom of heaven.

"Blessed are you when men revile you and persecute you and utter all kinds of evil against you falsely on my account. Rejoice and be glad, for your reward is great in heaven, for so men persecuted the prophets who were before you. . . .

. . . .

"You have heard that it was said, 'An eye for an eye and a tooth for a tooth.' But I say to you, Do not resist one who is evil. But if any one strikes you on the right cheek, turn to him the other also; and if any one would sue you and take your coat, let him have your cloak as well; and if any one forces you to go one mile, go with him two miles. Give to him who begs from you, and do not refuse him who would borrow from you.

"You have heard that it was said, 'You shall love your neighbor and hate your enemy.' But I say to you, Love your enemies and pray for those who persecute you, so that you may be sons of your Father who is in heaven; for he makes his sun rise on the evil and on the good, and sends rain on the just and on the unjust.

The Gospel of Matthew 5: 1–45, *Revised Standard Version of the Bible.* (New York: Thomas Nelson and Sons, 1946 and 1952).

Mark Describes the Resurrection of Jesus

Belief that Jesus rose from the dead after his Crucifixion (about A.D. 29) was and is central to traditional Christian doctrine. The record of the Resurrection in the Gospel of Mark, written a generation later (toward A.D. 65), is the earliest we have. The significance to most Christian groups revolves about the assurance given them that death and the grave are not final and that, instead, salvation for a future life is possible. The appeal of these views was to be nearly universal in the West during the Middle Ages. The church was commonly thought to be the means of implementing the promise of salvation; hence the enormous importance of the church's sacramental system, its rules, and its clergy.

AND *when evening had come, since it was the day of Preparation, that is, the day before the sabbath, Joseph of Arimathea, a respected member of the council, who was also himself looking for the kingdom of God, took courage and went to Pilate, and asked for the body of Jesus. And Pilate wondered if he were already dead; and summoning the centurion, he asked him whether he was already dead. And when he learned from the centurion that he was dead, he granted the body to Joseph. And he bought a linen shroud, and taking him down, wrapped him in the linen shroud, and laid him in a tomb which had been hewn out of the rock; and he rolled a stone against the door of the tomb. Mary Magdalene and Mary the mother of Joses saw where he was laid.*

And when the sabbath was past, Mary Magdalene, and Mary the mother of James, and Salome, bought spices, so that they might go and anoint him. And very early on the first day of the week they went to the tomb when the sun had risen. And they were saying to one another, "Who will roll away the stone for us from the door of the tomb?" And looking up, they saw that the stone was rolled back; for it was very large. And entering the tomb, they saw a young man sitting on the right side, dressed in a white robe; and they were amazed. And he said to them, "Do not be amazed; you seek Jesus of Nazareth, who was crucified. He has risen, he is not here, see the place where they laid him. But go, tell his disciples and Peter that he is going before you to Galilee; there you will see him, as he told you." And they went out and fled from the tomb; for trembling and astonishment had come upon them; and they said nothing to any one, for they were afraid.

Gospel of Mark, 15:42–47; 16:1–8, Revised Standard Version of the Bible. (New York: Thomas Nelson and Sons, 1946 and 1952).

The Rise of Christianity

The story of how Christianity emerged, spread, survived, and ultimately conquered the Roman Empire is one of the most remarkable in history. Its origin among poor people from an unimportant and remote province of the empire gave little promise of what was to come. Christianity faced the hostility of the established religious institutions of its native Judaea and had to compete not only against the official cults of Rome and the highly sophisticated philosophies of the educated classes but even against other "mystery" religions like the cults of Mithra, Isis and Osiris, and many others. (We shall return to them in the next chapter.) In addition to all this, the Christians faced the opposition of the imperial government and even formal persecution, yet Christianity achieved toleration and finally exclusive command as the official religion of the empire.

Jesus of Nazareth

An attempt to understand this amazing outcome must begin with Jesus of Nazareth, though there are many problems in arriving at a clear picture of his life and teachings. Apart from the question of sectarian prejudices that might affect the historian's judgment, the sources present special difficulties. The most important evidence is in the Gospel accounts. All of them were written well after the death of Jesus; the earliest, by Mark, is dated about A.D. 70, and the latest, by John, about A.D. 100. They are not, moreover, attempts at simply describing the life of Jesus with historical accuracy; they are statements of faith by true believers. The authors of the Gospels believed that Jesus was the son of God and that he came into the world to redeem mankind and to bring immortality to those who believed in him and followed his way; to the Gospel writers, Jesus' resurrection was striking proof of his teachings. At the same time, the Gospels regard Jesus as a figure in history, and they recount events in his life as well as his sayings. To distinguish historical fact from myth and religious doctrine is not easy, but there is agreement on some of the basic points.

There is no reason to doubt that Jesus was born in the province of Judaea in the time of Augustus and that he was a most effective teacher in the tradition of the prophets. This tradition promised the coming of a Messiah (in Greek, *christos*—so *Jesus Christ* means "Jesus the Messiah"), the redeemer who would make Israel triumph over its enemies and establish the kingdom of God on earth. In fact, Jesus seems to have insisted that the Messiah would not establish an earthly kingdom but would bring an end to the world as men knew it at the Day of Judgment. On that day God would reward the righteous with immortality and happiness in heaven and condemn the wicked to eternal suffering in hell. Until that day, which his followers believed would come very soon, Jesus taught the faithful to abandon sin and worldly concerns; to follow him and his way; to follow the moral code described in the Sermon on the Mount, which preached love, charity, and humility; and to believe in him and his divine mission.

Jesus had success and won a considerable following, especially among the poor. This success caused great suspicion among the upper classes. His novel message and his criticism of the current religious practices connected with the temple at Jerusalem and its priests provoked the hostility of the religious establishment. A misunderstanding of the movement made it easy to convince the Roman governor that Jesus and his followers might be dangerous revolutionaries. He was put to death in Jerusalem by the cruel and degrading device of crucifixion, probably in A.D. 30. His followers believed that he was resurrected on the third day after his death, and that belief became a critical element in the religion that they propagated throughout the Roman Empire and beyond.

Jesus was a Jew who followed the Jewish law. So did his followers, who, after his execution, were few and frightened. Although they differed from their fellow Jews in their belief that Jesus was the Messiah, who had come and would soon return, they had no intention of abandoning Judaism. However, some of their more radical ideas infuriated their coreligionists.

The conquest of Judaea by the Hellenistic monarchs and the spread of Jewish communities throughout the Greek-speaking eastern empire had produced a Hellenizing group of Jews whose ideas differed from those of the more conservative citizens of Judaea, who spoke Aramaic and held fast to traditional Jewish law. There were a good number of "Hellenists" among the early followers of Jesus. One of these, Stephen, was especially outspoken and critical of traditional ways; he was stoned to death by a mob in Jerusalem and became the first Christian martyr.

Although the new belief spread quickly to the Jewish communities of Syria and Asia Minor, there is reason to believe that it might have had only a short life as a despised Jewish heresy were it not for the conversion and career of Saint Paul.

Paul of Tarsus

Paul was born Saul, a citizen of the Cilician city of Tarsus in Asia Minor. Even though he was trained in Hellenistic culture and was a Roman citizen, he was a zealous member of the Jewish sect known as the Pharisees, the group that was most strict in its insistence on adherence to the Jewish law. He took a vigorous part in the persecution of the early Christians until his own conversion outside Damascus about A.D. 35. The great problem facing the early Christians was their relationship to Judaism. If the new faith was a version of Judaism, then it must adhere to the Jewish law and seek converts only among Jews. James, called the brother of Jesus, was a conservative who held to that view, whereas the Hellenist Jews tended to see it as a new and universal religion. To force all converts to adhere to Jewish law would have been fatal to the growth of the new sect, for its many technicalities and dietary prohibitions were strange to gentiles, and the necessity of circumcision—a frightening, painful, and dangerous operation for adults—would have been a tremendous deterrent to conversion. Paul, converted and with his new name, supported the position of the Hellenists and soon won many converts among the gentiles. After some conflict within the sect Paul won out, and the "apostle to the gentiles" deserves recognition as a crucial contributor to the success of Christianity.

The mind and personality of Paul had an important effect not only on the organization of the church but on its religious ideas as well. He combined the skills of a great leader and organizer with the transcendent vision of a mystic. He lived a celibate life, and his own rejection of sexual pleasure left its mark on Christianity. He appears to have been obsessed with a sense of his own sinfulness and guilt and of man's general impotence in relation to God. He believed that man had fallen from God's favor because of Adam's sin, provoked by the woman Eve, and that all men therefore were born with that inherited sin. To free man from sin, God had sent his own son, Jesus, as a sacrifice and an atonement, although mankind was unworthy.

Paul believed it important that the followers of Jesus be evangelists, messengers, to spread the gospel ("good news") of God's gracious gift, for he taught that Jesus would soon return for the Day of Judgment, and it was important that all who would should believe in him and accept his way. Faith in Jesus as the Christ was necessary but not sufficient for salvation, nor could good deeds alone achieve it. That final blessing of salvation was a gift of God's grace that would be granted to some but not to all.

There was another, to some a more attractive, side to Paul's vision, his emphasis on love:

If I speak in the tongues of men and of angels, but have not love, I am a noisy gong or a clanging cymbal. And if I have prophetic powers, and understand all mysteries and all knowledge, and if I have all faith, so as to remove mountains, but have not love, I am nothing. If I give away all I have, and if I deliver my body to be burned, but have not love, I gain nothing. . . . So faith, hope, love abide, these three; but the greatest of these is love.[3]

Organization

Paul and the other apostles did their work well, and the new religion spread throughout the Roman Empire and even beyond its borders. It had its greatest success in the cities and for the most part among the poor and uneducated. The rites of the early communities appear to have been simple and few. Baptism by water removed original sin and permitted participation in the community and its activities. The central ritual was a common meal called the *agape* ("love feast"), followed by the ceremony of the *eucharist* ("thanksgiving"), a celebration of the Lord's Supper in which unleavened bread was eaten and unfermented wine drunk. There were also prayers, hymns, and readings from the Gospels.

Not all the early Christians were poor, and it became customary for the rich to provide for the poor at the common meals. The sense of brotherhood and common love fostered in these ways focused the community's attention on the needs of the weak, the sick, the unfortunate, and the unprotected. This concern gave the early Christian communities a warmth and a human appeal that stood in marked contrast to the coldness and impersonality of the pagan cults. No less attractive were the promise of salvation, the importance to God of each individual human soul, and the spiritual equality of all men in the new faith. As Paul put it, "There is neither Jew nor Greek, there is neither slave nor free, there is neither male nor female: for you are all one in Christ Jesus."[4]

The future of Christianity depended on its communities' finding an organization that would preserve unity within the group and help protect it against enemies outside. At first the churches had little formal organization. Soon, it appears, affairs were placed in the hands of boards of *presbyters* ("elders") and *deacons* ("those who serve"). By the second century A.D., as their numbers

3 I Corinthians 13:1–3, 13. *Revised Standard Version of the Bible.*
4 Galatians 3:28. *Revised Standard Version of the Bible.*

grew the Christians of each city tended to accept the authority and leadership of bishops (*episkopoi*, or "overseers"), who were elected by the congregation to lead them in worship and supervise funds. As time passed bishops extended their authority over the Christian communities in outlying towns and the countryside. The power and almost monarchical authority of the bishops was soon enhanced by the doctrine of Apostolic Succession, which asserted that the powers that Jesus had given his original disciples were passed on from bishop to bishop by ordination.

The bishops kept in touch with one another, maintained communications between different Christian communities, and prevented doctrinal and sectarian splintering, which would have destroyed Christian unity. They maintained internal discipline and dealt with the civil authorities. After a time they began the practice of coming together in councils to settle difficult questions, to establish orthodox opinion, and even to expel as heretics those who would not accept it. It seems unlikely that Christianity could have survived the travails of its early years without such strong internal organization and government.

The Persecution of Christians

The new faith soon incurred the distrust of the pagan world and of the imperial government. At first Christians were thought of as Jewish sect and therefore protected by Roman law. It soon became clear, however, that they were something quite different. They seemed both mysterious and dangerous. They denied the existence of the pagan gods and so were accused of atheism. They refused to worship the emperor, which was judged to be treason. Because they mostly kept to themselves, took no part in civic affairs, engaged in secret rites, and had an organized network of local associations, they were misunderstood and suspected. The love feasts were erroneously reported to be scenes of sexual scandal, and the alarming doctrine of Jesus' body's actual presence in the eucharist was distorted into an accusation of cannibalism. The privacy and

secrecy of Christian life and worship ran counter to a traditional Roman dislike of any private association, especially any of a religious nature, and it earned the Christians the reputation of being "haters of humanity." Claudius expelled them from the city of Rome, and Nero

---

Pliny and Trajan Discuss the Christians in the Empire

Pliny the Younger was the governor of the province of Bithynia in Asia Minor about A.D. 112. The following exchange between him and the Emperor Trajan is important evidence for imperial policy toward the Christians at the time.

To the Emperor Trajan

Having *never been present at any trials of the Christians, I am unacquainted with the method and limits to be observed either in examining or punishing them.*

. . . .

In the meanwhile, the method I have observed towards those who have been denounced to me as Christians is this: I interrogated them whether they were Christians; if they confessed it, I repeated the question twice again, adding the threat of capital punishment; if they still persevered, I ordered them to be executed. For whatever the nature of their creed might be, I could at least feel no doubt that contumacy and inflexible obstinacy deserved chastisement. There were others also possessed with the same infatuation, but being citizens of Rome, I directed them to be carried thither. . . .

Trajan to Pliny

The *method you have pursued, my dear Pliny, in sifting the cases of those denounced to you as Christians is extremely proper. It is not possible to lay down any general rule which can be applied as the fixed standard in all cases of this nature. No search should be made for these people, when they are denounced and found guilty they must be punished; with the restriction, however, that when the party denies himself to be a Christian, and shall give proof that he is not (that is, by adoring our Gods he shall be pardoned on the ground of repentance, even though he may have formerly incurred suspicion. Informations without the accuser's name subscribed must not be admitted in evidence against anyone, as it is introducing a very dangerous precedent, and by no means agreeable to the spirit of the age.*

Pliny the Younger, *Letters,* trans. by W. Melmoth, revised by W. M. Hutchinson (London: William Heinemann, Ltd; Cambridge, Mass.: Harvard University Press, 1935), pp. 401, 403, 407.

The catacomb of Priscilla. The catacombs were secret Christian underground cemeteries and places of worship in Rome and along many of the roads leading from the city. The tomb chamber shown here is typical of many and a model for later Christian crypts. The wall paintings represent some of the earliest examples of Christian art. [SCALA/Editorial Photocolor Archives.]

tried to make them scapegoats for the great fire that struck the city in A.D. 64. By the end of the first century "the name alone"—that is, simple membership in the Christian community—was a crime.

But for the most part the Roman government did not take the initiative in attacking Christians in the first two centuries. When one of the emperor Trajan's governors sought instructions for dealing with the Christians, Trajan urged moderation: Christians were not to be sought out, anonymous accusations were to be disregarded, and anyone denounced could be acquitted merely by abjuring Christ and sacrificing to the emperor. Unfortunately no true Christian could meet the conditions, so there were some martyrdoms.

Most persecutions in this period, however, were instituted not by the government but by mob action. Though they lived quiet, inoffensive lives, some Christians must have seemed unbearably smug and self-righteous. Unlike the tolerant, easy going pagans, who were generally willing to accept the new gods of foreign people and add them to the pantheon, the Christians denied the reality of the pagan gods. They proclaimed the unique rightness of their own way and looked forward to their own salvation and the damnation of nonbelievers. It is not surprising, therefore, that pagans disliked these strange and unsocial people, tended to blame misfortunes upon them, and, in extreme cases, turned to violence. But even this adversity had its uses. It weeded out the weaklings among the Christians, brought greater unity to those who remained faithful, and provided the church with martyrs around whom legends could grow that would inspire still greater devotion and dedication.

Gnosticism

Division within the Christian church may have been an even greater threat to its existence than persecution from outside.

Gnosticism was a widespread heresy that took many forms. The name derives from the Greek word *gnosis* ("knowledge"), but it implies a special kind of mystical, supernatural wisdom through which those who shared in its mysteries could arrive at a true understanding of the universe and be saved from the evils of this world. It had much in common with the mystery religions and combined aspects of pagan religion and philosophy as well as magic and astrology. The Gnostics divided the universe in two: the good, ideal world beyond human experience, on the one hand, and the material world of experience, which is evil and from which one must escape, on the other. The material world, therefore, could not have been created by a good God but must have been made by an evil, or at least imperfect, deity. The figure of Jesus was appealing to the Gnostics because he seemed to come bringing a mystic wisdom that could free men from the bondage of the visible world.

Gnosticism led to a number of conclusions that created problems for orthodox Christians. Because the Old Testament God had created the world and it was evil, he must be the demiurge and evil or imperfect himself. Nor could the son of God have become a human being, for that would have spoiled his perfection. Finally, the Gnostics did not think that all Christians received the redeeming special knowledge but only some favored few—the "spiritual" capable of salvation, unlike the "material," who were beyond redemption. These ideas presented great dangers to the unity and survival of Christianity, and they opened questions about the nature of God that troubled the church for centuries to come.

The great majority of Christians never accepted such complex, intellectualized opinions but held to what even then were more traditional, simple, conservative beliefs. This body of majority opinion and the church that enshrined it came to be called *Catholic,* which means "universal." Its doctrines were deemed orthodox, whereas those holding contrary opinions were heretics.

The need to combat the Gnostics and other heretics compelled the orthodox to formulate their own views more clearly and firmly. By the end of the second century, an orthodox canon had been shaped that included the Old Testament, the Gospels, and the Epistles of Paul, among other writings. The process was not completed for a least two more centuries, but a vitally important start had been made. To resist the Gnostic idea of a secret teaching, the orthodox declared the church itself to be the depository of Christian teaching and the bishops to be its receivers. They also drew up creeds, brief statements of faith to which true Christians should adhere. In the first century all that was required of one to be a Christian was to be baptized, to partake of the eucharist, and to call Jesus the Lord. By the end of the second century an orthodox Christian—that is, a member of the Catholic Church—was required to accept its creed, its canon of holy writings, and the authority of the bishops. The loose structure of the apostolic church had given way to an organized body with recognized leaders able to define its faith and exclude those who did not accept it. Whatever the shortcomings of this development, there can be little doubt that it provided the clarity, unity, and discipline needed for survival.

Rome As a Center of the Early Church

During this same period the church in the city of Rome came to have special prominence. As the center of communications and the capital of the empire, Rome had natural advantages. After the Roman destruction of Jerusalem in 135 A.D., no other city had any convincing claim to primacy. Besides having the largest single congregation of Christians, Rome also benefited from the tradition that both Jesus' disciple Peter and the apostle Paul were martyred there. Peter, moreover, was thought to be the first bishop of Rome, and the Gospel of Matthew (16:18) reported Jesus' statement to Peter: "Thou art Peter [in Greek, *Petros*] and upon this rock [in Greek, *petra*] I will build my church." Eastern Christians might later point out that Peter had been leader of the Christian community at Antioch before he went to Rome, but in the second century the church at Antioch, along with the other Christian churches of Asia Minor, was fading in influence, and by 200 A.D. Rome was the most important center of Christianity. Because of the city's early influence and because of the Petrine doctrine derived from the Gospel of Matthew, later bishops of Rome claimed supremacy in the Catholic Church, but as the era of the "good emperors" came to a close, this controversy was far in the future.

SUGGESTED READINGS

J. P. V. D. BALSDON, *The Emperor Gaius (Caligula),* (Oxford, 1934). A good biography.

J. P. V. D. BALSDON, *Roman Women* (London, 1962).

A. BIRLEY, *Marcus Aurelius* (London, 1966).

J. CARCOPINO, *Daily Life in Ancient Rome,* tr. by E. O. Lorimer, (New Haven, 1940).

M. GRANT, *Nero* (New York, 1970).

M. HAMMOND, *The Augustan Principate* (Cambridge, Mass., 1933). A study of the Augustan constitution.

M. HAMMOND, *The Antonine Monarchy* (Rome, 1959). A study of the Roman imperial government in the second century A.D.

T. RICE HOLMES, *Architect of the Roman Empire,* 2 vols. (Oxford, 1928–1931). An account of Augustus' career in detail.

A. H. M. JONES, *Studies in Roman Government and Law* (New York, 1960). A collection of excellent essays on imperial constitutional questions.

M. L. W. LAISTNER, *The Greater Roman Historians* (Berkeley, 1963). Essays on the major Roman historical writers.

J. LEBRETON and J. ZEILLER, *History of the Primitive Church,* 3 vols. (New York, 1962). From the Catholic viewpoint.

H. LIETZMANN, *History of the Early Church,* 2 vols. (New York, 1961). From the Protestant viewpoint.

R. MACMULLEN, *Enemies of the Roman Order* (Cambridge, Mass., 1966). An original and revealing examination of opposition to the emperors.

F. B. MARSH, *The Founding of the Roman Empire* (Cambridge, 1959).

A. MOMIGLIANO, *Claudius, the Emperor and His Achievement* (New York, 1961).

M. REINHOLD, *Marcus Agrippa.* A fine biography of Augustus' best general and friend.

E. T. SALMON, *A History of the Roman World, 30 B.C. to A.D. 138* (London, 1968). A good survey.

C. G. STARR, *Civilization and the Caesars* (New York, 1965). A study of Roman culture in the Augustan period.

R. SYME, *The Roman Revolution* (Oxford, 1960). A brilliant study of Augustus, his supporters, and their rise to power.

L. R. TAYLOR, *The Divinity of the Roman Empire* (Middletown, Conn., 1931). A study of the imperial cult.

196

9
The Late Roman Empire

The Crisis of the Third Century

DIO CASSIUS, a historian of the third century, wrote of the Roman Empire after the death of Marcus Aurelius as a decline from "a kingdom of gold into one of iron and rust," and though we have seen that the gold contained more than a little dross, there is no reason to quarrel with Dio's assessment of his own time. Commodus (A.D. 180–192), the son of Marcus Aurelius, proved the wisdom of the "good emperors" in selecting their successors for their talents rather than for family ties, for Commodus was incompetent and autocratic. He reduced the respect in which the imperial office was held, and his assassination brought the return of civil war. Even an excellent emperor, however, would have had a difficult time as Rome's troubles, internal as well as external, grew.

Barbarian Invasions

The pressure on Rome's frontiers, already serious in the time of Marcus Aurelius, reached massive proportions in the third century. In the east the frontiers were threatened by a new power arising in the old Persian Empire. In the third century B.C. the Parthians had succeeded in making the Iranians independent of the Hellenistic kings and had established an empire of their own on the old foundations of the Persian Empire. Several Roman attempts to conquer them had failed, but as late as A.D. 198 the Romans were able to reach and destroy the Parthian capital and bring at least northern Mesopotamia under

Equestrian statue of Emperor Marcus Aurelius. In a setting in Rome arranged in the sixteenth century by Michelangelo stands the only remaining equestrian statue of an emperor. It was enormously influential during the Renaissance and thereafter. [Copyright by Leonard von Matt.]

their rule. In A.D. 224, however, a new Iranian dynasty, the Sassanians, seized control from the Parthians and brought new vitality to Persia. They soon recovered Mesopotamia and made raids deep into Roman provinces. In A.D. 260 they humiliated the Romans by actually taking the Emperor Valerian prisoner; he died in captivity.

On the western and northern frontiers the pressure came not from a well-organized rival empire but from an ever-increasing number of German tribes. Though they had been in contact with the Romans at least since the second century B.C., they had not been much affected by civilization. The men did no agricultural work, confining their activities to hunting, drinking, and fighting. They were organized on a family basis by clans, hundreds, and tribes led by chiefs, usually from a royal family, elected by the assembly of fighting men. The king was surrounded by a collection of warriors who were his personal retainers and warriors whom the Romans called his *comitatus*. These tough barbarians were always eager for plunder and were much attracted by the civilized delights they knew existed beyond the frontier of the Rhine and the Danube rivers.

The most aggressive of the Germans in the third century were the Goths. Centuries earlier they had wandered from their ancestral home near the Baltic Sea into the area of southern Russia. In the 220s and 230s they began to put pressure on the Danube frontier, and by about A.D. 250 they were able to penetrate into the empire and overrun the Balkan provinces. The need to meet this threat and the one posed by the Persian Sassanids in the east made the Romans weaken their western frontiers, and other Germanic peoples—the Franks and the Alemanni—broke through in those regions. There was a considerable danger that Rome would be unable to meet this challenge.

Changes in the Roman Army

Rome's perils were caused, no doubt, by the unprecedentedly numerous and simultaneous attacks against her,

ABOVE: Romans fighting barbarians. This relief on a sarcophagus shows a battle between the Romans and an army of unidentified barbarians. Its date is about 250, and the general in the central portion is thought to be the son of Emperor Decius. It is now in the Museo delle Terme in Rome. [Copyright by Leonard von Matt.]

LEFT: The Aurelian wall. This is part of the system of walls built around Rome by Emperor Aurelian beginning in A.D. 271. Intended to defend the city from Barbarian attack, it was made of brick, was twelve feet thick, and was equipped with sally ports and artillery towers. [Editorial Photocolor Archives.]

but Rome's internal weakness encouraged them. The Roman army was not what it had been in its best days. By the second century it was made up mostly of Romanized provincials. The pressure on the frontiers and epidemics of plague in the time of Marcus Aurelius forced the emperor to resort to the conscription of slaves, gladiators, barbarians, and brigands. These were emergency measures, but as time passed, the army was made up of an increasingly high percentage of soldiers who were barbarians in background and way of life. They were attracted less by the goal of achieving citizenship and a place in Roman society than by gifts from the emperors and the prospect of gaining wealth and power.

Septimius Severus (emperor A.D. 193–211) and his successors played a crucial role in the transformation of the character of the Roman army. Septimius was a mili-

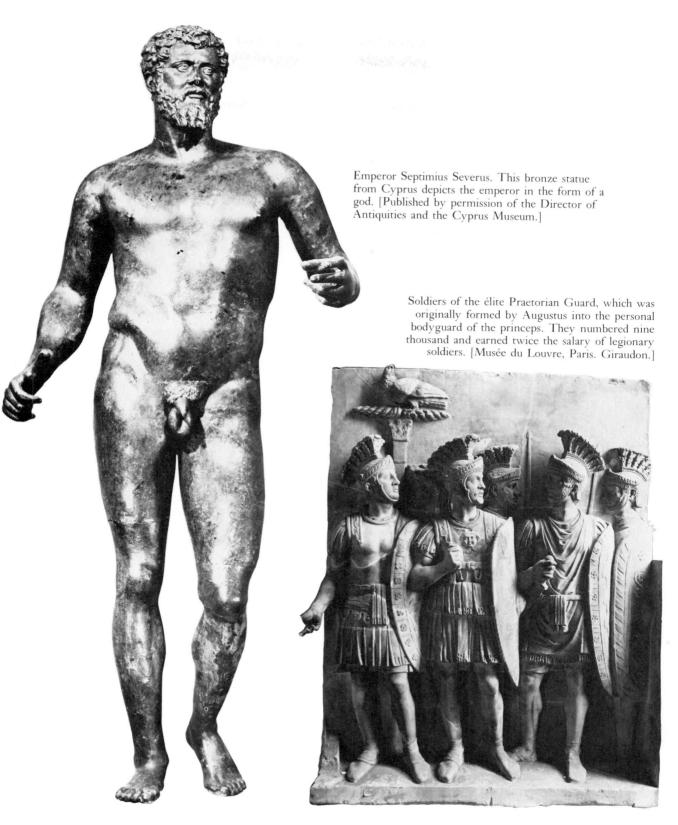

Emperor Septimius Severus. This bronze statue from Cyprus depicts the emperor in the form of a god. [Published by permission of the Director of Antiquities and the Cyprus Museum.]

Soldiers of the élite Praetorian Guard, which was originally formed by Augustus into the personal bodyguard of the princeps. They numbered nine thousand and earned twice the salary of legionary soldiers. [Musée du Louvre, Paris. Giraudon.]

tary usurper who owed everything to the support of his soldiers. He meant to establish a family dynasty, in contrast to the policy of the "good emperors" of the second century, and he was prepared to make Rome into an undisguised military monarchy. The Praetorian Guard, formerly recruited from Italians and thoroughly Romanized provincials, was now open to all. Being a praetorian was preliminary to receiving a commission as a centurion in the army, and veteran centurions and their sons became members of the equestrian class. Depending on one's point of view, the new policy opened the way either for a new democracy or for a new barbarism in the Roman army and state. Whatever the emperor's intention, the chief result was to barbarize the army. Its men were drawn increasingly from peasants from the less civilized provinces.

Septimius introduced other changes that were no less important. Soldiers were permitted to marry while still on active service and to form their own social clubs. Rather than being quartered in military camps, they were stationed in cities, where discipline was notoriously lax. Septimius used soldiers for nonmilitary purposes. They pastured their own flocks and grew their own crops. They manufactured bricks, timber, and weapons for the army's use and sold the surplus to civilians. They did police duty and served as administrators, judges, tax collectors, and civil servants of every description. The result was to reduce the number of troops fit for combat and to reduce the effectiveness even of those who were supposed to fight.

Economic Difficulties

These changes responded to the great financial needs caused by the barbarian attacks. Inflation had forced Commodus to raise the soldiers' pay, but the Severan emperors had to double it to keep up with prices, which increased the imperial budget by as much as 25 per cent. The emperors resorted to inventing new taxes, debasing the coinage, and even to selling the palace furniture, to raise money. Even then it was hard to recruit troops, and

Lactantius Denounces the Reforms of Diocletian

Lactantius (A.D. 256–330) was a North African Christian convert who became one of the most powerful defenders of and apologists for the growing religion. This selection, though full of a burning hatred for Emperor Diocletian, the instigator of a persecution of the Christians, is an important source for the reforms he introduced during his reign as emperor from 284 to 305.

WHILE *Diocletian, who was the inventor of wicked deeds and the contriver of evils, was ruining everything, he could not keep his hands even from God. This man, through both avarice and cowardice, overturned the whole world. For he made three men sharers of his rule; the world was divided into four parts, and armies were multiplied, each of the rulers striving to have a far larger number of soldiers than former emperors had had when the state was ruled by single emperors. The number of those receiving [pay from the state] was so much larger than the number of those paying [taxes] that, because of the enormous size of the assessments, the resources of the tenant farmers were exhausted, fields were abandoned, and cultivated areas were transformed into wilderness. And to fill everything with fear, the provinces also were cut into bits; many governors and more minor offices lay like incubi over each region and almost on every municipality, likewise many procurators of revenues, administrators, and deputy prefects. Very few civil cases came before all of these, but only condemnations and frequent confiscations, and there were not merely frequent but perpetual exactions of innumerable things, and in the process of exaction intolerable wrongs.*

Whatever was imposed with a view to the maintenance of the soldiery might have been endured; but Diocletian, with insatiable avarice, would never permit the treasury to be diminished. He was constantly accumulating extraordinary resources and funds so as to preserve what he had stored away untouched and inviolate. Likewise, when by various iniquities he brought about enormously high prices, he attempted to legislate the prices of commodities. Then much blood was spilled . . . nothing appeared on the market because of fear, and prices soared much higher. In the end, after many people had lost their lives, it became absolutely necessary to repeal the law.

Lactantius, *On the Death of the Persecutors*, in N. Lewis and M. Reinhold, *Roman Civilization*, Vol. 2 (New York: Columbia University Press, 1955), pp. 458–459.

the new style of military life introduced by Septimius—with its laxer discipline, more pleasant duties, and greater opportunity for advancement, not only in the army but in Roman society—was needed to attract men into the army. The policy proved effective for a short time but could not prevent the chaos of the late third century.

The same forces that caused problems for the army did great damage to society at large. The shortage of manpower reduced agricultural production. As external threats distracted the emperors, they were less able to preserve domestic peace. Piracy, brigandage, and the neglect of roads and harbors all hampered trade. So, too, did the debasement of the coinage and the inflation in general. Imperial exactions and confiscations of the property of the rich removed badly needed capital from productive use. More and more the government was required to demand services that had been given gladly in the past. Because the empire lived on a hand-to-mouth basis, with no significant reserve fund and no system of credit financing, the emperors were led to compel the people to supply food, supplies, money, and labor. The upper classes in the cities were made to serve as administrators without pay and to meet deficits in revenue out of their own pockets. Sometimes these demands caused provincial rebellions, as in Egypt and Gaul. More typically they caused peasants and even town administrators to flee to escape their burdens. The result of all these difficulties was to weaken Rome's economic strength when it was most needed.

The Social Order

The new conditions caused important changes in the social order. The Senate and the traditional ruling class were decimated by direct attacks from hostile emperors and by economic losses. Their ranks were filled by men coming up through the army. The whole state, began to take on an increasingly military appearance. Distinctions among the classes by dress had been traditional since the republic, but in the third and fourth centuries they developed to the point where one's everyday clothing was a kind of uniform that precisely revealed his status. Titles were assigned to ranks in society as to ranks in the army, although they were more grandiloquent. The most important distinction was the one formally established by Septimius Severus, which drew a sharp line between the *honestiores* (senators, equestrians, the municipal aristocracy, and the soldiers) and the lower classes or *humiliores*. In a sharp departure from the principle of Roman law that treated all men equally, Septimius gave the *honestiores* a privileged position before the law. They were given lighter punishments, could not be tortured, and alone had the right of appeal to the emperor.

As time passed, it became more difficult to move from the lower order to the higher, another example of the growing rigidity of the late Roman Empire. Peasants were tied to their lands, artisans to their crafts, soldiers to the army, merchants and shipowners to the needs of the state, and citizens of the municipal upper class to the collection and payment of increasingly burdensome taxes. Freedom and private initiative gave way before the needs of the state and its ever-expanding control of its citizens.

Civil Disorder

Commodus was killed on the last day of A.D. 192, and the succeeding year was like the year 69. Three emperors ruled in swift succession, Septimius Severus emerging, as we have seen, to establish firm rule and a dynasty. The death of Alexander Severus, the last of the dynasty, in A.D. 235 brought on a half century of internal anarchy and foreign invasion. In the endless civil wars, eighteen emperors ruled along with eight designated colleagues, and of the twenty-six only one died a quiet death. Perhaps the nadir of this period came in the reign of Gallienus (A.D. 253–268). He was co-emperor with his father, Valerian, until the latter's capture by the Persians in A.D. 260. As sole emperor Gallienus immediately faced uprisings by many pretenders to the throne in various provinces. Most of these so-called "thirty tyrants" were quickly put down, but one of them united Gaul with Spain and Britain and declared himself "Emperor of the

Emperor Gallienus (253–268). He was co-emperor with Valerian until the latter's defeat and capture by the Persians. His bust is in the Museo delle Terme, Rome. [Alinari/SCALA.]

Gauls," and Gallienus could do nothing about it. At the same time German tribes made their way into the empire.

The empire seemed on the point of collapse, but the two conspirators who overthrew and then succeeded Gallienus were able soldiers. Claudius II Gothicus (A.D. 268–270) and Aurelian (A.D. 270–275) drove back the barbarians and stamped out internal disorder. The soldiers who followed Aurelian on the throne were good fighters and made significant changes in Rome's system of defense. They built heavy walls around the city of Rome, Athens, and other cities that could resist barbarian attack. They drew back their best troops from the frontiers, relying chiefly on a newly organized heavy cavalry and a mobile army near the emperor's own residence. Hereafter the army was composed largely of mercenaries who came from among the least civilized provincials and even from among the Germans. The officers gave per-

sonal loyalty to the emperor rather than to the empire. These officers became a foreign, hereditary caste of aristocrats that increasingly supplied high administrators and even emperors. In effect, the Roman people hired an army of mercenaries, only technically Roman, to protect them.

The Fourth Century and Imperial Reorganization

The period from Diocletian (A.D. 284–305) to Constantine (A.D. 306–337) was one of reconstruction and reorganization after a time of civil war and turmoil. Diocletian was an Illyrian of undistinguished birth who rose to the throne through the ranks of the army. He knew that he was not a great general and that the job of defending and governing the entire empire was too great for one man. He therefore introduced the tetrarchy, the rule of the empire by four men with power divided on a territorial basis. Diocletian allotted the provinces of Thrace, Asia, and Egypt to himself. His co-emperor Maximian shared with him the title of Augustus and governed Italy, Africa, and Spain. In addition, two men were given the subordinate title of Caesar: Galerius, who was in charge of the Danube frontier and the Balkans, and Constantius, who governed Britain and Gaul. This arrangement not only provided a good solution to the military problem but also provided for a peaceful succession. Diocletian was recognized as the senior Augustus, but each was supreme in his own sphere. The Caesars were recognized as successors to each half of the empire, and their loyalty was enhanced by marriages to daughters

Emperor Valerian (253–260) surrendering to Shapur I. This is a relief carved into a rock near the ancient Persian city of Persepolis. It commemorates the victory in 260 over the Romans by Shapur I of the Sassanid dynasty of Persian kings. Kneeling before Shapur is the chained Roman emperor, who soon died in captivity. [AHM.]

The Historia Augusta Describes Third Century Military Discipline

Historia Augusta is the name given to a collection of lives of the Roman emperors from Hadrian to Numerian (A.D. 117–284). The collection dates from the fourth century and the authors are unknown. The following selection is from the life of Aurelian who reigned from 270 to 275.

Aurelian *was so feared by the soldiers that, under him, after offenses had once been punished by him in the camp with the utmost severity, no one offended again. . . . There is a letter of his, truly that of a soldier, written to his deputy as follows: "If you wish to be a tribune, or rather if you wish to remain alive, restrain the hands of your soldiers. None shall steal another's fowl or touch his sheep. None shall carry off grapes, or thresh out grain, or exact oil, salt, or firewood, and each shall be content with his own allowance. Let them have these things from the booty taken from the enemy and not from the tears of the provincials. Their arms shall be kept burnished, their implements bright, their boots stout. Let old uniforms be replaced by new. Let them keep their pay in their belts and not spend it in public houses. Let them wear their collars, arm rings, and finger rings. Let each man curry his own horse and baggage animal, let no one sell the fodder allowed him for his beast, and let them take care in common of the mule belonging to the century. Let one yield obedience to another as to a master, and no one as a slave, let them be attended by physicians without charge, let them give no fees to soothsayers, let them conduct themselves in their lodgings with propriety, and let anyone who begins a brawl be thrashed."*

"Historia Augusta," *Life of Aurelian,* in N. Lewis and M Reinhold, *Roman Civilization,* Vol. 2 (New York: Columbia University Press, 1955), p. 423.

The Tetrarchs. This porphyry sculpture on the corner of the church of San Marco in Venice depicts Emperor Diocletian (284–305) and his three imperial colleagues. They are in battle dress and clasp one another to express solidarity. This fourth-century sculpture was part of the booty brought back by the Venetians from their capture of Constantinople during the Fourth Crusade about nine hundred years later. [AHM.]

of the Augusti. It was a return, in a way, to the happy precedent of the "good emperors," who chose their successors from the ranks of the ablest men, and it seemed to promise orderly and peaceful transitions instead of assassinations, chaos, and civil war.

Each man established his residence and capital at a place convenient for frontier defense, and none chose Rome. The effective capital of Italy became the northern city of Milan. Diocletian beautified Rome by constructing his monumental baths, but he visited the city only once and made his own capital at Nicomedia in Bithynia. This was another step in the long leveling process that

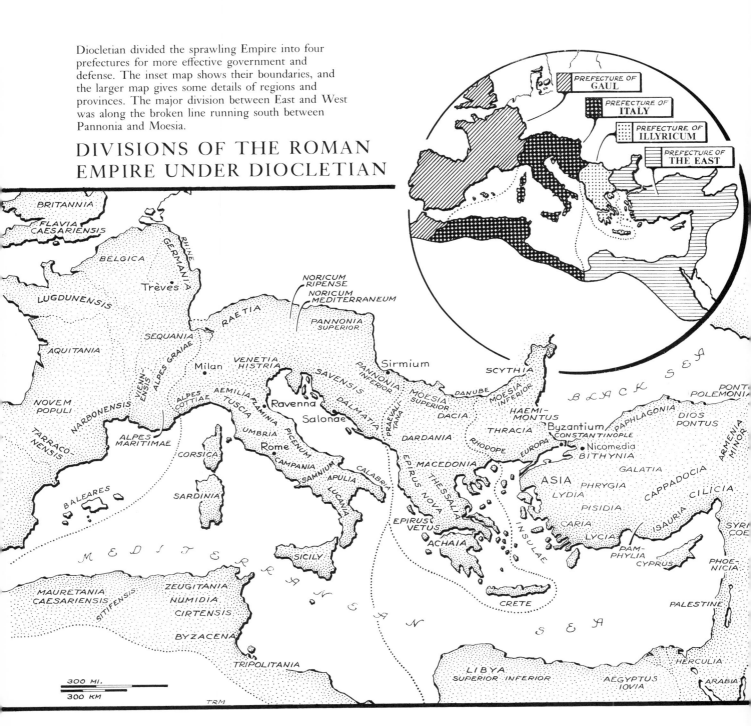

Diocletian divided the sprawling Empire into four
prefectures for more effective government and
defense. The inset map shows their boundaries, and
the larger map gives some details of regions and
provinces. The major division between East and West
was along the broken line running south between
Pannonia and Moesia.

DIVISIONS OF THE ROMAN
EMPIRE UNDER DIOCLETIAN

PREFECTURE OF
GAUL

PREFECTURE OF
ITALY

PREFECTURE OF
ILLYRICUM

PREFECTURE OF
THE EAST

BRITANNIA

FLAVIA
CAESARIENSIS

BELGICA

GERMANIA

RHINE

Trèves

LUGDUNENSIS

RAETIA

NORICUM
RIPENSE

NORICUM
MEDITERRANEUM

PANNONIA
SUPERIOR

SEQUANIA

AQUITANIA

ALPES GRAIAE

VIENN-
ENSIS

VENETIA
HISTRIA

Milan

SAVENSIS

PANNONIA
INFERIOR

Sirmium

SCYTHIA

BLACK SEA

DANUBE

MOESIA
SUPERIOR

MOESIA
INFERIOR

PONT
POLEMONIA

NOVEM
POPULI

NARBONENSIS

ALPES
COTTIAE

AEMILIA

FLAMINIA

TUSCIA

Ravenna

DALMATIA

PRAEVALI-
TANA

Salonae

DACIA

HAEMI-
MONTUS

PAPHLAGONIA

DIOS
PONTUS

ARMENIA
MINOR

TARRACO-
NENSIS

ALPES
MARITIMAE

UMBRIA

PICENUM

Rome

DARDANIA

RHODOPE

THRACIA

Byzantium
CONSTANTINOPLE

EUROPA

Nicomedia
BITHYNIA

GALATIA

CAPPADOCIA

CILICIA

CORSICA

CAMPANIA

SAMNIUM

APULIA

CALABRA

LUCANIA

MACEDONIA

ASIA

PHRYGIA

LYDIA

PISIDIA

ISAURIA

SYRI
COE

BALEARES

SARDINIA

EPIRUS
NOVA

THESSALIA

CARIA

LYCIA

PAM-
PHYLIA

CYPRUS

PHOE-
NICIA

MEDITERRANEAN

SICILY

EPIRUS
VETUS

ACHAIA

INSULAE

MAURETANIA
CAESARIENSIS

SITIFENSIS

ZEUGITANIA
NUMIDIA
CIRTENSIS

BYZACENA

CRETE

SEA

PALESTINE

TRIPOLITANIA

HERCULIA

300 MI.

300 KM

TRM

LIBYA
SUPERIOR   INFERIOR

AEGYPTUS
IOVIA

ARABIA

had reduced the eminence of Rome and Italy, and it was also evidence of the growing importance of the east.

In 305 Diocletian retired and compelled his co-emperor to do the same. But his plan for a smooth succession failed completely. In 310 there were five Augusti and no Caesars. Out of this chaos Constantine, son of Constantius, produced order. In 324 he defeated his last opponent and made himself sole emperor, uniting the empire once again; he reigned until 337. For the most part Constantine carried forward the policies of Diocletian. The one exception was his support of Christianity, which Diocletian had tried to suppress. In all other respects, however, the work of the two emperors is so complementary and continuous that our sources do not always tell us which emperor introduced each regulation.

The development of the imperial office toward autocracy was carried to the extreme by Diocletian and Constantine. The emperor ruled by decree, consulting only a few high officials whom he himself appointed. The Senate had no role whatever, and its dignity was further diminished by the elimination of all distinction between senator and equestrian.

The emperor was a remote figure surrounded by carefully chosen high officials. He lived in a great palace and was almost unapproachable. Those admitted to his presence had to prostrate themselves before him and kiss the hem of his robe, which was purple and had golden threads going through it. The emperor was addressed as *dominus* ("lord"), and his right to rule was not derived from the Roman people but from God. All this remoteness and ceremony had a double purpose: to enhance the dignity of the emperor and to safeguard him against assassination.

Constantine erected the new city of Constantinople on the site of ancient Byzantium on the Bosporus, which leads to both the Aegean and Black seas, and made it the new capital of the empire. Its strategic location was excellent for protecting the eastern and Danubian frontiers, and, surrounded on three sides by water, it was easily defended. It also made it easier to carry forward the policies of fostering autocracy and Christianity. Rome was full of tradition, the center of senatorial and even republican memories and of pagan worship. Constantinople was free from both, and its dedication in 330 marked the beginning of a new era. Until its fall to the Turks in 1453, it served as the bastion of civilization, the preserver of classical culture, a bulwark against barbarian attack, and the greatest city in Christendom.

The autocratic rule of the emperors was carried out by a civilian bureaucracy, which was carefully separated from the military service to reduce the chances of rebellion by anyone combining the two kinds of power. Below the emperor's court the most important officials were the praetorian prefects, each of whom administered one of the four major areas into which the empire was divided: Gaul, Italy, Illyricum, and the Orient. The four prefectures were subdivided into twelve territorial units called *dioceses*, each under a vicar who was subordinate to the prefect. The dioceses were further divided into almost a hundred provinces, each under a provincial governor.

The operation of the entire system was supervised by a vast system of spies and secret police, without whom the increasingly rigid totalitarian organization could not be trusted to perform. In spite of these efforts, the system was filled with corruption and inefficiency.

The cost of maintaining a 400,000-man army as well as the vast civilian bureaucracy, the expensive imperial court, and the imperial taste for splendid buildings put a great strain on an already weak economy. Diocletian's attempts at establishing a uniform and reliable currency failed and merely led to increased inflation. To deal with it, he resorted to price control with his Edict of Maximum Prices in 301. For each product and each kind of labor a maximum price was set, and violations were punishable by death. The edict failed despite the harshness of its provisions.

Peasants unable to pay their taxes and officials unable to collect them tried to escape, and Diocletian resorted to stern regimentation to keep everyone in his place and at the service of the government. The terror of the third

ABOVE: Diocletian's palace at Spalato. Emperor Diocletian (284–305) was a native of Dalmatia, the section of eastern Adriatic coast in what is now Yugoslavia. In the town now called Split he built a palace at the edge of the sea, to which he retired after his abdication in 305; this is a model of it. It is a fortress modeled on the Roman military camp. His mausoleum is the prominent octagonal structure in the right center. [Alinari/SCALA.]

RIGHT: Model of a late Roman fortress at Deuta, near Cologne, in Germany. It was built by Constantine in 310 to protect a bridge across the Rhine. The construction is strikingly similar to some medieval castles. [Alinari/SCALA.]

century had turned many peasants into *coloni*, tenant farmers who fled for protection to the *villa* ("country estate") of a large and powerful landowner. They were tied to the land, as were their descendants, as the caste system hardened.

Division of the Empire

The peace and unity established by Constantine did not last long. His death was followed by a struggle for succession that was won by Constantius II (337–361). His death left the empire to his young cousin Julian (361–363), called by the Christians "the Apostate" because of his attempt to stamp out Christianity and restore paganism. Julian undertook a campaign against Persia with the aim of putting a Roman on the throne of the Sassanids and ending the Persian menace once and for all. He penetrated deep into Persia but was killed in battle. His death put an end to the expedition and to the pagan revival.

The Germans in the west took advantage of the eastern campaign to attack along the Rhine River and the upper Danube River, but even greater trouble was brewing along the middle and upper Danube. That territory was occupied by the eastern Goths, the Ostrogoths. They were being pushed hard by their western cousins, the Visigoths, who in turn had been driven from their home in the Ukraine by the fierce Huns, a nomadic people from central Asia. The Emperor Valentinian (364–375) saw that he could not defend the empire alone and appointed his brother Valens (364–378) as co-ruler. (To provide for the succession, he appointed his own nine-year-old son, Gratian, as Caesar in the west.) Valentinian made his own headquarters at Milan and spent the rest of his life fighting successfully against the Franks and the Alemanni in the west. Valens was given control of the east. The empire was once again divided in two, never really to be united again. The two emperors maintained their own courts, and the two halves of the empire became increasingly separate and different. Latin was the language of the west and Greek of the east.

In 376 the hard-pressed Visigoths asked and received

[*Text continued on page 210*]

RIGHT: The Milvian bridge over the Tiber, built in the second century, where in A.D. 312 Constantine defeated Maxentius to gain control of Rome. [Editorial Photocolor Archives.]

BELOW: Arch of Constantine. The triumphal arch was a characteristic Roman imperial structure, and examples are found throughout the empire. This one at Rome was dedicated by Constantine in 315 in celebration of his victory over Maxentius at the Milvian Bridge. The best of its sculptural and architectural elements were reused from works of earlier centuries.

In the distance, through the center arch, note some remaining arches of a first-century aqueduct, the Aqua Claudia.

Such structures as this arch and the aqueduct illustrate a significant point: With control of their diverse and far-flung empire continually at stake, as an adjunct of its administration, maintenance, safety, and amusement the Romans were immensely practical—almost compulsive—builders and engineers. Their bridges and aqueducts, temples and altars, triumphal arches and columns, theatres and arenas, palaces and villas, roads and government buildings, baths and public housing, harbor facilities, defensive walls, and fortresses were to be found all over the Mediterranean world and set standards that long challenged the West. [Alinari/SCALA.]

The Late Roman Empire

LEFT: Emperor Constantine (307–337). The face, from his colossal statue, is characteristic of sculpture in the late Roman Empire. While often impressive, the work lacks the refinement of earlier periods.

OPPOSITE: Constantine placed a colossal statue of himself, nearly forty feet high, in his monumental basilica near the Roman Forum. These are the remaining pieces of it as displayed in the Palazzo dei Conservatori in Rome. [Copyright by Leonard von Matt.]

RIGHT: A Roman imperial triumph. This relief is from a panel on a triumphal arch erected in honor of Emperor Marcus Aurelius (161–180). The emperor stands in a chariot drawn by four horses and is crowned by the goddess Victory. A trumpeter goes before him on his way to the Capitol. [Alinari/SCALA.]

BELOW: A Roman triumph in the colonies, on a triumphal arch of the third century in the Roman colony of Leptis Magna in Lybia in North Africa. [The British School at Rome.]

permission to enter the empire to escape the Huns. Contrary to the bargain, the Goths kept their weapons and began to plunder the Balkan provinces. Without waiting for help from Gratian, the emperor in the west, Valens attacked the Goths and died, along with most of his army, at Adrianople in Thrace in 378. Gratian could not deal with the new challenge and named Theodosius (379–395), an able and experienced general, his co-ruler in the east. By a combination of military and diplomatic skills Theodosius pacified the Goths, giving them land and a high degree of autonomy and enrolling many of them in his army. He made important military reforms, putting greater emphasis on the cavalry. When Gratian proved unable to maintain his rule in the west, Theodosius reconquered that part of the empire. For a brief moment in 394 there seemed once again to be a unified empire, but in the next year Theodosius died, leaving the empire to be divided between his sons, Arcadius in the east and Honorius in the west.

For the future the two parts of the empire went their separate and different ways. The west became increasingly rural as barbarian invasions continued and grew in intensity. The *villa*, a fortified country estate, became the basic unit of life. There *coloni* gave their services to the local magnate in return for economic assistance and protection from both barbarians and imperial officials. Many cities shrank to no more than tiny walled fortresses ruled by military commanders and bishops. The upper classes moved to the country and asserted ever greater independence of imperial authority. The failure of the central authority to maintain the roads and the constant danger from robber bands sharply curtailed trade and communications, forcing greater self-reliance and a more primitive style of life. The new world emerging in the west by the fifth century and after was increasingly made up of isolated units of rural aristocrats and their dependent laborers. The only institution providing a high degree of unity was the Christian Church. The pattern for the early Middle Ages in the west was already formed.

In the east the situation was quite different. Constanti-

Ammianus Marcellinus Describes the People Called Huns

Ammianus Marcellinus was born about 330 in Syria where Greek was the language of his well-to-do family. After a military career and considerable travel, he lived in Rome and wrote an encyclopedic Latin history of the empire, covering the years 96 to 378 and giving special emphasis to the difficulties of the fourth century. Here he describes the Huns, one of the barbarous peoples pressing on the frontiers.

THE *people called Huns, barely mentioned in ancient records, live beyond the sea of Azof, on the border of the Frozen Ocean, and are a race savage beyond all parallel. At the very moment of birth the cheeks of their infant children are deeply marked by an iron, in order that the hair, instead of growing at the proper season on their faces, may be hindered by the scars; accordingly the Huns grow up without beards, and without any beauty. They all have closely knit and strong limbs and plump necks; they are of great size, and low legged, so that you might fancy them two-legged beasts or the stout figures which are hewn out in a rude manner with an ax on the posts at the end of bridges.*

They are certainly in the shape of men, however uncouth, and are so hardy that they neither require fire nor well-flavored food, but live on the roots of such herbs as they get in the fields, or on the half-raw flesh of any animal, which they merely warm rapidly by placing it between their own thighs and the backs of their horses.

They never shelter themselves under roofed houses, but avoid them, as people ordinarily avoid sepulchers as things not fit for common use. Nor is there even to be found among them a cabin thatched with reeds; but they wander about, roaming over the mountains and the woods, and accustom themselves to bear frost and hunger and thirst from their very cradles. . . .

There is not a person in the whole nation who cannot remain on his horse day and night. On horseback they buy and sell, they take their meat and drink, and there they recline on the narrow neck of their steed, and yield to sleep so deep as to indulge in every variety of dream.

And when any deliberation is to take place on any weighty matter, they all hold their common council on horseback. They are not under kingly authority, but are contented with the irregular government of their chiefs, and under their lead they force their way through all obstacles. . . .

Ammianus Marcellinus, *Res Gestae*, trans. by C. D. Yonge (London: George Bell and Son, 1862), pp. 312–314.

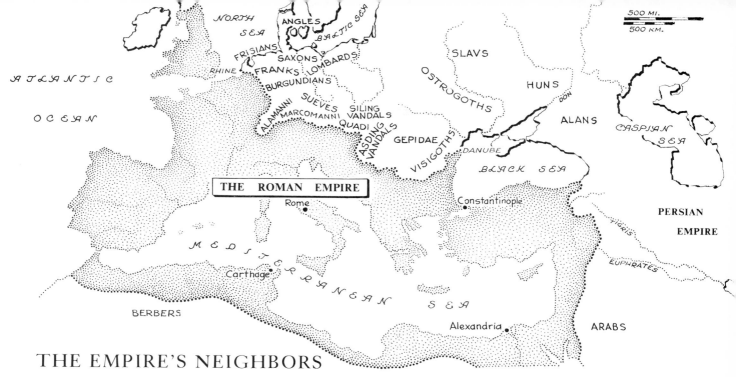

THE EMPIRE'S NEIGHBORS

In the fourth century the Roman Empire was nearly surrounded by ever more threatening neighbors. The map shows who these so-called barbarians were and where they lived before their armed contact with the Romans.

nople became the center of a vital and flourishing culture that we call *Byzantine* and that lasted until the fifteenth century. Because of its defensible location, the skill of its emperors, and the firmness and strength of its base in Asia Minor, it was able to deflect and repulse barbarian attacks. A strong navy allowed commerce to flourish in the eastern Mediterranean and, in good times, far beyond. Cities continued to prosper and the emperors made their will good over the nobles in the countryside. The civilization of the Byzantine Empire was a unique combination of classical culture, the Christian religion, Roman law, and eastern artistic influences. While the west was being overrun by barbarians, the Roman Empire, in altered form, persisted in the east. While Rome shrank to an insignificant ecclesiastical town, Constantinople flourished as the seat of empire, the "New Rome," and the Byzantines called themselves "Romans." When we contemplate the decline and fall of the Roman Empire in the fourth and fifth centuries we are speaking only of the west. A form of classical culture persisted in the Byzantine east for a thousand years more.

The Triumph of Christianity
Religious Currents in the Empire

The rise of Christianity to dominance in the empire was closely connected with the political and cultural experience of the third and fourth centuries. Political chaos and decentralization had religious and cultural consequences. In some of the provinces, native languages replaced Latin and Greek, sometimes even for official

purposes, and the classical tradition that had been the basis of imperial life became the exclusive possession of a small, educated aristocracy. In religion the public cults had grown up in an urban environment and were largely political in character. As the importance of the cities diminished, so did the significance of their gods. People might still take comfort in the worship of the friendly, intimate deities of family, field, hearth, storehouse, and craft, but these were too petty to serve their needs in a confused and frightening world. The only universal worship was of the emperor, but he was far off, and obeisance to his cult was more a political than a religious act.

In the troubled times of the fourth and fifth centuries people sought powerful, personal deities who would bring them safety and prosperity in this world and immortality in the next. Paganism was open and tolerant, and it was by no means unusual for men to worship new deities alongside the old and even to intertwine elements of several to form a new amalgam by the device called *syncretism*. In this way a number of "mystery" religions made their way to Rome, won many adherents, and achieved legitimacy. The cult of Cybele, the great mother (*Magna Mater*), came from Asia Minor and that of Isis from Egypt. Each had become popular by the third century by virtue of its universality and intensely per-

A mosaic from Carthage illustrating aspects of life on the manorial estate of a certain Julian in the province of Africa. His housing, provisions, and entertainment appear to have been opulent. [Musée National du Bardo, Tunis.]

sonal qualities. Anyone, regardless of class, race, or condition, could join and could observe and take part in rituals—often secret; hence the term "mystery"—that included dramatic reenactments of the suffering, death, and resurrection of the god. The mystery cults invited each initiate into a common fellowship and morality, encouraged prayer directly to the god without priestly intervention, and held out the hope of eternal life.

Somewhat different was the cult of Mithras, a religion of Persian origin that came to Rome by way of Asia Minor and achieved special popularity in the Roman army and eventually in the western provinces. Mithras is depicted in all his shrines as capturing and killing a bull, the source of all life. He then receives the homage of the sun god, with whom he shares a sacred meal. Members of the cult were initiated in an elaborate ceremony and shared common meals of bread and drink. They believed that Mithras had taken part in the creation of the world and would come back at the millennium. They followed a prescribed moral code and helped Mithras in the struggle against Ahriman, the god of evil. Mithras determined by their performance whether they would go to heaven or hell after death.

Manichaeism was an especially potent rival of Christianity. Named for its founder, Mani, a Persian who lived in the third century, it contained aspects of various religious traditions, including Zoroastrianism from Persia and both Judaism and Christianity. Like the Gnostics, the Manichaeans were dualists who pictured a world in which light and darkness, good and evil, were constantly at war. Good was spiritual and evil material; because man was made of matter, his body was a prison of evil and darkness, but he also contained an element of light and

The goddess Cybele. She was a mother-goddess from Asia Minor connected with fertility, agriculture, and ecstatic rites. Her cult was brought to Rome during the Republic and given official status. It flourished during the Empire and was one of several major competitors with Christianity for popular favor. This bronze sculpture from Rome shows the goddess enthroned on a cart drawn by lions—the usual representation of her. [Metropolitan Museum of Art, New York; gift of Henry B. Marquand, 1897.]

ABOVE: Mithras sacrificing a bull. The cult of Mithras originated among the Aryans of India and Iran, was brought to Rome late in the first century by the army, in which it was widespread, and became very popular in the second century. It is sometimes thought to have been the chief rival of Christianity. This relief shows Mithras in his central ritual act, killing the bull. Ths sun god is shown on the left. [Cincinnati Art Museum; gift of Mr. and Mrs. Fletcher E. Nyce.]

RIGHT: A shrine of Mithras, one of eleven found at Ostia, the port of the city of Rome. The statue of the god ritually killing the bull is at the far end. [Fototeca Unione.]

good. The "Father of Goodness" had sent Mani, among other prophets, to free man and gain his salvation. To achieve salvation, man must want to reach the realm of light and to abandon all physical desires. Manichaeans led an ascetic life and practiced a simple worship guided by a well-organized church. The movement reached its greatest strength in the fourth and fifth centuries, and some of its central ideas persisted into the Middle Ages.

Obviously Christianity had something in common with these cults and answered many of the same needs felt by their devotees. There can be no doubt that its success owed something to the same causes as accounted for their popularity, and they are often spoken of as its rivals. None of them, however, attained Christianity's universality, and none appears to have given the early Christians and the spokesmen for Christianity as much competition as the ancient philosophies or the state religion.

Christianity offered its adherents everything the mystery cults provided, and more: a god who suffered, died, and was resurrected; mystical and sacred rites; a moral code; community; a close, personal relationship with the deity; and the promise of immortality. Beyond that, the Christians had the Bible, a marvelous book that related the new religion to an ancient tradition, and they had reports of miracles with witnesses to attest to them. They also had an efficient organization under the bishops. Finally, Christianity had the profoundly attractive doctrines of love and the brotherhood of all men under a God represented as loving and forgiving.

Imperial Persecution

By the third century Christianity had taken firm hold in the eastern provinces and in Italy, though it had not made much headway in the west. Christian apologists pointed out that the Christians were good citizens who differed from others only in not worshiping the public gods. Until the middle of the third century the emperors tacitly accepted this view and were tolerant without granting official toleration. As times became bad and the Christians became more numerous and visible, that policy changed. Popular opinion blamed disasters, natural and military, on the Christians. About 250 the Emperor Decius (249–251) invoked the aid of the gods in his war against the Goths and required that all citizens worship the state gods publicly. True Christians could not obey, and Decius instituted a major persecution. Many Christians, even some bishops, yielded to threats and torture, but others held out and were killed. Valerian (253–260) resumed the persecutions, partly in order to confiscate the wealth of rich Christians. His successors, however, found other matters more pressing, and persecution lapsed until the end of the century.

By the time of Diocletian the number of Christians had grown still greater and included some high state officials. At the same time, hostility to the Christians grew on every level. Diocletian was not generous toward unorthodox intellectual or religious movements, and his own effort to bolster imperial power with the aura of divinity boded ill for the church, yet he did not attack the Chris-

tians for almost twenty years. In 303, however, he launched the most serious persecution inflicted on the Christians in the Roman Empire. He issued a series of edicts confiscating church property and destroying churches and their sacred books; he deprived upper-class Christians of public office and judicial rights, imprisoned clergymen, enslaved Christians of the lower classes, and placed heavy fines on anyone refusing to sacrifice to the public gods. A final decree required public sacrifices and libations. The decrees were harsh, and there were many Christian martyrs, but enforcement was by no means uniform. The edict against the upper classes was the one most easily and widely enforced, but the persecution horrified many pagans, and the plight and the demeanor of the martyrs often aroused pity and sympathy. For these reasons, as well as the incapacity of any large ancient state to carry out a program of terror with the thoroughness of modern totalitarian governments, the Christians and their church survived to enjoy what they must have considered a miraculous change of fortune. In 311 Galerius, who had been one of the most vigorous persecutors, was influenced, perhaps by his Christian wife, to issue an edict of toleration permitting Christian worship.

Constantine and Christianity

The victory of Constantine and his emergence as sole ruler of the empire changed the condition of Christianity from a precariously tolerated sect to the religion favored by the emperor and put it on the path to becoming the official and only legal religion in the empire.

It was not until 312, in the midst of his struggle against his rival Maxentius, that Constantine became a champion of Christianity. Before the climactic battle at the Milvian bridge in Rome, he had a dream that made him believe that his subsequent victory was owed to the Christian God. From then on his support of the Christian cause was unfailing. He went far beyond toleration, restoring property to bereft Christians, lending financial support, building churches, exempting the clergy from taxation, granting judicial authority to ecclesiastical courts, helping to define orthodox doctrine, and in many other ways showing his favor. He did not, however, abolish the imperial cult or any part of the pagan state religion. Christians remained a minority of the population.

Emergence of Christianity As the State Religion

The sons of Constantine continued to favor the new religion, but the succession of Julian the Apostate posed a new threat. He was a devotee of traditional classical pagan culture and, as a believer in Neoplatonism, an opponent of Christianity. Neoplatonism was a religious philosophy, or a philosophical religion, whose connection with Platonic teachings was distant. Its chief formulator was Plotinus (A.D. 205–270), who attempted to combine classical and rational philosophical speculation with the mystical spirit of his time. Plotinus' successors were bitter critics of Christianity, and Julian was influenced by their views. Though he refrained from persecution, he tried to undo the work of Constantine by withdrawing the privileges of the Church, removing Christians from high offices, and attempting to introduce a new form of pagan worship. His reign, however, was short, and his work did not last. In 375 the emperor Gratian abandoned the pagan title of *Pontifex Maximus;* later he withdrew financial support for the pagan festivals. Finally, amidst great controversy, he removed the altar of the goddess Victory from the Senate House in Rome. Argument about this symbolic act continued for years, but in 394 Theodosius forbade the celebration of pagan cults and abolished the pagan religious calendar. At the death of Theodosius, Christianity was the official religion of the Roman Empire.

The establishment of Christianity as the state religion did not put an end to the troubles of the Christians and their church; instead it created new ones and complicated some that were old. The favored position of the church attracted converts for the wrong reasons and diluted the moral excellence and spiritual fervor of its adherents. The

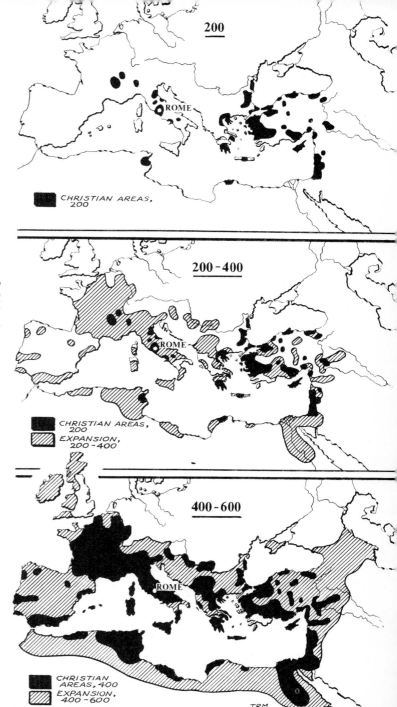

CHRISTIAN AREAS, 200

CHRISTIAN AREAS, 200
EXPANSION, 200-400

CHRISTIAN AREAS, 400
EXPANSION, 400-600

THE SPREAD OF CHRISTIANITY

Christianity grew swiftly in the third, fourth, fifth, and sixth centuries—especially after the conversion of the emperors in the fourth century. By 600, on the eve of the birth of Mohammed's new Moslem religion, Christianity was dominant throughout the Mediterranean world and most of Western Europe. But losses were in store in the next few centuries.

The Triumph of Christianity 215

problem of the relationship between church and state arose, presenting the possibility that religion would become subordinate to the state, as it had been in the classical world and in earlier civilizations. In the east that is what happened to a considerable degree. In the west the weakness of the emperors prevented such a development and permitted church leaders to exercise remarkable independence. In 390 Ambrose, bishop of Milan, excommunicated Emperor Theodosius for a massacre he had carried out, and the emperor did humble penance. This act provided an important precedent for future assertions of the church's autonomy and authority, but it did not put an end to secular interference and influence in the church by any means.

The Council of Nicaea. This painting in the Vatican by Giovanni Speranza, a sixteenth-century artist, is an imaginative and dramatic portrayal of the council of Christian bishops in 325 that established an orthodox creed and condemned the Arian heresy. Constantine himself presided. Nicaea is in Asia Minor not far from the place where Constantinople was to be built. [SCALA/Editorial Photocolor Archives.]

Arianism and the Council of Nicaea

Internal divisions proved to be even more troubling as new heresies emerged. Because they threatened the unity of an empire that was now Christian, they took on a political character and inevitably involved the emperor and the powers of the state. Before long the world could view Christians persecuting other Christians with a zeal at least as great as had been displayed against them by the most fanatical pagans.

Among the many controversial views that arose, the most important and the most threatening was Arianism, founded by a priest named Arius of Alexandria (ca. 280–336) in the fourth century. The issue creating difficulty was the relation of God the Father and God the Son. Arius argued that Jesus was a created being, unlike God the Father. He was, therefore, not made of the substance of God and was not eternal. "The Son has a beginning," he said, "but God is without beginning." For Arius, Jesus was neither fully man nor fully God but something in between. His view did away with the mysterious concept of the Trinity, the difficult doctrine that

God is three persons—the Father, the Son, and the Holy Spirit—at the same time that he is one in substance and essence. The Arian concept had the advantage of appearing simple, rational, and philosophically acceptable, but to its ablest opponent, Athanasius, it had serious shortcomings. Athanasius (ca. 293–373), later bishop of Alexandria, saw the Arian view as an impediment to any acceptable theory of salvation, to him the most important religious question. He adhered to the old Greek idea of salvation as involving the change of sinful mortality into divine immortality through the gift of "life." Only if Jesus were both fully man and fully God could the transformation of humanity to divinity have taken place in him and be transmitted by him to his disciples. "Christ was made man," he said, "that we might be made divine."

To deal with the growing controversy, Constantine called a council of Christian bishops at Nicaea, not far from Constantinople, in 325. For the emperor the question was essentially political, but for the disputants salvation was at stake. At Nicaea the view expounded by Athanasius won out and became orthodox and was embodied in the Nicene Creed. But Arianism persisted and spread. Some later emperors were either Arians or sympathetic to that view. Some of the most successful missionaries to the barbarians were Arians, with the result that many of the German tribes who overran the empire were Arians. The Christian emperors hoped to bring unity to their increasingly decentralized realms by imposing the single religion, and over time it did prove to be a unifying force, but it also introduced new divisions where none had existed before.

Arts and Letters in the Late Empire

The art and literature of the late empire reflect the confluence of pagan and Christian ideas and traditions as well as the conflict between them. Much of the literature is of a polemical nature and much of the art is propaganda. At the same time, the great social changes that began to accelerate in the third century had parallel effects.

The salvation of the empire from the chaos of the third century was accomplished by a military revolution based on and led by provincials whose origins were in the lower classes. They brought with them the fresh winds of cultural change, which blew out not only the dust of classical culture but much of its substance as well. Yet the new ruling class was not interested in leveling but wanted instead to establish itself as a new aristocracy. It thought of itself as effecting a great restoration rather than a revolution and sought to restore classical culture and absorb it. The confusion and uncertainty of the times were tempered in part, of course, by the comfort of

Christianity, but the new ruling class sought order and stability—ethical, literary, and artistic—in the classical tradition as well.

The culture of late antiquity has often been considered decadent and incompetent, and it is true that the disturbances of the troubled times must have interfered with patronage and brought about some decline in technique. But far more important in explaining the changes are the changed conditions of society, the changed needs of its people and of their outlook on the world. The culture of late antiquity was transitional, looking back to the classical heritage and forward to the medieval world.

The Preservation of Classical Culture

One of the main needs and accomplishments of this period was the preservation of classical culture and the discovery of ways to make it available and useful to the newly arrived ruling class. The great classical authors were reproduced in many copies, and their works were transferred from perishable and inconvenient papyrus rolls to sturdier codices that were as easy to use as modern books. Scholars also digested long works like Livy's *History of Rome* into shorter versions and wrote learned commentaries and compiled grammars. Original works by pagan writers of the late empire were neither numerous nor especially distinguished. The most noteworthy literary effort by a pagan in this period was the history of the Roman Empire from A.D. 96 to 378 written by Ammianus Marcellinus (born *ca.* 330). It is written in a lively narrative style and is remarkable for its honesty and dispassionate approach to recent and even contemporary events. Only the part covering the years 353–378 is extant.

Christian Writers

Of Christian writings, on the other hand, the late empire saw a great outpouring. There were many examples of Christian apologetics in poetry as well as in prose, and there were sermons, hymns, and biblical commentaries. Christianity could also boast important scholars. Jerome (348–420), thoroughly trained in both the east and the west in classical Latin literature and rhetoric, produced a revised version of the Bible in Latin, commonly called the Vulgate, which became the Bible used by the Catholic Church. Probably the most important eastern scholar was Eusebius of Caesarea (*ca.* 260–*ca.* 340). He wrote apologetics; an idealized, hagiographic biography of Constantine; and a valuable attempt to reconstruct the chronology of important events in the past. His most important contribution, however, was his *Ecclesiastical History*, an attempt to set forth the Christian view of history. He saw all of history as the working out of God's will. All of history, therefore, had a purpose and a direction, and Constantine's victory and the subsequent unity of empire and church were its culmination.

It must be emphasized that the great Christian writers were educated in the classical tradition, and they easily overcame qualms they may have felt in using classical writers for Christian purposes. Jerome used Cicero's works on law and ethics to bolster his own arguments, and Lactantius (*ca.* 250–317), the greatest of Latin apologists and himself called "the Christian Cicero," was a professor of classical rhetoric before his conversion to Christianity. In his *Divine Institutes,* a treatise aimed at educated pagans, he argued that far from being the enemy of classical civilization, Christian revelation was the only hope for its salvation and that of the Roman Empire from the attacks of the barbarians.

AUGUSTINE OF HIPPO. The closeness and also the complexity of the relationship between classical pagan culture and that of the Christianity of the late empire is nowhere better displayed than in the career and writings of Augustine (354–430), bishop of Hippo in north Africa. He was born at Carthage and was trained as a teacher of rhetoric. His father was a pagan, but his mother was a Christian and hers was ultimately the stronger influence. He passed through a number of intellectual way stations, skepticism and Neoplatonism among others, before his conversion to Christianity. His training and skill in pagan rhetoric and philosophy made him

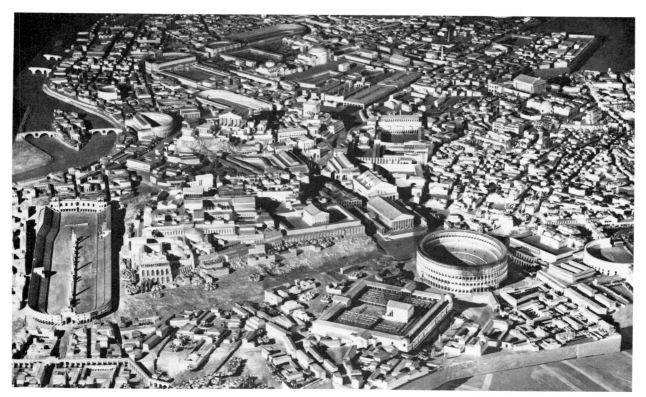

Imperial Rome. This is a model of a reconstruction of the city of Rome during the imperial period. At the left is the Circus Maximus; on the lower right is the Colosseum; and the Forum is just above the exact center of the picture. The model is in the Museo della Civiltà Romana. [Bettmann Archive.]

peerless among contemporaries as a defender of Christianity and as a theologian. His greatest works are his *Confessions,* an autobiography describing the road to his conversion, and *The City of God.* The latter was a response to the pagan charge that Rome's sack by the Goths in 410 was caused by the abandonment of the old gods and the advent of Christianity. The optimistic view held by some Christians that God's will worked its way in history and was easily comprehensible needed further support in the face of this disaster. Augustine sought to separate the fate of Christianity from that of the Roman Empire. He contrasted the secular world, the City of Man, with the spiritual, the City of God. The former was selfish, the latter unselfish; the former evil, the latter good. Augustine argued that history was moving forward, in the spiritual sense, to the Day of Judgment but that there was no reason to expect improvement before then in the secular sphere. The fall of Rome was neither surprising nor important, for all states, even a Christian Rome, were part of the City of Man and therefore corrupt and mortal. Only the City of God was immortal,

and it, consisting of all the saints on earth and in heaven, was untouched by earthly calamities.

Though the *Confessions* and the *City of God* are Augustine's most famous works, they emphasize only a part of his thought. His treatises *On the Trinity* and *On Christian Education* reveal the great skill with which he supported Christian belief with the learning, logic, and philosophy of the pagan classics. His writings constantly reveal the presence of both Christian faith and pagan reason and the tension between them, a legacy he left to the Middle Ages.

Problem of the Decline and Fall of the Empire in the West

Whether important to Augustine or not, the massive barbarian invasions of the fifth century put an end to effective imperial government in the west. For centuries people have speculated about the causes of the collapse of the ancient world. Every kind of reason has been put forward, and some suggestions seem to have nothing to do with reason at all. Soil exhaustion, plague, climatic change, and even poisoning caused by lead water pipes have been suggested as reasons for Rome's decline in manpower, vigor, and the capacity to defend herself. Some blame the institution of slavery and the failure to make advances in science and technology that they believe resulted from it. Others blame excessive government interference in the economic life of the empire, others the destruction of the urban middle class, the carrier of classical culture.

Perhaps a plausible explanation can be found that is more simple and obvious. It might begin with the observation that the growth of so mighty an empire as Rome's was by no means inevitable. Rome's greatness had come from conquests that provided the Romans with the means to expand still further, until there were not enough Romans to conquer and govern any more peoples and territory. When pressure from outsiders grew, the Romans lacked the resources to advance and defeat the enemy as in the past. The tenacity and success of their resistance for so long is remarkable. Without new conquests to provide the immense wealth needed for the defense and maintenance of internal prosperity, the Romans finally yielded to unprecedented onslaughts by fierce and numerous attackers.

To blame the ancients and the institution of slavery for the failure to produce an industrial and economic revolution like that of the modern world, one capable of producing wealth without taking it from another, is to stand the problem on its head. No one yet has a satisfactory explanation for those revolutions, so it is improper to blame any institution or society for not achieving what has been achieved only once in human history, in what are still mysterious circumstances. Perhaps we would do well to think of the problem as Gibbon did:

> The decline of Rome was the natural and inevitable effect of immoderate greatness. Prosperity ripened the principle of decay; the cause of the destruction multiplied with the extent of conquest; and, as soon as time or accident had removed the artificial supports, the stupendous fabric yielded to the pressure of its own weight. The story of the ruin is simple and obvious; and instead of inquiring why the Roman Empire was destroyed, we should rather be surprised that it had subsisted so long.[1]

1 Edward Gibbon, *Decline and Fall of the Roman Empire,* J. B. Bury, ed., 2nd ed., vol. 4 (London, 1909), pp. 173–174.

SUGGESTED READINGS

P. Brown, *Augustine of Hippo* (Berkeley, 1967). A splendid biography.

P. Brown, *The World of Late Antiquity, A.D. 150–750* (London, 1971). A brilliant and readable essay.

J. Burckhardt, *The Age of Constantine the Great* (New York, 1956). A classic work by the Swiss cultural historian.

J. B. Bury, *The Invasion of Europe by the Barbarians* (London, 1928).

C. M. Cochrane, *Christianity and Classical Culture* (New York, 1957). A study of intellectual change in the late empire.

S. Dill, *Roman Society in the Last Century of the Western Empire* (New York, 1958).

E. R. Dodds, *Pagan and Christian in an Age of Anxiety* (Cambridge, 1965). An original and perceptive study.

J. Ferguson, *The Religions of the Roman Empire* (Ithaca, 1970).

E. Gibbon, *The History of the Decline and Fall of the Roman Empire,* 7 vols., ed. by J. B. Bury, 2nd ed. (London, 1909–1914). One of the masterworks of the English language.

M. Grant, *The Fall of the Roman Empire: A Reappraisal* (London, 1976). An interesting interpretation of the fall of Rome that emphasizes social disunity as a cause.

A. H. M. Jones, *Constantine and the Conversion of Europe* (London, 1948).

A. H. M. Jones, *The Later Roman Empire,* 3 vols. (Oxford, 1964). A comprehensive study of the period.

D. Kagan (editor), *The End of the Roman Empire: Decline or Transformation?,* 2nd ed. (Lexington, Massachusetts, 1978). A collection of essays discussing the problem of the decline and fall of the Roman Empire.

F. Lot, *The End of the Ancient World and the Beginnings of the Middle Ages* (New York, 1961). A study that emphasizes gradual transition rather than abrupt change.

R. Macmullen, *Soldier and Civilian in the Later Roman Empire* (Cambridge, Mass., 1963). A study of the growing militarization of the whole society of the late empire.

R. Macmullen, *Constantine* (New York, 1970). A scholarly and readable biography.

F. G. B. Millar, *The Roman Empire and Its Neighbors* (New York, 1968).

A. Momigliano (editor), *The Conflict between Paganism*

and Christianity (Oxford, 1963). A valuable collection of essays.

A. D. NOCK, *Conversion* (Oxford, 1933). A fine study of an important phenomenon.

H. M. D. PARKER, *A History of the Roman World from A.D. 138 to 337* (New York, 1969). A good survey.

M. I. ROSTOVTZEFF, *Social and Economic History of the Roman Empire,* 2nd ed. (Oxford, 1957). A masterpiece whose main thesis has been much disputed.

E. A. THOMPSON, *The Early Germans* (Oxford, 1965). A study of the society of the people who destroyed the Roman Empire.

J. VOGT, *The Decline of Rome* (New York, 1967).

F. W. WALBANK, *The Awful Revolution: The Decline of the Roman Empire in the West* (Liverpool, 1969). Emphasizes the role of slavery and technological failure.

222

10

The Early Middle Ages (476–1000): The Birth of Europe

THE EARLY Middle Ages mark the birth of Europe. It was the period in which a distinctive western European culture began to emerge. In geography, government, religion, and language, western Europe became a land distinct from both the Eastern or Byzantine world and the Arab or Moslem world. It was a period of recovery from the collapse of Roman civilization, a time of forced experimentation with new ideas and institutions. Western European culture, as we know it today, was born of a unique, inventive mix of surviving Roman, new Germanic, and evolving Christian traditions.

The early Middle Ages have been called, and not with complete fairness, a "dark age." This is because it lost touch with classical, especially Greek, learning and science. In this period there were fierce invasions from the north and the east by peoples that the Romans somewhat arrogantly called barbarians, and to the south the Mediterranean was transformed by Arab dominance into an inhospitable "Moslem lake." A Europe thus surrounded and assailed from north, east, and south understandably became somewhat insular and even stagnant. On the other hand, being forced to manage by itself, western Europe also learned to develop its native resources. The early Middle Ages were not without a modest renaissance of antiquity during the reign of Charlemagne. And the distinctive social and political form of this period—feudalism—proved to be not only a successful way to cope with

unprecedented chaos on local levels but also a fertile seedbed for some of the truths Western men and women have always held to be self-evident.

On the Eve of the Frankish Ascendancy
Germanic and Arab Invasions

As we have already seen, by the late third century the Roman Empire was too large for a single sovereign to govern. For this reason the Emperor Diocletian (284–305) divided the empire, establishing an eastern and a western half, each with its own emperor and imperial bureaucracy. The Emperor Constantine the Great (306–337) reunited the empire by conquest and was sole emperor of the east and the west after 324. In 330 he created the city of Constantinople as the new administrative center of the empire. Constantinople was to be a "new Rome" and to replace the old, whose internal political quarrels and geographical distance from new military fronts in Syria and along the Danube River made it less appealing. Rome and the western empire were on the wane in the late third and fourth centuries well before the barbarian invasions in the west began. In 286 Milan had replaced Rome as the imperial residence; in 402 the seat of western government was moved still again, to Ravenna. When the barbarian invasions began in the late fourth century, the west was in disarray, and imperial power and prestige had shifted decisively to Constantinople and the east.

GERMAN TRIBES AND THE WEST. The German tribes did not burst upon the west all of a sudden. They were at first a token and benign presence. Before the great invasions from the north and the east, there had been a period of peaceful commingling of Germanic and Roman cultures. The Romans "imported" barbarians as domestics and soldiers before they came as conquerors. Barbarian soldiers rose to positions of high leadership and fame in Roman legions. In the late fourth century, however, this peaceful coexistence came to an end because of

The awesome interior of Hagia Sophia in Constantinople. The great sixth-century church is here seen in its Moslem guise. It was a mosque from 1453 to 1935, and the original Christian elements of decoration were replaced by Islamic ones. This mid-nineteenth-century drawing by the Italian architect Fossati better reveals the interior than photographs have been able to do. [Fossati, *Aya Sophia, Constantinople, as Recently Restored by Order of H. M. the Sultan Abdul Medjiel* (London, 1852).]

a great influx of Visigoths (west Goths) into the empire. They were stampeded there in 376 by the emergence of a new, violent people, the Huns, who erupted from the area of modern Mongolia. The Visigoths were a Christianized Germanic tribe, and the first of many waves of barbarian migrations into the west. In 378 they handily defeated Roman armies under the eastern emperor Valens at the Battle of Adrianople and won full rights of settlement and material assistance within the empire.

After Adrianople the Romans passively permitted settlement after settlement of barbarians within the very heart of western Europe. Why was there so little resistance to the German tribes? The invaders found a western empire weakened by decades of famine, pestilence, overtaxation, and the divisiveness of ambitious military commanders. The Roman world was literally impoverished, its will to resist simply sapped. The Roman Empire did not fall simply because of unprecedented moral decay and materialism, but because of a combination of political mismanagement, bad weather, disease, and sheer poverty.

The late fourth and early fifth centuries saw the invasion of still other tribes: the Vandals, the Burgundians, and the Franks. In 410 Visigoths revolted under Alaric (ca. 370–410) and sacked the "eternal city" of Rome. From 451 to 453 Italy suffered the invasions of Attila the Hun (d. 453), who was known to contemporaries as the "scourge of God." In 455 Rome was overrun by the Vandals.

By the mid-fifth century, power in western Europe had passed decisively from the hands of the Roman emperors to those of barbarian chieftains. In 476, the traditional date for the fall of the Roman Empire, the western emperor Romulus Augustulus was deposed and replaced by the barbarian Odoacer (ca. 434–493), who ruled as king of the Romans. Odoacer was recognized by the eastern emperor Zeno (emperor 474–491), to whom Odoacer ceded authority as sole emperor, being content to serve as his viceroy in the west. In a subsequent coup in 493 manipulated by Zeno, Theodoric, (ca. 454–526), king of the Ostrogoths (east Goths), defeated Odoacer

---

ᴿ Salvian the Priest Compares the Romans and the Barbarians

Salvian, a Christian priest writing around 440, found the barbarians morally superior to the Romans—indeed, truer to Roman virtues than the Romans themselves, whose failings are all the more serious because they, unlike the barbarians, have knowledge of Christianity.

Iɴ ᴡʜᴀᴛ *respects can our customs be preferred to those of the Goths and Vandals, or even compared with them? And first, to speak of affection and mutual charity, . . . almost all barbarians, at least those who are of one race and kin, love each other, while the Romans persecute each other. . . . The many are oppressed by the few, who regard public exactions as their own peculiar right, who carry on private traffic under the guise of collecting the taxes. . . . So the poor are despoiled, the widows sigh, the orphans are oppressed, until many of them, born of families not obscure, and liberally educated, flee to our enemies that they may no longer suffer the oppression of public persecution. They doubtless seek Roman humanity among the barbarians, because they cannot bear barbarian inhumanity among the Romans. And although they differ from the people to whom they flee in manner and in language; although they are unlike as regards the fetid odor of the barbarians' bodies and garments, yet they would rather endure a foreign civilization among the barbarians than cruel injustice among the Romans.*

It is urged that if we Romans are wicked and corrupt, that the barbarians commit the same sins. . . . There is, however, this difference, that if the barbarians commit the same crimes as we, yet we sin more grievously. . . . All the barbarians . . . are pagans or heretics. The Saxon race is cruel, the Franks are faithless . . . the Huns are unchaste,—in short there is vice in the life of all the barbarian peoples. But are their offenses as serious as [those of Christians]? Is the unchastity of the Hun so criminal as ours? Is the faithlessness of the Frank so blameworthy as ours?

Of God's Government, in James Harvey Robinson, *Readings in European History*, Vol. 1 (Boston: Athenaeum, 1904), pp. 28–30.

---

and thereafter ruled Italy with full acceptance by the Roman people and the Christian Church. By the end of the fifth century the western empire was thoroughly overrun by barbarians. The Ostrogoths settled in Italy, the Franks in northern Gaul, the Burgundians in Provence, the Visigoths in southern Gaul and Spain, the

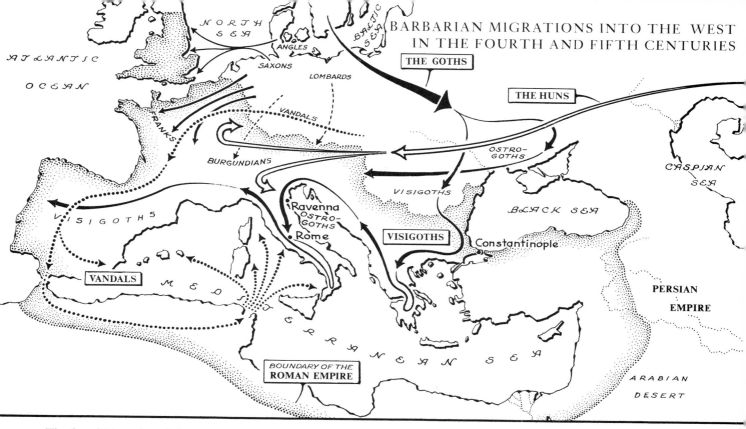

THE GOTHS

THE HUNS

OSTRO-GOTHS

VISIGOTHS

VISIGOTHS

VANDALS

VISIGOTHS

Ravenna
OSTRO-GOTHS
Rome

Constantinople

BOUNDARY OF THE
ROMAN EMPIRE

ATLANTIC OCEAN

NORTH SEA

BALTIC SEA

ANGLES

SAXONS

LOMBARDS

FRANKS

VANDALS

BURGUNDIANS

MED

CASPIAN SEA

BLACK SEA

PERSIAN EMPIRE

TERRANEAN SEA

ARABIAN DESERT

The forceful intrusion of Germanic and non-Germanic barbarians into the Empire from the last quarter of the fourth century through the fifth century made for a constantly changing pattern of movement and relations. However, the map shows the major routes taken by the usually unwelcome newcomers and the areas most deeply affected by the main groups.

BELOW: This is a partly conjectural reconstruction of the imperial palace complex in Constantinople as it existed in the early Middle Ages. The arena (Hippodrome)—its outlines are still easily visible —is at the upper left and is connected directly to the palace. Hagia Sophia is at the top right, and at the bottom are walls along the Sea of Marmora. [A. Vogt, *Le Livre des Cérémonies* (Paris, 1935).]

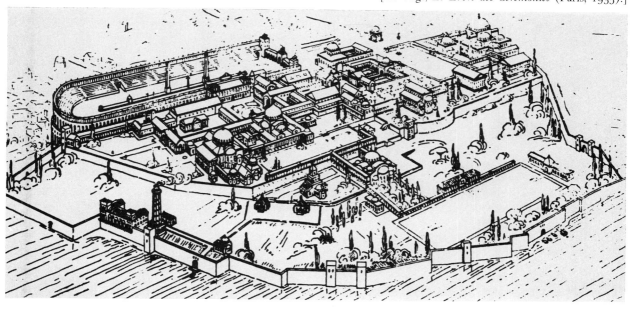

On the Eve of the Frankish Ascendancy **225**

ABOVE: Exterior of the Church of S. Apollinare in Classe near Ravenna, Italy. This sixth-century church is a good example of the style of early Christian church that evolved from the Roman basilica. [Fotocielo.]

LEFT: The interior of S. Apollinare in Classe. The adaptation of the secular pagan basilica to religious uses shows clearly here; at the far end is an apse gorgeously decorated with mosaics that provides a proper background for the altar. [Alinari/SCALA.]

Vandals in Africa and the Mediterranean, and the Angles and Saxons in England. Barbarians were the new western masters—but masters who were willing to learn from the people they conquered.

Western Europe was not transformed into a savage land. The military victories of the barbarians did not issue in a great cultural defeat of the Roman Empire. The barbarians were militarily superior, but the Romans retained their cultural strength. Apart from Britain and northern Gaul, Roman language, law, and government continued to exist side by side with the new Germanic institutions. In Italy under Theodoric, Roman law gradually replaced tribal custom. Only the Vandals and the Anglo-Saxons refused to profess at least titular obedience to the emperor in Constantinople.

Behind this accommodation of cultures was the fact that the Visigoths, the Ostrogoths, and the Vandals entered the west as Christianized people. They professed, however, a religious creed that was considered heretical in the west. They were Arian Christians, that is, Chris-

A Byzantine Emperor, possibly Justinian, from the leaf of an ivory diptych (Louvre, Paris). Justinian, who conquered barbarians and temporarily re-established control over the Western empire in the mid-sixth century, is here depicted as a conquering hero and defender of the faith. [Bettmann Archive.]

A mosaic portrait of Justinian's wife, the Empress Theodora (*ca.* 500–547), from the church of St. Vitale in Ravenna. She played a prominent role in the heated theological controversies of the time. [Bettmann Archive.]

tians who believed that Jesus Christ was not of one substance with God the Father—a point of view that had been condemned in 325 by the Council of Nicaea (see Chapter 9). Later, under Clovis, the founder of the Frankish dynasty, the Franks converted to "orthodox" or Nicene Christianity around the year 500 and, with the enthusiastic support of the church, proceeded in subsequent centuries to conquer and convert heterodox Goths and other barbarians.

All things considered, rapprochement and a gradual interpenetration of two strong cultures—a creative tension—marked the period of the Germanic migrations. The stronger culture was the Roman, and it became dominant in a later fusion. Despite western military defeat, it can still be said that the Goths and the Franks became far more Romanized than the Romans were Germanized. Latin language, Nicene Christianity, and Roman law and government were to triumph in the West during the Middle Ages.

CONTINUITY IN THE EAST. As western Europe succumbed to the Germanic invasions, Constantinople became the sole capital of the empire. The eastern empire, established in 330, was to last until May 29, 1453, when Constantinople finally fell to the Turks after centuries of unsuccessful siege. The early Middle Ages were a period of important political and cultural achievement in the east. The Emperor Justinian (527–565) collated and revised Roman law. His *Code,* issued in 533, was the first codification of Roman law and became the foundation of most European law. Justinian was assisted by his brilliant and powerful wife and empress, Theodora. She favored the Monophysite teaching that Jesus had only one nature, a composite of both human and divine nature. This view was not shared by Justinian, who supported the majority view that Jesus was of two separate natures, fully human and fully divine. Despite this theological disagreement, Justinian and Theodora succeeded in imposing an imperial theology on their subjects that made the emperor supreme in religious matters. These efforts laid the foundation for eastern Caesaropapism, a highly successful program of state control of the church that saved eastern emperors from such embarrassments as that suffered in 1077 by the excommunicated western emperor, Henry IV, who stood for days in the snow at Canossa in order to obtain Pope Gregory VII's absolution.

Justinian and Theodora did not forget the west. They took advantage of the political disunity of the German

[*Text continued on page 232*]

On the Eve of the Frankish Ascendancy **227**

Byzantine architecture—the architecture of the Roman Empire of the East after about the fifth century and of other areas strongly influenced by the East—is represented here by what are probably its two grandest remaining monuments.

The first one [OPPOSITE, TOP] is Emperor Justinian's Hagia Sophia (Church of the Holy Wisdom) in Constantinople, which was built between 532 and 537. With its great dome, 107 feet in diameter, several half domes, and richly decorated interior of marbles and mosaics, it was enormously influential on subsequent church architecture.

For a view of Hagia Sophia's vast central inside space see the chapter opening picture on page 222. Its exterior is now much changed from its original profile by Moslem minarets, tombs, and buttresses added at various times after the Turkish conquest of Constantinople in 1453. From that date the building was a mosque for nearly five hundred years. In modern, secular Istanbul, it has been a Turkish national museum since 1935. [AHM.]

After Hagia Sophia, the second greatest surviving example of Byzantine architecture—from a much later period of the style—is Saint Mark's in Venice [OPPOSITE, BOTTOM]. Most of the building dates from the eleventh century and was built to house the remains of the Apostle Mark, said to have been dramatically carried away from their earlier resting place in Alexandria in Egypt. The building carries the characteristic rounded arches, numerous domes, and mosaics of the Byzantine style. The ornamental pointed arches and pinnacles of the façade's upper story are later additions. [Italian Government Travel Office, New York.]

The interior of Saint Mark's [LEFT] is a dazzling display of Byzantine and Byzantine-influenced art. The most striking feature is the mosaics, reminiscent of those in Hagia Sophia that were covered over by the Moslems. [Editorial Photocolor Archives.]

230 The Early Middle Ages (467–1000): The Birth of Europe

Byzantine church decoration consisted predominantly of rigidly stylized mosaics. A theme repeated endlessly in these church mosaics is that of Christ Pantacrator (Christ the Ruler of All). The stern, bearded judge is quite different from the frequently encountered gentle figure in the West of Christ as the good shepherd and the suffering mortal. This example [OPPOSITE, TOP] from about 1100 is from the Church of St. Savior in Chora in Istanbul. [AHM.]

Frescoes also adorned Byzantine churches. St. Savior in Chora is also the locale of this powerful painting [OPPOSITE, BOTTOM] in which the triumphant Christ tramples on the gates of Hell while literally dragging a rather startled Adam and Eve from their tombs to join him. [AHM.]

Less refined—and often less well preserved—Byzantine frescoes are found in many places in the East. This one [BELOW], recently uncovered, pictures the miracle of the multiplication of loaves. It is in a church in the Black Sea town of Trebizond (modern Trabzon, Turkey), to which the imperial court of Constantinople fled when the city was captured and sacked by the Venetians in 1204 during the abortive Fourth Crusade. [AHM.]

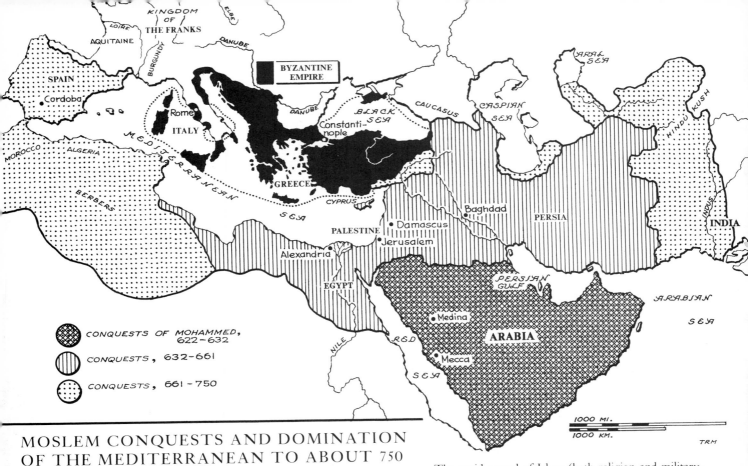

MOSLEM CONQUESTS AND DOMINATION OF THE MEDITERRANEAN TO ABOUT 750

The rapid spread of Islam (both religion and military-political power) is shown here. From the West's viewpoint, the important fact was that in the 125 years after Mohammed's rise Moslems came to dominate Spain and all areas south and east of the Mediterranean.

tribes and papal opposition to the Arian Ostrogoths briefly to reconquer the western empire in the mid-sixth century. Justinian's armies overcame the Vandals in Africa in 533 and marched invincibly through Spain and southern France into Italy, which Justinian also controlled by 533. But a revival and reunion of the old Roman Empire was not to be. In northern Europe the Franks were becoming the dominant western power, a power Justinian's armies were not strong enough to subdue. It was only the appearance and the firm entrenchment of the Lombards in northern Italy, as a buffer between the Franks and imperial forces, that prevented what would surely have been a fatal confrontation for the reviving empire of Justinian.

ISLAM AND ITS EFFECTS ON EAST AND WEST. A new drama was unfolding at this time, and it was to prove equally decisive for western Europe's future. In the south an enemy far more dangerous than the German tribes was on the march: the faith of Islam. During the lifetime of the prophet Mohammed (570–632) and thereafter, invading Arab armies absorbed the attention and resources of the emperors in Constantinople, who found themselves in a life-and-death struggle. Unlike the comparatively mild Germanic invaders, Arab armies did

not encourage a creative interpenetration of cultures. They carefully protected the purity of Arab religion, language, and law from foreign influences, imposing them on conquered peoples where they could.

Mohammed, an Arab trader who married a wealthy woman, received his call to be "the Prophet" at age forty. His religion, Islam, means "submission to the will of Allah," and Moslems (Arabic for "true believers") are people who obey the will of Allah as revealed to Mohammed. This will is contained in the Koran, a series of revelations received by Mohammed over a period of time. It recognized Jesus Christ as a prophet sent by God, but not one so great as Mohammed, and certainly not God's coequal son as the Christians believed. Indeed, Islam is uncompromisingly monotheistic. Among the things required of the faithful are prayer five times each day, generous almsgiving, fasting during daylight hours one month each year, and a pilgrimage to the holy city of Mecca, in what is now Saudi Arabia, at least once during one's lifetime. Moslems also permitted polygamy (each

Islam's most holy shrine, at Mecca in modern Saudi
Arabia. Pilgrims who are able come from all over
the world to pray at the Kaaba. They are required
to walk around the great symbolic stone seven times,
repeating appropriate prayers as they do. [Arab
Information Center, New York.]

man might have up to four wives) and envisioned heaven
to be a place of fleshly delights. Unlike Christianity, Islam
has no special priesthood and hence no distinction between clergy and laity. Another striking difference from
Christianity, especially Western Christianity, is the complete unity of religion and politics.

Mohammed preached his message unsuccessfully for
several years in pagan Mecca before fleeing the city in
622 for the neighboring and more receptive city of Me-
dina. This flight, known to Moslems as the *Hegira*, became a key event in the history of Islam—the beginning
of the new religion's successful expansion and the starting
point for its calendar. Thereafter, supported by growing
numbers of followers and by firm organization, Mohammed absolutely opposed any accommodation with pagans

and urged that his religion be imposed on fellow Arabs by
holy war. Mecca itself, a city of long association with
Arab pagan rites, was captured and made the center of
Moslem activity and government.

Within little more than a century following Mohammed's death, Moslems conquered the southern and eastern Mediterranean coastline (territories mostly still held
by Islamic states today) and occupied parts of Spain,
which they controlled until the fifteenth century. In
addition, their armies had pushed north and east through
Mesopotamia and Persia and beyond. These conquests
would not have been so rapid and thorough had the
contemporary Byzantine and Persian empires not been
exhausted by a long period of war. The Moslems struck
at the conclusion of the successful campaign of Byzantine
Emperor Heraclius (d. 641) against the Persian King
Chosroes II. Most of the population in the conquered area
was Semitic and more easily fired by hatred of the Byzantine Greek army of occupation than it was inspired to
unity by a common Christian tradition. The Christian
community was itself badly divided. The Egyptian (also

The Dome of the Rock in Jerusalem. A very early example of monumental Islamic architecture, it dates from the seventh century, during the first wave of Arab expansion, and derives its name from the rock from which Moslems believe Mohammed ascended to heaven. Jews believe the rock to be the one on which Abraham prepared to sacrifice Isaac. [Israel Government Tourist Office, New York.]

known as *Coptic*) and Syrian churches were Monophysitic. Heraclius' efforts to enforce doctrinal unity within these churches only increased the enmity between Greek and Semitic Christians. Many Egyptian and Syrian Christians came to look on the Arabs as deliverers from the Byzantine conquerors.

Moslems tolerated conquered Christians, whether orthodox or Monophysite, provided they paid taxes, kept their distance, and made no efforts to proselytize Moslem communities. It was tolerance strictly on a live-and-let-live basis. The Arabs were always extremely anxious to maintain the purity of their religion, culture, and language. Mixed marriages were forbidden, as was any conscious cultural interchange. Special taxes on conquered peoples encouraged them to convert to Islam. After the middle of the eighth century, by which time the seat of Islam had been moved from Arabia to Damascus in Syria and from there to the brand-new city of Baghdad in Mesopotamia, the huge Moslem empire tended to break into separate states. There states often had their own caliphs (or rulers), each claiming to be the true successor of Mohammed. Such division made Islam less tolerant of other religions.

Assaulted on both their eastern and their western frontiers and everywhere challenged in the Mediterranean, Europeans developed lasting fear and suspicion of the Moslems. In the east, during the reign of the Byzantine Leo III (717–740), the Arabs were stopped after a year's seige of Constantinople (717–718). Leo and his successors in the Isaurian dynasty of Byzantine rulers created a successful defensive organization against them. It was so effective that the rulers of the following Macedonian dynasty (867–1057) were able to expand militarily and commercially into Moslem lands. It was the later Turks, themselves Moslem, and the western Christians who proved more deadly foes of Byzantium than were the Arabs. In 1071 the Seljuk Turks from central Asia, by way of Persia and Mesopotamia, overran Armenia at the eastern end of the empire in the first of a long series of confrontations that would finally end with the fall of Constantinople in 1453 to the Seljuks' relatives, the Ottoman Turks. In 1096 the first crusaders from western Europe arrived in Constantinople in the first of a series of moves to the east that ended with the capture of Constantinople in 1204 and the establishment of a half century of western rule over Byzantium.

As for the west's own dangers, the ruler of the Franks, Charles Martel, defeated the Arabs on the western frontier of Europe at Poitiers (today in central France) in 732, a victory that ended Arab expansion into western Europe by way of Spain. From the end of the seventh century to the middle of the eleventh century, the Mediterranean still remained something of a Moslem lake. While trade of the western empire with the Orient was not cut off during these centuries, as some scholars have argued, it was significantly decreased because of Moslem dominance.

When trade wanes, cities decline, and with them those centers for the exchange of goods and ideas that enable a society to look and live beyond itself. The Arab invasions and domination of the Mediterranean during a crucial part of the early Middle Ages created the essential conditions for the birth of western Europe as a distinctive cultural entity. Arab belligerency forced western Europe to fall back on its own distinctive resources and to develop its peculiar Germanic and Roman heritage into a unique culture. The Arabs accomplished this by diverting the attention and energies of the eastern empire at a time of Frankish and Lombard ascendancy (thereby preventing Byzantium from imposing its will on the west) and by greatly reducing western navigation of the Mediterranean (thereby closing off much eastern trade and cultural influence).

The seeds of feudal and manorial society—the creation of warrior knights and the division of land and labor between lord and serf for the profit and protection of both—were sown in the wake of Arab encirclement and aggression. As western shipping was reduced in the Mediterranean, coastal urban centers declined. Populations that would otherwise have been engaged in trade-related work in the cities moved in great numbers into interior regions, there to work the farms of the great landholders. The latter needed their labor and welcomed the new emigrants, who were even more in need of the employment and protection that the landholders could provide. A mild serfdom evolved. As the demand for agricultural products diminished in the great urban centers and as traffic between town and country was reduced, the farming belts became regionally insular and self-contained. Production and travel were adjusted to local needs, and there was little incentive for bold experimentation and exploration. The domains of the great landholders became the basic social and political units of society, with local barter economies developing within them.

One institution remained firmly entrenched within the cities during the Arab invasions—the Christian Church. The church had long modeled its own structure on that of the imperial Roman administration. Like the latter, it was a centralized, hierarchical government with strategically placed viceroys (bishops) in European cities who were relatively loyal to their "sovereign," the pope in Rome. As the western empire crumbled and populations emigrated to the countryside after the barbarian and Arab invasions, local bishops and cathedral chapters filled the vacuum of authority left by the removal of Roman viceroys. The local cathedral became the center of urban life and the local bishop the highest authority for those who remained in the cities—just as in Rome, on a larger and more fateful scale, the pope took control of the city as the western emperors gradually departed and died out. Left to its own devices, western Europe soon discovered that the Christian Church was a rich repository of Roman administrative skills and classical culture.

The Developing Roman Church

The Christian church had been graced with special privileges, great lands, and wealth by Emperor Constantine and his successors. In 313 Constantine issued the Edict of Milan, giving Christians legal standing and a favored status within the empire. By the end of the century (391) Emperor Theodosius I (ca. 346–395), after whose death the empire was again divided into eastern and western parts, raised Christianity to the official religion of the empire. Both Theodosius and his predecessors acted as much for political effect as out of any religious conviction; in 313 Christians composed about one fifth of the population of the empire and were unquestionably the strongest of the competing religions. Mithraism, the religion popular among army officers and restricted to males, was its main rival.

The church survived the period of Germanic and Arab invasions as a weakened and compromised institution, yet it was still a most potent civilizing and unifying force. It had a religious message of providential purpose and individual worth that could give solace and meaning to life at its worst. Following the fall of Rome, this message was eloquently defined by Augustine (353–430) in his *City of God,* a favorite book of the Frankish king Charlemagne nearly four hundred years later. The church also had a ritual of baptism and a creedal confession that united people beyond the traditional barriers of social class, education, and sex. After the Germanic and Arab invasions the church alone possessed an effective hierarchical administration, scattered throughout the old empire, staffed by the best-educated minds in Europe, and centered in emperorless Rome. The church also had a growing army of monks, who were not only loyal to its mission but also objects of great popular respect. It was monastic culture especially that proved again and again to be the peculiar strength of the church during the Middle Ages.

MONASTIC CULTURE. Monks were originally hermits, individuals who withdrew from society to pursue a more perfect way of life. They were inspired by the Christian ideal of a life of complete self-denial in imitation of Christ, who had denied himself even unto death. The popularity of monasticism began to grow as Roman persecution of Christians waned in the mid-third century. As the Romans stopped feeding Christians to the lions—indeed, as Christianity became the favored religion of the empire—monasticism replaced martyrdom as the most perfect way to imitate Christ and to confess one's faith. Embracing the biblical "counsels of perfection" (chastity, poverty, and obedience), the monastic way, a form of dying in the midst of life, became the purest form of religious life in the Middle Ages. There developed among the monks, the Christian laity, and the secular clergy a view of monastic life as the superior religious life, beyond the baptism and creedal confession that identified ordinary believers. This view evolved during the Middle Ages into a belief in the general superiority of the clergy and the Church over the laity and the state—a belief that served the papacy in later confrontations with secular rulers.

Anthony of Egypt (*ca.* 251–356), the father of hermit monasticism, was inspired by Jesus' command to the rich young ruler: "If you will be perfect, sell all that you have, give it to the poor, and follow me" (Matthew 19:21). Anthony went into the desert to pray and work, setting an example followed by hundreds in Egypt, Syria, and Palestine in the fourth and fifth centuries. Anthony's hermit monasticism was soon joined by the development of communal monasticism. In southern Egypt in the first

quarter of the fourth century, Pachomius (*ca.* 286–346) organized monks into a highly directed common life. Hundreds shared a life together that was ordered and disciplined by a strict penal code and assigned manual labor. Such monastic communities grew to contain a thousand or more inhabitants; they were little "cities of God," separated from the collapsing Roman and the nominal Christian world. Basil the Great (329–379) popularized communal monasticism throughout the east, providing a rule that lessened the asceticism of Pachomius and directed monks beyond their enclaves of perfection into such social services as caring for orphans, widows, and the infirm in surrounding communities.

Monasticism was introduced into the west by Athanasius and Martin of Tours, but its great organizer was Benedict of Nursia (*ca.* 480–*ca.* 547). In 529 Benedict

Augustine of Hippo Describes His Conversion to Christianity

Augustine of Hippo (354–430) frankly confessed his utter sinfulness and domination by lust until Christianity gave him the will to resist.

Who *am I, and what am I? Is there any evil that is not found in my acts, or if not in my acts, in my words, or if not in my words, in my will? But you, O Lord, are good and merciful, and your right hand has had regard for the depth of my death, and from the very bottom of my heart it has emptied out an abyss of corruption. This was the sum of it: not to will what I willed and to will what you willed.*

But throughout these long years where was my free will? Out of what deep and hidden pit was it called forth in a single moment, wherein to bend my neck to your mild yoke and my shoulders to your light burden, O Christ Jesus, "my helper and my redeemer?" How sweet did it suddenly become to me to be free of the sweets of folly: things that I once feared to lose it was now joy to put away. You cast them forth from me, you the true and highest sweetness, you cast them forth, and in their stead you entered in, sweeter than every pleasure, but not to flesh and blood, brighter than every light, but deeper within me than any secret retreat, higher than every honor, but not to those who exalt themselves. Now was my mind free from the gnawing cares of favor-seeking, of striving for gain, of wallowing in the mire, and of scratching lust's itchy sore. I spoke like a child to you, my light, my wealth, my salvation, my Lord God.

The Confessions of St. Augustine, *trans. by John K. Ryan (New York: Doubleday, 1960), pp. 205–206.*

founded the mother monastery of the Benedictine Order at Monte Cassino in Italy, the foundation on which all western monasticism has been built. Benedict also wrote a sophisticated *Rule for Monasteries*, a comprehensive plan for every activity of the monks, even detailing how they were to sleep. The monastery was hierarchically organized and directed by an abbot, whose command was beyond question. Periods of devotion (about four hours each day were set aside for the work of God) and study alternated with manual labor—a program that permitted not a moment's idleness and carefully promoted the religious, intellectual, and physical growth of the cloistered.

THE DOCTRINE OF PAPAL PRIMACY. Constantine and his successors, especially the eastern emperors, ruled religious life with an iron hand, consistently looking upon the church as little more than a department of the state. Such "Caesaropapism"—Caesar acting as pope—involved the emperor directly in the church's affairs, even to the point of playing the theologian and imposing conciliar solutions upon its doctrinal quarrels. State con-

trol of religion was the original Church–State relation in the west. Roman popes never accepted such intervention and opposed it in every way they could. In the fifth and sixth centuries, taking advantage of imperial weakness and distraction, they developed for their own defense the fateful weaponry of the doctrine of "papal primacy." This teaching raised the Roman pontiff to an unassailable supremacy within the church; it also put him in a position to make important secular claims. The doctrine was destined to occasion repeated conflicts between church and state, pope and emperor, throughout the Middle Ages.

The notion of papal primacy was first conceived as a papal response to the decline of imperial Rome in favor of Milan and Ravenna and to the concurrent competitive claims of the patriarchs of the eastern Church. The latter looked upon the bishop of Rome as but a peer, not as a superior, after imperial power was transferred to Constantinople. In 381 the ecumenical Council of Constantinople declared the bishop of Constantinople to be of first rank after the bishop of Rome "because Constantinople is the new Rome." In 451 the ecumenical Council of Chalcedon recognized Constantinople as having the same religious primacy in the east as Rome had traditionally possessed in the west. By the mid-sixth century the bishop of Constantinople regularly described himself in correspondence as a "universal" patriarch.

Roman pontiffs were understandably jealous of such claims and resentful of the ecclesiastical interference of eastern emperors. A counteroffensive was launched. Pope Damasus I (366–384)[1] took the first of several major steps in the rise of the Roman church when he declared a Roman "apostolic" primacy. Pointing to Jesus' words to Peter in the Gospel of Matthew (16:18), the pope claimed to be in direct succession from Peter as the unique "rock" upon which the Christian church was built. Pope Leo I (440–461) took still another fateful step by assuming the title *pontifex maximus*—"supreme priest"—and he further proclaimed himself to be endowed

1 Papal dates give the years of each reign.

with a "plentitude of power." Already during Leo's reign an imperial decree recognized his exclusive jurisdiction over the western church.

The western church was favored by events as well as by ideology. It was the chief beneficiary of imperial adversity in the face of Germanic and Arab invasions. Islam may even be said to have saved the western church from eastern domination, while the emergent Lombards and Franks provided it with new political allies. The success of Arab armies removed eastern episcopal competition with Rome as the area of bishopric after bishopric fell to the Moslems in the east. The power of the exarch of Ravenna, who was the Byzantine emperor's regent in the west, was eclipsed by invading Lombards, who, thanks to Frankish prodding, became Nicene Christians loyal to Rome in the late seventh century. In an unprecedented act Pope Gregory I, "the Great" (590–604), negotiated an independent peace treaty with the Lombards, completely ignoring the emperor and the imperial government in Ravenna, who were at the time too weak to offer resistance.

THE DIVISION OF CHRISTENDOM. The division of Christendom into eastern and western churches has its roots in the early Middle Ages. From the start there was the difference in language (Greek in the east, Latin in the west) and culture. Compared with his western counterpart, the eastern Christian attributed little importance to life in this world. He was far more concerned about questions affecting his eternal destiny. This concern made him more receptive than the western Christian to Oriental mysticism and theological ideas. It was, after all, a combination of Greek, Roman, and Oriental elements that formed Byzantine culture. The strong mystical orientation to the next world also caused the eastern church to submit more passively than western popes could ever do to Caesaropapism.

As in the west, eastern church organization closely followed that of the secular state. A patriarch ruled over metropolitans and archbishops in the cities and provinces, and they in turn ruled over bishops, who were the au-

The Benedictine Order Sets Its Requirements for Entrance

The growing appeal of a religious life in a time of political and social uncertainty and religious enthusiasm could easily lead to such socially unproductive lives as those of the hermit monks or to communities of either unorganized or too strictly organized monks. Benedict's great contribution was to prescribe a balanced blend of religious, physical, intellectual, and societal lives for monks. His *Rule* makes clear the need first of all for careful selection of candidates.

WHEN *anyone is newly come for the reformation of his life, let him not be granted an easy entrance; but, as the Apostle says, "Test the spirits to see whether they are from God." If the newcomer, therefore, perseveres in his knocking, and if it is seen after four or five days that he bears patiently the harsh treatment offered him and the difficulty of admission, and that he persists in his petition, then let entrance be granted him, and let him stay in the guest house for a few days.*

After that let him live in the novitiate, where the novices study, eat, and sleep. A senior shall be assigned to them who is skilled in winning souls, to watch over them with the utmost care. Let him examine whether the novice is truly seeking God, and whether he is zealous for the Work of God, for obedience and for humiliations. Let the novice be told all the hard and rugged ways by which the journey to God is made.

If he promises stability and perseverance, then at the end of two months let this Rule be read through to him, and let him be addressed thus: "Here is the law under which you wish to fight. If you can observe it, enter; if you cannot, you are free to depart." If he still stands firm, let him be taken to the above-mentioned novitiate and again tested in all patience. And after the lapse of six months let the Rule be read to him, that he may know on what he is entering. And if he still remains firm, after four months let the same Rule be read to him again.

Then, having deliberated with himself, if he promises to keep it in its entirety and to observe everything that is commanded him, let him be received into the community. But let him understand that, according to the law of the Rule, from that day forward he may not leave the monastery nor withdraw his neck from under the yoke of the Rule which he was free to refuse or to accept during that prolonged deliberation.

St. Benedict's Rule for Monasteries, trans. by Leonard J. Doyle (Collegeville, Minn.: Liturgical Press, 1948), Chap. 58, p. 79–80.

thorities over local clergy. With the exception of the patriarch Michael Cerularius, who tried unsuccessfully to free the church from its traditional tight state control, the patriarchs were normally carefully regulated by the emperor.

Contrary to the evolving western tradition of universal clerical celibacy, the eastern church permitted the marriage of secular priests, while strictly forbidding bishops to marry. The eastern church also used leavened bread in the Eucharist, contrary to the western custom of using unleavened bread. Also unliked by the west was the tendency of the eastern church to compromise doctrinally with the politically powerful Arian and Monophysite Christians.

Beyond these issues the major factors in the religious break between east and west revolved around questions of doctrinal authority. From the start the eastern church put more stress on the authority of the Bible and of the ecumenical councils of the church than on "papal primacy." The seven councils and Holy Scripture were the ultimate authorities in the definition of orthodoxy. The claims of Roman popes to a special primacy of authority on the basis of the apostle Peter's commission from Jesus in Matthew 16:18 ("Thou art Peter, and upon this rock I will build my church") were completely unacceptable to the east, where the independence and autonomy of national churches was much preferred. As Steven Runciman has summarized, "The Byzantine ideal was a series of autocephalous state churches, linked by inter-communion and the faith of the seven councils."[2] This basic issue of authority in matters of faith was behind the mutual excommunication of Pope Nicholas I and Patriarch Photius in the ninth century and that of Pope Leo IX and Patriarch Michael Cerularius in 1054.

A second major issue in the separation of the two churches was the western addition of the *filioque* clause to the Nicene–Constantinopolitan Creed—an anti-Arian move that made the Holy Spirit proceed "also from the Son" (*filioque*) as well as from the Father. This addition

2 *Byzantine Civilization* (London: A. and C. Black, 1933), p. 128.

made clear the western belief that Christ was fully substantial with God the Father.

The final and most direct issue in the religious division of Christendom was the iconoclastic controversy of the first half of the eighth century. After 725 the eastern emperor, Leo III (717–740), attempted to force western popes to abolish the use of images in their churches. In opposing icons and images in the churches, the eastern church was influenced by Islam. This stand met fierce official and popular resistance in the west, where images were greatly cherished. Emperor Leo punished the disobedient west by confiscating papal lands in Sicily and Calabria (in southern Italy) and placing them under the jurisdiction of the subservient patriarch of Constantinople. Because these territories provided essential papal revenues, the western church could not but view the emperor's action as a declaration of war. Later the empress mother Irene (mother of Constantine VI) made peace with the Roman church on this issue and restored the use of images at the sixth ecumenical council in Nicea in 789.

Leo's direct challenge of the pope came almost simultaneously with still another agressive act against the western church: attacks by the heretofore docile Lombards of northern Italy. Assailed by both the emperor and the Lombards, the pope in Rome seemed surely doomed. But there has not been a more resilient and enterprising institution in Western history than the Roman papacy. Since the pontificate of Gregory the Great, Roman popes had eyed the Franks of northern Gaul as Europe's ascendant power and their surest protector. Imperial and Lombard aggression against the Roman pope in the first half of the eighth century provided the occasion for the most fateful political alliance of the Middle Ages. In 754 Pope Stephen II (752–757) enlisted Pepin III and his Franks as defenders of the church against the Lombards and as a western counterweight to the eastern emperor. This marriage of religion and politics created a new western church and empire; it also determined the course of Western history into the modern world.

The Kingdom of the Franks

Merovingians and Carolingians: From Clovis to Charlemagne

A warrior chieftain, Clovis (466?–511), founded the Frankish monarchy and its first ruling family, the Merovingian dynasty. A convert to Christianity around 500, Clovis and his successors subdued the pagan Burgundians and the Arian Visigoths and established within ancient Gaul the kingdom of the Franks. The Franks were a broad belt of people scattered throughout modern Belgium, the Netherlands, and western Germany, whose loyalties remained strictly tribal and local. The Merovingians attempted to govern this sprawling kingdom by pacts with landed nobility and by the creation of the royal office of count. The most persistent problem of medieval political history was the competing claims of the "one" and the "many"—on the one hand, the king, who struggled for a centralized government and transregional loyalty, and on the other, powerful local magnates, who were intent on preserving their regional autonomy and traditions. The Merovingian counts were men without possessions to whom the king gave great lands in the expectation that they would be, as the landed aristocrats often were not, loyal officers of the "state." But like local aristocrats the Merovingian counts also proved not to be good vassals. Once established in office for a period of time, they too became territorial rulers in their own right, with the result that the kingdom was progressively fragmented into independent regions and tiny principalities. This centrifugal tendency was further assisted by the Frankish custom of dividing the kingdom equally among the king's legitimate male heirs.

Rather than purchasing allegiance and unity within the kingdom, the Merovingian largess simply provided the occasion for the rise of competing magnates and petty tyrants, who became laws unto themselves within their regions. By the seventh century the Frankish king existed far more in title than in effective executive power. Real power came to be concentrated in an office known as the *mayor of the palace.* The mayor of the palace was the spokesman at the king's court for the great landowners of the three regions into which the Frankish kingdom was divided: Neustria, Austrasia, and Burgundy. It was through this office that the Carolingian dynasty rose to power.

The Carolingians controlled the office of the mayor of the palace from the ascent to that post of Pepin I of Austrasia (d. 639) until 751, at which time the Carolingians, with the enterprising connivance of the pope, simply expropriated the Frankish crown. Pepin II (d. 714) ruled in fact if not in title over the Frankish kingdom. His illegitimate son, Charles Martel ("the Hammer," d. 741), created a great cavalry by bestowing lands known as *benefices* or *fiefs* on powerful noblemen, who, in return, agreed to be ready to serve as the king's army. It was such an army that finally checked the Arab advance on the western front at Poitiers in 732—an important battle that helped to secure the borders of western Europe.

The fiefs so generously bestowed by Charles Martel to create his army came in large part from landed property that he usurped from the church, to the latter's undying resentment. His alliance with the landed aristocracy in this grand manner permitted the Carolingians to have some measure of political success where the Merovingians had failed. Carolingian counts were created almost entirely out of the landed nobility from which the Carolingians themselves had arisen. The Merovingians, in contrast, had tried to compete directly with these great aristocrats by raising landless men to great power. By playing to strength rather than challenging it, the Carolingians strengthened themselves, at least for the short term. Because the church was by this time completely dependent upon the protection of the Franks against the eastern emperor and the Lombards, it tolerated the fact that its savior was created in part with lands to which it held claim.

THE FRANKISH CHURCH. The church came to

Rising monastic activity and the popular cult of relics gave rise to elaborately bejeweled containers for religious objects and the bodily remains of holy persons. This reliquary is ascribed to Pepin, king of Aquitaine, grandson of Charlemagne (died 838). [Hirmer Fotoarchiv München.]

play a large and initially quite voluntary role in the Frankish government. By Carolingian times monasteries were a dominant force. Their intellectual achievements made them respected repositories of culture. Their religious teachings and example imposed order upon surrounding populations. Their relics and rituals made them magical shrines to which pilgrims came in great numbers. And, thanks to their internal discipline and industry, many became very profitable farms and landed estates, their abbots becoming rich and powerful magnates. Already in Merovingian times the higher clergy were employed in tandem with counts as royal agents. It was the policy of the Carolingians, perfected by Charles Martel and his successor, Pepin III ("the Short"; d. 768), to use the church to pacify conquered neighboring tribes—Frisians, Thüringians, Bavarians, and especially the Franks' archenemies, the Saxons. Conversion to Nicene Christianity became an integral part of the successful annexation of conquered lands and people. The cavalry broke their bodies, while the clergy won their hearts and minds. The Anglo-Saxon missionary Saint Boniface (born Wynfrith; 680?–755) was the most important of the German clergy who served Carolingian kings in this way. Christian bishops in missionary districts were made lords, appointed by and subject to the king—an ominous integration of secular and religious policy in which lay the seeds of the later Investiture Controversy of the eleventh and twelfth centuries.

The church served more than Carolingian territorial expansion. Pope Zacharias (741–752) also sanctioned Pepin the Short's removal of the vestigial Merovingian dynasty and the accession of the Carolingians to outright kingship of the Franks. With the pope's public blessing, Pepin was proclaimed king by the nobility in council in 751, while the last of the Merovingians, the puppet king Childeric III, was hustled off to a monastery and dynastic oblivion. According to legend, Pepin was annointed by Saint Boniface, thereby investing the Frankish rule from the very start with a certain sacral character.

Zacharias's successor, Pope Stephen II (752–757), did not let Pepin forget the favor of his predecessor. Driven from Rome in 753 by the Lombards, Pope Stephen appealed directly to Pepin to cast out the invaders and guarantee papal claims to central Italy, which was dominated at this time by the eastern emperor. In 754 the Franks and the church formed an alliance against the Lombards and the eastern emperor. Carolingian kings became the protectors of the Catholic Church and thereby "kings by the grace of God." Pepin was awarded the title *patricius Romanorum,* "father-protector of the Romans," a title heretofore borne only by the representative of the eastern emperor. In 755 the Lombards were defeated by the Franks, and the pope was given the lands surrounding Rome, an event that created what came to be known as the *Papal States.* The lands earlier appropriated by Charles Martel and parceled out to the Frankish nobility were never returned to the church, despite the appearance in this period of a most enterprising fraudulent document designed to win their return known as the *Donation of Constantine* (written between 750 and 800). This imperial parchment alleged that the Emperor Constantine had personally conveyed to the church his palace and "all provinces and districts of the city of Rome and Italy and of the regions of the West" as permanent possessions. It was believed by many to be a genuine document until definitely exposed as a forgery in the fifteenth century by the humanist Lorenzo Valla.

The papacy had looked to the Franks for an ally strong enough to protect it from the Caesaropapism of eastern emperors. It is an irony of history that the church found in the Carolingian dynasty a western imperial government that drew almost as slight a boundary between State and Church, secular and religious policy, as did eastern emperors. While eminently preferable to eastern domination, Carolingian patronage of the church proved in its own way to be no less Caesaropapist.

The Reign of Charlemagne (768–814)

Charlemagne continued his father, Pepin the Short's, role as papal protector in Italy and his policy of territorial conquest in the north. In 774 King Desiderius and the Lombards of northern Italy were decisively defeated, and Charlemagne took upon himself the title "King of the Lombards" in Pavia. He widened the frontiers of his kingdom further by subjugating surrounding pagan tribes, foremost among whom were the Saxons, who were brutally Christianized and dispersed in small groups throughout Frankish lands. The Avars (Huns) were practically annihilated, bringing the Danubian plains into the Frankish orbit. The Arabs were chased beyond the Pyrenees. By the time of his death on January 28, 814, Charlemagne's kingdom embraced modern France, Belgium, Holland, Switzerland, almost the whole of western Germany, much of Italy, a portion of Spain, and the island of Corsica—an area approximately equal to that of the modern Common Market.

THE NEW EMPIRE. Charlemagne harbored imperial designs; he desired to be not only king of the Germans but a universal emperor as well. His sacred palace city, Aachen (in French, Aix-la-Chapelle), was constructed in conscious imitation of the courts of ancient Roman and of contemporary eastern emperors. Although permitted its distinctiveness, the church was looked after by Charlemagne with a paternalism almost as great as that of any eastern emperor. He used the church above all to promote social stability and hierarchical order throughout the kingdom—as an aid in the creation of a great Frankish Christian tribe. Frankish Christians were ceremoniously baptized, professed the Nicene Creed (with the filioque clause), and were taught by the church to revere Charlemagne.

The Christian Church Fakes a Donation of the Empire

Among the ways the church fought to free itself from political domination was to assert its own sovereign territorial and political rights. One of the most ambitious of such assertions was the so-called Donation of Constantine (eighth century), a fraudulent document claiming papal succession to much of the old Roman Empire.

THE *Emperor Caesar Flavius Constantinus in Christ Jesus . . . to the most Holy and blessed Father of fathers, Silvester, Bishop of the Roman city and Pope; and to all his successors, the pontiffs, who shall sit in the chair of blessed Peter to the end of time. . . . Grace, peace, love, joy, long-suffering, mercy . . . be with you all. . . . For we wish you to know . . . that we have forsaken the worship of idols . . . and have come to the pure Christian faith. . . .*

To the holy apostles, my lords the most blessed Peter and Paul, and through them also to blessed Silvester, our father, supreme pontiff and universal pope of the city of Rome, and to the pontiffs, his successors, who to the end of the world shall sit in the seat of blessed Peter, we grant and by this present we convey our imperial Lateran palace, which is superior to and excels all palaces in the whole world; and further the diadem, which is the crown of our head; and the miter; as also the super-humeral, that is, the stole which usually surrounds our imperial neck; and the purple cloak and the scarlet tunic and all the imperial robes. . . .

And we decree that those most reverend men, the clergy of various orders serving the same most holy Roman Church, shall have that eminence, distinction, power and precedence, with which our illustrious senate is gloriously adorned; that is, they shall be made patricians and consuls. And we ordain that they shall also be adorned with other imperial dignities. Also we decree that the clergy of the sacred Roman Church shall be adorned as are the imperial officers. . . .

We convey to the oft-mentioned and most blessed Silvester, universal pope, both our palace, as preferment, and likewise all provinces, palaces and districts of the city of Rome and Italy and of the regions of the West; and, bequeathing them to the power and sway of him and the pontiffs, his successors, we do determine and decree that the same be placed at his disposal, and do lawfully grant it as a permanent possession to the holy Roman Church.

Henry Bettenson (Ed.), *Documents of the Christian Church* (New York: Oxford University Press 1961), pp. 137–141.

An equestrian figure of Charlemagne (or perhaps one of his sons) from the early ninth century. [Musée du Louvre, Paris. Giraudon.]

Carolingian architecture. The cathedral church at Aachen (now in modern West Germany) containing the Palatine Chapel of Charlemagne. The original parts were constructed between 792 and 805. [Bildarchiv Foto Marburg.]

In the 790s the formation of a peculiar Carolingian Christendom was made clear by the royal issuance of the so-called *Libri Carolini*. These documents were a blistering attack by Charlemagne on the second ecumenical Council of Nicaea, which had met in 787 to construct a new, approving eastern position on the use of images in churches—actually a friendly gesture toward the west. The height of Charlemagne's imperial pretension was reached, however, on Christmas Day, 800, when Pope Leo III (795–816), a contested pope whom Charlemagne had only a short time before forcibly restored to power, crowned Charlemagne emperor. This fateful coronation was in part an effort by the pope to enhance the church's stature and to gain a certain leverage over this king who seemed to dominate everything in his path. It was no papal *coup d'état*, however; Charlemagne's control over the church was as strong after as before the event. If the coronation benefited the church, as it certainly did, it also

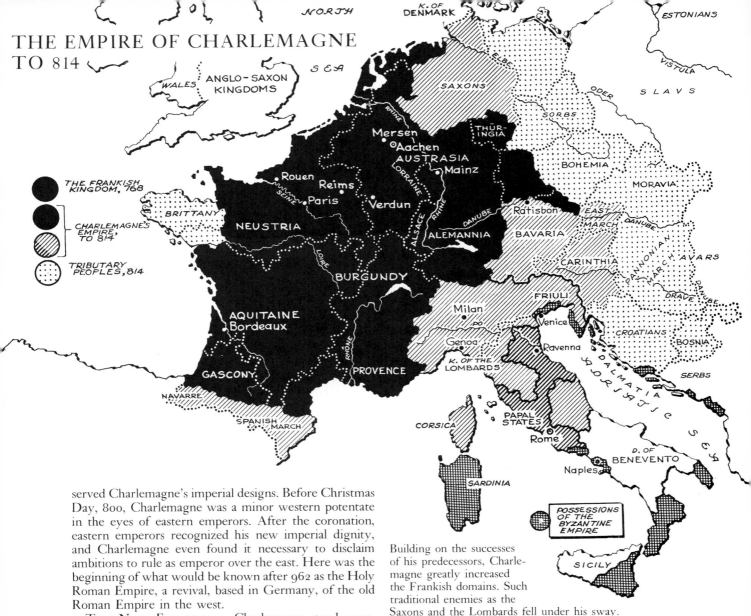

THE FRANKISH
KINGDOM, 768

CHARLEMAGNE'S
EMPIRE,
TO 814

TRIBUTARY
PEOPLES, 814

Building on the successes
of his predecessors, Charlemagne greatly increased
the Frankish domains. Such
traditional enemies as the
Saxons and the Lombards fell under his sway.

served Charlemagne's imperial designs. Before Christmas Day, 800, Charlemagne was a minor western potentate in the eyes of eastern emperors. After the coronation, eastern emperors recognized his new imperial dignity, and Charlemagne even found it necessary to disclaim ambitions to rule as emperor over the east. Here was the beginning of what would be known after 962 as the Holy Roman Empire, a revival, based in Germany, of the old Roman Empire in the west.

THE NEW EMPEROR. Charlemagne stood a majestic six feet, three and one-half inches tall—a fact secured when his tomb was opened and exact measurements were made in 1861. He was nomadic, ever ready for a hunt. Informal and gregarious, he insisted upon the presence of friends even when he bathed and was widely known for his practical jokes, lusty good humor, and warm hospitality. Aachen was a festive palace city to which people and gifts came from all over the world. In 802 Charlemagne even received from the caliph of Baghdad, Harun-al-Rashid, a white elephant, the transport of which across the Alps was as great a wonder as the creature itself.

Charlemagne had five official wives, possessed many mistresses and concubines, and sired numerous children. This connubial variety created special problems. His

oldest son by his first marriage, Pepin, jealous of the attention shown by his father to the sons of his second wife and fearing the loss of paternal favor, joined with noble enemies in a conspiracy against his father. He ended his life in confinement in a monastery after the plot was exposed.

PROBLEMS OF GOVERNMENT. Charlemagne governed his kingdom through counts, of whom there were perhaps as many as 250. They were strategically located within the administrative districts into which the kingdom was divided. The count had three main duties: to maintain a local army loyal to the king, to collect

Einhard Describes His Admired Emperor, Charlemagne

We are fortunate to have the eye-witness account of Charlemagne by a court scholar, Einhard. Here are his remarks on the king's features, habits, and aspirations.

CHARLES *was large and robust, of commanding stature and excellent proportions. . . . He took constant exercise in riding and hunting, which was natural for a Frank, since scarcely any nation can be found to equal them in these pursuits. He also delighted in the natural warm baths, frequently exercising himself by swimming, in which he was very skillful, no one being able to outstrip him. It was on account of the warm baths at Aix-la-Chapelle that he built his palace there and lived there constantly during the last years of his life and until his death. . . .*

He wore the dress of his native country, that is, the Frankish. . . . He thoroughly disliked the dress of foreigners, however fine; and he never put it on except at Rome. . . .

In his eating and drinking he was temperate; more particularly so in his drinking, for he had the greatest abhorrence of drunkenness in anybody, but more especially in himself and his companions. . . . While he was dining he listened to music or reading. History and the deeds of men of old were most often read. He derived much pleasure from the works of St. Augustine, especially from his book called The City of God.

He was ready and fluent in speaking, and able to express himself with great clearness. He did not confine himself to his native tongue, but took pains to learn foreign languages, acquiring such knowledge of Latin that he could make an address in that language as well as in his own. Greek he could better understand than speak. Indeed, he was so polished in speech that he might have passed for a learned man.

He was an ardent admirer of the liberal arts, and greatly revered their professors, whom he promoted to high honors. In order to learn grammar, he attended the lectures of the aged Peter of Pisa, a deacon; and for other branches he chose as his preceptor Alcuin, also a deacon,—a Saxon by race, from Britain, the most learned man of the day, with whom the king spent much time in learning rhetoric and logic, and more especially astronomy. He learned the art of determining the dates upon which the movable festivals of the Church fall, and with deep thought and skill most carefully calculated the courses of the planets.

Charles also tried to learn to write, and used to keep his tablets and writing book under the pillow of his couch, *that when he had leisure he might practice his hand in forming letters; but he made little progress in this task, too long deferred and begun too late in life.*

Life of Charlemagne, in James Harvey Robinson, *Readings in European History*, Vol. 1 (Boston: Athenaeum, 1904), pp. 126–128.

tribute and dues, and to administer justice throughout his district. This last responsibility was undertaken through a district law court known as the *mallus*. Difficult cases were settled by judicial duels or by such "divine" judgments as the length of time it took a defendant's hand to heal after it was immersed in boiling water. The *mallus* assessed *wergeld*, that is, the compensation paid to an injured party to bring an end to a feud, which was the most popular way of settling grievances. In Carolingian practice the count tended to be a local magnate, one who already possessed the armed might and the self-interest to enforce the will of a generous king.

As in Merovingian times many counts used their official position and new judicial powers to their own advantage, becoming little despots within their districts. As the strong were made stronger they became more independent. They looked upon the land grants with which they were paid as hereditary possessions rather than generous royal donations—a development that began to fragment Charlemagne's kingdom. Charlemagne tried to oversee his overseers and improve local justice by creating special royal envoys known as *missi dominici*. These were lay and clerical agents (counts and archbishops and bishops) who made annual visits to districts other than their own. But their impact was only marginal. Permanent provincial governors, bearing the title of prefect, duke, or margrave, were created in what was still another attempt to supervise the counts and organize the outlying region of the kingdom. But as these governors became established in their areas, they proved no less corruptible than the others. Charlemagne never solved the problem of a loyal

Charlemagne's amulet, a bejeweled reliquary, possibly containing a piece of the cross of Jesus. Such charms were thought to protect one. [Joubert/© Archives Photographiques, Paris/S.P.A.D.E.M.]

bureaucracy. Ecclesiastical agents proved no better than secular ones in this regard. Landowning bishops had not only the same responsibilities but also the same secular lifestyles and aspirations as the royal counts. Save for their attendance to the liturgy and to church prayers, they were largely indistinguishable. Capitularies or royal decrees were issued to discourage the more outrageous behavior of the clergy. But Charlemagne also sensed, rightly as the Gregorian reform of the eleventh century would prove, a danger to royal government in the emergence of a distinctive and reformed-minded class of ecclesiastical landowners. Charlemagne purposefully treated his bishops as he treated his counts, that is, as vassals who served at the king's pleasure.

Carolingian society lacked the developed feudal and urban structures necessary to the pursuit of the high Christian virtues of love and self-sacrifice. To be a Christian in this period was more a matter of ritual and doctrine, being baptized and reciting the Creed, than a prescribed ethical behavior and social service. For both the clergy and the laity it was a time when more primitive social goals were being contested. A legislative achievement of Charlemagne's reign, for example, was to give a free vassal the right to break his oath of loyalty to his lord if the lord tried to kill him, to reduce him to an unfree serf, to withhold promised protection in time of need, or to seduce his wife.

ALCUIN AND THE CAROLINGIAN RENAISSANCE. Charlemagne accumulated a great deal of wealth in the form of loot and land from conquered tribes. A substantial part of this booty was used to attract Europe's best scholars to Aachen, where they developed court culture and education. By making scholarship materially as well as intellectually rewarding, Charlemagne attracted such scholars as Theodulf of Orleans, Angilbert, his own biographer Einhard, and the reknowned Anglo-Saxon master Alcuin of York (735–804), who, at almost fifty, was persuaded in 782 to become director of the king's palace school. Alcuin brought classical and Christian learning to Aachen and was handsomely rewarded

for his efforts with several monastic estates, including that of Saint Martin of Tours, the wealthiest in the kingdom.

Although Charlemagne also appreciated learning for its own sake, this grand palace school was not created simply for love of antiquity. It was intended to upgrade the administrative skills of the clerics and officials who staffed the royal bureaucracy. By preparing the sons of noblemen to run the religious and secular offices of the realm, court scholarship served kingdom building. The school provided basic instruction in the seven liberal arts, with special concentration on grammar, logic, and mathematics, that is, training in reading, writing, speaking, and sound reasoning—the basic tools of bureaucracy. A clearer style of handwriting—the Carolingian miniscule—and accurate Latin appeared in the official documents. Lay literacy was also much increased. Through personal correspondence and visitations Alcuin created a genuine if limited community of scholars and clerics at court and did much to infuse the highest administrative levels with a sense of brotherhood and common purpose.

A modest renaissance or rebirth of antiquity occurred in the palace school as scholars collected and preserved many ancient manuscripts for a more curious posterity. Alcuin worked on a correct text of the Bible and made editions of the works of Gregory the Great and the monastic *Rule* of Saint Benedict. These scholarly activities aimed at concrete reforms and served official efforts to bring uniformity to church law and liturgy, to educate the clergy, and to improve moral life within the monasteries.

SERFDOM. Serfs were basically farmers who tended the lord's lands. By the time of Charlemagne the mold-board plow and the three-field system of land cultivation were in use, developments that improved agricultural productivity. Unlike the older "scratch" plow that criss-crossed the field with slight penetration, the moldboard cut deep into the soil and turned it so that it formed a ridge, providing a natural drainage system to the field.

Unlike the earlier two-field system of crop rotation, which simply alternated fallow with planted fields each

The invention of the moldboard plow around 900 greatly improved farming. The heavy plow cut deeply into the ground and furrowed it. This illustration from the Luttrell Psalter (*ca.* 1340) shows that the traction harness, which lessened the strangulating effect of the yoke on the animals, had not yet been adopted. Indeed, one of the oxen seems to be on the verge of choking. [Add. MS. 42130, f. 170. Reproduced by permission of the British Library Board, London.]

year, the three-field system increased the amount of cultivated land by leaving only one third fallow in a given year. It also better adjusted crops to seasons. In winter one field was planted with winter crops of wheat or rye; in the summer a second field was planted with summer crops of oats, barley, and lentils; and the third field was left fallow, to be planted in its turn with winter and summer crops.

Serfs were subject to so-called dues in kind: firewood for cutting the lord's wood, sheep for grazing their sheep on the lord's land, and the like. In this way the lord, by furnishing shacks and small plots of land from his vast domain, created an army of servants who provided him with everything from eggs to boots. The discontent of the common man is witnessed by the high number of recorded escapes. An astrological calendar from the period even marks the days most favorable for escaping. Escaped serfs roamed the land as beggars and vagabonds, vainly searching for new and better masters.

Serfdom is a desirable state in no age, but it was particularly gruesome in the Carolingian. Small landowners and freemen were subjected to many royal obligations: taxes, church tithes, military service, and forced labor on special occasions. An incautious freeman could find himself stripped of all power and possessions and entangled in a lifetime of military service to the king. Many had no alternative but to choose the lesser of two evils and surrender their modest allodial or hereditary property to a local magnate, giving up property and freedom to gain security. The local magnate became in turn their lord and agreed to be their advocate before the king. Freemen who were unable to find such patronage were virtually forced into the great mass of bonded serfs who had no realistic hopes of ever improving their lot. Such landless men were under the absolute authority of their masters. Fleeing to a monastery was often seen as preferable for weak freemen and peasants, and it was for that reason an avenue of escape eventually closed by law. Each estate was in need of every man's labor, and landowners acted to keep their servants firmly in their places.

RELIGION AND THE CLERGY. The lower clergy lived among and were drawn from the peasant class. They hardly fared better than peasants in Carolingian times. As owners of the churches on their lands, the lords had the right to raise chosen serfs to the post of parish priest, placing them in charge of the proprietary churches on the lords' estates. Although church law directed the lord to set a serf free before he entered the clergy, lords were reluctant to do this and risk thereby a later challenge to their jurisdiction over the ecclesiastical property with which the serf, as priest, was invested. Lords rather preferred a "serf-priest," one who not only said the mass on Sundays and holidays but who also continued to remain in his place during the week, waiting upon the lord's table and tending his steeds. Like Charlemagne with his bishops, Frankish lords cultivated a docile parish clergy.

The ordinary man looked to his religion for comfort and consolation. He considered his baptism and confession of the Creed a surety of future salvation. He baptized his children, attended mass, tried to learn the Lord's Prayer, and received extreme unction from the priest on his deathbed. This was done with more awe and simple faith than understanding. Religious instruction in the meaning of doctrine and practice remained at a bare minimum, and local priests on the manors were no better educated than their congregations. People understandably became particularly attached in this period to the more tangible veneration of relics and saints. Religious devotion to saints has been compared to secular subjection to powerful lords; both the saint and the lord were protectors whose honor the serf was bound to defend and whose favor and help in time of need he hoped to receive. Veneration of saints also had strong points of contact with old tribal religious customs, from which the common man was hardly detached, as Charlemagne's enforcement of laws against witchcraft, sorcery, and the ritual sacrifice of animals by monks makes all too clear. But it is also to be appreciated that religion has an intrinsic appeal and special meaning to those who, like the masses of medieval men and women, find themselves burdened, fearful, and with little hope of material betterment this side of eternity. Charlemagne shared many of the religious beliefs of his ordinary subjects. He collected and venerated relics, made pilgrimages to Rome, frequented the church of Saint Mary in Aachen several times a day, and directed in his last will and testament that all but a fraction of his great treasure be spent to endow masses and prayers for his departed soul.

Breakup of the Carolingian Kingdom

In the last years of his life an ailing Charlemagne knew that his empire was coming apart. The seeds of dissolution lay in regionalism. Despite his considerable skill and resolution, Charlemagne's realm was too fragmented among powerful regional magnates. Although they were his vassals, these same men were also great landholders and lords in their own right. They knew that their sovereignty lessened as Charlemagne's increased and accordingly became reluctant servants of the state. In feudal society there was a direct relationship between physical proximity to authority and loyalty to authority. Local people obeyed local lords more readily than they obeyed their glorious but distant king. Charlemagne had been forced to recognize and even to enhance the power of regional magnates in order to win needed financial and military support. But as in the Merovingian kingdom so also in the Carolingian, the tail came increasingly to wag the dog. Charlemagne's major attempt to enforce subordination to royal dictates and a transregional discipline—through the institution of the *missi dominici*—proved unsuccessful.

LOUIS THE PIOUS. Carolingian kings did not give up easily. Charlemagne's only surviving son and successor was Louis the Pious (814–840), so-called because of his close alliance with the church and his promotion of puritanical reforms. Before his death Charlemagne secured the imperial succession by raising Louis to "co-emperor" in a grand public ceremony. After Charlemagne's death Louis no longer referred to himself as "king of the Franks." He bore instead the single title of *emperor*. This reflected not only Carolingian pretense to an imperial dynasty, but also Louis's determination to unify his kingdom and raise its people above mere regional and tribal loyalties. Unfortunately Louis's own fertility and the weight of Salic law and Frankish custom prevented the achievement of this high goal.

Louis had three sons by his first wife. According to Salic or Germanic law, a ruler partitioned his kingdom

Carolingian architecture. In addition to Charlemagne's grander cathedral and mausoleum at Aachen (shown above on page 243), this simple and unpretentious oratory of Germigny-des-Prés, France, built about 806, exemplifies Western medieval building before the spread of a distinctive Romanesque style. [French Cultural Services, New York.]

equally among his surviving sons. Louis, who saw himself as an emperor and no mere German king, recognized that a tripartite kingdom would hardly be an empire and acted early in his reign, in the year 817, to break this legal tradition. This he did by making his eldest son, Lothar (d. 855), co-regent and sole imperial heir. Lothar's brothers were awarded important but much lesser appanages: Pepin (d. 838) became king of Aquitaine, and Louis "the German" (d. 876) became king of Bavaria or over the eastern Franks.

In 823 Louis's second wife, Judith of Bavaria, bore him still a fourth son, Charles, later called "the Bald" (d. 877). Mindful of Frankish law and custom and determined that her son should receive more than just a nominal inheritance, the queen incited the brothers Pepin and Louis to war against Lothar, who fled for refuge to the pope. More importantly, Judith was instrumental in persuading Louis to reverse his earlier decision and divide the kingdom equally among his four living sons. As their stepmother and the young Charles rose in their father's favor, the three brothers feared still further reversals. They decided to act against their father. Supported by the pope, they joined forces and defeated their father in a battle near Colmar (833).

As the bestower of crowns upon emperors, the pope had an important stake in the preservation of the revived western empire and the imperial title, which Louis's belated agreement to an equal partition of his kingdom threatened to undo. The pope condemned Louis and restored Lothar to his original inheritance. But Lothar's revived imperial dignity only stirred anew the resentments of his brothers, including his stepbrother, Charles, who reheated their war against him.

THE TREATY OF VERDUN AND ITS AFTERMATH. Peace finally came to the heirs of Louis the Pious in 843 in the Treaty of Verdun. But this agreement also brought about the disaster Louis had originally feared: the great Carolingian empire was partitioned according to Frankish law into three equal parts, Pepin having died in 838. Lothar received a middle section,

The Treaty of Verdun divided the kingdom of Louis the Pious among his three feuding children: Charles the Bald, Lothar, and Louis the German. After Lothar's death in 855 the middle kingdom was so weakened by division among *his* three sons that Charles the Bald and Louis the German divided it between themselves in the Treaty of Mersen in 870.

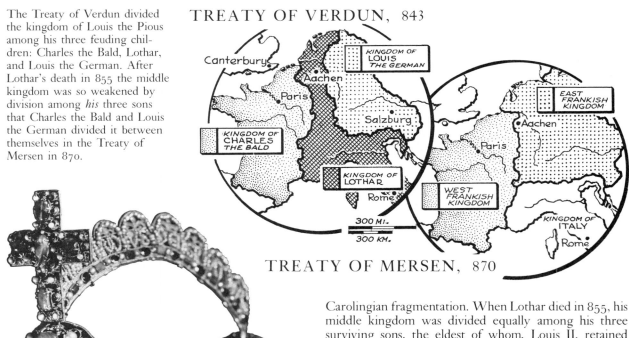

TREATY OF VERDUN, 843

Canterbury
Aachen
Paris
KINGDOM OF LOUIS THE GERMAN
Salzburg
KINGDOM OF CHARLES THE BALD
KINGDOM OF LOTHAR
Rome
300 MI.
300 KM.

EAST FRANKISH KINGDOM
Aachen
Paris
WEST FRANKISH KINGDOM
KINGDOM OF ITALY
Rome

TREATY OF MERSEN, 870

A crown of the emperor of the Holy Roman Empire from the early tenth century with a depiction of the Biblical King Solomon on the front section. The back sections of the crown bear depictions of King David and the prophet Isaiah. [Kunsthistorisches Museum, Vienna.]

which came to be known as Lotharingia and embraced roughly modern Holland, Belgium, Switzerland, Alsace-Lorraine, and Italy. Charles the Bald received the western part of the kingdom or roughly modern France. And Louis the German came into the eastern part or roughly modern Germany. Although Lothar retained the imperial title, the universal empire of Charlemagne and Louis the Pious was no more after Verdun. Not until the sixteenth century, with the election in 1519 of Charles I of Spain as the Holy Roman Emperor Charles V, would the world again see a kingdom so great as Charlemagne's.

The Treaty of Verdun proved but the beginning of Carolingian fragmentation. When Lothar died in 855, his middle kingdom was divided equally among his three surviving sons, the eldest of whom, Louis II, retained Italy and the imperial title. This partition of the partition left the middle or imperial kingdom much smaller and weaker than that of Louis the German and Charles the Bald. In fact it sealed the dissolution of the great empire of Charlemagne. Henceforth western Europe saw an eastern and a western Frankish kingdom—roughly Germany versus France—at war over the fractionalized middle kingdom, a contest that has continued into modern times.

In Italy the demise of Carolingian emperors enhanced for the moment the power of the popes, who had long been adept at filling vacuums. Popes were now strong enough to excommunicate and override the wishes of weak emperors. Pope Nicholas I (858–867) excommunicated Lothar II for divorcing his wife in a major church crackdown on the serial polygamy of the Germans. After the death of the childless emperor Louis II (875), Pope John VII (872–882) installed Charles the Bald as emperor against the express last wishes of Louis II.

When Charles the Bald died in 877, both the papal and the imperial thrones fell on especially hard times. Each became a pawn in the hands of powerful German and Italian magnates. Neither pope nor emperor was to know dignity and power again until a new western imperial dynasty—the Ottonians—attained dominance during the reign of Otto I (962–976). It is especially at this juncture in European history—the last quarter of the ninth and the first half of the tenth century—that one may speak with some justification of a "dark age." Simultaneously with the internal political breakdown of the empire and the papacy came new barbarian attacks, set off probably by overpopulation and famine in northern Europe. The late ninth and tenth centuries saw successive waves of Nor-

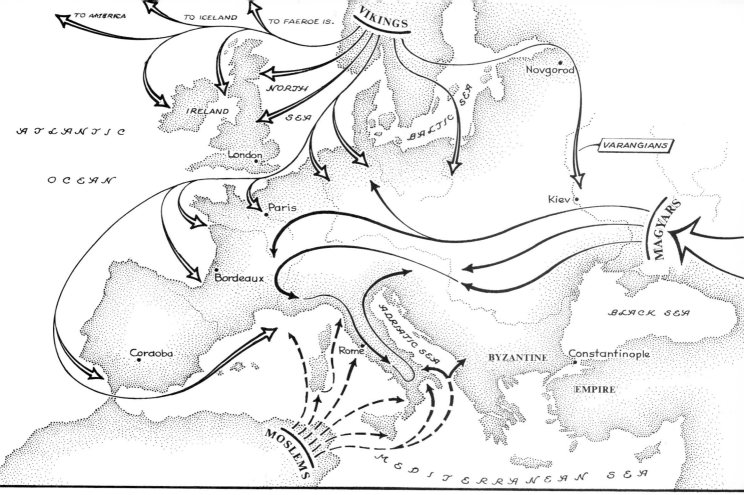

VIKING, MOSLEM, AND MAGYAR INVASIONS TO THE ELEVENTH CENTURY

Western Europe was sorely beset by new waves of outsiders from the ninth to the eleventh century. From north, east, and south a stream of invading Vikings, Magyars, and Moslems brought the West at times to near collapse and of course gravely affected institutions within Europe.

mans (North-men), better known as Vikings, from Scandinavia; Magyars or Hungarians, the great horsemen from the eastern plains; and Saracens from the south. In the 88os the Vikings penetrated to the imperial residence of Aachen and to Paris. Moving rapidly in ships and raiding coastal towns, they were almost impossible to defend against and kept western Europe on edge. The Franks built great fortified towns and castles in strategic locations, which served as refuges. When they could, they bought off the invaders with outright grants of land (for example, Normandy) and payments of silver. In this period local populations came to be more dependent than ever before upon local strongmen for life, limb, and livelihood. It was that brute fact of life that provided

the essential precondition for the maturation of feudal society.

Feudal Society

The Middle Ages were characterized by a chronic absence of effective central government and the constant threat of famine and foreign invasion. *Feudal society* is a term used to describe the adjustment to this breakdown of centralized government as the weaker sought protection from the stronger. The term refers to the social, political, and economic system that emerged from the repeatedly experienced fact that only those who could guarantee immediate protection from rapine and starvation were true lords and masters. Feudal society is a social order in which a regional prince or a local lord is dominant and the highest virtues are those of mutual trust and fidelity. In a feudal society what men most need is the firm assurance that others can be depended upon in time of dire need.

Medieval times saw the landed nobility become great lords who ruled over their domains as miniature fatherlands. They maintained their own armies and courts, regulated their area's tolls, even minted their own coins. Large warrior groups of vassals were created by extensive bestowals of land, and they developed into a prominent professional military class with its own code of knightly conduct. In feudal society most serfs docilely worked the land, clergy prayed and gave counsel, and the nobility—both landed and vassal—maintained law and order by swift steed and sword.

Origins

The main features of feudal government can be found in the divisions and conflicts of Merovingian society. In the sixth and seventh centuries there evolved the custom of individual freemen placing themselves under the protection of more powerful freemen. In this way the latter built up armies and became local magnates, and the former solved the problem of simple survival. Freemen who so entrusted themselves to others were known as *ingenui in obsequio* ("freemen in a contractual relation of dependence"). Those who so gave themselves to the king were called *antrustiones*. All men of this type came to be described collectively as *vassi* ("those who serve"), from which evolved the term *vassalage*, meaning the placement of oneself in the personal service of another who promises protection in return.

Landed nobility, like kings, tried to acquire as many such vassals as they could, because military strength in the early Middle Ages lay in numbers. As it proved impossible to maintain these growing armies within the lord's own household, as was the original custom, or to support them by special monetary payments, the practice evolved of simply granting them land as a "tenement." Such land came to be known as a *benefice* or a *fief*, and vassals were expected to dwell on it and maintain in good order their steeds and other accouterments of war. Originally vassals, therefore, were little more than gangs-in-waiting.

The Franks Formalize the Entrance into Vassalage

Entrance into vassalage involved a very formal and sacred ceremony in which the vassal pledged to serve and honor his lord and the lord to guard and protect his vassal from all his enemies. The following is a Frankish formula of commendation from the seventh century.

VASSAL:

To that *magnificent Lord* , I, , *Since it is known familiarly to all how little I have whence to feed and clothe myself, I have therefore petitioned your Piety, and your good will has permitted me to hand myself over or commend myself to your guardianship, which I have thereupon done; that is to say, in this way, that you should aid and succor me as well with food as with clothing, according as I shall be able to serve you and deserve it.*

And so long as I shall live I ought to provide service and honor to you, suitably to my free condition; and I shall not during my lifetime have the ability to withdraw from your power or guardianship, but must remain during the days of my life under your power or defense. Wherefore it is proper that if either of us shall wish to withdraw himself from these agreements, he shall pay shillings to his companion, and this agreement shall remain unbroken. . . .

LORD:

It is *right that those who offer to us unbroken fidelity should be protected by our aid. And since , a faithful one of ours, by the favor of God, coming here in our palace with his arms, has seen fit to swear trust and fidelity to us in our hand, therefore we herewith decree and command that for the future , above mentioned, be reckoned among the number of the antrustions [i.e. followers]. And if any one perchance should presume to kill him, let him know that he will be judged guilty of his weregild of six hundred shillings.*

James Harvey Robinson (Ed.), *Readings in European History*, Vol. 1 (Boston: Athenaeum, 1904), pp. 175–176.

Vassalage and the Fief

Vassalage involved "fealty" to the lord. To swear fealty was to promise to refrain from any action that might in any way threaten the lord's well-being and to perform personal services for him, upon his request. Chief among the expected services was military duty as a mounted

Bishop Fulbert Describes the Obligations of Vassal and Lord

Trust held the lord and vassal together. Their duties in this regard were carefully defined. Here are six general rules for vassal and lord, laid down by Bishop Fulbert of Chartres in a letter to William, Duke of Aquitaine, in 1020.

H E   W H O *swears fealty to his lord ought always to have these six things in memory: what is harmless, safe, honorable, useful, easy, practicable. Harmless, that is to say, that he should not injure his lord in his body; safe, that he should not injure him by betraying his secrets or the defenses upon which he relies for safety; honorable, that he should not injure him in his justice or in other matters that pertain to his honor; useful, that he should not injure him in his possessions; easy and practicable, that that good which his lord is able to do easily he make not difficult, nor that which is practicable he make not impossible to him.*

That the faithful vassal should avoid these injuries is certainly proper, but not for this alone does he deserve his holding; for it is not sufficient to abstain from evil, unless what is good is done also. It remains, therefore, that in the same six things mentioned above he should faithfully counsel and aid his lord, if he wishes to be looked upon as worthy of his benefice and to be safe concerning the fealty which he has sworn.

The lord also ought to act toward his faithful vassal reciprocally in all these things. And if he does not do this, he will be justly considered guilty of bad faith, just as the former, if he should be detected in avoiding or consenting to the avoidance of his duties, would be perfidious and perjured.

From James Harvey Robinson (Ed.), *Readings in European History,* Vol. 1 (Boston: Athenaeum, 1904), p. 184.

---

knight. This could involve a variety of activities: a short or long military expedition, escort duty, standing castle guard, and the placement of one's own fortress at the lord's disposal, if the vassal was of such stature as to have one. There was continuous bargaining and bickering over the terms of service. Limitations were placed on the number of days a lord could require services from a vassal. In France in the eleventh century about forty days of service were considered sufficient. It also became possible for vassals to buy their way out of military service by a monetary payment known as *scutage.* The lord in turn applied this payment to the hiring of mercenaries, who often proved more efficient than contract-conscious vassals. Beyond his military duty the vassal was also expected to give the lord advice when he requested it and to sit as a member of his court when the latter was in session.

Beginning with the reign of Louis the Pious (814–840), bishops and abbots were also required to swear fealty and to receive their offices from the king as a benefice. These clerics were formally "invested" in their offices by the king during a special ceremony in which he presented them with a ring and a staff, the symbols of high spiritual office. Louis's predecessors had earlier confiscated church lands with only modest and belated compensation to the church in the form of a tithe required of all Frankish inhabitants. Long a sore point for the church, the presumptuous practice of lay investiture of clergy provoked a world-shaking confrontation of church and state in the eleventh and twelfth centuries, when reform-minded clergy rebelled against what they then believed was involuntary clerical vassalage.

The lord's obligations to his vassals were very specific. He was, first of all, obligated to protect the vassal from physical harm and to stand as his advocate in public court. After fealty was sworn and homage paid, the lord was expected to provide for the vassal's physical maintenance by the bestowal of a benefice or fief. The fief was simply the physical or material wherewithal to meet the vassal's military and other obligations. It could take the form of liquid wealth as well as the more common grant of real property. There were so-called money fiefs, which empowered a vassal to receive regular payments from the lord's treasury. Such fiefs were potentially quite devilish because they made it possible for one country to acquire vassals among the nobility of another. Normally the fief consisted of a landed estate of anywhere from a few to several thousand acres. But it could also take the form of a castle.

In Carolingian times a benefice or fief varied in size from one or more small villas to several *mansi*, which were agricultural holdings of twenty-five to forty-eight acres. The king's vassals are known to have received benefices of at least thirty and as many as two hundred such holdings, truly a vast estate. Royal vassalage with benefice understandably came to be widely sought by the highest classes of Carolingian society. As a royal policy, however, it proved deadly to the king in the long run. Although Carolingian kings jealously guarded their rights over property granted in benefice to vassals, resident vassals were still free to dispose of their benefices as they pleased. Vassals of the king, strengthened by his donations, in turn created their own vassals. These in turn created still further vassals of their own—vassals of vassals of vassals—in a reverse pyramiding effect that fragmented land and authority from the highest to the lowest levels by the late ninth century.

Fragmentation and Divided Loyalty

In addition to the fragmentation brought about by the multiplication of vassalage, effective occupation of land led gradually to claims of hereditary possession. Hereditary possession became a legally recognized principle in the ninth century and laid the basis for claims to real ownership. Fiefs given as royal donations became hereditary possessions and, with the passage of time, the real property of the possessor. Further, vassal engagements came to be multiplied in still another way as enterprising freemen sought to accumulate as much land as possible. One man actually became a vassal to several different lords. It was this development that led in the ninth century to the concept of a "liege lord"—that one master whom the vassal must obey even to the harm of the others, should a direct conflict among them arise.

The problem of loyalty was reflected not only in the literature of the period, with its praise of the virtues of honor and fidelity, but also in the ceremonial development of the very act of "commendation" by which a freeman became a vassal. In the mid-eighth century an "oath of fealty" was added to the ceremony. One reinforced his promise of fidelity to the lord by swearing a special oath with his hand on a sacred relic or the Bible. In the tenth and eleventh centuries paying homage to the lord involved not only the swearing of such an oath but also the placement of the vassal's hands between the lord's and the sealing of the ceremony with a kiss.

As the centuries passed, personal loyalty and service became quite secondary to the acquisition of property. The fief overshadowed fealty; the benefice became more important than vassalage. Freemen proved themselves prepared to swear allegiance to the highest bidder—a development that signaled the waning of feudal society.

SUGGESTED READINGS

MARC BLOCH, *Feudal Society*, Vols. 1 and 2, trans. by L. A. Manyon (Chicago, 1971). A classic on the topic and as an example of historical study.

PETER BROWN, *Augustine of Hippo: A Biography* (1967). Late antiquity seen through the biography of its greatest Christian thinker.

HENRY CHADWICK, *The Early Church* (1967). Among the best treatments of early Christianity.

R. H. C. DAVIS, *A History of Medieval Europe: From Constantine to St. Louis* (1972), Part 1. Unsurpassed in clarity.

K. F. DREW (Ed.), *The Barbarian Invasions: Catalyst of a New Order* (1970). Collection of essays that focuses the issues.

HEINRICH FICHTENAU, *The Carolingian Empire: The Age of Charlemagne*, trans. by Peter Munz (1964). Strongest on political history of the era.

F. L. GANSHOF, *Feudalism*, trans. by Philip Grierson (1964). The most profound brief analysis of the subject.

A. F. HAVIGHURST (Ed.), *The Pirenne Thesis: Analysis, Criticism, and Revision* (1958). Excerpts from the scholarly debate over the extent of Western trade in the East during the early Middle Ages.

DAVID KNOWLES, *Christian Monasticism* (1969). Sweeping survey with helpful photographs.

M. L. W. LAISTNER, *Thought and Letters in Western Europe, 500 to 900* (1957). Among the best surveys of early medieval intellectual history.

JEAN LECLERCQ, *The Love of Learning and the Desire for*

God: A Study of Monastic Culture, trans. by Catherine Misrahi (1962). Lucid, delightful, absorbing account of the ideals of monks.

J. LECLERCQ, F. VANDENBROUCKE, and L. BOUYER, *The Spirituality of the Middle Ages* (1968). The best survey of medieval Christianity, East and West, to the eve of the Protestant Reformation.

PETER MUNZ, *The Age of Charlemagne* (1971). Penetrating social history of the period.

HENRI PIRENNE, *A History of Europe, I: From the End of the Roman World in the West to the Beginnings of the Western States,* trans. by Bernhard Maill (1958). Comprehensive survey, with now-controversial views on the demise of Western trade and cities in the early Middle Ages.

STEVEN RUNCIMAN, *Byzantine Civilization* (1970). Succinct, comprehensive account by a master.

PETER SAWYER, *The Age of the Vikings* (1962). The best account.

R. W. SOUTHERN, *The Making of the Middle Ages* (1973). Originally published in 1953, but still a fresh account by an imaginative historian.

CARL STEPHENSON, *Medieval Feudalism* (1969). Excellent short summary and introduction.

A. A. VASILIEV, *History of the Byzantine Empire 324–1453* (1952). The most comprehensive treatment in English.

LYNN WHITE, JR., *Medieval Technology and Social Change* (1962). Often fascinating account of the way primitive technology changed life.

I I

The High Middle Ages (1000–1300): Revival of Empire, Church, and Towns

THE HIGH Middle Ages mark a period of political expansion and consolidation and of intellectual flowering and synthesis. The noted medievalist Joseph Strayer has called it the age that saw "the full development of all the potentialities of medieval civilization."[1] Some even argue that as far as the development of Western institutions is concerned, this was a more creative period than the later Italian Renaissance and the German Reformation.

The high Middle Ages saw the borders of Europe largely secured against foreign invaders. Although there was intermittent Moslem aggression well into the sixteenth century, fear of assault from without diminished. A striking change occurred in the late eleventh century and the twelfth century. Western Europe, which had for so long been the hunted, became through the crusades and foreign trade the feared hunter within both the Eastern and the Arab world.

It was during the high Middle Ages that national monarchies emerged in France, England, and Germany. Parliaments and popular assemblies representing feudal interests—those of noblemen, the clergy, and townsmen—also appeared at this time to secure local rights and customs against the claims of the developing nation-state. The foundations of modern representative institutions can be found in this period.

The high Middle Ages saw a revolution in agriculture that increased both food supplies and populations. This period witnessed a great revival of trade and commerce,

[1] *Western History in the Middle Ages—A Short History* (New York: Appleton-Century-Crofts, 1955), pp. 9, 127.

the rise of towns, and the emergence of a "new rich" merchant class, the ancestors of modern capitalists. Urban culture and education flourished through the recovery of Greek manuscripts made possible by the revival of Eastern trade. Unlike the dabbling in antiquity during Carolingian times, the twelfth century enjoyed a true renaissance of classical learning.

The high Middle Ages were also the time of the distinctive Western separation of Church and State. This occurred during the Investiture Struggle of the late eleventh century and the twelfth century. It was in this confrontation between popes and emperors that a reformed papacy overcame its long subservience to Carolingian and Ottonian kings. The papacy won out, however, by becoming itself a monarchy among the world's emerging monarchies, thereby preparing the way for still more fateful confrontations between popes and emperors in the later Middle Ages. Religious reformers would later see in the Gregorian papacy of the high Middle Ages the fall of the church from its spiritual mission as well as its declaration of independence from secular power.

Otto I and Revival of the Empire

The fortunes of both the old empire and the papacy began to revive after the dark period of the late ninth century and early tenth century with the election in 918 of the Saxon Henry I ("the Fowler"; d. 936), the strongest of the German dukes and the first non-Frankish king of Germany. Henry rebuilt royal power by forcibly consolidating the duchies of Swabia, Bavaria, Saxony, Franconia, and Lotharingia. He secured imperial borders by checking the invasions of the Hungarians and the Danes. Although greatly reduced in size by comparison with Charlemagne's empire, Henry's German kingdom still placed his son and successor Otto I (936–973) in a strong territorial position.

The very able Otto maneuvered his own kin into positions of power in Bavaria, Swabia, and Franconia. He refused to treat each duchy as an independent hereditary

The fortified monastery of Mont-Saint-Michel in Normandy on the west coast of northern France was, in origin, a dramatic Romanesque complex of the twelfth century. It was later modified with Gothic additions and was much restored in the nineteenth century. [French Government Tourist Office, New York.]

Conspectus ecclesiæ Cluniacensis.

dukedom, as was the trend among the nobility. He dealt with each as a subordinate member of a unified kingdom. In a truly imperial gesture in 951, Otto invaded Italy and proclaimed himself its king. In 955 he won his most magnificent victory when he defeated the Hungarians at Lechfeld, a feat comparable to Charles Martel's earlier victory over the Saracens at Poitiers in 732. The victory at Lechfeld secured German borders against new barbarian attack, further unified the German duchies, and earned Otto the well-deserved title "the Great."

As part of a careful rebuilding program, Otto, following the example of his predecessors, enlisted the church. Bishops and abbots, men who possessed a sense of universal empire yet did not marry and found competitive dynasties, were made royal princes and agents of the king. Because these clergy, as royal bureaucrats, received great land holdings and immunity from local counts and dukes, they also found such vassalage to the king very attractive. The medieval church did not become a great territorial power reluctantly. It appreciated the blessings of receiving, although it taught the blessedness of giving.

In 961 Otto, who had long aspired to the imperial crown, responded to a call for help from Pope John XII (955–964), who was at this time being bullied by an Italian enemy of the German king, Berengar of Friuli. In recompense for this rescue Pope John crowned Otto emperor on February 2, 962, an event that proclaimed the Holy Roman Empire. At this time Otto also recognized the existence of the Papal States and proclaimed himself their special protector. But the church was now more than ever under royal control. Its bishops and abbots were Otto's appointees and bureaucrats, and the pope reigned in Rome only by the power of the emperor's sword. Pope John belatedly recognized the royal web in which the church was being entangled. As a countermeasure he joined Italian opposition to the new emperor. This turnabout brought Otto's swift revenge. In an ecclesiastical synod over which Otto personally presided, Pope John was deposed and a proclamation was made that henceforth no pope could take office without first

swearing an oath of allegiance to the emperor. In Otto I western Caesaropapism reached a peak, as popes ruled at the emperor's pleasure.

Otto had shifted the royal focus from Germany to Italy. His successors—Otto II (973–983), Otto III (994–1002), and Henry II (1002–1024)—became so preoccupied with running the affairs of Italy that their German base began to disintegrate, sacrificed to imperial dreams. They might have learned a lesson from the contemporary Capetian kings, the successor dynasty to the Carolingians in France, who wisely mended local fences and concentrated their limited resources on securing absolutely their immediate royal domain, which was never neglected for the sake of foreign adventure. The Ottonians, in contrast, reached far beyond their grasp when they tried to subdue Italy. As the briefly revived empire began to crumble in the first quarter of the eleventh century, the church, long unhappy with Carolingian and Ottonian domination, prepared to declare its independence and exact its own vengeance.

The Reviving Catholic Church
The Cluny Reform Movement

During the late ninth and early tenth centuries the clergy had been tools of kings and magnates and the

papacy a toy of Italian nobles. The Ottonians made bishops their servile princes, and popes served at their pleasure. A new day dawned for the church, however, thanks not only to the failing fortunes of the overextended empire but also to a new force for reform within the church itself. In a great monastery in Cluny in east central France a reform movement appeared to challenge political domination of the church at both the episcopal and the papal levels.

The reformers of Cluny were aided by widespread popular respect for the church. Most people admired clerics and monks. The church was medieval society's most democratic institution. In the Middle Ages any man could rise to the position of pope, and all were candidates for the church's grace and salvation. A better life to come was promised the great mass of ordinary people who found the present one brutish and without hope. Since the fall of the Roman Empire popular support for the church had been especially inspired by the example of the monks. Monasteries provided an important alternative style of life in an age when most people had very few options. The tenth and eleventh centuries saw an unprecedented boom in their construction. Monks remained the least secularized and most spiritual of the church's clergy. Their cultural achievements were widely admired, their relics and rituals considered magical, and their high religious ideals and sacrifices even imitated by the laity.

Cluny, the main source of the reform movement, was founded in 910 by William the Pious, duke of Aquitaine. It was a Benedictine monastery devoted to the strictest observance of Saint Benedict's *Rule for Monasteries*. Intent on creating a spiritual church, Cluny reformers absolutely rejected the subservience of clergy, especially that of German bishops, to royal authority. They taught that the pope in Rome was the sole ruler over all clergy. The Cluny reformers further resented the transgression of ascetic piety that the liaisons of secular clergy represented. (The secular clergy were all those who were active in the world [*saeculum*], as distinct from monks and

Pope Gregory VII Asserts the Power of the Pope

Church reformers of the high Middle Ages vigorously asserted the power of the pope within the church and his rights against emperors and all others who might transgress the papal sphere of jurisdiction. Here is a statement of the basic principles of the Gregorian reformers, known as the *Dictatus Papae*, which is attributed to Pope Gregory VII (1073–1085).

Tʜᴀᴛ *the Roman Church was founded by God alone.*

That the Roman Pontiff alone is rightly to be called universal.

That the Pope may depose the absent.

That for him alone it is lawful to enact new laws according to the needs of the time, to assemble together new congregations, to make an abbey of a canonry; and . . . to divide a rich bishopric and unite the poor ones.

That he alone may use the imperial insignia.

That the Pope is the only one whose feet are to be kissed by all princes.

That his name alone is to be recited in churches.

That his title is unique in the world.

That he may depose Emperors.

That he may transfer bishops, if necessary, from one See to another.

That no synod may be called a general one without his order.

That no chapter or book may be regarded as canonical without his authority.

That no sentence of his may be retracted by any one; and that he, alone of all, can retract it.

That he himself may be judged by no one.

That the Roman Church has never erred, nor ever, by the witness of Scripture, shall err to all eternity.

That the Pope may absolve subjects of unjust men from their fealty.

Church and State Through the Centuries: A Collection of Historic Documents, trans. and ed. by S. Z. Ehler and John B. Morrall (New York: Biblo and Tannen, 1967), pp. 43–44.

nuns, the regular clergy withdrawn from the world and living according to a special rule [*regula*]). The Cluny reformers resolved to free clergy from both kings and "wives," to create an independent and chaste clergy. The church alone was to be the clergy's sovereign and spouse. The distinctive Western separation of Church and State and the celibacy of Catholic clergy, both of which continue today, find their definitive origins in the Cluny reform movement.

Cluny rapidly became a center from which reformers were despatched to monasteries throughout France and Italy. Under its aggressive abbots, especially Saint Odo (926–946), it grew to embrace almost fifteen hundred dependent cloisters, each devoted to Cluny's program of desecularizing the church. In the last half of the eleventh century the Cluny reformers reached the summit when they captured the papacy itself.

Popes devoted to Cluny's reforms came to power during the reign of the Emperor Henry III (1036–1056). Pope Leo IX (1048–1054) promoted regional synods in opposition to simony (that is, the selling of spiritual things, such as church offices) and clerical concubinage. He also placed Cluniacs in key administrative posts in Rome. During the turbulent minority of Henry III's successor, Henry IV (1056–1106), reform popes began to assert themselves more openly. Pope Stephen IX (1057–1058) reigned without imperial ratification, contrary to the earlier declaration of Otto I. Pope Nicholas II (1059–1061) took the unprecedented step of establishing a College of Cardinals in 1059, and henceforth this body alone elected the pope. Only thirteen years earlier Henry III had deposed three schismatic popes, each a pawn of a Roman noble faction, and had installed a German bishop of his own choosing who ruled as Pope Clement I (1046–1047).

Such highhanded practices ended after 1059. With the creation of the College of Cardinals popes declared their full independence from both local Italian and distant royal interference, although rulers continued to have considerable indirect influence on the election of popes. Pope Nicholas II also embraced Cluny's strictures against simony and clerical concubinage and even struck his own political alliances with the Normans in Sicily and with France and Tuscany. His successor, Pope Alexander II (1061–1073), was elected solely by the College of Cardinals.

The Investiture Struggle: Gregory VII and Henry IV

It was Alexander's successor, Pope Gregory VII (1073–1085), a fierce Cluniac who had entered the papal bureaucracy a quarter century earlier during the pontificate of Leo IX, who put the church's declaration of independence to the test. Cluniacs had repeatedly inveighed against simony. A case had been built up by Cardinal Humbert against lay investiture of clergy as the supreme form of this evil practice. In 1075 Pope Gregory embraced these arguments and condemned under penalty of excommunication lay investiture of clergy at any level. He had primarily in mind the emperor's well-established custom of installing bishops by presenting them with the ring and staff that symbolized episcopal office. After Gregory's ruling, bishops no more than popes were to be the creatures of emperors. As popes were elected by the College of Cardinals and were not raised up by kings or nobles, so bishops were to be installed in their offices by the pope and none other.

Gregory's prohibition was a jolt to royal authority. Since the days of Otto I emperors had routinely passed out bishoprics to favored clergy. Bishops, who were recipients of royal estates, were their appointees and servants of the state. Henry IV's Carolingian and Ottonian predecessors had carefully nurtured the sacerdotal character of the empire in both concept and administrative bureaucracy. The church and religion were integral parts of government. Now Henry found himself ordered to secularize the empire by drawing a distinct line between the spheres of temporal and spiritual—royal and ecclesiastical—authority and jurisdiction. But if his key administrators were no longer to be his own carefully chosen and sworn servants, then was not his kingdom in jeopardy? Henry considered Gregory's action a direct challenge to his authority. The territorial princes, on the other hand, ever tending away from the center and eager to see the emperor weakened, were quick to see the advantages of Gregory's ruling: if the king did not have a bishop's ear, then a territorial prince might. They fully supported Gregory's edict.

The lines of battle were quickly drawn. Henry assembled his loyal German bishops at Worms in January, 1076, and had them proclaim their independence from Gregory. Gregory promptly responded with the church's heavy artillery: he excommunicated Henry and absolved all his subjects from loyalty to him. The German princes were delighted by this turn of events, and Henry found himself facing a general revolt led by the duchy of Saxony. He had no recourse but to come to terms with Gregory. In a famous scene Henry prostrated himself outside Gregory's castle retreat at Canossa on January 25, 1077. There he reportedly stood barefoot in the snow for three days before the pope absolved his royal penitent. Papal power had, at this moment, reached its pinnacle. But heights are also for descending, and Gregory's grandeur, as he must surely have known when he pardoned Henry and restored him to power, was very soon to fade.

Henry regrouped his forces, regained much of his power within the empire, and soon acted as if the humiliation at Canossa had never occurred. In March 1080 Gregory excommunicated him once again, but this time such action was ineffectual. (Historically, repeated excommunications of the same individual have proved to have diminishing returns.) In 1084 Henry, absolutely

Calixtus II and Henry V End the Investiture Controversy

The Concordat of Worms between Pope Calixtus II (1119-1124) and Emperor Henry V (1106-1125) on September 23, 1122 ended the Investiture Controversy. Calixtus acknowledged the emperor's right to be present as a judge and to bestow temporal rights and revenues (as distinct from ecclesiastical) on the candidate, while Henry acknowledged the exclusive right of the pope to invest clergy in their religious offices and further promised to restore previously usurped church possessions.

PRIVILEGE OF THE POPE:
I, BISHOP CALIXTUS, *servant of the servants of God, concede to you beloved son Henry—by the grace of God August Emperor of the Romans—that the election of those bishops and abbots in the German kingdom who belong to the kingdom [i.e., those in Germany, Italy, and Burgundy] shall take place in your presence without simony and without any violence; so that if any discord occurs between the parties concerned, you may —with the counsel or judgment of the metropolitan and the co-provincials—give your assent and assistance to the party which appears to have the better case. The candidate elected may receive the "regalia" [i.e., the temporal rights and revenues connected with the benefice] from you through the sceptre and he shall perform his lawful duties to you for them. But he who is elected in the other parts of the Empire shall, within six months, receive the "regalia" from you through the sceptre and shall perform his lawful duties for them, saving all things which are known as pertaining to the Church. If you complain to me in any of these matters and ask for help, I will furnish you the aid, if such is the duty of any office. I grant true peace to you and to all those who are or have been of your party during this discord.*

PRIVILEGE OF THE EMPEROR:
IN THE *name of Holy and Indivisible Trinity. I, Henry, by the grace of God August Emperor of the Romans, for the love of God and of the Holy Roman Church and of the lord Pope Calixtus and for the healing of my soul, do surrender to God, to the Holy Apostles of God, Peter and Paul, and to the Holy Roman Church all investiture through ring and staff; and do agree that in all churches throughout my kingdom and empire there shall be canonical elections and free consecration. I restore to the same Roman Church all the possessions and temporalities ("regalia") which have been abstracted until the present day either in the lifetime of my father or in my own and which I hold; and I will faithfully aid in*

the restoration of those which I do not hold. The posses-sions also of all other churches and princes and of every one else, either cleric or layman, which had been lost in that war, I will restore, so far as I hold them, according to the counsel of the princes or according to justice; and I will faithfully aid in the restoration of those that I do not hold. And I grant a true peace to the lord Pope Calixtus and to the Holy Roman Church and to all who are or have been on its side. In matters where the Holy Roman Church would seek assistance I will faithfully grant it; and in those where she shall complain to me, I will duly grant justice to her.

Church and State Through the Centuries: A Collection of Historic Documents, trans. and ed. by S. Z. Ehler and John B. Morrall (New York: Biblo and Tannen, 1967), pp. 48–49.

dominant, installed his own antipope, Clement III, and forced Gregory into exile, where he died the following year. It appeared as if the old practice of kings' control-ling popes had been restored, and with a vengeance. Clement, however, was never recognized within the church, and the Gregorian party, which retained wide popular support, regained power during the pontificates of Victor III (1086–1087) and Urban II (1088–1099).

The settlement of the investiture controversy came in 1122 with the Concordat of Worms. The Emperor Henry V (1106–1125), having long abandoned his pred-ecessors' practice of nominating popes and raising up antipopes, formally renounced his power to invest bishops with ring and staff. In exchange Pope Calixtus II (1119–1124) recognized the emperor's right to be pres-ent and to invest bishops with fiefs before or after their investment with ring and staff by the church. The old Church–State "back scratching" in this way continued, but now on very different terms. Clergy received their offices and attendant religious powers solely from ecclesi-astical authority and no longer from kings and emperors. Rulers continued to bestow lands and worldly goods on high clergy in the hope of influencing them; the Con-cordat of Worms made the clergy independent but not necessarily more moral.

The Gregorian party won the independence of the clergy at the price of encouraging the divisive feudal forces within the empire. The pope was made strong by making imperial authority weak. In the end those who profited most from the Investiture Controversy were the local princes.

The new Gregorian fence between temporal and spir-itual power did not prevent kings and popes from re-maining good neighbors if the will was present. Succeed-ing centuries demonstrated that royal and papal aspirations were too competitive for peaceful coexistence. The most bitter clash between Church and State was still to come. It would occur during the late thirteenth cen-tury and early fourteenth century in the confrontation between Pope Boniface VIII and King Philip IV of France.

The First Crusades

If an index of popular piety and support for the pope in the high Middle Ages is needed, the crusades amply provide it. What the Cluny reform was to the clergy, the First Crusade was to the laity: an outlet for the height-ened religious zeal of what was Europe's most religious century prior to the Protestant Reformation. Unlike the later crusades, which were undertaken for patently mer-cenary motives, the early crusades were largely motivated by genuine religious piety and were carefully orches-trated by the revived papacy. In November 1095 Pope Urban II proclaimed the First Crusade at the Council of Clermont in France, and the popular response was over-whelming. Participants in the crusade were promised a plenary indulgence should they die in battle, that is, a complete remission of the temporal punishment due them for their mortal sins and hence release from suffering for

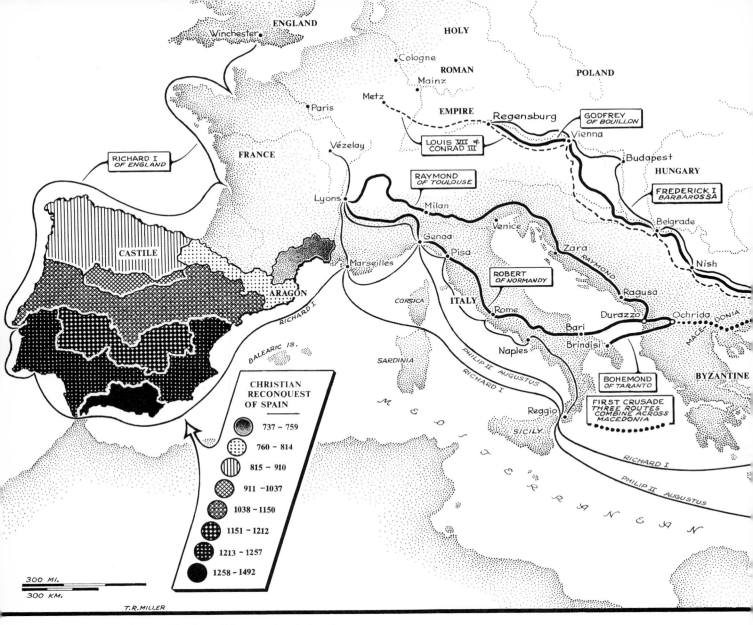

Routes and several leaders of the crusades during the first century of the movement. Indicated names of the great nobles of the First Crusade do not exhaust the list. The even showier array of monarchs of the Second and Third still left the crusades, on balance, ineffective in achieving their ostensible goals.

them in purgatory. But this spiritual reward was only part of the crusading impulse. Other factors were widespread popular respect for the reformed papacy and the existence of a nobility newly strengthened by the breakdown of imperial power and eager for military adventure. These elements combined to make the First Crusade a rousing success.

The eastern emperor had petitioned both Pope Greg-

ory VII and Pope Urban II for aid against advancing Moslem armies. The western crusaders did not, however, assemble for the purpose of defending Europe's borders against aggression. They freely took the offensive to rescue the holy city of Jerusalem, which had been in non-Christian hands since the ninth century, from the Seljuk Turks. To this end three great armies—tens of thousands of crusaders—gathered in France, Germany, and Italy. Following different routes, they reassembled in Constantinople in 1097. The convergence of these spirited soldiers upon the eastern capital was a cultural shock that only deepened eastern antipathy toward the west. The weakened eastern emperor was suspicious of their true motives, and the common people, who were forced

THE EARLY CRUSADES

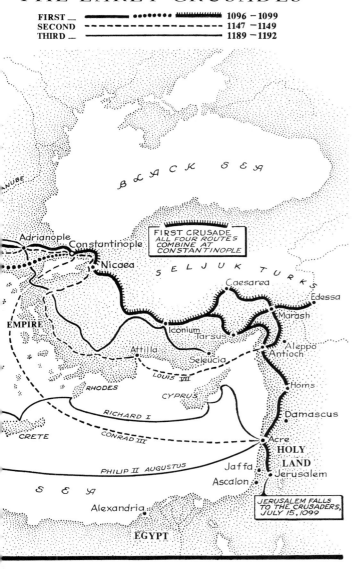

FIRST ___ ●━━━━●●●●●●━━━━━━ 1096 – 1099
SECOND ___ ------------------- 1147 – 1149
THIRD ___ ━━━━━━━━━━━━━ 1189 – 1192

FIRST CRUSADE
ALL FOUR ROUTES
COMBINE AT
CONSTANTINOPLE

JERUSALEM FALLS
TO THE CRUSADERS,
JULY 15, 1099

savages. The conquerors built defensive fortifications and received assistance from the new religious–military orders of the Knights Hospitalers (founded in 1113) and the Knights Templars (founded ca. 1119). But native persistence finally broke the crusaders around mid-century, and the forty-odd-year Latin presence in the east began to crumble. Edessa fell to Moslem armies in 1144. A second crusade, preached by the eminent Cistercian Bernard of Clairvaux (1091–1154), Christendom's most powerful monastic leader, was sent to the rescue, but it met with dismal failure. In October 1187 Jerusalem itself was reconquered by Saladin (1138–1193), king of Egypt and Syria, and remained thereafter in Islamic hands until modern times.

A third crusade in the twelfth century (1189–1192) attempted yet another rescue, enlisting as its leaders the most powerful western rulers: Emperor Frederick Barbarossa; Richard the Lion-Hearted, king of England; and Philip Augustus, king of France. But the Third Crusade proved a tragicomic commentary on the passing of the original crusading spirit. Frederick Barbarossa accidentally drowned in the Saleph River while en route to the Holy Land. Richard the Lion-Hearted and Philip Augustus reached the outskirts of Jerusalem, but their intense personal rivalry shattered the crusaders' unity. Philip Augustus returned to France and made war on English continental territories, and Richard fell captive to the Emperor Henry VI as he was returning to England. (Henry VI suspected Richard of plotting against him with Henry's mortal enemy, Henry the Lion, the duke of Saxony, who happened also to be Richard's brother-in-law.) The English were forced to pay a handsome ransom for their adventurous king's release. Popular resentment of taxes for this ransom became part of the background to the revolt against the English monarchy that led to royal recognition of Magna Carta in 1215.

The long-term achievement of the first crusades had little to do with their original purpose. Politically and religiously they were a failure; the Holy Land reverted as firmly as ever to Moslem hands. These crusades

to give them room and board, hardly considered them Christian brothers in a common cause. Nonetheless these fanatical crusaders accomplished what no eastern army had ever been able to do. They soundly defeated one Seljuk army after another in a steady advance toward Jerusalem, which fell to them on July 15, 1099.

The victorious crusaders divided the conquered territory into the feudal states of Jerusalem, Edessa, and Antioch, which they held as alleged fiefs from the pope. Godfrey of Bouillon, leader of the French–German army (and after him his brother Baldwin), ruled over the kingdom of Jerusalem. However, the crusaders remained only small islands within a great sea of Moslems, who looked upon the western invaders as hardly more than

were more important for the way they stimulated western trade with the east. The merchants of Venice, Pisa, and Genoa followed the crusaders' cross to lucrative new markets. The need to resupply the new Christian settlements in the Near East not only reopened old trade routes that had long been closed by Arab domination of the Mediterranean but also established new ones. It is a commentary on both the degeneration of the original intent of the crusades and their true historical importance that the Fourth Crusade became an enterprising commercial venture manipulated by the Venetians.

Medieval Universities and Scholasticism

Thanks to Spanish Moslem scholars the logical works of Aristotle, the writings of Euclid and Ptolemy, the basic works of Greek physicians and Arab mathematicians, and the larger texts of Roman law became available to western scholars in the early twelfth century. This renaissance of ancient knowledge in turn provided the occasion for the rise of universities.

BOLOGNA AND PARIS. The first important Western university was in Bologna. It received its formal grant of rights and privileges from the emperor Frederick Barbarossa in 1158. University members, like clergy, were granted royal immunity from local jurisdiction and were viewed by local townspeople as a group apart. It is in Bologna that we find the first formal organizations of students and professors and the first degree programs—the institutional foundations of the modern university. The "university" was at first simply a program of study that gave the student a license to teach others. Originally the term *university* meant no more than a group or corporation of individuals who were united by common self-interest and for mutual protection. It followed the model of a medieval trade guild. Bolognese students formed such a bloc in order to guarantee fair rents and prices from the townspeople and regular and high-quality teaching from their professors. Price gouging by towns-

Pope Eugenius III Promotes the Second Crusade

Full absolution and remission of all sins was but one of many benefits promised by the church to those who went on crusades to the Holy Land. Here are the inducements offered by Pope Eugenius III (1145–1153) in 1146.

IN VIRTUE *of the authority vested by God in us, we . . . have promised and granted to those who from a spirit of devotion have resolved to enter upon and accomplish this holy and necessary undertaking, that full remission of sins which our predecessor, Pope Urban, granted. We have also commanded that their wives and children, their property and possessions, shall be under the protection of the holy Church. . . . Moreover we ordain, by our apostolic authority, that until their return or death is fully proven, no lawsuit shall be instituted hereafter in regard to any property of which they were in peaceful possession when they took the cross.*

Those who with pure hearts enter upon this sacred journey, and who are in debt, shall pay no interest. And if they, or others for them, are bound by oath or promise to pay interest, we free them by our apostolic authority. And after they have sought aid of their relatives, or of the lords of whom they hold their fiefs, if the latter are unable or unwilling to advance them money, we allow them freely to mortgage their lands and other possessions to churches, ecclesiastics, or other Christians, and their lords shall have no redress.

Following the example of our predecessor, and through the authority of omnipotent God and St. Peter, prince of the apostles, which is vested in us by God, we grant absolution and remission of sins, so that those who devoutly undertake and accomplish this holy journey, or who die by the way, shall obtain absolution for all their sins which they confess with humble and contrite heart, and shall receive from him who grants to each his due reward the prize of eternal life.

James Harvey Robinson, *Readings in European History*, Vol. 1 (Boston: Athenaeum, 1904), pp. 337–338.

people was met with the threat to move the university to another town—a threat that could easily be carried out because the university at this time was not a great, fixed physical plant. Professors who failed to meet student expectations were boycotted. The mobility of the first universities gave them a unique independence.

Professors also formed protective associations and es-

Bernard of Clairvaux Recruits Members for the Second Crusade

The crusades had a great emotional appeal to religious noblemen. Here Bernard (1091–1153), the formidable abbot of Clairvaux, goads the West to undertake the second crusade (1146) and preserve the Holy Land for Christians.

BEHOLD, *brethren, now is the accepted time, now is the day of salvation. The earth also is moved and has trembled, because the God of heaven has begun to destroy the land which is his: his, I say, in which the word of the Father was taught, and where he dwelt for more than thirty years, a man among men; his, for he enlightened it with miracles, he consecrated it with his own blood; in it appeared the first fruits of his resurrection. And now, for our sins, the enemies of the Cross have raised blaspheming heads, ravaging with the edge of the sword the land of promise. They are almost on the point . . . of bursting into the very city of the living God, of overturning the sanctuaries of our redemption, of polluting the holy places of the spotless Lamb . . . . What are you going to do then, O brave men? What are you doing, O servants of the Cross?*

James Harvey Robinson, *Readings in European History*, Vol. I (Boston: Athenaeum, 1904), p. 330.

The "Castle of the Knights" (Krak-des-Chevaliers), the most magnificent of the many crusader castles built in the Holy Land in the twelfth and thirteenth centuries and whose ruins remain in modern Syria, Lebanon, and Jordan. It is situated in northern Syria a few miles from the Lebanese border. Its defense consisted of two massive walls, one overhanging the other, divided by a great moat. The Moslems of the same period used very similar military architecture. [Arab Information Center, New York.]

A medieval school scene as imagined by a later engraver. The teacher reads from his great manuscript, while a proctor maintains the students' attention. [Bettmann Archive.]

A modern engraving after an illumination of about 1400 showing scholars in discussion at the University of Paris. The scepters carried by the three standing scholars may contain relics or the consecrated host. [Bettmann Archive.]

tablished the procedures and standards for certification to teach within their ranks. The first academic degree was a certificate (*licentia docendi*) given by the professors' guild, which permitted graduates in the liberal arts program or in the higher professional sciences of medicine, theology, and law to "teach anywhere" (*ius ubique docendi*).

Bologna was distinguished as the center for the revival of Roman law. From the seventh to the eleventh centuries only the most rudimentary manuals of Roman law had survived and circulated. With the growth of trade and towns in the late eleventh century, western scholars were brought into contact with the larger and more important parts of the Roman *Corpus Juris Civilis*. The study and dissemination of this new material was directed by Irnerius. He and his students made authoritative commentaries or glosses on individual laws following their broad knowledge of the *Corpus Juris*. Around 1140 a monk named Gratian, also resident in Bologna, created the standard legal text in church or canon law, the *Concordance of Discordant Canons*, known more commonly as Gratian's *Decretum*.

As Bologna proved the model for southern European universities and the study of law, Paris became the model for northern Europe and the study of theology. Oxford, Cambridge, and Heidelberg were among Paris's early imitators. In all of these universities a foundation in the liberal arts was required for further study in the higher sciences of medicine, theology, and law. The arts program consisted of the *trivium* (grammar, rhetoric, and logic) and the *quadrivium* (arithmetic, geometry, astronomy, and music). Before the emergence of the universities, the liberal arts had been taught in the cathedral and monastery schools, that is, schools attached to cathedrals or monasteries for the purpose of training clergy. The most famous of the cathedral schools were those of Chartres, under the direction of such distinguished teachers as Saint Ivo and Saint Bernard, and Rheims, which rose to greatness in the last quarter of the tenth century under Gerbert, who later became Pope Sylvester II (999–1003). Gerbert was filled with enthusiasm for knowledge and promoted both logical and rhetorical studies. He was especially famous for his lectures on Boethius and did much to raise the study of logic to preeminence within the liberal arts, this despite his personal belief in the greater Christian relevance of rhetoric.

The University of Paris grew institutionally out of the cathedral school of Notre Dame, receiving its charter in 1200 from King Philip Augustus. Papal sanction and regulations, among them the right of faculty to strike, were issued in 1231 in the bull *Parens scientiarum* and gave the university freedom from local church control. At this time the University of Paris consisted of independent faculties of arts, canon law, medicine, and theology, with the masters of arts, who were grouped together in four national factions (French, Norman, English–German, and Picard), the dominant faculty.

It was at Paris that the college system originated. At first colleges were no more than hospices providing room and board for poor students. But the educational life of the university rapidly expanded into these fixed buildings and began to thrive on their sure endowments. In Paris the most famous college was the Sorbonne, founded around 1257 by Robert de Sorbon, chaplain to the king, for the purpose of educating advanced theological students. In Oxford and Cambridge the colleges became the basic unit of student life, indistinguishable from the university. By the fifteenth and sixteenth centuries colleges had tied the universities to physical plants and fixed foundations, greatly restricting their previous autonomy and freedom of movement.

THE CURRICULUM. Before the renaissance of the twelfth century the education available within the cathedral and monastic schools was quite limited. Students learned elementary geometry and astronomy. They used the Latin grammars of Donatus and Priscian and studied Saint Augustine's *On Christian Doctrine,* Cassiodorus's *On Divine and Secular Learning,* and the various writings of Boethius (d. 524). Boethius was important for instruction in arithmetic and music and especially for the transmission of the small body of Aristotle's logical works

known before the twelfth century. After the textual finds of the early twelfth century, Western scholars had the whole of Aristotle's logic, the astronomy of Ptolemy, the writings of Euclid, and many Latin classics. By the end of the twelfth century the ethical, physical, and metaphysical writings of Aristotle were in circulation in the West.

Logic and dialectic rapidly triumphed in importance over the other arts. They were tools designed to discipline knowledge and thought. Even before the twelfth century, cathedral schools had directed students to Boethius's translation and commentary on Porphyry's *Introduction to Aristotle* and to his translation and commentaries on Aristotle's *Categories* and *On Interpretation.* In the high Middle Ages the learning process was very basic. The student wrote commentaries on authoritative texts, especially those of Aristotle, and was not encouraged to strive independently for undiscovered truth. He was taught rather to organize and harmonize the accepted truth of tradition. The basic assumption was that truth already existed; it was not something to be discovered but something at hand requiring systematic organization and elucidation. Such conviction made logic and dialectic supreme within the liberal arts.

The scholastic program of study, based on logic and dialectic, reigned supreme in all the faculties—in law and medicine as well as in philosophy and theology. The student read the traditional authorities in his field, formed short summaries of their teaching, disputed it by elaborating arguments pro and con, and then drew his own modest conclusions. The twelfth century saw the rise of the "summa," a summary of all that was known about a topic, and works whose purpose was to conciliate traditional authorities. In canon law there was Gratian's *Concordance of Discordant Canons.* In theology Peter Lombard's *Four Books of Sentences,* published around 1150, embraced traditional opinion on God, the creation, Christ, and the sacraments. It also enumerated the seven sacraments, which became traditional in the high Middle Ages (baptism, confirmation, penance, the Eucharist, extreme unction, holy orders, and marriage). Lombard's work evolved from Peter Abelard's *Sic et Non*, a juxtaposition of seemingly contradictory statements on the same subject by revered authorities. Lombard's *Sentences* became the standard theological textbook until the Protestant Reformation in the sixteenth century. In biblical studies the *Glossa ordinaria* of Anselm of Laon (*ca.* 1120) was the authoritative summary. All these works were forerunners of Saint Thomas Aquinas's magnificent *Summa Theologica,* an ambitious summary of the whole of theological knowledge from the creation to the last day, which many consider the greatest theological work ever written.

In the first half of the twelfth century such prominent men as John of Salisbury (*ca.* 1120–1180) and Saint Bernard of Clairvaux (1090–1153) rejected the dialectic of the logicians, which they found to be heartless and presumptuous. The later humanist criticism of scholastic learning as "useless" can be heard in their complaints. Although grammar and eloquence were eclipsed by dialectic and logic in medieval universities, professional rhetoricians, known as *dictatores,* retained their places within the universities and continued to give practical instruction in the composition of letters and official documents. These professional rhetoricians were the forerunners of later humanists, and their skills as secretaries were much in private demand in the high Middle Ages. A famous allegorical poem was written in commentary on the domination of logic and dialectic within the universities. It was known as *The Battle of the Seven Arts* (1250). In the poem, which argues the rhetorician's position, vain logic is seen driving noble grammar into exile, where the latter patiently waits in confident expectation that a more enlightened age will demand her return.

PHILOSOPHY AND THEOLOGY: FRIENDS OR FOES? Scholastic thinkers in medieval universities quarreled over two basic problems: (1) the proper relation of philosophy, which was virtually identical with the writings of Aristotle, and theology, and (2) whether or not so-called universal concepts existed apart from the human mind.

Bishop Stephen Complains About the New Scholastic Learning

Scholasticism involved an intellectual, learned approach to religion and its doctrines rather than simple, uncritical piety. Many saw in it a threat to the study of the Bible and the Church Fathers, as doctrines that should simply be believed and revered were rationally dissected for their logical meaning by presumptuous and none-too-well-trained youths. Here is a particularly graphic description of the threat, replete with classical allusion, as perceived by Stephen, Bishop of Tournai, in a letter to the pope written between 1192 and 1203.

THE *studies of sacred letters among us are fallen into the workshop of confusion, while both disciples applaud novelties alone and masters watch out for glory rather than learning. They everywhere compose new and recent* summulae *[little summaries] and commentaries, by which they attract, detain, and deceive their hearers, as if the works of the holy fathers were not still sufficient, who, we read, expounded Holy Scripture in the same spirit in which we believe the apostles and prophets composed it. They prepare strange and exotic courses for their banquet, when at the nuptials of the son of the king of Taurus his own flesh and blood are killed and all prepared, and the wedding guests have only to take and eat what is set before them. Contrary to the sacred canons there is public disputation over the incomprehensible deity; concerning the incarnation of the Word, verbose flesh and blood irreverently litigate. The indivisible Trinity is cut up and wrangled over in the trivia, so that now there are as many errors as doctors, as many scandals as classrooms, as many blasphemies as squares.... Faculties called liberal having lost their pristine liberty are sunk in such servitude that adolescents with long hair impudently usurp their professorships, and beardless youths sit in the seat of their seniors, and those who don't yet know how to be disciples strive to be named masters. And they write their* summulae *moistened with drool and dribble but unseasoned with the salt of philosphers. Omitting the rules of the arts and discarding the authentic books of the artificers, they seize the flies of empty words in their sophisms like the claws of spiders. Philosophy cries that her garments are torn and disordered and, modestly concealing her nudity by a few specific tatters, neither is consulted nor consoles as of old. All these things, father, call for the hand of apostolic correction....*

Lynn Thorndike, *University Records and Life in the Middle Ages* (New York: Octagon Books, 1971), pp. 22–24.

Thomas Aquinas Defines the Nature of Christian Theology

Although its premises and data came from divine revelation rather than from empirical observation, theology was considered a "science" in its own right in the Middle Ages. Here Thomas Aquinas (*ca.* 1225–1274) defines Christian theology and explains its use of human reasoning to elucidate the truths of faith.

THE *premises of Christian theology are revealed truths, accepted on the word of the teacher who reveals them. Consequently its typical method is the appeal to authority. This does not impair its scientific dignity, for though to cite human authority is the poorest form of argument, the appeal to divine authority is the highest and most cogent.*

Nevertheless, Christian theology also avails itself of human reasoning to illustrate the truths of faith, not to prove them. Grace does not scrap nature, but improves it; reason subserves faith, and natural love runs through charity. Theology invokes great thinkers on matters where they are received authorities.... Theology treats them as sources of external evidence for its arguments. Its proper and indispensable court of appeal is to the authority of the canonical Scriptures. The writings of the Fathers of the Church are also proper sources, yet their authority is not final. Faith rests on divine revelation made through the prophets and apostles and set down in the canonical Scriptures, not on revelations, if there be any, made to other holy teachers.

From the *Summa Theologica*, Ia, i. 8, ad 2 in Thomas Gilby (Ed. and Trans.), *St. Thomas Aquinas: Theological Texts* (New York: Oxford University Press, 1955), pp. 22–23.

The first problem arose from the fact that there were manifestly heretical tenets in the corpus of Aristotle's writings, especially as his teaching was elaborated by the Islamic commentators. For example, Aristotle's belief in the eternality of the world called into question the Judeo-Christian teaching about the world's creation according to the book of Genesis. Aristotelian teaching that intellect was one seemed to deny all individuality, Christian teaching about individual responsibility, and the personal immortality of the soul.

When theologians began to adopt the logic and the metaphysics of Aristotle, some critics saw a mortal threat to biblical and traditional authority. Berengar of Tours (d. 1088) applied logic to the sacrament of the Eucharist and came to question the Church's teaching on transubstantiation. Peter Abelard (1079–1142) subjected the Trinity to logical examination. The curiosity of these new logicians shocked more conservative men, such as Lanfranc (d. 1089), the reformer of the Abbey of Bec, and especially the powerful Saint Bernard. The latter questioned whether the liberal arts course, dominated by Aristotelian logic, had become more a foe than an ally of theological study. A century of suspicion and criticism of Aristotle's influence on theological study culminated when the bishop of Paris condemned 219 philosophical propositions in 1277. This massive condemnation was directed against devotees of Aristotle, many of whom followed the Moslem authority Averroës (1126–1198), but it also caught in its net a few teachings of such orthodox Western theologians as Thomas Aquinas (d. 1274), who had tried to reconcile Aristotle, considered the highest human wisdom by medieval scholars, with traditional Christian teaching.

After this condemnation philosophy was never again to have such importance within theology. William of Ockham (d. 1349), who represented conservative opinion in this controversy, strictly limited the ability of reason, assisted by logic and dialectic, to fathom the nature and decisions of God independently of divine revelation. Ockham taught that one must abandon all such efforts to penetrate the divine mind in essential theological matters and be content with the Bible's teaching. Some have seen in his position a reliance on faith that foreshadowed the Protestant reformers.

THE PROBLEM OF UNIVERSALS: AQUINAS AND OCKHAM. The classical scholastic problem concerned the question whether or not universal concepts really exist apart from the human mind. Do words that signify a multitude of individual things, such as *man, dog, chair,* and so forth, refer to realities which have extramental existence? The question, perhaps strange at first to modern people, involved a very basic discussion of how one truly knows anything. Because the world of individual physical things is manifestly perishable—individual men,

Thomas Aquinas, siding with Aristotle against Plato, rejected the Platonic belief that knowledge occurred independently of sensory experience, although Aquinas still believed that universals, abstracted from things and existing in the mind as so-called "intelligible species," were essential to knowledge. Later, the more radical William of Ockham (*ca.* 1300–1349) rejected any hint of the extra-mental existence of human concepts. Universals were only contents of the mind and verbal conventions.

AQUINAS:

PLATO *held that the intellect differed from the senses and was a spiritual power making no use of a bodily organ in its thinking. Now since a spiritual thing cannot be changed by a bodily thing, he was convinced that intellectual knowledge does not come about because the intellect is transmuted by sense-objects, but because it shares in intelligible and bodiless ideas [universals]. . . . Aristotle, however, took a middle path. He agreed with Plato that intellect differs from sense, but he also maintained that there is no proper activity of sense into which the body does not enter; sensation is not the activity of soul alone, but of the body–soul compound. . . . Aristotle, however, taught that the intrinsic activity of mind was independent of intercourse with body. No corporeal thing can impress itself on an incorporeal thing. Therefore the mere impression of sensible bodies is not sufficient to cause intellectual activity. A nobler and higher force is required. . . . Not, however, in such a way that intellectual activity is caused in us by the sole influence of some higher being, as Plato held, but that there is a spiritual ability within us, called after Aristotle the active intellect, which by the process of abstraction renders actually intelligible images taken from sense [intelligible species]. As regards these images intellectual knowledge is caused by the senses. Yet because an image alone is not sufficient to transform the receptive mind until it has been heightened and made actually intelligible by an active intellect, we should not say that sense-knowledge is the total and perfect cause of intellectual knowledge. Let us say instead that sense-data are by way of offering the material for the cause.*

OCKHAM:

WE HAVE *to say that every universal is one singular thing. Therefore nothing is universal except by signification, that is, by being a sign of several things. . . . It must, however, be understood that there are two sorts of universal. There is one sort which is naturally universal; it is a sign naturally predicable of many things, in much*

dogs, and chairs pass away—philosophical realists, who closely followed the views of Plato, believed such a perishable world of particular things could not be directly known by an immaterial and immortal soul. They reasoned that like can know and be known only by like. What is immaterial and immortal can know directly only immaterial and immortal things. Hence, these realists argued, there must be a transcendent world of being in which perfect, imperishable, immaterial models of individual things exist. It is because the mind of man is privy to such a world that humans can know immediately the world of physical things. These models, existing in the transcendent world of being, are the "universals," and according to the realists they exist apart from the mind of man. They are the original models of the individual things of the world, and they function as the ultimate principles of being and intelligibility. It is because individual things participate in the universals that they exist and can be known.

The moderate realists, who followed Aristotle more than Plato on this question, agreed that universals were really distinct from individual things. But they argued that such universals existed only *within* individual things as intrinsic qualities that gave them form and intelligibility. According to this point of view, most clearly expressed perhaps by Thomas Aquinas, one came to know individual things truly by isolating and abstracting their intrinsic universal features. The universal, which is within individual things, is "extracted" from them by way of sensation and intellection and brought into the mind as a so-called "intelligible species." Aquinas continued to believe with the realists that only like can know like; intelligible species are immaterial realities "like" the mind of man. But contrary to the pure realists, Aquinas looked directly at empirical reality itself, and not introspectively beyond it to a pure world of being, in order to find the essential agency of knowledge. Universals were in things, not beyond them. His famous motto was "there is nothing in the mind that was not first in the senses."

The nominalists took the most radical position on the

Thomas Aquinas as imagined, and idealized, about a century and a half later by the Italian painter Fra Angelico (1387–1455). [The Granger Collection.]

the same way as smoke naturally signifies fire, or a groan the pain of a sick man, or laughter an inner joy. Such a universal is nothing other than a content of the mind; and therefore no substance outside the mind and no accident outside the mind is such a universal. . . . The other sort of universal is so by convention. In this way, an uttered word, which is really a single quality, is universal; for it is a conventional sign meant to signify many things. Therefore, just as the word is said to be common, so it can be said to be universal. But it is not so by nature, only by convention.

Aquinas: *Summa Theologica,* Ia, lxxxiv, 6, in Thomas Gilby (Ed. and Trans.), *St. Thomas Aquinas: Philosophical Texts* (New York: Oxford University Press, 1960), pp. 242–243.

Ockham: *Summa Totius Logicae,* Ic, xiv, in *Ockham: Philosophical Writings,* ed. and trans. by Philotheus Boehner (New York: Nelson, 1962), pp. 33–34.

question of universals. They looked on universal concepts as simply "names" or "terms" created by the mind and existing only within the mind. William of Ockham was the most famous nominalist. As a general principle he believed that the simpler explanation was always the more convincing explanation. This was his famous "razor." A special world of being and "intelligible species" were neither necessary nor helpful assumptions when one attempted to explain satisfactorily how one truly knows. Ockham felt that such speculations led only to greater confusion and skepticism. He rather taught that individual things were known directly and without mediation and that simple "intuitive knowledge" provided the foundation for the mind's formation of the universal concepts it used to aid its recall and verbal communication. Universals were a type of "abstractive knowledge" that was extrapolated from sensory experience and reflection. Universal concepts were "conventions," naturally formed by the mind as essential aids to knowledge, but really existing only in the mind and in words.

The revolutionary character of Ockhamism lay in its threat to the hierarchical order and harmony of God, man, and nature that most medieval thinkers believed to exist. The *Summa Theologica* of Thomas Aquinas was the most eloquent and comprehensive statement of this belief. It attempted to harmonize reason (philosophy) and revelation (theology), nature and grace, the state and the church within an all-embracing hierarchical order. Ockhamists declared nonexistent the traditionally assumed real connections between a divine sphere of being, the mind of man, and the external or created world. A pure realist, Anselm of Canterbury (1033–1109), had argued from the sheer idea of "that than which nothing could be greater" to postulate the real, extramental existence of a God who created the world. A moderate realist, Thomas Aquinas believed he could posit God's existence by simply examining created things and tracing them back to their ultimate origin. William of Ockham, however, could not move from either ideas or the finite things of the world to a declaration of God's existence. He found no grounds for the existence of God or the trustworthiness of his own perception of the world beyond faith in divine revelation and his own experience. Such a position seemed to threaten the medieval church. From the point of view of an Ockhamist the church was more an object of faith than a rationally provable passageway through which all life must necessarily travel en route to God. Realist philosophy, with its strong sense of hierarchy and belief in the superiority of the spiritual over the material world, had been congenial to the medieval church's claims to temporal power in the thirteenth and fourteenth centuries. The teaching of Ockham seemed to view the church theologically in a far more modest secular role— and at roughly the same time when kings were forcibly curtailing the political power of the pope. It may have been as much for the latter reason as for alleged skepticism that extreme nominalists were condemned by the church in the fourteenth century.

ABOVE: One of the problems discussed by medieval theologians was the fate of the damned, here portrayed rather gruesomely in a mosaic from the twelfth or thirteenth century in the former cathedral on the island of Torcello near Venice. [AHM.]

BELOW: In a society of limited literacy, church decoration often carried the burden of telling Bible stories to the laity and reminding them of the dread consequences of a sinful life. From the sculptures (ca. 1100) on the Romanesque Cathedral of Santiago de Compostela, Spain, whither hordes of medieval pilgrims went to venerate the remains of the Apostle James, we see [LEFT] the expulsion of Adam and Eve from Paradise and [RIGHT] a gathering of unpleasant creatures waiting to prey upon fallen souls after the day of judgment. [AHM.]

Trade and the Growth of Towns (1100–1300)

During the centuries following the collapse of the Roman Empire, western Europe became a closed and predominantly agricultural society, with small international commerce and even less urban culture. The great seaports of Italy were the exceptions. Venice, Pisa, and Genoa continued to trade actively with Constantinople and throughout the eastern Mediterranean, including Palestine, Syria, and Egypt, during the Middle Ages. The Venetians were Europe's most sober businessmen and jealously guarded their eastern trade, attacking western Christian competitors as quickly as Moslem predators. The latter were largely subdued by the success of the First Crusade, which proved a trade bonanza for Italian cities as the Mediterranean ceased to be dominated by the Arabs. Venice, Pisa, and Genoa maintained major trading posts throughout the Mediterranean by the twelfth century.

During the tenth, eleventh, and twelfth centuries,
the so-called Romanesque style characterized much
architecture in the West, especially church architecture. The Roman basilica was still taken as the
basis. In the churches, the addition of transepts,
as in the Byzantine style, made cross-shaped
buildings that were congenial with Christian
symbolism. Rounded arches were preferred, and sheer
height was not emphasized. As a result, sometimes
a feeling of earthbound heaviness resulted; but
conversely this sense of massiveness and closeness
also gave worshippers a sense of being enclosed and
protected.

A great many important examples of this style
survive throughout western Europe. We have already
illustrated the monastery churches at Cluny (on
pages 258–9) and at Mont-Saint-Michel (on page 256).
Here [ABOVE] is the Cathedral of Pisa, Italy, built
in the second half of the eleventh century. Nearby
is the cathedral bell tower of 1174—the "leaning Tower of
Pisa"—which has settled alarmingly out of line. [Italian
Government Travel Office, New York.]

Notre-Dame-la-Grande in Poitiers, France [RIGHT],
eleventh century received its name from the splendor of its elaborately carved façade; its proportions
are quite modest compared with many other Romanesque
churches. [French Government Tourist Office, New York.]

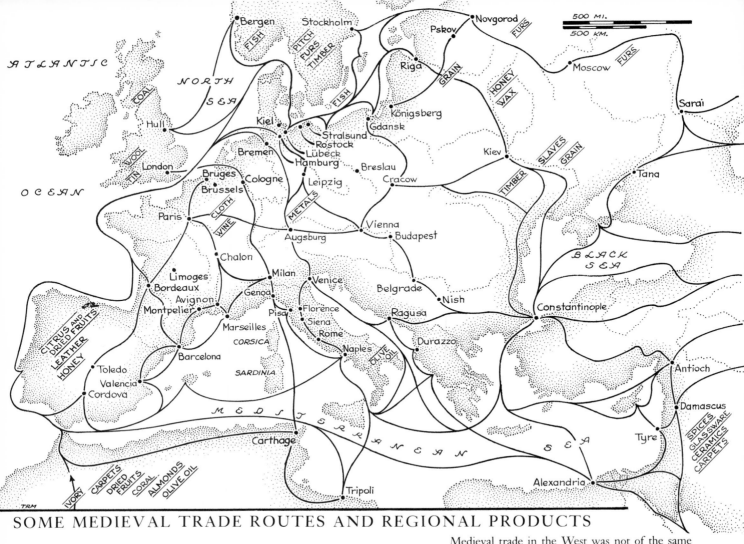

SOME MEDIEVAL TRADE ROUTES AND REGIONAL PRODUCTS

THE FOURTH CRUSADE. In an unintended chain reaction, crusades created trade, which in turn gave rise to new towns and industry, which in turn brought about major social upheavals. The enterprising way in which the Venetians turned the Fourth Crusade to their own advantage reveals the interdependence of religion and business in the later crusades. In 1202 crusaders, some 30,000 strong, arrived in Venice to set sail for Egypt. When they were unable to pay the price of transport, the Venetians negotiated as an alternative to payment the conquest of a rival Christian port city on the Adriatic: the city of Zara. To the shock of Pope Innocent III, the crusaders obligingly subdued Zara. This proved to be but the beginning of the crusaders' digression from their original goal. They were further persuaded to conquer Constantinople itself in support of disputed imperial claims made by the dethroned Greek prince Alexis. In July 1203 Constantinople fell, and by April 1204 it was completely in western hands. Venice acquired thereby new lands and maritime rights that assured its domination

Medieval trade in the West was not of the same intensity nor of the same geographical breadth in different periods. The map shows some of the channels that came to be used in interregional commerce. Labels tell part of what was carried in that commerce.

of the eastern Mediterranean. During the decades of its occupation, Constantinople was the center for western trade throughout the Near East.

THE NEW MERCHANT CLASS. The western commercial revival attendant upon these events repopulated the old Roman urban centers and gave birth to new industries. Trade put both money and ideas into circulation. New riches or the prospect thereof improved living conditions, raised hopes, and increased populations. In the twelfth century western Europe became a "boomtown." Among the most interesting creations were the traders themselves, who formed a new, distinctive social class. These prosperous merchants did not, as might first be suspected, spring from the landed nobility. They were, to the contrary, poor, landless adventurers who had abso-

276 *The High Middle Ages (1000–1300): Revival of Empire, Church, and Towns*

lutely nothing to lose and everything to gain by the risks of foreign trade. For mutual protection they traveled together in great armed caravans, buying their products as cheaply as possible at the source and selling them as dearly as possible in western marketplaces. They have been called the first western capitalists, men inspired by profit and devoted to little more than amassing fortunes. But their very greed and daring laid the foundations for western urban life as we have come to know it today.

Although in power, wealth, and privilege the great merchants were destined to join and eventually eclipse the landed aristocracy, they were initially misfits in traditional medieval society. They were freemen, often possessed of great wealth, yet they neither owned land nor tilled the soil. They did not value land and farming but were men of liquid wealth and constant movement. Aristocrats and clergy looked down on them as degenerates, and they were viewed by the common man with suspicion. They were intruders within medieval society, a new breed who did not fit into the neat hierarchy of clergy, nobility, and serfs.

Merchants fanned out from the great Flemish and Italian trading centers: Bruges, Ghent, Venice, Pisa, Genoa, Florence. Wherever they settled in large numbers, they lobbied for a degree of freedom necessary for successful commerce, opposing tolls, tariffs, and other petty restrictions that discouraged the flow of trade. This brought them initially into conflict with the norms of static agricultural society. But as they demonstrated the many advantages of vigorous trade, the merchants progressively won their case. They were able not only to remodel city government to favor their new industries and the free flow of trade, but also to impart to cities an aura of importance unknown during previous centuries. By the late Middle Ages cities commonly saw themselves as miniature states, even self-contained Christendoms. "God has become a citizen of Bern," wrote a Bernese chronicler in the fourteenth century, "and who can fight against God?"

As they grew and became prosperous, medieval cities also became very jealous of their good fortune. Every measure was taken to protect skilled industries, expand trade, and prevent competition from the surrounding countryside. Government remained in the hands of the rich and the few—patricians, *grandi,* the "old rich"—although wealthy merchants, aspiring to the noble style of life, began increasingly to find their way into the inner circles of government as money proved early that it could talk. By the thirteenth century city councils, operating on the basis of aristocratic constitutions and composed of patricians and wealthy merchants—the old rich *and* the new rich—internally controlled city life. These oligarchies were increasingly confronted by small artisans who demanded improved living conditions and a role in making policy. This latter group formed the far greater part of the new burgher class and organized to express its will through powerful corporations or craft guilds. The high and late Middle Ages also saw a deepening conflict between craft masters, who were determined to keep their numbers at an absolute minimum, and journeymen, who found themselves frozen at the lower levels of their trade. The self-protectiveness and internal conflicts of medieval cities did not, however, prevent them from forming larger trade associations, such as the famous German Hanseatic League, or Hansa, which kept Baltic trade a German monopoly well into the fifteenth century.

CHANGES IN SOCIETY. The rise of the merchant class was an important crack in the old social order. New-rich merchants, a class originally sprung from ordinary, landless people, broke into the aristocracy, and in doing so drew behind them the leadership of the new artisan class created by the urban industries that had grown up in the wake of the growth of trade. In the late Middle Ages and especially through the Protestant Reformation in the sixteenth century, the "middle classes" firmly established themselves; they have been enlarging their numbers ever since.

Although from one perspective medieval towns were overly self-protective and "egoistic," they also became a force for innovation and change far beyond their walls.

LEFT: A section of the walls that encircle the fortified medieval city of Avila in Spain. These are the north walls looking west and date from the twelfth century. [AHM.]

OPPOSITE: The fortified city of Carcassonne in southern France, whose defenses date from the period 1240-1285, during the reigns of Louis IX and Philip the Bold. Note the protective walls and towers. [Bildarchiv Foto Marburg.]

This fact is all the more remarkable when it is remembered that towns at this time made up hardly more than 5 per cent of the population. Townsmen became a major force in the breakup of feudal society, aiding both kings and the peasantry at the expense of the landed nobility. Generally speaking, towns and kings tended to ally against the great feudal lords. A notable exception may be seen in England, where the towns joined the barons against the oppressive monarchy of King John and became a part of the parliamentary opposition. Townsmen generally, however, found their autonomy better preserved by having one distant master rather than several nearer and factious overlords. Kings in turn courted the liquid wealth and administrative skills of the townsmen, who began to replace the clergy and the nobility in the royal bureaucracy. Urban money made it possible for kings to hire mercenary armies and thereby decrease their dependence on the noble cavalry—an important step in the consolidation of territories divided for centuries by feudal allegiances and customs.

It was from burgher ranks that kings drew the skilled lawyers who began the long process of replacing feudal custom with centralized Roman law. Kings in return gave towns political recognition and guaranteed their constitutions against territorial magnates. This was more easily done in the stronger coastal towns than in interior areas, where urban life was less vigorous and territorial power was on the rise. In France, towns became totally integrated into the royal government. In Germany and Austria, by contrast, towns were subjected to ever tighter control by territorial princes. In Italy towns uniquely grew to absorb their surrounding territory, becoming city-states.

Towns also aided the peasantry, to the detriment of the landed nobility. A popular maxim of the time in German cities was: *Stadtluft macht frei*—"City air makes one free." Cities passed legislation making serfs who spent a year and a day within their walls freemen. New urban industries provided lucky peasants vocations alternative to farming. The new money economy made it possible for serfs or their urban patrons to buy their freedom from feudal services and rents as the latter became translatable into direct money payments. A serf or his patron could simply buy up the "contract." The growth of a free peasantry was especially evident in the thirteenth century.

All of this worked against the landed nobility. As urban trade and industries put more money into circulation, its value decreased (inflation). The great landowners, whose wealth was static, found themselves confronted, on the one hand, by serfs who longed to flee to the city and, on the other, by rising prices. They were losing their free labor supply and facing diminished productivity; at the same time they had to pay more for their accustomed style of life. The nobility were not disciplined people, and many fell prey to money-wise urban merchants.

The new urban economy worked, then, to free both kings and peasants from dependence on feudal lords. As royal authority became centralized and kings were able to hire mercenary soldiers, the noble cavalry became militarily obsolescent, at most a minor part of the king's armed forces. And as towns and urban industries grew, attracting serfs from the farms, the nobility gradually lost its once all-powerful economic base. The long-term consequence was to strengthen the monarchy against the nobility.

SUGGESTED READINGS

JOHN W. BALDWIN, *The Scholastic Culture of the Middle Ages: 1000-1300* (1971). Best brief synthesis available.

M. W. BALDWIN (Ed.), *History of the Crusades*, I: *The First Hundred Years* (1955). Basic historical narrative.

GEOFFREY BARRACLOUGH, *The Medieval Papacy* (1968). Brief, comprehensive survey, with pictures.

F. C. COPLESTON, *Aquinas* (1965). Best introduction to Aquinas's philosophy.

FREDERICK COPLESTON, *A History of Philosophy*, III/1: *Ockham to the Speculative Mystics* (1963). The best introduction to Ockham and his movement.

ETIENNE GILSON, *Heloise and Abelard* (1968). Analysis and defense of medieval scholarly values.

CHARLES H. HASKINS, *The Renaissance of the Twelfth Century* (1927). Still the standard account.

CHARLES H. HASKINS, *The Rise of Universities* (1972). A short, minor classic.

GORDON LEFF, *Paris and Oxford Universities in the Thirteenth and Fourteenth Centuries: An Institutional and Intellectual History* (1968). Very good on Scholastic debates.

EMILE MÂLE, *The Gothic Image: Religious Art in France in the Thirteenth Century* (1913). A classic.

HANS EBERHARD MAYER, *The Crusades,* trans. by John Gilligham (1972). Extremely detailed, and best one-volume account.

ERWIN PANOFSKY, *Gothic Architecture and Scholasticism* (1951). A controversial classic.

HENRI PIRENNE, *Medieval Cities: Their Origins and the Revival of Trade,* trans. by Frank D. Halsey (1970). A minor classic.

HASTINGS RASHDALL, *The Universities of Europe in the Middle Ages,* Vols. 1–3 (1936). Dated but still standard comprehensive work.

FRITZ RÖRIG, *The Medieval Town,* trans. by D. J. A. Matthew (1971). Excellent on northern Europe.

BRIAN TIERNEY, *The Crisis of Church and State 1050–1300* (1964). Very useful collection of primary sources on key Church–State conflicts.

S. WILLIAMS (Ed.), *The Gregorian Epoch: Reformation, Revolution, Reaction* (1964). Variety of scholarly opinion on the significance of Pope Gregory's reign presented on debate forum.

R. L. WOLFF AND H. W. HAZARD (Eds.), *History of the Crusades,* II: *The Later Crusades 1189–1311* (1962).

280

12

The High Middle Ages: Society and Politics

The Order of Life

FOUR basic social groups were distinguished in the Middle Ages: those who fought (the landed nobility), those who prayed (the clergy), those who labored (the peasantry), and, after the revival of towns in the eleventh century, those who traded and manufactured (the townsmen). It would be false to view each of these groups as closed and homogenized. Throughout medieval society, like tended to be attracted to like regardless of social grouping. Barons, archbishops, rich farmers, and successful merchants had far more in common with each other than they did with the middle and lower strata of their various professions.

Nobles

When noblemen first appeared in the early Middle Ages, they came from the ranks of feudal vassals or warrior knights. The successful vassal attained a special social and legal status based on his landed wealth (accumulated fiefs), his exercise of authority over others, and his distinctive social customs—all of which set him apart from others in medieval society. By the late Middle Ages there had evolved a distinguishable higher and lower nobility living in both town and country. The higher were the great landowners and territorial magnates; the lower were petty landlords, descendants from minor knights, new-rich merchants who could buy country estates, and wealthy farmers patiently risen from ancestral serfdom.

It was a special mark of noblemen that they lived on the labor of others. Basically lords of manors, the nobility of the early and high Middle Ages neither tilled the soil like the peasantry nor engaged in the commerce of mer-

The Gothic town hall of Siena, Italy, built 1288–1309, with its magnificent tower and great bell to summon the citizenry. [Alinari/SCALA.]

chants—activities considered beneath their dignity. The nobleman resided in a country mansion or, if he were particularly wealthy, a castle. He was drawn to the countryside as much by personal preference as by the fact that his fiefs were usually rural manors. Arms were his profession; the nobleman's sole occupation and reason for living was waging war. His fief provided the means to acquire the expensive military equipment that his rank required, and he maintained his enviable position as he had gained it, by fighting for his chief.

The nobility celebrated the physical strength, courage, and constant activity of warfare. Warring was both the source of new riches and an opportunity to gain honor and glory. Knights were paid a share in the plunder of victory, and in time of war everything became fair game. Special war wagons, designed for the collection and transport of booty, followed them into battle. Periods of peace were greeted with great sadness, as they meant economic stagnation and boredom. Whereas peasants and townsmen counted peace the condition of their occupational success, the nobility despised it as unnatural to their profession. They looked down on the peasantry as cowards who ran and hid in time of war. Urban merchants, who amassed wealth by business methods strange to feudal society, were held in equal contempt, which increased as the affluence and political power of townsmen grew. The nobleman possessed as strong a sense of superiority over these "unwarlike" people as the clergy did over the general run of laity.

The nobleman's sense of distinctiveness within medieval society was nurtured by the chivalric ritual of dubbing to knighthood, a ceremonial entrance into the noble class that became almost a religious sacrament. The ceremony was preceded by a bath of purification, confession, communion, and a prayer vigil. Thereafter the priest blessed the knight's standard, lance, and sword. As prayers were chanted, the priest girded the knight with his sword and presented him his shield, enlisting him as much in the defense of the church as in the service of his lord. Dubbing raised the nobleman to a state as sacred in his sphere

The life of a late medieval aristocrat: the Duke of Berry at table. The tapestry battle in the background is from the contemporary Hundred Years' War between France and England, and appropriate zodiac signs appear above. This is the January scene from *Les très riches heures du duc de Berry* (1413–1416). [Musée Condé, Chantilly. Giraudon.]

as clerical ordination made the priest in his. This comparison is quite legitimate. The clergy and the nobility were medieval society's privileged estates. The appointment of noblemen to high ecclesiastical office and their eager participation in the church's crusades had strong ideological and social underpinnings as well as economic and political motives.

In peacetime the nobility had two favorite amusements: hunting and tournaments. Because of the threat to towns and villages posed by wild animals the great hunts actually aided the physical security of ordinary people while occupying restless noblemen. However, where they could, noblemen progressively monopolized the rights to game, forbidding the common man from hunting in the "lord's" forests. This practice built resentment among common people to the level of revolt. Free game, fishing, and access to wood were basic demands in the petitions of grievance and the revolts of the peasantry throughout the high and especially during the later Middle Ages.

The pastime of tournaments also sowed seeds of social disruption, but more within the ranks of the nobility itself. Tournaments were designed to provide the excite-

ment of war without the useless maiming and killing of prized vassals. But as regions competed fiercely with one another for victory and glory, even mock battles with blunted weapons proved to be deadly. Tournaments tended to get out of hand, ending with bloodshed and animosity among the combatants. Remnants survive today in the intense regional rivalry of European soccer. The church came to oppose tournaments as occasions of pagan revelry and senseless violence. Kings and princes also turned against them as sources of division within their realms. Henry II of England proscribed them in the twelfth century. They were ended in France in the mid-sixteenth century after Henry II of France received a mortal shaft through his visor during a tournament celebrating his daughter's marriage.

From the repeated assemblies in the courts of barons and kings, set codes of social conduct or "courtesy" developed in noble circles during the high Middle Ages. With the French leading the way, mannered behavior and court etiquette became almost as important as battlefield expertise. Knights became literate gentlemen, and lyric poets sang and moralized at court. The cultivation of a code of behaviour and a special literature to eulogize it was not unrelated to problems within the social life of the nobility. Noblemen were public philanderers; their illegitimate children mingled openly with their legitimate offspring in their houses. The advent of courtesy was in part an effort to reform this situation. Although the poetry of courtly love was sprinkled with frank eroticism and the beloved in these epics were married women pursued by those to whom they were not married, the love recommended by the poet was usually love at a distance, unconsummated by sexual intercourse. It was love without touching, a kind of sex without physical sex, and only as such was it considered to be ennobling. Those who did carnally consummate their illicit love were depicted as reaping at least as much suffering as joy from it.

In the twelfth century knighthood was legally restricted to those of high birth. This circumscription of noble ranks came in reaction to the growing wealth,

Aristocrats hunting outside the castle walls. Note the swimmers, probably peasants, in the stream. The August scene from *Les très riches heures du duc de Berry.* [Musée Condé, Chantilly. Giraudon.]

political power, and social climbing of the emergent urban patriciate. Kings remained free, however, to raise up knights at will and did not shrink from increasing royal revenues by selling noble titles to wealthy merchants. But law was building fences—fortunately not without gates—between town and countryside in the high Middle Ages.

For their part, merchants supported the passage of statutes prohibiting the nobility, who maintained houses and family businesses in the towns, from disrupting their carefully created monopolies by engaging in long-distance trade. Such jockeying to protect self-interests brought the lawyer into a prominence he has never lost in Western society.

No medieval social group was absolutely uniform—not the nobility, the clergy, townsmen, not even the peasantry. Not only was the nobility a class apart, it also had strong social divisions within its own ranks. Noblemen formed a broad social spectrum—from minor vassals without subordinate vassals to the mighty baron, the

A banquet scene from sculptured details of the banquet hall of the twelfth-century archbishop's palace in Santiago de Compostela, Spain. [AHM.]

principal vassal of a king or prince, who had many vassals of his own. Dignity and status within the nobility were directly related to the exercise of authority over others; a chief with many vassals obviously far excelled the small country nobleman who served another and was lord over none but himself.

Even among the domestic servants of the nobility a broad social hierarchy developed in accordance with assigned manorial duties. Although they were peasants in the eyes of the law, the chief stewards charged to oversee the operation of the lord's manor and entrusted with the care and education of his children became powerful "lords" within their "domains." Some freemen found the status of the steward enviable enough to surrender their own freedom and become domestic servants in the hope of obtaining it. In time the social superiority of the higher ranks of domestic servants was legally recognized as medieval law adjusted to acknowledge the privileges of wealth and power at whatever level the latter appeared.

In the late Middle Ages several factors forced the landed nobility into a steep economic and political decline, one from which it never recovered. These were the great population losses of the fourteenth century brought on by the great plague; the changes in military tactics occasioned by the use of infantry and heavy artillery during the Hundred Years War; and the alliance of the wealthy towns with the king. By the sixteenth century the old knightly class, the original nobility, waged desperate revolts in the hope of restoring its lost status. The Knight's Revolt of Franz von Sickingen and Ulrich von Hutten in 1523 is a touching example in Germany. In mid-seventeenth-century France the old feudal aristocracy allied with privileged leaders of the bourgeoisie to win a brief victory over the monarchy in an upper-class revolt known as the Fronde. But generally one can speak of a waning of the landed nobility after the fourteenth century. Thereafter the effective possession of land and wealth counted far more than parentage and family tree as qualification for entrance into the highest social class.

Clergy

Unlike the nobility and the peasantry the clergy was an open estate. Although clerical ranks reflected the social classes from which the clergy came and a definite clerical hierarchy formed, one was still a cleric by religious training and ordination, not simply by birth. There were two basic types of clerical vocation: the regular and the secular clergy. The former were the orders of monks, friars, and nuns who lived according to a special ascetic rule (*regula*) in cloisters separated from the world. They were the spiritual elite among the clergy. It was not a way of life lightly entered. Canon law required that one be at least twenty-one years of age before making a final profession of the monastic vows of poverty, chastity, and obedience. Their personal sacrifices and high religious ideals made the monks much respected in high medieval society. This popularity was a major factor in the success of the Cluny reform movement and of the crusades of the eleventh and twelfth centuries. Crusades became a way for the layman to embrace the admired life of asceticism and prayer. They were holy pilgrimages providing the opportunity to imitate the suffering of Jesus even unto death, just as the monks imitated his suffering and death by their retreat from the world and their severe self-denial.

Although many monks and nuns secluded themselves altogether, the regular clergy were never completely cut off from the secular world. They maintained frequent contact with laity through their charitable activities, through liberal arts instruction in monastic schools, through special pastoral commissions from the pope, and as supplemental preachers and confessors in parish churches during Lent and other peak religious seasons. Some monks, because of their learning and rhetorical skills, even rose to prominence as secretaries and private confessors to kings and queens.

The secular clergy were those who lived and worked directly among the laity in the world (*saeculum*). They formed a vast hierarchy. There were the high prelates— the wealthy cardinals, archbishops, and bishops, who were drawn almost exclusively from the nobility—the urban priests, the cathedral canons, and the court clerks; and, finally, there was the great mass of poor parish priests, who were neither financially nor intellectually very far above the common people they served (the basic educational requirement was an ability to say the Mass). Until the Gregorian reform in the eleventh century began to reverse the trend, parish priests lived with women in a relationship akin to marriage and their "wives" and children were accepted within the communities they served. Because of their relative poverty, it was not unusual for priests to "moonlight" as teachers, artisans, or farmers, a practice also accepted and even admired by their flocks.

One of the results of the Gregorian reform was the creation of new religious orders. The more important were the Canons Regular (founded, 1050–1100), Carthusians (founded, 1084), Cistercians (founded, 1098), and Praemonstratensians (founded, 1121). Carthusians, Cistercians, and Praemonstratensians were extremely puritanical in their quest to recapture the purer religious life of the early church. Cistercians were known as the

"White Monks" and the Praemonstratensians as the "White Order," both descriptions reflecting their all white attire—symbolic of the quest for apostolic purity—while the Carthusians were known to flagellate themselves. The Canons Regular were independent groups of secular clergy and also earnest laity, who, in addition to services to souls in the world, also adopted the Rule of Saint Augustine, a monastic guide dating from around A.D. 500, and practiced the virtues of regular clerics. As there were monks who renounced exclusive withdrawal from the world, so there were priests who renounced exclusive involvement in it. By merging the life of the cloister with traditional clerical duties, the Canons Regular foreshadowed the great mendicant orders of the thirteenth century, the Dominicans and the Franciscans.

Monasteries and nunneries recruited candidates from among the wealthiest social groups. A dowry came to be required upon entrance for the support of prospective monks and nuns. This requirement was no problem for the sons and daughters of the nobility and urban merchants. Fathers with many daughters often found a nun's dowry a bargain compared with that required for a proper noble marriage. However, expense tended to deny admission to those without a wealthy patron. Men with little means were forced into the ranks of the lower secular clergy. The absence of patronage was also a factor in the thirteenth-century growth of lay satellite convents known as *beguinages,* which housed religiously earnest unmarried women, mostly from the middle social strata. A number of these convents became heterodox in religious doctrine and practice, falling prey to the precepts of Catharism, a dualist heresy. Among the responsibilities of the new religious orders of Dominicans and Franciscans was the "regularization" of such convents.

By modern comparison medieval society severely constricted the options open to women. Although widowed noblewomen managed their own affairs and could move at will in the man's world of the Middle Ages, the cloister was the only vocational alternative for other unmarried women. There women received basic education, were able to associate with their social peers, and, as the sizeable mystical literature authored by women attests, developed considerable literary talents. The alleged emotional and seductive nature of woman, following the biblical example of Eve, was cited as unfitting her for political and ecclesiastical office. It was sincerely believed to be against both divine and natural law for women to have authority over men. This was the reason that medieval kings trembled at the thought of having no male heirs. Historical examples of successful women rulers, such as Deborah in the Old Testament, were explained away as special providential exceptions to the rule of male dominance. Late medieval ecclesiasts argued that the moral and mental inferiority of women made them more prone to witchcraft than men. In the fifteenth century the *Malleus Maleficarum* (1485–1486), the supreme medieval handbook for the detection and interrogation of witches—there were twenty-nine editions of this work by 1669—referred to witches exclusively in the feminine gender. Far more women than men were burned as witches, probably as a direct result of this prejudgment. In the twelfth century women who became nuns were praised as having done a more meritorious work than men who became monks. This was because women's alleged physical, mental, and moral inferiority were believed to make it far more difficult for them than for men to master the discipline of the cloistered life. Even as loyal wives and dutiful mothers women in the Middle Ages still fell short of their potential earthly purity. Only as virgins withdrawn to nunneries did they win the unqualified blessing of the church's theologians.

There was a far greater proportion of clergy within medieval than within modern society. It has been estimated that 1.5 per cent of fourteenth-century Europe was in clerical garb. The clergy were concentrated in urban areas, especially in towns with universities and cathedrals, where a wide variety of religious services were always in demand. In late fourteenth-century England there was one cleric for every seventy laymen, and in counties with a cathedral or a university the proportion rose to one cleric for every fifty laymen.[1] In large university towns the clergy could exceed 10 per cent of the population. One of the most popular reforms of the Protestant Reformation in the sixteenth century, a uniquely urban movement, was a sharp reduction of the proportion of clergy in society. An early Protestant pamphleteer, Eberlin von Günzburg, for example, reflected pervasive late-medieval lay sentiment when he proposed that there be but one cleric for every three hundred laymen.

Despite the moonlighting of poorer parish priests, the clergy as a whole, like the nobility, lived on the labor of others. Their income came from the regular collection of tithes and church taxes according to an elaborate system that evolved in the high and later Middle Ages. Monastic communities and high prelates amassed truly great fortunes; there was a popular saying that the granaries were always full in the monasteries. The immense secular power attached to high clerical posts can be seen in the intensity of the Investiture Struggle, when the loss of the right to present chosen clergy with the ring and staff of episcopal office seemed a direct threat to the emperor's control of his realm.

During the greater part of the Middle Ages the clergy were the first estate and theology the queen of the sciences. How did the clergy come into such prominence? It was basically popular reverence for the clergy's role as mediator between God and man that made this superiority possible. The priest was believed to bring the very Son of God down to earth when he celebrated the sacrament of the Eucharist; it was his absolution that released penitents from punishment for mortal sin. It was considered improper that mere laymen should sit in judgment on such a priest. The distinction between the clergy and the laity was elaborated very much to the clergy's benefit. The belief in the superior status of the clergy underlay the evolution of clerical privileges and immunities in both person and property. As holy persons, clergy could not

be taxed by secular rulers without special permission from the proper ecclesiastical authorities. Clerical crimes were under the jurisdiction of special ecclesiastical courts, not the secular courts. Because churches and monasteries were holy places, they too were deemed free from secular taxation and legal jurisdiction. Hunted criminals, lay and clerical, regularly sought asylum within them, disrupting the normal processes of law and order. Ecclesiastical authorities were quick to threaten excommunication and interdict, which medieval towns feared almost as much as they did criminals, when this privilege of asylum was violated by civil officials.

In the late Middle Ages townsmen came increasingly to resent the special immunities of the clergy. They complained that it was not proper for clergy to have greater privileges yet far fewer responsibilities than all others who lived within town walls. An early sixteenth-century lampoon reflected what had by then become a widespread sentiment:

Priests, monks, and nuns
Are but a burden to the earth.
They have decided
That they will not become citizens.
That's why they're so greedy—
They stand firm against our city
And will swear no allegiance to it.
And we hear their fine excuses:
"It would cause us much toil and trouble
Should we pledge our troth as burghers."[2]

Although the separation of church and state and the distinction between the clergy and the laity have persisted into modern times, after the fifteenth century the clergy ceased to be the superior class they had been for so much of the Middle Ages. In both Protestant and Catholic lands governments progressively subjected them to the basic responsibilities of citizenship.

1 Denys Hay, *Europe in the Fourteenth and Fifteenth Centuries* (New York: Holt, Rinehart, 1966), pp. 58–59.

2 Cited by S. Ozment, *The Reformation in the Cities* (New Haven: Yale University Press, 1975), p. 36.

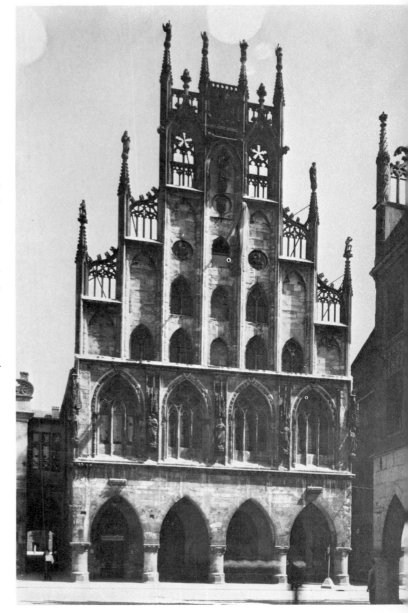

The Gothic town hall of Münster, West Germany, built about 1350. Note the treatment of windows and the open work in the upper stories, a later development of the Gothic style. [Bildarchiv Foto Marburg.]

Townsmen

In the eleventh century towns and cities held only about 5 per cent of Western Europe's population. Nonetheless one could find there the whole of medieval society: nobles visiting their townhouses, peasants living or working within the walls, resident monks and priests, university scholars, great merchants and poor journeymen, pilgrims en route to shrines, and beggars passing through. By modern comparison the great majority of medieval towns were but small villages. Of some three thousand late medieval German towns, for example, twenty-eight hundred had populations under 1,000 and only fifteen were in excess of 10,000 inhabitants. Only London, Paris, and the great merchant capitals of Italy—Florence, Venice, and Naples—approached 100,000 by the fifteenth century.

Women appear to have slightly outnumbered men. War, the perils of long-distance travel, and illnesses resulting from immoderation in food and drink combined to reduce male ranks. The frequent remarriage of widows, whose inheritances made them attractive mates, and the church's siphoning off of an already short supply of eligible bachelors into monasteries contributed to the large number of unmarried women. Those from the upper and middle classes entered nunneries and beguinages, and the very poor joined wandering bands of prostitutes. It has been speculated that the fact that unmarried women were an unproductive surplus contributed to the prejudice of late medieval society against them and made them the more vulnerable targets of the great witch hunts of the fifteenth and sixteenth centuries. Between 1250 and 1350 Cologne, the largest German city, established a hundred beguinages, each able to accommodate about ten women and open to all classes, although many Beguines also lived alone with their families. As the example of Cologne illustrates, medieval towns were conscientious about caring for the poor and unfortunate within their walls.

The term *bourgeois* first appeared in the eleventh century to describe a new addition to the three traditional social ranks: knight (noble), cleric, and serf. The term initially designated the merchant groups, who formed new communities or "bourgs" as bases of operation in or around the old Roman towns that were governed by the nobility. These men, whose business was long-distance trade and commerce, were at first highly suspect within traditional medieval society. Clerics condemned their profits as immoral usury and noblemen viewed their fluid wealth and mobility as politically disruptive. The merchants in turn resented the laws and customs of feudal society that gave the nobility and the clergy special privileges. Town life was often disrupted because regional laws permitted the nobility and the clergy to live beyond the rules that governed the activities of everyone else.

Merchants especially wanted an end to the arbitrary tolls and tariffs imposed by regional magnates over the surrounding countryside. Such regulations hampered and could even bring to a standstill the flow of commerce on which both merchants and craftsmen in the growing urban export industries depended. Townsmen needed simple, uniform laws and a government sympathetic to their business interests; they needed a government in which merchants and craftsmen had a major voice. That need created internal and external struggles with the old landed nobility. This was the basic conflict that led towns in the late Middle Ages to form their own independent communes and ally with kings against the nobility—developments that bespoke the dissolution of feudal society.

Manorial society actually contributed to the creation of its urban challenger. Nobles longed for finished goods and the luxuries that came from faraway places. They urged their serfs to become skilled craftsmen. In return for a fixed rent and proper subservience, they granted charters conveying rights and privileges to those who would create towns upon their land. By the eleventh century skilled serfs were beginning to pay their feudal dues in manufactured goods. Many serfs took their new skills to the growing urban centers, where there were greater freedom and profits that could catapult an industrious craftsman into higher social ranks. As the migration of serfs to the towns accelerated, the lords offered them greater freedom and more favorable terms of tenure to keep them on the land. The twelfth and thirteenth centuries saw a mass "freeing" of serfs in the sense of a formal contractual fixing of rights and required services—a privilege heretofore known only by freemen. But serfs simply could not be kept down on the farm after they had seen the opportunities of town life. Rural society not only gave the towns their craftsmen and day laborers, but the first merchants themselves appear to have been wandering, enterprising serfs.

Despite unified resistance to external domination, the medieval town was not an internally harmonious social unit. It was a collection of many selfish, competitive communities. Only families of long standing and those who owned property had the full rights of citizenship and a say in the town's government. Workers in the same trade lived together on streets that bore their name, apparently doing so as much to monitor one another's business practices as to dwell among peers. Sumptuary laws regulated not only the dress but even the architecture of the residences of the various social groups. Merchant guilds appeared in the eleventh century and were followed in the twelfth by the craft guilds (organizations of drapers, haberdashers, furriers, hosiers, goldsmiths, and so on). These organizations existed solely to protect the personal well-being and to advance the business interests of their members. They won favorable government policies and served as collection agencies for the unpaid accounts of individual members. The guilds also formed distinctive religious confraternities, inward-looking associations that ministered to the needs of member families in both life and death.

The merchants and the stronger craft guilds quickly won a role in town government. "New-rich" patricians married into the old nobility and aped their social customs. Sharing the power of government in the city councils, the craft guilds used their position in the most selfish way to limit their membership, to regulate their wages favorably, and to establish exacting standards of workmanship so that their products could not be copied by others (trademarks first made their appearance in the twelfth century). So rigid and exclusive did the dominant guilds become that they stifled their own creativity and inflamed the journeymen who were excluded from joining their ranks. In the fourteenth century unrepresented artisans and craftsmen, a true urban proletariat prevented by law from either forming their own guilds or entering the existing guilds, revolted in a number of places—Florence, Paris, and the cities of Flanders. Their main opponents were the merchant and craft guilds, which had

Peasant Wedding, by Pieter Brueghel
(*ca.* 1520–1569), the Flemish painter. Note the
bagpipes and the peacock feather on the cap of
the boy in the foreground. Artists are still
seeking the owner of one of the four feet under
the front edge of the door being used to carry
pies. [Kunsthistorisches Museum, Vienna.]

themselves risen to prominence by opposing the anti-
quated laws and privileges of the old nobility.

Peasants

The largest and, save for chattel slaves, lowest social
group in medieval society was the one on whose labor the
welfare of all others depended: the agrarian peasantry.
Landless men, the peasants knew most about the land.
They lived on and worked the manors of noblemen, the
primitive cells of rural social life. The manor was originally a plot of land within a village, ranging from twelve
to seventy-five acres in size, assigned to a certain member
by a settled tribe or clan. This member and his family
became lord of the land and those who came to dwell
there formed a smaller self-sufficient community within a
larger village community. In the early Middle Ages such
a manor consisted of the dwellings of the lord, the cottages of his peasant workers, agricultural sheds, and fields.

The landowner or lord of the manor required a certain
amount of produce (grain, eggs, and the like) and a
certain number of services from the peasant families who
came to dwell on and farm his land. The tenants were
free to divide the labor as they wished and what remained
after the lord's levies were met was their own. A powerful lord might own many such manors and kings later
based their military and tax assessments on the number of
manors owned by a vassal landlord.

There were both servile and free manors. The tenants
of the latter had originally been freemen known as *coloni*,
original inhabitants and petty landowners who swapped
their small possessions for a guarantee of security from a
more powerful lord who came to possess their land.
Unlike the pure serfdom of the servile manors, whose
tenants had no original claim to a part of the land, the
tenancy obligations on free manors were limited and their
rights carefully defined. Tenants of servile manors were
by comparison far more vulnerable to the whims of
landlords.

Marc Bloch, the modern authority on manorial society,
has vividly depicted the duties of tenancy:

On certain days the tenant brings the lord's steward
perhaps a few small silver coins or, more often, sheaves

The life of peasants, like that of the nobles, had many unchanging features throughout late medieval and early modern times. Here peasant women raise their dresses to catch the warmth of the fire while others gather wood. Note the beehives. The February scene from *Les très riches heures du duc de Berry.* [Musée Condé, Chantilly. Giraudon.]

of grain harvested on his fields, chickens from his farmyard, cakes of wax from his beehives or from the swarms of the neighboring forest. At other times he works on the arable or the meadows of the demesne [the lord's plot of land in the manoral fields, between one third and one half of that available]. Or else we find him carting casks of wine or sacks of grain on behalf of the master to distant residences. His is the labour which repairs the walls or moats of the castle. If the master has guests the peasant strips his own bed to provide the necessary extra bed-clothes. When the hunting season comes round he feeds the pack. If war breaks out he does duty as a foot-soldier or orderly, under the leadership of the reeve of the village.[3]

The lord also had the right to subject his tenants to exactions known as *banalities.* He could, for example,

force them to breed their cows with his bull (for a fee), grind their corn in his mill, bake their bread in his oven, make their wine in his wine press, buy their beer from his brewery, and even surrender to him the tongues of all animals slaughtered on his lands. He had the right to levy taxes at will.

Exploited as the serf may appear to have been from a modern point of view, his status was far from outright chattel slavery. It was to the lord's advantage to keep his serfs healthy and happy; his welfare, like theirs, depended on a successful harvest. Serfs had their own dwellings and modest strips of land. They lived by the produce of their own labor and organization. They were permitted to market for their own profit what surpluses might remain after the harvest. They were free to choose their spouses within the local village, although the lord's permission was required if a wife was sought from another village. And serfs were able to pass their property (their dwellings and field strips) and worldly goods on to their children.

Peasants lived in mud huts with thatched roofs and, with the exception of the higher domestic servants, seldom ventured beyond their own villages. The local priest was their window on the world and church festivals their major communal entertainment. Their religiosity was based in large part on the fact that the church was the only show in town. Despite the social distinctions between free and servile serfs—and, within these groups, between those who owned ploughs and oxen and those who possessed only hoes—the common dependence upon the soil forced close cooperation. As the ratio of seed to grain yield was consistently poor—about two bushels of seed were required to produce six to ten bushels of grain in good times—there was rarely an abundance of bread and ale, the staple peasant foods. There was no corn or potatoes in Europe until the sixteenth century. Pork was the major source of protein and every peasant household had its pigs. At slaughter time a family might receive a little tough beef. But basically everyone depended on the grain crops. When they failed or fell short, the peasantry

3 *Feudal Society,* trans. by L. A. Manyon (Chicago: University of Chicago Press 1968), p. 250.

Peasants plowing, planting, and clearing ground in the spring. Note the moldboard plow. The March scene from *Les très riches heures du duc de Berry*. The artists of this and the other paintings from this source were Pol de Limbourg and his two brothers. (Another illustration from this same work appears in the color album.) [Musée Condé, Chantilly. Giraudon.]

BELOW: For hundreds of years and over a great part of Europe the manor was basic for much of the population. Despite regional variation and changes that came with the revival of trade and the growth of towns, manors in the West had enough common features to justify this modern reconstruction of a characteristic example. Note the lord's hall and lands (demesne), the peasant village with common grounds and services, the church and its lands (glebe), peasant holdings in open fields, and areas for woodcutting and hunting. [The Granger Collection.]

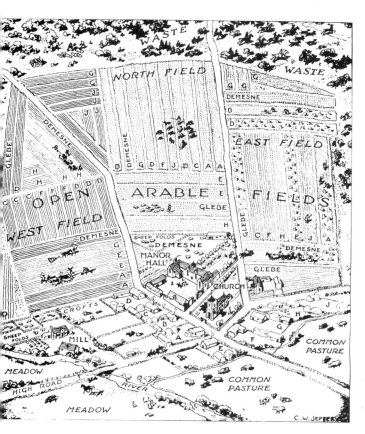

simply went hungry unless the lord had surplus stores to share.

Two basic changes occurred in the evolution of the manor from the early to the later Middle Ages. The first was the fragmentation of the manor and the rise to dominance of the single-family unit. As the lords parceled out their land to new tenants, their own plots became progressively smaller. The increase in tenants and the decrease in the lord's fields brought about a corresponding reduction in the labor services exacted from tenants. In France, by the reign of Louis IX (1214–1270), only a few days a year were required, whereas in the time of Charlemagne peasants had worked the lord's fields several days a week. By the twelfth century the manor was hopelessly fragmented. As the single-family unit replaced the clan as the basic nuclear group, assessments of goods and services fell on individual fields and households, no longer on manors as a whole. Family farms replaced manorial units. Children continued to live with their parents after marriage, and several generations of one family were normally found within a single household. It was this carefully nurtured communal life of peasant

This pair of illustrations shows the difference between [LEFT] the simple strap harness, which formed a collar around the horses' or oxen's necks and tended to choke them, and [RIGHT, OPPOSITE] the more advanced traction harness that came into use during the Middle Ages and permitted a swift gallop without discomfort to the animals. [Charles Singer, et al., *A History of Technology*, II (London: Oxford University Press, 1950), p. 553.]

families that laid the basis of mortmain, or the transfer of the land and the dwelling of a peasant to his family when he died. The family that stayed together had a certain security.

Throughout medieval society children were treated as adults, and nowhere was this truer than among the peasantry, who could ill afford idle hands. Children dressed like their parents, shared their work and conversation, and lived and slept in the same room. It has been speculated that the high mortality rate among infants prevented the growth of sentimental views about children and special care for them. The church considered children capable of mortal sin as early as age seven and expected them to attend confession at least once a year after they reached the age of twelve. The modern view of children as innocent, fragile creatures and of childhood as a distinct stage in life requiring special treatment did not develop until well into the seventeenth century.

The second change in the evolution of the manor was the translation of feudal dues into money payments, a change made possible by the revival of trade and the rise of towns. This development, which was completed by the thirteenth century, permitted serfs to hold their land as rent-paying tenants and to overcome their servile status. Although tenants thereby gained greater freedom, they were not necessarily better off materially. Whereas servile workers had been able to count on the benevolent assistance of their landlords in hard times, rent-paying workers were left by and large to their own devices, their independence causing indifference and even resentment among their landlords.

Lands and properties that had been occupied by generations of peasants and recognized as their own were always under the threat of the lord's claim to a prior right of inheritance and even outright usurpation. As their demesnes declined, the lords were increasingly tempted to encroach on such traditionally common lands. The peasantry fiercely resisted such efforts, instinctively clinging to the little they had. In many regions they successfully organized to win a role in the choice of petty rural officials. By the mid-fourteenth century a declining nobility in England and France, faced with the ravages of the great plague and the Hundred Years' War, attempted to turn back the historical clock by increasing taxes on the peasantry and passing laws to restrict their migration into the cities. The peasantry responded with armed revolts in the countryside. These were rural equivalents to the organization of late medieval cities in sworn communes to protect their self-interests against territorial rulers. The revolts of the agrarian peasantry, like those of the urban proletariat, were brutally crushed. They stand out at the end of the Middle Ages as violent testimony to the breakup of medieval society. As growing national sentiment would break its political unity and heretical movements—soon to peak in the Protestant Reformation—would end its nominal religious oneness, the revolts of the peasantry signaled the passage of medieval social unity.

England and France: Hastings (1066) to Bouvines (1214)
William the Conqueror

The most important change in English political life was occasioned in 1066 by the death of the childless Anglo-Saxon prince Edward the Confessor. Edward's mother was a Norman princess and this fact gave the duke of Normandy a hereditary claim to the English throne. Before his death Edward acknowledged this claim and even directed that his throne go to William of Normandy (d. 1087). But the Anglo-Saxon assembly, which customarily bestowed the royal power, had a mind of its own and vetoed Edward's last wishes. It chose instead Harold Godwinsson. This defiant action brought the swift conquest of England by the powerful Normans. William's forces defeated Harold's army at Hastings on October 13, 1066. Within weeks of the invasion William was crowned king of England in Westminster Abbey, both by right of heredity and by right of conquest.

Thereafter all of England became William's domain. Every landholder, whether large or small, was henceforth his vassal, holding his land legally as a fief from the king. William organized his new English nation shrewdly. On the one hand, he established a strong monarchy whose power was not fragmented by independent territorial princes. On the other hand, he was careful not to destroy Anglo-Saxon democratic traditions. The Norman king thoroughly subjected his noble vassals to the crown, yet he also consulted with them regularly about decisions of "state." The result was a unique blending of the "one" and the "many," a balance between monarchical and

William the Conqueror, on horseback, leads his Norman troops against the English at the Battle of Hastings (October 14, 1066). From the Bayeux Tapestry, about 1073–1083. (Another portion of the Bayeux Tapestry appears in the color album). [Musée de l'Évêché, Bayeux, France. Avec autorisation spéciale de la ville de Bayeux. Giraudon.

The effigy of Eleanor of Aquitaine, who had been queen of France as well as queen of England, is on her tomb at Fontevrault Abbey in France. [The Granger Collection.]

representative elements that has ever since characterized English government.

For the purposes of administration and taxation William commissioned a county-by-county survey of his new realm, a detailed accounting known as the *Domesday Book* (1080–1086). The title of the book reflects the thoroughness of the survey: just as none would escape the doomsday judgment of God, so none was overlooked by William's assessors.

Henry II

William's son, Henry I (ruled 1100–1135), died without a male heir and this threw England into virtual anarchy until Henry II (1154–1189), son of the duke of Anjou and Matilda, daughter of Henry I, mounted the throne as head of the new Plantagenet dynasty. Under Henry II the English monarchy began to drift toward an oppressive rule. Henry brought to the throne greatly expanded French holdings, partly by inheritance from his father (Burgundy and Anjou) and partly by his marriage to Eleanor of Aquitaine (1122?–1204), a union that created the so-called Angevin or English French empire. Eleanor married Henry while he was still the count of Anjou and not yet king of England. The marriage occurred only eight weeks after the annulment of her marriage to the French king, Louis VII, in March 1152. She bore Henry eight children, among them the future kings Richard the Lion-Hearted and John. Not only did England, under Henry, come to control most of the coast of France, but Henry also conquered a part of Ireland and made the king of Scotland his vassal.

The French king, Louis VII, who had lost both his wife and considerable French land to Henry, saw a mortal threat to France in this English expansion. He responded by adopting what came to be a permanent French policy of containment and expulsion of the English from their continental holdings in France—a policy that was not finally successful until the mid-fifteenth century, when English power on the Continent collapsed at the conclusion of the Hundred Years' War.

Eleanor of Aquitaine and Court Culture

Eleanor of Aquitaine was closely associated with the rise of court culture and literature in France and England. After marrying Henry, she settled in Angers, the chief town of Anjou, where she sponsored troubadours and poets at her lively court. There the troubadour Bernart de Ventadorn composed in Eleanor's honor many of the most popular love songs of high medieval aristocratic society. Eleanor spent the years 1154–1170 as Henry's queen in England. She separated from him in 1170, partly because of his public philandering. Thereafter she lived in Poitiers with her daughter Marie, the countess of Champagne, and the two made the court of Poitiers a famous center for the literature of courtly love.

This literary genre, with its thinly veiled eroticism, has been viewed as an attack on medieval ascetic values. Be that as it may, it was certainly a commentary on contemporary problems within the domestic life of the aristocracy. The code of chivalry that guided the relations between lords and their vassals looked upon the seduction of the wife of one's lord as the most heinous of offenses. In some areas such adultery was punished by castration and/or execution. The troubadours and minnesingers hardly promoted such promiscuity at court. They rather presented in a frank and entertaining way stories that satirized or depicted in tragic irony illicit carnal love, while glorifying the ennobling power of friendly or "courteous" love. The most famous courtly literature was Chretien de Troyes's stories of King Arthur and the Knights of the Round Table, which contained the tragic story of Sir Lancelot's secret and illicit love for Arthur's wife, Guinevere.

Popular Rebellion and Magna Carta

As Henry II acquired new lands abroad, he became more autocratic at home. He subjected his vassals more than ever to the royal yoke. He forced his will upon the clergy in the Constitutions of Clarendon (1164), measures that limited appeals to Rome, subjected the clergy to the civil courts, and gave the king control over the election of bishops. The result was strong political resistance from both the nobility and the clergy. The archbishop of Canterbury, Thomas à Becket (1118?-1170), once Henry's compliant chancellor, broke openly with the king and fled to Louis VII. Becket's subsequent assassination in 1170 and his canonization by Pope Alexander III in 1172 forced the king to retreat from his heavy-handed tactics, as popular resentment grew. Two hundred years later Geoffrey Chaucer, writing in an age made cynical by the Black Death and the Hundred Years' War, had the pilgrims of his *Canterbury Tales* journey to the shrine of Thomas à Becket.

English resistance to the king became outright rebellion under Henry's successors, the brothers Richard the Lion-Hearted (1189-1199) and John (1199-1216). Their burdensome taxation in support of unnecessary foreign crusades and a failing war with France left the English people no alternative. Richard had to be ransomed at a high price from the Holy Roman Emperor Henry VI, who had taken him prisoner during his return from the ill-fated Third Crusade. In 1209 King John was excommunicated and England was placed under interdict by Pope Innocent III. This humiliating experience saw the king of England declare his country a fief of the pope. But it was the defeat of the English by the French at Bouvines in 1214 that proved the last straw. With the full support of the clergy and the townsmen, the English barons revolted against John. The popular rebellion ended with the king's grudging recognition of Magna Carta in 1215.

This monumental document was a victory of feudal over monarchical power in the sense that it secured the rights of the many—the nobility, the clergy, and the townsmen—over the autocratic king; it was a restoration of the internal balance of power that had been the English experience since the Norman Conquest. The English people, at least the privileged English people, thereby preserved their right to be represented at the highest levels of government, especially in matters of taxation. The monarchy remained intact, however, and its legitimate powers and rights were duly recognized and preserved. This outcome contrasted with the experience on the Continent, where victorious nobility tended to humiliate kings and emperors and undo all efforts at centralization.

With a peculiar political genius the English consistently refused to tolerate either the absorption of the power of monarchy by the nobility or the abridgment of the rights of the nobility by the monarchy. Although King John continued to resist the Great Charter in every way he could, his son Henry III formally ratified it, and it has since remained a cornerstone of English law.

Philip II Augustus

During the century and a half between the Norman Conquest (1066) and Magna Carta (1215), a strong monarchy was never in question in England. The English struggle in the high Middle Ages was to secure the rights of the many, not the authority of the king. The French faced the reverse problem in this period. Powerful feudal princes dominated France for two centuries, from the beginning of the Capetian dynasty (987) until the reign of Philip II Augustus (1180-1223). During this period the Capetian kings wisely concentrated their limited resources on securing the royal domain, their uncontested territory round about Paris known as the Île-de-France. They did not rashly challenge the more powerful nobility. Aggressively exercising their feudal rights in this area, they secured absolute obedience and a solid base of power. By the time of Philip II, Paris had become the center of French government and culture and the Capetian dynasty a secure hereditary monarchy. Thereafter the kings of France were in a position to impose their will upon the French nobles, who were always in law, if not in political fact, their sworn vassals.

It was the Norman conquest of England that first stirred France to unity and made it possible for the Capetian kings to establish a truly national monarchy. The duke of Normandy, who after 1066 was master of the whole of England, was also among the vassals of the French king in Paris. Capetian kings understandably watched with alarm as the power of their Norman vassal grew. Other powerful vassals of the king also watched with alarm. King Louis VI (1108–1137) entered an alliance with Flanders, which had traditionally been a Norman enemy. King Louis VII (1137–1180), assisted by a brilliant minister, Suger, the abbot of St. Denis and famous for his patronage of Gothic architecture, sought alliances with the great northern French cities and used their wealth to build a royal army. Philip II Augustus, who was Louis VII's successor, inherited financial resources and an administrative bureaucracy capable of resisting the divisive French nobility and clergy and capable of pressing the contest with the English king.

Philip Augustus faced, at the same time, an internal and an international struggle and he was successful in both. His armies occupied all the English territories on the French coast, with the exception of Aquitaine. As the showdown with the English neared on the Continent, however, the Holy Roman Emperor Otto IV (1198–1215) entered the fray on the side of the English. The French found themselves assailed from both east and west. But when the international armies finally clashed at Bouvines on July 27, 1214, in what became the first great European battle in history, the French won handily over the English and the Germans. This victory unified France around the monarchy and thereby laid the foun-

The English Nobility Imposes Restraints on King John

The gradual building of a sound English constitutional system in the Middle Ages was in danger of going awry if a monarch overstepped the fine line dividing necessary strength from outright despotism. The danger became acute under the rule of King John. The English nobility, therefore, forced the king's recognition of Magna Carta (1215), which reaffirmed traditional rights and personal liberties of free men against royal authority. The document remained enshrined in English law.

A FREE *man shall not be fined for a small offense, except in proportion to the gravity of the offense; and for a great offense he shall be fined in proportion to the magnitude of the offense, saving his freehold; and a merchant in the same way, saving his merchandise; and the villein shall be fined in the same way, saving his wainage, if he shall be at our [i.e. the king's] mercy; and none of the above fines shall be imposed except by the oaths of honest men of the neighborhood....*

No constable or other bailiff of ours [i.e. the king] shall take anyone's grain or other chattels without immediately paying for them in money, unless he is able to obtain a postponement at the good will of the seller.

No constable shall require any knight to give money in place of his ward of a castle [i.e. standing guard] if he is willing to furnish that ward in his own person, or through another honest man if he himself is not able to do it for a reasonable cause; and if we shall lead or send him into the army he shall be free from ward in proportion to the amount of time which he has been in the army through us.

No sheriff or bailiff of ours [i.e. the king], or any one else, shall take horses or wagons of any free man, for carrying purposes, except on the permission of that free man.

Neither we nor our bailiffs will take the wood of another man for castles, or for anything else which we are doing, except by the permission of him to whom the wood belongs....

No free man shall be taken, or imprisoned, or dispossessed, or outlawed, or banished, or in any way injured, nor will we go upon him, nor send upon him, except by the legal judgment of his peers, or by the law of the land.

To no one will we sell, to no one will we deny or delay, right or justice.

James Harvey Robinson, *Readings in European History*, Vol. 1 (Boston: Atheneaum, 1904), pp. 236–237.

dation for French ascendancy in the later Middle Ages. Philip Augustus also gained control of the lucrative urban industries of Flanders. Otto IV was so weakened by the defeat that he fell from power in Germany.

The repercussions were still greater in England, where the defeat contributed to the popular rebellion against King John that culminated in the king's recognition of Magna Carta.

The Hohenstaufen Empire
(1152–1272)

During the twelfth and thirteenth centuries stable governments developed in both England and France. In England Magna Carta balanced the rights of the nobility against the authority of the king, while in France the reign of Philip II Augustus secured the authority of the king over the competitive claims of the nobility. The experience within the Holy Roman Empire, which embraced Germany, Burgundy, and northern Italy by the mid-thirteenth century, was a very different story. There, primarily because of the efforts of the Hohenstaufen dynasty to extend imperial power into southern Italy, disunity and blood feuding remained the order of the day for two centuries and left as a legacy the fragmentation of Germany until modern times.

Frederick I Barbarossa

The Investiture Struggle had earlier weakened imperial authority. After the Concordat of Worms the German princes held the dominant lay influence over episcopal appointments and within the rich ecclesiastical territories.

A new day seemed to dawn for imperial power, however, with the accession to the throne of Frederick I Barbarossa (1152–1190), the first of the Hohenstaufens, the successor dynasty within the empire to the Franks and the Ottonians. The Hohenstaufens not only reestablished imperial authority, but they also initiated a new phase in the contest between popes and emperors, one that was to prove even more deadly than the Investiture

GERMANY AND ITALY IN THE MIDDLE AGES

Medieval Germany and Italy were divided, factious lands. The Holy Roman Empire (Germany) embraced hundreds of independent territories that the emperor ruled only in name. The papacy controlled the Rome area and tried to enforce its will on Romagna. Under the Hohenstaufens (mid-12th to mid-13th century), internal German divisions and papal conflict reached new heights; German rulers sought to extend their power to southern Italy and Sicily.

Struggle had been. Never have kings and popes despised and persecuted one another more than during the Hohenstaufen dynasty.

As Frederick I surveyed his empire, he saw powerful feudal princes in Germany and Lombardy and a pope in Rome who believed that the emperor was the creature of the pope. There was, however, widespread popular disaffection with the incessant feudal strife of the princes and the turmoil caused by the theocratic pretensions of the papacy. Popular opinion was on the emperor's side. This gave Frederick a foundation upon which to rebuild imperial authority, and he was shrewd enough to take advantage of it. He championed Roman law, which was at the time enjoying a revival in Bologna under Irnerius. Roman law served Frederick on both his fronts: on the one hand, it enhanced centralized authority against the nobility; on the other, it stressed the secular foundation of imperial power against Roman election and papal coronation.

Switzerland became Frederick's base of operation. From there he attempted to hold the empire together by appealing to feudal bonds. He was relatively successful in Germany, thanks largely to the fall from power in 1180 and the exile to England of his strongest German rival, Henry the Lion (d. 1195), the duke of Saxony. Although realistically acknowledging the power of the German duchies, Frederick never missed the opportunity to apprise each of its prescribed duties as a fief of the king. If Frederick was not everywhere ruler in fact, he was clearly so in law, and no one was permitted to forget it. That was the same tactic employed by the Capetian kings of France when they faced superior noble forces.

Italy proved to be the great obstacle to imperial plans. In 1155 Frederick restored Pope Hadrian IV (1154–1159) to power in Rome after a religious revolutionary, Arnold of Brescia (d. 1155), had gained control of the city. For his efforts Frederick won a coveted papal coronation—and strictly on his terms, not on those of the pope. The door to Italy was thereby opened. Having won recognition of his rights of jurisdiction in Burgundy in 1157, Frederick attempted to secure the same recognition in Italy. Resistance to him became fiercest in Lombardy. The Milanese balked at the implementation of these rights, which were defined by the imperial Diet of Roncaglia, and refused to recognize Frederick's representatives within the city.

As this challenge to royal authority was occurring, Pope Alexander III (1159–1181), a pope inspired by Gregorian ideals of papal sovereignty, came to power, and Frederick found himself at war with a united front composed of the pope, Milan, and Sicily. In 1167 the combined forces of the north Italian communes drove him back into Germany. The final blow to imperial plans in Italy came a decade later in 1176, when Italian forces soundly defeated Frederick at Legnano. In the final Peace of Constance in 1183 Frederick recognized the claims of the Lombard cities to full rights of jurisdiction.

Henry VI and the Sicilian Connection

Frederick's reign ended with stalemate in Germany and defeat in Italy. At his death in 1190 he was not a ruler of the stature of the kings of England and France. After the Peace of Constance in 1183 he seems himself to have conceded as much, as he accepted the reality of the empire's indefinite division among the feudal princes of Germany. Concluding that future emperors would need a new territorial base of power, Frederick contracted in 1186 a most fateful marriage between his son, the future Henry VI (1190–1197), and Constance, heiress to the kingdom of Sicily. This alliance proved, however, to be but another well-laid political plan that went astray. The Sicilian connection became a fatal distraction for Hohenstaufen kings. They were led repeatedly to sacrifice their traditional territorial base in northern Europe to that temptress, imperialism. Equally ominous, this union of the empire with Sicily left Rome encircled, thereby ensuring the undying hostility of a papacy already thoroughly distrustful of the emperor. The marriage alliance with Sicily was the first step in what soon became a fight to the death between pope and emperor.

A marble head of Emperor Frederick II (1215–1250), whose preoccupation with Italy and Sicily led to the fragmentation of Germany until the nineteenth century. [Deutsches Archäologisches Institut, Rome.]

When Henry VI came to rule in 1190, he faced a multitude of enemies: a hostile papacy, still smarting from the refusal of his father to recognize territorial claims within the Papal States; supremely independent German princes, led by the archbishop of Cologne; and an England whose adventurous king, Richard the Lion-Hearted, was encouraged to plot against Henry by the exiled duke of Saxony, Henry the Lion.

It was into this divided kingdom that a son, the future Frederick II, was born in 1194. To stabilize his monarchy, Henry campaigned vigorously for the recognition of hereditary succession; he wanted birth alone to secure the imperial throne uncontestably. He won a large number of German princes to this point of view by granting them full hereditary rights to their fiefs—an appropriate exchange. But the encircled papacy was not disposed to secure Hohenstaufen power by supporting a hereditary right to the imperial throne. The pope wanted to return to the period before 1152, when imperial power was diffused among many princes. He accordingly joined dissident German princes against Henry.

Otto IV and the Welf Interregnum

Henry died in September 1197 and chaos proved his immediate heir. Between English intervention in its politics and the pope's deliberate efforts to sabotage the Hohenstaufen dynasty, Germany was thrown into anarchy and civil war. England gave financial support to anti-Hohenstaufen factions, and its candidate for the imperial throne, Otto of Brunswick of the rival Welf dynasty, the son of Henry the Lion, bested Philip of Swabia, Henry VI's brother. Otto was crowned Otto IV by his supporters in Aachen in 1198 and thereafter was recognized in Germany. With England supporting Otto, the French rushed in on the side of the fallen Hohenstaufen. This was the beginning of periodic French fishing in troubled German waters throughout the thirteenth century. Meanwhile Henry VI's four-year-old son, Frederick, was safely, and fatefully, tucked away as a ward of Pope Innocent III (1198–1215), a shrewd pope determined to break imperial power and restore papal power in Italy and willing to play one German dynasty against the other to do so.

Hohenstaufen support remained alive in Germany, however, and Otto was never more than the ruler of a divided kingdom. In October 1209 he received papal coronation as Emperor from Pope Innocent, recognition which enhanced his power. But the pope quickly moved from benefactor to mortal enemy when, following his coronation, Otto proceeded to reconquer Sicily and once again pursue an imperial policy that left Rome encircled. Within four months of his papal coronation Otto received a papal excommunication.

Frederick II

Pope Innocent, casting about for a counterweight to the treacherous Otto, joined the French, who had remained loyal to the Hohenstaufens, against the English–Welf alliance. His new ally, Philip Augustus, impressed upon Innocent the fact that a solution to their problems with Otto IV lay near at hand in Innocent's ward, Frederick of Sicily. Frederick, the son of the late Hohenstaufen Emperor Henry VI, was now of age and, unlike Otto, had an immediate hereditary claim to the imperial throne. In December 1212 the young Frederick, with papal, French, and German support, was crowned king of the Romans in Mainz. Within a year and a half Philip Augustus ended the Welf interregnum of Otto IV on the battlefield of Bouvines. Philip sent Frederick II Otto's fallen imperial banner from the battlefield, a bold gesture that suggests the extent to which Frederick's ascent to the throne was intended to be that of a French–papal puppet. In 1215 Frederick repeated his earlier crowning, this time in the imperial city of Aachen.

If Frederick was intended to be a puppet king, he soon proved to be one without strings to hold him up. His reign was an absolute disaster for Germany and may be credited with securing German fragmentation until modern times. Frederick was Sicilian and dreaded the very thought of travel beyond the Alps. Only nine of his thirty-eight years as emperor were spent in Germany, and six of those were before 1218. Frederick asked only one thing from the German princes, the imperial title for himself and his sons, and he was willing to give them anything they wanted to secure it. His eager compliance with their demands laid the foundation for six centuries of German division. In 1220 he recognized the jurisdictional claims of the ecclesiastical princes of Germany, and in 1232 he extended the same recognition to the secular princes. Thereafter the German princes were undisputed lords over their territories. These magnanimous concessions to the princes were nothing less than an abdication of imperial responsibility in Germany. They have been characterized as a German equivalent to *Magna Carta* in the sense that they secured the rights of the German nobility. Unlike *Magna Carta,* however, they did so without at the same time securing the rights of monarchy. *Magna Carta* placed the king and the nobility in England in a creative tension; the reign of Frederick II simply made the German nobility petty kings.

Frederick's relation with the pope was equally disastrous. He was excommunicated no less than four times, the first in 1227 for refusing to undertake a crusade at the pope's request. The papacy came to view Frederick as the Anti-Christ, the biblical beast of the Apocalypse whose persecution of the faithful signaled the end of the world. The basis of the conflict lay once again in an imperial policy that left Rome encircled. Although Frederick abandoned Germany, he was determined to control Lombardy. His efforts to establish a dominant Lombardy–Sicily axis in Italy brought his excommunication in 1238, an action that Frederick fiercely resisted as unwarranted papal interference in his secular rights as emperor.

The pope finally won the long struggle that ensued, although his victory proved in time to be a Pyrrhic one. In the contest with Frederick II, Pope Innocent IV (1243–1254) launched the church into European politics on a massive scale, and this wholesale secularization of the papacy made the church highly vulnerable to the criticism of religious reformers and royal apologists. Innocent

organized and led the German princes against Frederick, who—thanks to Frederick's grand concessions to them—were a superior force and in full control of Germany by the 1240s. German and Italian resistance kept Frederick completely on the defensive throughout his last years.

When Frederick died in 1250, the German monarchy died with him. The princes established an electoral college in 1257, which thereafter reigned supreme. The "king of the Romans" became their puppet, this time with firmly attached strings; he was elected and did not rule by hereditary right. Between 1250 and 1272 the Hohenstaufen dynasty slowly faded into oblivion. It finally died altogether after the dual defeat of Frederick's quarrelsome grandsons—Manfred in 1266 and Conradino in 1268—by Charles of Anjou, the adventurous brother of the sainted French King Louis IX.

The Hohenstaufen legacy was to make permanent the divisions within the empire. Independent princes now controlled Germany. Italy fell to local magnates. The connection between Germany and Sicily, established by Frederick I, was permanently broken. And the papal monarchy emerged as one of Europe's most formidable powers, soon to enter its most costly conflict with the French and the English.

The Pontificate of Innocent III (1198–1215)
The New Papal Monarchy

The reign of Innocent III was as important for the papacy of the thirteenth century and beyond as it was for the ill-fated Hohenstaufen dynasty. Innocent, a papal monarch in the Gregorian tradition, proclaimed and practiced as none before him the doctrine of the plenitude of papal power. In a famous statement he likened the relation of the pope and the emperor—or the Church and the State—to that of the sun and the moon. As the moon received its light from the sun, so the emperor received his brilliance (that is, his crown) from the hand of the

[*Text continued on page 306*]

Beginning in the mid-twelfth century, the Gothic style evolved from Romanesque architecture. The term itself was at first pejorative; it meant "barbaric" and was applied to the new style by its critics. Gothic was also often known in the Middle Ages as the "French style" because of its unusual popularity in France. Its most distinctive visible features are its ribbed, criss-cross vaulting, its pointed arches rather than rounded ones, and its frequent exterior buttresses. The result gives an essential impression of vertical lines. The vaulting made possible more height than the Romanesque style had sought, while the extensive addition of "flying" buttresses made even greater height possible. Because walls, therefore, did not have to carry all of a structure's weight, wide expanses of windows were possible—hence the extensive use of stained glass and the characteristic color that often floods Gothic cathedrals. Use of the windows to show stories from the Bible, saints' lives, and local events was similar to earlier use of mosaics. (See the Canterbury window in the color album.)

This diagram shows the typical vaulting, arches, and buttresses of a Gothic building. [*World Architecture,* Trewin Copplestone, General Editor (London: Hamlyn, 1963), p. 216.]

BELOW: Among the very earliest examples of Gothic is the abbey church of St. Denis near Paris, built 1137-1144. St. Denis became the burial place for the kings of France. [French Cultural Services, New York.]

The Pontificate of Innocent III (1198–1215) 301

OPPOSITE: Salisbury cathedral, built 1220-1265, an example of English Gothic. Note the flying buttresses, which permit greater height, and the soaring towers and spire. [British Tourist Authority, New York.]

BELOW: Reims Cathedral, thirteenth century, reveals French Gothic architecture in all its complex splendor. It was the traditional coronation place of the kings of France.
While the English cathedrals are mostly situated in large open areas and are surrounded by vast yards and gardens, French cathedrals typically are located in the centers of their towns and are crowded around by buildings that afford little or no vista. [SCALA/ Editorial Photocolor Archives.]

ABOVE: The ability of Gothic architecture to achieve a light, airy effect and, as it were, to lift the viewer heavenward, is illustrated by the whole of Milan cathedral, of which this illustration shows only one detail. Begun in 1386, the cathedral was not completed until the nineteenth century. This is the main spire, built in 1750, as seen from the roof. [AHM.]

ABOVE, LEFT: The interior of Salisbury cathedral, showing the vaulting and the pointed arches. [The National Monuments Record, London.]

BELOW, LEFT: the main portals of Reims Cathedral. [Ruth H. Cloudman.]

RIGHT: The cathedral at Amiens, France, is another splendid example of the thirteenth-century flowering of Gothic architecture. [Aerofilms Limited.]

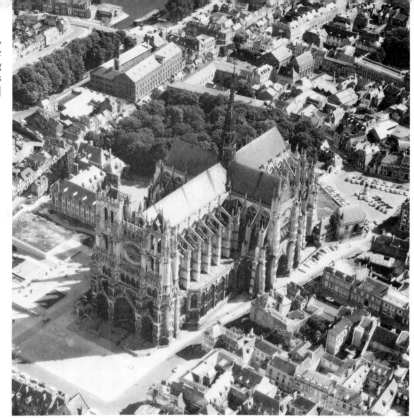

BELOW: Europe's largest Gothic church is the fifteenth-century cathedral at Seville, Spain. Here is a portion of the elaborate system of flying buttresses. [AHM.]

(Other Gothic structures, both religious and domestic, are illustrated in the color album.)

The Pontificate of Innocent III (1198–1215)

pope—an allusion to the famous precedent set on Christmas Day 800, when Charlemagne was crowned by Pope Leo III. Although this pretentious theory greatly exceeded Innocent's ability to practice it, he and his successors did not hesitate to act in the most forceful way. When Philip II tried unlawfully to annul his marriage, Innocent placed France under interdict, suspending all church services save baptism and the last rites. And the same punishment befell England with even greater force when King John refused to accept Innocent's nominee to the archbishopric of Canterbury.

Innocent made the papacy a great secular power, with financial resources and a bureaucracy equal to those of contemporary monarchs. It was during his reign that the papacy transformed itself into that efficient ecclesio-commercial complex attacked by reformers throughout the later Middle Ages. Innocent consolidated and expanded ecclesiastical taxes on the laity, the chief of which at this time was Peter's pence, long a levy on all but the poorest English houses, which was commuted to a lump-sum payment by the English crown in the twelfth century. He imposed an income tax of 2.5 per cent on the clergy. Annates (the payment of a portion or all of the first year's income received by the holder of a new benefice) and fees for the pallium (the symbol of episcopal office) became especially popular revenue-gathering devices employed by the pope. Innocent also reserved to the pope the absolution of many sins and religious crimes, forcing those desirous of pardons or exemptions to bargain directly with Rome. It was a measure of the degree to which the papacy had embraced the new money economy that Lombard merchants and bankers were employed to collect the growing papal revenues.

Crusades in France and the East

Innocent's predilection for power politics was also expressed by his use of the crusade, the traditional weapon of the church against Islam, to suppress internal heresy and dissent. In 1209 he launched a crusade against the Albigensians or Cathars ("pure ones"), advocates of

Innocent III Claims Primacy for Ecclesiastical Power

No pope held a higher view of papal power than Innocent III (1198–1216). Here he compares the relationship of ecclesiastical and royal power to that of the sun and the moon (1198).

Just as God, founder of the universe, has constituted two large luminaries in the firmament of Heaven, a major one to dominate the day and a minor one to dominate the night, so he has established in the firmament of the Universal Church, which is signified by the name of Heaven, two great dignities, a major one to preside, so to speak, over the days of the souls, and a minor one to preside over the nights of the bodies. They are the Pontifical authority and the royal power. Thus, as the moon receives its light from the sun and for this very reason is minor both in quantity and in quality, in its size and in its effect, so the royal power derives from the Pontifical authority the splendour of its dignity, the more of which [splendor] is inherent in it, the less is the light with which it is adorned [from itself], whereas the more it is distant from its reach, the more it benefits [from the] splendour [bestowed upon it]. Both these powers or leaderships have had their seat established in Italy, which country consequently obtained the precedence over all provinces by Divine disposition.

Letter "Sicut universitatis conditor," November 3, 1198, in *Church and State Through the Centuries: A collection of Historic Documents,* trans. and ed. by S. Z. Ehler and John B. Morrall (New York: Biblo and Tannen, 1967), p. 73.

an ascetic, dualist religion who were concentrated in the area of Albi in southern France, but who also had adherents among the laity in Italy and Spain. The Albigensians opposed Christian teaching on several points. They denied the Old Testament and its God of wrath as well as the Christian belief in God's incarnation in Jesus Christ, and many rejected human procreation. They sought instead a pure and simple religious life, following the model of the apostles of Jesus in the New Testament. It was against such sects, whose ascetical extremes even challenged the very propagation of the human species, that the church developed its social teachings on contraception and abortion.

The crusades against the heretics were carried out by powerful noblemen from northern France. These great magnates, led by Simon de Montfort, were as much attracted by the great wealth of the area of Languedoc, among the richest regions of Europe at the time, as they were moved by Christian conscience to stamp out heresy.

B. Picart. del.   C. Du Bofi. cx.

Under the name of auto-da-fé (Portuguese for "act
of the faith"), investigations and judgments on
cases of possible religious heresy and other offenses
were held by the Inquisition. Although by no means
alone, the Spanish Inquisition became the most famous
for the vigor of its prosecutions. The picture shows
a late example of the not infrequent result—the
public burning by government authorities of heretics
convicted by the courts of the Inquisition. [*The
Granger Collection.*]

A succession of massacres occurred, ending with a crusade led by King Louis VIII of France in 1225–1226,
which completely destroyed the Albigensians as a political entity. The Inquisition was introduced into the region
by Pope Gregory IX (1227–1241) to complete the work
of the crusaders. Henceforth the church responded to
heresy with fire and the sword.

It was also during Innocent's pontificate that the
Fourth Crusade to the Holy Land was launched (1202).
Innocent called for the crusade because he believed it
would stimulate religiosity and unite Christendom as the
first crusades had done in such striking fashion in the
preceding century. What was intended as a noble project
became instead a universal scandal, Christians against

Christians, as the crusaders were sidetracked into conquering Zara and eventually capturing the eastern capital
of Constantinople.

The stunning capture of Constantinople established
Latin control of the Eastern Empire until 1261, when the
eastern emperor Michael Paleologus, assisted by the
Genoese, who envied Venetian prosperity in the Eastern
Empire, finally recaptured the city. Innocent was initially
embarrassed by the fall of Constantinople to the crusaders. But the papacy soon adjusted to this unforeseen turn
of events and shared in the spoils. The eastern base gave
the Western church a unique opportunity. A confidant of
Innocent's, Tommaso Morosini, was made patriarch of
Constantinople and launched a mission to win the Greeks
and the Slavs back to the Roman Church. The almost
fifty-year occupation of Constantinople did nothing to
heal the political and religious divisions between east and
west. To the contrary, it only intensified eastern resentment of the west.

The Fourth Lateran Council

Under Innocent's direction the Fourth Lateran Council met in 1215 to establish hierarchical church discipline

from pope to parish. This council was a landmark in ecclesiastical legislation. It gave the controversial theory of transubstantiation full dogmatic sanction, and the Catholic Church has ever since taught that the bread and wine of the Lord's Supper becomes the true body and blood of Christ upon consecration by the priest. The council also made annual confession and Easter communion mandatory for every adult Christian. This latter legislation formalized the sacrament of Penance as the church's key instrument of religious education and discipline in the later Middle Ages.

Franciscans and Dominicans

No action of Pope Innocent was more important than his official sanction of the mendicant orders of the Franciscans and the Dominicans. Lay piety had swollen by the turn of the twelfth century. In addition to the heretical Albigensians, there were movements of Waldensians, Beguines, and Beghards, each of which stressed biblical simplicity in religion and aspired to a life of poverty in imitation of Christ. They were especially vocal in Italy and France. There were, however, heterodox teachings and a critical frame of mind within these movements that caused the pope deep concern that lay piety would turn against the church in militant fashion. The Franciscan and Dominican orders were a response to heterodox piety as well as an answer to lay criticism of the worldliness of the papal monarchy. The Franciscan Order was founded by Saint Francis of Assisi (1182–1226), the son of a rich Italian cloth merchant, who became disaffected with wealth and urged his followers to practice extreme poverty. Pope Innocent recognized the Order in 1210 and the official Rule was approved in 1223. The Dominican Order, the Order of Preachers, was founded by Saint Dominic (1170–1221), a well-educated Spanish cleric, and was sanctioned by the pope in 1216.

Pope Gregory IX (1227–1241) canonized Saint Francis only two years after his death. That was not only a fitting honor for Francis but also a stroke of genius on the part of the pope. By bringing the age's most popular

Francis of Assisi, the son of a rich merchant, rebelled against the materialism of his age, forsook his wealth, and early in the thirteenth century founded the begging order of Franciscans (Friars Minor). Here Francis is shown wedding Lady Poverty in a painting by the Sienese painter Stefano di Giovanni, called Sasetta (1392–1451). [Musée Condé, Chantilly. Giraudon.]

religious figure, one who had even received stigmata (bleeding wounds like those of the crucified Jesus), within the confines of the church, he enhanced papal authority over lay piety, for saints are distinguished by nothing so much as by their loyalty and obedience to the church.

Two years after the canonization Gregory canceled Saint Francis's own *Testament*, which had admonished a life of strictest poverty. The pope set it aside as an authoritative rule for Franciscans because the nonconventual life of nomadic poverty urged by Francis upon his followers conflicted with papal plans to enlist the order as

Saint Francis of Assisi (1182–1226) was the founder of the Franciscan Order of friars. Here are some of his religious principles as stated in the definitive Rule of the Order, approved by the pope in 1223; the Rule especially stresses the ideal of living in poverty.

Tʜɪs *is the rule and way of living of the Minorite brothers, namely, to observe the holy Gospel of our Lord Jesus Christ, living in obedience, without personal possessions, and in chastity. Brother Francis promises obedience and reverence to our lord Pope Honorius, and to his successors who canonically enter upon their office, and to the Roman Chruch. And the other brothers shall be bound to obey Brother Francis and his successors.*

I firmly command all the brothers by no means to receive coin or money, of themselves or through an intervening person. But for the needs of the sick and for clothing the other brothers, the ministers alone and the guardians shall provide through spiritual friends, as it may seem to them that necessity demands, according to time, place, and the coldness of the temperature. This one thing being always borne in mind, that, as has been said, they receive neither coin nor money.

Those brothers to whom God has given the ability to labor shall do so faithfully and devoutly, but in such manner that idleness, the enemy of the soul, being averted, they may not extinguish the spirit of holy prayer and devotion, to which other temporal things should be subservient. As a reward, moreover, for their labor, they may receive for themselves and their brothers the necessities of life, but not coin or money; and this humbly, as becomes the servants of God and the followers of most holy poverty.

The brothers shall appropriate nothing to themselves, neither a house, nor a place, nor anything; but as pilgrims and strangers in this world, in poverty and humility serving God, they shall confidently go seeking for alms. Nor need they be ashamed, for the Lord made Himself poor for us in this world.

A Source Book of Mediaeval History, edited by Frederic Austin Ogg (New York: Cooper Square Publishers, 1972), pp. 375–376.

sidered him almost a new Messiah, were condemned, and absolute poverty was declared a fictitious ideal that not even Christ endorsed.

The Dominicans were a more obedient order. They received the task of combating doctrinal error through visitations and preaching. They conformed convents of Beguines to the church's teaching, led the church's campaign against heretics in southern France, and staffed the offices of the Inquisition after its centralization by Pope Gregory IX in 1223. Their leading theologian, Thomas Aquinas, was canonized in 1322, and his teaching is still considered the most definitive statement of Catholic belief.

Both the Dominicans and the Franciscans strengthened the church among the laity. Through the institution of so-called Third Orders they provided ordinary men and women the opportunity to affiliate with the monastic life and pursue the highest religious ideals, while still remaining laymen and laywomen. Laity who joined such orders were known as tertiaries. Such organizations helped keep lay piety orthodox and within the church.

France in the Thirteenth Century: The Reign of Louis IX

If Innocent III realized the fondest ambitions of medieval popes, Louis IX (1226–1270), the grandson of Philip Augustus, embodied the medieval view of the perfect ruler. His reign was a striking contrast to that of his contemporary, Frederick II of Germany. Coming to power in the wake of the French victory at Bouvines (1214), Louis was heir to a unified and secure kingdom. He was also endowed with a moral character that far excelled that of his royal and papal contemporaries but that was also at times prey to naïveté. Not beset by the problems of sheer survival, and a reformer at heart, Louis found himself free to concentrate on what medieval people believed to be the business of civilization.

Magnanimity in politics is not always a sign of strength and Louis could be very magnanimous. Although in a

an arm of church policy. During the thirteenth century the order was progressively tamed in accordance with papal wishes. In the fourteenth century the Spiritual Franciscans, extreme followers of Saint Francis who con-

King Louis IX of France, shown in a thirteenth-century manuscript, riding off on a crusade with his knights and priests, as monks bless and bid him farewell. [Royal MS. 16 G. VI, f. 404v. Reproduced by permission of the British Library Board, London.]

position to make extensive territorial gains at the expense of England and Aragon, he refused to take such advantage. Had he done so and confiscated English territories on the French coast, he might have lessened, if not averted altogether, the conflict of the Hundred Years' War. Although he occasionally chastized popes for their crude ambitions, Louis remained neutral during the long struggle between Frederick II and the papacy, and his neutrality redounded very much to the pope's advantage. Louis also remained neutral when his brother, Charles of Anjou, intervened in Italy and Sicily against the Hohenstaufens. Urged on by the Welfs and the pope, Charles was crowned king of Sicily in Rome, and his subsequent defeat of the grandsons of Frederick II ended the Hohenstaufen dynasty. For their assistance, both by action and by inaction, the Capetian kings of the thirteenth century became the objects of many papal favors.

Louis's greatest achievements lay at home. He civilized France and made it a nation. The efficient French bureaucracy, which his predecessors had used to fleece their subjects, became under Louis an instrument of order and fair play in local government. He sent forth royal commissioners, reminiscent of Charlemagne's far less successful *missi dominici*, to monitor local bailiffs and to ensure that justice was truly meted out to all. These royal ambassadors were looked upon as genuine tribunes of the people. Louis further abolished private wars and serfdom within his royal domain, gave his subjects the judicial

right of appeal from local to higher courts, and made the tax system, by medieval standards, more equitable. The French people came to associate their king with justice, and national feeling, the glue of nationhood, grew very strong.

Respected by the kings of Europe, Louis became an arbiter among the world's powers, having far greater moral authority than the pope. During his reign French society and culture were an example to all of Europe, a pattern that would continue into the modern period. Northern France became the showcase of monastic reform, chivalry, and Gothic art and architecture. Louis's reign also coincided with the golden age of Scholasticism, which saw the convergence of Europe's greatest thinkers upon Paris, among them Saint Thomas Aquinas and Saint Bonaventura.

Louis's perfection remained, however, that of a medieval king. Like his father, Louis VIII (1223–1226), who had led the second Albigensian crusade, Louis was something of a religious fanatic. He sponsored the French Inquisition. He led two French crusades against the Arabs; these crusades were inspired by the purest religious motives but proved to be personal disasters. During the first (1248–1254) Louis was captured and had to be ransomed out of Egypt. He died of a fever during the second in 1270. It was especially for this selfless, but also quite useless, service on behalf of the church that Louis later received that rare church honor, sainthood.

SUGGESTED READINGS

PHILIPPE ARIES, *Centuries of Childhood: A Social History of Family Life,* trans. by Robert Baldick (1962). Provocative pioneer effort on the subject.

GEOFFREY BARRACLOUGH, *The Origins of Modern Germany* (1963). Penetrating political narrative.

MARC BLOCH, *French Rural Society,* trans. by J. Sondheimer (1966). A classic by a great modern historian.

ANDREAS CAPELLANUS, *The Art of Courtly Love,* trans. by J. J. Parry (1941). Documents from the court of Marie de Champagne.

M. CLAGETT, G. POST, AND R. REYNOLDS (Eds.), *Twelfth-Century Europe and the Foundations of Modern Society* (1966). Demanding but stimulating collection of essays.

R. H. C. DAVIS, *A History of Medieval Europe: From Constantine to St. Louis* (1972), Part 2.

GEORGES DUBY, *Rural Economy and Country Life in the Medieval West* (1968). Slice of life analysis.

ROBERT FAWTIER, *The Capetian Kings of France: Monarchy and Nation 987–1328,* trans. by L. Butler and R. J. Adam (1972). Detailed, standard account.

E. H. KANTOROWICZ, *The King's Two Bodies* (1957). Controversial analysis of political concepts in the high Middle Ages.

R. S. LOOMIS (Ed.), *The Development of Arthurian Romance* (1963). Basic study.

ROBERT S. LOPEZ AND I. W. RAYMOND (Eds.), *Medieval Trade in the Mediterranean World* (1955). Illuminating collection of sources, concentrated on southern Europe.

P. MANDONNET, *St. Dominic and His Work* (1944). For the origins of the Dominican Order.

JOHN MOORMAN, *A History of the Franciscan Order* (1968). The best survey.

JOHN B. MORRALL, *Political Thought in Medieval Times* (1962). Readable and illuminating account.

JOHN T. NOONAN, *Contraception: A History of Its Treatment by the Catholic Theologians and Canonists* (1967). Fascinating account of medieval theological attitudes toward sexuality and sex-related problems.

CHARLES PETIT-DUTAILLIS, *The Feudal Monarchy in France and England from the Tenth to the Thirteenth Century,* trans. by E. D. Hunt (1964). Political narrative.

J. M. POWELL, *Innocent III: Vicar of Christ or Lord of the World* (1963). Excerpts from the scholarly debate over Innocent's reign.

F. W. POWICKE, *The Thirteenth Century* (1962). Outstanding treatment of English political history.

R. W. SOUTHERN, *Medieval Humanism and Other Studies* (1970). Provocative and far-ranging essays on topics in intellectual history of high Middle Ages.

W. L. WAKEFIELD AND A. P. EVANS (Eds.), *Heresies of the High Middle Ages* (1969). A major document collection.

13
The Late Middle Ages and the Renaissance: Decline and Renewal (1300–1527)

The late Middle Ages and the Renaissance mark, on the one hand, a time of unprecedented calamity. There was the Hundred Years' War between England and France (1338–1453), an exercise in seemingly willful self-destruction, which was made even more terrible in its later stages by the invention of gunpowder and heavy artillery. There was almost universal bubonic plague, known to contemporaries as the Black Death. This reached a peak in 1348–1350, killing as much as one third of the population in many regions and transforming many pious Christians into believers in the omnipotence of death. There was a schism within the church that lasted thirty-seven years (1378–1415) and saw by 1409 the election of no less than three competing popes and colleges of cardinals. And there was the onslaught of the Turks, who in 1453 marched seemingly invincibly through Constantinople and toward the west. As their political and religious institutions buckled, as disease, bandits, and wolves ravaged their cities in the wake of war, and as Moslem armies gathered at their borders, Europeans beheld what seemed to be the imminent total collapse of Western civilization.

But if the late Middle Ages saw unprecedented chaos, it also witnessed bold new beginnings. Two modern

The Last Judgment by Michelangelo is part of the vast system of frescoes painted between 1536 and 1541 on the walls and ceiling of the Sistine Chapel in the Vatican. As the dead are raised and brought before the judgment seat, a youthful, athletic, Italianate Jesus, as judge, directs the damned into the hands of Satan's workers, who pack them into barges for the journey to Hell. The subject is medieval, but the classical treatment of bodies and the work's action and energy are of the Renaissance at its grandest. The emptied skin of an old man at right center may be a self portrait of the artist. [Bettmann Archive.]

Dutch scholars have employed the same word—*Herfsttij*, "harvesttide"—with different connotations to describe the period, one interpreting the word as a "waning" or "decline" (Johan Huizinga), the other as a true "harvest" (Heiko Oberman). If something was dying away, some ripe fruit and seed grain were also being gathered in. The late Middle Ages were a creative breaking up.

It was in this period that such scholars as Marsilius of Padua, William of Ockham, and Lorenzo Valla produced lasting criticisms of medieval assumptions about the nature of God, man, and society. It was a period in which kings worked through parliaments and clergy through councils to subdue the papal monarchy of the high Middle Ages and to establish lasting limits on the pope's temporal power. The accountability of a sovereign (in this case, the pope) to the body of which he is head was made clear. The arguments used by conciliarists to establish papal accountability to the body of the faithful also proved applicable in the secular sphere, as kings were reminded of their responsibility to the body politic.

The late Middle Ages also saw an unprecedented scholarly renaissance, as Italian humanists made a full recovery of classical knowledge and languages. In the process they invented, for all practical purposes, critical historical scholarship and exploited a new fifteenth-century invention, the "divine art" of printing with movable type. It was in this period that the vernacular, the local language, began to replace Latin, the international language, on a large scale. The independent nation-states of Europe progressively superseded the universal church as the community of highest allegiance, as patriotism and incipient nationalism became a major force. Nations henceforth transcended themselves not by journeys to Rome but by competitive voyages to the Far East and the Americas, as the age of global exploration opened.

A time of both waning and harvest, constriction (in the form of nationalism) and expansion (in the sense of world exploration), the late Middle Ages saw medieval culture grudgingly give way to the age of Renaissance and Reformation.

Political and Social Breakdown

The Hundred Years' War and the Rise of National Sentiment

CAUSES OF THE WAR. From May 1337 to October 1453 England and France periodically engaged in what was for both a futile and devastating war. The conflict was initiated by the English king Edward III (1327–1377), who held a strong claim to the French throne as the grandson of Philip the Fair (1285–1314). When Charles IV (1322–1328), the last of Philip the Fair's surviving sons died, Edward, who was only fifteen at the time, asserted his right to Capetian succession. The French barons, however, were not willing to place an English king on the French throne. They chose instead the first cousin of Charles IV, Philip VI of Valois (1328–1350), the first of a new French dynasty that was to rule into the sixteenth century. Edward, crying foul, used his hereditary higher claim to Capetian succession as the immediate pretext for starting the great war.

But there was much more to the Hundred Years' War than just a defense of Edward's prestige. In the background were other important factors that help to explain both Edward's success in gaining popular and parliamentary support after the war started and the determination of the English and the French people to endure the war to its bitter end. For one thing, the English king held Gascony, Anjou, Guyenne, and other French territories as fiefs from the French king. This made him in law a vassal of the French king—a problem that stretched back to the Norman Conquest. In May 1329 Edward journeyed to Amiens and, most insincerely, swore fealty to Philip VI. As Philip's vassal Edward was, theoretically if not in fact, committed to support policies detrimental to England, if his lord so commanded. If such vassalage was embarrassing to Edward, the English possession of French lands was even more repugnant to the French, especially inasmuch as the English presence was a constant distraction from the royal policy of centralization.

Still another factor that fueled the conflict was French support of the Bruces of Scotland, strong opponents of English overlordship of Scotland who had won a victory over the English in 1314. The French and the English were also at this time quarreling over Flanders, a French fief, yet also a country whose towns were completely dependent for their livelihood upon imported English wool. Edward III and his successors manipulated this situation to English advantage throughout the conflict; by controlling the export of wool to Flanders, England influenced its foreign policy. Finally, there were decades of prejudice and animosity between the French and the English people, who constantly confronted one another on the high seas and in port towns. Taken together, these various factors made the Hundred Years' War a struggle to the death for national sovereignty and identity.

FRENCH WEAKNESS. Throughout the conflict France was statistically the stronger; it had three times the population of England, was far the wealthier, and fought on its own soil. Yet for the greater part of the conflict, until 1415, the major battles ended in often stunning English victories. France was not so strong as it appeared. It was, first of all, internally disunited by social conflict and the absence of a centralized system of taxation to fund the war. French kings raised funds by depreciating the currency, taxing the clergy, and borrowing heavily from Italian bankers—practices that created a financial crisis by mid-century. Although the Estates-General, convened in 1355, levied new taxes at the king's request, the towns and the princes who made up the assembly used the king's plight to enhance their own regional rights. Just how successful they were is indicated by the creation in this period of the Burgundian state, a thorn in the sides of French kings throughout the fifteenth century. France, unlike England, was still struggling in the fourteenth century to make the transition from a fragmented feudal society to a centralized "modern" state.

Beyond this struggle, there was the clear fact of English military superiority, due to the greater discipline of her infantry and the rapid-fire and long-range capability of that ingeniously simple weapon, the English longbow. The longbow scattered the French cavalry and cross-bowmen in one engagement after the other. Only in the later stages of the war, with the introduction of heavy artillery, did the French alter their military tactics to advantage.

Finally, French weakness was related in no small degree to the comparative mediocrity of royal leadership during the Hundred Years' War. English kings were far the shrewder. As historians have pointed out, it is a telling commentary on the leadership ability of French kings in this period that the most memorable military leader on the French side is the peasant girl Joan of Arc.

Progress of the War

The war had three major stages of development: (1) during the reign of Edward III (d. 1377); (2) from Edward's death to the Treaty of Troyes (1420); and (3) from the appearance of Joan of Arc (1429) to the English retreat.

THE CONFLICT DURING THE REIGN OF EDWARD III. Edward prepared for the first stage of the war by securing allies in the Netherlands and a personal pledge of support from the emperor Louis IV of Bavaria (1314–1347). By slapping an embargo on English wool to Flanders, Edward sparked urban rebellions by merchants and the trade guilds. Inspired by a rich merchant, Jacob van Artevelde, the Flemish cities, led by Ghent, revolted against the French. Having at first taken as neutral a stand as possible in the conflict, these cities, whose economies faced total collapse without imported English wool, signed a half-hearted alliance with England in January 1340, acknowledging Edward as king of France.

Edward defeated the French fleet in the first great battle of the war in the Bay of Sluys on June 23, 1340. But his subsequent effort to invade France by way of Flanders failed, largely because his allies proved undependable. As a stalemate developed, a truce was struck

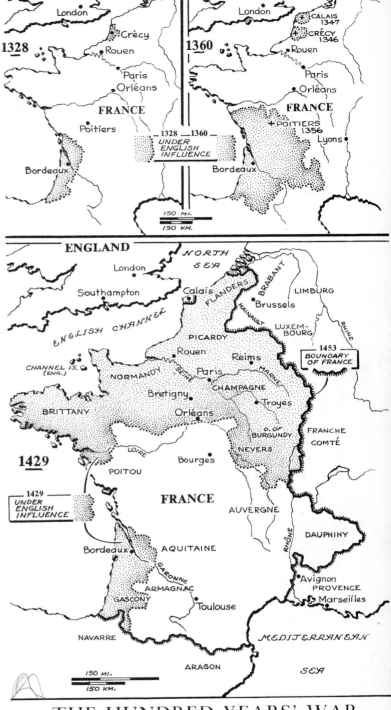

THE HUNDRED YEARS' WAR

The Hundred Years' War went on intermittently from the late 1330s until 1453. These maps show the remarkable English territorial gains up to the sudden and decisive turning of the tide of battle in favor of the French by the forces of Joan of Arc in 1429.

and was more or less observed until 1346. In that year Edward attacked Normandy and won a series of easy victories that were capped by that at Crécy in August. This was quickly followed by the seizure of Calais, which the English held thereafter for over two hundred years. Both sides employed scorched-earth tactics and completely devastated the areas of conflict.

Exhaustion and the onset of the Black Death forced a second truce in late 1347, and the war entered a lull that was not broken until 1355. On September 19, 1356, the English won their greatest victory near Poitiers, routing the noble cavalry and even taking the French king, John II the Good (1350–1364), captive back to England. After Poitiers there was a complete breakdown of political order in France. Disbanded soldiers from both sides became professional bandits, roaming the land, pillaging areas untouched by the war, and bringing disaster almost as great as the war itself.

Power in France lay with the privileged classes, who expressed their will through the representative assembly of the Estates-General. Convened in 1355 by the faltering king so that revenues might be provided to continue the war, the Estates-General, led by powerful merchants of Paris under Étienne Marcel, had demanded and received rights similar to those granted the English privileged classes in *Magna Carta*. Unlike the English Parliament, which represented the interests of a comparatively unified English nobility, the French Estates-General was a many-tongued lobby, a forum for the diverse interests of the new-rich urban commercial and industrial classes, the territorial princes, and the clergy. It was no instrument for effective government. To secure their rights, the privileged bullied the French peasantry, who were forced to pay ever-increasing taxes and to repair without compensation the war-damaged properties of the noblemen. The pressure became more than the peasantry could bear. Burdened by the Estates-General, terrified by the Black Death, and emboldened by the cowardly retreat of the French cavalry at Poitiers, the peasantry exploded in several regions in a series of bloody uprisings known as the *Jacquerie*. The revolt was quickly put down by the nobility, who matched "Jacques Bonhomme," as the peasant revolutionary was popularly known, atrocity for atrocity.

On May 9, 1360, another milestone of the war was reached when England forced the Peace of Bretigny upon the French. In this agreement Edward's vassalage to the king of France was declared ended, and his sovereignty over English territories in France (including Gascony, Guyenne, Poitou, Calais) was affirmed. The French king also agreed to pay the English three million gold crowns. In return for all this Edward renounced his claim to the French throne.

Such a partition of French territorial sovereignty was completely unrealistic, and sober observers on both sides knew it could not long continue. France became strong enough to strike back in the late 1360s, during the reign of John the Good's successor, Charles V (1364–1380). In 1369 Flanders came into the French fold when Charles's brother, Philip the Bold, who held the duchy of Burgundy as his appanage, married the daughter of the Count of Flanders. Backed by the Estates-General and blessed with a brilliant military commander in Bertrand du Guesclin, the French launched a successful counteroffensive. By the time of Edward's death in 1377 the English had been beaten back to coastal enclaves and the territory of Bordeaux.

FRENCH DEFEAT AND THE TREATY OF TROYES. After Edward's death the English war effort lessened considerably. This was partly because of domestic problems within England. During the reign of Richard II (1377–1399) England had its own version of the *Jacquerie*. To counter the economic strain of the war with France and the ravages of the Black Death, Parliament had reduced the wages of peasants and journeymen, imposed new tolls and taxes, and reasserted old domainal rights in an effort to keep the peasants bound to the land. Both the urban proletariat and the agarian peasantry greatly resented these measures, which were enforced by the king's uncle and regent, John of Gaunt, the Duke of

A highly romanticized nineteenth-century conception of Joan of Arc by the English painter W. B. Richmond. [Bettmann Archive.]

Lancaster. In June 1381 a great revolt of the unprivileged classes exploded under the leadership of John Ball, a secular priest, and Wat Tyler, a journeyman. As in France the revolt was short-lived, brutally crushed within the year. But it left the country divided for decades.

In 1396 France and England signed still another truce, this one backed up by the marriage of Richard II to the daughter of the French king, Charles VI (1380–1422). This truce lasted through the reign of Richard's successor, Henry IV of Lancaster (1399–1413). His successor, Henry V (1413–1422), reheated the war with France by taking advantage of the internal French turmoil created by the rise to power of the duchy of Burgundy. Charles VI had gone mad in the second half of his reign, and control of the French government had devolved on his brother, the duke of Orléans. Orléans struggled manfully but in vain to contain the aggressive duke of Burgundy, John the Fearless (1404–1419). The latter succeeded in having Orléans assassinated in 1407. Thereafter civil war enveloped France, with the count of Armagnac taking up the royal banner, while John the Fearless found allies in the French cities.

With France so divided, Henry V struck hard in Normandy. John the Fearless and the Burgundians foolishly watched from the sidelines while Henry's army overran the Armagnacs at Agincourt on October 25, 1415. In the years thereafter the Burgundians closed ranks behind the royal forces as they belatedly recognized that a divided France would remain an easy prey for the English. But this inchoate French unity, which promised to bring eventual victory, was shattered in September 1419. In a belated reprisal for the assassination of the duke of Orléans twelve years earlier, soldiers of Charles VI stabbed John the Fearless to death only hours after the two men had quarreled. This shocking turn of events led to a Burgundian alliance with the English under John's son, Philip the Good (1419–1467), who was determined to avenge his father's death at any price, even if it meant giving the English control of France.

With Burgundian support behind the English, France became Henry V's for the taking. The Treaty of Troyes in 1420 disinherited the legitimate heir to the French throne, the dauphin, the future Charles VII, and made Henry V successor to the mad Charles VI. When Henry V and Charles VI died within months of one another in 1422, the infant Henry VI of England was proclaimed in Paris to be king of both France and England under the regency of the duke of Bedford. The dream of Edward III, the pretext for the great war, was now, for the moment, realized: in 1422 an English king ruled as the king of France.

The dauphin went into retreat in Bourges, where, on the death of his father, he became Charles VII to most Frenchmen, who ignored the Treaty of Troyes. Although some years were to pass before he was powerful enough to take his crown in fact, the French people would not deny the throne to a legitimate successor, despite the terms dictated by the Treaty of Troyes. National sentiment, spurred to unprecedented heights by Joan of Arc, soon brought the French people together as never before in a victorious coalition.

JOAN OF ARC AND THE WAR'S CONCLUSION. Joan of Arc (1412–1431), a peasant from Domremy, presented herself to Charles VII in March 1429. When she declared that the King of Heaven had called her to deliver beseiged Orléans from the English, Charles was understandably skeptical. But the dauphin and his advisers, in retreat from what seemed to be a completely hopeless war, were desperate men, willing to try anything to reverse French fortunes on the battlefield. Charles's desperation overcame his skepticism, and he gave her his leave.

Circumstances worked perfectly to Joan's advantage. The English force was already exhausted by its six-month seige of Orléans and actually at the point of withdrawal when Joan arrived with fresh French troops. After the English were repulsed at Orléans, there followed a succession of French victories that were popularly attributed to Joan. Joan truly deserved much of the credit, not, however, because she was a military genius. She gave the French people and armies something military experts could not—a unique inspiration and an almost mystical confidence in themselves as a nation. Within a few months of the liberation of Orléans Charles VII received his crown in Rheims and ended the nine-year "disinheritance" prescribed by the Treaty of Troyes.

Charles forgot his liberator as quickly as he had embraced her. Joan was captured by the Burgundians in May 1430, and although he was in a position to secure her release, the French king did little to help her. She was turned over to the Inquisition at Rouen. It was important to the Burgundians and to the English that Joan be publically discredited; they believed that by such means they could also discredit her patron, Charles VII, and might demoralize French resistance. The skilled inquisitors broke the courageous "Maid of Orléans" in ten weeks of merciless interrogation, and she was executed as a relapsed heretic on May 30, 1431. Charles reopened Joan's trial at a later date, and she was finally declared innocent of all the charges against her on July 7, 1456, twenty-five years after her execution. In 1920 the church declared her a saint.

Charles VII and Philip the Good made peace in 1435, and a unified France, now at peace with Burgundy, progressively forced the English back. By 1453, the date of the war's end, the English held only their coastal enclave in Calais.

Joan of Arc Refuses to Recant Her Beliefs

Joan of Arc, threatened with torture, refused to recant her beliefs and instead defended the instructions she received from the voices that spoke to her. Here is a part of her self-defense from the contemporary trial record.

ON WEDNESDAY, *May 9th of the same year [1431], Joan was brought into the great tower of the castle of Rouen before us the said judges and in the presence of the reverend father, lord abbot of St. Cormeille de Compiegne, of masters Jean de Châtillon and Guillaume Erart, doctors of sacred theology, of André Marguerie and Nicolas de Venderes, archdeacons of the church of Rouen, of William Haiton, bachelor of theology, Aubert Morel, licentiate in canon law; Nicolas Loiseleur, canon of the cathedral of Rouen, and master Jean Massieu.*

And Joan was required and admonished to speak the truth on many different points contained in her trial which she had denied or to which she had given false replies, whereas we possessed certain information, proofs, and vehement presumptions upon them. Many of the points were read and explained to her, and she was told that if she did not confess them truthfully she would be put to the torture, the instruments of which were shown to her all ready in the tower. There were also present by our instruction men ready to put her to the torture in order to restore her to the way and knowledge of truth, and by this means to procure the salvation of her body and soul which by her lying inventions she exposed to such grave perils.

To which the said Joan answered in this manner: "Truly if you were to tear me limb from limb and separate my soul from my body, I would not tell you anything more: and if I did say anything, I should afterwards declare that you had compelled me to say it by force." Then she said that on Holy Cross Day last she received comfort from St. Gabriel; she firmly believes it was St. Gabriel. She knew by her voices whether she should submit to the Church, since the clergy were pressing her hard to submit. Her voices told her that if she desired Our Lord to aid her she must wait upon Him in all her doings. She said that Our Lord has always been the master of her doings, and the Enemy never had power over them. She asked her voices if she would be burned and they answered that she must wait upon God, and He would aid her.

The Trial of Jeanne D'Arc, trans. by W. P. Barrett (New York: Gotham House, 1932), pp. 303–304.

During the Hundred Years' War there were sixty-eight years of at least nominal peace and forty-four of hot war. The political and social consequences were lasting. The war awakened the giant of French nationalism and hastened the transition in France from feudal monarchy to a centralized state. Burgundy became a major European political power. The seesawing allegiance of the Netherlands throughout the conflict encouraged the English to develop their own clothing industry and foreign markets. In both France and England the on-again, off-again war devastated the peasantry, who were forced to bear its burden in taxes and services. After the *Jacquerie* of 1358 there was not to be another significant peasant uprising in France until the French Revolution in the eighteenth century.

The Black Death

PRECONDITIONS AND CAUSES. In the late Middle Ages nine tenths of the population were still farmers. The three-field system, in use in most areas since well before the fourteenth century, had increased the amount of arable land and thereby the food supply. The growth of cities and trade had also stimulated agricultural science and productivity. But as the food supply grew, so also did the population. It is estimated that Europe's population doubled between the years 1000 and 1300. By 1300 the balance between food supply and population growth was decisively tipped in favor of the latter. There were more people than food to feed them or jobs to employ them, and the average European faced the probability of extreme hunger at least once during his expected thirty-five-year life span.

Famines followed the population explosion in the first half of the fourteenth century. Between 1315 and 1317 crop failures produced the greatest famine of the Middle Ages. Great suffering was inflicted on densely populated urban areas like the industrial towns of the Netherlands. Decades of overpopulation, economic depression, famine, and bad health progressively weakened Europe's population and made it highly vulnerable to a virulent bubonic

So terrifying was the Black Death and so powerless the people before it that strange behavior was called forth. Here, in a fifteenth-century chronicle, a group don sackcloth and ashes, confess their sins, and flagellate themselves in a show of penance. [Bettmann Archive.]

(See also the stained glass Black Death window at Canterbury in the color album.)

plague that struck with full force in 1348. This "Black Death," so called by contemporaries because of the way it discolored the body, followed the trade routes into Europe. Appearing in Sicily in late 1347, it entered Europe through the port cities of Venice, Genoa, and Pisa in 1348, and from there swept rapidly through Spain and southern France and into northern Europe. Areas that lay outside the major trade routes, like Bohemia, appear to have remained virtually unaffected. By the end of the fourteenth century it is estimated that western Europe as a whole had lost as much as two fifths of its population, and a full recovery was not made until the sixteenth century.

POPULAR REMEDIES. In the Black Death people confronted a catastrophe against which they had neither understanding nor defense. Never have Western people stood so helpless against the inexplicable and the uncontrollable. Contemporary physicians did not even know that the disease was transmitted by rat- or human-transported fleas, and hence the most rudimentary prophylaxis was lacking. Popular wisdom held that a corruption in the atmosphere caused the disease. Some blamed poisonous fumes released by earthquakes and many adopted aromatic amulets as a remedy. According to the contemporary observations of Boccaccio, who recorded the varied reactions to the plague in the *Decameron* (1353), some sought a remedy in moderation and a temperate life; others gave themselves over entirely to their passions (sexual promiscuity among the stricken apparently ran high); and still others, "the most sound, perhaps, in judgment," chose flight and seclusion as the best medicine.

Among the most extreme social reactions were processions of flagellants. These were religious fanatics who beat their bodies in ritual penance until they bled, believing that such action would bring divine intervention. The Jews, who were hated by many because of centuries of Christian propaganda against them and the fact that they had become society's money lenders, a disreputable and resented profession, were made scapegoats. Pogroms occurred in several cities, sometimes incited by the advent

of flagellants. The terror created by the flagellants, whose dirty bodies may have actually served to transport the disease, became so socially disruptive and threatening even to established authority that the church finally outlawed such processions.

SOCIAL AND ECONOMIC CONSEQUENCES. Among the social and economic consequences of the plague were a shrunken labor supply and the devaluation of the estates of noblemen. Villages vanished in the wake of the plague. As the number of farm laborers decreased, their wages increased and those of skilled artisans soared. Agricultural prices fell because of the lowered demand, and the price of luxury and manufactured goods—the work of skilled artisans—rose. The noble landholders suffered the greatest decline in power from this new state of affairs. They were forced to pay more for finished products and for farm labor, and they received a smaller return on their agricultural produce. Everywhere their rents were in steady decline after the plague.

To recoup their losses, some landowners converted arable land to sheep pasture, substituting more profitable wool production for labor-intensive grain crops. Others abandoned the effort to farm their land and simply leased it to the highest bidder. Most ominously, legislation was sought to force land tenure and low wages on the peasantry, that is, to close off immediately the new economic opportunities opened for the peasantry by the demographic crisis. In France the direct tax on the peasantry, the *taille,* was increased, and opposition to it was prominent among the grievances behind the *Jacquerie.* A Statute of Laborers was passed by the English Parliament in 1351 that limited wages to preplague levels and restricted the ability of peasants to leave the land of their traditional masters. Opposition to such legislation was also a prominent factor in the English Peasants' Revolt of 1381.

Although the plague hit urban populations especially hard, the cities and their skilled industries came in time to prosper from it. Cities had always been careful to protect their interests; as they grew they passed legislation to regulate competition from rural areas and to control

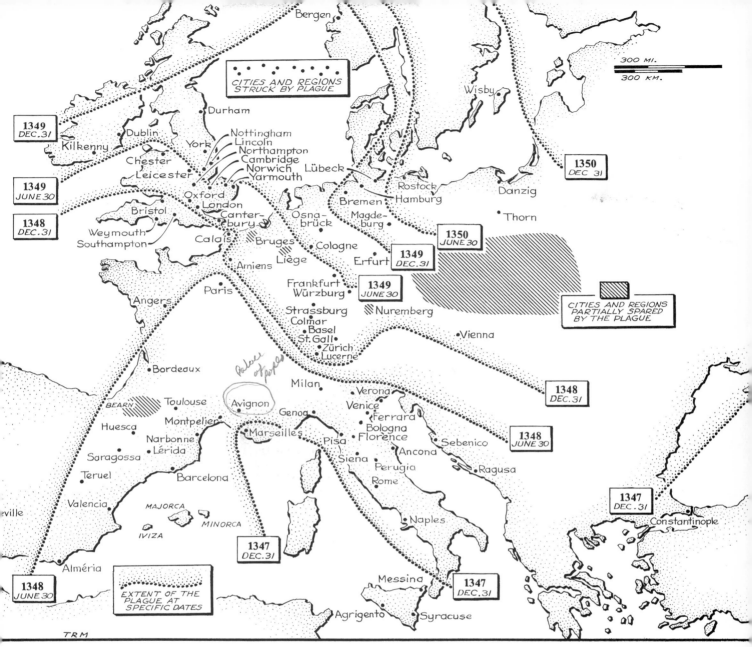

Cities and regions struck by plague

1349 DEC.31
1349 JUNE 30
1348 DEC.31

Bergen

Wisby

1350 DEC.31

Durham
Dublin
Kilkenny
York
Nottingham
Lincoln
Northampton
Cambridge
Norwich
Yarmouth
Lübeck
Rostock
Chester
Leicester
Danzig
Oxford
London
Canterbury
Osnabrück
Bremen
Hamburg
Magdeburg
Thorn
Bristol
Weymouth
Southampton
Calais
Bruges
Cologne
Erfurt
1349 DEC.31
Liège
Amiens
1350 JUNE 30
Angers
Paris
Frankfurt
Würzburg
1349 JUNE 30
Cities and regions partially spared by the plague
Nuremberg
Strassburg
Colmar
Basel
St.Gall
Zürich
Lucerne
Vienna
Bordeaux
Milan
1348 DEC.31
BEARN
Toulouse
Avignon
Genoa
Verona
Venice
Ferrara
Bologna
Florence
Sebenico
1348 JUNE 30
Huesca
Montpelier
Marseilles
Pisa
Ancona
Narbonne
Lérida
Siena
Perugia
Rome
Ragusa
Saragossa
Teruel
Barcelona
1347 DEC.31
Constantinople
Valencia
MAJORCA
MINORCA
IVIZA
Naples
eville
Alméria
1347 DEC.31
1348 JUNE 30
Extent of the plague at specific dates
Messina
1347 DEC.31
Agrigento
Syracuse

TRM

300 MI.
300 KM.

SPREAD OF THE BLACK DEATH

immigration. After the plague their laws were progressively extended over the surrounding lands of nobles and feudal landlords, many of whom were peacefully integrated into urban life on terms very favorable to the cities.

The basic unit of urban industry was the master and his apprentices (usually one or two). Their numbers were purposely kept low and jealously guarded. As the craft of the skilled artisan was only very slowly passed

Apparently introduced by sea-borne rats from Black Sea areas where plague-infested rodents have long been known, the Black Death brought huge human, social, and economic consequences. One of the lower estimates of Europeans dying is 25,000,000. The map charts its spread in the mid-fourteenth century. Generally following trade routes, the plague reached Scandinavia by 1350, and some believe it then went on to Iceland and even Greenland. Areas off the main trade routes were largely spared.

from master to apprentice, the first wave of plague created a short supply of skilled labor almost overnight. But this short supply also raised the prices of available manufactured and luxury items to new heights. The omnipresence of death whetted the appetite for the things that only skilled urban industries could produce. Expensive cloths and jewelry, furs from the north, and silks from the south were in great demand in the second half of the fourteenth century. Faced with life at its worst, people insisted on having the very best. Townsmen profited coming and going; as wealth poured into the cities and per capita income rose, the cost to urban dwellers of agricultural products from the countryside, which were now less in demand, actually declined.

The church also profited from the plague as gifts and bequests multiplied. Although the church, as a great landholder, also suffered losses, it had offsetting revenues from the vastly increased demand for religious services for the dead and the dying.

NEW CONFLICTS AND OPPORTUNITIES. By increasing the importance of skilled artisans, the plague contributed to new conflicts within the cities. The economic and political power of local artisans and trade guilds grew steadily in the late Middle Ages along with the demand for their goods and services. The merchant and patrician classes found it increasingly difficult to maintain their traditional dominance and grudgingly gave guild masters a voice in city government. As the guilds won political power, they encouraged restrictive legislation to protect local industries. These restrictions in turn brought confrontations between master artisans, who wanted to keep their numbers low and expand their industries at a snail's pace, and the many journeymen, who were eager to rise to the rank of master. To the conflict between the guilds and the urban patriciate was now added a conflict within the guilds themselves.

Another indirect effect of the great plague was to assist monarchies in the development of centralized states. The plague caused the landed nobility to lose much of its economic power in the same period when the military superiority of a paid professional army over the traditional noble cavalry was being demonstrated by the Hundred Years' War. The plague also killed large numbers of clergy—perhaps one third of the German clergy fell victim to it—at the same time that the residence of the pope in Avignon (1309–1377) and the Schism (1378–1415) were undermining much of the church's popular support. After 1350 the two traditional "containers" of monarchy—the landed nobility and the church—were in decline, to no small degree as a consequence of the plague. Kings took full advantage of the new situation, as they drew on growing national sentiment to centralize their governments and economies.

Ecclesiastical Breakdown and Revival: The Late Medieval Church
The Thirteenth-Century Papacy

Popes may appear to have been in a very favorable situation in the latter half of the thirteenth century. Frederick II had been vanquished and imperial pressure on Rome had been removed. The sainted French King Louis IX was an enthusiastic supporter of the church, as his two disastrous crusades testify. Although it lasted only seven years, a reunion of the eastern church with Rome was proclaimed by the Council of Lyons in 1274, as the western church took advantage of the Emperor Michael Palaeologus's request for aid against the Turks. Despite these positive events, the church was not in as favorable a situation as it appeared.

As early as the reign of Pope Innocent III (1198–1216), when papal power reached its height, there were ominous developments. Innocent had elaborated the doctrine of papal plenitude of power and on that authority had raised up saints, disposed of benefices, and created a centralized papal monarchy with a clearly political mission. Innocent's transformation of the papacy into a great secular power had the consequence of weakening the church religiously as he sought to strengthen it politically.

Thereafter the church as a papal monarchy and the church as the "body of the faithful" came increasingly to be differentiated. It was against the "papal church" and in the name of the "true Christian church" that both reformers and heretics raised their voices in protest until the Protestant Reformation.

What Innocent began, his successors perfected. Under Urban IV (1261–1264) the papacy established its own law court, the Rota Romana. The latter half of the thirteenth century saw an elaboration of the system of clerical taxation; what had begun in the twelfth century as an emergency measure to raise funds for the crusades became a fixed institution. In the same period papal power to determine appointments to major and minor church offices—so-called reservations—was greatly broadened. The thirteenth-century papacy became a political institution in which the pope was considered all-powerful. The papacy had an efficient international bureaucracy; it was governed by its own law and courts; and it was thoroughly preoccupied with secular goals.

Papal centralization of the church tended to undermine both diocesan authority and popular support. Rome's interests, not local interests, came to control church appointments, policies, and discipline. Discontented lower clergy appealed to the higher authority of Rome against the disciplinary measures of local bishops. In the second half of the thirteenth century bishops and abbots protested such undercutting of their power. Many now came to perceive the church in Rome as hardly more than a legalized, fiscalized, bureaucratic institution. As early as the late twelfth century heretical movements of Cathars and Waldensians had appealed to the biblical ideal of simplicity and separation from the world.

The church of the thirteenth century was being undermined by more than internal religious disunity. The demise of imperial power meant that the papacy in Rome was no longer the leader of anti-imperial (or Guelf) sentiment in Italy. Instead of being the center of Italian resistance to the emperor, popes now found themselves on the defensive against their old allies. That was the ironic price paid by the papacy to vanquish the Hohenstaufens.

Italian magnates now directed the intrigue formerly aimed at the emperor toward dominating the College of Cardinals. Charles of Anjou, for example, managed to create a French–Sicilian faction within the college. Such efforts to control the decisions of the college led Pope Gregory X (1271–1276) to establish the so-called conclave of cardinals. This was the practice of sequestering the cardinals immediately upon the death of the pope so that extraneous political influence on the election of new popes might be kept to a minimum. But the conclave proved to be of no avail, so politicized had the College of Cardinals become.

In 1294 it was such a college that in frustration during a prolonged deadlock chose a saintly but inept Calabrian hermit as Pope Celestine V. Celestine abdicated under suspicious circumstances after only a few weeks in office. His tragicomic reign shocked a majority of the college into unified affirmative action. He was quickly replaced by his very opposite, Pope Boniface VIII (1294–1303), a nobleman and a skilled politician, whose pontificate saw the beginning of the end of papal pretensions to great power status.

Boniface VIII and Philip the Fair

Boniface had the misfortune of coming to rule when England and France were maturing as nation–states. Monarchy and Parliament had come together in England during the reigns of Henry III (1216–1272) and Edward I (1272–1307) to create a unified kingdom. The reign of the French king Philip IV the Fair (1285–1314) saw France become an efficient centralized monarchy. Philip was no Saint Louis, but a ruthless politician intent on ending England's continental holdings, controlling wealthy Flanders, and establishing French hegemony within the Holy Roman Empire. Boniface had the further misfortune of bringing to the papal throne memories of the way earlier popes had brought kings and emperors to their knees. Very painfully he was to discover that the papal monarchy of the early thirteenth century was not equipped to survive amid the new political realities of the late thirteenth century.

France and England were on the brink of all-out war when Boniface became pope (1294). Only Edward I's preoccupation with rebellion in Scotland, which the French encouraged, prevented a full-scale English invasion of France around the turn of the century—a turn of events that would have started the Hundred Years' War a half-century earlier. As both countries mobilized for war, they used the pretext of preparing for a crusade to tax the clergy heavily. In 1215 Pope Innocent III had decreed that the clergy were to pay no taxes to rulers without prior papal consent. Viewing English and French taxation of the clergy as an assault on traditional clerical rights, Boniface took a strong stand against it. On February 5, 1296, he issued a bull, *Clericis Laicos,* which forbade lay taxation of the clergy without prior papal approval and took back all previous papal dispensations in this regard. Boniface further threatened to excommunicate any ruler who continued such policies.

In the late thirteenth century rulers were in a position to hurt the church far more than it could hurt them. In England Edward I retaliated by denying the clergy the right to be heard in royal court, in effect removing from them the protection of the king. But it was Philip the Fair who struck back with a vengeance. In August 1296 he forbade the exportation of money from France to Rome, thereby denying the papacy revenues without which it could not operate. Boniface had no choice but to come quickly to terms with Philip. In February 1297 he privately conceded Philip the right to tax French clergy "during an emergency." In July 1297 this agreement was made explicit in the bull *Etsi de Statu.* Also, and not coincidentally, Boniface canonized Louis IX in the same year.

Boniface was at this time also under seige by powerful Italian enemies, whom Philip did not fail to patronize. A noble family, the Colonnas, a rival of Boniface's family, the Gaetani, and the radical followers of Saint Francis of

---

Boniface VIII Reasserts the Church's Claim to Temporal Power

Defied by the French and the English, Pope Boniface VIII (1294–1303) boldly reasserted the temporal power of the church in the bull *Unam Sanctam* (November 1302). This document claimed that both spiritual and temporal power on earth were under the pope's jurisdiction, because, in the hierarchy of the universe, spiritual power both preceded and sat in judgment upon temporal power.

W E   A R E *taught by the words of the Gospel that in this church and in her power there are two swords, a spiritual one and a temporal one.... Certainly anyone who denies that the temporal sword is in the power of Peter has not paid heed to the words of the Lord when he said, "Put up thy sword into its sheath" (Matthew 26:52). Both then are in the power of the church, the material sword and the spiritual. But the one is exercised for the church, the other by the church, the one by the hand of the priest, the other by the hand of kings and soldiers, though at the will and suffrance of the authority subject to the spiritual power.... For, according to the blessed Dionysius, it is the law of divinity for the lowest to be led to the highest through intermediaries. In the order of the universe all things are not kept in order in the same fashion and immediately but the lowest are ordered by the intermediate and inferiors by superiors. But that the spiritual power excels any earthly one in dignity and nobility we ought the more openly to confess in proportion as spiritual things excel temporal ones. Moreover we clearly perceive this from the giving of tithes, from benediction and sanctification, from the acceptance of this power and from the very government of things. For, the truth bearing witness, the spiritual power has to institute the earthly power and to judge it if it has not been good. So it is verified the prophecy of Jeremias (1:10) concerning the church and the power of the church, "Lo, I have set thee this day over the nations and over kingdoms."*

From Brian Tierney, *The Crisis of Church and State 1050–1300* (Englewood Cliffs, N.J.: Prentice-Hall, 1964), pp. 188–189.

Assisi, the Spiritual Franciscans, were seeking to invalidate Boniface's election as pope on the grounds that Celestine V had resigned the office under coercion. Charges of heresy, simony, and even the murder of Celestine, who had died shortly after his abdication, were hurled against Boniface.

In the year 1300 Boniface's fortunes appeared to revive. Tens of thousands of pilgrims flocked to Rome in

John of Paris Separates Spiritual from Secular Power

Royal apologists responded to papal claims to temporal power like *Unam Sanctam* by confining ecclesiastical power to strictly spiritual matters and stressing the sovereignty of kings over all things temporal. Here John of Paris, in a treatise written in 1302–1303, points out that the spiritual power of the pope is superior to the secular power of the king only in religious matters, not also in temporal affairs.

A KINGDOM *is ordered to this end, that an assembled multitude may live virtuously, and it is further ordered to a higher end which is the enjoyment of God; and responsibility for this end belongs to Christ, whose ministers and vicars are the priests. Therefore the priestly power is of greater dignity than the secular and this is commonly conceded.... But if the priest is greater in himself than the prince and is greater in dignity, it does not follow that he is greater in all respects. For the lesser secular power is not related to the greater spiritual power as having its origin from it or being derived from it as the power of a proconsul is related to that of the emperor, which is greater in all respects since the power of the former is derived from the latter. The relationship is rather like that of a head of a household to a general of armies, since one is not derived from the other but both from a superior power. And so the secular power is greater than the spiritual in some things, namely in temporal affairs, and in such affairs it is not subject to the spiritual power in any way because it does not have its origin from it but rather both have their origin immediately from the one supreme power, namely the divine.*

Brian Tierney, *The Crisis of Church and State 1050–1300* (Englewood Cliffs, N.J.: Prentice-Hall, 1964), pp. 208–209.

that year for the Jubilee celebration. In a Jubilee year all Catholics who visited Rome and there fulfilled certain conditions received a special remission of their sins. Heady with this display of popular religiosity, Boniface reinserted himself into international politics. He championed Scottish resistance to England, for which he received a firm rebuke from an outraged Edward I and from Parliament.

But once again it was a confrontation with the king of France that proved the more costly. Philip, seemingly spoiling for another fight with the pope, arrested, with little provocation, Boniface's legate to Paris, Bernard Saisset, the bishop of Pamiers. Saisset, an outspoken defender of the pope's rights, was accused of heresy and

treason and was tried and convicted in the king's court. Thereafter Philip demanded that Boniface recognize the process against Saisset, something that Boniface could only do if he was prepared to surrender his jurisdiction over the French episcopate. This challenge could not be sidestepped and Boniface acted swiftly. He demanded Saisset's unconditional release, revoked all previous agreements with Philip in the matter of clerical taxation, and ordered the French bishops to convene in Rome within a year. A bull, *Ausculta Fili*—"Listen, My Son"—was sent to Philip in December 1301, pointedly informing him that "God has set popes over kings and kingdoms," and admonishing immediate subjection to the head of the ecclesiastical hierarchy.

UNAM SANCTAM (1302). Philip, backed by the Estates-General and popular sentiment, which he shrewdly managed, unleashed a ruthless antipapal campaign. Two royal apologists, Pierre Dubois and John of Paris, refuted papal claims to the right to intervene in temporal matters. Increasingly placed on the defensive, Boniface made a last-ditch stand against state control of national churches when on November 18, 1302, he issued the bull *Unam Sanctam*. This famous statement of papal power declared that temporal authority was "subject" to the spiritual power of the church, which was said both to "institute" and to "judge" it. On its face a bold assertion, *Unam Sanctam* was in truth the desperate act of a besieged papacy.

After *Unam Sanctam* the French and the Colonnas moved against Boniface with force. Guillaume de Nogaret, Philip's chief minister, denounced Boniface to the French clergy as a common heretic and criminal. An army, led by Nogaret and Sciarra Colonna, surprised the pope in mid-August 1303 at his retreat in Anagni. Boniface was badly beaten up and almost executed before an aroused populace liberated and returned him safely to Rome. But the ordeal proved too much for the pope, who died a few months later in October 1303.

Boniface's immediate successor, Benedict XI (1303–1304), excommunicated Nogaret for his despicable deed,

A sculpture of Pope Boniface VIII (1294–1303) who opposed the taxation of clergy by the kings of France and England and issued one of the strongest declarations of papal authority, the bull *Unam Sanctam*. The statue is in the Museo Civico, Bologna, Italy. [Alinari/SCALA.]

but there was to be no lasting papal retaliation. Benedict's successor, Clement V (1305–1314), was forced into French subservience. He renounced *Clericis Laicos* and rendered *Unam Sanctam* harmless. He released Nogaret from excommunication and condemned the Knights Templars, whose treasure Philip thereafter forcibly expropriated. Clement moved physically to Avignon on the southeastern border of France in 1309 and two years later made the city his permanent residence. There the papacy was to remain until 1377.

After Boniface's humiliation popes never again seriously threatened kings and emperors, despite continuing papal excommunications and political intrigue. In the future the relation between Church and State would tilt toward state control of religion within particular monarchies and the subordination of ecclesiastical to larger political purposes. Renaissance popes appealed to *Unam Sanctam* in the fifteenth century, but they did so not in opposition to secular rulers but against a movement within the church itself to subject popes to the rulings of councils.

The Avignon Papacy (1309–1377)

The Avignon papacy was in appearance, although not always in actual fact, under strong French influence. During Clement V's pontificate the French came to dominate the College of Cardinals. Clement also expanded papal taxes, especially the practice of collecting annates, the first year's revenue of a church office or benefice bestowed by the pope—a practice that contributed much to the Avignon papacy's reputation as materialistic and politically motivated.

POPE JOHN XXII. Pope John XXII (1316–1334), the strongest Avignon pope, tried to restore papal independence and return to Italy. This goal led him into war with the Visconti in Milan and a costly contest with Emperor Louis IV, whose election as emperor in 1314 John challenged in favor of the rival Hapsburg candidate. The result was a minor replay of the confrontation between Philip the Fair and Boniface VIII. When John

Palace of the popes in Avignon, France, the papal
residence from 1309 to 1377, following Boniface
VIII's defeat by the French king, Philip the Fair.
[French Government Tourist Office, New York.]

obstinately and without legal justification refused to recognize Louis's election, the emperor retaliated by declaring John deposed and setting in his place an antipope. As
Philip the Fair too had done, Louis enlisted the support of
the Spiritual Franciscans, whose views on absolute poverty John had condemned as heretical. Two outstanding
pamphleteers wrote lasting tracts for the royal cause:
William of Ockham, whom John excommunicated in
1328, and Marsilius of Padua (ca. 1290–1342/43), whose
teaching John declared heretical in 1327.

MARSILIUS OF PADUA. Marsilius of Padua was the
most important political thinker in the late Middle Ages.
His *Defender of Peace* (1324) stressed the independent
origins and autonomy of the state. Clergy were subjected
to the strictest apostolic ideals and purely spiritual functions, and all power of coercive judgment was denied the
pope. Marsilius argued that spiritual crimes must await an
eternal punishment. Transgressions of divine law, over
which the pope has jurisdiction, are to be punished in the
next life, not in the present one, unless the secular ruler
declares a divine law also a secular law. This was a direct
challenge of the power of the pope to excommunicate
rulers and place countries under interdict. The *Defender
of Peace* depicted the pope as a subordinate member of
a society over which the emperor ruled supreme and

temporal peace was the highest good. In the sixteenth
century the ministers of King Henry VIII translated and
disseminated the *Defender of Peace* as part of the justification for the English king's control of the English church.

John XXII made the papacy a sophisticated international agency and adroitly adjusted it to the growing
European money economy. The more the Curia (or
papal court) mastered the latter, however, the more
vulnerable it became to criticism. At John's death his
court held the respect of neither kings nor simple laymen.
Under his successor, Benedict XII (1334–1342), the
papacy became entrenched in Avignon. Seemingly for-
getting Rome altogether, Benedict began construction of
the great Palace of the Popes. His high-living French
successor, Clement VI (1342–1352), placed papal policy
in lockstep with the French. In this period the cardinals
became barely more than lobbyists for policies favorable
to their secular patrons. To many contemporaries it
seemed a fitting divine judgment that the Black Death
reached its height during the prodigal pontificate of
Clement VI.

NATIONAL OPPOSITION TO THE AVIGNON
PAPACY. As Avignon's fiscal tentacles probed new
areas, monarchies took strong action to protect their
interests. The latter half of the fourteenth century saw
legislation restricting papal jurisdiction and taxation in
France, England, and Germany. In England, where the
Avignon papacy was identified with the French enemy

after the outbreak of the Hundred Years' War, statutes of *provisors* and *praemunire,* which restricted appeals and payments to Rome, were several times passed between 1351 and 1393. In France ecclesiastical appointments and taxation were regulated by the so-called Gallican liberties. These national rights over religion were long exercised in fact and were legally acknowledged by the church in the Pragmatic Sanction of Bourges in 1438. This agreement recognized the right of the French church to elect its own clergy without papal interference, prohibited the payment of annates to Rome, and limited the right of appeals from French courts to the Curia in Rome. In German and Swiss cities in the fourteenth and fifteenth centuries local governments also took the initiative to limit and even overturn traditional clerical privileges and immunities.

The Great Schism (1378–1417) and the Conciliar Movement to 1449

URBAN VI AND CLEMENT VII. Pope Gregory XI (1370–1378) reestablished the papacy in Rome in January 1377, ending what had come to be known as the "Babylonian Captivity" of the church, the reference being to the biblical bondage of the Israelites. The return to Rome proved, however, a short-lived joy, as a fate worse than captivity in Babylon now befell the church. Upon Gregory's death on March 27, 1378, the cardinals elected a new pope, Urban VI (1378–1389), who immediately proclaimed his intention to reform the Curia. This came as an unexpected challenge to the cardinals, most of whom were French, and made them amenable to royal pressures to return the papacy to Avignon. The French king, Charles V, not wanting to surrender the benefits of a papacy located within the sphere of French influence, directly inspired a schism. Five months after Urban's election, on September 20, 1378, thirteen cardinals, all but one of whom was French, formed their own conclave and elected a cousin of the French king as Pope Clement VII (1378–1397). Thereafter the papacy became a "two-headed thing" and a scandal to Christendom. Alle-

---

John XXII Condemns Marsilius of Padua's Views on Power

In defending the sovereignty of rulers against popes, Marsilius of Padua (ca. 1275–1343) insisted not only that clergy were bound by divine and human law to obey the emperor, but also that all coercive power on earth lay in the hands of the emperor alone, who could judge and punish popes. These and other teachings of Marsilius were condemned by Pope John XXII (1316–1334) on October 23, 1327.

ERRORS OF
MARSILIUS OF PADUA
ON THE
CONSTITUTION OF THE CHURCH

1. T HAT *when his disciples found a silver coin in the mouth of a fish and Jesus told them to give it to Caesar [Matthew 17:26], he did this not in a condescending way, freely and out of piety, but because such homage was due Caesar. From this it is concluded that in the mind of Marsilius all the temporal things of the church are subservient to the emperor, and he can take them as his own.*

2. That the blessed apostle Peter had no more authority than the other apostles and was no more the head of the church than they were, nor was he the head of the other apostles. For Christ left no head of the church, nor did he make any one apostle his vicar.

3. That it is within the province of the emperor to correct, institute, destroy, and punish the pope.

4. That all priests, whether the pope, archbishop, or simple priest, are by Christ's institution of equal authority and jurisdiction.

5. That the pope or the whole church taken together can punish no man, however sinful he may be, coercively unless the emperor concede this power to them.

Henricus Denzinger and Adolfus Schönmetzer, *Enchiridion Symbolorum Definitionum et Declarationum de Rebus Fidei et Morum,* 32nd ed. (Freiburg im Breisgau: Herder, 1963), pp. 289–290.

---

giance to the two papal courts divided along political lines: England and its allies (the Holy Roman Empire, Hungary, Bohemia, and Poland) acknowledged Urban VI, whereas France and its orbit (Naples, Scotland, Castile, and Aragon) supported Clement VII. Only the Roman line of popes came to be recognized as official, however, in subsequent church history.

Two approaches were initially taken to end the schism. One tried to win the mutual cession of both popes, thereby clearing the way for a new election of a single pope. The other sought to secure the resignation of the one in favor of the other. Both proved completely fruitless, however. Each pope considered himself fully legitimate, and too much was at stake for a magnanimous concession on the part of either. There was one way left: the forced deposition of both popes by a special council of the church.

CONCILIAR THEORY OF CHURCH GOVERNMENT. Legally a church council could be convened only by a pope, and the competing popes were not inclined to summon a council for their own deposition. Also, the deposition of a legitimate pope against his will by a council of the church was as serious a matter for medieval people as the forced dethronement of a legally recognized hereditary monarch by a representative body.

The correctness of a conciliar deposition of a pope was debated a full thirty years before any direct action was taken. Conciliar theorists, chief among whom were the Parisians Conrad of Gelnhausen, Henry of Langenstein, Jean Gerson, and Pierre d'Ailly, challenged the popes' identification of the church's welfare with their own welfare and developed arguments in favor of a more representative government of the church. Conciliarists defined the church as the whole body of the faithful, a body of which the elected head, the pope, was but one part, and a part whose sole purpose was to maintain the unity and well-being of the body as a whole—something that the schismatic popes were far from doing. It was further argued that a council of the church, as a Holy Spirit–inspired spokesman for a majority of the faithful, acted with greater authority than the pope alone.

THE COUNCIL OF PISA (1409–1410). On the basis of such arguments, cardinals representing both sides convened on their own authority in Pisa in 1409. There they deposed both the Roman and the Avignon popes, and elected in their stead a new pope, Alexander V. To the council's consternation neither pope accepted its action, and after 1409 Christendom confronted the spectacle of three contending popes.

THE COUNCIL OF CONSTANCE (1414–1417). This intolerable situation ended when the emperor Sigismund prevailed upon Alexander V's Pisan successor, John XXIII (1410–1415), to summon a legal council of the church in Constance in 1414. In a famous declaration entitled *Sacrosancto* the council fathers asserted their supremacy and proceeded to conduct the business of the church. They made clear their authority by burning John Huss and Jerome of Prague at the stake for heresy in 1415. These executions were intended to end heresy in Bohemia, but they had the opposite result, only making it more militant. In November 1417 the council successfully accomplished its main business when it elected a new pope, Martin V (1417–1431), after the three contending popes had either resigned or, as in the case of John XXIII, were deposed. The council made provisions for regular meetings of church councils in the decree *Frequens* (1417), which scheduled a general council of the church for purposes of reform within five, then seven, and thereafter every ten years.

THE COUNCIL OF BASEL (1431–1449). Conciliar government of the church both peaked and declined during the Council of Basel, the church's last attempt at truly representative government. It was a far more egalitarian council than Constance had been, permitting clergy beneath the rank of bishop and abbot, university scholars, and certain laymen to vote. In 1432 the council invited the Hussites to send a delegation to Basel to make peace. The Hussites, whose armies were terrorizing central Europe, presented a doctrinal statement known as the *Four Articles of Prague*, which served as a basis for the negotiations. This document contained requests for (1) giving the laity the Eucharist with cup as well as bread (hence their name *Utraquists*, from the Latin word meaning "both," and *Calixtines*, from the Latin word for "cup"); (2) free, itinerant preaching; (3) the exclusion of the clergy from holding secular offices and possessing property; and (4) just punishment of clergy who have committed mortal sins. In November 1433 an agreement, the Compacts of Prague, was reached between the em-

Ecclesiastical Breakdown and Revival: The Late Medieval Church

The Chronicler Calls the Roll at the Council of Constance

The Council of Constance, in session for three years (1414–1417), not only drew many clergy and political representatives into its proceedings but also required a great variety of supporting personnel. Here is an inventory from the contemporary chronicle by Ulrich Richental.

Pope *John XXIII came with 600 men.*
Pope Martin, who was elected pope at Constance, came with 30 men.
5 patriarchs, with 118 men.
33 cardinals, with 3,056 men.
47 archbishops, with 4,700 men.
145 bishops, with 6,000 men.
93 suffragan bishops, with 360 men.
Some 500 spiritual lords, with 4,000 men.
24 auditors and secretaries, with 300 men.
37 scholars from the universities of all nations, with 2,000 men.
217 doctors of theology from the five nations, who walked in the processions, with 2,600 men.
361 doctors of both laws, with 1,260 men.
171 doctors of medicine, with 1,600 men.
1,400 masters of arts and licentiates, with 3,000 men.
5,300 simple priests and scholars, some by threes, some by twos, some alone.
The apothecaries who lived in huts, with 300 men. (16 of them were masters).
72 goldsmiths, who lived in huts.
Over 1,400 merchants, shopkeepers, furriers, smiths, shoemakers, innkeepers, and handworkers, who lived in huts and rented houses and huts, with their servants.
24 rightful heralds of the King, with their squires.
1,700 trumpeters, fifers, fiddlers, and players of all kinds.
Over 700 harlots in brothels came, who hired their own houses, and some who lay in stables and wherever they could, beside the private ones whom I could not count.
In the train of the Pope were 24 secretaries with 200 men, 16 doorkeepers, 12 beadles who carried silver rods, 60 other beadles for the cardinals, auditors and auditors of the camera, and many old women who washed and mended the clothes of the Roman lords in private and public.
132 abbots, all named, with 2,000 men.
155 priors, all recorded with their names, with 1600 men.
Our lord King, two queens, and 5 princely ladies.

39 dukes, 32 princely lords and counts, 141 counts, 71 barons, more than 1500 knights, more than 20,000 noble squires.
Embassies from 83 kings of Asia, Africa, and Europe, with full powers; envoys from other lords without number, for they rode in and out every day. There were easily 5,000.
472 envoys from imperial cities.
352 envoys from baronial cities.
72,460 persons.

Richental's *Chronicle of the Council, Constance,* in *The Council of Constance,* ed. by J. H. Mundy and K. M. Woodey, trans. by Louise R. Roomis (New York: Columbia University Press, 1961), pp. 189–190.

peror, the council, and the Hussites. The Bohemian church was granted jurisdictional rights similar to those already secured by France and England. Three of the four Prague articles were conceded: communion with cup, free preaching by ordained clergy, and like punishment of clergy and laity for mortal sins. The church firmly retained, however, the right to possess and dispose of property.

THE COUNCIL OF FERRARA–FLORENCE (1438–1439). The termination of the Hussite wars and reform legislation curtailing papal power of appointment and taxation were the high points of the Council of Basel. Heady with success, the Basel council asserted its powers beyond the original intention of the decrees of Constance and in doing so undermined much internal and external support. Original supporters of the council, prominent among them the philosopher Nicholas of Cusa, turned their backs on the council when Pope Eugenius IV (1431–1447) ordered it to transfer to Ferrara in 1437. The pope had a golden opportunity to upstage the Council of Basel by negotiating reunion with

The Council of Constance Declares Conciliar Supremacy

The decree *Sacrosancto* (April 1415) asserted the supremacy of councils over popes in time of emergency in the church. This was the legal basis on which the Council of Constance proceeded to remove the contending popes from power and end the schism by electing a new pope, Martin V (1417–1431).

THIS *holy Council of Constance ... declares, first that it is lawfully assembled in the Holy Spirit, that it constitutes a General Council, representing the Catholic Church, and that therefore it has its authority immediately from Christ; and that all men, of every rank and condition, including the pope himself, are bound to obey it in matters concerning the Faith, the abolition of the schism, and the reformation of the Church of God in its head and its members. Secondly, it declares that anyone, of any rank and condition, who shall contumaciously refuse to obey the orders, decrees, statutes or instructions, made or to be made by this holy Council ... or by any other lawfully assembled general council ... shall, unless he comes to a right frame of mind, be subjected to fitting penance and punished appropriately: and, if need be, recourse shall be had to the other sanctions of the law.*

From *Documents of the Christian Church*, ed. by Henry Bettenson (New York: Oxford University Press, 1961), pp. 192–193.

Pius II Condemns the Conciliar Theory of Church Government

After the restoration of papal power in the mid-fifteenth century Pope Pius II (1458–1464) condemned the conciliar theory of church government as defined by the Councils of Constance and Basel. The bull *Execrabilis* (January 18, 1460) condemned appeals beyond the pope to a council of the church as erroneous and abominable.

A HORRIBLE *and in earlier times unheard-of abuse has sprung up in our period. Some men, imbued with a spirit of rebellion ... suppose that they can appeal from the pope, vicar of Jesus Christ ... to a future council. ... Desirous of banishing this deadly poison from the Church of Christ, and concerned with the salvation of the sheep committed to us ... with the counsel and with the assent drawn from our venerable Fathers of the Holy Roman Church, all the cardinals and prelates and all those who interpret divine and human law in accordance with the curia, and being fully informed, we condemn appeals of this kind, reject them as erroneous and abominable, declare them to be completely null and void. ... And we lay down that from now on, no one should dare, regardless of his pretext, to make such an appeal from our decisions, be they legal or theological, or from any commands at all from us or our successors, to heed such an appeal made by another, or to make use of these in any fashion whatsoever.*

From Heiko A. Oberman, *Forerunners of the Reformation: The Shape of Late Medieval Thought* (New York: 1966), pp. 238–239.

---

the eastern church, which was once again bargaining for western aid against new Turkish advances. A majority of Basel's members refused to transfer to Ferrara, and their defiance made Basel a schismatic council. They watched helplessly while the reunion of the eastern and western churches was proclaimed in Florence, where the council of Ferrara had been transferred because of plague, in 1439. This agreement, although short-lived, restored papal prestige and signaled the demise of the conciliar movement.

After Eugenius's successful challenge of its power, the Council of Basel excommunicated him and elected a new pope, Felix V (1439–1449). But such action was too much too late; the tide had already turned in favor of a revived papal monarchy. By 1449 the Council of Basel, since removed to Lausanne, had received Felix's resignation and formally recognized Eugenius's Roman successor, Nicholas V (1447–1455), as the legitimate pope. Church councils have ever since been conducted strictly on the pope's terms. The notion of conciliar superiority suffered a mortal blow with the collapse of the Council of

Basel in 1449. The *coup de grâce* came a decade later with the publication of the papal bull *Execrabilis* in 1460. That decree condemned appeals to councils as not only "erroneous and abominable" but also "completely null and void."

If the conciliar movement died with Basel, the principles for which the conciliarists stood were to win their way in the early modern world—religiously through the Protestant Reformation and politically through the development of theories of representative government and tyrannicide. The conciliar age planted deep within the conscience of Western man the conviction that the leader of an institution must be responsive to its members and that the head exists to lead and serve, not to bring disaster upon, the body.

A second consequence of the conciliar movement was the devolving of religious responsibility on the laity. In the absence of papal leadership, secular control of national or territorial churches increased. Kings asserted power over the church in England and France. Magistrates and city councils reformed and regulated religious life in German, Swiss, and Italian cities. This development was not reversed by the powerful "restoration" popes of the high Renaissance. On the contrary, as the papacy was transformed into a limited territorial regime, national control of the church simply ran apace. Perceived as but one among several Italian states, the Papal States came to be opposed as much on the grounds of "national" policy and sentiment as for religious reasons. Both humanist critics and Protestant reformers looked upon the popes of the late fifteenth and the early sixteenth centuries as the rivals of secular princes in political scandal and international intrigue.

Revival of Monarchy: Nation Building in the Fifteenth Century

After 1450 there was a progressive shift from divided feudal to unified national monarchies as truly sovereign rulers emerged. This is not to say that the dynastic and chivalric ideals of feudal monarchy did not continue. Territorial princes did not pass from the scene, and representative bodies persisted and in some areas even grew in influence. But in the late fifteenth and early sixteenth centuries the old problem of the one and the many was decided clearly in favor of the interests of monarchy.

The feudal monarchy of the high Middle Ages was characterized by the division of the basic powers of government between the king and his semiautonomous vassals. The nobility and the towns acted with varying degrees of unity and success through such bodies as the English parliament, the French Estates-General, and the Spanish Cortes to thwart the centralization of royal power. Because of the Hundred Years' War and the schism in the church, the nobility and the clergy were in decline in the late Middle Ages. The increasingly important towns began to ally with the king. Loyal, business-wise townsmen, not the nobility and the clergy, staffed the royal offices and became the king's lawyers, bookkeepers, military tacticians, and foreign diplomats. It was this new alliance between king and town that finally broke the bonds of feudal society and made possible the rise of sovereign states.

In a sovereign state the power of taxation, war making, and law enforcement is no longer the local right of semiautonomous vassals but is concentrated in the monarch and is exercised by his chosen agents. Taxes, wars, and laws become national rather than merely regional matters. Only as monarchs were able to act independently of the nobility and the representative assemblies could they overcome the decentralization that had been the basic obstacle to nation building. Ferdinand and Isabella rarely called the Cortes into session. The French Estates-General did not meet at all from 1484 to 1560. Henry VII (1485–1509) of England managed to raise revenues without going begging to Parliament. Kings were also assisted by brilliant theorists, from Marsilius of Padua in the fourteenth century to Machiavelli and Jean Bodin in the sixteenth, who eloquently argued the sovereign rights of monarchy.

The many were of course never totally subjugated to the one, and still today the cry of "states' rights" is very distinct. But in the last half of the fifteenth century, rulers were able to demonstrate that the law was their creature. Royal offices were manned by civil servants whose vision was no longer local or regional. In Castile they were the *corregidores,* in England the justices of the peace, in France bailiffs operating through well-drilled lieutenants. These royal ministers and agents were not immune to becoming closely attached to the localities they administered in the king's name. And regions were able to secure congenial royal appointments. Throughout England local magnates served as representatives of Tudor kings. Nonetheless these new executives were truly *royal* executives, bureaucrats whose outlook was national and whose loyalty was to the "state."

Monarchies also began to create standing national armies in the fifteenth century. As the noble cavalry receded and the infantry and the artillery became the backbone of the armies, mercenary soldiers were recruited from Switzerland and Germany to form the major part of the "king's army." Professional soldiers who fought for pay and booty proved far more efficient than feudal vassals who fought simply for honor's sake. Kings who failed to meet their payrolls, however, faced a new danger of mutiny and banditry by alien troops.

The more expensive warfare of the fifteenth and sixteenth centuries increased the need to develop new national sources of royal inocme. The expansion of royal revenues was especially hampered by the stubborn belief among the highest classes that they were immune from government taxation. The nobility guarded their properties and traditional rights and despised royal taxation as an insult and a humiliation. Royal revenues accordingly grew at the expense of those least able to resist and to pay. The king had several options. As a feudal lord he could collect rents from his royal domain. He could also levy national taxes on basic food and clothing, such as the *gabelle* or salt tax in France and the *alcabala* or 10-percent sales tax on commercial transactions in Spain. The king could also levy direct taxes on the peasantry. This he did through agreeable representatives assemblies of the privileged classes in which the peasantry did not sit. The French *taille*, which kings independently determined from year to year after the Estates-General was suspended in 1484, was such a tax. Sale of public offices and issuance of high-interest government bonds appeared in the fifteenth century as innovative fund-raising devices. But kings did not levy taxes on the powerful nobility. They turned to rich nobles, as to the great bankers of Italy and Germany, for loans, bargaining with privileged classes, who in many instances remained as much their creditors and competitors as their subjects.

France

Charles VII (1422–1461) was a king made great by those who served him. His ministers created a professional army, which—thanks initially to the inspiration of Joan of Arc—drove the English out of France. And largely because of the enterprise of an independent merchant banker named Jacques Coeur, the French also developed a strong economy, diplomatic cours, and national administration during Charles VII's reign. These were the sturdy tools with which Charles' successor, the ruthless Louis XI (1461–1483), made France a great power.

There were two cornerstones of French nation-building in the fifteenth century. The first was the collapse of the English empire in France following the Hundred Years' War. The second was the defeat of Charles the Bold and the duchy of Burgundy. Perhaps Europe's strongest political power in the mid-fifteenth century, Burgundy aspired to dwarf both France and the Holy Roman Empire as the leader of a dominant middle kingdom. It might have succeeded in doing so had not the continental powers joined together in opposition. When Charles the Bold died in defeat in a battle at Nancy in 1477, the dream of Burgundian empire died with him. Louis XI and the Hapsburg Emperor Maximilian I divided the conquered Burgundian lands between them, with the treaty-wise Hapsburgs getting the better part. The dissolution of Burgundy ended its constant intrigue against the French king and left Louis XI free to secure the monarchy. The newly acquired Burgundian lands and his own Angevin inheritance permitted the king to end his reign with a kingdom almost twice the size of that with which he had started. Louis successfully harnessed the nobility, expanded the trade and industry so carefully nurtured by Jacques Coeur, created a national postal system, and even established a lucrative silk industry at Lyons (later transferred to Tours). Such deliberate and farsighted national economic planning, known as *mercantilism*, is a mark of a centralized nation-state.

But a strong nation is a two-edged sword. It was because Louis's successors inherited such a secure and efficient government that France was able to pursue Italian conquests in the 1490s and to fight a long series of losing wars with the Hapsburgs in the first half of the sixteenth century. By the mid-sixteenth century France was again a defeated nation and almost as divided internally as during the Hundred Years War.

Spain

Spain too became a strong country in the late fifteenth century. Both Castile and Aragon had been poorly ruled and divided kingdoms in the mid-fifteenth century. The union of Isabella of Castile (1474–1504) and Ferdinand of Aragon (1478–1516) changed that situation. The two future sovereigns married in 1469, despite strong protests from neighboring Portugal and France, both of which foresaw the formidable European power such a union would create. Castile was by far the richer and more populous of the two, having an estimated five million inhabitants to Aragon's population of under one million. Castile was also distinguished by its lucrative sheep-farming industry, which was run by a government-backed organization called the Mesta, another example of developing centralized economic planning. Although the two kingdoms were dynastically united by the marriage of Ferdinand and Isabella in 1469, they remained constitutionally separated, as each retained its respective government agencies—separate laws, armies, coinage, and taxation—and cultural traditions.

Ferdinand and Isabella could do together what neither was able to accomplish alone: subdue their realms, secure their borders, and venture abroad militarily. Between 1482 and 1492 they conquered the Moors in Granada. Naples became a Spanish possession in 1504. By 1512 Ferdinand had secured his northern borders by conquering the kingdom of Navarre. Internally Ferdinand and Isabella won the allegiance of the Hermandad, a powerful league of cities and towns, which served them against stubborn landowners. Townsmen allied with the crown and progressively replaced the nobility within the royal administration. The crown also extended its authority over the wealthy chivalric orders, a further circumscription of the power of the nobility.

Spain was the prime example of state-controlled religion. Ferdinand and Isabella exercised almost total control over the Spanish church as religion was placed in the service of national unity. They appointed the higher clergy and the officers of the Inquisition. The Inquisition, run by Tomás de Torquemada (d. 1498), Isabella's confessor, was a key national agency established in 1479 to monitor the activity of converted Jews (*conversos*) and Moslems (*Moriscos*) in Spain. In 1492 Torquemada exiled the Jews and confiscated their properties. In 1502 non-converting Moors in Granada were driven into exile by Cardinal Francesco Ximenes (1436–1517), the great spiritual reformer and educator. On the eve of the Protestant Reformation Spanish religious life was largely uniform and successfully controlled—a major reason for Spain's remaining a loyal Catholic country throughout the sixteenth century and providing a base of operation for the European Counter Reformation.

Despite a certain internal narrowness Ferdinand and Isabella were rulers with wide horizons. They contracted anti-French marriage alliances that came to determine a large part of European history in the sixteenth century. In 1496 their eldest daughter Joanna, later known as "the Mad," married Archduke Philip, the son of Emperor Maximilian I. The fruit of this union, Charles I of Spain, came by his inheritance and election as emperor in 1519 to rule over a European kingdom almost equal in size to that of Charlemagne. A second daughter, Katherine of Aragon, wed Arthur, the son of the English King Henry VII, and after Arthur's premature death, she married his brother, the future King Henry VIII. The failure of this latter marriage became the key factor in the emergence of the Anglican Church and the English Reformation.

Ferdinand and Isabella also promoted overseas exploration. Their patronage of the Genoese adventurer Christopher Columbus (1446–1506), who discovered the islands of the Caribbean while sailing west in search of a shorter route to the spice markets of the Far East, led to the creation of the Spanish Empire in Mexico and Peru, whose gold and silver mines helped to make Spain Europe's dominant power in the sixteenth century.

England

The last half of the fifteenth century was a period of especially difficult political trial for the English. Following the Hundred Years War, a defeated England was subjected to internal warfare between two rival branches of the royal family, the house of York and the House of Lancaster. This conflict, known to us today as the War of the Roses (as York's symbol was a white rose and Lancaster's a red rose) kept England in turmoil from 1455 to 1485.

The Lancastrian monarchy of Henry VI (1422–1461) was consistently challenged by the duke of York and his supporters in the prosperous southern towns. In 1461 Edward IV (1461–1483), son of the duke of York, successfully seized power and instituted a strong-arm rule that lasted over twenty years, being only briefly interrupted in 1470–1471 by Henry VI's short-lived restoration. Edward, assisted by loyal and able ministers, effectively bent Parliament to his will. His brother and successor was Richard III (1483–1485). During the reign of the Tudors a tradition arose that painted Richard III as an unprincipled villain who murdered Edward's sons in the Tower of London to secure the throne. The best known version of this—perhaps unjust—characterization is found in Shakespeare's *Richard III*. Be that as it may, Richard's reign saw the growth of support for the exiled Lancastrian Henry Tudor. Henry returned to England to defeat Richard on Bosworth Field in August 1485.

Henry Tudor ruled as Henry VII (1485–1509), the first of the new Tudor dynasty that would dominate England throughout the sixteenth century. In order to bring the rival royal families together and to make the hereditary claim of his offspring to the throne uncontestable, Henry married Edward IV's daughter, Elizabeth of York. He succeeded in subduing the English nobility through a highly undemocratic instrument of the royal will known as the Court of Star Chamber. Created in 1487, the court had the power to control royal patronage to the nobility and thereby bring factious noblemen to heel. Henry shrewdly construed legal precedents to the advantage of the crown, using English law to further his own ends. He managed to confiscate noble lands and fortunes with such success that he governed without dependence on Parliament for royal funds, always a cornerstone of strong monarchy. In these ways Henry began to shape a dynasty that would develop into one of early modern Europe's most exemplary governments during the reign of his granddaughter, Elizabeth I.

The Holy Roman Empire

Germany and Italy are the striking exceptions to the steady development of centralized nation-states in the last half of the fifteenth century. Unlike France, Spain, and England, the empire saw the many thoroughly repulse the one. In Germany territorial rulers and cities resisted every effort at national consolidation. As in Carolingian times, rulers continued to partition their kingdoms, however small, among their sons, and by the late fifteenth century Germany was hopelessly divided into some three hundred autonomous political entities.

The princes and the cities did work together to create the machinery of law and order, if not of union, within the divided Empire. An agreement reached in 1356, known as the Golden Bull, established a seven-member electoral college consisting of the archbishops of Mainz, Trier, and Cologne; the duke of Saxony; the margrave of Brandenburg; the count Palatine; and the king of Bohemia. This group also functioned as an administrative body. They elected the emperor and, in cooperation with him, provided what transregional unity and administration existed. The figure of the emperor gave the Empire a single ruler in law, if not in actual fact, as the conditions of his rule and the extent of his powers over his subjects, especially the seven electors, were renegotiated with every imperial election and always the rights of the many (the princes) were balanced against the power of the one (the emperor). In the fifteenth century an effort was made to control incessant feuding by the creation of an imperial diet (*Reichstag*). This was a national assembly of the seven electors, the nonelectoral princes, and the sixty-five imperial free cities. The cities were the weakest of the three bodies represented at the diet. During such an assembly in Worms in 1495 the members won from the emperor, Maximilian I (1493–1519), concessions that had been successfully resisted by his predecessor, Frederick III (1440–1493). Led by Berthold of Henneberg, the archbishop of Mainz, the Diet of Worms secured an imperial ban on private warfare, a court of justice (the *Reichskammergericht*) to enforce internal peace, and an imperial Council of Regency (the *Reichsregiment*) to coordinate imperial and internal German policy. The latter was very grudgingly conceded by the emperor because it gave the princes a share in executive power.

Although important, these reforms were still a poor substitute for true national unity. This most disunified of late medieval countries was soon, however, to be also the most Protestant of European countries. It was in the cities and towns of still feudal, fractionalized, backward Germany that the Protestant Reformation broke out.

The Renaissance in Italy to 1527

When we think of medieval Europe, we think of a fragmented feudal society, an agricultural economy, and thought and culture dominated by the church. In contrast, Renaissance Europe is characterized by growing national consciousness and centralization, an urban economy based on commerce, and lay influence on thought and culture. In these terms one may see the transition from medieval to Renaissance Europe beginning as early as the eleventh century with the revival of trade and the rapid growth of cities and towns.

Renaissance society was no simple cultural transformation. It first took distinctive shape within the cities of late medieval Italy. Italy had always had a cultural advantage over the rest of Europe because its geography made it the natural gateway between east and west. Venice, Genoa,

---

The Golden Bull Tells How to Elect the Holy Roman Emperor

The Golden Bull, named for its gold seal, or *bulla*, was a stabilizing compromise between central and regional authorities in the Holy Roman Empire. It was promulgated by Charles IV in 1356 and in exchange for regularizing election arrangements for emperors it recognized rights and powers of the seven traditional electors. It also excluded popes from what thereafter was an all-German administration of the Empire.

1. Mass shall be celebrated on the day after the arrival of the electors. The archbishop of Mainz administers this oath, which the other electors repeat:

2. "I, archbishop of Mainz, archchancellor of the empire for Germany, electoral prince, swear on the holy gospels here before me, and by the faith which I owe to God and to the holy Roman empire, that with the aid of God, and according to my best judgment and knowledge, I will cast my vote, in this election of the king of the Romans and future emperor, for a person fitted to rule the Christian people. I will give my voice and vote freely, uninfluenced by any agreement, price, bribe, promise, or anything of the sort, by whatever name it may be called. So help me God and all the saints."

3. After the electors have taken this oath, they shall proceed to the election, and shall not depart from Frankfort until the majority have elected a king of the Romans and future emperor, to be ruler of the world and of the Christian people. If they have not come to a decision within thirty days from the day on which they took the above oath, after that they shall live upon bread and water and shall not leave the city until the election has been decided.

4. Such an election shall be as valid as if all the princes had agreed unanimously and without difference upon a candidate. . . . According to the ancient and approved custom, the king of the Romans elect, immediately after his election and before he takes up any other business of the empire, shall confirm and approve by sealed letters for each and all of the electoral princes, ecclesiastical and secular, the privileges, charters, rights, liberties, concessions, ancient customs, and dignities, and whatever else the princes held and possessed from the empire at the time of the election; and he shall renew the confirmation and approval when he becomes emperor.

Oliver J. Thatcher and Edgar H. McNeal, *A Source Book for Medieval History: Selected Documents Illustrating the History of Europe in the Middle Ages* (New York: Scribner's, 1905), pp. 288–289.

Emperor Maximilian (1493–1519) and his family, painted in 1515 by Bernard Strigel. Note the prominent Hapsburg chin of the middle child. [Kunsthistorisches Museum, Vienna.]

and Pisa traded uninterruptedly with the Near East throughout the Middle Ages and maintained vibrant urban societies. When commerce revived on a large scale in the eleventh century, Italian merchants quickly mastered the business skills of organization, bookkeeping, scouting new markets, and securing monopolies. By the thirteenth century independent city-states dominated central and northern Italy; in the fourteenth and fifteenth centuries the great Italian cities had become the bankers of Europe.

The Italian City-State: Social Conflict and Despotism

The growth of Italian cities and urban culture was assisted by the endemic warfare between the emperor and the pope. Either of these might have subdued the cities had they permitted the other to concentrate on it. They chose instead to weaken one another and thus strengthened the cities. Unlike northern Europe, where the cities tended to be dominated by kings and territorial princes, the great Italian cities were left free to expand into states. They became independent states absorbing the surrounding countryside and assimilating area nobility in a unique urban meld of old and new rich. There were five such major, competitive states in Italy: the duchy of Milan; the republics of Florence and Venice; the Papal States; and the kingdom of Naples.

The transition to Renaissance society was so often accompanied by internal turmoil that most city-states, for sheer survival's sake, evolved into despotisms by the fifteenth century. Venice, ruled by a successful merchant

RENAISSANCE ITALY

The city-states of Renaissance Italy were self-contained principalities whose internal strife was monitored by their despots and whose external aggression was long successfully controlled by treaty.

The Renaissance in Italy to 1527

338 *The Late Middle Ages and the Renaissance: Decline and Renewal* (*1300–1527*)

Some homes of the rich and powerful in Renaissance Europe.

OPPOSITE, TOP: Villa of Lorenzo de' Medici (1449–1492), "Lorenzo the Magnificent," ruler of Florence, at Poggio a Caiano near Florence. [Alinari/SCALA.]

OPPOSITE, BOTTOM: The Villa Farnesina, Rome, home of the banker and patron of artists, Agostino Chigi (ca. 1465–1520). It was built between 1509 and 1511. [Alinari/SCALA.]

RIGHT, TOP: The home in Bourges of the brilliant French merchant and finance minister, Jacques Coeur (1395–1456), who helped transform France into a strong nation state. Built between 1443 and 1451, it has two false windows above and flanking the entrance that seem to frame insiders looking out. [French Cultural Services, New York.]

RIGHT, BOTTOM: The courtyard of the so-called Casa de Pilatos in Seville, Spain, the home of the duke of Medinaceli. It dates from about 1500. [AHM.]

oligarchy, was the notable exception to this general rule. Elsewhere rapid urban growth produced new social classes and divisions within society that led to near-anarchic conflict.

Florence is the most striking example. There were four distinguishable social groups within the city. The first was the old rich or *grandi*, the nobles and merchants who traditionally ruled the city. The second group was the emergent new-rich merchant class, capitalists and bankers known as the *populo grasso* or "fat people." They began to challenge the old rich for political power in the late thirteenth and early fourteenth centuries. Then there were the middle-burgher ranks of guildmasters, shopkeepers, and professionals, those small businessmen who, in Florence as elsewhere, tended to take the side of the new rich against the conservative policies of the old rich. Finally, there was the omnipresent *populo minuto,* the poor masses who lived literally from hand to mouth. In 1457 one third of the population of Florence, about thirty-thousand people, were officially listed as paupers.

These social divisions produced conflict at every level of society, to which was added the every-present fear of foreign intrigue. In 1378 feuding between the old and the new rich combined with the social pressures of the Black Death, which cut the city's population almost in half, and with the collapse of the banking houses of Bardi and Peruzzi to ignite a great revolt by the poor. It was known as the Ciompi Revolt and established a chaotic four-year reign of power by the lower Florentine classes. True stability did not return to Florence until the ascent to power in 1434 of Cosimo de' Medici (1389–1464), who began three centuries of Medici rule.

Cosimo de' Medici was the wealthiest Florentine and an astute statesman. He controlled the city internally

A terra cotta bust of Lorenzo de' Medici by the sculptor Andrea del Verrocchio (*ca.* 1435–1488). [National Gallery of Art, Washington; Samuel H. Kress Collection.]

from behind the scenes, skillfully manipulating the constitution and influencing elections. As head of the Office of Public Debt, he was able to favor congenial factions. His grandson, Lorenzo the Magnificent (1449–1492), ruled Florence in almost totalitarian fashion during the last quarter of the fifteenth century, having been made cautious by the assassination of his brother in 1478 by a rival Florentine family, the Pazzi, who plotted with the pope against Medici rule.

Despotism was less subtle elsewhere. In order to prevent internal social conflict and foreign intrigue from paralyzing their cities, old and new rich cooperated to install a hired strongman, known as a *podesta,* for the purpose of maintaining law and order. He was given executive, military, and judicial authority and his mandate was direct and simple: to permit, by whatever means required, the normal flow of business activity without which neither the old rich, the new rich, nor the poor of a city could long survive. Because these *despots* could not depend on the divided populace, they operated through mercenary armies, which they obtained through military brokers known as *condottieri.* It was a hazardous job. Despots were not only subject to dismissal by the oligarchies that hired them, but they were also popular objects of assassination attempts. The spoils of success very great. In Milan it was as *despots* that the Visconti family came to power in 1278 and the Sforza family in 1450. The latter produced one of Machiavelli's heroes, Ludovico il Moro.

Whether within the comparatively tranquil republic of Venice, the strong-arm democracy of Florence, or the undisguised despotism of Milan, the disciplined Italian city proved a most congenial climate for an unprecedented flowering of thought and culture. Italian Renaissance culture was promoted as vigorously by despots as by republicans and by secularized popes as enthusiastically as by the more spiritually minded. This support was related to the fact that the main requirement for patronage of the arts and letters was the one thing that Italian cities of the high Renaissance had in abundance: great wealth.

Humanism

There are several schools of thought on the essence of Humanism. Those who follow the nineteenth-century historian Jacob Burckhardt, who saw the Italian Renaissance as the birth of modernity, view it as an unchristian philosophy that stressed the dignity of man and championed individualism and secular values. Others argue that Humanists were the very champions of authentic Catholic Christianity, who opposed the pagan teaching of Aristotle and the ineloquent Scholasticism his writings nurtured. Still others see Humanism as a form of scholarship consciously designed to promote a sense of civic responsibility and political liberty. One of the most authoritative modern commentators, Paul O. Kristeller, has accused all these views of dealing more with the secondary effects than with the essence of Humanism. Humanism, he believes, was no particular philosophy or value system but simply an educational program concentrated on rhetoric and sound scholarship for their own sake.

There is truth in each of these definitions. Humanism was the scholarly study of the Latin and Greek classics and the ancient Church Fathers both for their own sake and in the hope of a rebirth of ancient norms and values. Humanists were advocates of the *studia humanitatis,* a liberal arts program of study that embraced grammar, rhetoric, poetry, history, politics, and moral philosophy. These subjects were not only considered a joy in themselves; they were also seen as celebrating the diginity of man and preparing him for a life of virtuous action. The Florentine Leonardi Bruni (1370–1444) first gave the name *humanitas* ("humanity") to the learning that resulted from such scholarly pursuits.

The first Humanists were orators and poets. They wrote original literature, inspired by and modeled on the newly discovered works of the ancients, and they taught rhetoric within the universities. Their rivals, both for professorial chairs and for the hearts and minds of the students, were the Scholastics. When Humanists were not employed as teachers of rhetoric, their talents were

Dante Aligheri as seen by his contemporary, Giotto.
[The Granger Collection.]

sought as secretaries, speech writers, and diplomats in princely and papal courts.

The study of classical and Christian antiquity existed before the Italian Renaissance. There were recoveries of ancient civilization during the Carolingian renaissance of the ninth century, within the cathedral school of Chartres in the twelfth century, during the great Aristotelian revival in Paris in the thirteenth century, and among the Augustinians in the early fourteenth century. However, these precedents only partially compare with the grand achievements of the Italian Renaissance of the late Middle Ages. The latter was far more secular and lay-dominated, possessed much broader interests, was blessed with far more recovered manuscripts, and was endowed with far superior technical skills than had been the case in the earlier "rebirths" of antiqutiy. There is a kernel of truth in the arrogant boast of the Humanists that the period between themselves and classical civilization was a "dark middle age."

PETRARCH, DANTE, BOCCACIO. Francesco Petrarch (1304–1374) is known as the father of Humanism. Although most of his life was spent in and around Avignon, he became caught up in Cola di Rienzo's popular revolt and two-year reign (1347–1349) in Rome as "tribune" of the Roman people. He also served the Visconti family in Milan in his later years. Petrarch celebrated ancient Rome in his *Letters to the Ancient Dead*, fancied personal letters to Cicero, Livy, Vergil, and Horace. His critical textual studies, elitism, and contempt for the allegedly useless learning of the Scholastics were features that many later Humanists shared. Petrarch's most famous contemporary work was a collection of highly introspective love sonnets to a certain Laura, a married woman whom he romantically admired from a safe distance. Classical and Christian values coexist, not always harmoniously, in his work, and this uneasy coexistence too is true of many later Humanists. Medieval Christian values can be seen in his imagined dialogues with Saint Augustine and in tracts written to defend the personal immortality of the soul against the Aristotelians.

Petrarch was, however, far more secular in orientation than his famous contemporary Dante Alighieri (1265–1321), whose *Vita Nuova* and *Divine Comedy* form with Petrarch's sonnets the cornerstones of Italian vernacular literature. Petrarch's student and friend, Giovanni Boccaccio (1313–1375), author of the *Decameron*, one hundred bawdy tales told by three men and seven women in a country retreat from the plague that ravaged Florence in 1348, was also a pioneer of Humanist studies.

EDUCATIONAL REFORMS AND GOALS. The goal of Humanist studies was to be wise and to speak eloquently, both to know what is good and to practice virtue. Learning was not to remain abstract. "It is better to will the good than to know the truth," Petrarch had taught, and this became a motto of many later Humanists. The ideal of a useful education and well-rounded people inspired far-reaching reforms in traditional Scholastic methods and subject matter. Quintilian's *Education of the Orator*, the full text of which was discovered by Poggio Bracciolini (d. 1459) in 1416, became the basic classical guide for the Humanist revision of the traditional curriculum. The most influential Renaissance tract on education, Pietro Paolo Vergerio's (d. 1444) *On the Morals That Befit a Free Man*, was written directly from classical models. Vittorino da Feltre (d. 1446) was a teacher who not only directed his students to a highly disciplined reading of Pliny, Ptolemy, Terence, Plautus, Livy, and Plutarch but also combined vigorous physical exercise and games with intellectual pursuits. Another educator, Guarino da Verona (d. 1460), rector of the new University of Ferrara and a student of the Greek scholar Manuel Chrysoloras, streamlined the study of classical languages and gave it systematic form. A mastery of Latin and Greek was the surgeon's tool of the Humanist.

Humanists were not bashful scholars. They delighted in going directly to the primary sources themselves and reading them in the original languages. They refused to be slaves of tradition, satisfied, as they felt their Scholastic rivals to be, with the commentaries of the accepted masters. Such an attitude made Humanists not only innovative educators but also restless manuscript hunters, ever in search of new sources of information. Poggio and Francesco Filelfo (d. 1481) assembled magnificent manuscript collections.

THE FLORENTINE ACADEMY AND THE REVIVAL OF PLANTONISM. Of all the important recoveries of the past made during the Italian Renaissance none stands out more than the revival of Greek studies, especially the works of Plato, in fifteenth-century Florence. Many factors combined to bring this revival about. An important foundation was laid in 1397 when the city invited Manuel Chrysoloras to come from Constantinople and promote Greek learning. A half-century later (1439) the ecumenical Council of Ferrara–Florence, having convened to negotiate the reunion of the eastern and western churches, opened the door for many Greek scholars and manuscripts to enter the west. After the fall of Constantinople to the Turks in 1453, Greek scholars fled to Florence for refuge. This was the background against which the Florentine Platonic Academy evolved under the patronage of Cosimo de' Medici and the supervision of Marsilio Ficino (1433–1499) and Pico della Mirandola (1463–1494).

Although the thinkers of the Renaissance were interested in every variety of ancient wisdom, they seemed to be especially attracted to the Platonic tradition and those Church Fathers who tried to synthesize Platonic philoso-phy and Christian teaching. The Florentine Academy, a small villa designed for comfortable discussion, became both a cultic and a scholarly center for the revival of Plato and the Neoplatonists—Plotinus, Proclus, Porphyry, and Dionysius the Areopagite. There Fincino edited and saw to the publication of the complete works of Plato.

The appeal of Platonism lay in its flattering view of human nature. This can be seen in Pico's *Oration on the Dignity of Man,* considered the most famous Renaissance statement on the nature of man. Pico wrote the *Oration* as an introduction to a pretentious collection of nine hundred theses, which were published in Rome in December 1486 and intended to serve as the basis for a public debate on all of life's important topics. The *Oration* drew on Platonic teaching to depict man as the one creature in the world who possessed the freedom to be whatever he chose, able at will to rise to the height of angels or to descend to the level of pigs.

CRITICAL WORK OF THE HUMANISTS: LORENZO VALLA. Because they were guided by a scholarly ideal of philological accuracy and historical truthfulness, the Humanists could become critics of tradition even when that was not their intention. Dispassionate critical scholarship shook long-standing foundations, not the least of which were those of the medieval church.

The work of Lorenzo Valla (1407–1457), author of the standard Renaissance text in Latin philology, the *Elegances of the Latin Language* (1444), reveals the explosive character of the new learning. Although a good Catholic, Valla became a hero to later Protestants. His popularity among Protestants stemmed from his defense of predestination against the advocates of free will and especially from his exposé of the Donation of Constantine, a fraudulent document written in the eighth century alleging that the Emperor Constantine had given vast territories to the pope. The exposé of the Donation was not intended by Valla to have the devastating force that Protestants attributed to it. He only demonstrated in a careful, scholarly way what others had long suspected. Using the most rudimentary textual analysis and histori-

Pico della Mirandola States the Renaissance Image of Man

One of the most eloquent descriptions of the Renaissance image of man comes from the Italian Humanist Pico della Mirandola (1463–1494). In his famed *Oration on the Dignity of Man* (*ca.* 1486) Pico describes man as free to become whatever he chooses.

THE *best of artisans* [*God*] *ordained that that creature* (*man*) *to whom He had been able to give nothing proper to himself should have joint possession of whatever had been peculiar to each of the different kinds of being. He therefore took man as a creature of indeterminate nature and, assigning him a place in the middle of the world, addressed him thus: "Neither a fixed abode nor a form that is thine alone nor any function peculiar to thyself have we given thee, Adam, to the end that according to thy longing and according to thy judgment thou mayest have and possess what abode, what form, and what functions thou thyself shalt desire. The nature of all other beings is limited and constrained within the bounds of laws prescribed by Us. Thou, constrained by no limits, in accordance with thine own free will, in whose hand We have placed thee, shall ordain for thyself the limits of thy nature. We have set thee at the world's center that thou mayest from thence more easily observe whatever is in the world. We have made thee neither of heaven nor of earth, neither mortal nor immortal, so that with freedom of choice and with honor, as though the maker and molder of thyself, thou mayest fashion thyself in whatever shape thou shalt prefer. Thou shalt have the power to degenerate into the lower forms of life, which are brutish. Thou shalt have the power, out of thy soul's judgment, to be reborn into the higher forms, which are divine." O supreme generosity of God the Father, O highest and most marvelous felicity of man! To him it is granted to have whatever he chooses, to be whatever he wills.*

From Giovanni Pico della Mirandola, *Oration on the Dignity of Man*, in *The Renaissance Philosophy of Man*, ed. by E. Cassirer et al. (Chicago: Phoenix Books, 1961), pp. 224–225.

cal logic, Valla proved that the document was filled with such anachronistic terms as "fief" and made references that were meaningless in the fourth century. In the same dispassionate way Valla also pointed out errors in the Latin Vulgate, still the authorized version of the Bible for the Roman Catholic Church.

Such discoveries did not make Valla any less Catholic, nor did they prevent his faithful fulfillment of the office of Apostolic Secretary in Rome under Pope Nicholas V. Nonetheless, historical criticism of this type served those less loyal to the medieval church, and it was no accident that young Humanists formed the first identifiable group of Martin Luther's supporters.

CIVIC HUMANISM. Italian Humanists were exponents of applied knowledge; their basic criticism of traditional education was that much of its learning was useless. Education, they believed, should promote individual virtue and public service. This ideal inspired what has been called *civic Humanism,* by which is meant examples of Humanist leadership of the political and cultural life, the most striking instance of which was the city of Florence. There three Humanists served as chancellors: Colluccio Salutati (1331–1406), Leonardo Bruni (*ca.* 1370–1444), and Poggio Bracciolini (1380–1459). Each used his rhetorical skills to rally the Florentines against the aggression of Naples and Milan. Bruni and Poggio also wrote adulatory histories of the city. Another accomplished Humanist scholar, Leon Battista Alberti (1402–1472), was a noted architect and builder in the city.

On the other hand, many Humanists became clubbish and snobbish, an intellectual elite concerned only with pursuing narrow, antiquarian interests and writing pure, classical Latin in the quiet of their studies. It was in reaction against this elitist trend that the Humanist historians Niccolò Machiavelli and Francesco Guicciardini adopted the vernacular and made contemporary history their primary source and subject matter.

Renaissance Art

In Renaissance Italy, as in Reformation Europe, the values and interests of the laity were no longer subordinated to those of the clergy. In education, culture, and religion the laity assumed a leading role and established models for the clergy to imitate. This was a development due in part to the breakdown of the church and its international bureaucracy during the great crises of the late Middle Ages. But it was also encouraged by the rise of national sentiment, the creation of competant national

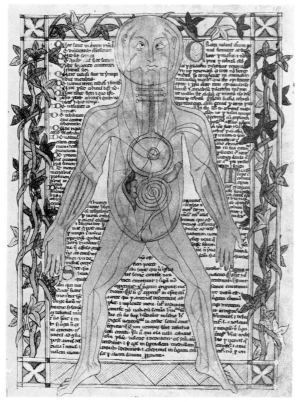

A

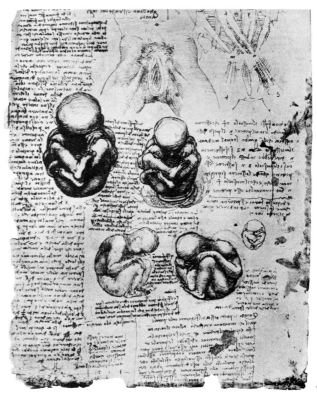

C

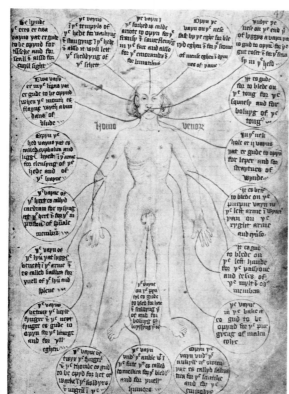

B

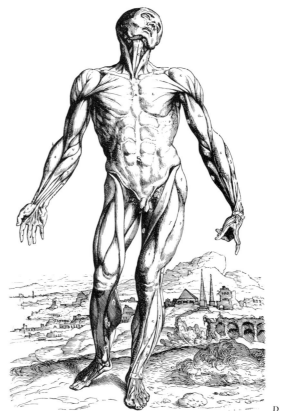

D

OPPOSITE: The developing knowledge of human anatomy and physiology.

A: Medieval conception of the human body, from a manuscript of about 1292, depicting the venous system and what purport to be a few internal organs. Since post-mortems were forbidden, medieval renderings of the human body were based on a combination of speculation and animal dissection. [The Bodleian Library, Oxford.]

B: A chart showing the points of blood-letting, long an accepted medical practice. From the *Guidebook of the Barber Surgeons of York* (fifteenth century), now in the British Museum. [Egerton MS. 2572, f. 50. Reproduced by permission of the British Library Board.]

C: Leonardo da Vinci's drawings of the human fetus. Renaissance artists and scientists, in contrast to medieval artists, began to base their portrayal of the human body on the actual study of it. [Bettmann Archive.]

D: A woodcut illustration by John of Carcar from *De Humanis corporis fabrica* (*Structure of the Human body*) (Basel, 1543), by the great Flemish anatomist, Andreas Vesalius (1514–1564), the foundation work of modern knowledge of human anatomy. [Bettmann Archive.]

(See also Rembrandt's The Anatomy Lesson of Dr. Nicolaas Tulp in the color album.)

The Stigmatization of St. Francis (early fourteenth century) by Giotto.

In a vision on Mt. Alverna, St. Francis is said to have received the wounds of Christ (the stigmata) in his own body and to have borne them for almost two years before his death in 1226. The small lower panels show Francis saving the church, receiving with his followers the Franciscans' charter from the pope, and—characteristically—preaching to the birds. [Musée du Louvre, Paris. Cliché des Musées Nationaux.]

(See also Giotto's painting of the death of St. Francis in the color album.)

bureaucracies, and the rapid growth of lay education during the fourteenth and fifteenth centuries. Medieval Christian values were adjusting to a more this-worldly spirit. One of the most read vernacular books of the high Renaissance was Baldasar Castiglione's *Book of the Courtier,* written between 1508 and 1528 and intended as a treatise on individual self-improvement and good manners at court. Men and women began again to appreciate and even glorify the secular world, education, and purely human things as ends in themselves.

This new perspective on life is very prominent in the painting and sculpture of the high Renaissance. Whereas Byzantine and Gothic art had been religious and idealized in the extreme, Renaissance art, especially in the fifteenth century, achieved the highest realism. The direction was signaled by Giotto (1266–1336), who is considered the father of Renaissance painting. Inspired by Saint Francis of Assisi, whose love of nature Giotto shared, Giotto painted a more natural world than his Byzantine and Gothic predecessors. Though still filled with religious seriousness, his work was no longer an abstract and unnatural depiction of the world.

Renaissance artists were equipped with new technical skills developed during the fifteenth century. In addition to the availability of oil paints, the techniques of using shading to enhance realism (*chiaroscuro*) and adjusting the size of figures so as to give the viewer a feeling of continuity with the painting (linear perspective) were perfected. Compared with their flat Byzantine and

LEFT: The expulsion of Adam and Eve from Paradise, fresco by Masaccio in the Chiesa del Carmine in Florence. [Alinari/SCALA.]
(Another contemporary representation of the expulsion by Pol de Limbourg and his brothers is in the color album and an earlier one is on page 274.)

OPPOSITE: Equestrian statue of Gattemelata (about 1440) by Donatello, in Padua, Italy, a work that began the Renaissance revival of such statues. [SCALA/Editorial Photocolor Archives.]

BELOW: A possible self-portrait by Leonardo da Vinci. [Alinari/SCALA.]

Gothic counterparts, Renaissance paintings were filled with energy and life and stood out from the canvas in three dimensions.

Masaccio (1401–1428) carried Giotto's naturalism to a new maturity. His painting was almost a direct slice of life. What Masaccio was to painting, Donatello (1386–1466) was to sculpture. His famous equestrian statue of the Venetian *condottiere* Gattamelata seems to pulsate with life. The realism of Masaccio and Donatello was the point of departure for the greatest masters of the high Renaissance: Leonardo da Vinci (1452–1519), Raphael (1483–1520), and Michelangelo Buonarroti (1475–1564).

LEONARDO DA VINCI. More than any other person in the period Leonardo exhibits the Renaissance ideal of the universal man, one who is not only a jack-of-all-

The Late Middle Ages and the Renaissance: Decline and Renewal (1300–1527)

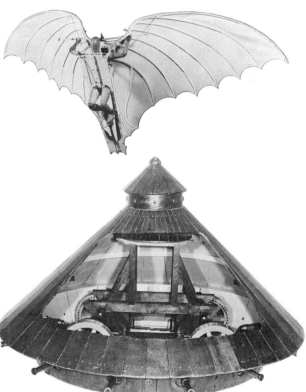

LEFT AND BELOW: Models of some of Leonardo da Vinci's military inventions, which were creative but sometimes beyond the capacity of late fifteenth century technology. [International Business Machines.]

LEFT: Attempt at a flying machine based on the principle of flight by birdlike flapping of flexible wings. The aviator worked the wings by pulleys connected with stirrups moved by his feet.

LEFT BELOW: An armored tank, equipped with breech-loading cannons and maneuverable from the inside.

BELOW: A triple-tier machine gun, with eleven barrels in each tier. While one is being fired, the tier just fired is cooling, and the third one is being loaded.

The Renaissance in Italy to 1527 **347**

ABOVE: The School of Athens, fresco by Raphael in the Vatican in Rome, painted *ca.* 1510–1511. The symmetry and organic unity of the painting, as well as its theme of antiquity, make it one of the most telling examples of Renaissance classicism. [Bettmann Archive.]

RIGHT: The Sistine Madonna, by Raphael, painted about 1521. Note how the haunting, sensuous poetry of this painting is interrupted by the admiring angels. It is now in Dresden, East Germany. [Alinari/SCALA.]

(A portrait by Raphael will also be found in the color album.)

trades but also a true master of many. One of the greatest painters of all time, Leonardo was also a military engineer for Ludovico il Moro in Milan, Cesare Borgia in Romagna, and the French king Francis I, who became the owner of Leonardo's famous portrait of the Mona Lisa. Leonardo advocated scientific experimentation, dissected corpses to learn anatomy, and was an accomplished, self-taught botanist. His inventive mind foresaw such modern machines as airplanes and submarines.

RAPHAEL. Raphael, an unusually sensitive man, was apparently loved by contemporaries as much for his person as for his work. He is famous for his tender madonnas, the best known of which graces the monastery of San Sisto in Piacenza. Art historians praise his fresco, *The School of Athens,* an involved portrayal of the great mas-

ABOVE: Moses, by Michelangelo. This statue was planned as part of the tomb of Pope Julius II (1503–1513) but is now in the church of S. Pietro in Vincoli, Rome. [Bettmann Archive.]

LEFT: David, by Michelangelo. One of the most famous—and popular—of all the world's sculptures, it was made in the period 1501–1504 and now stands in the Galleria dell' Accademia in Florence. [Alinari/SCALA.]

ters of Western philosophy, as one of the most perfect examples of Renaissance artistic theory and technique.

MICHELANGELO. The melancholy genius Michelangelo also excelled in a variety of arts and crafts. His eighteen-foot David, which long stood majestically in the great square of Florence, is a perfect example of Renais-

[Text continued on page 353]

[*The legends for this group are on page 352.*]

The Late Middle Ages and the Renaissance: Decline and Renewal (1300–1527)

The Renaissance in Italy to 1527 351

The Baptism of Christ, by El Greco (ca. 1541–1614). Elongated figures and somber religious mood mark his work. [Museo del Prado, Madrid.]
(Another El Greco is in the color album.)

The Crucifixion of Christ, the center panel of the Isenheim Altar by Mathis Grünewald (*ca.* 1470–1528). Another example of Renaissance realism, it depicts Christ's tortured body covered with wounds and sores, visually like those seen by Grünewald in a hospital for syphilitics. [Musée d'Unterlinden, Colmar, France. Fellmann.]

sance classicism. Four different popes commissioned works by Michelangelo, the most famous of which are the frescoes for the Sistine chapel, painted during the pontificate of Pope Julius II (1503–1513). They originally covered 10,000 square feet and involved 343 figures, over half of which exceeded ten feet in height. This labor of love and piety, painted while Michelangelo was lying on his back or stooping, took four years to complete and left Michelangelo partially crippled.

His later works are more complex and suggest deep personal changes within the artist himself. They mark, artistically and philosophically, the passing of high Renaissance painting and the advent of a new, experimental style known as *Mannerism*. A reaction against the simplicity and symmetry of high Renaissance art, mannerism made room for the strange and even abnormal and gave freer reign to the subjectivity of the artist. Tintoretto (d. 1594) and especially El Greco (d. 1614) became its supreme representatives. Mannerism also found expression in literature and music.

Italy's Political Decline: The French Invasions (1494-1527)

THE TREATY OF LODI. As a nation of autonomous city-states, Italy's peace and safety from foreign invasion, especially from invasion by the Turks, had always depended upon internal cooperation. Such had been maintained during the fifteenth century, thanks to a carefully constructed political alliance known as the Treaty of Lodi (1454-1455). The terms of the treaty brought Milan and Naples, long traditional enemies, into alliance with Florence. These three stood together for decades against Venice, which was frequently joined by the Papal States—an internal balance of power that also made possible a unified front against external enemies.

Around 1490, following the rise to power of the Milanese despot Ludovico il Moro, hostilities between Milan and Naples were rekindled. The peace made possible by the Treaty of Lodi ended in 1494 when Naples, supported by Florence and the Borgia Pope Alexander VI (1492-1503), prepared to attack Milan. Ludovico made what proved to be a fatal response to these new political alignments: he appealed for aid to the French. French kings had ruled Naples from 1266 to 1435, before they were driven out by Duke Alfonso of Sicily. Breaking a wise Italian rule, Ludovico invited the French to reenter Italy and revive their dynastic claim to Naples. In his haste to check his rival, Naples, Ludovico did not consider sufficiently that France also had dynastic claims to Milan, nor did he foresee how insatiable the French appetite for Italian territory would become once the Alps were crossed.

CHARLES VIII'S MARCH THROUGH ITALY. The French king, Louis XI, had resisted the temptation to invade Italy, while nonetheless keeping French dynastic claims in Italy alive. His successor, Charles VIII (1483-1498), an eager youth in his twenties, responded to Ludovico's siren call with lightning speed. Within five months he had crossed the Alps (August 1495) and raced as conqueror through Florence and the Papal States into Naples. As Charles approached Florence, The Florentine ruler, Piero de' Medici, who had allied with Naples against Milan, tried to placate the French king by handing over Pisa and other Florentine possessions. Such appeasement only brought about Piero's forced exile by a population that was revolutionized at this time by the radical preacher Girolamo Savonarola (1452-1498). Savonarola convinced a majority of the fearful Florentines that the French king's advent was a long-delayed and fully justified divine vengeance on their immorality.

Charles entered Florence without resistance and, thanks to Savonarola's flattery and the payment of a large ransom, spared the city a threatened destruction. Savonarola continued to rule Florence for four years after Charles's departure. The Florentines proved, however, not to be the stuff theocracies are made of. Savonarola's puritanism and antipapal policies made it impossible for him to survive indefinitely. This was especially true after the Italian cities reunited and the ouster of the French invader, whom Savonarola had praised as a godsend, became national policy. Savonarola was imprisoned and executed in May 1498.

Charles's lightning march through Italy also struck terror in non-Italian hearts. Ferdinand of Aragon, whose native land and self-interests as king of Sicily were now made vulnerable to a French–Italian axis, took the initiative to form a counteralliance. This was the League of Venice, formed in March 1495, with Venice, the Papal States, and the Emperor Maximilian I joining Ferdinand against the French. The stage was here set for a conflict between France and Spain that would not end until 1559.

Ludovico il Moro meanwhile recognized that he had sown the wind. He had desired a French invasion only so long as it weakened his enemies. As he now saw Milan threatened by the whirlwind of events that he had created, he joined the League of Venice. The alliance proved sufficiently strong to send Charles into retreat by May, and he remained thereafter on the defensive until his death in April 1498.

POPE ALEXANDER VI AND THE BORGIA FAMILY. The French returned to Italy under Charles's successor Louis XII (1498–1515), this time assisted by a new Italian ally, Pope Alexander VI (1492–1503). Alexander, whom some consider the most corrupt pope ever to have sat on the papal throne, openly promoted the political careers of the children he had before he became pope, Cesare and Lucrezia, as he placed the efforts of the Borgia family to secure a political base in Romagna in tandem with papal policy there.

In Romagna several principalities had fallen away from the church during the Avignon papacy, and Venice, the pope's ally within the League of Venice, continued to contest the Papal States for their loyalty. Seeing that a French alliance could give him the opportunity to reestablish control over the region, Alexander took steps to secure French favor. He annulled Louis XII's marriage to Charles VIII's sister so that Louis could marry Charles's widow, Anne of Brittany—a popular move designed to keep Brittany French. The pope also bestowed a cardinal's hat on the archbishop of Rouen, Louis's favorite cleric. But most importantly, Alexander agreed to abandon the League of Venice, a withdrawal of support that made the league too weak to resist a French reconquest of Milan. In exchange, Cesare Borgia received the sister of the king of Navarre, Charlotte d'Albret, in marriage, a union that greatly enhanced Borgia military strength. Cesare also received land grants from Louis XII and the promise of French military aid in Romagna.

All in all it was a scandalous tradeoff, but one that made it possible for the French king and the pope to realize their ambitions within Italy. Louis successfully invaded Milan in August 1499. Ludovico il Moro, who had originally opened the Pandora's box of French invasion, spent his last years languishing in a French prison. In 1500 Louis and Ferdinand of Aragon divided Naples between them, while the pope and Cesare Borgia conquered the cities of Romagna without opposition. Alexander awarded his victorious son the title "duke of Romagna."

POPE JULIUS II. All dynasties end and that of the Borgias was no exception. Cardinal Giulano della Rovere, a strong opponent of the Borgia family, became Pope Julius II (1503–1513). He suppressed the Borgias and placed their newly conquered lands in Romagna under papal jurisdiction. Julius came to be known as the "warrior pope" because he brought the Renaissance papacy to a peak of military prowess and diplomatic intrigue. Shocked as were other contemporaries by his throughly secular papacy, the Humanist Erasmus (1466?–1536) authored a popular anonymous satire entitled *Julius Excluded from Heaven.* This humorous account purported to describe the pope's unsuccessful efforts to convince Saint Peter that he was worthy of admission to heaven.

Assisted by his powerful allies, Pope Julius succeeded in driving the Venetians out of Romagna in 1509, thereby ending Venetian claims in the region and fully securing the Papal States. Having realized this long-sought papal goal, Julius turned to the second major undertaking of his pontificate: ridding Italy of his ally, the French invader. Julius, Ferdinand of Aragon, and Venice formed a second Holy League in October 1511, and within a short period they were joined by the Emperor Maximilian I and the Swiss. By 1512 the League had the French in full retreat, and they were soundly defeated by the Swiss in 1513 at Novara.

The French were nothing if not persistent. They invaded Italy still a third time under Louis's successor, Francis I (1515–1547). French armies massacred Swiss soldiers of the Holy League at Marignano in September 1515, revenging the earlier defeat at Novara. The victory won from the pope the Concordat of Bologna in August 1516, an agreement that gave the French king control over the French clergy in exchange for French recognition of the pope's superiority over church councils and his right to collect annates in France. This was an important compromise that helped keep France Catholic after the outbreak of the Protestant Reformation. But the new French entry into Italy also led to the first of five major wars with Spain in the first half of the sixteenth cen-

A bust of Niccolò Machiavelli (1469–1527), who advised Renaissance princes to practice artful deception if necessary and to inspire fear in their subjects if they wished to be successful. [Bettmann Archive.]

tury—the Hapsburg—Valois wars—none of which France won.

NICCOLÒ MACHIAVELLI. The period of foreign invasions made a shambles of Italy. The same period that saw Italy's cultural peak in the work of Leonardo, Raphael, and Michelangelo also witnessed her political tragedy. One who watched as French, Spanish, and German armies wreaked havoc upon his country was Niccolò Machiavelli (1469–1527). The more he saw, the more convinced he became that Italian political unity and independence were ends that justified any means. A Humanist and a careful student of ancient Rome, Machiavelli was impressed by the deliberate and heroic acts of ancient Roman rulers, what Renaissance people called *Virtù*. Stories of the unbounded patriotism and self-sacrifice of the old Roman citizenry were his favorites, and he lamented the absence of such traits among his countrymen. The juxtaposition of what Machiavelli believed men had been in ancient Rome with his experience of their contemporary failure made him the famous cynic we know in the popular epithet *Machiavellian*. Only an unscrupulous strongman, he concluded, could impose order on so divided and selfish a people; the moral revival of the Italians required an unprincipled dictator.

Some believe that Machiavelli wrote *The Prince* in 1513 as a cynical satire on the way rulers actually did behave and not as a serious recommendation of unprincipled despotic rule. They see his advocacy of tyranny as a contradiction of both his earlier works and his own strong family tradition of republican service. But Machiavelli seems to have been in earnest when he advised rulers to discover the advantages of fraud and brutality. He apparently hoped to see a strong ruler emerge from the Medici family, which had captured the papacy in 1513 with the pontificate of Leo X (1513–1521). At the same time the Medici family retained control over the powerful territorial state of Florence—a situation similar to that of Machiavelli's hero Cesare Borgia and his father Pope Alexander VI, who had earlier brought factious Romagna to heel by placing secular family goals and religious policy in tandem. *The Prince* was pointedly dedicated to Lorenzo de' Medici, duke of Urbino and grandson of Lorenzo the Magnificent.

Whatever Machiavelli's hopes may have been, the Medicis were not destined to be Italy's deliverers. The second Medici pope, Clement VII (1523–1534), watched helplessly as Rome was sacked by the army of Emperor Charles V in 1527, also the year of Machiavelli's death.

For all its spectacular cultural achievements it was not the Italian Renaissance but the Protestant Reformation in northern Europe, beginning in Germany in 1517 and

ABOVE: The town hall of Antwerp, Belgium, built between 1561 and 1565. Here, Gothic has given way to Renaissance styling, with high belfries and elaborate carvings. On the right are guild halls. [Belgian National Tourist Office, New York.]

BELOW: Children's Games, by Pieter Brueghel, painted in 1560. How many games can you find? [Kunsthistorisches Museum, Vienna.]

ABOVE: The Legend of Saint Eligius and Godeberta, by the Flemish painter Petrus Christus (*ca.* 1420–1473), painted 1449. Eligius, the patron saint of goldsmiths, sells a ring to a bridal couple. [Metropolitan Museum of Art, New York; Robert Lehman Collection, 1975.]

ABOVE: A Banker and His Wife, by Quentin Massys (*ca.* 1466–1530), painted 1514. While the wife thumbs an illustrated Bible, her husband counts his money. Note also the pearls on the table and the neighbors in conversation outside the door. [Musée du Louvre, Paris. Cliché des Musées Nationaux.]

SCENES OF FIFTEENTH- AND SIXTEENTH-CENTURY URBAN LIFE

BELOW: The Butcher's Stall, by Pieter Aertsen (*ca.* 1508–*ca.* 1575), painted 1551. Everything from fish to fowl could be purchased from the butcher. [Universitetets Konstmuseum, Uppsala, Sweden.]

BELOW: The Weightmaster, by the German sculptor Adam Krafft, made 1497. The weightmaster establishes a just price, while the buyer, on the right, digs into his purse to pay. [Bildarchiv Foto Marburg.]

Members of a Gun Club, by Kirck Barends, painted
1562. The note held by the man in the far left
corner reads, "In wine, truth"—an informal touch
in this very sober group. Also note the member
holding an arrow. [Stedelijk Museum, Amsterdam.]

Loose Company, by Jan Sanders von Hemessen. Here
a man is about to be robbed in the parlor of a bawdy
house, another in the background receives services,
and a third is enticed to enter. [Staatliche Kunst-
halle, Karlsruhe, West Germany.]

extending throughout Europe by the end of the century,
that changed contemporary history in the most fundamental ways. The religious revolution that gripped Europe in the sixteenth century was to embrace and preserve many Renaissance values, divide Christendom
permanently, and reshape the social and political structures of Europe in lasting ways.

SUGGESTED READINGS

MARGARET ASTON, *The Fifteenth Century: The Prospect of
Europe* (1968). Crisp social history, with pictures.

HANS BARON, *The Crisis of the Early Italian Renaissance*,
Vols. 1 and 2 (1966). A major work, setting forth the civic
dimension of Italian humanism.

BERNARD BERENSON, *Italian Painters of the Renaissance*
(1901).

JACOB BURCKHARDT, *The Civilization of the Renaissance in
Italy* (1867). The old classic that still has as many defenders
as detractors.

WALLACE K. FERGUSON, *The Renaissance* (1940). A brief,
stimulating summary of the Renaissance in both Italy and
northern Europe.

WALLACE K. FERGUSON, *Europe in Transition 1300–1520*
(1962). A major survey that deals with the transition from
medieval to Renaissance society.

MYRON GILMORE, *The World of Humanism 1453–1517*
(1952). A comprehensive survey, especially strong in intellectual and cultural history.

J. R. HALE, *Renaissance Europe: The Individual and Society,
1480–1520* (1971). Many-sided treatment of social history.

DENYS HAY, *Europe in the Fourteenth and Fifteenth Centuries*
(1966). Many-sided treatment of political history.

JOHAN HUIZINGA, *The Waning of the Middle Ages: A
Study of the Forms of Life, Thought, and Art in France and
the Netherlands in the Dawn of the Renaissance* (1924). A
classic study of "mentality" at the end of the Middle Ages.

PAUL O. KRISTELLER, *Renaissance Thought: The Classic,
Scholastic, and Humanist Strains* (1961). A master shows the
many sides of Renaissance thought.

ROBERT E. LERNER, *The Age of Adversity: The Fourteenth
Century* (1968). Brief, comprehensive survey.

HARRY A. MISKIMIN, *The Economy of Early Renaissance
Europe 1300–1460* (1969). Shows interaction of social,
political, and economic change.

HEIKO A. OBERMAN, *The Harvest of Medieval Theology*
(1963). A demanding synthesis and revision.

EDOUARD PERROY, *The Hundred Years War*, trans. by
W. B. Wells (1965). The most comprehensive one-volume
account.

YVES RENOVARD, *The Avignon Papacy 1305–1403*, trans.
by D. Bethell (1970). Standard narrative.

J. W. THOMPSON, *Economic and Social History of Europe in
the Later Middle Ages 1300–1530* (1958). A bread-and-
butter account.

BRIAN TIERNEY, *Foundations of the Conciliar Theory*
(1955). Important study showing origins of conciliar theory
in canon law.

BRIAN TIERNEY, *The Crisis of Church and State 1050–1300*
(1964). Part IV provides the major documents in the clash
between Boniface VIII and Philip the Fair.

WALTER ULLMANN, *Origins of the Great Schism* (1948). A
basic study by a controversial interpreter of medieval political thought.

CHARLES T. WOOD, *Philip the Fair and Boniface VIII*
(1967). Excerpts from the scholarly debate over the significance of this confrontation.

PHILIP ZIEGLER, *The Black Death* (1969). Highly readable
journalistic account.

14
The Age of Reformation: I

For Europe the sixteenth century was a period of unprecedented territorial expansion and ideological experimentation. Permanent colonies were established within the Americas, and the exploitation of the New World's human and seemingly endless mineral resources was begun. The American gold and silver imported into Europe spurred scientific invention and the modern weapons industry and touched off an inflationary spiral that produced a revolution in prices by the end of the century. The new bullion also created international traffic in African slaves, who were needed to work the mines and the plantations of the New World as American natives were killed in great numbers by forced labor and European diseases. This period further saw social engineering and political planning on a large scale as nations were forced as never before to develop long-range economic policies, a practice that came to be known as *mercantilism*.

It was during the Age of Reformation that the first wide-scale use of the printing press occurred, assisted by the development of a process of cheap paper manufacture and publishers greedy to exploit a fascinating new technology. Printing with movable type, invented by Johannes Gutenberg (d. 1468) in the mid-fifteenth century in Mainz, brought vernacular literacy and primary education, as well as revolutionary new ideas, to Europe's growing cities and towns. This period also saw the beginning of the vernacular education of women in large numbers, as Protestants set out to teach every girl how to read the Bible in her native tongue—in the hope that women would thereby become model housewives.

Luther and the Wittenberg reformers with Elector John Frederick of Saxony (1532–1547), painted about 1543 by Lucas Cranach the Younger (1515–1586). Luther is on the far left, Philip Melanchthon in the front row on the far right. [Toledo Museum of Art, Toledo, Ohio; gift of Edward Drummond Libbey.]

It is especially in terms of changes in religious thought, practice, and institutions that we think of the Age of Reformation. The Protestant movement of the sixteenth century has with justification been described as an early Western enlightenment. It was a major and lasting criticism of what were believed to be psychologically and financially burdensome "superstitions." In a relatively short span of time hundreds of thousands of people set aside the beliefs of centuries, replacing them with a more simplified religious practice. The result was a revolution in ideas and institutions without parallel until the modern American, French, and Russian revolutions.

Voyages of Discovery and Changes in Society

Spices, Gold, and Silver

On the eve of the Reformation the geographical as well as the intellectual horizons of Western people were broadening. The fifteenth century saw the beginning of western Europe's global expansion and the transference of commercial supremacy from the Mediterranean and the Baltic to the Atlantic seaboard. Mercenary motives, reinforced by traditional missionary ideals, inspired Prince Henry the Navigator (1394–1460) to sponsor Portuguese exploration of the African coast. His main object was the gold trade, which for centuries had been an Arab monopoly. By the last decades of the fifteenth century, gold from Guinea was entering Europe by way of Portuguese ships calling at the port cities of Lisbon and Antwerp, rather than by Arab land routes. Antwerp became the financial center of Europe, a commercial crossroads where the enterprise and derring-do of the Portuguese and the Spanish met the capital funds of the German banking houses of Fugger and Welser.

The rush for gold quickly expanded into a rush for the spice markets of India. In the fifteenth century the diet of most Europeans was a dull combination of bread and gruel, cabbage, turnips, peas, lentils, and onions, together

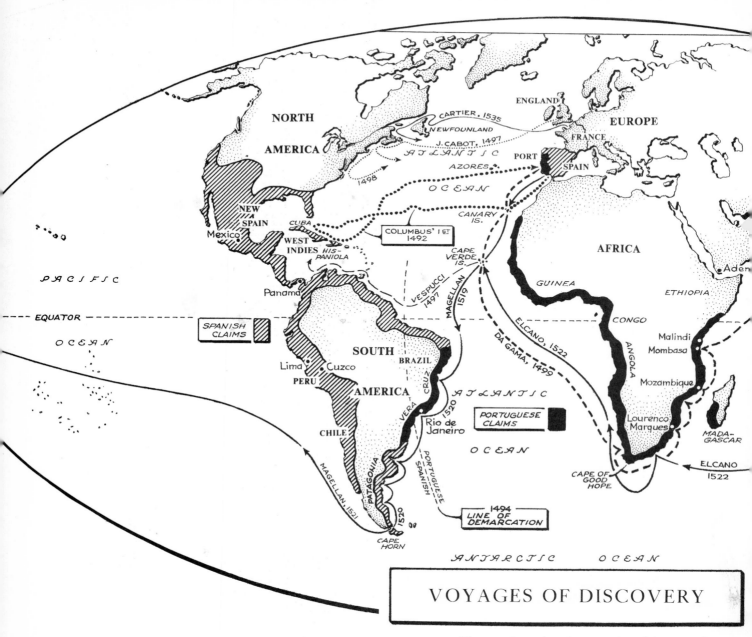

VOYAGES OF DISCOVERY

The map dramatizes the expansion of the area of European interest in the fifteenth and sixteenth centuries. Not until today's "space age" has a comparable widening of horizons been possible.

with what meat became available during seasonal periods of slaughter. Spices, especially pepper and cloves, were in great demand both to preserve and to enhance the taste of food. Bartholomew Dias (d. 1500) opened the Portuguese Empire in the East when he rounded the Cape of Good Hope at the tip of Africa in 1487. A decade later, in 1498, Vasco da Gama (d. 1524) reached the coast of India. In subsequent years the Portuguese dominated the Malabar Coast with established colonies in Goa and Calicut, successfully challenging the Arabs and the Venetians for control of the European spice trade.

While the Portuguese concentrated on the Indian Ocean, the Spanish set sail across the Atlantic. They did so in the hope of establishing a shorter route to the rich spice markets of the East Indies. Rather than beating the Portuguese at their own game, however, Christopher Columbus (1451–1506) discovered the Americas instead.

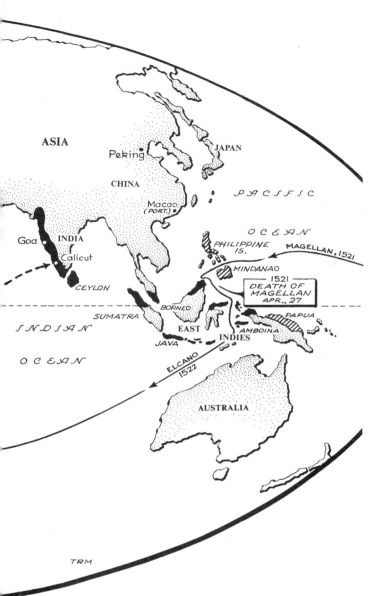

ASIA
Peking
JAPAN
CHINA
Macao (PORT.)
PACIFIC
OCEAN
Goa
INDIA
Calicut
PHILIPPINE IS.
MAGELLAN, 1521
CEYLON
MINDANAO
1521 DEATH OF MAGELLAN APR., 27
BORNEO
SUMATRA
INDIAN
EAST INDIES
JAVA
AMBOINA
PAPUA
OCEAN
ELCANO 1522
AUSTRALIA
TRM

The Monument to Discoveries, a sculpture in the harbor of Lisbon, Portugal, on the site from which Portuguese explorers set sail for over 400 years. Prince Henry the Navigator (1394–1460) stands at the helm. [Portuguese National Tourist Office, New York. Heyward Associates, Inc.]

Model of the Portuguese caravel, a light, fast ship used extensively in trade and exploration. [National Maritime Museum, London.]

Amerigo Vespucci (1451–1512) and Ferdinand Magellan (1480–1521) demonstrated that these new lands were not the outermost territory of the Far East, as Columbus died believing, but an entirely new continent that opened upon the still greater Pacific Ocean. Magellan died in the Philippines.

The discovery of gold and silver in vast quantities more than compensated for the disappointment of failing to find a shorter route to the Indies. Still greater mines were opened in the 1520s and the 1530s when Hernando Cortes (1485–1547) conquered the Aztecs of Mexico

Voyages of Discovery and Changes in Society 363

Detail of a portrait of Christopher Columbus by Sebastiano del Piombo (1485–1547). It shows Columbus, who died in 1506, late in life. [Metropolitan Museum of Art, New York; gift of J. Pierpont Morgan, 1900.]

BELOW: A quadrant (seventeenth century) and early compass (sixteenth century) of the types that made possible the long voyages of discovery. [National Maritime Museum, London.]

OPPOSITE: The world as shown on Martin Behaim's globe of 1492, the first such representation that we know of, clearly reflecting awareness that the earth was round and not flat. This two-dimensional adaptation of the globe's surface was made by J. G. Doppelmayer in the eighteenth century. Note the absence of the North and South American continents—a gap on the map leaving Columbus free to assume that he could go west from Spain (in the upper left) to reach the Indies. The original of Behaim's "earth-apple," as he called his globe, is in a museum in Nuremberg, West Germany.

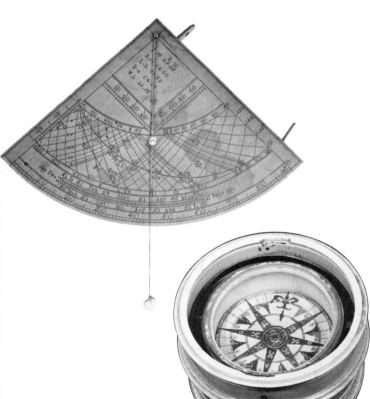

and Francisco Pizarro (*ca.* 1470–1541) conquered the Incas of Peru, enslaving the native Indian populations and forcing them to work the new mines. As the forced labor and the new European diseases against which American natives had no immunity decimated their numbers, a boom in still another item of trade was created: African slaves. In the sixteenth century they came in great numbers to replace faltering native populations in the mines and on the sugar cane plantations of the New World.

Rise in Prices and the Development of Capitalism

The influx of spices and precious metals into Europe was not an unmixed blessing. It contributed to a steady rise in prices during the sixteenth century. The new supply of bullion from the Americas joined with enlarged European production to increase greatly the amount of coinage in circulation, and this increase in turn fed inflation. Fortunately the increase in prices was spread over a long period of time and was not sudden. Prices doubled in Spain by mid-century, quadrupled by 1600. In Luther's Wittenberg, however, the cost of basic food and clothing increased almost 100 per cent between 1519 and 1540. Generally wages and rents remained well behind the rise in prices.

The new wealth enabled governments and private

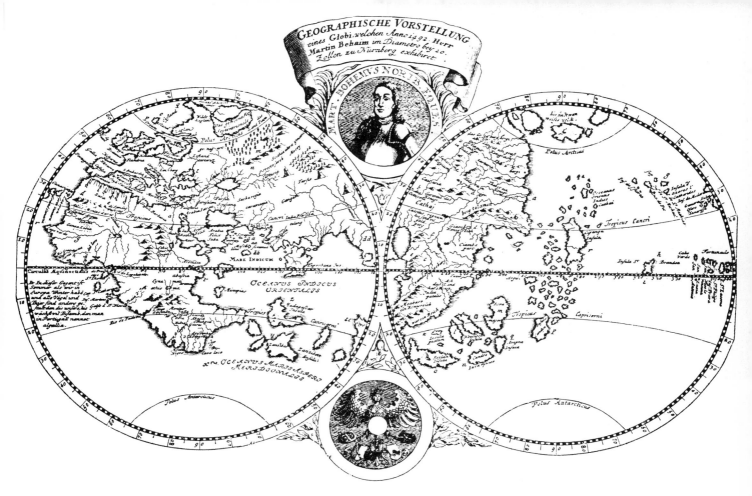

entrepreneurs to sponsor basic research and expansion in the printing, shipping, mining, textile, and weapons industries—the growth industries of the Age of Reformation. There is also evidence of mercantilism or large-scale government planning in such ventures as the French silk industry and the Hapsburg–Fugger development of mines in Austria and Hungary. As early as the thirteenth and fourteenth centuries there had been great accumulations of capital in the Italian cities—one may cite the Florentine banking houses of Bardi and Peruzzi—and the development of capitalist institutions and practices. The latter entailed the following: a division between those who owned the means of production and those who operated them; the creation of monopolies; the charging of interest on loans; actual, if not legal, usury; and the practice of the virtues of thrift, industry, and orderly planning.

The late fifteenth and sixteenth centuries saw the maturation of such capitalism together with its peculiar social problems. The new wealth and industrial expansion raised the expectations of the poor and the ambitious and heightened the reactionary tendencies within the established and wealthy classes. There was great aggravation

of the traditional social divisions between the clergy and the laity, the higher and the lower clergy, the urban patriciate and the guilds, masters and journeymen, and the landed nobility and the agrarian peasantry.

The far-flung transactions created by the new commerce increased the demand for lawyers and bankers. The Medici of Florence grew very rich as bankers of the pope, as did the Fuggers of Augsburg as bankers of Hapsburg rulers. The Fuggers lent Charles I of Spain over 500,000 florins to buy his election as Holy Roman Emperor in 1519, and they later boasted that they had created the emperor. But those who paid out their money also took their chances. Both the Fuggers and the Medicis were later bankrupted by popes and kings who defaulted on their heavy debts.

Northern Renaissance

In addition to the favorable sentiment of popular piety and the social agitation created by the influx of wealth from the New World, a further factor preparing the way for the Protestant Reformation was the work of the northern Humanists. Northern Humanist culture was

Desiderius Erasmus, the prince of the northern humanists, as painted about 1523 by Hans Holbein the Younger (*ca.* 1497–1543). Erasmus influenced all the reform movements of the sixteenth century and was popularly said to have "laid the egg that Luther hatched." [Bettmann Archive.]

largely imported from the south by students who had studied in Italy and by such intermediaries as the Brothers of the Common Life. Northern Humanists tended to be both more socially diversified and religious than their Italian counterparts. They put their scholarship in the service of religious reform, writing for lay audiences as well as for a narrow intelligentsia.

Erasmus

The Christian Humanism of Desiderius Erasmus (1466–1536) is a good example of much of northern Humanism. His ideal was a simple, ethical piety in imitation of Jesus—what he summarized as the *"philosophia Christi."* Erasmus set this ideal in starkest contrast to what he believed to be the abstract, ceremonial, and factious religion of the later Middle Ages. He wrote satirical and didactic tracts in support of basic religious reforms and made critical editions of the New Testament and the Church Fathers—scholarly tools that became weapons against the old church in the hands of Protestant reformers.

Luder, Agricola, Celtis, Von Hutten

Peter Luder (d. 1474) and Rudolf Agricola (1444–1485) brought Italian learning to Germany. Agricola, known as the father of German Humanism, spent ten years in Italy. Like later German Humanists, he aspired to outdo the Italians in classical learning, adding a nationalist motivation to German scholarship. Conrad Celtis (d. 1508), the first German poet laureate, was a strong exponent of romantic cultural nationalism, and an even stronger exponent was the intemperate knight Ulrich von Hutten (1488–1523). The life and work of Von Hutten especially illustrates the union of Humanism, German nationalism, and Luther's religious reform. A poet who attacked Scholasticism and bad Latin, Von Hutten was also a member of the fading landed nobility who aspired to a revival of ancient German virtue—he died in 1523 in a hopeless knights' revolt against the princes—and an advocate of religious reform who attacked indulgences

and published an edition of Valla's exposé of the Donation of Constantine.

THE REUCHLIN AFFAIR. The *cause célèbre* that brought Von Hutten onto the historical stage and unified German humanists was the Reuchlin affair. Johann Reuchlin (1455–1522) was Europe's foremost Christian authority on Hebrew and Jewish learning. He had written the first reliable Hebrew grammar by a Christian scholar and was personally attracted to Jewish mysticism. Around 1506 a converted Jew named Pfefferkorn, supported by the Dominican Order in Cologne (known as "the German Rome"), began a movement to suppress Jewish writings. Long an exponent of Jewish learning, Reuchlin came under attack by the fanatical Pfefferkorn. In the name of academic freedom and good scholarship, not for any pro-Jewish sentiment, many German Humanists rushed to Reuchlin's defense. The controversy, which lasted several years, produced one of the great satires of the period, the *Letters of Obscure Men* (1515), a hilarious and merciless satire of monks and Scholastics, particularly those in Cologne, written by Crotus Rubeanus and Ulrich von Hutten. When Luther came under attack after his famous ninety-five theses against indulgences in 1517, many German Humanists tended to see in his plight a repetition of the Scholastic attack on Reuchlin. Religious reform and academic freedom were again at stake. Although, following Erasmus's lead, many of these same men ceased to support Luther when the revolutionary direction of his theology became clear, German Humanists still formed the first identifiable group of Luther's supporters, and many young Humanists became Lutheran pastors.

Humanism in England

Humanists also promoted basic educational and religious reforms in England and France. English scholars and merchants and Italian prelates brought Italian learning to England. The Oxford lectures of William Grocyn (d. 1519) and Thomas Linacre (d. 1524) and the Cambridge lectures of the visiting Erasmus (1510–1513)

Thomas More by Hans Holbein the Younger, painted in 1527. The English statesman and author was beheaded by Henry VIII for his refusal to recognize the king's sovereignty over the English church. [The Frick Collection.]

marked the scholarly maturation of English Humanism. John Colet (1467–1519), after 1505 dean of St. Paul's Cathedral, was renowned for his sermons and commentaries on the New Testament and his patronage of Humanist studies for the young.

THOMAS MORE. Thomas More (1478–1535) was the best known of early English Humanists. His *Utopia* (1516), a criticism of contemporary society, still rivals the plays of Shakespeare as the most-read sixteenth-century English work. It was while visiting More that Erasmus wrote his most famous work, *The Praise of Folly*, an amusing exposé of human gullibility. A bureaucrat under Henry VII, More became one of Henry VIII's most trusted diplomats, succeeding Cardinal Wolsey as Lord Chancellor in 1529. More resigned that position in May 1532 because he could not in good conscience support the Act of Supremacy, which made Henry head of the English church—a refusal for which More paid with his head in July 1535.

Although More remained staunchly Catholic, Humanism in England, as in Germany, played an important role in preparing the way for the English Reformation. It was a circle of English Humanists under the direction of Henry VIII's minister Thomas Cromwell that translated and disseminated, to the king's advantage, such pertinent works as Marsilius of Padua's condemned *Defender of Peace*, a work that exalted the sovereignty of rulers over popes.

Humanism in France

It was through the French invasions of Italy that Italian learning penetrated France. Guillaume Budé (1468–1540), an accomplished Greek scholar, and Jacques Lefèvre d'Étaples (1454–1536) were the leaders of French Humanism. Lefèvre's two main works—the *Quincuplex Psalterium*, five Latin versions of the psalms arranged in parallel columns, and a translation and commentary on Saint Paul's Epistle to the Romans—not only exemplified the new critical scholarship but also influenced the theology of Martin Luther. The chief patrons

of French Humanism were Guillaume Briçonnet (1470–1533), after 1516 the bishop of Meaux, and Marguerite d'Angoulême (1492–1549), sister of Francis I and the future queen of Navarre, who made her own reputation as a writer. The future Protestant reformer John Calvin was a product of this native reform circle. Calvin was the first of three major vernacular writers with Humanist backgrounds who created the modern French language. The others were the physician François Rabelais (1494–1553), an ex-Franciscan and Benedictine monk whose *Gargantua* and *Pantagruel* satirized his age, and the skeptical essayist Michel de Montaigne (1533–1592), who ridiculed the authoritarian Scholastic mind.

Humanism in Spain

Whereas in Germany, England, and France Humanism prepared the way for Protestant reforms, in Spain it entered the service of the Catholic Church. Here the key figure was Francesco Ximenes de Cisneros (1436–1517), a confessor to Queen Isabella, and after 1508 Grand Inquisitor—a position from which he was able to enforce the strictest religious orthodoxy. Ximenes was a conduit for Humanist scholarship and learning. He founded the University of Alcalá in 1500, printed a Greek edition of the New Testament, and translated many religious tracts that aided clerical reform and control of lay religious life. His greatest achievement, taking fifteen years to complete, was the *Complutensian Polyglot Bible,* a six-volume work that placed the Hebrew, Greek, and Latin versions of the Bible in parallel columns. Such scholarly projects and internal church reforms were joined with the repressive measures of Ferdinand and Isabella to keep Spain strictly Catholic throughout the Age of Reformation.

Popular Piety and Heresy
Popular Religious Movements and Criticism of the Church

The Protestant Reformation could not have occurred without the monumental crises of the medieval church during the "exile" in Avignon, the Great Schism, the conciliar period, and the Renaissance papacy. But the late medieval church was a failing institution not only in the political sense of its internal division and the conflict between popes and kings and national assemblies. For increasing numbers the medieval church had ceased also to provide a viable religious piety. There was a crisis in the traditional teaching and spiritual practice of the church among many of its intellectuals and laity. Between the secular pretensions of the papacy and the dry teaching of Scholastic theologians, laymen and clerics alike began to seek a more heartfelt, idealistic, and—in the eyes of the pope—increasingly heretical religious piety. The late Middle Ages were marked by independent lay and clerical efforts to reform local religious practice and by widespread experimentation with new religious forms.

A variety of factors contributed to the growth of lay criticism of the church. In the cities the laity were far more knowledgeable about the world and those who controlled their lives. Laymen traveled—as soldiers, pilgrims, explorers, and traders. In the fifteenth century new postal systems and the printing press increased the information at their disposal. The fourteenth and fifteenth centuries also saw a boom in colleges and universities. The age of books and libraries raised literacy and heightened curiosity. Humanists and religious reformers taught laymen to use their new power and wealth to promote virtue, inculcating in them a sense of civic duty. Laymen were increasingly in a position to take the initiative in shaping the religious and cultural life of their communities.

Already in the thirteenth century lay piety had begun to build against the official church in such diverse movements as the Albigensians, the Waldensians, and the Beguines and the Beghards, each in its zeal susceptible to church criticism. The Albigensians embraced an unchristian dualism, which divided the world into spheres of demonic darkness and godly light. The Waldensians of southeastern France translated and disseminated portions of the New Testament, contrary to church prohibitions. The Beguines and the Beghards were accused of having claimed a more than human perfection. All these movements shared a common goal of religious simplicity in imitation of Jesus. Practically without exception the religious movements from the thirteenth century until the Protestant Reformation were inspired by an ideal of apostolic poverty in religion; all wanted a religion more like that of Jesus and the first disciples. The laity sought a more egalitarian church, one that gave the members as well as the head of the church a voice, and a more spiritual church, one that lived manifestly according to its New Testament model.

The papacy, fearing utopian ideals and divisive criticism, took a progressively harder stand against new religious movements and heterodox opinion and practice. By the early fourteenth century it had crushed the Albigensians with crusades, prohibited the biblical translations of the Waldensians, and condemned the Beguines and Beghards as "Free Spirit" heretics. The pontificate of Pope John XXII (1316–1334) became a high point of ecclesiastical censures and condemnations, as the pope enforced his version of orthodoxy throughout the church. Pope John condemned the Fraticelli, millenarian followers of Saint Francis of Assisi; William of Ockham and the General of the Franciscan Order, Michael of Cesena (d. 1342); all the writings of Marsilius of Padua and his collaborator John of Jandun (d. 1328); and the teaching of the Cologne mystical theologian Meister Eckhart (d. 1326). With the exception of Eckhart, all these thinkers took refuge in Munich with Louis IV of Bavaria, whose election as emperor had been contested by Pope John.

The pope had legitimate fears in suppressing these men. The poverty ideal of the Fraticelli seemed to demand the church's disendowment; Ockham's theology seemed to make the church and revelation questionable objects of faith; Marsilius's *Defender of Peace* seemed to reduce the church to purely sacramental functions; and Meister Eckhart seemed to identify the church's means of grace with special divine powers within each individual soul. Pope John and his successors much preferred the hierarchical world view of Saint Thomas Aquinas (d. 1274), which subordinated temporal to spiritual power and the laity to clerical authority. In 1309 the teaching of Aquinas became binding within the Dominican Order, and it has grown ever since in influence and authority within the Catholic Church. In 1879, after the Catholic Church's repudiation of Modernism, the theology of Aquinas became the guideline for all Catholics.

THE MODERN DEVOTION. The Franciscan and Dominican orders, founded in the early thirteenth century, did much to channel lay piety in orthodox directions. They regularized convents of Beguines and Beghards and rekindled lay respect for the church. One of the most constructive lay religious movements of the late Middle Ages—also from the church's point of view—was the Modern Devotion or the Brothers of the Common Life. The brothers fostered the religious life outside formal ecclesiastical offices and religious vows. Established by Gerard Groote (1340–1400) and centered at Zwolle and Deventer in the Netherlands, the brother and sister houses of the Modern Devotion spread rapidly throughout northern Europe. In these houses clerics and laymen came together to share a common life, stressing individual piety and practical religion. The laity were not expected to take special vows or to wear special religious dress, nor did they abandon their ordinary secular vocations. A strict-observance wing of the brothers did form in 1386 around the brother house of Windesheim, and they adopted the Augustinian Rule—but they were an exception and not the norm.

The brothers were very active in education. They worked as copyists, sponsored many religious and a few classical publications, built hospices for poor students, and conducted schools for the young, especially for boys preparing for the priesthood or a monastic vocation. As youths, Nicholas of Cusa, Johannes Reuchlin, and Desiderius Erasmus were among the prominent northern Humanists looked after by the brothers. The philosophy of the brothers was summarized in the most popular religious book of the period: Thomas à Kempis' (d. 1471) *Imitation of Christ,* a semimystical guide to the inner life intended primarily for monks and nuns, but widely appropriated by laity who also wanted to pursue the ascetic life.

The Modern Devotion has been seen as the source of Humanist, Protestant, and Catholic reform movements in the sixteenth century. Other scholars believe that it represented an individualistic approach to religion, indifferent to the sacramental piety of the church. It was actually a very conservative movement, having no direct connection with the Protestant Reformation. The brothers retained the old clerical doctrines and values, while placing them within the new framework of an active common life. They clearly met a need for a more personal piety and a better-informed religious life. Their movement appeared at a time when the laity were demanding good preaching in the vernacular and were even taking the initiative to endow special preacherships to ensure it. It was an age of popular preachers—such men as Saint Vincent Ferrer, Jean Gerson, Saint John of Capestrano, Saint Bernardino of Siena, and Geiler of Kaisersberg. The Modern Devotion permitted laity to be so to speak, "weekend ascetics," to practice the religious life to the fullest, yet without at the same time having to surrender their life in the world.

John Wycliffe and John Huss

The popular lay movements that most directly assailed the late medieval church were those of the Lollards in England and the Hussites in Bohemia. Both John Wycliffe (d. 1348) and John Huss (d. 1415) would have disclaimed these extremists who revolted in their name, yet Wycliffe's writings gave theological justification to the demands of the Lollards and Huss' writings to the programs of both moderate and extreme Hussites.

Wycliffe's work initially served the anticlerical policies of the English government. An Oxford theologian and a philosopher of high standing, Wycliffe became within England what William of Ockham and Marsilius of Padua had been at the Bavarian court of Emperor Louis IV—a major intellectual spokesman for the rights of royalty against the secular pretensions of popes. After 1350 English kings greatly reduced the power of the Avignon papacy to make ecclesiastical appointments and collect taxes within England, a position that Wycliffe strongly supported. His views on clerical poverty followed original Franciscan ideals and, more by accident than by design, gave justification to government restriction and even confiscation of church properties within England. Wycliffe argued that the clergy "ought to be content with food and clothing." He also maintained that personal merit, not rank and office, was the only basis of religious authority—a dangerous teaching because it raised allegedly pious laymen above allegedly corrupt ecclesiasts, regardless of the latter's official stature. There was a threat in such teaching to secular as well as ecclesiastical dominion and jurisdiction. At his posthumous condemnation by the pope, Wycliffe was accused of the ancient heresy of Donatism—the teaching that the efficacy of the church's sacraments did not lie in their sheer performance but also depended upon the moral character of the clergy who administered them.

Wycliffe anticipated certain Protestant criticisms of the medieval church by challenging papal infallibility, the sale of indulgences, and the dogma of transubstantiation. Had he not written in a period when England was politically opposed to the papacy and the church in deep schism, he would surely not have died peacefully in bed.

English advocates of Wycliffe's teaching were called *Lollards*. Like the Waldensians, they preached in the vernacular, disseminated translations of Holy Scripture, and championed clerical poverty. At first they came from every social class, being especially prominent among groups who had something tangible to gain from the confiscation of clerical properties (the nobility and the gentry) or who had suffered most under the current church system (the lower clergy and the poor people). After the English Peasant's Revolt of 1381, an uprising filled with egalitarian notions that could find support in Wycliffe's teaching, Lollardy was officially viewed as subversive. Opposed by an alliance of church and crown, it became a capital offense in England by 1401.

Heresy was not so easily harnessed in Bohemia, where it coalesced with a strong national movement. The University of Prague, founded in 1348, became the center for both Czech nationalism and a native religious reform movement. The latter began within the bounds of orthodoxy and was led by local intellectuals and preachers, the most famous of whom was John Huss, the rector of the university after 1403. The reformers supported vernacular translations of the Bible and were critical of traditional ceremonies and allegedly superstitious practices, particularly those relating to the sacrament of the Eucharist. They advocated lay communion with cup as well as bread, taught that bread and wine remained bread and wine after priestly consecration, and questioned the validity of sacraments performed by priests in mortal sin. Wycliffe's teaching appears to have influenced the movement very early. Regular traffic between England and Bohemia had existed for decades, ever since the marriage in 1381 of Anne of Bohemia to King Richard II. Czech students studied at Oxford and many returned with copies of Wycliffe's writings.

In 1403 the German faculty within the University of Prague acted to end the circulation of Wycliffe's writings. Twenty-four articles from his works had been condemned in London in 1382. The German faculty now added twenty-one, making a grand total of forty-five allegedly heretical tenets, which were forbidden topics in university classrooms and Prague pulpits. It was at this time that Huss stepped forward as the leader of the pro-Wycliffe faction. A bitter division resulted within the university that finally led to the departure of the German

Martin Luther in 1521, near the beginning of his career as a reformer. The portrait is by Lucas Cranach the Elder (1472–1553). [Metropolitan Museum of Art, New York; gift of Robert Lehman, 1955.]

and other foreign masters, leaving the native reform party in complete control. Thereafter the University of Prague was looked upon as an international center of heresy.

In 1410 Pope John XXIII excommunicated Huss and placed Prague under interdict. In late 1412 a harried Huss went into retreat in the countryside, remaining in seclusion until he was summoned in 1414 to appear before the Council of Constance. Huss naïvely believed that he could convince his strongest critics of the truth of his teaching, and he departed for Constance armed with a safe-conduct from the emperor Sigismund and a letter from the Archbishop of Prague attesting his orthodoxy on the issue of transubstantiation. It was especially because of his denial of the latter that John Wycliffe had been posthumously condemned.

Within weeks of his arrival in early November 1414, Huss was formally accused of heresy and imprisoned, Sigismund's safe-conduct proving a paper shield. In the summer of 1415, after months of house arrest, Huss received the hearing he had so long desired, shocking the assembled council by obstinately defending certain condemned teachings of Wycliffe. To the end, Huss refused to recant all the articles of Wycliffe, sufficient proof of his guilt in the eyes of his executioners. Jean Gerson, who was prominent among the latter, singled out Huss' denial of authority to reprobate and wicked men as the most pernicious of all his errors because it made the rule of law uncertain and insecure.

John Huss died at the stake on July 6, 1415, and was followed there less than a year later by his colleague Jerome of Prague (March 30, 1416). The reaction in Bohemia to the execution of these national heroes was a fierce revolution. Two religious factions formed: moderate Hussites, known as Utraquists or Calixtines, and militant Hussites, known as Taborites, who set out to transform Bohemia by force into a religious and social paradise. The Hussites fielded formidable armies under the leadership of John Ziska. In November 1420 they defeated armies of the hated Emperor Sigismund, who had assumed power in Bohemia in 1419. By the late

1420's Hussite armies were marching invincibly east and west. In 1431 a Bohemian delegation was invited to the Council of Basel to negotiate their grievances, a process that led to the granting of significant religious reforms and the creation of a strong national church in Bohemia. It was with such national independence and basic religious reforms in mind that Martin Luther later described himself and his followers as "Hussites."

Martin Luther and German Reformation to 1525

Unlike France and England, late medieval Germany lacked the political unity to enforce national religious reforms during the late Middle Ages. There were no lasting Statutes of Provisors and *praemunire*, as in England, nor a Pragmatic Sanction of Bourges, as in France, limiting papal jurisdiction and taxation on a national scale. What happened on a unified national level in England and France occurred only locally and piecemeal within German territories and towns. As popular resentment of clerical immunities and ecclesiastical abuses, especially the selling of indulgences, spread among German cities and towns, an unorganized "national" opposition to Rome formed. German Humanists had long given voice to such criticism, and by 1517 it was pervasive enough to provide a solid foundation for Martin Luther's reform.

Luther (1483–1546) was the son of a successful Thüringian miner. He was educated in Mansfeld, Magdeburg, where the Brothers of the Common Life were his teachers, and Eisenach. Between 1501 and 1505 he attended the University of Erfurt, where the nominalist teachings of William of Ockham and Gabriel Biel (d. 1495) prevailed within the Philosophical Faculty. After receiving his master of arts degree in 1505, Luther registered with the Law Faculty in accordance with his parents' wishes. But he never began the study of law. To the shock and disappointment of his family, he instead entered the Order of the Hermits of Saint Augustine in Erfurt on July 17, 1505. This decision had apparently been building for some time and was resolved during a lightning storm in which a terrified Luther, crying out to Saint Anne for assistance, as was customary for endangered travelers, promised to enter a monastery if he escaped death.

Ordained in 1507, Luther pursued a traditional course of study, becoming a *baccalaureus biblicus* and *sententiarius* in 1509. In 1510 he journeyed to Rome on the business of his order, finding there justification for the many criticisms of the church he had heard in Germany. In 1511 he was transferred to the Augustinian monastery in Wittenberg, where he earned his doctorate in theology in 1512, thereafter becoming a leader within the monastery, the new university, and the religious life of the city.

JUSTIFICATION BY FAITH ALONE. Reformation theology grew out of a problem common to many clerics and laymen at this time: the failure of traditional medieval religion to provide either full personal or intellectual satisfaction. Luther was especially plagued by the disproportion between his own sense of sinfulness and the perfect righteousness that medieval theology taught that God required for salvation. Traditional church teaching and the sacrament of penance proved to be of no consolation. Luther wrote that he came to despise the phrase "righteousness of God," for it seemed to demand of him a perfection he knew neither he nor any other man could ever achieve. Probably during his first lectures on the Psalms, between 1513 and 1515, he attained the insight of "Justification by faith alone." The righteousness God demands of men, he concluded, was not one that came from many religious works and ceremonies but was present in full measure in those who simply believed and trusted in the work of Jesus Christ, who alone was the perfect righteousness satisfying to God. To believe in Christ was to stand before God clothed in Christ's sure righteousness.

THE ATTACK ON INDULGENCES. An indulgence was a remission of the temporal penalty imposed by the priest upon penitents as a "work of satisfaction" for confessed mortal sins. According to medieval theology,

Martin Luther Discovers Justification by Faith Alone

Eighteen years after the fact, Martin Luther describes his discovery that God's righteousness is not an active, punishing righteousness but a passive, transforming righteousness, which makes those who believe in him righteous as God himself is righteous.

THOUGH *I lived as a monk without reproach, I felt that I was a sinner before God with an extremely disturbed conscience. I could not believe that he was placated by my satisfaction. I did not love, yes, I hated the righteous God who punishes sinners, and secretly, if not blasphemously, certainly murmuring greatly, I was angry with God, and said, "As if, indeed, it is not enough, that miserable sinners, eternally lost through original sin, are crushed by every kind of calamity by the law of the decalogue, without having God add pain to pain by the gospel and also by the gospel threatening us with his righteousness and wrath!" Thus I raged with a fierce and troubled conscience. Nevertheless, I beat importunately upon Paul at that place, most ardently desiring to know what St. Paul wanted.*

At last, by the mercy of God, meditating day and night, I gave heed to the context of the words, namely, "In it the righteousness of God is revealed, as it is written, 'He who through faith is righteous shall live.'" [Romans 1:17] There I began to understand that the righteousness of God is that by which the righteous lives by a gift of God, namely by faith. And this is the meaning: the righteousness of God is revealed by the gospel, namely, the passive righteousness with which merciful God justifies us by faith, as it is written, "He who through faith is righteous shall live." Here I felt that I was altogether born again and had entered paradise itself through open gates. There a totally other face of the entire Scripture showed itself to me. Thereupon I ran through the Scriptures from memory. I also found in other terms an analogy, as, the work of God, that is, what God does in us, the power of God, with which he makes us strong, the wisdom of God, with which he makes us wise, the strength of God, the salvation of God, the glory of God.

And I extolled my sweetest word with a love as great as the hatred with which I had before hated the word "righteousness of God." Thus that place in Paul was for me truly the gate to paradise.

Preface to the Complete Edition of Luther's Latin Writings (1545), in *Luther's Works,* Vol. 34, ed. by Lewis W. Spitz (Philadelphia: Muhlenberg Press, 1960), pp. 336–337.

Pope Leo X (1513–1521), of the Medici family, with two cardinals, as painted about 1517–18 by Raphael. Leo was pope when the Reformation began and condemned Luther for heresy in 1520. [Alinari/SCALA.]

when one was absolved of guilt for his sins, he still remained under an eternal penalty, a punishment God justly imposed on him for his sins. After absolution, however, this eternal penalty was said to be transformed into a temporal penalty, a manageable "work of satisfaction" the penitent could perform here and now (for example, prayers, fasting, almsgiving, retreats, pilgrimages, and so on). Penitents who defaulted on such prescribed works of satisfaction could expect to suffer for them in purgatory.

It was at this point that indulgences came into play as an aid to laity made genuinely anxious by the belief in a future suffering in purgatory for neglected penances or unrepented sins. In 1343 Pope Clement VI (1342–1352) had proclaimed the existence of a "treasury of merit," an infinite reservoir of good works in the church's possession that could be dispensed at the pope's discretion. It was on the basis of this declared treasury that the church sold so-called "letters of indulgence," which covered the works of satisfaction owed by penitents. In 1476 Pope Sixtus IV (1471–1484) extended indulgences also to purgatory. Originally indulgences had been given only for the true self-sacrifice of going on a crusade to the Holy Land. By Luther's time they were regularly dispensed for small cash payments and were presented to the laity as remitting not only their own punishments, but also those of their dead relatives presumed to be suffering in purgatory.

In 1517 a Jubilee indulgence, proclaimed during the pontificate of Pope Julius II (1503–1512) to raise funds for the rebuilding of St. Peter's in Rome, was revived and preached on the borders of Saxony in the territories of Archbishop Albrecht of Mainz. Albrecht was much in need of revenues because of large debts he had incurred to hold, contrary to church law, three ecclesiastical appointments: the archbishoprics of Mainz and Magdeburg in addition to the bishopric of Halberstadt. The selling of the indulgence was a joint venture by Albrecht, the Augsburg banking-house of Fugger, and Pope Leo X, half the proceeds going to the pope and half to Albrecht

and his creditors. The infamous indulgence preacher John Tetzel (d. 1519) was enlisted to preach the indulgence in Albrecht's territories because he was a seasoned professional who knew how to stir ordinary people to action. As he exhorted on one occasion:

> Don't you hear the voices of your dead parents and other relatives crying out, "Have mercy on us, for we suffer great punishment and pain. From this you could release us with a few alms. . . . We have created you, fed you, cared for you, and left you our temporal goods. Why do you treat us so cruelly and leave us to suffer in the flames, when it takes only a little to save us?"[1]

When on October 31, 1517, Luther posted his ninety-five theses against indulgences, he protested especially against the impression created by Tetzel that indulgences actually remitted sins and released the dead from punishment in purgatory—claims he believed went far beyond the traditional practice and seemed to make salvation something that could be bought and sold.

ELECTION OF CHARLES V. The ninety-five theses were embraced by Humanists and other proponents of reform. They made Luther famous overnight and

1 *Die Reformation in Augenzeugen berichten,* ed. by Helmar Junghaus (Karl Rauch Verlag, Düsseldorf, 1967), p. 44.

Francis I, king of France (1515–1547), by the Flemish painter Joos van Cleve (*ca.* 1485–1541). France was the counterweight to Spanish Hapsburg power in the first half of the sixteenth century. Francis fought four unsuccessful wars against Emperor Charles V. [Philadelphia Museum of Art; John G. Johnson Collection.]

The young Charles I of Spain about 1517. Charles was elected emperor as Charles V two years later at age 19 and reigned until 1556 when, weary and disillusioned by the success of Protestantism, he retired to a monastery. The wooden bust shown here is attributed to Conrad Meit. [Stedelijke Musea, Bruges, Belgium. Copyright A.C.L., Brussels.]

prompted official proceedings against him. In April 1518 he was summoned to appear before the general chapter of his order in Heidelberg, and the following October he was called before the papal legate and general of the Dominican Order, Cardinal Cajetan in Augsburg. As sanctions were being prepared against Luther, Emperor Maximilian I died (January 12, 1519), and this event, fortunate for the Reformation, turned all attention from heresy in Saxony to the contest for a new emperor.

The Pope backed the French king, Francis I. However, Charles I of Spain, a youth of nineteen, succeeded his grandfather and became Emperor Charles V. Charles was assisted by both recent tradition and a massive Fugger campaign chest, which secured the votes of the seven electors. The electors, who traditionally enhanced their power at every opportunity, wrung new concessions from Charles for their votes. The emperor agreed to a revival of the Imperial Supreme Court and the Council of Regency and promised to consult with a diet of the empire on all major domestic and foreign affairs; these measures also helped the development of the Reformation.

LUTHER'S EXCOMMUNICATION AND THE DIET OF WORMS. In the same month in which Charles was elected emperor, Luther began the famous Leipzig Debate (June 27, 1519) with the Ingolstadt professor John Eck. During this contest Luther challenged the infallibility of the pope and the inerrancy of church councils, appealing, for the first time, to the sovereign authority of Scripture alone. All his bridges to the old church were burned when he further defended certain teachings of

John Huss condemned by the Council of Constance. In 1520 Luther signaled his new direction with three famous pamphlets: the *Address to the Christian Nobility of the German Nation,* which urged the German princes to force reforms upon the Roman Church; the *Babylonian Captivity of the Church,* which attacked the traditional seven sacraments, arguing that only two were proper; and the eloquent *Freedom of a Christian,* which summarized the new teaching of salvation by faith alone. On June 15, 1520, the papal bull *Exsurge Domine* condemned Luther for heresy and gave him sixty days to retract. The final bull of excommunication, *Decet Pontificem Romanum,* was issued on January 3, 1521.

In April 1521 Luther presented his views before a diet of the empire in Worms, over which the newly elected Emperor Charles V presided. Ordered to recant, Luther declared that to do so would be to act against Scripture, reason, and his own conscience. On May 26, 1521, he was placed under the imperial ban and thereafter became an "outlaw" to secular as well as to religious authority. For his own protection friends hid him in Wartburg Castle, where he spent almost a year in seclusion, from April 1521 to March 1522. During his stay, he translated the New Testament into German using Erasmus' new Greek text, and he attempted by correspondence to oversee the first stages of the Reformation in Wittenberg.

IMPERIAL DISTRACTIONS: FRANCE AND THE TURKS. The Reformation was greatly assisted in these early years by the emperor's war with France and the advance of the Ottoman Turks into eastern Europe. Against both adversaries Charles V, who also remained a

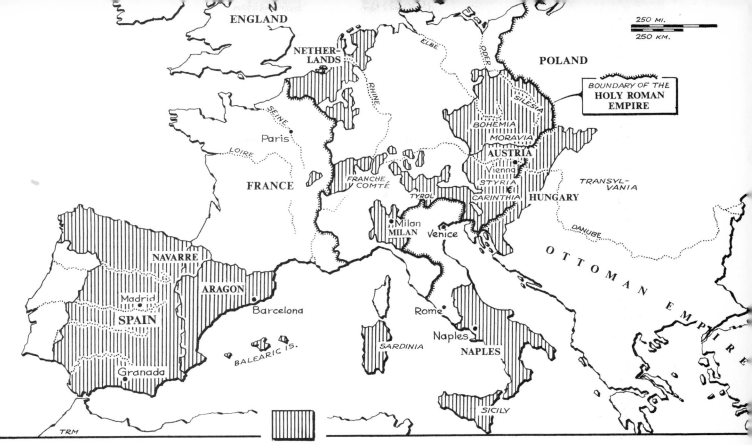

THE EMPIRE OF CHARLES V

Dynastic marriages and simple chance concentrated into Charles's hands rule over the lands shown here, plus Spain's overseas possessions. Crowns and titles rained in on him; election in 1519 as emperor gave him new burdens and responsibilities.

Frederick the Wise (1463–1525), the Elector of Saxony and Luther's protector. Etching by Albrecht Dürer.

Spanish king with dynastic responsibilities outside the Empire, needed German troops, and to that end he promoted friendly relations with the German princes. In 1526 the Turks overran Hungary at the Battle of Mohacs, while in western Europe the French-led League of Cognac formed against Charles for the second Hapsburg–Valois war. Thus preoccupied, the emperor agreed through his representatives at the German Diet of Speyer in 1526 that each German territory was free to enforce the Edict of Worms (1521) against Luther "so as to be able to answer in good conscience to God and the emperor." That concession in effect gave the German princes territorial sovereignty in religious matters and the Reformation time to put down deep roots.

INTERNAL DIVISIONS IN THE PROTESTANT MOVEMENT. In its first decade the Protestant movement suffered more from internal division than from

Martin Luther and German Reformation to 1525 375

imperial interference. By 1525 Luther had become as much an object of protest within Germany as was the pope in Rome. Original allies, sympathizers, and fellow travelers declared their independence from him. Erasmus led conservative humanist opposition, attacking Luther's views on the bondage of the will.

Like the German humanists, the German peasantry also had at first believed Luther to be an ally. The peasantry had been organized since the late fifteenth century against efforts by territorial princes to override their traditional laws and customs and to subject them to new regulations and taxes. During the Peasants' Revolt of 1524–1525, which Luther condemned in the strongest terms as "unchristian," the peasants discovered that Luther's concept of freedom was completely different from their own. Tens of thousands (estimates run between 70,000 and 100,000) died in the abortive revolt. At the same time radical Protestants—Anabaptists and Spiritualists—and the Swiss reformers also found it necessary to distinguish themselves from Luther's movement. The 1520s saw the beginning of an even larger proliferation of Protestant denominations and sects.

Ulrich Zwingli and the Swiss Reformation

Switzerland was a loose confederacy of thirteen autonomous cantons and allied areas. Some cantons (*e.g.* Zurich, Bern, Basel, Schaffhausen) became Protestant, some (especially around the Lucerne heartland) remained Catholic, and a few other cantons and regions managed to effect a compromise. Among the preconditions of the Swiss Reformation were the growth of national sentiment occasioned by opposition to foreign mercenary service and a desire for church reform that had persisted in Switzerland since the councils of Constance (1414–1417) and Basel (1431–1449).

THE REFORMATION IN ZURICH. Ulrich Zwingli (1484–1531), the leader of the Swiss Reformation, had been humanistically educated in Bern, Vienna, and Basel.

Erasmus and Luther Debate the Freedom of the Will

Erasmus and Luther finally broke with each other in 1524–1525 over the issue of whether man had free will in matters of salvation. Erasmus believed that salvation depended on how each individual chose to live his life. Luther argued that man had such freedom only in earthly matters, not in regard to his eternal salvation.

ERASMUS:

L ET *us assume the truth of what Wycliffe has taught and Luther asserted, namely, that everything we do happens not on account of our free will, but out of sheer necessity. What could be more useless than to publish this paradox to the world? . . . Let us assume that it is true . . . that God causes both good and evil in us, and that he rewards us for his good works wrought in us and punishes us for the evil deeds done in us. What a loophole . . . this opinion would open to godlessness. . . . What wicked fellow would henceforth try to better his conduct? . . . People are universally ignorant and carnal-minded. They tend towards unbelief, wickedness and blasphemy. There is nothing to be gained from pouring oil upon the fire.*

LUTHER:

IF WE *do not want to drop this term [free will] altogether, which would be the safest and most Christian thing to do, we may still use it in good faith to denote free will in respect not of what is above man, but of what is below him. This is to say, man should know in regard to his goods and possessions that he has the right to use them, to do or to leave undone, according to his free will. Although at the same time, that free will may be overruled by the free will of God, just as he pleases. However, with regard to salvation or damnation, man has no free will, but is a captive, servant and bondslave, either to the will of God or to the will of the Devil.*

From *Erasmus-Luther: Discourse on Free Will*, trans. and ed. by E. F. Winter (New York: F. Ungar, 1961), pp. 11–12, 113.

He was strongly influenced by Erasmus. He served as chaplain with Swiss mercenaries during the disastrous Battle of Marignano in 1515 and thereafter became an eloquent critic of mercenary service. He believed that this policy threatened both the political sovereignty and the moral well-being of the Swiss confederacy. By 1518 Zwingli was also widely known for opposition to the sale of indulgences and to religious superstition. In 1519 he entered the competition for the post of people's priest in the main church of Zurich. His candidacy was contested

German Peasants Protest Rising Feudal Exactions

In the late fifteenth and early sixteenth centuries German feudal lords, both secular and ecclesiastical, tried to increase the earnings from their lands by raising demands on their peasant tenants. As the personal freedoms of peasants were restricted, their properties confiscated, and their traditional laws and customs overridden, massive revolts occurred in southern Germany in 1525. Not a few historians, especially those of Marxist persuasion, see this uprising and the social and economic conditions that gave rise to it, as the major historical force in early modern history. The following, from Memmingen, in modern West Germany, is the most representative and well known statement of peasant grievances.

Thomas Müntzer (died 1525), Luther's fiercest opponent and a leader of the Peasants' Revolt of 1525. His name became synonymous with rebellion and anarchy. He is seen here in a woodcut portrait of about 1600 by Christoffel van Sichem the Elder. [Bildarchiv Preussischer Kulturbesitz.]

THE FIRST ARTICLE. *It is our humble petition and desire, as also our will and resolution, that in the future we should have power and authority so that each community should choose and appoint a pastor, and that we should have the right to depose him should he conduct himself improperly. . . .*

The Second Article. *According as the just tithe is established by the Old Testament and fulfilled in the New, we are ready and willing to pay the fair tithe of grain. . . . The small tithes, whether ecclesiastical or lay, we will not pay at all, for the Lord God created cattle for the free use of man. . . .*

The Third Article. *. . . We . . . take it for granted that you will release us from serfdom as true Christians, unless it should be shown us from the Gospel that we are serfs.*

The Fourth Article. *. . . It has been the custom heretofore that no poor man should be allowed to catch venison or wildfowl or fish in flowing water, which seems to us quite unseemly and unbrotherly as well as selfish and not agreeable to the Word of God. . . .*

The Fifth Article. *. . . We are aggrieved in the matter of woodcutting, for the noble folk have appropriated all the woods to themselves. . . .*

The Sixth Article. *. . . In regard to the excessive services demanded of us which are increased from day to day, we ask that this matter be properly looked into so that we shall not continue to be oppressed in this way. . . .*

The Seventh Article. *We will not hereafter allow ourselves to be further oppressed by our lords, but will let them demand only what is just and proper according to the word of the agreement between the lord and the peasant. The lord should no longer try to force more*

services or other dues from the peasant without payment. . . .

The Eighth Article. *. . . We are greatly burdened by holdings which cannot support the rent exacted from them. . . . We ask that the lords may appoint persons of honor to inspect these holdings and fix a rent in accordance with justice. . . .*

The Ninth Article. *. . . We are burdened with a great evil in the constant making of new laws. . . . In our opinion we should be judged according to the old written law. . . .*

The Tenth Article. *. . . We are aggrieved by the appropriation . . . of meadows and fields which at one time belonged to a community. These we will take again into our own hands. . . .*

The Eleventh Article. *. . . We will entirely abolish the due called* Todfall [*that is, heriot or death tax, by which the lord received the best horse, cow, or garment of a family upon the death of a serf*] *and will no longer endure it, nor allow widows and orphans to be thus shamefully robbed against God's will, and in violation of justice and right. . . .*

Conclusion. *In the twelfth place it is our conclusion and final resolution, that if any one or more of the articles here set forth should not be in agreement with the Word of God, as we think they are, such article we will willingly recede from when it is proved really to be against the Word of God by a clear explanation of the Scripture.*

Translations and Reprints from the Original Sources of European History, Vol. II. Department of History, University of Pennsylvania (Philadelphia, 1897).

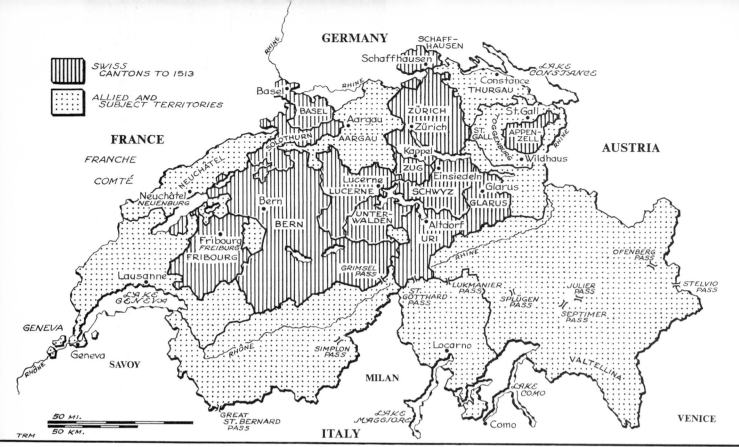

THE SWISS CONFEDERATION

because of his acknowledged fornication with a barber's daughter, an affair he minimized in a forcefully written self-defense. Actually his conduct was less scandalous to his contemporaries, who sympathized with the plight of celibate clergy, than it may be to the modern reader. One of Zwingli's first acts as a reformer was to petition for an end to clerical celibacy and for the institution of priestly marriage, a practice that quickly succeeded in all Protestant lands.

From his new position as people's priest in Zurich, Zwingli engineered the Swiss Reformation. In March 1522 he was party to the breaking of the Lenten fast—an act of protest analogous to burning the flag today. Zwingli's reform guideline was very simple and very effective: whatever lacked literal support in Scripture was to be neither believed nor practiced. That test soon raised questions about such honored traditional teachings and practices as fasting, transubstantiation, the worship of saints, pilgrimages, purgatory, clerical celibacy, and certain sacraments. A disputation held on January 29, 1523, concluded with the city government's sanction of Zwingli's Scripture test. Thereafter Zurich became, to all intents and purposes, a Protestant city and the center of the Swiss Reformation.

THE MARBURG COLLOQUY. Landgrave Philip of

While nominally still a part of the Holy Roman Empire, Switzerland grew from a loose defensive union of the central "forest cantons" in the thirteenth century to a fiercely independent association of regions with different languages, histories, and, finally, religions.

Hesse (1504–1567) sought to unite Swiss and German Protestants in a mutual defense pact, a potentially significant political alliance. His efforts were spoiled, however, by theological disagreements between Luther and Zwingli over the nature of Christ's presence in the Eucharist. Zwingli maintained a symbolic interpretation of Christ's words, "This is my body"; Christ, he argued, was only spiritually, not also bodily, present in the bread and wine of the Eucharist. Luther, to the contrary, insisted that Christ's human nature could share the properties of his divine nature; hence, where Christ was spiritually present, he could also be bodily present. Luther wanted no part of an abstract, spiritualized Christ. Zwingli, on the other hand, feared that Luther had not broken sufficiently with medieval sacramental theology.

Philip of Hesse brought the two Protestant leaders together in his castle in Marburg in early October 1529, but they were unable to work out their differences on this issue. Luther left thinking Zwingli a dangerous fanatic. Although cooperation between the two sides did not

Zwingli Lists the Errors of the Roman Church

Religious argument can become confusing. A clear summary of issues is often helpful—both to the disputants and to interested bystanders. Prior to the first Zurich Disputation (1523), which effectually introduced the Protestant Reformation in Zurich, the reformer Zwingli prepared such a summary of the errors of the Roman Church, known as the *Sixty-Seven Articles*. Here are some of them.

ALL *who consider other teachings equal to or higher than the Gospel err, and they do not know what the Gospel is.*

In the faith rests our salvation, and in unbelief our damnation; for all truth is clear in Christ.

In the Gospel one learns that human doctrines and decrees do not aid in salvation.

That Christ, having sacrificed himself once, is to eternity a certain and valid sacrifice for the sins of all faithful, wherefrom it follows that the Mass is not a sacrifice, but is a remembrance of the sacrifice and assurance of the salvation which Christ has given us.

That God desires to give us all things in his name, whence it follows that outside of this life we need no [intercession of the saints or any] mediator except himself.

That no Christian is bound to do those things which God has not decreed, therefore one may eat at all times all food, where from one learns that the decree about cheese and butter is a Roman swindle.

That no special person can impose the ban upon anyone, but the Church, that is, the congregation of those among whom the one to be banned dwells, together with their watchman, i.e. the pastor.

All that the spiritual so-called state [i.e., the papal church] claims to have of power and protection belongs to the lay [i.e., the secular magistracy], if they wish to be Christians.

Greater offence I know not than that one does not allow priests to have wives, but permits them to hire prostitutes.

Christ has borne all our pains and labor. Hence whoever assigns to works of penance what belongs to Christ errs and slanders God.

The true divine Scriptures know naught about purgatory after this life.

The Scriptures know no priests except those who proclaim the word of God.

Ulrich Zwingli (1484–1531): Selected Works, ed. by Samuel M. Jackson (Philadelphia: University of Pennsylvania Press, 1972), pp. 111–117.

The Swiss reformer Ulrich Zwingli (1484–1531), by Hans Holbein the Younger. Zwingli was a great patriot as well as a religious activist. "If I seek the salvation of the fatherland through sacred dogma while cut off from the fatherland, I fall by the sword as an ungrateful person." [Alinari/SCALA.]

cease, the disagreement splintered the Protestant movement theologically and politically. Separate defense leagues formed, and Zwinglian theological views came to be embodied in the *Confessio Tetrapolitana,* a confession of faith prepared by the Strasbourg reformers Martin Bucer and Caspar Hedio for presentation to the Diet of Augsburg (1530) as a Protestant alternative to the Lutheran *Augsburg Confession.*

SWISS CIVIL WARS. As the Swiss cantons divided between Protestantism and Catholicism, civil wars began. There were two major battles, both at Kappel, one in June 1529 and a second in October 1531. The first ended in a Protestant victory, which forced the Catholic cantons to break their foreign alliances and to recognize the rights of Swiss Protestants. During the second battle Zwingli was captured and executed. The subsequent treaty confirmed the right of each canton to determine its own religion. Heinrich Bullinger (1504–1575), who was Zwingli's son-in-law, became the new leader of the Swiss Reformation and guided its development into an established religion.

Anabaptists and Radical Protestants

The moderate pace and seemingly low ethical results of the Lutheran and Zwinglian reformations discontented many people, among them some of the original co-workers of Luther and Zwingli. Many desired a more rapid and thorough implementation of primitive Christianity and accused the major reformers of entering into deadly compromises. The most important of these radical groups were the Anabaptists, sixteenth-century ancestors of

The circular courtyard of the palace of Emperor Charles V in Granada, Spain, built in Roman imperial style—a commentary on Charles's ambitions. [Editorial Photocolor Archives.]

modern Mennonites and Amish. Anabaptists were especially distinguished by their rejection of infant baptism and their insistence upon only adult baptism, believing that the latter conformed to Scripture and was more respectful of human freedom.

CONRAD GREBEL AND THE SWISS BRETHREN. Conrad Grebel (1498–1526), with whom Anabaptism may be said to have originated, performed the first adult rebaptism in Zurich in January 1525. Initially a co-worker with Zwingli and an even greater biblical literalist, Grebel broke openly with Zwingli after a religious disputation in October 1523 in which Zwingli supported the city government's plea for a gradual removal of traditional religious practices. The alternative of the Swiss Brethren, as Grebel's group came to be called, was set forth in the *Schleitheim Confession* of 1527. This document distinguished Anabaptists not only by their practice of adult baptism but also by their refusal to go to war, swear oaths, and participate in the offices of secular government. Anabaptists physically separated from society to form a more perfect community in imitation of what they believed to be the example of the first Christians. Because of the close connection between religious and civic life in this period, such separatism was viewed by the political authorities as a dire threat to basic social bonds.

THE ANABAPTIST REIGN IN MÜNSTER. At first, Anabaptism drew its adherents from all social classes. But as Lutherans and Zwinglians joined with Catholics in opposition to the Anabaptists, a more rural, agrarian class came to make up the great majority. In 1529 an ancient law of the Emperor Justinian against rebaptism as a capital offense was revived throughout the Holy Roman Empire. It has been estimated that at least one thousand and perhaps as many as five thousand men and women were executed for this practice between 1525 and 1618. Brutal measures were universally applied against sectarians after Anabaptist extremists came to power in the city of Münster in 1534–1535. Led by a baker, Jan Matthys of Haarlem, and a tailor, Jan Beukelsz

of Leiden, the Anabaptist majority in this city forced Lutherans and Catholics either to convert or to emigrate. As the Lutherans and Catholics left, Münster was transformed into an Old Testament theocracy, replete with charismatic leaders and the practice of polygamy. The outside world was deeply shocked. Protestant and Catholic armies united to crush the radicals, and the skeletons of their leaders long hung in public view as a warning to all who would so offend traditional Christian sensitivities. In the wake of the Münster debacle, moderate, pacifistic Anabaptism on the model of the Swiss Brethren became the norm among most Protestant sectarians. The moderate Anabaptist leader Menno Simons (1496–1561), the founder of the Mennonites, set the example for the future.

SPIRITUALISTS. In addition to the Anabaptists there were radicals known as *Spiritualists*. These were mostly isolated individuals distinguished by their disdain of all traditions and institutions. They believed that the only religious authority was God's spirit, which spoke here and now to every individual. Among them were several Lutherans: Thomas Müntzer (d. 1525), who had close contacts with Anabaptist leaders in Germany and Switzerland and died as a leader of a peasants' revolt; Sebastian Franck (d. 1541), a free-lance critic of all dogmatic religion and considered by some to be among the most modern thinkers of the period; and Caspar Schwenckfeld (d. 1561), a prolific writer and wanderer after whom the Schwenckfeldian Church is named.

ANTITRINITARIANS. A final group of radical Protestants was the Antitrinitarians, exponents of a common-sense, rational, and ethical religion. Chief among this group were the Spaniard Michael Servetus (1511–1553), executed in 1553 by John Calvin for "blasphemies against the Holy Trinity," and the Italians Lelio (d. 1562) and Faustus Sozzini (d. 1604), the founders of Socinianism. These thinkers were the strongest opponents of Calvinism, especially its belief in original sin and predestination, and have a deserved reputation as defenders of religious toleration.

Sieben Köpffe Martini Luthers
Vom Hochwirdigen Sacrament des Altars / Durch
Doctor Jo. Cocleus.

A Catholic caricature of Martin Luther as a seven-headed monster. This picture served as the title page of a pamphlet by one of Luther's strongest Catholic critics, Johannes Cochlaeus.

BELOW: A Protestant caricature of the pope as a monster with the characteristics of several beasts. Note in the background the flag with the pope's "keys" to heaven and hell.

Political Consolidation of the Lutheran Reformation

THE DIET OF AUGSBURG. Charles V returned to the empire in 1530 to direct the Diet of Augsburg, a meeting of Protestant and Catholic representatives assembled for the purpose of imposing a settlement of the religious divisions. With its terms dictated by the Catholic emperor, it adjourned with a blunt order to all Lutherans to revert to Catholicism. The Reformation was by this time too firmly established for that to occur, and in February 1531 the Lutherans responded with the formation of their own defensive alliance, the Schmalkaldic League. The league took as its banner the *Augsburg Confession,* a moderate statement of Protestant beliefs that had been spurned by the emperor at the Diet of Augsburg. In 1538 Luther drew up a more strongly worded Protestant confession known as the *Schmalkaldic Articles.* Under the leadership of Landgrave Philip of Hesse, the league achieved a stalemate with the emperor, who was again distracted by renewed war with France and the ever-resilient Turks.

The Reformation Grows

In the 1530s German Lutherans formed regional consistories, judicial bodies composed of theologians and lawyers, which oversaw and administered the new Protestant churches. These consistories replaced the old Catholic episcopates. Under the leadership of Philip Melanchthon, the "praeceptor of Germany," educational reforms were enacted that provided for compulsory primary education, schools for girls, a Humanist revision of the traditional curriculum, and catechetical instruction of the laity in the new religion.

The Reformation dug in elsewhere. Introduced into Denmark by Christian II (ruled 1513–1523), Danish Lutheranism throve under Frederick I (1523–1533), who joined the Schmalkaldic League. Under Christian III (1536–1559) Lutheranism became the state religion, and

Ein grausam Meerwunder / den Bapst
bedeutende / zu Rom gefunden / und zu Wittemberg erstlich Anno
23. und darnach abermal Anno 46. mit der auslegung Philippi gedruckt.
Mit einer Vorrede Matthiæ Flacij Illyrici.

Political Consolidation of the Lutheran Reformation 381

the Wittenberg preacher Johannes Bugenhagen arrived to organize the Danish Lutheran church.

In Sweden Gustavus Vasa (1523–1560), supported by a Swedish nobility greedy for church lands, confiscated church property and subjected the clergy to royal authority at the Diet of Vesteras (1527).

In politically splintered Poland, Lutherans, Anabaptists, Calvinists, and even Antitrinitarians found room to practice their beliefs, as Poland, primarily because of the absence of a central political authority, became a model of religious pluralism and toleration in the second half of the sixteenth century.

REACTION AGAINST PROTESTANTS; THE INTERIM. Charles V made abortive efforts in 1540–1541 to enforce a compromise agreement between Protestants and Catholics. As these and other conciliar efforts failed, he turned to a military solution. In 1547 imperial armies crushed the Protestant Schmalkaldic League. John Frederick of Saxony was defeated in April 1547, and Philip of Hesse was taken captive shortly thereafter.

The emperor established puppet rulers in Saxony and Hesse and issued as imperial law the *Augsburg Interim*, a new order that Protestants everywhere readopt old Catholic beliefs and practices. There were a few cosmetic Protestant concessions, for example, clerical marriage (with papal approval of individual cases) and communion in both kinds (that is, bread *and* wine). Although the *Interim* met only surface acceptance within Germany, it forced many Protestant leaders into exile. The Strasbourg reformer Martin Bucer, for example, departed to England, where he played an important role in the drafting of the religious documents of the English Reformation during the reign of Edward VI. In Germany, Magdeburg became a refuge for persecuted Protestants and the center of Lutheran resistance.

The Peace of Augsburg

The Reformation was too entrenched by 1547 to be ended even by brute force. Maurice of Saxony, who had been hand-picked by Charles V to rule Saxony, recog-

The Empire Recognizes the Legality of Lutheranism

The Peace of Augsburg recognized the legality of Lutheran religious belief (the Augsburg Confession). In return, Lutheran territories agreed to recognize the rights of those who wished to continue in the old faith. An attempt was made to prevent converting Catholic clergy from taking their benefices into the Lutheran fold. Those unhappy with the religion of their region could migrate.

H*IS Imperial Majesty, Ourself, the Electors, Princes, and Estates of the Holy Empire shall not invade, damage or assault any Estate of the Empire because of the [Lutheran] Augsburg Confession, its doctrine, religion and faith, or otherwise press such Estate by violent acts and by attacking it in its principalities and lands to abandon, against its own will and conscience, the Augsburg Confession, religion, faith, rites, regulations and ceremonies, as these are established now or may be established in the future, or trouble it or penalize it by mandate or in any other form; but they shall be left to enjoy quietly and peacefully their religion, faith, rites, regulations and ceremonies, keeping their property, both movable and immovable goods, land, subjects, lordships, jurisdictions and magistracies. . . .*

Likewise the Estates espousing the Augsburg Confession shall let His Roman Imperial Majesty, Ourself, the Electors, Princes, and other Estates of the Holy Empire who are keeping and supporting the old religion, enjoy undisturbed our religion, faith, rites, regulations and ceremonies. . . .

Where an archbishop, bishop, prelate, or another priest shall abandon the old religion, he shall abandon immediately, without any objection and delay, his archbishopric, bishopric, prelacy or other benefice, and all fruits and incomes drawn from them; and he shall do so without detriment to his honour. . . .

If our subjects or those of the Electors, Princes, and Estates, belonging either to the old religion or to the Augsburg Confession, would like to move with their wives and children, because of their religion, from our territories . . . in order to settle down in another place, free egress and ingress without hindrance shall be conceded and allowed to everybody as also the sale of their goods and property, after payment of a moderately adequate compensation for their serfdom and tax arrears as it is in each particular locality fixed by tradition. . . .

Church and State Through the Centuries: A Collection of Historic Documents, trans. and ed. by S. Z. Ehler and John B. Morrall (New York: Biblo and Tannen, 1967), pp. 167–170.

nized the inevitability of Protestantism and shifted his allegiance to the Protestants. Confronted by fierce Protestant resistance and weary from three decades of war, the emperor was forced to relent. He reinstated John Frederick and Philip of Hesse and guaranteed Lutheran religious freedoms in the Peace of Passau (August 1552), a declaration that effectively surrendered his lifelong quest for European religious unity.

The division of Christendom was made permanent by the Peace of Augsburg in September 1555. This agreement recognized in law what had already been well established in practice: *cuius regio, eius religio,* "the ruler of a land shall determine the religion of the land." Lutherans were permitted to retain all church lands forcibly seized before 1552. An "ecclesiastical reservation" was added, however, that was intended to prevent newly converting Catholic higher clergy from retaining their lands, titles, and privileges. Those discontent with the religion of their region were permitted to migrate to another.

Calvinism and Anabaptism were not among the legal religions recognized by the Peace of Augsburg. Anabaptists had long adjusted to such exclusion by forming their own separatist communities. Calvinists, however, were not separatists and could not choose this route; they remained determined not only to secure the right to worship publicly as they pleased but also to shape society according to their own religious convictions. While Anabaptists retreated and Lutherans enjoyed the security of an established religion, Calvinists organized to lead national revolutions throughout northern Europe in the second half of the sixteenth century.

SUGGESTED READINGS

ROLAND H. BAINTON, *Erasmus of Christendom* (1969). Charming presentation.

CHARLES BOXER, *Four Centuries of Portuguese Expansion 1415–1825* (1961). Comprehensive survey by a leading authority.

OWEN CHADWICK, *The Reformation* (1964). Among best short histories and especially strong on theological and ecclesiastical issues.

NORMAN COHN, *The Pursuit of the Millennium* (1957). Traces millennial speculation and activity from the Old Testament to the sixteenth century.

G. R. ELTON, *Reformation Europe 1517–1559* (1966). Among the best short treatments and especially strong on political issues.

ERIK ERIKSON, *Young Man Luther: A Study in Psychoanalysis and History* (1962). Controversial study that has opened a new field of historiography.

WERNER L. GUNDERSHEIMER (Ed.), *French Humanism 1470–1600* (1969). Collection of essays that both summarize and provoke.

ROBERT M. KINGDON, *Transition and Revolution: Problems and Issues of European Renaissance and Reformation History* (1974).

STEVEN E. OZMENT (Ed.), *The Reformation in Medieval Perspective* (1971). Difficult but rewarding essays in late medieval intellectual history.

J. H. PARRY, *The Age of Reconnaissance* (1964). A comprehensive account of explorations from 1450 to 1650.

R. R. POST, *The Modern Devotion* (1968). Currently the authoritative interpretation.

EUGENE F. RICE, JR., *The Foundations of Early Modern Europe 1460–1559* (1970). Broad, succinct narrative.

E. GORDON RUPP, *Patterns of Reformation: Oecolampadius, Karlstadt, Müntzer* (1969). Effort to demonstrate the variety within early Protestantism.

MATTHEW SPINKA, *John Hus' Concept of the Church* (1966).

LEWIS SPITZ, *The Religious Renaissance of the German Humanists* (1963). Comprehensive and entertaining.

JAMES STAYER, *Anabaptists and the Sword* (1972).

GERALD STRAUSS (Ed. and trans.), *Manifestations of Discontent in Germany on the Eve of the Reformation* (1971). Rich collection of sources for both rural and urban scenes.

ROBERT C. WALTON, *Zwingli's Theocracy* (1968). Deals with origins and nature of Zwingli's reforms in Zurich.

GEORGE H. WILLIAMS, *The Radical Reformation* (1962). Broad survey of the varieties of dissent within Protestantism.

H. B. WORKMAN, *John Wyclif,* Vols. 1 and 2 (1926). Dated but still standard biography.

ANNO ·ÆTATIS ·   · SVÆ · XLIX ·

384

15
The Age of Reformation: II

John Calvin and the Genevan Reformation

I N THE second half of the sixteenth century Calvinism, absorbing the earlier Zwinglian tradition, replaced Lutheranism as the dominant Protestant force in Europe. Calvinism was the religious ideology that inspired or accompanied massive political resistance in France, the Netherlands, and Scotland. It established itself within the Palatinate during the reign of Elector Frederick III (1559–1576). Believing strongly in both divine predestination and the individual's responsibility to reorder society according to God's plan, Calvinists became zealous reformers. They were determined to transform and order society in such a way that men and women would act externally as they believed, or should believe, internally and were destined to live eternally. The German sociologist Max Weber argued that this peculiar combination of confidence and self-disciplined activism produced an ethic that stimulated and reinforced the spirit of emergent capitalism, bringing Calvinism and later Puritanism into close association with the development of modern capitalist societies.

The founder of Calvinism, John Calvin (1509–1564), was born into a well-to-do family, the son of the secretary to the bishop of Noyon in Picardy. He received a church benefice at age twelve, which financed the best possible education at Parisian colleges and a law degree at Orléans. Calvin associated with members of the indigenous French reform party, a group of Catholic Humanists led by Jacques Lefèvre d'Étaples and Marguerite d'Angoulême, the queen of Navarre after 1527. Although Calvin finally rejected this group as ineffectual, its members contributed to his preparation as a religious reformer. Their sincere but largely hortatory approach to

Henry VIII, king of England 1509–1547, as portrayed in 1540 by Hans Holbein the Younger. This picture has wandered far afield and is now in the Galleria Nazionale in Rome. [Alinari/SCALA.]

reform was portrayed in Calvin's first work, a commentary on Seneca's *De Clementia* in 1533.

It was probably in the spring of 1534 that Calvin experienced that conversion to Protestantism by which he says his "long stubborn heart" was "made teachable" by God—a personal model he would later apply to the recalcitrant citizenry of Geneva. In May 1534 he dramatically surrendered the benefice he had held for so long and at such profit and joined the Reformation.

Political Revolt and Religious Reform in Geneva

Whereas in Saxony religious reform paved the way for a political revolution against the emperor, in Geneva a political revolution against the local prince-bishop laid the foundation for a change in religious polity. Genevans successfully revolted against the House of Savoy and their resident prince-bishop in the late 1520s. Assisted by the Swiss Confederacy—the city-states of Fribourg and Bern were Geneva's allies—the Genevans drove out the prince-bishop in August 1527, his legal and political powers being thereafter assumed by the city councils. In late 1533 Bern dispatched the Protestant reformers Guillaume Farel (1489–1565) and Antoine Froment (1508–1581) to Geneva. In the summer of 1535, after much internal turmoil, the Protestants triumphed, and the traditional Mass and other religious practices were removed. On May 21, 1536, the city voted officially to adopt the Reformation: "to live according to the Gospel and the Word of God . . . without . . . any more masses, statues, idols, or other papal abuses."

CALVIN AND FAREL. Calvin arrived after these events, in July 1536, having been forced by the third Hapsburg–Valois war to detour through Geneva while en route to a scholarly refuge in Strasbourg. Farel successfully pleaded with him to stay and assist in the implementation of the Reformation, threatening Calvin with divine vengeance if he turned away from this task.

Before a year had passed, Calvin had drawn up articles for the governance of the new church as well as a cate-

The Genevan reformer and Protestant theologian, John Calvin (1509–1564). [Musée Historique de la Réformation et Bibliothèque Calvinienne, Geneva. H. Pattusch.]

chism to guide and discipline the people, both of which were presented for approval to the city councils in early 1537. Because of the strong measures proposed to govern Geneva's moral life, Calvin and Farel were suspected by many of desiring to create a "new papacy." Their orthodoxy was attacked and Geneva's powerful Protestant ally, Bern, which had adopted a more moderate Protestant reform, pressured Geneva's magistrates to restore traditional religious ceremonies and holidays abolished by Calvin and Farel. Both within and outside Geneva Calvin and Farel were perceived as going too far too fast. In February 1538 the four syndics chosen in the annual election opposed them and reinstated the controversial ceremonies desired by Bern.

Two months later the defiant reformers were exiled from the city, Calvin stalking off to Strasbourg, where he became pastor to several hundred French exiles. During his long stay in Strasbourg Calvin wrote biblical commentaries and a second edition of his masterful and eloquent *Institutes of the Christian Religion,* which many consider to be the definitive theological statement of the Protestant faith. Calvin also married and participated in the ecumenical discussions urged upon Protestants and Catholics by Charles V. Most importantly, he learned from the Strasbourg reformer Martin Bucer how to implement successfully the Protestant Reformation.

CALVIN'S GENEVA. In 1540 Geneva elected syndics who were both favorable to Calvin and determined to establish full Genevan political and religious independence from Bern. They knew Calvin would be a valuable ally in the latter project and invited him to return. This he did in September 1540, never to leave the city again. Within months of his arrival new ecclesiastical ordinances were implemented that provided for cooperation between the magistrates and the clergy in matters of internal discipline. Following the Strasbourg model, the Genevan church was organized into four offices: (1) pastors, of which there were five; (2) teachers or doctors to instruct the populace in and to defend true doctrine; (3) elders, a group of twelve laymen chosen by and from the Genevan councils and empowered to "oversee the life of everybody;" and (4) deacons to dispense church goods and services to the poor and the sick.

The Consistory became Calvin's instrument of power. This body was composed of the elders and the pastors and was presided over by one of the four syndics. It enforced the strictest moral discipline, meting out punishments for a broad range of moral and religious transgressions, from missing church services (a fine of 3 sous) to fornication (six days on bread and water and a fine of 60 sous) and, as time passed, increasingly for criticism of Calvin and the Consistory. Calvin ridiculed his opponents as undisciplined "Libertines."

Among the many personal conflicts in Geneva that gave Calvin his reputation as a stern moralist, none proved more damaging than his active role in the capture and execution of the Spanish physician and amateur theologian Michael Servetus in 1553. After 1555 the city's syndics were all devout Calvinists, and Geneva was home to thousands of exiled Protestants who had been driven out of France, England, and Scotland. Refugees (more than five thousand), most of them utterly loyal to Calvin, came to make up over one third of the population of Geneva. From this time until his death in 1564, Calvin's position in the city was greatly strengthened and the syndics were very cooperative.

Catholic Reform and Counter Reformation

THE FIFTH LATERAN COUNCIL. The Protestant Reformation did not take the medieval church completely by surprise. There were much internal criticism and many efforts at internal reform before there was a Counter Reformation in reaction to Protestant successes. Before the Reformation ambitious proposals had been set forth to bring about the long-demanded reform of the church in head and members. One of the boldest attempts came on the eve of the Fifth Lateran Council (1513–1517), the last reform council before the Reformation, and was drafted by two Venetian monks, Tommaso Giustiniani and Vincenzo Quirini. Their program went so far as to call for a revision of the *Corpus Juris Canonici,* the massive body of church law that authorized papal practices and ensured papal prerogatives. Sixteenth-century popes, ever mindful of the way the councils of Constance and Basel had stripped the pope of his traditional powers, quickly squelched such efforts to bring about basic changes in the laws and institutions of the church. High Renaissance popes preferred the charge given to the Fifth Lateran Council in the keynote address by Giles of Viterbo, the superior general of the Hermits of Saint Augustine: "Men are to be changed by, not to change, religion." The Fifth Lateran Council remained a regional council completely within the pope's control and brought about no significant reforms. The very month after its adjournment Martin Luther posted his ninety-five theses.

New Sources of Catholic Reform

The most important Catholic reform initiatives did not come from the papal court but from such movements as the Modern Devotion and the Oratory of Divine Love (founded in 1517); the new religious orders of Capuchins (1528), Barnabites (1530), Theatines (1534), Ursulines (1535), Jesuits (1540), and Oratorians (1576); and the Spanish mystics, Saint Teresa of Avila (1515–1582) and Saint John of the Cross (1542–1591).

Ignatius of Loyola and the Jesuits

It was especially the Jesuits, members of the Society of Jesus, who led the Catholic counterattack against Protestantism. Constituted as an order of the church in 1540 by Pope Paul III, the Jesuits became to Catholic reform what the Calvinists were to Protestant reform. They were the educators of Catholic youth and clergy in the second half of the sixteenth century, establishing colleges and forming Catholic "fifth columns" throughout Protestant Europe. By 1624 the Society, sixteen thousand strong, had missions in India, Japan, and the Americas.

Ignatius of Loyola, founder of the Society of Jesus. After a painting by Peter Paul Rubens (1577–1640). [Bettman Archive.]

The Jesuit philosophy is contained in the *Spiritual Exercises* of Saint Ignatius of Loyola (1491–1556), the founder of the Society of Jesus. This psychologically perceptive manual contains mental and emotional exercises designed to teach one absolute self-mastery. Its origin lay in Ignatius' own experience, both as a soldier who had endured repeated settings of a shattered leg and as a hermit who had created a new self by severe ascetic practice.

Whereas Protestants were distinguished by disobedience and innovation, the exercises of Ignatius were intended to teach good Catholics to deny themselves and submit without question to higher authority. Perfect discipline and self-control were the conditions of obedience. According to the famous thirteenth rule for "Thinking with the Church" in the *Spiritual Exercises:* "I will believe that the white that I see is black, if the hierarchical church so defines it." To such obedience was added the enthusiasm of traditional spirituality and mysticism—a potent combination that effectively countered Calvinism and won many Protestants back to the Catholic fold.

The Council of Trent (1545–1563)

The broad success of the Reformation and the insistence of the Emperor Charles V forced Pope Paul to call a general council of the church to define religious doctrine. The pope, delaying as long as he could, appointed a reform commission, chaired by Caspar Contarini (1483–1542). Contarini was considered by many to be "semi-Lutheran" and his committee consisted of some very liberal Catholic clergy. Their report, presented to the pope in February 1537, bluntly criticized the fiscality and simony of the papal Curia as the primary source of the church's loss of esteem. It was so critical in fact that

---

The Jesuits State the Principle of Obedience

As leaders of the Counterreformation the Jesuits attempted to live by and to instill in Catholics the strictest self-discipline and obedience. Here is a statement from the *Constitutions of the Order* by which the Jesuits were governed.

Lᴇᴛ *us with the utmost pains strain every nerve of our strength to exhibit this virtue of obedience, firstly to the Highest Pontiff, then to the Superiors of the Society; so that in all things, to which obedience can be extended with charity, we may be most ready to obey his voice, just as if it issued from Christ our Lord . . . directing to this goal all our strength and intention in the Lord, that holy obedience may be made perfect in us in every respect, in performance, in will, in intellect; by submitting to whatever may be enjoined on us with great readiness, with spiritual joy and perseverance; by persuading ourselves that all things [commanded] are just; by rejecting with a kind of blind obedience all opposing opinion or judgment of our own; and [let us do so] in all things which are ordained by the Superior where it cannot be clearly held that any kind of sin intervenes. And let each one persuade himself that they that live under obedience ought to allow themselves to be borne and ruled by divine providence working through their Superiors exactly as if they were a corpse which suffers itself to be borne and handled in any way whatsoever; or just as an old man's stick which serves him who holds it in his hand wherever and for whatever purpose he may wish to use it. . . .*

From the *Constitutions of the Order,* in *Documents of the Christian Church,* ed. by Henry Bettenson (New York: Oxford University Press, 1961), p. 366.

Pope Paul attempted unsuccessfully to suppress its publication. Protestants reprinted and circulated it as justification of their criticism.

The long-delayed council of the church met in 1545 in the city of Trent in the Austrian Tyrol. There were three sessions, spread over eighteen years, with long interruptions due to war, plague, and imperial and papal politics. The council met from 1545 to 1547, from 1551 to 1552, and from 1562 to 1563, a period that spanned the careers of four different popes.

Unlike the general councils of the fifteenth century, Trent was strictly under the pope's control, with high Italian prelates and Jesuits, especially Diego Lainez and Alfonso Salmeron, very prominent in the proceedings. Voting was limited to high churchmen; university theo-

The Council of Trent in session. The Council met in three separate sessions over an eighteen-year period beginning in 1545 and formed the Catholic response to the theological divisions of the later Middle Ages and to the Protestant Reformation. This painting is possibly by the Venetian painter Titian (1477–1576). [Musée du Louvre, Paris. Cliché des Musées Nationaux.]

logians, the lower clergy, and the laity were not permitted to share in the council's decisions.

The council's most important reforms concerned internal church discipline. Steps were taken to curtail the selling of church offices and other religious goods. Many bishops who resided in Rome rather than within their diocese were forced to move to their appointed seats of authority. The council created new seminaries, made provisions for upgrading clerical education, and passed new regulations to monitor clerical morality.

Not a single doctrinal concession was made to the Protestants, however. In the face of Protestant criticism the Council of Trent gave a ringing reaffirmation to the traditional Scholastic education of the clergy; the role of good works in man's salvation; the authority of tradition; the seven sacraments; transubstantiation; the withholding of the Eucharistic cup from the laity; clerical celibacy; the reality of purgatory; the veneration of saints, relics, and sacred images; and the granting of letters of indulgence. The council resolved medieval Scholastic quarrels in favor of the theology of Saint Thomas Aquinas, further enhancing his authority within the church. The strongest resistance was thereafter offered to groups like the Jansenists, who represented the medieval Augustinian tradition, a source of alternative Catholic as well as many Protestant doctrines.

The English Reformation to 1553
The Preconditions of Reform

Late medieval England had a reputation for maintaining the rights of the crown against the pope in Rome. Edward I (d. 1307) had rejected efforts by Pope Boniface VIII to prevent secular taxation of the clergy. Parliament passed the first Statutes of Provisors and *Praemunire* in the mid-fourteenth century, curtailing

payments and judicial appeals to Rome. The English Franciscan William of Ockham defended the rights of royalty against Pope John XXII, and John Wycliffe even sanctioned secular confiscation of clerical property in support of the principle of apostolic poverty. Lollardy, Humanism, and widespread anticlerical sentiment prepared the way intellectually for Protestant ideas, which began to enter England in the early 1520s.

William Tyndale (*ca.* 1492–1536), who translated the New Testament into English in 1526, and other future Protestant reformers met regularly in the White Horse Inn in Cambridge to mull over Lutheran writings. Cardinal Thomas Wolsey (*ca.* 1475–1530), the chief minister of King Henry VIII, and Sir Thomas More (1478–1535), Wolsey's successor, guided royal opposition to incipient Protestantism. The king himself defended the seven sacraments against Luther, receiving as a reward the title "Defender of the Faith" from Pope Leo X. Following Luther's intemperate reply to Henry's amateur theological attack, More wrote a lengthy *Response to Luther* in 1523.

THE KING'S AFFAIR. As important as the other preconditions were, the key precondition of the English Reformation lay elsewhere, in what came to be known as the *king's affair*. Henry was married to Catherine of Aragon (d. 1536), elder daughter of Ferdinand and Isabella of Spain and the aunt of Emperor Charles V. By 1527 the union had produced no male heir to the throne and only one surviving child, a daughter, Mary. Henry was justifiably concerned about the political consequences of leaving only a female heir. People in this period believed it unnatural for women to rule over men; at best a woman ruler meant a contested reign, at worst, turmoil and revolution. Henry even came to believe that his

union with Catherine had been cursed by God, because prior to their marriage Catherine had been the wife of his brother, Arthur. Henry's father, King Henry VII, had passed Catherine on to Henry after Arthur's untimely death in order to keep the English alliance with Spain intact. Marriage to the wife of one's brother was against both canon and biblical law (see Leviticus 18:16, 20:21), and a special dispensation had been required from Pope Julius II before Henry married Catherine in 1509, also the year Henry became king.

By 1527 Henry was thoroughly enamoured of Anne Boleyn, one of Catherine's ladies in waiting, and determined to put Catherine aside and take Anne to wife. This could not occur in Catholic England without papal annulment of the marriage to Catherine. And therein lay a special problem. The year 1527 was also the year of the infamous sack of Rome, and the reigning Pope Clement VII was at the time a prisoner of Charles V, Catherine's nephew. Even if this had not been the case, it would have been virtually impossible for the pope to grant an annulment of a marriage that had not only survived for eighteen years but had been made possible in the first place by a special papal dispensation.

Cardinal Wolsey, who aspired to become pope, was placed in charge of securing the royal annulment. Lord Chancellor since 1515 and papal legate since 1518, Wolsey had long been Henry's "heavy" and the object of much popular resentment. When he failed to secure the annulment, through no fault of his own, he was dismissed in disgrace in 1527. Thomas Cranmer (1489–1556) and Thomas Cromwell (1485–1546), both of whom harbored Lutheran sympathies, thereafter became the king's closest advisers. Finding the way to a papal annulment closed, Henry's new advisers struck a different course:

OPPOSITE: Hampton Court Palace, a major home to the English kings after it was taken over by Henry VIII from Cardinal Wolsey, its builder, early in the sixteenth century. In the seventeenth century, Sir Christopher Wren, the great architect of the Restoration period, made additions not shown here. [British Tourist Authority, New York.]

RIGHT: A lion—one of the so-called "Queen's Beasts"—stands guard at Hampton Court Palace. [British Tourist Authority, New York.]

Catherine of Aragon, the first wife of Henry VIII, in a portrait by an unknown artist. [National Portrait Gallery, London.]

Why not simply declare the king supreme in English spiritual affairs as he was in English temporal affairs? Then the king himself could settle the king's affair.

The Reformation Parliament

In 1529 Parliament was convened for what would be a seven-year session that earned it the title "Reformation Parliament." During this period, it passed a flood of legislation that harassed and finally placed royal reins upon the clergy. In January 1531 the clergy in Convocation (a legislature assembly representing the English clergy) publicly recognized Henry as head of the church in England "as far as the law of Christ allows." In 1532 the Supplication of the Commons Against the Ordinaries was passed, a list of grievances against the church ranging from indifference to the needs of the laity to an excessive number of religious holidays. In the same year the Submission of the Clergy was passed, effectively placing canon law under royal control and thereby the clergy under royal jurisdiction. The Act in Conditional Restraint of Annates further gave the English king the power to withhold from Rome these lucrative "first fruits" of new ecclesiastical appointments.

In January 1533 Henry wed the pregnant Anne Boleyn, with Thomas Cranmer officiating. In February 1533 the Act for the Restraint of Appeals made the king the highest court of appeal for all Englishmen. In March 1533 Cranmer was elevated to archbishop of Canterbury and led Convocation in invalidating the king's marriage to Catherine. In 1534 Parliament ended all payments by the English clergy and laity to Rome and gave Henry sole jurisdiction over high ecclesiastical appointments. The Act of Succession in the same year made Anne Boleyn's children legitimate heirs to the throne, and the Act of

Supremacy declared Henry "the only supreme head in earth of the church of England." Refusal to recognize these two acts brought the execution of Thomas More and John Fischer, bishop of Rochester—events that made clear the king's determination to have his way regardless of cost. In 1536 came the first Act for Dissolution of Monasteries, which affected only the smaller. Three years later a second act dissolved all English monasteries and turned their endowments over to the king.

WIVES OF HENRY VIII. Henry's domestic life proved to lack the consistency of his political life. In 1536 Anne Boleyn was executed for adultery and her daughter, Elizabeth, was declared illegitimate. Henry had four further marriages. His third wife, Jane Seymour, died in 1537 shortly after giving birth to the future Edward VI. Henry wed Anne of Cleves sight unseen on the advice of Cromwell, the purpose being to create by the marriage an alliance with the Protestant princes. Neither the alliance nor Anne—whom Henry found to have a remarkable resemblance to a horse—proved worth the trouble; the marriage was annulled by Parliament and Cromwell dismissed and executed. Catherine Howard, Henry's fifth wife, was beheaded for adultery in 1542. His last wife, Catherine Parr, for whom Henry was her third marriage, survived him to marry still a fourth time—obviously she was a match for the English king.

THE KING'S RELIGIOUS CONSERVATISM. Henry's political and domestic boldness was not carried over to the religious front. Despite his political break with Rome, he remained decidedly conservative in his religious beliefs, and Catholic teaching remained prominent in a country seething with Protestant sentiment. Despite his many wives and amorous adventures, Henry absolutely forbade the English clergy to marry and threatened clergy who were twice caught in concubinage with execution. The Ten Articles of 1536 prescribed Catholic doctrine with only mild Protestant concessions. Angered by the growing popularity of Protestant views even among his chief advisers, Henry struck directly at them in the Six Articles of 1539. These reaffirmed transubstantiation, denied the Eucharistic cup to the laity, enforced clerical celibacy, declared monastic vows inviolable, provided for private masses, and ordered the continuation of auricular confession. Although William Tyndale's English New Testament grew into the Coverdale Bible (1535) and the Great Bible (1539) and the latter was mandated for every English parish during Henry's reign, England had to await Henry's death before it could become a genuinely Protestant country.

The Protestant Reformation Under Edward VI

When Henry died, his son and successor Edward VI (1547–1553) was only ten years old. Edward reigned under the successive regencies of Edward Seymour, the duke of Somerset (1547–1550), and the earl of Warwick, known as the duke of Northumberland (1550–1553), during which time England fully enacted the Protestant Reformation. The new king and Somerset corresponded directly with John Calvin. During Somerset's regency, Henry's Six Articles and laws against heresy were repealed, and clerical marriage and communion with cup were sanctioned.

In 1547 the chantries, places where endowed masses had traditionally been said for the dead, were dissolved. In 1549, the Act of Uniformity imposed Thomas Cranmer's *Book of Common Prayer* on all English churches. Images and altars were removed in 1550. Still more radical Protestant reforms were carried out by Somerset's usurper, the duke of Northumberland. After Charles V's victory over the German princes in 1547, German Protestant leaders fled to England for refuge, and several directly assisted the completion of the English Reformation, Martin Bucer being prominent among them. The Second Act of Uniformity, passed in 1552, imposed a revised edition of the *Book of Common Prayer* on all English churches. A forty-two-article confession of faith, also authored by Thomas Cranmer, was adopted, setting forth a moderate Protestant doctrine. It taught justification by faith and the supremacy of Holy Scripture, de-

---

The English Monarch Becomes Head of the Anglican Church

The parliamentary Act of Supremacy (1534) recognized Henry VIII, and his successors, as head of the Church of England, thereby sealing the separation of the Church from the pope in Rome and fixing a foundation for the English Reformation.

ALBEIT *the King's Majesty justly and rightfully is and oweth to be the Supreme Head of the Church of England, and so is recognized by the clergy of this realm in their Convocations, yet nevertheless for corroboration and confirmation thereof, and for increase of virtue in Christ's religion within this realm of England, and to repress and extirp all errors, heresies, and other enormities and abuses heretofore used in the same; be it enacted by authority of this present Parliament, that the King our Sovereign Lord, his heirs and successors, kings of this realm, shall be taken, accepted, and reputed the only Supreme Head in earth of the Church of England, called* Anglicana Ecclesia, *and shall have and enjoy, annexed and united to the imperial Crown of this realm, as well the title and style thereof, as all honours, dignities, preeminences, jurisdictions, privileges, authorities, immunities, profits, and commodities, to the said dignity of Supreme Head of the same Church belonging and appertaining; and that our said Sovereign Lord, his heirs and successors, kings of this realm, shall have full power and authority from time to time to visit, repress, redress, reform, order, correct, restrain, and amend all such errors, heresies, abuses, offences, contempts and enormities, whatsoever they be, which by any manner spiritual authority or jurisdiction ought or may lawfully be reformed, repressed, ordered, redressed, corrected, restrained, or amended, most to the pleasure of Almighty God, the increase of virtue in Christ's religion, and for the conservation of the peace, unity and tranquillity of this realm; any usage, custom, foreign laws, foreign authority, prescription, or any other thing or things to the contrary hereof notwithstanding.*

The Reformation in England: To the Accession of Elizabeth I, ed. by A. G. Dickens and Dorothy Carr (New York: St. Martin's Press, 1968), pp. 64–65.

---

nied transubstantiation (although not real presence), and recognized only two sacraments.

All these changes were short-lived, however. In 1553 Catherine's daughter, Mary, succeeded Edward to the English throne and proceeded to restore Catholic doctrine and practice with a singlemindedness that rivaled

THE RELIGIOUS SITUATION ABOUT 1560

Most of Europe

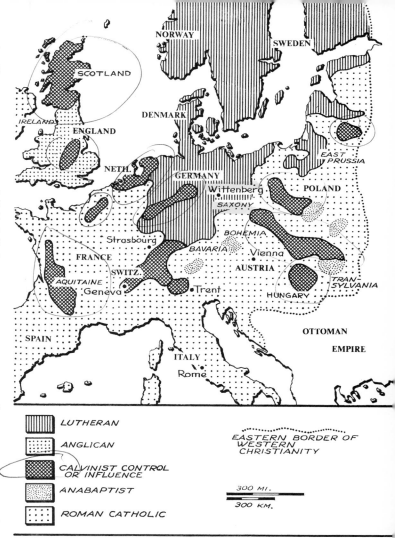

By 1560 Luther, Zwingli, and Loyola were dead, Calvin near the end of his life, the English break from Rome fully accomplished, and the last session of the Council of Trent about to assemble. Here is the religious geography of Western Europe at this time.

that of her father. It was not until the reign of Anne Boleyn's daughter, Elizabeth (1558–1603), that a lasting religious settlement was achieved in England.

The Social Significance of the Reformation in Western Europe

It was a common feature of the Lutheran, Zwinglian, and Calvinist reforms to work within the framework of reigning political power. Luther, Zwingli, and Calvin saw themselves and their followers as citizens of the world, subject to definite civic responsibilities and obligations. Their adjustments in this regard have led scholars to characterize them as "magisterial reformers," meaning not only that they were the leaders of the major Protestant movements but also that they succeeded by the force of the magistrate's sword. It was probably not a matter of compromising the principles of the Gospels and choosing the way of brute force, as some have argued. The reformers never contemplated a reform outside or against the societies of which they were members. They wanted a reform that took shape within the laws and institutions of the sixteenth century, and to that end they remained highly sensitive to what was politically and socially possible in their age.

Some scholars believe that they were too conscious of the historically possible, that their reforms went forward with such caution that they not only changed late medieval society very little but actually encouraged acceptance of the sociopolitical *status quo*. Those who so argue follow the work of the late German historian and sociologist Ernst Troeltsch, who has influenced modern interpretation of the Reformation more than any single scholar. In his view Protestantism was a "church-type" of religion, one in which salvation was considered a pure gift independent of all individual efforts, having only to be appropriated by faith. From this point of view it was only a slight variation of the church civilization of the Middle Ages and less progressive in political and social theory

than contemporary Humanists, Anabaptists, and Spiritualists.

For every positive feature of the Reformation, scholars influenced by Troeltsch point to a corresponding negative feature.

Protestants replaced the Catholic doctrine of salvation with a religious individualism that anticipated modern religion, but they also attempted to regulate state and society, science and education, and law and commerce according to the standards of a supernatural revelation. Protestants transformed the other-worldliness of monasticism into an inner attitude of self-denial, a "worldly asceticism," but they also attempted to create a society run according to puritanical biblical norms. Protestants created new patterns of family life, making marriage a more ethical and personal matter and recognizing a mutual right of divorce, yet they also enforced the medieval patriarchical ideal with its complete subordination of wife and children to the man of the house.

Protestants championed the legal rights of secular rulers against the claims of popes to temporal power, yet the

Lutheran church became a staunch supporter of Prussian absolutism. Calvinists were famous for their defense of the right of citizens to resist tyrants who denied them the freedom to worship as they chose, but John Calvin also erected an intolerant near theocracy in Geneva. Protestants, rejecting medieval belief in the superiority of clergy and special religious works, enhanced secular callings and ordinary work in the world, yet Lutherans clung to agrarian society values despite a more positive view of new economic institutions on the part of Calvinists.

Finally, Protestants embraced humanist educational reforms and rejected much traditional Scholastic education. Yet here too they fell short of the ideal of universal education and intellectual autonomy that characterized the Enlightenment of the eighteenth century, as a narrow confessionalism came to dominate many Protestant universities in the sixteenth and seventeenth centuries. All things considered, it is argued, the effect of Protestantism was to perpetuate the "medieval spirit" until the new science and philosophy of the seventeenth and eighteenth centuries finally secured the victory of modern values.

Whether the Reformation was more medieval than modern is an issue that will continue to be debated by scholars. Its continuance does not distract, however, from the changes brought about by the Reformation in religious life, education, and the image and role of women.

The Revolution in Religious Life

The Protestant Reformation was basically a change in the religious life of people; in its essence it was a transvaluation of the concept, practice, and institutions of religion.[1] Because the Age of Reformation was a period when religion embraced so much of life, the changes in religious belief penetrated into the political, social, and economic spheres in ways quite foreign to the modern world. When the Protestant reformers rejected such popular revenue-gathering devices of the medieval church as indulgences, pilgrimages, and annates of benefices, or

[1] Much of what follows is elaborated in Ozment, *The Reformation in the Cities.*

when they reduced the number of feast and fast days or dissolved monasteries and the episcopal system of church government, there were profound repercussions in the nonreligious spheres. The reformers, pursuing late medieval reform efforts shook the foundations of a traditional ecclesiocommercial complex in which bankers and politicians were as heavily invested as the Roman Curia.

LAY CONTROL OF RELIGION. A desire to simplify religion and make it more socially responsible had been expressed throughout the later Middle Ages. It was being achieved on the higher political levels by royal circumscription of papal and episcopal jurisdiction in England and France as early as the fourteenth century. In the cities and towns of Germany we find the religious life increasingly regulated by magistrates and city councils. There were determined efforts at both the higher and the lower levels of society to make the religious life of the laity less psychologically and financially burdensome and the activities of the clergy more socially constructive.

This extension of "civilian" control over religion was impelled by the evident corruption and inefficiency of many local ecclesiastical authorities. On the eve of the Reformation, Rome's international network of church offices, which had religiously unified Europe during the Middle Ages, began to fall apart in many areas, hurried along by a growing sense of regional identity—incipient nationalism—and local secular administrative competence. A widespread attitude of "Mother Church, we would rather do it ourselves" is evident. As early as the fourteenth century vernacular languages had made their appearance at official levels. This inclination toward official use of the vernacular rather than Latin reflected the growth of regional and national self-consciousness, a centrifugal force that worked against the traditional perception of Europe as a religiously unified body of Christians. One of the indices of the Reformation's victory in cities and towns was the transition from "papist" Latin to the vernacular in the city records. Luther and Calvin, respectively, were very prominent in the formation of modern German and French.

SAD STATE OF THE CLERGY. The long-entrenched benefice system of the medieval church, which had permitted important ecclesiastical posts to be sold to the highest bidders and left residency requirements in parishes unenforced, did not make for a vibrant local religious life. The substitutes hired by nonresident holders of benefices, who lived elsewhere (mostly in Rome) and milked the revenues of their offices, performed their chores mechanically and had neither first-hand knowledge of nor much sympathy with local needs and problems. Rare is the late medieval German town that did not have complaints about the maladministration, concubinage, and/or fiscalism of their clergy, especially the higher clergy (i.e., bishops, abbots, and prelates). Parish priests in the lowest echelons were often as much victims as perpetrators of the church's inefficiency, an important factor in their relatively high level of participation in the Reformation. The majority of Protestant clergy, like most late medieval parish priests, had lower-middle-class origins. A high percentage came from the families of craftsmen.

Lower clergy had two basic sources of income: a portion of the tithes paid by parishioners and the modest fees they received for performing such pastoral duties as confessions, marriages, baptisms, and burials. Although the situation can be exaggerated, many unbeneficed parish priests lived as a proletariat, moonlighting in menial tasks and even wandering from church to church in search of additional fees. We find city ordinances listing the types of secular employment permitted priests who needed to supplement their income. Ordinary people tended to sympathize with them, in part because the lower clergy were more like their parishioners than were the higher clergy. Laymen lent support to the complaints of the lower clergy against rich higher clergy and against the "poaching" of the mendicant orders among their congregations (i.e. performing religious services for fees).

Concubinage fees are a prime example of the way the higher clergy burdened the lives of parish priests. It had been part of the Gregorian reform of the eleventh cen-tury to make the secular clergy as celibate as the regular clergy. There were special fines for the sins of clerical concubinage and parenthood (the so-called "cradle tax"), as well as fees for baptizing the children of priests and making them legitimate heirs. These fees were levied as punishment and penance for the departure from clerical vows. The *Reformatio Sigismundi*, an important anonymous reform tract that circulated widely in the fifteenth century, complained about this exploitation of lower clergy and strongly urged clerical marriage. Protestants, who fully shared this late medieval reform sentiment, gave clerical marriage an overwhelming endorsement and came by this route to enhance the importance of women, as mothers and housewives, and family life.

ATTACK ON FINANCIAL ABUSES. Communities loudly protested the financial abuses of the medieval church long before Luther published his famous summary of economic grievances in the *Address to the Christian Nobility of the German Nation*. The sale of indulgences, a practice that was greatly expanded on the eve of the Reformation, had also been repeatedly attacked before Luther came on the scene. Rulers and magistrates had little objection to and could even encourage the sale of indulgences as long as a generous portion of the income remained within the local coffers. Bishops and secular authorities profited from the sale. Indulgences were an aid in financing local projects as well as an answer to the genuine religious anxiety of people who wished to reduce or avoid punishment for unresolved sins in purgatory. It is clear that when an indulgence was preached primarily for the benefit of distant interests, as was the case with the St. Peter's indulgence protested by Luther, there could be resistance for strictly financial reasons, because their sale drained away local revenues.

Indulgences could not pass from the scene until rulers found new ways to profit from religion and a more effective popular remedy for religious anxiety was at hand. The Reformation provided the former by sanctioning the secular dissolution of monasteries and the confiscation of ecclesiastical properties. And it also held out the latter in its new theology of justification by faith.

PREACHERSHIPS. City governments also undertook to improve local religious life on the eve of the Reformation by endowing preacherships. These were beneficed positions that provided for well-trained and dedicated pastors and regular preaching and pastoral care, which went beyond the routine performance of the Mass and traditional religious functions. In many instances these preacherships became platforms for Protestant preachers, who made the preaching of the Word, rather than the celebration of the Mass, the central religious moment in the service of worship.

RESTRICTIONS ON THE CLERGY. Magistrates also very carefully restricted the growth of ecclesiastical properties and clerical privileges. During the Middle Ages special clerical rights in both property and person had come to be recognized by canon and civil law. Because they were holy places, churches and monasteries were exempted from the taxes and laws that affected others. They were treated as special places of "sacral peace" and asylum. It was considered inappropriate for holy persons (clergy) to be burdened with such "dirty jobs" as military service, compulsory labor, standing watch at city gates, and other normal obligations of citizenship. Nor was it thought right that laymen, of whatever rank, should sit in judgment on those who were their shepherds and intermediaries with God. Secular and regular clergy, accordingly, came to enjoy an immunity of place (which exempted ecclesiastical properties from taxes and recognized their right of asylum) and an immunity of person (which exempted the clergy from the jurisdiction of civil courts).

On the eve of the Reformation we find many examples of lay-inspired measures to restrict these privileges and end their abuses—efforts to regulate ecclesiastical acquisition of new property, to circumvent the right of asylum in churches and monasteries (a practice that posed a threat to the normal administration of justice), and to bring the clergy under the local tax code. Governments were understandably tired of ecclesiastical interference in what seemed to them to be strictly political spheres of competence and authority.

Between the fourteenth and the sixteenth centuries there was a significant fusion of the religious and secular spheres and a leveling of clergy and laity. These were the popular foundations on which the religious revolution of the sixteenth century occurred. Most Protestant cities and towns required the clergy to swear allegiance, pay taxes, and defend the city. Protestant clergy either formally became citizens or pledged to fulfill, in one form or another, most of the basic obligations of citizenship. Protestant clergy surrendered the traditional immunities and privileges of the medieval clergy and undertook a greater degree of civic responsibility. However, they never became citizens as other citizens were citizens. They were, for example, excluded from holding high political office. Still Protestant reforms consummated late medieval efforts to integrate the religious life more effectively into the civic life.

PROTESTANTISM: A BURDENSOME RELIGION? There are those who argue that Catholicism, in contrast to all forms of Protestantism, was the more tolerant religion, possessing a greater understanding of human frailty and a greater flexibility in regard to the practices and lifestyles permitted believers. In the tradition of scholarship influenced by the German sociologist and religious historian Max Weber, Protestantism is seen as the more burdensome and anxiety-producing of the two Western forms of Christianity. In a famous summary, Weber described the Reformation as

the repudiation of a control over everyday life which was very lax, at that time scarcely perceptible in practice, and hardly more than formal, in favor of a regulation of the whole of conduct which, penetrating to all departments of private and public life, was infinitely burdensome and earnestly enforced.[2]

2 *The Protestant Ethic and the Spirit of Capitalism*, trans. by Talcott Parsons (New York: Charles Scribner's Sons, 1958) p. 36.

Those who agree with this assessment have pointed out that one could not, as a good Protestant, become a monk or a nun, invoke the aid of saints, treasure relics, buy indulgences, and generally indulge in a broad spectrum of popular religious activity. The medieval Catholic Church, this argument continues, was not a stern disciplinarian father but an overly indulgent mother, forgiving and tolerant even to the point of permitting glaring doctrinal contradictions, liturgical irregularities, and gross moral indiscipline as long as basic obedience to her authority was observed. From this point of view the Protestant Reformation is seen to be a grand effort to "shape up" religious life, not to make it any freer and less burdensome. Protestants are seen as having narrowed religious options, carefully defining true doctrine and fanatically enforcing moral discipline.

The Protestant Reformation was only in part a reform movement against a failing institution. It was also a challenge to a vibrant religious practice that had prevailed for centuries despite the irregularities and shortcomings of the medieval church. The Protestant reformers contested the best as well as the worst of medieval religious life. A prominent motive of the Protestant reformers was their belief in the inadequacy of even a *reformed* medieval church. This was strikingly indicated by Luther's statement that even if Rome and its clergy had observed traditional religion with the rigor and discipline of the hermits, and such saintly figures as Jerome, Augustine, Gregory, Bernard, Francis, and Dominic, its "false doctrine" would still have necessitated the Reformation.

PROTEST AGAINST CONFESSION AND PENANCE. Despite often frenzied religious activities, large numbers of people appear to have been disinclined to go frequently to confession and to hear Mass on the eve of the Reformation. From one point of view this may look like religious laxity and indiscipline. From another, however, it may be seen as weariness with a religious practice that had lost the ability to satisfy the basic religious needs of many people.

A case in point is the sacrament of Penance, or confession. This particular sacrament was the centerpiece of late medieval lay religious practice. Belief in purgatory, relics, pilgrimages, and indulgences was closely tied to this key sacrament. It became the first object of attack by Protestants.

Church law required people to confess their sins at least once each year and without fail during Lent. They were expected to examine themselves and itemize all conscious mortal sins. According to a confessional guide of 1504, the penitent was to confess all sins committed directly by deed and indirectly by counsel or inaction (so-called sins of commission and omission). He was also expected to narrate the exact circumstances of each, taking account of such things as with what persons and where the sin was committed (if clergy and church property were involved, a special absolution was required); at what time the sin was committed (if the sin occurred on Sunday or a religious holiday, its seriousness was compounded); how often the sin was committed; why it was committed (certain motives being worse than others); and the consequences of the sin. As this example indicates, going to confession could be an unpleasant undertaking that required considerable forethought and preparation on the part of the penitent.

The burdensome requirements of late medieval religion can also be seen in the most popular late medieval German catechism for laity, Dietrich Coelde's *Mirror of the Christian Man*, a guide to the religious life that went through twenty-nine editions between 1480 and 1520. This catechism carefully modeled lay religious life upon clerical life, directing the good lay Christian to live as much like a cleric as he could in the world. The medieval belief in the superiority of the spiritual estate over the lay estate encouraged such modeling of lay upon clerical religiosity. When Coelde cited things that assured one of good standing with God, they were the kinds of things monks and clerics were preoccupied with. The twenty-four articles of *The Mirror of the Christian Man* covered every conceivable "sin," from oversleeping to masturbation, and admonished the laity to meditate daily on their ten or twelve most committed sins.

LUTHER'S SMALL CATECHISM. The revolution in individual religious practice brought about by the Reformation can be illustrated if one contrasts Martin Luther's *Small Catechism* for laity with such medieval confessional guides and catechisms as those just described. There were only nine articles in Luther's catechism. The first stated the Ten Commandments, the second the Apostles' Creed, and the third the Lord's Prayer. Articles four to six took up the sacraments, which were reduced in number from seven to three: baptism, confession, and communion.

Article five, "How Simple People Should Be Taught to Confess," set forth the Protestant alternative to the medieval sacrament of penance. Protestants did not consider confession to a priest a proper sacrament; it was an ecclesiastical ordinance, a voluntary matter advised in place of the traditional requirement of an annual auricular confession of all conscious mortal sins. In Protestant churches this confession came normally to be transacted by congregational recitation of a formalized confession of sin. Luther taught that one should forthrightly acknowledge guilt to God for every sin, as these are quickly discovered in the mirror of the Ten Commandments. But he believed that one need bring before the priest only those individual sins that have proved to be particularly distressing. The priest who hears such a voluntary confession is instructed to respond: "As you believe, so it will happen. I, by the command of our Lord Jesus Christ, forgive you your sin in the name of the Father, the Son, and the Holy Spirit. Amen. Go in peace." There were no judicial interrogation, cataloguing of sins, or imposed works of penance. One supposedly left confession with his sins resolved; he did not have the threat of purgatory hanging over his head if he failed to perform works of satisfaction.

In article seven of Luther's catechism there were morning and evening prayers for the father of the house and in article eight blessings for before and after meals.

The final article described the daily responsibilities of what Luther called the "holy orders and stations in life." Here Luther illustrated the Protestant repudiation of the medieval distinction between clergy and laity, a rejection that transformed the expectations of lay religious life by no longer patterning it on monastic and clerical practice. Luther's "holy orders" were not special religious bodies but the following groups: (1) bishops, pastors, preachers, and magistrates; (2) husbands, wives, and parents; (3) children; (4) servants, maids, day laborers, and workers; (5) masters and mistresses of households; (6) youth; (7) widows; and (8) the community as a whole. Their religious duties were not deduced from clerical ideals but carefully tailored to the particular estate involved.

THE CHANGES IN RELIGIOUS LIFE. As it developed, the Reformation eliminated or put severe restrictions upon such traditional practices as mandatory fasting; auricular confession; the veneration of saints, relics, and images; indulgences; pilgrimages and shrines; vigils; weekly, monthly, and annual Masses for the dead; the belief in purgatory; Latin worship services; the sacrifice of the Mass; numerous religious ceremonies, festivals, and holidays; the canonical hours; monasteries and mendicant orders; the sacramental status of marriage, extreme unction, confirmation, holy orders, and penance; clerical celibacy; clerical immunity from civil taxation and criminal jurisdiction; nonresident benefices; excommunication and interdict; canon law; episcopal and papal authority; and the traditional Scholastic education of the clergy.

It may be argued that by the second half of the sixteenth century Protestant religion had become just as burdensome as medieval religion had ever been. As Protestants won power in cities and towns, they tended to use their new position to erect what critics called "new papacies." In its first decades, however, the Reformation was presented and perceived by those who embraced it as a profound simplification of religious life. It was freeing precisely because it required less rather than more from those who wanted to be pious Christians and gave clearer focus to their ethical obligations.

Philip Melanchthon (1497–1560), by Lucas Cranach the Elder (1472–1553). Melanchthon was professor of Greek at the University of Wittenberg, one of Luther's closest friends, author of the major Lutheran Confessions, and is known as the "Educator of Germany" because of his pedagogical reforms. [Bettmann Archive.]

The Reformation and Education

An important cultural achievement of the Reformation was its implementation of many of the educational reforms of Humanism. Many Protestant reformers in Germany, France, and England were Humanists. Even when their views on church doctrine and the nature of man separated them from the Humanist movement, Protestant reformers continued to share with Humanists a common opposition to Scholasticism and belief in the unity of wisdom, eloquence, and action. Religious reform went hand in hand with educational reform in Protestant cities and towns. The Humanist program of studies, which gave men the language skills to deal authoritatively with original sources, clearly proved to be a more appropriate tool for the defense of Protestant doctrine than did Scholastic dialectic.

The connections between Humanism and the Reformation were recognized by the Catholic counterreformers. Ignatius of Loyola observed the way the new learning had been embraced by and served the Protestant cause. In his *Spiritual Exercises* he insisted that when the Bible and the Church Fathers were read directly, they be read under the guidance of the authoritative Scholastic theologians: Peter Lombard, Bonaventura, and Thomas Aquinas. The latter, Ignatius argued, being "of more recent date," had the clearer understanding of what Scripture and the Fathers mean and therefore should guide the study of the past.

When in August 1518 Philip Melanchthon, a young Humanist and professor of Greek, arrived at the University of Wittenberg, his first act was to implement curricular reforms on the Humanist model. This he undertook with Luther's blessing. In his inaugural address, entitled *On Improving the Studies of the Young,* Melanchthon presented himself as a defender of good letters and classical studies against "barbarians who practice barbarous arts." By the latter he meant the Scholastic theologians of the later Middle Ages. Such men, he argued, had risen to power after the fall of good letters, during the long dark night of the Middle Ages. Their dominance in the uni-

versities was seen by Melanchthon to have bred contempt for the Greek language and learning and to have encouraged neglect of the study of mathematics, sacred studies, and the art of oratory. Melanchthon urged the careful study of history, poetry, and other humanist disciplines.

The following year (1519) Luther wrote of the traditional theological curriculum, "I have learned nothing in scholastic theology except ignorance of sin, righteousness, baptism, and the whole Christian life. . . . Everything I learned was something I have had to unlearn."[3]

Together Luther and Melanchthon completely restructured the University of Wittenberg's curriculum. Commentaries on Lombard's *Sentences* were dropped, as was canon law. The old scholastic lectures on Aristotle were replaced by straightforward historical study based on the most recent translations. Students read primary sources directly, not by way of accepted Scholastic commentators. Candidates for theological degrees were made to defend their views on the basis of their own exegesis of the Bible. New chairs of Greek and Hebrew were created. Luther and Melanchthon also pressed for universal compulsory education so that both boys and girls could reach vernacular literacy in the Bible.

In Geneva John Calvin and his successor, Theodore Beza, founded the Genevan Academy, which later evolved into the University of Geneva. This institution, created primarily for the purpose of training Calvinist ministers, pursued ideals similar to those set forth by Luther and Melanchthon. Calvinist refugees trained in the academy carried Protestant educational reforms to France, Scotland, England, and the New World. It was due to such efforts that a working knowledge of Greek and Hebrew became commonplace in the sixteenth and seventeenth centuries.

The Humanist curriculum was placed in the strict service of the new Protestant doctrine. Some contemporaries decried what they saw as a narrowing of the origi-

3 *Documente zu Luthers Entwicklung,* edited by Otto Scheel (Tübingen: J. C. B. Mohr, 1929) no. 27, p. 14.

nal Humanist program as Protestants took it over. Erasmus, for example, came to fear the Reformation as a threat to the liberal arts and good learning and Sebastian Franck pointed to parallels between Luther's and Zwingli's debates over Christ's presence in the Eucharist and such old Scholastic disputations as that over the Immaculate Conception of the Virgin.

Humanist culture and learning nonetheless remained indebted to the Reformation. The Protestant endorsement of the Humanist program of studies remained as significant for the Humanist movement as the latter had been for the Reformation. Protestant schools and universities consolidated and preserved for the modern world many of the basic pedagogical achievements of Humanism. There the *studia humanitatis,* albeit often as little more than a handmaiden to theological doctrine, found a permanent home, one that remained hospitable even in the heyday of Protestant Scholasticism.

The Reformation and the Changing Role of Women

The Protestant reformers took a positive stand on clerical marriage and strongly opposed monasticism and the celibate life. From this position they challenged the medieval tendency alternately to degrade women as temptresses (following the model of Eve) and to exalt them as virgins (following the model of Mary). Protestants opposed the popular antiwomen and antimarriage literature of the Middle Ages. They praised woman in her own right but especially in her biblical vocation as mother and housewife. Although relief of sexual frustration and a remedy of fornication were motives behind Protestant pro-marriage arguments, and although motherhood and housewifery were considered woman's true vocation, the reformers also viewed their wives as indispensable companions in their work, and this not solely because they took domestic cares off their husbands' minds. Luther, who married in 1525 at the age of forty-one, wrote of women:

Imagine what it would be like without women. The home, cities, economic life, and government would virtually disappear. Men cannot do without women. Even if it were possible for men to beget and bear children, they still could not do without women.[4]

John Calvin wrote at the death of his wife:

I have been bereaved of the best companion of my life, of one who, had it been so ordered, would not only have been the willing sharer of my indigence, but even of my death. During her life she was the faithful helper of my ministry.[5]

Such tributes were intended in part to overcome Catholic criticism of clerical marriage as a distraction from one's ministry. They were primarily the expression of a new value placed upon the estate of marriage and family life.

Protestant doctrines were as attractive to women as they were to men. Women who had been maligned as the concubines of priests came to know a new dignity as the "honorable wives" of Protestant ministers. Renegade nuns wrote exposés of the nunnery in the name of Christian freedom and justification by faith. Women in the higher classes, who were enjoying new social and political freedoms during the Renaissance, found in Protestant theology a religious complement to their greater independence in other walks of life.

Because of their desire to have women become pious housewives, Protestants also encouraged the education of girls to vernacular literacy, expecting them thereafter to model their lives on the Bible. Women came in the course of such study, however, to find in the Bible passages that made them the equals to men in the presence of God. Such education further gave them a role in the Reforma-

4 *Luther's Works,* Vol. 54: Table Talk, ed. and trans. by Theodore G. Tappert (Philadelphia: Fortress Press, 1967), p. 161.
5 *Letters of John Calvin,* Vol. 2, trans. by J. Bonnet (Edinburgh: T. Constable and Co., 1858), p. 216.

tion as independent authors. These may seem like small advances from a modern perspective, but they were significant, if indirect, steps in the direction of the emancipation of women.

SUGGESTED READINGS

S. T. BINDHOFF, *Tudor England* (1950). Basic political narrative.

A. G. DICKENS, *The Counter Reformation* (1969). Brief narrative with pictures.

A. G. DICKENS, *The English Reformation* (1974). The best one-volume account.

G. DONALDSON, *The Scottish Reformation* (1960). Dependable, comprehensive narrative.

H. OUTRAM EVENNETT, *The Spirit of the Counter Reformation* (1968). Essay on the continuity of Catholic reform and its independence from the Protestant Reformation.

RENE FÜLOP-MILLER, *The Jesuits: A History of the Society of Jesus,* trans. by F. S. Flint and D. F. Tait (1963). A critical survey, given to psychological analysis.

HAROLD GRIMM, *The Reformation Era: 1500–1650* (1973). Very good on later Lutheran developments.

HUBERT JEDIN, *A History of the Council of Trent,* Vols. 1 and 2 (1957–1961). Comprehensive, detailed, authoritative account.

WILBUR K. JORDAN, *Edward VI: The Young King* (1968). The basic biography.

JOHN H. LEITH, *The Reformed Tradition* (1977). Beliefs and confessions of the Zwinglian–Calvinist tradition.

JOHN T. MCNEILL, *The History and Character of Calvinism* (1954). The most comprehensive account and very readable.

E. W. MONTER, *Calvins Geneva* (1967). Dependable sketch derived from authoritative studies.

DONALD NUGENT, *Ecumenism in the Age of Reformation: The Colloquy of Poissy* (1974). Study of the last ecumenical council of the sixteenth century.

STEVEN E. OZMENT, *Mysticism and Dissent* (1973). Treats dissenters from Lutheranism and Calvinism.

STEVEN E. OZMENT, *The Reformation in the Cities* (1975). An essay on why people thought they wanted to be Protestants.

JASPAR G. RIDLEY, *Thomas Cranmer* (1962). The basic biography.

J. J. SCARISBRICK, *Henry VIII* (1968). Comprehensive and entertaining.

R. H. TAWNEY, *Religion and the Rise of Capitalism* (1947). Advances beyond Weber's arguments relating Protestantism and capitalist economic behavior.

ERNST TROELTSCH, *The Social Teaching of the Christian Churches,* trans. by Olive Wyon I–II (1960).

MAX WEBER, *The Protestant Ethic and the Spirit of Capitalism,* trans. by Talcott Parsons, (1958). First appeared in 1904–1905 and has continued to stimulate debate over the relationship between religion and society.

FRANCOIS WENDEL, *Calvin: The Origins and Development of His Religious Thought,* trans. by Philip Mairet (1963). The best treatment of Calvin's theology.

402

16
The Age of Religious Wars

THE LATE sixteenth century and the first half of the seventeenth century are described as an "age of religious wars" because of the bloody opposition of Protestants and Catholics across the length and breadth of Europe. Politically and religiously inspired Calvinists fought Catholic rulers for basic civil rights in France, the Netherlands, England, and Scotland in the second half of the sixteenth century. In the first half of the seventeenth century Lutherans, Calvinists, and Catholics marched against one another in central and northern Europe during the Thirty Years' War. And by the middle of the seventeenth century English Puritans had successfully revolted against the Stuart monarchy and the Anglican Church settlement. In the second half of the sixteenth century the political conflict, which had previously been confined to central Europe and a struggle for Lutheran rights and freedoms, shifted to western Europe—to France, the Netherlands, England, and Scotland—and became a struggle for Calvinist recognition. War-weary German Lutherans and Catholics agreed to live and let live in the Peace of Augsburg (1555): *cuius regio, eius religio,* "he who controls the land may determine its religion." Lutheranism thereafter became a contented, established religion within the Empire. Non-Lutheran Protestants, however, were not recognized by the Peace of Augsburg. Both sides scorned Anabaptists and other sectarians as anarchists,

St. Peter's in Rome was built in the sixteenth and seventeenth centuries replacing Emperor Constantine's early Christian basilica of the fourth century on the probable site of the saint's tomb. The great church had many architects, among them Michelangelo, who designed the great dome. The vast piazza in front was designed by Bernini; note how the thrown-open arms extend to embrace pilgrims and draw them into the church. A portion of the pope's residence, the Vatican palace, is at the right center. [Foto-cielo.]

and Calvinists were not yet strong enough to demand legal standing.

If German Lutherans had reason to take quiet satisfaction, Protestants elsewhere obviously did not. The struggle for religious freedom had intensified in most countries outside the Empire by the mid-16th century. The Council of Trent adjourned in 1563 with the declaration of an international Catholic counteroffensive against Protestants to be led by the Jesuits. At the time of John Calvin's death in 1564, Geneva had become both a refuge for Europe's persecuted Protestants and an international school for Protestant resistance, producing leaders fully equal to the new Catholic challenge. Genevan Calvinism and Tridentine Catholicism were two equally dogmatic, aggressive, and irreconcilable church systems. Calvinism was a religion committed to changing societies, whereas the Catholicism of the Counter Reformation was devoted to traditional ways of doing things. Although Calvinists looked like "new papists" to critics when they dominated cities like Geneva, they were firebrands and revolutionaries when, as minorities, they found their civil and religious rights denied. Calvinism was characterized by a presbyterian organization that magnified regional and local religious authority. By contrast, Catholicism sponsored a centralized episcopal church system, hierarchically arranged from pope to parish priest, which stressed absolute obedience to the person at the top. Calvinism proved very attractive to proponents of political decentralization in contest with totalitarian rulers, whereas Catholicism was congenial to the proponents of absolute monarchy determined to maintain "one king, one church, one law" throughout the land.

The opposition between the two religions has been seen even in the art and architecture each came to embrace. The Catholic Counter Reformation found the Baroque style congenial. A successor to Mannerism, Baroque art is a three-dimensional display of grandeur, energy, and sheer fleshiness. Great Baroque artists like Peter Paul Rubens (1571–1640) and Gianlorenzo Ber-

[*Text continued on page 406*]

The Apennine (a mountain god), by Giovanni da Bologna, called Giambologna (1529–1608). The colossal construction is a magnificent example of Baroque sculpture. It is in a private park near Florence. [Alinari/SCALA.]

The Ecstasy of Saint Teresa, by Gianlorenzo Bernini (1598–1680). This depiction of the saint in mystical rapture is one of the most famous Baroque sculptures. It is in the church of Santa Maria della Vittoria in Rome. [Bettmann Archive.]

That seventeenth-century art was not wholly dominated by Baroque splendor is seen in the contrast between the etching [RIGHT] by Rembrandt called Christ Preaching the Forgiveness of Sins, with its gentleness, peace, and quiet, and the vast painting [OPPOSITE] by Rubens, The Crucifixion of Saint Peter. The latter, based on the tradition that Peter was crucified head-downwards, is an example of the intense energy of much Baroque painting. [REMBRANDT: Reproduced by courtesy of the Trustees of the British Museum, London. RUBENS: Municipal Museums, Cologne.] (In addition to the Rembrandt etching here, a painting by him is reproduced in the color album.)

The splendor of a Baroque church. This is the interior of the eighteenth-century cloister church at Ottobeuren in Bavaria, West Germany. The architect was Johann Michael Fischer. Note how the atmosphere is charged with energy and action. [Bettmann Archive.]

The interior of St. Paul's Cathedral in London, by Sir Christopher Wren (1632–1723). Although elaborately decorated, the interior is subdued in effect. [Bettmann Archive.]

nini (1598–1680) were Catholics. Protestants by contrast seemed to opt for a simpler, almost self-effacing art and architecture. This can be seen in the English churches of Christopher Wren (1632–1723) and the gentle, searching portraits of the Dutch Mennonite Rembrandt van Rijn (1606–1669).

As religious wars engulfed Europe, the intellectuals perceived the wisdom of religious pluralism and toleration more quickly than did the politicians. A new skepticism, relativism, and individualism in religion became respectable in the sixteenth and seventeenth centuries. Sebastian Castellio's (1515–1563) pithy censure of John Calvin for executing the Antitrinitarian Michael Servetus summarized a sentiment that was to grow in early modern Europe: "To kill a man is not to defend a doctrine, but to kill a man."[1] As a new skepticism greeted the failure of the great reform movements, the French essayist Michel

1 *Contra libellum Calvini* (N.P., 1562), p. E 2 a.

de Montaigne (1533–1592) asked in scorn of the dogmatic mind: "What do I know?" The Lutheran Valentin Weigel (1533–1588), surveying a half-century of religious strife in Germany, advised men to look within themselves for religious truth and no longer to churches and creeds.

Such views gained currency in larger political circles only by the most painful experiences. Where religious strife and its attendant civil war were best held in check, rulers tended to subordinate theological doctrine to political unity, urging tolerance, moderation, and compromise, even indifference, in religious matters. Such rulers came to be known as *politiques,* and the most successful among them was Elizabeth I of England. By contrast, rulers like Mary I of England, Philip II of Spain, and Oliver Cromwell, who tended to take their religion with utmost seriousness and refused every compromise, did not maintain political unity in the long run.

The French Wars of Religion (1562–1598)
Anti-Protestant Measures and the Struggle for Political Power

French Protestants were known as *Huguenots,* a term derived from Besançon Hugues, the leader of the political revolt against the House of Savoy that preceded the Calvinist Reformation in Geneva in the mid-1530s. As early as the 1520s the Sorbonne was vigilant against Lutheran writings and doctrines.

The capture of the French king Francis I by the forces of Charles V at the Battle of Pavia in 1525 provided a motive for the first wave of Protestant persecution in France. Hoping to pacify their Spanish conqueror and win their king's swift release, the French government took repressive measures against the native reform movement, led by Jacques Lèfevre d'Étaples and Bishop Briçonnet of Meaux, that had proved a seedbed of Protestant sentiment.

A second major crackdown came after a rectorial address, laced with Lutheran and Erasmian sentiments, by Nicholas Cop, a friend of John Calvin, at the University of Paris in November 1533. When Protestants plastered Paris and other cities with anti-Catholic placards on October 18, 1534, there was a mass arrest of suspected Protestants. Government retaliation for this action drove John Calvin and other members of the French reform party into exile and permanent Protestantism. In 1540 the Edict of Fontainebleau subjected French Protestants to the Inquisition. Henry II (1547–1559) established legal procedures against Protestants in the Edict of Chateaubriand in 1551. Save for a few brief interludes, the French monarchy remained a staunch Catholic foe of the Protestants until the ascension to the throne of Henry of Navarre in 1589.

The Hapsburg–Valois wars ended with the Treaty of Cateau-Cambrésis in 1559, and Europe experienced a moment of peace. But only a moment. The same year marked the beginning of internal French conflict and the shift of the European balance of power in favor of Spain. It began with an accident. During a tournament held to celebrate the marriage of his thirteen-year-old daughter, Elizabeth, to Philip II, the son of Charles V and heir to the Spanish Hapsburg lands, the French king, Henry II, was mortally wounded. This unforeseen event brought to the throne Henry's sickly fifteen-year-old son, Francis II, under the regency of the queen mother, Catherine de' Medici. With the monarchy so weakened by Henry's death, three powerful families saw their chance to control France and began to compete for the young king's ear. They were the Bourbons, whose power lay in the south and west; the Montmorency-Chatillons, who controlled the center of France; and the Guises, who were dominant in eastern France.

The Guises were far the strongest and had little trouble establishing firm control over the young king. Francis, duke of Guise, had been Henry II's general, and his brothers, Charles and Louis, were cardinals of the church. Mary Stuart, queen of Scots, was their niece. Throughout the latter half of the sixteenth century the name of Guise was interchangeable with militant, reactionary Catholicism. The Bourbon and Montmorency-Chatillon families, in contrast, developed strong Huguenot sympathies, largely for political reasons. The Bourbon Louis I, prince of Condé (d. 1569), and the Montmorency-Chatillon Admiral Gaspard de Coligny (1519–1572) became the political leaders of the French Protestant resistance. They collaborated early in an abortive plot to kidnap Francis II from his Guise advisers. This was the famous Conspiracy of Amboise in 1560. It was strongly condemned by John Calvin, who considered such tactics a disgrace to the Reformation.

Appeal of Calvinism

Often for quite different reasons ambitious aristocrats and discontented townsmen joined Calvinist churches in opposition to the Guise-dominated French monarchy. In 1561 there were over two thousand Huguenot congregations scattered throughout France, although Huguenots were a majority of the population in only two regions, Dauphiné and Languedoc. Although they made up only about one fifteenth of the population at this time, Huguenots were in important geographic areas and heavily represented among the more powerful segments of French society. Over two fifths of the French aristocracy became Huguenots. Many apparently hoped to establish within France a principle of territorial sovereignty akin to that secured within the Empire by the Peace of Augsburg (1555). In this way Calvinism served the forces of political decentralization.

John Calvin and Theodore Beza consciously sought to advance their cause by currying the favor of powerful aristocrats. Beza converted Jeanne d'Albret, the mother of the future Henry IV. The Prince of Condé was apparently converted in 1558 by the influence of his Calvinist wife. For many aristocrats—Condé seems clearly to have been among them—Calvinist religious convictions were attractive primarily as aids to long-sought political goals. The military organization of Condé

and Coligny progressively merged with the religious organization of the French Huguenot churches, creating a potent combination that benefited both sides. Calvinism gave political resistance justification and inspiration, and the forces of political resistance made Calvinism a viable religious alternative in Catholic France. Each side had much to gain from the other. The confluence of secular and religious motives, although beneficial to aristocratic resistance and Calvinist religion alike, tended to cast suspicion on the religious appeal of Calvinism. Clearly religious conviction was neither the only nor always the main reason for becoming a Calvinist in France in the second half of the sixteenth century.

Catherine de' Medici and the Guises

Following Francis II's death in 1560, Catherine de' Medici continued as regent for her minor son, Charles IX (1560–1574). At a colloquy in Poissy she endeavored to reconcile the Protestant and Catholic factions, but her efforts were quite unsuccessful. Fearing the power and guile of the Guises, Catherine, whose first concern was always to preserve the monarchy, sought allies among the Protestants. In 1562, after conversations with Beza and Coligny, she issued the January Edict, a measure that granted Protestants freedom to worship publicly outside towns—although only privately within them—and to hold synods. In March this royal honeymoon with Protestantism came to an abrupt end when the duke of Guise surprised a Protestant congregation at Vassy in Champagne and proceeded to massacre several score—an event that is considered formally to mark the beginning of the French wars of religion.

Had Condé and the Huguenot armies rushed immediately to the queen's side after this atrocity, Protestants might well have secured an alliance with the crown, so great was the queen mother's fear of Guise domination at this time. But the hesitation of Protestant leaders, which was due primarily to indecisive leadership on the part of Condé, placed the young king and the queen mother, against their deepest wishes, in firm Guise control, as such cooperation became the only alternative to capitulation.

During the first French war of religion, fought between April 1562 and March 1563, the duke of Guise was assassinated. It is a measure of the international character of the struggle in France that troops from Hesse and the Palatinate fought alongside the Huguenots. A brief resumption of hostilities in 1567–1568 was followed by the bloodiest of all the wars, between September 1568 and August 1570. It was in this period that Condé was killed and Huguenot leadership passed to Coligny—actually a blessing in disguise for the Protestants because Coligny was far the better military strategist. In the Peace of St. Germain-en-Laye (1570), which ended the third war, the crown, acknowledging the power of the Protestant nobility, granted the Huguenots religious freedoms within their territories and the right to fortify their cities.

Perpetually caught between fanatical Huguenot and Guise extremes, Queen Catherine had always sought to balance the one side against the other. Like the Guises, she wanted a Catholic France; she did not, however, desire a Guise-dominated monarchy. After the Peace of St. Germain-en-Laye the crown tilted manifestly toward the Bourbon faction and the Huguenots, and Coligny became Charles IX's most trusted adviser. Unknown to the king, Catherine began at this time to plot with the Guises against the ascendant Protestants. As she had earlier sought Protestant support when Guise power threatened to subdue the monarchy, so she now sought Guise support as Protestant influence grew.

There was reason for Catherine to fear Coligny's hold on the king. Louis of Nassau, the leader of Protestant resistance to Philip II in the Netherlands, had gained Coligny's ear, and Coligny was using his position of influence to win the king of France over to a planned French invasion of the Netherlands in support of Dutch Protestants. Such a course of action would have placed France squarely on a collision course with almighty Spain. Catherine recognized far better than her son that

Catherine de' Medici (1519–1589). Following the death of her husband, King Henry II of France, in 1559, Catherine, as Queen Mother, exercized much power during the reigns of her three sons, Francis II (1559–1560), Charles IX (1560–1574), and Henry III (1574–1589). She is most remembered for her role in the Saint Bartholomew's Day Massacre in 1572. [Bettmann Archive.]

France stood little chance in such a contest. She and her advisers had been much sobered in this regard by news of the stunning Spanish victory over the Turks at Lepanto in October 1571.

THE SAINT BARTHOLOMEW'S DAY MASSACRE. When Catherine supported the infamous Saint Bartholomew's Day Massacre of Protestants, she did so out of a far less reasoned judgment. Her decision appears to have been made in a state of near panic. On August 22, 1572, four days after the Huguenot Henry of Navarre had married the king's sister, Marguerite of Valois—still another sign of growing Protestant power—Coligny was struck down, although not killed, by an assassin's bullet. Catherine had been party to this Guise plot to eliminate Coligny. After its failure she feared both the king's reaction to her complicity and the Huguenot response under a recovered Coligny. Summoning all her motherly charm and fury, Catherine convinced Charles that a Huguenot *coup* was afoot, inspired by Coligny, and

The Catholic massacre of Huguenots in Paris on Saint Batholomew's Day, August 24, 1572, as remembered by François Dubois, a Huguenot eyewitness. [The Granger Collection.]

that only the swift execution of Protestant leaders could save the crown from a Protestant dictatorship. On Saint Bartholomew's Day, 1572, Coligny and three thousand fellow Huguenots were butchered in Paris, the Guise stronghold. Before the day ended, an estimated twenty thousand Huguenots were executed in coordinated attacks throughout France. It is a date that has ever since lived in infamy for Protestants.

Pope Gregory XIII and Philip II of Spain reportedly greeted the news of the Protestant massacre with special religious celebrations. Philip especially had good reason to rejoice, for the massacre ended for the moment any planned French opposition to his grand design to subjugate the Netherlands. But the massacre of thousands of Protestants also gave the discerning Catholic world cause for new alarm. The event changed the nature of the struggle between Protestants and Catholics both within and beyond the borders of France. It was thereafter no longer an internal contest between Guise and Bourbon factions for French political influence, nor was it simply a Huguenot campaign to win basic religious freedoms. Henceforth, in Protestant eyes, it became an international struggle to the death for sheer survival against an

adversary whose cruelty now justified any means of resistance.

PROTESTANT RESISTANCE THEORY. Only as Protestants faced suppression and sure defeat did they begin to sanction active political resistance. At first they tried to practice the biblical precept of obedient subjection to worldly authority (Romans 13:1).

Luther only grudgingly approved resistance to the emperor after the Diet of Augsburg in 1530. In 1550 Lutherans in the city of Magdeburg published their highly influential defense of the right of lower authorities to oppose the emperor's order that all Lutherans return to the Catholic fold.

Calvin, who never faced the specter of political defeat after his return to Geneva in 1541, always condemned willful disobedience and rebellion against lawfully constituted governments as unchristian. But he also taught that lower magistrates, as part of the lawfully constituted government, had the right and duty to oppose tyrannical higher authority.

The exiled Scottish reformer John Knox, who had seen his cause crushed by Mary, queen of Scots, and Mary I of England, pointed the way for later Calvinists in his famous *Blast of the Trumpet Against the Terrible Regiment of Women* (1558). Knox declared that the removal of a heathen tyrant was a Christian duty. He had the Catholic queen of England in mind.

Theodore Beza Defends the Right to Resist Tyranny

One of the oldest problems in political and social theory has been that of knowing when resistance to repression in matters of conscience is justified. Since Luther's day Protestant reformers, although accused by their Catholic critics of fomenting social division and revolution, had urged their followers to strict obedience to established political authority. After the 1572 massacre of Saint Bartholomew's day, however, Protestant pampheteers urged Protestants to resist tyrants and persecutors with armed force. Here, in 1574, Theodore Beza points out the obligation of rulers to their subjects and the latter's right to resist rulers who fail to meet the conditions of their office.

IT IS *apparent that there is a mutual obligation between the king and the officers of a kingdom; that the government of the kingdom is not in the hands of the king in its entirety, but only the sovereign degree; that each of the officers has a share in accord with his degree; and that there are definite conditions on either side. If these conditions are not observed by the inferior officers, it is the part of the sovereign to dismiss and punish them. . . . If the king, hereditary or elective, clearly goes back on the conditions without which he would not have been recognized and acknowledged, can there be any doubt that the lesser magistrates of the kingdom, of the cities, and of the provinces, the administration of which they have received from the sovereignty itself, are free of their oath, at least to the extent that they are entitled to resist flagrant oppression of the realm which they swore to defend and protect according to their office and their particular jurisdiction? . . .*

We must now speak of the third class of subjects, which though admittedly subject to the sovereign in a certain respect, is, in another respect, and in cases of necessity the protector of the rights of the sovereignty itself, and is established to hold the sovereign to his duty, and even, if need be, to constrain and punish him. . . . The people is prior to all the magistrates, and does not exist for them, but they for it. . . . Whenever law and equity prevailed, nations neither created nor accepted kings except upon definite conditions. From this it follows that when kings flagrantly violate these terms, these who have the power to give them their authority have no less power to deprive them of it.

Constitutionalism and Resistance in the Sixteenth Century: Three Treatises by Hotman, Beza, and Mornay, trans. and ed. by Julian H. Franklin (New York: Pegasus, 1969), pp. 111–114.

After the great massacre of French Protestants on Saint Bartholomew's Day, 1572, Calvinists everywhere came to appreciate the need for active defense of their religious rights. Classical Huguenot theories of resistance appeared in three major works of the 1570s. The first was the *Franco-Gallia* of François Hotman (1573), a Humanist argument that the representative Estates-General of France was historically of higher authority than the French king. The second was Theodore Beza's *On the Right of Magistrates over Their Subjects* (1574), which, going beyond Calvin's views, justified the correction and even the deposing of tyrannical rulers by lower authorities. Finally, there was Philippe du Plessis Mornay's *Defense of Liberty Against Tyrants* (1579), which directly urged princes, nobles, and magistrates, as guardians of the rights of the body politic, to take up arms against tyranny.

The Rise to Power of Henry of Navarre

Henry III (1574–1589), who was the last of Henry II's three sons, found the monarchy wedged between a radical Catholic League, formed in 1576 by Henry of Guise, and vengeful Huguenots. Neither group was reluctant to assassinate a ruler whom they considered heretical and a tyrant. Like the queen mother, Henry sought to steer a middle course, and in this effort he received support from a growing body of neutral Catholics and Huguenots who put the political survival of France above its religious unity. Such people were known as *politiques*, and they were prepared to compromise religious creeds as may be required to save the nation.

The Peace of Beaulieu in May 1576 granted the Huguenots almost complete religious and civil freedom. France was not, however, at this time ready for such sweeping toleration. Within seven months of the Peace of Beaulieu, the Catholic League forced Henry to return again to the illusory quest for absolute religious unity in France during a meeting of the Estates-General in Blois. In October 1577 the king issued the Edict of Poitiers, which truncated the Peace of Beaulieu, and once again

Henry of Navarre (king of France as Henry IV). Henry brought religious peace to France when he promulgated the Edict of Nantes in 1598. This gave French Protestants freedom of worship in selected places and permitted them to maintain garrisons for their own protection. The seventeenth-century painter is not known. [Château de Versailles. Giraudon.]

OPPOSITE: This is Rubens's sketch for his allegorical picture of Henry IV's triumphal entry into Paris to take the throne of France in 1589. Unlike the irreality behind various other such works, this one truly anticipates the actual long-lasting affection for and popularity of the new king. [Reproduced by permission of the Trustees of the Wallace Collection, London.]

circumscribed areas of permitted Huguenot worship. Thereafter Huguenot and Catholic factions quickly returned to their accustomed anarchical military solutions, the Protestants now under the leadership of Henry of Navarre, who was the next recognized legal heir to the French throne.

In the mid-1580s the Catholic League, supported by the Spanish, became completely dominant in Paris. In what came to be known as the Day of the Barricades, Henry III attempted to rout the league with a surprise attack in 1588. The effort failed badly and the king had to flee Paris. Forced by his weakened position into unkingly guerrilla tactics, and also emboldened by news of the English victory over the Spanish Armada in 1588, Henry successfully plotted the assassination of both the duke and the cardinal of Guise. These assassinations sent France reeling once again. Led by still another Guise brother, Charles, duke of Mayenne, the Catholic League reacted with a fury that matched the earlier Huguenot response to the Massacre of Saint Bartholomew's Day. The king now had only one course of action: he struck an alliance with the Protestant Henry of Navarre in April 1589.

As the two Henries prepared to attack the Guise stronghold of Paris, however, a fanatical Jacobin friar stabbed Henry III to death. Thereupon the Bourbon Huguenot Henry of Navarre succeeded the childless Valois king to the French throne as Henry IV (1589–1610). Pope Sixtus V and Philip II were aghast at the sudden prospect of a Protestant France. They had always wanted France to be religiously Catholic and politically weak, and they now acted to achieve that end. Spain rushed troops to support the beseiged Catholic League. Philip II apparently even harbored hopes of placing his eldest daughter, Isabella, who was the granddaughter of Henry II and Catherine de' Medici, on the French throne.

Direct Spanish intervention in the affairs of France seemed only to strengthen Henry IV's grasp on the crown. The French people viewed his right to hereditary succession more seriously than his espoused Protestant confession. Henry was also widely liked. Notoriously informal in dress and manner—a factor that made him especially popular with the soldiers—Henry also had the wit and charm to neutralize the strongest enemy in a face-to-face confrontation. He came to the throne as a *politique,* weary with religious strife and prepared to place political peace above absolute religious unity. He believed a royal policy of tolerant Catholicism would be the best way to achieve such peace. On July 25, 1593, he publically abjured the Protestant faith and embraced the traditional and majority religion of his country. "Paris is worth a mass," he is reported to have said.

It was in fact a decision he made only after a long period of personal agonizing. The Huguenots were understandably horrified by this turnabout and Pope Clement VIII remained skeptical of Henry's sincerity. But the majority of the French church and people, having known internal strife too long, rallied to the king's side. By 1596 the Catholic League was dissolved, its ties with

Spain were broken, and the wars of religion in France to all intents and purposes had ground to a close.

The Edict of Nantes

On April 13, 1598, a formal religious settlement was proclaimed in Henry IV's famous Edict of Nantes, and the following month, on May 2, 1598, the Treaty of Vervins ended hostilities between France and Spain. The Edict of Nantes was a politique recognition of minority religious rights within what was to remain an officially Catholic country. Already in the earlier Edict of Mantes (1591) Henry IV had assured the Huguenots of at least qualified religious freedoms. The Edict of Nantes made good that promise. This religious truce—and it was never more than that—granted the Huguenots, who by this time numbered well over one million, freedom of public worship, the right of assembly, admission to public offices and universities, and permission to maintain fortified towns. The latter concession reveals the continuing distrust between French Protestants and Catholics. As significant as it was, the edict only transformed a long hot war between irreconcilable enemies into a long cold war.

Henry IV was assassinated by a Catholic fanatic in May 1610. Although he is remembered most for the religious settlement of the Edict of Nantes, it was he and his finance minister, the duke of Sully, who laid the foundations for the later transformation of France into the absolute state of Cardinal Richelieu and Louis XIV. It would be in pursuit of the political and religious unity that had escaped Henry IV that Louis XIV, calling for "one king, one church, one law," would revoke the Edict of Nantes in 1685 and force France and Europe to learn again by bitter experience the hard lessons of the wars of religion. Rare is the politician who has preferred to learn from the lessons of history rather than to repeat its mistakes.

Imperial Spain and the Reign of Philip II (1556–1598)

Pillars of Spanish Power

Until the English defeated his mighty Armada in 1588, no one person stood larger in the second half of the sixteenth century than Philip II of Spain. Philip was heir to the intensely Catholic and militarily supreme western Hapsburg kingdom. The eastern Hapsburg lands of Austria, Bohemia, and Hungary had been given over by his father, Charles V, to Philip's uncle, the Emperor Ferdinand I, and they remained, together with the imperial title, in the possession of the Austrian branch of the family. Populous and wealthy Castile gave Philip a solid home base. Additional wealth was provided by the regular arrival in Seville of bullion from the Spanish colonies in the New World. In the 1540s great silver mines had been opened in Potosí in present-day Bolivia and in Zacatecas in Mexico. These gave Philip the great sums needed to pay his bankers and mercenaries. He nonetheless never managed to erase the debts left by his father and to finance his own foreign adventures fully. He later

---

Henry IV Recognizes Huguenot Religious Freedom

By the Edict of Nantes (April 13, 1598) Henry IV recognized Huguenot religious freedoms and the rights of Protestants to participate in French public institutions. Here are some of its provisions.

WE HAVE *by this perpetual and irrevocable Edict pronounced, declared, and ordained and we pronounce, declare and ordain:*

Art. I. Firstly, that the memory of everything done on both sides from the beginning of the month of March, 1585, until our accession to the Crown and during the other previous troubles, and at the outbreak of them, shall remain extinct and suppressed, as if it were something which had never occurred. . . .

Art. II. We forbid all our subjects, of whatever rank and quality they may be, to renew the memory of these matters, to attack, be hostile to, injure or provoke each other in revenge for the past, whatever may be the reason and pretext . . . but let them restrain themselves and live peaceably together as brothers, friends, and fellow-citizens. . . .

Art. III. We ordain that the Catholic, Apostolic, and Roman religion shall be restored and re-established in all places and districts of this our kingdom and the countries under our rule, where its practice has been interrupted. . . .

Art. VI. And we permit those of the so-called Reformed religion to live and dwell in all the towns and districts of this our kingdom and the countries under our rule, without being annoyed, disturbed, molested or constrained to do anything against their conscience, or for this cause to be sought out in their houses and districts where they wish to live, provided that they conduct themselves in other respects to the provisions of our present Edict. . . .

Art. XXI. Books dealing with the matters of the aforesaid so-called Reformed religion shall not be printed and sold publicly, except in the towns and districts where the public exercise of the said religion is allowed. . . .

Art. XXII. We ordain that there shall be no difference or distinction, because of the aforesaid religion, in the reception of students to be instructed in Universities, Colleges, and schools, or of the sick and poor into hospitals, infirmaries, and public charitable institutions.

Art. XXVII. In order to reunite more effectively the wills of our subjects, as is our intention, and to remove all future complaints, we declare that all those who profess

or shall profess the aforesaid so-called Reformed religion are capable of holding and exercising all public positions honours, offices, and duties whatsoever . . . in the towns of our kingdom . . . notwithstanding all contrary oaths.

Church and State Through the Centuries: A Collection of Historic Documents, trans. and ed. by S. Z. Ehler and John B. Morrall (New York: Biblo and Tannen, 1967), pp. 185–187.

contributed to the bankruptcy of the Fuggers when, at the end of his life, he defaulted on his enormous debts.

The new American wealth brought dramatic social change to the second half of the sixteenth century. As Europe became richer, it was also becoming more populous, especially in the economically and politically active towns of France, England, and the Netherlands, where populations tripled and quadrupled by the early seventeenth century. Europe's population approached an estimated 100 million by 1600.

The combination of increased wealth and population triggered a serious inflation. As there were more people and coinage in circulation, but less food and fewer jobs, wages stagnated while prices doubled and tripled in much of Europe. This was especially the case in Spain. Because the new wealth was concentrated in the hands of a few, the traditional gap between the "haves"—the propertied, privileged, and educated classes—and the "have-nots" greatly widened. Nowhere did the unprivileged suffer more than in Spain, where the Castilian peasantry, the backbone of Philip II's great empire, became the most heavily taxed people of Europe. Those who contributed most to making possible the Spanish hegemony in Europe in the second half of the sixteenth century were to prosper least from it.

A subjugated peasantry and wealth from the New World were not the only pillars of Spanish strength. Philip shrewdly organized the lesser nobility into a loyal and efficient national bureaucracy. A reclusive man, he managed his kingdom by pen and paper rather than by personal presence. He was also a learned and pious Catholic, although some popes suspected that he used religion as much for political as for devotional purposes. That he was a generous patron of the arts and culture can be seen in his unique retreat outside Madrid, the Escorial, which was a combination of palace, church, tomb, and monastery. Philip also knew personal sorrows. He was plagued by a mad and treacherous son, Don Carlos, who died under suspicious circumstances in 1568—some contemporaries suspected that Philip had him quietly executed—only three months before the death of the queen.

During the first half of Philip's reign, attention was focused almost exclusively on the Mediterranean and the Turkish threat, a constant European preoccupation. By history, geography, and choice Spain had traditionally been Catholic Europe's champion against Islam. During the 1560s, the Turks advanced deep into Austria, while their fleets dominated the Mediterranean. Between 1568 and 1570 armies under Philip's half-brother, Don John of Austria, the illegitimate son of Charles V, suppressed and dispersed the Moors in Granada. In May 1571 a Holy League of Spain, Venice, and the pope, again under Don John's command, formed to check Turkish belligerence in the Mediterranean. In what became the largest naval battle of the sixteenth century, Don John's fleet engaged the Ottoman navy under Ali Pasha off Lepanto in the Gulf of Corinth on October 7, 1571. Before the engagement ended, thirty thousand Turks had died and over one third of the Turkish fleet was sunk or captured. The Mediterranean belonged thereafter to Spain, and the Europeans had only themselves to fear. Philip's armies were equally successful in putting down resistance in neighboring Portugal, which Spain annexed in 1580. The conquest of Portugal not only added to Spanish seapower but also brought the magnificent Portuguese overseas empire in Africa, India, and the Americas into the Spanish orbit.

[Text continued on page 418]

Philip II of Spain (1556–1598) at age 24, by Titian.
Philip controlled the dominant political power of
the second half of the sixteenth century. However,
he was finally denied victory over the two areas in
which he most sought to impose his will, the Netherlands and England. [Museo del Prado, Madrid.]

The Escorial, Philip II's massive, sternly simple,
and rather gloomy palace-monastery-mausoleum complex
near Madrid. The engraving by Franz Hogenberg is
contemporary with the early years of the structure
in the late sixteenth century and appeared in Georg
Braun, *Civitates Orbis Terrarum.*

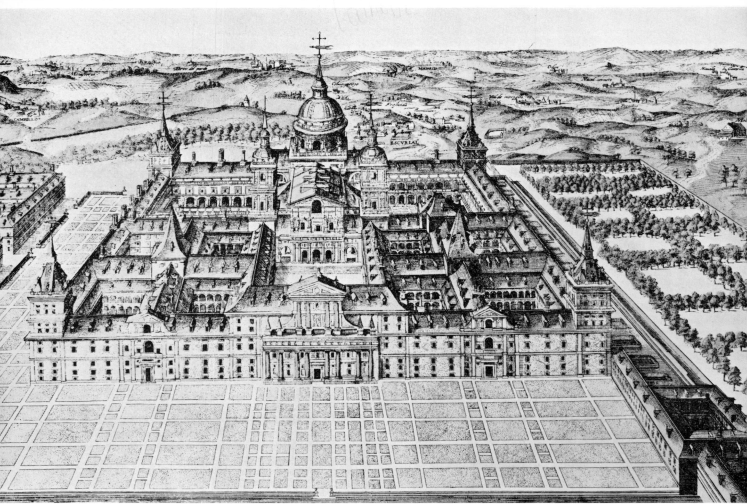

The great naval battle of Lepanto (in the Gulf of Corinth in Greece), October 7, 1571, the largest pitched sea fight of the sixteenth century, in which the Spanish and their allies defeated the Ottoman Turkish fleet. It ended the threat of Ottoman sea power in the Mediterranean Sea. [National Maritime Museum, London.]

The mosque of Ottoman Sultan Suleiman the Magnificent (1520–1566) in Constantinople (modern Istanbul). It was built by Suleiman's architect Sinan at the height of the Ottoman Empire's glory. Like many Ottoman mosques, it was clearly inspired by neighboring Hagia Sophia built by Byzantine Emperor Justinian a thousand years earlier. [Turkish Government Tourism and Information Office, New York.]

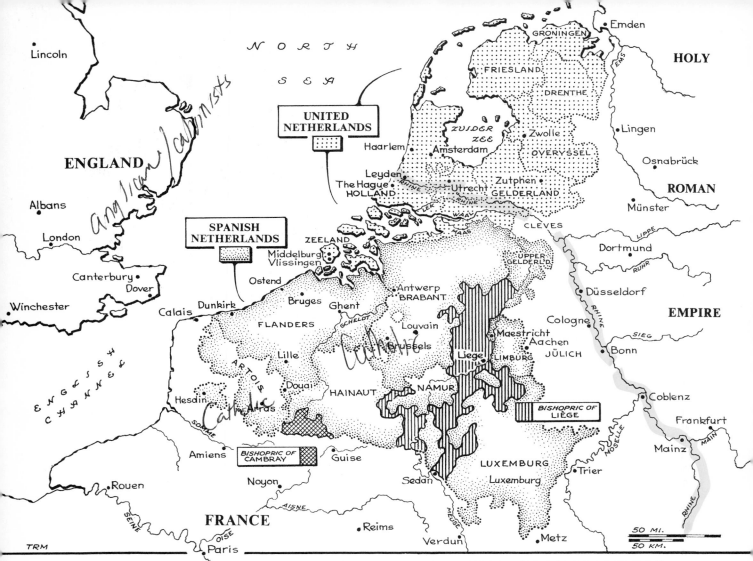

THE NETHERLANDS DURING THE REFORMATION

The northern and southern provinces of the Netherlands. The former, the United Provinces, were mostly Protestant in the second half of the sixteenth century, while the southern, the Spanish Netherlands, made peace with Spain and remained largely Catholic.

The Revolt in the Netherlands

The spectacular Spanish military success in southern Europe was not repeated in northern Europe. When Philip attempted to impose his will upon the Netherlands, England, and France, he learned the lessons of defeat. It was especially the resistance of the Netherlands that proved the undoing of Spanish dreams of world empire.

CARDINAL GRANVELLE. In 1559 Philip had departed the Netherlands for Spain, never again to return. His half-sister, Margaret of Parma, assisted by a special council of state, was made regent in his absence. The council was headed by Philip's hand-picked lieutenant, the extremely able Antoine Perrenot (1517–1586); after 1561 he was Cardinal Granvelle. Granvelle hoped to check Protestant gains by internal church reforms, and he planned to break down the traditional local autonomy of the seventeen Netherlands provinces by stages and establish in its place a centralized royal government directed from Madrid. A politically docile and religiously uniform country was the Spanish objective.

The merchant towns of the Netherlands were, however, Europe's wealthiest and most independent; many, like magnificent Antwerp, were also Calvinist strong-

418 *The Age of Religious Wars*

The Duke of Alba (*ca.* 1508–1583), who was sent into the Netherlands by Philip II to crush the Dutch civil and religious revolt against Spanish rule. Engraving from the sixteenth century. [The Granger Collection.]

holds. By tradition and temperament the people of the Netherlands were far more inclined toward variety and toleration than toward obeisant conformity and hierarchical order. Two members of the Council of State recognized the Spanish design and formed a stubborn opposition. They were the Count of Egmont (1522–1568) and William of Nassau, the Prince of Orange (1533–1584), known as "the Silent" because of his extremely small circle of confidants.

Like other successful rulers in this period, William of Orange was a *politique* who placed the Netherlands' political autonomy and well-being above religious creeds. He personally passed through successive Catholic, Lutheran, and Calvinist stages. In 1561 he married Anne of Saxony, the daughter of the Lutheran Elector Maurice and the granddaughter of the late Landgrave Philip of Hesse. He maintained his Catholic practices until 1567, at which time he turned Lutheran. After the Saint Bartholomew's Day Massacre (1572), Orange became an avowed Calvinist.

In 1561 Cardinal Granvelle proceeded with a planned ecclesiastical reorganization of the Netherlands that was intended to tighten the control of the Catholic hierarchy over the country and to accelerate its consolidation as a Spanish ward. Orange and Egmont, organizing the Dutch nobility in opposition, succeeded in gaining Granvelle's removal from office in 1564, with Regent Margaret's blessing. But aristocratic control of the country after Granvelle's departure proved woefully inefficient, and popular unrest continued to grow, especially among urban artisans, who joined the congregations of radical Calvinist preachers in increasing numbers.

THE COMPROMISE. The year 1564 also saw the first fusion of political and religious opposition to Margaret's government. This opposition resulted from Philip II's unwise insistence that the decrees of the Council of Trent be enforced throughout the Netherlands. The opposition was led by William of Orange's younger brother, Louis of Nassau, who had been raised a Lutheran, and it received support from the Calvinist-

inclined lesser nobility and townsmen. A national covenant was drawn up called the *Compromise*. This was a solemn pledge to resist the decrees of Trent and the Inquisition. Grievances were loudly and persistently voiced, and when Margaret's government spurned the protesters as "beggars" in 1566, Calvinists ran riot through the country. Louis called upon French Huguenots and German Lutherans to send aid to the Netherlands, and a full-scale rebellion against the Spanish regency appeared imminent.

THE DUKE OF ALBA. The rebellion failed to materialize, however, because the Netherlands' higher nobility would not support it. Their shock at Calvinist iconoclasm and anarchy was as great as their resentment of Granvelle's more subtle repression. Philip, determined to make an example of the Protestant rebels, despatched the duke of Alba to suppress the revolt. Having assembled an army of ten thousand men in Milan, Alba marched ostentatiously northward in 1567, in a show of combined Spanish and papal might. A special tribunal, known to the Spanish as the Council of Troubles and among the Netherlanders as the Council of Blood, was set up to police the land. The counts of Egmont and Horn and several thousand suspected heretics were publicly executed before Alba's reign of terror ended.

New taxes were levied forcing the Netherlands to pay for the suppression of its own revolt. One of these, the "tenth penny," a 10 per cent sales tax, met such resistance from merchants and artisans that it remained uncollectable in some areas even after its reduction to 3 per cent. Combined persecution and taxation sent tens of thousands fleeing from the Netherlands during Alba's cruel six-year rule. Alba came to be more hated than Granvelle or the radical Calvinists had ever been.

William I of Orange (1533–1584), known as "the Silent." Founder of the Dutch Republic, he spoiled Philip II's designs on the Netherlands. [Bettmann Archive.]

RESISTANCE AND UNIFICATION.   William of Orange was an exile in Germany during these turbulent years. He now emerged as the leader of a broad movement for the Netherlands' independence from Spain. The northern, Calvinist-inclined provinces of Holland, Zeeland, and Utrecht, of which Orange was the *stadholder*, became his base. As in France, political resistance in the Netherlands gained both organization and inspiration by merging with Calvinism.

The early victories of the resistance attest the popular character of the revolt. A case in point is the capture of the port city of Brill by the "Sea Beggars." These men were an international group of anti-Spanish exiles and criminals, among them many Englishmen. William of Orange did not hesitate to enlist their services. Their brazen piracy, however, had forced Queen Elizabeth to disassociate herself from them and to bar their ships from English ports. In 1572 the Beggars captured Brill and other seaports in Zeeland and Holland. Mixing with the native population, they quickly sparked rebellions against Alba in town after town and spread the resistance southward. In 1574 the people of Leiden heroically resisted a long Spanish siege. The Dutch did not hesitate to open the dikes and flood their own country to repulse the hated Spanish. The faltering Alba had by that time ceded power to Don Luis de Requesens, who replaced him as commander of Spanish forces in the Netherlands in November 1573.

THE PACIFICATION OF GHENT.   The greatest atrocity of the war came after Requesens's death in 1576. Spanish mercenaries, leaderless and unpaid, ran amuck in Antwerp on November 4, 1576, and they left seven thousand people dead in the streets. The event came to be known as the Spanish Fury.

These atrocities accomplished in four short days what neither religion nor patriotism had previously been able to do. The ten largely Catholic southern provinces (what is roughly modern Belgium) now came together with the seven largely Protestant northern provinces (what is roughly the modern Netherlands) in unified opposition to Spain. This union, known as the Pacification of Ghent, was accomplished on November 8, 1576. It declared internal regional sovereignty in matters of religion, a key clause that permitted political cooperation among the signatories who were not agreed over religion. It was a Netherlands version of the territorial settlement of religious differences brought about in the Holy Roman Empire in 1555 by the Peace of Augsburg. Four provinces initially held out, but they soon made the resistance unanimous two months later by joining the all-embracing Union of Brussels in January 1577. Thereafter the Netherlands was unified and determined.

Don John, the victor over the Turks at Lepanto in 1571, had taken command of Spanish land forces in November 1576. He was now to experience his first defeat. Confronted by unified Netherlands resistance, he signed the Perpetual Edict in February 1577, a humiliating treaty that provided for the removal of all Spanish troops from the Netherlands within twenty days. This withdrawal of troops not only gave the country to William of Orange, but it also effectively ended for the present whatever plans Philip may have had for using the Netherlands as a staging area for an invasion of England.

THE UNION OF ARRAS AND THE UNION OF UTRECHT.   The Spanish, however, were nothing if not persistent. Don John and Alessandro Farnese of Parma, the Regent Margaret's son, revived Spanish power in the southern provinces, where constant fear of Calvinist extremism moved the leaders to break the Union of Brussels. In January 1579 the southern provinces formed the Union of Arras, and within five months they made peace with Spain. These provinces later served the cause of the Counter Reformation. The northern provinces responded with the formation of the Union of Utrecht.

NETHERLANDS INDEPENDENCE.   Seizing what now appeared to be a last opportunity to break the back of Netherlands resistance, Philip II declared William of Orange an outlaw and placed a bounty of 25,000 crowns on his head. The act predictably stiffened the resistance of the northern provinces. In a famous defiant speech to

William of Orange Defends Himself to the Dutch Estates

Branded an outlaw by Philip II of Spain, the Protestant Dutch Prince William of Orange defended himself to his countrymen in an eloquent address known as the *Apology* (1581).

WHAT *could be more gratifying in this world, especially to one engaged in the great and excellent task of securing liberty for a good people oppressed by evil men, than to be mortally hated by one's enemies, who are at the same time enemies of the fatherland, and by their mouths to receive a sweet testimony to one's fidelity to his people and to his obstinate opposition to tyrants and disturbers of the peace? Such is the pleasure that the Spaniards and their adherents have prepared for me in their anxiety to disturb me. They have but gratified me by that infamous proscription by which they sought to ruin me. Not only do I owe to them this favor, but also the occasion to make generally known the equity and justice of my enterprises. . . .*

My enemies object that I have "established liberty of conscience." I confess that the glow of fires in which so many poor Christians have been tormented is not an agreeable sight to me, although it may rejoice the eyes of the duke of Alba and the Spaniards; and that it has been my opinion that persecutions should cease in the Netherlands. . . .

They denounce me as a hypocrite, which is absurd enough. . . . As their friend, I told them quite frankly that they were twisting a rope to hang themselves when they began the barbarous policy of persecution. . . .

As for me personally . . . it is my head that they are looking for, and that they have vowed my death by offering such a great sum of money. They say that the war can never come to an end so long as I am among you. . . .

If, gentlemen, you believe that my exile, or even my death, may serve you, I am ready to obey your behests. Here is my head, over which no prince or monarch has authority save you. Dispose of it as you will for the safety and preservation of our commonwealth. But if you judge that such little experience and energy as I have acquired through long and assiduous labors, if you judge that the remainder of my possessions and of my life can be of service to you, I dedicate them to you and to the fatherland.

James Harvey Robinson, *Readings in European History*, Vol. 2 (Boston: Ginn and Co., 1906), pp. 177–179.

the Estates-General of Holland in December 1580, known as the *Apology*, Orange publicly denounced Philip as a heathen tyrant whom the Netherlands need no longer obey. On July 22, 1581, the member provinces of the Union of Utrecht met in The Hague and formally declared Philip no longer their ruler. They turned in his stead to the French duke of Alençon, who was Catherine de' Medici's youngest and least satisfactory son, a man to whom the southern provinces had also earlier looked as a possible middle way between Spanish and Calvinist overlordship. Alençon was accepted as "sovereign" by all the northern provinces save Holland and Zeeland, which distrusted him almost as much as they did Philip II. It was intended that Alençon would be no more than a titular sovereign. But Alençon, an ambitious failure, saw this as his one chance at greatness. When he rashly attempted to take actual control of the provinces in 1583, he was deposed and returned to France.

Spanish efforts to reconquer the Netherlands continued into the 1580s. William of Orange was assassinated in July 1584 and was succeeded by his seventeen-year-old son, Maurice (1567–1625), who, with the assistance of England and France, was able to maintain Dutch resistance. Fortunately for the Netherlands Philip II began at this time to meddle directly in French and English affairs. He signed a secret treaty with the Guises (the Treaty of Joinville in December 1584) and sent armies under Farnese into France in 1590. Hostilities with the English increased, gradually building toward the climax of 1588, when Philip's great Armada was defeated in the English channel. These new Spanish fronts strengthened the Netherlands as Spain became badly overextended. Spanish preoccupation with France and England permitted the northern provinces to drive out all Spanish soldiers by 1593. In 1596 France and England formally recognized the independence of these provinces. Peace was not, however, concluded with Spain until 1609, when the Twelve Years Truce gave the northern provinces their virtual independence. Full recognition came finally in the Peace of Westphalia in 1648.

Mary I. During her five-year reign as queen of England, she reversed protestant gains and reimposed the Catholic religion on England. Her execution of Protestant leaders won her the title "Bloody Mary" among Protestants. [Bettmann Archive.]

Spain and England (1553–1603)

Mary I

Before Edward VI died in 1553, he agreed to a device to make Lady Jane Grey, the teen-age daughter of a niece of Henry VIII and a powerful Protestant nobleman, his successor in place of the Catholic Mary Tudor (1553–1558). But popular support for the principle of hereditary monarchy was too strong to deprive Mary of her rightful rule. Jane Grey was dethroned within days and eventually beheaded (1554).

Once enthroned Mary proceeded to act even beyond the worst fears of the Protestants. In 1554 she entered a highly unpopular marriage with Philip II of Spain and pursued at his direction a foreign policy that in 1558 cost England its last enclave on the Continent, Calais.

Mary's domestic measures were equally shocking and even more divisive. During her reign Parliament repealed the Protestant statutes of Edward and reverted to the strict Catholic practice of her father, Henry VIII. The great Protestant leaders of the Edwardian age—John Hooper, Hugh Latimer, Miles Coverdale, and Thomas Cranmer—were executed. Hundreds of Protestants either joined them in martyrdom or took flight to the Continent. These "Marian exiles," prominent among whom was the future leader of the Reformation in Scotland, John Knox, settled in Germany and Switzerland, forming especially large communities in Frankfurt, Strasbourg, and Geneva. There they worshiped in their own congregations, wrote tracts justifying armed resistance, and waited for the time when a Protestant counteroffensive could be launched in their homelands.

Elizabeth I

Mary's successor was her half-sister Elizabeth I (1558–1603), the daughter of Henry VIII and Anne Boleyn, and probably the most astute politician of the sixteenth century in both domestic and foreign policy. Assisted by a shrewd adviser, Sir William Cecil (1520–1598), known as Lord Burghley after 1571, Elizabeth built a true kingdom upon the ruins of Mary's reign. Between 1559 and 1563 she and Cecil guided a religious settlement through Parliament that prevented England from being torn asunder by religious differences in the sixteenth century. A *politique* who subordinated religious to political unity, Elizabeth merged a centralized episcopal system, which she firmly controlled, with broadly defined Protestant doctrine and traditional Catholic ritual. In the resulting Anglican Church inflexible extremes were not permitted in religion.

In 1559 an Act of Supremacy was passed repealing all the anti-Protestant legislation of Mary Tudor and asserting Elizabeth's right as "supreme governor" over both spiritual and temporal affairs. An Act of Uniformity in the same year mandated a revised version of the second *Book of Common Prayer* (1552) for every English parish. The issuance of the Thirty-Nine Articles on Religion in 1563—which were a revision of Thomas Cranmer's original forty-two—made a moderate Protestantism the official religion within the Church of England.

CATHOLIC AND PROTESTANT EXTREMISTS. Elizabeth hoped to avoid both Catholic and Protestant extremism at the official level by pursuing a middle way. Her first archbishop of Canterbury, Matthew Parker (d. 1575), represented this ideal. But Elizabeth was not able to prevent the emergence of subversive Catholic and Protestant zealots. When she ascended the throne, Catholics were in the majority in England, and the extremists among them, encouraged by the Jesuits, plotted against her. They were also encouraged and later directly assisted by the Spanish, who were piqued both by Elizabeth's Protestant sympathies and by her refusal to follow the example of her half-sister Mary and take Philip II's hand in marriage. Elizabeth remained unmarried throughout her reign, using the possibility of a marriage alliance very much to her diplomatic advantage.

Catholic extremists hoped eventually to replace Elizabeth with Mary, queen of Scots. Unlike Elizabeth, who had been declared illegitimate during the reign of her father, Mary Stuart had an unblemished claim to the

Elizabeth I of England. She is considered by many the most successful ruler of the sixteenth century. This portrait, celebrating the defeat of the Spanish Armada (1588), is by Marcus Gheeraerts (*ca.* 1525–1599). [The Granger Collection.]

throne by way of her grandmother Margaret, who was the sister of Henry VIII. Elizabeth acted swiftly against Catholic assassination plots and rarely let emotion override her political instincts. Despite proven cases of Catholic treason and even attempted regicide, however, she executed fewer Catholics during her forty-five years on the throne than Mary Tudor had executed Protestants during her brief six-year reign.

Elizabeth dealt cautiously with the Puritans, who were Protestants working within the national church to "purify" it of every vestige of "popery" and to make its Protestant doctrine more precise. The Puritans had two special grievances: (1) the retention of Catholic cere-mony and vestments within the Church of England, which made it appear to the casual observer that no Reformation had occurred, and (2) the continuation of the episcopal system of church governance, which conceived of the English church theologically as the true successor to Rome, while placing it politically under the iron hand of the queen and her compliant archbishop.

Sixteenth-century Puritans were not separatists. Enjoying wide popular support and led by widely respected men like Thomas Cartwright (d. 1603), they worked through Parliament to create an alternative national church of semiautonomous congregations governed by representative presbyteries, following the model of Calvin and Geneva. Elizabeth wisely bent with this group, letting them lobby at the tops of their voices but conceding absolutely nothing that lessened the hierarchical unity of the Church of England and her control over it.

The more extreme Puritans wanted every congregation to be autonomous, a law unto itself, with neither higher episcopal nor presbyterian control. They came to be known as *congregationalists*. Elizabeth and her second archbishop of Canterbury, John Whitgift (d. 1604), refused to tolerate this group, whose views on independence seemed to them to be patently subversive. The Conventicle Act of 1593 gave such separatists the option of either conforming to the practices of the Church of England or facing exile or death.

DETERIORATION OF RELATIONS WITH SPAIN. A series of events led inexorably to war between England and Spain, despite the sincerest desires on the part of both Philip II and Elizabeth to avoid a direct confrontation. In 1567 the Spanish duke of Alba marched his mighty army into the Netherlands, which was, from the English point of view, simply a convenient staging area for a Spanish invasion of England. Pope Pius V (1556–1572), who favored a military conquest of Protestant England, "excommunicated" Elizabeth for heresy in 1570—a mischievous act that only encouraged both internal resistance and international intrigue against the queen. Two years later the piratical Sea Beggars, many of whom were Englishmen, occupied the port city of Brill in the Netherlands and aroused the surrounding countryside against the Spanish.

Following Don John's demonstration of Spain's awesome seapower at the famous naval battle of Lepanto in 1571, England signed a mutual defense pact with France. Also in the 1570s, Elizabeth's famous seamen, John Hawkins (1532–1595) and Sir Francis Drake (1545?–

An Unknown Contemporary Describes Queen Elizabeth

No sixteenth-century ruler governed more effectively than Elizabeth of England (1558–1603), who was both loved and feared by her subjects. An unknown contemporary has left the following description, revealing not only her intelligence and shrewdness but also something of her tremendous vanity.

I WILL *proceed with the description of the queen's disposition and natural gifts of mind and body, wherein she either matched or exceeded all the princes of her time, as being of a great spirit yet tempered with moderation, in adversity never dejected, in prosperity rather joyful than proud; affable to her subjects, but always with due regard to the greatness of her estate, by reason whereof she was both loved and feared.*

In her later time, when she showed herself in public, she was always magnificent in apparel; supposing haply thereby that the eyes of her people (being dazzled by the glittering aspect of those her outward ornaments) would not so easily discern the marks of age and decay of natural beauty; and she came abroad the more seldom, to make her presence the more grateful and applauded by the multitude, to whom things rarely seen are in manner as new.

She suffered not, at any time, any suitor to depart discontented from her, and though ofttimes he obtained not that he desired, yet he held himself satisfied with her manner of speech, which gave hope of success in the second attempt. . . .

Latin, French, and Italian she could speak very elegantly, and she was able in all those languages to answer ambassadors on the sudden. . . . Of the Greek tongue she was also not altogether ignorant. She took pleasure in reading of the best and wisest histories, and some part of Tacitus' Annals *she herself turned into English for her private exercise. She also translated Boethius'* On the Consolation of Philosophy *and a treatise of Plutarch,* On Curiosity, *with divers others. . . .*

It is credibly reported that not long before her death she had a great apprehension of her own age and declination by seeing her face (then lean and full of wrinkles) truly represented to her in a glass, which she a good while very earnestly beheld; perceiving thereby how often she had been abused by flatterers (whom she held in too great estimation) that had informed her the contrary.

James Harvey Robinson, *Readings in European History*, Vol. 2 (Boston: Ginn and Co., 1906), pages 191–193.

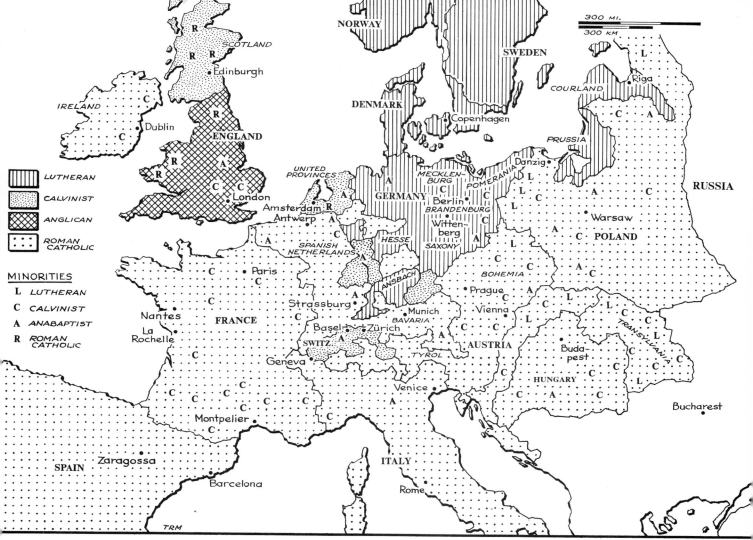

RELIGIOUS DIVISIONS ABOUT 1600

By 1600 few could seriously expect Christians to return to a uniform religious allegiance. In Spain and southern Italy Catholicism remained relatively unchallenged, but note the existence of large religious minorities, both Catholic and Protestant, elsewhere.

1596), began to prey regularly on Spanish shipping in the Americas. Drake's circumnavigation of the globe between 1577 and 1580 was one in a series of dramatic demonstrations of English ascendancy on the high seas.

After the Saint Bartholomew's Day Massacre, Elizabeth's was the only bosom to which Protestants in France and the Netherlands could cleave. In 1585 she signed the Treaty of Nonsuch, which provided English soldiers and cavalry to the Netherlands. Funds that had previously been funneled covertly to support Henry of Navarre's army in France were now given openly.

MARY, QUEEN OF SCOTS. These events made a tinderbox of English–Spanish relations. The spark that finally touched it off was Elizabeth's reluctant but necessary execution of Mary, queen of Scots (1542–1587).

Mary was the daughter of King James V and Mary of

Guise and had resided in France from the time she was six years old. This thoroughly French and Catholic queen had returned to Scotland after the death of her husband, the French king Francis II, in 1561, there to find a successful, fervent Protestant Reformation that had won legal sanction the year before in the Treaty of Edinburgh (1560). As hereditary heir to the throne of Scotland, Mary remained queen by divine and human right. She was not intimidated by the Protestants who controlled her realm. She established an international French court culture the gaiety and sophistication of which impressed

Engravings based on tapestries that hung in the British House of Lords try to show two phases of the running battle of the Spanish Armada with the English fleet in the summer of 1588.

many Protestant noblemen, whose religion tended to make their lives exceedingly dour.

Mary was closely watched by the ever-vigilant eye of John Knox, who fumed publicly and always with effect against the queen's private Mass and Catholic practices, which Scottish law made a capital offense for everyone else. Knox was supported in his role of watchdog by Elizabeth and Cecil. Elizabeth personally despised Knox and never forgave him for writing the *First Blast of the Trumpet Against the Terrible Regiment of Women,* a work aimed at provoking a revolt against Mary Tudor but published in the year of Elizabeth's ascension to the throne. Elizabeth and Cecil tolerated Knox because he served their foreign policy, never permitting Scotland to succumb to the young Mary and her French and Catholic ways.

In 1568 a public scandal forced Mary's abdication and flight to her cousin Elizabeth in England. Mary's reputed lover, the earl of Bothwell, was, with cause, suspected of having killed her legal husband, Lord Darnley. When Bothwell was acquitted by a packed court, and then abducted Mary and married her, the outraged reaction from Protestant nobles forced Mary to surrender the throne to her one-year-old son, who became James VI of Scotland. He was also destined to be Elizabeth's successor as the future James I of England. Because of Mary's clear claim to the English throne, she remained an international symbol of a possible Catholic England. Her presence in England, where she resided under mild house arrest for nineteen years, was a constant discomfort to Elizabeth.

In 1583 Elizabeth's vigilant secretary, Sir Francis Walsingham, uncovered a plot against Elizabeth involving the Spanish ambassador Mendoza, a frequent companion of Mary Stuart. After Mendoza's deportation in January 1584, popular antipathy toward Spain and support for Protestant resistance in France and the Netherlands became massive throughout England.

In 1586 Walsingham uncovered still another plot against Elizabeth, the so-called Babington plot, and this time he had uncontestable proof of Mary's complicity.

Elizabeth believed that the execution of a sovereign, even a dethroned sovereign, weakened royalty everywhere. She was also aware of the outcry that Mary's execution would create throughout the Catholic world. But she really had no choice in the matter and consented to Mary's execution on February 18, 1587. This event dashed all Catholic hopes for a bloodless reconversion of Protestant England. After the execution of the Catholic queen of Scotland, Pope Sixtus V (1585–1590), who feared Spanish domination almost as much as he abhorred English Protestantism, could no longer withhold public support for a Spanish invasion of England. Philip II ordered his Armada to make ready.

THE ARMADA. Spain's war preparations were interrupted in the spring of 1587 by Sir Francis Drake's successful shelling of the port city of Cadiz, an attack that inflicted heavy damage on Spanish ships and stores. The success of this strike forced the Spanish to postpone their planned invasion of England until the spring of 1588. On May 30 of that year, a mighty fleet of 130 ships bearing twenty-five thousand sailors and soldiers under the command of the duke of Medina-Sidonia set sail for England. But the day belonged completely to the English. The invasion barges that were to transport Spanish soldiers from the galleons onto English shores were prevented from leaving Calais and Dunkirk. The swifter English and Netherlands ships, assisted by what came to be known as an "English wind," dispersed the waiting Spanish fleet, over one third of which never returned to Spain.

The news of the Armada's defeat gave heart to Protestant resistance everywhere. Although Spain continued to win impressive victories in the 1590s, it never fully recovered from this defeat. Spanish soldiers faced unified and inspired French, English, and Dutch armies. By the time of Philip's death on September 13, 1598, his forces had been successfully rebuffed on all fronts. His seventeenth-century successors—Philip III (1598–1621), Philip IV (1621–1665), and Charles II (1665–1700)— were all inferior leaders who never knew responsibilities

equal to Philip's. Nor did Spain ever again know such imperial grandeur. The French soon dominated the Continent, while in the New World the Dutch and the English progressively whittled away Spain's once glorious overseas empire.

Elizabeth died on March 23, 1603, knowing few national wounds and leaving behind her a strong nation, soon to become an empire upon which the sun would not set.

The Thirty Years' War (1618–1648)
Preconditions for War

FRAGMENTED GERMANY. In the second half of the sixteenth century Germany (the Holy Roman Empire) was an almost ungovernable land of three hundred autonomous political entities. There were independent secular principalities (duchies, landgravates, and marches); ecclesiastical principalities (archbishoprics, bishoprics, and abbeys); numerous free cities; and castle regions dominated by knights. The Peace of Augsburg (1555) had made each supreme within its own borders. Each levied its own tolls and tariffs and coined its own money, practices that made land travel and trade between the various regions difficult, if not impossible. In addition, many of these little "states" were filled with great power pretensions. Political decentralization and fragmentation characterized Germany as the seventeenth century opened; it was not a unified nation like Spain, England, or even strife-filled France.

Germany had always been Europe's highway; during the Thirty Years' War it became its stomping ground. Europe's rulers pressed in on Germany both for reasons of trade and because some of them held lands or legal privileges within certain German principalities. German princes, in their turn, looked to import and export markets beyond German borders. They were quick to oppose any efforts to consolidate the Holy Roman Empire, lest their territorial rights, confirmed by the Peace of Augsburg in the principle *cuius regio, eius religio*, be

overturned. German princes were not loath to turn to Catholic France or to the kings of Denmark and Sweden for allies against the Hapsburg emperor. The latter's dynastic connections with Spain generated policies that were perceived to be against the best interests of the empire. Even the pope found political reasons for supporting Bourbon France against the menacing international Hapsburg kingdom.

After the Council of Trent, Protestants in the empire gravely suspected that an imperial and papal conspiracy was operating to re-create the Catholic Europe of pre-Reformation times. The imperial diet, which was controlled by the German princes, demanded that the constitutional rights of Germans be strictly observed, and it effectively countered every move by the emperor to impose his will in the empire. In the late sixteenth century the emperor ruled in the empire only as much as he was prepared to use force of arms against his subjects.

RELIGIOUS DIVISION. Religious conflict accentuated the international and internal political divisions. During this period the population within the Holy Roman Empire was about equally divided between Catholics and Protestants, the latter having perhaps a slight numerical edge by 1600. The terms of the Peace of Augsburg (1555) had attempted to freeze the territorial holdings of the Lutherans and the Catholics. In the intervening years, however, the Lutherans had gained political control in some Catholic areas, as had the Catholics in a few previously Lutheran areas. Such territorial reversals, or the threat of them, only increased the suspicion and antipathy between the two sides.

The Lutherans had been far more successful in securing their rights to worship in Catholic lands than the Catholics had been in securing such rights in Lutheran lands. The reason was that the Catholic rulers, who were in a weakened position after the Reformation, had no choice but to make concessions to Protestant communities within their territories. Such communities were increasingly a sore point. Also the Catholics wanted a strict enforcement of the "Ecclesiastical Reservation" of the

Peace of Augsburg; they demanded that all ecclesiastical princes, electors, archbishops, bishops, and abbots who deserted the Catholic for the Protestant side be immediately deprived of their religious offices and positions. The Lutherans and especially the Calvinists in the Palatinate ignored this stipulation at every opportunity.

There was religious strife in the empire not only between Protestants and Catholics but also between pietistical and conservative Lutherans and between Lutherans and growing numbers of Calvinists. The last half of the sixteenth century was the heyday of Protestant Scholasticism in German universities. In addition to the heightened religious strife, the anxiety of religious people of all persuasions was increased by the new scientific and material culture that was becoming ascendant in important intellectual and political circles. The age of religious wars was an age of growing preoccupation with magic, mysticism, witchcraft, and the occult, as doubts and suspicions stampeded religious feeling.

CALVINISM AND THE PALATINATE. As elsewhere in Europe, Calvinism was the political and religious leaven within the Holy Roman Empire on the eve of the Thirty Years' War. Unrecognized as a legal religion by the Peace of Augsburg, it had established a strong foothold within the empire when Frederick III (1559–1576), a devout convert to Calvinism, had made it the official religion of his land when he became Elector Palatine or ruler within the Palatinate in 1559. Heidelberg became a German Geneva in the 1560s, both a great intellectual center of Calvinism and a staging area for Calvinist penetration into the empire. By 1609 Palatine Calvinists were at the head of a Protestant defensive alliance that received outside support from Spain's sixteenth-century enemies: England, France, and the Netherlands. The Lutherans came to fear the Calvinists almost as much as they did the Catholics. The Palatine Calvinists seemed to the Lutherans directly to threaten the Peace of Augsburg—and hence the legal foundation of the Lutheran states—by their bold missionary forays into the empire. The more religiously conservative Lutherans were also shocked by outspoken Calvinist criticism of the doctrine of Christ's real presence in the Eucharist. The Elector Palatine once expressed his disbelief in transubstantiation by publicly shredding the host and mocking it as a "fine God." To Lutherans, such religious disrespect and aggressiveness were a disgrace to the Reformation.

MAXIMILIAN OF BAVARIA AND THE CATHOLIC LEAGUE. If the Calvinists were active within the Holy Roman Empire, so also were their Catholic counterparts, the Jesuits. Staunchly Catholic Bavaria, supported by Spain, became militarily and ideologically for the Counter Reformation what the Palatinate was for Protestantism. From there the Jesuits launched successful missions throughout the empire, winning such major cities as Strasbourg and Osnabrück back to the Catholic fold by 1600. In 1609 Maximilian, duke of Bavaria, organized a Catholic League to counter a new Protestant alliance that had been formed in the same year under the leadership of the Calvinist Elector Palatine, Frederick IV (1583–1610). When the league fielded a great army under the command of Count Johann von Tilly, the stage was set, internally and internationally, for the worst of the religious wars, the Thirty Years' War.

Four Periods of War

The war went through four distinguishable periods, and during its course it drew in every major western European nation—at least diplomatically and financially if not in terms of direct military involvement. The four periods were the Bohemian (1618–1625); the Danish (1625–1629); the Swedish (1630–1635); and the Swedish–French (1635–1648).

THE BOHEMIAN PERIOD. The war broke out in Bohemia after the ascent to the Bohemian throne in 1618 of the Hapsburg Ferdinand, the archduke of Styria, who was also in the line of succession to the imperial throne. Educated by the Jesuits and a fervent Catholic, Ferdinand was determined to restore the traditional faith throughout Austria, Bohemia, and Poland—the eastern Hapsburg lands.

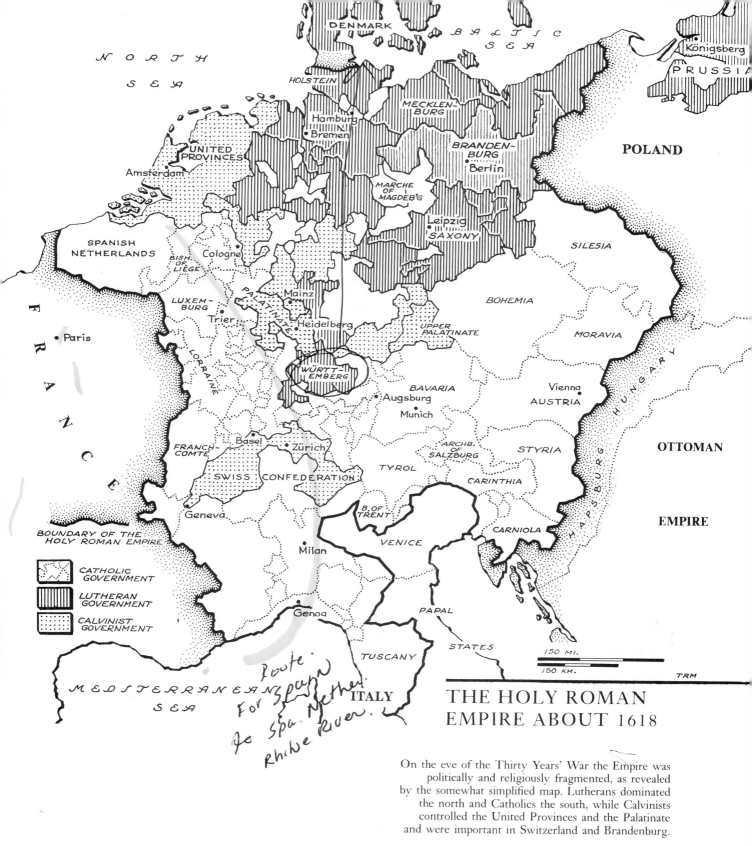

DENMARK

BALTIC SEA

NORTH SEA

HOLSTEIN

Königsberg

PRUSSIA

MECKLEN-BURG

Hamburg
Bremen

BRANDEN-BURG
• Berlin

POLAND

UNITED PROVINCES

Amsterdam

MARCHE OF MAGDEB'G

SPANISH NETHERLANDS

BISH. OF LIÈGE

Cologne

Leipzig
SAXONY

SILESIA

LUXEM-BURG

Trier

PALATINATE

Mainz

Heidelberg

BOHEMIA

MORAVIA

FRANCE

• Paris

LORRAINE

UPPER PALATINATE

WÜRTT-EMBERG

BAVARIA

Augsburg
Munich

Vienna
AUSTRIA

HUNGARY

OTTOMAN

FRANCH-COMTE

Basel

• Zürich

ARCHB. OF SALZBURG

STYRIA

SWISS CONFEDERATION

TYROL

CARINTHIA

EMPIRE

Geneva

B. OF TRENT

CARNIOLA

• Milan

VENICE

BOUNDARY OF THE HOLY ROMAN EMPIRE

PAPAL

STATES

CATHOLIC GOVERNMENT

LUTHERAN GOVERNMENT

CALVINIST GOVERNMENT

Genoa

150 MI.

150 KM.

TRM

MEDITERRANEAN SEA

Route for Spain to Spa. Nether. Rhine River.

ITALY

TUSCANY

THE HOLY ROMAN EMPIRE ABOUT 1618

On the eve of the Thirty Years' War the Empire was
politically and religiously fragmented, as revealed
by the somewhat simplified map. Lutherans dominated
the north and Catholics the south, while Calvinists
controlled the United Provinces and the Palatinate
and were important in Switzerland and Brandenburg.

The Thirty Years' War (1618–1648) 429

A musket fire drill for the seventeenth-century infantryman. This is a portion of a manual for English soldiers engraved by Thomas Cockson. The complexity of it all is indicated by the opening lines of the accompanying text: "In the instruction for the musket, there are six points to be considered, 51 postures, and 123 words of command . . ." [Reproduced by courtesy of the Trustees of the British Museum.]

who found more immediate allies in Maximilian of Bavaria and the opportunistic Lutheran Elector John George I of Saxony (1611–1656). John George saw a sure route to territorial gain by joining in an easy victory over the weaker Elector Palatine. This was not the only time politics and greed would overshadow religion during this long conflict, although Lutheran–Calvinist animosity also overrode a common Protestantism. We shall find other instances of such conflicts.

Frederick V's troops were routed by Ferdinand's army under Von Tilly at the Battle of White Mountain in 1620. By 1622 Ferdinand had managed not only to subdue and re-Catholicize Bohemia but to conquer the Palatinate as well. While he and his allies enjoyed the spoils of these victories, fighting was extended into northwestern Germany by the duke of Bavaria. Laying claim to land as he went, he continued to pursue Ernst von Mansfeld, one of Frederick's surviving mercenary generals, into the north.

THE DANISH PERIOD. The emperor's subjugation of Bohemia and the Palatinate and Maximilian's forays into northwestern Germany raised new fears that a reconquest of the whole empire was planned. This was in fact precisely Ferdinand II's design. Encouraged by the English, the French, and the Dutch, the Lutheran King Christian IV (1588–1648) of Denmark, who already held territory within the empire as the duke of Holstein, picked up the Protestant banner of resistance, opening the Danish period of the conflict (1625–1629). Christian's forces were not, however, up to the challenge. Entering Germany with his army in 1626, he was quickly humiliated by Maximilian and forced to retreat back into Denmark.

As military success made Maximilian stronger and more difficult to control, Ferdinand II sought a more pliant tool for his policies by hiring a powerful, complex mercenary, Albrecht of Wallenstein (1583–1634). Wallenstein was another opportunistic Protestant who had gained a great deal of territory by joining Ferdinand during the conquest of Bohemia. A brilliant and ruthless

No sooner had Ferdinand become king of Bohemia than he revoked the religious freedoms of Bohemian Protestants. These freedoms had been in force since 1575 and had even been recently broadened by the Emperor Rudolf II (1576–1612) in his Letter of Majesty in 1609. The Protestant nobility in Prague responded to Ferdinand's act by literally defenestrating his regents; this happened in May 1618. When in the following year Ferdinand became Holy Roman Emperor as Ferdinand II, by the unanimous vote of the seven electors, the Bohemians defiantly deposed him in Prague and declared the Calvinist Elector Palatine, Frederick V (1616–1623), their overlord.

What had begun as a revolt of Protestant nobility against an unpopular king of Bohemia thereafter escalated into an international war. Spain sent troops to Ferdinand,

Marauding armies during the Thirty Years' War, by Jan Brueghel (1568–1625) and Sebastien Vrancx (1573–1647), both Flemish artists. During breaks in the fighting, mercenary armies pillaged local villages and towns. [Kunsthistorisches Museum, Vienna.]

military strategist, Wallenstein not only completed Maximilian's work by bringing the career of the elusive Ernst von Mansfeld to an end, but he also penetrated into Denmark with an occupying army. By 1628 Wallenstein was in command of a crack army of over 100,000 men. Running afoul of Ferdinand's best-laid plans, he became a law unto himself within the empire, completely outside the emperor's control. Pandora's box had now been fully opened.

Wallenstein broke Protestant resistance so successfully that Ferdinand was able to issue the Edict of Restitution in 1629. This proclamation dramatically reasserted the Catholic safeguards of the Peace of Augsburg (1555). It reaffirmed the illegality of Calvinism—a completely unrealistic move in 1629—and it ordered the return of all church lands acquired by Lutherans since 1552, an equally unrealistic mandate. Compliance with the latter would have involved the return of no less than sixteen bishoprics and twenty-eight cities and towns to Catholic allegiance. While based on legal precedent and certainly within Ferdinand's power to command, the expectations of the edict were not adjusted to the political realities of 1629. It struck panic into the hearts of Protestants and Hapsburg opponents everywhere, who now saw clearly the emperor's plan to re-create a Catholic Europe. Resistance quickly refueled.

THE SWEDISH PERIOD. Gustavus Adolphus of Sweden (1611–1632), a deeply pious king of a unified Lutheran nation, became the new leader of Protestant forces within the empire, opening the Swedish period of the war (1630–1635). He was handsomely bankrolled by two very interested bystanders: the French minister Cardinal Richelieu, whose foreign policy was to protect French interests by keeping Hapsburg armies tied down in Germany, and the Dutch, who had not forgotten Spanish Hapsburg domination in the sixteenth century. The Swedish king found ready allies in the electors of Brandenburg and Saxony and soon won a smashing victory at Breitenfeld in 1630. The Protestant victory at Breitenfeld so dramatically reversed the course of the war that it has been regarded as the most decisive, although far from the final, engagement of the long conflict. Gustavus Adolphus was later killed by the forces of Wallenstein during the Battle of Lützen (November 1632)—a very costly engagement for both sides that created a brief standstill.

Ferdinand had long been resentful of Wallenstein's independence, despite the fact that he was the major factor in imperial success. In 1634 he had Wallenstein assassinated. By that time Wallenstein had not only served his purpose for the emperor, but, ever opportunistic, he was even trying openly to strike bargains with the Protestants for his services. The Wallenstein episode is a telling commentary on this war without honor.

In the Peace of Prague in 1635 the German Protestant states, led by Saxony, reached a compromise agreement with Ferdinand. The Swedes, however, received continued support from France and the Netherlands. Desiring to maximize their investment in the war, they refused to join the agreement. Their resistance to settlement plunged the war into its fourth and most devastating phase, the Swedish–French period (1635–1648).

THE SWEDISH–FRENCH PERIOD. The French openly entered the war in 1635, sending men and munitions as well as financial subsidies. After their entrance the war dragged on for thirteen years, with French, Swedish, and Spanish soldiers looting the length and breadth of Germany—warring, it seemed, simply for the sake of warfare itself. The Germans, long weary of the devastation, were too disunited to repulse the foreign armies; they simply watched and suffered. By the time peace talks began in the Westphalian cities of Münster and Osnabrück in 1644, an estimated one third of the German population had died as a direct result of the war. It was the worst European catastrophe since the Black Death of the fourteenth century.

The Treaty of Westphalia

The Treaty of Westphalia in 1648 brought all hostilities within the Holy Roman Empire to an end. It rescinded Ferdinand's Edict of Restitution and firmly reasserted the major feature of the religious settlement of the Peace of Augsburg (1555), as the ruler of each land was again permitted to determine the religion of his land. The treaty also gave the Calvinists their long-sought legal recognition. The independence of the Swiss Confederacy and the United Provinces of Holland, long recognized in fact, was now proclaimed in law. Finally, the treaty elevated Bavaria to the rank of an elector state.

France and Spain remained at war outside the empire until 1659, when French victories forced upon the Spanish the humiliating Treaty of the Pyrenees. Thereafter France became Europe's dominant power, and the once vast Hapsburg kingdom waned.

By confirming the territorial sovereignty of Germany's many political entities, the Treaty of Westphalia perpetuated German division and political weakness into the modern period. Only two German states attained any international significance during the seventeenth century. These were Austria and Brandenburg–Prussia. The petty regionalism within the empire also reflected on a small scale the drift of larger European politics. In the seventeenth century distinctive nation-states, each with its own political, cultural, and religious identity, reached maturity and firmly established the competitive nationalism of the modern world.

C. V. Wedgwood has described the outcome of the Thirty Years' War:

> After the expenditure of so much human life to so little purpose, men might have grasped the essential futility of putting the beliefs of the mind to the judgment of the sword. Instead, they rejected religion as an object to fight for and found others. . . . The war solved no problem. Its effects, both immediate and indirect, were either negative or disastrous. Morally subversive, economically destructive, socially degrading, confused in its causes, devious in its course, futile in its result, it is the outstanding example in European history of meaningless conflict.[2]

2 In T. K. Rabb, *The Thirty Years' War: Problems of Motive, Extent and Effect* (Boston: D. C. Heath 1964), pp. 18–19.

SUGGESTED READINGS

FERNAND BRAUDEL, *The Mediterranean and the Mediterranean World in the Age of Philip the Second*, Vols. 1 and 2 (1976). Widely acclaimed work of a French master historian.

RICHARD DUNN, *The Age of Religious Wars 1559–1689* (1970). Excellent brief survey of every major conflict.

J. H. ELLIOTT, *Europe Divided 1559–1598* (1968). Direct, lucid narrative account.

G. R. ELTON, *England Under the Tudors* (1955). Masterly account.

JULIAN H. FRANKLIN (Ed. and Trans.), *Constitutionalism and Resistance in the Sixteenth Century: Three Treatises by Hotman, Beza, and Mornay* (1969). Three defenders of the right of people to resist tyranny.

PIETER GEYL, *The Revolt of the Netherlands, 1555–1609* (1958). The authoritative survey.

JOHN LYNCH, *Spain Under the Hapsburg I: 1516–1598* (1964). Political narrative.

J. RUSSELL MAJOR, *Representative Institutions in Renaissance France* (1960). An essay in French constitutional history.

GARRETT MATTINGLY, *The Armada* (1959). A masterpiece and novel-like in style.

J. E. NEALE, *The Age of Catherine de Medici* (1962). Short concise summary.

JOHN NEALE, *Queen Elizabeth I* (1934). Superb biography.

THEODORE K. RABB (Ed.), *The Thirty Years' War* (1972). Excerpts from the scholarly debate over the war's significance.

JASPER G. RIDLEY, *John Knox* (1968). Large, detailed biography.

J. H. M. SALMON, (Ed.), *The French Wars of Religion: How Important Were the Religious Factors?* (1967). Scholarly debate over the relation between politics and religion.

J. H. M. SALMON, *Society in Crisis: France in the Sixteenth Century* (1976).

ALFRED SOMAN (Ed.), *The Massacre of St. Batholomew's Day: Reappraisals and Documents* (1974). Results of an international symposium on the anniversary of the massacre.

C. V. WEDGWOOD, *The Thirty Years' War* (1939). The authoritative account.

C. V. WEDGWOOD, *William the Silent* (1944). Excellent political biography.

LVDOVICVS XIIII DEI GRATIA FRANCIÆ
ET NAVARRÆ REX CHRISTIANISSIMVS.

W. Vaillant ad vivum faciebat cum Privilegio Regis   P. Van Schuppen Sculpebat 1660.

17
England and France in the Seventeenth Century

Constitutional Crisis and Settlement in Stuart England

BETWEEN 1603 and 1715 England experienced the most tumultuous years of its long history. In this period Puritan resistance to the Elizabethan religious settlement merged with fierce Parliamentary opposition to the aspirations to absolute monarchy of the Stuart kings. During these years no less than three foreigners occupied the English throne, and between 1649 and 1660 England was without a king altogether. Yet by the end of this century of crisis England was a model to Europe of limited monarchy, parliamentary government, and measured religious toleration.

James I

The first of England's foreign monarchs was James VI of Scotland, the son of Mary Stuart, queen of Scots, who in 1603 succeeded the childless Elizabeth as James I of England. This first Stuart king inherited not only the crown but also a royal debt of almost one-half million pounds, a fiercely divided church, and a Parliament already restive over the extent of his predecessor's claims to royal authority. Under James each of these problems worsened. The new king utterly lacked tact, was ignorant of English institutions, and strongly advocated the divine right of kings, a subject on which he had written a book in 1598 entitled *A Trew Law of Free Monarchies.* Both

King Louis XIV of France (1643–1715) at the age of twenty-two. Louis was the dominant European political figure in the second half of the seventeenth century, and the culture of his court was imitated throughout Europe. This rare 1660 portrait is by the engraver Van Schuppen after a painting by W. Vaillant. Its subject should be compared with the aged Louis shown on page 459. [Charles Farrell Collection.]

Parliament and the politically powerful Puritans were rapidly alienated.

The breach with Parliament was opened by James's seeming usurpation of the power of the purse. Royal debts and his own extravagance made it necessary for the king to be constantly in quest of additional revenues. These he sought to a large degree by levying—solely on the authority of an ill-defined royal prerogative—new custom duties known as tonnage and poundage. Parliament resented such independent efforts to raise revenues as an affront to its power, and the result was a long and divisive court struggle between the king and Parliament.

As the distance between the king and Parliament widened, the religious problems also worsened. The Puritans, who were prominent among the lesser landed gentry and within Parliament, had hoped that James's experience with the Scottish Presbyterian Church would incline him to favor their efforts to purify the Anglican Church. Since the days of Elizabeth the Puritans had sought to eliminate elaborate religious ceremonies and to replace the hierarchical episcopal system of church governance with a more representative presbyterian form like that of the Calvinist churches on the Continent. In January 1604 they had their first direct dealing with the new king. James responded in that month to a statement of Puritan grievances, the so-called Millenary Petition, at a special religious conference at Hampton Court. To the dismay of the Puritans the king firmly declared his intention to maintain and even enhance the episcopacy. "A Scottish presbytery," he snorted, "agreeth as well with monarchy as God and the devil." Nonconformists were clearly forewarned.

Both sides departed the conference with their worst suspicions of one another largely confirmed, and as the years passed the distrust between them only deepened. It was during James's reign in 1620 that Puritan separatists founded Plymouth Colony in Cape Cod Bay, preferring flight from England to Anglican conformity. The Hampton Court conference did, however, sow one fruitful seed. A commission was appointed to render a new

435

EUROPE IN 1648

SWEDISH DOMINIONS

BRANDENBURG-PRUSSIA

SPANISH MONARCHY

AUSTRIA HAPSBURGS

CHURCH LANDS

NORWAY

Bergen

Christiana

SWEDE

FINLAND

Reval

ESTONIA

Stockholm

SCOTLAND

Edinburgh

Stavanger

KINGDOM OF DENMARK AND NORWAY

LIVONIA

Riga

COURLAND

Memel

Belfast

Dublin

York

NORTH SEA

DENMARK

Copenhagen

Danzig

EAST PRUSSIA

IRELAND

ENGLAND

BOUNDARY OF THE EMPIRE

SCHLESWIG

HOLSTEIN

Cork

WALES

London

ATLANTIC

Bristol

Plymouth

UNITED PROVINCES

SPANISH NETH.

BRANDEN-BURG

Posen

PO

Warsaw

Rouen

Reims

Brussels

MINOR GERMAN STATES

HESSE

SAXONY

Breslau

SILESIA

Prague

Cracow

GA

BOHEMIA

MORAVIA

Paris

Orleans

BAVARIA

AUSTRIA

HUNGARY

Pressburg

Budapest

Vienna

OCEAN

Nantes

Tours

FRANCHE COMTÉ

SWITZ.

FRANCE

Lyons

SAVOY

VENICE

Venice

HUNGAR

SLAVONIA

SAVE

Belgrade

Bordeaux

PIED-MONT

MILAN

PAR.

MOD.

Bologna

BOSNIA

SERVIA

Spalato

Toulouse

LANGUEDOC

AVIGNON

Genoa

LUCCA

PAPAL STATES

Cattaro

MONTE-NEGRO

Marseilles

TUSCANY

Oporto

León

NAVARRE

Burgos

CORSICA (GEN.)

ITALY

Rome

ALBANIA

Salamanca

Saragossa

Capua

Bari

PORTUGAL

Madrid

Barcelona

Naples

Lisbon

Toledo

SPAIN

BALEARIC IS.

SARDINIA (SP.)

KINGDOM OF THE TWO SICILIES

Cordova

Seville

Granada

SICILY

Cadiz

MEDITE

Tangier (PORT.)

Ceuta (SP.)

FEZ & MOROCCO

Algiers

ALGERIA

Tunis (OTT.)

RANEAN

James VI (of Scotland) and I (of England, 1603–1625), the first of the ill-fated Stuart line of England's monarchs. The artist is unknown. [The Granger Collection.]

OPPOSITE: At the end of the Thirty Years' War Spain still had extensive possessions, Austria and Branden-burg-Prussia were prominent, the independence of the United Provinces and Switzerland was recognized, and Sweden held important river mouths in north Germany.

translation of the Bible, a mission fulfilled in 1611 when the Authorized or King James Version of the Bible was published.

Though he inherited major political and religious difficulties, James also created special problems for himself. His court became a center of scandal and corruption. He governed by favorites, the most influential of whom was the duke of Buckingham, whom rumor made the king's homosexual lover. Buckingham controlled royal patronage and openly sold peerages and titles to the highest bidders—a practice that angered the nobility, who found that it cheapened their rank. James's pro-Spanish foreign policy also displeased Englishmen. In 1604 he concluded a much needed peace with Spain, England's chief adversary of the

Portrait of King Charles I of England hunting, by Anthony van Dyck (1599–1641). Charles was executed by order of Parliament in 1649 following the rise to power of Oliver Cromwell who, among other things, then sold the royal picture collection, so that this portrait is now in France. [Musée du Louvre, Paris. Cliché des Musées Nationaux.]

extra-Parliamentary measures. He levied new imposts, attempted to collect discontinued taxes, and even subjected the English people to a so-called forced loan (a tax theoretically to be repaid), imprisoning those who refused to pay. Troops in transit to war zones were quartered in private English homes.

When Parliament met in 1628, its members were furious. Taxes were being illegally collected for a war that was going badly for England and that now, through royal blundering, involved France as well as Spain. Parliament expressed its displeasure by making the king's request for new funds conditional upon his recognition of the Petition of Right. This major document of constitutional freedom declared that henceforth there should be no forced loans or taxation without the consent of Parliament, that no free man should be imprisoned without due cause, and that troops should not be billeted in private homes. Though Charles agreed to the petition, there was little confidence that he would keep his word.

In January 1629 Parliament further underscored its resolve to circumscribe royal prerogative. It declared religious innovations leading to "popery"—Charles's high-church policies were meant—and the levying of taxes without Parliamentary consent acts of treason. Perceiving that things were getting out of hand, Charles promptly dissolved Parliament and did not recall it again until 1640, when war with Scotland forced him to do so.

To conserve his limited resources, Charles made peace with France and Spain in 1629 and 1630, respectively. His finance minister, Thomas Wentworth, earl of Stafford, instituted a policy of "thorough," that is, strict efficiency and administrative centralization in government. This policy aimed at absolute royal control of England and required for its success the king's ability to operate independently of Parliament. Every legal fund-raising device was exploited to the full. Neglected laws suddenly came to be enforced, and existing taxes were extended into new areas. An example of the latter tactic was the inland collection of "ship money." This tax was normally levied only on coastal areas to pay for naval protection, but after

sixteenth century. His subjects viewed it as a sign of pro-Catholic sentiment on his part. Suspicions were further increased when James attempted unsuccessfully to relax the penal laws against Catholics. Englishmen had not forgotten the brutal reign of Mary Tudor and the acts of treason by Catholics during Elizabeth's reign. In 1618 James hesitated, not unwisely, to rush English troops to the aid of Protestants in Germany at the outbreak of the Thirty Years' War. This hesitation caused his loyalty to the Anglican Church to be openly questioned. In the king's last years, as his health failed and the reins of government were increasingly given over to his son Charles and Buckingham, Parliamentary power and Protestant sentiment combined to undo his pro-Spanish foreign policy. In 1624 England entered a continental war against Spain.

Charles I

Charles I (1625–1649) flew even more brazenly in the face of Parliament and the Puritans than did his father. Unable to receive adequate funds from Parliament to prosecute the Spanish war, Charles also resorted to

Parliament Attacks Charles I's Royal Abuses of His Subjects

The tension between King Charles I (1625–1649) and Parliament had very few causes that did not go back to earlier reigns. The Petition of Right can, therefore, be seen as a general catalogue of reasons for opposing arbitrary royal power. Specifically, angered by Charles and his levying of new taxes and other revenue-gathering devices, his coercion of freemen, and his quartering of troops in transit in private homes, Parliament refused to grant the king any funds until he rescinded such practices by recognizing the Petition of Right (June 7, 1628). Here is the Petition and the king's reply.

[THE Lords Spiritual and Temporal, and Commons in Parliament assembled] do humbly pray your Most Excellent Majesty, that no man hereafter be compelled to make or yield any gift, loan, benevolence, tax, or such like charge, without common consent by Act of Parliament; and that none be called to make answer, or take such oath, or to give attendance, or be confined, or otherwise molested or disquieted concerning the same, or for refusal thereof; and that no freeman, in any such manner as is before-mentioned, be imprisoned or detained; and that your Majesty will be pleased to remove the said soldiers and mariners [who have been quartered in private homes], and that your people may not be so burdened in time to come; and that the foresaid commissions for proceeding by martial law, may be revoked and annulled; and that hereafter no commissions of like nature may issue forth to any person or persons whatsoever, to be executed as aforesaid, lest by colour of them any of your Majesty's subjects be destroyed or put to death, contrary to the laws and francise of the land.

All which they most humbly pray of your Most Excellent Majesty, as their rights and liberties according to the laws and statutes of this realm.

[THE KING'S REPLY: The King willeth that right be done according to the laws and customs of the realm; and that the statutes be put in due execution, that his subjects may have no cause to complain of any wrong or oppressions, contrary to their just rights and liberties, to the preservation whereof he holds himself as well obliged as of his prerogative.]

The Constitutional Documents of the Puritan Revolution, ed. by Samuel R. Gardiner (Oxford, England: Clarendon Press, 1889), pp. 4–5.

1634 it was gradually applied to the whole of England, interior and coastal towns alike. A great landowner named John Hampden unsuccessfully challenged its extension in a close legal contest. Although the king prevailed, it was a costly victory, for it deepened the animosity toward him among the powerful landowners, who both elected Parliament and sat in Parliament.

Charles had neither the royal bureaucracy nor the standing army to rule as an absolute monarch. This became abundantly clear when he and his religious minister, William Laud (1573–1645; after 1633 the archbishop of Canterbury), provoked a war with Scotland. They tried to impose the English episcopal system and the Anglican prayer book upon the Scots as they had done throughout England. From his position within the Court of High Commission, Laud had already radicalized the Puritans by denying them the right to publish and preach.

When the Presbyterian Scots invaded England in 1640, Charles was forced to seek assistance from a Parliament that opposed his policies almost as much as the foreign invaders. Led by John Pym (1584–1643), Parliament refused even to consider funds for war until the king agreed to redress a long list of political and religious grievances. The result was the king's immediate dissolution of Parliament—hence its name, the Short Parliament (April–May 1640). But by November 1640 Charles was forced to reconvene Parliament, this time on the latter's terms and for what would be a long and most fateful duration.

THE LONG PARLIAMENT. The landowners and the merchant classes represented by Parliament had resented the king's financial measures and paternalistic rule for some time. To this resentment was added the fervent Puritan opposition. Hence the Long Parliament (1640–1660) acted with widespread support and general unanimity when it convened in November 1640. Disgraced and convicted by a Parliamentary bill of attainder, Charles's chief minister, Thomas Wentworth, was executed in 1641. Archbishop Laud was imprisoned and executed in 1645. The Court of Star Chamber and the

The House of Commons in session in 1648 toward the end of the Civil War, as seen in a contemporary engraving. [The Granger Collection.]

Court of High Commission, royal instruments of political and religious "thorough," respectively, were abolished. The levying of new taxes without consent of Parliament and the inland extension of ship money were declared illegal. Finally, it was resolved that no more than three years should elapse between meetings of Parliament and that Parliament could not be dissolved without its own consent.

There remained division within Parliament, however, over the precise direction of religious reform. Extremists—the Independents—wanted the complete abolition of the episcopal system and the *Book of Common Prayer*. The more moderate Puritan majority—the Presbyterians—wanted rather to reshape both along Calvinist State-Church lines. There were also a considerable number of conservatives in both houses who were determined to preserve the English church in its current form.

The division within Parliament was further intensified in October 1641, when a rebellion erupted in Ireland requiring an army to suppress it. Pym and his followers, loudly reminding the House of Commons of the king's past misdeeds, argued that Charles could not be trusted with an army and that Parliament should become the

commander-in-chief of English armed forces. Parliamentary conservatives, who had winced once at Puritan religious reforms, winced thrice at this bold departure from English practice.

Charles saw the division within Parliament as a last chance to regain power. In January 1642 he invaded Parliament with his soldiers. He intended to arrest Pym and the other leaders, but they had been forewarned and managed to escape. Shocked by the king's action, a majority of the House of Commons thereafter passed the Militia Ordinance, a measure that gave Parliament control of the army.

The die was now cast. Charles assembled his forces at Nottingham, and in August the civil war began to determine whether England would be ruled by an absolute monarchy or by a parliamentary government and whether English religion would be conformist high Anglican and controlled by the king's bishops or tempered by a significant degree of decentralization and pluralism. Charles's supporters, known as *Cavaliers,* were located in the northwestern half of England. The Parliamentary opposition, known as *Roundheads,* had its stronghold in the southeastern half of the country. The nobility, identifying the power of their peerage with the preservation of the current form of the monarchy and the church, became prominent supporters of the king, whereas the townsmen were conspicuous in support of the Parliamentary army.

Oliver Cromwell and the Puritan Republic

Two factors led finally to Parliament's victory. The first was an alliance with Scotland in 1643 consummated when Pym signed the Solemn League and Covenant. The second was the reorganization of the Parliamentary army under Oliver Cromwell (1599–1658), a middle-aged country squire of iron discipline and strong Independent religious sentiment. Cromwell and his "godly men" favored neither the episcopal system of the king nor the presbyterian system of the Solemn League and Covenant.

Oliver Cromwell who, following the execution of Charles I, transformed England into a Puritan Republic and ruled as "Lord Protector" from 1553 until his death. The painting is by Samuel Cooper and is at Sidney Sussex College, Cambridge. [Bettmann Archive.]

The bleeding head of Charles I is exhibited to the crowd after his execution on a cold day in January 1649. The contemporary Dutch artist also professed to see the immediate ascension of Charles's soul to heaven. In fact, to many the king was seen as a martyr. [The Granger Collection.]

They wanted instead to let every congregation be its own master. The allies won the Battle of Marston Moor in 1644, the largest engagement of the war, and in June 1645 Cromwell's New Model Army, which fought with a disciplined fanaticism, decisively defeated the king at Naseby.

Though defeated militarily, Charles again took advantage of the deep divisions within Parliament, this time seeking to win the Presbyterians and the Scots over to the royalist side. But Cromwell's army firmly imposed its will. In December 1648 Colonel Pride physically barred the Presbyterians, who made up a majority of Parliament, from taking their seats. After "Pride's Purge," only a "rump" of less than fifty members remained. Though small in numbers, this Independent Rump Parliament had supreme military power within England. It did not hesitate to use this power. On January 30, 1649, after trial by a special court, it executed Charles as a public criminal and thereafter abolished the monarchy, the House of Lords, and the Anglican Church. The revolution was consummated.

From 1649 to 1660 England was officially a Puritan republic under Oliver Cromwell. Cromwell's army conquered Ireland and Scotland, creating the single political entity of Great Britain. Cromwell, however, was a military man and no politician. He was increasingly frustrated by what seemed to him to be pettiness and dawdling on the part of Parliament. When in 1653 the House of Commons entertained a motion to disband the expensive army of fifty thousand men, Cromwell responded by marching in and disbanding Parliament. He ruled thereafter as Lord Protector.

But his military dictatorship proved no more effective and became just as harsh and hated as Charles's rule had been. Cromwell's great army and foreign adventures inflated his budget to three times that of Charles's. Trade and commerce suffered throughout England, as near chaos reigned in many places. Puritan regulation of the moral life, which forbade such pastimes as theaters, dancing, and drunkenness, was resented. Cromwell's treatment of

Anglicans came to be just as intolerant as Charles's treatment of Puritans had been. And Cromwell was unable to get along even with the new Parliaments that were elected under the auspices of his army. By the time of his death in 1658, a majority of Englishmen were ready to end the Puritan experiment and return to the traditional institutions of government.

Charles II and Restoration of the Monarchy

The Stuart monarchy was restored in 1660 when Charles II (1660–1685) returned to England amid great rejoicing. A man of considerable charm and political skill, Charles set a refreshing new tone after eleven years of somber Puritanism. Politically and religiously his restoration returned England to the status quo of 1642.

Because of his secret Catholic sympathies the king favored a policy of religious toleration. He wanted to allow all persons outside the Church of England, Catholics as well as Puritans, to worship freely so long as they remained loyal to the throne. But the ultraroyalist Anglicans—the Tories—in Parliament decided otherwise. They did not believe patriotism and religion could be so disjointed. Between 1661 and 1665, through a series of laws known as the Clarendon Code, Parliament excluded Roman Catholics, Presbyterians, and Independents from the religious and political life of the nation. Penalties were imposed for attending non-Anglican worship services, strict adherence to the *Book of Common Prayer* and the Thirty-Nine Articles was required, and all who desired to serve in local government were made to swear oaths of allegiance to the Church of England. The Whigs in Parliament opposed this suppression of the Puritans, but they were not strong enough to override the Tory majority.

Under Charles II England also launched a bold new foreign policy, challenging the Dutch to become Europe's commercial and business center. Navigation Acts were passed that required all imports into England to be carried either in English ships or in ships registered to the same country as the imports they carried. Because the Dutch were original suppliers of hardly more than tulips and cheese, these laws struck directly at their lucrative role as Europe's commercial middlemen. A series of naval wars between England and Holland ensued. Charles also undertook at this time to subdue the rich English colonies in North America and the Caribbean that had been settled and developed by separatist Puritans and had broken away from English rule—a most enterprising move.

Although Parliament strongly supported the monarchy, Charles, following the habit of his predecessors, required greater revenues than Parliament appropriated. To fund his ventures fully, he became a secret client of the French king, Louis XIV. England and France formally allied against the Dutch in the Treaty of Dover in 1670. In a secret portion of this treaty Charles pledged to announce

Charles II of England in a portrait from an unknown hand. [The Granger Collection.]

his conversion to Catholicism as soon as conditions in England permitted. In exchange for this promise he received a French war chest that came to exceed 700,000 pounds.

In an attempt to unite the English people behind the war with Holland, and as a sign of good faith to Louis XIV, Charles issued a Declaration of Indulgence in 1672 suspending all laws against Roman Catholics and Protestant nonconformists. But again the Tory Parliament proved less generous than the king and refused to grant money for the war until Charles rescinded the measure. After Charles withdrew the declaration, Parliament passed the Test Act, which required all officials of the crown, civil and military, to swear an oath against the doctrine of transubstantiation—a requirement that no loyal Roman Catholic could honestly meet.

The Test Act was aimed in large measure at the king's brother, James, duke of York, who was heir to the throne and a recent, devout convert to Catholicism. A notorious liar named Titus Oates swore before a magistrate that Charles's Catholic wife was plotting with Jesuits to poison the king so that James could assume the throne. The matter was taken before Parliament, where it was believed. In the ensuing hysteria several people, including an Irish bishop, were tried and executed. In 1680–1681, riding the crest of anti-Catholic sentiment, Whig mem-

James II of England, the fourth Stuart, was painted about the time of his accession by Sir Godfrey Kneller (1646-1723). [The Granger Collection.]

bers of Parliament, led by the earl of Shaftsbury (1621–1683), made an impressive but unsuccessful effort to enact a bill excluding James from succession to the throne.

More suspicious than ever of Parliament, Charles II turned again to Louis XIV for extra income and was able to rule from 1681 to 1685 without recalling Parliament. In these years Charles suppressed much of his opposition, driving the earl of Shaftsbury into exile, executing several Whig leaders for treason, and bullying local corporations into electing members of Parliament submissive to the royal will. When Charles died in 1685 after a deathbed conversion to Catholicism, he left James the prospect of a Parliament filled with royal friends.

James II and Renewed Fears of a Catholic England

James II (1685–1688) did not know how to make the most of a good thing. He alienated Parliament by insisting upon the repeal of the Test Act. When Parliament balked, he dissolved it and proceeded openly to appoint known Catholics to high positions in both his court and the army. In 1687 James issued a Declaration of Indulgence, which suspended all religious tests and permitted free worship. Local candidates for Parliament who opposed the declaration were removed from their offices by the king's soldiers and were replaced by Catholics. In June 1688 James went so far as to imprison seven Anglican bishops who had refused to publicize his suspension of laws against Catholics.

Under the guise of a policy of enlightened toleration James was actually seeking to subject all English institutions to the power of the monarchy. His goal was absolutism, and even the Tories could not abide this. Englishmen had reason to fear that James planned to imitate the policy of Louis XIV, who in 1685 had revoked the Edict of Nantes (which had protected French Protestants for almost a century) and reconverted France to Catholicism by use of dragoons. A national consensus very quickly formed against the monarchy of James II.

The direct stimulus for Parliamentary action came when on June 20, 1688, James's second wife, a Catholic, gave birth to a son, a male Catholic heir to the English throne. Englishmen had hoped that James would die without a male heir and that the throne would revert to his Protestant eldest daughter, Mary. Mary was the wife of William III of Orange, *stadholder* of the Netherlands, great-grandson of William the Silent, and the leader of European opposition to Louis XIV's imperial designs. Within days of the birth of a Catholic male heir, Whig and Tory members of Parliament formed a coalition and invited Orange to invade England to preserve "traditional liberties," that is, the Anglican Church and parliamentary government.

The "Glorious Revolution."

In the face of sure defeat James fled to France and the protection of Louis XIV. When William of Orange arrived with his army in November 1688, he was received without opposition from the English people. With James gone, Parliament declared the throne vacant and on its own authority proclaimed William and Mary the new monarchs in 1689, completing a successful bloodless revolution. William and Mary in turn recognized a Bill of Rights that limited the powers of the monarchy and guaranteed the civil liberties of the English privileged classes. It also pointedly prohibited Roman Catholics from occupying the English throne. The Toleration Act of 1689 permitted worship by all Protestants and outlawed Roman Catholics and antitrinitarians.

The final measure closing the century of strife was the Act of Settlement in 1701. This bill provided for the English crown to go to the Protestant House of Hanover in Germany if Queen Anne (1702–1714), the second daughter of James II and the last of the Stuart monarchs, was not survived by her children. Consequently in 1715 the Elector of Hanover became King George I of England, the third foreign monarch to occupy the English throne in just over a century.

The "Glorious Revolution" of 1688 established a framework of government by and for the governed. It

With her husband already in exile and William and Mary about to be proclaimed sovereigns, the ex-queen, wife of James II, is pictured fleeing London in December 1688. [The Granger Collection.]

The bloodless revolution of 1688–1689 yielded the only instance of joint sovereigns in English history. Here are William III and Mary II as shown on a popular ballad sheet of 1689. [The Granger Collection.]

received classic philosophical justification in John Locke's *Second Treatise on Government* (1690), wherein Locke described the relationship of a king and his people in terms of a bilateral contract. If the king broke that contract, the people, by whom Locke meant the privileged and powerful, had the right to depose him. Although it was, neither in fact nor in theory, a popular revolution such as would occur in France and America a hundred years later, the Glorious Revolution did establish in England a permanent check on monarchical power by the classes represented in Parliament. Thereby it established a model for subsequent Western political history.

The joint monarchs' coronation medal, designed by George Bower. [The Granger Collection.]

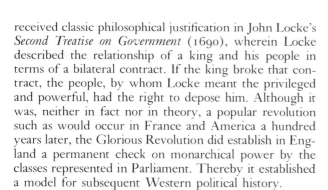

Queen Anne was the last Stuart monarch of Great Britain. Because she outlived her numerous children, she was succeeded by George I of the new house of Hanover. This is a medal by John Croker. [The Granger Collection.]

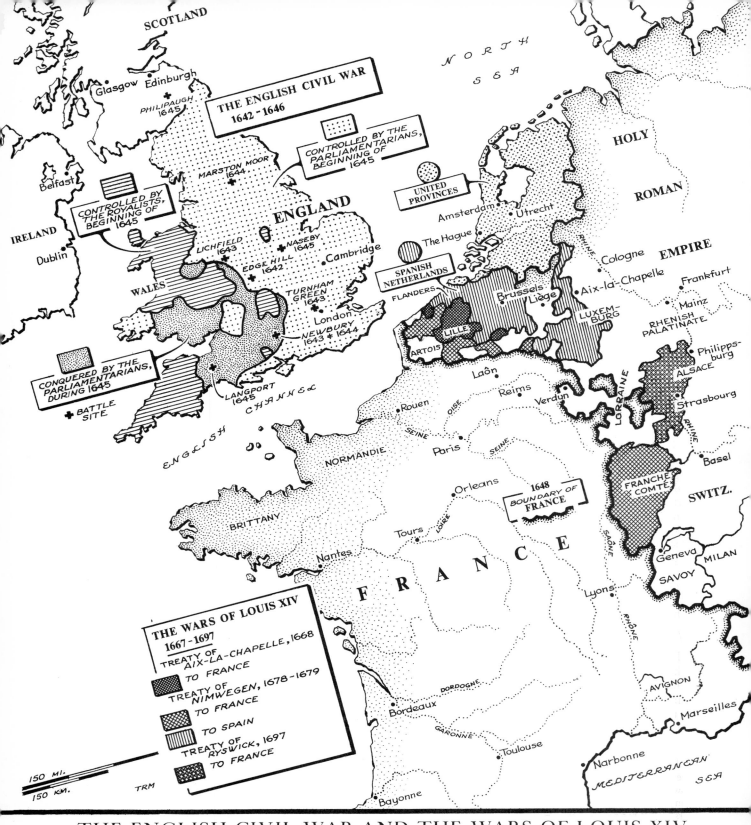

SCOTLAND

Glasgow · Edinburgh
+ PHILIPAUGH
1645

THE ENGLISH CIVIL WAR
1642 - 1646

Belfast

IRELAND

Dublin

MARSTON MOOR
1644

CONTROLLED BY THE
PARLIAMENTARIANS,
BEGINNING OF 1645

CONTROLLED BY
THE ROYALISTS,
BEGINNING OF
1645

ENGLAND

LICHFIELD
1643 · NASEBY
1645

EDGE HILL
1642 · Cambridge

WALES

TURNHAM
GREEN
1643

London

NEWBURY
1643 + 1644

CONQUERED BY THE
PARLIAMENTARIANS,
DURING 1645

LANGPORT
1645

+ BATTLE
SITE

ENGLISH CHANNEL

NORTH SEA

UNITED
PROVINCES

Amsterdam · Utrecht

The Hague

SPANISH
NETHERLANDS

FLANDERS

ARTOIS

LILLE

Brussels · Liège

Rouen

SEINE

NORMANDIE

Paris

SEINE

Orleans

LOIRE

Tours

BRITTANY

Nantes

FRANCE

HOLY

ROMAN

Cologne · EMPIRE

Aix-la-Chapelle · Frankfurt

LUXEM-
BURG · Mainz

RHENISH
PALATINATE

Philipps-
burg
ALSACE

Verdun · Strasbourg

Reims

Laôn

OISE

LORRAINE

RHINE

RHINE

1648
BOUNDARY OF
FRANCE

Basel

FRANCHE
COMTÉ

SWITZ.

Geneva

Lyons

SAÔNE

MILAN

SAVOY

THE WARS OF LOUIS XIV
1667 - 1697
TREATY OF
AIX-LA-CHAPELLE, 1668
TO FRANCE
TREATY OF
NIMWEGEN, 1678-1679
TO FRANCE
TO SPAIN
TREATY OF
RYSWICK, 1697
TO FRANCE

150 MI.

150 KM.

TRM

DORDOGNE

Bordeaux

GARONNE

Toulouse

RHÔNE

AVIGNON

Marseilles

Narbonne

MEDITERRANEAN SEA

Bayonne

THE ENGLISH CIVIL WAR AND THE WARS OF LOUIS XIV

England and France in the Seventeenth Century

Rise of Absolutism in France

Regional rights and a degree of religious diversity were recognized within the Holy Roman Empire, England, and the Netherlands during the seventeenth century. The assertion of local autonomy by the numerous member states and cities of the Holy Roman Empire made a strong central government there unthinkable. In England and the Netherlands centuries of parliamentary practice permitted regional freedoms to coexist with a strong central government.

Following the devastation of the Thirty Years War, the Peace of Westphalia (1648) reaffirmed religious pluralism within the Holy Roman Empire. A degree of religious diversity, long a Netherlands tradition, received final confirmation also in England after decades of dogged Puritan resistance, when the Toleration Act of 1689 granted rights of worship to protestant nonconformists.

Seventeenth-century France, in contrast to these developments, saw both representative government and religious pluralism crushed by the absolute monarchy and the closed Catholic state of Louis XIV (1643-1715). Louis XIV was determined to export abroad as well as to impose at home his motto of "One king, one law, one faith."

Henry IV and Sully

The foundation was well laid for Louis's grand reign by his predecessors and their exceptional ministers. It was Henry IV (1589-1610) who began in earnest the curtailment of the privileges of the French nobility necessary for the creation of a strong centralized state. His target was the provincial governors and the regional *parlements*,

In the English Civil War, 1645 was a crucial year; here the rapidly deteriorating Royalist position is shown. A bit later in France we see the territorial changes resulting from Louis XIV's first three major wars. The War of the Spanish Succession was yet to come.

especially the powerful *Parlement* of Paris, where the divisive feudal spirit still lived on. Here were to be found the old privileged groups, tax-exempt magnates whose sole preoccupation was to prevent royal laws from infringing upon their self-interests. During Louis XIV's reign their powers were completely usurped by royal civil servants known as *intendants*, who implemented the king's will in the provinces.

It was also during Henry IV's reign that a government-controlled economy emerged as part of the task of reconstruction after the long decades of religious and civil war. Henry and his finance minister, the duke of Sully (1560-1641), prepared the way for the later mercantilist policies of Louis XIV and his minister Colbert. They established government monopolies on gunpowder, mines, and salt. A canal system was begun to link the Atlantic and the Mediterranean by joining the Saône, the Loire, the Seine, and the Meuse rivers. An involuntary national labor force was created by the introduction of a royal *corvée*, and this drafting of workers provided the manpower to improve roads and the conditions of internal travel. Sully even dreamed of the political and commercial organization of the whole of Europe in a kind of common market.

Louis XIII and Richelieu

Henry IV was assassinated in 1610, and the following year Sully retired. Because Henry's successor, Louis XIII (1610-1643), was only nine years old when his father was assassinated, the task of governing fell to the queen mother, Marie de' Medici (d. 1642). Finding herself in a vulnerable position, she sought security abroad by signing a ten-year mutual defense pact with arch-rival Spain in the Treaty of Fontainebleau (1611), an alliance that also arranged for the later marriage of Louis XIII to the Spanish infanta as well as for the marriage of the queen's daughter Elizabeth to the heir to the Spanish throne. Internal security against the French nobility was obtained by the queen's promotion of the career of Cardinal Richelieu (1585-1642) as the king's chief adviser. Richelieu,

loyal and shrewd, aspired to make France a supreme European power and more than any one person was the secret of French success in the first half of the seventeenth century.

Strongly Catholic in religion, Richelieu was just as strongly anti-Hapsburg in politics. On the one hand, he supported the Spanish alliance of the queen and Catholic religious unity within France; on the other, he was determined to contain Spanish power and influence, even when that meant aiding and abetting Protestant Europe. It is an indication both of Richelieu's awkward political situation and of his diplomatic agility that he could pledge funds to the Protestant army of Gustavus Adolphus in the Treaty of Barwälde, in 1631, while at the same time insisting on the condition that Catholic Bavaria be spared from attack and that Catholics in conquered countries be permitted to practice their religion.

At home Richelieu pursued his policies utterly without sentiment. Supported by the king, whose best decision was to let his chief minister make all the decisions of state, Richelieu stepped up the campaign against the separatist provincial governors and *parlements*. He made it clear to all that there was but one law, that of the king, and that none could stand above it. When disobedient noblemen defied his edicts, they were imprisoned and even executed. Louis XIV had Richelieu to thank for the fact that the French nobility became docile beggars at his court. Such treatment of the princes of the blood won Richelieu much enmity, even from the queen mother, who was not prepared to place the larger interests of the state above the pleasure of favorite princes. But the king let no criticism weaken his chief minister, not even that of his mother. The queen mother had largely ignored Louis during his youth—his education came mostly at the hands of his falconer—and they remained estranged and ill at ease in each other's presence. This was doubtless a factor in the king's firm support of Richelieu when his mother became Richelieu's accuser.

Richelieu began the campaign against the Huguenots that would end in 1685 with Louis XIV's shocking revo-

cation of the Edict of Nantes. Royal armies conquered major Huguenot cities in 1629 and the subsequent Peace of Alais (1629) truncated the Edict of Nantes by denying Protestants the right to maintain garrisoned cities, separate political organizations, and independent law courts. Only Richelieu's foreign policy prevented the earlier implementation of the extreme intolerance of Louis XIV. In the same year that the independent status of Huguenots was rescinded, Richelieu also entered negotiations to make Gustavus Adolphus his counterweight to the expansion of Hapsburg power within the Holy Roman Empire. By 1635 the Catholic soldiers of France fought openly with Swedish Lutherans against the emperor's army in the final phase of the Thirty Years War.

In the best Machiavellian tradition Richelieu employed the arts and the printing press to defend his actions and to indoctrinate Frenchmen in the meaning of *raison de'état* ("reasons of state")—again setting a precedent for Louis XIV's elaborate use of royal propaganda and spectacle. It is one measure of Richelieu's success that France made substantial gains in land and political influence when hostilities were ended in the Holy Roman Empire by the Treaty of Westphalia (1648) and peace with Spain was sealed in the Treaty of the Pyrenees (1659).

Young Louis XIV and Mazarin

Richelieu's immediate legacy, however, was strong resentment of the monarchy on the part of the French aristocracy and the privileged bourgeoisie. He and Louis XIII died within months of one another in 1643.

During the minority of Louis XIV, who was only five years old at the time of Louis XIII's death, the queen mother, Anne of Austria (d. 1666), placed the reins of government in the hands of Cardinal Mazarin (1602–1661), who happened also to be her lover and, some report, her secret husband. Mazarin continued Richelieu's pitiless policy of centralization. During his regency the long-building backlash occurred, and France was shaken to its foundations by the Fronde (1649–1652).

Named after the slingshot used by street urchins to

Cardinal Mazarin, in whose hands lay the real power in France during the minority of Louis XIV. [The Granger Collection.]

strike the carriages of the rich, the Fronde was a series of widespread rebellions by segments of the French nobility and townsmen aimed at reversing the drift toward absolute monarchy—a last-ditch effort to preserve their local autonomy. These privileged groups saw their traditional position in French society thoroughly undermined by the crown's steady multiplication of royal offices, replacement of local with "state" agents, and reduction of the patronage they received.

The *Parlement* of Paris initiated the revolt in 1649 and the nobility at large soon followed. The latter were urged on by the influential wives of princes who had been imprisoned by Mazarin for treason. The many briefly triumphed over the one when Mazarin was forced to release the imprisoned princes in February 1651. He and Louis XIV thereafter entered a short exile and were unable to return to Paris until October 1652, when the inefficiency and near anarchy of government by the nobility made them very welcome. The period of the Fronde convinced a majority of Frenchmen that being left to the mercy of a strong king was preferable to being subjected to the competing claims of many regional magnates. After 1652 the French were ready to experiment in earnest with absolute rule.

The World of Louis XIV

UNITY AT HOME. Thanks to the forethought of Mazarin, Louis XIV was well prepared to rule France. The turbulent periods of his youth seem also to have made an indelible impression. Louis wrote in his memoires that the Fronde caused him to loathe "kings of straw" and made him determined never to become one. Indoctrinated with a strong sense of the grandeur of his crown, he never missed an opportunity to impress it upon the French people. When the dauphin was born in 1662, for example, Louis appeared for the celebration dressed as a Roman emperor. Although his rule became the prototype of the modern centralized state, its inspiration was a very narrow medieval ideal of personal glory.

KING BY DIVINE RIGHT. Reverence for the king and the personification of government in his person had been nurtured in France since Capetian times. It was a maxim of French law and popular opinion as early as the late Middle Ages that "The king of France is emperor in his realm," that the king's wish is the law of the land.

An important theorist for Louis's even grander concept of royal authority was the Jesuit tutor of the dauphin, Bishop Jacques-Bénigne Bossuet (1627–1704). An ardent champion of the Gallican Liberties—the traditional rights of the French king and church in matters of ecclesiastical appointments and taxation—Bossuet defended what he called the "divine right of kings." He cited the Old Testament example of rulers divinely appointed by and answerable only to God. Against the claims to power of princes and *parlements* Bossuet enunciated a secular version of an argument earlier used by medieval popes to secure their authority against the competitive claims of bishops and church councils. As medieval popes had insisted that only God could judge a pope, so Bossuet argued that none save God could sit in judgment on the king. Although kings remained duty-bound to reflect God's will in their rule—and in this sense Bossuet considered them always subject to a higher authority—as God's regents on earth they could not be bound to the dictates of mere princes and parliaments. Such were the assumptions that lay behind Louis XIV's alleged declaration: "L'état, c'est moi" ("I am the state").

VERSAILLES. The palace court at Versailles on the outskirts of Paris became Louis's permanent residence

[*Text continued on page 452*]

Versailles as it appeared in 1668 in a painting by
Pierre Patel the Elder (1605–1676). The central
building is the hunting lodge built for Louis XIII
earlier in the century, and some of the first
expansion undertaken by Louis XIV appears as wings.
The painting is in the Versailles museum. [Cliché
des Musées Nationaux, Paris.]

The sumptuous Salon de la Guerre in the Palace of
Versailles. It was begun in 1678. Several rooms
of the palace were badly damaged by a terrorist's
bomb in June 1978. [French Embassy Press and
Information Division, New York.]

A full view of Versailles as it appears today. Louis XIV
vastly enlarged his father's hunting lodge into a palace
estate beginning in 1661. It became not only the royal
residence but the seat of the French government, a
symbol of royal and national power, and the frequently
imitated model for other seventeenth- and eighteenth-
century monarchs. This photograph is from the opposite
direction to Patel's painting; the coaches in his picture
are arriving on the diagonal road at the top left of the
photograph. [French Government Tourist Office, New
York.]

after 1682 and was a true temple to royalty, architecturally designed and artistically decorated to proclaim the glory of the Sun King, as Louis was known. A spectacular estate with magnificent fountains and acres of orange groves, it became home to thousands of aristocrats, royal officials, and servants. Although its physical maintenance and new additions, which continued throughout Louis's lifetime, consumed over half his annual revenues—around five million livres a year—Versailles paid political dividends well worth the investment.

Life at court was organized around the king's daily routine.

His rising and dressing was a time of rare intimacy, when nobles, who entered their names on waiting lists to be in attendance, whispered their special requests in Louis's ear.

After the morning Mass, which Louis always observed, there followed long hours in council with the chief ministers, assemblies from which the nobility was carefully excluded. Louis's ministers and councillors were hand-picked townsmen, servants who owed everything they had to the king's favor and were for that reason inclined to serve faithfully and without question. There were three main councils: the Council of State, a small group of four or five who met thrice weekly to rule on all matters of state, but especially on foreign affairs and war policy; the Council of Despatches, which regularly assessed the reports from the *intendants* in the towns and provinces, a boring business that the king often left to his ministers; and finally, the Council of Finances, which handled matters of taxation and commerce.

The afternoons were spent hunting, riding, or strolling about the lush gardens. Evenings were given over to planned entertainment in the large salons (plays, concerts, gambling, and the like), followed by supper at 10:00 P.M.

Even the king's retirement was a part of the day's spectacle. Fortunate nobles were permitted briefly to hold his night candle as they accompanied him to his bed.

Although only five feet, four inches in height, the king

Bishop Bossuet Defends the Divine Right of Kings

The revolutions of the seventeenth century caused many to fear anarchy far more than tyranny, among them the influential French bishop, Jacques Bénigne Bossuet (1627–1704). Bossuet owed his rise to power as virtual leader of French Catholicism in the second half of the seventeenth century to his oratorical, literary, and historical skills. Louis XIV made him court preacher and tutor to his son, for whom Bossuet wrote a celebrated *Universal History*. Here he defends the divine right and absolute power of kings, who are depicted as embracing in their person the whole body of the state and the will of the people they govern and, as such, as being immune from judgment by any man.

THE *royal power is absolute. . . . The prince need render account of his acts to no one. "I counsel thee to keep the king's commandment, and that in regard of the oath of God. Be not hasty to go out of his sight; stand not on an evil thing for he doeth whatsoever pleaseth him. Where the word of a king is, there is power: and who may say unto him, What doest thou? Whoso keepeth the commandment shall feel no evil thing" [Eccles. 8:2–5]. Without this absolute authority the king could neither do good nor repress evil. It is necessary that his power be such that no one can hope to escape him, and finally, the only protection of individuals against the public authority should be their innocence. This confirms the teaching of St. Paul: "Wilt thou then not be afraid of the power? Do that which is good" [Rom. 13:3].*

God is infinite, God is all. The prince, as prince, is not regarded as a private person: he is a public personage, all the state is in him; the will of all the people is included in his. As all perfection and all strength are united in God, so all the power of individuals is united in the person of the prince. What grandeur that a single man should embody so much! . . .

Behold an immense people united in a single person; behold this holy power, paternal and absolute; behold the secret cause which governs the whole body of the state, contained in a single head: you see the image of God in the king, and you have the idea of royal majesty. God is holiness itself, goodness itself, and power itself. In these things lies the majesty of God. In the image of these things lies the majesty of the prince.

From *Politics Drawn from the Very Words of Holy Scripture*, in James Harvey Robinson, *Readings in European History*, Vol. 2 (Boston: Ginn and Co., 1906), pp. 275–276.

Bishop Cornelis Jansen (1585–1638) was the author of the intellectual and theological foundations of what came to be called Jansenism. Several of his key beliefs were eventually declared heretical by the Catholic Church. [The Granger Collection.]

The abbey of Port Royal near Paris in the seventeenth century, the main center of Jansenist theological activity. Its picture gives a good impression of the layout of a religious community of the time. [The Granger Collection.]

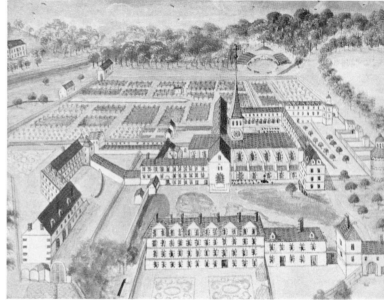

had presence and was always engaging in conversation. An unabashed ladies' man, he encouraged the belief at court that it was an honor to lie with the king. Louis was a bee who gathered nectar from many flowers. Married to the Spanish Infanta Marie Thérèse for political reasons in 1660, he kept many mistresses. After Marie's death in 1683 he settled down in secret marriage with one, Madame de Maintenon, and apparently became thereafter much less the philanderer.

All this ritual and play served the political purpose of keeping an impoverished nobility, barred by law from high government positions, busy and begging so that they had no time to plot revolt. The dress codes and the high-stakes gaming at court contributed to the indebtedness and dependency of noblemen on the king. Court life was a carefully planned and successfully executed domestication of the nobility.

Suppression of the Jansenists

Like Richelieu before him, Louis believed that political unity required religious conformity. To that end he suppressed two groups of religious dissenters: the Catholic Jansenists, who were opponents of the Jesuits, and the Protestant Huguenots.

Although the king and the French church had always jealously guarded their traditional independence from Rome, the years following the conversion of Henry IV to Catholicism saw a great influx of Catholic religious orders into France, prominent among which were the Jesuits. Because of their leadership at the Council of Trent and their close Spanish connections, Catherine de' Medici had earlier banned the Jesuits from France. Henry IV lifted the ban in 1603, with certain conditions: there was to be a limitation on the number of new colleges they could open; special licenses were required for activities outside their own buildings; and each member of the order was subjected to an oath of allegiance to the king. The Jesuits were not, however, easily harnessed. They rapidly monopolized the education of the upper classes, and their devout students promoted the religious reforms and doctrine of the Council of Trent throughout France. It is a measure of their success that Jesuits served as confessors to Henry IV, Louis XIII, and Louis XIV.

In the 1630s an intra-Catholic opposition to both the theology and the political influence of the Jesuits formed: the Jansenists. They were Catholics who adhered to the Augustinian tradition out of which many Protestant teachings had also come. Serious and uncompromising in their religious doctrine and practice, they were especially distinguished by belief in the utter bondage of man's will to sin without the special assistance of divine grace. Their namesake, Cornelis Jansen (d. 1638), a Flemish theologian and the bishop of Ypres, was the author of a posthumously published book entitled *Augustinus* (1640), which assailed Jesuit teaching on grace and salvation.

Jean du Vergier de Hauranne (1581–1643), the abbot of Saint-Cyran and Jansen's close friend, was instrumental in bringing into the Jansenist fold a Parisian family, the Arnaulds, who were prominent in the Gallican opposition to the Jesuits. The Arnauld family, like many other Frenchmen, believed that the Jesuits had been behind the assassination of Henry IV in 1610 and constantly suspected their intentions. Arnauld support added a strong political element to the Jansenists' theological opposition to the Jesuits. Jansenist communities in Port Royal and Paris were dominated by the Arnaulds during the 1640s. In 1643 Antoine Arnauld published a work entitled *On Frequent Communion* in which Jesuits were criticized for confessional practices that permitted easy redress of almost any sin. The Jesuits in turn condemned the Jansenists as "crypto-Calvinists" in their theology.

On May 31, 1653, Jansenism was declared a heresy. On that day five Jansenist theological propositions on grace and salvation, earlier condemned by the Sorbonne, were deemed heretical by Pope Innocent X. In 1656 the Pope banned Jansen's *Augustinus* and the Sorbonne censured Antoine Arnauld. It was in this same year that the latter's friend, Blaise Pascal (d. 1662), the most famous of Jansen's followers, published the first of his *Provincial Letters* in defense of Jansenism. A deeply religious man,

Louix XIV Revokes the Edict of Nantes

Believing that a country could not be under one king and one law unless it was also under one religious system, Louis XIV stunned Europe in October 1685 by revoking the Edict of Nantes, which had protected the religious freedoms and civil rights of French Reformed Protestants since 1598.

ART. 1. *Know that we . . . with our certain knowledge, full power and royal authority, have by this present, perpetual and irrevocable edict, suppressed and revoked the edict of the aforesaid king our grandfather, given at Nantes in the month of April, 1598, in all its extent . . . together with all the concessions made by [this] and other edicts, declarations, and decrees, to the people of the so-called Reformed religion, of whatever nature they be . . . and in consequence we desire . . . that all the temples of the people of the aforesaid so-called Reformed religion situated in our kingdom . . . should be demolished forthwith.*

Art. 2. We forbid our subjects of the so-called Reformed religion to assemble any more for public worship of the above-mentioned religion. . . .

Art. 3. We likewise forbid all lords, of whatever rank they may be, to carry out heretical services in houses and fiefs . . . the penalty for . . . the said worship being confiscation of their body and possessions.

Art. 4. We order all ministers of the aforesaid so-called Reformed religion who do not wish to be converted and to embrace the Catholic, Apostolic, and Roman religion, to depart from our kingdom and the lands subject to us within fifteen days from the publication of our present edict . . . on pain of the galleys.

Art. 5. We desire that those among the said [Reformed] ministers who shall be converted [to the Catholic religion] shall continue to enjoy during their life, and their wives shall enjoy after their death as long as they remain widows, the same exemptions from taxation and billeting of soldiers, which they enjoyed while they fulfilled the function of ministers. . . .

.   .   .   .

Art. 8. With regard to children who shall be born to those of the aforesaid so-called Reformed religion, we desire that they be baptized by their parish priests. We command the fathers and mothers to send them to the churches for that purpose, on penalty of a fine of 500 livres or more if they fail to do so; and afterwards, the children shall be brought up in the Catholic, Apostolic, and Roman religion. . . .

.   .   .   .

Art. 10. All our subjects of the so-called Reformed religion, with their wives and children, are to be strongly and repeatedly prohibited from leaving our aforesaid kingdom . . . or of taking out . . . their possessions and effects. . . .

.   .   .   .

The members of the so-called Reformed religion, while awaiting God's pleasure to enlighten them like the others, can live in the towns and districts of our kingdom . . . and continue their occupation there, and enjoy their possessions . . . on condition . . . that they do not make public profession of [their religion].

Church and State Through the Centuries: A Collection of Historic Documents, trans. and ed. by S. Z. Ehler and John B. Morrall (New York: Biblo and Tannen, 1967), pp. 209–213.

Pascal tried to reconcile the "reasons of the heart" with growing seventeenth-century reverence for the clear and distinct ideas of the mind. He found Jesuit moral theology to be not only lax and shallow, but also a rationalized approach to religion that did injustice to religious experience.

In 1660 Louis permitted the enforcement of the papal bull *Ad Sacram Sedem* (1656), which banned Jansenism, and he closed down the Port Royal community. Thereafter Jansenists either capitulated by signing retractions or went underground. At a later date (1710) the French king lent his support to a still more thorough Jesuit purge of Jansenist sentiment. With the fall of the Jansenists went any hope of a Catholicism broad enough to attract Huguenots.

Revocation of the Edict of Nantes

Since 1598, when the Edict of Nantes was proclaimed, a cold war had existed between the great Catholic majority (nine tenths of the French population remained Catholic) and the Protestant minority. Despite their respecta-

ble numbers, about 1.75 million by the 1660s, the Huguenots were in decline in the second half of the seventeenth century. Government harrassment had forced the more influential members to withdraw their support. Officially the French Catholic Church had long denounced Calvinists as heretical and treasonous and had supported their persecution as both a pious and a patriotic act. Following the Peace of Nijmegen in 1678–1679, which halted for the moment Louis's aggression in Europe, a methodical government campaign was launched against French Huguenots as Louis became determined to unify France religiously. The Huguenots were hounded out of public life, banned from government office, and excluded from such professions as printing and medicine. Subsidies and selective taxation were used to encourage their conversion to Catholicism. In 1681 dragoons were quartered in Huguenot towns. The final stage of the persecution came in October 1685, when Louis revoked the Edict of Nantes. In practical terms the revocation meant the closing of Protestant churches and schools, the exile of Protestant ministers, the placement of nonconverting laymen in galleys as slaves, and the ceremonial baptism of Protestant children by Catholic priests.

The revocation of the Edict of Nantes was the major blunder of Louis's reign. Thereafter he was viewed throughout Europe as a new Philip II, intent on a Catholic reconquest of the whole of Europe, who must be resisted at all costs. Internally the revocation of the Edict of Nantes led to the voluntary emigration of over a quarter million Frenchmen, who formed new communities and joined French resistance in England, Germany, Holland, and the New World. Thousands of French Huguenots served in the army of Louis's arch foe, William III of the Netherlands, later King William III of England. Those who remained in France became an uncompromising guerrilla force. But despite the many domestic and foreign liabilities created for France by the revocation of the Edict of Nantes, Louis to his death considered it his most pious act, one that placed God in his debt.

Jean-Baptiste Colbert, the strongly nationalistic finance minister and sponsor of mercantilism under Louis XIV. His portrait is by Pierre Mignard. [The Granger Collection.]

War Abroad

War was the normal state for seventeenth-century rulers and for none more so than for Louis XIV, who confessed on his deathbed that he had "loved war too much." Periods of peace were viewed as opportunities for the discontented in town and countryside to plot against the king. By the 1660s France was the superior of any other nation in administrative bureaucracy, armed forces, and national unity. It had a population of nineteen million, prosperous farms, vigorous trade, and much taxable wealth. By every external measure Louis was in a position to dominate Europe.

LOUVOIS, VAUBAN, COLBERT. The great French war machine was the work of three ministers: Louvois, Vauban, and Colbert. The army, which maintained a strength of about a quarter of a million men, was the creation of Michel le Tellier and his more famous son, the marquis of Louvois (1641–1691). The latter was the supreme military tactician of the age before the emergence of the English duke of Marlborough. He served as Louis's war minister from 1677 to 1691.

Before Louvois the French army had been a medley of local recruits and mercenaries, uncoordinated groups whose loyalty could not always be counted upon. Louvois disciplined the French army and made it a respectable profession. He placed a limit on military commissions and introduced a system of promotion by merit, moves that brought dedicated fighting men into the ranks. Enlistment was for four years and was restricted to single men. The pay was good and regular. *Intendants*, those ubiquitous civil servants, carried out regular inspections, monitoring conduct at all levels and reporting to the king.

What Louvois was to military organization Sebastien Vauban (1633–1707) was to military engineering. He perfected the arts of fortifying and besieging towns. He also devised the system of trench warfare and developed the concept of defensive frontiers that remained basic military tactics through World War I.

War cannot be successful without financing, and here Louis had the guidance of his most brilliant minister, Jean-Baptiste Colbert (1619–1683). Colbert centralized the French economy with the same rigor that Louis had centralized the French government. He put the nation to work under state supervision and carefully regulated the flow of imports and exports through tariffs. He created new national industries and organized factories around a tight regimen of work and ideology. Administrative bureaucracy was simplified, unnecessary positions abolished, and the number of tax-exempt nobles reduced. Colbert also increased the *taille* on the peasantry, the chief source of royal wealth. This close government control of the economy came to be known as *mercantilism*. Its aim was to maximize foreign exports and the internal reserves of bullion, the gold and silver necessary for war making. Modern scholars argue that Colbert overcontrolled the French economy and cite his paternalism as a major reason for French failures in the New World. Be that as it may, Colbert unquestionably transformed France into a major industrial and commercial power, with foreign bases in Africa, India, and the Americas from Canada to the Caribbean.

THE WAR OF DEVOLUTION. Louis's first great foreign adventure was the War of Devolution (1667–1668). It was fought, as still a later and greater war would be, over Louis's claim to a Spanish inheritance through his wife, Marie Thérèse (1638–1683). According to the terms of the Treaty of the Pyrenees (1659), Marie had renounced her claim to the Spanish succession on condition that a 500,000 crown dowry be paid to Louis within eighteen months of the marriage, a condition that was not met. When Philip IV of Spain died in September 1665, he left all his lands to his sickly four-year-old son by a second marriage, Charles II (1665–1700), and explicitly excluded his daughter Marie from any share. Louis had always harbored the hope of turning the marriage to territorial gain and argued even before Philip's death that Marie was entitled to a portion of the inheritance.

Louis had a legal argument on his side, which gave the

war its name. He maintained that because in certain regions of Brabant and Flanders, which were part of the Spanish inheritance, property "devolved" to the children of a first marriage rather than to those of a second, Marie had a higher claim than Charles II to these regions. The argument was not accepted—such regional laws could hardly bind the king of Spain—but Louis was not deterred from moving his armies, under vicomte de Turenne, into Flanders and the Franche-Comté in 1667. It was in response to this aggression that England, Sweden, and the United Provinces of Holland formed the Triple Alliance, a force sufficient to bring Louis to peace terms in the Treaty of Aix-la-Chapelle (1668).

INVASION OF THE NETHERLANDS. In 1670 England and France became allies against the Dutch by signing the Treaty of Dover, a move that set the Stuart monarchy of Charles II on a new international course. With the departure of the English from membership in it, the Triple Alliance crumbled. This left Louis in a stronger position to invade the Netherlands for a second time, which he did in 1672. This second invasion was aimed directly at Holland, the organizer of the Triple Alliance in 1667 and the country held accountable by Louis for foiling French designs in Flanders. Louis had been mightily offended by Dutch boasting after the Treaty of Aix-la-Chapelle; cartoons like one depicting the sun (Louis was the "Sun King") eclipsed by a great moon of Dutch cheese cut the French king to the quick. It was also clear that there could be no French acquisition of land in the Spanish Netherlands, nor European hegemony beyond that, until Holland was neutralized.

Louis's successful invasion of the United Provinces in 1672 brought the downfall of Jan and Cornelius De Witt, Dutch statesmen who were blamed for the French success. In their place came the twenty-seven-year-old William III, Prince of Orange (1650–1702), the great-grandson of William the Silent, who had successfully repulsed Philip II and dashed Spanish hopes of dominating the Netherlands in the sixteenth century.

After 1689 William III became King William III of England and proved more than any one man to be Louis's undoing. This unpretentious Calvinist, who was in almost every way Louis's opposite, galvanized the seven provinces into a fierce fighting unit that did not shrink from opening the dikes on French armies. In 1673 he united the Holy Roman Emperor, Spain, Lorraine, and Brandenburg in an alliance against Louis, who was now seen by his enemies to be "the Christian Turk," a menace to the whole of western Europe, Catholic and Protestant alike. Subsequent battles saw Louis lose his ablest generals, Turenne and Condé, in 1675, while the defeat of the Dutch fleet by Admiral Duquesne established French control of the Mediterranean in 1676. The Peace of Nimwegen, signed with different parties in successive years, ended the hostilities of this second war. In 1678 France entered agreements with Holland and Spain and in 1679 with the Holy Roman Emperor, Brandenburg, and Denmark. The settlements were not unfavorable to France—Spain, for example, surrendered the Franche-Comté—but France still fell far short of the European empire to which Louis aspired.

THE LEAGUE OF AUGSBURG. Between the Treaty of Nimwegen and the renewal of full-scale war in 1689, Louis restlessly probed his perimeters. The army was maintained at full strength. In 1681 it conquered the free city of Strasbourg, setting off the formation of new defensive coalitions against Louis. The League of Augsburg was created in 1686 to resist French expansion into Germany and grew by 1689 to include the Emperor Leopold, Spain, Sweden, the United Provinces, the electorates of Bavaria, Saxony, and the Palatinate, and the England of William and Mary. That year saw the beginning of the Nine Years' War (1689–1697) between France and the League. For the third time stalemate and exhaustion forced the combatants to an interim settlement. The Peace of Ryswick in September 1697 was a personal triumph for William, now William III of England, and the Emperor Leopold, as it secured Holland's borders and thwarted Louis's expansion into Germany. During this same period England and France fought for

The first duke of Marlborough (1650–1722) was the military genius of England and its allies in the War of the Spanish Succession. For him a grateful country built Blenheim Palace near Oxford, named for one of his famous battles, and still one of the grandest country estates of England. The portrait is by Sir Godfrey Kneller. [The Granger Collection.]

OPPOSITE: In 1701, at age 63—when this famous portrait was painted by Hyacinthe Rigaud (1659–1743)—Louis XIV was at the height of his power, despite wars past and future that did not always go well for him. The contrast between the portrait of the youthful, watchful king that opens this chapter and the present portrait shows only too clearly the effects of forty years of absolute authority. Rigaud's picture is in the Louvre. [The Granger Collection.]

The nations of Europe were far more fearful of a union of the French and Spanish crowns than they were of a union of the imperial and Spanish crowns. Indeed, they were determined that the former alliance not occur. Hence, before Charles's death negotiations began to partition the inheritance in such a way that the current balance of power would be maintained.

Charles II upset all plans by leaving the entire Spanish inheritance to Philip of Anjou, Louis's grandson. At a stroke the Spanish inheritance had fallen to France. Although Louis had been party to the partition agreements in advance of Charles's death, he now saw God's hand in Charles's will and chose to enforce its terms fully rather than abide by those of the partition treaty. Philip of Anjou moved to Madrid and became Philip V of Spain, and Louis, in what was interpreted as naked French aggression, sent his troops once again into Flanders, this time to remove Dutch soldiers from Spanish territory in the name of the new French king of Spain.

In September 1701 the Grand Alliance of England, Holland, and the Holy Roman Emperor formed against Louis in The Hague. Its intent was to preserve the balance of power by once and for all securing Flanders as a neutral barrier between Holland and France and by gaining for the emperor his fair share of the Spanish inheritance. After the formation of the alliance, Louis increased the stakes of battle by recognizing the son of James II of England as James III, king of England.

Once again total war enveloped western Europe as the twelve-year War of the Spanish Succession (1702–1714) began. This time, and for the first time, France went to war with inadequate finances, a poorly equipped army, and mediocre military leadership. John Churchill, the duke of Marlborough, who succeeded William of Orange as leader of the alliance, bested Louis's soldiers in every major engagement. French armies were routed at Blenheim in August 1704 and on the plain of Ramillies in 1706—two decisive battles of the war. In 1708–1709 famine, revolts, and uncollectable taxes tore France apart internally. Despair pervaded the French court, and Louis

control of North America in what came to be known as King William's War (1689–1697).

WAR OF THE SPANISH SUCCESSION: TREATIES OF UTRECHT–RASTADT. After Ryswick, Louis, who seemed to thrive on partial success, made still a fourth attempt to realize his grand design of French European domination, this time assisted by an unforeseen turn of events. On November 1, 1700, Charles II of Spain, known as "the Sufferer" because of his genetic deformities and lingering illnesses, died. Both Louis and the Austrian Emperor Leopold had claims to the Spanish inheritance through their grandsons: Louis through his marriage to Maria Thérèse and Leopold through his marriage to her younger sister, Margaret Thérèse. Although the dauphin had the higher blood claim, it was assumed that the inheritance would go to the grandson of the emperor. The French painted the specter of a belligerent Hapsburg kingdom like that of Charles V in the sixteenth century should Spain come under the imperial crown. Maria Thérèse, however, had renounced any right to the Spanish inheritance in the Treaty of the Pyrenees (1659).

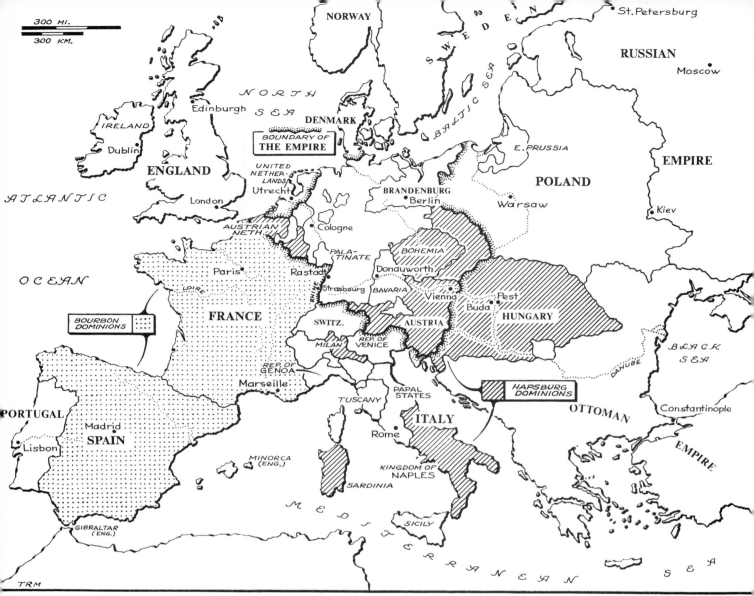

EUROPE IN 1714

The War of the Spanish Succession ended in the year before the death of the aged Louis XIV. By then France and Spain, although not united, were ruled by members of the Bourbon family, and Spain had lost her non-Iberian possessions. Austria had continued to grow.

wondered aloud how God could forsake one who had done so much for Him.

Though ready to make peace in 1709, Louis could not bring himself to accept the stiff terms of the alliance, which included the demand that he transfer all Spanish possessions to the emperor's grandson Charles and remove Philip V from Madrid. An immediate result of this failure to come to terms was a clash of forces at Mal-

plaquet (September 1709), which left carnage on the battlefield unsurpassed until modern times.

Under the English minister Bolingbroke the allies renewed peace talks in 1711. France signed an armistice with England at Utrecht in July 1712, and hostilities were concluded with Holland and the emperor in the treaty of Rastadt in March 1714. These agreements confirmed Philip V as king of Spain. They gave England Gibraltar, which made England thereafter a Mediterranean power, and won Louis's recognition of the House of Hanover's right of accession to the English throne.

Politically the eighteenth century would belong to England as the sixteenth had belonged to Spain and the seventeenth to France. The emperor received control of the Spanish Netherlands, which was established as a barrier between France and Holland, with Dutch troops stationed in key towns. France kept the cities of Strasbourg and Lille. Although France remained intact and quite strong, the realization of Louis XIV's ambition had to await the rise of Napoleon Bonaparte. On his deathbed on September 1, 1715, a dying Louis fittingly warned the dauphin not to imitate his love of buildings and his liking for war.

SUGGESTED READINGS

MAURICE ASHLEY, *The Greatness of Oliver Cromwell* (1966). Detailed biography.

TREVOR ASTON (Ed.), *Crisis in Europe 1560–1660* (1965). Essays by major scholars focused on social and economic forces.

WILLIAM F. CHURCH (Ed.), *The Greatness of Louis XIV: Myth or Reality?* (1959). Excerpts from the scholarly debate over Louis's reign.

C. H. FIRTH, *Oliver Cromwell and the Rule of the Puritans in England* (1900). Old but still very authoritative work.

WILLIAM HALLER, *The Rise of Puritanism* (1957). Interesting study based largely on Puritan sermons.

CHRISTOPHER HILL, *The Century of Revolution 1603–1714* (1961). Bold, imaginative synthesis by a controversial master.

W. H. LEWIS, *The Splended Century* (1953). Focuses on society, especially in the age of Louis XIV.

DAVID OGG, *Europe in the Seventeenth Century* (1925). Among the most authoritative syntheses.

SUART E. PRALL, *The Puritan Revolution: A Documentary History* (1968). Comprehensive document collection.

LAWRENCE STONE, *The Causes of the English Revolution 1529–1642* (1972). Brief survey stressing social history and ruminating over historians and historical method.

G. R. R. TREASURE, *Seventeenth Century France* (1966). Broad, detailed survey of entire century.

MICHAEL WALZER, *The Revolution of the Saints: A Study in the Origins of Radical Politics* (1965). Effort to relate ideas and politics that depicts Puritans as true revolutionaries.

C. V. WEDGWOOD, *Richelieu and the French Monarchy* (1950). Fine biography.

JOHN B. WOLF, *Louis XIV* (1968). Very detailed political biography.

net, in quo terram cum orbe lunari tanquam epicyclo contineri diximus. Quinto loco Venus nono mense reducitur. Sextum deniæ locum Mercurius tenet, octuaginta dierum spacio circu currens. In medio uero omnium residet Sol. Quis enim in hoc

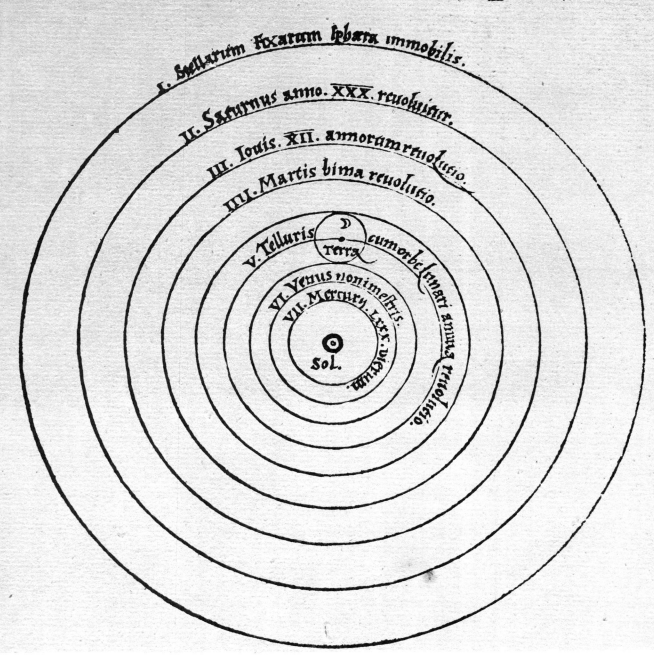

18
New Directions in Science and Thought in the Sixteenth and Seventeenth Centuries

The Scientific Revolution
New Departures

THE SIXTEENTH and seventeenth centuries witnessed a sweeping change in the scientific view of the universe. An earth-centered picture of the universe gave way to one in which the earth was only another planet orbiting about the sun. The sun itself became one of millions of stars. This transformation of humankind's perception of its place in the larger scheme of things led to a vast rethinking of moral and religious matters as well as scientific theory. At the same time the new scientific concepts and the methods of their construction became so impressive that subsequent knowledge in the Western world has been deemed correct only as it has approximated knowledge as defined by science. Perhaps no single intellectual development proved to be more significant for the future of European and Western civilization.

The process by which this new view of the universe and of scientific knowledge came to be established is normally termed the *Scientific Revolution.* However, care must be taken in the use of this metaphor. The word *revolution* normally denotes fairly rapid changes in the political world involving large numbers of people. The Scientific Revolution was not rapid, nor did it involve more than a few hundred human beings. It was a complex movement with many false starts and many brilliant people with wrong as well as useful ideas. It took place in the studies and the crude laboratories of thinkers in Po-

land, Italy, Bohemia, France, and Great Britain. It stemmed from two major tendencies. The first, as illustrated by Nicolaus Copernicus, was the imposition of important small changes on existing models of thought. The second, as embodied by Francis Bacon, was the desire to pose new kinds of questions and to use new methods of investigation. In both cases, scientific thought changed the current and traditional opinions in other fields.

Nicolaus Copernicus

Copernicus (1473–1543) was a Polish astronomer who enjoyed a very high reputation throughout his life. He was neither an obscure nor an unknown figure. He had been educated in Italy and corresponded with other astronomers throughout Europe. However, he had not been known for strikingly original or unorthodox thought. In 1543, the year of his death, Copernicus published *On the Revolutions of the Heavenly Spheres.* Because he died near the time of publication, the fortunes of his work are not the story of one person's crusade for progressive science. Copernicus's book was "a revolution-making rather than a revolutionary text."[1] What Copernicus did was to provide an intellectual springboard for a complete criticism of the then dominant view of the position of the earth in the universe.

At the time of Copernicus the standard explanation of the earth and the heavens was that associated with Ptolemy and his work entitled the *Almagest* (A.D. 150). There was not just one Ptolemaic system but rather several versions had been developed over the centuries by commentators on the original work. Most of these systems assumed that the earth was the center of the universe. Above the earth lay a series of crystalline spheres, one of which contained the moon, another the sun, and still others the planets and the stars. This was the astron-

Nicolaus Copernicus's view of the universe with the sun in the center. The basis of the scientific and intellectual revolution initiated by the Polish astronomer (1473–1543) is summarized in this diagram printed in his *De Revolutionibus Orbium Coelestium* (*On the Revolutions of Heavenly Bodies*) of 1543. [The British Library, London.]

1 Thomas S. Kuhn, *The Copernican Revolution: Planetary Astronomy in the Development of Western Thought* (New York: Vintage, 1959), p. 135.

Hypothetical reconstruction of the printing press of Johannes Gutenberg of Mainz (in what is now West Germany). Between about 1435 and 1455, Gutenberg worked out the complete technology of making individual rectangular metal types, composing the type into pages held together by pressure, and printing from those on an adaptation of the wooden standing press with ink of lampblack mixed with oil varnish. This new technology for the first time made it possible to manufacture numerous identical copies of written works and was basic to the intellectual development of the West. [Gutenberg-Museum, Mainz.]

omy found in such works as Dante's *Divine Comedy*. At the outer regions of these spheres lay the realm of God and the angels. Aristotelian physics provided the intellectual underpinnings of the Ptolemaic systems. The earth had to be the center because of its heaviness. The stars and the other heavenly bodies had to be enclosed in the crystalline spheres so that they could move. Nothing could move unless something was actually moving it. The state of rest was natural; motion was the condition that required explanation.

Numerous problems were associated with this system, and these had long been recognized. The most important was the observed motions of the planets. Planets could be seen moving in noncircular patterns around the earth. At certain times the planets actually appeared to be making backward or retrograde motion. The Ptolemaic systems explained these strange motions through *epicycles*. The planets were said to make a second revolution in an orbit tangent to their primary orbit around the earth. The epicycle was compared to a jewel on a ring. Other intellectual but nonobservational difficulties related to the immense speed at which the spheres had to move around the earth. To say the least, the Ptolemaic systems were cluttered. However, they were effective explanations as long as one assumed Aristotelian physics and the Christian belief that the earth rested at the center of the created universe.

Copernicus's *On the Revolutions of the Heavenly Spheres* challenged this picture in the most conservative manner possible. It suggested that if the earth were supposed to move about the sun in a circle, many of the difficulties with the Ptolemaic systems would disappear or become simpler. Although not wholly eliminated, the number of epicycles would be somewhat fewer. The motive behind this shift away from an earth-centered universe was to find a solution to the problems of planetary motion. By allowing the earth to move around the sun, Copernicus was able to construct a more mathematically elegant basis for astronomy. He had been discontented with the traditional system because it was mathematically clumsy and inconsistent. The primary appeal of his new system was its mathematical aesthetics. He wanted to put the sun at the center of the universe so that mathematical astronomy would make more sense. A change in the conception of the position of the earth meant that the planets were actually moving in circular orbits and only seemed to be doing otherwise because of the position of the observers on earth.

Except for the modification in the position of the earth, most of the other parts of Copernicus's book were Ptolemaic. The path of the planets remained circular. Genuine epicycles still existed in the heavens. His system was no more accurate than the existing ones for predicting the location of the planets. He had employed no new evidence. The major impact of his work was to provide another way of confronting some of the difficulties inherent in Ptolemaic astronomy. This work did not immedi-

View of the universe as described by Claudius Ptolemy, an astronomer of Alexandria, Egypt, in the second century. Ptolemy's view, which put the earth unmoving in the center with the other heavenly objects circling it (the sun being in the fourth circle), dominated astronomy until the sixteenth century. The illustration is from a book by Gregor Reisch, *Margarita Philosophica* (1515). [The British Library, London.]

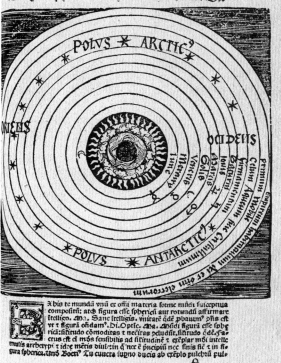

ately replace the old astronomy, but it did allow other people who were also discontented with the Ptolemaic systems to think in new directions.

Copernicus's concern for mathematics provided an example of the single most important factor in the developing new science. Mathematics became the model to which the new emerging scientific thought would conform. However, from the late sixteenth century onward there was added to the mathematical bias a desire for scientific thought to conform to empirical observation. The major spokesman for this position was Francis Bacon.

Francis Bacon

Bacon (1561–1626) was an Englishman of almost universal accomplishment. He was a lawyer, a high royal official, and the author of histories, moral essays, and philosophical discourses. Traditionally he has been regarded as the Father of Empiricism and of the idea of experimentation in science. Much of this reputation is unearned. Nor was Bacon a scientist except in the most amateur fashion. His accomplishment was setting a tone and helping to create a climate in which other scientists worked. In books such as *The Advancement of Learning* (1605), the *Novum Organum* (1620), and the *New Atlantis* (1627), Bacon attacked Scholastic philosophy and reverence for intellectual authority in general. He believed that Scholastic thinkers paid too much attention to tradition and to knowledge achieved by the ancients. He urged contemporaries to strike out on their own in search of a new understanding of nature. He wanted seventeenth-century Europeans to have confidence in themselves and their own abilities rather than in the people and methods of the past. Bacon was one of the first major European writers to champion the desirability of innovation and change.

Bacon believed that human knowledge should produce useful results. In particular, knowledge of nature should be brought to the aid of the human condition. Those goals required the modification or abandonment of Scho-

The Scientific Revolution 465

Francis Bacon here muses in Trinity College Chapel, Cambridge University, as sculptured by Henry Weekes. [By courtesy of The Courtauld Institute of Art, London.]

flowers of the garden and of the field, but transforms and digests it by a power of its own. Not unlike this is the true business of philosophy.[3]

By directing scientists toward an examination of empirical evidence, Bacon hoped that they would achieve new knowledge and thus new capabilities for humankind.

Bacon compared himself to Columbus plotting a new route to intellectual discovery. The comparison is significant, because it displays the consciousness of a changing world that appears so often in writers of the late sixteenth and early seventeenth centuries. They were rejecting the past not from simple hatred but rather from a firm understanding that the world was much more complicated than their medieval forebears had thought.

Neither Europe nor European thought could remain self-contained. There were not only new worlds on the globe but also new worlds of the mind. Most of the people in Bacon's day, including intellectuals, thought that the best era of human history lay in the past. Bacon dissented vigorously from that point of view. He looked to a future of material improvement achieved through the empirical examination of nature. His own theory of induction from empirical evidence was quite faulty, but his insistence upon appeal to experience influenced others whose methods were more productive. His great achievement was to persuade increasing numbers of thinkers that scientific thought must conform to empirical experience.

Bacon gave science a progressionist bias: it was to have a practical purpose and the goal of human improvement. Some scientific investigation does possess this character. Much pure research does not. However, Bacon linked in the public mind the concepts of science and material progress. This was a powerful idea and has continued to influence Western civilization to the present day. It has made science and those who can appeal to the authority of science major forces for change and innovation. Thus,

lastic modes of learning and thinking. Bacon contended, "The [scholastic] logic now in use serves more to fix and give stability to the errors which have their foundation in commonly received notions than to help the search after truth."[2] Scholastic philosophers could not escape from their syllogisms to examine the foundations of their thought and intellectual presuppositions. Bacon urged that philosophers and investigators of nature examine the evidence of their senses before constructing logical speculations. In a famous passage he divided all philosophers into "men of experiment and men of dogmas." He observed;

> The men of experiment are like the ant, they only collect and use; the reasoners resemble spiders, who make cobwebs out of their own substance. But the bee takes a middle course: it gathers its materials from the

2 Quoted in Franklin Baumer, *Main Currents of Western Thought,* 4th ed. (New Haven: Yale, 1978), p. 281.

3 Quoted in ibid., p. 288.

though not making any major scientific contribution himself, Bacon directed investigators of nature to a new method and a new purpose.

Working Out a New Scientific World View

The key to the future development of the Copernican revolution lay in the fusion of mathematical astronomy with further empirical data and observation. Mathematics provided the foundation for the new scientific model; the new empirical evidence helped to persuade the learned public.

Tycho Brahe and Johannes Kepler

The next major step toward the conception of a sun-centered system was taken by Tycho Brahe (1546–1601). He actually spent most of his life opposing Copernicus and advocating a different kind of earth-centered system. He suggested that the moon and the sun revolved around the earth and that the other planets revolved around the sun. However, in attacking Copernicus he gave the latter's ideas more publicity. More important, this Danish astronomer's major weapon against Copernican astronomy was a series of new naked-eye astronomical observations. Brahe constructed the most accurate tables of observations that had been drawn up for centuries.

When Brahe died, these tables came into the possession of Johannes Kepler (1571–1630), a German astronomer. Kepler was a convinced Copernican, but his reasons for taking that position were not scientific. Kepler was deeply influenced by Renaissance Neoplatonism and its honoring of the sun. These Neoplatonists were also determined to discover mathematical harmonies in those numbers that would support a sun-centered universe. After much work Kepler discovered that to keep the sun at the center of things, he must abandon the Copernican concept of circular orbits. The mathematical relationships that emerged from consideration of Brahe's observations

Galileo Galilei, the Florentine whose observational work helped mightily to confirm Copernicus's theories. The Ptolemaic view of the universe was thus destroyed and the foundations of modern astronomy were laid. The portrait is from 1624. [Reproduced by courtesy of the Trustees of the British Museum.]

suggested that the orbits of the planets were elliptical. Kepler published his findings in 1609 in a book entitled *On the Motion of Mars*. He had solved the problem of planetary orbits by using Copernicus's sun-centered universe and Brahe's empirical data.

Galileo Galilei

From Copernicus to Brahe to Kepler there had been little new information about the heavens that might not have been known to Ptolemy. However, in the same year that Kepler published his volume on Mars, an Italian scientist named Galileo Galilei (1564–1642) first turned a telescope on the heavens. Through that recently invented instrument he saw stars where none had been known to exist, mountains on the moon, spots moving across the sun, and moons orbiting Jupiter. The heavens were far more complex than anyone had formerly suspected. None of these discoveries proved that the earth orbited the sun, but they did suggest the complete inade-

Galileo, working at first from others' suggestions, effectively invented the telescope. This is his 1609 instrument. His observations of the physical features on earth's moon and of the cyclical phases of the planet Venus and his discovery of the most prominent moons of the planet Jupiter were the first major astronomical observations since antiquity and had revolutionary intellectual and theological implications. [Istituto e Museo de Storia della Scienza, Florence.]

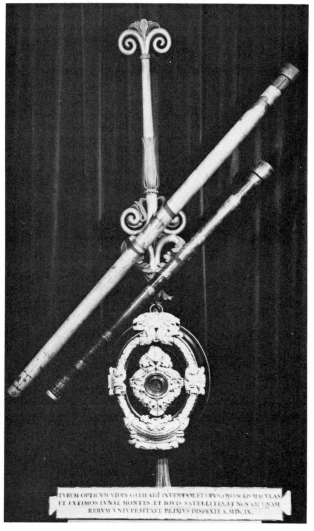

TVBVM OPTICVM VIDES GALILAEI INVENTVM ET OPVS, QVO SOLIS MACVLAS
ET EXTIMOS LVNAE MONTES, ET IOVIS SATELLITES, ET NOVAM QVASI
RERVM VNIVERSITATE PRIMVS DISPEXIT A. MDCIX.

Spectacles were an earlier optical aid. They were known at least as early as the fourteenth century, and by the sixteenth they appear fairly frequently in portraits. Here the sixteenth-century German painter Hermann Tom Ring imagines the classical Roman author Vergil reading with spectacles. [Bettmann Archive.]

quacy of the Ptolemaic system. It simply could not accommodate itself to all of these new phenomena. Some of Galileo's colleagues at the university of Padua were so unnerved that they refused to look through the telescope. Galileo publicized his findings and arguments for the Copernican system in numerous works, the most famous of which was his *Dialogues on the Two Chief Systems of the World* (1632). This book brought down upon him the condemnation of the Roman Catholic Church. He was compelled to recant his opinions. However, he is reputed to have muttered after the recantation, "E pur si muove" ("It [the earth] still moves").

Galileo's discoveries and his popularization of the Copernican system were of secondary importance in his life

The microscope was the telescope's companion as a major optical invention of the seventeenth century. Several people, including Galileo, had a hand in its development, but the greatest progress—and the most amazing results—came from the Hollander Anton van Leeuwenhoek (1632–1723) who, using only primitive simple instruments made by himself, was the first person actually to see protozoa and bacteria, and the Englishman Robert Hooke (1635–1703). Hooke's fairly elaborate microscope is shown here. [Courtesy Bausch and Lomb, Inc.]

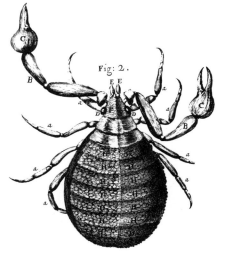

Robert Hooke carefully drew the startling results of his microscopic explorations. From his book *Micrographia* (1665) comes this rendering of the body louse; even such familiar small creatures had not been seen before in this detail.

work. His most important achievement was to articulate the concept of a universe totally subject to mathematical laws. More than any other writer of the century he argued that nature in its most minute details was mathematical. He once wrote:

> Philosophy is written in that great book which ever lies before our eyes—I mean the universe—but we cannot understand it if we do not first learn the language and grasp the symbols in which it is written. This book is written in the mathematical language, and the symbols are triangles, circles, and other geometrical figures, without whose help it is impossible to comprehend a single word of it; without which one wanders through a dark labyrinth.[4]

4 Quoted in E. A. Burtt, *The Metaphysical Foundations of Modern Physical Science* (Garden City, N.Y.: Anchor-Doubleday, 1954), p. 75.

The universe was rational; however, its rationality was not that of Scholastic logic but of mathematics. Copernicus had thought that the heavens conformed to mathematical regularity; Galileo saw this regularity throughout physical nature. He believed that the smallest atom behaved with the same mathematical precision as the largest heavenly sphere.

Galileo's thought meant that a world of quantity was replacing one of qualities. Mathematical quantities and relationships would henceforth increasingly be used to describe nature. Color, beauty, taste, and the like would be reduced to numerical relationships. And eventually social relationships would be envisioned in a mathematical model. Nature was cold, rational, mathematical, and mechanistic. What was real and lasting in the world was what was mathematically measurable. Few intellectual shifts have wrought such momentous changes for Western civilization.

René Descartes

No writer of the seventeenth century more fully adopted the geometric spirit of contemporary mathematics than René Descartes (1596–1650). He was a gifted mathematician who invented analytic geometry, and he was the author of major works on numerous scientific topics. However, his most important contribution was to scientific method. Unlike Bacon he wanted to proceed by deduction rather than by empirical observation and induction.

René Descartes, the reputed father of modern philosophy. He was famed for his declaration, "Cogito, ergo sum" ("I think, therefore I am"), which was for Descartes the point of departure for all human knowledge. [Bettmann Archive.]

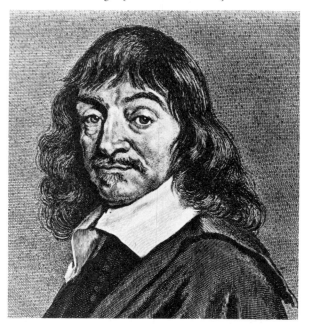

In 1637 Descartes published a *Discourse on Method* in which he attempted to provide a basis for all thinking based on a mathematical model. He published the work in French rather than in Latin because he wanted it to have wide circulation and application. He commenced by saying that he would doubt everything except those propositions about which he could have clear and distinct ideas. This approach rejected all forms of intellectual authority except the conviction of his own reason. He concluded that he could not doubt his own act of thinking and his own existence. From this base he proceeded to deduce the existence of God. The presence of God was important to Descartes because God was the guarantor of the correctness of clear and distinct ideas. Because God was not a deceiver, the ideas of God-given reason could not be false.

Descartes believed that this powerful human reason could fully comprehend the world. He divided existing things into mind and body. Thinking was the characteristic of the mind, extension of the body. Within the material world, mathematical laws reigned supreme. These could be grasped by the human reason. Because the laws were mathematical, they could be deduced from each other and constituted a complete system. The world of extension was the world of the scientist. The area of mind related to theology and philosophy. In the material world there was no room for spirits, divinity, or anything nonmaterial. Descartes had separated mind from body in order to banish the former from the realm of scientific speculation. He wanted to resurrect the speculative use of reason, but in a limited manner. It was to be applied only to the mechanical and mathematical realm of matter.

Descartes's emphasis on deduction and rational speculation exercised broad influence. Well into the eighteenth century European thinkers appealed to Descartes's method. However, it was eventually overcome by the force of Baconian induction. The chief reason for the demise of Descartes's influence was the association of the achievements of Sir Isaac Newton with the empirical method.

Sir Isaac Newton, the Englishman who discovered
the mathematical and physical laws governing
the force of gravity in the universe. The portrait
is by Sir Godfrey Kneller. [National Portrait
Gallery, London.]

Isaac Newton

Isaac Newton (1642–1727) drew upon the work of his
predecessors and his own brilliance to solve the major
remaining problem of planetary motion and to establish a
basis for physics that endured more than two centuries.
The question that continued to perplex seventeenth-century scientists who accepted the theories of Copernicus,
Kepler, and Galileo was how the planets and other heavenly bodies moved in an orderly fashion. The Ptolemaic
and Aristotelian answer had been the crystalline spheres
and a universe arranged in the order of the heaviness of
its parts. Numerous unsatisfactory theories had been set
forth to deal with the question.

In 1687 Newton published *The Mathematical Principles
of Natural Philosophy,* better known by its Latin title of
Principia Mathematica. Much of the research and thinking
for this great work had taken place more than fifteen
years earlier. Newton was heavily indebted to the work
of Galileo and particularly to the latter's view that inertia
could exist in either a state of motion or a state of rest.
Galileo's mathematical bias permeated Newton's thought.

Newton reasoned that the planets and all other physical
objects in the universe moved through mutual attraction.
Every object in the universe affected every other object
through gravity. The attraction of gravity explained why
the planets moved in an orderly rather than in a chaotic
manner. He had found that "the force of gravity towards
the whole planet did arise from and was compounded of
the forces of gravity towards all its parts, and towards
every one part was in the inverse proportion of the
squares of the distances from the part." [5] Newton demonstrated this relationship mathematically. He made no
attempt to explain the nature of gravity itself.

Newton was a great mathematical genius, but he also
upheld the importance of empirical data and observation.
He believed, in good Baconian fashion, that one must
observe phenomena before attempting to explain them.
The final test of any theory or hypothesis for him was
whether it described what could actually be observed. He
was a great opponent of Descartes's rationalism, which he
believed included insufficient guards against error. As
Newton's own theory of universal gravitation became
increasingly accepted, the Baconian bias also became
more fully popularized.

With the work of Newton the natural universe became a realm of law and regularity. Spirits and divinities
were no longer necessary to explain its operation. The
Scientific Revolution in that manner liberated human
beings from the fear of a chaotic or haphazard universe.
Most of the scientists were very devout people. They saw
the new picture of physical nature as suggesting a new
picture of God. The Creator of this rational, lawful
nature must also be rational. To study nature was to come
to a better understanding of that Creator. Science and
religious faith were not only compatible but mutually
supporting. As Newton wrote, "The main Business of
Natural Philosophy is to argue from Phaenomena without feigning Hypothesis, and to deduce Causes from

5 Quoted in A. Rupert Hall, *From Galileo to Newton, 1630–1720*
(London: Fontana, 1970), p. 300.

William Blake's Newton is, of course, not a portrait of an individual. Instead, it dramatizes and glorifies the detached, almost God-like scientist who can solve the mysteries of the universe and display the results with mathematical precision. [The Tate Gallery, London.]

Effects, till we come to the very first Cause, which certainly is not mechanical."[6]

This reconciliation of faith and science allowed the new physics and astronomy to spread rapidly. At the very time when Europeans were finally tiring of the wars of religion, the new science provided the basis for a view of God that might lead away from irrational disputes and wars over religious doctrine. Faith in a rational God encouraged faith in the rationality of human beings and in their capacity to improve their lot once liberated from the traditions of the past. The Scientific Revolution provided the great model for the desirability of change and of criticism of inherited views. Yet at the same time the new science caused some people to feel that the mystery had been driven from the universe and that the rational Creator was less loving and near to humankind than the God of earlier ages.

Writers and Philosophers

The end of the sixteenth century saw weariness with religious strife and incipient unbelief as many could no longer embrace either old Catholic or new Protestant absolutes. Intellectually as well as politically the seventeenth century was a period of transition. It was a transition already well prepared by the thinkers of the Renaissance, who had reacted strongly against medieval intellectual traditions, especially those informed by Aristotle and Scholasticism.

Even as they sought a purer culture behind the Middle

Ages in pagan and Christian antiquity, however, Humanists and Protestants continued to share much of the medieval vision of a unified Christendom. Few were prepared to embrace the secular values and preoccupations of the growing scientific movement, which found its models in mathematics and the natural sciences, not in the example and authority of antiquity. Some strongly condemned the work of Copernicus, Kepler, and Galileo, whose theories seemed to fly in the face of common-sense experience as well as to question hallowed tradition.

The thinkers of the Renaissance and the Reformation nonetheless prepared the way for the new science and philosophy both by their attacks on tradition and by their own failure to implement radical reforms. Humanist revival of interest in ancient skepticism proved an effective foundation for attacks on traditional views of authority and rationality in both religion and science. Already such thinkers as the Italian Pico della Mirandola (1463–1494), the German Agrippa of Nettisheim (1486–1535), and the Frenchman François Rabelais (1494–1553) had questioned the ability of reason to obtain certitude. Sebastian Castellio (1515–1563), Michel de Montaigne (1533–1592), and Pierre Charron (1541–1603) had been as much repulsed by the new Calvinist religion as John Calvin had been by medieval religion. It was in the wake of such criticism that Francis Bacon and René Descartes developed a more modest, yet surer, definition of rationality as the tool of the new scientific philosophy.

The writers and philosophers of the seventeenth century were aware that they lived in a period of transition. Some embraced the new science wholeheartedly (Hobbes and Locke), some tried to straddle the two ages (Cervantes, Shakespeare, and Milton), and still others ignored or opposed the new developments that seemed mortally to threaten traditional values (Pascal and Bunyan).

Miguel de Cervantes Saavedra (1547–1616)

Spanish literature of the sixteenth and seventeenth centuries was influenced by the peculiar religious and

6 Quoted in Baumer, p. 323.

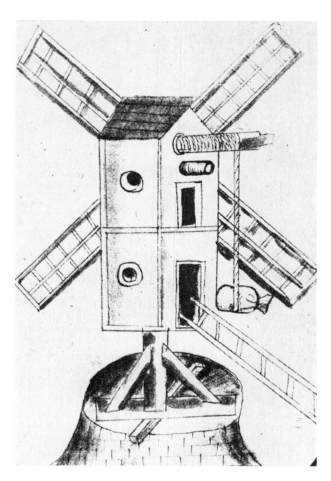

Don Quixote's windmill was not a new invention. Instead, it was an important item of rural technology from at least as early as the twelfth century. The one shown here is equipped with an automatic winch to raise bags of grain for grinding. The mill itself is on a post that can be turned with the direction of the wind. This illustration is probably from the fifteenth century. [Bettmann Archive.]

political history of Spain in this period. Spain was dominated by the Catholic Church. Since the joint reign of Ferdinand and Isabella (1479–1504) the church had received the unqualified support of reigning political power. Although there was religious reform in Spain, there was never a Protestant Reformation, thanks largely to the abiding power of the church and the Inquisition.

The second influence was the aggressive piety of the Spanish rulers Charles I (who was also the Holy Roman Emperor Charles V) (1516–1556) and Philip II (1556–1598). The intertwining of Catholic piety and Spanish political power underlay the third major influence on Spanish literature: preoccupation with medieval chivalric virtues—in particular, questions of honor and loyalty. The novels and plays of the period almost invariably focus on a special decision involving a character's reputation as his honor or loyalty is tested. In this regard Spanish literature may be said to have remained more Catholic and medieval than that of England and France, both of which saw major Protestant movements. Two of the most important Spanish writers in this period became priests (Lope de Vega and Pedro Calderón de la Barca), and the one

generally acknowledged to be the greatest Spanish writer of all time, Cervantes, was preoccupied in his work with the strengths and weaknesses of religious idealism.

Cervantes was born in Alcalá, the son of a nomadic physician. Having received only a smattering of formal education, he educated himself by insatiable reading in vernacular literature and immersion in the "school of life." As a young man he worked in Rome for a Spanish cardinal. In 1570 he became a soldier and was even decorated for gallantry in the Battle of Lepanto (1571), an engagement that also left one of his hands paralyzed for life. When he was returning to Spain in 1575, his ship was captured by pirates and Cervantes was forced to spend five years as a slave in Algiers. Upon his release and return to Spain he held many odd jobs, among them that of a tax collector. He was several times imprisoned for padding his accounts. *Don Quixote*, his most famous work, was conceived and begun in 1603, while he languished in prison.

The first part of *Don Quixote* appeared in 1605 and a second part followed in 1615. If, as many argue, the intent of this work was to satirize the chivalric romances so popular in Spain, Cervantes was nonetheless also unable to conceal his deep affection for the character he created as an object of ridicule, Don Quixote. The work is satire only on the surface and has remained as much an object of study by philosophers and theologians as by students of Spanish literature. Don Quixote, a none too stable middle-aged man, is presented by Cervantes as one driven mad by reading too many chivalric romances. He comes finally to believe that he is an aspirant to knighthood and must prove by brave deeds his worthiness of initiation into knightly rank. To this end he acquires a rusty suit of armor, mounts an aged steed (named Rozinante), and chooses for his inspiration a quite unworthy peasant girl, Dulcinea, whom he fancies to be a noble lady to whom he can, with honor, dedicate his life.

Don Quixote's foil in the story—Sancho Panza, a clever, worldly-wise peasant, who serves as Don Quixote's squire—is an equally fascinating character. Sancho

Panza watches with bemused skepticism, but also with genuine sympathy, as his lord does battle with a windmill (which he mistakes for a dragon) and repeatedly makes a fool of himself as he gallops across the countryside. The story ends tragically with Don Quixote's humiliating defeat by a well-meaning friend, who, disguised as a knight, bests Don Quixote in combat and forces him to renounce his quest for knighthood. The humiliated Don Quixote does not, however, come thereafter to his senses. He returns sadly to his village to die a shamed and broken-hearted old man.

Throughout *Don Quixote* Cervantes juxtaposed the down-to-earth realism of Sancho Panza with the old-fashioned religious idealism of Don Quixote. The reader perceives that Cervantes really admired the one as much as the other and meant to portray both as representing attitudes necessary for a happy life. Like his English counterpart William Shakespeare, Cervantes understood the complexity of human nature. He wanted his readers to remember that if they are to be truly happy, men and women need dreams, even impossible ones, just as much as they need a sense of reality.

The other major Spanish writers of the period had a far less universal vision than Cervantes. Lope Felix de Vega Carpio (1562–1635), the author of an incredible number of epics, romances, novels, lyrics, and plays, pandered to popular Spanish tastes and remained content to meet the contemporary demand for entertainment rather than venturing profound and lasting works. He never wanted for variety in his work, however, and almost singlehandedly created the Spanish national theater. Pedro Calderón de la Barca (1600–1681) wrote court dramas, comedies and highly sentimental "point of honor" plays that spoke to current national interests and became favorites among later Romantic writers.

William Shakespeare (1564–1616)

Shakespeare, to many the greatest playwright in the English language, was born in Stratford-on-Avon, where he lived almost all of his life. There is much less factual

The English dramatist and poet, William Shakespeare. This engraving by Martin Droeshout appears on the title page of the collected edition of his plays published in 1623 and is probably as close as we shall come to knowing what he looked like.

knowledge about him than one would expect of such an important figure. Shakespeare was married in 1582, at the early age of eighteen, and he and his wife, Anne Hathaway, had three children (two were twins) by 1585. He was apparently employed as a schoolteacher for a time and in this capacity acquired his broad knowledge of Renaissance learning and literature. The argument of

Planities siue arena.

Ex obseruationibus Londinensibus Johannis De witt

This 1596 sketch of the interior of the Swan Theater in London by Johannis de Witt, a Dutch visitor, is the only known contemporary view of an Elizabethan playhouse. In this kind of setting the plays of Marlowe, Shakespeare, Jonson, and their fellows were first seen. [The Granger Collection.]

some scholars that he was an untutored natural genius is highly questionable. His own learning and his enthusiasm for the education of his day are manifest in the many learned allusions that appear in such plays as *A Midsummer-Night's Dream* (1594–1595).

Shakespeare was a man of the country as well as of the town and manifestly enjoyed the life of a country gentleman. There is none of the Puritan distress over worldliness in his work. He took the new commercialism and the bawdy pleasures of the Elizabethan Age in stride and with amusement. The few allusions to the Puritans that exist in his works appear to be more critical than complementary. In matters of religion, as in those of politics, he was very much a man of his time and not inclined to offend his queen.

That Shakespeare was interested in politics is apparent from his history plays and the references, to contempo-

rary political events that fill all his plays. He seems to have viewed government simply, however, through the character of the individual ruler, whether Richard III or Elizabeth Tudor, not in terms of ideal systems. By modern standards he was a political conservative, accepting the social rankings and the power structure of his day and demonstrating unquestioned patriotism.

Shakespeare knew the theatre as one who participated in every phase of its life—as a playwright, an actor, and a part owner of a theater. He was a member and principal dramatist of a famous company of actors known as the King's Men. During the tenure of Edmund Tilney, who was the Master of Revels during the greater part of Shakespeare's active period (1590–1610), many of Shakespeare's plays were performed at court before the queen, who was a most enthusiastic patron of plays and pageants.

Elizabethan drama was already a distinctive form when Shakespeare began writing. Unlike French drama of the seventeenth century, which was dominated by the court and classical models, English drama developed in the sixteenth and seventeenth centuries as a blending of many extant forms, ranging from classical comedies and tragedies to contemporary Italian short stories. In Shakespeare's own library were to be found Holinshed's and other English chronicles; the works of Plutarch, Ovid, and Vergil, among other Latin authors; Arthurian romances and popular songs and fables; the writings of Montaigne and Rabelais; and the major English poets and prose writers.

Shakespeare's tragedies were especially influenced by the work of two of his contemporaries: Thomas Kyd and Christopher Marlowe. Kyd (1558–1594) was the author of the first dramatic version of *Hamlet* and a master at weaving together motive, plot, and tragic intensity. The tragedies of Marlowe (1564–1593) set a model for character, poetry, and style that only Shakespeare among the English playwrights of the period surpassed. Shakespeare's work is an original synthesis of the best past and current achievements.

Shakespeare mastered the psychology of human motivation and passion. He had a unique talent for psychological penetration, one rivalled only by the French Jansenist dramatist Jean Racine (1639–1699), who, however, remained confined to classical forms and rules. Later romantic writers claimed Shakespeare as one of their own and contrasted his work sharply with the neo-classicism of Pierre Corneille and Racine, who they found by comparison to be narrow and mechanical.

Shakespeare wrote histories, comedies, and tragedies. *Richard III* (1593), a very early play, stands out among the examples of the first genre, although historians have criticized as historically inaccurate his patriotic depiction of Richard, the foe of Henry Tudor, as an unprincipled villain. Shakespeare's comedies, while not attaining the heights of his tragedies, surpass in originality his history plays. Save for the *Tempest* (1611), his last play and his farewell to the stage, the comedies most familiar to modern readers were written between 1598–1602: *Much Ado About Nothing* (1598/99), *As You Like It* (1598–1600), and *Twelfth Night* (1602).

The tragedies are considered his unique achievement. Four of these were written within a three year period: *Hamlet* (1603), *Othello* (1604), *King Lear* (1605), and *Macbeth* (1606). The most original and independent of the tragedies, *Romeo and Juliet* (1597), transformed an old popular story into a moving drama of "star-cross'd lovers." Both Romeo and Juliet, denied a marriage by their factious families, die tragic deaths. Romeo, finding Juliet and thinking her dead after she had taken a sleeping potion, poisons himself. Juliet, awakening to find her Romeo dead, stabs herself to death with his dagger.

Throughout his lifetime and ever since Shakespeare has been immensely popular with both the play-goer and the play-reader. As Ben Jonson, a contemporary classical dramatist who created his own school of poets, aptly put it in a tribute affixed to the First Folio edition of Shakespeare's plays (1623): "He was not of an age, but for all time."

Ioannis Miltoni Effigies Ætat: 62.
1670.

Gul. Faithorne ad Vivum.   *Delin. et sculpsit.*

The English writer and poet John Milton in an engraving by William Faithorne—one of the few authentic contemporary likenesses of him. [The Granger Collection.]

John Milton (1608–1674)

John Milton was the son of a devout Puritan father. Educated at St. Paul's School and Christ's College, Cambridge, he became a careful student of Christian and pagan classics. In 1638, he traveled to Italy, where he found the lingering Renaissance to be a very congenial intellectual atmosphere. The Phlegraean Fields near Naples, a volcanic region, later became the model for hell in *Paradise Lost,* and the Villa d'Este is suspected by some scholars to have provided the model for paradise in *Paradise Regained.* Milton remained throughout his life a man more at home in the Italian Renaissance, with its high ideals and universal vision, than in the strife-torn England of the seventeenth century.

Milton was a man of deep inner conviction and principle; standing a test of character was uppermost in his own personal life and in the subjects of his literary work. An early poem, *Lycidas*, was a pastoral elegy dealing with one who lived well but not long. Edward King, a close college friend who tragically drowned. In 1639 Milton joined the Puritan struggle against Charles I and Archbishop Laud. Employing his literary talents as a pamphleteer, he defended the presbyterian form of church government against the episcopacy and supported other Puritan reforms. After a month-long unsuccessful marriage in 1642 (a marriage later reconciled), he wrote several tracts in defense of the right to divorce. These writings became a factor in Parliament's passage of a censorship law in 1643, against which Milton wrote an eloquent defense of the freedom of the press, *Areopagitica* (1664).

Until the upheavals of the civil war moderated his views, Milton believed that government should have the least possible control over the private lives of individuals. When Parliament divided into Presbyterians and Independents, he took the side of the latter, who wanted to dissolve the national church altogether in favor of the local autonomy of individual congregations. He further defended the execution of Charles I in a tract on the *Tenure of Kings and Magistrates* and later served as secretary to the executive committee of Parliament during Cromwell's protectorate. It was after his intense labor on this tract that his eyesight failed. Milton wrote his acclaimed masterpieces as one totally blind.

Paradise Lost, Milton's masterpiece of English blank verse, was completed in 1665 and published in 1667. A study of the destructive qualities of pride and the redeeming possibilities of humility, it elaborates in traditional Christian language and concept the revolt of Satan in heaven and the fall of Adam on earth. Milton was throughout preoccupied with the motives of Satan and all who rebel against God. His proud but tragic Satan, one of the great figures of all literature, represents the absolute corruption of potential greatness.

In *Paradise Lost* Milton aspired to give England a lasting classic like that given Greece in Homer's *Iliad* and ancient Rome in Vergil's *Aeneid*. In choosing biblical subject matter, he revealed the influence of contemporary theology on his work. Milton tended to agree with the Arminians, who, unlike the extreme Calvinists, did not believe that all worldly events, including the Fall of Man, were immutably fixed in the eternal decree of God. Milton shared the Arminian belief that man must take responsibility for his fate and that human efforts to improve character could, with God's grace, bring man to salvation.

Perhaps his own blindness, joined with the hope of making the best out of a failed religious revolution, inclined Milton to sympathize with those who urged men to make the most of what they had, even in the face of seemingly sure defeat. That is a manifest concern of his last works, *Samson Agonistes*, which recounts the biblical story of Samson, and *Paradise Regained*, the story of Christ's temptation in the wilderness, both published in 1671.

John Bunyan (1628–1688)

Bunyan was the author of two classics of sectarian Puritan spirituality: *Grace Abounding* (1666) and *The Pilgrim's Progress* (1678). A Bedford tinker, his works speak especially for the seventeenth-century working man and popular religious culture. Bunyan received only the most basic education before taking up his father's craft. He was drafted into Oliver Cromwell's revolutionary army in 1644 and served for two years, although without seeing actual combat. The visionary fervor of the New Model Army and the imagery of warring abound in Bunyan's work.

After the restoration of the monarchy in 1660 Bunyan was arrested for his fiery preaching and remained in prison for twelve years. Had he been willing to agree to give up preaching, he might have been released much sooner. But Puritans considered the compromise of one's beliefs a tragic flaw and Bunyan steadfastly refused all such suggestions.

It was during this period of imprisonment that Bunyan wrote his famous autobiography, *Grace Abounding*, for his separated friends. It is both a very personal statement and a model for the faithful. Like *The Pilgrim's Progress,* Bunyan's later masterpiece, *Grace Abounding* expresses Puritan piety at its most fervent. Puritans believed that the individual could do absolutely nothing to save himself and this made them extremely restless and introspective. The individual believer could only trust that God had placed him among the elect and try each day to live a life that reflected such a favored status. So long as he struggled successfully against the flesh and the world, he had presumptive evidence that he was among God's elect. To falter or to become complacent in the face of temptation, was to cast doubt upon ones' faith and salvation and even raise the specter of eternal damnation.

This anxious questing for salvation came to classic expression in *The Pilgrim's Progress,* a work unique in its contribution to Western religious symbolism and imagery. The story of the journey of Christian and his friends Hopeful and Faithful to the Celestial City, it teaches that one must deny wife, children, and all earthly security and go in search of "Life, life, eternal life." During the long journey, the travelers must resist the temptations of Worldly-Wiseman and Vanity Fair, pass through the Slough of Despond, and endure a long dark night in Doubting Castle, their faith being tested at every turn. Bunyan later wrote a work tracing the progress of Christian's opposite, entitled *The Life and Death of Mr. Badman* (1680), the story of a man so addicted to the bad habits of Restoration society, of which Bunyan strongly disapproved, that he journeyed steadfastly not to heaven but to hell.

The loss of national unity during the Puritan struggle against the Stuart monarchy and the Anglican Church took its toll on English literature and drama during the seventeenth century. In 1642 the Puritans had closed the theaters of London. They were reopened after the Restoration of Charles II in 1660, and drama revived following the long Puritan interregnum.

Literary thought thereafter became less experimental and adopted proven classical forms as a new movement to subject reality to the strict rules of reason began. During the so-called Augustan Age, from John Dryden (1631–1700) to Alexander Pope (1688–1744), classicism was the literary rule. There was a preoccupation with the world of mundane facts, rather than with that of universal ideals, and a waning of the transcendental concerns of the Elizabethans and the Puritan divines. As in France, where the French comedy writer Molière (1622–1673) is the outstanding example, English writers tried to please the royal court and aristocracy by turning to more earthy and entertaining popular topics.

Blaise Pascal (1623–1662)

Pascal was a mathematician and a physical scientist widely acclaimed by his contemporaries. He was also a most devout man, who surrendered all his wealth so that he might more easily pursue an austere, self-disciplined life. Torn between the continuing dogmatism and the new skepticism of the seventeenth century, he aspired to write a work that would refute both the Jesuits, whose casuistry (i.e., confessional tactics designed to minimize and even excuse sinful acts) he considered a distortion of Christian teaching, and the skeptics of his age, who either denied religion altogether (atheists) or accepted it only as it conformed to reason (Deists). Such a definitive work was never realized, and his views on these matters exist only in piecemeal form. He wrote against the Jesuits in his *Provincial Letters* (1656–1657), and he left behind a provocative collection of reflections on man and religion that were published posthumously under the title *Pensées.*

Pascal was early influenced by the Jansenists, seventeenth-century Catholic opponents of the Jesuits. His sister was a member of the Jansenist community of Port Royal near Paris, and after 1654 Pascal himself was closely identified with this community. The Jansenists shared with the Calvinists St. Augustine's belief in man's total sinfulness, his eternal predestination by God, and his

The arithmetical machine invented in 1642 by Blaise Pascal, the French philosopher and mathematician. Its main feature was the automatic carry-forward. The wheels, each divided into nine sections, were connected in such a way that the complete rotation of one of them caused the wheel on the left of it to move forward by one digit. The foundations of adding machines and other mechanical calculators were thus laid by this device. [Culver Pictures.]

complete dependence on faith and grace for knowledge of God and salvation.

Pascal believed that reason and science, although attesting man's dignity, remained of no avail in matters of religion. Here only the reasons of the heart and a "leap of faith" could prevail. Pascal saw two essential truths in the Christian religion: that a loving God, worthy of man's attainment, exists, and that man, because he is corrupted in his nature, is utterly unworthy of God. Pascal believed that the atheists and the Deists of the age had spurned the lesson of reason. For him rational analysis of the human condition attested man's utter mortality and corruption and exposed the weakness of reason itself in resolving the problems of human nature and destiny. Reason should rather drive those who truly heed it to faith and dependence on divine grace.

Pascal made a famous wager with the skeptics. It is a better bet, he argued, to believe that God exists and to stake everything on his promised mercy than not to do so, because if God does exist everything will be gained by the believer, whereas the loss incurred by having believed in him should he prove not to exist is by comparison very slight.

Pascal was convinced that belief in God measurably improved man's present life psychologically and disciplined it morally, regardless of whether or not God proved in the end to exist; great danger lay in the surrender of traditional religious belief. Pascal urged his contemporaries to seek self-understanding by "learned ignorance" and to discover man's greatness by recognizing his

Even before Pascal's day, of course, there was a tradition of elaborate mechanical devices throughout Europe. For example, by 1500 there were public clocks in practically every town. One of the most famous is the astronomical clock of Strasbourg's cathedral in France, which presents a parade of allegorical figures every day at noon. [French Government Tourist Office, New York.]

OPPOSITE: The Glockenspiel, or clock performance, occurring hourly at the Munich city hall, is another ingenious time-keeping device. [German Information Center, New York.]

misery. Thereby Pascal hoped to counter what he believed to be the false optimism of the new rationalism and science.

Baruch Spinoza (1632–1677)

The most controversial thinker of the seventeenth century was Baruch Spinoza, the son of a Jewish merchant of Amsterdam. Spinoza's philosophy caused his excommunication by his own synagogue in 1656. In 1670 he published his *Treatise on Religious and Political Philosophy*, a work that criticized the dogmatism of Dutch Calvinists and championed freedom of thought. During his lifetime both Jews and Protestants attacked him as an atheist.

Spinoza's most influential writing, the *Ethics*, was published after his death in 1677. Religious leaders universally condemned it for its apparent espousal of pantheism. God and nature were so closely identified by Spinoza that little room seemed left either for divine revelation in Scripture or for the personal immortality of the soul, denials equally repugnant to Jews and Christians. The *Ethics* was a very complicated work, written in the spirit of the new science as a geometrical system of definitions, axioms, and propositions. It was divided into five parts, which dealt with God, the mind, emotions, human bondage, and human freedom.

The most controversial part of the *Ethics* dealt with the nature of substance and of God. According to Spinoza, there is but one substance, which is self-caused, free, and infinite, and God is that substance. From this definition it follows that everything that exists is in God and cannot even be conceived apart from him. Such a doctrine is not literally pantheistic because God is still seen to be more than the created world that he, as primal substance, embraces. It may perhaps best be described as *panentheism*: the teaching that all that is is within God, yet God remains more than and beyond the natural world. Nonetheless, in Spinoza's view, statements about the natural world are also statements about divine nature. Mind and matter are seen to be extensions of the infinite substance of God; what transpires in the world of man and nature is a necessary outpouring of the divine.

Such teaching clearly ran the danger of portraying the world as eternal and human actions as unfree and inevitable, the expression of a divine fatalism. Such points of view have been considered heresies by Jews and Christians because they deny the creation of the world by God in time and destroy any voluntary basis for personal reward and punishment.

Spinoza found enthusiastic supporters in the German philosopher Georg Wilhelm Friedrich Hegel and in romantic writers of the nineteenth century, especially Johann Wolfgang von Goethe and Percy Bysshe Shelley. Modern thinkers unable to accept traditional religious language and doctrines have continued to find in Spinoza a congenial rational religion.

Thomas Hobbes (1588–1679)

Thomas Hobbes is incontestably the most original political philosopher of the seventeenth century. The son of a clergyman, he was educated at Magdalen College, Oxford, during a period when Puritanism was dominant there. Although he never broke with the Church of England, he came to share basic Calvinist beliefs, especially the low view of human nature and the ideal of a commonwealth based on a covenant, both of which find eloquent expression in Hobbes's political philosophy.

Hobbes was an urbane and much-traveled man and one of the most enthusiastic supporters of the new scientific movement. He worked as tutor and secretary to three earls of Devonshire over a fifty-year period. During the 1630s he visited Paris, where he came to know Descartes, and after the outbreak of the Puritan Revolution in 1640, he lived as an exile in Paris until 1651. In 1646 Hobbes became the tutor of the Prince of Wales, the future Charles II, and remained on good terms with him after the restoration of the Stuart monarchy. Hobbes also spent time with Galileo in Italy and took a special interest in the works of William Harvey (1578–1657). Harvey was a physiologist famed for the discovery of how blood circulated through the body; his scientific writings influenced Hobbes own tracts on bodily motions. Hobbes became an expert in geometry and optics. Also highly trained in classical languages, his first published work was a translation of Thucydides' *History of the Peloponnesian War,* the first English translation of this work and one that is still reprinted today.

Hobbes was driven to the vocation of political philosopher by the English civil war. In 1651 his *Leviathan* appeared. Written as the concluding part of a broad philosophical system that analyzed physical bodies and human nature, the work established Hobbes as a major European thinker. Its subject was the political consequences of human passions and its originality lay in (1) its making natural law, rather than common law (i.e., custom or precedent), the basis of all positive law and (2) its

defense of a representative theory of absolute authority against the theory of the divine right of kings. Hobbes maintained that statute law found its justification only as an expression of the law of nature and that political authority came to rulers by way of the consent of the people.

Hobbes viewed man and society in a thoroughly materialistic and mechanical way. Man is defined as a collection of material particles in motion. All his psychological processes begin with and are derived from bare sensation, and all his motivations are egoistical, intended to increase his pleasure and minimize his pain. His power of reasoning, which Hobbes defined unspectacularly as a process of adding and substracting the consequences of agreed-upon general names of things, develops only after years of concentrated industry.

Despite this seemingly low estimate of man, Hobbes believed much could be accomplished by the reasoned use of science. All was contingent, however, on the correct use of that greatest of all human powers, one compounded of the powers of most men: the commonwealth, in which men are united by their consent in one all-powerful person.

The key to Hobbes's political philosophy is a brilliant myth of the original state of mankind. According to this myth, man in his natural state is absolutely insatiable; mankind is generally inclined to a "perpetual and restless desire of power after power that ceases only in death."[7] As all men desire and in the state of nature have a natural right to everything, their equality breeds enmity; competition, diffidence, and the desire for glory beget perpetual quarreling—"a war of every man against every man."[8] As Hobbes put it in a famous summary:

In such condition there is no place for industry, because the fruit thereof is uncertain; and consequently

7 *Leviathan Parts I and II,* ed. by H. W. Schneider (Indianapolis: Bobbs-Merrill, 1958), p. 86.
8 Ibid., p. 106.

The English philosopher Thomas Hobbes, author of *Leviathan*. Hobbes believed that once established in office rulers held an absolute power over their subjects, the alternative being the chaos of a brutish state of nature. The portrait is from a painting in The Royal Society, London. [Bettmann Archive.]

The famous title-page illustration for Hobbes's *Leviathan*. The ruler is pictured as absolute lord of his lands, but note that the ruler incorporates the mass of individuals whose self-interests are best served by their willing consent to accept him and cooperate with him.

no culture of the earth; no navigation nor use of the commodities that may be imported by sea; no commodious building; no instruments of moving and removing such things as require much force; no knowledge of the face of the earth; no account of time; no arts; no letters; no society; and, which is worst of all, continual fear and danger of violent death; and the life of man solitary, poor, nasty, brutish, and short.[9]

Whereas earlier and later philosophers saw man's original state as a paradise from which he had fallen, Hobbes saw it as a corruption from which only society had delivered him. Contrary to the views of Aristotle and Christian thinkers like Thomas Aquinas, man in the view of Hobbes is not by nature a sociable, political animal; he is a self-centered beast, a law unto himself, utterly without a master unless one is imposed on him by force.

According to Hobbes, men escape the impossible state of nature only by entering a social contract that creates a commonwealth tightly ruled by law and order. They are driven to this solution by their fear of death and their desire for "commodious living." The social contract obliges every man, for the sake of peace and self-defense, to agree to set aside his right to all things and be content with as much liberty against others as he would allow others against himself. All agree to live according to a secularized version of the golden rule: "Do not that to another which you would not have done to yourself."[10]

Because words and promises are insufficient to guarantee this state, the social contract also establishes the coercive force necessary to compel compliance with the covenant. Hobbes believed that the dangers of anarchy were far greater than those of tyranny and conceived of the ruler as absolute and unlimited in his power, once established in office. There is no room in Hobbes's political philosophy for political protest in the name of individual conscience, nor for resistance to legitimate authority by private individuals—features of the *Leviathan* criticized by contemporary Catholics and Puritans alike. To his critics, who lamented the loss of their individual liberty in such a government, Hobbes pointed out the alternative:

The greatest that in any form of government can possibly happen to the people in general is scarce sensible in respect of the miseries and horrible calamities that accompany a civil war or that dissolute condition of masterless men, without subjection to laws and a coercive power to tie their hands from rapine and revenge.[11]

It is puzzling why Hobbes believed that absolute rulers would be more benevolent and less egoistic than all other men. He simply placed the highest possible value on a strong, efficient ruler who could save men from the chaos attendant upon the state of nature. In the end it mattered little to Hobbes whether this ruler was Charles I, Oliver Cromwell, or Charles II, each of whom received Hobbes's enthusiastic support, once he was established in power.

John Locke (1632–1704)

Locke has proved to be the most influential political thinker of the seventeenth century. His political philosophy came to be embodied in the Glorious Revolution of 1688–1689. Although he was not as original as Hobbes, his political writings were a major source for the later Enlightenment criticism of absolutism, and they gave inspiration to both the American and the French revolutions. A direct line has been drawn between the political philosophy of Locke, whose works circulated in the American colonies in the eighteenth century, and that of Thomas Jefferson.

Locke was reared in a family whose sympathies lay with the Puritans and the Parliamentary forces that challenged the Stuart monarchy. His father fought with the

9 Ibid., p. 107.
10 Ibid., p. 130.

11 Ibid., p. 152.

The English philosopher John Locke, who influenced modern representative government by insisting that the people had inalienable rights of life, liberty, and property, which rulers overrode only at their peril. The portrait is from a painting at Christ Church, Oxford. [Bettmann Archive.]

Parliamentary army during the English civil war. Locke read deeply in the works of Francis Bacon, René Descartes, and Isaac Newton and was a close friend of the English physicist and chemist Robert Boyle (1627–1691). Some argue that Locke was the first philosopher to be successful in synthesizing the rationalism of Descartes and the experimental science of Bacon, Newton, and Boyle.

Locke was for a brief period strongly influenced by the conservative political views of Hobbes. This influence changed, however, after his association with Anthony Ashley Cooper, the earl of Shaftesbury. In 1667 Locke moved into Shaftesbury's London home, where he served as physician, secretary, and traveling companion. A zealous Protestant, Shaftesbury was considered by his contemporaries to be a radical in both religion (he is known as the father of Deism) and politics. He organized an unsuccessful rebellion against Charles II in 1682 in the hope of excluding Charles's Catholic brother, James, from the English throne and putting the king's bastard son, the earl of Monmouth, in James's place. Although Locke had no part in the plot, both he and Shaftesbury were forced to flee to Holland after its failure.

Locke's two most famous works were the *Essay on Human Understanding*, completed during his exile in Holland, and the *Two Treatises on Civil Government*. In the *Essay on Human Understanding* Locke stressed the creative function of the human mind. He believed that the mind at birth was a blank tablet. In Locke's view, contrary to that of much medieval philosophy, there are no innate ideas; all knowledge is derived from actual sensual experience. Human ideas are either simple (that is, passive receptions from daily experience) or complex (that is, products of sustained mental exercise). What people know is not the external world in itself but the results of the interaction of the mind with the outside world. Locke also denied the existence of innate moral norms. Moral ideals are the product of man's subjection of his self-love to his reason—a freely chosen self-disciplining of natural desires so that conflict in conscience may be avoided and

happiness attained. Locke also believed that the teachings of Christianity were identical with what uncorrupted reason taught about the good life. A rational man would therefore always live according to simple Christian precepts. Although Locke firmly denied toleration to Catholics and atheists—both were considered subversive in England—he otherwise sanctioned a variety of Protestant religious practice.

The *Two Treatises on Civil Government* was written during the reign of Charles II and was directed against the argument that rulers were absolute in their power. According to the preface of the published edition, which appeared after the Glorious Revolution, the treatises were written "to justify to the world the people of England, whose love of their just and natural rights, with their resolution to preserve them, saved the nation when it was on the brink of slavery and ruin."[12] Locke opposed particularly the views of Sir Robert Filmer and Thomas Hobbes.

Filmer had written a work entitled *Patriarcha, or the Natural Power of Kings* (published in 1680), in which the rights of kings over their subjects were compared to the rights of fathers over their children. Locke devoted the entire first treatise to a refutation of Filmer's argument,

12 *The Second Treatise of Government*, ed. T. P. Peardon (Indianapolis: Bobbs Merrill, 1952), preface.

maintaining that the analogy was not only inappropriate, but that even the right of a father over his children could not be construed as absolute but was subject to a higher natural law. Both fathers and rulers, Locke argued, remain bound to the law of nature, which is the voice of reason, teaching that "all mankind [are] equal and independent, [and] no one ought to harm another in his life, health, liberty, or possessions,"[13] inasmuch as all men are the images and property of God. According to Locke, men enter into social contracts, empowering legislatures and kings to "umpire" their disputes, precisely in order to preserve their natural rights, and not to give rulers an absolute power over them. Rulers are rather "entrusted" with the preservation of the law of nature and transgress it at their peril.

> Whenever that end [namely, the preservation of life, liberty, and property for which power is given to rulers by a commonwealth] is manifestly neglected or opposed, the trust must necessarily be forfeited and the power devolve into the hands of those that gave it, who may place it anew where they think best for their safety and security.[14]

From Locke's point of view absolute monarchy was "inconsistent" with civil society and could be "no form of civil government at all."

Locke's main differences with Hobbes stemmed from the latter's well-known views on the state of nature. Locke believed that man's natural state was one of perfect freedom and equality. Here the natural rights of life, liberty, and property were enjoyed, in unregulated fashion, by all. The only thing lacking in the state of nature was a single authority to judge among men when disputes inevitably arose because of the natural freedom and equality possessed by all. Contrary to Hobbes, men in their natural state were not creatures of monomaniacal passion but were possessed of extreme goodwill and rationality. They did not surrender their natural rights unconditionally when they entered the social contract; they rather established a means whereby these rights could be better preserved. The state of warfare that Hobbes believed characterized the state of nature emerged for Locke only when rulers failed in their responsibility to preserve the freedoms of the state of nature and attempted to enslave men by absolute rule, that is, to remove them from their "natural" condition. Only then was the peace, good-will, mutual assistance, and preservation in which men naturally live and socially ought to live undermined and a state of war created.

SUGGESTED READINGS

V. M. BRITTAIN, *Valiant Pilgrim: The Story of John Bunyan and Puritan England* (1950). Illustrated historical biography.

HERBERT BUTTERFIELD, *The Origins of Modern Science 1300–1800*, (1949). An authoritative survey.

JOHN CAIRD, *Spinoza* (1971). Intellectual biography by a philosopher.

NORMAN F. CANTOR (Ed.), *Seventeenth Century Rationalism: Bacon and Descartes* (1969).

CERVANTES, *The Portable Cervantes*, ed. and trans. by Samuel Putman (1969).

HARDIN CRAIG, *Shakespeare: A Historical and Critical Study With Annotated Texts of Twenty-one Plays* (1958).

MAURICE CRANSTON, *Locke* (1961). Brief biographical sketch.

MANUEL DURÁN, *Cervantes* (1974). Detailed biography.

GALILEO GALILEI, *Discoveries and Opinions of Galileo*, ed. and trans. by Stillman Drake (1957).

A. R. HALL, *The Scientific Revolution 1500–1800: The Formation of the Modern Scientific Attitude* (1966). Traces undermining of traditional science and rise of new sciences.

THOMAS HOBBES, *Leviathan. Parts I & II*, ed. by H. W. Schneider (1958).

T. E. JESSOP, *Thomas Hobbes* (1960), Brief biographical sketch.

H. KEARNEY, *Science and Change 1500–1700* (1971). Broad survey.

---

13 Ibid., Ch. 2, sects. 4–6, pp. 4–6.
14 Ibid., Ch. 13, sect. 149, p. 84.

ALEXANDER KOYRÉ, *From the Closed World to the Infinite Universe* (1957). Treated from perspective of the historian of ideas.

THOMAS S. KUHN, *The Copernican Revolution* (1957). A scholarly treatment.

JOHN LOCKE, *The Second Treatise of Government,* ed. by T. P. Peardon (1952).

JOHN D. NORTH, *Isaac Newton* (1967). Brief biography.

BLAISE PASCAL, *The Essential Pascal,* ed. by R. W. Gleason (1966).

E. M. W. TILLYARD, *Milton* (1952). Brief biographical sketch.

488

19
The Waxing and Waning of States (1686–1740)

THE LATE seventeenth and early eighteenth centuries witnessed significant shifts of power and influence among the states of Europe. Previously strong nations lost their status as significant military and economic units. Other countries that had in some cases figured only marginally in international relations came to the fore. Great Britain, France, Austria, Russia, and Prussia emerged during this period as the powers that would dominate Europe until at least World War I. The establishment of their political and economic dominance occurred at the expense of Spain, the United Netherlands, Poland, Sweden, and the Ottoman Empire. Equally essential to their rise was the weakness of the Holy Roman Empire after the Treaty of Westphalia (1648).

The successful competitors for international power were those states that in differing fashions created strong central political authorities. Farsighted observers in the late seventeenth century already understood that in the future those domains that would become or remain great powers must imitate the political and military organization of Louis XIV. Monarchy alone could impose unity of purpose on the state. The turmoil of seventeenth-century civil wars and aristocratic revolts had impressed people with the value of the monarch as a guarantor of minimum domestic tranquillity. Imitation of French absolutism involved other factors besides belief in strong monarchy. It usually required building a standing army, organizing an efficient tax structure to support the army, and establishing a bureaucracy to collect the taxes. Moreover the political classes of the country and especially the nobles had to be converted to a sense of duty and loyalty to the central government that was more intense than their

loyalty to other competing political and social institutions.

The waning powers of Europe were those whose leaders failed to achieve such effective organization. They were unable to employ their political, economic, and human resources to foil external aggression or to overcome forces of domestic dissolution. The internal and external failures were closely related. If a state failed to maintain or establish a central political authority with sufficient power over the nobility, cities, guilds, and the church, it could not raise a strong army to defend its borders or its economic interests. More often than not the key element leading to success or failure was the character, personality, and energy of the monarch.

The Maritime Powers

In western Europe, Britain and France emerged as the dominant powers. This development represented a shift of influence against Spain and the United Netherlands. Both the latter countries had been quite strong and important during the sixteenth and seventeenth centuries, but they became negligible during the course of the eighteenth century. However, neither disappeared from the map. Both retained considerable economic vitality and influence. The difference was that France and Britain attained so much more power and economic strength.

Spain

Spanish power had depended on the influx of wealth from the Americas and on the capacity of Spanish monarchs to rule the still largely autonomous provinces of Spain. Within Castile, Aragon, Navarre, the Basque province, and other districts, there were strong noble and clerical estates without whose cooperation royal government was impossible. From the defeat of the Spanish Armada in 1588 to the Treaty of the Pyrenees in 1659, Spain had experienced a series of foreign policy reverses that harmed the prestige of the monarchy. Numerous treasure fleets from the New World were captured.

Peter the Great of Russia, through his centralization of tsarist power and his military exploits, epitomized the state-building monarchs of the late seventeenth and early eighteenth centuries. This portrait was painted in 1711 by I. Kupetsky. [The Granger Collection.]

The reign of Charles II of Spain (1665–1700) saw the power of the crown greatly weaken. He was the last Hapsburg king of the country, for in him the line at last failed; deformed (the Hapsburg jaw carried to parody made it almost impossible for him to eat), dull, and impotent, he left no heir. Louis XIV's successful determination to have his grandson succeed Charles led to the War of the Spanish Succession. [The Granger Collection.]

Dutch shipbuilding remained important throughout the seventeenth and eighteenth centuries, although not as prosperous as in the sixteenth. Ships, such as this one being constructed at Amsterdam in 1694, were the sinews of trade during the period. The building in the background is the headquarters of the Dutch West Indies Company, which settled New Amsterdam (subsequently New York). [The Granger Collection.]

The Duke of Orleans was regent of France during the minority of Louis XV, years marked by financial scandal and weak administration. [The Granger Collection.]

Between 1665 and 1700 the physically malformed, dull-witted, and sexually impotent Charles II was monarch. Throughout his reign the local provincial estates and the nobility increased their power. On his death the War of the Spanish Succession had seen the other powers of Europe contesting the issue of the next ruler of Spain.

The Treaty of Utrecht (1713) gave the Spanish crown to Philip V (1700–1746), who was a Bourbon and the grandson of Louis XIV. The new king should have attempted to consolidate his internal power and to protect Spanish overseas trade. However, his second wife, Elizabeth Farnese, wanted to use Spanish power to carve out interests for her sons on the Italian peninsula. Such machinations diverted government resources and allowed the nobility and the provinces to continue to assert their privileges against the authority of the monarchy. Not until the reign of Charles III (1759–1788) did Spain possess a monarch concerned with efficient administration and internal improvement. By the third quarter of the century the country was better governed, but it could no longer effectively compete in power politics.

The Netherlands

The demise of the United Netherlands occurred wholly within the eighteenth century. After the death of William III in 1702, the various local provinces successfully prevented the emergence of another strong *stadtholder*. Unified political leadership therefore vanished. During the earlier long wars of the Netherlands with Louis XIV and England, naval supremacy slowly but steadily had passed to the British. The fishing industry declined, and the Dutch lost their technological superiority in shipbuilding. Countries between which Dutch ships had once carried goods now came to trade directly with each other. For example, the British began to use more and more of their own vessels in the Baltic traffic with Russia. Similar stagnation overtook Dutch domestic industries, such as textile finishing, paper making, and glass blowing. The disunity of the provinces and the absence of vigorous leadership hastened this economic decline and

prevented action that might have slowed or halted it. What saved the United Netherlands from becoming completely insignificant in European matters was their continued dominance of the financial community. Their banks continued well past the middle of the century to provide loans and financing for European trade.

France After Louis XIV

Despite its military losses in the War of the Spanish Succession, France remained a great power. It was less strong in 1715 than in 1680, but it still possessed a large population, an advanced if troubled economy, and the administrative structure bequeathed it by Louis XIV. Moreover, even if France and its resources had been badly drained by the last of Louis's wars, the other major states of Europe emerged from the conflict similarly debilitated. What the country required was a period of economic recovery and consolidation and better, wiser, and less ambitious political leadership. It enjoyed a period of recovery, but the quality of its leadership was at best indifferent. Louis XIV was succeeded by his five-year-old great-grandson Louis XV (1715–1774). Within two years the young boy's uncle, the duke of Orléans, had become regent and remained so until 1720. The regency further undermined the already faltering prestige of the monarchy.

The duke of Orléans was a gambler, and for a time he

John Law, a wily Scots speculator,
became Controller General of Finances in France
and was responsible for the Mississippi Company
scandal (the Mississippi Bubble) that came to a
head in 1719. [The Granger Collection.]

Saint-Simon Shows the French Nobility's Incapacity to Govern

The regent under the young Louis XV hoped that the nobility of France might assume an active role in the government of the nation in place of the passive role assigned to them by Louis XIV. This plan involved displacing many non-noble bureaucrats. As described by the duke of Saint-Simon (1675-1755), the plan failed because the nobles proved unequal to their new duties.

THE *design was to begin to put the nobility into the ministry, with the dignity and authority befitting them, at the expense of the high civil servants and nobles of the robe, and by degree and according to events to guide affairs wisely so that little by little those commoners would lose all those administrative duties that are not purely judicial . . . in order to submit to the nobility all modes of administration. The difficulty was the ignorance, the frivolity, and the lack of diligence of the nobility who were accustomed to being good for nothing except getting killed, succeeding at war only by seniority, and romping around for the rest of the time in the most mortal uselessness. As a result they were devoted to idleness and disgusted with all knowledge outside war by their conditioned incapacity for being able to provide themselves with anything useful to do. It was impossible to make the first step in this direction without overturning the monster that had devoured the nobility, the controller general and the secretaries of state.*

Duc de Saint-Simon, *Memoires,* trans. by Frank M. Turner, cited in John Lough, *An Introduction to Eighteenth Century France* (New York: David MacKay Company, Inc., 1964), pp. 135-136.

turned over the financial management of the kingdom to John Law (1671-1729), a fellow gambler and a Scottish mathematician. Law believed that an increase in the paper money supply would stimulate the postwar economic recovery of the country. With the permission of the regent he established a bank in Paris that issued paper money. Law then organized the Mississippi Company, which was to possess a monopoly on trading privileges with the French colony of Louisiana in North America.

The Mississippi Company also assumed the management of the French national debt. The company issued shares of its own stock in exchange for government bonds, which had greatly fallen in value. In order to redeem large quantities of bonds, Law encouraged speculation in Mississippi Company stock. In 1719 the price of the stock rose handsomely. However, smart investors took their profits by selling their stock in exchange for money from Law's bank. Then they sought to exchange the currency for gold. To make the second transaction they went to Law's bank, but that institution lacked sufficient gold to redeem all the money brought to it.

In February 1720 all gold payments were halted in France. Soon thereafter Law himself fled the country. The "Mississippi Bubble," as the affair was called, had burst. The fiasco brought disgrace upon the government that had made Law its controller general. The Mississippi Company was later reorganized and functioned quite profitably, but fear of paper money and speculation marked French economic life for the rest of the century.

The duke of Orléans made a second departure that also lessened the power of the monarchy. He attempted to draw the French nobility once again into the decision-making processes of the government. Louis XIV had downgraded the nobility and had filled his ministries and

bureaucracies with persons of nonnoble families. The regent was seeking to restore a balance. He adopted a system of councils on which the nobles were to serve along with the bureaucrats. However, the years of noble domestication at Versailles had worked too well, and the nobility seemed to lack both the talent and the desire to govern. The experiment failed.

The failure of the great French nobles to function as satisfactory councilors did not mean that they had surrendered their ancient ambition to assert their rights, privileges, and local power over those of the monarchy. The chief feature of French political life from this time until the French Revolution was the attempt of the nobility to impose its power on the monarchy. The most effective instrument in this process was the *parlements,* or

In 1722 the young great-grandson of Louis XIV was crowned the new King of France as Louis XV in the Cathedral of Rheims. He was then twelve years old and had already been king for seven years. This painting by J. B. Martin shows the moment in the darkened cathedral when the young king was anointed. It is now in the museum at Versailles. [Cliché des Musées Nationaux.]

courts dominated by the nobility of the robe. The most important of these was the Parlement of Paris. These bodies could refuse to recognize the legality of an act or law promulgated by the monarch. By long tradition their approval had been required to make a law valid. Louis XIV had often overridden stubborn, uncooperative *parlements*. However, the financial and moral weakness of the eighteenth-century monarchy allowed these judicial institutions to reassert their authority. One of the major blunders of the duke of Orléans had been to approve the reinstitution of the *parlements'* power to allow or disallow laws.

By 1726 the chief minister of the French court was Cardinal Fleury (1653–1743). He was the last of those great churchmen who had so loyally and effectively served the French monarchy. Like his seventeenth-century predecessors, Cardinals Richelieu and Mazarin, Fleury was a realist. He understood the political ambition and incapacity of the nobility and worked quietly to block their undue influence. Fleury was also aware of the precarious financial situation in which the wars of Louis XIV had left the royal treasury.

The Maritime Powers 493

Madame de Pompadour (1721–1764) was the first
official mistress of Louis XV and a person of
beauty, cultivation, and ambition. After her death
the king had an increasing number of mistresses,
both unofficial and official, but none were as
cultured as she, and inevitably, the increasingly
low moral tone of the French court did much to
undermine the loyalty of the general public for
the throne. This lovely portrait of his patroness
is by one of the eighteenth century's masters,
François Boucher (1703–1770). It is now in the
National Gallery of Scotland in Edinburgh. [The
Granger Collection.]

The cardinal, who was seventy-three years old when
he came to office, was determined to give the country a
period of peace. He surrounded himself with generally
able assistants who attempted to solve the financial problems. Part of the national debt was repudiated. New
industries enjoying special privileges were established,
and new roads and bridges were built. On the whole the
nation prospered, but Fleury was never able to draw from
the nobles or the church sufficient tax revenues to put the
state on a stable financial footing.

Fleury died in 1743, having unsuccessfully attempted
to prevent France from intervening in the war then
raging between Austria and Prussia. All of his financial
pruning and planning had come to nought. Another
failure must also be credited to this elderly churchman.
Despite his best efforts he had not trained Louis XV to
become an effective monarch. Louis XV possessed most
of the vices and almost none of the virtues of his grandfather. He wanted to hold on to absolute power but was
unwilling to work the long hours required. He did not
choose many wise advisers after Fleury. He was tossed
about by the gossip and intrigues of the court nobles. His
personal life was scandalous. His reign became more
famous for his mistress, Madame de Pompadour, than for
anything else. Louis XV was not an evil person but a
mediocre one. And in a monarch the latter fault was
unfortunately often a greater failure than the former.

Despite this political drift France remained a great
power. Its army remained at mid-century the largest and
strongest military force on the Continent. Its commerce
and production expanded. Its colonies produced wealth
and spurred domestic industries. Its cities grew and prospered. The wealth of the nation waxed as the absolutism
of the monarchy waned. France did not lack sources of
power and strength, but it did lack political leadership
that could organize, direct, and inspire its people.

George I of Great Britain was originally the Elector of Hanover in Germany. He succeeded to the British throne in 1714. The painting is from Godfrey Kneller's studio, and the medal is by John Croker. [The Granger Collection.]

Great Britain: The Age of Walpole

Britain in 1713 had emerged as a victor over Louis XIV, but the nation required a period of recovery. As an institution the British monarchy was not in the degraded state of the French monarchy, but its stability was not certain. In 1714 the Hanoverian dynasty came to the throne. Almost immediately George I (1714–1727) confronted a challenge to his new title. The Stuart pretender James Edward (1688–1766), the son of James II,

Sir Robert Walpole (1676–1745) brought political stability to eighteenth-century Britain by achieving the trust of the king and by using government patronage in a very skillful and sometimes ruthless manner. [Culver Pictures.]

landed in Scotland in December 1715. His forces marched southward but met defeat less than two months later.

Although militarily successful against the pretender, the new dynasty, designated by the Act of Settlement (1701), and its supporters saw the need for consolidation. During the seventeenth century England had been one of the most politically restive countries in Europe. The closing years of Queen Anne's reign (1702–1714) had seen sharp clashes between the political factions of Whigs and Tories over the coming Treaty of Utrecht. The Tories had urged a rapid peace settlement and after 1710 had opened negotiations with France. During the same period the Whigs were seeking favor from the Elector of Hanover, who would soon be their monarch. His concern for his domains in Hanover made him less than happy with the Tory peace policy. In the final months of Anne's reign some Tories, fearing loss of power under the waiting Hanoverian dynasty, opened channels of communication with the Stuart pretender; and a few even rallied to his losing cause.

Under these circumstances it was little wonder that George I, upon arrival in Britain, clearly favored the Whigs and proceeded with caution. Previously the differences between Whigs and Tories had been vaguely related to principle. The Tories emphasized a strong monarchy, low taxes for landowners, and firm support of the Anglican Church. The Whigs supported monarchy but wanted Parliament to retain final sovereignty. They tended to favor urban commercial interests as well as the prosperity of the landowners. They encouraged a policy of religious toleration toward the Protestant nonconformists in England. Socially both groups supported the *status quo*. Neither was organized in any way like a

This etching by William Hogarth is a satire of
the South Sea Bubble scandal in Great Britain in
1720. The Bubble was attended by the same kind of
frenzied financial speculation, corruption, and
crash that had gone on in the French Mississippi
scheme in 1719. [The Granger Collection.]

See here ẏ Causes why in London,
So many Men are made & undone,
That Arts, & honest Trading drop,
To Swarm about ẏ Devils Shop (A)
Who cuts out (B) Fortunes Golden Haunches

Trapping their Souls with Lotts & Chances,
Sharing em from Blue Garters down
To all Blue Aprons in the Town.
Here all Religions flock together
Like Tame & Wild Fowl of a Feather.

Leaving their strife Religious bustle,
Kneel down to play at pitch & Hussle (C)
Thus when the Sheepherds are at play,
Their flocks must surely go Astray,
The woeful cause ẏ in these Times

(E) Honour, & honesty, are Crimes
That publickly are punish'd by
(G) Self Interest and (F) Vilany;
So much for Monys, magick power
Guess at the Rest you find out more.

modern political party. However, after the Hanoverian accession and the Whig success in achieving the confidence of George I, the difference between Whig and Tory meant primarily that one group was in office and the other was out.

The political situation remained in a state of flux until Robert Walpole (1676–1745) took over the helm of government. This Norfolk squire had been active in the House of Commons since the reign of Queen Anne, and he had served as a cabinet minister. What gave him special prominence under the new dynasty was a British financial scandal similar to the French Mississippi Bubble.

Management of the British national debt had been assigned to the South Sea Company, which exchanged government bonds for company stock. As in the French case, the price of the stock flew high, only to crash in 1720 when prudent investors sold their holdings and took their speculative profits. Parliament intervened and under Walpole's leadership adopted measures to honor the national debt. To most contemporaries Walpole had saved the financial integrity of the country and in so doing had proved himself a person of immense administrative capacity and political ability.

George I gave Walpole his full confidence. For this reason Walpole has often been regarded as the first prime minister of Great Britain and the originator of the cabinet system of government. However, unlike a modern prime minister he was not chosen by the majority of the House of Commons. His power largely depended upon the good will of George I and later of George II (1727–1760). Walpole generally demanded that all of the ministers in the cabinet agree on policy, but this did not prevent frequent public differences on policy. The real source of Walpole's power was the combination of the personal support of the king, his ability to handle the House of Commons, and his iron-fisted control of government patronage. To oppose Walpole on either minor or more substantial matters was to risk the almost certain loss of government patronage for oneself, one's family, or one's

friends. Through skillful patronage Walpole bought support for himself and his policies from people who wanted to receive jobs, appointments, favors, and government contracts. Such corruption supplied the glue of political loyalty. By 1730 to be a Whig meant essentially to be a supporter of Walpole.

Walpole's favorite slogan was *quieta non movere* ("let sleeping dogs lie"). To that end he pursued a policy of peace abroad and promotion of the *status quo* at home. In this regard he and Cardinal Fleury were much alike. The structure of the eighteenth-century British House of Commons aided Walpole in his pacific policies. It was neither a democratic nor a representative body. Each of the counties elected two members. But if the more powerful landed families in a county agreed on the candidates, there would be no election. Other members were elected from districts called *boroughs*, of which there were a considerable variety. A few were large enough for elections to be relatively democratic. However, most boroughs had a very small number of electors. For example, a local municipal corporation or council of only a dozen members might have the legal right to elect a member of Parliament. In Old Sarum, one of the most famous corrupt or "rotten" boroughs, the Pitt family for many years simply bought up those pieces of property to which a vote was attached and thus in effect owned a seat in the House of Commons. Through proper electoral management, which involved favors to the electors, the House of Commons could be controlled.

The structure of Parliament and the manner in which it was elected meant that the government of England was dominated by the owners of property and by especially wealthy nobles. They did not pretend to represent people and districts or to be responsive to what would later be called public opinion. They regarded themselves as representing various economic and social interests, such as the West Indian interest, the merchant interest, or the landed interest. These owners of property were suspicious of an administrative bureaucracy controlled by the crown or its ministers. For this reason they or their

William Hogarth's etching, Chairing the Member, after his own painting, illustrates the ritual of "chairing" the victorious candidate in an eighteenth-century English parliamentary election. These elections were frequently quite rowdy and involved much drinking and fighting; in this instance, the triumphal procession has run into opposition, with resulting loss of dignity for the newly elected member. In this role Hogarth portrayed an actual candidate named Bub Doddington. [Charles Farrell Collection.]

agents served as local government administrators, judges, militia commanders, and tax collectors. In this sense the British nobility and other substantial landowners actually did govern the nation. And because they regarded the Parliament as the political sovereign, there was no absence of central political authority and direction. Conse-

quently the supremacy of Parliament provided Britain with the kind of unity that elsewhere in Europe was sought through the institutions of absolutism.

There were limits in Britain to the power of Robert Walpole and to the unresponsiveness of Parliament. Newspapers and public debate flourished. Free speech was a reality, as was freedom of association. In 1733 Walpole presented to the House of Commons a scheme for an excise tax that would have raised revenue somewhat in the fashion of a modern sales tax. The public outcry in the press, on the public platform, and in the streets was so great that he eventually withdrew the measure. What the English regarded as their traditional political rights raised a real and potent barrier to the power of the government. Again, in 1739, public outcry over the Spanish treatment

Blackstone States the Virtues of the English Constitution

William Blackstone (1723–1780) was an important English jurist. In this passage, written in 1765, he explains how the various parts of the English government checked and balanced each other. These relationships were considered the reason for the stability of eighteenth-century British politics.

AND *herein indeed consists the true excellence of the English government, that all the parts of it form a mutual check upon each other. In the legislature, the people are a check upon the nobility, and the nobility a check upon the people; by the mutual privilege of rejecting what the other has resolved: while the king is a check upon both, which preserves the executive power from encroachments. And this very executive power is again checked and kept within due bounds by the two houses, through the privilege they have of inquiring into, impeaching and punishing the conduct (not indeed of the king, which would destroy his constitutional independence; but, which is more beneficial to the public,) of his evil and pernicious counsellors. Thus every branch of our civil polity supports and is supported, regulates and is regulated, by the rest. . . . Like three distinct powers in mechanics, they jointly impel the machine of government in a direction different from what either, acting by itself, would have done; but at the same time in a direction partaking of each, and formed out of all; a direction which constitutes the true line of the liberty and happiness of the community.*

William Blackstone, *Commentaries on the Laws of England,* 15th ed. (London: Cadell and Davies 1809), Vol. 1, p. 153.

---

of British merchants in the Caribbean pushed Britain into the War of Jenkins's Ear, which Walpole opposed and deplored.

Walpole's ascendancy, which lasted until 1742, did little to raise the level of British political morality, but it brought the nation a kind of stability that it had not enjoyed for well over a century. Its foreign trade grew steadily and spread from New England to India. Agriculture improved its productivity. All forms of economic enterprise seemed to prosper. The navy became stronger. As a result of this political stability and economic growth, Great Britain became a European power of the first order and stood at the beginning of its era as a world power. Its government and economy during the next generation became a model for all progressive Europeans.

Central and Eastern Europe

The major factors in the shift of political influence among the maritime nations were naval strength, economic progress, foreign trade, and sound domestic administration. The conflicts among them occurred less in Europe than on the high seas and in their empires. Their nations already existed in well-defined geographical areas with established borders. Their populations generally accepted the authority of the central government.

The situation in central and eastern Europe was rather different. Except for the cities on the Baltic, the economy was agrarian. There were fewer cities and many more large estates populated by serfs. The states in this region did not possess overseas empires. Changes in the power structure normally involved changes in borders or at least in the prince who ruled a particular area. Their military conflicts took place at home rather than overseas. The political structure of this region, which lay largely east of the Elbe River, was very "soft." The almost constant warfare of the seventeenth century had led to a habit of temporary and shifting political loyalties. The princes and aristocracies of small states and principalities were unwilling to subordinate themselves voluntarily to a central monarchical authority. Consequently the political life of the region and the kind of states that emerged there were rather different from those of western Europe.

Beginning in the last half of the seventeenth century, eastern and central Europe began to assume the political and social contours that would characterize it for the next two hundred years. After the Peace of Westphalia, the Austrian Hapsburgs recognized the basic weakness of the title of Holy Roman Emperor and began a new consolidation of their power. At the same time the state of Prussia emerged as a factor in north German politics and as a major challenger to Hapsburg domination of Germany. Most importantly, Russia at the opening of the eighteenth century burst upon the eastern horizon as a military power of the first order. These three states achieved their new status largely as a result of the political

In this rather fanciful nineteenth-century engraving Charles XII of Sweden, in the upper right, leads his troops in battle even though he has himself been wounded. The Swedish king was known for such bravery, which most of his contemporaries considered simple foolhardiness. In 1718 he was finally killed in a battle. [Bildarchiv Preussischer Kulturbesitz.]

but one that eventually led to the defeat of Sweden. In 1700 he defeated the Russians at the battle of Narva, but then he turned south to invade Poland. The conflict dragged on, and the Russians were able to strengthen their forces. In 1708 the Swedish monarch began a major invasion of Russia but became bogged down in the harsh Russian winter. The next year his army was decisively defeated at the battle of Poltava. Thereafter the Swedes could maintain only a holding action. Charles himself sought refuge with the Ottoman army and then eventually returned to Sweden in 1714. He was shot four years later while fighting the Norwegians.

The Great Northern War came to a close in 1721. Sweden had exhausted its military and economic resources and had lost its monopoly on the Baltic coast. Russia had conquered a large section of the eastern Baltic, and Prussia had gained a portion of Pomerania. Internally, after the death of Charles XII, the Swedish nobles were determined to reassert their power over that of the monarchy. They did so but then fell into quarrels among themselves. Sweden played a very minor role in European affairs thereafter.

decay or military defeat of Sweden, Poland, and the Ottoman Empire.

Sweden: The Ambitions of Charles XII

Under Gustavus Adolphus II (1611–1632) Sweden had played an important role as a Protestant combatant in the Thirty Years' War. During the rest of the seventeenth century Sweden had consolidated its control of the Baltic, preventing Russian possession of a Baltic port and permitting Polish and German access to the sea only on Swedish terms. The Swedes also possessed one of the better armies in Europe. However, Sweden's economy, based primarily on export of iron, was not strong enough to ensure continued political success.

In 1697 Charles XII (1697–1718) came to the throne. He was headstrong, to say the least, and perhaps insane. In 1700 Russia began a drive to the west against Swedish territory. The Russian goal was a foothold on the Baltic. In the resulting Great Northern War (1700–1721), Charles XII led a vigorous and often brilliant campaign,

The Ottoman Empire

At the southeastern extreme of Europe, the Ottoman Empire lay as a barrier to the territorial ambitions of the Austrian Hapsburgs and of Poland and Russia. The empire in the late seventeenth century still controlled most of the Balkan peninsula and the entire coastline of the Black Sea. It was an aggressive power that had for two centuries attempted to press its control further westward in Europe. The Ottoman Empire had probably made its greatest military impression on Europe in 1683, when it laid siege to the city of Vienna.

However, the Ottomans had overextended themselves politically, economically, and militarily. The major domestic political groups resisted any substantial strengthening of the central government in Constantinople. Rivalries for power among army leaders and nobles weakened the effectiveness of the government. In the

A contemporary Dutch print views the 1683 Turkish siege of Vienna from a remarkably revealing position in the hills west of the city. We are fortunate to capture the scene on the point of the Turkish forces deciding to give up the summer-long attack; their commanders, the Ottoman Grand Vizier and the Pasha of Adrianople, lower left, are just beginning their flight back toward the Ottoman homelands. Polish and other Christian aid for the beleaguered Hapsburg forces had arrived, and the battle was clearly going against the Turks. Vienna was not captured, and never again did the progressively weakening Moslem Ottoman Empire penetrate so far west.

In the picture, note the Danube River toward the top, the elaborate zig-zag fortifications outside the walls, and bursts of artillery fire at several points. Most details inside the walled city are omitted, but the central cathedral and the imperial palace, toward the bottom, are shown. The walls themselves, when later torn down, made space for the Ring, the famous boulevard still encircling central Vienna.

One unforeseen lasting social result of the siege was the further boost given to coffee drinking by the Viennese discovery of the beverage in the deserted Turkish camps around the city. [The Granger Collection.]

Belegeringe En Onset Der Stadt WEENEN,

DONAU

Flur

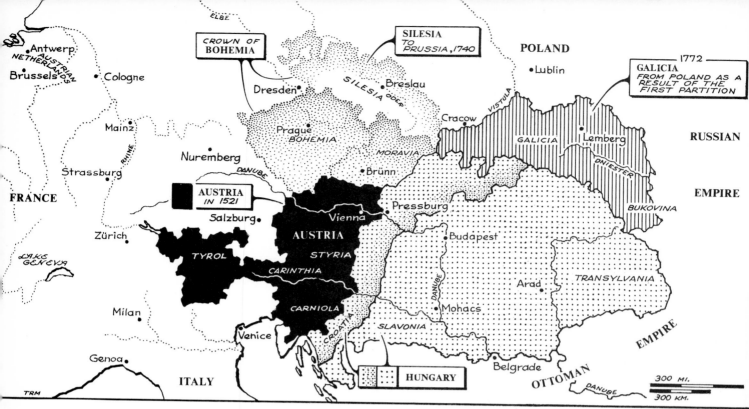

THE AUSTRIAN HAPSBURG EMPIRE, 1521–1772

The Empire had three main units—Austria, Bohemia, Hungary. Expansion was mainly eastward: east Hungary from the Ottomans (17th century) and Galicia from Poland (1772). Meantime, Silesia was lost, but Hapsburgs retained German influence as Holy Roman Emperors.

outer provinces, such as Transylvania, Wallachia, and Moldavia (all parts of modern Romania), the empire depended upon the goodwill of local rulers, who never submitted themselves fully to the imperial power. The empire's economy was weak, and its exports were primarily raw materials. Moreover, the actual conduct of most of its trade had been turned over to representatives of other nations.

By the early eighteenth century the weakness of the Ottoman Empire meant that on the southeastern perimeter of Europe there existed an immense political vacuum. In 1699 the Turks concluded a treaty with their longtime Hapsburg enemy and surrendered all pretensions of control over Hungary, Transylvania, Croatia, and Slavonia. From this time onward Russia attempted to extend its territory and influence at the expense of the empire. For almost two hundred years the decay of the Ottoman Empire constituted a major factor in European international relations. The area always proved tempting to the major powers, but their distrust of each other and their conflicting rivalries as well as a considerable residual

strength on the part of the Turks prevented the dismemberment of the empire.

Poland

In no other part of Europe was the failure to maintain a competitive political position so complete as in Poland. In 1683 King John III Sobieski (1673–1696) had led a Polish army to rescue Vienna from the Turkish siege. But following that spectacular effort, Poland became little more than a byword for the dangers of aristocratic independence. In Poland as nowhere else on the Continent the nobility became the single most powerful political factor in the country. Unlike the British nobility and landowners, the Polish nobility would not even submit to a central authority of their own making. There was no effective central authority in the form of either a king or a parliament.

The Polish monarchy was elective, but the deep distrust and divisions among the nobility prevented their electing a king from among their own numbers. Sobieski was a notable exception. Most of the Polish monarchs came from outside the borders of the kingdom and were tools of foreign powers. The Polish nobles did have a central legislative body called the Diet. It included only the nobles and specifically excluded representatives from corporate bodies, such as the towns. In the Diet, however, there existed a practice known as the *liberum veto*, whereby the staunch opposition of any single member could require the body to disband. Such opposition was termed "exploding" the Diet.

Government as it was developing elsewhere in Europe simply was not tolerated in Poland. Localism reminiscent of the Middle Ages continued to hold sway as the nobles used all their energy to maintain their traditional "Polish liberties." There was no way to collect sufficient taxes to build up an army. The price of this noble liberty was eventually the disappearance of Poland from the map of Europe during the last half of the eighteenth century.

The Hapsburg Empire and the Pragmatic Sanction

The Hapsburgs in Austria came out of the Thirty Years' War much weaker than they had entered it. Their lands had been desolated by the conflict, and the Holy Roman Emperorship—the traditional base of Hapsburg political power—had been rendered a hollow title. The Treaty of Westphalia had recognized the political autonomy of the more than three hundred corporate entities of the empire. These included large political units, such as Saxony, Hanover, Bavaria, and Brandenburg, but they also included scores of small cities, bishoprics, principalities, and territories of independent knights. The role and power of the Holy Roman Emperor henceforth depended upon the cooperation he could elicit from these various political bodies. The Diet of the empire sat perpetually at Regensburg without new elections from 1663 until its dissolution in 1806. The Diet and the empire generally regulated the daily economic and political life of Germany. The post-Westphalian Holy Roman Empire in many ways resembled Poland with its lack of central authority. However, unlike its Polish neighbor, the Holy Roman Empire was reorganized from within as the Hapsburgs attempted to regain their authority and, as will be seen shortly, as Prussia set out on its course toward European power.

In addition to retaining the emperorship of the Holy Roman Empire, the Hapsburgs also held hereditary possession of the kingdom of Bohemia (in modern Czechoslovakia), which included Silesia and Moravia, and the Crown of Saint Stephen, which ruled Hungary and Transylvania. They also possessed stretches of northern Italy and the Austrian Netherlands, which is present-day Belgium. They confronted immense problems in all these territories. In each they ruled by virtue of a different title and had to gain the cooperation of the local nobility. The most problematic province in this regard was Hungary, where the Magyar nobility seemed ever ready to rebel.

There was practically no common basis for political unity among peoples of such diverse languages, customs, and geography. Even the Hapsburg zeal for Roman Catholicism no longer proved a bond for unity when they confronted the equally zealous Calvinism of the Magyar nobles. The Hapsburgs established various central councils to chart common policies for their farflung domains. None of these proved effective because the dynasty repeatedly had to bargain with nobles in one part of Europe in order to maintain their position in another part of the Continent. Consequently, for all practical purposes, not until well into the nineteenth century did the Vienna government directly affect the lives of any social group below the nobility.

Despite all these internal difficulties Leopold I (1657–1705) rallied his domains to resist the advances of the Turks and to resist the aggression of Louis XIV. He achieved Ottoman recognition of his sovereignty over Hungary in 1699 and suppressed the long rebellion of his new Magyar subjects between 1703 and 1711. He also extended his territorial holdings over much of what is today Yugoslavia and western Romania. These eastward extensions allowed the Hapsburgs to hope to develop Mediterranean trade through the port of Trieste. The expansion at the cost of the Ottoman Empire also helped the Hapsburgs to compensate for their loss of domination over the Holy Roman Empire. Strength in the east gave them greater political leverage in Germany. Leopold was succeeded by Joseph I (1705–1711), who continued his policies.

Charles VI of Austria (Holy Roman Emperor) devoted most of his life to securing approval of the Pragmatic Sanction, which would guarantee the succession of his daughter Maria Theresa to the various Hapsburg domains. The portrait, of which this is a detail, is by Johann Gottfried Auerbach, and is in Vienna. [Bettmann Archive.]

Schönbrunn Palace of the Austrian Hapsburgs stands outside Vienna. Like many royal palaces of the eighteenth century, it was modeled after Louis XIV's palace of Versailles. [Austrian Information Service, New York.]

The Waxing and Waning of States (1686–1740)

Maria Theresa Discusses One Weakness of Her Throne

Scattered subjects of the multi-language Austrian Empire (Germans, Hungarians, Czechs, Slovaks, Slovenes, Croatians, Poles, Romanians, for example) made impossible the unifying of the Empire into a strong centralized monarchy. Maria Theresa, writing in 1745, explains how previous Hapsburg rulers had impoverished themselves by attempting with little success to purchase the political and military support of the nobles in different provinces. The more privileges they gave the nobles the more they were expected to give.

To RETURN *once again to my ancestors, these individuals not only gave away most of the crown estates, but absorbed also the debts of those properties confiscated in time of rebellion, and these debts are still in arrears. Emperor Leopold [1658–1705] found little left to give away, but the terrible wars he fought no doubt forced him to mortgage or pawn additional crown estates. His successors did not relieve these burdens, and when I became sovereign, the crown revenues barely reached eighty thousand gulden. Also in the time of my forebears, the ministers received enormous payments from the crown and from the local Estates because they knew not only how to exploit selfishly the good will, grace, and munificence of the Austrian house by convincing each ruler that his predecessor had won fame by giving freely but also how to win the ears of the provincial lords and clergy so that these ministers acquired all that they wished. In fact they spread their influence so wide that in the provinces they were more feared and respected than the ruler himself. And when they had finally taken everything from the sovereign, these same ministers turned for additional compensation to their provinces, where their great authority continuously increased. Even though complaints reached the monarch, out of grace and forebearance toward the ministers, he simply allowed the exploitations to continue. . . .*

This system gave the ministers such authority that the sovereign himself found it convenient for his own interests to support them because he learned by experience that the more prestige enjoyed by the heads of the provinces, the more of the sovereign's demands these heads could extract from their Estates.

Maria Theresa, *Political Testament*, cited in Karl A. Roider (Ed. and Trans.), *Maria Theresa* (Englewood Cliffs, N.J.: Prentice-Hall, 1973), pp. 32–33.

When Charles VI (1711–1740) succeeded Joseph he added a new problem to the old chronic one of territorial diversity. It was that he had no male heir, and there was only the weakest of precedents for a female ruler of the Hapsburg domains. Charles feared that upon his death the Austrian Hapsburg lands might fall prey to the surrounding powers as had those of the Spanish Hapsburgs in 1700. He was determined to prevent that disaster and to provide his domains with the semblance of legal unity. To those ends, he devoted most of his reign to seeking the approval of his family, the estates of his realms, and the major foreign powers for a curious document called the Pragmatic Sanction.

This instrument provided the legal basis for a single line of inheritance within the Hapsburg dynasty through Charles VI's daughter Maria Theresa (1740–1780). Other members of the Hapsburg family recognized her as the rightful heir. The nobles of the various domains did likewise after extracting various concessions from Charles. The major states of Europe followed a similar course. Consequently, when Charles VI died in October 1740, he believed he had secured legal unity for the Hapsburg Empire and a safe succession for his daughter. Less than two months after his death the fragility of such a paper agreement became all too apparent. In December 1740 Frederick II of Prussia invaded the Hapsburg province of Silesia. Maria Theresa would have to fight to defend her inheritance.

Prussia and the Hohenzollerns

The Hapsburg achievement was to draw together into an uncertain legal unity a collection of domains possessed by dint of separate feudal titles. The achievement of the Hohenzollerns of Brandenburg-Prussia was to acquire a similar collection of titular holdings and then to forge them into a centrally administered unit. In spite of the geographical separation of their territories and the paucity of their natural economic resources, they transformed feudal ties and structures into bureaucratic ones. They subordinated every social class and most economic

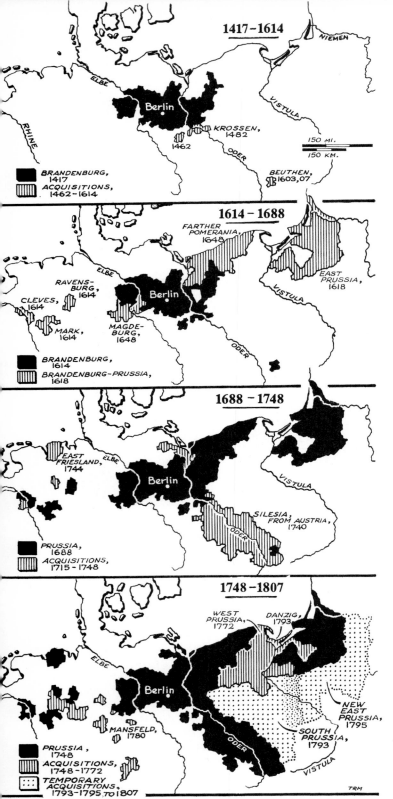

1417-1614

RHINE · ELBE · NIEMEN · VISTULA · ODER

Berlin

KROSSEN, 1482

1462

150 MI.
150 KM.

BEUTHEN, 1603,07

■ BRANDENBURG, 1417
▨ ACQUISITIONS, 1462-1614

1614-1688

FARTHER POMERANIA, 1648

EAST PRUSSIA, 1618

ELBE · VISTULA · ODER

RAVENS-BURG, 1614

CLEVES, 1614

MARK, 1614

Berlin

MAGDE-BURG, 1648

■ BRANDENBURG, 1614
▨ BRANDENBURG-PRUSSIA, 1618

1688-1748

EAST FRIESLAND, 1744

ELBE · VISTULA · ODER

Berlin

SILESIA, FROM AUSTRIA, 1740

■ PRUSSIA, 1688
▥ ACQUISITIONS, 1715-1748

1748-1807

WEST PRUSSIA, 1772

DANZIG, 1793

ELBE

Berlin

MANSFELD, 1780

NEW EAST PRUSSIA, 1795

SOUTH PRUSSIA, 1793

ODER · VISTULA

■ PRUSSIA, 1748
▥ ACQUISITIONS, 1748-1772
⣿ TEMPORARY ACQUISITIONS, 1793-1795 TO 1807

TRM

EXPANSION OF BRANDENBURG-PRUSSIA

pursuits to the strengthening of the one institution that united their far-flung realms: the army. In so doing they made the term *Prussian* synonymous with administrative rigor and military discipline.

The rise of Prussia occurred within the German power vacuum created by the Peace of Westphalia. It is the story of the extraordinary Hohenzollern family, which had ruled the German territory of Brandenburg since 1417. Through inheritance the family had acquired the Duchy of Cleves and the counties of Mark and Ravensburg in 1609, the Duchy of East Prussia in 1618, and the Duchy of Pomerania in 1637. Except for Pomerania, none of these lands was contiguous with Brandenburg. East Prussia lay inside Poland and outside the authority of the Holy Roman Emperor. All of the territories lacked endowment of good natural resources, and many of them were devastated during the Thirty Years' War. At Westphalia the Hohenzollerns lost part of Pomerania to Sweden but were compensated by receiving three more bishoprics and the promise of the archbishopric of Magdeburg when it became vacant, as it did in 1680. By the late seventeenth century the scattered Hohenzollern holdings represented a block of territory within the Holy Roman Empire second in size only to that of the Hapsburgs.

Despite its size the Hohenzollern conglomerate was weak. The areas were geographically separate. There was no mutual sympathy or common concern among them. In each there existed some form of local noble estates that limited the power of the Hohenzollern prince. They were exposed to foreign aggression.

The person who began to forge these areas and nobles into a modern state was Frederick William (1640-1688), who became known as the Great Elector. He established

Seventeenth-century Brandenburg-Prussia expanded mainly by acquiring dynastic titles in geographically separated lands. Eighteenth-century expansion occurred through aggression to the east: Silesia seized in 1740 and various parts of Poland in 1772, 1793, and 1795.

Frederick William I of Prussia ruthlessly forged the Prussian army into a major instrument of state. But he also attempted to avoid committing his valuable troops to warfare. [The Granger Collection.]

himself and his successors as the central uniting power by breaking the estates, organizing a royal bureaucracy, and establishing a strong army.

Between 1655 and 1660 Sweden and Poland engaged in a war that endangered the Great Elector's holdings in Pomerania and East Prussia. Frederick William had neither an adequate army nor the tax revenues to confront this threat. In 1655 the Brandenburg estates refused to grant him new taxes; however, he proceeded to collect the required taxes by military force. In 1659 a different grant of taxes, originally made in 1653, elapsed; Frederick William continued to collect them as well as those he had imposed by his own authority. He used the money to build up an army, which allowed him to continue to enforce his will without the approval of the nobility. Similar processes of threats and coercion took place against the nobles in his other territories.

However, there was a political and social trade-off between the elector and his various nobles. These *Junkers,* or German noble landlords, were allowed almost complete control over the serfs on their estates. In exchange for their obedience to the Hohenzollerns the *Junkers* received the right to demand obedience from their serfs. Frederick William also tended to choose as the local administrators of the tax structure men who would normally have been members of the noble estates. In this fashion, he coopted potential opponents into his service. The taxes fell most heavily on the backs of the peasants and the urban classes. As the years passed, sons of *Junkers* increasingly dominated the army officer corps, and this practice became even more pronounced during the eighteenth century. All officials and army officers took an oath of loyalty directly to the elector. The army and the elector thus came to embody the otherwise absent unity of the state. The existence of the army made Prussia a valuable potential ally and a state with which other powers needed to curry favor.

Yet even with the considerable accomplishments of the Great Elector, the house of Hohenzollern did not possess a crown. The achievement of a royal title was one of the

few state-building accomplishments of Frederick I (1688–1713). This son of the Great Elector was the least "Prussian" of his family during these crucial years. He built palaces, founded Halle University (1694), patronized the arts, and lived luxuriously. However, in 1700 at the outbreak of the War of the Spanish Succession he put his army at the disposal of the Hapsburg Holy Roman Emperor. In exchange for this loyal service, the emperor permitted Frederick to assume the title of "King in Prussia." Thereafter Frederick became Frederick I, and he passed the much-desired royal title to his son Frederick William I in 1713.

Frederick William I (1713–1740) was both the most eccentric personality to rule the Hohenzollern domains and one of its most effective monarchs. After giving his father a funeral that matched the luxury of his life, Frederick William I immediately imposed policies of strict austerity. In some cases jobs were abolished, and in others salaries were lowered. His political aims seem to have been nothing else than the consolidation of an obedient, compliant bureaucracy and the expansion of the army. He initiated a policy of *Kabinett* government, which meant that lower officials submitted all relevant documents to him in his office or *Kabinett.* Then he alone examined the papers, made his decision, and issued his orders. Frederick William I thus skirted the influence of ministers and ruled alone.

Frederick William organized the bureaucracy along the lines of military discipline. All departments were united under the *GeneraloberfinanzKriegsundDomain-Direktorium,* which is more happily known to us as the General Directory. He imposed taxes on the nobility and changed most remaining feudal dues into money payments. He sought to transform feudal and administrative loyalties into a sense of duty to the monarch as a political institution rather than as a person. He once described the perfect royal servant as

an intelligent, assiduous, and alert person who after God values nothing higher than his king's pleasure and serves him out of love and for the sake of honor rather than money and who in his conduct solely seeks and constantly bears in mind his king's service and interests, who, moreover, abhors all intrigues and emotional deterrents.[1]

Service to the state and the monarch was to become impersonal, mechanical, and in effect unquestioning.

The discipline that Frederick William applied to the army was little less than fanatical. During his reign the size of the military force grew from about thirty-nine thousand in 1713 to over eighty thousand in 1740. It was the third or fourth largest army in Europe, whereas Prussia ranked thirteenth in size of population. Rather than using recruiters, the king made each canton responsible for supplying a certain number of soldiers.

After 1725 Frederick William always wore an officer's uniform. He built one regiment from the tallest soldiers he could find in Europe. Separate laws applied to the army and to civilians. Laws, customs, and royal attention made the officer corps the highest social class of the state. Military service attracted the sons of *Junkers*. In this fashion, the army, the *Junker* nobility, and the monarchy became forged into a single political entity. Militarism became a style of life and of governing. Military priorities and values dominated Prussian society and daily life as in no other state of Europe. It has often been said that whereas other nations possessed armies, the Prussian army possessed its nation.

Although Frederick William I built the best army in Europe, he followed a consistent policy of avoiding conflict. He wanted to drill his soldiers but not to order them into battle. Although Frederick William terrorized his family and associates and on occasion knocked out teeth with his walking stick, he was not a militarily aggressive person. The army for him was a symbol of Prussian power and unity, not an instrument to be used for foreign

adventures or aggression. At his death in 1740 he passed to his son Frederick II (1740–1786; Frederick the Great) this superb military machine, but he could not pass to his son the wisdom to refrain from using it. Almost immediately upon coming to the throne, Frederick II upset the Pragmatic Sanction and invaded Silesia. He thus crystallized the Austrian–Prussian rivalry for control of Germany that would dominate central European affairs for over a century.

Russia and Peter the Great

Though ripe with consequences for the future, the rise of Prussia and the new consolidation of the Austrian Hapsburg domains seemed to many at the time only one more shift in the long-troubled German scene. However, the emergence of Russia as an active European power constituted a wholly new factor in European politics. Previously Russia had been considered a part of Europe only by courtesy. Geographically and politically it lay on the periphery of Europe. Hemmed in by Sweden on the Baltic and by the Ottoman Empire on the Black Sea, the country had no warm-water ports. Its chief outlet to the west was Archangel on the White Sea, which was open to ships during only part of the year. There was little trade. What Russia did possess was a vast reserve of largely undeveloped natural and human resources.

Religion also set off Russia from the rest of Europe. The Russian Orthodox Church was separated from Latin Christendom and was also frequently at odds with other sectors of the Eastern Orthodox communion. The church opposed the scientific as well as the theological thought of the West. In the mid-seventeenth century a sort of reformist movement led by Patriarch Nikon arose in the Russian church. In 1667 certain changes were made in the texts and the ritual of the church. These reforms caused great unrest because the Russian church had always claimed to be the great protector of true ritual. The Old Believers were a group of Russian Christians who strongly opposed these changes. They were condemned by the hierarchy, but they persisted in their opposition.

1 Quoted in Hans Rosenberg, *Bureaucracy, Aristocracy, and Autocracy* (Boston: Beacon Press 1958), p. 93.

Bishop Burnet Looks Over a Foreign Visitor

In 1797 and 1798 Peter the Great of Russia toured western Europe to discover how Russia must change its society and economy in order to become a great power. As this description by Bishop Gilbert Burnet in England indicates, the west Europeans found the tsar a curious person in his own right.

HE CAME *this winter over to England, and stayed some months among us. . . . I had good interpreters, so I had much free discourse with him; he is a man of a very hot temper, soon inflamed, and very brutal in his passion; he raises his natural heat, by drinking much brandy, . . . he is subject to convulsive motions all over his body, and his head seems to be affected with these; he wants not capacity, and has a larger measure of knowledge, than might be expected from his education, which was very indifferent; a want of judgment, with an instability of temper, appear in him too often and too evidently; he is mechanically turned, and seems designed by nature rather to be a ship-carpenter, than a great prince. This was his chief study and exercise, while he stayed here: he wrought much with his own hands, and made all about him work at the models of ships. . . . He was . . . resolved to encourage learning, and to polish his people, by sending some of them to travel in other countries, and to draw strangers to come and live among them. . . . After I had seen him often, and had conversed much with him, I could not but adore the depth of the providence of God, that had raised up such a furious man to so absolute an authority over so great a part of the world.*

Bishop Burnet's History of His Own Time (Oxford, England: Clarendon Press, 1823), Vol. 4, pp. 396–397.

Late in the century thousands of them committed suicide rather than submit to the new rituals. The Old Believers' movement represented a rejection of change and innovation; its presence discouraged the rest of the church hierarchy from making any further substantial moves toward modern thought.

The political structure of Russia had also contributed to its isolation. During the "time of troubles" in the early seventeenth century, it had experienced considerable conflict between the nobles, or *boyars,* and the tsar. In 1613, in hopes of resolving that tension, an assembly of nobles had elected a seventeen-year-old boy named Michael Romanov (1613–1645) to be tsar. Thus was established the dynasty that in spite of palace revolutions, military conspiracies, assassinations, and family strife ruled Russia until 1917. However, during the rest of the seventeenth century constant turmoil surrounded the tsars. The Moscow guards, or *streltsi,* made and unmade rulers; and the nobility fought to retain its privileges.

In 1682 another boy—ten years old at the time—ascended the fragile Russian throne as co-ruler with his half brother. His name was Peter (1682–1725), and Russia would never be the same after him. He and his ill half brother, Ivan V, had come to power on the shoulders of the *streltsi,* who expected rewards from the persons they favored. Much violence and bloodshed had surrounded the disputed succession. Matters became even more confused when their sister Sophia was named regent. Peter's followers overthrew her in 1689. From that date onward Peter ruled personally, although in theory he shared the crown with the unwell Ivan, who died in 1696. The dangers and turmoil of his youth convinced Peter of two things. First, the power of the tsar must be made secure from the jealousy of the *boyars* and the greed of the *streltsi.* Second, the military power of Russia must be increased.

Peter I, who became Peter the Great, was fascinated by western Europe. He particularly admired the military resources of those kingdoms. He was an imitator of the first order. The products and workmen from the West who had filtered into Russia impressed and intrigued him. In 1697 he made a famous visit in rather weak disguises throughout western Europe. There he dined and talked with the great and the powerful, who considered this almost seven-foot-tall ruler both crude and rude. However, his happiest moments on the trip were spent inspecting shipyards, docks, and the manufacture of military hardware. He returned to Moscow determined by whatever means necessary to copy what he had seen abroad, for he knew that warfare would be necessary to make Russia a great power. The tsar's drive toward westernization, though unsystematic, had four general areas of concern: taming the *boyars* and the *streltsi,*

After Peter the Great of Russia returned from his journey to western Europe, he personally cut off the traditional and highly prized long sleeves and beards of the Russian nobles. His action symbolized his desire to see Russia become more powerful and more modern. [SLEEVES: Culver Pictures; BEARDS: The Granger Collection.]

achieving secular control of the church, reorganizing internal administration, and developing the economy. Peter pursued each of these goals with violence and ruthlessness.

He made a sustained attack on the Russian *boyars*. In 1698, immediately upon his return from abroad, he personally shaved the long beards of the court *boyars* and sheared off the long sleeves of their shirts and coats, which had made them the butt of jokes throughout Europe. More important, he demanded that the nobles provide his state with their services. The *boyars* resisted these demands. Throughout Peter's reign that struggle continued. His strongest action to engage their service came in 1722. That year he published a Table of Ranks, which henceforth equated a person's social position and privileges with his rank in the bureaucracy or the army rather than with his position in the nobility. However, unlike the case in Prussia, the Russian nobility never became perfectly loyal to the state. They repeatedly sought to reassert their independence and control of the Russian imperial court.

The fate of the *streltsi* was less fortunate than that of the *boyars*. In 1698 they had rebelled while Peter was on his European tour. When he returned and put down the revolt of these Moscow troops, he directed massive violence and brutality against both leaders and followers. There were private tortures and public executions, in which Peter's own ministers took part. Almost twelve hundred of the rebels were put to death, and their corpses long remained on public display to discourage future disloyalty.

Peter dealt with the potential political independence of the Russian church with similar ruthlessness. The reformist theological policies that had created the Old Believers had also, of course, created a political problem for the tsar. Such was not to occur in the future. In 1721 Peter simply abolished the position of patriarch of the Russian church. In its place he established a synod to rule the church in accordance with secular requirements. The head of the synod was to be a layman. So far as changing a traditional institution was concerned, the policy toward the church was the most radical of Peter's reign. It produced further opposition from the Old Believers, who saw the tsar as leading the church into further heresy.

In his reorganization of domestic administration, Peter looked to institutions then used in Sweden. These were "colleges" or bureaus composed of several persons rather than departments headed by a single minister. These colleges, which he imposed on Russia, were to look after matters such as the collection of taxes, foreign affairs,

war, and economic matters. This new organization was
an attempt to breathe life into the generally stagnant and
inefficient administration of the country. In 1711 he
created a central senate of nine members who were to
direct the Moscow government when the tsar was away
with the army. The purpose of these and other local
administrative reforms was to establish a bureaucracy that
could collect and spend tax revenues to support an efficient army.

The economic development advocated by Peter the
Great was closely related to his military needs. He encouraged the establishment of an iron industry in the
Ural Mountains, and by mid-century Russia was the
largest iron producer in Europe. He sent prominent
young Russians abroad to acquire technical and organizational skills. He attempted to attract west European
craftsmen to live and work in Russia. Except for the
striking growth of the iron industry, which later languished, all these efforts had only marginal success.

The purpose of these internal reforms and political
departures was to support a policy of warfare. Peter was
determined to secure warm-water ports that would allow
Russia to trade with the West and to have a greater
impact on European affairs. This policy led him into wars
with the Ottoman Empire and with Sweden. His armies

commenced fighting the Turks in 1695 and captured
Azov on the Black Sea in 1696. It was a temporary
victory, for in 1711 he was compelled to return the port.

Peter was more successful against Sweden, where the
inconsistency and irrationality of Charles XII were no
small aid. In 1700 Russia moved against the Swedish
territory on the Baltic. The Swedish king's failure to
follow up his victory at Narva in 1700 allowed Peter the
Great to regroup his forces and hoard his resources. In
1709, when Charles XII returned to fight Russia again,
Peter was ready and the battle of Poltava sealed the fate
of Sweden. In 1721, at the Peace of Nystad, which ended
the Great Northern War, Russian conquest of Estonia,
Livonia, and part of Finland was confirmed. Henceforth
Russia possessed warm-water ports and a permanent
influence on European affairs.

At one point the domestic and foreign policies of Peter
the Great literally intersected. This was at the spot on the
Gulf of Finland where Peter founded his new capital city

of St. Petersburg (now Leningrad). There he built government structures and compelled his *boyars* to construct townhouses. In this fashion he imitated those west European monarchs who had copied Louis XIV by constructing smaller versions of Versailles. However, the founding of St. Petersburg went beyond the construction of a central court. It symbolized a new western orientation of Russia and Peter's determination to hold his position on the Baltic coast. He had commenced construction of the city and had moved the capital there in 1703, even before victory over Sweden was assured.

Despite the notable success on the Baltic, Peter's reign ended with a great question mark. He had long quarreled with his only son, Alexis. Peter was jealous of the young man and fearful that he might undertake sedition. In 1718 Peter had his son imprisoned, and during this imprisonment the presumed successor to the throne died mysteriously. Thereafter Peter claimed for himself the right of naming a successor, but he could never bring himself to designate the person orally or in writing. Consequently, when he died in 1725, there was no firmer policy on succession to the throne than when he had acceded to the title. For over thirty years, once again soldiers and nobles would determine who ruled Russia. Peter had laid the foundations of a modern Russia, but he had failed to lay the foundations of a stable state.

Eighteenth-Century European States

The major European powers by the second quarter of the eighteenth century were not yet nation-states. They were still monarchies in which the personality of the ruler and the personal relationships of the great noble families exercised considerable influence over public affairs. The monarchs had generally succeeded in making their power greater than the nobility's. However, the power of the aristocracy and its capacity to resist or obstruct the policies of the monarchs were not destroyed. In Britain, of course, the nobility had tamed the monarchy, but even

there tension between nobles and monarchs would continue through the rest of the century.

In foreign affairs the new arrangement of military and diplomatic power established during the early years of the century prepared the way for two long-term conflicts. The first was a commercial rivalry for trade and overseas empire between France and Great Britain. During the reign of Louis XIV these two nations had collided over the French bid for dominance in Europe. During the eighteenth century they dueled for control of commerce on other continents. The second arena of warfare was central Europe, where Austria and Prussia fought for the leadership of the states of Germany.

However, behind these international conflicts and the domestic rivalry of monarchs and nobles, the society of eighteenth-century Europe began to experience momentous change. The character and structures of the society over which the monarchs ruled were beginning to take on some features associated with the modern age. These economic and social developments would in the long run produce transformations in the life of Europe beside which the achievements of the early eighteenth-century state-building monarchs paled.

SUGGESTED READINGS

M. S. ANDERSON, *Europe in the Eighteenth Century, 1713–1783* (1961). The best one-volume introduction.

F. L. CARSTON, *The Origins of Prussia* (1954). Discusses the groundwork laid by the Great Elector in the seventeenth century.

A. COBBAN, *A History of Modern France*, Vol. 1, 2nd ed. (1961). A lively and opinionated survey.

R. R. ERGANG, *The Potsdam Führer* (1941). The biography of Frederick William I.

S. B. FAY AND K. EPSTEIN, *The Rise of Brandenburg-Prussia to 1786* (1937, rev. 1964). A brief outline.

M. T. FLORINSKY, *Russia: A History and an Interpretation*, 2 vols. (1953). A useful and far-ranging work.

G. P. GOOCH, *Maria Theresa and Other Studies* (1951). A sound introduction to the problems of the Hapsburgs.

G. P. Gooch, *Louis XV, The Monarchy in Decline* (1956). A discussion of the problems of France after the death of Louis XIV.

H. Holborn, *A History of Modern Germany, 1648–1840* (1966). The best and most comprehensive survey in English.

V. K. Klyuchevsky, *Peter the Great*, tr. by Liliana Archibald (1958). A standard biography.

Dorthy Marshall, *Eighteenth-Century England* (1962). Emphasizes social and economic background.

L. B. Namier and J. Brooke, *The History of Parliament: The House of Commons, 1754–1790*, 3 vols. (1964). A detailed examination of the unreformed British House of Commons and electoral system.

L. J. Oliva (Ed.), *Russia and the West from Peter the Great to Khrushchev* (1965). An anthology of articles tracing an important and ambiguous subject.

J. H. Plumb, *Sir Robert Walpole*, 2 vols. (1956, 1961). A masterful biography ranging across the sweep of European politics.

P. Roberts, *The Quest for Security, 1715–1740* (1947). Very good on the diplomatic problems of the period.

H. Rosenberg, *Bureaucracy, Aristocracy, and Autocracy: the Prussian Experience, 1660–1815* (1960). Emphasizes the organization of Prussian administration.

B. H. Summer, *Peter the Great and the Emergence of Russia* (1950). A brief but well-organized discussion.

B. Williams, *The Whig Supremacy, 1714–1760* (1939). A general survey.

E. N. Williams, *The Ancien Regime in Europe* (1972). A state by state survey of very high quality.

A. M. Wilson, *French Foreign Policy During the Administration of Cardinal Fleury, 1726–1743* (1936). The standard account.

J. B. Wolf, *The Emergence of the Great Powers, 1685–1715* (1951). A comprehensive survey.

514

20
Society Under the Old Regime

DURING the French Revolution and the turmoil spawned by that upheaval it became customary to refer to the patterns of social, political, and economic relationships that had previously existed in France as the *ancien régime,* or the old regime. The term has come to be applied generally to the life and institutions of prerevolutionary Europe. Politically the term indicated the rule of theoretically absolute monarchies with growing bureaucracies and aristocratically led armies. Economically the old regime was characterized by scarcity of food, predominance of agriculture, slow transport, a low level of iron production, rather unsophisticated financial institutions, and in some cases competitive commercial overseas empires. Socially prerevolutionary Europe was based on aristocratic elites possessing a wide variety of inherited legal privileges, established Roman Catholic and Protestant churches intimately related to the state and the aristocracy, an urban labor force usually organized into guilds, and a rural peasantry subject to high taxes and feudal dues. However, it should be remembered that the men and women living during this period did not know it was the *old* regime. In most cases they earned their livelihoods and went through the various stages of life as their forebears had done for generations before them and as they expected their children to do after them.

Probably the most striking feature of the old regime was the marked contrasts in the lives and experiences of people in different social ranks, different countries, and even different regions of the same country. The bonds created by rapid transport and communication that have

today led to similar patterns of life throughout the Western world simply did not yet exist.

Within the major monarchies there was usually no single standard of uniform law, money, or weights and measures. Except in Britain there were internal tolls that hampered the passage of goods. The nobility of Great Britain lived in the most magnificent luxury the order had ever known. On the Continent some groups of nobles were also very wealthy, but other members of the continental nobility were little better off than wealthier peasants. So far as the peasantry was concerned, it tended to prosper in western Europe while reaching new depths of social and economic degradation east of the Elbe River.

In Britain, Holland, and parts of France there was a healthy and growing middle class, but such an order hardly existed in the German principalities, the Austrian Empire, or Russia. Finally, there was a stark contrast between the refinement of taste, fashion, and manners of the upper levels of society and the simultaneous presence of public whipping, torture, and executions inflicted upon the lower classes. Historians often point to the difficulties of life and the differences in wealth in our industrial society, but these were hardly lacking in the society of the old regime.

Eighteenth-century society was traditional. The past weighed more heavily on people's minds than did the future. Few persons outside the government bureaucracies and the writers of the Enlightenment considered innovation to be desirable. This was especially true of social relationships. Both nobles and peasants, for very different reasons, repeatedly called for the restoration of traditional or customary rights. The nobles asserted what they considered their ancient rights against the intrusion of the expanding monarchical bureaucracies. The peasants in petitions and revolts called for the revival or the maintenance of customary manorial rights that provided access to particular lands, courts, or grievance procedures.

With the exception of the early industrial development in Britain, the eighteenth-century economy was also quite traditional. The quality and quantity of the harvest re-

Agriculture, basic to society, is illustrated in this plate from the mid-eighteenth-century French *Encyclopédie, ou Dictionnaire Raisonné des Sciences, des Arts et des Métiers* (hereafter the *Encyclopedia*). New machinery, such as the plows shown at the bottom, helped to increase yield from the land and thus the food supply for Europe.

mained the single most important fact of life for the overwhelming majority of the population and the gravest concern of the governments.

Closely related to this traditional social and economic outlook was the hierarchical structure of the society. The medieval sense of rank and degree not only persisted but became more rigid in the course of the century. In several continental cities *sumptuary* laws regulating the dress of the different classes remained on the books. The hierarchy was enforced through the corporate nature of social relationships. Each state or society was considered a community of numerous smaller communities. People in eighteenth-century Europe did not enjoy what Americans consider to be individual rights. A person enjoyed such rights and privileges as were guaranteed to the particular communities or groups of which he was a part. The "community" might include the village, the municipality, the nobility, the church, the guild, or the parish. In turn each of these bodies enjoyed certain privileges, some of which were great and some small. The privileges might involve exemption from taxation or from some especially humiliating punishment, the right to practice a trade or craft, the right for one's children to pursue a particular occupation, or in the case of the church the right to collect the tithe.

Tradition, hierarchy, corporateness, and privilege were the chief social characteristics of the old regime. Yet it was by no means a static society. Factors of change and innovation were fermenting in its midst. There was a strong demand from the colonies in the Americas for European goods and manufactures. Merchants in seaports and other cities were expanding their businesses. By preparing their states for war, the various governments put new demands on the resources and the economic organizations of their nations. The spirit of rationality that had been so important to the Scientific Revolution of the seventeenth century continued to manifest itself in the economic life of the eighteenth century. Perhaps most important, the population of Europe grew rapidly. The old regime itself fostered the changes that eventually transformed it into a very different kind of society.

The Land and Its Tillers

Land constituted the economic basis of eighteenth-century life. Well over three fourths of all Europeans lived in the country, and few of these people ever traveled beyond a ten-mile radius of their birthplace. Male children tended to follow the occupation of their fathers.

At the opposite end of the social scale from Castle Howard is the mid-eighteenth-century rural laborer's hut far to the east in Austria. However proper a subject for the artist, Franz Edmund Weirotter (1730–1771), the scene is probably a realistic one of the wretched housing endured by many. [Charles Farrell Collection.]

Village families tended to intermarry; there were only occasional marriages between men and women from neighboring villages. The lot of women continued to be circumscribed by family duties, the family economy, and the burden of child bearing and rearing. With the exception of the nobility and the wealthier nonaristocratic landowners, the dwellers on the land were poor, and by any modern standard their lives were difficult. They lived in various modes of economic and social dependency, exploitation, and vulnerability.

Peasants and Serfs

The major forms of rural social dependency related directly to the land. Those who worked the land were subject to immense control from the landowners. This situation was true for free peasants, such as English tenants and most French cultivators, and for the serfs of Germany, Austria, and Russia, who were legally bound to a particular plot of land and a particular lord. In all cases the class who owned most of the land also controlled the local government and the courts. For example, in

Great Britain all farmers and smaller tenants had the legal rights of English citizens. But the justices of the peace who presided over the county courts and who could call out the local militia were always substantial landowners, as were also the members of Parliament, who made the laws.

The intensity of landlord power increased as one moved from west to east. In France the situation differed somewhat from province to province. Most French peasants owned some land, but there were a few serfs. However, practically all peasants were subject to certain feudal dues, called *banalités,* that included required use for payment of the lord or seigneur's mill to grind grain and his oven to bake bread. The seigneur could also require a certain number of days each year from the peasant's labor. This practice was termed the *corvée.* Because even landowning French peasants rarely possessed enough land to support their families, they were also subject to feudal dues related to the plots of land they rented. In Prussia and Austria, despite attempts by the monarchies late in the century to improve the lot of serfs, the landlords continued to exercise almost complete control over them. In Austria law and custom required serfs to provide service or *robot* to the lords. Moreover, throughout continental Europe in addition to these feudal services, the burden of state taxation fell on the tillers of the soil. Through various legal privileges and the ability to demand further concessions from the monarchs, the

Society Under the Old Regime

William Coxe Describes Serfdom in Eighteenth-Century Russia

William Coxe was an Englishman who travelled widely in eastern Europe. His description of Russian serfdom portrays the brutality of the institution. It also illustrates his amazement at the absence in Russia of civil liberties such as he and more humble citizens enjoyed in England.

Peasants *belonging to individuals are the private property of the landholders, as much as implements of agriculture, or herds of cattle; and the value of an estate is estimated, as in Poland, by the number of boors [serfs], and not by the number of acres. . . . If the Polish boor is oppressed, and he escapes to another master, the latter is liable to no pecuniary penalty for harbouring him; but in Russia the person who receives another's vassal is subject to an heavy fine. With respect to his own demands upon his peasants, the lord is restrained by no law, either in the exaction of any sum, or in the mode of employing them. He is absolute master of their time and labour: some he employs in agriculture: a few he makes his menial servants, and perhaps without wages; and from others he exacts an annual payment.*

Each vassal, therefore, is rated according to the arbitrary will of his master. Some contribute four or five shillings a year; others, who are engaged in traffic or trade, are assessed in proportion to their supposed profits. . . . . With regard to any capital which they may have acquired by their industry, it may be seized, and there can be no redress. . . .

[S]ome of the Russian nobility send their vassals to Moscow or Petersburg for the purpose of learning various handcraft trades: they either employ them on their own estates; let them out for hire; sell them at an advanced price; or receive from them an annual compensation for the permission of exercising trade for their own advantage.

William Coxe, *Travels into Poland, Russia, Sweden, and Denmark,* 4th ed. (London: T. Cadell 1972, first printed 1784), Vol. 3, pp. 174–181.

OPPOSITE, TOP: Lunchtime on an eighteenth-century French farm. The softened style of drawing gives a somewhat romanticized cast to the scene, but farm workers did usually work in the kind of group shown here. [The Granger Collection.]

OPPOSITE: J. J. De Boissieu's 1780 etching of the interior of a French dairy barn associates the life of the land with the life of the family. [Charles Farrell Collection.]

landlords escaped payment of numerous taxes. They also presided over the manorial courts.

The condition of serfs was worst in Russia. The contrast is best revealed by the Russian custom of enumerating the number of "souls," that is male serfs, owned rather than the acreage possessed. The serfs were merely economic commodities. Russian landlords could demand as much as six days a week of labor, and like Prussian and Austrian landlords they enjoyed the right to punish serfs. They could even exile a serf to Siberia on their own authority. The serfs had no legal recourse against the orders and whims of their lords. There was actually little difference between Russian serfdom and slavery.

The Russian monarchy itself contributed to the degradation of the serfs. Peter the Great gave whole villages to favored nobles. Later in the century Catherine the Great (1762–1796) granted nobles even more authority over their serfs in exchange for the political cooperation of the landowners. The situation in Russia led to considerable unrest. There were well over fifty peasant revolts between 1762 and 1769. These culminated between 1771 and 1775 in Pugachev's rebellion, during which all of southern Russia experienced intense unrest. Emelyan Pugachev (1726–1775) promised the serfs land of their own and freedom from their lords. The rebellion was brutally suppressed. Thereafter any thought of liberalizing or improving the condition of the serfs was set aside for a generation.

Pugachev's was the greatest rebellion in Russian history and the largest peasant uprising of the eighteenth century. Smaller peasant revolts or disturbances occurred elsewhere. Rebellions took place in Bohemia in 1775, in Transylvania in 1784, in Moravia in 1786, and in Austria in 1789. Revolts in western Europe were almost nonexistent, but England experienced numerous local enclosure riots. Rural rebellions were violent, but the peasants and serfs normally directed their wrath against property rather than persons. The rebels usually sought to reassert traditional or customary rights against practices they perceived as innovations. Their targets were carefully

Emelyan Pugachev (1726–1775) led the largest peasant revolt in Russian history. Here in a contemporary propaganda picture he is shown in chains. An inscription in Russian and German was printed below the picture discussing the evil of revolution and insurrection. [Bildarchiv Preussischer Kulturbesitz.]

Catherine the Great Issues a Proclamation Against Pugachev

Against a background of longstanding human degradation, and even increasing landowner authority, the greatest serf rebellion in Russian history was led by a Don Cossack named Emelyan Pugachev from 1773 to 1775. Empress Catherine the Great's proclamation of 1773 argues that he was alienating the serfs from their natural and proper allegiance to her and their masters.

BY THE *grace of God, we Catherine II . . . make known to our faithful subjects, that we have learnt, with the utmost indignation and extreme affliction, that a certain Cossack, a deserter and fugitive from the Don, named Emelyan Pugachev, after having traversed Poland, has been collecting, for some time past, in the districts that border on the river Irghis, in the government of Orenburg, a troop of vagabonds like himself; that he continues to commit in those parts all kinds of excesses, by inhumanly depriving the inhabitants of their possessions, and even of their lives. . . .*

In a word, there is not a man deserving of the Russian name, who does not hold in abomination the odious and insolent lie by which Pugachev fancies himself able to seduce and to deceive persons of a simple and credulous disposition, by promising to free them from the bonds of submission, and obedience to their sovereign, as if the Creation of the universe had established human societies in such a manner as that they can subsist without an intermediate authority between the sovereign and the people.

Nevertheless, as the insolence of this vile refuse of the human race is attended with consequences pernicious to the provinces adjacent to that district; as the report of the flagrant enormities which he has committed, may affright those persons who are accustomed to imagine the misfortunes of others as ready to fall upon them, and as we watch with indefatigable care over the tranquillity of our faithful subjects, we inform them . . . that we have taken . . . such measures as are the best adapted to stifle the sedition. . . .

We trust . . . that every true son of the country will unremittedly fulfill his duty, of the contributing to the maintenance of good order and of public tranquillity, by preserving himself from the snares of seduction, and by discharging his obedience to his lawful sovereign.

William Tooke, *Life of Catherine II, Empress of Russia,* Fourth Edition (London: T. N. Longman and O. Rees, 1800), Vol. 2, pp. 460–461 (spelling modernized).

chosen and included unfair pricing, onerous new or increased feudal dues, changes in methods of payment or land use, unjust officials, or extraordinarily brutal overseers and landlords. In this respect the peasant revolts were quite conservative in nature.

The main goal of peasant society was stability that would ensure the local food supply. In western Europe most rural society was organized into villages. The owners of the individual plots or strips would decide communally what crops would be planted. In eastern Europe, with its great estates of hundreds or thousands of acres, the landlords decided how to use the land. But in either case the tillers resisted change that might endanger the sure supply of food that they believed to be promised by traditional cultivation. However, throughout the eighteenth century landlords across the Continent began to search for higher profits from their holdings. They embraced innovation in order to increase their own prosper-

Failure of the grain crop and other plantings could bring both hunger and social disruption during the eighteenth century. Turgot (1727–1781), who later became finance minister of France, emphasizes the role of private charity and government policy in relieving the suffering. His description, written in 1769, also provides a brief survey of the diet of the French peasant.

Everyone *has heard of the terrible dearth that has just afflicted this generality [a local administrative district]. The harvest of 1769 in every respect proved to be one of the worst in the memory of man. The dearths of 1709 and 1739 were incomparably less cruel. To the loss of the greatest part of the rye was added the total loss of the chestnuts, of the buckwheat, and of the Spanish wheat—cheap food stuffs with which the peasant sustained himself habitually a great part of the year, reserving as much as he could of his corn [grain], in order to sell it to the inhabitants of the towns. . . . The people could exist only by exhausting their resources, by selling at a miserable price their articles of furniture and even their clothes. Many of the inhabitants have been obliged to disperse themselves through other provinces to seek work or to beg, leaving their wives and children to the charity of the parishes. It has been necessary for the public authority to require the proprietors and inhabitants in better circumstances in each parish to assess themselves for the relief of the poor people; nearly a fourth of the population is dependent upon charitable contributions. After these melancholy sufferings which the province has already undergone, and with the reduced condition in which it was left by the dearth of last year, even had the harvest of the present year been a good one, the poverty of the inhabitants would have necessitated the greatest efforts to be made for their relief. But we have now to add the dismal fact of our harvest being again deficient. . . .*

W. W. Stephens (Ed.), *The Life and Writings of Turgot* (London: Longmans, Green, and Co., 1895), p. 50.

The Revolution in Agriculture

Even more basic than the social dependency of peasants and small tenant farmers was their dependency upon the productiveness of nature. The quantity and quality of the annual grain harvest was the most fundamental fact for their lives. On the Continent bread was the primary component of the diet for the lower classes. The food supply was never certain, and the farther east one traveled, the more uncertain it became. Failure of the harvest meant not only hardship but actual death from either outright starvation or protracted debility. Quite often people living in the countryside encountered more difficulty finding food than did city dwellers, whose local government usually stored reserve supplies of grain.

Poor harvests also played havoc with prices. Smaller supplies or larger demand raised grain prices. Even small increases in the cost of food could exert heavy pressure on peasant or artisan families. If prices increased sharply, many of those families would fall back on poor relief from their local municipality or county or the church. What made the situation of food supply and prices so difficult was the peasants' sense of helplessness before the whims of nature and the marketplace.

Over the course of the century, historians now believe, there occurred a slow but steady inflation of bread prices spurred largely by population growth. This inflation put pressure on all of the poor. The prices rose faster than urban wages and brought no appreciable advantage to the very small peasant producer. On the other hand, the rise in grain prices benefited landowners and those wealthier peasants who had surplus grain to sell.

The increasing price of grain presented landlords with the opportunity to improve their incomes and life style. To those ends they began a series of innovations in farm production that are known as the *agricultural revolution*. This movement commenced in the Low Countries and England but spread in varying degrees eastward.

The revolution in agriculture included new methods of farming, new crops, and new modes of land holding, all

ity. They commercialized agriculture and thereby challenged traditional peasant ways of production. Peasant revolts and disturbances resulted. However, the governments of Europe, hungry for new taxes and dependent on the goodwill of the nobility, used their armies and militias to smash the peasants who defended the past.

of which eventually led to greater productivity. This advance in food production was necessary for the development of industrial society. It assured food to people living in cities and freed agricultural labor for use in industrial production. The changing modes of agriculture sponsored by the landlords undermined the assumptions of traditional peasant production. Farming now took place not only for the local food supply but also to assure the landlord a handsome profit. The latter goal meant that the landlords began to exert new pressures on their tenants and serfs.

Landlords in Great Britain provided the most striking examples of the improving spirit. Jethro Tull (1674–1741) contributed a willingness to experiment and to finance the experiments of others. Many of his ideas, such as the refusal to use manure as fertilizer, were wrong. Others, however, such as using iron plows to overturn earth more deeply and planting wheat by a drill rather than by casting, were excellent. His methods permitted land to be cultivated for longer periods without having to be left fallow.

Charles "Turnip" Townsend (1674–1738) encouraged even more important innovations. He learned from the Dutch how to cultivate sandy soil with fertilizers. He also instituted crop rotation, using wheat, turnips, barley, and clover. This system abolished the fallow field and produced more food for both animals and human beings.

A third British agricultural improver was Robert Bakewell (1725–1795), who pioneered new methods of animal breeding that produced more and better animals and more milk and meat.

These and other innovations received widespread discussion in the works of Arthur Young (1741–1820), who edited the *Annals of Agriculture* and who in 1793 became secretary of the British Board of Agriculture. Young traveled widely across Europe, and his books are among the most important documents of life during the second half of the eighteenth century.

Many of these innovations, which were adopted only very slowly, were incompatible with the existing organi-zation of the land in Britain. Most of the soil was still farmed by small cultivators who lived in village communities. Each farmer tilled an assortment of unconnected strips. The two- or three-field systems of rotation left large portions of land annually fallow and unproductive. Animals grazed on the common land in the summer and on the stubble of the harvest in the winter. Until at least the middle of the century the decisions as to what crops would be planted were made communally. The entire system discouraged improvement and favored the poorer farmers, who needed the common land and stubble fields for their animals. The village method provided little possibility for expanding pasture to raise more animals that would in turn produce more manure, which could be used for fertilizer. Thus, the methods of traditional production aimed at a steady but not a growing supply of food.

In 1700 approximately half the arable land in Britain was farmed by this open-field method. By the second half of the century the rising price of wheat encouraged landlords to consolidate or enclose their lands to increase production. The enclosures were intended to use land more rationally to achieve greater commercial profits. The process involved the fencing of common lands, the reclamation of previously untilled waste, and the transformation of strips into block fields. These procedures brought turmoil to the economic and social life of the countryside. Riots often ensued. Because many British farmers either owned their strips or rented them in a manner that amounted to ownership, the larger landlords had to resort to parliamentary acts to legalize the enclosure of the land, which they owned but rented to farmers. Because large landowners controlled Parliament, there was little difficulty in obtaining such measures. Between 1761 and 1792 almost 500,000 acres were enclosed through parliamentary act as compared with 75,000 acres between 1727 and 1760. In 1801 a general enclosure act streamlined the process.

The enclosures were at the time and have remained a very controversial topic. They permitted the extension of both farming and innovation. In that regard they increased food production on larger agricultural units. At the same time they disrupted small traditional communities. They forced off the land some independent farmers, who had needed the common pasturage, and very poor cottagers, who had lived on the reclaimed waste land. However, the enclosures did not depopulate the countryside. In some counties where the enclosures took place the population increased. New soil had come into production, and services subsidiary to farming also expanded.

The enclosures did not create the labor force for the British Industrial Revolution. What the enclosures most conspicuously display is the introduction of the entrepreneurial or capitalistic attitude of the urban merchant into the countryside. This commercialization of agriculture, which spread from Britain very slowly across the Continent during the next century, led to a breakdown of paternal relationships between the governing and governed classes. Previously the landlords had somewhat looked after the welfare of the lower orders through price controls or alleviation of rents during depressed periods. However, as the landlords became increasingly concerned about profits, they began to leave peasants to the mercy of the marketplace.

Improving agriculture tended to characterize farm production west of the Elbe. Dutch farming was quite efficient. In France, despite efforts of the government to improve agriculture, enclosures were restricted. Yet there was much discussion in France about improving methods. These new procedures benefited the ruling classes because better agriculture increased their incomes and assured a larger food supply, which tended to discourage social unrest.

In Russia, Prussia, Poland, and Austria only limited improvement took place. There the chief method of increasing production was to extend farming to previously untilled lands. The management of the farms was under the direction of the landlords or their agents rather than villages. By extending tillage, the great landlords sought to squeeze more labor from their serfs rather than

greater productivity from the soil. However, as in the West, the goal was increased profits.

Population Expansion

The assault on human dependence upon nature through improved farming was both a cause and a result of an immense expansion in the population of Europe. The population explosion with which the entire world must today contend seems to have had its origins in the eighteenth century. Prior to this time Europe's population had experienced dramatic increases, but plagues, wars, or harvest failures had in time decimated the increase. Beginning in the second quarter of the eighteenth century, the population began to grow without decimation.

Exact figures are lacking but the best estimates suggest that in 1700 Europe's population, excluding the European provinces of the Ottoman Empire, stood between 100 and 120 million people. By 1800 the figures had risen to almost 190 million, and by 1850 to 260 million. The population of England and Wales rose from 6 million in 1750 to 9 million in 1800. France grew from 18 million in 1715 to approximately 26 million in 1789. Russia's population increased from 19 million in 1722 to 29 million in 1766. Such extraordinary, sustained growth put new demands on all resources and considerable pressure on existing social organization.

The population expansion occurred across the Continent in both the country and the cities. There exists only a limited consensus of opinion about the causes of this growth. There was a clear decline in the death rate. There were fewer wars and somewhat fewer epidemics in the eighteenth century. Hygiene and sanitation also improved. Better medical knowledge and techniques were once thought to have contributed to the decline in deaths. This factor is now discounted because the more important medical advances came after the initial population explosion or would not have contributed directly to it. Rather, changes in the food supply itself may have provided the chief factor that allowed the population

these pressures and demands continued to increase. The society and the social practices of the old regime literally outgrew their traditional bounds.

The Industrial Revolution of the Eighteenth Century

The second half of the eighteenth century witnessed the beginning of the industrialization of the European economy. The Industrial Revolution constituted the achievement of sustained economic growth. Previously production had been of a limited character. The economy of a province or a country might grow, but it soon reached a plateau. However, since the late eighteenth century the economy of Europe has managed to expand in a relatively uninterrupted manner. Depressions and recessions have been of a temporary nature, and even during such economic downturns the Western economy has continued to grow. Industrialism at considerable social cost made possible more goods and more services than ever before in human history. Industrialism in Europe eventually overcame the economy of scarcity. Whether that process has in our own day brought the West to a new confrontation with resource scarcity is a question and problem for the present generation.

NEW METHODS OF TEXTILE PRODUCTION. Although eighteenth-century society was primarily devoted to agriculture, manufacturing permeated the countryside. The same peasants who tilled the land in spring and summer often spun thread or wove textiles in the winter. Under what is termed the *domestic* or *putting-out system*, agents of urban textile merchants took wool or other unfinished fibers to the homes of peasants, who spun it into thread. The agent then transported the thread to other peasants, who wove it into the finished product. The merchant sold the wares. In literally thousands of peasant cottages from Ireland to Austria, there stood either a spinning wheel or a handloom. Sometimes the spinner or weaver owned his own equipment, but more often than not by the middle of the century the

growth to become sustained. The improved and expanding grain production made one contribution. Another and even more important modification was the cultivation of the potato. This tuber was a product of the New World and came into widespread European production during the eighteenth century. On a single acre a peasant could raise enough potatoes to feed his family for an entire year. With such an assured food supply more children could be reared, and more could survive.

The impact of the population explosion can hardly be underestimated. It created new demands for food, goods, jobs, and services. It provided a new pool of labor. Traditional modes of production and living had to be devised. More people came to live in the countryside than could find employment there. Migration increased. There were also more people to be socially and politically discontent. And because the population growth fed on itself, all of

La Rochefoucault-Liancourt Sees the Domestic System in France

In the domestic system of production different peasants were responsible for separate processes in the manufacture of cloth. Some spun and others wove, but all worked in their own homes. Merchants then sold the finished cloth all over Europe and the New World. The production of cloth was undertaken by peasants in addition to their farming. La Rochefoucault observed the system in France in the 1780s.

I THEN *saw the material called cotton check* [cotonnades]. *There are all sorts of cotton manufacture made up at Rouen and in the area 15 leagues around it. The peasant who returns to the plough to work his fields, sits at his cotton frame and makes either* siamoises [common cotton goods] *or ticking or even white, very fine, cotton cloth. One must admire the activity of the Normans. This activity does not interfere at all with their daily work. Land is very dear and consequently very well cultivated. The farmer works on the land during the day and it is in the evening by the light of the lamp that he starts his other task. His workers and his family have to help. When they have worked all week they come into the town with horses or carts piled up with material. Goods are sold in the Hall, which is all that remains of the palace of the former Dukes of Normandy, on Thursdays. It is truly a wonderful sight. It takes place at surprising speed. Almost 800,000 francs worth of business is transacted between 6:00 and 9:00 in the morning. Among those who do the buying there are many agents who buy for merchants and then the goods pass to America, Italy and Spain. The majority goes to America.*

Francois De La Rochefoucauld-Liancourt, *Voyages en France* (1781–1783), cited and trans. in S. Pollard and C. Holmes (Eds.), *Documents of European Economic History* (London: Edward Arnold, 1968), Vol. 1, p. 91.

family by his own labor alone. It was necessary not merely for comfort but for economic survival that his wife spin or weave or knit and that his children be set to work as soon as they were physically able. The subsistence of these families depended upon their capacity to find makeshift ways of earning income beyond that from farming. Certain members of the family, including women, might migrate with the harvest. Children might ultimately go to the city to seek employment. If any of these sources of income failed, the entire family might fall into dependence on some form of charity or crime. As Olwen Hufton has written, it was a life in which "one lived daily from hand to mouth without provision for old age, sickness, incapacity to work, or disasters such as harvest failure or even the arrival of a baby."[1]

The domestic system of textile production was a basic feature of this family economy. However, by mid-century a series of production bottlenecks had developed within the domestic system. Demand for cotton textiles was growing more rapidly than production. This demand was felt particularly in Great Britain, where there existed a large domestic demand for cotton textiles from the growing population. There was a similar foreign demand upon British production from its colonies in North America. It was in response to this consumer demand for cotton textiles that the most famous inventions of the Industrial Revolution were devised.

Cotton textile weavers had the technical capacity to produce the quantity of fabric that was in demand. However, the spinners did not possess the equipment to produce as much thread as the weavers needed and could use. This imbalance had been created during the 1730s by James Kay's invention of the flying shuttle, which increased the productivity of the weavers. Thereafter various groups of manufacturers and merchants offered prizes for the invention of a machine to eliminate this bottleneck. About 1764 James Hargreaves (d. 1778)

[1] Allan Mitchell and Istvan Deak (Eds.), *Everyman in Europe: Essays in Social History* (Englewood Cliffs, N.J.: Prentice-Hall, 1974), vol. 2, p. 82.

merchant capitalist owned the machinery as well as the raw material.

What must be kept constantly in mind is the rather surprising fact that eighteenth-century industrial development took place within a rural setting. The peasant family living in a one- or two-room cottage was the basic unit of production rather than the factory. The family economy rather than the industrial factory economy characterized the century.

The small married farmer or peasant burdened by taxes and feudal dues could not support himself and his

invented the spinning jenny. Initially this machine allowed 16 spindles of thread to be spun, but by the close of the century its capacity had been increased to as many as 120 spindles.

The spinning jenny broke the bottleneck between the productive capacity of spinners and weavers, but it was still a piece of machinery that was used in the cottage. The invention that took cotton textile manufacture out of the home and put it into the factory was Richard Arkwright's (1732–1792) water frame, patented in 1769. It was a water-powered device designed to permit production of a purely cotton fabric rather than a cotton fabric containing linen fiber for durability. Eventually Arkwright lost his patent rights, and other manufacturers were able to use his invention freely. As a result, numerous factories sprang up in the countryside near streams that provided the necessary water power. From the 1780s onward the cotton industry could meet an ever-expanding demand. In the last two decades of the century cotton output increased by 800 per cent over the production of 1780. By 1815 cotton composed 40 per cent of the value of British domestic exports, and by 1830 just over 50 per cent.

The Industrial Revolution had commenced in earnest by the 1780s, but the full economic and social ramifica-tions of this unleashing of human productive capacity were not really felt until the early nineteenth century. The expansion of industry and the incorporation of new inventions often occurred rather slowly. For example, Edmund Cartwright (1743–1822) invented the power loom for machine weaving in the late 1780s. Yet not until the 1830s were there more power-loom weavers than hand-loom weavers in Britain. Nor did all of the social ramifications of industrialism appear immediately. The first cotton mills used water power, were located in the country, and rarely employed more than two dozen workers. Not until the late-century application of the steam engine, perfected by James Watt (1736–1819) in 1769, to the running of textile machinery could factories easily be located in or near existing urban centers. The steam engine not only vastly increased and regularized the available energy but also made possible the combination of urbanization and industrialization.

IRON PRODUCTION. Certain inventions and manufacturing improvements also had to await the next century for realization of their economic potential. The best example is that of the iron industry. Production of iron has been basic to modern industrial development. It constitutes the chief element for all heavy industry and has been the material out of which most productive machin-

OPPOSITE: This landscape painting by an unknown contemporary British artist portrays the pithead of an eighteenth-century coal mine in England. The machinery on the left included a steam engine that powered equipment either to bring the mined coal to the surface or to pump water from the mine. [Walker Art Gallery, Liverpool.]

ABOVE: Throughout most of the eighteenth century nearly all industrial manufacture took place in relatively small workshops such as the lead-casting shop illustrated in this print from the French *Encyclopedia*. Very large factories became established only quite late in the eighteenth century and early in the nineteenth.

ery itself has been manufactured. During the early eighteenth century British ironmongers produced somewhat less than twenty-five thousand tons annually. Three factors held back the production of the metal. Charcoal rather than coke was used to smelt the ore. Until the perfection of the steam engine, insufficient blasts could be achieved in the furnaces. Finally, the demand for iron was limited. The elimination of the first two problems eliminated the third.

In the course of the century British ironmongers began to use coke, and the steam engine provided new power for the blast furnaces. In 1784 Henry Cort (1740–1800) introduced a new puddling process that allowed more slag to be removed and a purer iron to be produced. These innovations achieved a better product at a lower cost. The demand for iron grew as its price became cheaper. By the early years of the nineteenth century British iron production amounted to over a million tons annually. The lower cost of iron in turn lowered the cost of steam engines and allowed them to be used more widely.

Industrial Leadership of Great Britain

Great Britain was the home of the Industrial Revolution and until the middle of the nineteenth century maintained the industrial leadership of Europe. Several factors contributed to the early start in Britain. The nation constituted the single largest free-trade area in Europe. The British possessed good roads and waterways without internal tolls or internal trade barriers. The country was endowed with rich deposits of coal and iron ore. The political structure was stable, and property was absolutely secure. Taxation was not especially heavy. In addition to existing domestic consumer demand, the British economy was also influenced by demand from the colonies in North America.

Finally, British society was relatively mobile by the standards of the time. Assuming a person had money or could earn money, he could rise socially. The British aristocracy would receive into its midst people who had amassed very large fortunes. No one of these factors preordained the British advance toward industrialism. However, the combination of them plus the progressive state of British agriculture provided the nation with the marginal advantage in the creation of a new mode of economic production.

While this economic development was occurring, people did not call it a *revolution*. That term came to be applied to the British economic phenomena only after the French Revolution. Then continental writers observed that what had taken place in Britain was the economic equivalent of the political events in France; hence the concept of an *industrial* revolution. It was revolutionary less in its speed, which was on the whole rather slow, than in its implications for the future of European society.

The means of production demanded new kinds of skills, new discipline in work, and a large labor force. The goods produced both met immediate consumer demand and created new demands. In the long run, industrialism clearly raised the standard of living and overcame the poverty experienced by the overwhelming majority of Europeans who lived during the eighteenth century and earlier. Industrialization provided human beings greater control over the forces of nature than ever known before. The wealth produced by industrialism upset the political structures of the old regime and led to reforms. The economic elite of the emerging industrial society would eventually challenge the political dominance of the aristocracy.

The Aristocracy

Despite the emerging Industrial Revolution, the eighteenth century remained par excellence the age of the aristocracy. The nobility of every country was the single wealthiest sector of the population; possessed the widest degree of social, political, and economic power; and set the tone of polite society. Land continued to provide the aristocracy with its largest source of income, but the role of the aristocrat was not limited to his estate. The influence of aristocrats was felt in every area of life. To be an aristocrat was a matter of birth and legal privilege. This much they had in common across the Continent. In almost every other respect they differed markedly from country to country.

The smallest, wealthiest, best-defined, and most socially responsible aristocracy resided in Great Britain. It consisted of about four hundred families whose eldest male member sat in the House of Lords. Through the corruptions of the electoral system these families also controlled a large number of seats in the House of Com-

---

Josiah Tucker Praises the New Use of Machinery in England

The extensive use of recently invented machines made the Industrial Revolution possible in England. This passage from a 1757 travel guide illustrates how the application of machines in various manufacturing processes was regarded by contemporaries as new and exciting.

Few *countries are equal, perhaps none excel, the English in the number of contrivances of their Machines to abridge labour. Indeed the Dutch are superior to them in the use and application of Wind Mills for sawing Timber, expressing Oil, making Paper and the like. But in regard to Mines and Metals of all sorts, the English are uncommonly dexterous in their contrivance of the mechanic Powers; some being calculated for landing the Ores out of the Pits, such as Cranes and Horse Engines; others for draining off superfluous Water, such as Water Wheels and Steam Engines; others again for easing the Expense of Carriage such as Machines to run on inclined Planes or Roads downhill with wooden frames, in order to carry many Tons of Material at a Time. And to these must be added the various sorts of Levers used in different processes; also the Brass Battery works, the Slitting Mills, Plate and Flatting Mills, and those for making Wire of different Fineness. Yet all these, curious as they may seem, are little more than Preparations or Introductions for further Operations. Therefore, when we still consider that at Birmingham, Wolverhampton, Sheffield and other manufacturing Places, almost every Master Manufacturer hath a new Invention of his own, and is daily improving on those of others; we may aver with some confidence that those parts of England in which these things are seen exhibit a specimen of practical mechanics scarce to be paralleled in any part of the world.*

Josiah Tucker, *Instructions to Travellers* (London: Privately Printed, 1757), p. 20

---

mons. The estates of the British nobility ranged from a few thousand to fifty thousand acres, from which they received rents. The nobles owned approximately one fourth of all the arable land in the country. Increasingly the money of the aristocracy was being invested in commerce, canals, urban real estate, mines, and sometimes in industrial ventures. Because only the eldest son inherited the title and the land, younger sons moved into commerce, the army, the professions, and the church. The British aristocracy levied taxes in Parliament and also paid

This famous portrait painting, Robert Andrews and His Wife, by the British artist Thomas Gainsborough (1728–1788) illustrates the peaceful and prosperous life of an English landowner. As the gun and dog indicate, he enjoyed considerable leisure time for sports such as hunting. [Reproduced by courtesy of the Trustees, The National Gallery, London.]

taxes. It had practically no significant legal privileges, but its direct or indirect control of local government gave it immense political power and social influence. The aristocracy quite simply dominated the society and the politics of the English counties.

The situation of the continental nobilities was less clear-cut. In France the nobility was divided between nobles of the sword and those of the robe. The former families enjoyed privileges deriving from military service; the latter had either received their titles from serving in the bureaucracy or had purchased them. The two groups had frequently quarreled in the past but tended to cooperate during the eighteenth century to defend their common privileges.

The French nobility was also divided between those who held office or favor with the royal court at Versailles and those who did not. The court nobility reaped the immense wealth that could be gained from holding high offices. The noble hold on such offices intensified over the course of the century. By the late 1780s appointments to the church, the army, the bureaucracy, and other profitable positions tended to go to nobles already established in court circles. Whereas these well-connected aristocrats were quite rich, other nobles who lived in the provinces were often rather poor. These *hobereaux*, as the poverty-stricken nobles were called, were sometimes little or no better off than wealthy peasants.

Despite differences in rank, origin, and wealth, all French aristocrats enjoyed certain hereditary privileges that set them apart from the rest of society. They were exempt from many taxes. For example, most French nobles did not pay the *taille*, which was the basic tax of the old regime. The nobles were technically liable for payment of the *vingtième*, or the twentieth, which resembled an income tax. However, by virtue of protests and legal procedures, the nobility rarely felt the entire weight of this tax. The nobles were not liable for the royal *corvées*, or labor donations, which fell on the peas-

The Aristocracy 529

ants. In addition to these exemptions, the approximately four hundred thousand French nobles could collect feudal dues from their tenants and enjoyed hunting and fishing privileges denied their tenants.

East of the Elbe River the character of the nobility became even more complicated and repressive. In Poland there were thousands of nobles, or *szlachta*, who after 1741 were entirely exempt from taxes. Until 1768 these Polish aristocrats possessed the right of life and death over their serfs. Most of the Polish nobility were relatively poor. The political power of the fragile Polish state resided in the few very rich nobles.

In Austria and Hungary the nobility continued to possess broad judicial powers over the peasantry through manorial courts.

In Prussia after the accession of Frederick the Great in

1740, the position of the *Junker* nobles became much stronger. Frederick's various wars required the support of his nobles. He drew his officers almost wholly from the *Junker* class. The bureaucracy was also increasingly composed of nobles. As in other parts of eastern Europe, the Prussian nobles enjoyed extensive judicial authority over the serfs.

In Russia the eighteenth century saw what amounted to the creation of the nobility. Peter the Great's linking of state service and noble social status through the Table of Ranks (1722) established among Russian nobles a self-conscious class identity that had not previously existed. Thereafter they stood united in their determination to resist compulsory state service. In 1736 Empress Ann reduced such service to a period of twenty-five years. In 1762 Peter III removed the liability for compulsory serv-

VXORI · OPTIMAE
ALBERTVS

OPPOSITE: The Scots brothers Adam dominated British decorative taste in the late eighteenth century. About 1770, Robert, the more important, planned this elegant drawing room for Home House in London. [The Courtauld Institute of Art and *Country Life,* London.]

ABOVE: The tomb of Countess Maria Christina in a church in Vienna by the Italian sculptor Antonio Canova (1757–1822). It represents the kind of artistic extravagance the European aristocracy could command in the late eighteenth century. [Eva Frodl-Kraft.]

ice entirely from the greatest nobles. In 1785, in the Charter of the Nobility, Catherine the Great granted an explicit legal definition of noble rights and privileges in exchange for assurances of voluntary state service from the nobility. The noble privileges included the right of transmitting noble status to one's wife and children, judicial protection of noble rights and property, considerable power over serfs, and exemption from personal taxes.

The Russian Charter of the Nobility constituted one aspect of the broader European-wide development termed the *aristocratic resurgence.* Throughout the century the various nobilities felt their social position and privileges threatened by the expanding power of the monarchies and the growing wealth of merchants, bankers, and other commercial groups. All nobilities attempted to preserve their exclusiveness by making entry into their

ranks and institutions more difficult. They also pushed for exclusively noble appointments to the officer corps of the armies, the bureaucracies, government ministries, and the church. In that manner nobles hoped to control the power of the monarchies.

On a third level the nobles attempted to use the authority of existing aristocratically controlled institutions against the power of the monarchies. These institutions included the British Parliament and on the Continent the French courts or *parlements,* local aristocratic estates, and provincial diets. Economically the aristocratic resurgence took the form of pressing the peasantry for higher rents or collecting long-forgotten feudal dues. There was a general tendency for the nobility to shore up its position by various appeals to traditional and often ancient privileges that had lapsed over the course of time. To contem-

The Aristocracy 531

bles controlled the municipal government and sat as judges in municipal courts.

There also existed a two-way migration of people between the country and the city. In many cities, especially of central and eastern Europe, rural day laborers lived in the towns and traveled outward to find their work. Other cities witnessed what has become a common modern phenomenon—migration of people from the countryside into the town to find work, better wages, and possibly a more exciting life. Thousands of men and women born in the country moved to the city to become domestic servants or artisans.

Fernand Braudel has rightly described cities as "so many electric transformers," which "increase tension, accelerate the rhythm of exchange and ceaselessly stir up men's lives."[2] The eighteenth century witnessed a considerable growth of towns. The tumult of the day and the revolutions with which the century closed had no small relationship to that urban expansion. London grew from about 700,000 inhabitants in 1700 to almost a million in 1800. By the time of the French Revolution the population of Paris stood over a half million. Berlin's population tripled over the course of the century, reaching 170,000 in 1800. St. Petersburg, founded in 1703, numbered over a quarter million inhabitants a century later. In addition to the growth of these capitals, the number of smaller urban units of 20,000–50,000 people increased considerably. However, this urban growth must be kept in perspective. Even in France and Great Britain probably somewhat less than 20 per cent of the population lived in cities. And the town of 10,000 inhabitants was much more common than the giant urban center.

Practically all of these urban conglomerates were nonindustrial cities. They grew and expanded for reasons other than the location of factories or other large manufacturing establishments. Only Manchester in England had experienced such industrial growth, and even its most spectacular expansion occurred after 1800.

2 Fernand Braudel, *Capitalism and Material Life, 1400–1800* (New York: Harper Torchbooks, 1973), p. 373.

poraries this aristocratic challenge to the monarchies and to the rising commercial classes constituted one of the most fundamental political facts of the day.

Cities

The Urban Setting

The influence of land and landed society extended to the cities of the old regime. The cities of the eighteenth century, like those of today, were dependent on the countryside for their food supply. The specter of famine or food shortages haunted cities. Their governments took great care to ensure adequate supplies of grain by building granaries and by paying careful attention to the fluctuation of bread prices. The nobility were not absent from the cities. They owned homes in the urban centers and often possessed large blocks of city real estate, which they developed as sources of new rents. Frequently no-

Eighteenth-century cities fall into three broad and rather imperfect categories. The first and most common were market centers for the exchange of goods, most of which were produced locally. These relatively small provincial centers might also provide the location for local courts and state administration. The second category consisted of commercial, trading, shipping, and financial centers. These included the major sea and river ports. Finally, there were the great capital cities, which were also frequently commercial centers. In a sense both of the latter kind of cities were the creation of the expanding bureaucratic states. All of their rulers wished to see trade and commerce prosper. The great taxing power of those monarchies meant that vast wealth flowed into the capitals.

With the exception of St. Petersburg, the cities of the

The Royal Crescent in Bath, England, is an example of fashionable eighteenth-century town planning. The elliptical crescent contained luxury housing for wealthy families who vacationed in Bath, which is on the site of a Roman town of the first century B.C. [British Tourist Authority, New York.]

eighteenth century were largely unplanned. A few urban developers might create elegant squares for the wealthy merchants or urban-dwelling aristocrats, but most cities simply expanded on the base of their medieval precursors. London had burned in 1666. Its reconstruction benefited from the planning and architecture of Sir Christopher Wren (1632–1723), but expansion was still quite haphazard. On the Continent many cities retained their medieval walls, within which and beyond which growth occurred. There was usually a central square with civic buildings or a cathedral or a fortress nearby. Quite often urban expansion pressed beyond the original city border and onto territory of non-urban landlords. The authority of the latter would then extend over that part of the city. Consequently some urban areas were governed by manorial courts and other institutions of the countryside.

There existed visible segregation between the urban rich and the urban poor. The former lived in fashionable townhouses, often constructed around newly laid-out green squares. The poorest town dwellers usually congregatated along the rivers. Small merchants and craftsmen lived above their shops. Whole families might live in a single room. Sanitary facilities such as now exist were still unknown. There was little pure water. Cattle, pigs, goats, and other animals walked the streets with the people. All reports on the cities of Europe during this period emphasize both the striking grace and beauty of the dwellings of the wealthy and the dirt, filth, and stench that filled the streets.

Despite the more obvious drawbacks, it was still in the cities that men and women from all walks and stations of life found entertainment and excitement. There were more modes of recreation in cities than in the countryside. The cities provided more opportunities for theater, gambling, womanizing, and husband hunting. The season of parties in London drew noble and upper-gentry families from all over England. Here marriages were sought, and friendships were renewed. The French nobility had learned to enjoy Paris after Louis XIV had initially forced them to come to his court at nearby Versailles. And many Russian nobles came to crave life in St. Petersburg after having first arrived under the compulsion of Peter the Great. The eighteenth-century townhouse as much as the country house provided the aristocracy with its public stage.

There was, however, another side to urban life. This was the lot of the poor, who often depended on charity in the city. Poverty was not a city problem; it was usually worse in the countryside. But in the city poverty more visibly manifested itself in terms of crime, prostitution, vagrancy, begging, and alchoholism. Many a young man or woman from the countryside migrated to the nearest city to seek a better life, only to discover poor housing, little food, disease, degradation, and finally death. It did not require the Industrial Revolution and the urban factory to make the cities into hellholes for the poor and the dispossessed. The full darkness of London life during the mid-century "gin age" when consumption of that liquor blinded and killed many poor people can be seen in the engravings of William Hogarth (1697–1764). Also contrasting with the serenity of the aristocratic and upper commercial-class life style were the public executions that took place all over Europe, the breaking of men and women on the wheel in Paris, and the public floggings in Russia. Brutality condoned and carried out by the ruling classes was quite simply a fact of everyday life.

Urban Classes

Social divisions were as marked in the cities of the eighteenth century as they were in the industrial centers of the nineteenth. At the top of the urban social structure was a generally small group of nobles, large merchants, bankers, financiers, clergy, and government officials. These men (and they were always men) controlled the political and economic affairs of the town. Normally they constituted a self-appointed and self-electing oligarchy who governed the city through its corporation or city council. These rights of self-government had normally been granted by some form of royal charter that gave the city corporation its authority and the power to select its

GIN LANE.

S. GRIPE PAWN. BROKER

KILMAN DISTILLER

GIN ROYAL

Gin cursed Fiend, with Fury fraught,
    Makes human Race a Prey.
It enters by a deadly Draught,
    And steals our Life away.

Virtue and Truth, driv'n to Despair,
    It's Rage compells to fly.
But cherishes, with hellish Care,
    Theft, Murder, Perjury.

Damn'd Cup! that on the Vitals preys,
    That liquid Fire contains,
Which Madness to the Heart conveys,
    And rolls it thro' the Veins.

In late eighteenth-century Vienna, apprehended prostitutes had to appear before courts, as in this print, where they were ordered to have their hair shorn and then sent out to sweep the streets. [Österreichische Nationalbibliothek, Vienna]

own members. In a few cities on the Continent, artisan guilds controlled the corporations, but more generally the councils were under the influence of the local nobility and the wealthiest commercial people.

THE MIDDLE CLASS. Another group in the city were the prosperous but not immensely wealthy merchants, tradesmen, bankers, and professional people. These were the most dynamic element of the urban population and constituted the persons traditionally regarded as the middle class or *bourgeoisie*. The concept of the middle class was much less clear-cut than that of the nobility. They had less wealth than most nobles but more than urban artisans. The middle-class people lived in the cities and towns, and their sources of income had little or nothing to do with the land. The middle class normally stood on the side of reform, change, and economic growth. The middle-class commercial figures—traders, bankers, manufacturers, and lawyers—often found their pursuit of both profit and prestige blocked by the privileges of the nobility and its social exclusiveness. The bourgeoisie also wanted more rational regulations for trade and commerce, as did some of the more progressive aristocrats.

During the eighteenth century the middle class and the aristocracy were on a collision course. The former often imitated the life style of the latter, and the nobles were increasingly embracing the commercial spirit of the middle class. The bourgeoisie was not rising to challenge the nobility; both were seeking to add new dimensions to their existing power and prestige. However, tradition and political connection gave the advantage to the nobility. Consequently, as the century passed, members of the middle class felt and voiced increasing resentment toward the aristocracy. That resentment became more bitter as the wealth and numbers of the *bourgeoisie* increased and the aristocratic control of political and ecclesiastical power became tighter. The growing influence of the nobility seemed to mean that the middle class would continue to be excluded from the political decisions of the day.

On the other hand, the middle class in the cities tended to fear the lower urban classes as much as they resented the nobility. The lower orders constituted a potentially violent element in the society, a potential threat to property, and in their poverty a drain on national resources. However, the lower orders were much more varied than either the city aristocracy or the middle class cared to admit.

Several examples of non-agricultural working-class skills can be shown. Printing shops produced the flood of eighteenth-century publications. Type was set and presses operated by hand, and the workmen were among the most highly skilled urban craftsmen. The picture is from the *Encyclopedia*. [Charles Farrell Collection.]

ARTISANS. The segment of the urban population that suffered from both the grasping of the middle class and the oligarchy of the nobility was that made up of the shopkeepers, the artisans, and the wage earners. These people constituted the single largest group in any city. The lives and experience of this class were very diverse. They included grocers, butchers, fishmongers, carpenters, cabinetmakers, smiths, printers, hand-loom weavers, and tailors, to give but a few examples. They had their own culture, values, and institutions. Like the peasants of the countryside, they were in many respects very conservative. Their economic position was highly vulnerable. If a poor harvest raised the price of food, their own businesses suffered.

The entire life of these artisans and shopkeepers centered on their work. They usually lived near or at their place of employment. Most of them worked in shops with fewer than a half dozen other craftsmen. Their primary institution had historically been the guild. By the eighteenth century the guilds rarely possessed the influence of their predecessors in medieval or early modern Europe.

Nevertheless the guilds were not to be ignored. They played a conservative role. They did not seek economic growth or innovation. They attempted to preserve the jobs and the skills of their members. The guilds still were able in many countries to determine who might and might not pursue a particular craft. They attempted to prevent too many people from learning a particular skill. The guilds also provided a framework for social and economic advancement. A boy might at an early age become an apprentice to learn a craft or a trade. After several years he would be made a journeyman. Still later, if successful and sufficiently competent, he might become a master. The artisan could also receive certain social benefits from the guilds. These might include aid for his family during sickness or the promise of admission for his son. The guilds constituted the chief protection for artisans against the operation of the commercial market. They were particularly strong in central Europe.

The artisan class with its generally conservative outlook maintained a rather fine sense of social and economic justice. These ideals were based largely on traditional practice. If the collective sense of what was economically "just" became offended, artisans frequently manifested their displeasure through the instrument of the riot. The most sensitive area was the price of bread. If a baker or a

grain merchant announced a price that was considered unjustly high, a bread riot might well ensue. Artisan leaders would confiscate the bread or grain and sell it for what the urban crowd considered a "just price." They would then give the money paid for the bread or grain to the baker or merchant. The possibility of bread riots acted as a restraint on the greed of merchants. Such disturbances represented a collective method of imposing the "just price" in place of the price set by the commercial marketplace. In other words, bread and food riots were not irrational acts of screaming hungry people but rather were highly ritualized social phenomena of the old regime and its economy of scarcity.

Other kinds of riots were also a basic characteristic of eighteenth-century society and politics. The riot was a way in which people excluded in every other way from the political processes could make their will known. Sometimes urban rioters were incited by religious bigotry. For example, in 1753 London Protestant mobs compelled the government ministry to withdraw an act for Jewish naturalization. In 1780 the same rabidly Protestant spirit manifested itself in the Gordon riots, named

[Text continued on page 542]

ABOVE: Barrel makers were included among the craftsmen of the eighteenth-century city. Jean Jacques De Boissieu of Lyons (1736–1810) made the etching. [Charles Farrell Collection.]

OPPOSITE: The skills of the blacksmith were required in both city and countryside. It is noteworthy that when Joseph Moxon, an English publisher and map-maker, wrote a series of *Mechanick Exercises: Or, the Doctrine of Handy-works,* published in parts between 1677 and 1683 and the first textbooks in any language on several of the major crafts, he began with the smith's trade because, as he said, "without the Invention of *Smithing* primarily, most other Mechanick Inventions would be at a stand: The Instruments or Tools that are used in them being either made of Iron, or of some other matter form'd by the help of Iron. But pray take notice, that by Iron I also mean Steel, it being originally Iron. . . . Some perhaps would have thought it more Policy to have introduced these *Exercises* with a more curious and less Vulgar Art than that of *Smithing*; but I am not of their opinion; for *Smithing* is (in all its parts) as curious a Handy-craft as any is . . ." This striking painting is by Joseph Wright of Derby (1734–1797). [Yale Center for British Art, New Haven.]

The fire and smoke in this contemporary drawing are billowing out of the furnace being used to produce sulphuric acid in an eighteenth-century Italian precursor of an industrial laboratory. The artist was Louis-Jacques Durambeau, and the original is in the Louvre. [Courtesy Charles Farrell.]

Bread was the single most important foodstuff in the eighteenth century, and its relative availability and price were constant social, economic, and political problems. This etching of an urban bakery from the *Encyclopedia* illustrates, from right to left, the kneading of the dough, the weighing of the loaves, the shaping of the loaves, and the baking of the bread. [The Granger Collection.]

Torture and public executions were still quite common during the eighteenth century. In some places, weights, as shown here, were used as a torture to extract information. Pressing was also a mode of execution for prisoners who refused to plead to the charges. [Bettmann Archive.]

The burning of Newgate Prison, London, in June 1780 during the anti-Catholic Gordon riots, which raged for several days. It is said that some three hundred prisoners were released and the unfortunate warden, Mr. Akerman, lost all his furniture in the fire. [The Granger Collection.]

after Lord George Gordon, who had raised the specter of an imaginary Catholic plot against England. In these riots and in food riots, violence was normally directed against property rather than against people. The rioters themselves were not "riffraff" but usually small shopkeepers, freeholders, craftsmen, and wage earners. They usually had no other purpose than to restore a traditional right or practice that seemed endangered. Nevertheless considerable turmoil and destruction could result from their actions.

During the last half of the century urban riots increasingly involved political ends. Though often simultaneous with economic disturbances, the political riot always had nonartisan leadership or instigators. In fact, the "crowd" of the eighteenth century was often the tool of the upper classes. In Paris the aristocratic Parlement often urged crowd action in their disputes with the monarchy. In Geneva middle-class citizens supported artisan riots against the local urban oligarchy. In Great Britain in 1792 the government turned out mobs to attack English sympathizers of the French Revolution. All of these and other various outbursts of popular unrest suggest that the crowd or mob did not first enter the European political and social arena during the Revolution in France.

A Society on the Edge of Modern Times

This chapter opened by describing eighteenth-century society as traditional, hierarchical, corporate, and privileged. These features had characterized Europe for hundreds of years. However, by the close of the eighteenth century each of these facets of European life had been undermined or challenged in a fundamental fashion from developments within the society itself. Europe stood on the brink of a new era in which the social, economic, and political relationships of centuries would be burst.

The society had remained traditional and corporate largely because of the economy of scarcity. The agricul-

tural and industrial revolutions would eventually overcome most scarcity in Europe and the West generally. The commercial spirit and values of the marketplace clashed with the traditional values and practices of peasants and guilds. The desire to make money and accumulate profits was hardly new, but beginning in the eighteenth century, it was permitted fuller play than ever before in European history. The commercial spirit was a major vehicle of social change and by the early nineteenth century led increasingly to conceiving of human beings as individuals rather than as members of communities.

The expansion of population provided further stimulus for change and challenge to tradition, hierarchy, and corporateness. Economic and social organization had presupposed a stable or declining population. The additional numbers of people meant new ways had to be devised to solve old problems. More people also meant more labor, more energy, and more minds contributing to the creation and solution of social difficulties. The improvements in health and the longer life span may have given that larger population a new sense of confidence. The social hierarchy had to accommodate itself to more people. Corporate groups, such as the guilds, had to confront the existence of an expanded labor force. Moreover the products and industries rising from the Industrial Revolution made the society and the economy much more complicated. Class structure and social hierarchy remained, but the boundaries became blurred. New wealth meant that birth would eventually become less and less of a determining factor in social relationships except in regard to the social role assigned to the two sexes.

Finally, the conflicting political ambitions of the monarchs, the nobilities, and the middle class generated innovation. The monarchs wanted to make their nations rich enough to wage war. As will be seen, this goal led them to attempt to interfere further with the privileges of the nobles. In the name of ancient rights the nobles attempted to secure and expand their existing social privileges by achieving further political power in the state. By making their privileges so exclusive, they helped to undermine the principle of privilege itself. The middle class in all of its diversity was growing wealthier from trade, commerce, and the practice of the professions. They wanted social prestige and political influence equal to their wealth. And they wanted the government to function in an efficient and businesslike manner. They resented privileges, frowned at hierarchy, and rejected tradition.

All of these factors meant that the society of the eighteenth century stood at the close of one era in European history and at the opening of another. What began to make contemporaries aware of that fact were the great wars of mid-century, the revolt of the British colonies in North America, and the intellectual currents of the Enlightenment.

SUGGESTED READINGS

C. B. A. BEHRENS, *The Ancien Régime* (1967). A brief account of life in France with excellent illustrations.

J. BLUM, *Lord and Peasant in Russia from the Ninth to the Nineteenth Century* (1961). A thorough and wide-ranging discussion.

F. BRAUDEL, *Capitalism and Material Life, 1400–1800* (1974). An investigation of the physical resources and human organization of preindustrial Europe.

P. DEANE, *The First Industrial Revolution* (1965). A well-balanced and systematic treatment.

F. FORD, *Robe and Sword: The Regrouping of the French Aristocracy After Louis XIV* (1953). An important treatment of the growing social tensions within the French nobility during the eighteenth century.

R. FORSTER, *The Nobility of Toulouse in the Eighteenth Century* (1960). A local study that displays the variety of noble economic activity.

R. FORSTER AND E. FORSTER, *European Society in the Eighteenth Century* (1969). An excellent collection of documents.

D. GEORGE, *London Life in the Eighteenth Century* (1925). A lively account.

D. V. GLASS AND D. E. C. EVERSLEY (Ed.), *Population in History: Essays in Historical Demography* (1965). Fundamental for an understanding of the eighteenth-century increase in population.

A. GOODWIN, *The European Nobility in the Eighteenth Century* (1953). Essays on the nobility in each state.

P. GOUBERT, *The Ancien Régime: French Society, 1600–1750*, tr. by Steve Cox (1974). A superb account of the peasant social order.

H. J. HABAKKUK AND M. POSTAN (Eds.), *The Cambridge Economic History of Europe* (1965). Separate chapters by different authors on major topics.

DOUGLAS HAY et al., *Albion's Fatal Tree: Crime and Society in Eighteenth-Century England* (1976). Separate essays on a previously little explored subject.

O. H. HUFTON, *The Poor of Eighteenth-Century France, 1750–1789* (1975). A brilliant study of poverty and the family economy.

E. L. JONES, *Agriculture and Economic Growth in England, 1650–1815* (1968). A good introduction to an important subject.

JOHN LOUGH, *An Introduction to Eighteenth-Century France* (1960). A systematic survey with good quotations (in French) from contemporaries.

S. POLLARD AND C. HOLMES, *Documents of European Economic History: The Process of Industrialization, 1750–1870* (1968). A very useful collection.

G. RUDÉ, *The Crowd in History, 1730–1848* (1964). This and the following work were pioneering studies.

G. RUDÉ, *Paris and London in the Eighteenth Century* (1973).

G. RUDÉ, *Europe in the Eighteenth Century* (1972). A survey with emphasis on social history.

C. WILSON, *England's Apprenticeship, 1603–1763* (1965). A broad survey of English economic life on the eve of industrialism.

A Declaration by the Representatives of the UNITED STATES OF AMERICA, in General Congress assembled.

When in the course of human events it becomes necessary for one people to dissolve the political bands which have connected them with another, and to assume among the powers of the earth the separate and equal station to which the laws of nature & of nature's god entitle them, a decent respect to the opinions of mankind requires that they should declare the causes which impel them to the separation.

We hold these truths to be self-evident; that all men are created equal, that they are endowed by their creator with equal rights, that among these are life, & liberty, & the pursuit of happiness; that to secure these rights, governments are instituted among men, deriving their just powers from the consent of the governed; that whenever any form of government becomes destructive of these ends, it is the right of the people to alter or to abolish it, & to institute new government, laying it's foundation on such principles & organising it's powers in such form, as to them shall seem most likely to effect their safety & happiness. prudence indeed will dictate that governments long established should not be changed for light & transient causes: and accordingly all experience hath shewn that mankind are more disposed to suffer while evils are sufferable than to right themselves by abolishing the forms to which they are accustomed. but when a long train of abuses & usurpations [begun at a distinguished period, &] pursuing invariably the same object, evinces a design to reduce them under absolute Despotism, it is their right, it is their duty, to throw off such government & to provide new guards for their future security. such has been the patient sufferance of these colonies; & such is now the necessity which constrains them to [expunge] their former systems of government. the history of the present king of Great Britain is a history of [unremitting] injuries and usurpations, [among which appears no solitary fact to contradict the uniform tenor of the rest [but all have] in direct object the establishment of an absolute tyranny over these states. to prove this, let facts be submitted to a candid world [for the truth of which we pledge a faith yet unsullied by falsehood]

544

21

Empire, War, and Colonial Rebellion

THE MIDDLE of the eighteenth century witnessed a renewal of European warfare on a worldwide scale. The conflict involved two separate but interrelated rivalries. Austria and Prussia fought for dominance in central Europe while Great Britain and France dueled for commercial and colonial supremacy. The wars were long, extensive, and very costly in both men and money. They resulted in a new balance of power on the Continent and on the high seas. Great Britain gained a world empire, and Prussia achieved the recognized status of a great power. Moreover the expense of these wars led every major European government after the Peace of Paris of 1763 to reconstruct in an extensive fashion their policies of taxation and finance. Those revised fiscal programs produced internal conditions for the monarchies of Europe that had most significant results for the rest of the century. They included the American Revolution, enlightened absolutism on the Continent, and a continuing financial crisis for the French monarchy.

Eighteenth-Century Empires
Periods of European Overseas Empires

Since the Renaissance, European contacts with the rest of the world have gone through four distinct stages. The first period was that of discovery, exploration, and initial conquest and settlement of the New World. It had closed by the end of the seventeenth century. The second era,

The American Revolution, proclaimed to the world through the Declaration of Independence, marked the climax of the eighteenth-century colonial wars and the beginning of a new democratic age in the West. This is the first page of Thomas Jefferson's rough draft of the declaration, with changes made by Benjamin Franklin and John Adams. [The Granger Collection.]

which is largely the concern of this chapter, was one of colonial trade rivalry among Spain, France, and Great Britain. The Anglo-French side of the contest has often been compared to a second hundred years' war. During this second period, which may be said to have closed during the 1820s, both the British colonies of the North American seaboard and the Spanish colonies of Central and South America emancipated themselves from European control. The third stage of European contact with the non-European world occurred in the late nineteenth century, when new formal empires involving European administration of indigenous peoples were carved out in Africa and Asia. Those nineteenth-century empires also included new areas of European settlement, such as Australia, New Zealand, and South Africa. The bases of these empires were trade, national honor, and military strategy. The last period of European empire came in the present century with the decolonization of peoples previously under European colonial rule.

During the four and one-half centuries before decolonization, Europeans exerted political dominance over much of the rest of the world. They frequently treated other peoples as social, intellectual, and economic inferiors. They ravaged existing cultures because of greed, religious zeal, or political ambition. These actions are major facts of European history and significant factors in the contemporary relationship of Europe and its former colonies. What allowed Europeans to exert such influence and domination for so long over so much of the world was not any innate cultural superiority but rather a technological supremacy closely related to naval power and gunpowder. Ships and guns allowed Europeans to exercise their will almost wherever they chose.

Mercantile Empires

Navies and merchant shipping were the keystone of the mercantile empires of the eighteenth century. These empires were meant to bring profit to a nation rather than to provide areas for settlement. The Treaty of Utrecht (1713) established the boundaries of empire

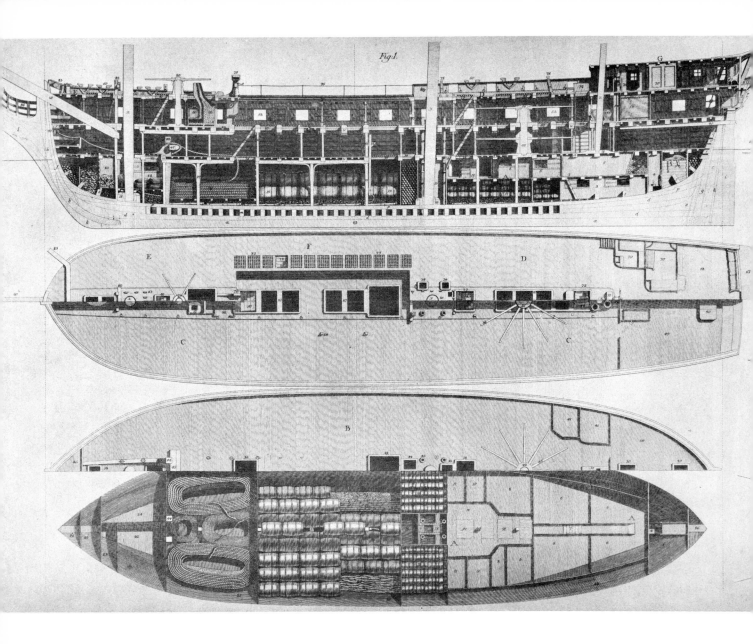

during the first half of the century. Except for Brazil, which was governed by Portugal, Spain controlled all the mainland of South America and in North America controlled Florida, Mexico, and California. The Spanish also governed the island of Cuba and half of Hispaniola. The British Empire consisted of the colonies along the North Atlantic seaboard, Nova Scotia, Newfoundland, Jamaica, and Barbados. Britain also possessed a few trading stations on the Indian subcontinent. The French domains covered the St. Lawrence River valley; the Ohio and Mississippi river valleys; the West Indian islands of St. Domingue, Guadeloupe, and Martinique; and stations in India. All

three powers also possessed numerous smaller islands in the Caribbean.

So far as any formal theory lay behind the conduct of these empires, it was mercantilism, that practical creed of hardheaded businessmen. The colonies were to provide markets and natural resources for the industries of the home country. In turn, the latter was to furnish military security and political administration for the colonies. For decades both sides assumed that the colonies were the inferior partner in the relationship. The mercantilist statesmen and traders regarded the world as an arena of scarce resources and economic limitation. They assumed

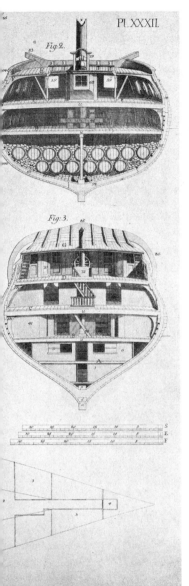

This is the group of plans of a typical frigate of the mid-eighteenth century included by the Swede Frederik Henrik af Chapman in his monumental album of ship plans, *Architectura Navalis Mercatoria* (Stockholm, 1768) as plate 32. Although frigates were primarily planned as small fighting ships—note the single row of gun ports on the main deck—they could also be adapted for storing the goods of trade. (It is virtually impossible to find a cutaway view of a purely merchant vessel before the nineteenth century.) [Courtesy of George Campbell.]

that one national economy could grow only at the expense of others. Colonies and the home country were to trade only with each other. To that end they attempted to forge trade-tight systems of national commerce through navigation laws, tariffs, bounties to encourage production, and prohibitions against trading with subjects of other monarchs. National monopoly was the ruling principle.

Mercantilist ideas had always been neater on paper than in practice. By the early eighteenth century these assumptions were held only in the vaguest manner. They stood too far removed from the economic realities of the colonies and perhaps from human nature. The colonial

and home markets simply failed to mesh. Spain could not produce sufficient goods for South America. Economic production in the British North American colonies challenged English manufacturing and led to British attempts to limit certain colonial industries, such as iron and hat making. Colonists of different countries wished to trade with each other. English colonists could buy sugar more cheaply from the French West Indies than from English suppliers. Traders and merchants from one nation always hoped to break the monopoly of another. For all these reasons the eighteenth century became the "golden age of smugglers."[1] The governments could not control the activities of all their subjects. Clashes among colonists could and did bring about conflict between governments.

Areas of Rivalry and Conflict

The Spanish Empire stood on the defensive throughout the century. It was a sprawling expanse of territory over which the Spanish government wished to maintain a commercial monopoly without possessing the capacity to do so. Spanish colonists looked to illegal imports from French and British traders to supply needed goods. Both France and Britain assumed a very aggressive stance toward the Spanish Empire because they viewed it as a vast potential market and a major source of gold. Their rivalry for intrusion into the mainland Spanish markets were matched by other conflicts in North America, India, and the West Indies.

Neither the French nor the British colonies of North America fit particularly well into the mercantile pattern of empire. Trade with these areas during the early part of the century was smaller than with the West Indies. These mainland colonies were settlements rather than arenas for economic exploitation. The French lands of Canada were quite sparsely populated. Relations with the Indians were troublesome. The economic interests and the development of the colonies were not wholly com-

1 Walter Dorn, *Competition for Empire, 1740–1763* (New York: Harper, 1940), p. 266.

patible with those of the home countries. Nevertheless flash points existed between France and Britain on the North American continent. Their colonists quarreled endlessly with each other. Both groups of settlers were jealous over rights to the lower St. Lawrence River valley, upper New England, and later the Ohio River valley. There were other rivalries over fishing rights, fur trade, and relationships with the Indians.

Unlike North America or the West Indies, India was neither the home of migrating Europeans nor an integral part of their imperial schemes. The Indian subcontinent was an area where both France and Britain traded through privileged, chartered companies that enjoyed a legal monopoly. The East India Company was the English institution; the French equivalent was the Compagnie des Indes. The trade of India and Asia figured only marginally in the economics of empire. Some bullion gained by trade or piracy in the West Indies was shipped to India, where it was used to purchase cotton cloth that was shipped to England and then used to purchase slaves in Africa for the West Indies. The commercial problem with the states of India was that Europeans produced little or nothing wanted in the region.

Nevertheless throughout the century trade and involvement on the subcontinent continued. Enterprising Europeans always hoped that in some fashion profitable commerce with India might be developed. Others regarded India as a springboard into the even larger potential market of China. The original European footholds in India were trading posts called *factories*. They existed through privileges granted by the various Indian governments. Two circumstances arose during the middle of the eighteenth century to change this situation. First, in several of the Indian states there occurred decay in the indigenous administration and government. Second, Joseph Dupleix (1697–1763) for the French and Robert Clive (1725–1774) for the British saw these developments as opportunities for expanding the control of their companies. To maintain their own security and to expand their privileges, the companies began to fill the power

---

An English Mercantilist Views Trade Between Nations

It is not difficult for us to see mercantilism as a selfish and limited idea of what commerce should be. But seventeenth- and eighteenth-century theorists found it quite defensible. Its major tenet was the desirability of increasing the exports of a nation. This British pamphlet of 1721 praises the kind of trade that allows exports to grow and creates employment at home. It criticizes the trade that creates imports or that imports goods like those already produced at home or that could be produced at home.

I. THAT Trade which exports Manufactures made of the sole Product or Growth of the Country, is undoubtedly good . . . as much as those Exports amount to, so much is the clear Gain of the Nation.

II. That Trade which helps off the Consumption of our Superfluities, is also visibly advantageous . . . so much as the exported Superfluities amount unto, so much also is the clear National Profit.

III. The importing of foreign Materials to be manufactured at home, especially when the Goods, after they are manufactured, are mostly sent abroad, is also, without dispute, very beneficial. . . .

. . . .

VI. A Trade may be call'd good which exchanges Manufactures for Manufactures, and Commodities for Commodities. . . . [B]y this means numbers of People are employ'd on both sides, to their mutual Advantage.

. . . .

*VIII. The carrying of Goods from one foreign Country to another, is a profitable Article in Trade. . . .
But a Trade is disadvantageous to a Nation,*

1. Which brings in things of mere Luxury and Pleasure, which are entirely, or for the most part, consumed among us. . . .

2. Much worse is that Trade which brings in a Commodity that is not only consumed amongst us, but hinders the consumption of the like quantity of ours. . . .

3. That Trade is eminently bad, which supplies the same Goods as we manufacture ourselves, especially if we can make enough for our Consumption. . . .

4. The Importation upon easy Terms of such Manufactures as are already introduc'd in a Country, must be of bad consequence, and check their progress. . . .

The British Merchant: A Collection of Papers, Charles King, (Ed.), cited in D. B. Horn and Mary Ransome, *English Historical Documents, 1715–1783* (London: Eyre and Spottiswoode, 1957), pp. 492–493.

The Custom House in Dublin, Ireland, is one of the most elegant political buildings of Europe. Its fine architecture suggests the importance that eighteenth-century governments attached to trade and the regulation of trade. [Irish Tourist Board, New York.]

vacuum and in effect took over the government of some regions. Each group of Europeans hoped to checkmate the other.

STRUGGLE FOR THE WEST INDIES. The heart of the eighteenth-century colonial rivalry was the West Indies. These islands, close to the American continents, constituted the jewels of empire. Here the colonial powers pursued their greedy ambitions in close proximity to each other. The West Indies raised tobacco, cotton, indigo, coffee, and sugar, for which there existed strong markets in Europe. Sugar in particular had become a product of standard consumption rather than a luxury. It was used in coffee, tea, and cocoa, for making candy and preserving fruits, and in the brewing industry. There seemed no limit to its uses. Sugar was also important to the domestic economy of Europe. Sugar refining had become a major industry in France. Sugar and tobacco figured prominently in the reexport industry. For example, large quantities of tobacco were shipped from Scotland to the Continent.

Basic to the economy of the West Indies as well as to that of South America and the British colonies on the south Atlantic seaboard of North America was the institution of slavery. Hundreds of thousands of slaves were imported into the Americas during the eighteenth century. Planters could not attract sufficient quantities of free labor to these areas. They became wholly dependent upon slaves. Slavery and the slave trade touched most of the economy of the transatlantic world. Cities such as Newport, Rhode Island; Liverpool, England; and Nantes,

France, enjoyed prosperity that rested almost entirely on the slave trade. All of the shippers who handled cotton, tobacco, and sugar were dependent on slavery, though they might have no direct contact with the institution. There was a general triangle of trade that consisted of carrying goods to Africa to be traded for slaves, who were then taken to the West Indies, where they were traded for sugar and other tropical produce, which were then shipped to Europe. Not all ships necessarily covered all three legs of the triangle. Another major trade pattern existed between New England and the West Indies. New England rum or ship stores were traded for sugar.

Within the rich commerce and agriculture of the West Indies there existed three varieties of colonial rivalry. Producers of different nations were intensely jealous of each other. The quantity of sugar being raised had expanded so as to depress the price in Europe. Consequently one group of planters hoped not to conquer the lands of their competitors but rather to destroy the productive capacity of those islands. There was a second form of rivalry among shippers in the Caribbean. Every captain hoped to transport as much sugar as possible to Europe. Finally, the West Indies possessions of France and Britain provided excellent bases for penetration of the trade of the Spanish Empire. Many French and British

Eighteenth-Century Empires 549

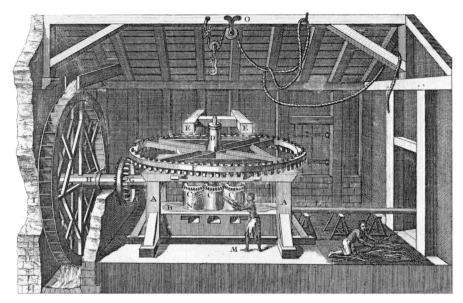

An eighteenth-century sugar press in Cuba. At this period it was tended by slaves. Most of the sugar would eventually end up in Europe where there was a growing market for the product. [Bettmann Archive.]

On a French West Indian plantation slaves pick cotton on the right while other slaves on the left remove the seeds from the fiber. The particular variety of cotton shown in this engraving grew on shrubs rather than on the bushes grown in the American south. [The Granger Collection.]

ship captains in the West Indies were admitted smugglers, and some were little better than pirates.

The close interrelationship of the West Indies and European economies meant that significant numbers of British, French, and Spanish subjects had an interest in the area. This "West Indian Interest," as it was called in England, consisted of absentee plantation owners, shippers, insurers, merchants, bankers, owners of domestic industry dependent on West Indian products, and all of those involved in the slave trade. In Great Britain it was an articulate and well-organized pressure group. In 1739 the West India Interest and political enemies of Robert Walpole succeeded in driving Britain into war with Spain, the War of Jenkins' Ear.

The Treaty of Utrecht (1713) included two special privileges for Great Britain in regard to the Spanish Empire. The British received a thirty-year contract known as the *asiento* to furnish slaves to the Spanish. Britain was also given the right to send one ship each year to the trading fair at Portobello, a major Caribbean seaport on the Panamanian coast. These two privileges allowed British traders and smugglers potential inroads into the Spanish market. Little but friction arose from these rights. The annual ship to Portobello was often supplied with additional goods during the night as it lay in port. Much to the chagrin of the British, the Spanish government took its own alleged trading monopoly seriously and maintained coastal patrols, which boarded and searched English vessels to look for contraband.

In 1731 during one such boarding operation there was a fight, and an English captain named Robert Jenkins had his ear cut off by the Spaniards. Thereafter he carried about his severed ear preserved in a jar of brandy. This incident was of little importance until 1738, when Jenkins appeared before the British Parliament, reportedly brandishing his ear as an example of Spanish atrocities to British merchants in the West Indies. The British merchant and West Indies interests put great pressure on Parliament to do something about Spanish intervention in their trade. Robert Walpole attempted to reach a solution through negotiations. However, Parliament—and especially members who believed that the war would drive Walpole from office—refused all accommodation. In late 1739 Great Britain went to war with Spain.

At the outbreak of hostilities France under the administration of Cardinal Fleury stood ready to profit from the British–Spanish conflict. They expected to see British trade harmed and eventually to receive Spanish commercial favors for aid. None of the major European powers except Britain had any present grudge against France. The years of Fleury's cautious policy were about to pay off. Then quite literally overnight the situation on the Continent changed.

Mid-Century Wars
The War of the Austrian Succession (1740–1748)

In December 1740, after possessing the throne of Prussia for less than seven months, Frederick II ordered his troops to occupy the Austrian province of Silesia. The invasion shattered the provisions of the Pragmatic Sanction and upset the continental balance of power as established by the Treaty of Utrecht. The young king of Prussia had treated the House of Hapsburg simply as another German state rather than as the leader of the Holy Roman Empire. The province of Silesia itself rounded out Prussia's possessions, and Frederick was determined to keep his ill-gotten prize. In 1740 the other European states were not sure whether to consider the Prussian invasion the act of a great power or that of a mere aggressive upstart. The wars of the next quarter century affirmed the former judgment.

Maria Theresa was twenty-three years old and had succeeded to the Austrian crown only two months before Frederick's move. Her army was weak, her bureaucracy inefficient, and the loyalty of her subjects uncertain. She herself was inexperienced and was more usually guided by the values of piety than by hardheaded statecraft. Yet she succeeded in rallying to her side the Magyars of Hungary and the aristocratic leaders of her other domains. They were genuinely sympathetic to her plight and inspired by her courage. Maria Theresa's great achievement was not the reconquest of Silesia, which eluded her, but rather the preservation of the Hapsburg Empire as a major political power.

The seizure of Silesia could have marked the opening of a general hunting season on Hapsburg holdings and the beginning of revolts by Hapsburg subjects. Instead it proved the occasion for new political allegiances. Those new loyalties, particularly between the Magyars and the empress, were not gained merely through heroism but more specifically by grants of privileges to the nobilities of the realm. The empress recognized Hungary as the most important of her crowns and promised the Magyars considerable local autonomy. However, the Hapsburg state was preserved at great cost to the power of the central monarchy. It would never become a unified modern political entity.

The war over the Austrian succession and the British–Spanish commercial conflict could have remained separate disputes. They were neither logically nor necessarily politically related. What ultimately united them was the role of France. Cardinal Fleury understood that the long-range interests of France lay in the direction of commercial growth. However, just as British merchant interests had pushed Robert Walpole into war, a group of court aristocrats led by the Comte de Belle Isle compelled the elderly Fleury to abandon his planned attack on British trade and to support the Prussian aggression against Austria. This proved to be one of the most fateful decisions in French history.

Even though the Hapsburgs had been the historic enemy of France, a war against Austria was not in the French interest in 1741. In the first place, aid to Prussia had the effect of consolidating a new powerful state in Germany. That new power could, and indeed later did, endanger France. Second, the French move against Austria brought Great Britain into the continental war. The

Prince Frederick Discusses Statecraft and European Affairs

King Frederick William I of Prussia thought at times he had reason for concern about the qualities of his flute-playing, philosophizing son, Prince Frederick. He need not have worried. The young prince was already able to write this hardnosed essay in 1738, two years before he became King Frederick II. He states the view common at the time that a monarch normally seeks to increase the power of his state. He also suggests that the major states of Europe were not in a healthy balance. Two years later he would follow up these thoughts by invading Silesia.

"IT IS *an unshaken principle among kings to aggrandize themselves as much as their power will permit; and, though such aggrandizement must be subject to different modifications, and infinitely varied according to the situation of princes, the power of neighboring states, or fortunate opportunities, the principle is not the less unchangeable, and is never abandoned by monarchs. Their pretended fame is part of this system. In a word, it is necessary they should increase in greatness."*

.   .   .   .

From what has been said, it will be easy to perceive that the political body of Europe is in a perilous situation. It is deprived of its due equilibrium, and is in a state in which it cannot long remain, without great risk. The political body resembles the human body, which can only subsist by a mixture of equal quantities of the acid and the alkali. Whenever one of these two substances predominates, the body is made sensible of it, and the health is considerably injured: should that substance continue to increase, it may finally cause the destruction of the machine. Thus, whenever the policy and prudence of the princes of Europe lose sight of the maintenance of a just balance, between the principal powers, it is felt by the constitution of the whole body-politic. Violence on the one side, weakness on the other; the desire of invading on the one, and on the other the inability to prevent invasion. The most puissant [powerful] gives law, and the feeble are under the necessity of adding their signature. All finally concur in augmenting disorder and confusion. Force acts like an impetuous torrent, passes its bounds, carries everything with it, and exposes this unfortunate body-politic to the most fatal revolutions.

Frederick the Great, "Considerations on the Present State of the Body-Politic of Europe" (1738), in *Posthumous Works of Frederic II, King of Prussia*, trans. by Thomas Holcroft (London: G. G. J. and J. Robinson 1789), Vol. 4, pp. 364–365, 381–382.

Maria Theresa of Austria (seated right) and her husband, Emperor Francis I (seated left), with their very large family. Her son and successor, Joseph II, is the tall adolescent near her. The artist was Martin Meytens (1695–1770), court painter in Vienna. [Kunsthistorisches Museum, Vienna.]

British as usual wanted to see the Low Countries remain in friendly hands. In the eighteenth century that policy required continued Hapsburg control of the Austrian Netherlands. In 1744 the British–French conflict expanded beyond the Continent, as France decided to support Spain against Britain. As a result, French military and economic resources became badly divided. France could not bring sufficient strength to the colonial struggle. Having chosen to continue a struggle from the past with Austria, France lost the struggle for the future against Great Britain.

By 1748 the war had become a military stalemate for

all concerned. Austria had not been able to regain Silesia, but it had fended off further aggression from other German states. The French army, led by Marshal Maurice de Saxe (1696–1750), won a series of splendid victories over the British and Austrians in the Netherlands during 1747 and 1748. Britain, for its part, had pursued a very suc-

Empire, War, and Colonial Rebellion

cessful colonial campaign. Forces in America captured the fortress of Louisburg at the mouth of the St. Lawrence River. The British more than held their own on the Indian subcontinent. Warfare on French commerce had been highly effective. These victories overseas compensated for the poor showing on the Continent. Consequently the war was brought to a close by the Treaty of Aix-la-Chapelle (1748). In effect it restored conditions that had existed prior to the war, with the exception that Prussia retained Silesia. Spain renewed the *asiento* agreement with Great Britain. All observers believed that the treaty constituted a truce rather than a permanent peace.

The Diplomatic Revolution of 1756

Before the rivalries again erupted into war, a dramatic shift of alliances took place. In 1756 Prussia and Great Britain signed the Convention of Westminster. It was a defensive alliance aimed at preventing the entry of foreign troops into the Germanies. Frederick II feared invasions by both Russia and France. The convention meant that Great Britain, the ally of Austria since the wars of Louis XIV, had now joined forces with Austria's major eighteenth-century enemy.

Maria Theresa was despondent over this development. However, her foreign minister, Count Wenzel Anton Kaunitz (1711–1794), was delighted. This brilliant diplomat and servant of the Hapsburg dynasty had long hoped for an alliance between Austria and France for the dismemberment of Prussia. The Convention of Westminster made this alliance, unthinkable a few years earlier, possible. France was agreeable because Frederick had not consulted it before coming to his understanding with Britain. Consequently later in 1756 France and Austria signed a defensive alliance. Kaunitz had succeeded in completely reversing the direction of French foreign policy from Richelieu through Fleury. France would now fight to restore Austrian supremacy in central Europe. But the French monarchy, though having changed its German ally, would remain diverted from its commercial interests on the high seas.

Frederick the Great of Prussia in his later years displayed in his face the burden of personal hardship that his ambitious wars had brought to him and to his nation. Yet he did succeed in making Prussia a major power. [Culver Pictures.]

The Seven Years' War (1756–1763)

The Treaty of Aix-la-Chapelle had brought peace in Europe, but the conflict between France and Great Britain continued unofficially on the colonial front. There were continuous clashes between American and French settlers in the Ohio River valley and in upper New England. These were the prelude to what is known as the French and Indian War in American history. These colonial skirmishes would certainly have led in time to a broader conflict. However, once again the factor that opened a general European war that extended into a colonial theater was the action of the king of Prussia.

In August 1756 Frederick II invaded the kingdom of

Both the British general James Wolfe and the French general Montcalm died at the Battle of Quebec in September 1759, in which the British forces won the crucial encounter and thus drove the French out of their North American empire. The picture of the death of Wolfe is an engraving from a famous painting by the American artist Benjamin West (1738–1820). [Culver Pictures.]

Saxony. He regarded this invasion as a continuation of the defensive strategy of which the Convention of Westminster had been a part. Frederick believed that there existed an international conspiracy on the part of Saxony, Austria, and France to undermine and destroy Prussian power. The attack on Saxony was in Frederick's mind a preemptive strike. The invasion itself created the very destructive alliance that Frederick feared. In the spring of 1757 France and Austria made a new alliance dedicated to the destruction of Prussia. They were eventually joined by Sweden, Russia, and the smaller German states.

Prussia was surrounded by enemies, and Frederick II confronted the gravest crisis of his career. It was after these struggles that he came to be called Frederick the Great. He won several initial battles, the most famous of which was Rossbach, on November 5, 1757. Thereafter, however, the Prussians experienced a long series of defeats that might have destroyed the state. Two factors in addition to Frederick's stubborn leadership saved Prussia. The first was major financial aid from Great Britain. The British contributed as much to the Prussian war effort as did the Prussian treasury itself. Second, in 1762 Empress Elizabeth of Russia died. Her successor was Tsar Peter III (he also died in the same year), whose admiration for Frederick knew almost no bounds. He immediately made peace with Prussia, thus relieving the country of one enemy and allowing it to hold its own against Austria and France. The treaty of Hubertusburg of 1763 closed the continental conflict with no significant changes in prewar borders. Silesia remained Prussia's province, and Prussia clearly stood in the ranks of the great powers.

The survival of Prussia was less impressive to the rest of Europe than the victories of Great Britain over France in every theater of conflict. The architect of this victory was William Pitt the Elder (1708–1778). He came from a family that had made its fortune from commerce. His grandfather, "Diamond" Pitt, had laid the foundations of the family's wealth by commercial ventures in India. The grandson was no less dedicated to the growth of British trade and economic interests. Pitt was a person of colossal ego and administrative genius. From the time of the War of Jenkins' Ear he had criticized the government as being too timid in its colonial policy. He had been strongly critical of all continental involvement, including the Convention of Westminster. During the 1750s he had gained the favor of the London merchant interest. Once war had commenced again, these groups clamored for his appointment to the cabinet. In 1757 he was named prime minister, and he drew into his own hands all the power he could grasp. He was confident, as he told friends, that he and only he could lead the nation to victory.

Once in office Pitt changed his attitude toward British involvement on the Continent. He came to regard the German conflict as a way to divert French resources and attention from the colonial struggle. He pumped huge financial subsidies to Frederick the Great and later boasted of having won America on the plains of Germany. North America was the center of Pitt's real concern. Put quite simply, he wanted all of North America east of the Mississippi for Great Britain, and that was exactly what he won. In 1759 on the Plains of Abraham at Quebec the British army under General James Wolfe decisively defeated the French under Marshal Louis Joseph Montcalm. The French Empire in Canada had come to an end.

However, Pitt's colonial vision extended beyond the St. Lawrence valley and the Great Lakes basin. The major islands of the French West Indies fell to the British fleets. Income from the sale of captured sugar helped finance the British war effort. British slave interests captured the bulk of the French slave trade. Between 1755

France Turns Over French Canada to Great Britain

The Treaty of Paris (1763) concluded the French and English portion of the Seven Years' War. In this particular clause the previously French portion of Canada was turned over to Great Britain.

His *Most Christian Majesty [the King of France] renounces all pretensions which he has heretofore formed or might have formed to Nova Scotia or Acadia in all its parts, and guarantees the whole of it, and with all its dependencies, to the King of Great Britain: Moreover, His Most Christian Majesty cedes and guarantees to his said Britannic Majesty, in full right, Canada, with all its dependencies, as well as the island of Cape Breton, and all the other islands and coasts in the gulf and river of St. Laurence, and in general, everything that depends on the said countries, land, islands, and coasts, with the sovereignty, property, possession, and all rights acquired by treaty, or otherwise, which the Most Christian King and the Crown of France have had till now over the said countries, lands, islands, places, coasts, and their inhabitants, so that the Most Christian King cedes and makes over the whole to the said King, and to the Crown of Great Britain, and that in the most ample manner and form, without restriction, and without any liberty to depart from the said cession and guarantee under any pretence, or to disturb Great Britain in the possessions above mentioned. His Britannic Majesty, on his side, agrees to grant the liberty of the Catholic Religion, to the inhabitants of Canada: he will, in consequence, give the most precise and effectual orders, that his new Roman Catholic subjects may profess the worship of their religion according to the rights of the Romish Church, as far as the laws of Great Britain permit.*

H. Butterfield (Ed.), *Select Documents of European History, 1715–1920* (London: Methuen, 1931), pp. 29–30.

William Pitt the Elder guided the armies and navies of Great Britain to a stunning victory in the Seven Years' War. His portrait is from the studio of the artist Richard Brompton. [The Granger Collection.]

George II (1727–1760) was the British monarch during the great wars of the mid-century. The painting is by Thomas Worlidge, and the medal is by E. Hannibal. [The Granger Collection.]

and 1760 the value of the French colonial trade fell from thirty million to four million livres. On the Indian subcontinent the British forces under the command of Robert Clive defeated the French in 1757 at the Battle of Plassey. This victory opened the way for the eventual conquest of Bengal and later all of India by the British East India Company. Never had Great Britain or any other European power experienced such a complete worldwide military victory.

The Peace of Paris of 1763 reflected somewhat less of

a victory than Britain had won in the battle field. Pitt was no longer in office. George III (1760–1820) had succeeded to the British throne in 1760. He and Pitt had quarreled over policy, and the minister had departed. His replacement was the earl of Bute, a favorite of the new monarch. The new minister was responsible for the peace settlement. Britain received all of Canada, the Ohio River valley, and the eastern half of the Mississippi River valley. Britain partially surrendered the conquest in India by giving France footholds at Pondichéry and Chandernagore. The sugar islands of Guadeloupe and Martinique were restored to the French. Britain could have gained more territory only with further war involving more taxation, against which the country was already complaining.

The Seven Years' War had been a great conflict. Tens of thousands of soldiers had been killed or wounded. Major battles had been fought around the globe. At great internal sacrifice Prussia had permanently wrested Silesia from Austria and had turned the Holy Roman Empire into an empty shell. Hapsburg power now depended on the Hungarian domains. France, though still possessing sources of colonial income, was no longer a great colonial power. The Spanish Empire remained largely intact, but the British were still determined to penetrate its markets. On the Indian subcontinent the British East India Company was in a position to continue to press against the decaying indigenous governments and to impose its own authority. The results of that situation would be felt until the middle of the twentieth century. In North America the British government faced the task of organizing its new territories. From this time until World War II, Great Britain assumed the status not simply of a European but also of a world power.

The quarter century of warfare also caused a long series of domestic crises among the European powers. The French defeat impressed many people in the nation with a new sense of the necessity for political and administrative reform. The financial burdens of the wars had astounded all contemporaries. Every power had to begin to find ways to increase revenues to pay the war debt and to finance preparation for the next combat. Nowhere did this search for revenue lead to more far-ranging consequences than in the British colonies in North America.

The American Revolution and Europe
Events in the British Colonies

The revolt of the British colonies in North America was an event in transAtlantic and European history. It erupted from problems of revenue collection common to all the major powers after the Seven Years' War. The War of the American Revolution was a continuation of the conflict between France and Great Britain. The French support for the Americans deepened the existing financial and administrative difficulties of the monarchy.

The political ideals of the Americans had roots in the thought of John Locke and other English political theorists. The colonists raised questions of the most profound nature about monarchy, political authority, and constitutionalism. These questions had ramifications for all European states. Part of the difficulties from the British side arose because of the characteristic European political friction between the monarch and the aristocracy. Finally, the Americans were seen by many Europeans as inaugurating a new era in the history of European peoples and indeed of the world.

After the Treaty of Paris of 1763 the British government faced three imperial problems. The first was the sheer cost of empire, which the British felt they could no longer carry alone. The national debt had risen considerably and taxation had done likewise. The American colonies had been the chief beneficiaries of the conflict. It made rational sense that they should henceforth bear part of the cost of their protection and administration. The second problem was the vast expanse of new territory in North America that the British had to organize. There was all the land from the mouth of the St. Lawrence River to the Mississippi River with its French settlers and, more important, its Indian possessors.

The "Boston Massacre" of March 5, 1770 was depicted in an engraving quickly made and put on sale by Paul Revere. [The Granger Collection.]

The BLOODY MASSACRE perpetrated in King—Street BOSTON on March 5th 1770 by a party of the 29th REGT

Unhappy Boston! see thy Sons deplore,
Thy hallow'd Walks besmear'd with guiltless Gore.
While faithless P—n and his savage Bands,
With murd'rous Rancour stretch their bloody Hands;
Like fierce Barbarians grinning o'er their Prey,
Approve the Carnage and enjoy the Day.

If scalding drops from Rage from Anguish Wrung
If speechless Sorrows lab'ring for a Tongue,
Or if a weeping World can ought appease
The plaintive Ghosts of Victims such as these;
The Patriot's copious Tears for each are shed,
A glorious Tribute which embalms the Dead.

But know Fate summons to that awful Goal,
Where Justice strips the Murd'rer of his Soul:
Should venal C—ts the scandal of the Land,
Snatch the relentless Villain from her Hand,
Keen Execrations on this Plate inscrib'd,
Shall reach a Judge who never can be brib'd.

The unhappy Sufferers were Messrs. Sam. Gray, Sam. Maverick, Jam. Caldwell, Crispus Attucks & Pat. Carr
Killed. Six wounded; two of them (Christr. Monk & John Clark) Mortally

Engrav'd Printed & Sold by Paul Revere Boston

As the British ministers pursued solutions to these difficulties, a third and more serious issue arose. The British colonists in North America resisted the taxation and were suspicious about the imperial policies toward the western lands. Consequently the British had to search for new ways to exert their authority over the colonies. The Americans became increasingly resistant because their economy had outgrown the framework of mercantilism, because the removal of the French relieved them of dependence on the British army, and because they believed that their liberty was in danger.

The British drive for revenue commenced in 1764 with the passage of the Sugar Act under the ministry of George Grenville (1712–1770). The measure was designed to produce more revenue from imports into the colonies. Smugglers who violated the law were to be tried in admiralty courts without juries. The next year Parliament passed the Stamp Act, which put a tax on legal documents and certain other items such as newspapers. The British considered these taxes legal because they had been passed by Parliament. The taxes seemed just because the money was to be spent in the colonies. The Americans responded that they had the right to tax themselves and that they were not represented in Parliament. Moreover, because most of the colonial charters had been granted by the king, the Americans claimed that their legal connection to Britain was through the monarch rather than the Parliament. The expenditure in the colonies of the revenue levied by Parliament did not reassure the colonists. They feared that if colonial government was financed from outside, they would lose control over their government. In October 1765 the Stamp Act Congress met in America and drew up a protest to the crown. There was much disorder in the colonies, particularly in Massachussetts. The colonists agreed to refuse to import British goods. In 1766 Parliament repealed the Stamp Act, but through the Declaratory Act it said that Parliament had the power to legislate for the colonies.

The Stamp Act crisis set the pattern for the next ten years. Parliament under the leadership of a royal minister would approve a piece of revenue or administrative legislation. The Americans would then resist by reasoned argument, economic pressure, and violence. Then the legislation would be repealed, and the process would commence again. Each time tempers on both sides became more frayed and positions more irreconcilable. In 1767 the ministry of Charles Townshend (1725–1767) passed a series of revenue acts relating to colonial imports. The colonists again resisted. The ministry sent over its own customs agents to administer the laws. To protect these new officers, British troops were sent to Boston in 1768. Tensions obviously resulted, and in March 1770 the Boston Massacre, in which British troops killed five citizens, took place. That same year all of the Townshend duties except for the one on tea were repealed.

In May 1773 Parliament passed a new law relating to the sale of tea by the East India Company. The measure permitted direct importation into the American colonies. It actually lowered the price of tea while retaining the tax. In some cities the colonists refused to permit the unloading of the tea; in Boston a shipload of tea was thrown into the harbor. The British ministry of Lord North (1732–1790) was determined to assert the authority of Parliament over the resistent colonies. During

COMMON SENSE;

ADDRESSED TO THE

INHABITANTS

OF

AMERICA,

On the following interesting

SUBJECTS.

I. Of the Origin and Design of Government in general, with concise Remarks on the English Constitution.

II. Of Monarchy and Hereditary Succession.

III. Thoughts on the present State of American Affairs.

IV. Of the present Ability of America, with some miscellaneous Reflections.

Man knows no Master save creating HEAVEN,
Or those whom choice and common good ordain.
THOMSON.

PHILADELPHIA;

Printed, and Sold, by R. BELL, in Third-Street.
MDCCLXXVI.

Common Sense, written by Tom Paine, was the most important political pamphlet published during 1776 when the American colonies were deciding to make a final break with Great Britain. [The Granger Collection.]

1774 Parliament passed a series of laws known in American history as the Intolerable Acts. These measures closed the port of Boston, reorganized the government of Massachussetts, allowed troops to be quartered in private homes, and removed trials of royal customs officials to England. The same year Parliament approved the Quebec Act for the future administration of that province. It extended the boundaries of Quebec to include the Ohio River valley. The Americans regarded the Quebec Act as an attempt to prevent the extension of their mode of self-government westward beyond the mountains.

During these years committees of correspondence composed of citizens critical of Britain had been established throughout the colonies. They made the various sections of the eastern seaboard aware of common problems and aided united action. In September 1774 these committees organized the gathering of the First Continental Congress in Philadelphia. This body hoped to persuade Parliament to restore self-government in the colonies and to abandon its attempt at direct supervision of colonial affairs. However, conciliation was not forthcoming. By April 1775 the battles of Lexington and Concord had been fought. In June the colonists had been defeated at the Battle of Bunker Hill. The colonial assemblies soon began to meet under their own authority rather than under that of the king.

The Second Continental Congress met in May 1775. It still sought conciliation with Britain, but the pressure of events led that assembly to begin to conduct the government of the colonies. By August 1775 George III had declared the colonies in rebellion. During the winter Thomas Paine's pamphlet *Common Sense* galvanized public opinion in favor of separation from Great Britain. A colonial army and navy were organized. In April 1776

Lord Cornwallis surrenders to General George Washington at Yorktown, Virginia, October 19, 1781. This is a romanticized nineteenth-century reconstruction of a scene that no contemporary pencil portrayed. [Culver Pictures.]

George III of Great Britain was distrusted by politicians at home and American colonists abroad. The 1767 portrait is by Allan Ramsay (1713–1784) and the medal is by C. H. Küchler. [Painting: Culver Pictures; medal: The Granger Collection.]

the Continental Congress opened American ports to the trade of all nations. And on July 4, 1776, the Continental Congress adopted the Declaration of Independence. Thereafter the war of the American Revolution continued until 1781, when the forces of George Washington defeated those of Lord Charles Cornwallis at Yorktown. However, early in 1778 the war had widened into a European conflict when Benjamin Franklin persuaded the French government to support the rebellion. In 1779 the Spanish also came to the aid of the colonies. In 1783 the Peace of Paris concluded the conflict, and the thirteen American colonies had established their independence.

This series of events is generally familiar to American readers. The relationship of the American Revolution to European affairs and the European roots of the American revolutionary ideals are less familiar.

The political theory of the American Declaration of Independence derived from the writings of seventeenth-century English Whig theorists, such as John Locke, and eighteenth-century Scottish moral philosophers, such as Francis Hutcheson. Their political ideas had in large measure arisen out of the struggle of seventeenth-century English aristocrats and gentry against the absolutism of the Stuarts. The American colonists looked to the English Revolution of 1688 as having established many of their own fundamental political liberties as well as those of England. The colonists claimed that through the measures imposed from 1763 to 1776 George III and the British parliament had attacked those liberties and dissolved the bonds of moral and political allegiance that had formerly united the two peoples. Consequently the Americans employed a theory developed to justify an aristocratic rebellion to support a popular revolution.

These Whig political ideas were only a part of the English ideological heritage that affected the Americans. Throughout the eighteenth century the colonists had become familiar with a series of British political writers called the *Commonwealthmen*. They held republican political ideas and had their intellectual roots in the most radical thought of the Puritan revolution. During the early eighteenth century these writers had relentlessly criticized the government patronage and parliamentary management of Robert Walpole and his successors. They argued that such government was corrupt and that it undermined liberty. They regarded much parliamentary taxation as simply a means of financing corruption. They also attacked standing armies, which they considered instruments of tyranny. In Great Britain this political tradition had only a marginal impact. The writers were largely ignored because most British subjects regarded themselves as the freest people in the world. However, four thousand miles away in the colonies, these radical books and pamphlets were read widely and were often accepted at face value. The events in Great Britain following the accession of King George III made many colonists believe that the worst fears of the Commonwealth writers were coming true.

Events in Great Britain

George III (1760–1820) believed that his two immediate royal predecessors had been improperly bullied and controlled by their ministers. Royal power had in effect amounted to little more than the policies carried out by a few powerful Whig families. The new king intended to rule through Parliament, but he was determined to have ministers of his own choice. Moreover George III believed that Parliament should function under royal rather than under aristocratic management. When William Pitt resigned after disagreement over war policy, the king appointed the earl of Bute as his first minister. In doing so, he ignored the great Whig families that had run the country since 1715. The king sought the aid of politicians whom the Whigs hated. Moreover he attempted to use the same kind of patronage techniques developed by Walpole to achieve royal control of the House of Commons.

Between 1761 and 1770 George tried one minister after another, but each in turn failed to gain sufficient support from the various factions in the House of Com-

John Wilkes Esq
Drawn from the Life and Etch'd in Aquafortis by Willm Hogarth.
Publish'd according to Act of Parliament May 16 1763.

which he had been arrested was illegal. However, the House of Commons ruled that issue Number 45 of *The North Briton* was a libel and expelled Wilkes from the Commons. He soon fled the country and was outlawed. Throughout these procedures there was very widespread support for Wilkes, and many demonstrations were held in his cause.

In 1768 Wilkes returned to England and again stood for election to Parliament. He won the election, but the House of Commons, under the influence of George III's friends, refused to seat him. He was elected three more times. After the fourth election the House of Commons simply ignored the election results and seated the government-supported candidate. As earlier in the decade, large popular demonstrations of shopkeepers, artisans, and small property owners supported Wilkes. He was also aided by some aristocratic politicians who wished to humiliate George III. Wilkes himself contended during all of his troubles that his cause was the cause of English liberty. "Wilkes and Liberty" became the slogan of all political radicals and many noble opponents of the monarch. Wilkes was finally seated in 1774, after having become the lord mayor of London.

The American colonists followed all of these developments of the 1760s very closely. The contemporary events in Britain confirmed their fears about a monarchical and parliamentary conspiracy against liberty. The king, as their Whig friends told them, was behaving like a tyrant. The Wilkes affair displayed the arbitrary power of the monarch, the corruption of the House of Commons, and the contempt of both for popular electors. That same monarch and Parliament were attempting to overturn the traditional relationship of Great Britain to its colonies by imposing parliamentary taxes. The same government had then landed troops in Boston, changed the government of Massachussetts, and undermined the traditional right of jury trial. All of these events fulfilled too exactly the portrait of political tyranny that had developed over the years in the minds of articulate colonists.

mons. Finally, in 1770 he turned to Lord North (1732–1792), who remained the king's first minister until 1782. The reaction of the Whig families and political spokesmen was to proclaim that George III was attempting to impose a tyranny. What they meant was that the king was attempting to curb the power of a particular group of the aristocracy. George III certainly was seeking to restore more royal influence to the government of Great Britain, but he was not attempting to make himself a tyrant.

THE CHALLENGE OF JOHN WILKES. Then in 1763 began the affair of John Wilkes (1725–1797). This London political radical and member of Parliament published a newspaper called *The North Briton*. In issue Number 45 of this paper Wilkes strongly criticized Lord Bute's handling of the peace negotiations with France. Wilkes was arrested under authority of a general warrant issued by the secretary of state. He pled the privileges of a member of Parliament and was released. The courts also later ruled that the vague kind of general warrant by

Major John Cartwright (1740–1824) was the first English political reformer to call for universal manhood suffrage in parliamentary elections. [The Granger Collection.]

ical structure. Colonial arguments could be used by British subjects at home who were no more directly represented in the House of Commons than were the Americans. The colonial questioning of the taxing authority of the House of Commons was not unrelated to the protest of John Wilkes. Both the Americans and Wilkes were challenging the power of the monarch and the authority of Parliament. Moreover both the colonial leaders and Wilkes appealed over the head of legally constituted political authorities to popular opinion and popular demonstrations. Both were protesting the power of a largely self-selected aristocratic political body. The British ministry was fully aware of these broader implications of the American troubles.

The American colonists also demonstrated to Europe how a politically restive people in the old regime could fight tyranny and protect political liberty. They established revolutionary but orderly political bodies that would function outside the existing political framework. These revolutionary political institutions were the congress and the convention. These began with the Stamp Act Congress of 1765 and culminated in the Constitutional Convention of 1787. The legitimacy of those congresses and conventions lay not in existing law but rather with the alleged consent of the governed. This approach represented a new way to found a government.

Toward the end of the War of the American Revolution, calls for parliamentary reform were heard in Britain itself. The method proposed for changing the system was the extralegal Association Movement.

By the close of the 1770s there was much resentment

MOVEMENT FOR PARLIAMENTARY REFORM IN BRITAIN. The political influences between America and Britain operated both ways. The colonial demand for no taxation without representation and the criticism of the adequacy of the British system of representation struck at the core of the eighteenth-century British politin Britain about the mismanagement of the war, the high taxes, and Lord North's ministry. In northern England in 1778 Christopher Wyvil (1740–1822), a landowner and retired clergyman, organized the Yorkshire Association Movement. Property owners or freeholders of Yorkshire met in a mass meeting to demand rather moderate changes in the corrupt system of parliamentary elections. They organized corresponding societies elsewhere. They intended that the Association examine, and suggest reforms for, the entire government. The Association Movement was thus a popular attempt to establish an extralegal institution to reform the government. The movement collapsed during the early 1780s because its supporters, unlike Wilkes and the American rebels, were not willing to appeal for broad popular support. Nonetheless the agitation of the Association Movement provided many people with experience in political protest. Several of its younger figures lived to raise the issue of parliamentary reform after 1815.

Parliament was not insensitive to the demands of the Association Movement. In April 1780 the Commons passed a resolution that called for lessening the power of the crown. In 1782 Parliament adopted a measure for "economical" reform, which abolished some patronage at the disposal of the monarch. However, these actions did not prevent George III from appointing a minister of his own choice. In 1782 Lord North had to form a ministry with Charles James Fox (1749–1806), a long-time critic of George III. The monarch was most unhappy with the arrangement. In 1783 he approached William Pitt the Younger (1759–1806), son of the victorious war minister, to manage the House of Commons. During the election of 1784 Pitt received immense patronage support from the crown and constructed a House of Commons favorable to the king. Thereafter Pitt sought to formulate trade policies that would give his ministry broad popularity. He attempted in 1785 one measure of modest parliamentary reform. When it failed, the young prime minister, who had been only twenty-two at the time of his appointment, abandoned the cause of reform.

By the mid-1780s George III had achieved what he sought beginning in 1761. He had restored the influence of the monarchy in political affairs. It proved a temporary victory because his own mental illness, which would finally require a regency, weakened the royal power. The cost of his years of dominance had been very high. On both sides of the Atlantic the issue of popular sovereignty had been raised and widely discussed. The American colonies had been lost. Economically this loss did not prove disastrous. American trade after independence actually increased. However, the Americans—through the state constitutions, the Articles of Confederation, and the federal Constitution—had demonstrated to Europe the possibility of government without kings and without aristocracies. They had established the example of a nation in which written documents based on popular consent and popular sovereignty rather than upon divine law, natural law, tradition, or the will of kings stood as the highest political and legal authority. Writers throughout western Europe sensed that a new kind of political era was dawning. It was to be an age of constituent assemblies, constitutions, and declarations of rights.

Colonies founded to serve the economic requirements of Britain and Europe repaid the debt by serving as examples of new political ideals and institutions. The ideas had generally been developed in Europe, but America was the first place where most of them were initially put into practice. America for a time served as an experiment station for the advanced political ideas of Europe. Soon the ideas would find their way back to the lands of their origins.

SUGGESTED READINGS

B. BAILYN, *The Ideological Origins of the American Revolution* (1967). An important work illustrating the role of English radical thought in the perceptions of the American colonists.

C. BECKER, *The Declaration of Independence: A Study in the History of Political Ideas* (1922). An examination of the political and imperial theory of the Declaration.

H. Butterfield, *George III, Lord North, and the People, 1779–1780* (1949). Explores the domestic unrest in Britain during the American Revolution.

Walter Dorn, *Competition for Empire, 1740–1763* (1940). Still one of the best accounts of the mid-century struggle.

L. H. Gipson, *The British Empire Before the American Revolution,* 13 vols. (1936–1967). A magisterial account of the mid-century wars from an imperial viewpoint.

R. Lodge, *Great Britain and Prussia in the Eighteenth Century* (1923). The standard account.

E. Morgan and H. Morgan, *The Stamp Act Crisis* (1953). A lively account of the incident from the viewpoint of both the colonies and England.

R. Pares, *War and Trade in the West Indies* (1936). Relates the West Indies to Britain's larger commercial and naval concerns.

R. Pares, *King George III and the Politicians* (1953). An important analysis of the constitutional and political structures.

J. H. Parry, *Trade and Dominion: The European Overseas Empires in the Eighteenth Century* (1971). A comprehensive account with attention to the European impact on the rest of the world.

C. D. Rice, *The Rise and Fall of Black Slavery* (1975). An excellent survey of the subject with careful attention to the numerous historiographical controversies.

C. G. Robertson, *Chatham and the British Empire* (1948). A brief study.

G. Rudé, *Wilkes and Political Liberty* (1962). A close analysis of popular political behavior.

J. S. Watson, *The Reign of George III, 1760–1815* (1960). Covers the British domestic political scene.

G. Wills, *Inventing America: Jefferson's Declaration of Independence* (1978). An important new study that challenges much of the analysis in the Becker volume noted above.

566

22

The Age of Enlightenment: Eighteenth-Century Thought

DURING the eighteenth century the conviction began to spread throughout the literate sectors of European society that change and reform were both possible and desirable. This attitude is now commonplace, but it came into its own only after 1700. It represents one of the primary intellectual inheritances from that age. The movement of people and ideas that fostered such thinking is called the *Enlightenment*. Its leading voices combined confidence in the human mind inspired by the Scientific Revolution and faith in the power of rational criticism to challenge the intellectual authority of tradition and the Christian past. These writers stood convinced that human beings could comprehend the operation of physical nature and mold it to the ends of material and moral improvement. The rationality of the physical universe became a standard against which the customs and traditions of society could be measured and criticized. Such criticism penetrated every corner of contemporary society, politics, and religious opinion. As a result the spirit of innovation and improvement came to characterize modern European and Western society.

The *Philosophes*

The writers and critics who forged this new attitude and who championed change and reform were the *philosophes*. They were not usually philosophers in a formal

Sir Isaac Newton's tomb in Westminster Abbey, London (1731) was the work of William Kent and Michael Rysbrack. With Newton, classically draped and with his books and the globe itself accompanying him, it both symbolizes the Enlightenment's mathematical and philosophical concerns and honors the man who defined some of nature's most important basic laws. There was hardly a thinker of the Enlightenment to whom Newton was not an intellectual hero. [By courtesy of the Dean and Chapter of Westminster.]

sense but rather were people who sought to apply the rules of reason and common sense to practically all the major institutions and social practices of the day. The most famous of their number included Voltaire, Montesquieu, Diderot, Rousseau, Hume, Gibbon, Smith, Bentham, Lessing, and Kant. A few of them occupied professorships in universities, but most were free agents who might be found in London coffeehouses, Edinburgh drinking spots, the salons of fashionable Parisian ladies, the country houses of reform-minded nobles, or the courts of the most powerful monarchs on the Continent. They were not an organized group; they disagreed on many issues. Their relationship with each other and with lesser figures of the same turn of mind has been quite appropriately compared to that of a family, in which despite quarrels and tensions a basic unity still remains.[1]

The chief unity of the *philosophes* lay in their desire to reform thought, society, and government for the sake of human liberty. As Peter Gay has suggested, this goal included "freedom from arbitrary power, freedom of speech, freedom of trade, freedom to realize one's talents, freedom of aesthetic response, freedom, in a word, of moral man to make his way in the world."[2] No other single set of ideas has done so much to shape the modern world. The literary vehicles through which the *philosophes* delivered their message included books, pamphlets, plays, novels, philosophical treatises, encyclopedias, newspapers, and magazines. During the Reformation and the religious wars the printed word had been used to debate the proper mode of faith in God. The *philosophes* of the Enlightenment employed the printed word to proclaim a new faith in the capacity of humankind to improve itself without the aid of God.

Most of the *philosophes* were middle class in their social origins. The bulk of their readership were also drawn from the prosperous commercial and professional people

1 Peter Gay, *The Enlightenment: An Interpretation* (New York: Alfred A. Knopf, 1967), Vol. 1, p. 4.
2 Ibid., 1, p. 3.

Edward Jenner (1749–1823), an English physician, discovered that by inoculating human beings with the relatively mild disease of cowpox he could make them immune to the dread disease of smallpox. That discovery eventually led to the practically complete removal of the danger of smallpox. [Culver Pictures.]

of the eighteenth-century towns and cities. These people discussed the reformers' writings and ideas in local philosophical societies, Freemason lodges, and clubs. They had sufficient income and leisure time to buy and read the *philosophes'* works. However, the writers of the Enlightenment did not consciously champion the goals or causes of the middle class. Nevertheless they did provide an intellectual ferment and a major source of ideas that could be used to undermine existing social practices and political structures. They taught their contemporaries how to pose pointed, critical questions. Moreover the *philosophes* generally supported the economic growth, the expansion of trade, and the improvement of transport that were transforming the society and economy of the eighteenth century.

Formative Influences

The Newtonian world view, the stability and prosperity of Great Britain after 1688, and the degradation that the wars of Louis XIV brought to France were the chief factors that favored discussion of reform throughout Europe.

Isaac Newton (1642–1727) and John Locke (1632–1704) were the major intellectual forerunners of the Enlightenment. Newton's formulation of the laws of universal gravitation exemplified the power of the human mind. His example and his writing encouraged Europeans to approach the study of nature directly and to avoid metaphysics and supernaturalism. Newton had formulated general laws but had always insisted upon a foundation of specific empirical evidence for those laws. Empirical experience had provided the constant check upon his

rational speculation. This emphasis on concrete experience became a keystone for Enlightenment thought. Moreover Newton had discerned a pattern of rationality in natural physical phenomena. During the eighteenth century the ancient idea of following nature became transformed under the Newtonian influence into the idea of following reason. Because nature was rational, society should be organized in a rational manner.

As explained in Chapter 18, Newton's scientific achievement had inspired his fellow countryman John Locke to seek a human psychology based on experience. In *An Essay Concerning Human Understanding* (1690), Locke argued that each human being enters the world as a *tabula rasa*, or blank page. His or her personality is consequently the product of the sensations that impinge from the external world throughout the course of life. The significant conclusion that followed from this psychology was that human nature is changeable and can be molded by modification of the surrounding physical and social environment. Locke's was a reformer's psychology. It suggested that improvement in the human situation was possible. Locke also in effect rejected the Christian view of humankind as creatures permanently flawed by sin. Human beings need not wait for the grace of God or other divine aid to better their lives.

Newton's physics and Locke's psychology provided the theoretical basis for reform. The domestic stability of Great Britain after the Revolution of 1688 furnished a living example of a society in which enlightened reforms functioned for the benefit of all concerned. England permitted religious toleration to all creeds except Unitarianism and Roman Catholicism, whose believers were not actually persecuted. Relative freedom of the press and free speech prevailed. The monarchy was limited in its authority, and political sovereignty resided in Parliament. Courts protected citizens from arbitrary government action. The army was quite small. These liberal policies had produced not disorder and instability but economic prosperity and loyalty to the political system. The continental view of England was somewhat idealized; never-

Voltaire challenged the authorities of eighteenth-century Europe with his mockery and bitter satire. Many of the *philosophes* considered him the leading figure in their effort to liberate European thought from the burden of the past. The statue is in the Théâtre Français in Paris. [Culver Pictures.]

theless the country was sufficiently freer than any other nation to make the point the reformers sought.

If the example of Great Britain proved that change need not be disastrous to a nation and society, France exhibited many of the practices and customs of European politics and society that needed to be reformed. Louis XIV had built his power on the grounds of absolute monarchy, religious unity involving persecution, a large standing army, and heavy taxation. However, the nation had been defeated in war by its enemies. Its people were miserable, and celebrations had marked the death of the great king. His successors had been unable to reform the state. Critics of the monarchy could be arbitrarily arrested. There was no freedom of worship. Political and religious censorship was frequently exercised over the press and other literary productions. Offending authors could be imprisoned, although some achieved co-operative relations with the authorities. State regulations hampered economic growth. Many aristocrats regarded themselves as a military class and upheld militaristic values. Yet throughout the French social structure there existed people who wanted to see changes brought about. These people read and supported the *philosophes* of their nation and of other countries. Consequently France became the major center for the Enlightenment. For there more than in any other state the demand for reform daily confronted writers and political thinkers.

Stages of the Enlightenment

The movement that came to be known as the Enlightenment evolved over the course of the century and involved a number of writers living at different times in various countries. Its early spokesmen popularized the rationalism and scientific ideas of the seventeenth century. They worked to expose contemporary social and political abuses and argued that reform was necessary and possible. The advancement of their cause and ideas was anything but steady. They confronted the obstacles of vested interests, political oppression, and religious con-

demnation. Yet by mid-century enlightened ideas had been brought to the public in a variety of formats. The *philosophes'* family had come into being. They corresponded with each other, wrote for each other as well as for the general public, and defended each other against the political and religious authorities.

By the second half of the century they were sufficiently safe to quarrel among themselves on occasion. They had stopped talking in generalities, and their major spokesmen were addressing themselves to specific abuses. Their books and articles had become more specialized and more practical. Having convinced Europeans that change was a good idea, they began to suggest exactly what changes were most desirable. They had become honored figures.

Voltaire

One of the earliest and by far the most influential of the *philosophes* was François Marie Arouet, known to posterity as Voltaire (1694–1778). During the 1720s Voltaire had offended the French authorities by certain of his writings. He was arrested and put in prison for a brief time.

Later Voltaire went to England, where he visited in the best literary circles, observed the tolerant intellectual and religious climate, felt free in its atmosphere of moderate politics, and admired its science and economic prosperity. In 1733 he published *Letters on the English*, which appeared in French the next year. The book praised the virtues of the English and indirectly criticized the abuses of French society. In 1738 he published *Elements of the Philosophy of Newton*, which popularized the thought of the great scientist. Both works were well received and gave Voltaire a reputation as an important writer.

Thereafter Voltaire lived part of the time in France and part near Geneva, just across the French border, where royal authorities could not bother him. He wrote essays, history, plays, stories, and letters that made him the literary dictator of Europe. He brought the bitter venom of his satire and sarcasm against one evil after another in French and European life. His most famous satire was *Candide* (1759), in which he attacked war, religious persecution, and unthinking optimism about the human condition. Like most *philosophes,* Voltaire believed that improvement of human society was necessary and possible. But he was never certain that reform, if achieved, would be permanent. The optimism of the Enlightenment constituted a tempered hopefulness rather than a glib certainty. Pessimism provided an undercurrent to most of the works of the period.

Montesquieu

Among the other pioneers of the early Enlightenment Charles de Secondat, Baron de Montesquieu (1689–1755) was outstanding. He was a lawyer, a noble of the robe, and a member of a provincial *parlement.* He also belonged to the Bordeaux Academy of Science, before which he presented papers on scientific topics. Although living comfortably within the bosom of French society, he saw the need for reform. In 1721 he published *The Persian Letters* to satirize contemporary institutions. The book consisted of letters purportedly written by two Persians visiting Europe. They explained to friends at home how European behavior contrasted with Persian life and customs. Behind the humor lay the cutting edge of criticism and an exposition of the cruelty and irrationality of much contemporary European life. In his most enduring work, *The Spirit of the Laws* (1748), Montesquieu held up the example of the British constitution as the wisest model for regulating the power of government. (We shall examine *The Spirit of the Laws* more closely later in this chapter.)

The Encyclopedia

The mid-century witnessed the publication of one of the greatest monuments of the Enlightenment. Under the heroic leadership of Denis Diderot (1713–1784), and Jean le Rond d'Alembert (1717–1783), the first volume of the *Encyclopedia* appeared in 1751. The project reached completion in 1772 with seventeen volumes of

---

The Encyclopedia *Discourses on Reason and Faith*

As illustrated in this passage from the *Encyclopedia* article on "Reason and Faith," the writers of the Enlightenment in the mid-eighteenth century wished to see human reason limit the excesses and fanaticism associated with religion. They wished to see reason as well as faith determine the practical character of religion.

E VERYTHING *within the province of revelation must prevail over our opinions, our prejudices and our interests, and is entitled to demand complete assent from the mind. But such submission of our* reason *to faith does not thereby reverse the limits of human knowledge and does not shake the foundations of* reason; *it allows us the freedom to employ our faculties in the areas of application for which they were given to us.*

If we are not careful in distinguishing between the different jurisdictions of faith and reason *by means of these limits,* reason *will have no place in matters of religion, and we shall have no right to mock the extravagant opinions and ceremonies that we notice in most religions of the world. Who does not see that this opens a wide field to the most excessive fanaticism and the most insane superstition? With such a principle there is nothing so absurd that will not be believed. Hence it happens that religion, which is to the credit of humanity and the most excellent prerogative of our nature over the animals, is often the area in which men seem to be the most irrational.*

Stephen J. Gendzier (Ed. and Trans.), *The Encyclopedia: Selections* (New York: Harper Torchbook, 1967), pp. 212–213.

OPPOSITE, LEFT: The title page of the first volume of the *Encyclopedia.* The early volumes of the text received the approval of the royal censor, as noted on the last line, but when it became evident that the work challenged many widely held religious and political views, its opponents obtained withholding of approval for later volumes which were eventually published. [The Mansell Collection.]
OPPOSITE, RIGHT: Denis Diderot, the principal editor who saw it through to the end; d'Alembert withdrew when the opposition turned nasty. [The Granger Collection.]
OPPOSITE, TOP: An extraordinary feature of the set was the plates, which set out the entire spectrum of contemporary technology in thousands of detailed etchings. This typical figure shows the contents of a chemical laboratory. [Giraudon.]

ENCYCLOPÉDIE,
OÙ
DICTIONNAIRE RAISONNÉ
DES SCIENCES,
DES ARTS ET DES MÉTIERS,
PAR UNE SOCIÉTÉ DE GENS DE LETTRES.

Mis en ordre & publié par M. *DIDEROT*, de l'Académie Royale des Sciences & des Belles-
Lettres de Prusse ; & quant à la PARTIE MATHÉMATIQUE, par M. *D'ALEMBERT*,
de l'Académie Royale des Sciences de Paris, de celle de Prusse, & de la Société Royale
de Londres.

Tantùm feries juncturaque pollet,
Tantum de medio fumptis accedit honoris ! HORAT.

TOME PREMIER.

A PARIS,

Chez
BRIASSON, *rue Saint Jacques, à la Science.*
DAVID l'aîné, *rue Saint Jacques, à la Plume d'or.*
LE BRETON, *Imprimeur ordinaire du Roy, rue de la Harpe.*
DURAND, *rue Saint Jacques, à Saint Landry, & au Griffon.*

M. DCC. LI.
AVEC APPROBATION ET PRIVILEGE DU ROY.

Gotthold Lessing (1729-1781) was a German dramatist and literary critic whose works made strong pleas for religious toleration. His 1760 portrait is by J. H. Tischbein. [The Granger Collection.]

text and eleven of plates. The *Encyclopedia* was the product of the collective effort of more than one hundred authors, and its editors had at one time or another solicited articles from all the major French *philosophes*. The project reached fruition only after numerous attempts to censor it and halt its publication. The *Encyclopedia* set forth the most advanced critical ideas in religion, government, and philosophy. This criticism often had to be hidden in obscure articles or under the cover of irony. The articles represented a collective plea for freedom of expression. However, the large volumes also provided important information on manufacturing, canal building, ship construction, and improved agriculture.

Between fourteen and sixteen thousand copies of various editions of the *Encyclopedia* were sold before 1789. The project had been constructed to secularize learning and to undermine the intellectual assumptions remaining from the Middle Ages and the Reformation. The articles on politics, ethics, and society ignored concerns about divine law and concentrated on humanity and its immediate well-being. The encyclopedists looked to antiquity rather than to the Christian centuries for their intellectual and ethical models. The future welfare of humankind lay not in pleasing God or following divine commandments but rather in harnessing the power of the earth and its resources and in living at peace with one's fellow human beings. The good life lay here and now and was to be achieved through the application of reason to human relationships.

With the publication of the *Encyclopedia*, enlightened thought was diffused over the Continent. Enlightened ideas penetrated German and Russian intellectual and political circles. The *philosophes* of the latter part of the century turned from championing the general cause of reform and discussed specific areas of practical application. Gotthold Lessing (1729-1781) wrote plays to plead for religious toleration. Adam Smith (1723-1790) attacked the mercantile system. Cesare Beccaria (1738-1794) and Jeremy Bentham (1748-1832) called for penal and legal reforms. By this time the concepts of

reform and the rationalization of existing institutions had become deeply impressed on European thinking and society. The issue then became and would remain for over a century how best to implement those reforms.

The Enlightenment and Religion

Throughout the century, in the eyes of the *philosophes* the chief enemy of the improvement of humankind and the enjoyment of happiness was the existence and influence of ecclesiastical institutions. The hatred of the *philosophes* for the church and Christianity was summed up in Voltaire's cry of "Crush the Infamous Thing." Almost all varieties of Christianity, but especially Roman Catholicism, invited the criticism of the *philosophes*. Intellectually the churches perpetuated a religious rather than a scientific view of humankind and physical nature. The clergy taught that human beings were basically depraved and that they required divine grace to become worthy creatures. The doctrine of original sin in either its Catholic or its Protestant formulation suggested that meaningful improvement in human nature on earth was impossible. Religious concerns turned human interest away from this world to the world to come. The concept of predestination suggested that the condition of the human soul after death had little or no relationship to virtuous living during this life. Through disagreements over obscure doctrines the various churches favored the politics of intolerance and bigotry that caused human suffering, torture, and war.

To attack the Christian churches in this manner was to raise major questions about the life and society of the old regime. Politically and socially the churches were deeply enmeshed in the power structure. They owned large amounts of land and collected tithes from peasants before any other taxes were collected. Most of the clergy were legally exempt from taxation, and made only annual voluntary grants to the government. The upper clergy in most countries were relatives of aristocrats. Churchmen were actively involved in politics, serving in the British

House of Lords and on the Continent advising princes. In Protestant countries the local clergyman of a particular parish was usually appointed by the local major landowner. Across the Continent membership in the predominant denomination of the kingdom gave certain subjects political advantages. Nonmembership often excluded other subjects from political participation. Clergymen of all faiths preached the sinfulness of political disobedience, and they provided the intellectual justification for the social and political status quo. They were active where possible in exerting religious and literary censorship. The churches were thus privileged and powerful corporate bodies of the old regime. The *philosophes* chose to attack both their ideas and their power.

Deism

The *philosophes* believed that religion should be reasonable and should lead to moral behavior. The Newtonian world view had convinced many writers that nature was rational. Therefore the God who had created nature must be rational and the religion through which that God was worshiped should also be rational. Moreover Lockean psychology, which limited human knowledge to empirical experience, raised the question whether such a thing as divine revelation to humankind was after all possible. These considerations gave rise to a movement for enlightened rational religion known as *deism*. The tenor of this religion is displayed in the title of one of its earliest expositions: *Christianity Not Mysterious* (1696) by John Toland. He and later writers wished to consider religion as a natural and rational rather than a supernatural phenomenon.

There were two major points in the deists' creed. The first was the belief in the existence of God. They thought that this belief could be empirically deduced from the contemplation of nature. Joseph Addison's poem on the spacious firmament (1712), illustrates this idea:

> The spacious firmament on high,
> With all the blue ethereal sky,

> And spangled heav'n, a shining frame,
> Their great Original proclaim:
> Th' unwearied Sun, from day to day,
> Does his Creator's power display,
> And publishes to every land
> The work of an Almighty hand.

Because nature provided evidence of a rational God, that deity must also favor rational morality. Consequently the second point in the deists' creed was the belief in life after death, when rewards and punishments would be meted out according to the virtue of the life a person led on this earth.

Deism was empirical, tolerant, reasonable, and capable of encouraging virtuous living. It was the major positive religious component of the Enlightenment. Voltaire declared:

> The great name of Deist, which is not sufficiently revered, is the only name one ought to take. The only gospel one ought to read is the great book of Nature, written by the hand of God and sealed with his seal. The only religion that ought to be professed is the religion of worshiping God and being a good man.[3]

If such a faith became widely accepted, the fanaticism and rivalry of the various Christian sects might be overcome. Religious conflict and persecutions encouraged by that fulsome zeal would end. There would also be little or no necessity for a priestly class to foment fanaticism, denominational hatred, and bigotry.

The *philosophes* did not rest with the formulation of a rational religious alternative to Christianity. They also attacked the churches and the clergy with great vehemence. Voltaire repeatedly questioned the truthfulness of priests and the morality of the Bible. In his *Philosophical Dictionary* (1764) he humorously pointed out inconsist-

---

3 Quoted in J. H. Randall, *The Making of the Modern Mind*, rev. ed. (New York: Houghton Mifflin, 1940), p. 292.

David Hume (1711–1776), a Scotsman, was one of the foremost philosophers of the Enlightenment. His essay on miracles was one of the key examples of religious scepticism. The painting is by Allan Ramsay. [The Granger Collection.]

Edward Gibbon (1737–1794), the English historian, was the author of *The History of the Decline and Fall of the Roman Empire*, published between 1776 and 1788. He is shown here as painted by Henry Walton.

encies in biblical narratives and immoral acts of the biblical heroes. In an *Essay on Miracles* (1748) the Scottish *philosophe* David Hume (1711–1776) argued that miracles, in which the churches put great store, were logically and naturally impossible. The greatest miracle was to believe in miracles. Edward Gibbon (1737–1794), the English historian, in *The Decline and Fall of the Roman Empire* (1776) examined the early history of Christianity and explained the rise of that faith in terms of natural causes rather than the influence of miracles and piety. A few *philosophes* went further. Baron d'Holbach (1723–1789) and Julien Offroy de La Mettre (1709–1751) embraced positions very near to atheism and materialism. Theirs was distinctly a minority position, however. Most of the *philosophes* sought not the abolition of religion but its transformation into a humane force that would encourage good living.

Toleration

A primary social condition for such a life was the establishment of religious toleration. Again Voltaire took the lead in championing this cause. In 1762 the Roman Catholic political authorities in Toulouse ordered the execution of a Huguenot named Jean Calas. He stood accused of having murdered his son to prevent him from converting to Roman Catholicism. Calas had been viciously tortured, broken on the wheel, and finally strangled to death without ever having confessed his guilt. The confession would not have saved his life, but it would

OPPOSITE: The elaborate Baroque splendor of the Kaisersaal in the episcopal, or bishop's, palace at Würzburg, West Germany, built in the early eighteenth century, displays the vast wealth and influence of the church in the society and the political structure of the old regime. The complex frescos were painted by the celebrated Italian artist Giovanni Battista Tiepolo and assistants in 1751. A close-up of the scene between the two circular windows is included in the color album. [Photo-Gundermann.]

Cesare Beccaria was an Italian advocate of the rational reform of criminal law and punishments. [The Granger Collection.]

Beccaria Objects to Capital Punishment as Unenlightened

Beccaria Objects to Capital Punishment as Unenlightened

In the eighteenth century the death penalty was commonly applied throughout Europe for small as well as great crimes. The young north Italian nobleman Cesare Beccaria thought the penalty was unproductive of law and order and also unenlightened. *On Crimes and Punishments* appeared when he was only 26, and Voltaire, Bentham, and Catherine the Great professed to admire the work. His 1764 comments are a good example of the Enlightenment application of the criteria of reason and utility to social problems.

Is the death penalty really useful and necessary for the security and good order of society? Are torture and torments just, and do they attain the end for which laws are instituted? What is the best way to prevent crimes? Are the same punishments equally effective for all times? What influence have they on customary behavior? These problems deserve to be analyzed with that geometric precision which the mist of sophisms, seductive eloquence, and timorous doubt cannot withstand. . . . If, by defending the rights of man and of unconquerable truth, I should help to save from the spasm and agonies of death some wretched victim of tyranny or of no less fatal ignorance, the thanks and tears of one innocent mortal in his transports of joy would console me for the contempt of all mankind.

.   .   .   .

If one were to cite against me the example of all the ages and of almost all the nations that have applied the death penalty to certain crimes, my reply would be that the example reduced itself to nothing in the face of truth, against which there is no prescription; that the history of men leaves us with the impression of a vast sea of errors; among which, at great intervals, some rare and hardly intelligible truths appear to float on the surface. Human sacrifices were once common to almost all nations, yet who will dare to defend them? That only a few societies, and for a short time only, have abstained from applying the death penalty, stands in my favor rather than against me, for that conforms with the usual lot of great truths, which are about as long-lasting as a lightning flash in comparison with the long dark night that envelops mankind. The happy time has not yet arrived in which truth shall be the portion of the greatest number, as error has heretofore been.

Cesare Beccaria, *On Crimes and Punishments*, trans. by Henry M. Paolucci (Indianapolis: Bobbs Merrill, Inc., 1963), pp. 10, 51.

have given the Catholics good propaganda to use against Protestants.

Voltaire learned of the case only after Calas's death. He made the dead man's cause his own. In 1763 he published a *Treatise on Tolerance* and hounded the authorities for a new investigation. Finally, in 1765, the judicial decision against the unfortunate man was reversed. For Voltaire the case illustrated the fruits of religious fanaticism and the need for rational reform of judicial processes. Somewhat later in the century the German playwright and critic Gotthold Lessing (1729–1781) wrote *Nathan the Wise* (1779) as a plea not only for toleration of different Christian sects but also of religious faiths other than Christianity. All of these calls for toleration stated in effect that life on earth and human relationships should not be subordinated to religion. Secular values and considerations were more important than religious ones.

The Enlightenment and Society

Although the *philosophes* wrote much on religion, humanity was the center of their interest. As one writer in the *Encyclopedia* observed, "Man is the unique point to which we must refer everything, if we wish to interest and please amongst considerations the most arid and

Jeremy Bentham applied the principle of "the greatest good for the greatest number" to his criticism of and attempts to reform English law. [The Granger Collection.]

details the most dry."[4] They believed that the application of human reason to society would reveal laws in human relationships similar to those found in physical nature. Although the term did not appear until later, the idea of social science originated with the Enlightenment. The purpose of discovering social laws was the removal of inhumanity that existed through ignorance of them. These concerns became especially evident in the work of the *philosophes* on law and prison procedures.

Beccaria

In 1764 Cesare Beccaria (1738–1794), an Italian *philosophe,* published *On Crimes and Punishments,* in which he applied critical analysis to the problem of making punishments both effective and just. He wanted the laws of monarchs and legislatures—that is, positive law— to conform with the rational laws of nature. He rigorously and eloquently attacked both torture and capital punishment. He thought that the criminal justice system should ensure speedy trial, sure punishment, and punishment intended to deter further crime. The purpose of law was not to impose the will of God or some other ideal of perfection; its purpose was to secure the greatest good or happiness for the greatest number of human beings. This utilitarian philosophy based on happiness in this life permeated most of the Enlightenment writing on practical reforms.

Bentham

Although utilitarianism did not originate with him, it is particularly associated with the English legal reformer Jeremy Bentham (1748–1832). He sought to create codes of scientific law that were founded on the principle of utility, that is, the greatest good for the greatest number. In the *Fragment on Government* (1776) and *The Principles of Morals and Legislation* (1789), Bentham explained that the application of the principle of utility

4 Quoted in F. L. Baumer, *Main Currents of Western Thought,* 4th ed. (New Haven: Yale University Press, 1978), p. 374.

would overcome the special interests or privileged groups who prevented rational government. Bentham regarded the existing legal and judicial systems as burdened by traditional practices that harmed the very people whom the law should serve. The application of reason and utility would remove the legal clutter that prevented justice from being realized.

The Physiocrats

Another area of social relationships where the *philosophes* saw existing legislation and administration preventing the operation of natural social laws was the field of economic policy. They believed trade, manufacture, and bountiful agriculture were hampered by the mercantilist legislation and labor regulations established by various governments and guilds. In France these economic reformers were called the *physiocrats.* Their leading spokesmen were François Quesnay (1694–1744) and Pierre Du Pont de Nemours (1739–1817). They believed that the primary role of government was to protect property and to permit freedom in the use of property. They particularly felt that all economic production was dependent on sound agriculture, and they favored the consolidation of small peasant holdings into larger, more efficient farms.

Adam Smith

The most important of Enlightenment discussions of economics was Adam Smith's (1723–1790) *Inquiry into the Nature and Causes of the Wealth of Nations* (1776). Smith, who was a professor at Edinburgh, urged that the mercantile system of England—including the navigation acts, the bounties, most tariffs, special trading monopolies, and the domestic regulation of labor and manufacture—be abolished. Smith believed that these modes of economic regulation by the state interfered with the natural system of economic liberty. They were intended to preserve the wealth of the nation, to capture wealth from other nations, and to preserve a minimum amount of work for the laborers of the country. However, Smith saw such regu-

Adam Smith was one of the most important members of what may be called the Class of 1776—the astonishing outburst of British historical writing that centered on that year. In addition to Smith's *Inquiry into the Nature and Causes of the Wealth of Nations*, Gibbon published the first volume of *The Decline and Fall*, Dr. Charles Burney (1726–1814) published the first volume of *A General History of Music* (completed in 1789), and Sir John Hawkins (1719–1789) managed to publish the entire five volumes of his *A General History of the Science and Practice of Music*. Moreover, in 1774, Thomas Warton (1728–1790) published the first volume of *The History of English Poetry* (third volume, 1781; never completed), while in 1777 the Scottish historian William Robertson (1721–1793) finished his career with the publication of his *History of America*. [Culver Pictures.]

Adam Smith Argues for Individual Industry and Wealth

Adam Smith (1723–1790) wanted to see a general, though not complete, application of individual self-interest to economic activity in place of existing mercantilist policies of state regulation. As he explains in this famous passage from *The Wealth of Nations* (1776), he thought that basically unregulated individual economic actions would produce more goods and services than mercantilist policy.

THE *annual revenue of every society is always precisely equal to the exchangeable value of the whole annual produce of its industry, or rather is precisely the same thing with that exchangeable value. As every individual, therefore, endeavours as much as he can both to employ his capital in the support of domestic industry, and so to direct that industry that its produce may be of the greatest value; every individual necessarily labours to render the annual revenue of the society as great as he can. He generally, indeed, neither intends to promote the public interest, nor knows how much he is promoting it. By preferring the support of domestic to that of foreign industry, he intends only his own security; and by directing that industry in such a manner as its produce may be of the greatest value, he intends only his own gain, and he is in this, as in many other cases, led by an invisible hand to promote an end which was no part of his intention. Nor is it always the worse for the society that it was no part of it. By pursuing his own interest he frequently promotes that of the society more effectually than when he really intends to promote it. I have never known much good done by those who affected to trade for the public good.*

Adam Smith, *The Wealth of Nations* (New York: Modern Library, 1965), p. 423.

lations as preventing the wealth and production of the country from growing. He wanted to see economic growth and a consumer-oriented economy. The means to those ends was the unleashing of individuals to pursue their own selfish economic interest. Free pursuit of economic self-interest would ensure economic expansion as each person attempted to enrich himself by meeting the demands of the marketplace. Consumers would find their wants met as manufacturers and merchants sought their business.

Smith's book challenged the concept of scarce goods and resources that lay behind mercantilism and the guilds. Smith saw the realm of nature as a boundless expanse of water, air, soil, and minerals. The physical resources of the earth seemed to demand exploitation for the enrichment and comfort of humankind. In effect, Smith was saying that the nations and peoples of Europe need not be poor. The idea of the infinite use of nature's goods for the material benefit of humankind—a concept that has dominated Western life until recent years—stemmed directly from the Enlightenment. When Smith wrote, the population of the world was smaller, its people were poorer,

Charles de Secondat, Baron de Montesquieu (1689–1755) was the author of *L'Esprit des Lois* (*The Spirit of the Laws*) (1748), which may have been the single most influential book of the Enlightenment, both in Europe and in America. The bust is the work of the sculptor LeComte. [Musée de Versailles. Cliché des Musées Nationaux.]

and the quantity of undeveloped resources per capita was much greater. For people of the eighteenth century it was in the uninhibited exploitation of natural resources that the true improvement of the human condition seemed to lie.

Smith is usually regarded as the founder of *laissez-faire* economics. However, the *Wealth of Nations* was a very complex book. Smith was no simple dogmatist. For example, he was not opposed to all government activity touching upon the economy. The state should provide schools, armies, navies, and roads. It should also undertake certain commercial ventures, such as the opening of dangerous new trade routes, that were economically desirable but the expense or risk of which discouraged private enterprise. His reasonable tone and recognition of the complexity of social and economic life displayed a very important point about the *philosophes*. Most of them were much less rigid and doctrinaire than any brief summary of their thought may tend to suggest. They recognized the passions of humanity as well as its reason. They adopted reason and nature as tools of criticism through which they might create a climate of opinion that would allow the fully developed human personality to flourish.

Political Thought of the *Philosophes*

Nowhere did the appreciation of the complexity of the problems of contemporary society become more evident than in the *philosophes*' political thought. Nor did any other area of their reformist enterprise so clearly illustrate the tension and conflict within the "family" of the Enlightenment. Most *philosophes* were discontent with certain political features of their countries, but they were especially discontent in France. There the corruptness of the royal court, the blundering of the bureaucracy, the less than glorious mid-century wars, and the power of the church compounded all problems. Consequently it was in France that the most important political thought of the Enlightenment occurred. However, the French *philo-*

sophes stood quite divided as to the proper solution. Their attitudes spanned the whole spectrum from aristocratic reform to democracy to constitutional monarchy.

The Spirit of the Laws

Montesquieu's *The Spirit of the Laws* (1748) may well have been the single most influential book of the century. It was a work that exhibited the internal tensions of the Enlightenment. Montesquieu pursued an empirical method, taking illustrative examples from the political experience of both ancient and modern nations. From these he concluded that there could be no single set of political laws that applied to all peoples at all times and in all places. Rather there existed a large number of political variables, and the good political life depended upon the relationship of those variables. Whether a monarchy or a republic was the best form of government was a matter of the size of the political unit and its population, the social and religious customs, the economic structure, the traditions, and the climate. Only a careful examination and evaluation of these elements could reveal what mode of government would prove most beneficial to a particular people. A century later such speculations would have been classified as sociology.

So far as France was concerned, Montesquieu had some rather definite ideas. He believed in monarchical government, but with a monarchy whose power was tempered and limited by various sets of intermediary institutions. The latter included the aristocracy, the towns, and the other corporate bodies that enjoyed particular liberties that the monarch must respect. These corporate bodies might be said to represent various segments of the general population and thus of public opinion. In France he regarded the aristocratic courts or *parlements* as the major example of an intermediary association. Their role was to limit the power of the monarchy and thus preserve the liberty of subjects. In championing these aristocratic bodies and the general role of the aristocracy, Montesquieu was a political reactionary. However, he adopted that stance in the hope of achieving

The writings of Jean Jacques Rousseau raised some of the most profound social and ethical questions of the Enlightenment. [Bettmann Archive.]

reform. For in his opinion it was the oppressive and inefficient absolutism of the monarchy that accounted for the degradation of French life.

One of Montesquieu's most influential ideas was that of division of power within any government. For his model of a government with power wisely separated among different branches, he took contemporary Great Britain. There he believed he had found a system in which executive power resided in the king, legislative power in the Parliament, and judicial power in the courts. He thought any two branches could check and balance the power of the other. His perception of the eighteenth-century British constitution was incorrect because he failed to see how patronage and electoral corruption allowed a handful of powerful aristocrats to dominate the government. Moreover, he was also unaware of the emerging cabinet system, which meant that the executive power was slowly becoming a creature of the Parliament. Nevertheless the analysis illustrated Montesquieu's strong sense of the need to limit the exercise of power through constitutionalism and the formation of law by legislatures rather than by monarchs. In this manner, although Montesquieu set out to defend the political privileges of the French aristocracy, his ideas had a profound and still lasting effect upon the liberal democracies of the next two centuries.

Rousseau

Jean Jacques Rousseau (1712–1778) held a view of the exercise and reform of political power quite different from Montesquieu's.

Rousseau was a strange isolated genius who never felt particularly comfortable with the other *philosophes*. Yet perhaps more than any other writer of the mid-eighteenth century he transcended the thought and values of his own time. Rousseau held a deep antipathy toward the world and the society in which he dwelled. It seemed impossible for human beings living according to contemporary commercial values to achieve moral, virtuous, or sincere lives. In 1750, in his *Discourse on the Moral Effects of the Arts and Sciences,* he contended that the process of civilization and enlightenment had corrupted human nature. Human beings in the state of nature had been more dignified. In 1755, in a *Discourse on the Origin of Inequality,* Rousseau blamed much of the evil in the world on maldistribution of property.

In both works Rousseau brilliantly and directly challenged the social fabric of the day. He drew into question the concepts of material and intellectual progress and the morality of a society in which commerce and industry were regarded as the most important of human activities. He felt that the real purpose of society was to nurture better people. In this respect Rousseau's vision of reform was much more radical than that of other contemporary writers. The other *philosophes* believed that human life would be improved if people could enjoy more of the fruits of the earth or could produce more goods. Rousseau raised the more fundamental question of what the good life is. This question has haunted European social thought ever since the eighteenth century. Much of the criticism of Europe's post-World War II society is rooted in this Rousseauean approach.

Rousseau carried these same concerns into his political thought. His most extensive discussion of politics appeared in *The Social Contract* (1762). Although the book attracted rather little immediate attention, it had by the end of the century become widely read in France. *The Social Contract,* as compared to Montesquieu's *Spirit of the Laws,* was a very abstract book. It did not propose specific reforms but outlined the kind of political structure that Rousseau believed would overcome the evils of contemporary politics and society.

Rousseau Argues that Inequality Is Not Natural

Jean Jacques Rousseau was one of the first writers to assert the social equality of human beings. He argued, as in this 1755 passage, that inequality had developed through the ages and was not "natural." He directly questioned the sanctity of property based on the assumed natural inquality of human beings.

I HAVE *endeavoured to trace the origin and progress of inequality, and the institution and abuse of political societies, as far as these are capable of being deduced from the nature of man merely by the light of reason, and independently of those sacred dogmas which give the sanction of divine right to sovereign authority. It follows from this survey that, as there is hardly any inequality in the state of nature, all the inequality which now prevails owes its strength and growth to the development of our faculties and the advance of the human mind, and becomes at last permanent and legitimate by the establishment of property and laws. Secondly, it follows that moral inequality, authorized by positive right alone, clashes with natural right, whenever it is not proportionate to physical inequality—a distinction which sufficiently determines what we think of that species of inequality which prevails in all civilized countries; since it is plainly contrary to the law of nature, however defined, that children should command old men, fools wise men, and that the privileged few should gorge themselves with superfluities while the starving multitude are in want of the bare necessities of life.*

Jean Jacques Rousseau, *The Social Contract and Discourses*, trans. by G. D. H. Cole, (New York: E. P. Dutton, 1950), pp. 271–272.

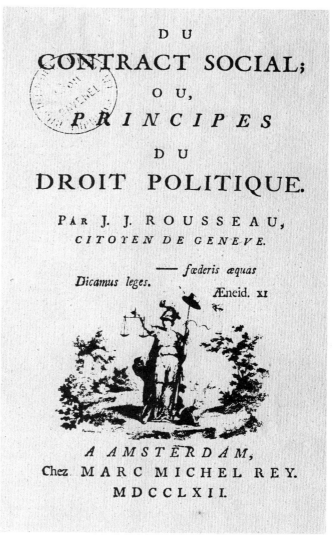

DU
CONTRACT SOCIAL;
OU,
PRINCIPES
DU
DROIT POLITIQUE.

PAR J. J. ROUSSEAU,
CITOYEN DE GENEVE.

Dicamus leges. —— *fœderis æquas*
Æneid. XI

A AMSTERDAM,
Chez MARC MICHEL REY.
MDCCLXII.

Rousseau's *Social Contract* (1762) challenged the political thought of an aristocratic age by calling for radical political equality. Note that, like many other unorthodox works, it was published in relatively free Amsterdam. [The Granger Collection.]

Most eighteenth-century political thinkers, in the tradition of Thomas Hobbes and John Locke, regarded human beings as individuals and society as a collection of such independent individuals pursuing personal selfish goals. These writers wished to liberate these individuals from the undue bonds of government. Rousseau picked up the stick from the other end. His book opens with the declaration, "All men are born free, but everywhere they are in chains."[5] The rest of the volume constitutes a *defense* of the chains of society over its members. Rousseau suggested that society is more important than its individual members, because they are what they are only because of their relationship to the larger community. Independent human beings living alone can achieve very little. Through their relationship to the larger community, they become moral creatures capable of significant action. The question then becomes what kind of community allows people to behave morally. In his two previous discourses Rousseau had explained that contemporary European society was not such a community. It was rather merely an aggregate of competing individuals

5 Jean Jacques Rousseau, *The Social Contract and Discourses*, trans. by G. D. H. Cole (New York: E. P. Dutton, 1950), p. 3.

Political Thought of the Philosophes 581

whose chief social goal was to preserve selfish independence in spite of all potential social bonds and obligations.

Rousseau sought to project the vision of a society in which each person could maintain his own personal freedom while at the same time behaving as a loyal member of the larger community. To that end Rousseau drew upon the traditions of Plato and Calvin to define freedom as obedience to law. In his case the law to be obeyed was that created by the general will. This concept normally meant the will of the majority of citizens as expressed through voting. Democratic participation in decision making would bind the individual citizen to the community. Rousseau believed that the general will must always be right and that to obey the general will was to be free. This argument led him to the notorious conclusion that under certain circumstances some people must be forced to be free. Rousseau's politics thus constituted a justification for radical direct democracy and for collective action against individual citizens.

Rousseau had in effect launched an assault on the eighteenth-century cult of the individual and the fruits of selfishness. He stood at odds with the commercial spirit that was transforming the society in which he lived. Rousseau would have disapproved the main thrust of Adam Smith's *Wealth of Nations,* which he may or may not have read, and would no doubt have preferred a study on the virtue of nations. Smith wanted people to be prosperous; Rousseau wanted them to be good even if that meant that they might remain economically poor. He saw human beings not as independent individuals but as creatures enmeshed in necessary social relationships. He believed that loyalty to the community should be encouraged. As one device to that end he suggested a civic religion based on the creed of Deism. Such a shared tolerant religious faith would provide unity for the society. Rousseau's chief intellectual inspiration arose from his study of Plato and the ancient Greek *polis.* Especially in Sparta he thought he had discovered human beings dwelling in a moral society inspired by a common purpose. He hoped that modern human beings might also create such a moral commonwealth in which virtuous living would become subordinate to commercial profit.

Rousseau's thought had only a marginal impact on his own time. The other *philosophes* questioned his critique of material improvement. Aristocrats and royal ministers could hardly be expected to welcome his proposal for radical democracy. Too many people were either making or hoping to make money to pay attention to his criticism of commercial values. However, he proved to be a figure to whom later generations returned. Many leaders in the French Revolution were familiar with his writing. Thereafter his ideas were important for most writers who felt called upon to criticize the general tenor and direction of Western culture. Rousseau hated much about the emerging modern society in Europe, but he contributed much to modernity by exemplifying for later generations the critic who dared to call into question the very foundations of social thought and action. Whatever our opinions of Rousseau, we have not yet escaped him.

Enlightened Absolutism

Most of the *philosophes* favored neither Montesquieu's reformed and revived aristocracy nor Rousseau's democracy as a solution to contemporary political problems. Like other thoughtful people of the day in other stations and occupations, they looked to the existing monarchies. The *philosophes* hoped in particular that the French monarchy might assert really effective power over the aristocracy and the church to bring about significant reform. Voltaire was a very strong monarchist. He and others—such as Diderot, who visited Catherine II of Russia, and physiocrats who were ministers to the French kings—did not wish to limit the power of monarchs but sought to redirect that power toward the rationalization of economic and political structures and the liberation of intellectual life. Most *philosophes* were not opposed to power if they could find a way of using it for their own purposes.

During the last third of the century it seemed to some

observers that several European rulers had actually embraced many of the reforms set forth by the *philosophes.* *Enlightened absolutism* is the term used to describe this phenomenon. The phrase indicates monarchical government dedicated to the rational strengthening of the central absolutist administration at the cost of other lesser centers of political power. However, the monarchs most closely associated with it—Frederick II of Prussia, Joseph II of Austria, and Catherine II of Russia—were neither genuinely enlightened nor truly absolute in the exercise of royal power. Their enlightenment was a veneer, and their absolutism was limited by the realities of political and economic life. Frederick II corresponded with the *philosophes,* for a time provided Voltaire with a place at his court, and even wrote history and political tracts. Catherine II, who was a master of what would later be called public relations, consciously sought to create the image of being enlightened. She read the works of the *philosophes,* became a friend of Diderot and Voltaire, and made frequent references to their ideas, all in the hope that her nation might seem more modern and Western. Joseph II undertook a series of religious, legal, and social reforms that contemporaries believed he had derived from suggestions of the *philosophes.*

Despite such appearances the policies of these monarchs were directed by the requirements of state security and political ambition rather than by the humanitarian and liberating zeal of the Enlightenment. They sought the rational economic and social integration of their realms so that they could wage more efficient future wars—a policy profoundly hateful to the *philosophes.* All of the states of Europe had emerged from the Seven Year's War understanding that they would require stronger armed forces for the next conflict and looking for new sources of taxation to finance those armies. The search for new revenues and further internal political support for their rule led these eastern monarchs to make "enlightened" reforms. They and their advisors used rationality to further what the *philosophes* considered irrational militarism.

Frederick the Great of Prussia

After the mid-century wars, during which Prussia had suffered badly and had almost been defeated, Frederick II (1740–1786) hoped to achieve recovery and consolidation. At grave cost he had succeeded in retaining Silesia, which he had seized from Austria in 1740. He worked to stimulate its potential as a manufacturing district. Like his Hohenzollern forebears he continued to import workers from outside Prussia. He directed new attention to Prussian agriculture. Under state supervision, swamps were drained, new crops introduced, and peasants encouraged and sometimes compelled to migrate. For the first time in Prussia potatoes and turnips came into general production. Frederick established a Land-Mortgage Credit Association to aid landowners in raising money for agricultural improvements.

Throughout this process, the impetus for development came from the state. The monarchy and its bureaucracy were the engine for change. Despite new policies and personal exhortations the general populace of Prussia did not prosper under Frederick's reign. The burden of taxation still fell disproportionally on peasants and townspeople.

In less material areas Frederick pursued enlightened policies with somewhat more success. He allowed Catholics and Jews to settle in his predominately Lutheran country, and he protected the Catholics residing in Silesia. He ordered a new codification of Prussian law, which was completed after his death. The policy of toleration allowed foreign workers to contribute to the economic growth of the state. The new legal code was to rationalize the existing system, to make it more efficient, to eliminate regional peculiarities, and to eliminate excessive aristocratic influence. The enlightened monarchs were very concerned about legal reforms, primarily as a means of extending and strengthening royal power.

Frederick liked to describe himself as "the first servant of the State." That image represented an important change in the European conception of monarchy. The idea of an impersonal state was beginning to replace the concept of a personal monarchy. Kings might come and go, but the impersonal apparatus of government—the bureaucracy, the armies, the rational laws, the courts, and the citizens' loyalty arising from fear and from appreciation of state services and protection—remained. The state as an entity separate from the personality of the ruler came into its own after the French Revolution, but it was born in the monarchies of the old regime.

Joseph II of Austria

No eighteenth-century ruler so embodied rational, impersonal force as the emperor Joseph II of Austria. He was the son of Maria Theresa and co-ruler with her from 1765 to 1780. During the next ten years he ruled alone. He has been aptly described as "an imperial puritan and a good deal of a prig."[6] During much of his life he slept on straw and ate little but beef. He prided himself on a narrow, passionless rationality, which he sought to impose by his own will on the various Hapsburg domains. The ultimate result of his well-intentioned efforts was a series of aristocratic and peasant rebellions extending from Hungary to the Austrian Netherlands.

As explained in Chapter 21, of all the rising states of the eighteenth century Austria was the most diverse in its people and problems. Robert Palmer has likened it to a "a vast holding company."[7] The Hapsburgs never succeeded in creating either a unified administrative structure or strong aristocratic loyalty. The price of the preservation of the monarchy during the War of the Austrian Succession (1740–1748) had been guarantees of considerable aristocratic independence. Joseph sought to overcome the pluralism of his holdings by increasing the power of the central monarchy. He also wished to expand

6 R. J. White, *Europe in the Eighteenth Century* (New York: St. Martin's, 1965), p. 214.
7 Robert R. Palmer, *The Age of Democratic Revolution* (Princeton: Princeton University Press, 1959), Vol. 1, p. 103.

Joseph II of Austria Promotes Toleration in His Realm

Toleration was frequently an important policy of enlightened absolutism. As shown in this 1787 passage, Joseph II of Austria believed toleration would remove religious fanaticism from his realms, lead to greater human knowledge, and at the same time make his subjects more loyal.

TILL *now the Protestant religion has been opposed in my states; its adherents have been treated like foreigners; civil rights, possession of estates, titles, and appointments, all were refused them.*

I determined from the very commencement of my reign to adorn my diadem with the love of my people, to act in the administration of affairs according to just, impartial, and liberal principles; consequently, I granted toleration, and removed the yoke which had oppressed the protestants for centuries.

Fanaticism shall in future be known in my states only by the contempt I have for it; nobody shall any longer be exposed to hardships on account of his creed; no man shall be compelled in future to profess the religion of the state, if it be contrary to his persuasion, and if he have other ideas of the right way of insuring blessedness. . . .

Tolerance is an effect of that beneficent increase of knowledge which now enlightens Europe, and which is owing to philosophy and the efforts of great men; it is a convincing proof of the improvement of the human mind, which has boldly reopened a road through the dominions of superstition, which was trodden centuries ago by Zoroaster and Confucius, and which, fortunately for mankind, has now become the highway of monarchs.

"Letters of Joseph II," *The Pamphleteer*, Vol. 19 (1822), pp. 289–290.

the borders of his territory in the direction of Poland and the Ottoman Empire.

The first target of Joseph's reassertion of royal absolutism was the church. From the reign of Charles V in the sixteenth century to that of Maria Theresa, the Hapsburgs had been the single most important dynastic champion of Roman Catholicism. Maria Theresa had surrounded herself with pious and sometimes very superstitious advisers. Joseph changed these policies. He was a practicing and perhaps even a believing Catholic, but he rid himself of priestly advisers. He extended genuine toleration to all Christians and relieved Jews living in

Emperor Joseph II of Austria encouraged
improved farming and industry in his domains. This
propaganda painting portrayed him plowing a field
and providing a good example to his subjects.
[Austrian Information Service, New York.]

Austria of many special taxes and signs of degradation.
He sought to undermine in every possible way the influence of the papacy in his lands. He drove monks and nuns
from monasteries and reduced the number of religious
holidays. While encouraging the construction of
churches, he confiscated ecclesiastical lands. He considered church use of that property unproductive. Revenues
traditionally going to the church were redirected to the
state. Priests in effect became the employees of the state.
The influence of the Roman Catholic Church as an
independent institution came to a close. Joseph was willing for religious faith and practice to flourish, but religious institutions and the people they employed must
stand subordinate to the power of the government. In
many respects the ecclesiastical policies of Joseph II pre-
figured those of the French Revolution.

Like Frederick of Prussia, Joseph sought to improve
the economic life of his domains. He abolished many
internal tariffs and encouraged road building and the
improvement of river transport. He went on personal
inspection tours of farms and manufacturing districts.

Joseph also reconstructed the judicial system to make laws
more uniform and rational and to lessen the influence of
local landlords. National courts with power over landlord
courts were established. All of these improvements were
expected to bring new unity to the state and more taxes
into the coffers at Vienna.

The most revolutionary of Joseph's departures was his
attitude toward serfdom and the land. The emperor
believed that if the peasantry were legally free and to
some extent liberated from the special feudal payments to
landlords, they would become more productive and industrious. However, to interfere with the landlord–serf
relationship was to breach what had been one of the
foundation stones of eastern European absolutism: the
tradeoff of aristocratic support for the monarchy in exchange for a free hand with the serfs.

In 1781, 1783, and 1785 Jospeh issued a series of
decrees giving legal freedom to serfs in Bohemia, Austria,
Transylvania, and Hungary. They could marry and migrate without the permission of their landlords and could
appeal decisions from manorial courts to the civil courts of
the state. Between 1783 and 1789 Joseph went even
further and drew up a tax list on which all occupiers of
land were enumerated. Henceforth, all proprietors of the
land were to be taxed regardless of social status. In 1789
by royal decree the emperor abolished *robot* or services

Empress Catherine the Great of Russia, born Sophia Augusta Frederica in the tiny German state of Anhalt-Zerbst, cultivated the friendship of the *philosophes* but pursued many policies of which they disapproved, including warfare and censorship. The artist represented here is Boroviloosky. [John R. Freeman.]

due landlords from serfs. The service was commuted to a tax, only part of which went to the landlord while the remainder reverted to the state. These measures brought turmoil to the Hapsburg domains. Peasants revolted against their landlords over the interpretation of their newly granted rights. Then the nobles of the various realms also rose up in rebellion over the emperor's decrees.

Having sowed the wind, Joseph died in 1790. His brother and successor Leopold II (1790–1792) reaped the noble whirlwind. Although quite sympathetic with Joseph's goals, Leopold repealed most of the reformist decrees to shore up the stability of his own rule. Serfdom persisted in the Austrian lands until 1848. Joseph II had possessed a narrow vision attached to an unbending will. For all his intellectual brilliance and hard work, he had failed to understand that except for a few royal bureaucrats his policies enjoyed no supporters. He had ruled without consulting any political constituency. The nobles, the church, the towns with their chartered liberties, and the absence of a strong bureaucracy or army stood as barriers to his absolutism. His was a mind of classical rationalism in conflict with political and social realities of baroque complexity.

Catherine the Great of Russia

Joseph II never grasped the practical necessity of cultivating political support for his policies. Catherine II (1762–1796) who had been born a German princess but who became empress of Russia understood only too well the fragility of the Romanov dynasty's base of power.

After the death of Peter the Great in 1725 the Russian succession had repeatedly been determined by court nobles and the army. The crown fell primarily into the hands of people with little talent. Peter's wife, Catherine I, ruled for two years (1725–1727) and was succeeded for three years by Peter's grandson Peter II. In 1730 the crown devolved on Anna, who was a niece of Peter the Great. During 1740 and 1741 a child named Ivan VI, who was less than a year old, was the nominal

The overriding territorial aim of Peter the Great in the first quarter and of Catherine the Great in the last half of the eighteenth century was the securing of northern and southern navigable-water outlets for the vast Russian Empire. Hence Peter's push to the Baltic Sea and Catherine's to the Black Sea. Catherine also managed to acquire large areas of Poland through the partitions of that country.

(See pages 588–589.)

RUSSIAN EMPIRE, 1689

TERRITORIES ADDED, 1725–1762

TERRITORIES ADDED UNDER PETER THE GREAT, 1689–1725

TERRITORIES ADDED UNDER CATHERINE THE GREAT, 1762–1796

500 MI.

500 KM.

EXPANSION OF RUSSIA, 1689–1796

ruler. Finally, in 1741 Peter the Great's daughter Elizabeth came to the throne. She held the title of empress until 1762, but she did not rule. Her court was a shambles of political and romantic intrigue. Needless to say, much of the power possessed by the tsar at the opening of the century had vanished.

At her death in 1762 Elizabeth was succeeded by Peter III, one of her nephews. He was a weak ruler whom many contemporaries considered mad. He immediately exempted the nobles from compulsory military service and then made rapid peace with Frederick the Great, for whom he held unbounded admiration. That decision probably saved Prussia from military defeat. The one positive feature of this unbalanced creature's life was his marriage in 1745 to a young German princess born in Pomerania. This was the future Catherine the Great, who for almost twenty years lived in misery and frequent danger at the court of Elizabeth. During that time she befriended important nobles and read widely in the books of the *philosophes*. She was a shrewd person whose experience in a court crawling with rumors, intrigue, and conspiracy had taught her how to survive. She had neither love nor loyalty for her demented husband. After a few months of rule Peter III was deposed and murdered with the approval, if not the aid, of Catherine. On his death she was immediately proclaimed empress.

Catherine's familiarity with the Enlightenment and the general culture of Western Europe convinced her that Russia was very backward and that it must make major reforms if it were to remain a great power. She understood that any major reform must have a wide base of political and social support. In 1767 she summoned a Legislative Commission to revise the law and government of Russia. There were over five hundred delegates from all sectors of Russian life. Prior to the convening of the Commission she issued a set of *Instructions* partly written by herself. They contained numerous ideas drawn from the political writings of the *philosophes*. The Commission considered the *Instructions* as well as other ideas and complaints raised by its members. The revision of Rus-

sian law, however, did not occur for more than a half-century. In 1768 Catherine simply dismissed the Commission, which had reached few concrete decisions. Yet the meeting had not been useless, for considerable information had been gathered about the condition of the realm. The inconclusive debates and the absence of programs from the delegates themselves suggested that most Russians saw no alternative to an autocratic monarchy.

Catherine proceeded to carry out limited reforms on

her own authority. She gave strong support to the rights and local power of the nobility. In 1775 she reorganized local government to solve problems brought to light by the Legislative Commission. She put most local offices into the hands of nobles rather than creating a royal bureaucracy. In 1785 Catherine issued the Charter of the Nobility, which guaranteed many noble rights and privileges. In part the empress had no choice but to favor the nobles. They had the capacity to topple her from the throne. There were too few educated subjects in her realm to establish an independent bureaucracy. The treasury could not afford an army strictly loyal to the crown. So Catherine wisely made a virtue of necessity. She strengthened the stability of her crown by making convenient friends with her nobles.

Part and parcel of Catherine's program was a continuation of the economic development commenced under Peter the Great. She attempted to suppress internal barriers to trade. Exports of grain, flax, furs, and naval stores grew dramatically. She also favored the expansion of the small Russian middle class. Russian trade required such a vital urban class. And through all of these departures Catherine attempted to maintain ties of friendship and correspondence with the *philosophes*. She knew that if she treated them kindly, they would be sufficiently flattered and would give her a progressive reputation throughout Europe.

The limited administrative reforms and the policy of economic growth had a counterpart in the diplomatic sphere. The Russian drive for warm-water ports continued. This goal required warfare with the Turks. In 1769, as a result of a minor Russian incursion, the Ottoman Empire declared war on Russia. The Russians responded in a series of strikingly successful military moves. During 1769 and 1770 the Russian fleet sailed all the way from the Baltic Sea into the eastern Mediterranean. The Russian army won several major victories that by 1771 gave Russia control of Ottoman provinces on the Danube River and the Crimean coast of the Black Sea. The conflict dragged on until 1774, when it was closed by the Treaty of Kuchuk–Kainardji. The treaty gave Russia a direct outlet on the Black Sea, free navigation rights in its waters, and free access through the Bosporus. Moreover, the province of the Crimea became an independent state, which Catherine painlessly annexed in 1783.

The Partition of Poland

These military successes obviously brought the empress much domestic political support. However, they made the other states of eastern Europe uneasy. These anxieties were overcome by an extraordinary division of Polish territory known as the First Partition of Poland. The Russian victories along the Danube River were most unwelcome to Austria, which also harbored ambitions for territorial expansion in that direction. At the same time, the Ottoman Empire was pressing Prussia for aid against Russia. Frederick the Great made a proposal to Russia and Austria that would give each something it wanted, prevent conflict among the powers, and save appearances. After long, complicated, secret negotiations the three powers agreed that Russia would abandon the conquered Danubian provinces. In compensation Russia received a large portion of Polish territory with almost two million inhabitants. As a reward for remaining neutral Prussia annexed most of the territory between East Prussia and Prussia proper. This land allowed Frederick to unite two previously separate sections of his realm. Finally, Austria took Galicia, with its important salt mines, and other Polish territory with over two and one-half million inhabitants. In September 1773 the helpless Polish aristocracy, paying the price for the maintenance of their internal liberties, ratified this seizure of their territory. The Polish state had lost approximately one third of its territory.

There were two additional partitions of Poland by Russia, Prussia, and Austria. These occurred in 1793 and 1795 and removed Poland from the map of Europe. Each time the great powers contended that they were saving themselves and by implication the rest of Europe from Polish anarchy. The fact of the matter was that the

PARTITIONS OF POLAND, 1772–1793–1795

	FIRST PARTITION 1772	SECOND PARTITION 1793	THIRD PARTITION 1795
TO PRUSSIA			
TO AUSTRIA			
TO RUSSIA			

The callous eradication of Poland from the map displayed eighteenth-century power politics at its most extreme. Poland, without strong central governmental institutions, fell victim to those states in central and eastern Europe that *had* developed such institutions.

This French engraving is a satirical comment on the first partition of Poland (1772) by Russia, Austria, and Prussia. The distressed monarch attempting to retain his crown is Stanislaus of Poland. Catherine of Russia, Joseph of Austria, and Frederick of Prussia point out their respective shares of the loot.

political weakness of Poland made the country and its resources a rich field for plunderous aggression. The last two partitions took place during the French Revolution. The three eastern absolute monarchies objected to certain reforms undertaken by Polish nobles for fear that even minor Polish reform might endanger the stability of their own societies.

The End of the Eighteenth Century in Eastern Europe

During the last quarter of the eighteenth century all three regimes based on enlightened absolutism had become more repressive. Frederick lived much removed from his people during his old age. The aristocracy, looking out for its own self-interest, filled the major Prussian military and administrative posts. As Joseph II

Enlightened Absolutism 589

confronted growing frustration and political unrest over his plans for restructuring the society of his realms, he used more and more censorship and secret police. Catherine the Great never fully recovered from the fears raised by Pugachev's rebellion. Once the French Revolution broke out in 1789, the Russian empress censored books based on Enlightenment thought and sent offensive authors into Siberian exile.

By the close of the century all three states were characterized by autocracy, censorship, increasingly downtrodden serf populations, grasping nobilities, and fear of change permeating all the ruling classes. These attitudes had come into existence prior to 1789, but the events in France froze those points of view for almost half a century. Paradoxically nowhere did the humanity and liberalism of the Enlightenment ultimately have a more difficult time surviving and entering the mainstream of life and thought than in those states that had experienced "enlightened" rulers.

Although the enlightened absolute monarchs lacked the humanity of the *philosophes,* they had embraced the Enlightenment spirit of innovation. They wanted to change the political, social, and economic structures of their realms. From the close of the Seven Years' War (1763) until the opening of the French Revolution in 1789, the monarchies of both western and eastern Europe had been the major forces working for significant institutional change. In every case they had stirred up considerable aristocratic and some popular resistance and resentment. George III of Britain for years fought with Parliament and lost the colonies of North America in the process. Frederick II of Prussia carried out his program of reform only because he accepted new aristocratic influence over the bureaucracy and army. Catherine II of Russia had come to terms with her nobility. Joseph II had left his domains in turmoil by imposing changes without consulting the nobility.

These monarchs pushed for innovations because of their desires for increased revenue. The same problem existed in France. There the royal drive for adequate fiscal resources also led to aristocratic rebellion. However, in France neither the monarchy nor the aristocracy could control the social and political forces unleashed by their quarrel.

SUGGESTED READINGS

C. BECKER, *The Heavenly City of the Eighteenth Century Philosophers* (1932). An influential, but very controversial discussion.

P. P. BERNARD, *Joseph II* (1968). A brief biography.

T. BESTERMANN, *Voltaire* (1969). A recent biography by the editor of Voltaire's letters.

E. CASSIRER, *The Philosophy of the Enlightenment* (1951). A brilliant but difficult work by one of the great philosophers of the twentieth century.

G. R. CRAGG, *The Church and the Age of Reason* (1961). A general survey of eighteenth-century religious life.

P. FUSSELL, *The Rhetorical World of Augustan Humanism* (1969). Examines English writers during the Enlightenment.

J. GAGLIARDO, *Enlightened Despotism* (1967). A discussion of the subject in its European context.

P. GAY, *The Enlightenment: An Interpretation,* 2 vols. (1966, 1969). The most important and far-reaching recent treatment.

P. GAY, *The Enlightenment: A Comprehensive Anthology* (1973). A large, well-edited set of documents.

L. GERSHOY, *From Despotism to Revolution, 1763–1793* (1944). A sound treatment of the political background.

N. HAMPSON, *A Cultural History of the Enlightenment* (1969). A useful introduction.

P. HAZARD, *The European Mind: The Critical Years, 1680–1715* (1935), and *European Thought in the Eighteenth Century from Montesquieu to Lessing* (1946). The two volumes portray the century as the turning point for the emergence of the modern mind in Europe.

L. KRIEGER, *Kings and Philosophers, 1689–1789* (1970). A survey that relates the social and political thought of the Enlightenment writers to their immediate political setting.

K. MARTIN, *French Liberal Thought in the Eighteenth Century,* rev. ed. (1954). Surveys the political ideas of the French *philosophes.*

R. R. Palmer, *Catholics and Unbelievers in Eighteenth Century France* (1939). A discussion of the opponents of the *philosophes.*

G. Ritter, *Frederick the Great* (trans. 1968). A useful biography.

R. O. Rockford (Ed.), *Carl Becker's Heavenly City Revisited* (1958). Important essays qualifying Becker's thesis.

G. S. Thomson, *Catherine the Great and the Expansion of Russia* (1947). A short study that sets Catherine in the arena of general European politics.

A. M. Wilson, *Diderot* (1972). A splendid biography of the person behind the project for the *Encyclopedia* and other major Enlightenment publications.

592

23
The French Revolution

I N T H E spring of 1789 the long-festering conflict between the French monarchy and aristocracy erupted into a new political crisis. This dispute, unlike earlier ones, quickly outgrew the issues of its origins and produced the wider disruption of the French Revolution. The quarrel that began as a struggle between the most exclusive elements of the political nation soon involved all sectors of French society and eventually every major state in Europe. Before the turmoil settled, small-town provincial lawyers and Parisian street orators exercised more influence over the fate of the Continent than did aristocrats, royal ministers, or monarchs. Armies commanded by persons of low birth and filled by conscripted village youths emerged victorious over forces composed of professional soldiers and directed by officers of noble birth. The very existence of the Roman Catholic faith in France was challenged. Politically and socially neither France nor Europe would ever be quite the same after these events.

The Crisis of the French Monarchy

The French Revolution constituted one of the central turning points in modern European history, but it originated from the basic tensions and problems that characterized practically all late eighteenth-century states. From the Seven Years' War (1756–1763) onward, the French monarchy was unable to handle its finances on a sound basis. It emerged from the conflict both defeated and in debt. The French support of the American revolt against

This nineteenth-century relief from the Arch of Triumph in Paris represents the spirit of the "Marseillaise" and the militant height in 1792 of the French Revolution. In contrast to earlier sculpture, its heroes are not aristocrats or mercenary soldiers but the people themselves, in bits of heroic antique armor, prepared to fight for liberty. The sculptor was François Rude (1784–1855). [Bettmann Archive.]

Great Britain further deepened the financial difficulties of the government. On the eve of the revolution the interest and payments on the royal debt amounted to just over one half of the entire budget. The annual deficit was in the vicinity of 126 million livres. Given the economic vitality of the nation, this debt was neither overly large nor disproportionate to those of other European powers. The problem lay with the inability of the royal government to tap the wealth of the French nation through taxes to service and repay the debt. Paradoxically France was a rich nation with an impoverished government.

The debt was symptomatic of the failure of the eighteenth-century French monarchy to come to terms with the resurgent social and political power of the aristocracy. For twenty-five years after the Seven Years' War there was a standoff between them. The monarchy attempted to pursue a program somewhat resembling that associated with enlightened absolutism in eastern Europe. However, both Louis XV (1715–1774) and Louis XVI (1774–1792) lacked the character and resolution for such a departure. The moral corruption of the former and the indecision of the latter meant that the monarchy could not rally the French public to its side. Generally speaking, the aristocratic *parlements* won the battle for public opinion. Whenever the king's ministers attacked the privileges or wealth of the nobility, the *parlements* represented themselves as the protectors of French liberty against the intrusion of absolute monarchical power.

In place of a consistent policy to deal with the growing debt, the monarchy gave way to hesitancy, retreat, and even duplicity. In 1763 the monarchy issued a new set of tax decrees that would have extended the collection of certain taxes that were supposed to have been discontinued at the close of the war. There were also new tax assessments. This search for revenue was not unlike the one that led the British government to attempt to tax the American colonies. Several of the provincial *parlements* and finally the Parlement of Paris—all controlled by nobles—declared the taxes illegal. During the ensuing dispute the aristocratic *parlements* set themselves up as the

Louis XVI of France (1774–1792) was unable to regain control of the political situation in France after the summer of 1789. The drawing is by Ducreux. [French Cultural Services, New York.]

spokesmen of the nation against the illegal assertion of monarchical power. Such was one of the political functions of the nobility that Montesquieu had outlined in *The Spirit of the Laws* (1748).

In 1770 Louis XV appointed René Maupeou (1714–1792) as chancellor. The new minister was determined to break the *parlements* and impose a greater part of the tax burden on the nobility. He abolished the *parlements* and exiled their members to different parts of the country. He then commenced an ambitious program of reform and efficiency. What ultimately doomed Maupeou's policy was less the resistance of the nobility than the death of Louis XV in 1774. His successor, Louis XVI, in an attempt to regain what he conceived to be popular support, restored all the *parlements* and confirmed their old powers. This action in conjunction with the later aid to the American colonies locked the monarchy into a continuing financial bind. Thereafter meaningful fiscal or political reform through existing institutions was probably doomed.

Louis XVI's first minister was the physiocrat Jacques Turgot (1727–1781), who attempted various economic reforms, including the removal of restrictions on the grain trade and the abolishment of the guilds. He transformed the *corvée* or road-working obligation of peasants into money payments. Turgot also intended to restructure the taxation system in order to tap the wealth of the nobility. These and other ideas represented a program of bold new departures for the monarchy. They proved too bold for the tremulous young king, who dismissed Turgot in 1776. By 1781 the debt, as a result of the aid to America, was larger and the sources of revenues unchanged. However, the new finance minister, Jacques Necker (1732–1804), a Swiss banker, produced a public report which suggested that the situation was not so bad as feared. He argued that if the expenditures for the American war were removed, the budget was in surplus. Soon after issuing this optimistic document, Necker left office. His financial sleight of hand made it more difficult for later ministers to claim the need for new taxes.

The Parlement *of Paris Makes Claims to Political Power*

The *Parlement* of Paris was a judicial court dominated by the French nobility. From the mid-eighteenth century until the French Revolution this court attempted to assert its power as a curb on the power of the monarchy. In this 1755 document, the Parlement argues that from time immemorial monarchs submitted their laws for the approval of the court and that stability and political harmony resulted. The Parlement has to appeal to very early times because under Louis XIV it had lost much power.

Sire, *the monarchy has existed thirteen centuries. For thirteen centuries your* Parlement, *under whatever name it has been known by, always constituted the same tribunal and exercised the same functions in the State. Its administration, in regard to the management of the laws, has never ceased to be the same up to this moment. It has always preserved the glorious benefit of being the true Court of France because it was born with the empire of the French to be a branch of the essential pattern of government.*

. . . .

It is in accordance with this view, sire, that in order to enlighten and moderate the absolute power of sovereignty by the prudence of advisers, our monarchs in the past have always wisely granted their first magistrates [that is, the Parlement] *the right to check the possible extravagance of one man [that is, the monarch] against the fairness of princes [that is, the nobles of the* Parlement]. *Monarchs have perceived, they have recognized, that such ministers of their authority serve only to make monarchs rule justly and to win more and more people over to them.*

And what advantages have resulted, sire, from the birth of the monarchy to this day, from the happy mixture of sovereignty and prudence and from that wise moderation of one by the other? Constant and essential harmony as ancient as the French Empire and to which it is indebted for its progress and grandeur. Harmony is the principle and the pledge of the Empire's preservation. Harmony maintains authority without effort and assures sovereignty by justice.

Remonstrances du Parlement de Paris au XVIIIe Siècle, ed. by J. Flamermont. (Paris, 1898), Vol. 2, pp. 26, 86–87, cited in John Lough, *An Introduction to Eighteenth-Century France* (New York: David MacKay Company, 1964), pp. 174–175 (passage translated by Frank M. Turner).

Queen Marie Antoinette (1755–1793) was the daughter of Empress Maria Theresa of Austria and the wife of Louis XVI. Around her gathered many of the popularly believed unfavorable stories of the French court. The painting is by Elisabeth Vigée-Lebrun (1755–1842). [The Granger Collection.]

The monarchy hobbled along until 1786. By this time Charles Alexandre de Calonne (1734–1802) was the minister of finance. He was probably the most able administrator to serve Louis XVI. More carefully than previous ministers he charted the size of the debt and the deficit. He submitted a program for reform quite similar to that presented by Turgot a decade earlier. Calonne proposed to encourage internal trade, to lower some taxes such as the *gabelle* on salt, and to transform peasants' services to money payments.

More important, Calonne urged the introduction of a new land tax that would require payments from all landowners regardless of their social status. If this tax could be imposed, the monarchy would be able to abandon other indirect taxes. The government would also rarely have to seek approval for further new taxes from the aristocratically dominated *parlements*. Calonne also intended to establish new local assemblies to approve land taxes in which voting power would depend upon the amount of land owned rather than upon the social status of the owner. All of these proposals would have undermined both the political and the social power of the French aristocracy.

A new clash with the nobility was unavoidable, but the monarchy had very little room for maneuver. The creditors were at the door, and the treasury was nearly empty. Consequently, in 1787 Calonne met with an Assembly of Notables drawn from the upper ranks of the aristocracy and the church to seek support and approval for his plan. The assembly adamantly refused any such action. Rather

they demanded that the aristocracy be allowed a greater share in the government of the kingdom. They also called for the reappointment of Necker, whom they believed had left the country in sound fiscal condition. Finally, they demanded the convocation of the ancient Estates-General of France, which had not met since 1614.

Again Louis XVI backed off. He dismissed Calonne and replaced him with Étienne Charles Loménie de Brienne (1727–1794), who was archbishop of Toulouse and the chief opponent of Calonne at the Assembly of Notables. Once in office Brienne found to his astonishment that the situation was as bad as his predecessor had asserted. Brienne himself now sought to impose the land tax. However, the Parlement of Paris took the new position that it lacked authority to authorize the tax and said that only the Estates-General could do so. Shortly thereafter Brienne appealed to the Assembly of the

In the parks of the palace of Versailles was built an idealized farm village for Queen Marie Antoinette. There she and her friends could go to pretend for an afternoon that they were shepherds and milkmaids. Such extravagance was one of the reasons for resentment of the monarchy. This is a recent photograph of her restored hamlet. [The Granger Collection.]

Clergy to approve a large subsidy to allow funding of that part of the debt then coming due for payment. The clergy, like the Parlement dominated by aristocrats, not only refused the subsidy, but also reduced their existing contribution or *don gratuit* to the government. As these unfruitful negotiations were transpiring at the center of political life, local aristocratic *parlements* and estates in the provinces were demanding restoration of the privileges they had enjoyed during the early seventeenth century before Richelieu and Louis XIV had crushed their independent power. Consequently, in July 1788 the king, through Brienne, agreed to convoke the Estates-General the next year. Brienne resigned and was replaced by Necker. The institutions of the aristocracy and to a lesser degree of the church had brought the French monarchy to its knees. In the country of its origin, royal absolutism had been defeated.

The Revolutions of 1789

The Estates-General Becomes the National Assembly

The aristocratic triumph proved to be quite brief. It unloosed social and political forces that neither the nobles nor the monarchy could control. The new difficulties arose from clashes among the groups represented in the Estates-General. The body was composed of three divisions: the First Estate of the clergy, the Second Estate of the nobility, and the Third Estate, which represented everyone else in the kingdom. During the widespread public discussions preceding the meeting of the Estates-General, it became clear that the Third Estate, which included all the professional, commercial, and middle-class groups of the country, would not permit the monarchy and the aristocracy to decide the future course of the nation. Their spirit was best displayed in a pamphlet published during 1789 in which the Abbé Sieyès (1748–1836) declared, "What is the Third Estate? Everything. What has it been in the political order up to

1789

May 5	The Estates General opens at Versailles.
June 17	The Third Estate declares itself the National Assembly.
June 20	The National Assembly takes the Tennis Court Oath.
July 14	Fall of the Bastille in the city of Paris.
Late July	The Great Fear spreads in the countryside.
August 4	The nobles surrender their feudal rights in a meeting of the National Assembly.
August 27	Declaration of the Rights of Man and Citizen.
October 5–6	Parisian women march to Versailles and force Louis XVI and his family to return to Paris.

1790

July 12	Civil Constitution of the Clergy adopted.
July 14	A new constitution is accepted by the king.

1791

June 20–25	Louis XVI and his family attempt to flee France and are stopped at Varennes.
August 27	The Declaration of Pillnitz.
October 1	The Legislative Assembly meets.

1792

April 20	France declares war against Austria.
August 10	The Tuileries palace is stormed, and Louis XVI takes refuge with the Legislative Assembly.
September 2–7	The September Massacres.
September 20	France wins the battle of Valmy.
September 21	The Convention meets, and the monarchy is abolished.

1793

January 21	Louis XVI is executed.
February 1	France declares war against Great Britain.
March	Counterrevolution breaks out in the Vendée.
April	The Committee of Public Safety is formed.

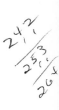

The Estates-General opened at Versailles in 1789 with much pomp and splendor. In the old French print shown here, Louis XVI is on the throne. The First Estate, the clergy, is at the left; the Second Estate, the nobility, sits at the upper right; and the more numerous Third Estate, dressed in black suits and capes, sits at the lower right. [Culver Pictures.]

June 22	The Constitution of 1793 is adopted but not put into operation.
July	Robespierre enters the Committee of Public Safety.
August 23	*Levée en masse* proclaimed.
September 17	Maximum prices set on food and other commodities.
October 16	Queen Marie Antoinette is executed.
November 10	Worship of God is abolished, and the Cult of Reason is proclaimed.
	The revolutionary calendar beginning on September 22, 1792 is adopted.

1794

March 24	Execution of the Hébertist leaders of the *sans-culottes*.
April 6	Execution of Danton.
June 8	Robespierre leads the celebration of the Festival of the Supreme Being.
June 10	The Law of 22 Prairial is adopted.
July 27	The ninth of Thermidor and the fall of Robespierre.
July 28	Robespierre is executed.

1795

| August 22 | The Constitution of 1795 is adopted establishing the Directory. |

the present? Nothing. What does it ask? To become something."[1]

The split between the aristocracy and the Third Estate occurred before the Estates-General gathered. Debate over the proper organization of the body drew the lines of basic disagreement. Members of the aristocracy demanded an equal number of representatives for each estate. In September 1788 the Parlement of Paris ruled that voting in the Estates-General should be conducted by order rather than by head, that is, that each estate, or order, should have one vote, rather than that each member should have one vote. That procedure would ensure that the aristocratic First and Second Estates could always outvote the Third. Both moves on the part of the aristocracy unmasked its alleged concern for French liberty and exposed it as a group determined to maintain its privileges. After much public debate and private consultation, however, Louis XVI announced that the Third Estate would elect twice as many representatives as either the nobles or the clergy. This so-called doubling of the Third meant that the Third Estate could easily dominate the

1 Quoted in Leo Gershoy, *The French Revolution and Napoleon* (New York: Appleton, Century, Crofts, 1964), p. 102.

This well-known painting by Jacques Louis David (1748–1825) portrays the Tennis Court Oath, June 20. The emotion of the scene should be compared with the calm shown in the previous picture of the opening of the Estates-General. In the center foreground are members of *different* Estates joining hands in cooperation as equals. The presiding officer leading the oath is Jean Sylvain Bailly, soon to become mayor in a reorganized government of the city of Paris. The painting is in the Musée Carnavalet in Paris. [French Embassy Press and Information Division, New York.]

Estates-General if voting were allowed by head rather than by order. It was properly assumed that some liberal nobles and clergy would support the Third Estate. The method of voting was not settled until after the Estates-General gathered at Versailles in May 1789.

When the representatives came to the royal palace, they brought with them *cahiers*, or lists of grievances, registered by the local electors and to be presented to the king. Large numbers of these have survived to provide considerable information about the state of the country on the eve of the revolution. But those complaints could not be discussed until the questions of organization and voting had been decided. From the beginning, the Third Estate, whose members consisted largely of local officials, professional men, and lawyers, refused to sit as a separate order as the king desired. For several weeks there was a standoff. Then on June 1 the Third Estate invited the clergy and the nobles to join them in organizing a new legislative body. A few members of the lower clergy did so. On June 17 that body declared itself the National Assembly.

Three days later, locked out of their usual meeting place, the National Assembly moved to a nearby tennis court, where its members made an oath to continue to sit until they had given France a constitution. This was the famous "Tennis Court Oath." Louis XVI ordered the National Assembly to desist from their actions, but shortly afterward a majority of the clergy and a large group of nobles joined the Assembly. On June 27 the king capitulated and formally requested the First and Second Estates to meet with the National Assembly. Had

The fall of the Bastille on July 14, 1789 is recreated, possibly a bit romantically, in an early nineteenth-century French engraving. [The Granger Collection.]

nothing further occurred, the government of France would have been transformed. Government by privileged orders had come to an end. For the National Assembly, which renamed itself the National Constituent Assembly, was composed of persons from all three orders who possessed shared liberal goals for the administrative, constitutional, and economic reform of the country.

Fall of the Bastille

Two new factors soon intruded upon the scene. The first was Louis XVI himself, who attempted to regain the initiative by mustering royal troops in the vicinity of Versailles and Paris. It appeared that he might be contemplating the disruption of the National Constituent Assembly. Such was the advice of Queen Marie Antoinette, his brothers, and the most conservative nobles, with whom he had begun to consult. On July 11, without consultation with the Assembly leaders, Louis abruptly dismissed Necker. These actions marked the beginning of a steady, but consistently poorly executed, royal attempt to undermine the Assembly and halt the revolution. Most of the Constituent Assembly wished to create some form of constitutional monarchy, but from the start that effort was thwarted by Louis's refusal to cooperate. The king fatally decided to throw his lot in with the aristocracy against the nation.

The second new factor to impose itself on the events at Versailles was the populace of Paris. The mustering of royal troops created anxiety in the city, where throughout the winter and spring of 1789 there had been several riots. The Parisians who had elected their representatives to the Third Estate had continued to meet after the elections. By June they were organizing a citizen militia and collecting arms. They regarded the dismissal of Necker as the opening of a royal offensive against the National Constituent Assembly and the city. On July 14 somewhat over eight hundred people, most of whom were small shopkeepers, tradesmen, craftsmen, and wage earners, marched to the Bastille in search of weapons for

The Revolutions of 1789 **599**

the militia. This great fortress, with ten-foot-thick walls, had once held political prisoners. Through miscalculations and ineptitude on the part of the governor of the fortress, the troops in the Bastille fired into the crowd, killing ninety-eight people and wounding many others. Thereafter the crowd stormed the fortress and eventually gained entrance. They released the seven prisoners, none of whom were there for political reasons, and killed several troops and the governor. They found no weapons.

The attack on the Bastille marked the first of many crucial *journées*, or days, when the populace of Paris would redirect the course of the revolution. The fall of the fortress signaled that the political future of the nation would not be decided solely by the National Constituent Assembly. As the news of the Bastille spread, similar disturbances took place in the provincial cities. A few days later Louis XVI again bowed to the force of events and went to Paris, where he wore the revolutionary cockade and recognized the organized electors as the legitimate government of the city. The king also recognized the citizen militia, which under the command of Lafayette became the National Guard. The citizens of Paris were for the time being satisfied.

The Great Fear and the Surrender of Feudal Privileges

Simultaneous with the popular urban disturbances a movement known as the Great Fear swept across much of the French countryside. Rumors had spread that royal troops would be sent into the rural districts. The result was an intensification of peasant disturbances that had begun earlier during the spring. The Great Fear witnessed the burning of chateaux, the destruction of records and documents, and the refusal to pay feudal dues. The peasants were determined to take possession of food supplies and land that they considered to be rightfully theirs. They were reclaiming rights and property that they had lost through the aristocratic resurgence of the last quarter-century, as well as venting their general anger against the injustices of rural life.

On the night of August 4, 1789, aristocrats in the National Constituent Assembly attempted to halt the spreading disorder in the countryside. By prearrangement a number of liberal nobles and churchmen rose in the Assembly and renounced their feudal rights, dues, and tithes. In a scene of great emotion, hunting and fishing rights, judicial authority, and special exemptions were surrendered. In a sense these nobles gave up what they had already lost and what could not be regained without civil war in the rural areas. They would also in many cases receive compensation for their losses. Nonetheless, after the night of August 4 all Frenchmen were subject to the same and equal laws. That dramatic session of the Assembly paved the way for the legal and social reconstruction of the nation. Without those renunciations the constructive work of the National Constituent Assembly would have been much more difficult.

Both the attack on the Bastille and the Great Fear displayed varieties of rural and urban riots that had characterized much of eighteenth-century political and social life. Louis XVI first thought that the turmoil over the Bastille was simply another bread riot. The popular disturbances also were only partly related to the events at Versailles. A deep economic downturn had struck France during 1788 and had continued into 1789. The harvests for both years had been poor, and food prices in 1789 stood higher than at any time since 1703. Wages had not kept up with the rise in prices. Throughout the winter of 1788–1789, an unusually cold one, many people suffered from hunger. Several cities had experienced wage and food riots. These economic difficulties helped the revolution reach such vast proportions. The political, social, and economic grievances of numerous sections of the country became combined. The National Constituent Assembly could look to the popular forces as a source of strength against the king and the conservative aristocrats. As the various elements of the Assembly later fell into quarrels among themselves, their factions succumbed to the temptation of appealing to the politically sophisticated and well-organized shopkeeping and artisan classes for support. When this turn of events came to pass, the popular classes could demand a price for their cooperation.

The Declaration of the Rights of Man and Citizen

During late August 1789 the National Constituent Assembly decided that prior to the writing of a new constitution a statement of broad principles should be set forth. This task was accomplished on August 27 in the Declaration of the Rights of Man and Citizen. The declaration drew together much of the political language of the Enlightenment and was also influenced by the Declaration of Rights adopted by Virginia in America in June 1776. The French declaration proclaimed that all men were "born and remain free and equal in rights." The natural rights of men and citizens were "liberty, property, security, and resistence to oppression." Governments existed to protect those rights. All political sovereignty resided in the nation and its representatives. All citizens were to be equal before the law and were to be "equally admissible to all public dignities, offices and employments, according to their capacity, and with no other distinction than that of their virtues and talents." There were to be due process of law and presumption of innocence until proof of guilt. Freedom of religion was affirmed. Taxation was to be apportioned equally according to capacity to pay. Property constituted "an inviolable and sacred right."[2] Although these statements were rather abstract, practically all of them were directed against specific abuses of the old aristocratic and absolutist regime. If any two principles of the future governed the declaration, they were civic equality and protection of property. The Declaration of the Rights of Man and Citizen has often been considered the death certificate of the old regime.

Louis XVI stalled before ratifying both the declaration and the aristocratic renunciation of feudalism. The longer he hesitated, the larger existing suspicions grew that he might again try to resort to the use of troops. Moreover bread continued to be in short supply. On October 5 a large crowd of Parisian women marched to Versailles demanding more bread. They milled about the palace, and many stayed the night. Under this pressure the king agreed to sanction the decrees of the Assembly. The next day he and his family appeared on a balcony before the

2 Quoted in Georges Lefebvre, *The Coming of the French Revolution*, trans. by R. R. Palmer (Princeton, N.J.: Princeton University Press, 1967), pp. 221–223.

crowd. Finally, to satisfy the demands of the women, the monarch left Versailles for the last time and rode with his family to Paris, where they settled in the Tuileries Palace. The National Constituent Assembly soon followed. Thereafter both Paris and France remained relatively stable and peaceful until the summer of 1792.

An unknown contemporary German depicted the march of the women of Paris on the palace of Versailles in October 1789. On their return to the city they were accompanied by Louis XVI and his family. [The Granger Collection.]

The Reconstruction of France

Once established in Paris, the National Constituent Assembly set about reorganizing France. In government it pursued a policy of constitutional monarchy; in administration, rationalism; in economics, unregulated freedom; and in religion, anticlericalism. Throughout its proceedings the Assembly was determined to protect property and to limit the impact upon national life of the unpropertied elements of the nation and even of possessors of small amounts of property. While championing civic equality before the law, the Assembly spurned social equality and extensive democracy. In all these areas the Assembly charted a general course that to a greater or lesser degree nineteenth-century liberals across Europe would follow.

Political Reorganization

The Constitution of 1791, which was the product of the National Constituent Assembly's deliberations, established a constitutional monarchy. There was to be a unicameral Legislative Assembly in which all laws would originate and in which the major political authority of the

nation would reside. The monarch was allowed a suspensive veto that could delay but not halt legislation. Powers of war and peace were vested in the Assembly. The constitution provided for an elaborate system of indirect elections intended to thwart direct popular pressure on the government. The citizens of France were divided into active and passive categories. Only active citizens—that is, men paying annual taxes equal to three days of local labor wages—could vote. They chose electors who then in turn voted for the members of the legislature. At the levels of electors or members still further property qualifications were imposed. Only about fifty thousand citizens of a population of about twenty-five million could qualify as electors or members of the Legislative Assembly.

In reconstructing the local and judicial administration, the National Constituent Assembly applied the rational spirit of the Enlightenment. It abolished the ancient French provinces, such as Burgundy and Brittany, and established in their place eighty-three departments (*départements*) of generally equal size named after rivers, mountains, and other geographical features. The departments in turn were subdivided into districts, cantons, and communes. Most local elections were also indirect. The

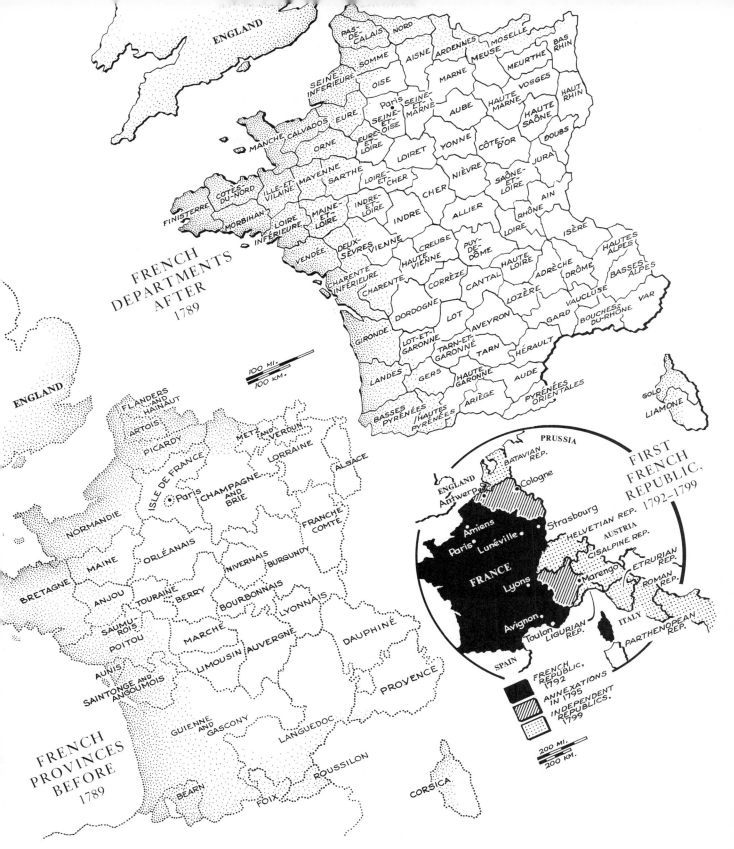

ENGLAND

FRENCH
DEPARTMENTS
AFTER
1789

PAS-DE-CALAIS
NORD
SOMME
AISNE
ARDENNES
MOSELLE
MEUSE
BAS-RHIN
SEINE-INFÉRIEURE
OISE
Paris
SEINE-ET-MARNE
MARNE
MEUSE
MEURTHE
VOSGES
HAUT-RHIN
MANCHE
CALVADOS
EURE
SEINE-ET-OISE
AUBE
HAUTE-MARNE
HAUTE-SAÔNE
ORNE
EURE-ET-LOIRE
YONNE
CÔTE-D'OR
DOUBS
CÔTES-DU-NORD
ILLE-ET-VILAINE
MAYENNE
SARTHE
LOIRE-ET-CHER
LOIRET
NIÈVRE
SAÔNE-ET-LOIRE
JURA
FINISTÈRE
MORBIHAN
LOIRE-INFÉRIEURE
MAINE-ET-LOIRE
INDRE-ET-LOIRE
CHER
ALLIER
RHÔNE
AIN
VENDÉE
DEUX-SÈVRES
VIENNE
INDRE
CREUSE
PUY-DE-DÔME
LOIRE
ISÈRE
HAUTES-ALPES
CHARENTE-INFÉRIEURE
CHARENTE
HAUTE-VIENNE
CORRÈZE
CANTAL
HAUTE-LOIRE
ARDÈCHE
DRÔME
BASSES-ALPES
DORDOGNE
LOT
AVEYRON
LOZÈRE
GARD
VAUCLUSE
BOUCHES-DU-RHÔNE
VAR
GIRONDE
LOT-ET-GARONNE
TARN-ET-GARONNE
TARN
HÉRAULT
LANDES
GERS
HAUTE-GARONNE
AUDE
BASSES-PYRÉNÉES
HAUTES-PYRÉNÉES
ARIÈGE
PYRÉNÉES-ORIENTALES

GOLO
LIAMONE

100 MI.
100 KM.

ENGLAND

FRENCH
PROVINCES
BEFORE
1789

FLANDERS AND HAINAUT
ARTOIS
PICARDY
METZ AND VERDUN
LORRAINE
ALSACE
ISLE DE FRANCE
Paris
CHAMPAGNE AND BRIE
FRANCHE-COMTÉ
NORMANDIE
MAINE
ORLÉANAIS
NIVERNAIS
BURGUNDY
BRETAGNE
ANJOU
TOURAINE
BERRY
BOURBONNAIS
LYONNAIS
SAUMU-ROIS
POITOU
MARCHE
AUVERGNE
DAUPHINÉ
AUNIS
LIMOUSIN
SAINTONGE AND ANGOUMOIS
PROVENCE
GUIENNE AND GASCONY
LANGUEDOC
BÉARN
FOIX
ROUSSILON
CORSICA

FIRST
FRENCH
REPUBLIC,
1792–1799

PRUSSIA
BATAVIAN REP.
ENGLAND
Antwerp
Cologne
Amiens
Paris
Lunéville
Strasbourg
HELVETIAN REP.
AUSTRIA
CISALPINE REP.
FRANCE
Lyons
Marengo
ETRURIAN REP.
ROMAN REP.
Avignon
Toulon
LIGURIAN REP.
ITALY
PARTHENOPEAN REP.
SPAIN

FRENCH REPUBLIC, 1792
ANNEXATIONS IN 1795
INDEPENDENT REPUBLICS, 1799

200 MI.
200 KM.

departmental reconstruction proved one of the most permanent achievements of the Assembly. The departments exist to the present day. All of the ancient judicial courts, including the seigneurial courts and the *parlements,* were also abolished. In their place were organized uniform courts with elected judges and prosecutors. Procedures were simplified, and the most degrading punishments were removed from the books.

Economic Policy

In economic matters the Assembly continued the policies attempted by Louis XVI's reformist ministers. The suppression of the guilds and the liberation of the grain trade were supported. The metric system was established to provide the nation with uniform weights and measures. These policies of economic freedom and uniformity disappointed both peasants and urban workers caught in the cycle of inflation. By decrees of 1790 the Assembly placed the burden of proof on the peasants to rid themselves of residual feudal dues for which compensation was to be paid. On June 14, 1791, the Assembly crushed the attempts of urban workers to protect their wages by enacting the Chapelier Law, which forbade worker associations. Peasants and workers were to be left to the freedom and mercy of the marketplace.

While these various reforms were put into effect, the original financial crisis that had occasioned the calling of the Estates-General persisted. The royal debt was not repudiated because it was owed to the bankers, the merchants, and the commercial traders of the Third Estate. The National Constituent Assembly had suppressed many of the old hated indirect taxes and had substituted new land taxes, but these proved insufficient. Moreover there were not enough officials to collect them. The continuing financial problem led the Assembly to take what may well have been for the future of French life and society its most decisive action. The Assembly decided to finance the debt by confiscating and then selling the land and property of the Roman Catholic Church in France. The results were further inflation, religious schism, and

The *assignats* were government bonds that were backed by confiscated church lands. They circulated as money. When the government printed too many of them, inflation resulted and their value fell. [Bettmann Archive.]

civil war. In effect, the National Constituent Assembly opened a new chapter in the relations of church and state in Europe.

Having chosen to plunder the land of the church, the Assembly in December 1790 authorized the issuance of *assignats,* or government bonds, the value of which was guaranteed by the revenue to be generated from the sale of church property. Initially a limit was set on the quantity of *assignats* to be issued. However, the bonds proved so acceptable to the public that they began to circulate as currency. The Assembly decided to issue an ever larger number of them to liquidate the national debt and to create a large body of new property owners with a direct stake in the revolution. However, within a few months the value of the *assignats* began to fall. Inflation increased and put new stress on the lives of the urban poor.

The Civil Constitution of the Clergy

The confiscation of church lands required an ecclesiastical reconstruction. In July 1790 the National Constituent Assembly issued the Civil Constitution of the Clergy, which transformed the Roman Catholic Church in France into a branch of the secular state. The number of bishoprics was reduced from 135 to 83, and the borders of the dioceses were brought into conformity with those of the new departments. Priests and bishops were to be elected and were henceforth regarded as salaried employees of the state. Neither the pope nor the clergy of France were consulted about these broad changes. The king approved the measure only with the greatest reluctance.

The Civil Constitution of the Clergy was the major blunder of the National Constituent Assembly. The measure created immense opposition within the French

Here, as seen by a contemporary Dutchman, Louis XVI and his family are being led back to Paris by armed escort after their attempt to flee France in June 1791 was foiled near Varennes. [The Granger Collection.]

church even from bishops who had long championed Gallican liberties over papal domination. In the face of this resistance, the assembly unwisely ruled that all clergy must take an oath to support the Civil Constitution. Only seven bishops and about half the regular clergy did so. In reprisal the Assembly designated the clergy who had not taken the oath as "refractory" and removed them from their clerical functions.

Further reaction was swift. Refractory priests attempted to celebrate mass. In February 1791 the pope condemned not only the Civil Constitution of the Clergy but also the Declaration of the Rights of Man and Citizen. That condemnation marked the opening of a Roman Catholic offensive against the revolution and liberalism that continued throughout the nineteenth century. Within France itself the pope's action created a crisis of conscience and political loyalty for all sincere Catholics. Religious devotion and revolutionary loyalty became incompatible for many people. French citizens were divided between those who supported the constitutional priests and those who resorted to refractory clergy. Louis XVI and his family favored the latter.

Counterrevolutionary Activity

The revolution had other enemies besides the pope and devout Catholics. As it became clear that the old political and social order was undergoing fundamental and probably permanent change, considerable numbers of aristocrats left France. Known as the *émigrés*, they settled in countries near the French border, where they sought to foment counterrevolution. Among the most important of their number was the king's younger brother, the Count of Artois (1757–1836). In the summer of 1791 he and the queen persuaded Louis XVI to attempt to flee the country. On the night of June 20, 1791, Louis and his immediate family, disguised as servants, left Paris. They traveled as far as Varennes on their way to Metz. At Varennes the king was recognized, and his flight was halted. On June 24 a company of soldiers escorted the royal family back to Paris. The leaders of the National Constituent Assembly, determined to save the constitutional monarchy, announced that the king had been abducted from the capital. However, such a convenient public fiction could not cloak the reality that the chief counterrevolutionary in France sat on the throne.

Two months later, on August 27, 1791, under pressure from a group of *émigrés*, Emperor Leopold II of Austria, who was the brother of Marie Antoinette, and Frederick William II the king of Prussia, issued the Declaration of Pillnitz. The two monarchs promised to intervene in

France to protect the royal family and to preserve the monarchy *if* the other major European powers agreed. The latter provision rendered the statement meaningless because at the time Great Britain would not have given its consent. However, the declaration was not so read in France, where the revolutionaries saw the nation surrounded by aristocratic and monarchical foes.

The National Constituent Assembly drew to a close in September 1791. Its task of restructuring the government and administration of France had been completed. One of its last acts was the passage of a measure disallowing any of its own members to sit in the Legislative Assembly then being elected. The new body met on October 1 and had to confront the immense problems that had emerged during the earlier part of the year. Within the Legislative Assembly there also soon developed a major political divisions about the future course of the nation and the revolution.

A Second Revolution
End of the Monarchy

The issues of the Civil Constitution of the Clergy and the trustworthiness of Louis XVI undermined the unity of the revolution. Much factionalism displayed itself throughout the short life of the Legislative Assembly (1791–1792). Ever since the original gathering of the Estates-General, deputies from the Third Estate had organized themselves into clubs composed of politically like-minded persons. The most famous and best organized of these were the Jacobins, whose name derived from the fact that Dominican friars were called Jacobins, and the group met in a Dominican monastery in Paris. The Jacobins had also established a network of local clubs throughout the provinces. They had constituted the most advanced political group in the National Constituent Assembly and had pressed for a republic rather than a constitutional monarchy. The events of the summer of 1791 led them to renew those demands.

In the Legislative Assembly a group of Jacobins known as the *Girondists* assumed leadership.[3] They were determined to oppose the forces of counterrevolution. They passed measures ordering the *émigrés* to return or suffer loss of property and requiring the refractory clergy to support the Civil Constitution or lose their state pensions. The king vetoed both acts. On April 20, 1792, the Girondists led the Assembly to declare war on Austria, by this time governed by Francis II (1768–1835) and allied to Prussia. The Girondists believed that the war would preserve the revolution from domestic enemies and bring the most advanced revolutionaries to power. Paradoxically Louis XVI and other monarchists also favored the war. They thought that the conflict would strengthen the executive. The king also entertained the hope that French forces might be defeated and the old regime restored. Both sides were playing dangerously foolish politics.

The war radicalized the revolution and led to what is usually called the second revolution, which overthrew the constitutional monarchy and established a republic. Initially the war effort went quite poorly. Both the country and the revolution seemed in danger. In July 1792 the Duke of Brunswick, commander of the Prussian forces, issued a manifesto promising the destruction of Paris if harm came to the French royal family. This statement stiffened support for the war and increased the already significant distrust of the king.

Late in July the government of the city of Paris passed from the elected council to a committee or commune of representatives from the sections of Paris. On August 10, 1792, a very large Paris crowd invaded the Tuileries Palace and forced Louis XVI and Marie Antoinette to take refuge in the Legislative Assembly itself. The crowd fought with the royal Swiss guards. When Louis was finally able to call off the troops, several hundred of them and a large number of Paris citizens lay dead. The monarchy itself was also a casualty of that melee. Thereafter

3 The Girondists are also frequently called the *Brissotins* after Jacques-Pierre Brissot (1754–1793), who was their chief spokesman in early 1792.

This pamphlet is a 1793 description of a *sans-culotte*
written either by one or by a sympathizer. It describes the *sans-culotte* as a hardworking, useful,
patriotic citizen who bravely sacrifices himself to the
war effort. It contrasts those virtues to the lazy and
unproductive luxury of the noble and the personally
self-interested plottings of the politician.

A sans-culotte *you rogues? He is someone who always
goes on foot, who has no millions as you would all like to
have, no chateaux, no valets to serve him, and who lives
simply with his wife and children, if he has any, on a
fourth or fifth storey.*

*He is useful, because he knows how to work in the
field, to forge iron, to use a saw, to use a file, to roof a
house, to make shoes, and to shed his last drop of blood
for the safety of the Republic.*

*And because he works, you are sure not to meet his
person in the Café de Chartres, or in the gaming houses
where others conspire and game; nor at the National
theatre . . . nor in the literary clubs. . . .*

*In the evening he goes to his section, not powdered or
perfumed, or smartly booted in the hope of catching the
eye of the citzeneses in the galleries, but ready to support
good proposals with all his might, and to crush those
which come from the abominable faction of politicians.*

*Finally, a sans-culotte always has his sabre sharp, to
cut off the ears of all enemies of the Revolution; sometimes he even goes out with his pike; but at the first
sound of the drum he is ready to leave for the Vendée, for
the army of the Alps or for the army of the North. . . .*

"Reply to an Impertinent Question: What Is a *sans-culotte?*" April
1793. Reprinted in Walter Markov and Albert Soboul (eds.), *Die
Sansculotten von Paris,* and republished translated by Clive Emsley
in Merryn Williams (ed.), *Revolutions: 1775–1830* (Baltimore:
Penguin Books, in association with The Open University, 1971),
pp. 100–101.

the royal family was imprisoned in comfortable quarters,
but the king was allowed to perform none of his functions.

The Convention and the Role of
the Sans-Culottes

Early in September the Paris crowd again made its will
felt. During the first week of the month, in what are
known as the September Massacres, the Paris Commune
summarily executed or murdered about twelve hundred
people who were in the city jails. Many of these people
were aristocrats or priests, but the majority were simply
common criminals. The crowd had assumed that the
prisoners were all counterrevolutionaries. The Paris
Commune then compelled the Legislative Assembly to
call for the election by universal manhood suffrage of a
new assembly to write a democratic constitution. That
body, called the *Convention* after its American counterpart of 1787, met on September 21, 1792. The previous
day the French Army had halted the Prussian advance at
the battle of Valmy in eastern France. The victory of
democratic forces at home had been confirmed by victory
on the battlefield.

As its first act, the Convention declared France a
republic, that is, a nation governed by an elected assembly without a king. The second revolution had been the
work of Jacobins more radical than the Girondists and of
the people of Paris known as the *sans-culottes.* The name
of the latter means "without breeches" and derived from
the long trousers that as working people they wore instead of aristocratic knee breeches. The sans-culottes
were shopkeepers, artisans, wage earners, and in a few
cases factory workers. The persistent food shortages and
the revolutionary inflation had made their generally difficult lives even more burdensome. The politics of the old
regime had ignored them, and the policies of the National
Constituent Assembly had left them victims of unregulated economic liberty. However, the nation required
their labor and their lives if the war was to succeed. From
the summer of 1792 until the summer of 1794 their
attitudes, desires, and ideals were the primary factors in
the internal development of the revolution.

The sans-culottes generally knew what they wanted.
The Paris tradesmen and craftsmen sought immediate
relief from food shortages and rising prices through the
vehicle of price controls. They believed that all people
had a right to subsistence and profoundly resented most
forms of social inequality. This attitude led them to
intense hostility toward the aristocracy and toward the

original leaders of the revolution who might have taken over the social privileges of the aristocracy. Their hatred of inequality did not go so far as a demand for the abolition of property. Rather they advocated a community of relatively small property owners. In politics they were strongly republican and even suspicious of representative government. In Paris, where their influence was most important, the sans-culottes' political experience had been gained in meetings of the Paris sections. Those gatherings exemplified direct community democracy and were not unlike a New England town meeting. The economic hardship of their lives made them impatient to see their demands met.

The goals of the sans-culottes were not wholly compatible with those of the Jacobins. The latter were republicans who sought representative government. Jacobin hatred of the aristocracy did not extend to a general suspicion of wealth. Basically the Jacobins favored an unregulated economy. However, from the time of the flight to Varennes onward, the more extreme Jacobins began to cooperate with leaders from the Paris sans-culottes and the Paris Commune for the overthrow of the monarchy. Once the Convention began its deliberations, these advanced Jacobins, known as the Mountain because of their seats high in the assembly hall, worked with the sans-culottes to carry the revolution forward and to win the war. This willingness to cooperate with the forces of the popular revolution separated the Mountain from the Girondists, who were also members of the Jacobin Club.

By the spring of 1793 several issues had brought the Mountain and its sans-culottes allies to domination of the Convention and the revolution. In December 1792 Louis XVI was put on trial as mere "Citizen Capet," the family name of extremely distant forebears of the royal family. The Girondists looked for some way to spare his life, but the Mountain defeated the effort. Louis was convicted by a very narrow majority, condemned to death, and beheaded on January 21, 1793. The next month the Convention declared war on Great Britain, Holland, and Spain. Soon thereafter the Prussians re-newed their offensive and drove the French out of Belgium. To make matters worse, General Dumouriez, the Girondist victor of Valmy, deserted to the enemy. Finally, in March 1793 a royalist revolt led by aristocratic officers and priests erupted in the Vendée in western France and roused much popular support. Consequently the revolution found itself at war with most of Europe and much of the French nation. The Girondists had led the country into the war but had proved themselves incapable of winning it and suppressing the enemies of revolution at home. The Mountain stood ready to take up the task. Every major European power was now hostile to the revolution.

The Revolution and Europe at War

Initially the attitude of the rest of Europe toward the revolutionary events in France had been ambivalent. Those people who favored political reform regarded the revolution as wisely and rationally reorganizing a corrupt and inefficient government. The major foreign governments thought that the revolution meant that France would cease to be an important factor in European affairs for several years. In 1790, however, the Irish-born writer and British statesman Edmund Burke (1729–1797) argued a different position in *Reflections on the Revolution in France*. Burke regarded the reconstruction of French administration as the application of a blind rationalism that ignored the historical realities of political development and the complexities of social relations. He also forecast further turmoil as persons without political experience attempted to govern France. As the revolutionaries proceeded to attack the church, the monarchy, and finally the rest of Europe, Burke's ideas came to have many admirers, and his *Reflections* became the handbook of European conservatives for decades.

By the time of the commencement of the war with Austria in April 1792, the other European monarchies recognized the danger of both the ideas and the aggression of revolutionary France. The ideals of the Rights of

Burke Condemns the Work of the French National Assembly

Burke was undoubtedly the most important and articulate foreign critic of the French Revolution. He believed that governments could not be quickly created or organized, as seemed to have occurred in France. He was also deeply opposed to democracy, which he thought would lead to unwise, extreme actions on the part of government. Burke left a legacy of brilliantly argued conservative thought that remained a comfort to many followers, a serious challenge to liberals in nineteenth-century Europe, and an important statement in political theory. This passage is from his 1790 *Reflections on the Revolution in France.*

To MAKE *a government requires no great prudence. Settle the seat of power; teach obedience: and the work is done. To give Freedom is still more easy. It is not necessary to guide; it only requires to let go the rein. But to form a free government; that is, to temper together these opposite elements of liberty and restraint in one consistent work, requires much thought, deep reflection, a sagacious, powerful, and combining mind. This I do not find in those who take the lead in the National Assembly. Perhaps they are not so miserably deficient as they appear. I rather believe it. It would put them below the common level of human understanding. But when the leaders choose to make themselves bidders at an auction of popularity, their talents, in the construction of the state, will be of no service. They will become flatterers instead of legislators; the instruments, not the guides, of the people. If any of them should happen to propose a scheme of liberty, soberly limited, and defined with proper qualifications, he will be immediately outbid by his competitors, who will produce something more splendidly popular. Suspicions will be raised of his fidelity to his cause. Moderation will be stigmatized as the virtue of cowards; and compromise as the prudence of traitors; until, in hopes of preserving the credit which may enable him to temper, and moderate, on some occasions, the popular leader is obliged to become active in propagating doctrines, and establishing powers, that will afterwards defeat any sober purpose at which he ultimately might have aimed.*

. . . The improvements of the National Assembly are superficial, their errors fundamental.

Edumund Burke, *Reflections on the Revolution in France,* in *The Works of the Right Honourable Edmund Burke* (London: Henry G. Bohn, 1864), Vol. 2, pp. 515–516.

Edmund Burke. The portrait is from the studio of Joshua Reynolds. [National Portrait Gallery, London.]

Man and Citizen were highly exportable and applicable to the rest of the Continent. One government after another turned to repressive domestic policies. In Great Britain William Pitt the Younger (1759–1806), who had unsuccessfully supported moderate reform of Parliament during the 1780s, turned against both reform and popular movements. The government suppressed the London Corresponding Society founded in 1792 as a working-class reform group. In Birmingham the government sponsored mob action to drive Joseph Priestley (1733–1804), the chemist and radical political thinker, out of the country. In early 1793 Pitt secured parliamentary approval for acts suspending habeas corpus and making it possible to commit treason in writing. With less success Pitt attempted to curb freedom of the press. All political groups who dared to oppose the action of the government were in danger of becoming associated with revolutionary sedition.

In eastern Europe the revolution brought to a close the life of enlightened absolutism. The aristocratic resistance to the reforms of Joseph II in the Hapsburg lands led his brother Leopold II to come to terms with the landowners. Leopold's successor, Francis II (1792–1835) became a major leader of the counterrevolution. In Prussia Frederick William II (1786–1797), the son of Frederick the Great, looked to the leaders of the Lutheran Church and the aristocracy to discourage any potential popular uprisings, such as those of the downtrodden Silesian weavers. In Russia Catherine the Great burned the works of her onetime friend Voltaire and exiled Alexander Radishchev (1749–1802) to Siberia for publishing *Journey from St. Petersburg to Moscow,* a work critical of Russian social conditions.

In 1792 and 1793 the three eastern powers once again combined against Poland. In that unhappy land aristocratic reformers had finally achieved the abolition of the

liberum veto and had organized a new constitutional monarchy in 1791. Russia and Prussia, which already had designs on Polish territory, saw or pretended to see a threat of revolution in the new Polish constitution. In 1792 they annexed large sections of the country; in 1795 Austria joined the two other powers in a final partition that removed Poland from the map of Europe until after World War I. The governments of eastern Europe had used the widely shared fear of further revolutionary disorder to justify old-fashioned eighteenth-century aggression.

Consequently, in a paradoxical fashion the very success of the revolution in France brought to a rapid close reform movements in the rest of Europe. The French invasion of the Austrian Netherlands and the revolutionary reorganization of that territory roused the rest of Europe to the point of active hostility. In November 1792 the Convention declared that it would aid all peoples who wished to cast off the burdens of aristocratic and monarchical oppression. The Convention had also proclaimed the Scheldt River in the Netherlands open to the commerce of all nations and thus had broken a treaty that Great Britain had made with Austria and Holland. The British were on the point of declaring war on France over this issue when the Convention issued its own declaration of hostilities. By April 1793, when the Mountain began

to direct the French government, the nation stood at war with Austria, Prussia, Great Britain, Spain, Sardinia, and Holland. The governments of those nations were attempting to protect their social structures, political systems, and economic interests against the aggression of the revolution.

The Reign of Terror
The Republic Defended

In April 1793 the Convention established a Committee of General Security and a Committee of Public Safety to perform the executive duties of the government. The latter committee became more important and eventually enjoyed almost dictatorial power. The most prominent leaders of the Committee of Public Safety were Jacques Danton (1759–1794), who had provided heroic leadership in September 1792; Maximilien Robespierre (1758–1794), who became for a time the single most powerful member of the committee; and Lazare Carnot (1753–1823), who was in charge of the military. All of these men and the other figures on the committee were

The French Convention Calls Up the Entire Nation

This proclamation for the *levée en masse*, August 23, 1793, marked the first time in European history that all citizens of a nation were called to contribute to a war effort. The decree set the entire nation on a wartime footing under the centralized direction of the Committee of Public Safety.

1. From this moment until that in which the enemy shall have been driven from the soil of the Republic, all Frenchmen are in permanent requisition for the service of the armies.

The young men shall go to battle; the married men shall forge arms and transport provisions; the women shall make tents and clothing and shall serve in the hospitals; the children shall turn old linen into lint; the aged shall betake themselves to the public places in order to arouse the courage of the warriors and preach the hatred of kings and the unity of the Republic.

2. The national buildings shall be converted into barracks, the public places into workshops for arms, the soil of the cellars shall be washed in order to extract therefrom the saltpetre.

3. The arms of the regulation calibre shall be reserved exclusively for those who shall march against the enemy; the service of the interior shall be performed with hunting pieces and side arms.

4. The saddle horses are put in requisition to complete the cavalry corps; the draught-horses, other than those employed in agriculture, shall convey the artillery and the provisions.

5. The Committee of Public Safety is charged to take all the necessary measures to set up without delay an extraordinary manufacture of arms of every sort which corresponds with the ardor and energy of the French people. . . .

.   .   .   .

8. The levy shall be general. . . .

Frank Maloy Anderson (Ed. and Trans.), *The Constitutions and Other Select Documents Illustrative of the History of France, 1789–1907*, 2nd ed., rev. and enlarged (Minneapolis: The H. W. Wilson Company, 1908), pp. 184–185.

Maximilien Robespierre was the dominant member of the Committee of Public Safety during the Reign of Terror. [Bettmann Archive.]

The major problem was to wage the war and to secure domestic support for the effort. In early June 1793 the Paris sans-culottes invaded the Convention and successfully demanded the expulsion of the Girondist members. That action further radicalized the Convention and gave the Mountain complete control. On June 22 the Convention approved a fully democratic constitution but suspended its operation until the conclusion of the war emergency. On August 23 Carnot began a mobilization for victory by issuing a *levée en masse*, which conscripted males into the army and directed economic production for military purposes. On September 17 a maximum on prices was established in accord with sans-culotte demands. During these same months the armies of the revolution also successfully crushed many of the counter-revolutionary disturbances in the provinces.

Never before had Europe seen a nation organized in this way nor one defended by a citizen army. Other events within France astounded Europeans even more. The Reign of Terror had begun. Those months of quasi-judicial executions and murders stretching from the autumn of 1793 to the midsummer of 1794 are probably the most famous or infamous period of the revolution. They can be understood only in the context of the war on the one hand and the revolutionary expectations of the Convention and the sans-culottes on the other.

The Republic of Virtue

The presence of armies closing in upon the nation created a situation in which it was relatively easy to dispense with legal due process. However, the people who sat in the Convention and composed the Committee of Public Safety also believed that they had made a new departure in world history. They had established a republic in which civic virtue rather than aristocratic and

strong republicans and had opposed the weak policies of the Girondists. They conceived of their task as saving the revolution from mortal enemies at home and abroad. They generally enjoyed a working political relationship with the sans-culottes of Paris, but this was an alliance of expediency on the part of the committee.

monarchical corruption might flourish. The republic of virtue manifested itself in the renaming of streets from the egalitarian vocabulary of the revolution, in republican dress copied from that of the sans-culottes or the Roman Republic, in the absence of powdered wigs, in the suppression of plays that were insufficiently republican, and in a general attack against crimes, such as prostitution, that were supposedly characteristic of aristocratic society.

The most dramatic departure of the republic of virtue and one that illustrates the imposition of political values that would justify the terror was an attempt by the Convention to dechristianize France. In November 1793 the Convention proclaimed a new calendar dating from the first day of the French Republic. There were twelve months of thirty days with names associated with the seasons and climate. Every tenth day rather than every seventh was a holiday. Many of the most important events of the next few years became known by their dates on the revolutionary calendar.[4] Also in November 1793 the convention abolished the worship of God and established a Cult of Reason. The legislature then sent trusted members known as *deputies on mission* into the provinces to enforce dechristianization by closing churches, persecuting clergy and believers, and occasionally forcing priests to marry. Needless to say, this religious policy roused much opposition and deeply separated the French provinces from the revolutionary government in Paris.

During the crucial months of late 1793 and early 1794 the person who emerged as the chief figure on the Committee of Public Safety was Robespierre. He was a complex person who has remained controversial to the present day. He was utterly selfless and from the earliest days of the revolution had favored a republic. The Jacobin Club provided his primary forum and base of power. A shrewd and sensitive politician, he had opposed the war in 1792 as a measure that might aid the monarchy. He largely depended upon the support of the sans-culottes of

Paris, but he continued to dress as he had prior to the revolution and opposed dechristianization as a political blunder. For him the republic of virtue meant wholehearted support of republican government and the renunciation of selfish gains from political life. He once told the Convention, "If the mainspring of popular government in peacetime is virtue, amid revolution it is at the same time virtue and *terror:* virtue, without which terror is fatal; terror, without which virtue is impotent. Terror is nothing but prompt, severe, inflexible justice; it is therefore an emanation of virtue."[5] He and those who supported his policies were among the first apostles of secular ideologies who in the name of humanity would bring so much suffering to European politics of the left and the right in the next two centuries.

Progress of the Terror

The Reign of Terror manifested itself through a series of revolutionary tribunals established by the Convention during the summer of 1793. They were to try the enemies of the republic, but the definition of *enemy* remained uncertain and shifted as the months passed. The enemies included those who might aid other European powers, those who endangered republican virtue, and finally good republicans who opposed the policies of the dominant faction of the government. In a very real sense the terror of the revolutionary tribunals systematized and channeled the popular resentment that had manifested itself in the September Massacres of 1792. The first victims were Marie Antoinette, other members of the royal family, and some aristocrats, who were executed in October 1793. They were followed by certain Girondist politicians who had been prominent in the Legislative Assembly.

By the early months of 1794 the Terror had moved to the provinces, where the deputies on mission presided over the summary execution of thousands of people who had allegedly supported internal opposition to the revolution. One of the most infamous incidents occurred in

4 From summer to spring the months on the revolutionary calendar were Messidor, Thermidor, Fructidor, Vendémiaire, Brumaire, Frimaire, Nivôse, Pluviôse, Ventôse, Germinal, Floréal, and Prairial.

5 Quoted in Richard T. Bienvenu, *The Ninth of Thermidor: The Fall of Robespierre* (New York: Oxford University Press, 1968), p. 38.

Marie Antoinette on the way to her execution, sketched from life by David, as her tumbril passed his window. [Bettmann Archive.]

Nantes, where several hundred people were simply tied to rafts and drowned in the river. By early 1794 the victims of the Terror came from every social class, including the sans-culottes.

In Paris during the late winter Robespierre began to orchestrate the Terror against republican political figures of the left and right. On March 24 he secured the execution of certain extreme sans-culottes leaders known as the *enragés*. They had wanted further measures regulating prices, securing social equality, and pressing dechristianization. Robespierre then turned against more conservative republicans, who included Danton. They were insufficiently militant on the war and had profited monetarily from the revolution. Danton was executed during the first week in April. In this fashion, Robespierre exterminated the leadership from both groups that might have threatened his position. Finally, on June 10, he secured passage of the Law of 22 Prairial, which permitted the revolutionary tribunal to convict suspects without even hearing evidence. The number of executions was growing steadily.

In June 1794, at the height of his power, Robespierre, considering the Cult of Reason too abstract for most citizens, abolished it and established the Cult of the Supreme Being. This deistic cult was in line with Rousseau's idea of a civic religion that would induce morality among citizens. However, Robespierre did not long preside over his new religion. On July 26 he made an ill-tempered speech in the Convention declaring there existed among other leaders of the government a conspiracy against himself and the revolution. Such accusations against unnamed persons had usually preceded his earlier attacks. On July 27—the Ninth of Thermidor—by prearrange-

Although many of the victims of the Reign of Terror were executed by other methods, the guillotine became the symbol of those frightening months in 1793 and 1794. Here prisoners are being prepared for decapitation, as the heads of those already executed are displayed to the crowd. [Bettmann Archive.]

ment, members of the Convention shouted him down when he rose to make another speech. That night Robespierre was arrested, and the next day he was executed. The revolutionary sans-culottes of Paris could not save him because he had deprived them of their chief leaders. The other Jacobins turned against him because after Danton's death they feared becoming the next victims. Robespierre had destroyed rivals for leadership without creating supporters for himself. In that regard he was the selfless creator of his own self-image.

The fall of Robespierre might simply have been one more shift in the turbulent politics of the revolution. Those who brought about his demise were motivated by instincts of self-preservation rather than by major policy differences. They had fully supported the Terror and the executions. Yet within a short time the Reign of Terror, which ultimately claimed over twenty-five thousand victims, did come to a close. The largest number of executions had involved peasants and sans-culottes who joined rebellions against the revolutionary government. By the late summer of 1794 those provincial uprisings had been crushed, and the war against foreign enemies was also going well. Those factors, combined with the feeling in Paris that the revolution had consumed enough of its children, brought the Terror to an end.

The Thermidorian Reaction
The End of the Terror and Establishment of the Directory

A tempering of the revolution called the *Thermidorian Reaction* began in July 1794. It consisted of the destruction of the machinery of terror and the institution of a new constitutional regime. Within days and weeks of Robespierre's execution the Convention allowed the Girondists who had been in prison or hiding to return to their seats. There was a general amnesty for political prisoners. The Committee of Public Safety was restructured under closer control of the Convention, and the notorious Law of 22 Prairial was repealed. Some, though by no means all, of the people responsible for the Terror were removed from public life. Leaders of the Paris Commune and certain deputies on mission were executed. The Paris Commune itself was outlawed. The Paris Jacobin Club was closed, and Jacobin clubs in the provinces were forbidden to correspond with each other.

One of the major events during the Thermidorian Reaction was the closing in November 1794 of the Jacobin Club in Paris. The structure was part of a former convent in the center of the city. [The Granger Collection.]

The executions of former terrorists marked the beginning of "the white terror." Throughout the country people who had been involved in the Reign of Terror were attacked and often murdered. Jacobins were executed with little more due process than they had extended to their victims a few months earlier. The Convention itself approved some of these trials. In other cases gangs of youths who had aristocratic connections or who had avoided serving in the army roamed the streets striking and beating known Jacobins. In Lyons, Toulon, and Marseilles these "bands of Jesus" dragged suspected terrorists from prisons and murdered them much as alleged royalists had been murdered during the September Massacres.

The republic of virtue gave way, if not to one of vice, at least to one of frivolous pleasures. The dress of the sans-culottes and the Roman Republic disappeared among the middle class and the aristocracy. New plays appeared in the theaters, and prostitutes again roamed the streets of Paris. Families of victims of the Reign of Terror gave parties in which they appeared with shaved necks like the victims of the guillotine and red ribbons tied about them. Although the Convention continued to favor the Cult of the Supreme Being, it allowed Catholic services to be held. Many refractory priests returned to the country. One of the unanticipated results of the Thermidorian Reaction was a genuine revival of Catholic worship.

The Thermidorian Reaction also involved a political reconstruction. The fully democratic constitution of 1793, which had never gone into effect, was abandoned. The Convention issued in its place the Constitution of the Year III, which reflected the Thermidorian determination to reject both constitutional monarchy and democracy. The new document provided for a legislature of two houses. Members of the upper body, or Council of Elders, were to be men over forty years of age who were either husbands or widowers. The lower Council of Five Hundred was to consist of married or single men at least thirty years old. The executive body was to be a five-person Directory chosen by the Elders from a list submitted by the Council of Five Hundred. Property qualifications limited the franchise except for soldiers, who even without property were permitted to vote.

Thermidor became a term associated with political reaction. However, if the French Revolution had originated in political conflicts characteristic of the eighteenth century, it had by 1795 become something very different. A society and a political structure based on rank and birth had given way to one based on civic equality and social status stemming from ownership or nonownership of property. People who had never been allowed direct, formal access to political power had to differing degrees been admitted to those activities. Their entrance had given rise to questions of property distribution and economic regulations that could not again be totally ignored. Representation had been established as a principle of practical politics. Henceforth the question before France and eventually before all of Europe would be which new groups would be admitted to representation. In the *levée en masse* the French had demonstrated to Europe the power of the secular ideal of nationhood.

All of these stunning changes in the political and social contours of Europe are not to be forgotten in a consideration of the post-Thermidorian course of the French Revolution. What triumphed in the Constitution of the Year III was the revolution of the holders of property. For this reason the French Revolution has usually been considered the victory of the bourgeoisie or middle class. However, the property that won the day was not industrial wealth but the wealth stemming from commerce and the professions. Moreover the largest new propertied class to emerge from the revolutionary turmoil was the peasantry, who as a result of the destruction of feudal privileges had achieved personal ownership of the land. Unlike peasants liberated from feudalism in other parts of Europe during the next century, French peasants had to pay no monetary compensation.

The most decisively reactionary element in the Thermidorian Reaction and the new constitution was the removal of the sans-culottes from political life. With the war effort succeeding, the Convention severed its ties with the sans-culottes. True to their belief in an unregulated economy, the Thermidorians repealed the ceiling on prices. As a result, the winter of 1794–1795 brought the worst food shortages of the period. There were numerous food riots, which the Convention put down with force to prove that the era of the sans-culottes *journées* had come to a close. On October 5, 1795—13 Vendémiaire—the sections of Paris rose up against the Convention. For the first time in the history of the revolution, artillery was turned against the people of Paris. A general named Napoleon Bonaparte (1769–1821) commanded the cannon, and with a "whiff of grapeshot" he dispersed the crowd.

By the Treaty of Basel in March 1795, the Convention concluded peace with Prussia and Spain. However, the legislators feared a resurgence of both radical democrats and royalists in the upcoming elections for the Council of Five Hundred. Consequently the Convention ruled that at least two thirds of the new legislature must have been members of the older body. The Thermidorians did not even trust the property owners as voters. The next year the newly established Directory again faced social unrest. In Paris Gracchus Babeuf (1760–1797) led the Conspiracy of Equals. He and his followers called for more radical democracy and for more equality of property. Babeuf was arrested, tried, and executed. This quite minor plot became famous many decades later when European socialists attempted to find their historical roots in the French Revolution.

The suppression of the sans-culottes, the narrow franchise of the constitution, the rule of the two thirds, and the Catholic royalist revival presented the Directory with problems that it never succeeded in overcoming. It lacked any broad base of meaningful political support. It particularly required active loyalty because France remained at war with Austria and Great Britain. Consequently the Directory came to depend upon the power of the army rather than upon constitutional processes for governing the country. All of the soldiers could vote. Moreover, within the army, created and sustained by the revolution, stood officers who were eager for power and ambitious for political conquest. The results of the instability of the Directory and the growing role of the army held profound consequences not only for France but for the entire Western world.

SUGGESTED READINGS

C. Brinton, *The Jacobins: An Essay in the New History* (1930). An examination of the social background of these revolutionaries.

C. Brinton, *A Decade of Revolution, 1789–1799* (1934). A general survey of Europe during the revolutionary years.

A. Cobban, *Edmund Burke and the Revolt against the Eighteenth Century* (1929). Sets Burke's thought in a broader intellectual context.

A. Cobban, *Aspects of the French Revolution* (1970). Essays on numerous subjects.

C. Cone, *The English Jacobins: Reformers in Late Eighteenth Century England* (1968). The fortunes of English radicals during the repression following the outbreak of war with France.

K. Epstein, *The Genesis of German Conservatism* (1966). A major study of antiliberal forces in Germany before and during the revolution.

D. M. Greer, *The Incidence of the Terror During the French Revolution: A Statistical Interpretation* (1935). A study of what people in which regions became the victims of the Terror.

N. Hampson, *A Social History of the French Revolution* (1963). A clear account with much interesting detail.

G. Lefebvre, *The Coming of the French Revolution* (trans., 1947). An examination of the crisis of the French monarchy and the events of 1789.

G. Lefebvre, *The French Revolution*, 2 vols. (1962–1964). A major study by one of the most important modern writers on the subject.

R. R. Palmer, *Twelve Who Ruled: The Committee of Public Safety During the Terror* (1941). A clear narrative and analysis of the policies and problems of the committee.

R. R. Palmer, *The Age of Democratic Revolution: A Political History of Europe and America, 1760–1800*, 2 vols. (1959, 1964). An impressive survey of the political turmoil in the transAtlantic world.

G. Rudé, *The Crowd in the French Revolution* (1959). Examines who composed the revolutionary crowds and why.

Albert Soboul, *The French Revolution* (trans., 1975). An important work by a Marxist scholar.

J. H. Stewart, *A Documentary Survey of the French Revolution* (1951). Major sources in translation.

J. M. Thompson, *Robespierre,* 2 vols. (1935). The best biography.

C. Tilly, *The Vendée* (1964). A significant sociological investigation.

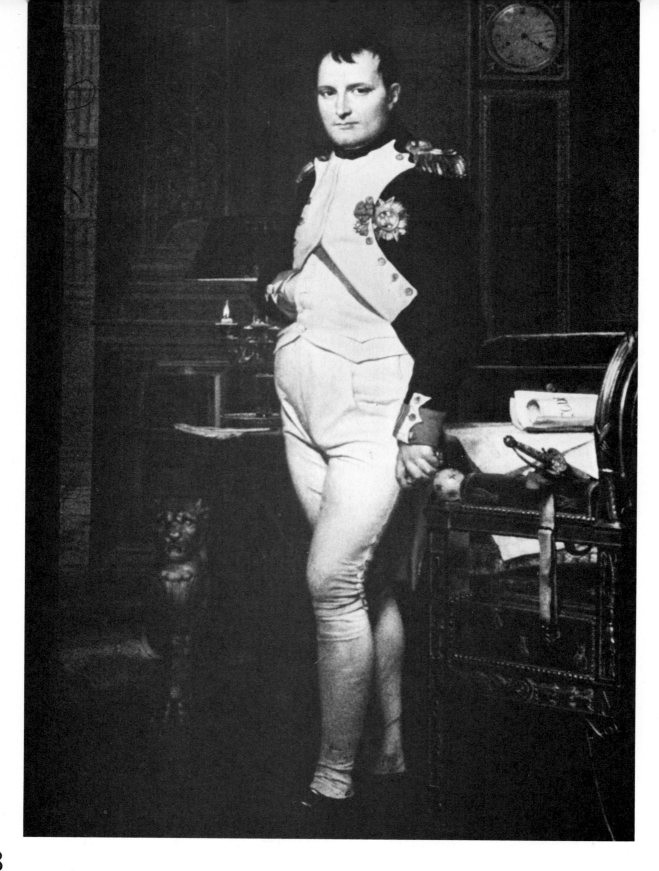

618

24
The Age of Napoleon and the Triumph of Romanticism

THE GOVERNMENT of the Directory represented a new class made up of politicians, merchants, bankers, war speculators, and profiteers sprung from the nonaristocratic order of the old regime, as well as a few undistinguished nobles. Together they formed a society of recently enriched and powerful people whose chief goal was to halt the revolutionary movement without rolling it back. They wanted to perpetuate their own rule. They sought to achieve peace and quiet in order to gain more wealth and to establish a society in which money would become the only requirement for eminence and power. They and their goals confronted a host of enemies.

The Rise of Napoleon Bonaparte

The chief danger to the Directory came from the royalists, who hoped to restore the Bourbon monarchy by legal means. Many of the *émigrés* had drifted back into France. Their plans for a restoration drew support from devout Catholics and from those citizens who had been disgusted by the excesses of the revolution. Monarchy seemed to hold the promise of stability. The spring elections of 1797 turned out most of the incumbents and replaced them with a majority of constitutional monarchists and their sympathizers. To prevent an end to the republic and a peaceful restoration of monarchy, the antimonarchist Directory staged a *coup d'état* on 18 Fructidor (September 4, 1797). They put their own supporters into the legislative seats won by their opponents. They then imposed censorship and exiled some of their enemies. These actions had been made possible by Napo-

leon Bonaparte who was the general in charge of the Italian military campaign. At the request of the Directors, he had sent one of his subordinates to Paris to guarantee the success of the *coup*. In 1797, as in 1795, the army and Bonaparte had saved the day for the government.

Napoleon Bonaparte was born in 1769 to a poor family of lesser nobles at Ajaccio, Corsica. Because France had annexed Corsica in the previous year, he went to French schools, pursued a military career, and in 1785 obtained a commission as a French artillery officer. He strongly favored the revolution and was a fiery Jacobin. In 1793 he played a leading role in recovering the port of Toulon from the British. In reward for his service the government appointed him a brigadier general. His radical associations threatened his career during the Therimidorian Reaction, but his defense of the new regime on 13 Vendémiaire restored him to favor and won him another promotion and a command in Italy.

By 1795 French arms and diplomacy had shattered the enemy coalition, but France's annexation of Belgium guaranteed continued fighting with Britain and Austria. The attack on Italy was aimed at depriving Austria of the provinces of Lombardy and Venetia. In a series of lightning victories Bonaparte crushed the Austrian and Sardinian armies. On his own initiative, and in many ways contrary to the wishes of the government in Paris, he concluded the treaty of Campo Formio in October 1797. The treaty took Austria out of the war and crowned Napoleon's campaign and independent policy with success. Before long all of Italy and Switzerland had fallen under French domination.

In November 1797 the triumphant Bonaparte returned to Paris to be hailed as a hero and to confront France's only remaining enemy, Britain. He judged it impossible to cross the channel and invade England at that time. Instead he chose to capture Egypt from the Ottoman Empire and thereby to drive the British fleet from the Mediterranean, cut off British communication with India, damage British trade, and threaten the British empire. The invasion of Egypt was a failure. Admiral

This portrait of Napoleon by the artist David illustrates the ruler as liberal reformer. Napoleon is shown working early into the morning on affairs of state. The *Code Napoléon* lies on the table at the right of the picture. [Bettmann Archive.]

Horatio Nelson (1758–1805) destroyed the French fleet at Abukir on August 1, 1798. The French army could then neither accomplish anything of importance in the Near East nor get home. To make matters worse, the situation in Europe was deteriorating. Russia, which also had ambitions in the Near East, was alarmed by the French invasion of Egypt. The Russians, the Austrians, and the Ottomans soon joined Britain to form the Second Coalition. In 1799 the Russian and Austrian armies defeated the French in Italy and Switzerland and threatened to invade France.

Economic troubles and the dangerous international situation eroded the already fragile support for the Directory. One of the Directors, the Abbé Sieyès, proposed a new constitution. The author of the pamphlet *What Is the Third Estate?* (1789) wanted to establish a vigorous executive body independent of the whims of electoral politics, a government based on the principle of "confidence from below, power from above." The change would require a *coup d'état* with military support. News of France's misfortunes had reached Napoleon in Egypt. Without orders and leaving his doomed army behind, he returned to France in October 1799. He received much popular acclaim, although some people thought he deserved a court-martial for desertion. He soon joined Sieyès. On 18 Brumaire (November 9, 1799) his troops drove out the legislators and permitted the success of the *coup*.

Sieyès appears to have thought Napoleon could be used and then dismissed, but if so he badly misjudged his man. The proposed constitution divided executive authority among three consuls. Bonaparte pushed it aside, as he did Sieyès, and in December 1799 put forth the Constitution of the Year VIII. Behind a screen of universal manhood suffrage that suggested democratic principles, a complicated system of checks and balances that appealed to republican theory, and a Council of State that evoked memories of Louis XIV, the constitution in fact established the rule of one man, the First Consul, Bonaparte. To find a reasonably close historical analogy one must go back to Caesar and Augustus and the earlier Greek

tyrants. The career of Bonaparte, however, pointed forward to the dictators of the twentieth century. He was the first modern political figure to employ the rhetoric of revolution and nationalism, to back it with military force, and to combine these elements into a mighty weapon of imperial expansion in the service of his own power and ambition.

The Consulate in France (1799–1804)

The establishment of the Consulate may be regarded as the end of the revolution in France. The leading elements of the Third Estate—that is, officials, landowners, doctors, lawyers, and financiers—had achieved most of their goals by 1799. Hereditary privilege had been abolished, and the career open to talent allowed them to achieve the wealth and status they sought. The peasants also were satisfied. They had acquired the land they had always wanted and had destroyed oppressive feudal privileges as well. The newly established dominant classes were profoundly conservative. They had little or no desire to share their recently won privileges with lower social orders. Bonaparte seemed just the person to give

Napoleon Describes Conditions Leading to the Consulate

November 1799 as described by Bonaparte.

ON MY *return to Paris I found division among all authorities, and agreement upon only one point, namely, that the Constitution was half destroyed and was unable to save liberty.*

All parties came to me, confided to me their designs, disclosed their secrets, and requested my support; I refused to be the man of a party.

The Council of Elders summoned me; I answered its appeal. A plan of general restoration had been devised by men whom the nation has been accustomed to regard as the defenders of liberty, equality, and property; this plan required an examination, calm, free, exempt from all influence and all fear. Accordingly, the Council of Elders resolved upon the removal of the Legislative Body to Saint-Cloud; it gave me the responsibility of disposing the force necessary for its independence. I believed it my duty to my fellow citizens, to the soldiers perishing in our armies, to the national glory acquired at the cost of their blood, to accept the command. . . .

I presented myself at the Council of Five Hundred, alone, unarmed, my head uncovered, just as the Elders had received and applauded me; I came to remind the majority of its wishes, and to assure it of its power.

The stilettos which menaced the deputies were instantly raised against their liberator; twenty assassins threw themselves upon me and aimed at my breast. The grenadiers of the Legislative Body whom I had left at the door of the hall ran forward, placed themselves between the assassins and myself. One of these brave grenadiers had his clothes pierced by a stiletto. They bore me out.

At the same moment cries of "Outlaw" were raised against the defender of the law. It was the fierce cry of assassins against the power destined to repress them.

They crowded around the president, uttering threats, arms in their hands; they commanded him to outlaw me; I was informed of this; I ordered him to be rescued from their fury, and six grenadiers of the Legislative Body secured him. Immediately afterwards some grenadiers of the Legislative Body charged into the hall and cleared it. The factions, intimidated, dispersed and fled. . . .

Frenchmen, you will doubtless recognize in this conduct the zeal of a soldier of liberty, a citizen devoted to the Republic. Conservative, tutelary, and liberal ideas have been restored to their rights through the dispersal of the rebels who oppressed the Councils. . . .

J. H. Stewart, *A Documentary Survey of the French Revolution* (New York: Macmillan, 1951), pp. 763–765.

them security. When he submitted his constitution to the voters in a plebiscite, they approved it by 3,011,077 votes to 1,567.

Bonaparte quickly justified the public's confidence by setting about achieving peace with France's enemies. Russia had already quarreled with its allies and left the Second Coalition. A campaign in Italy brought another victory over Austria at Marengo in 1800. The Treaty of Lunéville early in 1801 took Austria out of the war and confirmed the earlier settlement of Campo Formio. Britain was now alone and, in 1802, concluded the Treaty of Amiens, which brought peace to Europe. Bonaparte was equally effective in restoring peace and order at home. He employed generosity, flattery, and bribery to win over some of his enemies. He issued a general amnesty and employed in his own service persons from all political factions. He required only that they be loyal to him. Some of the highest offices were occupied by persons who had been extreme radicals during the Reign of Terror, another by a person who had fled the Terror and favored constitutional monarchy, and still another by a former high official of the old regime.

On the other hand, Bonaparte was ruthless and efficient in suppressing opposition. He established a highly centralized administration in which all departments were managed by prefects directly responsible to the central government in Paris. He employed secret police. He stamped out the royalist rebellion in the west and made the rule of Paris effective in Brittany and the Vendée for the first time in many years. Nor was he above using or even inventing opportunities to destroy his enemies. When a bomb aimed at him exploded in 1804, he used the event as an excuse to attack the Jacobins, even though the bombing was the work of royalists. In 1804 his forces invaded the sovereignty of Baden to seize the Bourbon Duke of Enghien. The duke was accused of participation in a royalist plot and put to death, even though Bonaparte knew him to be innocent. The action was a flagrant violation of international law and of due process. Charles Maurice de Talleyrand-Périgord (1754–1838), Bona-

Charles Maurice de Talleyrand-Périgord, known to history as Talleyrand, was one of the most talented—or adaptable—political survivors of the Revolution. Before 1789 he had been a Roman Catholic bishop. Later he became a major diplomat, first for the revolutionary government, and then for Napoleon. Finally, in 1815, he represented the restored Bourbon government at the Congress of Vienna. The portrait is by Pierre-Paul Prud'hon. [The Granger Collection.]

parte's foreign minister, later termed the act "worse than a crime—a blunder," for it helped to provoke foreign opposition. On the other hand, it was popular with the former Jacobins, for it precluded the possibility of a Bourbon restoration. The person who killed a Bourbon was hardly likely to restore the royal family. The execution seems to have put an end to royalist plots.

A major obstacle to internal peace was the continued hostility of French Catholics. Refractory clergy continued to advocate counterrevolution. The religious revival that dated from the Thermidorian Reaction continued to increase discontent with the secular state created by the revolution. Bonaparte viewed religion as a political matter. He approved its role in preserving an orderly society but was suspicious of any such power independent of the state.

In 1801 Napoleon concluded a concordat with Pope Pius VII to the shock and dismay of his anticlerical supporters. The settlement gave Napoleon what he most wanted. Both refractory clergy and those who had accepted the revolution were forced to resign. Their replacements were given their spiritual investiture by the pope, but the state named the bishops and paid their salaries and the salary of one priest in each parish. In return the church gave up its claims on its confiscated property. The concordat declared that "Catholicism is the religion of the great majority of French citizens." This was merely a statement of fact and fell far short of what the pope had wanted, religious dominance for the Roman Catholic Church. Clergy had to swear an oath of loyalty to the state, and the Organic Articles of 1802 established the supremacy of State over Church. Similar laws were applied to the Protestant and Jewish religious communities as well, reducing still further the privileged position of the Catholic Church.

Peace and efficient administration brought prosperity and security to the French and gratitude and popularity to Bonaparte. In 1802 a plebiscite appointed him consul for life, and he soon produced still another new constitution that granted him what amounted to full power. The years of the Consulate were employed in reforming and establishing the basic laws and institutions of France. The settlement imposed by Napoleon was an ambiguous combination of liberal principles derived from the Enlightenment and the early years of the revolution and conservative principles and practices going back to the old regime or adapted to the conservative spirit that had triumphed at Thermidor.

The abolition of all privileges based on birth, the establishment of equality before the law, the disappearance of all authority except that of the national state and all legal distinctions based on class or locality, the end of all purchased offices and the substitution of salaried officials chosen for merit represented the application of rationality and the achievement of goals sought by the people who had made the revolution. Most of these were embodied in the general codification of laws carried out under Bonaparte's direction. This was especially true of the Civil Code, usually called the Napoleonic Code. However, these laws stopped far short of full equality advocated by liberal rationalists. Fathers were granted extensive control over their children and men over their wives. Labor unions were still forbidden, and the rights of workers were inferior to those of their employers.

In the political arena and in administration Napoleonic institutions ran contrary to the tendencies of the revolution. They aimed at a kind of enlightened absolutism that was similar to but more effective than what had existed in the old regime. Representative government, local auton-

Napoleon Makes Peace with the Papacy

The following is part of the Concordat of 1802 between Napoleon's France and the papacy of Pius VII. It was announced in France on April 8, 1802 and was the cornerstone of Napoleon's religious settlement following the upheavals of the French Revolution.

THE *government of the French Republic recognizes that the Roman, catholic and apostolic religion is the religion of the great majority of French citizens.*

His Holiness likewise recognizes that this same religion has derived and in this moment again expects the greatest benefit and grandeur from the establishment of the catholic worship in France and from the personal profession of it which the consuls of the Republic make.

In consequence, after this mutual recognition, as well for the benefit of religion as for the maintenance of internal tranquility, they have agreed as follows:

1. The catholic, apostolic and Roman religion shall be freely exercised in France: its worship shall be public, and in conformity with the police regulations which the government shall deem necessary for the public tranquility.

. . . .

4. The First Consul of the Republic shall make appointments, within the three months which shall follow the publication of the bull of His Holiness, to the archbishoprics and bishoprics of the new circumscription. His Holiness shall confer the canonical institution, following the forms established in relation to France before the change of government.

. . . .

6. Before entering upon their functions, the bishops shall take directly, at the hands of the First Consul, the oath of fidelity which was in use before the change of government, expressed in the following terms:

"I swear and promise to God, upon the holy scriptures, to remain in obedience and fidelity to the government established by the constitution of the French Republic. I also promise not to have any intercourse, nor to assist by any counsel, nor to support any league, either within or without, which is inimical to the public tranquility; and if, within my diocese or elsewhere, I learn that anything to the prejudice of the state is being contrived, I will make it known to the government."

F. M. Anderson, *The Constitutions and Other Select Documents Illustrative of the History of France 1789–1907*, 2nd ed. (Minneapolis: H. W. Wilson Company, 1908), pp. 296–297.

omy, and personal freedom were rejected in favor of the centralization of all power and the subordination of personal rights and political freedom to the needs of the state as interpreted by the first consul. All of this was acceptable to the dominant bourgeoisie and the peasantry. They accepted censorship, the arbitrary and sometimes brutal suppression of dissent, and even the restoration of a new quasi nobility in the Legion of Honor so long as order, prosperity, and security of property were preserved.

In 1804 Bonaparte seized on the bomb attack on his life to make himself emperor. He argued that the establishment of a dynasty would make the new regime secure and make further attempts on his life useless. Another new constitution was promulgated in which Napoleon Bonaparte was called Emperor of the French, as well as First Consul of the Republic. This constitution was also overwhelmingly ratified in a plebiscite.

To conclude the drama, Napoleon invited the pope to Notre Dame to take part in the coronation. But at the last minute Napoleon snatched the crown away and placed it on his own head. Henceforth, he was called Napoleon I. This act was the natural goal of his career. His aims had always been profoundly selfish: power and glory for himself and his family. There was, moreover, a romantic streak in Napoleon. He thought of himself as a rival of Alexander the Great and Caesar, a conqueror as well as a ruler. Had Napoleon wished it, Europe might well have had peace; but his ambition would not permit it.

Napoleon's Empire (1804–1814)

In the decade between his coronation as emperor and his final defeat at Waterloo (1815), Napoleon conquered most of Europe in a series of campaigns that astonished the world. France's victories changed the map of Europe, put an end to the old regime and its feudal trappings in the west, and forced the eastern European states to reorganize themselves to resist Napoleon's armies. Everywhere Napoleon's advance unleashed the powerful force of nationalism. The French nation in arms, the invention of the revolution, was Napoleon's weapon. He could put as many as 700,000 men under arms at one time, risk as many as 100,000 troops in a single battle, endure heavy losses, and come back to fight again. He could conscript citizen soldiers in unprecedented numbers thanks to their loyalty to the nation and to their remarkable leader. No single enemy could match such resources, and even coalitions were unsuccessful until Napoleon at last overreached himself and made mistakes that led to his own defeat.

Napoleon deserves his reputation as one of the great commanders of all time. His genius did not lie in strategic or tactical invention, for the French military commanders of the eighteenth century had already pointed the course in that direction. Rather his brilliance lay in execution and leadership. His strategy depended on mobility and timing. He liked to divide his forces into units of moderate size, disperse them across the country, and use their superior speed and his skill in planning to unite them at the critical point at the right time. Self-sufficiency was an important Napoleonic principle that enabled him to disperse and reunite his armies swiftly as well as to outmaneuver his opponents.

The whole army, moreover, traveled light. By living off the country in which it fought, it was free of the need to establish and follow a chain of supply depots. This was a great advantage in fertile areas like western and central Europe but later proved a problem in the vast expanse of Russia during the winter and against guerrilla fighters in Spain. All of this speed of maneuver had a single goal: to bring the hostile armies together in a major battle swiftly. Napoleon departed from the usual eighteenth-century tactics, which emphasized maneuver and strategic position, fighting a battle only as a last resort. His aim was not to control territory nor to gain strong points but to destroy the enemy army. After that the rest would follow. So long as conditions permitted such warfare, Napoleon was unbeatable.

The Peace of Amiens (1802) was doomed to be merely a truce. Any hope that it might last was shattered

by Napoleon's unlimited ambitions. He sent an army to restore the rebellious island of Haiti to French rule. This move aroused British fears that he was planning the renewal of a French Empire in America, because Spain had restored Louisiana to France in 1800. More serious were his interventions in the Dutch Republic, Italy, and Switzerland and his role in the reorganization of Germany. The Treaty of Campo Formio had required a redistribution of territories along the Rhine River, and the petty princes of the region engaged in a shameful scramble to enlarge their holdings. Among the results were the reduction of Austrian influence in Germany and the emergence of a smaller number of larger German states in the west, all dependent on Napoleon.

The British found all of these developments alarming enough to justify an ultimatum. When Napoleon ignored it, Britain declared war in May 1803. William Pitt the Younger returned to office as prime minister in 1804 and began to construct the Third Coalition. By August 1805 he had persuaded Russia and Austria once again to move against French aggression. A great naval victory soon raised the fortunes of the allies. On October 21, 1805, the British admiral Lord Horatio Nelson (1758–1805) destroyed the combined French and Spanish fleets at the Battle of Trafalgar just off the Spanish coast. Nelson died in the battle, but the British lost no ships. The victory of Trafalgar put an end to all French hope of an invasion of Britain and guaranteed British control of the sea for the rest of the war.

On land the story was very different. Even before Trafalgar Napoleon had marched to the Danube River to

attack his continental enemies. In mid-October he forced a large Austrian army to surrender at Ulm and soon occupied Vienna. On December 2, 1805, in perhaps his greatest victory, Napoleon defeated the combined Austrian and Russian forces at Austerlitz. The Treaty of Pressburg that followed took Russia out of the war and won major concessions from Austria. The Austrians withdrew from Italy and left Napoleon in control of everything north of Rome. He was recognized as king of Italy.

Extensive changes also came about in Germany. In July 1806 Napoleon organized the Confederation of the Rhine, which included most of the western German princes. The withdrawal of these princes from the Holy Roman Empire led Francis II of Austria to dissolve that ancient political body and hencefore to call himself only emperor of Austria.

Prussia, which had carefully remained neutral up to this point, was now provoked into war against France. The famous Prussian army was quickly crushed at the battles of Jena and Auerstädt in 1806. Two weeks later Napoleon was in Berlin. On June 13, 1807, Napoleon defeated the Russians at Friedland and was able to occupy Königsburg, the capital of East Prussia. The French emperor was master of all Germany.

Unable to fight another battle and unwilling to retreat into Russia, Tsar Alexander I (1801–1825) was ready to make peace. The two rulers met on a raft in the middle of the Niemen River while the two armies and the nervous king of Prussia watched. On July 7, 1807, they signed the Treaty of Tilsit, which confirmed France's gains. Moreover the Prussian state was reduced to half its size and was saved from extinction only by the support of Alexander. Prussia openly and Russia secretly became allies of Napoleon in his war against Britain.

Napoleon organized Europe much like the domain of a great Corsican family. The great French Empire was ruled directly by the head of the clan, Napoleon. On its borders were a number of satellite states carved out as the portions of the several family members. His stepson ruled

This painting of Napoleon and his officers at the battle of Eylau in 1807 clearly shows the vast number of troops that he customarily used in combat—although in this picture the troops are included only as a backdrop for a romantic rendering of the emperor and his aides on the field of battle. The artist was Antoine Jean Gros (1771–1835). [The Granger Collection.]

In 1807 Tsar Alexander I of Russia (center left) and Napoleon (center right) met on a raft in the Niemen River near Tilsit (on the Lithuanian border). At that conference they signed a treaty in which they divided Europe into spheres of French and Russian influence. The scene is imagined here by the artist Ludwig Wolf. [Bildarchiv Preussischer Kulturbesitz.]

Italy for him, while three of his brothers and his brother-in-law were made kings of other conquered states. Napoleon denied a kingdom to his brother Lucien because he disapproved of his wife. The relatives were expected to take orders without question. When they failed to do so, they were rebuked and even punished. The establishment of the Napoleonic family as the collective sovereign of Europe was offensive to the growing

Napoleon's Empire (1804–1814) **627**

national feeling in many states and helped to create it in others. The rule of puppet kings was unpopular and provoked opposition that needed only encouragement and assistance to flare up into serious resistance.

After the Peace of Tilsit such assistance could come only from Britain, and Napoleon knew he must defeat the British before he could feel safe. Unable to compete with the British navy, he turned to economic warfare. His plan was to cut off all British trade with the European continent. In this manner he hoped to cripple the commercial and financial power on which Britain depended, to cause domestic unrest and revolution, and so to drive the British from the war. For a time it appeared that this Continental System might work. British exports dropped, and riots broke out in England. But in the end the system failed and may even have contributed significantly to Napoleon's defeat.

The British economy survived because of its access to the growing markets of North and South America and of the eastern Mediterranean. At the same time, the Continental System did great harm to the European economies. The system was meant not only to hurt Britain but also to help France economically. Napoleon resisted advice to turn his empire into a free-trade area. Such a policy would have been both popular and helpful. Instead, his tariff policies favored France, increased the resentment of foreign merchants, and made them less willing to enforce the system and more ready to engage in smuggling. It was in part to prevent smuggling that Napoleon invaded Spain in 1808, and the resulting peninsular campaign in Spain and Portugal helped to bring on his ruin.

European Response to the Empire

Napoleon's conquests stimulated the two most powerful forces in nineteenth-century Europe: liberalism and nationalism. The export of his version of the French Revolution directly and indirectly spread the ideas and values of the Enlightenment and the principles of 1789. Wherever Napoleon ruled, the Napoleonic Code was imposed and class distinction abolished. Feudal dues disappeared and the peasants were freed from serfdom and manorial dues. In the towns the guilds and the local oligarchies that had dominated for centuries were dissolved or deprived of their power. New freedom thus came to serfs, artisans, workers, and entrepreneurs outside the privileged circles. Church monopoly of religion was replaced by general toleration. The established churches were deprived of their traditional independence, and made subordinate to the state.

These reforms were not undone by the fall of Napoleon and, along with the demand for representative, constitutional government, remained the basis for later liberal reforms. However, at the same time it became increasingly clear that Napoleon's policies were intended first and foremost for his own glory and that of France. The Continental System demonstrated that France rather than Europe generally was to be enriched by Napoleon's rule. Consequently, before long the conquered states and peoples became restive.

German Nationalism and Prussian Reform

The German response to Napoleon's success was particularly interesting and important. There had never been a unified German state. The great German writers of the Enlightenment, such as Kant, Schiller, and Lessing, were neither political nor nationalistic.

At the beginning of the nineteenth century the Romantic Movement had begun to take hold. One of its basic features in Germany was the emergence of nationalism. This movement went through two distinct stages. Initially, nationalistic writers emphasized the unique and admirable qualities of German culture, which, they argued, arose from the peculiar history of the German people. Such cultural nationalism prevailed until Napoleon's humiliation of Prussia at Jena in 1806. At that point many German intellectuals began to urge resistance to Napoleon on the basis of German nationality. The French conquest endangered the independence and achievements of the German people. Many nationalists

Baron Heinrich von Stein (1757–1831), on the left, and Prince Karl von Hardenberg (1750–1822) guided the reform of Prussia after the defeat by Napoleon at Jena in 1806. [The Granger Collection.]

were also critical of the German princes, who ruled selfishly and inefficiently and who seemed ever ready to lick the boots of Napoleon. No less important in forging a German national sentiment was the example of France, which had attained greatness by enlisting the active support of the entire people in the patriotic cause. Henceforth many Germans sought to solve their internal political problems by establishing a unified German state, reformed to harness the energies of the entire people.

After Tilsit only Prussia could arouse such patriotic feelings. Elsewhere German rulers were either under Napoleon's thumb or actively collaborating with him. Defeated, humiliated, and shrunken in size, Prussia continued to resist, however feebly. To Prussia fled German nationalists from other states, calling for reforms and unification that were, in fact, feared and hated by Frederick William III and the *Junker* nobility. Reforms came about in spite of such opposition because the defeat at Jena had made clear the necessity of new departures for the Prussian state.

The Prussian administrative and social reforms were the work of Baron von Stein (1757–1831) and Count von Hardenberg (1750–1822). The architects of military reform were General Gerhard von Scharnhorst (1755–

1813) and Count von Gneisenau (1760–1831). None of their reforms was intended to reduce the autocratic power of the Prussian monarch or to put an end to the dominance of the *Junkers,* who formed the bulwark of the state and of the army officer corps. Rather they aimed at fighting the revolution and French power with their own version of the French weapons. As Hardenburg declared:

> Our objective, our guiding principle, must be a revolution in the better sense, a revolution leading directly to the great goal, the elevation of humanity through the wisdom of those in authority. . . . Democratic rules of conduct in a monarchical administration, such is the formula . . . which will conform most comfortably with the spirit of the age.[1]

Although the reforms came from the top, they brought important changes in Prussian society.

Stein's reforms put an end to the existing system of Prussian landownership. The *Junker* monopoly of landholding was broken. Serfdom was generally abolished.

1 Quoted in Geoffrey Brunn, *Europe and the French Imperium* (New York: Harper and Row, 1938), p. 174.

Arthur Wellesley, the duke of Wellington, first led troops against Napoleon in Spain and later defeated him at the battle of Waterloo, June 18, 1815. Unlike his great naval contemporary, Nelson, he lived to become an elder statesman of Britain. The portrait is by the celebrated Spanish painter Francisco Goya (1746–1828), another example of whose work is reproduced in the color album. [The Granger Collection.]

However, the power of the *Junkers* did not permit the total end of the system, as in the western principalities of Germany. Peasants remaining on the land were forced to continue manorial labor although they were free to leave the land if they chose. They could obtain the ownership of the land they worked only at the price of forfeiting a third of it to the lord. The result was that *Junker* holdings grew larger. Some peasants went to the cities to find work; others became agricultural laborers; and some did actually become small freeholding farmers. Serfdom had come to an end, but new social problems that would fester for another half century had been created as a landless labor force emerged.

The military reforms sought to increase the supply of soldiers and to improve their quality. Jena had shown that an army of free patriots commanded by officers chosen on merit rather than by birth could defeat an army of serfs and mercenaries commanded by incompetent nobles. To remedy the situation, the Prussian reformers abolished inhumane punishments, sought to inspire patriotic feelings in the soldiers, opened the officer corps to commoners, gave promotions on the basis of merit, and organized war colleges that developed new theories of strategy and tactics. These reforms soon put Prussia in a condition to regain its former power. However, because Napoleon had put a strict limit on the size of the Prussian army, universal conscription could not be introduced until 1813. Before that date the Prussians got around the limit of 42,000 men in arms by training one group each year, putting them into the reserves, and then training a new group the same size. In this manner Prussia could boast an army of 270,000 by 1814.

The Wars of Liberation

In Spain more than elsewhere in Europe national resistance to France had deep social roots. Spain had achieved political unity as early as the sixteenth century. The Spanish peasants were devoted to the ruling dynasty and especially to the Roman Catholic Church. France and Spain had been allies since 1796. In 1807, however, a French army came into the Iberian Peninsula to force Portugal to abandon its traditional alliance with Britain. The army stayed in Spain to protect lines of supply and communication. When a revolt broke out in Madrid in 1808, Napoleon used it as a pretext to depose the Spanish Bourbon dynasty and place his brother Joseph on the Spanish throne. Public outrage was increased by attacks on the privileges of the church. Many members of the upper classes were prepared to collaborate with Napoleon, but the peasants, urged on by the lower clergy and the monks, rose in a general rebellion.

Napoleon faced a new kind of warfare not vulnerable to his usual tactics. Guerrilla bands cut lines of communication, killed stragglers, destroyed isolated units, and then disappeared into the mountains. The British landed an army under Sir Arthur Wellesley (1769–1852), later the duke of Wellington, to support the Spanish insurgents. Thus began the long peninsular campaign that would drain French strength from elsewhere in Europe and play a critical role in Napoleon's eventual defeat.

The French troubles in Spain encouraged the Austrians to renew the war in 1809. Since their defeat at Austerlitz they had sought a war of revenge. The Austrians counted on Napoleon's distraction in Spain, French war weariness, and aid from other German princes. However, Napoleon was fully in command in France;

When their marriage failed to produce a male heir, Napoleon divorced his first wife, Joséphine de Beauharnais (1763–1814) [LEFT]. Many considered the action one aspect of Napoleon's betrayal of the Revolution, especially because he then married Marie Louise (1791–1847) [RIGHT], daughter of the Hapsburg Emperor, who bore him a son. It was clear that Napoleon hoped to establish a new imperial dynasty in France. Joséphine's portrait is by F. P. Gérard and Marie Louise's is by J. B. Isabey. [The Granger Collection.]

and the German princes did not move. The French army marched swiftly into Austria and won the battle of Wagram. The resulting Peace of Schönbrunn deprived Austria of much territory and three and a half million subjects. Another spoil of victory was the Austrian Archduchess Marie Louise, daughter of the emperor. Napoleon's wife, Josephine de Beauharnais, was forty-six and had borne him no children. His dynastic ambitions, as well as the desire for a marriage matching his new position as master of Europe, led him to divorce his wife and to marry the eighteen-year-old Austrian heiress. Napoleon had also considered the sister of Tsar Alexander but had been politely rebuffed.

The failure of Napoleon's marriage negotiations with Russia emphasized the shakiness of the Franco-Russian alliance concluded at Tilsit. The alliance was unpopular with Russian nobles because of the liberal politics of France and because of the prohibition of the Continental System on timber sales to Britain. Only French aid in gaining Constantinople could justify the alliance in their eyes, but Napoleon gave them no help against the Ottoman Empire. The organization of the Grand Duchy of Warsaw as a Napoleonic satellite on the Russian doorstep and its enlargement in 1809 after the battle of Wagram angered Alexander I. Napoleon's annexation of Holland in violation of the Treaty of Tilsit, his recognition of the French Marshal Bernadotte as King Charles XIV of Sweden, and his marriage to an Austrian princess further

disturbed the tsar. At the end of 1810 Russia withdrew from the Continental System and began to prepare for war.

Napoleon was determined to put an end to the Russian military threat. He amassed an army of over 600,000 men, including a core of Frenchmen and over 400,000 other soldiers drawn from the rest of his empire. He intended the usual short campaign crowned by a decisive battle, but the Russians disappointed him by retreating before his advance. His vast superiority in numbers—the Russians had only about 160,000 troops—made it foolish for them to risk a battle. Instead they followed a "scorched-earth" policy, destroying all food and supplies as they retreated. The so-called Grand Army of Napoleon could not live off the country, and the expanse of Russia made supply lines too long to maintain. Terrible rains, fierce heat, shortages of food and water, and the courage of the Russian rear guard defending their country against the invader eroded the morale of Napoleon's army. Napoleon's advisers urged him to abandon the venture, but he feared that an unsuccessful campaign would undermine his position in the empire and in France. He pinned his faith on the Russians' unwillingness to abandon Moscow without a fight.

In September 1812 Russian public opinion forced the army to give Napoleon the battle he wanted in spite of the canny Russian General Kutuzov's wish to avoid the fight and to let the Russian winter defeat the invader. At

THE
CONTINENTAL
SYSTEM
1806 - 1810

NORWAY
SWEDEN
DENMARK
ENGLAND
PRUSSIA
POLAND
RHINE
CONF.
RUSSIA
FRANCE
AUSTRIA
PORT.
ITALY
SPAIN

AREAS IN WHICH
BRITISH EXPORTS
WERE PROHIBITED

THE
FRENCH EMPIRE

THE
GRAND EMPIRE

ALLIED WITH
NAPOLEON

300 MI.

300 KM.

BATTLE
SITES

NORWAY
Christiana

SWEDEN
Stockholm

GOTHLAND

KINGDOM OF
DENMARK
AND
NORWAY

Gothenburg

SCOTLAND

Edinburgh

NORTH

SEA

DENMARK   Copenhagen

BALTIC SEA

SWEDISH
POMERANIA

HELIGO-
LAND
(U.K.)

Lübeck

MECK.

PRUSSIA

THORN
GRAN

York

Hamburg

BERLIN

Posen

UNITED
KINGDOM

WALES

London

Dover

Boulogne

HOLLAND

OLDEN-
BURG

WEST-
PHALIA

HESSE

BERG
Cologne

SAXONY
LEIPZIG

DRESDEN

BAUTZEN

Breslau

Brussels

WATERLOO

Amiens

Reims

Mainz

JENA

CONFEDERATION
OF THE
RHINE

Prague
BOHEMIA
AUSTERLITZ

Brest

Paris

Versailles

VALMY

BADEN

ULM

RATISBON

WAGRAM

Fontainebleau

Strasbourg

Munich

ASPERN

QUIBERON

Nantes

Orléans

HOHENLINDEN

BAVARIA
INNSBRUCK

Vienna

VENDÉE

FRANCE

SWITZ.
ST. GOTTHARD

VENETIA
SACILE

EMPIRE

Rochefort

Lyons

SAVOY

LOMBARDY
Milan
LODI

Trieste

BAY OF

BISCAY

Turin

MARENGO
Genoa

ITALY

BOS

Avignon

Marseilles

Nice

LUCCA
Leghorn

Urbino

ILLYRIAN PROVINCE

ADRIATIC

Bordeaux

TOULOUSE

Toulon

CAPE
FINISTERRE

Corunna

VITORIA

Burgos

SALAMANCA

CIUDAD
RODRIGO

SARAGOSSA

GERONA

ELBA

CORSICA

Rome

Bari

Oporto

ALMEIDA

Madrid

Barcelona
TARRAGONA

Naples

PORTUGAL

VIMEIRO
CINTRA

Lisbon

TALAVERA

SPAIN

OCAÑA

VALENCIA

VALENCIA

K. OF
NAPLES

ELVAS

BADAJOZ

CIUDAD
REAL

BAYLEN

K. OF
SARDINIA

BALEARIC IS.

Cordova

MURCIA

Cagliari

Seville

ANDALUCIA

Cadiz

TRAFALGAR

GIBALTAR
(U.K.)

MEDITERRANEAN

K. OF
SICILY

Algiers

Tunis

632   *The Age of Napoleon and the Triumph of Romanticism*

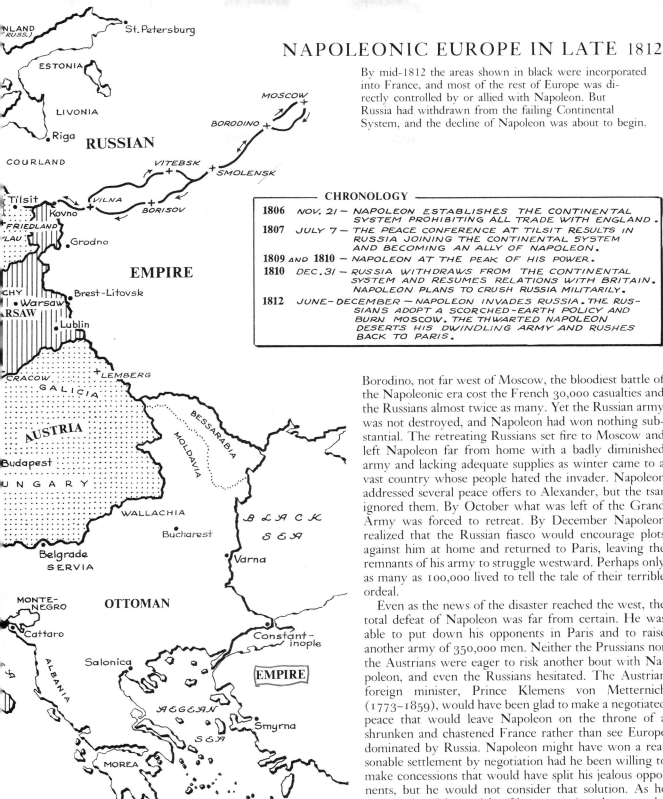

NAPOLEONIC EUROPE IN LATE 1812

By mid-1812 the areas shown in black were incorporated into France, and most of the rest of Europe was directly controlled by or allied with Napoleon. But Russia had withdrawn from the failing Continental System, and the decline of Napoleon was about to begin.

CHRONOLOGY

1806	*NOV. 21 — NAPOLEON ESTABLISHES THE CONTINENTAL SYSTEM PROHIBITING ALL TRADE WITH ENGLAND.*
1807	*JULY 7 — THE PEACE CONFERENCE AT TILSIT RESULTS IN RUSSIA JOINING THE CONTINENTAL SYSTEM AND BECOMING AN ALLY OF NAPOLEON.*
1809 AND 1810	*— NAPOLEON AT THE PEAK OF HIS POWER.*
1810	*DEC. 31 — RUSSIA WITHDRAWS FROM THE CONTINENTAL SYSTEM AND RESUMES RELATIONS WITH BRITAIN. NAPOLEON PLANS TO CRUSH RUSSIA MILITARILY.*
1812	*JUNE — DECEMBER — NAPOLEON INVADES RUSSIA. THE RUSSIANS ADOPT A SCORCHED-EARTH POLICY AND BURN MOSCOW. THE THWARTED NAPOLEON DESERTS HIS DWINDLING ARMY AND RUSHES BACK TO PARIS.*

Borodino, not far west of Moscow, the bloodiest battle of the Napoleonic era cost the French 30,000 casualties and the Russians almost twice as many. Yet the Russian army was not destroyed, and Napoleon had won nothing substantial. The retreating Russians set fire to Moscow and left Napoleon far from home with a badly diminished army and lacking adequate supplies as winter came to a vast country whose people hated the invader. Napoleon addressed several peace offers to Alexander, but the tsar ignored them. By October what was left of the Grand Army was forced to retreat. By December Napoleon realized that the Russian fiasco would encourage plots against him at home and returned to Paris, leaving the remnants of his army to struggle westward. Perhaps only as many as 100,000 lived to tell the tale of their terrible ordeal.

Even as the news of the disaster reached the west, the total defeat of Napoleon was far from certain. He was able to put down his opponents in Paris and to raise another army of 350,000 men. Neither the Prussians nor the Austrians were eager to risk another bout with Napoleon, and even the Russians hesitated. The Austrian foreign minister, Prince Klemens von Metternich (1773–1859), would have been glad to make a negotiated peace that would leave Napoleon on the throne of a shrunken and chastened France rather than see Europe dominated by Russia. Napoleon might have won a reasonable settlement by negotiation had he been willing to make concessions that would have split his jealous opponents, but he would not consider that solution. As he explained to Metternich, "Your sovereigns born on the throne can let themselves be beaten twenty times and return to their capitals. I cannot do this because I am an

The leading figures of the Congress of Vienna are here portrayed in a single group. Talleyrand has his arm on the table at right, and Metternich, in white breeches, stands toward the left. The actual work of the Congress took place in small meetings, with only a few of these statesmen present. The artist was Isabey. [Austrian Information Service, New York.]

upstart soldier. My domination will not survive the day when I cease to be strong, and therefore feared."[2]

In 1813 patriotic pressure and national ambition brought together the last and most powerful coalition against Napoleon. The Russians drove westward and were joined by Prussia and then Austria. All were assisted by vast amounts of British money. From the west Wellington marched his peninsular army into France. Napoleon's new army was inexperienced and poorly equipped. His generals had lost confidence and were tired. The emperor himself was worn out and sick. Still he was able to wage a skillful campaign in central Europe and to defeat the allies at Dresden. In October, however, he met the combined armies of the enemy at Leipzig in what the Germans called the Battle of the Nations and was decisively defeated. At the end of March 1814 the allied army marched into Paris, and a few days later Napoleon abdicated and went into exile on the island of Elba off the coast of northern Italy.

2 Quoted in Felix Markham, *Napoleon and the Awakening of Europe* (New York: Macmillan, 1965), pp. 115–116.

The Congress of Vienna and the European Settlement

The victorious coalition had been held together by fear of Napoleon and hostility to his ambitions. As soon as he was removed, the allies began to pursue their own separate ambitions. The key person in achieving agreement was Robert Stewart Viscount Castlereagh (1769–1822), the British foreign secretary. Even before the victorious armies had entered Paris, he brought about the signing of the Treaty of Chaumont on March 9, 1814. It provided for the restoration of the Bourbon dynasty to the French throne and the contraction of France to its frontiers of 1792. Even more important was the agreement by Britain, Austria, Russia, and Prussia to form a Quadruple Alliance for twenty years to guarantee the peace terms and to act together to preserve whatever settlement they later agreed upon. Remaining problems, and they were many, and final details were left for a conference to be held at Vienna.

The Congress of Vienna assembled in September 1814, and its work was not concluded until November 1815. Although it was attended by a glittering array of heads of state, the important work of the conference was carried out by the four great powers. The only full session of the congress met to ratify the arrangements made by the big four. The easiest problem facing the great powers was France. All the victors were agreed that no single state should be allowed to dominate Europe, and all were determined to see that France should be pre-

Napoleon Looks Back from Exile on St. Helena

The following remarks are from the ex-emperor's final period of exile on St. Helena, 1815–1821.

FRANCE, *by her geographical situation, the fertility of her soil, the energy and intelligence of her inhabitants, is the arbitress of European states. She is among the nations of Europe what the lion is amongst the other animals....*

Those who are called to hold the reins of such a kingdom should comprehend the full value and bearing of the favourable position which France enjoys, and never suffer a nation which was destined to be a sun, to degenerate into a satellite.

The whole of my policy was uniformly directed by this opinion, both during the consulate and the empire....

Had I reigned twenty years longer, I would have shown the difference between a constitutional emperor and a king of France. The kings of France have never done anything save in the interests of their dynasty, and with a view [to] increasing their feudal power by the depression of the high nobility, the extinction of the great fiefs and their reunion with the crown.... I would have changed the face of France and of Europe. Archimedes promised to move the world, if they only furnished him with a fulcrum for his lever; I would have made a fulcrum for myself, wherever I could have [put into action] my energy, my perseverance, and my budgets. With budgets well employed, a world may be regenerated.

Napoleon, ed. by Maurice Hutt (Englewood Cliffs, N.J.: Prentice-Hall, 1972), pp. 55–56.

vented from doing so again. The restoration of the French Bourbon monarchy, which was again popular, and a nonvindictive boundary settlement kept France calm and satisfied. In addition the powers constructed a series of states to serve as barriers to any new French expansion. They established the kingdom of the Netherlands, including Belgium, in the north and added Genoa to Piedmont in the south. Prussia, whose power was increased by accessions in eastern Europe, was given important new territories in the west along the Rhine River to deter French aggression in that area. Austria was given full control of northern Italy to prevent a repetition of Napoleon's conquests there. As for the rest of Germany, most of Napoleon's arrangements were left un-

touched. The venerable Holy Roman Empire, which had been dissolved in 1806, was not revived. In all these areas the congress established the rule of legitimate monarchs and rejected any hint of the republican and democratic politics that had flowed from the French Revolution.

On these matters agreement was not difficult, but the settlement of eastern Europe sharply divided the victors. Alexander I of Russia wanted all Poland under his rule. Prussia was willing if she herself received all of Saxony. But Austria was unwilling to surrender its share of Poland or to see the growth of Prussian power and the penetration of Russia deeper into central Europe. The Polish–Saxon question brought the congress to a standstill and almost brought on a new war among the victors, but defeated France provided a way out. The wily Talleyrand, now representing France at Vienna, suggested that the weight of France added to that of Britain and Austria might bring Alexander to his senses. When news of a secret treaty among the three leaked out, the tsar agreed to become ruler of a smaller Poland, and Frederick William III of Prussia agreed to accept only part of Saxony. Thereafter France was included as a fifth great power in all deliberations.

Unity among the victors was further restored by Napoleon's return from Elba on March 1, 1815. The French army was still loyal to the former emperor, and many Frenchmen thought that their fortunes might be safer under his rule than under that of the restored Bourbons. The coalition seemed to be dissolving in Vienna. Napoleon seized the opportunity, escaped to France, and was soon restored to power. He promised a liberal constitution and a peaceful foreign policy. The allies were not convinced. They declared Napoleon an outlaw, a new device under international law, and sent their armies to crush him. Wellington, with the crucial help of the Prussians under Field Marshal von Blücher, defeated Napoleon at Waterloo in Belgium on June 18, 1815. Napoleon again abdicated and was sent into exile to St. Helena, a tiny Atlantic island off the coast of Africa, where he spent the rest of his life.

EUROPE
IN 1815

NORWAY
AND
SWEDEN
1814

FINLAND
RUSS., 1809

Bergen

Christiania

Stockholm

SCOTLAND

Belfast
Edinburgh

DENMARK

NORTH

SEA

BALTIC SEA

Rig

PRUSSIA

Danzig

IRELAND

Dublin
Liver-
pool

Manchester

BOUNDARY OF THE
GERMAN
CONFEDERATION

SCHLESWIG

HOLSTEIN

EAST
PRUSSIA

UNITED
KINGDOM

London

(FORMER
DUTCH
REP.)

(FORMER
AUSTR.
NETHS.)

HANOVER

K. OF THE NETHERLANDS

Berlin

Cologne

Warsaw

K. OF
POLAND
(RUSS.)

Breslau

ATLANTIC

Brussels

Prague

BOHEMIA

Cracow

Brest

Rouen

MORAVIA

AUSTRIAN

Rennes

Paris

Reims

LORRAINE

Strassburg

BAVARIA

Munich

Vienna

AUSTRIA

HUNGARY

AUSTRIA

Orléans

OCEAN

Nantes

FRANCE

Berne

SWITZ.

Budapest

EMPIRE

Lyons

SAVOY

TYROL

VENETIA

Trieste

Agram

CROATIA

Bordeaux

LOM-
BARDY

Montpelier

PIEDMONT

PAR.

MOD.

Bologna

BOSNIA

Belgrade

Oviedo

XXX &
NICE

LUCCA

Sarajevo

SERBIA

MONTE-
NEGRO

Marseilles

ANDORRA

TUSCANY

STATES
OF THE
CHURCH

ADRIATIC SEA

Burgos

PORTUGAL

Madrid

ELBA

KINGDOM OF
SARDINIA

CORSICA
(FR.)

ITALY

Rome

Ochrid

Lisbon

SPAIN

Barcelona

Naples

Janin

Valencia

BALEARIC IS.
(SP.)

SARDINIA

Cordova

MEDIT

KINGDOM OF THE
TWO SICILIES

Cosenza

Seville

Tangier

GIBRALTAR (U.K.)
Ceuta
(SP.)

THE BARBARY STATES

Algiers

SICILY

Fez

MOROCCO

Tunis

ALGERIA
TURK TO 1830

TUNISIA
(TURK.)

MALTA
(U.K.)

T R MILLER

The Age of Napoleon and the Triumph of Romanticism

BOUNDARY OF THE
GERMAN
CONFEDERATION
1815

OLDEN-
BURG
HOLSTEIN
MECKLENBURG
SCHWERIN
NETHERLANDS
HANOVER
BRANDENBURG
WESTPHALIA
BRUNSWICK
ANHALT
RHINE
PROVINCES
HESSE-
CASSEL
SAXONY
LUX.
NASSAU
THÜRINGIA
HESSE
AUSTRIA
PALA-
TINATE
BAVARIA
WÜRT-
TEMBERG
BADEN

PRUSSIAN

100 MI.
100 KM.

The Congress of Vienna achieved the post-Napoleonic
territorial adjustments shown on the map. The most
notable arrangements dealt with areas along France's
borders (Netherlands, Prussia, Switzerland, and Piedmont) and in Poland and northern Italy.

The Hundred Days, as the period of Napoleon's return is called, frightened the great powers and hardened
the peace settlement for France. In addition to some
minor territorial adjustments, the victors imposed a war
indemnity and an army of occupation on France. The
Quadruple Alliance was renewed. Alexander also proposed a Holy Alliance, whereby the monarchs promised
to act in accordance with Christian principles. Austria
and Prussia signed; but Castlereagh thought it absurd,
and England abstained. The tsar, who was then embracing mysticism, thought his proposal a valuable tool for
international relations. The Holy Alliance soon became a
symbol of extreme political reaction.

The chief aims of the Congress of Vienna were to
prevent a recurrence of the Napoleonic nightmare and to
arrange an acceptable settlement for Europe that might
produce lasting peace. In achieving these goals it was
remarkably successful. France accepted the new situation
without undue resentment. The victorious powers settled
difficult problems in a reasonable way. They established a
legalistic balance of power and methods for adjusting to
change. The work of the congress has been criticized for
failing to recognize and provide for the great forces that
would stir the nineteenth century—nationalism and democracy—but such criticism is inappropriate. The settlement, like all such agreements, was aimed at solving past
ills, and in that it succeeded. If the powers failed to
anticipate future problems or to yield to forces of which
they disapproved, they would have been more than
human to have done so. Perhaps it was unusual enough to
produce a settlement that remained essentially intact for
almost half a century and that allowed Europe to suffer no
general war for one hundred years.

The Congress of Vienna and the European Settlement 637

The Romantic Movement

The years of the French Revolution and the conquests of Napoleon saw the emergence of a new and very important intellectual movement throughout Europe. Romanticism in its various manifestations was a reaction against much of the thought of the Enlightenment. Romantic writers opposed what they considered the excessive scientific narrowness of the eighteenth-century *philosophes*. The latter stood accused of subjecting everything to geometrical and mathematical models and thereby demeaning the world of the feelings and of imagination. Romantic thinkers refused to conceive of human nature as primarily rational. They wanted to interpret both physical nature and human society in organic rather than in mechanical terms and categories. Where the Enlightenment spokesmen had often criticized religion and faith, the Romantics saw religion as basic to human nature and faith as a means to knowledge. Expressing this reaction to the rationalism of the previous century the German Romantic composer Franz Schubert (1797–1828) called the Enlightenment "that ugly skeleton without flesh or blood."

Some historians, most notably Arthur O. Lovejoy, have warned against speaking of a single European-wide Romantic Movement. They have pointed out that a variety of such movements, occurring almost simultaneously in Germany, England, and France, arose independently and had their own particular courses of development. Such considerations have not, however, prevented the designation of a specific historical period, dated roughly from 1780 to 1830, as the Age of Romanticism or the Romantic Movement. Despite national differences a shared reaction to the Enlightenment marked all of these writers and artists. They generally saw the imagination or some such intuitive intellectual faculty supplementing the reason as a means of perceiving and understanding the world. They urged a revival of Christianity such as had permeated Europe during the Middle Ages. And unlike the *philosophes*, the Romantics liked the art, the literature, and the architecture of medieval times. They were also deeply interested in folklore, folk songs, and fairy tales. The Romantics were also fascinated by dreams, hallucinations, sleepwalking, and other phenomena that suggested the existence of a world beyond that of empirical observation, sensory data, and discursive reasoning.

Several historical streams fed the Romantic movement. These included the individualism of the Renaissance and the Reformation and the Pietism of the seventeenth century and the eighteenth-century English Methodist movement, which encouraged a heartfelt, practical religion in place of dogmatism, rationalism, and deism. The sentimental novels of the eighteenth century, such as Samuel Richardson's *Clarissa*, also paved the way for thinkers who would emphasize feeling and emotion. The so-called *Sturm und Drang* ("storm and stress") period of German literature and German idealist philosophy were important for the Romantics. However, two writers who were also closely related to the Enlightenment provided the immediate intellectual foundations for Romanticism. They were Rousseau and Immanuel Kant, both of whom raised questions about the sufficiency of the rationalism so dear to the *philosophes*.

It has already been pointed out in Chapter 22 that Jean Jacques Rousseau, though sharing in some of the reformist spirit of the Enlightenment, opposed many of its other facets. What Romantic writers especially drew from Rousseau was his conviction that society had corrupted human nature. In the two *Discourses* and others of his works Rousseau had portrayed humankind as created happy and good by nature and originally living in a state of equilibrium, able to do what it desired and desiring only what it was able to do. For humankind to become happy again, it must remain true to its natural being, while still attempting to realize the new moral possibilities of life in society.

In the *Social Contract* (1762) Rousseau had provided his prescription for the reorganization of political life that would achieve that goal.

Immanuel Kant was the most important German philosopher of the late eighteenth century. His thought was the capstone of the philosophy of the Enlightenment and paved the way for Romanticism. [Bettmann Archive.]

Rousseau set forth his view on the individual's development toward the good and happy life in a novel entitled *Émile* (1762). Initially this treatise on education was far more influential than the *Social Contract*. In *Émile* Rousseau stressed the difference between children and adults. He distinguished the stages of human maturation and urged that in rearing children one must give them maximum individual freedom. Each child should be allowed to grow freely, like a plant, and to learn by trial and error what reality is and how best to deal with it. The parent or teacher would help most by providing the basic necessities of life and warding off what was manifestly harmful. Otherwise the adult should stay completely out of the way, like a gardener who waters and weeds his garden but otherwise lets nature take its course.

This was a revolutionary concept of education in an age accustomed to narrow, bookish, and highly regimented vocational education and learning. Rousseau thought that the child's sentiments as well as its reason should be permitted to flourish. To Romantic writers this concept of human development vindicated the rights of nature over those of artificial society and would eventually lead to a natural society. In its fully developed form this view of life led the Romantics to place a high value on the uniqueness of each individual person and to explore in great detail the experiences of childhood. Like Rousseau, the Romantics saw humankind, nature, and society as organically related to each other.

Immanuel Kant (1724–1804) wrote the two greatest philosophical works of the late eighteenth century: *The Critique of Pure Reason* (1781) and *The Critique of Practical Reason* (1788). He sought to accept the rationalism of the Enlightenment and still to preserve a belief in human freedom, immortality, and the existence of God. Against Locke and other philosophers who saw knowledge rooted in sensory experience alone, Kant successfully argued for the subjective character of human knowledge. For Kant the human mind did not simply reflect the world around it like a passive mirror: rather it actively imposed on the world of sensory experience "forms of sensibility" and "categories of understanding." These categories were generated by the mind itself. In other words, the human mind perceives the world as it does because of its own internal mental categories. What this meant was that human perceptions were radically subjective and as much the product of the mind's own activity as of sense experience.

Kant found the sphere of reality that was accessible to pure reason to be quite limited. However, he believed that beyond the phenomenal world over which "pure reason" was master there existed what he called the "noumenal" world. The latter was a sphere of moral and aesthetic reality known by "practical reason" and conscience. Kant thought that all men possessed an innate sense of moral duty or an awareness of what he called a "categorical imperative." This term referred to an inner command to act in every situation as one would have all other people always act in the same situation. The existence of this imperative of conscience was regarded by Kant as incontrovertible proof of humankind's natural freedom. On the basis of humankind's moral sense Kant went on to postulate the existence of God, eternal life, and future rewards and punishments. He believed that these transcendental truths could not be proved by discursive reasoning. Still he was convinced that they were realities to which every reasonable person could attest.

To many Romantic writers Kantian philosophy was a decisive refutation of the narrow rationality of the Enlightenment. Whether they called it "practical reason," "fancy," "imagination," "intuition," or simply "feeling," the Romantics believed in the presence of a special power in the human mind that could penetrate beyond the limits of human understanding as set forth by Hobbes, Locke, and Hume. Most of them also believed that poets and artists generally possessed these powers in particular abundance. Other Romantic writers appealed to the limits of human reason to set forth new religious ideas or political thought often at odds with that of Enlightenment writers.

The Romantic Movement

An illustration made in 1825 for the Biblical book of Job by the English Romantic poet and engraver William Blake. [The Granger Collection.]

Romantic Literature

The term *romantic* appeared in English and French literature as early as the seventeenth century. Neoclassical writers used the word at that time to describe literature that they considered to be unreal, sentimental, or excessively fanciful. In the eighteenth century the English writer Thomas Warton associated *romantic* with medieval romances. In Germany, a major center of the Romantic literary movement, Johann Gottfried Herder used the terms *romantic* and *Gothic* interchangeably. In both England and Germany the term came to be applied to all literature that failed to observe classical forms and rules and gave free play to the imagination. English Romantic poets and essayists looked on the period of literature from John Dryden to Alexander Pope, roughly 1670–1750, as a classical "dark age." For both English and German Romantics the French Neoclassicists of the seventeenth century, such as Pierre Corneille and Jean Racine, were slavish imitators of the classics and represented all that literature should not be.

As an alternative to such dependence on the ancients August Wilhelm von Schlegel (1767–1845) praised the "romantic" literature of Dante, Petrarch, Boccaccio, Shakespeare, the Arthurian legends, Cervantes, and Calderón. According to Schlegel, Romantic literature was to classical literature what the organic and living were to the merely mechanical. He set forth his views in *Lectures on Dramatic Art and Literature* (1809–1811).

The Romantic Movement had peaked in Germany and England before it became a major force in France under the leadership of Madame de Staël (1766–1817) and Victor Hugo (1802–1885). So influential was the classical tradition in France that not until 1816 did a French writer openly declare himself a Romantic. That was Henri Beyle, who wrote under the pseudonym Stendahl (1783–1842). He praised Shakespeare and Lord Byron and criticized his own countryman, the seventeenth-century classical dramatist Racine.

The English Romantics believed that poetry was en-

hanced by freely following the creative impulses of the mind. In this belief they directly opposed Lockean psychology, which regarded the mind as a passive receptor and poetry a mechanical exercise of "wit" following prescribed rules. For William Blake and Samuel Taylor Coleridge the artist's imagination was God at work in the mind. As Blake expressed his views, the imagination was "a repetition in the finite mind of the eternal act of creation in the infinite I AM." Percy Bysshe Shelley believed that "A poet participates in the eternal, the infinite, and the One." So conceived, poetry could not be considered idle play. It was the highest of human acts, man's self-fullfillment in a transcendental world.

William Blake (1757–1827) considered the poet a seer and poetry translated vision. He thought it a great tragedy that so many people understood the world only rationally and could perceive no innocence or beauty in it. In the 1790s he experienced a period of deep personal depression, which seems to have been related to his own inability to perceive the world as he believed it to be. The better one got to know the world, the more the life of the imagination and its spiritual values seemed to recede. Blake saw this problem as evidence of the materialism and injustice of English society. He was deeply impressed by

William Wordsworth was among the earliest and most influential of the English Romantic poets. He was particularly noted for his nature poetry. [Culver Pictures.]

the strong sense of contradiction between a true childlike vision of the world and conceptions of it based on actual experience. Through his own poetry he sought to bring childlike innocence and experience together and to transform experience by imagination. The conflict of which he was so much aware can be seen in *Songs of Innocence* (1789) and *Songs of Experience* (1794). In "The Tyger," published in the latter, he asked:

Tyger, Tyger, burning bright
In the forests of the night,
. . . .
When the stars threw down their spears
And watered heaven with their tears,
Did He smile His work to see?
Did He who made the lamb make thee?

Samuel Taylor Coleridge (1772–1834) was the master of Gothic poems of the supernatural. His three poems, "Christabel," "The Ancient Mariner," and "Kubla Khan," are of this character. "The Ancient Mariner" relates the story of a sailor cursed for killing an albatross. The poem treats the subject as a crime against nature and God and raises the issues of guilt, punishment, and the redemptive possibilities of humility and penance. At the end of the poem the mariner discovers the unity and beauty of all things and, having repented, is delivered from his awful curse, which has been symbolized by the dead albatross hung around his neck:

O happy living things! no tongue
Their beauty might declare:
A spring of love gushed from my heart,
And I blessed them unaware . . .
The self-same moment I could pray;
And from my neck so free
The Albatross fell off, and sank
Like lead into the sea.

Coleridge also made major contributions to romantic literary criticism in his lectures on Shakespeare and in *Biographia Literaria* (1817), which presents his theories of poetry.

William Wordsworth (1770–1850) was Coleridge's closest friend. Together they published *Lyrical Ballads* in 1798 as a manifesto of poetry that rejected the rules of eighteenth-century criticism. Among Wordsworth's most important later poems is his "Ode on Intimations of Immortality" (1803), written in part to console Coleridge, who was in the midst of a deep personal crisis. Its subject is the loss of poetic vision, something Wordsworth also keenly felt at this time in himself. Nature, which he had worshiped, no longer spoke freely to him, and he feared that it might never speak to him again:

There was a time when meadow, grove, and stream,
The earth, and every common sight,
    To me did seem
    Appareled in celestial light,
The glory and the freshness of a dream.
It is not now as it hath been of yore—
    Turn whereso'er I may,
        By night or day,
The things which I have seen I now can see no more.

What he had lost was the vision that he believed all human beings lose in the necessary process of maturation: their childlike vision and closeness to spiritual reality. For both Wordsworth and Coleridge childhood was the bright period of creative imagination. Wordsworth held a theory of the soul's preexistence in a celestial state prior to its creation. The child, being closer in time to its eternal origin and undistracted by much worldly experience, recollects the supernatural world much more easily. Aging and urban living corrupt and deaden the imagination and make one's inner feelings and the beauty of nature less important. Yet Wordsworth took consolation in the occasional moments of later life when he still found in nature "intimations of immortality," a brief glimpse of humankind's eternal origin and destiny:

George Gordon, Lord Byron not only wrote important Romantic poetry but also became a romantic hero in his own right by his death in the Greek revolution in 1824. The portrait by Richard Westall is itself a bit of Romanticism. [The Granger Collection.]

> O joy! that in our embers
> Is something that doth live,
> That Nature yet remembers
> What was so fugitive!

In his book-length poem *The Prelude* (1850) Wordsworth presented a long autobiographical account of the growth of the poet's mind.

Percy Bysshe Shelley (1792–1822), a very philosophical poet, lived in a Platonic world of ideas more real to him than anything in the sensible world. One of his greatest poetic works, *Prometheus Unbound* (1820), was written in Rome when he was twenty-seven years old. It was stimulated by Aeschylus's *Prometheus Bound*, the story of a defiant Titan who stole fire from the gods and paid for his crime by being eternally bound to a rock and attacked by savage birds. For Shelley, Prometheus was a symbol of all that was good in life, the principle of life itself. He was the friend of humanity, who like Christ suffered because he tried to improve humankind. He was the soul's unconquerable desire to create harmony in the world through reasonableness and love. In the poem Prometheus struggles against Jupiter, who represents tyranny and the power of evil in the world. He receives assistance in his struggle from Asia, a symbol of unspoiled nature, and from Mother Earth. In the end Jupiter is overthrown by his own son, Demogorgon, who rewards Prometheus's patience and endurance by setting him free. Demogorgon summarizes the poem's romantic message:

> To suffer woes which Hope thinks infinite;
> To forgive wrongs darker than death or night;
>   To defy Power, which seems omnipotent;
> To live, and bear; to hope til Hope creates
> From its own wreck the thing it contemplates;
>   Neither to change, nor falter, nor repent;
> This, like thy glory, Titan, is to be
> Good, great and joyous, beautiful and free;
> This alone Life, Joy, Empire, and Victory.

A true rebel among the Romantic poets was Lord Byron (1788–1824). At home even the other Romantic writers distrusted and generally disliked him. He had little sympathy for their views of the imagination. However, outside England Byron was regarded as the embodiment of the new person of the French Revolution. He rejected the old traditions (he was divorced and famous for his amours) and championed the cause of personal liberty. Byron was outrageously skeptical and mocking, even of his own beliefs. In *Childe Harold's Pilgrimage* (1812) he created the the figure of a brooding, melancholy romantic hero. In *Don Juan* (1819) he wrote with ribald humor, acknowledged nature's cruelty as well as its beauty, and even expressed admiration for urban life. Byron tended to be content with the world as he directly knew it. He found his own experience of nature and love, objectively described and reported without embellishment, sufficient for poetic inspiration. He had the rare ability to encompass in his work the whole of his age and to write on subjects other Romantics considered unworthy of poetry.

The major figures of the early Romantic movement in Germany are August Wilhelm Schlegel and his brother Friedrich (1772–1829); Friedrich von Hardenberg, known under the pseudonym Novalis (1772–1801); Ludwig Tieck (1773–1853), famous for the story *Puss-in-Boots*; and Heinrich Wackenroder (1773–1798). In 1798 this group, under the leadership of the Schlegels, founded the principal organ of German Romanticism, the journal *Athenäum*. Their principles were derived from Shakespeare, Calderón, Johann Wolfgang von Goethe (1749–1832), Johann Christoph Friedrich von Schiller (1759–1805), and Friedrich Gottlieb Klopstock (1724–1803). *Athenäum* featured the most definitive Romantic views on art, literature, philosophy, and life, with contributions that were original, provocative, and seminal.

Much romantic poetry was also written on the continent, but almost all major German Romantics wrote at least one novel. Romantic novels tended to be highly sentimental and often borrowed material from medieval

The poetry of the German Johann Wolfgang von Goethe illustrated humankind striving with physical nature and attempting to discover the possibility of moral life on earth. The picture is a detail of a 1786 painting by Tischbein. [Bettmann Archive.]

romances. Novalis's *Heinrich von Ofterdingen* (1802), for example, was the story of a brooding poetical knight in search of a blue flower, symbolic of truth. The characters of Romantic novels were treated as symbols of the larger truth of life. Purely realistic description was avoided. The first German Romantic novel, Ludwig Tieck's *William Lovell* (1793–1795), contrasted the young Lovell, whose life is built on love and imagination, with those who live by cold reason alone and who thus become an easy prey to unbelief, misanthrophy, and egoism. As the novel rambles to its conclusion, Lovell is ruined by a mixture of philosophy, materialism, and skepticism, which are administered to him by two women he naively loves.

Friedrich Schlegel wrote a very progressive early Romantic novel, *Lucinde* (1799), which attacked contemporary prejudices against women as capable of being little more than lovers and domestics. Schlegel's novel reveals the ability of the Romantics to become involved in the social issues of their day. He depicted Lucinde as the perfect friend and companion, as well as the unsurpassed lover, of the hero. Like other early Romantic novels, the work shocked contemporary morals by frankly discussing sexual activity and by describing Lucinde as equal in all ways to the male hero.

Another important early Romantic novelist, E. T. A. Hoffmann (1776–1822), in *the Devil's Elixer* (1815–1816), traced in psychological detail the moral downfall of a monk aroused by sexuality. In these and other similiar works the Romantics attempted to repudiate many of the more widespread social values of their day. Their writings often reflect the world of dissolving certainties brought about by the continent-wide turmoil of the French Revolution and Napoleonic wars. What began as a movement in rebellion against literary norms became a movement in rebellion against social prejudices.

During the first three decades of the nineteenth century the Romantic Movement, begun in Berlin and Jena, established itself in major universities throughout Germany. Among other important nineteenth-century Romantics were Clemens Brentano (1778–1842) and

Achim von Arnim (1781–1831), famous for their collection of folk songs; the Grimm brothers, Jakob (1785–1863) and Wilhelm (1786–1859), famous for their collection of fairy tales; the tragic dramatist Heinrich von Kleist (1777–1811); and Heinrich Heine (1797–1856), the German master of satire and sarcasm.

Religion in the Romantic Period

During the Middle Ages the foundation of religion had been the church. The Reformation leaders had appealed to the authority of the Bible. Then, later Enlightenment writers had attempted to derive religion from the rational nature revealed by Newtonian physics. Romantic religious thinkers, on the other hand, appealed to the inner emotions of humankind for the foundation of religion. Their forerunners were the mystics of Western Christianity. One of the first great examples of a variety of Romantic religion—Methodism—occurred in England.

Methodism originated in the middle of the eighteenth century as a revolt against deism and rationalism in the Church of England. The Methodist revival formed an important part of the background of English Romanticism. The leader of the Methodist movement was John Wesley (1703–1791). His education and religious development had been carefully supervised by a remarkable mother, Susannah Wesley, who bore eighteen children in addition to John.

While at Oxford, Wesley organized a religious group known as the "Holy Club". He soon left England to give himself to missionary work in Georgia in America, where he arrived in 1735. While crossing the Atlantic, he had been deeply impressed by a group of German Moravians on the ship. These German pietists exhibited unshakable faith and confidence during a violent storm at sea while Wesley despaired of his life. Wesley concluded that they knew far better then he the meaning of justification by faith. When he returned to England in 1738 after an unhappy missionary career, Wesley began to worship with Moravians in London. There in 1739 he underwent a conversion experience that he described in the words,

John Wesley was the founder of the Methodist movement in Great Britain. His preaching, teaching, and revivals constituted—and expressed—one of the major impulses toward Romantic religion. [The Granger Collection.]

François René de Chateaubriand was the author of *The Genius of Christianity*, one of the key documents of the Roman Catholic revival of the Romantic period. The portrait is by the Marquise de Custine. [The Granger Collection.]

"My heart felt strangely warmed." From that point on he felt assured of his own salvation.

Wesley discovered that he could not preach his version of Christian conversion and practical piety in Anglican Church pulpits. Therefore, late in 1739 he began to preach in the open fields about the cities and towns of western England. Literally thousands of humble people responded to his message of repentance and good works. Soon he and his brother Charles, who became famous for his hymns, began to organize Methodist societies. By the late eighteenth century the Methodists had become a separate church. They ordained their own clergy and sent missionaries to America, where the Methodists eventually achieved their greatest success and most widespread influence.

The essence of Methodist teaching lay in its stress on inward, heartfelt religion and the possibility of Christian perfection in this life. John Wesley described Christianity as "an inward principle . . . the image of God impressed on a created spirit, a fountain of peace and love springing up into everlasting life." True Christians were those who were "saved in this world from all sin, from all unrighteousness . . . and now in such a sense perfect as not to commit sin and . . . freed from evil thoughts and evil tempers."[3] Many people, weary of the dry rationalism that derived from deism, found Wesley's ideal relevant to their own lives. The Methodist preachers emphasized the role of enthusiastic emotional experience as part of Christian conversion. After Wesley, religious revivals became highly emotional in style and content.

3 Quoted in Albert C. Outler (Ed.), *John Wesley: A Representative Collection of His Writings* (New York): Oxford University Press, 1964), p. 220.

Similar religion based on feeling appeared on the Continent. After the Thermidorian reaction a strong Roman Catholic revival took place in France. Its followers were people who had disapproved both the religious policy of the revolution and the anticlericalism of the Enlightenment. The most important book to express these sentiments was *The Genius of Christianity* (1802) by Vicomte François René de Chateaubriand (1768–1848). In this work, which became known as the "Bible of Romanticism," Chateaubriand argued that the essence of religion was "passion." The foundation of faith in the church was the emotion that its teachings and sacraments inspired in the heart of the Christian.

Against the Newtonian view of the world and of a rational God, the Romantics found God immanent in nature. No one stated the Romantic religious ideal more eloquently or with greater impact on the modern world than Friedrich Schleiermacher (1768–1834). In 1799 he published *Speeches on Religion to Its Cultured Despisers*. It was a response to Lutheran orthodoxy, on the one hand, and to Enlightenment rationalism on the other. The advocates of both were the "cultured despisers" of real or heartfelt religion. According to Schleiermacher, religion was neither dogma nor a system of ethics. It was an intuition or feeling of absolute dependence on an infinite reality. Religious institutions, doctrines, and moral activity expressed that primal religious feeling only in a secondary or indirect way.

Although Schleiermacher considered Christianity the "religion of religion," he also believed that every world religion was unique in its expression of the primal intuition of the infinite in the finite. He thus turned against the universal natural religion of the Enlightenment, which he termed "a name applied to loose, unconnected

Friedrich Schleiermacher of Germany was
the most important Protestant theologian of the
Romantic period. [The Granger Collection.]

impulses," and defended the meaningfulness of the numerous world religions. Every such religion was seen to
be a unique version of the emotional experience of dependence on an infinite being. In so arguing, Schleiermacher interpreted the religions of the world in the same
way that other Romantic writers interpreted the variety
of unique peoples and cultures.

Romantic Views of Nationalism and History

One of the most distinctive features of Romanticism,
especially in Germany, was its glorification of both the
individual person and individual cultures. Behind these
views lay the philosophy of German idealism, which
understood the world as the creation of subjective egos.
J. G. Fichte (1762–1814), an important German philosopher and nationalist, identified the individual ego with
the Absolute that underlay all existing things. According
to him and other similar philosophers, the world is truly
the creation of humankind. The world is as it is because
especially strong persons conceive of it in a particular way
and impose their wills on the world and other people.
Napoleon served as the contemporary example of such a
great person. This philosophy has ever since served to
justify the glorification of great people and their actions in
overriding all opposition to their wills and desires.

In addition to this philosophy the influence of new
historical studies lay behind the German glorification of
individual cultures. German Romantic writers went in
search of their own past in reaction to the copying of
French manners in eighteenth-century Germany, the
impact of the French Revolution, and the imperialism of
Napoleon. An early leader in this effort was Johann
Gottfried Herder (1744–1803). Herder had early resented the French cultural preponderance in Germany.

This feeling became widespread among German intellectuals after the arrival of Napoleon's armies. In 1778
Herder published an influential essay entitled "On the
Knowing and Feelings of the Human Soul." In it he
vigorously rejected the mechanical explanation of nature
so popular with Enlightenment writers. He saw human
beings and societies as developing organically over time.
Human beings were different at different times and
places.

Herder revived German folk culture by urging the
collection and preservation of distinctive German songs
and sayings. His most important followers in this regard
were the Grimm brothers. Believing that each language

Johann Gottfried von Herder was one of
the founders of nationalism in Europe. He thought
that each nationality had a particular contribution
to offer to the cultural life of the human race.
[Bettmann Archive.]

Georg W. F. Hegel introduced the most influential philosophy of history written in the nineteenth century. [Bettmann Archive.]

and culture was the unique expression of a people, Herder opposed both the concept and the use of a "common" language, such as French, and "universal" institutions, such as those imposed on Europe by Napoleon. These, he believed, were forms of tyranny over the individuality of a people. Herder's writings led to a broad revival of interest in history and philosophy. While initially directed toward the identification of German origins, such work soon expanded to embrace other world cultures as well. Eventually the ability of the Romantic imagination to be at home in any age or culture spurred the study of non-Western religion, comparative literature, and philology.

Perhaps the most important person to write about history during the Romantic period was the German Georg Wilhelm Friedrich Hegel (1770–1831). He is one of the most difficult philosophers in the history of Western civilization. He is also one of the most important.

Hegel believed that ideas develop in an evolutionary fashion that involves conflict. At any given time a predominant set of ideas, which he termed the *thesis,* holds sway. They are challenged by other conflicting ideas, which he termed the *antithesis.* As these patterns of thought clash, there emerges a *synthesis,* which eventually becomes the new thesis. Then the process commences all over. Periods of world history receive their character from the patterns of thought predominating during them. A number of important philosophical conclusions followed from this analysis. One of the most significant was the belief that all periods of history have been of practically equal value because each was by definition necessary for the achievement of the civilization that came latter. Also all cultures are valuable because each contributes to the necessary clash of values and ideas that allows humankind to develop. Hegel discussed these concepts in *The Phenomenology of Mind* (1806), *Lectures on the Philosophy of History* (1822–1831), and numerous other works, many of which were published only after his death. During his lifetime his ideas became widely known through his university lectures at Berlin.

These various Romantic ideas made a major contribution to the emergence of nationalism, which proved to be one of the strongest motivating forces of the nineteenth and twentieth centuries. The writers of the Enlightenment had generally championed a cosmopolitan outlook on the world. But the emphasis of the Romantic thinkers was on the individuality and worth of each separate people and culture. The factors that helped to define a people or a nation were common language, common history, a homeland that possessed historical associations, and common customs. This cultural nationalism gradually became transformed into a political creed. It came to be widely believed that every people or nation should constitute a separate political entity and that only when it so existed could the nation be secure in its own character.

The example of France under the revolutionary government and then Napoleon had demonstrated the power of nationhood. Other peoples came to desire similar strength and confidence. Napoleon's toppling of ancient political structures, such as the Holy Roman Empire, demonstrated the need for new political organization in Europe. By 1815 these were the aspirations of only a few Europeans, but as time passed, such yearnings came to be shared by scores of peoples from Ireland to the Ukraine. The Congress of Vienna could ignore such feelings, but for the rest of the nineteenth century, statesmen had to confront the growing reality of their power.

SUGGESTED READINGS

MEYER H. ABRAMS, *The Mirror and the Lamp: Romantic Theory and the Critical Tradition* (New York, 1958). A standard text on Romantic literary theory that looks at English Romanticism in the context of German Romantic idealism.

C. M. BOWRA, *The Romantic Imagination* (Cambridge, 1949). Penetrating individual sketches of the major English romantics.

C. BRINTON, *The Lives of Talleyrand* (New York, 1932). A biography of the diplomat.

G. BRUUN, *Europe and the French Imperium, 1799–1814* (New York, 1938). A good survey.

D. G. CHANDLER, *The Campaigns of Napoleon* (New York, 1966). A good military study.

O. CONNELLY, *Napoleon's Satellite Kingdoms* (New York, 1965). The rule of Napoleon and his family in Europe.

H. C. DEUTSCH, *The Genesis of Napoleon's Imperialism, 1801–1805.* (Cambridge, 1938). Basic for foreign policy.

Dictionary of the History of Ideas, Vol. 4 (New York, 1973), pp. 198–208. Contributions by Rene Wellek, "Romanticism in Literature"; Franklin L. Baumer, "Romanticism (ca. 1780–ca. 1830)"; and Jacques Droz, "Political Romanticism in Germany." Excellent and succinct.

P. GEYL, *Napoleon: For and Against* (New Haven, Conn.: 1949). A fine survey of the historical debate.

E. HECKSCHER, *The Continental System: An Economic Interpretation* (Oxford, 1922). Napoleon's commercial policy.

J. C. HEROLD, *The Age of Napoleon* (New York, 1968). A lively, readable account.

R. HOLTMAN, *The Napoleonic Revolution* (Baton Rouge, La.: 1950). Good on domestic policy.

G. LEFEBVRE, *Napoleon,* 2 vols., trans. by H. Stockhold, (New York, 1969). The fullest and finest biography.

ARTHUR O. LOVEJOY, *"The Meaning of Romanticism for the Historian of Ideas," in Franklin L. Baumer, (Ed.), Intellectual Movements in Modern European History* (New York, 1965). A very influential summary of the basic characteristics of Romanticism.

F. MARKHAM, *Napoleon and the Awakening of Europe* (London, 1954). Emphasizes the growth of nationalism.

F. MARKHAM, *Napoleon* (New York, 1963). A good biography strong on military questions.

H. NICOLSON, *The Congress of Vienna* (London, 1946). A good, readable account.

SIEGBERT PRAWER (Ed.), *The Romantic Period in Germany* (London, 1970). Contributions covering all facets of the movement.

J. L. TALMON, *Romanticism and Revolt: Europe, 1815–1848* (London, 1967). An effort to sketch the Romantic movements and relate them to one another and to the larger political history of the period.

E. TARLE, *Napoleon's Invasion of Russia* (New York, 1942).

J. M. THOMPSON, *Napoleon Bonaparte: His Rise and Fall* (Oxford, 1952). A sound biography.

L. A. WILLOUGHBY, *The Romantic Movement in Germany* (London, 1930). An older but still very useful treatment.

648

25
Restoration, Reaction, and Reform
(1815–1832)

THE DEFEAT of Napoleon and the diplomatic settlement of the Congress of Vienna restored a conservative political and social order in Europe. Legitimate monarchies, landed aristocracies, and established churches constituted the major pillars of conservatism. The institutions themselves were ancient, but the self-conscious alliance of throne, land, and altar was new. Throughout the eighteenth century these groups had been in frequent conflict. Only the upheaval of the French Revolution and the Napoleonic era transformed them into natural, if sometimes reluctant, allies. They retained their former arrogance but neither their former privileges nor their old confidence. They knew they could be toppled by the political groups who hated them. They understood that revolution in one country could spill over into another. The conservatives regarded themselves as surrounded by enemies and as standing permanently on the defensive against the forces of liberalism, nationalism, and popular sovereignty. These potential sources of unrest had to be confronted both at home and abroad.

Conservative Governments on the Domestic Scene

The course of nineteenth-century history is frequently associated with the emergence of the liberal, national state and industrial society. But the staying power of the restored conservative institutions, especially in Great Britain and eastern Europe, is an equally and perhaps even more striking feature of the century. Actually not

Greece Expiring on the Ruins of Missolonghi, by Eugène Delacroix (1799–1863) illustrates the manner in which small nationalities were idealized in sentimental liberal art in Western Europe. Greece is pictured as a beautiful, defenseless woman appealing for help against the dangers surrounding her. [Musée des Beaux-Arts, Bordeaux. A. Danvers.]

until World War I did their power and pervasive influence come to an end. One need not admire these institutions or the policies and personalities associated with them. Yet one must admit that their persistence constituted one of the most important features of nineteenth-century political and social life. To ignore or to disparage their relatively successful attempts at self-preservation is to underestimate the grave obstacles that confronted liberals and nationalists.

The more refined political and religious ideas of the conservative classes were associated with Romantic thinkers, such as Burke and Hegel. Conservatives shared other, less formal attitudes forged by the revolutionary experience. The fate of Louis XVI convinced most monarchs that they could trust only aristocratic governments or governments of aristocrats in alliance with the very wealthiest middle-class and professional people. The European aristocracies believed that their property and influence would rarely be safe under any form of genuinely representative government. All conservatives spurned the idea of a written constitution unless they were permitted to promulgate the document themselves. Even then some could not be reconciled to the concept.

The churches were equally apprehensive of popular movements except their own revivals. The ecclesiastical leaders throughout the Continent regarded themselves as entrusted with the educational task of supporting the social and political *status quo*. They also feared and hated most of the ideas associated with the Enlightenment because those rational concepts and reformist writings enshrined the critical spirit and undermined revealed religion. Conservative Europeans came to consider as *liberal* any idea or institution that they opposed. However, as will be seen, that word had rather different meanings in different countries.

Russia and Alexander I

The pursuit of Napoleon's army across Europe after the burning of Moscow created a new image of vast Russian power. The image remained until the Crimean

Tsar Alexander I of Russia began his reign with the reputation of a somewhat liberal reformer, but by the time of his death in 1825 he had become one of the most reactionary rulers in Europe. His portrait is by Gérard. [Bettmann Archive.]

War (1854–1856). In Vienna Tsar Alexander I had played a more important personal role than any other participating monarch. Both in those negotiations and in his governance of Russia, Alexander was and has remained an enigmatic figure. He was torn between an intellectual attraction to the doctrines of the Enlightenment and reform and a very pragmatic adherence to traditional autocracy. His own development as a person and as a ruler reflected the turn of eastern European states from enlightened absolutism to rigid conservatism and defense of the *status quo*.

Alexander I came to the Russian throne in 1801 after the murder of his father, Tsar Paul. The son had condoned the palace revolution. Paul had been an unstable person who ruled in an arbitrary and unpredictable manner. Paul had attempted to reverse the policies of his mother, Catherine the Great, whom he loathed. He attacked the privileges of the nobility. The result was a *coup d'état* led by court nobles and the army. Alexander I intended to return to the reformist policies of his grandmother. He confirmed the privileges of the nobles and abolished the security police. He was well educated in the ideas of the Enlightenment. In 1801 he appointed a government reform committee composed of liberal friends. Little came from the plans submitted by this group, and by 1803 Alexander declared that no group had a right to challenge the legality of the decrees of the tsar.

Once Alexander had led Russia into war against Napoleon, even the mild reformist tendencies began to wane. In 1807 the security police were, in effect, reestablished. Yet the military reverses of the campaign and his personal admiration for Napoleon's administrative genius convinced the tsar that a reconstruction of the Russian government was necessary. In 1808 he turned to Michael Speransky (1772–1839) to guide his thinking on matters of administrative reform. This enlightened minister, who held a series of government appointments, drew up a plan for constitutional government that included an elected legislative body. He even dared talk about an eventual,

Prince Klemens von Metternich (1773–1859), Foreign Minister, then Chancellor, of Austria, was the chief architect of reactionary politics in Europe between 1815 and 1848. [Culver Pictures.]

gradual abolition of serfdom. The tsar could not support such bold departures. Speransky had to be satisfied with a restructuring of the ministries and the bureaucracy. In 1812 he introduced new progressive taxes on landed income. Each of these policies alienated the nobility. In March 1812 Alexander dismissed his once-trusted minister. Again reform came to a close almost without having begun.

Thereafter Alexander, though occasionally using liberal rhetoric, became an increasingly hardened conservative. In the renewed struggle against Napoleon he needed the support of his nobility and the army. Also during this post-Speransky period he became deeply drawn to those mystical religious feelings that lay behind his project for the Holy Alliance. The tsar came to regard the Enlightenment, the French Revolution, and Napoleon as one vast attack on Christianity. His new chief adviser was Alexis Arakcheiev (1769–1834), a general and the opponent of Speransky. This reactionary military figure became the most powerful person in the country except for Alexander himself. Together they pursued a consistently conservative policy. Censorship and religiously dominated education became the order of the day. They also established "military farms." These institutions transformed whole districts of the country into military establishments where the army farmed and supported itself when not fighting. There was little or no toleration of political opposition or criticism of the regime. By the early 1820s the tsar, whose early years had been seen as holding the possible promise of reform, had become a leading symbol of conservative reaction.

Austria and the Germanies

The early nineteenth-century statesman who more than any other epitomized conservatism was the Austrian Prince Metternich whom we have already met at the Congress of Vienna. This devoted servant of the Hapsburg emperor had been, along with Castlereagh, the chief architect of the Vienna settlement. It was he who seemed to hold chief control over the forces of the European reaction. The conservative foreign and domestic policy that he forged for Austria stemmed from the pragmatic needs of that peculiar state rather than from ideology. To no other country were the programs of liberalism and nationalism potentially more dangerous. The Austrian government could make no serious compromises with the new political forces in Europe. Recognition of the rights and aspirations of the various national groups would mean probable dissolution of the empire. The Hapsburg domains were peopled with Poles, Hungarians, and several Slavic nationalities. Through puppet governments Austria also dominated the Italian peninsula. Hapsburg dynastic integrity required Austrian domination of the German Confederation to prevent the formation of a German national state that might absorb the heart of the empire. If Austria permitted representative government, Metternich and others feared that the national groups would fight their battles internally at the probable cost of Austrian international influence.

During the immediate postwar years Metternich's primary concern lay with Germany. The German Confederation had been created by the Congress of Vienna to replace the defunct Holy Roman Empire. It consisted of thirty-nine states under Austrian leadership. Each state remained more or less autonomous, but Austria was determined to prevent any movement toward constitutionalism in as many of them as possible.

The major victory for this holding policy came in Prussia. In 1815 Frederick William III (1797–1840), during the exhilaration after the War of Liberation, had promised his people some mode of constitutional government. However, he immediately stalled on keeping his pledge. In 1817 he formally reneged and created a new Council of State, which did bring about more efficient administration but which was not a constitutional mode of government. In 1819 the king moved further away from thoughts of reform. After a major disagreement over the organization of the army, his chief reform-minded ministers resigned. The monarch replaced them with hardened conservatives. On their advice in 1823

Frederick William III established eight provincial estates or diets, which were dominated by the *Junkers* and which exercised only an advisory function. The old alliance between the Prussian monarchy, the army, and the land-holders stood reestablished. This conservative alliance opposed German nationalist aspirations that seemed to threaten the social and political order.

Only two German states, Bavaria and Württemberg, enjoyed constitutional government. But the nationalist and liberal aspirations raised by the experience of defeating the French armies remained alive in the hearts and minds of many young Germans. The most important of these groups was university students. They had grown up during the days of the reforms of Stein and Hardenburg

and the initial circulation of the writings of Fichte and other German nationalists. Many of them had fought Napoleon. When they went to the universities, they continued to dream their dream of a united Germany. They formed various student clubs known as *Burschen-schaften*. Like student groups today, these clubs served numerous social functions, but one of them was severing old provincial loyalties and replacing them with loyalty to the concept of a united German state.

In 1817 in Jena one such student club organized a large celebration of the fourth anniversary of the battle of Leipzig and of the tercentenary of Luther's Ninety-five Theses. There were bonfires, songs, and processions as more than five hundred people gathered for the festivities. The event made German rulers uneasy, for it was known that some republicans were involved with the student clubs. Two years later, in March 1819, a young man named Karl Sand, who was a *Burschenschaft* member assassinated the conservative dramatist August von Kotzebue. Sand, who was tried, condemned, and publicly executed, became a martyr. Although the assassin had acted alone, Metternich decided to use the incident to suppress the student clubs and other potential institutions of liberalism.

In August 1819 Metternich persuaded representatives of the major German states to issue the Carlsbad Decrees, which dissolved the *Burschenschaften*. The decrees also provided for university inspectors and press censors. The next year the German governments promulgated the Final Act, which limited the subjects that might be discussed in the constitutional chambers of Bavaria and Württemberg. The measure also asserted the right of the

In 1817 on the fourth anniversary of the defeat of Napoleon by Prussians, Austrians, and Russians at Leipzig, German students held a nationalist festival near the Wartburg Castle. Such meetings were considered very dangerous by conservative statesmen who opposed nationalism in Germany. [Bildarchiv Preussischer Kulturbesitz.]

Metternich Comments on Students and Professors

Metternich was the chief minister of the Austrian emperor and the leader of reactionary political policy after the Congress of Vienna. In 1819 he was attempting to suppress political activity in the universities. As he explained in this letter, he did not fear students but the later adults who during their student days had been taught liberal political ideas.

THAT *the students' folly declines or turns to some other side than that of politics does not surprise me. This is in the nature of things. The student, taken in himself, is a child, and the* Burschenshaft *is an unpractical puppet-show. Then, I have never . . . spoken of the students, but all my aim has been directed at the professors. Now, the professors, singly or united, are most unsuited to be conspirators. People only conspire profitably against things, not against theories. . . . Where they are political, they must be supported by deed, and the deed is the overthrow of existing institutions. . . .*

This is what learned men and professors cannot manage, and the class of lawyers is better suited to carry it on. I know hardly one learned man who knows the value of property; while, on the contrary, the lawyer class is always rummaging about in the property of others. Besides, the professors are, nearly without exception, given up to theory; while no people are more practical than the lawyers.

Consequently, I have never feared that the revolution would be engendered by the universities; but that at them a whole generation of revolutionaries must be formed, unless the evil is restrained, seems to me certain. I hope that the most mischievous symptoms of the evil at the universities may be met, and that perhaps from its own peculiar sources, for the measures of the Government will contribute to this less than the weariness of the students, the weakness of the professors, and the different direction which the studies may take. . . .

The greatest and consequently the most urgent evil now is the press.

Memoirs of Prince Metternich, trans. by Mrs. Napier (New York: Scribner, 1880–1881), Vol. 3, pp. 286–288.

aristocracy to protect monarchs from demands of constitutionalists. Thereafter, for many years the secret police of the various German states harassed potential dissidents. In the eyes of the princes these included practically anyone who sought even moderate social or political change.

Great Britain

The years 1819 and 1820 marked a high tide for conservative influence and repression in western as well as eastern Europe. After 1815 Great Britain experienced two years of poor harvests. There was also considerable industrial unemployment, to which discharged sailors and soldiers added their numbers.

The Tory ministry of Lord Liverpool (1770–1828) was unprepared to deal with these problems of postwar dislocation. Instead, it sought to protect the interests of the landed and other wealthy classes. In 1815 the Parliament passed a Corn Law to maintain high prices for domestically produced grain through import duties on foreign grain. The next year Parliament reduced the income tax and replaced it with excise taxes on consumer goods. These laws represented a continuation of previous legislation through which the British ruling class had abandoned its traditional role of paternalistic protector of the poor. In 1799 Parliament had passed the Combination Acts forbidding workers' organizations or unions. During the war, wage protection had been removed. The tax-paying classes grumbled about supporting the poor law; many people called for its abolition.

In light of these policies and the postwar economic downturn, it is hardly surprising that the lower social orders began to doubt the wisdom of their rulers and to call for a reform of the political system. Mass meetings calling for the reform of Parliament were held. Reform clubs were organized. Radical newspapers, such as William Cobbett's *Political Registrar,* demanded political change. In the hungry, restive agricultural and industrial workers the government could see only images of continental sans-culotte crowds ready to hang aristocrats from the nearest lamppost. Radical leaders, such as Cobbett (1763–1835), Major John Cartwright (1740–1824), and Henry "Orator" Hunt (1773–1835), were considered demagogues who were seducing the people away from allegiance to their natural leaders. The answer of the government to the discontent was repression. In Decem-

As regent and then monarch, George IV of Great Britain (1820–1830) allowed scandal to come close to the British crown and lower its prestige among the general public. The medal by George Mills is from the year of the king's accession. [The Granger Collection.]

BELOW: The riots that occurred in London in 1815 at the time of the passage of the Corn Laws to protect the interests of British landlords marked the beginning of five years of political discontent, with popular uprisings and demonstrations. This contemporary picture shows an unruly crowd at the entrance to the House of Commons in 1815. [The Granger Collection.]

Scott Comments Unhappily on the New Industrial Labor Force

Sir Walter Scott (1771–1832) was a famous Scottish novelist. He was deeply disturbed by the conflict between workers and employers. In this passage from 1820 he blames that conflict largely on the steam engine. That new energy supply took manufacturing out of the countryside and into the cities where Scott believed employer-worker relations were much more impersonal.

The *unhappy dislocation which has taken place betwixt the Employer and those in his employment has been attended with very fatal consequences. Much of this is owing to the steam engine. When the machinery was driven by water, the manufacturer had to seek out some sequestered spot where he could obtain a suitable fall of water, and then his workmen formed the inhabitants of a village around him, and he necessarily bestowed some attention, less or more, on their morals and on their necessities, had knowledge of their persons and characters, and exercised a salutary influence as over men depending on and intimately connected with him and his prospects. This is now quite changed; the manufacturers are transferred to great towns, where a man may assemble five hundred workmen one week and dismiss them the next, without having any further connection with them than to receive a week's work for a week's wages, nor any further solicitude about their future fate than if they were so many old shuttles. A superintendance of the workers considered as moral and rational beings is thus a matter totally unconnected with the employer's usual thoughts and cares. They have now seen the danger of suffering a great population to be thus entirely separated from the influence of their employers, and given over to the management of their own societies, in which the cleverest and most impudent fellows always get the management of the others, and become bell-wethers in every sort of mischief.*

Walter Scott, *Familiar Letters* (Boston: Houghton, Mifflin, 1894), Vol. 2, p. 78.

ber 1816 a very unruly mass meeting took place at Spa Fields near London. This disturbance provided an excuse to pass the Coercion Acts of March 1817. These measures temporarily suspended habeas corpus and extended existing laws against seditious gatherings.

This initial repression, accompanied by improved harvests, brought calm for a time to the political landscape. However, by 1819 the people were restive again. Throughout the industrial north a large number of well-organized mass meetings were held to demand the reform of Parliament. Major radical leaders gave speeches to thousands of people. The radical reform campaign culminated on August 16, 1819, with a meeting in Manchester at St. Peter's Fields. Royal troops and the local militia were on hand to ensure order. Just as the speeches were about to begin, a local magistrate ordered the militia to move into the audience. The result was panic and death. At least eleven people in the crowd were killed; scores were injured. The event became known as the "Peterloo" Massacre through a contemptuous comparison with the victory at Waterloo.

Peterloo had been the act of the local Manchester officials. However, the Liverpool ministry felt that those officials must be supported. The Cabinet also decided to act once and for all to end these troubles. Most of the radical leaders were arrested and thus taken out of circulation. In December 1819, a few months after the German Carlsbad Decrees, Parliament passed a series of laws called the Six Acts. These forbade large meetings, raised the fines for seditious libel, speeded up the trials of political agitators, increased newspaper taxes, prohibited the training of armed groups, and allowed local officials to search homes in certain disturbed counties. In effect the Six Acts attempted to remove the instruments of agitation from the hands of radical leaders and to provide the authorities with new powers.

Two months after passage of the Six Acts, the Cato Street Conspiracy was unearthed. Under the guidance of a possibly demented figure named Thistlewood, a group of extreme radicals plotted to blow up the entire British Cabinet. The plot was foiled. The leaders were arrested and tried, and four of them were executed. The conspiracy was little more than a half-baked plot, but it provided new support for the repression of the government. More important, the conspiracy helped further to discredit the movement for parliamentary reform.

This contemporary print depicting the "Peterloo"
Massacre of 1819 in Manchester, England, was intended
to evoke sympathy for political radicalism. Note that
in addition to being dedicated to Henry "Orator"
Hunt, it is also dedicated to women who supported
political reform. A large number of women and
children had been present at the political rally
the authorities turned into a massacre. [The Mansell
Collection.]

TO HENRY HUNT, ESQ.ᴿ

As CHAIRMAN of the Meeting assembled on St. Peter's Field, Manchester on the 16.ᵀᴴ of AUGUST, 1819.
and to the **Female Reformers** of MANCHESTER and the adjacent TOWNS who were exposed to and suffered from
THE WANTON and FURIOUS ATTACK MADE ON THEM BY THAT BRUTAL ARMED FORCE THE MANCHESTER and CHESHIRE YEOMANRY CAVALRY.

Louis XVIII of France. After his elevation to the throne of his executed brother, Louis XVI, he attempted to rule with moderation. [Bettmann Archive.]

Bourbon Restoration in France

The abdication of Napoleon in 1814 opened the way for a restoration of Bourbon rule in the homeland of the great revolution. The new king was the former Duke of Provence and brother of Louis XVI. The son of the executed monarch had died in prison. Royalists regarded the dead boy as Louis XVII, so his uncle became Louis XVIII (1814–1824). This fat, awkward man had become a political realist during his more than twenty years of exile. He understood that he could not govern if he attempted to turn back the clock. France had undergone too many irreversible changes. Consequently Louis XVIII agreed to become a constitutional monarch, but under a constitution of his own making.

The constitution of the French restoration was the Charter. It provided for a hereditary monarchy and a bicameral legislature. The upper house was appointed by the monarch. The lower chamber was elected according to a very narrow franchise that upheld a high property qualification. The Charter guaranteed most of the rights enumerated by the Declaration of the Rights of Man and Citizen. There was to be religious toleration, but Roman Catholicism was designated as the official religion of the nation. Most important for thousands of Frenchmen at various stations of life who had profited from the revolution, the Charter promised not to disturb the property changes brought about by the confiscation and sale of aristocratic and church land. In this manner Louis XVIII attempted to reconcile to his restored regime those classes who had benefited from the revolution.

This moderate spirit was not widely shared within the ranks of royalist supporters. Their families had suffered much at the hands of the revolution. They now demanded their revenge. The king's brother, the Count of Artois (1757–1836), served as a rallying point for those people who were more royalist than the monarch. In the months after Napoleon's final defeat at Waterloo, royalists in the south and west carried out a White Terror against former revolutionaries and supporters of the de-posed emperor. The king could do little or nothing to halt this bloodbath of royalist revenge. Similar extreme royalist sentiment existed in the Chamber of Deputies. The ultraroyalist majority elected in 1816 proved so dangerously reactionary that the king soon dissolved the chamber. The majority returned by the second election were more moderate. Under the ministry of the Duke of Richelieu the country paid off the war indemnity to the allies, and the occupation troops were removed in 1818. Yet royalist discontent remained. Louis XVIII attempted to pursue a policy of mild accommodation with liberals through his minister Decazes, who took office in 1818, but the king's younger brother, the Count of Artois, pushed for reactionary departures.

This give and take might have continued for some time. However, in February 1820 the Duke of Berri, son of Artois and heir to the throne after his father, was murdered by a lone assassin. The ultraroyalists persuaded Louis XVIII that the murder was the result of Decazes's cooperation with liberal politicians. The Duke of Richelieu was recalled. The electoral laws were revised to give wealthy electors two votes. Press censorship was imposed. Persons suspected of dangerous political activity could be easily arrested. By 1821 the direction of secondary education in France was put under the control of the Roman Catholic bishops. All of these actions revealed the basic contradiction of the French restoration. There had been no intention of creating a genuinely parliamentary system. The king rather than the Chamber of Deputies chose the ministers. The government constantly tinkered with the electoral apparatus to disqualify opponents from voting. By the early 1820s the veneer of constitutionalism had worn away. Liberals were being driven out of legal political life and into near-illegal activity.

The Conservative International Order

The Congress System

At the Congress of Vienna the major powers—Russia, Austria, Prussia, and Great Britain—had agreed to consult

CENTERS OF REVOLUTION, 1820–1830

Conservative governments and cooperation among repressive great powers in post-Napoleonic Europe were challenged by uprisings and revolutions, beginning in 1820–1821 in Spain, Naples, and Greece and appearing in Russia, France, and Belgium later in the decade.

with each other from time to time on matters affecting Europe as a whole. The vehicle for this consultation was a series of postwar congresses. Later, as differences arose among the powers, consultation became more informal. This mode of working out issues of foreign policy was known as the Concert of Europe. It meant that no major move could be taken in international affairs by one nation without the assent of the others. The major goals of the Concert of Europe were to maintain the balance of power against new French aggression and against the military might of Russia. The Concert of Europe continued to function on large and small issues until the third quarter of the century.

The years that witnessed the domestic conservative consolidation of power also saw a generally successful functioning of the congress system. The first congress was held in 1818 at Aix-la-Chapelle. There the four major powers decided to remove their troops from France and to readmit that nation to good standing among European nations. Despite unanimity on these decisions, problems did arise during the conference. Tsar Alexander I, displaying his full reactionary colors, suggested that the Quadruple Alliance agree to uphold the borders and existing governments of all European countries. Britain, represented by Castlereagh, flatly rejected the proposal. He contended that the Quadruple Alliance was intended only to prevent future French aggression.

THE SPANISH REVOLUTION OF 1820. These disagreements appeared somewhat academic in 1818. But two years later a series of revolutions commenced in southern Europe. The Spanish rebelled against Ferdinand VII (1814–1833). When placed on his throne at the time of Napoleon's downfall, this Bourbon monarch had promised to govern according to a written constitution. Once securely in power Ferdinand simply ignored that pledge. He dissolved the parliament (the Cortes) and ruled alone. In 1820 a group of army officers about to be sent to suppress revolution in Spain's Latin American colonies rebelled. In March Ferdinand once again announced that he would abide by the provisions of the

constitution. For the time being the revolution had succeeded. Almost at the same time, in July 1820, the revolutionary spirit erupted in Naples where the King of the Two Sicilies very quickly accepted a constitution. There were other, lesser revolts in Italy, but none of them succeeded.

These events frightened the ever-nervous Metternich. Italian disturbances were especially troubling to him. Austria hoped to dominate the peninsula to provide a buffer against the spread of revolution on its southern flank. The other powers were divided on the best course of action. Britain opposed joint intervention in either Italy or Spain. Metternich turned to Prussia and Russia for support. The three eastern powers, along with unofficial delegations from Britain and France, met at the Congress of Troppau in late October 1820. The members of the Holy Alliance, led by Alexander of Russia, issued the Protocol of Troppau. This declaration asserted that stable governments might intervene to restore order in countries experiencing revolution. Yet even Russia hesitated to authorize Austrian intervention in Italian affairs. That decision was finally reached in January 1821 at the Congress of Laibach. Shortly thereafter Austrian troops marched into Naples and restored the King of the Two Sicilies to unconstitutional government.

The final postwar congress took place in October 1822 at Verona. Its primary purpose was to resolve the situation in Spain. Once again Britain balked at joint action. Shortly before the meeting Castlereagh had committed suicide. George Canning (1770–1827), the new foreign minister, was much less sympathetic to Metternich's goals. At Verona Britain, in effect, withdrew from continental affairs. Austria, Prussia, and Russia agreed to support French intervention in Spain. In April 1823 the French army crossed the Pyrenees and within a few months suppressed the Spanish revolution. Liberals and revolutionaries were tortured, executed, and driven from the country. The intervention in Spain in 1823 was one of the most bloody examples of reactionary politics during the entire century.

There was a second diplomatic result of the Congress of Verona and the Spanish intervention. George Canning was much more interested in the fate of British commerce and trade than Castlereagh had been. Consequently Canning sought to prevent the politics of European reaction from being extended to the Spanish colonies then revolting in Latin America. He intended to use those South American revolutions as the occasion for British penetration of the old Spanish trading monopoly in that area. To that end the British foreign minister supported the American Monroe Doctrine in 1823, prohibiting further colonization and intervention by European powers in the Americas. Britain soon recognized the Spanish colonies as independent states. Through the rest of the century British commercial interests dominated Latin America. In this fashion Canning may be said to have brought to a successful conclusion the War of Jenkins' Ear (1739).

The Greek Revolution of 1821

While the powers were plotting the new restorations in Italy and Spain, a third Mediterranean revolt had erupted in Greece. The Greek revolution became one of the most famous of the century because it attracted the support and participation of many illustrious literary figures. Liberals throughout Europe who were seeing their own hopes crushed at home imagined that ancient Greek democracy was being reborn. "The world's great age begins anew," wrote Shelley. Lord Byron went to fight and in 1824 died in the cause of Greek liberty. Philhellenic societies were founded in practically every major country.

The Greeks were rebelling against the Ottoman Empire. The weakness of that empire troubled Europe for the entire century and raised what was known as "the eastern question." The residue of the problem remains alive today in the tensions between Greece and Turkey and in the instability in the Middle East. Most of the major powers were interested in what happened to the Ottoman holdings for reasons less idealistic than the poets'. Russia and Austria coveted land in the Balkans. France and Britain were concerned with the empire's commerce and with control of key naval positions in the eastern Mediterranean. There was also the issue of protection of Christian access to the shrines in the Holy Land.

These conflicting interests, as well as mutual distrust, prevented any direct intervention in Greek affairs for several years. In 1827 a joint British, French, and Russian fleet supported the Greek revolt. The fleet was enforcing the Treaty of London of 1827, in which those powers demanded Turkish recognition of Greek independence. They had decided that their domestic security would not be endangered by an independent Greek state and that their several foreign policy concerns in the area would prosper from such a new nation. In 1828 Russia sent troops against the Ottoman holdings in what is today Romania. By the treaty of Adrianople of 1829 Russia gained effective control of that territory. The treaty further stipulated that the Turks would allow Britain, France, and Russia to decide the future of Greece.

In 1830 by a second Treaty of London Greece was declared an independent kingdom. Two years later Otto I (1832–1862), the son of the king of Bavaria, was chosen as the first king of the new Greek royal dynasty. The Greek revolt was the only successful national revolution of the first quarter of the century. Elsewhere the conservative powers had defeated the attempts at revolution.

Liberalism in the Early Nineteenth Century

The nineteenth century is frequently considered the great age of *isms*. Throughout the Western world secular ideologies began to take hold of the popular and learned imagination in opposition to the political and social *status quo*. These included liberalism, nationalism, socialism, republicanism, and communism. Other *isms* included conservatism, industrialism, and imperialism. One noted historian has called all such words "trouble-breeding and usually thought-obscuring terms."[1] They are just that if one uses them as an excuse to avoid thinking or if one fails to see the variety of opinions concealed beneath each word.

It was just such intellectual laziness that characterized European conservatives as they faced their political opposition after the Napoleonic wars. They tended to call "liberal" almost anything or anyone who drew into question their own political, social, or religious values. Moreover, the word *liberal* for twentieth-century Americans carries with it meanings and connotations that have little or nothing to do with its significance for nineteenth-century Europeans. European conservatives of the last century saw liberals as more radical than they actually were; present-day Americans consider them to be more conservative than they were.

Liberal Goals and Their Circumstances

POLITICS.   The political ideas of liberals derived from the writers of the Enlightenment, the example of English liberties, and the so-called principles of 1789 as embodied in the French Declaration of the Rights of Man and Citizen. Liberal political figures sought to establish a framework of legal equality, religious toleration, and

1 Arthur O. Lovejoy, *The Great Chain of Being: A Study in the History of an Idea* (New York: Harper Torchbook, 1936), p. 6.

freedom of the press. Their general goal was a political structure that would limit the arbitrary power of the goverment against the persons and property of individual citizens. They generally believed that the legitimacy of government emanated from the freely given consent of the governed. The popular basis of such government was to be expressed through elected representative or parliamentary bodies. Most important, free government required that state or crown ministers must be responsible to the representatives rather than to the monarch.

These goals may seem very limited, and they were. However, such responsible government existed in none of the major European countries in 1815. Even in Great Britain the Cabinet ministers were at least as responsible to the monarch as to the House of Commons. The kinds of people who espoused these changes in government tended to be those who were excluded from the existing political processes but whose wealth and education made them feel that such exclusion was unjustified. Liberals tended to be academics, members of the learned professions, and people involved in the rapidly expanding commercial and manufacturing segments of the economy. They believed in and were products of the career open to talent. The existing monarchical and aristocratic regimes often failed to recognize sufficiently their new status and to provide for their economic and professional interests.

However, liberals were *not* advocates of democracy. Second only to their hostility to privileged aristocracies was their general contempt for the lower, unpropertied classes. Liberals transformed the eighteenth-century concept of aristocratic liberty into a new concept of privilege based on wealth and property instead of on birth. As the French liberal theorist Benjamin Constant (1767–1830) wrote in 1814:

Those whom poverty keeps in eternal dependence are no more enlightened on public affairs than children, nor are they more interested than foreigners in national prosperity, of which they do not understand the basis and of which they enjoy the advantages only indirectly. Property alone, by giving sufficient leisure, renders a man capable of exercising his political rights.[2]

By the middle of the century this widely shared attitude meant that throughout Europe liberals had separated themselves from both the rural and the urban working class.

ECONOMICS. The economic goals of liberals also furthered that important future split in European politics and society. Here again the pattern was set by the Enlightenment and by the economic thought deriving from Adam Smith. The manufacturers of Great Britain, the landed and manufacturing middle class of France, and the commercial interests of Germany and Italy sought the removal of the economic restraints associated with mercantilism. They wanted to be able to manufacture and sell goods freely. To that end they favored the general removal of internal barriers to trade and of international tariffs. Economic liberals opposed the old paternalistic legislation that established wages and labor practices by government regulation or by guild privileges. Labor was simply one more commodity to be bought and sold freely. Liberals sought an economic structure in which people were at liberty to use whatever talents and property they possessed to enrich themselves. By this means, they contended, there would be more goods and more services for everyone at lower prices. Such a system of economic liberty was to provide the basis for material progress.

NATIONALISM. Another major ingredient of liberalism as it developed in Germany, Italy, and the Austrian Empire was nationalism. The idea of nationhood was not necessarily or logically linked to liberalism. There were conservative nationalists. However, liberalism and nationalism were often complementary. Behind the concept of a people joined naturally together by the bonds of common language, customs, culture, and history lurked the idea of popular sovereignty. The idea of the career open to talent could be applied to suppressed national

2 Quoted in Frederick B. Artz, *Reaction and Revolution, 1814–1832* (New York: Harper, 1934), p. 94.

This poster is evidence of the industrial discontent that spread in some parts of Britain during the Napoleonic wars. That discontent became even sharper during the years of unemployment that followed Waterloo. [The Granger Collection.]

Protection
FOR THE
INDUSTRIOUS
Weavers.

INFORMATION having been received that a great number of industrious Weavers have been deterred by threats and acts of violence from the pursuit of their lawful occupations, and that in many instances their Shuttles have been taken, and their Materials damaged by persons acting under the existing Combinations:

Notice is hereby Given,

That every Protection will be afforded to persons so injured, upon giving Information to the Constables of Stockport: And a Reward of

FIFTY GUINEAS

Will be paid, on conviction, to the person who will come forward with such evidence as may be the means of convicting any one or more of the offences mentioned in the Act of Parliament, of which an Extract is subjoined: And a Reward of

TWENTY GUINEAS

Will be paid, on conviction, to the person who will come forward and inform of any person being guilty of assaulting or molesting industrious and honest Weavers, so as to prevent them from taking out or bringing in their Work peaceably.

PETER BROWN,
T. CARTWRIGHT, }CONSTABLES.

Stockport, June 17th, 1808.

By the 22nd, Geo. 3, C. 40, S. 3.

It is enacted, " That if any person enter, by force, into any House or Shop, with intent to Cut and Destroy any Linen or Cotton, or Linen and Cotton mixed with any other Materials, in the Loom, or any Warp or Shute, Tools, Tackle, and Utensils, or shall Cut or Destroy the same, or shall Break and Destroy any Tools, Tackle, or Utensils, for Weaving, Preparing, or Making any such Manufactures, every such Offender shall be guilty of FELONY, without Benefit of Clergy".

groups who were not permitted to realize their cultural or political potential. The efficient government and administration required by commerce and industry would mean the replacement of the petty dynasties of the small German and Italian states with larger political units. Moreover nationalist groups in one country could gain the sympathy of liberals in other nations by espousing the cause of representative government and political liberty.

Because the social and political circumstances of various countries differed, the specific programs of liberals also differed. Great Britain already possessed institutions, such as Parliament, that could be reformed to provide more nearly representative government. The monarchy was already limited, and most individual liberties had been secured. Links between land, commerce, and industry existed. French liberals possessed a code of modern law in the Napoleonic Code. They could appeal to the widely accepted "principles of 1789." As in England, representatives of the different economic interests had worked together. Their problem was to protect the civil liberties by law and to define the respective powers of the monarch and the elected representative body.

The situation in Germany was quite different and very complex. Distinct social divisions existed between the aristocratic landowning classes, who filled the bureaucracies and officer corps, and the small middle-class commercial and industrial interests. There was little or no precedent for the latter groups' participating in the government or the army. There was no strong tradition of civil or individual liberty. From the time of Martin Luther through Kant and Hegel, freedom in Germany had meant conformity to a higher moral law rather than participation in politics. Consequently the mainstream of German liberalism differed from its British and French counterparts. There was much greater opposition from both the monarchs and the aristocracies. German liberals had little direct access to political influence. Most of them favored a united Germany that was to be created through the instrument of the Prussian monarchy. This policy meant that they tended to stress the power of the state

and the monarchy rather more than did other liberals. Once unification had been achieved, a freer social and political order might be established. The great difficulty for German liberals was the refusal of the Prussian monarchy to cooperate. Thus in Germany liberals were generally frustrated and had to remain satisfied with the lowering of internal trade barriers.

Between 1819 and 1822 the institutions of the restored conservative order had held back the forces of liberalism. In the Germanies, Austria, and Italy the liberal challenge was smothered for at least another twenty-five years. However, during the twenties the conservative governments of Russia, France, and Great Britain faced new stirrings of political discontent. In Russia the result was suppression; in France, revolution; and in Britain, accommodation.

Russia: The Decembrist Revolt of 1825 and the Autocracy of Nicholas I

During the mid-twenties Russia took the lead in suppressing both liberal and nationalistic tendencies within its domains. In the process of driving Napoleon's army across Europe and then of occupying defeated France, many officers in the Russian army were introduced to the ideas of the French Revolution and the Enlightenment. They realized how economically backward and politically stifled their own nation remained. The domestic repression in Russia hardened as Alexander I became more conservative. Under these conditions secret societies were formed within the army officer corps. One such reformist coterie was the Southern Society. Led by an officer named Pestel, these men sought a representative government and the abolition of serfdom. Pestel himself favored democracy and a moderately independent Poland. The Northern Society was a second, more moderate group. It favored constitutional monarchy and the abolition of serfdom but with protection for the interests of the aristocracy. Both societies were very small; there was much friction between them. They agreed only that there must be a change in the government of Russia. Sometime

Tsar Nicholas I of Russia was the most conservative major ruler of the early nineteenth century. He resisted practically all attempts to reform Russia and offered the use of Russian troops to other European nations endangered by revolutionary disturbances. [Culver Pictures.]

during 1825 they seem to have decided to carry out a *coup d'état* in 1826.

Other events intervened. In late November 1825 Tsar Alexander I suddenly and unexpectedly died. His death created two crises. The first was a dynastic one. Alexander had no direct heir. His brother Constantine stood next in line to the throne. However, Constantine had been ruling Poland and did not want the Russian crown. Through a series of instructions made public after his death, Alexander had named his younger brother Nicholas (1825–1855) as the new tsar. However, Constantine had neither publicly repudiated the throne nor acknowledged Nicholas. Under these circumstances the Russian Senate declared Constantine to be the tsar, but he still would not refuse the throne. Moreover Constantine was so angered by the general ineptitude of the officials that he declined to come to St. Petersburg to proclaim Nicholas. The family muddle continued for about three weeks. Then during the early days of December, the army command reported to Nicholas the existence of a conspiracy among certain officers. Able to wait no longer for the working out of legal niceties, Nicholas had himself declared tsar.

The second crisis now proceeded to unfold. There was a plot devised by a number of junior officers intent upon rallying the troops under their command to the cause of reform. On December 26, 1825, the army was to take the oath of allegiance to Nicholas. Nearly all of the regiments did so. But the Moscow regiment, whose chief officers surprisingly were not secret society members, marched into the Senate Square in St. Petersburg and refused to swear allegiance. Rather they called for Constantine and a constitution. Attempts to settle the situation peacefully failed. Late in the afternoon Nicholas ordered the cavalry and artillery to attack the insurgents. Over sixty people were killed. Early in 1826 Nicholas himself presided over the commission that investigated the Decembrist Revolt and the secret army societies. Five of the plotters were executed and over one hundred other officers were exiled to Siberia.

Although the Decembrist Revolt completely failed, it was the first rebellion in modern Russian history whose instigators had specific political goals. They wanted constitutional government and the abolition of serfdom. As the century passed, the Decembrists in their political martyrdom came to symbolize the yearnings of all Russian liberals, whose numbers were always quite small. The more immediate result of the revolt was the crushing of liberalism as even a moderate political influence in Russia. Nicholas I was determined that never again would his power come under question. He eventually epitomized the most extreme form of nineteenth-century autocracy.

Nicholas was neither an ignorant nor a bigoted reactionary. He was quite simply afraid of change. He knew that Russia required reforms for economic growth and social improvement. In 1842 he told his State Council, "There is no doubt that serfdom, in its present form, is a flagrant evil which everyone realizes, yet to attempt to remedy it now would be, of course, an evil more disastrous."[3] To remove serfdom would necessarily in his

3 Quoted in Michael T. Florinsky, *Russia: A History and an Interpretation* (New York: Macmillan, 1953), Vol. 2, p. 755.

view have undermined the nobles' support for the tsar. Consequently Nicholas turned his back on this and practically all other reforms. Literary and political censorship and a widespread system of secret police flourished throughout his reign. There was little attempt to forge even an efficient and honest administration. The only significant reform of his rule was a codification of Russian law published in 1833.

In place of reform Nicholas and his closest advisers embraced a program called Official Nationalism. Its slogan, published repeatedly in government documents, newspapers, journals, and schoolbooks, was "Orthodoxy, Autocracy, and Nationalism." The Russian Orthodox faith was to provide the basis for morality, education, and intellectual life. The church, which since the days of Peter the Great had been an arm of the secular government, controlled the schools and universities. Young Russians were taught to accept their place in life and to spurn rising in the social structure. The program of autocracy championed the unrestrained power of the Tsar as the only authority that could hold the vast expanse of Russia and its peoples together in an orderly fashion. Political writers stressed that only under the autocracy of Peter the Great, Catherine the Great, and Alexander I had Russia prospered and exerted a major influence on world affairs. Through the glorification of Russian nationality, the country was urged to see its religion, language, and customs as a source of perennial wisdom that separated the nation from the moral corruption and political turmoil of the West. The person who presided over the program of Official Nationalism was Count S. S. Uvarov, minister of education from 1833 to 1849. The result of his efforts and those of the Tsar was the profound alienation of serious Russian intellectual life from the tsarist government.

Nicholas I also manifested extreme conservatism in foreign affairs. After the Congress of Vienna, Poland had been given a constitutional government but within the limits of the Russian domination that dated back to the eighteenth-century partitions of Poland. Grand Duke

Uvarov Praises the Policy of Official Nationality

Uvarov was the Russian minister of education under Nicholas I. In that capacity he was largely responsible for the policy of Official Nationality with its program of orthodoxy, autocracy, and nationality. In 1843 he explains that this ideology is to prevent Russia from experiencing the political turmoil that had occurred in western Europe.

I N T H E *midst of rapid collapse in Europe of religious and civil institutions, at the time of a general spread of destructive ideas, at the sight of grievous phenomena surrounding us on all sides, it was necessary to establish our fatherland on firm foundations upon which is based the well-being, strength, and life of a people; it was necessary to find the principles which form the distinctive character of Russia, and which belong only to Russia; it was necessary to gather into one whole the sacred remnants of Russian nationality and to fasten to them the anchor of our salvation. Fortunately, Russia had retained a warm faith in the sacred principles without which she cannot prosper, gain in strength, live. Sincerely and deeply attached to the church of his fathers, the Russian has of old considered it the guarantee of social and family happiness. Without a love for the faith of its ancestors a people, as well as an individual must perish. A Russian devoted to his fatherland, will agree as little to the loss of a single dogma of our Orthodoxy as to the theft of a single pearl from the tsar's crown. Autocracy constitutes the main condition of the political existence of Russia. The Russian giant stands on it as on the cornerstone of his greatness. An innumerable majority of the subjects of Your Majesty feel this truth; they feel it in full measure although they are placed on different rungs of civil life and although they vary in education and in their relations to the government. The saving conviction that Russia lives and is protected by the spirit of a strong, humane, and enlightened autocracy must permeate popular education and must develop with it. Together with these two national principles there is a third, no less important, no less powerful:* nationality.

Cited in Nicholas Riasanovsky, *Nicholas I and Official Nationality in Russia, 1825–1855* (Berkeley: University of California Press, 1959), pp. 74–75.

Constantine, the brother of Alexander I and Nicholas I, was in charge of the Polish government by authority delegated by the tsars. Although both tsars frequently infringed upon the constitutional arrangement and quar-

Some of his subjects considered King Charles X of France to be the handsomest person in the nation. His reactionary policies prepared the way for the Revolution of 1830. [The Granger Collection.]

reled with the Polish Diet, the constitution itself remained. Nevertheless Polish nationalists continued to agitate for change.

In late November 1830, after the news of the French and Belgian revolutions of that summer had penetrated Poland, a small military insurrection broke out in Warsaw. Disturbances soon spread throughout the rest of the country. On December 18 the Polish Diet declared the revolution to be a nationalist movement. In early January 1831 the Diet voted to depose Nicholas as ruler of Poland. The tsar reacted by sending troops into the country. After several months the revolt was thoroughly suppressed. In February 1832 Nicholas issued the Organic Statute, which declared Poland to be an integral part of the Russian empire. The statute guaranteed certain Polish liberties, but they were systematically ignored. The Polish uprising had confirmed all the tsar's worst fears. Henceforth Russia and Nicholas became the gendarme of Europe, ever ready to provide troops to suppress liberal and nationalist movements.

Revolution in France (1830)

The Polish revolt was the most distant of several disturbances that flowed from the overthrow of the Bourbon dynasty in France during July 1830. In 1824 Louis XVIII had died. He was succeeded by his brother, the Count of Artois, who became Charles X (1824–1830). The new king, who had been the chief leader of the ultraroyalists at the time of the restoration, considered himself a monarch by divine right. He was crowned with elaborate ceremony and ritual at the Cathedral of Reims. At long last in power, he intended to roll back as much of the revolution as possible and to repay the loyalty of the French royalists.

His first action was to have the Chamber of Deputies in 1824 and 1825 provide for the indemnification of aristocrats who had lost their lands in the revolution. The existing land settlement was confirmed. However, by lowering the interest rates on government bonds, the Chamber created a fund from which the survivors of the

émigrés who had forfeited land would be paid, on the average, 1377 francs annually. This move was naturally resented by the middle-class bondholders, who lost income. Another measure restored the rule of primogeniture, whereby only the eldest son of an aristocrat inherited the family domains. Charles X supported the Roman Catholic Church by a law punishing sacrilege with sentences of imprisonment or death. Liberals disapproved of all of these measures.

The results of the elections of 1827 compelled Charles X to appease the liberals, who in conjunction with more moderate royalists could muster a majority in the Chamber of Deputies. He appointed a less conservative ministry. Laws directed against the press and those allowing the government to dominate education were eased. Yet the liberals, who wanted a genuinely constitutional regime, remained unsatisfied. In 1829 the king decided his policy of accommodation had failed. He dismissed his ministers and in their place appointed an ultraroyalist ministry headed by the Prince de Polignac (1780–1847). The opposition was now forced to the desperate action of opening negotiations with the liberal Orleanist branch of the royal family.

In 1830 Charles X called for new elections, in which the liberals scored a stunning victory. He might have relented and tried to accommodate the new Chamber of Deputies. Instead the king and his ministers decided to attempt a royalist seizure of power. In June and July 1830 Polignac had sent a naval expedition against Algeria. On July 9 reports of its victory reached Paris. The foundation of a French Empire in North Africa had been laid. On July 25, 1830, under the euphoria of this foreign diversion, Charles X issued the Four Ordinances, which amounted to a royal *coup d'état*. The ordinances restricted freedom of the press, dissolved the recently elected

LES POIRES,

Faites à la cour d'assises de Paris par le directeur de la CARICATURE.

Vendues pour payer les 6,000 fr. d'amende du journal le *Charivari.*

(CHEZ AUBERT, GALERIE VERO-DODAT.)

Si, pour reconnaître le monarque dans une caricature, vous n'attendez pas qu'il soit désigné autrement que par la ressemblance, vous tomberez dans l'absurde. Voyez ces croquis informes, auxquels j'aurais peut-être dû borner ma défense :

Ce croquis ressemble à Louis-Philippe, vous condamnerez donc ?

Alors il faudra condamner celui-ci, qui ressemble au premier.

Puis condamner cet autre, qui ressemble au second

Et enfin, si vous êtes conséquens, vous ne sauriez absoudre cette poire, qui ressemble aux croquis précédens.

Ainsi, pour une poire, pour une brioche, et pour toutes les têtes grotesques dans lesquelles le hasard ou la malice aura placé cette triste ressemblance, vous pourrez infliger à l'auteur cinq ans de prison et cinq mille francs d'amende!! Avouez, Messieurs, que c'est là une singulière liberté de la presse!!

Political cartoonists found a superb subject in Louis Philippe. In this series of caricatures he is shown being transformed by progressive stages into a pear. The surrounding text and this group of drawings are primarily a satire on the so-called freedom of the press under which publishers were still in danger of heavy fines and the individual cartoonists liable to imprisonment for up to five years for lack of respect to the king. [The Granger Collection.]

Chamber of Deputies, restricted the franchise to the wealthiest people in the country, and called for new elections under the new royalist franchise.

The Four Ordinances provoked swift and decisive popular political reactions. Liberal newspapers called upon the nation to reject the monarch's actions. The laboring populace of Paris, burdened since 1827 by an economic downturn, took to the streets and erected barricades. The king called out troops, and over eighteen hundred people died during the ensuing battles in the city. On August 2 Charles X abdicated and left France for exile in England. The liberals in the Chamber of Deputies named a new ministry composed of constitutional monarchists. They proclaimed Louis Philippe (1830–1848), the Duke of Orleans, as the new monarch. The July Days had brought to a final close the rule of the Bourbon dynasty in France.

In the Revolution of 1830 the liberals of the Chamber of Deputies filled a power vacuum created by the popular Paris uprising and the failure of effective royal action. Had Charles X provided himself with sufficient troops in Paris, the outcome could have been quite different. Moreover had the liberals, who favored constitutional monarchy, not acted quickly, the workers and shopkeepers of Paris might have formed a republic. By seizing the moment, the middle class, the bureaucrats, and the moderate aristocratic liberals overthrew the restoration monarchy and still avoided a republic. These liberals feared a new popular revolution such as had swept France in 1792 on the overthrow of the old monarchy. They had no desire for another sans-culotte republic. However, the basic tension that existed between hard-pressed laborers and prosperous middle-class persons who had in a temporary alliance achieved the revolution continued to mark the new monarchy.

Politically the July Monarchy, as it was called, was more liberal than the restoration government. Louis Philippe was called the king of the French rather than of France. The tricolor flag of the revolution replaced the white flag of the Bourbons. The Charter was regarded as a right of the people rather than a concession of the monarch. Catholicism became the religion of the majority

Louis Philippe became King of the French by the Revolution of 1830 and was deposed by the Revolution of 1848. [The Granger Collection.]

of the people rather than the official religion. Censorship was abolished. The franchise became somewhat wider but remained on the whole restricted. The king had to cooperate with the Chamber of Deputies; he could not dispense with laws on his own authority.

Socially, however, the Revolution of 1830 proved quite conservative. The hereditary peerage was abolished in 1831, but the everyday economic, political, and social influence of the landed oligarchy continued. Money was the path to power and influence in the government. There was much corruption. Most important, the liberal monarchy displayed little or no sympathy for the lower and working classes. The Paris workers in 1830 had called for the protection of jobs, better wages, and the preservation of the traditional crafts rather than for the usual goals of political liberalism. The government of Louis Philippe ignored their demands and their plight. The laboring classes of Paris and the provincial cities seemed just one more possible source of disorder. In late 1831 a workers' revolt in the city of Lyons was suppressed by troops. In July 1832 an uprising occurred in Paris during the funeral of a popular Napoleonic general. Again troops were called out, and over eight hundred people were killed or wounded. In 1834 a very large strike of silkworkers in Lyons was crushed. Such discontent might be smothered for a time, but without attention to the social and economic conditions creating that tension new turmoil would eventually erupt.

Belgium Becomes Independent (1830)

The July Days in Paris sent sparks into other political tinder on the continent. The revolutionary fires first lighted in neighboring Belgium. The former Austrian Netherlands had in 1815 been merged with the kingdom of Holland. The upper classes of Belgium had never reconciled themselves to rule by a country with a different language, religion, and economic life. On August 25, 1830, disturbances broke out in Brussels following the performance of an opera that portrayed a rebellion of Naples against Spanish rule. To put an end to the rioting,

the municipal authorities and persons from the propertied classes formed a provisional national government. When compromise between the Belgians and the Dutch failed, William of Holland sent troops and ships against Belgium. By November 10, 1830, the Dutch had been defeated. A National Congress then wrote a liberal Belgian constitution, which was promulgated in 1831.

The major powers saw the revolution in Belgium as upsetting the boundaries established by the Congress of Vienna. Russia could not intervene because of the Polish revolt. Prussia and the other German states were suppressing small risings in their own domains. The Austrians were busy putting down disturbances in Italy. France under Louis Philippe favored an independent Belgium and hoped to dominate it. Britain felt that it could tolerate a liberal Belgium so long as it was free of foreign domination. In December 1830 Lord Palmerston (1784–1865), the British foreign minister, gathered representatives of the powers in London. Through skillful negotiations he persuaded them to recognize Belgium as an independent and neutral state. In July 1831 Leopold of Saxe-Coburg (1831–1865) became king of the Belgians. By the Convention of 1839 the great powers guaranteed the neutrality of Belgium. For almost a century Belgian neutrality remained one of the articles of faith in European international relations. In 1914 it was German violation of the neutrality convention that technically brought Great Britain into World War I.

The Great Reform Bill in Britain (1832)

The revolutionary year of 1830 saw in Great Britain the election of the House of Commons that passed the first major bill to reform Parliament. The death of George IV (1820–1830) and the accession of William IV (1830–1837) required the calling of an election. It was once believed that the July revolution in France had influenced the British elections in the summer of 1830. This theory has been shown to be incorrect through a close analysis of the time and character of individual county and borough elections. The passage of the great reform bill, which became law in 1832, was the result of a series of events very different from those that occurred on the continent. In Britain the forces of conservatism and reform made accommodations with each other.

Several factors made this situation possible and meant that Great Britain would become "the chief laboratory of liberal thought during the century."[4] First, there was a larger commercial and industrial class in Britain than in other countries. No matter what group might control the government, British prosperity required attention to those economic interests. Second, there existed in Britain the long tradition of liberal Whig aristocrats, who regarded themselves as the protectors of constitutional liberty. They saw their role as that of making moderate political changes that would render revolutionary changes unnecessary. Their influence had been harmed by early sympathy for the French Revolution. However, after 1815 they reentered the political arena and waited to be recalled to power. Finally, there also existed in British law, tradition, and public opinion a strong respect for the civil liberties.

In 1820, the year after the passage of the notorious Six Acts, Lord Liverpool shrewdly moved to change his cabinet. New faces began to appear. They included George Canning, Robert Peel (1788–1850), and William Huskisson (1770–1830). These men, sometimes called "liberal Tories," favored conservative politics but also knew that the nation and government must accommodate themselves to the new economic and political forces of the day. Canning introduced the more liberal foreign policy that led to the recognition of the Latin American republics. Peel set about reforming the criminal law and reducing the number of capital offenses. Huskisson was an economic liberal who commenced a slow process of lowering tariffs for the benefit of the commercial classes. In 1824 the Combination Acts were repealed, and labor organization became possible.

4 George L. Mosse, *The Culture of Western Europe: The Nineteenth and Twentieth Centuries* (New York: Rand McNally, 1965), p. 97.

Daniel O'Connell was the most dynamic and effective Irish nationalist leader in the first half of the nineteenth century. His portrait is by George Hayter and was made in 1834 when O'Connell was 59. [The Granger Collection.]

Economic considerations had generally led to these moderate reforms. English determination to maintain its union with Ireland brought about another key reform. England's relationship to Ireland was not unlike that of Russia's to Poland or Austria's to its several national groups. In 1800, fearful that Irish nationalists might again rebel as they had in 1798 and perhaps turn Ireland into a base for a French invasion, William Pitt the Younger had Parliament enact the Act of Union between England and Ireland. Ireland now sent more than eighty members to the House of Commons. However, because of the religious scruples of King George III, Pitt was unable to secure passage of a law to permit Roman Catholics to sit in the House of Commons. Consequently only Protestant Irishmen, who usually had close ties to England, could be elected to represent overwhelmingly Catholic Ireland.

During the 1820s, under the leadership of Daniel O'Connell (1775–1847), Irish nationalists organized the Catholic Association to agitate for Catholic emancipation. In 1828 O'Connell secured his own election to Parliament, where he could not legally take his seat. The British ministry of the Duke of Wellington realized that henceforth an entirely Catholic delegation might be elected from Ireland. If they were not seated, civil war

Charles, Earl Grey was the prime minister under whose leadership the British Parliament passed the Great Reform Bill. [The Granger Collection.]

might erupt across the Irish Sea. Consequently, in 1829 Wellington and Robert Peel steered the Catholic Emancipation Act through Parliament. Roman Catholics could now become Members of Parliament. This measure, together with the repeal in 1827 of restrictions against Protestant nonconformists, meant that the Anglican monopoly on British political life was over.

Catholic emancipation was a liberal measure that was passed for the conservative purpose of preserving order in Ireland. It included a provision raising the franchise in

Thomas Babbington Macaulay Defends the Great Reform Bill

Macaulay (1800–1859) was a member of the House of Commons that twice passed the Parliamentary Reform Bill in 1831 only to have it rejected by the House of Lords before a third measure was successfully enacted in 1832. His speeches in support of the bill derived from his views on the need for Parliament to give balanced representation to major elements in the population. Specifically, he supported the Reform Bill because it allowed the middle class to obtain political influence without creating a democratic government. He saw the reform of Parliament as a way to prevent political revolution in England. His argument had wide appeal.

[THE principle of the ministers] is plain, rational, and consistent. It is this,—to admit the middle class to a large and direct share in the Representation, without any violent shock to the institutions of our country. . . . I hold it to be clearly expedient, that in a country like this, the right of suffrage should depend on a pecuniary qualification. Every argument . . . which would induce me to oppose Universal Suffrage, induces me to support the measure which is now before us. I oppose Universal Suffrage, because I think that it would produce a destructive revolution. I support this measure, because I am sure that it is our best security against a revolution. . . . I . . . do entertain great apprehension for the fate of my country. I do in my conscience believe, that unless this measure, or some similar measure, be speedily adopted, great and terrible calamities will befall us. Entertaining this opinion, I think myself bound to state it, not as a threat, but as a reason. I support this measure as a measure of Reform: but I support it still more as a measure of conservation. That we may exclude those whom it is necessary to exclude, we must admit those whom it may be safe to admit. . . . All history is full of revolutions, produced by causes similar to those which are now operating in England. A portion of the community which had been of no account, expands and becomes strong. It demands a place in the system, suited, not to its former weakness, but to its present power. If this is granted, all is well. If this is refused, then comes the struggle between the young energy of one class, and the ancient privileges of another. . . . Such . . . is the struggle which the middle classes in England are maintaining against an aristocracy of mere locality. . . .

Hansard's Parliamentary Debates, 3rd series, Vol. 2, pp. 1191–1197.

When King William IV (1830–1837) agreed to create enough new peers to pass the Reform Bill, the House of Lords at last accepted the measure. His portrait is by an unknown artist, and his medal is by William Wyon. [The Granger Collection.]

Ireland so that only the wealthier Irish could vote. Nonetheless this measure alienated many of Wellington's Anglican Tory supporters in the House of Commons. In the election of 1830 a large number of supporters of parliamentary reform were returned to Parliament. Even some Tories believed that parliamentary reform was necessary because they had concluded that Catholic emancipation could have been passed only by a corrupt House of Commons. The Wellington ministry soon fell. The Tories were badly divided. Consequently King William IV turned to the Whigs under the leadership of Earl Grey (1764–1845) to form a government.

The Whig ministry soon presented the House of Commons with a major reform bill that had two broad goals. The first was to abolish "rotten" boroughs, which had small numbers of voters, and to replace them with representatives for the previously unrepresented manufacturing districts and cities. Second, the number of voters was about doubled through a series of new franchises. In 1831 the House of Commons passed the bill, but the measure was defeated in the House of Lords. Grey called for a new election, in which another majority in favor of the bill was returned. The House of Commons passed the reform bill a second time, and again the House of Lords rejected it. Mass meetings were held throughout the country. Riots broke out in several cities. Finally, William IV agreed to create enough new peers to give a third reform bill a majority in the House of Lords. Under this pressure the House of Lords yielded, and in 1832 the measure became law.

The Great Reform Bill expanded the size of the British electorate, but it was not a democratic measure. The number of voters was increased by over 200,000 persons or by almost 50 per cent. However, the basis of voting remained a property qualification. Some working-class voters actually were disenfranchised because of the abolition of certain old franchise rights. New urban boroughs were created to allow the growing cities to have a voice in the House of Commons. Yet the passage of the reform act did not, as it was once thought, constitute the triumph of

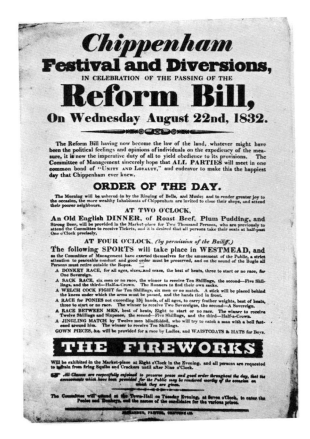

While less clamorous than the vigorous earlier demands for the Reform Bill, the celebrations after its passage in 1832 were none the less lively. These contemporary posters announce the different manners in which two English towns decided to mark the event. At Woodbridge the sobersided inhabitants elected to give a dinner to the poor. At Chippenham, however, they decided to give a vast "Old English Dinner" for two thousand of themselves, the menu for which they proudly announce, the dinner to be followed by a fine program of various sports and, finally, fireworks. [Courtesy Charles Farrell.]

the middle-class interest in Britain. For every new urban electoral district, a new rural district was also drawn. It was expected that the aristocracy would dominate the rural elections.

The success of the reform bill was its reconciliation of previously unrepresented property owners and economic interests to the existing political institutions of the country. The act created a political situation in which further reforms of the church, the municipal government, and commercial policy could be achieved in an orderly fashion. Revolution in Britain was unnecessary because the people who sought change had been admitted to the political forum that could legislate those changes. In this manner the historic institutions of Great Britain were maintained while the persons and groups who influenced them became more diverse.

SUGGESTED READINGS

F. B. Artz, *Reaction and Revolution, 1814–1832* (1934). A useful introduction.

A. Briggs, *The Making of Modern England* (1959). The best survey of English history during the first half of the nineteenth century.

M. Brock, *The Great Reform Act* (1974). The standard work.

G. A. Craig, *The Politics of the Prussian Army, 1640–1945* (1955). A splendid study of the conservative political influence of the army on Prussian development.

D. Dakin, *The Struggle for Greek Independence* (1973). An excellent explanation of the intricacies of the Greek independence question.

G. de Bertier de Sauvigny, *The Bourbon Restoration* (trans., 1966), and *Metternich and His Times* (1962). Sympathetic, but not uncritical studies of the forces of political conservatism.

G. de Ruggiero, *The History of European Liberalism* (1927). The major treatment of the subject.

J. Droz, *Europe between Revolutions, 1815–1848* (1967). An examination of Europe as created by the Vienna settlement.

Carlton J. Hayes, *Essays on Nationalism* (1926). Pioneering, but still useful studies.

E. J. Hobsbawm, *The Age of Revolution, 1789–1848* (1962). A very comprehensive survey emphasizing the social ramifications of the liberal democratic and industrial revolutions.

H. Kohn, *The Idea of Nationalism: A study in Its Origin and Background* (1944). An examination of the roots of nationalism in Western culture.

L. Krieger, *The German Idea of Freedom* (1957). A far-ranging examination of the problems and ideology of German liberalism.

J. Merriman (Ed.), *1830 in France* (1976). A collection of important essays on the Revolutions of 1830.

M. Raeff, *The Decembrist Movement* (1966). An examination of the unsuccessful uprising, with documents.

N. V. Riasanovsky, *Nicholas I and Official Nationality in Russia, 1825–1855* (1959). A lucid discussion of the conservative ideology that made Russia the major opponent of liberalism.

D. Thomson, *Europe Since Napoleon* (1962). A survey of political developments during the past century and a half.

Mack Walker, *Metternich's Europe* (1968). A useful collection of documents.

P. S. Wandycz, *The Lands of Partitioned Poland, 1795–1918* (1974). The best study of Poland during the nineteenth century.

674

26

Economic Advance and Social Unrest (1830–1850)

By 1830 Europe was headed toward an industrial society. Only Great Britain had already attained that status, but the pounding of new machinery and the grinding of railway engines soon began to echo across the entire continent. Further urbanization, the disintegration of traditional social bonds and work habits, and eventually class conflict became part and parcel of the economic development. However, what characterized the second quarter of the century was not the triumph of industrialism but the final gasps of those groups who opposed it. Intellectually the period saw the formulation of the major creeds supporting and criticizing the new society. These were years of uncertainty for almost everyone. Even the most confident businessman knew that the trade cycle might bankrupt him in a matter of weeks. For industrial workers and the artisans unemployment became a haunting and recurring problem. For the peasants the question was sufficiency of food. It was a period of self-conscious transition that culminated in 1848 with a continentwide outbreak of revolution. People knew that one mode of life was passing, but they were uncertain what would replace it.

Toward an Industrial Society

Population and Migration

The Industrial Revolution had begun in eighteenth-century Great Britain with the advances in textile production described in Chapter 20. Natural resources, adequate capital, native technological skills, a growing food supply, a social structure that allowed considerable mobility, and strong foreign and domestic demand for goods had given Britain an edge in achieving a vast new capacity for production in manufacturing. Its factories and recently invented machines allowed British producers to furnish customers with more products and better products at lower prices than any competitors. The wars of the French Revolution and of Napoleon brought about the collapse of the French Atlantic trade. The same conflicts had destroyed capital, led to inflated currencies, and killed off much of the labor supply in continental countries. The restored conservative governments were fearful of the social and political unrest that might accompany major economic change. Consequently Britain's initial lead became further extended, so that in 1850 the nation still remained a generation ahead of its future continental competitors.

Despite the economic lag the continental nations were beginning to make material progress. By the 1830s in Belgium, France, and Germany the number of steam engines in use was growing steadily. Exploitation of the coalfields of the Ruhr and the Saar basins had commenced. Coke was replacing charcoal in iron and steel production. Industrial areas were generally less concentrated than in Britain. Large manufacturing districts, such as the British Midlands, did not yet exist across the English Channel. There were major pockets of production, such as the cities of Lyons, Rouen, Liège, and Lille, but most continental manufacturing still took place in the countryside. New machines were integrated into the existing domestic system. The extreme slowness of continental imitation of the British example meant that at mid-century peasants and urban artisans remained more important politically than industrial factory workers.

While the process of industrialization spread, the population of Europe continued to grow upon the base of the eighteenth-century population explosion. The number of people in France rose from 32.5 million in 1831 to 35.8 million in 1851. The population of Germany rose from

After 1830 railroads began to destroy the peace and quiet of the countryside. Here, in an 1837 illustration by John G. Bourne for his *Drawings of the London and Birmingham Railway,* rocks are being blasted to make way for new tracks. Once the railroads penetrated the countryside, people at last could move easily to the city and to other parts of the country, a factor that helped to undermine the stability of rural society and to modify the character of the cities themselves.

675

The Clifton Bridge, a great iron suspension bridge over the Avon River gorge near Bristol, England, was one of the many spectacular engineering accomplishments of the early nineteenth century. It was designed in 1831 by Isambard Kingdom Brunel (1806–1859), possibly the greatest engineer of his era. Construction began in 1836, and the bridge was completed in 1864. It is still in use. The bridge epitomizes the modern breakthrough in building such structures, as well as railways, subways, massive ships, and others—all dependent on new technologies. [British Tourist Authority, New York.]

26.5 million to 33.5 million during approximately the same period. That of Britain grew from 16.3 million to 20.8 million. More and more of the people of Europe lived in cities. By mid-century one half of the population of England and Wales had become town dwellers; the proportion for France and Germany was about one quarter. The sheer numbers of human beings put considerable pressure on the physical resources of the cities. Migration from the countryside meant that existing housing, water, sewers, food supply, and lighting were completely inadequate. Slums with indescribable filth grew, and disease, especially cholera, ravaged the population. Crime increased and became a way of life for those who could make a living in no other manner. Human misery and

degradation in numerous early nineteenth-century cities seemed to have no bounds.

The situation in the countryside was little or no better. During the first half of the century, land ownership and its productive use still remained the overwhelming facts of life for the majority of Europeans. The enclosures of the late eighteenth century, the land redistribution of the French Revolution, and the emancipation of serfs in Prussia and later in central Europe (Austria, 1848; Russia, 1861) commercialized landholding. Liberal reformers had hoped that the legal revolution in ownership would transform peasants into progressive, industrious farmers. Most of them had instead become very conservative landholders who possessed too little soil to innovate or in many cases even to support themselves. The specter of poor harvests still haunted Europe. The worst such experience of the century was the Irish famine of 1845–1847. Tens of thousands of Irish peasants with no land or small plots simply starved when disease blighted the potato crop. Hundreds of thousands emigrated. By mid-century the revolution in landholding had led not to greater agricultural production but to vast uprootings of peoples from the countryside into cities and from Europe into the rest of the world.

Railways

Industrial advance itself had also contributed to this migration. The decades of the thirties and forties were the great age of railway building. The Stockton and Darlington Line opened in England in 1825. By 1830 another major line had been built between Manchester and Liverpool with several hundred daily passengers. Belgium had undertaken railway construction by 1835. The first French line opened in 1832, but serious construction came only in the forties. Germany entered the railway age in 1835. At mid-century Britain had 9,797 kilometers of railway; France, 2,915; and Germany, 5,856. The railroads plus canals and improved regular roads meant that people could leave the place of their birth more easily than ever before. The improvement in transportation also allowed cheaper and more rapid passage of raw materials and finished products.

Railways epitomized the character of the industrial economy during the second quarter of the century. They represented investment in capital rather than in consumer goods. There was consequently somewhat of a shortage of consumer goods at cheap prices. This favoring of capital over consumer production was one reason that the working class often found itself able to purchase so little for its wages. The railways in and of themselves also brought about still more industrialization. They created a sharply increased demand for iron and steel and then for a more skilled labor force. The new iron and steel capacity soon permitted the construction of ironclad ships and iron rather than wooden machinery. These great capital industries led to the formation of vast industrial fortunes that would be invested in still newer enterprises. Industrialism had begun to grow upon itself.

Railroads literally cut into the cities of Europe. Here in Camden Town in London retaining walls are being built in a deep cut on either side of the newly laid tracks. The picture was made in 1838 by John G. Bourne.

The "Penny Black" with a portrait of Queen Victoria was the world's first adhesive postage stamp. Issued on May 6, 1840, it signified one small part of a world of more rapid communication. The engraver was Frederick Heath. [The Granger Collection.]

The Middle Classes

It was the age of the career open to talent. The middle class of businessmen, traders, shippers, factory owners, doctors, lawyers, shopkeepers, and schoolteachers benefited most from the economic and material progress. Their incomes, unlike those of laborers, allowed them to buy consumer goods. Their skills and education permitted them to rise socially. They often had sufficient savings to make either large or small investments in the railroads and other heavy industries. Many of them were able to rise well above the social status of their birth.

The middle *classes*—for the group was very diverse—believed that merit and competition should replace good birth and patronage as avenues to social position and political influence. In place of the former aristocratic value of leisure, they raised the values of thrift and hard work. They tended to measure success and respectability in terms of money. This attitude made them very unsympathetic toward the plight of the poor. They believed that the poor experienced poverty from either lack of ability or laziness. The middle classes were the people whom the English novelist Charles Dickens (1812–1870) pilloried in *Hard Times* and other novels and whose amoral existence the French novelist Honoré de Balzac (1799–1850) dissected in his fiction. But the confidence of the middle classes was a reflection of the new economic order that their members had created. They were also arrogant because they had learned from the aristocracy that pride and self-confidence were the marks of socially superior people.

Charles Dickens was the most popular novelist of mid-Victorian England. His works included many memorable, moving, and comic characters, but he was also deeply committed to exploring the evils of industrial and commercial society in which money and production had replaced love and imagination. The photograph was made during an American tour in the 1860s. [The Granger Collection.]

Frances Trollope, mother of the popular novelist Anthony Trollope, was herself an English novelist who wrote books portraying the harsh conditions in factories. The painting from the 1830s is by Augusta Hervieu. [The Granger Collection.]

Yet for all their economic success and apparent self-certainty, in several countries the middle classes at mid-century still generally lacked effective political power. They were best off in Britain, where aristocratic leaders did listen to them and where they were being absorbed into the political process, as the careers of Robert Peel, Richard Cobden, John Bright, and William Gladstone demonstrated.

In France, by contrast, a very small group of extremely wealthy persons affected politics. During the July Monarchy only about 250,000 persons had the right to vote. In the states of Germany, the Hapsburg Empire, and Russia the small middle classes were relatively powerless. Throughout Europe these people were coming increasingly to resent the lack of political influence equal to their wealth and ability. Their enemies were the aristocracy and inefficient royal administrations. Through philosophical and scientific societies, chambers of commerce, and where possible newspapers, they were by the late forties voicing their complaints and ambitions.

The early nineteenth-century middle class, however, was critical of the social conditions arising from industrialism as well as eager to enjoy economic profits. During the second quarter of the century numerous physicians who had to enter working-class districts to treat disease wrote books describing the suffering of the poor. Novelists—such as Dickens, Elizabeth Gaskell (1810–1865), Frances Trollope (1780–1863), and Benjamin Disraeli (1804–1881), who was also a notable statesman—featured the plight of the British working class in works such as *Mary Barton* and *Sybil*. Social commentators, such as Thomas Carlyle (1795–1881) in *Past and Present*, denounced the sacrifice of social welfare to the naked profit motive. Henry Mayhew (1812–1887), a reporter for the London *Morning Chronicle*, wrote a long series of articles in 1849–1850 about the life of the laboring poor in the city. He revealed a world of which middle-class readers had neither knowledge nor experience. Edwin Chadwick (1800–1890), a pioneer of sanitary reform, presented government reports on the degradation of urban and industrial life in Britain. Various parliamentary commissions also published papers describing the harsh realities of the conditions of the working class. All of these materials provided Karl Marx (1818–1883) with some of the most important sources for his denunciation of capitalism.

The Labor Force

The composition and experience of the early nineteenth-century labor force was quite varied. No single description could include all of the factory workers, urban artisans, domestic system craftsmen, household servants, countryside peddlers, farm workers, or railroad navvies. The work force was composed of some persons who were reasonably well off, enjoying steady employment and decent wages. It also numbered the "laboring poor," who held jobs but whose wages allowed them little more than subsistence. The condition of any particular working-class family depended upon the skills of its members, the nature of the local labor market, and the trade cycle. But all of these working people faced possible unemployment with little or no provision for their security. They confronted over the course of their lives the dissolution of many of the traditional social ties of custom and community. Most of the economic relationships in their lives became that of the marketplace, or as Thomas Carlyle said of the "cash nexus."

Within the variety of workers there are two broad categories about whom some general statements can be made: factory workers and artisans. The former were on the side of the future; the latter tried to hold onto the past. During the second quarter of the century the skilled artisans were more likely than the factory workers to be vocally discontent about their situation.

FACTORY WORKERS. Throughout the period there was a relative shortage of factory labor. Most of the new industries paid their workers higher wages than they would have received elsewhere. Moreover, contrary to opinions once held, the factory did not destroy the working-class family. For some time spinners and weavers working in factories were able to employ their own

Machinery in early mechanized cotton mills was often tended by women and children, as shown in this 1835 picture. If this picture is reasonably accurate, this mill, with its windows and the wide aisles between the machines, would have been considered a fairly good place to work. However, note that there are few safety devices on the machines to prevent injury to workers. [Bettmann Archive.]

The drabness of the exterior of the factory and the filth of the smoke from its stacks symbolized to many social critics the dark side of the industrial revolution. Nevertheless, factories, like this one in Manchester, England, also symbolized the vast new productive potential of European society. [E. Bains, *History of the Cotton Manufacture in Great Britain.* Courtesy Frank Cass & Co., London.]

children as helpers. In this manner to a certain extent the old family economy was transported into the mills. Only later on, when a laboring family became prosperous enough to send its own children to school, did it employ children outside its own family to tend the machines, thus splitting up a less prosperous family. There were also some factory owners who really cared about the lives and welfare of their employees.

Nonetheless there were many factories that were dangerous and unhealthy. Women and children were frequently employed for long hours at low wages. Factory laws were passed in Great Britain, France, and Prussia, but for many years they had only a marginal impact.

The harshest aspect of factory life, with the exception of the long hours, was the discipline of the machinery itself. Workers could no longer, as in the domestic system, set their own hours or speed of production. All work became determined by the machine. The closing of fac-

Friedrich Engels Describes the Plight of English Workers

As the most industrially advanced country, England offered a vast object lesson for study by social critics like Karl Marx and Friedrich Engels. Engels (1820–1895) had visited England where his father owned a factory. At age twenty-five he already believed the major difficulty confronting industrial workers was the almost total lack of security in their lives. They seemed to be the victims of chance and of the economic interest of the middle class.

Insecurity *is even more demoralising than poverty. English wage-earners live from hand to mouth, and this is the distinguishing mark of their proletarian status. The lower ranks of the German peasantry are largely filled with men who are also poor, and often suffer want, but they are less subject to that sort of distress which is due solely to chance. They do at least enjoy some measure of security. But the proletarian is in quite a different position. He possesses nothing but his two hands and he consumes to-day what he earned yesterday. His future is at the mercy of chance. He has not the slightest guarantee that his skill will in the future enable him to earn even the bare necessities of life. Every commercial crisis, every whim of his master, can throw him out of work. He is placed in the most revolting and inhuman position imaginable. A slave is at least assured of his daily bread by the self-interest of his master. . . . Slaves and serfs are both guaranteed a basic minimum existence. The proletarian on the other hand is thrown wholly upon his own resources, and yet at the same time is placed in such a position that he cannot be sure that he can always use those resources to gain a livelihood for himself and his family. Everything that the factory worker can do to try and improve his position vanishes like a drop in the bucket in face of the flood of chance occurrences to which he is exposed and over which he has not the slightest control. He is the passive sufferer from every possible combination of mishaps, and can regard himself as fortunate if he keeps his head above water even for a short time. . . . He may fight for survival in this whirlpool; he may try to maintain his dignity as a human being. This he can do only by fighting the middle classes, who exploit him so ruthlessly and then condemn him to a fate which drives him to live in a way unworthy of a human being.*

Friedrich Engels, *The Condition of the Working Class in England*, trans. by W. O. Henderson and W. H. Chaloner (Stanford, Calif.: Stanford University Press, 1970), p. 131.

tory gates to late workers, the fines for such lateness, the dismissals for drunkenness, and the public scolding of faulty laborers constituted attempts to create human discipline and regularity that would match the demands of the cables, wheels, and pistons. To this psychological hardship in the plant must be added the haunting specter of unemployment.

URBAN ARTISANS. The plight of the urban artisans or craftsmen was different. They were attempting to maintain a traditional mode of life rather than adjusting to a new one. At mid-century there were still many more artisans working in small shops with fewer than ten employees than there were factory laborers. Often the introduction of new power machinery, such as the power loom, occurred so slowly that the artisan believed that he could still maintain his livelihood. By the time the true situation dawned on him, it was often too late for him to change skills.

The migration of rural domestic craftsmen into the cities created excessive hardship for urban artisans, such as weavers, metal workers, and construction laborers. The urban artisan already felt endangered by machines, and the new city dwellers increased the competition. Where possible, the guilds became more exclusive. Apprentices had difficulty becoming journeymen, and the latter found the ranks of the masters increasingly closed. The old framework of government control of wages and quality had been undermined by the economics of the middle class. With their skills threatened by machinery and with the old economic and social protections gone, these hard-pressed artisans, whose social forebears had been the revolutionary sans-culottes, became the most politically radical element in European society.

Early in the century the workers in traditional industries had attempted to protect their position by destroying the machines. These attacks on property failed, and swift repression often followed. By the twenties artisans and a few less-skilled workers were turning to unions. These efforts were only marginally successful during the first half of the century. In Germany liberal reformers

For a time it appeared that Chartism would become a violent political movement. However, riots, such as this one at Newport in 1839, eventually gave way to more peaceful demonstrations and mass petitions to Parliament to enact the Six Points of the Charter. [The Granger Collection.]

had attempted to break up the guilds. They succeeded in several states but not in Prussia. There the guilds remained effective until the middle of the forties and were legal until the sixties. In France the revolutionary legislation against workers' organizations remained on the books.

Workers' organizations again became legal in Great Britain after 1824. They made considerable headway until the early thirties. They then collapsed because they lacked sufficient funds to support long strikes. Equally important, the Whig government that passed the liberal Reform Act was most unsympathetic to organized labor. In 1833 that ministry mercilessly suppressed a revolt of farm workers called the Captain Swing uprising. In 1834 it transported to Australia four poor laborers, known as the Tolpuddle Martyrs, for attempting some vague kind of labor organization.

CHARTISM IN GREAT BRITAIN. By the late thirties, the British working class turned to direct political activity. They linked the solution of their economic plight to a program of political reform known as *Chartism*. In 1836 William Lovett (1800–1877) and other London radical artisans formed the London Working Men's Association. In 1838 the group issued the Charter, demanding six specific reforms. The Six Points of the Charter included universal manhood suffrage, annual election of the House of Commons, the secret ballot, equal electoral districts, abolition of property qualifications for Members of Parliament, and payment of members. For over ten years the Chartists, who were never tightly organized, agitated for their reforms. On three occasions the Charter was presented to Parliament, which refused to pass it. Mass petitions were presented to the House of Commons with millions of signatures. Strikes were called. A Chartist newspaper called *The Northern Star* was published. Feargus O'Connor (1794–1855), the most important Chartist spokesmen, made speeches up and down the island. Despite this vast activity Chartism as a national movement failed. Its ranks were split between those who favored violence and those who wanted to use peaceful tactics. However, locally the Chartists scored several successes and controlled the city councils in Leeds and Sheffield.

The economic foundation of Chartism had been the depression of the late thirties and early forties. As prosperity returned, many working people abandoned the movement. Chartism came to a close in March 1848. A mass march on Parliament planned for that month fizzled. The reviving economy took care of the rest of the problem. Nevertheless the Chartist movement constituted the first large-scale working-class political movement. It had specific goals and largely working-class leadership. Henceforth the British ruling classes knew that they could never again ignore the working class as a political factor. And eventually several of the Six Points were enacted into law. Continental working-class observers saw in Chartism the kind of mass movement that workers must eventually adopt if they were to improve their situation.

Intellectual Responses to Industrial Society

Classical Economics

Economists whose thought largely derived from Adam Smith's *Wealth of Nations* (1776) dominated private and public discussions of industrial and commercial policy. Their ideas are generally associated with the phrase *laissez-faire*. Although they thought that the government should perform many important functions, the classical economists favored economic growth through competitive free enterprise. Most economic decisions should be made through the mechanism of the marketplace. They distrusted government action, believing it to be mischievous and corrupt. The government should maintain a sound currency, enforce contracts, protect property, impose low tariffs and taxes, and leave the remainder of economic life to private initiative. The economists naturally assumed that the state would maintain sufficient armed forces and naval power to protect the economic structure and foreign trade of the nation.

The economists conceived of society as consisting of atomistic individuals from whose competitive efforts the demands of the consumers in the marketplace were met. Their theories supported the self-confidence of the middle class. The capitalist was the keystone of the whole economic system. The manufacturer or merchant, by making his capital produce, created jobs, goods, and income for other people. In contrast, the aristocrat or large landowner had a lazy, unproductive existence, as he lived off the rents from his land. The landlords had to do nothing to make their capital produce income. The logical conclusion of this theory was a seizure and redistribution of land. The economists, however, did not carry their ideas that far because the seizure of land would lead to ideas about seizing middle-class capital.

What the classical economists said about the working class was more complicated and very pessimistic. Thomas Malthus (1766–1834) and David Ricardo (1772–1823), probably the most influential of all these writers, suggested in effect that the condition of the working class could not be improved. In 1798 Malthus published the first edition of his *Essay on Population*. His ideas have haunted the world ever since. He contended that population must outstrip the food supply. Although the human population grows geometrically, the food supply can expand only arithmetically. There was little hope of averting the disaster, in Malthus's eyes, except through late marriage, chastity, and contraception, the last of which he considered a vice. It took three quarters of a century before contraception became a socially acceptable method of containing the population explosion.

Malthus contended that the immediate plight of the working class could only become worse. If wages were raised, the workers would simply produce more children, who would in turn consume both the extra wages and more food. Later in his life Malthus suggested in a more optimistic vein that if the working class could be persuaded to adopt a higher standard of living, their increased wages might be spent on consumer goods rather than upon more children.

In the *Principles of Political Economy* (1817) David Ricardo transformed the concepts of Malthus into the Iron Law of Wages. If wages were raised, more children would be produced. They in turn would enter the labor market, thus expanding the number of workers and lowering wages. As wages fell, working people would produce fewer children. Wages would then rise, and the process would start all over. Consequently, in the long run wages would always tend toward a minimum level. These arguments simply confirmed employers in their natural hesitancy to raise wages. These concepts also provided strong theoretical support to opposition to labor unions. The ideas of the economists were spread to the

Harriet Martineau (1802–1876) was one of the most important popularizers of the ideas of the British classical economists. She illustrated their principles through moral tales [The Granger Collection.]

public during the thirties through journals, newspapers, and even short stories, such as Harriet Martineau's series of *Illustrations of Political Economy*.

The working class of France and Great Britain, needless to say, resented these attitudes, but the governments embraced them. Louis Philippe and his minister Francois Guizot (1787–1874) told Frenchmen to go forth and enrich themselves. If a person simply displayed sufficient energy, he need not be poor. A goodly number of the French middle class did just that. The July Monarchy saw the construction of major social overhead capital, such as roads, canals, and railways. Little was done about the poverty in the cities and the countryside.

In Germany the middle classes made less headway. However, the Prussian reformers after the Napoleonic wars had seen the desirability of abolishing internal tariffs that impeded economic growth. In 1834 all the major German states, with the exception of Austria, formed the *Zollverein* or free trading union.

Britain was the home of the major classical economists, and their policies were widely accepted. In 1834 the reformed House of Commons passed a new Poor Law. This measure established a Poor Law Commission, which set out to make poverty the most undesirable of all social situations. Government poor relief was to be dispersed only in workhouses. Life in the workhouse was consciously designed to be more unpleasant than life outside. Husbands and wives were separated. The food was bad, and the work assigned in the house was distasteful. The social stigma of the workhouse was even worse. The law and its administration presupposed that people would not work because they were lazy. The laboring class not unjustly regarded the workhouses as new "bastilles."

The second British monument to applied classical economics was the repeal of the Corn Laws in 1846. The Anti-Corn Law League, organized by manufacturers, had sought this goal for over six years. The league wanted the tariffs protecting the domestic price of grain to be abolished. That change would lead to lower food prices, which would then allow lower wages at no real

cost to the workers. In turn the prices on British manufactured goods could be lowered to allow a stronger competitive position in the world market. The actual reason for Robert Peel's repeal of the Corn Laws in 1846 was the Irish famine. He had to open British ports to foreign grain to feed the starving Irish. He realized that the Corn Laws could not be reimposed. Peel accompanied the abolition measure with a program for government aid to modernize British agriculture and to make it more efficient. The repeal of the Corn Laws was the culmination of the lowering of British tariffs that had begun during the 1820s. The repeal marked the opening of an era of free trade that continued until late in the century.

UTILITARIANISM. Closely related to the classical economists were the British utilitarians. Their major figures included Jeremy Bentham (1748–1832), James Mill (1773–1836), John Stuart Mill (1806–1873), and Sir Edwin Chadwick (1800–1890). They were a set of radical political reformers who urged that the principle of utility—the greatest good for the greatest number—should constitute the guiding principle of public policy. They lacked all reverence for tradition. They felt that political, economic, and social problems should be addressed rationally and without reference to the sinister interests of special or privileged groups. They have frequently been considered spokesmen for the middle class, but it would be more correct to see them as forerunners of an efficient bureaucracy. The utilitarians and their disciples were often civil servants, and they frequently worked on governmental commissions. They were the actual authors of much reform legislation, such as the Factory Act of 1833, the Poor Law of 1834, and the Sanitation Act of 1848.

The utilitarians have achieved a bad reputation for lacking an understanding of humanity and emotion. Some of this reputation is deserved. However, their most distinguished spokesman, John Stuart Mill, was anything but doctrinaire. As a young man he revolted against the rigid Benthamite education imposed on him by his father, James Mill. In his *Principles of Political Economy* (1848)

John Stuart Mill advocated the education of the working class as a means of raising their standard of living. He believed workers capable of as high moral existence as any other social group. He urged the formation of labor cooperatives. In 1859 Mill published *On Liberty* to plead for freedom of thought and expression and for the protection of the individual against the intrusion of the state. In 1869 he took up the cause of women's rights in a pioneering essay on *The Subjection of Women*. If utilitarianism had been narrow in its origins, by the close of Mill's life in 1873 the creed had proved itself capable of considerable moderation.

Socialism

Today the socialist movement, in the form of either communist or social democratic political parties, constitutes one of the major political influences in Europe. Less than 150 years ago the spokesmen for socialism lacked any meaningful political following. Their doctrines were blurred and often seemed silly to their contemporaries. The confusion in early socialist thought reflected its pioneering nature. The social and economic conditions being analyzed were new, and the exact problems to be solved still had to be defined. The early socialists generally applauded the new productive capacity of industrialism, but they denied that the free market could produce and distribute goods in the fashion claimed by the classical economists. The socialists saw primarily mismanagement, low wages, maldistribution of goods, and suffering emanating from the unregulated industrial system. Moreover the socialists thought that human society should be organized as a community rather than merely as a conglomerate of atomistic, selfish individuals.

UTOPIAN SOCIALISM.   Among the earliest people to define the social question were a group of writers called the *utopian socialists*. They were considered utopian because their ideas were often visionary, and they frequently advocated the creation of ideal communities. They were called socialists because they questioned the structures and values of the existing capitalistic framework. In some cases they actually deserved neither description.

Claude Henri, Count of Saint-Simon (1760–1825), was the earliest of the socialist pioneers. As a young liberal French aristocrat he had fought in the American Revolution. Later he welcomed the French Revolution, during which he made and lost a fortune. By the time of Napoleon's ascendancy he had turned to a career of writing and social criticism. Saint-Simon believed that history oscillated between organic and critical periods. During organic periods, such as the Middle Ages, order, harmony, and shared values prevailed. During critical periods, such as the Reformation, the structures, values, and customs of a society underwent severe criticism and disintegration. He saw the late eighteenth and early nineteenth centuries as a critical age. He hoped to set forth a body of ideas and to organize a group of disciples that could project a social blueprint for the inevitable new organic period.

Above all else Saint-Simon believed that modern society would require rational management. Private wealth, property, and enterprise should be subject to administration other than that of its owners. His ideal government would have consisted of a large board of directors organizing and coordinating the activity of individuals and groups to achieve social harmony. In a sense he was the ideological father of technocracy. Not the redistribution of wealth but its management by experts would alleviate the poverty and social dislocation of the age. His faith in experts was similar to the Enlightenment *philosophes'* advocacy of political absolutism. Like his eighteenth-century forebears Saint-Simon had little sympathy with democracy. The order and harmony of the new organic age was to come from the genius of great thinkers such as himself. When Saint-Simon died in 1825, he had persuaded only a handful of people that his ideas were correct. Interestingly enough several of those disciples later became leaders in the French railway industry during the 1850s.

The major British contributor to the early socialist

THE CRISIS,

OR THE CHANGE FROM ERROR AND MISERY, TO TRUTH AND HAPPINESS

1832.

IF WE CANNOT YET   RECONCILE ALL OPINIONS,

LET US ENDEAVOUR   TO UNITE ALL HEARTS.

IT IS OF ALL TRUTHS THE MOST IMPORTANT, THAT THE CHARACTER OF MAN IS FORMED FOR—NOT BY HIMSELF.

Design of a Community of 2,000 Persons, founded upon a principle, commended by Plato, Lord Bacon, Sir T. More, & R. Owen

EDITED BY
ROBERT OWEN AND ROBERT DALE OWEN

London:
PRINTED AND PUBLISHED BY J. EAMONSON, 15, CHICHESTER PLACE
GRAY'S INN ROAD.
STRANGE, PATERNOSTER ROW; PURKISS, OLD COMPTON STREET,
AND MAY BE HAD OF ALL BOOKSELLERS

Robert Owen hoped to organize industrial society into a series of small communities such as that pictured on the cover of his publication. He thought such communities would lead people to live by cooperation rather than by competition. [Bettmann Archive.]

tradition was Robert Owen (1771–1858), a self-made cotton manufacturer. In his early twenties Owen became a partner in New Lanark, one of the largest cotton factories in Britain. Owen was a firm believer in the environmentalist psychology of the Enlightenment. If human beings were placed in the correct surroundings, they and their character could be improved. Moreover Owen saw no incompatibility between creating a humane industrial environment and making a good profit. At New Lanark he put his ideas into practice. Workers were provided with good quarters. Recreational possibilities abounded, and the children were educated. There were several churches, although Owen himself was a notorious freethinker on matters of religion and sex. In the factory itself various rewards were given for good work. His plant made a fine profit. Visitors flocked from all over Europe to see what Owen had accomplished through enlightened management.

Robert Owen Attacks the Economic Ideal of Competition

Robert Owen owned a cotton mill in Scotland—a model of good working conditions for employees. In 1820, he argued, as throughout his life, that the principle of cooperation must replace self-interested competition in economic relationships. He saw competition as one of the chief causes of human suffering.

I T H A S *been, and still is, a received opinion among theorists in political economy, that man can provide better for himself, and more advantageously for the public, when left to his own individual exertions, opposed to and in competition with his fellows, than when aided by any social arrangement which shall unite his interests individually and generally with society. . . .*

Yet when they shall know themselves, and discover the wonderful effects which combination and union can produce, they will acknowledge that the present arrangement of society is the most anti-social, impolitic, and irrational, that can be devised; that under its influence all the superior and valuable qualities of human nature are repressed from infancy, and that the most unnatural means are used to bring out the most injurious propensities; in short, that the utmost pains are taken to make that which by nature is the most delightful compound for producing excellence and happiness, absurd, imbecile, and wretched. . . .

From this principle of individual interest have arisen all the divisions of mankind, the endless errors and mischiefs of class, sect, party, and of national antipathies, creating the angry and malevolent passions, and all the crimes and misery with which the human race have been hitherto afflicted.

In short, if there be one closet doctrine more contrary to truth than another, it is the notion that individual interest, as that term is now understood, is a more advantageous principle on which to found the social system, for the benefit of all, or of any, than the principle of union and mutual cooperation.

Robert Owen, *Report to the County of Lanark*, in V. A. C. Gatrell (Ed.), Robert Owen, *A New View of Society and Report to the County of Lanark* (Baltimore: Penguin Books, 1970), pp. 231–232.

In numerous articles and pamphlets as well as in letters to influential people, Owen pleaded for a reorganization of industry based on his own successful model. He envisioned a series of communities shaped like parallelograms in which factory and farm workers might live together and produce their goods in cooperation. During the

no one under 10 could work

work days were only 10 hours

no fines for breaking rules.

Owen's town had hospitals, shops, schools, etc.

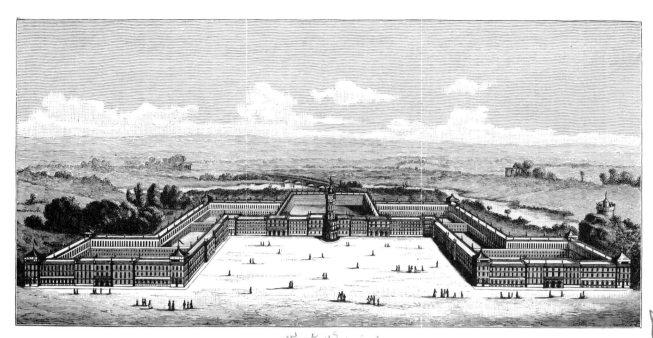

1820s Owen sold New Lanark and then went to the United States, where he established a community at New Harmony, Indiana. When it failed, he refused to give up his reformist causes. He returned to Britain, where he became the moving force behind the organization of the Grand National Union. This was an attempt to draw all British trade unions into a single body. It collapsed with other labor organizations during the early thirties. Owen possessed an exaggerated sense of his own importance and was a difficult person. His version of socialism amounted to little more than old-fashioned paternalism transported to the industrial setting. However, he contributed to the socialist tradition a strong belief in the practicality of cooperative production and proof that industrial production and humane working conditions were compatible.

Charles Fourier (1772–1837) was the French intellectual counterpart of Owen. He was a commercial salesman who never succeeded in attracting the same kind of public attention as Owen. He wrote his books and articles and returned home each day at noon, hoping to meet a patron who would undertake his program. No one ever arrived to meet him. Fourier believed that the industrial order ignored the passionate side of human nature. Social discipline ignored all the pleasures that human beings naturally seek. Fourier advocated the construction of communities, called *phalanxes,* in which liberated living would replace the boredom and dullness of industrial existence. Agrarian rather than industrial activity would predominate in these communities. Sexual activity would be relatively free, and marriage was to be reserved only for later life. Fourier also urged that no person be re-

Charles Fourier [BELOW], the French utopian socialist, believed that so far as possible work should be less boring and more pleasurable. His schemes for the ideal society were aimed at achieving this end.

A model for one of Fourier's phalansteries, in which the inhabitants would both live and work, is illustrated in this contemporary German print. [ABOVE]. [Both: The Granger Collection.]

quired to perform the same kind of work for the entire day. People would be both happier and more productive if they moved from one task to another. Through his emphasis on the problem of boredom Fourier isolated one of the key difficulties of modern economic life. Both he and Owen had raised the whole issue of the quality of life within the processes of industrial production.

Saint-Simon, Owen, and Fourier expected some existing government to carry out their ideas. They failed to confront the political difficulties of their envisioned social transformations. Other figures paid more attention to the politics of the situation. In 1839 Louis Blanc (1811–1882) published *The Organization of Labor*. Like other socialist writers this Frenchman demanded an end to competition, but he did not seek a wholly new society. He called for political reform that would give the vote to the working class. Once so empowered, workers could use the vote to turn the political processes to their own economic advantage. A state controlled by a working class electorate would finance workshops to employ the poor. In time such workshops might replace private enterprise. Industry could be organized to ensure jobs. Blanc recognized the power of the state to improve life and the conditions of labor. It could become the great employer of labor.

ANARCHISTS. Other writers and activists of the forties, however, rejected both industry and the dominance of government. These were the anarchists. They are usually included in the socialist tradition although they do not exactly fit. Some favored programs of violence; others were peaceful. Auguste Blanqui (1805–1881) was a major spokesman for terror and was one of Europe's earliest professional revolutionaries. He spent most of his adult life in jail. Blanqui urged the development of a professional revolutionary vanguard to attack capitalist society. He sought the abolition of both capitalism and the state. His ideas for the new society were quite vague, but in his call for professional revolutionaries he foreshadowed Lenin.

Pierre Joseph Proudhon (1809–1865) represented the other strain of anarchism. In his most famous work, *What Is Property?* (1840), Proudhon attacked the banking system, which so rarely extended credit to small property owners or the poor. He wanted credit expanded to allow such people to engage in economic enterprise. Society should be organized on the basis of mutualism, which amounted to a system of small businesses. There would be peaceful cooperation and exchange of goods among these groups. With such a social system the state as it then existed would be unnecessary. His ideas later influenced the French labor movement, which generally avoided political activity.

Pierre Joseph Proudhon, here portrayed with his children by the French realist painter Gustave Courbet (1819–1877), was the most important French contributor to anarchist thought. [The Granger Collection.]

These various strains of early socialist thought provided the background and the context for the emergence of Marxist socialism. But they did more than that. They influenced the ideas and activities of European socialists and trade unions well into the third quarter of the century. Too often the history of socialism is regarded as a linear development leading naturally or necessarily to the triumph of Marxism. Nothing could be further from the truth. Marxism did eventually triumph over much though not all of Europe but only through competition with other socialist formulas. At mid-century the ideas of Karl Marx were simply one more contribution to a heady mixture of concepts and programs criticizing the emerging industrial society. Marxist ideology differed from its competitors in the brilliance of its author, its claim to rigorous scientific accuracy, and its message of the inevitable collapse of the capitalistic order.

Marxism

Karl Marx was born in 1818 in the Rhineland. His Jewish middle-class parents sent him to the University of Berlin, where he became deeply involved with Hegelian philosophy and radical politics. During 1842 and 1843 he edited the radical *Rhineland Gazette* (*Rheinische Zeitung*). Soon the German authorities drove him from his native land. He lived as an exile in Paris, then in Brussels, and finally after 1847 in London.

In 1844 Marx met Friedrich Engels (1820–1895), another young middle-class German, whose father owned a textile factory in Manchester, England. The next year Engels published *The Condition of the Working Class in England*, which presented a devastating picture of industrial life. The two men became fast friends. Late in 1847 they were asked to write a pamphlet for a newly organized and ultimately short-lived secret Communist League. *The Communist Manifesto*, published in German, appeared early in 1848. This work of less than fifty pages would become the most influential political document of modern European history, but that development lay in the future. At the time it was simply one more political

The socialist philosophy of Karl Marx eventually triumphed over most alternative versions of socialism in Europe—even though varying interpretations, criticisms, and revisions of his monumental work continue to today. [Bettmann Archive.]

tract. Moreover neither Marx nor his thought had any effect on the revolutionary events of 1848.

The major ideas of the *Manifesto* and of Marx's later work, including *Capital* (1867), were derived from German Hegelianism, French socialism, and British classical economics. Marx applied to social and economic development Hegel's concept that thought develops from the clash of thesis and antithesis into a new intellectual synthesis. For Marx the conflict between dominant and lesser social groups generated conditions that led to the emergence of a new dominant social group. These new social relationships in turn generated new discontent, conflict, and development.

The French socialists provided Marx with a portrayal of the evils of capitalist society and had raised the issue of property redistribution. Both Hegel and Saint-Simon had led Marx to see society and economic conditions as developing through historical stages. The classical economists

The title page of the *Manifesto of the Communist Party* (February 1848), by Marx and Engels, called for the proletariat of all lands to unite. Although written in German, the *Manifesto* was printed in London where there was no political censorship. [Culver Pictures.]

had produced the analytical tools for empirical, scientific examination of industrial capitalist society. Marx later explained to a friend:

> What I did that was new was to prove: (1) that the *existence of classes* is bound up with *particular historical phases in the development of production*; (2) that the class struggle necessarily leads to the *dictatorship of the proletariat*; (3) that this dictatorship itself only constitutes the transition to the *abolition of all classes and to a classless society*.[1]

In *The Communist Manifesto* Marx and Engels contended that human history must be understood rationally and as a whole. It is the record of humankind coming to grips with physical nature to produce the goods necessary for survival. That basic productive process determines the structures, values, and ideas of a society. The organization of the means of production have historically always involved conflict between the classes who owned and controlled the means of production and those classes who work for them. That necessary conflict has provided the engine for historical development; it is not an accidental by-product of mismanagement or bad intentions. Consequently piecemeal reforms cannot eliminate the social and economic evils that are inherent in the very structures of production. What is required is a radical social transformation. Such a revolution will occur as the inevitable outcome of the development of capitalism.

In Marx's and Engels's eyes, during the nineteenth century the class conflict that had characterized previous Western history had become simplified into a struggle between the bourgeoisie and the proletariat, or between the middle class and the workers. The character of capitalism ensured the sharpening of the struggle. Capitalist production and competition would steadily increase the

---

1 Albert Fried and Ronald Sanders (Eds.), *Socialist Thought: A Documentary History* (Garden City, N.Y.: Anchor Doubleday, 1964), p. 295.

size of the unpropertied proletariat. Large-scale mechanical production crushed both traditional and smaller industrial producers into the ranks of the proletariat. As the business structures grew larger and larger, smaller middle-class units would be squeezed out by the competitive pressures. Competition among the few remaining giant concerns would lead to more intense suffering on the part of the proletariat. As the workers suffered increasingly from the competition among the ever-enlarging firms, they would eventually begin to foment revolution and finally overthrow the few remaining owners of the means of production. For a time the workers would organize the means of production through a dictatorship of the proletariat, which would eventually give way to a propertyless and classless communist society.

This proletarian revolution was inevitable, according to Marx and Engels. The structure of capitalism required competition and consolidation of enterprise. Although the class conflict involved in the contemporary process resembled that of the past, it differed in one major respect. The struggle between the capitalistic bourgeoisie and the industrial proletariat would culminate in a wholly new society that would be free of class conflict. The victorious proletariat by its very nature could not be a new oppressor class: "The proletarian movement is the self-conscious, independent movement of the immense majority, in the interest of the immense majority." [2] The result of the proletarian victory would be "an association, in which the free development of each is the condition for the free development of all." [3] The victory of the proletariat over the bourgeoisie represented the culmination of human history. For the first time in human history one group of people would not be oppressing another.

Marx's analysis was conditioned by his own economic environment. The 1840s had been a period of much unemployment and deprivation. However, capitalism did not collapse as he predicted, nor did the middle class during the rest of the century become proletarianized. Rather, more and more people came to benefit from the industrial system. Nonetheless, within a generation Marxism had captured the imagination of many socialists and large segments of the working class. The doctrines were based on the empirical evidence of hard economic fact. This scientific aspect of Marxism helped the ideology as science became more influential during the second half of the century. Marx had made the ultimate victory of socialism seem certain. His writings had also portrayed for the first time the actual magnitude of the revolutionary transformation. Those works also suggested that the path to socialism lay with revolution rather than with reform. The days of the utopians were over.

Conservative Paternalism Reasserted

The socialists were not alone in their criticism of the liberal, capitalistic order. Many conservative Europeans also hated the atomistic view of society set forth by the classical economists and the liberal politicians. These conservatives saw that philosophy as undermining the influence of the aristocracy and the landowning classes. The middle-class concept of the poor was also at odds with the traditional Christian view of charity. These conservatives had much paternalistic sympathy for the working class. The writers who upheld this position were generally less brilliant than the liberals and the socialists. Their view of society had developed during the Romantic movement and harkened back to an idealized view of the Middle Ages. In many ways it was an obsolete view of social problems. However, their opinions permitted a temporary political alliance to be forged for a time between workers caught in the pressures of the labor market and spokesmen for political reaction.

England again provides important examples of this attitude. The movement to enact the first meaningful and enforceable factory legislation was led by Richard Oastler (1789–1861), Michael Sadler (1780–1835), and Lord Shaftesbury (1801–1885). These figures were conserva-

2 Robert C. Tucker (Ed.), *The Marx–Engels Reader* (New York: W. W. Norton, 1972), p. 344.

3 Ibid., p. 353.

Lord Shaftesbury (1801–1885) was one of the liberal Victorian philanthropists and reformers. He sought improvement in factory and mining conditions, a shorter working day, and better sanitation. The photograph was made about 1876. [The Granger Collection.]

tive politically and upheld the position of the church and the aristocracy. After attaining the Factory Act of 1833, Oastler led the Anti-Poor Law movement, which protested the stark utilitarian measures for the relief of the unemployed. In 1843 Lord Shaftesbury fought for the passage of the Mines Act, which removed women and children from appalling labor conditions beneath the earth. In 1847 Shaftesbury and Oastler were again active in the campaign for the Ten Hours Act, which limited the length of the workday.

Continental conservatives often adopted similar attitudes. In 1846 Joseph Maria von Radowitz (1797–1853) published *Contemporary Talks on State and Church,* in which he attacked competition. Conservatives used paternalistic social arguments against the demands of liberals for free trade and industrial development. The conservatives could pose as the protectors of the poor and the industrial classes. They favored the preservation of guilds, the regulation of industry, and the paternalistic relief of poverty. The price of such protection, however, was nonparticipation in politics by the industrial and rural working classes. For sometime the working classes were willing to accept that political cost because political liberals repeatedly ignored the social question.

March 23	Piedmont is defeated, and Charles Albert abdicates the crown of Piedmont in favor of Victor Emmanuel II.
March 27	The Frankfurt Parliament completes a constitution for Germany.
March 28	The Frankfurt Parliament elects Frederick William IV of Prussia to be emperor of Germany.
April 21	Frederick William IV of Prussia rejects the crown offered by the Frankfurt Parliament.
June 18	The remaining members of the Frankfurt Parliament are dispersed by troops.
July 3	Collapse of the Roman Republic after invasion by French troops.
August 9–13	The Hungarian forces are defeated by Austria aided by the troops of Russia.

1850

November 29	The Punctuation of Olmütz.

1851

December 2	*Coup d'état* of Louis Napoleon.

1848: Year of Revolutions

In 1848 a series of liberal and nationalistic revolutions spread across the Continent. No single factor caused this general revolutionary ground swell; rather, a number of similar conditions existed in several countries. Severe food shortages had prevailed since 1846. The harvests of grain and potatoes had been very poor. The famine in Ireland was simply the worst example of a more widespread situation. The commercial and industrial economy was also in a period of downturn. Unemployment was very widespread. All systems of poor relief were overburdened. These difficulties, added to the wretched living conditions in the cities, heightened the sense of frustration and discontent of the urban artisan and laboring classes.

However, the dynamic force for change in 1848 originated not with the working classes but with the political liberals, who were generally drawn from the middle classes. Throughout the Continent liberals were pushing for their program of more representative government, civil liberty, and an unregulated economic life. They had received much encouragement from the repeal of the English Corn Laws and the example of peaceful agitation by the Anti-Corn Law League. The liberals on the Continent wanted to pursue similar peaceful tactics. However, to put additional pressure on their governments, they began to appeal for the support of the urban working classes. The goals of the latter were improved working and economic conditions rather than a liberal framework of government. Moreover the tactics of the working classes were frequently violent rather than peaceful. The temporary alliance of liberals and workers in several states overthrew the old order; then the allies commenced to fight between themselves.

Finally, outside France nationalism was an important common factor in the uprisings. Germans, Hungarians, Italians, and smaller national groups in eastern Europe sought to create national states that would reorganize or replace existing political entities. The Austrian Empire was the state most profoundly endangered by nationalism. The nationalists were also frequently liberal and sometimes benefited from lower- and working-class economic discontent in the major cities.

The immediate results of the 1848 revolutions were quite stunning. The French monarchy fell, and many of the others were badly shaken. Never in a single year had

Conditions leading to revolutions in the 1820s and 1830s remained and by 1848 were fuelled by new nationalist and liberal political demands, as well as by severe economic conditions among the poor. Following Paris's lead, violence erupted in the centers shown here.

CENTERS OF REVOLUTION, 1848–1849

Europe known so many major uprisings. Yet the revolutions proved a false spring for progressive Europeans. Without exception they failed to establish new liberal or national states. The conservative order proved stronger and more resilient than anyone had expected. Moreover the liberal middle-class political malcontents in each country discovered that they could no longer push for political reform without at the same time raising the social question. The liberals refused to follow political revolution with social reform and thus isolated themselves from the working classes. Once separated from potential mass support, the liberal revolutions became an easy prey to the armies of the reactionary classes.

France: The Second Republic and Louis Napoleon

As twice before, the revolutionary tinder first blazed in Paris. The liberal political opponents of the corrupt regime of Louis Philippe and his minister Guizot had organized a series of political banquets. These occasions were used to criticize the government and to demand further middle-class admission to the political process. The poor harvests of 1846 and 1847 and the resulting high food prices and unemployment brought working-class support to the liberal campaign. On February 21, 1848, the government forbade further banquets. A very large one had been scheduled for the next day. On February 22 disgruntled Parisian workers paraded through the streets demanding reform and Guizot's ouster. The next morning the crowds grew, and by afternoon Guizot had resigned. Barricades had been erected, and numerous clashes had occurred between the citizenry and the mu-

nicipal guard. On February 24, 1848, Louis Philippe abdicated and fled to England.

The liberal opposition, led by the poet Alphonse de Lamartine (1790–1869), organized a provisional government. They intended to call an election for an assembly that would write a republican constitution. The various working-class groups in Paris had other ideas; they wanted a social as well as a political revolution. Led by Louis Blanc, they demanded representation in the Cabinet. Blanc and two other radical leaders were made ministers. Under their pressure the provisional government organized national workshops to provide work and relief for thousands of unemployed workers.

On Sunday, April 23, an election based on universal manhood suffrage chose the new National Assembly. The result was a legislature dominated by moderates and conservatives. In the French provinces there had been much resentment against the Paris radicals. The church and the local notables still exercised considerable influence. Small landowning peasants feared possible confiscation of their holdings by Parisian socialists. The new conservative National Assembly had little sympathy for the national workshops, which they incorrectly perceived to be socialistic. Throughout May government troops and the Parisian crowd of unemployed workers and artisans clashed. Late that month the assembly closed the workshops to new entrants and planned the removal of many enrolled workers. By the latter part of June barricades again appeared in Paris. On June 24, under orders from the government, General Cavaignac, with troops drawn largely from the conservative countryside, moved to destroy the barricades and to quell potential disturbances.

Paris Workers Complain About the Actions of their Government

In the late spring of 1848 the government of the recently formed French Republic abolished the national workshops that it had created a few weeks earlier to provide aid for the unemployed. The first selection below illustrates the anger caused by the abolition of the workshops and the sense of betrayal felt by the workers. The second document describes the experience of a cabinet-maker who had for a time enrolled in one of the workshops.

TO THE FINANCE MINISTER OF THE REPUBLIC

Are you really the man who was the first finance minister of the Republic, of the Republic won at the cost of blood thanks to the workers' courage, of this Republic whose first vow was to provide bread every day for all its children by proclaiming the universal right to work. Work, who will give it to us if not the state at a time when industry has everywhere closed its workshops, shops and factories? Yesterday martyrs for the Republic out on the barricades, today its defenders in the ranks of the national guard, the workers might consider it owed them something. . . .

Why do the national workshops so rouse your reprobation . . . ? You are not asking for their reform, but for their total abolition. But what is to be done with this mass of 110,000 workers who are waiting each day for their modest pay, for the means of existence for themselves and their families? Are they to be left a prey to the evil influences of hunger and of the excesses that follow in the wake of despair?

A LETTER TO A NEWSPAPER EDITOR

I live in the fauborg; by trade I am a cabinet-maker and I am enrolled in the national workshops, waiting for trade to pick up again.

I went into the workshops when I could no longer find bread elsewhere. Since then people have said we were given charity there. But when I went in I did not think that I was becoming a beggar. I believed that my brothers who were rich were giving me a little of what they had to spare simply because I was their brother.

I admit that I have not worked very hard in the national workshops, but then I have done what I could. I am too old now to change my trade easily—that is one explanation. But there is another: the fact is that, in the national workshops, there is absolutely nothing to do.

Roger Price (Ed. and Trans.), *1848 in France* (Ithaca, N.Y.: Cornell University Press, 1975), pp. 103–104.

During the next two days over four hundred people were killed. Thereafter troops hunted down another three thousand persons in street-to-street fighting. The drive for social revolution had come to an end.

The so-called June Days confirmed the political predominance of conservative property holders in French life. They wanted a republic, but a republic safe for small property. This search for social order received further confirmation late in 1848. The victor in the presidential election was Prince Louis Napoleon Bonaparte (1808–1873), a nephew of the great emperor. For most of his life he had been an adventurer living outside France. Twice he had unsuccessfully attempted to lead a *coup* against the July Monarchy. The disorder of 1848 provided him a new opportunity to enter the French political scene. After the corruption of Louis Philippe and the turmoil of the early months of the Second Republic, the voters turned to the name of Bonaparte as a source of stability and greatness.

The election of the "Little Napoleon" doomed the Second Republic. Louis Napoleon was dedicated to his own fame rather than to republican institutions. He was the first of the modern dictators who by playing upon unstable politics and social insecurity have so changed European life. He constantly quarreled with the National Assembly and claimed that he rather than they represented the will of the nation. In 1851 the assembly refused to amend the constitution to allow the president to succeed himself. Consequently, on December 2, 1851, the anniversary of the great Napoleon's victory at Austerlitz, Louis Napoleon seized personal power. Troops dispersed the assembly, and the president called for new elections. Over two hundred people died resisting the *coup*, and over twenty-six thousand persons were arrested. Yet in the plebiscite of December 21, 1851, over $7\frac{1}{2}$ million voters supported Louis Napoleon, who, as a result, became Emperor Napoleon III. Only about 600,000 opposed him. For the second time in just over fifty years France had turned from republicanism to caesarism.

In 1848 the populace of Paris erected barricades
at strategic points throughout the city to halt
the movement of troops used against revolutionaries.
This picture of one in the Montmartre section
purports to be by an eyewitness and appeared in a
London newspaper. [The Granger Collection.]

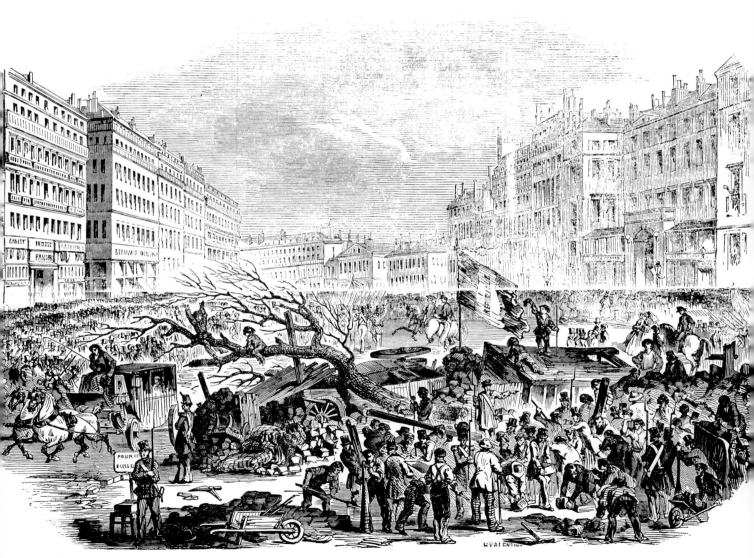

Economic Advance and Social Unrest (1830–1850)

De Tocqueville Analyzes the June Revolution in Paris

Alexis de Tocqueville (1805–1859) was a French liberal politician, historian, political scientist and also a keen social observer. By the time of the 1848 uprising in Paris he had lived two years in the United States in the 1830s; *Democracy in America* is still an important analysis of our early institutions. In this passage from his memoirs he describes the manner in which the conflict of the June Days of 1848 in Paris differed from earlier political upheavals in France. He understood that what had occurred was a mode of class warfare and that it might characterize European political life for many decades to come.

I COME *at last to the insurrection of June. . . .*

What distinguished it also, among all the events of this kind which have succeeded one another in France for sixty years, is that it did not aim at changing the form of government, but at altering the order of society. . . . It was not, strictly speaking, a political struggle, in the sense which until then we have given to the word, but a combat of class against class, a sort of Servile War. It represented the facts of the Revolution of February in the same manner as the theories of Socialism represented its ideas; or rather it issued naturally from these ideas, as a son does from his mother. We beheld in it nothing more than a blind and rude, but powerful, effort on the part of the workmen to escape from the necessities of their condition, which had been depicted to them as one of unlawful oppression, and to open up by main force a road towards that imaginary comfort with which they had been deluded. It was this mixture of greed and false theory which first gave birth to the insurrection and then made it so formidable. These poor people had been told that the wealth of the rich was in some way the produce of a theft practised upon themselves. They had been assured that the inequality of fortunes was as opposed to morality and the welfare of society as it was to nature. Prompted by their needs and their passions, many had believed this obscure and erroneous notion of right, which, mingled with brute force, imparted to the latter an energy, a tenacity and a power which it would never have possessed unaided.

It must be observed that this formidable insurrection was not the enterprise of a certain number of conspirators, but the revolt of one whole section of the population against another.

Alexis de Tocqueville, *Recollections*, trans. by A. T. de Mattos (New York: Macmillan, 1896), pp. 187–188.

The Hapsburg Empire: Nationalism Resisted

The events of February 1848 in Paris immediately reverberated throughout the Hapsburg domains. The empire was susceptible to revolutionary challenge on every score. Its government eschewed liberal institutions. Its geographical borders ignored the principle of nationalism. Its society perpetuated serfdom. During the forties even Metternich had urged reform, but none was forthcoming. In 1848 the regime confronted major rebellions in Vienna, Prague, Hungary, and Italy. It was also intimately involved in the disturbances that broke out in Germany.

The Hapsburg troubles commenced on March 3, 1848, when Louis Kossuth (1802–1894), a Hungarian Magyar nationalist, attacked Austrian domination of Hungary. He called for Hungarian independence and a responsible ministry under the Hapsburg crown. Ten days later, inspired by Kossuth's demands, students led a series of major disturbances in Vienna. The army failed to restore order. Metternich resigned and fled the country. The feeble-minded Emperor Ferdinand (1835–1848) promised a moderately liberal constitution. Unsatisfied, the radical students then formed democratic clubs to press the revolution further. On May 17 the emperor and the imperial court fled to Innsbruck. The government of Vienna at this point lay in the hands of a committee of over two hundred persons primarily concerned with alleviating the economic plight of Viennese workers.

What the Hapsburg government most feared was not the urban rebellions but rather a potential uprising of the serfs. Already there had been isolated instances of peasants invading manor houses and burning records. Almost immediately after the Vienna uprising the imperial government had emancipated the serfs in large areas of Austria. The Hungarian Diet also abolished serfdom in March 1848. These actions smothered the most serious potential threat to order in the empire. The emancipated serfs now had little reason to support the revolutionary movement in the cities.

Louis Kossuth, a Hungarian nationalist, helped to lead the revolution of 1848 in Budapest. The portrait was made the following year. [The Granger Collection.]

The Vienna revolt had given encouragement to the Hungarians. The leaders of the Hungarian March revolution were primarily liberal Magyars supported by Magyar nobles who wanted their aristocratic liberties guaranteed against the central government in Vienna. The Hungarian Diet passed a series of March Laws that ensured equality of religion, jury trials, the election of a lower chamber, a relatively free press, and payment of taxes by the nobility. Emperor Ferdinand approved these measures because in the spring of 1848 he was in a position to do little else.

The Hungarian Magyars also hoped to establish a separate Hungarian state within the Hapsburg domains. They would retain considerable local autonomy while Ferdinand remained their emperor. As part of this scheme for a partially independent state, the Hungarians attempted to annex Transylvania, Croatia, and other territories on the eastern border of the Hapsburg Empire. That policy of annexation would bring Romanians, Croatians, and Serbs under Magyar government. These national groups resisted the drive toward Magyarization. They believed that they had a better chance of maintaining their identity and self-interest under Hapsburg control. Consequently they turned against Hungary. In late March the Vienna government sent Baron Joseph Jellachich to aid the national groups who were rebelling against the rebellious Hungarians. By early September 1848 he was leading an invasion force against Hungary.

In the middle of March, 1848, with Vienna and Budapest in revolt, Czech nationalists had demanded that Bohemia, Moravia, and Silesia be permitted to constitute an autonomous Slavic state within the empire similar to that just constituted in Hungary. Conflict immediately developed, however, between the Czechs and the Germans living in these areas. The Czechs summoned a congress of the Slavs, which met in Prague during early

June. On June 12, the day the congress closed, a radical insurrection broke out in the city. General Alfred Windischgratz, whose wife had been killed by a stray bullet, moved his troops to repress the uprising. The local middle class was happy to see the radicals suppressed. The Germans in the area approved the smothering of Czech nationalism. The policy of divide and conquer had succeeded.

While confronting the Hungarian and Czech bids for autonomy, the Hapsburg government also faced war in northern Italy. A revolution commenced in Milan on March 18. Five days later the Austrian commander General Joseph Wenzel Radetzky retreated from the city. King Charles Albert of Piedmont (1831–1849), who wanted to expand the influence of his kingdom in the area, aided the rebels in Lombardy. The Austrian force faired badly until July, when Radetzky, reenforced by new troops, defeated Piedmont and suppressed the revolution. For the time being Austria had held its position in northern Italy.

Vienna and Hungary remained to be recaptured. In midsummer the emperor returned to the capital. A newly elected assembly was attempting to write a constitution. However, within the city the radicals continued to press for further concessions. The imperial government decided to reassert its control. When a new insurrection occurred in October, it was crushed by the imperial army, which bombarded Vienna. On December 2 Emperor Ferdinand abdicated in favor of his young nephew Francis Joseph (1848–1916). The real power now lay with Prince Felix Schwarzenberg (1800–1852), who intended to use the army with full force. On January 5, 1849, Budapest was occupied. By March the triumphant Austrian forces had imposed military rule over Hungary, and the new emperor repudiated the recent constitution. The Magyar nobles attempted one last revolt. It was crushed by Austrian troops reenforced by 200,000 soldiers happily furnished by Tsar Nicholas I of Russia. The imperial Hapsburg government had survived its gravest internal challenge because of the divisions among its

In this Dutch lithograph Pope Pius IX (1846–1878) is pictured as a vicious reactionary hiding behind the mask of the suffering Jesus. After 1848 the pope, who had once been thought liberal, followed a strongly reactionary policy in Italy and the Roman Catholic Church. [John R. Freeman.]

enemies and its own willingness to use military force with vengeance.

Italy: Republicanism Defeated

The brief Piedmont–Austrian war of 1848 marked only the first stage of the Italian revolution. Many Italians hoped that Piedmont would drive Austria from the peninsula and thus prepare the way for Italian unification. The defeat of Piedmont was a sharp disappointment. Liberal and nationalist hopes then shifted to the pope. Pius IX (1846–1878), who had become pope in 1846, had a liberal reputation. He had reformed the administration of the Papal States. Nationalists believed that some form of a united Italian state might emerge under the leadership of this pontiff.

In Rome, however, as in other cities, political radicalism was on the rise. On November 15, 1848, a democratic radical assassinated Count Pelligrino Rossi, the liberal minister of the Papal States. The next day popular demonstrations forced the pope to appoint a radical ministry. Shortly thereafter Pius IX fled to Naples for refuge. In February 1849 the radicals proclaimed the Roman Republic. Republican nationalists from all over Italy, including Giuseppe Mazzini (1805–1872) and Giuseppe Garibaldi (1807–1882), two of the most prominent nationalists, flocked to Rome. They hoped to use the new republic as a base of operations to unite the rest of the peninsula under a republican government.

In March 1849 radicals in Piedmont forced Charles Albert to renew the patriotic war against Austria. The almost immediate defeat at the battle of Novara gave the king an opportunity to abdicate in favor of his son, Victor Emmanuel II (1849–1878). The defeat of Piedmont meant that the Roman Republic must defend itself alone. The troops that attacked Rome and restored the pope came from France. The French wanted to prevent the rise of a strong, unified state on their southern border. Moreover protection of the pope was good domestic politics for the French Republic and its president, Louis Napoleon. In early June 1849 ten thousand French sol-

diers laid siege to the Eternal City. By the end of the month the Roman Republic had dissolved. Garibaldi attempted to lead an army north against Austria but was defeated. On July 3 Rome fell to the French forces, which continued to occupy it as protection for the pope until 1870. Pius IX returned, having renounced his previous liberalism. He became one of the archconservatives of the next quarter century. Leadership toward Italian unification would have to come from another direction.

Germany: Liberalism Frustrated

The revolutionary contagion had also spread rapidly through numerous states of Germany. Württemberg, Saxony, Hanover, and Bavaria all experienced insurrections calling for liberal government and greater German unity. The major revolution, however, occurred in Prussia. By March 15, 1848, large popular disturbances had erupted in Berlin. Frederick William IV (1840–1861), believing that the trouble stemmed from foreign conspirators, refused to turn his troops on the Berliners. He even announced certain limited reforms. Nevertheless, on March 18, several citizens were killed when troops cleared a square near the palace. The next day Frederick

King Frederick William IV of Prussia (1840–1861) disappointed the hopes of German nationalists by refusing to accept the crown of a united Germany offered by the Frankfurt Parliament. His portrait is by Franz Krüger. [Bildarchiv Preussischer Kulturbesitz.]

William IV was forced to salute the corpses of his slain subjects. He made further concessions and implied that henceforth Prussia would aid the movement toward German unification. The king also called for a Prussian constituent assembly to write a constitution. For all practical purposes the Prussian monarchy had capitulated.

Frederick William IV appointed a cabinet headed by David Hansemann (1790–1864), a widely respected moderate liberal. However, the Prussian constituent assembly proved to be radical and democratic. As time passed, the king and his conservative supporters decided that they would ignore the assembly. The liberal ministry resigned and was replaced by a conservative one. In April 1849 the assembly was dissolved, and the monarch proclaimed his own constitution. One of its key elements was a system of three-class voting. All adult males were allowed to vote. However, they voted according to three classes arranged by ability to pay taxes. Thus the largest taxpayers, who constituted only about 5 per cent of the population, elected one third of the Prussian Parliament. This system prevailed in Prussia until 1918. In the finally revised Prussian constitution of 1850, the ministry was responsible to the king alone. Moreover, the Prussian army and officer corps swore loyalty directly to the monarch.

While Prussia had moved from revolution to reaction, other events had unfolded in Germany as a whole. On May 18, 1848, representatives from all the German states had gathered in St. Paul's Church in Frankfurt to revise the organization of the German Confederation. The Frankfurt Parliament intended to write a moderately liberal constitution for a united Germany. The liberal character of the Frankfurt Parliament alienated both German conservatives and the German working class. The offense to the conservatives was simply the challenge to the existing political order. The Frankfurt Parliament lost the support of the industrial workers and artisans by refusing to restore the protection once afforded by the guilds. The liberals were too much attached to the concept of a free labor market to offer meaningful legislation to workers. This failure marked the beginning of a profound split between German liberals and the German working class. For the rest of the century German conservatives would be able to play upon that division.

As if to demonstrate its disaffection from workers, the Frankfurt Parliament in September, 1848, called in troops of the German Confederation to suppress a radical insurrection in the city. The liberals in the parliament wanted nothing to do with workers who erected barricades and threatened the safety of property.

The Frankfurt Parliament floundered on the issue of unification as well as upon the social question. Members differed over the inclusion of Austria in the projected united Germany. The large German (*grossdeutsch*) solution favored inclusion while the small German (*kleindeutsch*) solution advocated exclusion. The latter formula prevailed because Austria rejected the whole notion of German unification. It raised too many other nationality problems within the Hapsburg domains. Consequently the Frankfurt Parliament looked to Prussian leadership. On March 27, 1849, the parliament produced its constitution. Shortly thereafter its delegates offered the crown of a united Germany to Federick William IV of Prussia. He rejected the offer, asserting that kings ruled by the grace of God rather than by the wisdom of man-made constitutions. Upon his refusal the Frankfurt Parliament began to dissolve. Not long afterwards troops drove off the remaining members.

German liberals never fully recovered from this defeat. The Frankfurt Parliament had alienated the artisans and the working class without gaining any compensating support from the conservatives. The liberals had proved themselves to be awkward, hesitant, unrealistic, and ultimately dependent on the armies of the monarchies. They

The Frankfurt Parliament met in a church in that city in September 1848. Its deputies wanted to create a liberal, united Germany. However, as their debates dragged out, the forces of reaction regained strength and the parliament failed. [Bettmann Archive.]

had failed to unite Germany or to confront effectively the realities of political power in the German states. What was achieved through the various revolutions was an extension of the franchise in some of the German states and the establishment of conservative constitutions. The gains were not negligible, but they were a far cry from the hopes of March 1848.

The events of 1848 and 1849 had one important footnote for Frederick William IV. He gave much more thought to possible German unification under Prussia. In 1850 he attempted to create a German federation, which would have been a union of princes headed by the king of Prussia and excluding Austria. The Austrian Empire firmly rejected the proposal, which would have diminished Hapsburg influence in Germany. In November 1850, in what is known as the Punctuation of Olmütz, the Prussian monarch renounced his scheme at the demand of Austria. Prussian historians later called this event the Humiliation of Olmütz.

The turmoil of 1848 through 1850 brought to a close the era of liberal revolution that had begun in 1789. Liberals and nationalists had discovered that rational argument and small insurrections would not achieve their goals. The political initiative passed for a time to the conservative political groups. Nationalists henceforth were less romantic and more hardheaded. Railways, commerce, guns, soldiers, and devious diplomacy rather than language and cultural heritage became the weapons of national unification. The working class also adopted new tactics and organization. The day of the riot and urban insurrection were coming to a close. In the future, workers would turn to trade unions and political parties to achieve their political and social goals. Perhaps most important, after 1848 the European middle class ceased to be revolutionary. It became increasingly concerned about the protection of its property against radical political and social movements. The middle class remained politically liberal only so long as liberalism seemed to promise economic stability and social security for its own style of life.

Schurz Explains the Failure of the Frankfurt Parliament

Carl Schurz (1829–1906) was a German liberal who had witnessed and daringly participated in the uprisings of 1848 while still a student. He later moved to the United States, became a citizen, entered politics in Wisconsin, and served as a diplomat, Union Army general, cabinet member, senator from Missouri, and journalist. In his memoirs he attempted to explain why the German Frankfurt Parliament had been unable to provide Germany with a viable constitution and national unity. The Parliament had possessed no bureaucracy or military forces of its own, and its members had missed the opportunity to move rapidly to achieve their goals. By prolonging debate, the Parliament gave its opponents time to organize and permitted divisions to develop in its own ranks and in those of its supporters.

FACE *to face with the princes and their parties stood the national parliament in Frankfurt, that child of the revolution which might then have almost been called the orphan of the revolution. It had at its immediate disposal no administrative machinery, no army, no treasury, only its moral authority; all the rest was in the hands of the different German state governments. The only power of the national parliament consisted in the will of the people; and this power was sufficient for the fulfillment of its mission so long as the will of the people proved itself strong enough, even through revolutionary action in case of necessity, to counteract the adverse interests of the princes. The Parliament would have been sure of success in creating a constitutional German Empire, if it had performed that task quickly and elected and put into office its Kaiser while the revolutionary prestige of the people was still unbroken. . . .*

But that Parliament was laboring under an overabundance of learning and virtue and under a want of . . . political experience and sagacity. . . . The world has probably never seen a political assembly that contained a larger number of noble, learned, conscientious and patriotic men. . . . But it did not possess the genius that promptly discerns opportunity and with quick resolution takes fortune by the forelock; it was not mindful of the fact that in time of great commotion the history of the world does not wait for the theoretical thinker. And thus it failed.

The Reminiscences of Carl Schurz (New York: The McClure Company, 1907), Vol. 1, pp. 162–163.

SUGGESTED READINGS

S. Avineri, *The Social and Political Thought of Karl Marx* (1969). An advanced treatment.

I. Berlin, *Karl Marx: His Life and Environment* (1948). An excellent introduction.

A. Briggs (Ed.), *Chartist Studies* (1959). An anthology of significant studies.

S. G. Checkland, *The Rise of Industrial Society in England, 1815–1885* (1964). Strong on economic institutions.

G. D. H. Cole, *A History of Socialist Thought,* 5 vols. (1953–1960). An essential work that spans the entire nineteenth century.

G. Duveau, *The Making of a Revolution* (trans., 1968). A lively book that explores the attitudes of the various French social classes.

E. Halevy, *The Growth of Philosophic Radicalism* (1928). The basic discussion of utilitarianism.

T. Hamerow, *Restoration, Revolution, and Reaction: Economics and Politics in Germany, 1815–1871* (1958). Traces the forces that worked toward the failure of revolution in Germany.

J. F. C. Harrison, *Quest for the New Moral World: Robert Owen and the Owenites in Britain and America* (1969).

R. Heilbroner, *The Wordly Philosophers,* rev. ed. (1972). A useful, elementary introduction to nineteenth-century economic thought.

W. O. Henderson, *The Industrialization of Europe, 1780–1914* (1969). Emphasizes the Continent.

D. Landes, *The Unbound Prometheus: Technological Change and Industrial Development in Western Europe from 1750 to the Present* (1969). The best one-volume treatment of technological development in a broad social and economic context.

W. L. Langer, *Political and Social Upheaval, 1832–1852* (1969). A remarkably thorough survey strong in both social and intellectual history as well as political narrative.

F. Manuel, *The Prophets of Paris* (1962). A stimulating treatment of French utopian socialism and social reform.

H. Perkin, *The Origins of Modern English Society, 1780–1880* (1969). A provocative attempt to look at the society as a whole.

P. Robertson, *Revolutions of 1848: A Social History* (1952). Covers the developments in each nation.

P. Stearns, *Eighteen Forty Eight: The Tide of Revolution in Europe* (1974). A good discussion of the social background.

A. J. Taylor (Ed.), *The Standard of Living in Britain in the Industrial Revolution* (1975). A collection of major articles on the impact of industrialism.

E. P. Thompson, *The Making of the English Working Class* (1964). An important, influential, and controversial work.

704

27
The Age of Nation States

THE REVOLUTIONS of 1848 collapsed in defeat for both liberalism and nationalism. Throughout the early fifties authoritarian regimes entrenched themselves across the Continent. Yet only a quarter century later many of the major goals of early nineteenth-century liberals and nationalists stood accomplished. Italy and Germany were at long last united under constitutional monarchies. The Hapsburg emperor had accepted constitutional government; the Hungarian Magyars had attained recognition of their liberties. In Russia the serfs had been emancipated. France was again a republic. Liberalism and even democracy flourished in Great Britain.

Paradoxically, most of these developments occurred under the direction and leadership of conservative statesmen. Events within European international affairs compelled some of them to pursue new policies at home as well as abroad. They had to find novel methods of maintaining the loyalty of their subjects. In some cases conservative leaders preferred to carry out a popular policy on their own terms so that they rather than the liberals would receive credit. Finally, some political leaders moved as they did because they had no choice.

The Crimean War (1854–1856)

As has so often been true in modern European history, the impetus for change originated in war. The Crimean War (1854–1856) was rooted in the longstanding rivalry

The Victor Emmanuel Monument in Rome (completed 1911) honors the king under whose rule Italy was united. The massiveness of the grandiose structure may well have reminded some people that the large-scale nation-state had become the most important political institution of modern times. Note the contrasting ruined splendor of ancient Rome in the foreground—Emperor Trajan's forum and column. [Italian Government Travel Office, New York.]

between Russia and the Ottoman Empire. Russia wanted to extend its control over the provinces of Moldavia and Walachia (now in Romania). The tsar's duty to protect Orthodox Christians in the empire furnished the pretext for Russian aggression. The Ottoman Empire had recently granted Catholic France rather than Orthodox Russia oversight of shrines in the Holy Land. Russia occupied the provinces in the summer of 1853, and the other great powers soon became involved. Both France and Great Britain opposed Russian expansion in the eastern Mediterranean, where they had extensive naval and commercial interests. Napoleon III also thought that an activist foreign policy would shore up domestic support for his regime. On March 28, 1854, France and Britain declared war on Russia. Much to the chagrin of Tsar Nicholas I, Austria and Prussia remained neutral. The Austrians had their own ambitions in the Balkans, and Prussia after the Humiliation of Olmütz followed in the Austrian train.

The war was ineptly waged on both sides. The ill-equipped and poorly commanded armies became bogged down along the Crimean coast of the Black Sea. In September 1855, after a long siege, the Russian fortress of Sevastopol finally fell. In March 1856 the peace conference in Paris concluded a treaty highly unfavorable to Russia. It was required to surrender territory near the mouth of the Danube River, to recognize the neutrality of the Black Sea, and to renounce claims of protection over Christians in the Ottoman Empire. Even before the conference Austria had forced Russia to withdraw from Moldavia and Walachia. The image of an invincible Russia that had prevailed across Europe since the close of the Napoleonic wars was totally shattered.

Also shattered was the Concert of Europe as a means of dealing with international relations on the Continent. There was much less fear of revolution than in the early part of the century and consequently much less reverence for the Vienna settlement. As Gordon Craig has commented, "After 1856 there were more powers willing to fight to overthrow the existing order than there were to

Florence Nightingale (1820–1910) was a strong-willed English nurse who organized hospitals for English troops during the Crimean War and left an indelible influence on nursing as a profession. [The Granger Collection.]

take up arms to defend it."[1] Louis Napoleon had little respect for the Congress of Vienna and favored redrawing the map along lines of nationality. The Austrians hoped to compensate for the poor figure they had cut during the conflict by asserting more influence within the German Confederation. Prussia became increasingly discontented with a role in Germany subordinate to Austria's. Russia, who had been among the chief defenders of the Vienna settlement, now sought to overcome the disgrace of the 1856 Treaty of Paris. The mediocre display of British military prowess led that nation to hesitate about future continental involvement.

Consequently, for about twenty-five years after the Crimean War instability prevailed in European affairs. It allowed a largely unchecked adventurism in foreign policy. Without the restraining influence of the Concert of Europe, each nation believed that only the limits of its military power and diplomatic influence should act as constraints on its international ambitions. Moreover, foreign policy increasingly became an instrument of domestic policy. The two most significant achievements to result from this new international situation were the unifications of Italy and Germany. Those events in turn generated further pressures on neighboring countries.

Italian Unification

Nationalists had long wanted the small, absolutist principalities of the Italian peninsula united into a single state. However, during the first half of the century there had existed broad differences of opinion about the manner and goals of unification.

One approach to the issue had been that of romantic republicans. After the Congress of Vienna numerous secret republican societies were founded, the most famous of which was the *Carbonari*. They were singularly ineffective.

Following the failure of nationalist uprisings in 1831, the leadership of romantic republican nationalism passed to Giuseppe Mazzini (1805–1872). He became the most important nationalist leader in all Europe and brought to the cause of nationalism new emotional fervor. He once declared, "Nationality is the role assigned by God to a people in the work of humanity. It is its mission, its task on earth, to the end that God's thought may be realized in the world."[2] In 1831 he founded the Young Italy Society for the purposes of driving Austria from the peninsula and establishing an Italian republic. During the thirties and forties Mazzini and fellow republican Giuseppe Garibaldi (1807–1882) led insurrections. Both were deeply involved in the ill-fated Roman Republic of 1849. Throughout the next decade they continued to conduct what amounted to guerrilla warfare. Because both men spent much time in exile, they became well known across the Continent and in the United States.

Republican nationalism frightened the more moderate Italians, who wanted to rid themselves of Austrian domination but not at the cost of establishing a republic. For a time these people had looked to the pope as a possible vehicle for unification. That solution became impossible after the experience of Pius IX with the Roman Republic in 1849. Consequently, at mid-century "Italy" remained a geographical expression rather than a political entity. However, between 1854 and 1860 the area was transformed into a national state. The process was carried out not by Romantic republican nationalists but rather by Count Camillo Cavour (1810–1861), the moderately liberal and almost conservative prime minister of Piedmont. The method of unification was that of force of

1 *The New Cambridge Modern History*, Vol. 10 (Cambridge: Cambridge University Press, 1967), p. 273.

2 Quoted in William L. Langer, *Political and Social Upheaval, 1832–1852* (New York: Harper Torchbook, 1969), p. 115.

LEFT: Giuseppe Mazzini supported the cause of Italian unification with both pen and sword. His books and articles were widely read in nationalist circles. He also led guerilla bands of Italian nationalists against the petty princes of the Italian peninsula before unification. [The Granger Collection.]

LEFT BELOW: Garibaldi represented the popular forces of romantic Italian nationalism more than did anyone else. The landing of his Redshirts on Sicily and their subsequent invasion of southern Italy in 1860 forced Cavour to unite the entire peninsula sooner than he had intended. [Culver Pictures.]

BELOW: Cavour was the moderately liberal prime minister of the Kingdom of Piedmont. He was determined to make the idea of a united Italy respectable and acceptable to the rest of Europe. [Culver Pictures.]

arms tied to secret diplomacy. The spirit of Machiavelli must have smiled over the enterprise.

Cavour's Policy

Piedmont, in northwestern Italy, was the most independent state on the peninsula. The kingdom had been restored by the Congress of Vienna as a buffer between French and Austrian ambitions in the area. As we have seen, during 1848 and 1849 King Charles Albert, after having promulgated a conservative constitution, twice unsuccessfully fought Austria. Following the second defeat, he abdicated in favor of his son, Victor Emmanuel II. In 1852 the new monarch chose as his prime minister Count Camillo Cavour. This cunning statesman had begun political life as a strong conservative but had gradually moved toward a moderately liberal position. He made a personal fortune by investing in railroads, re-

forming agricultural methods on his own estates, and editing a newspaper. He was deeply embued with the ideas of the Enlightenment, classical economics, and utilitarianism. Cavour was a nationalist of a new breed who had no respect for Mazzini's ideals. A strong monarchist, Cavour rejected republicanism. It was economic and material progress rather than romantic ideals that required a large, unified state on the Italian peninsula.

Cavour believed that if Italians proved themselves to be efficient and economically progressive, the great powers might decide that Italy could govern itself. He joined the Piedmontese Cabinet in 1850 and became premier two years later. He worked for free trade, railway construction, credit expansion, and agricultural improvement. He felt that such material and economic bonds rather than fuzzy romantic yearnings must unite Italians. However, Cavour also recognized the need to capture the loyalties of the Italians who possessed other varieties of nationalistic feelings. To that end, he fostered the Nationalist Society, which established chapters in other Italian states to press for unification under the leadership of Piedmont. Finally, the prime minister believed that Italy could be unified only with the aid of France. The recent accession of Napoleon III in France seemed to open the way for such aid at some time in the future.

Cavour used the outbreak of the Crimean War to enter the larger European picture. In 1855 Piedmont joined the conflict on the side of France and Britain and sent ten thousand troops to the front. This small but significant participation in the war allowed Cavour to raise the Italian question at the Paris conference. He left Paris with no diplomatic reward, but he had impressed everyone with his intelligence and political capacity. Cavour also gained the sympathy of Napoleon III. During the rest of the decade Cavour achieved further international respectability for Piedmont by opposing various plots of Mazzini, who was still attempting to lead nationalist uprisings. By the close of the decade Cavour represented a moderate, conservatively liberal alternative to both republicanism and reactionary absolutism in Italy.

The Piedmontese prime minister continued to bide his time. Then in January 1858 an Italian named Orsini attempted to assassinate Napoleon III. The incident made the French emperor, who had once belonged to a nationalist group, newly aware of the Italian issue. He began to fancy himself as continuing his more famous uncle's liberation of the peninsula. He also saw Piedmont as a potential ally against Austria. In July 1858 Cavour and Napoleon III met at Plombiers. Riding alone in a carriage, with the emperor at the reins, the two men plotted

Cavour Explains Why Piedmont Should Enter the Crimean War

As Prime Minister of Piedmont, Cavour attempted to prove that Italians were capable of progressive government. In 1855 he urged entry into the Crimean War so that Europeans would also consider Piedmont a military power. Earlier politics in Italy had been characterized by petty absolute princes and romantic nationalist conspiracies, both of which Cavour scorned. He understood that in the nineteenth century a nation must possess good government, economic prosperity, and a strong army.

THE *experience of recent years and previous centuries has proved (at least in my opinion) how little Italy has benefited by conspiracies, revolutions and disorderly uprisings. Far from helping her, they have been a tremendous calamity for this beautiful part of Europe. And not only, gentlemen, because individual people so often suffered from them, not only because revolutions became the cause or pretext for repression, but above all because continual conspiracies, repeated revolutions and disorderly uprisings damaged the esteem and, up to a certain point, the sympathy that other European peoples cherished for Italy.*

Now, gentlemen, I believe that the principal condition for the improvement of Italy's fate, the condition that stands out above all others, is to lift up her reputation once more, so to act that all the peoples of the world, those governing and those governed, may do justice to her qualities. And for this two things are necessary: first, to prove to Europe that Italy has sufficient civic sense to govern herself freely and according to law, and that she is in a condition to adopt the very best forms of government; second, to prove that her military valor is as great as that of her ancestors.

You [the Parliament of Piedmont] have done Italy one service by your conduct over the last seven years. You have shown Europe in the most luminous way that Italians are capable of governing themselves with wisdom, prudence, and trustworthiness. But it still remains for you to do Italy an equal, if not a greater, service; it is our country's task to prove that Italy's sons can fight valiantly on battlefields where glory is to be won. And I am sure, gentlemen, that the laurels that our soldiers will win in Eastern Europe will help the future state of Italy more than all that has been done by those people who hoped to regenerate her by rhetorical speeches and writings.

Denis Mack Smith (Ed. and Trans.), *The Making of Italy, 1796–1870* (New York: Walker and Company, 1968), pp. 199–200.

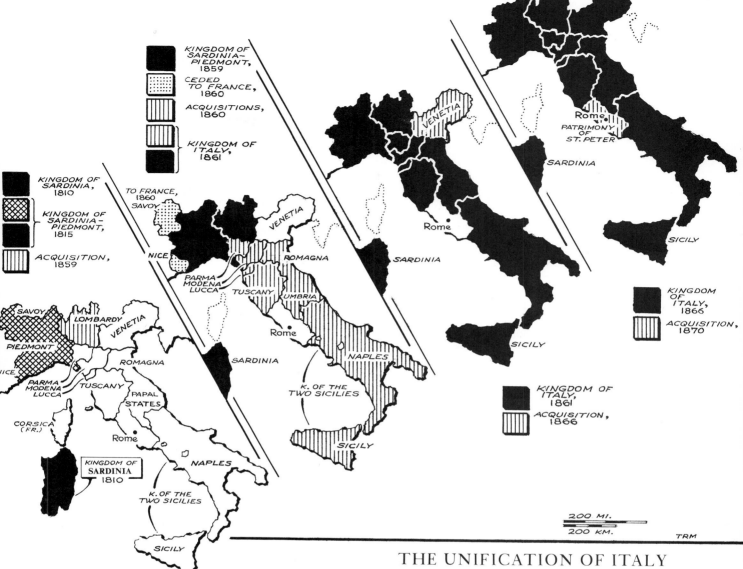

KINGDOM OF SARDINIA-PIEDMONT, 1859
CEDED TO FRANCE, 1860
ACQUISITIONS, 1860
KINGDOM OF ITALY, 1861

KINGDOM OF SARDINIA, 1810
KINGDOM OF SARDINIA-PIEDMONT, 1815
ACQUISITION, 1859

KINGDOM OF ITALY, 1866
ACQUISITION, 1870

KINGDOM OF ITALY, 1861
ACQUISITION, 1866

SAVOY LOMBARDY VENETIA
PIEDMONT
NICE PARMA MODENA LUCCA ROMAGNA TUSCANY
CORSICA (FR.) PAPAL STATES
Rome
KINGDOM OF SARDINIA 1810
NAPLES
K. OF THE TWO SICILIES
SICILY

TO FRANCE, 1860 SAVOY
NICE PARMA MODENA LUCCA VENETIA
ROMAGNA TUSCANY UMBRIA
Rome SARDINIA
NAPLES
K. OF THE TWO SICILIES
SICILY

VENETIA
Rome
SARDINIA
SICILY

Rome
PATRIMONY OF ST. PETER
SARDINIA
SICILY

200 MI.
200 KM.
TRM

THE UNIFICATION OF ITALY

Beginning with the association of Sardinia and Piedmont by the Congress of Vienna in 1815, unification was achieved through the expansion of Piedmont between 1859 and 1870. Both Cavour's statesmanship and the campaigns of ardent nationalists played large roles.

to provoke a war in Italy that would permit their two nations to intervene against Austria. A formal treaty in December 1858 confirmed the agreement. France was to receive Nice and Savoy for its aid.

During the winter and spring of 1859 tension grew between Austria and Piedmont as the latter country mobilized its army. On April 22 Austria presented Piedmont with an ultimatum ordering a halt to mobilization. That demand provided sufficient grounds to claim that Austria was provoking a war. France intervened to aid its ally. On June 4 the Austrians were defeated at Magenta and on June 24 at Solferino. In the meantime revolutions had broken out in Tuscany, Modena, Parma, and Romagna. With the Austrians in retreat and the new revo-

lutionary states calling for union with Piedmont, Napoleon III feared too extensive a Piedmontese victory. On July 11 he independently concluded a peace with Austria at Villafranca. Piedmont received Lombardy, but Venetia remained under Austrian control. Cavour felt betrayed by France, but nonetheless Austria had been driven from most of northern Italy. Later that summer Parma, Modena, Tuscany, and Romagna voted to unify with Piedmont.

Italian Unification 709

At this point the forces of romantic republican nationalism entered the picture and compelled Cavour to pursue complete unification of northern and southern Italy. In May 1860 Garibaldi landed in Sicily with more than a thousand troops, who had been outfitted in the north. He captured Palermo and prepared to attack the mainland. By September the city and kingdom of Naples, probably the most corrupt example of Italian absolutism, lay under Garibaldi's control. The popular leader had for over two decades hoped to form a republican Italy, but Cavour moved to forestall that possibility. He rushed Piedmontese troops south to confront Garibaldi. On the way they conquered the Papal States. Garibaldi's nationalism won out over his republicanism, and he unhappily accepted the Piedmontese domination. In late 1860 the southern Italian states joined the northern union forged by Piedmont.

The New Italian State

In March 1861 Victor Emmanuel II was proclaimed king of Italy. Three months later Cavour died. The new state more than ever needed his skills because Italy had in effect been more nearly conquered than united by Piedmont. Republicans resented the treatment of Garibaldi. Clericals resented the conquest of the Papal States. In the south armed resistance continued until 1866 against the intrusion of Piedmontese administration. The economies of the two areas were incompatible. The south was rural, poor, and backward. In the north industrialism was under way. The social structures reflected those differences.

The political framework of the united Italy did little to help overcome the problems. The constitution, which was that promulgated for Piedmont in 1848, provided for a rather conservative constitutional monarchy. The Senate was appointed, and the Chamber of Deputies was elected on a very narrow franchise. Ministers were responsible to the monarch. These arrangements did not foster a vigorous parliamentary life. The major problems of the nation were often simply avoided by the political leaders. In place of efficient, progressive government such

as Cavour had brought to Piedmont, a system of *transformiso* developed. This process meant the transformation of political opponents into government supporters through bribery and favors. Italian politics became a byword for corruption.

There also remained territories that many Italians believed should be added to their nation. The most important of these were Venetia and Rome. The former was gained in 1866 as one result of the Austro-Prussian War. Rome and the papacy continued to be guarded by French troops, first sent there in 1849, until the Franco-Prussian War of 1870 forced the withdrawal of the garrison. The Italian state then annexed Rome and transferred the capital there from Florence. By 1870 only the small territories of Trent and Trieste remained outside the state. In and of themselves these areas were not important, but they served to fuel the continued hostility of Italian patriots toward Austria. The desire to bring *Italia Irredenta* or "Unredeemed Italy" into the nation was one reason for the Italian support of the Allies against Austria and Germany in 1915. The papacy continued to remain at odds with the new secular state until the Lateran Accord of 1929.

German Unification

The construction of a united German nation was the single most important political development in Europe between 1848 and 1914. It transformed the balance of economic, military, and international power. Moreover, the character of the united German state was largely determined by the method of its creation. Germany was united by the conservative army, monarchy, and prime minister of Prussia among whose chief motives was the outflanking of Prussian liberals. The goal of a unified Germany sought for two generations by German liberals was actually achieved for the most illiberal of reasons.

During the 1850s German unification still seemed very far away. The major states continued to trade with each other through the *Zollverein,* and railways linked the

Bismarck was the most influential German and European statesman of the last half of the nineteenth century. [Culver Pictures.]

various economic regions. However, Frederick William IV of Prussia had given up his short-lived thoughts of unification under Prussian leadership. Austria continued to oppose any mode of closer union that might lessen its influence. Liberal nationalists had not recovered from the humiliating experiences of 1848 and 1849. What modified this situation rather quickly was a series of domestic political changes and problems within Prussia.

In 1858 Frederick William IV was adjudged insane, and his brother William assumed the regency. William I (1861–1888), who became king in his own right in 1861, was less of an idealist than his brother and rather more of a Prussian patriot. In the highest tradition of the Hohenzollern dynasty his first concern was for the strength of the Prussian army. In 1860 his war minister and chief of staff proposed to enlarge the army, to increase the number of officers, and to extend the period of conscription from two to three years. The Prussian Parliament, created by the Constitution of 1850, refused to approve the taxes necessary for the military expansion. The liberals, who dominated the body, did not wish to place so much additional power in the hands of the monarchy. A deadlock continued for two years between the monarch and the Parliament.

Bismarck

In September 1862 William I turned for help to the person who more than any other single individual shaped the next thirty years of European history: Otto von Bismarck (1815–1898). Born in 1815, Bismarck came from *Junker* stock. He attended the university, joined a *Burschenschaft,* and had for a time taken an interest in German unification. Then he retired to his father's estate. During the forties he had been elected to the local provincial diet. At the time of the revolutions of 1848 his stand was so reactionary as to disturb even the king and the leading state ministers. Yet he had made his mark. From 1851 to 1859 Bismarck was the Prussian minister to the Frankfurt Diet of the German Confederation. Later he served as Prussian ambassador to St. Petersburg.

Just before William I called him to become prime minister of Prussia, Bismarck had been transferred to the post of ambassador to Paris.

Although Bismarck entered public life as a reactionary, he had mellowed into a conservative. He opposed parliamentary government but not constitutionalism that provided a strong monarch. His origins were those of a *Junker,* but he understood that Prussia—and later, Germany—must have a strong industrial base. He was a strong Prussian patriot. His years in Frankfurt arguing with his Austrian counterpart had only hardened that patriotism. In politics he was a pragmatist who put more trust in power and action than in ideas. As he declared in his first speech as prime minister, "Germany is not looking to Prussia's liberalism but to her power. . . . The great questions of the day will not be decided by speeches and majority decisions—that was the mistake of 1848–1849—but by iron and blood."[3] Yet this same minister, after having led Prussia into three wars, spent the next nineteen years seeking to ensure peace.

After being appointed prime minister in 1862, Bismarck immediately moved against the liberal Parliament. He contended that in the absence of new levies the Prussian constitution permitted the government to carry out its functions on the basis of previously granted taxes. Therefore taxes could be collected and spent despite the parliamentary refusal to vote them. The army and most of the bureaucracy supported this outrageous interpretation of the constitution. However, in 1863 new elections

3 Quoted in Otto Pflanze, *Bismarck and the Development of Germany: The Period of Unification: 1815–1871* (Princeton: Princeton University Press, 1963), p. 177.

THE UNIFICATION OF GERMANY

Under Bismarck's leadership, and with the strong support of its royal house, Prussia used most of the available diplomatic and military means, on both the German and international stages, to force the unification of German states into a strong national entity.

sustained the liberal majority in the Parliament. Bismarck had to find some way to attract popular support away from the liberals and toward the monarchy and the army. To that end Bismarck set about uniting Germany through the conservative institutions of Prussia. The tactic amounted to diverting public attention from domestic matters to foreign affairs.

THE DANISH WAR (1864). Bismarck pursued a *kleindeutsch* or small German solution to the question of unification. Austria was to be excluded from German affairs. This maneuver required highly complex diplomacy. The Schleswig–Holstein problem provided the handle for Bismarck's policy. These two duchies had long been administered by Denmark without being incorpo-

rated into that kingdom. Their populations were a mixture of Germans and Danes. Holstein, where Germans predominated, belonged to the German Confederation. In 1863 the Danes moved to annex both duchies. The smaller states of the German Confederation proposed an all-German war to halt the annexation. Bismarck wanted Prussia to act alone or only in cooperation with Austria. Together the two large states defeated Denmark in a short war in 1864. They took over the joint administration of the provinces.

The Danish defeat gave Bismarck new personal prestige. The joint holding of the duchies allowed him to prod Austria into war with Prussia. In August 1865 the two powers negotiated the Convention of Gastein, which put Austria in charge of Holstein and Prussia in charge of Schleswig. Bismarck then moved to mend other diplomatic fences. He had gained Russian sympathy by supporting the 1863 suppression of the Polish revolt. Conversations with Napoleon III achieved promises of neutrality in case of an Austro-Prussian conflict. In April 1866 Bismarck concluded a treaty with Italy that provided for Italian annexation of Venetia in exchange for support of Prussia should war break out with Austria. Now the issue became provocation of hostilities.

THE AUSTRO-PRUSSIAN WAR (1866). There had been constant Austro-Prussian tension over the administration of Schleswig and Holstein. Bismarck ordered the Prussian forces to do whatever was necessary to be obnoxious to the Austrians. On June 1, 1866, Austria appealed to the German Confederation to intervene in the dispute. Bismarck claimed that the request violated the terms of the 1864 alliance and the Convention of Gastein. The Seven Weeks' War of the summer of 1866 led to the decisive defeat of Austria at Königgrätz. However, the Treaty of Prague, which ended the conflict on August 23, was quite lenient toward Austria. It lost no territory except Venetia, which was ceded to Napoleon III, who in turn ceded it to Italy. The exchange could not be direct because Austria had actually defeated Italy when the latter honored its commitment to Prussia. The defeat of Austria and the treaty permanently excluded the Hapsburgs from German affairs. Prussia had become the only major power among the German states.

THE NORTH GERMAN CONFEDERATION. The states of Hanover, Hesse, and Nassau, and the city of Frankfurt, which had supported Austria during the war, were incorporated into Prussia, and their ruling dynasties were deposed. Prussia and these newly incorporated territories plus Schleswig and Holstein constituted the North German Confederation. The constitution of this state provided for a federation under Prussian leadership. Each province retained its own local government, but the military forces were under federal control. The president of the federation was the king of Prussia, represented by his chancellor. There was a federal council or *Bundesrat* composed of nominated members. The lower house or *Reichstag* was chosen by universal manhood suffrage. Bismarck had little fear of this broad franchise because he sensed that the peasants would tend to vote conserva-

tively. Moreover the *Reichstag* had little real power because ministers were responsible only to the monarch. Even legislation did not originate in the *Reichstag*. The legislature did have the right to approve military budgets, but they were usually submitted to cover several years at a time. The constitution of the confederation, which after 1871 became the governing document of the German Empire, possessed some of the appearances but none of the substance of liberalism. Germany was in effect a military monarchy.

The spectacular success of Bismarck's policy overwhelmed the liberal opposition in the Prussian Parliament. The liberals split between those who prized liberalism and those who supported unification. In the end nationalism proved more attractive than liberalism. In 1866 the Prussian Parliament passed an indemnity measure that retroactively approved the earlier military budget. Bismarck had crushed the Prussian liberals by making the monarchy and the army the most popular institutions in the country. The drive toward unification had achieved Bismark's domestic political goal.

The Franco-Prussian War and the German Empire (1870–1871)

Bismarck now awaited an opportunity to complete unification by bringing the states of southern Germany into the confederation. Events in Spain provided the excuse. In 1868 a revolution led by conservatives deposed the corrupt Bourbon queen of Spain. In searching for a new monarch, the Spaniards chose Prince Leopold of Hohenzollern-Sigmaringen, a cousin of William I of Prussia. On June 19, 1870, Leopold accepted the Spanish crown with Prussian blessings. Bismarck knew that France would react strongly against the idea of a second bordering state ruled by a Hohenzollern. On July 2 the Spanish publicized Leopold's acceptance, and the French reacted as expected. France sent Count Vincent Benedetti (1817–1900) to consult with William I, who was vacationing at Bad Ems. They discussed the matter at several meetings. On July 12 William persuaded Leopold's father to renounce his son's candidacy for the Spanish throne.

There the matter might have rested had it not been for the impetuosity of the French and the guile of Bismarck. On July 13 the French government instructed Benedetti to ask William I for assurances that he would tolerate no future Spanish candidacy for Leopold. The king refused but said that he might take the question under further consideration. Later that day he sent Bismarck, who was in Berlin, a telegram reporting the substance of the meeting. The chancellor, who desperately wanted a war with France to complete unification, had been disappointed by the peaceful solution to the Spanish candidacy question. The telegram provided a new opportunity. Bismarck released an edited version of the dispatch. The revised Ems telegram made it appear that William I had insulted the French ambassador. The idea was to goad France into a declaration of war.

The French quickly fell for Bismarck's bait, and on July 19 they declared war. The armies of the south German states eagerly joined the northern cause against France whose defeat was not long in coming. On September 1 at the Battle of Sedan the Germans not only beat the French army but also captured the French emperor, Napoleon III. By late September Paris stood besieged; it finally capitulated on January 28, 1871. Ten days earlier, in the Hall of Mirrors at the Palace of Versailles, the German Empire had been declared. During the war the states of south Germany had joined the North German Confederation, and their princes had requested William I to accept the imperial title. The princes of the southern states retained their positions as heads of their respective states within the new federation. From the peace settlement with France, Germany received the additional territory of Alsace and Lorraine.

Both the fact and manner of German unification produced long-range effects in Europe. A powerful new state had been created in north central Europe. It was rich in natural resources and talented citizens. Militarily and

Bismarck Edits William I: The Two Versions of the Ems Telegram

On July 13, 1870 William I of Prussia sent Bismarck a telegram reporting his meeting with Benedetti, the French Ambassador, at Ems, a watering place in north-west Germany. Before releasing the dispatch to the press, Bismarck edited it so that the telegram appeared to report that the King of Prussia had treated the French ambassador in a brusque and insulting fashion. Bismarck thus hoped to goad France into a declaration of war. In the text of both telegrams "His Majesty" is William I, and "the Prince" is Charles Anthony, the father of Prince Leopold, the candidate for the Spanish throne. Throughout the negotiations Charles Anthony had spoken on behalf of his son.

THE ORIGINAL MESSAGE SENT BY WILLIAM I TO BISMARCK

M. BENEDETTI *intercepted me on the Promenade in order to demand of me most insistently that I should authorize him to telegraph immediately to Paris that I shall obligate myself for all future time never again to give my approval to the candidacy of the Hohenzollerns should it be renewed. I refused to agree to this, the last time somewhat severely, informing him that one dare not and cannot assume such obligations* à tout jamais [*forever*]. *Naturally, I informed him that I had received no news as yet, and since he had been informed earlier than I by way of Paris and Madrid, he could easily understand why my government was once again out of the matter.*

Since then His Majesty has received a dispatch from the Prince. As His Majesty has informed Count Benedetti that he was expecting news from the Prince, His Majesty himself, in view of the above-mentioned demand and in consonance with the advice of Count Eulenburg and myself, decided not to receive the French envoy again but to inform him through an adjutant that His Majesty had now received from the Prince confirmation of the news which Benedetti had already received from Paris, and that he had nothing further to say to the Ambassador. His Majesty leaves it to the judgement of Your Excellency whether or not to communicate at once the new demand by Benedetti and its rejection to our ambassadors and to the press.

BISMARCK'S EDITED VERSION RELEASED TO THE PRESS

AFTER *the reports of the renunciation by the Hereditary Prince of Hohenzollern had been officially transmitted by the Royal Government of Spain to the Imperial Govern-*

ment of France, the French Ambassador presented to His Majesty the King at Ems the demand to authorize him to telegraph to Paris that His Majesty the King would obligate himself for all future time never again to give his approval to the candidacy of the Hohenzollerns should it be renewed.

His Majesty the King thereupon refused to receive the French envoy again and informed him through an adjutant that His Majesty had nothing further to say to the Ambassador.

Louis L. Snyder (Ed. and Trans.), *Documents of German History* (New Brunswick, N.J. Rutgers University Press, 1958), pp. 215–216.

economically the German Empire would be stronger than Prussia had been alone. The unification of Germany was also a blow to European liberalism because the new state was a conservative creation. Conservative politics was now backed not by a weak Austria or an economically retrograde Russia but rather by the strongest state on the Continent. The two nations most immediately affected by German and also Italian unification were France and Austria. The emergence of the two new unified states revealed the weakness of both France and the Hapsburg Empire. Change had to come in each. France returned to republican government, and the Hapsburgs organized a dual monarchy.

France: From Liberal Empire to the Third Republic

The reign of Emperor Napoleon III (1851–1870) is traditionally divided into the years of the authoritarian empire and those of the liberal empire. The point of division is 1860. Initially, after the *coup* in December 1851, Napoleon III had kept a close rein on the legisla-

ture, had strictly controlled the press, and had made life difficult for political dissidents. His support came from property owners, the French Catholic Church, and businessmen. They approved the security he brought to property, his protection of the pope, and his aid to commerce and railroad construction. The French victory in the Crimean War had further confirmed the emperor's popularity.

From the late fifties onward Napoleon III began to modify his policy. In 1860 he concluded a free trade treaty with Britain and permitted the legislature to discuss matters of state more freely. By the late sixties he had relaxed the press laws. In 1870 he allowed the leaders of the moderates in the legislature to form a ministry. That same year Napoleon III agreed to a liberal constitution that made ministers responsible to the legislature. All of these liberal moves were closely related to problems in foreign policy. He had lost control of the diplomacy of Italian unification. Between 1861 and 1867 he had supported a military expedition against Mexico led by Archduke Maximilian of Austria. The venture ended in defeat and the execution of the archduke. In 1866 Napoleon III and France rather sat on the sideline while Bismarck and Prussia reorganized German affairs. The liberal concessions on domestic matters were attempts to compensate for an increasingly unsuccessful foreign policy.

Whether Napoleon III would have succeeded in sustaining liberal government or his own position became a moot point. The Second Empire, but not the war, came to an inglorious end with the Battle of Sedan in September 1870. The emperor was captured, imprisoned, and then allowed to go to England, where he died in 1873. Shortly after news of the Sedan disaster reached Paris, a republic was proclaimed and a Government of National Defense established. Paris itself was soon under Prussian siege. During the siege of Paris the French government was transferred to Bordeaux. Paris finally surrendered in January 1871, but the rest of France had been ready to sue for peace long before the capital.

[*Text continued on page 719*]

Emperor Napoleon III of France is here pictured with his wife and son. [Culver Pictures.]

At an exhibition in Paris in 1867 Napoleon III inspected cannons manufactured in Germany by the Krupp company. Three years later such weapons were used by Germany against France. [The Granger Collection.]

Walter Bagehot Analyzes the Power of Napoleon III

Walter Bagehot (1826–1877) was an astute English observer. This 1863 passage explains the manner in which Napoleon III had to please the various elements in French politics in order to remain in power.

THE *Emperor is the Crowned Democrat of Europe. The position is no doubt one of great elevation and of enormous power, but it is also one full of peril and full of exigencies. "The Masses," though an effective, and under many circumstances, an almost resistless servant make a capricious, exacting, and relentless master. Both at home and abroad Napoleon III has a contract with the agencies that have made him what he is and that sustain him where he is, the terms of which must be rigidly fulfilled. At home he rules over the middle classes,* in defiance *of the educated classes, and by the support of the lower classes and the army. In ultimate resort he may be said to reign by the right of numbers and by the instrumentality of bayonets. It is true that he has done much—perhaps as much as lay in his power—to widen the basis of his throne, and to make all classes interested in maintaining him. He has tentatively and modestly allowed the intellectual classes to raise their heads; he has conciliated the* bourgeoisie *by the material prosperity which he has so sagaciously and indefatigably fostered; and he has cancelled or moderated the hostility once felt towards him by the rich and great by convincing them that property was in habitual danger from the* Rouges [Reds], *and that his was the only hand that could avert that danger. So that beyond dispute the number of those who wish to overthrow him has largely diminished, and the number of those who desire to maintain him has largely increased, each year since 1852. Still it remains true that to retain his popularity and prestige with* FRANCE, . . . *he must be sedulous to please, or at all events careful not to offend, the populace, the peasantry, and the army.*

The Collected Works of Walter Bagehot, ed. Norman St. John-Stevas (Cambridge, Mass.: Harvard University Press, 1968), Vol. 4, p. 105.

The siege of Paris during the Franco-Prussian War led to extreme food shortages. Animals in the zoo were slaughtered, and domestic dogs and cats were butchered, to feed the hungry citizens. The sketches made early in 1871 were published in London newspapers after being sent from Paris by balloon post. [The Granger Collection.]

In October 1870 Gambetta, who was then chief of the new French government, and his secretary escaped by balloons from beseiged Paris. The city was surrounded by Prussian troops who attempted unsuccessfully to shoot down the balloons, the second of which was said to carry three wealthy Americans also fleeing the city. Gambetta eventually established a governmental headquarters in Tours and prepared to negotiate terms of surrender with Prussia. The drawing was made by an eye-witness, J. C. Palmuri, for the American periodical, *Leslie's Weekly*. [Culver Pictures.]

The Paris Commune

The division between the provinces and Paris became even more decided after the fighting stopped. The new National Assembly elected in February was dominated by monarchists. For the time being, executive power was turned over to Adolphe Thiers (1797–1877), who had been active in French politics since 1830. He negotiated a settlement with Prussia (the Treaty of Frankfurt) whereby France was charged with a large indemnity, remained occupied by Prussian troops until it had been paid, and surrendered the provinces of Alsace and Lorraine. The city of Paris, which had suffered much during the siege, resented what it regarded as a betrayal by the monarchist National Assembly sitting in Versailles. Thiers, familiar with a half-century of Parisian political turmoil, ordered the disarmament of the Paris National Guard on March 17. The attempt to seize the guard's cannon was bungled. Paris then regarded the National Assembly as its new enemy.

On March 26, 1871, a new government, called the Commune, was elected in Paris. Its goal was to administer the city separately from the rest of the country. Political radicals and socialists of all stripes participated in the Commune at one time or another. The National Assembly moved rapidly. By early April Paris was again a besieged city, but this time it was surrounded by a French army. On May 8 Paris was bombarded. On May 21, the day on which the formal treaty with Prussia was signed, the National Assembly forces broke through the city's defenses. During the next seven days the troops restored order to Paris and in the process killed about twenty thousand inhabitants. The communards claimed their own victims as well.

The short-lived Paris Commune very quickly became a legend throughout France and Europe. Marxists regarded it as a genuine proletarian government that had been suppressed by the troops of the French bourgeoisie. This interpretation is incorrect. The Commune, though of shifting composition, was dominated by petty bourgeois members. The socialism that was a part of the Commune had its roots in Blanqui and Proudhon rather than in Marx. The goal of the Commune was not a workers' republic but a nation composed of relatively independent, radically democratic enclaves. The suppression of the Commune consequently represented not only the protection of property but also the triumph of the centralized nation state over an alternative mode of political organization. Just as the armies of Piedmont and Prussia had united the small states of Italy and Germany, the army of the French National Assembly destroyed the particularistic political tendencies of Paris and by implication those of any other French community.

The Third Republic

The National Assembly put down the Commune directly, but it backed into a republican form of government indirectly and much against its will. The monarchists, who constituted its majority, were divided in loyalty between the House of Bourbon and the House of Orleans. This problem could have been surmounted because the Bourbon claimant had no children. He could have become king on the condition that the Orleanist heir would follow him to the throne. However, the Bourbon Duke of Chambord refused to become king if the revolutionary tricolor flag were retained. Even the conservative monarchists would not return to the white flag of the Bourbons, which symbolized extreme political reaction.

While the monarchists quarreled over the proper heir, and the heir over the proper flag, time passed and events marched on. By September 1873 the indemnity had been paid and the Prussian occupation troops withdrawn. Thiers was ousted from office because he had displayed clear republican sentiments. The monarchists wanted a more certain person to be executive. They elected as president Marshal MacMahon (1808–1893), who was conservative and who was expected to prepare for an eventual monarchist restoration. In 1875 the National Assembly, still monarchist in sentiment but unable to find a candidate for the throne, decided to regularize the

This English cartoon of 1889 portrays General Georges Boulanger as a mock-heroic Napoleon who might attempt to seize power in Paris. The expected Boulangerist coup never took place. [The Granger Collection.]

political system. It adopted a law that provided for a Chamber of Deputies elected by universal manhood suffrage, a Senate chosen indirectly, and a president elected by the two legislative houses. This relatively simple republican system had resulted from the bickering and frustration of the monarchists.

MacMahon remained as president. He would have liked to transform that office into a new emperorship. After numerous quarrels with the Chamber of Deputies, he resigned in 1879. His departure meant that people dedicated to a republic generally controlled the national government. But France remained an uncertain and unconfident republic. A considerable body of public opinion within the army, the church, and the wealthy families still favored government by a single strong figure. During the late eighties they looked to General Georges Boulanger (1837–1891) as such a leader. In 1886 and 1887 he had been a popular minister of war who initiated a number of military reforms. When a financial scandal touched several major political figures, Boulanger became all the more appealing for his honesty and integrity. He was elected to the Chamber of Deputies from numerous districts though afterwards he sat for only one. In 1889 there was much talk and expectation of his carrying out a *coup d'état*. Nothing came of these speculations. The good general had talked with too many different political

groups to be trusted by any. He also lacked real drive and political ambition. In the end he left France for life with his Belgian mistress and in 1891 committed suicide on her grave in Brussels.

The political structure of the Third Republic proved much stronger than many citizens suspected at the time. It was able to survive a series of major scandals. In the late eighties the son of the president was discovered to be selling positions in the Legion of Honor. Early in the next decade a number of ministers and deputies were implicated in the Panama affair. Ferdinand De Lesseps, who had constructed the Suez Canal, organized a company to build a canal in Panama. Various people in authority in France accepted bribes for their public support of the venture. These two *causes célèbres* made the republic look rather sleazy in the eyes of its conservative enemies. But the institutions of the republic allowed new ministers to replace those whose corruption was exposed.

THE DREYFUS AFFAIR. The greatest trauma of the republic occurred over the Dreyfus affair. On December 22, 1894, a French military court found Captain Alfred Dreyfus (1859–1935) guilty of passing secret information to the German army. The evidence supporting his guilt was at best flimsy and was later revealed to have been forged. Someone in the officer corps had been passing documents to the Germans, and it suited the army investigators to accuse Dreyfus, who was Jewish. However, after Dreyfus had been sent to Devil's Island, secrets continued to flow to the German army. In 1896 a new head of French counterintelligence reexamined the Dreyfus file and found evidence of forgery. A different officer was implicated, but a military court quickly acquitted him of all charges. The officer who had discovered the forgeries was transferred to a distant post. By then the matter had become one of widespread public interest. The army, the church, the anti-Semitic press, and political conservatives opposed Dreyfus. Liberals, radicals, and socialists demanded a new trial. They saw the conservative institutions of the nation as having denied Dreyfus the rights belonging to any citizen of the

The Palace of Justice in Brussels (completed in 1883), heavy and imposing, symbolizes the general assumption of police and judicial power by the modern central state. The architect was Joseph Poelaert. [Copyright A.C.L., Brussels.]

Captain Alfred Dreyfus was falsely accused of passing French military secrets to Germany. His several trials during the 1890s became the occasion for major clashes, with strong anti-Semitic overtones, between the political left and right in the Third French Republic. [Culver Pictures.]

republic. Moreover Dreyfus had been singled out in order to protect the guilty persons in the army. In August 1898 further evidence of forged material came to light. A new military trial took place, but Dreyfus was again convicted by officers who refused to admit the original mistake. The president of France immediately pardoned the captain, and in 1906 a civilian court set aside the results of both trials.

The Dreyfus case divided France as no issue had done since the Commune. But it also for the first time created broad popular political support for the republic. Liberals, radicals, republicans, and socialists developed an informal alliance that outlived the fight over Dreyfus himself. These groups realized that republican institutions must be preserved if the political left were to achieve any of its goals. Outside political circles ever larger numbers of French citizens understood that their rights and liberties were safer under a republic than under some alternative mode of conservative government.

The Hapsburg Empire: Formation of the Dual Monarchy

After 1848 the Hapsburg Empire remained a problem both to itself and to the rest of Europe. An ungenerous critic remarked that the empire was supported by a standing army of soldiers, a kneeling army of priests, and a crawling army of informers. In the age of national

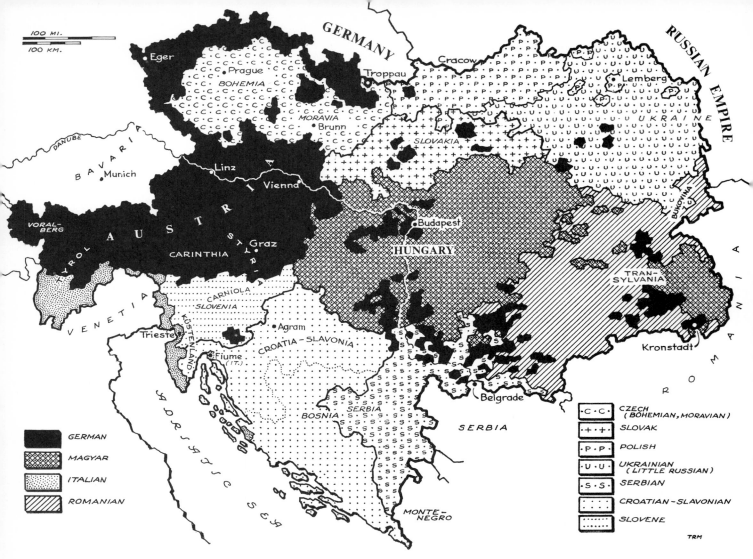

Map legend:

- GERMAN
- MAGYAR
- ITALIAN
- ROMANIAN

- C·C — CZECH (BOHEMIAN, MORAVIAN)
- +·+·+ — SLOVAK
- P·P — POLISH
- U·U — UKRAINIAN (LITTLE RUSSIAN)
- S·S — SERBIAN
- .·.·. — CROATIAN—SLAVONIAN
- .... — SLOVENE

NATIONALITIES WITHIN THE HAPSBURG EMPIRE

The patchwork appearance reflects the unusual problem of the numerous ethnic groups that the Hapsburgs could not, of course, meld into a modern national state. Only the Magyars were recognized in 1867, leaving nationalist Czechs, Slovaks, and the others chronically dissatisfied.

states, liberal institutions, and industrialism, the Hapsburg domains remained primarily dynastic, absolutist, and agrarian. The response to the revolts at the end of the forties had been the reassertion of absolutism. Francis Joseph, who became emperor in 1848 and ruled until 1916, was honest, hard-working, and unimaginative. He reacted to events but rarely commanded them.

During the 1850s his ministers attempted to impose a centralized administration on the empire. The system amounted to military and bureaucratic government dominated by German-speaking Austrians. All internal tariffs

were abolished. Hungary was divided into military districts. Education was put under the control of the Roman Catholic Church. Although creating much domestic resentment, this system of neoabsolutism actually floundered on a series of foreign policy setbacks. Austrian refusal to support Russia during the Crimean War meant that the new tsar would not help to preserve Hapsburg rule in Hungary as Nicholas I had done in 1849. The Austrian defeat in 1859 at the hands of France and Piedmont and the subsequent loss of territory in Italy pointed to the need for new structures of domestic government. For seven years the emperor, civil servants, aristocrats, and politicians attempted to construct a viable system of government.

In 1860 Francis Joseph issued the October Diploma, which created a federation among the states and provinces of the empire. There were to be local diets domi-

The Austrian Prime Minister Explains the Dual Monarchy

The multinational character of the Austrian Empire had long been a source of internal weakness and political discontent. After the defeat of Austria by Prussia in 1866, the Austrian government attempted to regain the loyalty of the Hungarians by making Hungary a separate kingdom within a dual monarchy known thereafter as Austria-Hungary.

THE *dangers which Austria has to face are of a two-fold nature. The first is presented by the tendency of her liberalminded German population to gravitate toward that larger portion of the German-speaking people. . . . the second is the diversity of language and race in the empire. Of Austria's large Slav population, the Poles have a natural craving for independence after having enjoyed and heroically fought for it for centuries; while the other nationalities are likely at a moment of dangerous crisis to develop pro-Russian tendencies.*

Now my object is to carry out a bloodless revolution—to show the various elements of this great empire that it is to the benefit of each of them to act in harmony with its neighbor. . . . But to this I have made one exception. Hungary is an ancient monarchy, more ancient as such than Austria proper. . . . I have endeavoured to give Hungary not a new position with regard to the Austrian empire, but to secure her in the one which she has occupied. The Emperor of Austria is King of Hungary; my idea was that he should revive in his person the Constitution of which he and his ancestors have been the heads. The leading principles of my plan are . . . the resuscitation of an old monarchy and an old Constitution; not the separation of one part of the empire from the other, but the drawing together of the two component parts by the recognition of their joint positions, the maintenance of their mutual obligations, their community in questions affecting the entire empire, and their proportional pecuniary responsibility for the liabilities of the whole State. It is no plan of separation that I have carried out: on the contrary, it is one of closer union, not by the creation of a new power, but by the recognition of an old one. . . .

Memoirs of Friedrich Ferdinand Count von Beust, Baron Henry de Worms (Ed.) (London: Remington 1887), Vol. 1, pp. xx–xxvi.

nated by the landed classes and a single imperial parliament. The Magyar nobility of Hungary rejected the plan. Consequently in 1861 the February Patent was promulgated. Technically it interpreted the Diploma, but in point of fact it constituted an entirely different form of government. It established a bicameral imperial parliament or *Reichsrat* with an appointed upper chamber and an indirectly elected lower chamber. Again the Magyars refused to cooperate in a system designed to permit German-speaking Austrian domination. The Hungarians sent no delegates to the legislature. Nevertheless, for six years, the February Patent governed the empire, and it prevailed in Austria proper until World War I. There was no ministerial responsibility to the *Reichsrat*. Few genuine guarantees existed for civil liberties. Armies could be levied and taxes raised without parliamentary consent. When the *Reichsrat* was not in session, the emperor could simply promulgate laws on his own authority.

Meanwhile negotiations continued between the emperor and the Magyars. These produced no concrete result until the defeat of Austria by Prussia in the summer of 1866 and the consequent exclusion of Austria from German affairs. The military disaster compelled Francis Joseph to come to terms with the Magyars. Through the *Ausgleich*, or Compromise, of 1867 the Hapsburg Empire was transformed into a dual monarchy. Francis Joseph was separately crowned king of Hungary in Budapest. Except for the common monarch, Austria and Hungary became almost wholly separate states. They shared ministers of foreign affairs, defense, and finance, but the other ministers were different for each state. There were also separate parliaments. Each year delegations of sixty parliamentary delegates from each state were to discuss matters of mutual interest. Every ten years Austria and Hungary were to renegotiate their trade relationship. By this cumbersome machinery, unique in all European history, the Hungarian Magyars were reconciled to Hapsburg rule. They had achieved the free hand they had long wanted in local Hungarian matters.

Many of the other national groups within the empire—including the Czechs, the Ruthenians, the Romanians, and the Serbo-Croatians—opposed the Compromise of 1867. The dual monarchy in effect permitted the

Tsar Alexander II of Russia emancipated the serfs in 1861 and began numerous other major reforms of the Russian government and army. He was assassinated by radicals who sought even more fundamental reforms of Russian life. [Culver Pictures.]

German-speaking Austrians and the Hungarian Magyars to dominate all other nationalities in their respective states. The most vocal critics were the Czechs of Bohemia. They favored a policy of trialism or triple monarchy. In 1871 Francis Joseph was willing to accept this concept. However, the Hungarian Magyars vetoed the proposal for fear they might have to make similar concessions to their own subject nationalities.

For over twenty years the Czechs were conciliated by an extension of generous Austrian patronage and admission to the Austrian bureaucracy. By the nineties Czech nationalism had again become more vocal. In 1897 a series of ordinances gave the Czechs and the Germans equality of language in various localities. The Germans in the Austrian *Reichsrat* set out on a course of parliamentary disruption to oppose these measures. The Czechs replied in kind. By the turn of the century this obstructionist activity had paralyzed parliamentary life. The emperor ruled by imperial decree with the support of the bureaucracy. In 1907 universal manhood suffrage was introduced into Austria, but it did not change the situation in the *Reichsrat*. In effect, by 1914 constitutionalism was a dead letter in Austria. It flourished in Hungary at the cost of Magyar political supremacy over all other national groups.

Russia: Emancipation and Revolutionary Stirrings
Reforms of Alexander II

The defeat in the Crimean War and the humiliation of the Treaty of Paris compelled the Russian government to reconsider its domestic situation. Nicholas I had died in 1855 during the conflict. Because of extensive travel in Russia and an early introduction to government procedures, Nicholas's son Alexander II (1855–1881) was quite familiar with the chief difficulties facing the nation. The debacle of the war had created a situation in which reform was both necessary and possible. Alexander II

took advantage of this turn of events to institute the most extensive restructuring of Russian society and administration since Peter the Great. Like Peter, Alexander imposed his reforms from the top.

In every area of economic and public life a profound cultural gap existed between Russia and the rest of Europe. Nowhere was this fact more true than in the matter of serfdom. Everywhere else on the Continent it had been abandoned. In Russia the institution had changed very little since the eighteenth century. Landowners had a very free hand with their serfs, and the serfs had little recourse against the lords. In March 1856, at the conclusion of the Crimean War, Alexander II announced his intention to abolish serfdom. For over five years government commissions wrestled over the way to implement the tsar's desire. Finally, in February 1861, against much opposition from the nobility and the landlords, Alexander II promulgated the long statute ending serfdom in Russia.

The technicalities of the emancipation statute meant that freedom was often more theoretical than practical. The procedures were so complicated and the results so limited that many serfs believed that real emancipation was still to come. Serfs immediately received the personal rights to marry, to purchase and sell property, to engage in court actions, and to pursue trades without securing their landlord's permission. What they did not receive

The harsh treatment of Russian serfs by their land-lords prior to emancipation was frequently criticized in the rest of Europe. This French cartoon of 1854 portrays Russian landlords using bundles of their serfs as stakes for a card game. [The Granger Collection.]

Even after emancipation, the life of Russian peasants was difficult. They attempted to secure a livelihood partly from farming and partly from small handcraft industries, such as those seen in this picture of a Russian village in the late nineteenth century. [Culver Pictures.]

immediately was free title to their land. They were to pay for frequently insufficient allotments of land over a period of forty-nine years. They were also charged interest during this period. The serfs made the payments to the government, which had already reimbursed the landlords for their losses. The serfs did not receive title to the land until the debt was paid. The redemption payments led to almost unending difficulty. Poor harvests caused the debts to fall into arrears. The situation was not remedied until 1906. With widespread unrest following the Japanese defeat of Russia in 1905, the government grudgingly completed the process of emancipation by canceling the remaining debts.

Abolition of serfdom required reorganization of local government and the judicial system. The authority of village communes replaced that of the landlord over the peasant. The village elders settled family quarrels, imposed fines, issued internal passports, and collected taxes. In many cases also, the land of the emancipated serfs was owned communally rather than individually. The nobility were permitted a larger role in local administration through a system of provincial and county *zemstvos,* or councils, organized in 1864. These councils were to oversee local matters such as bridge and road repair, education, and agricultural improvement. However, because the councils were not adequately funded, local government never became vigorous.

The flagrant inequities and abuses of the preemancipation judicial system could not continue. In 1864 Alexander II promulgated a new statute on the judiciary. For the first time principles of west European legal systems were introduced into Russia. These included equality before the law, impartial hearings, uniform procedures, judicial independence, and trial by jury. The new system was far from perfect. Judges were not genuinely independent, and the tsar could increase as well as reduce sentences. For certain offenses, such as those involving the press, jury trials were not held. Nonetheless the system was an improvement both in its efficiency and in its relative lack of the old corruption.

Reforms were also instituted in the army. Russia possessed the largest military establishment on the Continent, but it had floundered badly in the Crimea. The usual period of recruitment was twenty-five years. Villages had to provide quotas of serfs. Often recruiters had come to villages and simply seized serfs from their families. Once in the army, the recruits rarely saw their homes again. Life in the army was exceedingly harsh, even by the usually brutal standards of most mid-century armies. In the sixties the period of recruitment was lowered to fifteen years, and disciplinary procedures were slightly relaxed. In 1874 the enlistment period was lowered to six years of active duty, followed by nine years in the reserves. All males twenty years old were subject to military service.

Alexander's reformist departures came to a close shortly after the Polish Rebellion of 1863. As in 1830, Polish nationalists attempted to flout Russian dominance. Once again the Russian army suppressed the rebellion. Alexander II then moved to "russify" Poland. In 1864 he emancipated the Polish serfs as a move against the restive Polish nobility. Russian law, language, and administration were imposed on all areas of Polish life. Henceforth, until the close of World War I, Poland was treated merely as one other Russian province.

As revealed by the Polish suppression, Alexander II was a reformer only within the limits of his own autocracy. His changes in Russian life failed to create new loyalty or gratitude among his subjects. The serfs felt that emancipation had been inadequate. The nobles and the wealthier educated segments of Russian society resented the tsar's persistent refusal to allow them a meaningful role in government and policy making. Consequently, although Alexander II became known as the Tsar Liberator, he was never a popular ruler. He could be very indecisive and was rarely open to new ideas. These characteristics became more pronounced after 1866, when an attempt was made on his life. Thereafter Russia increasingly became a police state. This new repression fueled the activity of radical groups within Russia. Their actions in turn made the autocracy more reactionary.

Revolutionaries

The tsarist regime had long had its critics. One of the most prominent was Alexander Herzen (1812–1870),

---

George Kennan Describes Siberian Exile in Alexander III's Russia

Under Alexander III the police-state character of the Russian monarchy intensified. Exile was the most extreme form of punishment short of death. In effect it robbed the person exiled not only of legal rights but almost of his identity, as pointed out in this account by a noted American observer who spent long periods in Siberia in the 1860s and 1880s.

EXILE *by administrative process means the banishment of an obnoxious person from one part of the empire to another without the observance of any of the legal formalities that, in most civilized countries, precede the deprivation of rights and the restriction of personal liberty. The obnoxious person may not be guilty of any crime, and may not have rendered himself amenable in any way to the laws of the state, but if, in the opinion of the local authorities, his presence in a particular place is "prejudicial to public order," or "incompatible with public tranquillity," he may be arrested without a warrant, may be held from two weeks to two years in prison, and may then be removed by force to any other place within the limits of the empire and there be put under police surveillance for a period of from one year to ten years. He may or may not be informed of the reasons for this summary proceeding, but in either case he is perfectly helpless. He cannot examine the witnesses upon whose testimony his presence is declared to be "prejudicial to public order." He cannot summon friends to prove his loyalty and good character, without great risk of bringing upon them the same calamity that has befallen him. He has no right to demand a trial, or even a hearing. He cannot sue out a writ of habeas corpus. He cannot appeal to his fellow-citizens through the press. His communications with the world are so suddenly severed that sometimes even his own relatives do not know what has happened to him. He is literally and absolutely without any means whatever of self-defense.*

George Kennan, *Siberia and the Exile System* (London: Century Co., 1891), Vol. 1, pp. 242–243.

---

who lived in exile. From London he published a newspaper called *The Bell* in which he set forth reformist positions. The initial reforms of Alexander II had raised great hopes among Russian students and intellectuals, but they soon became discontented with the limited character of the restructuring. Drawing upon the ideas of Herzen and

other radicals, these students formed a revolutionary movement known as Populism. They sought a social revolution based on the communal life of the Russian peasants. The chief radical society was called Land and Freedom. In the early 1870s hundreds of young Russians, including both men and women, took their revolutionary message into the countryside. They intended to live with the peasants, to gain their trust, and to teach them about the peasant role in the coming revolution. The bewildered and distrustful peasants turned most of the youths over to the police. In the winter of 1877–1878 almost two hundred students were tried. Most were acquitted or given very light sentences. Alexander II then changed the sentences and sent many of the defendants to Siberia.

Thereafter the revolutionaries decided that the tsarist regime must be attacked directly. They adopted a policy of terrorism. In January 1878 Vera Zasulich attempted to assassinate the military governor of St. Petersburg. At her trial the jury acquitted her. This verdict encouraged the terrorists. In 1879 Land and Freedom split into two groups. One held to the idea of educating the peasants, and it soon dissolved. The other, known as People's Will, was dedicated to the overthrow of the autocracy. Its members decided to assassinate the tsar himself. Several assassination attempts failed, but on March 1, 1881, a bomb hurled by a member of People's Will killed Tsar Alexander II. Four men and two women were sentenced to death for the deed. All of them had been willing to die for their cause. The emergence of such dedicated revolutionary opposition constituted as much a part of the reign of Alexander II as did his reforms, for the limited character of those reforms convinced many people from various walks of life that the autocracy could never truly redirect Russian society.

Alexander III, whose reign (1881–1894) further underscored that pessimistic conviction, possessed all the autocratic and repressive characteristics of his grandfather Nicholas I and none of the better qualities of his father. Some slight attention was directed toward the improvement of life in the Russian factories, but primarily Alexander III sought to roll back the reforms of the third quarter of the century. He favored centralized bureaucracy over the new limited modes of self-government. He strengthened the secret police and increased press censorship. In effect, he confirmed all the evils that the revolutionaries saw inherent in autocratic government. His son, Nicholas II, who became tsar in 1894, would discover that autocracy could not survive the pressures of the twentieth century.

Alexander III (1881–1894) attempted to reimpose arbitrary rule after the reforms of Alexander II. The future Tsar Nicholas II (1894–1917) is standing directly behind his father. [The Granger Collection.]

Great Britain: Toward Democracy

While continental nations became unified and struggled toward internal political restructuring, Great Britain continued to symbolize the confident liberal state. Britain was not without its difficulties and domestic conflicts, but it seemed able to deal with these through existing political institutions. The general prosperity of the third quarter of the century took the edge off the class hostility of the forties. A large body of shared ideas emphasizing competition and individualism was accepted by the members of all classes. Even the leaders of trade unions during these years asked for little more than to receive a portion of the fruits of prosperity and to prove their own social respectability. Parliament itself continued to provide an institution that permitted the absorption of new groups and interests into the existing political processes. In short, the British did not have to create new liberal institutions and then learn how to live within them.

The major political figure of mid-century was Henry John Temple, Lord Palmerston (1784–1865). He became prime minister early in 1855 as the nation became weary of blunders in the conduct of the Crimean War. Except for a seventeen-month interlude in 1858 and 1859, he governed until late 1865. Palmerston was a liberal Whig, whose chief interest was foreign policy. He generally championed free trade and the right of European nationalities to determine their own political destinies. His bombastic patriotism made him very popular with voters; he rarely hesitated to parade British naval power before the world. Yet Palmerston was a person of the past. He had little sympathy with those political and working-class figures who wanted to extend the franchise beyond the limits of the Reform Act of 1832. By the time of his death in 1865 Palmerston had become the chief obstacle to further political and social reform.

The Second Reform Act (1867)

By the early sixties it had become clear to most observers that in one way or another the franchise would again

The young Queen Victoria is shown on a medal
by J. S. Wyon at the time of her accession.
[The Granger Collection.]

Prince Albert and Queen Victoria (1837–1901) of
Great Britain successfully accommodated the British
monarchy to new liberal democratic political
structures. Prince Albert died in 1861. The photograph, by Roger Fenton, is from 1854. [The Mansell
Collection.]

The new British Houses of Parliament in London were completed in the middle of the nineteenth century. The architectural style was that of the Gothic revival. Until at least after World War II these buildings symbolized political liberalism in the West. [British Tourist Authority, New York.]

have to be expanded. The prosperity and the social respectability of the working class convinced many politicians that workers truly deserved the vote. Organizations such as the Reform League, led by John Bright (1811–1889), were agitating for parliamentary action. In 1866 Lord John Russell's Liberal ministry introduced a reform bill that was defeated by a coalition of traditional Conservatives and antidemocratic liberals. Russell resigned, and the Tory Lord Derby replaced him. What then occurred surprised everyone.

The Conservative ministry, led in the House of Commons by Benjamin Disraeli (1804–1881), introduced its own reform bill in 1867. As the debate proceeded, Disraeli accepted one amendment after another and expanded the electorate well beyond the limits earlier proposed by the Liberals. When the final measure was passed, the number of voters had been increased from approximately 1,430,000 to 2,470,000. Britain had taken

a major step toward democracy. Large numbers of working-class voters had been admitted to the electorate. Disraeli hoped that by sponsoring the measure the Conservatives would receive the gratitude of the new voters. Because reform was bound to come, it was best for the Conservatives to enjoy the credit. Disraeli thought that eventually the working class would support Conservative candidates who proved themselves responsive to social issues. In the long run, his intuition proved correct, for in the past century the Conservative Party has dominated British politics.

In the immediate election of 1868, however, Disraeli's hopes were dashed. William Gladstone (1809–1898) became the new prime minister. Gladstone had begun political life in 1833 as a strong Tory, but over the next thirty-five years he moved steadily toward liberalism. He had supported Robert Peel, free trade, repeal of the Corn Laws, and efficient administration. As chancellor of the exchequer during the fifties and early sixties, he had lowered taxes and government expenditure. He had also championed Italian nationalism. For many years he continued to oppose a new reform bill. Yet by the early sixties he had also modified his position on that issue. In 1866 he had been Russell's spokesman in the House of Commons for the unsuccessful liberal reform bill.

Gladstone Praises the Education Act of 1870

The British Education Act of 1870 marked the creation of the first national system of schools. Prime Minister Gladstone and others admired the measure because it still permitted private religious schools, because it was relatively inexpensive, and because it depended largely on the initiative of local government. In other words, it permitted the liberty and the low taxes that liberals prized.

The great object of all was to make education universal and effective. This was to be done, and doing it we sought, and I think reason and common sense required us to seek, to turn to account for that purpose the vast machinery of education already existing in the country, which had been devised and mainly provided by the Christian philanthropy and the voluntary action of the people. That was the second condition under which the Act was framed. The third was, and I think it was not less wise than the two former, that we should endeavour to separate the action of the State in the matter of education, and the application of State funds, in which I include funds raised by rate [taxes], from all subjects on which, unhappily, religious differences prevail. Those, I may say, were three of the principles of the measure; and the fourth principle, not less important than the others, was this: that we should trust for the attainment of these great objects, as little as possible to the central Government, and as much as possible to the local authorities and the self-governing power of the people. And let me say in passing, that in my opinion if there be one portion of our institutions more precious in my view than another, it is that portion in which the people are locally organized for the purposes of acquiring the habits and instincts of political action, and applying their own free consciences and free understandings to dealing with the affairs of the community.

A. T. Bassett (Ed.), *Gladstone's Speeches* (London: Methuen, 1916), pp. 412–413.

Gladstone's Great Ministry (1868–1874)

Gladstone's ministry of 1868–1874 witnessed the culmination of classical British liberalism. Those institutions that still remained the preserve of the aristocracy and the Anglican Church were opened to people from other classes and religious denominations. By an Order in Council of 1870 competitive examinations replaced patronage as a means of entering the civil service. In 1871 the purchase of officer ranks in the army was abolished. The same year saw the removal of religious texts from Oxford and Cambridge universities. The Ballot Act of 1872 introduced voting by secret ballot. The most momentous measure of Gladstone's first ministry was the Education Act of 1870. For the first time in British history the government assumed the responsibility for establishing and running elementary schools. Previously British education had been a task relegated to the religious denominations, which received small amounts of state support for the purpose.

All of these reforms were typically liberal. They sought to remove longstanding abuses without destroying existing institutions and to permit all able citizens to compete on the grounds of ability and merit. They attempted to protect the state from the potential dangers of democracy by providing for a literate citizenry. These reforms also constituted a mode of state building because they created new bonds of loyalty to the nation by abolishing many sources of present and future discontent. They made increasing numbers of people benefit positively from being British citizens.

Disraeli in Office (1874–1880)

The liberal policy of creating popular support for the nation through the extension of political liberty and reform of abuses had its conservative counterpart in concern about social reform. Disraeli succeeded Gladstone as prime minister in 1874. The two men had stood on different sides of most issues for over a quarter century. Whereas Gladstone looked to individualism, free trade, and competition to solve social problems, Disraeli had believed that the ruling classes of the country must confront those matters through paternalistic legislation. Disraeli believed in state action to protect weak groups of citizens. In his view such paternalistic legislation would alleviate class antagonism.

Disraeli personally talked a better line than he pro-

William Gladstone was on four separate occasions the Liberal Party Prime Minister of Great Britain in the period from the 1860s to the 1890s. He was one of the most effective orators of his day. He pursued policies of peace, low government spending, and reform of major British political institutions. The 1869 caricature, for the British periodical *Vanity Fair,* is by "Ape" (Carlo Pellegrini). [The Granger Collection.]

duced. He had very few specific programs or ideas. The significant social legislation of his ministry stemmed primarily from the efforts of his Home Secretary Richard Cross. The Public Health Act of 1875 consolidated previous sanitary legislation and reaffirmed the duty of the state to interfere with private property on matters of health and physical well-being. Through the Artisans Dwelling Act of 1875 the government became actively involved in providing housing for the working class. The same year, in an important symbolic gesture, the Conservative majority in Parliament passed a law that gave new protection to British trade unions and allowed them to raise picket lines. The Gladstone ministry, although recognizing the legality of unions, had refused such extensive protection.

The Irish Question

In 1880 a second Gladstone ministry took office as an agricultural depression and unpopular foreign policy undermined Disraeli's popularity. In 1884, with Conservative cooperation, a third reform act extending the vote to most male farm workers was passed. However, the major issue of the decade was Ireland. From the late sixties onward Irish nationalists had sought to achieve home rule for Ireland, by which they meant more Irish control of local government. During his first ministry Gladstone had addressed the Irish question through two major pieces of legislation. In 1869 he carried a measure to disestablish the Church of Ireland, which was the Irish

Benjamin Disraeli was the Conservative Party leader of the House of Commons in 1867 at the time of the passage of the Second Reform Act. As Prime Minister between 1874 and 1880 he led the government in early efforts to improve the condition of the working class. The 1869 caricature is by "Ape." [The Granger Collection.]

branch of the Anglican Church. Henceforth Irish Roman Catholics would not pay taxes to support the hated Protestant church, to which only a small fraction of the population belonged. Second, in 1870 the Liberal ministry sponsored a land act that provided compensation to evicted Irish tenants and loans for tenants who wished to purchase their land.

Throughout the seventies the Irish question continued to fester. Land remained the center of the agitation. Today, the matter of Irish economic development seems more complicated and who owned the land seems less important than the methods of management and cultivation. Nevertheless the organization of the Irish Land League in the late seventies brought a period of intense agitation and intimidation against the landlords, who were often English. The leader of the Irish movement for a just land settlement and for home rule was Charles Stewart Parnell (1846–1891). In 1881 the second Gladstone ministry passed another Irish land act, which provided further guarantees of tenant rights. This measure only partly satisfied Irish opinion because it was accompanied by a Coercion Act intended to restore law and order to Ireland.

By 1885 Parnell had organized the eighty-five Irish members of the House of Commons into a tightly disciplined party that often voted as a bloc. They pursued disruptive tactics to gain attention for the cause of home rule. They bargained with the two English parties. In the election of 1885 the Irish Party emerged with the balance

Charles Stewart Parnell, shown here in an 1880 *Vanity Fair* drawing by Theobald Chartran, was the leader of the Irish members of Parliament during the Home Rule crisis of the 1880s. [The Granger Collection.]

of power between the English Liberals and Conservatives. The Irish could decide which party would take office. In December 1885 Gladstone announced support of home rule for Ireland. Parnell gave his votes to the formation of a Liberal ministry. However, the issue split the Liberal Party. In 1886 a group of Liberals known as the Liberal Unionists joined with the Conservatives to defeat Gladstone's Home Rule Bill. Gladstone called for a new election, in which the Liberals were defeated. They remained a permanently divided party.

The new Conservative ministry of Lord Salisbury (1830–1903) attempted to reconcile the Irish to English government through public works and administrative reform. The policy, which was tied to further coercion, had only marginal success. In 1892 Gladstone returned to power. A second Home Rule Bill passed the House of Commons but was defeated in the House of Lords. There the Irish question stood until after the turn of the century. The Conservatives sponsored a land act in 1903 that carried out the final transfer of land to tenant ownership. Ireland became a country of small farms. In 1911 a Liberal ministry passed the third Home Rule Bill. Under the provisions of the House of Lords Act of 1911, which curbed the power of that body, the bill had to pass the Commons three times over the Lords veto to become law. The third passage occurred in the summer of 1914, and the operation of the bill was suspended for the duration of World War I.

The Irish question affected British politics in a manner not unlike that of the Austrian nationalities problem. Normal British domestic issues could not be adequately addressed because of the political divisions created by Ireland. The split of the Liberal Party proved especially harmful to the cause of further social and political reform. The people who could agree on matters of reform could not agree on Ireland, and the latter problem seemed more important. As the two traditional parties failed to deal with the social questions, by the turn of the century a newly organized Labor Party began to fill the vacuum.

The European Political Scene: 1850–1875

Between 1850 and 1875 the major contours of the political systems that would dominate Europe until World War I had been drawn. Those systems and political arrangements solved, so far as such matters can be solved, many of the political questions and problems that had troubled the Europeans during the first half of the nineteenth century. The concept of the nation state had on the whole triumphed. Support for governments no longer stemmed from loyalty to dynasties but from various degrees of citizen participation. Moreover the unity of nations was no longer based on dynastic links but on cultural, linguistic, and historical bonds. The parliamentary governments of western Europe and the autocracies of eastern Europe were quite different, but both political systems had been compelled to recognize the force of nationalism and the larger role of citizens in political affairs. Only Russia failed to make such concessions, but the emancipation of the serfs had constituted a concession to a mode of popular opinion. The major sources of future discontent would arise from the demands of labor to enter the political processes and the still unsatisfied aspirations of subject nationalities. Those two areas of unrest would trouble Europe for the next forty years and would eventually undermine the political structures created during the third quarter of the nineteenth century.

SUGGESTED READINGS

G. F. A. BEST, *Mid-Victorian Britain* (1972). A good book on the social structure.

R. C. BINKLEY, *Realism and Nationalism, 1852–1871* (1935). A useful, though somewhat dated survey.

R. BLAKE, *Disraeli* (1967). The best recent biography.

J. BLUM, *Lord and Peasant in Russia from the Ninth to the Nineteenth Century* (1961). A clear discussion of emancipation in the later chapters.

W. L. BURN, *The Age of Equipoise* (1964). A thoughtful and convincing discussion of Victorian social stability.

G. KITSON CLARK, *The Making of Victorian England* (1962). The best introduction.

G. CRAIG, *Germany, 1866–1945* (1978). An excellent new survey.

R. A. KANN, *The Multinational Empire*, 2 vols. (1950). The basic treatment of the nationality problem of Austria–Hungary.

P. MAGNUS, *Gladstone: A Biography* (1955). A readable biography.

A. J. MAY, *The Hapsburg Monarchy, 1867–1914* (1951). Narrates in considerable detail and with much sympathy the fate of the dual monarchy.

W. N. MEDLICOTT, *Bismarck and Modern Germany* (1965). An excellent brief biography.

W. E. MOSSE, *Alexander II and the Modernization of Russia* (1958). A brief biography.

C. C. O'BRIEN, *Parnell and His Party* (1957). An excellent treatment of the Irish question.

O. PFLANZE, *Bismarck and the Development of Germany* (1963). Carries the story through the achievement of unification.

N. RICH, *The Age of Nationalism and Reform*, rev. ed. (1976). A sound volume based on recent research.

D. MACK SMITH, *Cavour and Garibaldi in 1860: A Study in Political Conflict* (1954). Explores the two key personalities in Italian unification.

D. MACK SMITH, *The Making of Italy, 1796–1870* (1968). A narrative that incorporates the major documents.

A. J. P. TAYLOR, *The Hapsburg Monarchy, 1809–1918* (1941). An opiniated but highly readable work.

D. THOMSOM, *Democracy in France since 1870*, rev. ed. (1969). A clear guide to a complex problem.

J. M. THOMSON, *Louis Napoleon and the Second Empire* (1954). A straightforward account.

VENTURI, *The Roots of Revolution* (trans., 1960). A major treatment of late nineteenth-century revolutionary movement.

H. SETON WATSON, *The Russian Empire, 1801–1917* (1967). A far-ranging narrative.

A. J. WHYTE, *The Evolution of Modern Italy* (1965). An interesting survey of the Italian problem in nineteenth-century diplomacy.

R. WILLIAMS, *The World of Napoleon III*, rev. ed. (1965). Examines the cultural setting.

C. B. WOODHAM-SMITH, *The Reason Why* (1953). A lively account of the Crimean War and the charge of the Light Brigade.

T. ZELDIN, *France: 1848–1945*, 2 vols. (1973, 1977). Emphasizes the social developments.

736

28

The Building of European Supremacy: Society and Politics to World War I

ETWEEN 1860 and 1914 European political, economic, and social life assumed many of the features characteristic of our world today. Nation states with large electorates, political parties, centralized bureaucracies, and universal military service emerged. Business adopted large-scale corporate structures, and the labor force organized itself into trade unions. Large numbers of white-collar workers appeared. Urban life came to predominate throughout western Europe. Socialism became a major ingredient in the political life of all nations. The foundations of the welfare state and of vast military establishments were laid. Taxation increased accordingly.

During this half century the extensive spread of industrialism created an unparalleled productive capacity in Europe. The age of the automobile, the airplane, the bicycle, the refrigerated ship, the telephone, the wireless, the typewriter, and the electric light bulb dawned. The world's economies, based on the gold standard, became increasingly interdependent. European goods flowed into markets all over the globe. In turn, foreign products, raw materials, and food stuffs were imported. Europe had also quietly become dependent on the resources and markets of the rest of the world. Changes in the weather conditions in Kansas, Argentina, or New Zealand might now effect the European economy. However, prior to World War I the dependence was concealed by Europe's industrial, military, and financial supremacy. At the time people rather assumed that such supremacy was a natural

situation, but the twentieth century would reveal it to have been quite temporary. Nevertheless, while that condition prevailed, Europeans were able to dominate most of the other peoples of the earth and to display the most extreme self-confidence.

Population Trends

There seem to have been more Europeans proportionally about 1900 than ever before or since. Europe then contained just under one quarter of the estimated world population. The demographic expansion to which so much attention has already been paid continued through the second half of the century. The number of Europeans rose from approximately 266 million in 1850 to 401 million in 1900 and 447 million in 1910. However, the rate of European growth began to slow while the population expansion elsewhere did not recede. Depending on the country in Europe, the birth rate either fell or remained stationary. The death rate did likewise. In the long run that ratio meant a more slowly growing population. This situation also meant that the grave demographic differential between the developed and the undeveloped world—which is so much a part of the present food and resource crisis—had been established.

During the second half of the nineteenth century the small family of two or three children became "normal." Knowledge about and means of contraception became more fully dispersed and its practice more widespread. The desire to maintain a high standard of living, the cost of rearing children, the smaller number of children in the work force, and the desire of women to limit the number of births contributed to the stabilization of population. It seems that more and more couples decided that they wanted to spend their incomes on consumer goods rather than on children. Moreover children brought fewer economic advantages to their parents than in the past. Further improvements in sanitation, housing, food processing, and medicine tended to lower the death rate at the

During the last half of the nineteenth century, thousands of Europeans lived in slums such as this one in Glasgow, Scotland, photographed about 1870. Such conditions stood as a living condemnation of the failure of Western industrial society to achieve a just distribution of its goods and services. As time passed, the socialist movement and government welfare programs would begin to address this problem —with results that many continued to feel were less than satisfactory. [The Mansell Collection.]

[Text continued on page 740]

737

After the street fighting of the revolutions of 1848, the old wall fortifications of Vienna were torn down. (See the illustration on page 501 which shows them.) In their place were built broad boulevards lined with fine buildings. The new streets were more beautiful—and were also better suited for rapid movement of troops against possible insurrection. This is an early photograph of a portion of the Ringstrasse, the street replacing the walls. [Austrian Information Service, New York.]

BELOW: The building of sewers for the disposal of urban waste was one of the great accomplishments of nineteenth-century sanitary engineering. This picture was made inside one of the sewers of Paris. [French Cultural Services, New York.]

A fashionable Paris boulevard in the late nineteenth century. Note the various kinds of horsedrawn carriages and the doubledecked horsedrawn bus. [French Cultural Services, New York.]

Pollution was one of the earliest results of industrialization and the resulting rapid population growth, and it became a major problem for nineteenth-century governments, as it has remained for those of today. This English cartoon of 1858 was published near the time of the passage by Parliament of an act to clean the River Thames. [The Granger Collection.]

THE "SILENT HIGHWAY"-MAN.
"YOUR *MONEY* OR YOUR *LIFE!*"

The first subway in the world was built in London between 1860 and 1863 and, although powered with steam-driven locomotives, was a success. However, subways did not become truly practicable until electricity was available as the source of power, and the great age of subway building began with the second London subway, opened in 1890. Within the next thirty years many of the great cities of Europe and America had subway systems in operation. This print shows construction work on the London Underground. The Houses of Parliament are in the background. [Mary Evans Picture Library.]

The great town halls, such as this one in Copenhagen, Denmark, built between 1905 and 1911, illustrate both civic pride and the important administrative and political role that cities acquired during the nineteenth century. [Danish Information Office, New York.]

same time. This vast, but stabilizing European population provided a large consumer market and an increasingly healthy work force.

Europe's peoples were on the move in the last half of the century as never before. Legal movement and migration became easier as the role of the landlords lessened. Railways, steamships, and better roads allowed greater physical mobility. The development of the European economy and those of North America, Latin America, and Australia meant better wages and cheap land, which enticed people to move. Within Europe the movement continued toward the cities.

GROWTH OF MAJOR EUROPEAN CITIES
(FIGURES IN THOUSANDS)

	1850	1880	1910
Berlin	419	1,122	2,071
Birmingham	233	437	840
Frankfurt	65	137	415
London	2,685	4,470	7,256
Madrid	281	398	600
Paris	1,053	2,269	2,888
Vienna	444	1,104	2,031

By about 1900 in all the major west European nations approximately 50 per cent of the people lived in urban areas. These city populations were largely uprooted from traditional social ties. They confronted poor housing, social anonymity, and potential unemployment. The migrants to cities in the last half of the century rarely possessed the artisan skills of urban immigrants fifty years earlier. Their problems and their social setting made them ripe for new kinds of political and economic organization. The failure of people to mix socially and the competition for too few jobs generated new varieties of urban discontent such as were experienced by the thousands of Russian Jews who migrated to western Europe. Much of the political anti-Semitism of the latter part of the century had its social roots in these problems of urban migration.

Europeans also migrated out of their continent in record numbers. Between 1846 and 1932 over fifty million Europeans left their homelands. The major areas to benefit from this movement were the United States, Canada, Australia, South Africa, Brazil, and Argentina. At midcentury most of the emigrants left from Great Britain (and especially Ireland), Germany, and Scandinavia. After 1885 the migration drew its numbers from southern and eastern Europe. This exodus helped to relieve the social and population pressures on the Continent. The outward movement of peoples in conjunction with Europe's economic and technological superiority contributed heavily to the Europeanization of the world. Not since the sixteenth century had European civilization produced such an impact on other cultures.

The Second Industrial Revolution

As David Landes has suggested, "The period from 1850 to 1873 was the Continental industry's coming-of-age."[1] The gap that had existed for half a century between British and continental economic development was closed. The basic heavy industries of Belgium, France, and Germany underwent major expansion. French development was relatively slow, but steady. The rate of growth became more rapid after the Franco-Prussian War. The expansion of German industry was stunning. Coal mining, iron and steel production, and the chemical industry made rapid progress. German steel production surpassed that of Britain in 1893 and had almost doubled the British effort by the outbreak of World War I. This emergence of an industrial Germany was the major fact of European economic and political life at the turn of the century.

The systematic spread of railways continued to make a key contribution to economic development during the third quarter of the century. Railways cheapened transport costs and made wider regional and continental marketing possible. Railway building by Europeans in other parts of the globe created new overseas markets. The money spent on railways created demand elsewhere in the economy. Rail transportation, besides fostering capital industry and investment, put new pressure on European

1 David S. Landes, *The Unbound Prometheus: Technological Change and Industrial Development in Western Europe from 1750 to the Present* (Cambridge, England: Cambridge University Press, 1969), p. 193.

agriculture. Trains running into the great plains of the United States lowered the cost of grain imported into Europe. Continental producers now faced foreign competition for the market in food.

Factors other than continued railway construction also accounted for the prosperity that followed hard on the heels of the economic troubles of the 1840s. From the fifties to the early seventies numerous countries negotiated treaties lowering tariffs. Goods could flow more easily and cheaply from one nation to another. New laws permitting the formation of joint stock companies and easier business incorporation allowed the garnering of vast capital funds for investment. Such legal reforms favoring capital expansion were enacted in Britain in 1856, in France in 1863, and in Prussia in 1870. The gold standard, whereby any major currency could be exchanged for gold, brought new confidence to international trade. Throughout Europe the various national currencies became more uniform. Currency rationalization was a major achievement of German unification. Finally, large banks, such as the French Crédit Mobilier and the German Darmstäder Bank, channeled funds into capital investment rather than commerce. Finance capitalism had the power to determine to a large extent what enterprises would and would not be undertaken. Banks rather than individual entrepreneurs now seemed to guide the economy.

New Industries

Initially the economic expansion of the third quarter of the century constituted the spread of industries similar to those pioneered earlier in Great Britain. Thereafter, however, wholly new industries emerged. It is this latter development that is usually termed the *Second Industrial Revolution*. The first Industrial Revolution was associated with textiles, steam, and iron; the second with steel, chemicals, electricity, and oil. Steel began to replace iron in manufacture and construction. It was stronger, more flexible, and more adaptable. Its uses seemed infinite. In the 1850s Henry Bessemer (1830–1898) discovered a

The Eiffel Tower built for a late-nineteenth-century exhibition in Paris seemed to symbolize the material confidence of the age. It dominated the skyline of Paris when it was built—as clearly shown in this 1900 photograph—and still does so today. [The Granger Collection.]

new process, named after him, for manufacturing steel cheaply in large quantities. In 1860 Great Britain, Belgium, France, and Germany had produced 125,000 tons of steel. By 1913 the figure had risen to 32,020,000 tons. Tied to the increased production were new processes for rolling and forming the molten metal for use in shipbuilding, machinery, and automobiles.

The chemical industry came of age during this period. The Solway process of alkali production replaced the older Leblanc process. More sulfuric acid could be produced and so could more laundry soap. New dyestuffs and plastics were also developed. The chemical industry, which has been so fundamental to the quality of life in the twentieth century, represented the earliest example of a combination of scientific and industrial development. Formal scientific research had played only the most minimal role in early industrial development. Trial-and-error amateurism was then the order of the day. By late in the second half of the century chemists and physicists were increasingly called upon to solve the problems of industry. This alliance of science, technology, and industry proved to be fundamental to economic development from the nineties onward. As in so many other fields of the Second Industrial Revolution, Germany led the way in fostering scientific research and education.

The most significant change for industry and eventually for everyday life was the application of electrical energy to production. Electricity was the most versatile and transportable source of power ever discovered. It could be employed to run either large or small machines and to make factory construction more efficient. Electricity was a mode of energy that could be taken to the machinery. The first major public power plant was constructed in Great Britain in 1881. Soon electric poles, lines, and generating stations dotted the European landscape. Electric lights were beginning to be used in homes. Streetcar and subway systems were electrified. The industries powered by electricity in turn produced more and more products that were run by electricity, so that the electrical industry grew rapidly on itself. Probably no

J. M. Keynes Describes Late-Nineteenth-Century Capitalism

In this passage, the great modern economist Keynes (1883–1946) describes the economy disrupted by World War I, with special attention to the inequality of wealth that had contributed to industrial development.

EUROPE *was so organized socially and economically as to secure the maximum accumulation of capital. While there was some continuous improvement in the daily conditions of life of the mass of the population, society was so framed as to throw a great part of the increased income into the control of the class least likely to consume it. The new rich of the nineteenth century were not brought up to large expenditures, and preferred the power which investment gave them to the pleasures of immediate consumption. In fact, it was precisely the inequality of the distribution of wealth which made possible those vast accumulations of fixed wealth and of capital improvements which distinguished that age from all others. Herein lay, in fact, the main justification of the capitalist system. If the rich had spent their new wealth on their own enjoyments, the world would long ago have found such a regime intolerable. But like bees they saved and accumulated, not less to the advantage of the whole community because they themselves held narrower ends in prospect.*

The immense accumulations of fixed capital, which to the great benefit of mankind, were built up during the half century before the [First World] war, could never have come about in a society where wealth was divided equitably. The railways of the world, which that age built as a monument to posterity, were, not less than the pyramids of Egypt, the work of labour which was not free to consume in immediate enjoyment the full equivalent of its efforts.

Thus this remarkable system depended for its growth on a double bluff or deception. On the one hand the labouring classes accepted from ignorance or powerlessness, or were compelled, persuaded, or cajoled by custom, convention, authority, and the well-established order of society into accepting, a situation in which they could call their own very little of the cake that they and nature and the capitalists were co-operating to produce. And on the other hand the capitalist classes were allowed to call the best part of the cake theirs and were theoretically free to consume it, on the tacit underlying conditions that they consumed very little of it in practice. . . .

J. M. Keynes, *The Economic Consequences of the Peace* (New York: Harcourt, Brace and Howe, 1919), pp. 18–20.

single late nineteenth-century development has so influenced the material life style of this century.

The turn of the century also saw the emergence of the first large European demand for petroleum. The internal combustion engine was invented in 1876. When the German engineer Gottlieb Daimler (1834–1900) put it on four wheels and obtained a French patent in 1885, the automobile was born. France initially took the lead in auto manufacture, but for many years the car remained a novelty item that only the wealthy could afford. It was the American Henry Ford (1863–1947) who later made the automobile accessible to large numbers of people. The automobile and the new industrial and chemical uses for oil greatly expanded the demand for petroleum. Before the nineties petroleum had been used primarily for lighting; soon it became the basis for transportation and much of the new chemical industry. Europe, then as now, was almost wholly dependent on imported oil. The major supplying companies were Standard Oil of the United States, British Shell Oil, and Royal Dutch.

The Second Industrial Revolution witnessed a shift in the European economic balance of power. In almost all areas of the new industrial expansion Great Britain, which had pioneered the first Industrial Revolution, fell behind the continent and especially Germany. Britain ceased to be a leader and became simply one more competitor. There was no lack of invention on the part of individual British citizens, but the early industrial lead meant that the nations's industries were often locked into existing productive processes and could not easily incorporate new techniques. The British did too little to encourage scientific and technical education. Its managers put too much faith in the inventive amateur, who had so brilliantly fostered the early Industrial Revolution. British investors put too little capital into new industry. Management was immensely complacent. There was too much dependence on old marketing techniques. Attempts to improve the situation came only after the lead had been lost. All of these factors meant that by 1900, while still a great industrial power, Britain was falling behind Ger-

In the 1890s bicycles rapidly became a popular and low-cost means of transportation. They have remained so among the working class in Europe to the present day. Here women workers are inflating the rubber tubes. Since rubber does not grow in Europe, the rubber for the tires often came from colonial holdings. [Bettmann Archive.]

man competition. This situation had much to do with the international rivalry of the two powers.

Wider Economic Trends

Business Difficulties

The second half of the century was not a period of uninterrupted or smooth economic growth. The years from 1850 to 1873 saw a general boom in both industry and agriculture. The last quarter of the century witnessed economic advance but of a much slower nature. Bad weather and foreign competition put grave pressures on European agriculture. Grain producers suffered the most. In Britain thousands of acres of land went out of tillage. In eastern Europe the landlords demanded new protective tariffs. There were moves to specialize farming. Denmark, for example, at this time changed to dairy production. Other countries adopted more scientific and mechanized modes of agriculture. Fertilizers were more frequently used, and steam engines were taken into fields to aid plowing. These techniques made farming more costly, and the size of farms became larger. From the consumers' standpoint these developments meant lower food prices. Nevertheless the difficulties of the agricultural sector put a drag on the general economy.

During 1873 a number of major banks failed, and the rate of capital investment slowed. The major railway systems had been built. During the next two decades stagnation occurred in several industries. Prices and profits fell. Wages also became lower, but the simultaneous fall in prices meant that real wages generally held firm and in some countries even improved. There were pockets of unemployment. (In fact the word *unemployment* was coined during this period.) Despite the stagnation, the general standard of living in the industrialized nations improved, although many workers still lived and labored in abysmal conditions. What made this depression less cruel and disruptive than the turmoil of the forties was the greater availability of consumer goods and the assurance of a food supply. By the turn of the century the demand for consumer goods and the development of new employing industries made possible by the Second Industrial Revolution had lifted Europe from its economic doldrums.

What brought the economy out of the depression was a new expansion of demand from three primary sources. These were changes in marketing, the reorganization of economic enterprise, and imperialism. The lower food prices eventually allowed all classes to spend a marginally larger amount of their income on consumer goods. Urbanization in and of itself created a larger market. People living in cities simply saw more things that they wanted to buy than they would have if still dwelling in the countryside. The new industries of the late century were largely directed toward consumer goods. Retailing techniques changed. Department stores, retail chains, new packaging, mail-order catalogues, and advertising were developed. Marketing itself was creating new demand. The foundations of a consumer economy were being laid.

Drift away from Competition and Free Trade

The economic pressures of the last quarter of the century brought about a shift from economic competition to business consolidation. Big business firms and corporations were organized. They had no desire to compete

The first telephone exchange in Berlin exhibits the role of both communication and electricity in the second industrial revolution. In this picture men are attending the switchboard; soon, however, women took over these jobs. Telephone companies eventually opened a large area of employment for women. [Bettmann Archive.]

RIGHT: A scene in the Great Hall of the Berlin Stock Exchange at the turn of the century. Holdings of and income from stock had become a major feature of wealthy middle-class life in Western Europe. [Ullstein Bilderdienst.]

because they had far too much to lose. Cartels and trade associations, which were the European version of the American trusts, were organized. They attempted to divide markets and to fix prices so as not to drive each other out of business. The great examples of these were the German General Electric Company, the German Siemens Electric Company, the I. G. Farben chemical concern, and the British Glass Manufacturers' Association. Other industries, such as the Krupp armaments company, organized vertically in order to control the sources of raw materials and marketing as well as manufacturing. These new forms of business organization tended to stabilize industries, to make jobs more secure, and to increase consumer demand in that fashion. They did not, however, necessarily produce the lowest consumer prices.

The mid-century ideal of free trade also came under increasing attack as both farming and manufacturing interests sought to ensure a monopoly in their national markets. Protective tariffs were raised across the Continent. Austria and Russia turned to this device in 1874 and in 1877, respectively. In 1879 Bismarck imposed a tariff to protect German industry and the *Junker* landlords. Italy moved to protection in 1887, and the Third French Republic passed the Meline Tariff in 1892. Each of these measures was passed to bring new domestic political support to the various governments. Great Britain remained true to free trade. Yet even there, after the turn of the century Joseph Chamberlain (1836–1914) led a campaign for tariff reform. The drive for tariffs meant that business was seeking the kind of government aid that it had largely spurned half a century earlier.

Europeans also looked outside their continent for markets. The late century age of imperialism was closely related to internal economic problems. European bankers invested large amounts of money in the rest of the world, with the largest portion going to the development of the United States. But traders and investors also hoped to reap profits from Latin America, Asia, and Africa. The early British textile industry had depended to a great extent on foreign markets. Britain's emulators in the latter part of the century also believed they must penetrate those areas. They needed both raw materials and new outlets for finished goods.

It was once argued that Europeans carved out their colonies in order to create those needed markets. The process is now considered more complicated. In establishing sources for raw materials and in forging markets, Europeans undermined existing governments and traditional societies in the underdeveloped portions of the globe. The result was political instability in those areas. It was after such turmoil had been created that European governments moved in to protect the already existing commercial presence of their nationals. The foreign markets never proved to be as profitable as their promoters hoped. Right up to World War I, Europe itself was the single largest market for its own goods.

At the close of the nineteenth century Europe clearly predominated in the world economy. It had the most capital and its industries provided it with the military might to control other areas. However, within Europe two distinct economic zones had come into existence. One consisted of advanced industrial states, including Britain, Belgium, France, Germany, northern Italy, and the western part of Austria. These areas enjoyed a relatively high standard of living, good transport systems, and healthy, educated populations. The second area consisted of Ireland, the Iberian Peninsula, southern Italy, the Balkans, most of Austria–Hungary, and Russia. There agricultural production and education were backward. These areas exported grain and foodstuffs to the industrialized sector. This European economic division, which came into being in the late nineteenth century, was not overcome until after World War II and even then only partially.

Social Ramifications of the Second Industrial Revolution
The Middle Classes

The sixty years prior to World War I were definitively the age of the middle classes. The Great Exhibition of 1851 held in the Crystal Palace in London had displayed the products and the new material life they had forged. Thereafter the middle classes became the arbiter of taste and the defender of the *status quo*. After the revolutions of 1848 the middle classes ceased to be a revolutionary group. Most of their political goals had been attained, even if imperfectly. Once the question of social equality had been raised, large and small property owners across

The Crystal Palace, erected to house the Great Exhibition of 1851, was a fabulous structure of glass and iron designed by the horticulturist and architect Sir Joseph Paxton (1801–1865) and modeled after his greenhouses for the Duke of Devonshire. It originally stood in Hyde Park, London, but after the exhibition it was dismantled and re-erected at Sydenham, the location shown here. It was destroyed by fire in 1936. The Great Exhibition itself was an abundant display of the vast material accomplishments of the industrial revolution and liberal society. [The Granger Collection.]

the Continent moved to protect what they possessed. The drive toward protective tariffs, new business organization, militarism, and empire suggested that bourgeois Europeans had come to use the power of the state to look out for their own interests as the aristocracy had done before them.

DIVISIONS WITHIN THE MIDDLE CLASS. The middle classes, which had never been perfectly homogeneous, now became even more diverse. Their most prosperous members were the owners and managers of great businesses and banks. They lived in a splendor that rivaled and sometimes excelled that of the aristocracy. Some, such as W. H. Smith, the owner of railway newsstands in England, were made peers. The Krupp family of Germany were pillars of the state. Only a few hundred families acquired such wealth. Beneath them were the comfortable small businessmen and professional people, whose incomes permitted private homes, large quantities

of furniture, pianos, pictures, books, journals, education for their children, and vacations. There were also the shopkeepers, the schoolteachers, the librarians, and others who had either a bit of property or a skill derived from education that provided respectable, nonmanual employment. Finally, there was a wholly new element in the white-collar workers. These included factory foremen, secretaries, retail clerks, and lower-level bureaucrats in business and government. The white-collar labor force was often working class in its origins and might even belong to unions, but its aspirations for life style were middle class. All of these middle-class groups yearned to consume the products made possible by the Second Industrial Revolution.

Considerable tension began to exist among the various strata of middle-class society during the latter part of the century. The small businessmen and shopkeepers, whose numbers rose steadily until shortly after 1900, often resented the power of the great capitalists. The little people of the middle class feared being edged out of the marketplace by large companies, with whom they could not hope to compete. The shopkeeping class always had to work very hard simply to maintain their life style and were often dependent upon banks for commercial credit. Department stores and mail-order catalogues endangered their livelihood. There is also good reason to believe that the learned professions were becoming overcrowded. To be a professional man no longer ensured a sound income. The new white-collar work force had just attained re-

The Gatling gun was a forerunner of the modern machine gun. It greatly increased the destructive power of a small military force. Its invention and incorporation into warfare illustrates the impact of technology on military power in the nineteenth century. In the picture, the American Professor Richard Jordon Gatling (1818–1903) demonstrates his invention. [Culver Pictures.]

The Krupp works at Essen, Germany, was one of the largest military manufacturing establishments in Europe. This late nineteenth-century photograph is taken in the gun shop. The massive production of such arms meant that in the early twentieth century Europeans would be able to turn on themselves more sheer physically destructive force than at any previous time in history. [Culver Pictures.]

spectability and a non-working-class status. They profoundly feared slipping back to their social origins.

Prior to World War I these social groups were reasonably secure but remained quite apprehensive. The business cycle might turn against them. The small supplementary incomes from stocks, bonds, or interest from savings might disappear. Somehow the socialists might confiscate their property. After World War I many of those fears were realized. The profound insecurity that the middle classes then experienced became one of the most significant factors of twentieth-century political life.

THE MIDDLE CLASS FAMILY AND WOMEN. During the late nineteenth century the life style of the middle classes set the tone of the day. Machine-made clothes allowed them to dress well and alike. Machine-made furniture and wallpaper allowed their homes to appear similar. The productive processes they directed allowed the world of everyday life to assume a regularity and a conformity never before quite so possible. At the center of their lives was the family. Although equality and independence were the keynotes of their politics, the opposite qualities predominated in their homes. The bourgeois father presided over his household as a patriarch. Throughout the Continent he controlled most of his wife's property. He could still generally determine whom his daughter married. His son depended on his allowance. He and his sons maintained a double standard of sexual morality, demanding chastity from their sisters and fidelity from their wives while perhaps frequenting brothels themselves. Women in the family setting were supposed to remain what the English poet Coventry Patmore termed "the angel of the house." Perhaps the middle-class male needed that firm structure of home life and domestic values because he knew that the business world in which he dwelled might collapse with the next trade cycle or bank panic.

Whatever the hypocrisy involved in this domestic situation, the nineteenth-century middle-class family, by providing a point of departure for social criticism, has proved a powerful force in forging the conscience of the modern world. There was little or no role in that family and home for an active, articulate, thinking woman. By allowing men to provide sufficient income for the entire family, the new industry and its related enterprises gave women only the most minimal economic role. Smaller families lessened child-rearing duties. The more idle the wife or daughter, the greater the evidence of the success of the husband and father. Yet both the ideology and the structures of liberal society generated a weakening of that situation.

Liberal society and its values neither automatically nor inevitably improved the lot of women. Those who pioneered female entry into the professions, activity on government commissions and school boards, or dispersal of birth control information faced grave social obstacles, personal humiliation, and often outright bigotry. However, the intellectual and political tools for their social critique were present in the society itself.

The rationalism and penchant for self-criticism that have characterized modern Western society manifested themselves in the movement to emancipate women. As early as 1792 in Britain Mary Wollstonecraft (1759–1797), in *The Vindication of the Rights of Woman*, had applied the revolutionary doctrines of the rights of man to the predicament of members of her own sex. John Stuart Mill (1806–1873), in conjunction with the thought of his wife, Harriet Taylor, had applied the logic of liberal freedom to the position of women in *The Subjection of Women* (1869). The arguments for utility and efficiency so dear to middle-class liberals could be used to expose the human and social waste implicit in the inferior role assigned to women. That waste was becoming increasingly demonstrated as women pursued jobs in the professions, schoolteaching, social work, and other employment formerly the preserves of men. New areas of female employment were also opened in clerical jobs. The growing consumer orientation of the economy gave women new indirect power while they were still in the home. Moreover the socialist critique of capitalist society also included

Mary Wollstonecraft (1759–1797) was one of the first writers to call for equal rights for women. Shortly before her early death she was married to William Godwin, the English political writer and novelist. Their child was the future Mary Shelley, author of *Frankenstein* and wife of the Romantic poet. The portrait by John Opie is in the National Portrait Gallery, London. [The Granger Collection.]

a harsh indictment of the social and economic position to which women had been relegated.

Much of the discussion of the social position of women remained merely theory and talk. Some women did gain meaningful employment, but their numbers were small. Women did not rise rapidly through the work force. However, to some extent theory was transformed into practice, or at least protest, so far as political life was concerned. The political tactics used by men to expand the electoral franchise and to influence the governing processes could be and were employed by women toward the same end. The claims to political participation set forth by the respectable, prosperous, and educated working class applied equally well to women.

The most important prewar example of such activity was the British women's suffrage movement led by Mrs. Emmeline Pankhurst (1858–1928). Her husband,

J. S. Mill Analyzes the Causes of the Subjection of Women

John Stuart Mill (1806–1873) was one of the key nineteenth-century spokesmen for women's rights. In this 1869 essay he was concerned that society benefit from the various talents and capacities that women could bring to the social, political, and intellectual problems of the day. He attempted to explain how custom, public opinion, and traditional education not only denied women their rightful place in society but also cunningly convinced them in numerous subtle ways that they could not achieve such a place.

MEN *do not want solely the obedience of women, they want their sentiments. . . . They have therefore put everything in practice to enslave their minds. . . . The masters of women wanted more than simple obedience, and they turned the whole force of education to effect their purpose. All women are brought up from the very earliest years in the belief that their ideal of character is the very opposite to that of men; not self-will, and government by self-control, but submission, and yielding to the control of others. All the moralities tell them that it is the duty of women, and all the current sentimentalities that it is their nature, to live for others; to make complete abnegation of themselves, and to have no life but in their affections. And by their affections are meant the only ones they are allowed to have—those to the men with whom they are connected, or to the children who constitute an additional and indefeasible tie between them and a man. When we put together three things—first, the natural attraction between opposite sexes; secondly, the wife's entire dependence on the husband, every privilege or pleasure she has being either his gift, or depending on his will; and lastly, that the principal object of human pursuit, consideration, and all objects of social ambition, can in general be sought or obtained by her only through him—it would be a miracle if the object of being attractive to men had not become the polar star of feminine education and formation of character. And, this great means of influence over the minds of women having been acquired, an instinct of selfishness made men avail themselves of it to the utmost as a means of holding women in subjection, by representing to them meekness, submissiveness, and resignation of all individual will into the hands of a man, as an essential part of sexual attractiveness.*

John Stuart Mill, *On Liberty, Representative Government, The Subjection of Women* (London: Oxford University Press, 1960), pp. 443–444.

A photograph of John Stuart Mill and his stepdaughter Helen Taylor. Mill was the foremost English rationalist philosopher of the nineteenth century. He was also one of the earliest outspoken advocates of women's rights. [Radio Times Hulton Picture Library.]

BELOW: In 1911 Mrs. Emmeline Pankhurst led major demonstrations of British suffragettes in favor of the vote for women. Several ended in violence. Here Mrs. Pankhurst is literally being carried off to jail. [Culver Pictures.]

who died near the close of the century, had been active in labor and Irish nationalist politics. In 1903 Mrs. Pankhurst and her daughters, Christabel and Sylvia, founded the Women's Social and Political Union. For several years they and their followers, known derisively as the *Suffragettes,* lobbied publicly and privately for the extension of the vote to women. By 1910, having failed to move the government, they turned to the violent tactics of arson, window breaking, and sabotage of postal boxes. They marched en masse on Parliament. The Liberal government of Henry Asquith imprisoned many of the women and force-fed those who went on hunger strikes in jail. The government refused to extend the franchise. Only in 1918 did some British women receive the vote as a result of their contribution to the war effort. Prior to the conflict women could vote only in Norway and Finland. It required the social and emotional upheaval of World War I to bring women in significant numbers to a place of prominence and acceptance in European political life.

The Working Classes

The late century industrial expansion wrought further changes in the life of the labor force. In all industrializing continental countries the numbers of the urban proletariat rose. Like the middle class, the working class became more differentiated in its composition. Proportionally there were many fewer artisans, craftsmen, and highly skilled workers. For the first time factory wage-earners came to predominate. The increasingly mechanized factories often required less highly technical skills from its operatives. There also occurred considerable growth in the very unskilled work associated with shipping, transportation, and building. Work assumed a more impersonal character. Factories were located in cities, and practically all links between factory or day-labor employment and home life dissolved. Large corporate enterprise meant less personal contact between employers and their workers.

On the whole, the standard of living improved throughout the second half of the century. However, that improvement was often more statistical than real. There still existed widespread poverty, poor housing, sweatshop working conditions, and the haunting fears of accident, disability, unemployment, and old age. Between 1900 and World War I, industrial labor discontent was distinctly on the rise as wages failed to keep up with rising prices. During the latter years of the nineteenth century a

This print by Gustave Doré from the third quarter of the nineteenth century portrays an institution in London where homeless persons might spend the night. The gentleman in the middle is reading the Bible to the derelicts who have come in off the street. Many such charitable institutions were closely connected to Christian churches.

few big businesses attempted to provide some security for their employees through company housing and pension plans. Although these efforts were in a few cases pioneering, they could not prove adequate for the mass of the labor force.

TRADE UNIONISM. Workers still had to look to themselves for improvement of their situation. However, after 1848 European workers ceased taking to the streets to voice their grievances in the form of riots. They also stopped trying to revive the paternal guilds and similar institutions of the past. After mid-century the labor force accepted the fact of modern industrial production and its general downgrading of skills and attempted to receive more benefits from that system. Workers turned to new institutions and ideologies. Chief among these were trade unions, democratic political parties, and socialism.

Trade unionism came of age as legal protections were extended throughout the second half of the century. Unions became legal in Great Britain in 1871 and were allowed to picket in 1875. In France Napoleon III had first used troops against strikes, but as his political power waned, he allowed weak labor associations in 1868. The Third French Republic fully legalized unions in 1884. After 1890 they could function in Germany with little disturbance. Initially most trade unions entered the political process in a rather marginal fashion. So long as representatives of the traditional governing classes looked after labor interests, members of the working class rarely sought office themselves.

The mid-century organizational efforts of the unions were directed toward skilled workers. The goal was immediate improvement of wages and working conditions. By the close of the century, industrial unions for unskilled workers were being organized. They were very large and included thousands of workers. They confronted extensive opposition from employers, and longer strikes were frequently required to bring about employer acceptance. In the prewar decade there were an exceedingly large number of strikes thoughout Europe as the unions attempted to raise wages to keep up with inflation.

However, despite the advances of unions and the growth of memberships in 1910 to approximately 3 million in Britain, 2 million in Germany, and 977,000 in France, they never included a majority of the industrial labor force. What the unions did represent was a new collective fashion in which workers could associate to confront the economic difficulties of their lives and to attain better security.

DEMOCRACY AND POLITICAL PARTIES. The democratic franchise provided workers with direct political influence, which meant that they could no longer be ignored. With the exception of Russia all the major European states adopted broad-based, if not perfectly democratic, electoral systems. Great Britain passed its second reform act in 1867 and its third in 1884. Bismarck brought universal manhood suffrage to the German Empire in 1871. The French Chamber of Deputies was democratically elected. Universal manhood suffrage was adopted in Switzerland in 1879, in Spain in 1890, in Belgium in 1893, in the Netherlands in 1896, and in Norway in 1898. Italy finally fell into line in 1912. Democracy brought new modes of popular pressure to bear on all governments. It meant that discontented groups could now voice their grievances and advocate their programs within the institutions of government rather than from the outside.

The advent of democracy witnessed the formation for the first time in Europe of organized mass political parties. These had existed throughout the nineteenth century in the United States. In the liberal European states of narrow electoral bases most voters had been people of property who knew what they had at stake in politics. Organization had been minimal. The new expansion of the electorate brought into the political processes many people whose level of political consciousness, awareness, and interest was quite low. This electorate had to be organized and taught the nature of power and influence in the liberal democratic state. The organized political party—with its workers, newspapers, offices, social life, and discipline—was the vehicle that mobilized the new voters. The largest single group in these mass electorates was the working class. The democratization of politics presented the socialists with opportunities and caused the traditional ruling classes to vie with the socialists for the support of the new voters.

Labor, Socialism, and Politics to World War I

Along with new opportunities, the trade unions and the democratic electorates created ideological and practical problems for European socialists. Early socialist doctrines had been conditioned by both the economic dislocation of early industrialization and the exclusion of the workers from politics. Socialists of various kinds had called for major social changes, often involving violent revolution. However, unions, democracy, and rising standards of living meant that the ends of socialism might be attained within the existing political framework and without violent revolution. Moreover, as the labor force began to receive direct benefits from the expanding economy, they were less likely to desire its destruction. It was while working out these ideological and tactical problems that European socialists entered the mainstream of European politics. The internal socialist conflicts of these years have continued to influence the movement in Europe and elsewhere to the present day.

Marx and the First International

Karl Marx himself made considerable accommodation to the new practical realities that developed during the third quarter of the century. He did not abandon the revolutionary doctrines of *The Communist Manifesto,* and in *Capital* (1867) he continued to predict the disintegration of capitalism. His private thoughts as revealed in his letters also remained quite revolutionary, but his practical, public political activity reflected a somewhat different approach.

In 1864 a group of British and French trade unionists founded the International Working Men's Association.

Known as the First International, its membership encompassed a vast array of radical political types, including socialists, anarchists, and Polish nationalists. The First International allowed Marx, who was by then quite active in the London radical community, to write its Inaugural Address. In it he urged radical social change and the economic emancipation of the working class, but he also supported and approved efforts by workers and trade unions to reform the conditions of labor within the existing political and economic processes. He urged revolution but tempered the means. Privately he often criticized such reformist activity, but those writings were not made public till near the end of the century, and after his death.

During the late sixties the First International gathered statistics, kept labor groups informed of mutual problems, provided a forum for debate of socialist doctrine, and extravagantly proclaimed its own size and influence. From these debates and activities Marxism emerged as the single most important strand of socialism. In 1872 Marx and his supporters drove the anarchists out of the International. Marx was determined to preserve the role of the state against the anarchist attack on authority and large political organizations. Through the meetings and discussions of the First International, German socialists became deeply impressed with Marx's thought. Because, as will be seen, they became the most important socialist party in Europe, they became the chief channel for the preservation and development of Marxist thought.

The First International proved to be a very fragile structure. The events surrounding the Paris Commune presented the final blow to its existence. Few socialists and no real Marxists were involved with the Commune. However, Marx in a major pamphlet glorified the Commune as a genuine proletarian uprising. British trade unionists, who in 1871 were finally receiving new legal protection, wanted no connection with the crimes of the Parisians. The French authorities used the uprising to suppress socialist activity. Throughout Europe the events in Paris cast a pall over socialism. The First International held its last European congress in 1873. Its offices were then transferred to the United States, where it was dissolved in 1876. Thereafter the fate of socialism and the labor movement depended largely on the economic and political conditions of the individual European countries.

Great Britain: Fabianism and Early Welfare Programs

Neither Marxism nor any other form of socialism made significant progress in Great Britain, the most advanced industrial society of the day. There trade unions grew steadily and members normally supported Liberal Party candidates. The "new unionism" of the late eighties and the nineties organized the dock workers, the gas workers, and similar unskilled groups. Employer resistance to unions heightened class antagonism. In 1892 Kier Hardie became the first independent working man to be elected to Parliament. The next year the small, socialist Independent Labor Party was founded, but it remained ineffective.

Until 1901 general political activity on the part of labor remained quite limited. The Taff Vale decision in that year by the House of Lords, however, removed the legal protection previously accorded union funds. The Trades Union Congress responded by launching the Labor Party. In the election of 1906 the fledgling party sent twenty-nine members to Parliament. Their goals as trade unionists did not yet encompass socialism. Along with this new political departure the British labor movement became more militant. There were scores of strikes before the war as workers fought for wages to meet the rising cost of living. The government took a larger role than ever before in mediating these strikes, which in 1911 and 1912 involved the railways, the docks, and the mines.

British socialism itself remained primarily the preserve of intellectuals. H. M. Hyndman (1842–1921), a wealthy graduate of Eton, and William Morris (1834–1896), the poet and designer, read Marx's works avidly, but their Social Democratic Federation, founded in 1881, never had more than a handful of members. The socialists who exerted the most influence were the Fabian Society, founded in 1884. Their leading members were Sydney (1859–1947) and Beatrice (1858–1943) Webb, H. G. Wells (1866–1946), Graham Wallas (1858–1932), and George Bernard Shaw (1856–1950). Many of the Fabians were civil servants who believed that the problems of industry, the expansion of ownership, and the state direction of production could be achieved gradually, peacefully, and democratically. They sought to educate the country to the rational wisdom of socialism. They were particularly interested in modes of collective ownership on the municipal level, the so-called gas and water socialism.

The British government and the major political parties responded slowly to these various pressures. In 1903 Joseph Chamberlain launched his unsuccessful tariff reform campaign to finance social reform through higher import duties. The campaign badly split the Conservative Party. After 1906 the Liberal Party, led by Henry Campbell-Bannerman (1836–1908) and after 1908 by Herbert Asquith (1852–1928), pursued a two-pronged policy. Fearful of losing seats in Parliament to the new Labor Party, they restored the former protection of unions. Then after 1909, with David Lloyd George (1863–1945) as the guiding light, the Liberal ministry undertook a broad program of social legislation. This included the establishment of labor exchanges, the regulation of the sweated labor trades, such as tailoring and lacemaking, and the National Insurance Act of 1911 to provide unemployment benefits and health care. The financing of these programs brought the House of Commons into conflict with the Conservative-dominated House of Lords. The result was the House of Lords Act of 1911, which allowed the Commons to override the legislative veto of the upper chamber. The new taxes and social programs meant that in Britain, the home of nineteenth-century liberalism, the state was taking on an expanded role in the life of its citizens. The early welfare legislation was only marginally satisfactory to labor, many of whose members still thought they could gain more from the direct action of strikes.

Sidney Webb Relates Socialism to Democracy

Members of the Fabian Society represented a major force in British socialism. They believed that through democracy the great social questions of the day could be addressed. They hoped to replace individualism by state action. In their view the goals of socialism could be achieved without revolution. Sidney Webb, whose views follow, and his wife Beatrice were frequent voices for the Fabians.

T*HE main stream which has borne European society towards Socialism during the past 100 years is the irresistible progress of Democracy. . . .*

In the present Socialist movement these two streams are united: advocates of social reconstruction have learnt the lesson of Democracy, and know that it is through the slow and gradual turning of the popular mind to new principles that social reorganization bit by bit comes. All students of society who are abreast of their time, Socialists as well as Individualists, realize that important organic changes can only be (1) democratic, and thus acceptable to a majority of the people, and prepared for in the minds of all; (2) gradual, and thus causing no dislocation, however rapid may be the rate of progress; (3) not regarded as immoral by the mass of the people, and thus not subjectively demoralizing to them; and (4) in this country at any rate, constitutional and peaceful. Socialists may therefore be quite one with Radicals in their political methods. Radicals, on the other hand, are perforce realizing that mere political levelling is insufficient to save a State from anarchy and despair. Both sections have been driven to recognize that the root of the difficulty is economic; and there is every day a wider consensus that the inevitable outcome of Democracy is the control by the people themselves, not only of their own political organization, but, through that, also of the main instruments of wealth production; the gradual substitution of organized cooperation for the anarchy of the competitive struggle. . . . The economic side of the democratic ideal is, in fact, Socialism itself.

Sidney Webb, in *Fabian Essays in Socialism* (Gloucester, Mass.: Peter Smith, 1967, originally published 1889), pp. 50–52.

Beatrice and Sidney Webb, a photograph from the late 1920s. These most influential British Fabian Socialists wrote many books on governmental and economic matters, served on special parliamentary commissions, and agitated for the enactment of socialist policies. [Radio Times Hulton Picture Library.]

France: "Opportunism" Rejected

French socialism gradually revived after the suppression of the Paris Commune. The institutions of the Third Republic provided a framework for legal activity. The major problem for French socialists was their own internal division rather than government opposition. There were no fewer than five separate parties, plus other independent socialists. They managed to elect approximately forty members to the Chamber of Deputies by the early nineties. Despite their lack of common policy, the socialist presence aided the passage of measures to relieve workers from carrying identity cards and to provide for factory inspection and limited working hours and health care. In 1910 the republic inaugurated a scheme for voluntary pensions. However, the most important developments of French labor and socialism were not legislative.

At the turn of the century the two major factions of French socialism were led by Jean Jaurès (1859–1914) and Jules Guesde (1845–1922). The former believed that socialists should cooperate with radical middle-class ministries to ensure the enactment of needed social legislation. Guesde opposed this policy, arguing that socialists could not with integrity support a bourgeois cabinet that they were theoretically dedicated to overthrow. The quarrel came to a head as a by-product of the Dreyfus affair. In 1899, as a means of uniting all supporters of Dreyfus, Prime Minister René Waldeck-Rousseau (1846–1904) appointed the socialist Allexander Millerand to the Cabinet. By 1904 the issue of "opportunism," as such cabinet participation by socialists was termed, came to be debated at the Amsterdam Congress of the Second International. This organization has been founded in 1889 in a new effort to unify the various national socialist parties and

Under a Dutch banner calling for the proletariat of all lands to unite, a congress of the Second Socialist International meets in Amsterdam in 1904 to debate ideology and practical tactics. [Internationaal Instituut voor Sociale Geschiedenis, Amsterdam.]

trade unions. The Amsterdam Congress condemned "opportunism" in France and ordered the French socialists to form a single party. Jaurès, believing socialist unity the most important issue in France, accepted the decision. French socialists began to work together, and by 1914 the United Socialist Party was the second largest group in the Chamber of Deputies. However, Socialist Party members would not again serve in a French cabinet until the Popular Front Government of 1936.

The French labor movement, with deep roots in the Proudhonian doctrines of anarchism, was uninterested in both politics and socialism. French workers tended to vote socialist, but the unions avoided active political participation. The Confédération Générale du Travail was founded in 1895 and regarded itself as a rival to the socialist parties. Its leaders sought to improve the workers' conditions through direct action. They embraced the doctrines of syndicalism, which were most persuasively expounded by Georges Sorel (1847–1922) in *Reflections on Violence* (1908). This book enshrined the idea of the general strike as a means of generating worker unity and power. The strike tactic was quite different from the socialist idea of aiding the situation of labor through the action of the state. Strike action on the part of unions flourished between 1905 and 1914, and the radical ministry on more than one occasion used troops against the strikers. Consequently, in France the forces of labor were suppressed by the liberal state, and the Socialist Party was locked into a doctrine of nonparticipation in the Cabinet, which effectively undermined its potential political influence.

Germany: Social Democrats and Revisionism

The hostile judgment rendered by the Second International against French socialist participation in bourgeois ministries reflected the policy previously adopted by the German Social Democratic Party, or SPD. The organizational success of this party more than any other single factor kept Marxist socialism alive into the latter part of the century. The party was founded in 1869. Its origins

 ## The German Empire Legislates Against the Socialists

Through these 1878 laws Bismarck hoped to destroy the young Social Democratic Party. The measures were intended to make it difficult for the SPD to hold meetings, publish newspapers and pamphlets, and collect money to support its activities. The Anti-Socialist Laws remained in effect until 1891.

1. Associations *which aim, by Social Democratic, Socialistic, or Communistic endeavours, at the destruction of the existing order in State or society, are to be forbidden. . . .*

.   .   .   .   .   .

9. *Meetings in which Social Democratic, Socialistic, or Communistic tendencies, directed to the destruction of the existing order in State or society, make their appearance, are to be dissolved.*

Meetings, of which facts justify the assumption that they are destined to further such tendencies, are to be forbidden.

Public festivities and processions are placed under the same restrictions.

.   .   .   .   .   .

11. *Printed matter, in which Social Democratic, Socialistic, or Communistic tendencies, directed to the destruction of the existing order in State and society in a manner dangerous to the peace, and, in particular, to the harmony between different classes of the population, make their appearance, is to be forbidden.*

In the case of periodical literature, the prohibition can be extended to any further issue, as soon as a single number has been forbidden under this law.

.   .   .   .   .   .

16. *The collection of contributions for the furthering of Social Democratic, Socialistic, or Communistic endeavours, directed toward the destruction of the existing order in State or society, as also the public instigation to the furnishing of such contributions, are [sic] to be forbidden by the police.*

.   .   .   .   .   .

28. *For districts or localities which are threatened, by the above-mentioned endeavours, with danger to the public safety, the following provisions can be made, for the space of a year at most, by the central police of the state in question, and subject to the permission of the* Bundesrath [*the upper chamber of the Parliament*].

(1) That meetings may only take place with the previous permission of the police; this prohibition does not extend to meetings for an election to the Reichstag *or the Diet.*

(2) That the distribution of printed matter may not

take place in public roads, streets, or places, or other public localities.

(3) That residence in such districts or localities can be forbidden to all persons from whom danger to the public safety or order is to be feared.

(4) That the possession, import, or sale of weapons is forbidden, limited, or confined by certain conditions.

Bertrand Russell, *German Social Democracy* (London: Longmans, Green, 1896), pp. 100–102.

lay in the labor agitation of Ferdinand Lasalle (1825–1864), who wanted worker participation in German politics. His followers were joined by Wilhelm Liebknecht (1826–1900) and August Bebel (1840–1913), who were Marxists. Consequently the party was divided from its founding between those who wanted reformist political activity and those who advocated revolution.

The forging experience of the SPD was twelve years of persecution by Bismarck. The iron chancellor believed that socialism would undermine German politics and society. Less than a decade after its founding, he moved against the young SPD. In 1878 there was an attempt to assassinate William I. Although the socialists were not involved, Bismarck used the opportunity to steer an antisocialist law through the *Reichstag*. The organization, meetings, newspapers, and other public activities of the SPD were suppressed. To remain a socialist meant to remove oneself from the mainstream of respectable German life and possibly to lose one's job. The antisocialist legislation proved politically counterproductive. From the early eighties onward the SPD steadily polled more and more votes in elections to the *Reichstag*.

As simple repression failed to separate German workers from socialist loyalties, Bismarck undertook a program of social welfare legislation. In 1883 the German Empire adopted a health insurance measure. The next year saw the enactment of accident insurance legislation. Finally, in 1889 Bismarck sponsored a plan for old age and disability pensions. These programs, to which both workers and employers contributed, represented a paternalistic, conservative alternative to socialism. The state itself would organize a system of social security that did not require any change in the system of property holding or politics. Germany became the first major industrial nation to enjoy this kind of welfare program.

In 1890, after forcing Bismarck's resignation, Emperor William II (1888–1918) allowed the antisocialist legislation to expire in hope of thus building new support for the monarchy among the working class. Even under the repressive laws members of the SPD could sit in the *Reichstag*. Now, however, the question became what attitude the recently legalized party should assume toward the German Empire. The answer came in the Erfurt Program of 1891, formulated under the political guidance of Bebel and the ideological tutelage of Karl Kautsky (1854–1938). In good Marxist fashion the program declared the imminent doom of capitalism and the necessity of socialist ownership of the means of production. However, these goals were to be achieved by legal political participation rather than by revolutionary activity. Because by its very nature capitalism must fall, the immediate task of socialists was to work for the improvement of workers' lives rather than for the revolution, which was inevitable. In theory the SPD was vehemently hostile to the German Empire, but in practice the party functioned within its institutions. The SPD members of the *Reichstag* maintained clear consciences by refusing to enter the Cabinet, to which they were not invited anyway, and by refraining for many years from voting for the military budget.

The situation of the SPD, however, generated the most important internal socialist challenge to the orthodox Marxist analysis of capitalism and the socialist revolution. Eduard Bernstein (1850–1932) was the author of this socialist heresy. He had spent over a decade of his life in Great Britain and was quite familiar with the Fabians.

Labor, Socialism, and Politics to World War I **759**

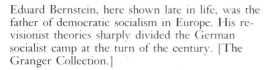

The German Social Democratic Party Presents a Program

After the Anti-Socialist Laws were repealed in 1891, the German Social Democratic Party could once more operate legally. Through the Erfurt Program of the same year the party again asserted a basically revolutionary program for the working class. In theory the Erfurt Program rejected the idea of compromising the goals of socialism with the existing social and economic structures of the German Empire. However, despite its rhetoric the SPD did not undertake revolutionary activity. Here is the important part of the Erfurt Program.

PRIVATE *property in the means of production, which was formerly the means of securing to the producer the possession of his own product, has to-day become the means of expropriating peasants, handicraftsmen and small producers, and of putting the non-workers, capitalists and great landlords in possession of the product of the workers. Only the conversion of capitalistic private property in the means of production . . . into common property, and the change of the production of goods into a socialistic production, worked for and through society, can bring it about that production on a large scale, and the ever-growing productiveness of human labour, shall develop, for the hitherto exploited classes, from a source of misery and oppression, into a source of the highest well-being and perfect universal harmony.*

This social change betokens the emancipation, not only of the proletariat, but of the whole human race, which is suffering under the present conditions. But it can only be the work of the working classes. . . .

The struggle of the working class against capitalistic exploitation is of necessity a political struggle. . . .

To give to this fight of the working class a conscious and unified form, and to show it its necessary goal—that is the task of the Social Democratic Party.

The interests of the working classes are the same in all countries with a capitalistic mode of production. . . . In recognition of this, the Social Democratic Party of Germany feels and declares itself to be one with the class-conscious workmen of all other countries.

The Social Democratic Party of Germany does not fight, accordingly, for new class-privileges and class-rights, but for the abolition of class-rule and of classes themselves, for equal rights and equal duties of all, without distinction of sex or descent.

Bertrand Russell, *German Social Democracy* (London: Longmans, Green, 1896), pp. 138–139.

Eduard Bernstein, here shown late in life, was the father of democratic socialism in Europe. His revisionist theories sharply divided the German socialist camp at the turn of the century. [The Granger Collection.]

Rosa Luxemburg (1870–1919) was a German radical who strongly supported the revolutionary concept of socialism. She was assassinated while in prison. [The Granger Collection.]

Bernstein questioned whether Marx and his later ortho-dox followers, such as Kautsky, had been correct in their pessimistic appraisal of capitalism and the necessity of revolution. In *Evolutionary Socialism* (1899) Bernstein pointed to the rising standard of living in Europe. Own-ership of capitalist industry was becoming more wide-spread through stockholding. The middle class was not being forced into the ranks of the proletariat and was not identifying its problems with those of the workers. The inner contradictions of capitalism as expounded by Marx had simply not developed. Moreover the opening of the franchise to the working class meant that revolutionary change might be achieved through parliamentary meth-ods. What was required to realize a humane socialist society was not revolution but more democracy and social reform.

Bernstein's doctrines, known as *revisionism*, were widely debated among German socialists and were finally condemned as theory. His critics argued that evolution toward social democracy might be possible in liberal, parliamentary Britain, but not in authoritarian, militaristic Germany, with its basically powerless *Reichstag*. The critics were probably correct about the German political scene. Nonetheless, while still calling for revolution, the SPD pursued a course of action similar to that advocated by Bernstein. Its trade union members prospering with the German economy did not want revolution. Its grass-roots members wanted to consider themselves patriotic Germans as well as good socialists. Its leaders feared any actions that might renew the persecution that they had experienced under Bismarck. Consequently the party worked at elections, membership expansion, and short-term political and social reform. It prospered and became one of the most important institutions of imperial Ger-many. Even some middle-class Germans voted for it as a means of opposing the illiberal institutions of the empire. And in August 1914, after long debate among them-selves, the SPD members of the *Reichstag* abandoned their former stance and unanimously voted for the war credits that would finance World War I.

Russia: Industrial Development and the Birth of Bolshevism

During the last decade of the nineteenth century Rus-sia entered the industrial age and confronted many of the problems that the more advanced nations of the Conti-nent had experienced fifty or seventy-five years earlier. Unlike those other countries Russia had to deal with major political discontent and economic development simultaneously. Russian socialism reflected that peculiar situation.

WITTE'S PROGRAM FOR INDUSTRIAL GROWTH. The emancipation of the serfs in 1861 had brought little agricultural progress. The peasants were burdened with redemption payments, local taxes, excessive national taxes, and falling grain prices. There were few attempts to educate the peasantry in the more advanced techniques of farming. Most of the land held by free peasants was owned communally through the *mir*, or village. This system of ownership was extremely inefficient and em-ployed strip farming and the farming of small plots. Between 1860 and 1914 the population of European Russia rose from approximately 50 million to approxi-mately 103 million people. Land hunger spread among the peasants. There was intense agrarian discontent.

Count Sergei Witte was the major planner of industrialism in late nineteenth-century Russia. [The Granger Collection.]

Peasants with too little land still had to work on larger noble estates or for more prosperous peasant farmers known as *kulaks*. Uprisings in the countryside were a frequent problem. The agricultural sector benefited little from the late-century industrialism.

Alexander III and Nicholas II were determined that Russia should become an industrial power. Only by this means could the country maintain its military position and its diplomatic role in Europe. The person who led Russia into the industrial age was Sergei Witte (1849–1915). After a career in railways and other private business, he was appointed finance minister in 1892. Witte epitomized the nineteenth-century modernizer who pursued a policy of planned economic development, protective tariffs, high taxes, the gold standard, and efficiency. He established a strong financial link with the French money market, which led to later diplomatic cooperation between Russia and France.

Witte favored heavy industries. Between 1890 and 1904 the Russian railway system grew from 30,596 kilometers to 59,616 kilometers. The 5000-mile Trans-Siberian Railroad was almost completed. Coal output more than tripled during the same period. There was a vast increase in pig-iron production, from 928,000 tons in 1890 to 4,641,000 tons in 1913. During the same period steel production rose from 378,000 tons to 4,918,000 tons. The textile industry continued to expand and still constituted the single largest industry. The factory sys-tem began to be used more extensively throughout the country.

Industrialism brought considerable social discontent to Russia, as it had elsewhere. Landowners felt that foreign capitalists were earning too much of the profits. The peasants saw their grain exports and tax payments finance development that did not measurably improve their lot. A small but significant industrial proletariat arose. At the turn of the century there were approximately three million factory workers in Russia. Their working and living conditions were very bad by any standard. They enjoyed little state protection, and trade unions were illegal. In 1897 Witte did enact a measure providing for an $11\frac{1}{2}$-hour workday. But needless to say, discontent and strikes continued.

The economic development was accompanied by new political departures. In 1901 the Social Revolutionary Party was founded. Its members and intellectual roots went back to the Populists of the seventies. The party was opposed to industrialism and looked to the communal life of rural Russia as a model for the future. In 1903 the Constitutional Democratic Party, or Cadets, was formed. They were liberal in outlook and were drawn from people who participated in the local *zemstvos*. They wanted a parliamentary regime with responsible ministries, civil liberties, and economic progress. The Cadets hoped to model themselves on the liberal parties of western Europe.

LENIN'S EARLY THOUGHT AND CAREER. The situation for Russian socialists differed radically from that in other major European countries. Russia had no representative institutions and only a small working class. The compromises and accommodations achieved elsewhere were meaningless in Russia, where socialism in both theory and practice had to be revolutionary. The Russian Social Democratic Party had been established in 1898, but the repressive policies of the tsarist regime meant that the party had to function in exile. It was Marxist and greatly admired the German Social Democratic Party.

The leading late nineteenth-century Russian Marxist

was Gregory Plekhanov (1857–1918), who wrote from his exile in Switzerland. At the turn of the century his chief disciple was Vladimir Illich Ulyanov (1870–1924), who later took the name of Lenin. The future leader of the Communist Revolution had been born in 1870 as the son of a high bureaucrat. His older brother while a student in St. Petersburg had become involved in radical politics. He was arrested for participating in a plot against Alexander III and was executed in 1887. In 1893 Lenin moved to St. Petersburg, where he studied to become a lawyer. Soon he too became drawn to the revolutionary groups among factory workers. He was arrested in 1895 and exiled to Siberia. In 1900, after his release, Lenin left Russia for the West. He spent most of the next eighteen years in Switzerland.

Once in Switzerland Lenin became deeply involved in the organizational and policy disputes of the exiled Russian Social Democrats. They all considered themselves Marxists, but they held differing positions on the proper nature of a Marxist revolution in primarily rural Russia and on the structure of their own party. Unlike the backward-looking Social Revolutionaries, the Social Democrats were modernizers who favored further industrial development. The majority believed that Russia must develop a large proletariat before the revolution could come. This same majority hoped to mold a mass political party like the German SPD.

Lenin dissented from both positions. In *What Is To Be Done?* (1902) he condemned any accommodations, such as those practiced by the German SPD. He also criticized trade unionism that settled for short-term gains rather than true revolutionary change for the working class. Lenin further rejected the concept of a mass party composed of workers. Revolutionary consciousness would not arise spontaneously from the working class. It must be carried to them by "people who make revolutionary activity their profession." [2] Only a small elite party would

possess the proper dedication to revolution and be able to resist penetration by police spies. The guiding principle of that party should be "the strictest secrecy, the strictest selection of members, and the training of professional revolutionaries." [3]

In 1903, at the London Congress of the Russian Social Democratic Party, Lenin forced a split in party ranks. The more moderate democratic revolutionary faction became known as the *Mensheviks,* or "minority," although they really constituted a majority of the congress. Lenin's faction assumed the name *Bolsheviks,* meaning "majority." In 1912 the Bolsheviks organized separately. In 1905 Lenin complemented his organizational theory with a program for revolution in Russia. *Two Tactics of Social Democracy in the Bourgeois-Democratic Revolution* urged that the socialist revolution unite the proletariat and the peasants. Lenin grasped better than any other revolutionary the profound discontent in the Russian countryside. He knew that an alliance of workers and peasants in rebellion probably could not be suppressed. Lenin's two principles of an elite party and a dual social revolution allowed the Bolsheviks in late 1917 to capture leadership of the Russian Revolution and to transform the political face of the modern world.

THE REVOLUTION OF 1905 AND ITS AFTERMATH. The quarrels among the Russian socialists and Lenin's doctrines had no immediate influence on events in their country itself. Industrialization proceeded and continued to stir resentment in many sectors. In 1903 Nicholas II dismissed Witte in hope of quelling the criticism. The next year Russia went to war with Japan, partly in expectation that public opinion would rally to the tsar. However, the result was Russian defeat and political crisis. The Japanese captured Port Arthur early in 1905. A few days later, on January 22, a priest named Father Gapon led several hundred workers to present a petition to the tsar for the improvement of industrial life. As the petitioners approached the Winter Palace in St. Petersburg, the tsar's troops opened fire. About one hundred

2 Quoted in Albert Fried and Ronald Sanders (Eds.), *Socialist Thought: A Documentary History* (Garden City, N.Y.: Anchor Doubleday, 1964), p. 459.

3 Ibid., p. 468.

people were shot down in cold blood, and many more were wounded. Never again would the Russian people see the tsar as their protector and "little father."

During the next ten months revolutionary disturbances spread throughout Russia. Sailors mutinied. Peasant revolts erupted, and property was attacked. The uncle of Nicholas II was assassinated. Liberal Constitutional Democrat leaders from the *zemstvos* demanded political reform. Student strikes occurred in the universities. Social Revolutionaries and Social Democrats were active among urban working groups. In early October 1905 strikes broke out in St. Petersburg, and for all practical purposes worker groups called *soviets* controlled the city. Nicholas II recalled Witte and issued the October Manifesto, which promised Russia constitutional government. Early in 1906 Nicholas II announced the election of a Duma with two chambers. However, he reserved to himself the appointment of ministers, financial policy, military matters, and foreign affairs. The April elections returned a very radical group of representatives. The tsar dismissed Witte and replaced him with P. A. Stolypin (1862–1911), who had little sympathy for parliamentary government. Within four months Stolypin persuaded Nicholas to dissolve the Duma. A second assembly was elected in February 1907. Again cooperation proved impossible, and dissolution came in June of that year. The tsar then changed the franchise to ensure a conservative parliament. The third Duma elected on the new basis in late 1907 proved sufficiently pliable for the tsar and his minister. Thus within two years of the 1905 Revolution, Nicholas II had recaptured much of the ground he had conceded.

Stolypin set about repressing rebellion, removing some causes of the revolt, and rallying property owners behind the tsarist regime. Early in 1907 special field courts-martial tried rebellious peasants, with almost seven hundred executions resulting. Before turning to this repression, the minister had canceled the redemptive payments that peasants still owed to the government from the emancipation of the serfs in 1861. This step, undertaken in

---

Russian Workers Attempt to Present a Petition to the Tsar

Growing unrest in Russia led, among other things, to organization in 1903 of the Assembly of Russian Factory and Mill Workers of St. Petersburg under a priest, Father Gapon. On January 22, 1905 the Assembly was able to muster a large crowd of workers to converge on Tsar Nicholas II's Winter Palace in the hope of peacefully presenting a petition detailing urban grievances and outlining a program of widespread industrial, political, and economic reform. Rather than allow access to the tsar, security forces, commanded by the tsar's uncle, fired on the crowd. This is the petition's preamble.

WE, WORKING *men and inhabitants of St. Petersburg of various classes, our wives and our children and our helpless old parents, come to Thee, Sire, to seek for truth and defence. We have become beggars; we have been oppressed; we are burdened by toil beyond our powers; we are scoffed at; we are not recognized as human beings; we are treated as slaves who must suffer their bitter fate and who must keep silence. We suffered, but we are pushed farther into the den of beggary, lawlessness, and ignorance. We are choked by despotism and irresponsibility, and we are breathless. . . . The first request which we made was that our masters should discuss our needs with us; but this they refused, on the ground that no right to make this request is recognized by law. They also declared to be illegal our requests to diminish the working hours to eight hours daily, to agree with us about the prices for our work, to consider our misunderstandings with the inferior administration of the mills, to increase the wages for the labour of women and of general labourers, so that the minimum daily wage should be one ruble per day, to abolish overtime work, to give us medical attention without insulting us, to arrange the workshops so that it might be possible to work there, and not find in them death from awful draughts and from rain and snow. All these requests appeared to be, in the opinion of our masters and of the factory and mill administrations, illegal. Everyone of our requests was a crime, and the desire to improve our condition was regarded by them as impertinence, and as offensive to them.*

. . . In reality in us, as in all Russian people, there is not recognized any human right, not even the right of speaking, thinking, meeting, discussing our needs, taking measures for the improvement of our condition.

James Mavor, *An Economic History of Russia* (London: J. M. Dent & Sons, 1914), pp. 469–470.

On "Bloody Sunday," January 22, 1905, troops of Tsar Nicholas II fired on a peaceful procession of workers who sought to present a petition at the Winter Palace in St. Petersburg. After this day there was little chance that the Russian working class could be reconciled with the existing government. [*Soviet Life* from Sovfoto.]

Grigori Rasputin was the sinister Russian monk who claimed the power to heal the ill son of Tsar Nicholas II and acquired great influence at court. His presence alienated many politically important persons from support of Nicholas. Rasputin was finally assassinated by a group of Russian noblemen. [The Granger Collection.]

November 1906, was part of a more general policy to eradicate communal land ownership. The peasants were encouraged to assume individual proprietorship of their land holdings and to abandon the communal system associated with the *mirs*. Stolypin believed that farmers working for themselves would be more productive. Agriculture did improve through this policy and through instruction of the peasants in better farming methods. The very small peasant proprietors who sold their land increased the size of the industrial labor force.

Russian moderate liberals who sat in the Duma approved of the new land measures. They liked the idea of competition and individual property ownership. The Constitutional Democrats wanted a more genuinely parliamentary mode of government, but they compromised out of fear of new revolutionary disturbances. There still existed widespread hatred of Stolypin among the older conservative groups in the country. The industrial workers were antagonistic to the tsar. In 1911 Stolypin was shot by a Social Revolutionary, who may have been a police agent in the pay of conservatives. Nicholas II found no worthy successor. His government simply continued to muddle along. At court the monk Grigori Efimovich Rasputin (1871?–1916) came into ascendancy because of his alleged power to heal the tsar's hemophilic son. The undue influence of this strange and uncouth man, the continued social discontent, and the conservative resistance rendered the position and policy of the tsar uncertain after 1911. Once again, as in 1904, he and his ministers thought that some bold move on the diplomatic front might bring the regime the broad popular support that it so desperately needed.

The domestic political situation in Russia was only the most extreme version of a pattern that appeared in several of the major European states. Potential or actual political and social unrest existed in Great Britain, France, Germany, Austria, and Russia. It was not at all certain that moderate political concessions could quiet the unrest of the working classes. Conservative governments were looking for some means whereby they might overcome social divisions and avoid further social change and revolution. From the French Revolution onward, war had been the one vehicle that had overcome the social and political cleavages in nations. It would be incorrect to say that this desire for national unity led governments to adopt war policies in 1914, but those anxieties may have made them less eager to turn back from the wider conflict. In other words, the social problems experienced by the major governments of Europe were closely related to their diplomatic policy.

SUGGESTED READINGS

A. ASHWORTH, *A Short History of the International Economy Since 1850*, rev. ed. (1967). An introductory survey.

R. E. CAMERON, *France and the Industrial Development of Europe, 1800–1914*, rev. ed. (1968). The best treatment of the subject.

C. M. CIPOLLA, *The Economic History of World Population* (1962). A basic introduction.

P. GAY, *The Dilemma of Democratic Socialism: Eduard Bernstein's Challenge to Marx* (1952). A clear presentation of the problems raised by Bernstein's revisionism.

H. GOLDBY, *A Life of Jean Jaurés* (1962). A splendid biography that explains the problems of the French socialists.

O. J. HALE, *The Great Illusion, 1901–1914* (1971). An excellent treatment based on the most recent scholarship.

S. HARCAVE, *First Blood: The Russian Revolution of 1905* (1964). A useful introduction.

C. J. H. HAYES, *A Generation of Materialism, 1871–1900* (1941). A classic account of the close of the century.

W. HENDERSON, *The Rise of German Industrial Power* (1976). A straightforward account.

E. J. HOBSBAWM, *The Age of Capital* (1975). Explores the consolidation of middle-class life after 1850.

L. JENKS, *The Migration of British Capital to 1875* (1927). The basic discussion of a key topic in European economic history.

J. JOLL, *The Second International* (1954). A straightforward treatment of the divisions among socialists before World War I.

D. LANDES, *The Unbound Prometheus: Technological Change and Industrial Development in Western Europe from 1750 to the Present* (1969). Includes excellent discussions of late-century development.

G. LICHTHEIM, *Marxism: An Historical and Critical Study* (1961). Perhaps the clearest one-volume discussion of the development of Marxist thought.

A. H. MCBRIAR, *Fabian Socialism and English Politics, 1884–1918* (1962). The standard discussion.

H. MOLLER (Ed.), *Population Movements in Modern European History* (1964). A collection of helpful and important articles.

H. PELLING, *The Origins of the Labour Party, 1880–1900* (1965). Examines the sources of the party in the activities of British socialists and trade unionists.

C. E. SCHORSKE, *German Social Democracy, 1907–1917* (1955). A brilliant study of the difficulties of the Social Democrats under the empire.

A. B. ULLAM, *The Bolsheviks: The Intellectual and Political History of the Triumph of Communism in Russia* (1965). Early chapters discuss prewar developments and the formation of Lenin's doctrines.

T. H. VON LAUE, *Sergei Witte and the Industrialization of Russia* (1963). A useful account of the last great minister of tsarist Russia.

ON

THE ORIGIN OF SPECIES

BY MEANS OF NATURAL SELECTION,

OR THE

PRESERVATION OF FAVOURED RACES IN THE STRUGGLE
FOR LIFE.

By CHARLES DARWIN, M.A.,

FELLOW OF THE ROYAL, GEOLOGICAL, LINNÆAN, ETC., SOCIETIES;
AUTHOR OF 'JOURNAL OF RESEARCHES DURING H. M. S. BEAGLE'S VOYAGE
ROUND THE WORLD.'

LONDON:
JOHN MURRAY, ALBEMARLE STREET.
1859.

The right of Translation is reserved.

29
The Birth of
Contemporary European Thought

D URING the same period that the modern nation state developed and the Second Industrial Revolution laid the foundations for the modern material life style, the contours of the European mind assumed what has become a familiar cast. Like previous intellectual changes, these arose from earlier patterns of thought. The Enlightenment provided late nineteenth-century Europeans with a heritage of rationalism, toleration, cosmopolitanism, and appreciation for science. Romanticism led them to value the feelings, imagination, national identity, and the autonomy of the artistic experience. By 1900 these strands of thought had become woven into a new fabric. Many of the traditional intellectual signposts were disappearing. The death of God had been proclaimed. Christianity had undergone the most severe attack in its history. The picture of the physical world that had dominated since Newton underwent major modification. The work of Darwin and Freud challenged the special place Western thinkers had assigned to humankind. The value long ascribed to rationality became questioned. The political and humanitarian ideals of liberalism and socialism for a time gave way to new aggressive nationalism. At the turn of the century European intellectuals were more daring than ever before, but they were also probably less certain and less optimistic.

Charles Darwin's *On the Origin of Species* revolutionized thought about the character and development of living organisms. As the subtitle indicates, struggle came to be seen as taking place throughout all the natural world; and validly or not this idea was soon picked up by some social scientists for use in their fields. Darwin had drafted an essay on the origin of species as early as 1842 but long hesitated to publish. He completed his final version only after learning that Alfred Russel Wallace had independently reached the same conclusions. This is the title page of his epoch-making work's first edition.

The New Reading Public

The social context of intellectual life changed in the last half of the nineteenth century. For the first time in Europe a mass reading public came into existence. In 1850 approximately half the population of western Europe and a much higher proportion of Russians were illiterate. Even those people who might technically be capable of reading and writing did so very poorly. The literacy of the Continent improved steadily, as from the sixties onward one government after another undertook state-financed education. Hungary provided elementary education in 1868; Britain, in 1870; Switzerland, in 1874; Italy, in 1877; and France, between 1878 and 1881. The already advanced education system of Prussia was extended in various ways throughout the German Empire after 1871. The attack on illiteracy proved most successful in Britain, France, Belgium, the Netherlands, Germany, and Scandinavia, where by 1900 approximately 85 per cent or more of the people could read. Italy, Spain, Russia, Austria–Hungary, and the Balkans lagged well behind, with illiteracy rates of between 30 and 60 percent.

The new primary education in the basic skills of reading and writing and elementary arithmetic both reflected and generated social change. Both liberals and conservatives regarded such minimal training as necessary for orderly political behavior on the part of the newly enfranchised voters. There was also hope that literacy might help the poor to help themselves and to create a better, more productive labor force. This side of the educational crusade embodied the rationalist faith that right knowledge will lead to right action. However, literacy and its extension soon became forces in their own right. The schoolteaching profession grew rapidly in numbers and prestige. Those people who learned to read the little they were taught could continue to read much more on their own. They soon discovered that the education that led to better jobs and political influence was still open only to those who could afford it. Having created systems of primary education, the major nations had to give further attention to secondary education by the time of World War I. In yet another generation the question would become one of democratic university instruction.

The expanding literate population created a vast market for new reading material. There was nothing less than an explosion of printed matter. Advances in printing and paper technology lowered production costs. The number of newspapers, books, quantities of editions, and libraries grew rapidly. Cheap mass-circulation newspapers, such as *Le Petit Journal* of Paris and the *Daily Mail* and *Daily Express* of London, enjoyed their first heyday. Newspapers with very specialized political or religious viewpoints were also published. The number of monthly and quarterly journals for families, women, and free-thinking intellectuals increased. Probably more people with more different kinds of ideas could get into print in the late nineteenth century than ever before in European history. And more people could read their ideas than ever before.

The quantity of readers and reading material did not ensure quality. The cheap newspapers prospered on sensational crimes, political scandal, and pages of advertising. Religious journals depended upon denominational bigotry. A brisk market existed for pornography. There was much cutthroat journalism as portrayed in George Gissing's (1857–1903) novel, *New Grub Street* (1892). Newspapers became major factors in the emerging mass politics. The news could be managed, but in central Europe more often by the government censor than by the publisher. Editorials appeared on the front page.

The mass audience and the new literary world created problems for the literary artist. Much of the contempt for democracy and for the "people" found in late nineteenth-century literature arose in reaction to the recently established conditions for publication. The new sense of distance between the artist and his public was in part a result of the changed character of the literate public. As publishers sought to make profits, they often feared offending the sensibilities of their potential readership.

Some writers accepted this situation and happily wrote harmless verbiage that supported current moral and political opinion. Others, such as Matthew Arnold (1822–1888), worked to raise the level of popular taste. Still others, such as the French novelist Émile Zola (1840–1902), self-consciously offended the values of their readers. These anxieties and tensions were closely related to writers' criticism of democracy, and the artist and his middle-class audience became the subjects of novels, such as James Joyce's (1882–1941) *Portrait of the Artist As a Young Man* (1914).

Because many of the new readers were only marginally literate and still quite ignorant on many scores, the books and journals catering to them seemed and often were thoroughly mediocre. Social and artistic critics were correct in pointing out this low level of public taste. Nevertheless the new education, the new readers, and the hundreds of new books and journals permitted a monumental popularization of knowledge that has become a hallmark of the contemporary world. The new literacy was the intellectual equivalent of the railroad and the steamship. People could leave their original intellectual surroundings.

Literacy is not an end in itself. It leads to other skills and the acquisition of other knowledge. People who can read may not necessarily change their world for the better, but they have a better chance to do so than those who remain illiterate.

Science at Mid-Century

In about 1850 Voltaire would still have felt at home in a general discussion of scientific concepts. The basic Newtonian picture of physical nature that he had popularized still prevailed. Scientists continued to believe that nature operated as a vast machine according to mechanical principles. During the first half of the century mechanistic explanation had been extended into several important areas. John Dalton (1766–1844) had formulated the modern theory of chemical composition. However, at

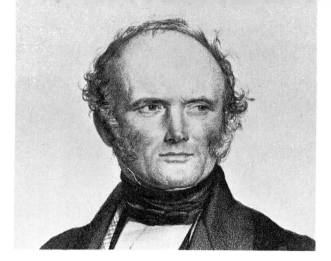

The geological theories of Sir Charles Lyell vastly expanded human understanding of the age of the earth and of the natural—and continuing—processes that have formed its geography. [Culver Pictures.]

BELOW, TOP: Charles Darwin, here portrayed at the age of forty, was the co-discoverer of the principle of evolution through natural selection. [Sidney W. Fox and Klaus Dose, *Molecular Evolution and the Origin of Life*. San Francisco: W. H. Freeman and Company. Copyright © 1972.]

BELOW, BOTTOM: Alfred Russel Wallace, here photographed in his later years, also came upon the principle of evolution by natural selection while working independently from Darwin. [The Granger Collection.]

mid-century and long thereafter atoms and molecules were considered to resemble billiard balls. During the 1840s several independent researchers had arrived at the concept of the conservation of energy, according to which energy is never lost in the universe but is simply transformed from one form to another. The principles of mechanism had been extended to geology through the work of Charles Lyell (1797–1875), whose *Principles of Geology* (1830) postulated that various changes in geological formation were the result of the mechanistic operation of natural causes over great spans of time.

At mid-century the physical world was thus regarded as rational, mechanical, and dependable. Its laws could be ascertained objectively through experiment and observation. Scientific theory purportedly described physical nature as it really existed. Moreover practically all scientists also believed like Newton and the Deists of the eighteenth century that their knowledge of nature demonstrated the existence of a God or a Supreme Being.

Darwin

In 1859 Charles Darwin (1809–1882) published *The Origin of Species*, which carried the mechanical interpretation of physical nature into the world of living things. The book proved to be one of the seminal works of Western thought and earned Darwin the honor of being regarded as the Newton of biology. Both Darwin and his book have been much misunderstood. He did not originate the concept of evolution, which had been discussed widely before he wrote. What he and Alfred Russel Wallace (1823–1913) did, working independently, was to formulate the principle of natural selection, which explained how species had changed or evolved over time. Earlier writers had believed that evolution might occur; Darwin and Wallace explained how it could occur.

Drawing upon Malthus, the two scientists contended that more seeds and living organisms came into existence than could survive in their environment. Those organisms possessing some marginal advantage in the struggle for existence lived long enough to propagate their kind. This

The Thinker, by the French sculptor Auguste Rodin (1840–1917), was completed in the late nineteenth century. The face and other physical features suggest one aspect of the impact of Darwinian thought, which taught that humankind developed from earlier forms of life, while the pose and serious expression affirm that despite lowly origins humankind is composed of thinking, rational creatures. [Bettmann Archive.]

principle of survival of the fittest Darwin called *natural selection*. The principle was naturalistic and mechanistic. Its operation required no guiding mind behind the development and change in organic nature. What neither Darwin nor anyone else in his day could explain was the origin of those chance variations that provided some living things with the marginal chance for survival. Only when the work of the Austrian monk Gregor Mendel (1822–1884) received public attention after 1900, several years following his death, did the mystery of heredity begin to be unraveled.

Darwin's and Wallace's theory represented the triumph of naturalistic explanation, which removed the idea of purpose from organic nature. Eyes were not made for seeing according to the rational wisdom and purpose of God but had developed mechanistically over the course of time. In this manner the theory of evolution through natural selection not only contradicted the biblical narrative of creation but also undermined the Deistic argument for the existence of God from the design of the universe. Moreover Darwin's work undermined the whole concept of fixity in nature or the universe at large. The world was a realm of flux and change. The fact that physical and organic nature might be constantly changing allowed people in the late nineteenth century to believe that society, values, customs, and beliefs should also change.

In 1871 Darwin carried his work a step further. In *The Descent of Man* he applied the principle of evolution by natural selection to human beings. Darwin was hardly the first person to treat human beings as animals, but his arguments brought greater plausibility to that point of view. He contended that humankind's moral nature and religious sentiments, as well as their physical frame, had developed naturalistically in response largely to the requirements of survival. Neither the origin nor the character of humankind on earth required the existence or role of God for their explanation. Not since Copernicus had removed the earth from the center of the universe had the pride of Western human beings received so sharp a blow.

The Prestige of Science

Darwin's ideas remained highly controversial. They were widely debated in popular and scientific journals. He changed some of them in the course of his writings. However, at issue was not only the correctness of the theory and the place of humankind in nature but also the role of science and scientists in society. The prestige of Darwin's achievement, progress in medicine, and the links of science to the technology of the Second Industrial Revolution made the general European public aware of science as never before. The British Fabian Socialist Beatrice Webb recalled from her youth:

Who will deny that the men of science were the leading British intellectuals of that period; that it was they who stood out as men of genius with international reputations; that it was they who were the self-confident militants of the period; that it was they who were routing the theologians, confounding the mystics, imposing their theories on philosophers, their inventions on capitalists, and their discoveries on medical men; whilst they were at the same time snubbing the artists, ignoring the poets, and even casting doubts on the capacity of the politicians?[1]

Contemporaries spoke of a religion of science that would explain all without resort to supernaturalism. Popularizers, such as Thomas Henry Huxley (1825–1895) and John Tyndall (1820–1893) in Britain and Ernst Haeckel (1834–1919) in Germany, wrote and lectured widely on scientific topics. They urged that science held the answer to the major questions of life and government. They worked for government support of scientific research and for inclusion of science in the schools and universities.

Scientific knowledge and theories became models for thought in other fields. The French philosopher Auguste

1 Beatrice Webb, *My Apprenticeship* (London: Longmans, Green, and Co., 1926), pp. 130–131.

Auguste Comte was the founder of Positivism. He urged that all knowledge be modeled on the empirical knowledge of science. Because he wanted the understanding of human society to assume a scientific character, he is often regarded as the founder of sociology. [French Cultural Services, New York.]

Comte (1798–1857), a late child of the Enlightenment and a onetime follower of Saint-Simon, developed a philosophy of human intellectual development that culminated in science. In *The Positive Philosophy* (1830–1842) Comte argued that human thought had gone through three stages of development. In the theological stage, physical nature was explained in terms of the action of divinities or spirits. In the second or metaphysical stage, abstract principles became regarded as the operative agencies of nature. In the final or positive stage, explanations of nature became matters of exact description of phenomena, without recourse to an unobservable operative principle. Physical science had, in Comte's view, entered the positive stage, and similar thinking should penetrate other areas of analysis. In particular Comte thought that positive laws of social behavior could be discovered in the same fashion as laws of physical nature. For this reason he is generally regarded as the father of sociology. Works like Comte's helped to convince learned Europeans that genuine knowledge in any area must resemble scientific knowledge. This belief had its roots in the Enlightenment and continues to permeate Western thought to the present day.

Theories of ethics became modeled upon science during the last half of the century. The concept of the struggle for survival was widely applied to human social relationships. The phrase "struggle for survival" predated Darwin and reflected the competitive outlook of classical economics. Darwin's use of the phrase gave it the prestige associated with advanced science.

The most famous advocate of evolutionary ethics was Herbert Spencer (1820–1903), the British philosopher. Spencer, a strong individualist, believed that human society progressed through competition. If the weak received too much protection, the rest of humankind was the loser. In Spencer's work, struggle against one's fellow human beings became a kind of ethical imperative. The concept could be applied to justify the avoidance of aiding the poor and the working class or to justify the domination of colonial peoples or to urge aggressively competitive rela-

tionships among nations. Evolutionary ethics often came very close to saying that might makes right.

Interestingly enough, one of the chief opponents of such thinking was Thomas Henry Huxley, the great defender of Darwin. In 1893 Huxley declared that the physical cosmic process of evolution was at odds with the process of human ethical development. The struggle in nature held no ethical implications except to demonstrate how human beings should not behave.

Scientific thought even affected the way in which authors wrote novels. The movement to literary realism, which is considered more fully later in this chapter, was a product of the influence of science. Certain writers wanted to portray the world as they observed it. In France, Gustave Flaubert's (1821–1880) *Madame Bovary* (1857); in England, George Eliot's (1819–1880) *Adam Bede* (1859); and in Russia, Ivan Turgenev's (1818–1883) *A Sportsman's Sketches* (1852) paid new attention to minute physical and natural details. Emile Zola (1840–1902) found artistic inspiration in Claude Bernard's (1813–1878) *An Introduction to the Study of Experimental Medicine* (1865). Zola, a French novelist, believed that he could write an experimental novel in which the characters and their actions would be observed and reported upon as the scientist might relate events within a laboratory experiment. Zola and others believed that absolute physical (and psychological) determinism ruled human events, just as in the physical world determinism prevailed.

Scientists and their admirers enjoyed a supreme confidence during the last half of the century. They genuinely believed that they had for all intents and purposes discovered all that might be discovered. The issues for science in the future would be the extension of acknowledged principles and the refinement of measurement. However, the turn of the century held a much more brilliant future for science. That confident, self-satisfied world of late nineteenth-century science and scientism vanished. A much more complicated picture of nature developed. Before examining those new departures, we must see how the cult of science affected religious thought and practice.

Christianity and the Church Under Siege

The nineteenth century was one of the most difficult periods in the history of the organized Christian churches. Many European intellectuals left the faith. The secular, liberal nation states attacked the political and social influence of the church. The expansion of population and the growth of cities challenged its organizational capacity to meet the modern age. Yet during all of this turmoil the Protestant and Catholic churches made considerable headway at the popular level.

The intellectual attack on Christianity arose on the grounds of its historical credibility, its scientific accuracy, and its pronounced morality. The *philosophes* of the Enlightenment had delighted in pointing out contradictions in the Bible. The historical scholarship of the nineteenth century brought new issues to the fore.

In 1835 David Friederich Strauss (1808–1874) published a *Life of Jesus* in which he questioned whether the Bible provided any genuine historical evidence about Jesus. Strauss contended that the story of Jesus was a myth that had arisen from the particular social and intellectual conditions of first-century Palestine. Jesus' character and life represented the aspirations of the people of that time and place rather than events that had occurred. Other skeptical lives of Jesus were written and published elsewhere.

During the second half of the century scholars such as Julius Wellhausen (1844–1918) in Germany, Ernst Renan (1823–1892) in France, and William Robertson Smith (1847–1894) in Great Britain contended that the books of the Bible had been written and revised as the problems of Jewish society and politics changed. They were not inspired books but had, like the Homeric epics, been written by normal human beings in a primitive society. This questioning of the historical validity of the

Matthew Arnold Contemplates the Loss of Intellectual Certainties

In this poem, written in 1867, Matthew Arnold (1822–1888) portrays a man and a woman looking across the waters of the English Channel on a moonlit night. The speaker in the poem notes that Sophocles, the ancient Greek dramatist, had drawn lessons about the misery of life from the ebb and flow of the Aegean Sea. The speaker then compares the movement of the sea to the withdrawal of the Christian faith from the lives of nineteenth-century men and women. Finally, he says that the world that seems so beautiful is really a place where there can be no certainty, love, light, or peace. This pessimism reflects the state of mind of many writers who were no longer sure of the truth of the Christian faith.

THE *sea is calm to-night.*
The tide is full, the moon lies fair
Upon the Straits;—on the French coast the light
Gleams and is gone; the cliffs of England stand,
Glimmering and vast, out in the tranquil bay,
Come to the window, sweet is the night air!
Only, from the long line of spray
Where the sea meets the moon-blanch'd land,
Listen! you hear the grating roar
Of pebbles which the waves draw back, and fling,
At their return, up the high strand,
Begin, and cease, and then again begin,
With tremulous cadence slow, and bring
The eternal note of sadness in.

Sophocles long ago
Heard it on the Aegean, and it brought
Into his mind the turbid ebb and flow
Of human misery; we
Find also in the sound a thought,
Hearing it by this distant northern sea.

The Sea of Faith
Was once, too, at the full, and round earth's shore
Lay like the folds of a bright girdle furl'd.
But now I only hear
Its melancholy, long, withdrawing roar,
Retreating, to the breath
Of the night-wind, down the vast edges drear
And naked shingles of the world.

Ah, love, let us be true
To one another! for the world, which seems
To lie before us like a land of dreams,
So various, so beautiful, so new,

> *Hath really neither joy, nor love, nor light,*
> *Nor certitude, nor peace, nor help for pain;*
> *And we are here as on a darkling plain*
> *Swept with confused alarms of struggle and flight,*
> *Where ignorant armies clash by night.*

Matthew Arnold, "Dover Beach." In Donald J. Gray and G. B. Tennyson: *Victorian Literature: Poetry* (New York: Macmillan, 1976), pp. 479–480.

Bible caused more literate men and women to lose faith in Christianity than any other single cause.

The march of science also undermined Christianity. This blow was particularly cruel because eighteenth-century Deists had led Christians to believe that the scientific examination of nature provided a strong buttress for their faith. This belief had been enshrined in works such as William Paley's (1743–1805) *Natural Theology* (1802) and in books by numerous scientists. The geology of Charles Lyell (1797–1875) suggested that the earth was much older than the biblical records contended. By appealing to natural causes to explain floods, mountains, and valleys, Lyell removed the miraculous hand of God from the physical development of the earth. Darwin's theory cast doubt on the doctrine of the Creation. His ideas and those of other writers suggested that the moral nature of humankind could be explained without appeal to the role of God. Finally, anthropologists, psychologists, and sociologists suggested that religion itself and the religious sentiments were just one more set of natural phenomena.

Other intellectuals questioned the morality of Christianity. The old issue of immoral biblical stories was again raised. Much more important, the moral character of the Old Testament God came under fire. His cruelty and unpredictability did not fit well with the progressive, tolerant, rational values of liberals. They also wondered about the morality of the New Testament God, who would sacrifice to his own satisfaction the only perfect being ever to walk the earth. Many clergymen began to ask themselves if they could honestly preach doctrines they felt to be immoral.

During the last quarter of the century this moral attack on Christianity came from another direction. Writers like Friederich Nietzsche (1844–1900) in Germany portrayed Christianity as a religion of sheep that glorified weakness rather than the strength that life required. Christianity demanded a useless and debilitating sacrifice of the flesh and spirit rather than full-blooded heroic living and daring. Nietzsche once observed, "War and courage have accomplished more great things than love of neighbor." [2]

These widespread skeptical intellectual currents seem to have directly influenced only the upper levels of educated society. Yet they created a climate in which Christianity lost much of its intellectual respectability. Fewer educated people became clergymen. More and more people found that they could lead their lives with little or no reference to Christianity. The secularism of everyday life proved as harmful to the faith as the direct attacks. This situation especially prevailed in the cities, which were growing faster than the capacity of the churches to meet the challenge. There was not even enough room in urban churches for the potential worshipers to sit. Whole generations of urban poor grew up with little or no experience with the church as an institution or with Christianity as a religious faith.

Conflict of Church and State

The secular state of the nineteenth century clashed with both the Protestant and the Roman Catholic churches. Liberals generally disliked the dogma and political privileges of the established churches. National states were often suspicious of the supranational character

---

2 Walter Kaufman (Ed. and Trans.), *The Portable Nietzsche* (New York: Viking, 1967), p. 159.

of the Roman Catholic Church. However, the primary area for conflict between the state and the churches was the expanding systems of education. The churches feared that future generations would emerge from the schools without the rudiments of religious teaching. The advocates of secular education feared the production of future generations more loyal to religion or the church than to the nation. From 1870 through the turn of the century the issue of religious education was heatedly debated in every major country.

GREAT BRITAIN. In Great Britain the Education Act of 1870 provided for the construction of state supported-school-board schools. They were to be built in areas where the religious denominations failed to provide satisfactory education. There was rivalry not only between the Anglican Church and the state but also between the Anglican Church and the Nonconformist denominations. There was intense local hostility among all these groups. The churches of all denominations had to oppose improvements in education because these increased the costs of their own schools. In the Education Act of 1902 the government decided to provide state support for both religious and nonreligious schools but imposed the same standards on each.

FRANCE. The British conflict was relatively calm compared to that in France, where there existed a dual system of Catholic and public schools. Under the Falloux Law of 1850 the local priest provided religious education in the public schools. The very conservative French Catholic Church and the Third French Republic were mutually hostile to each other. Between 1878 and 1886 the government passed a series of educational laws sponsored by Jules Ferry (1832–1893). The Ferry Laws replaced religious instruction in the public schools with civic training. Members of religious orders were no longer permitted to teach in the public schools, the number of which was to be expanded. After the Dreyfus affair the French Catholic Church again paid a price for its reactionary politics. The religious orders were sup-

pressed. In 1905 the Napoleonic Concordat was terminated, and Church and State were totally separated.

GERMANY AND THE KULTURKAMPF. The most extreme example of Church–State conflict occurred in Germany during the 1870s. At the time of unification the German Catholic hierarchy had wanted freedom for the churches guaranteed in the constitution. Bismarck left the matter to the discretion of each federal state, but he soon felt the activity of the Roman Catholic Church and the Catholic Center Party to be a threat to the new state. Through administrative orders in 1870 and 1871 Bismarck removed both Catholic and Protestant clergy from overseeing local education and set education under state direction. The secularization of education was merely the beginning of a concerted attack on the independence of the Catholic Church in Germany.

The "May Laws" of 1873 required German priests to have attended German schools and universities and to pass state-administered examinations. The state could veto appointments of priests. The disciplinary power of the pope and the church over the clergy was abolished and transferred to the state. When the bishops and many of the clergy refused to obey these laws, Bismarck used the police against them. In 1876 he had either arrested or driven from the country all the Catholic bishops. In the end Bismarck's Kulturkampf ("cultural struggle") against the Catholic Church failed. Not for the first time Christian martyrs had aided resistance to persecution. By the close of the decade the chancellor had abandoned his attack. He had gained only state control of education and civil laws governing marriage at the price of lingering Catholic resentment against the German Empire. The Kulturkampf was probably the greatest blunder of Bismarck's career.

AREAS OF RELIGIOUS REVIVAL. The successful German Catholic resistance to the intrusions of the secular state illustrates the continuing vitality of Christianity during this period of intellectual and political hardship. In Great Britain both the Anglican Church and the Non-

conformist denominations experienced considerable growth in membership. Vast sums of money were raised for new churches and schools. In Ireland the seventies saw a widespread Catholic devotional revival. Priests in France after the defeat by Prussia organized special pilgrimages by trains for thousands of penitents who believed that France had lost because of their sins. The cult of the miracles of Lourdes originated during these years. There were efforts by churches of all denominations to give more attention to the urban poor.

In effect, the last half of the nineteenth century witnessed the final great effort to Christianize Europe. It was well organized, well led, and well financed. It failed not from want of effort but rather because the population had simply outstripped the resources of the churches. This persistent liveliness of the church accounts in part for the intense hostility of its enemies.

The Roman Catholic Church and the Modern World

Perhaps the most striking feature of this religious revival amidst turmoil and persecution was the resilience of the papacy. The brief hope for a liberal pontificate from Pope Pius IX (1846–1878) vanished on the night in 1848 when he fled the turmoil in Rome. In the sixties Pius IX, embittered by the mode of Italian unification, launched a counteroffensive against liberalism in thought and deed. In 1864 he issued the *Syllabus of Errors,* which condemned all the major tenets of political liberalism and modern thought. He set the Roman Catholic Church squarely against the worlds of contemporary science, philosophy, and politics. In 1869 the pope called into session the First Vatican Council of the church. The next year, through the political manipulations of the pontiff and against much opposition from numerous members, the council promulgated the dogma of the infallibility of the pope when speaking officially on matters of faith and morals. No earlier pope had gone so far. The First Vatican Council came to a close in 1870, when Italian troops invaded Rome at the outbreak of the Franco-Prussian War.

The First Vatican Council met in 1869–1870 and proclaimed the dogma of the pope's infallibility when speaking in his official position on matters of faith and morals. This event marked the high water mark of papal influence in the Roman Catholic Church. The council was the first general one of the church since that at Trent in the sixteenth century. As shown in this painting from the Vatican, its main sessions took place in one of the transepts of Saint Peter's in Rome, with Pope Pius IX presiding. [Archivio Fotografico, Musei Vaticani.]

Pius IX died in 1878 and was succeeded by Leo XIII (1878–1903). The new pope, who was sixty-eight years old at the time of his election, sought to make accommodation with the modern age and to address the great social questions. He looked to the philosophical tradition of Thomas Aquinas to reconcile the claims of faith and reason. His encyclicals of 1888 and 1890 permitted Catholics to participate in the politics of liberal states.

Leo XIII's most important pronouncement on public issues was the encyclical *Rerum Novarum* (1891). In that document Leo XIII defended private property, religious education, and religious control of marriage laws, and he condemned socialism and Marxism. However, he also declared that employers should treat their employees justly, pay them proper wages, and permit them to organize labor unions. He supported laws and regulations to protect the conditions of labor. The Pope urged that modern society be organized according to corporate groups, including people from various classes, which might cooperate according to Christian principles. The corporate society, derivative of medieval social organization, was to be an alternative to both competitive capitalism and socialism. On the basis of Leo XIII's pronouncements democratic Catholic parties and Catholic trade unions were founded throughout Europe.

The emphasis of Pius X, who reigned from 1903 to 1914 and who has been proclaimed a saint, was intellectually reactionary. He hoped to restore traditional devo-

Leo XIII Considers the Social Question in European Politics

In this 1891 encyclical Pope Leo XIII addressed the social question in European politics. It was the answer of the Catholic Church to secular calls for social reforms. The pope denied the socialist claim that class conflict was the natural state of affairs. He urged employers to seek just and peaceful relations with workers.

THE great mistake that is made in the matter now under consideration is to possess oneself of the idea that class is naturally hostile to class; that rich and poor are intended by Nature to live at war with one another. So irrational and so false is this view that the exact contrary is the truth. . . . Each requires the other; capital cannot do without labour, nor labour without capital. Mutual agreement results in pleasantness and good order; perpetual conflict necessarily produces confusion and outrage. Now, in preventing such strife as this, and in making it impossible, the efficacy of Christianity is marvellous and manifold. . . . Religion teaches the labouring man and the workman to carry out honestly and well all equitable agreements freely made; never to injure capital, or to outrage the person of an employer; never to employ violence in representing his own cause, or to engage in riot or disorder; and to have nothing to do with men of evil principles, who work upon the people with artful promises and raise foolish hopes which usually end in disaster and in repentance when too late. Religion teaches the rich man and the employer that their work people are not their slaves; that they must respect in every man his dignity as a man and as a Christian; that labour is nothing to be ashamed of, if we listen to right reason and to Christian philosophy, but is an honourable employment, enabling a man to sustain his life in an upright and creditable way; and that it is shameful and inhuman to treat men like chattels to make money by, or to look upon them merely as so much muscle or physical power. Thus, again, Religion teaches that, as among the workman's concerns are Religion herself and things spiritual and mental, the employer is bound to see that he has time for the duties of piety; that he be not exposed to corrupting influences and dangerous occasions; and that he be not led away to neglect his home and family or to squander his wages. Then, again, the employer must never tax his work people beyond their strength, nor employ them in work unsuited to their sex or age. His great and principal obligation is to give every one that which is just.

F. S. Nitti, *Catholic Socialism*, trans. by Mary Mackintosh (London: S. Sonnenschein & Co., 1895), p. 409.

tional life. Between 1903 and 1907 he condemned Catholic Modernism, a movement of modern biblical criticism within the church, and in 1910 he required an anti-Modernist oath from all priests. By these actions Pius X set the church squarely against the intellectual currents of the day, and the struggle between Catholicism and modern thought continued. However, Pius X did not retreat measurably from the social policy of Leo XIII, so the Catholic Church continued to permit its members active participation in social and political movements.

Pope Leo XIII led the Roman Catholic Church toward a limited recognition of the social and political problems brought on by industrial democracy. His encyclical *Rerum Novarum* was the major statement of the Church on the issues of social justice and class conflict. [Culver Pictures.]

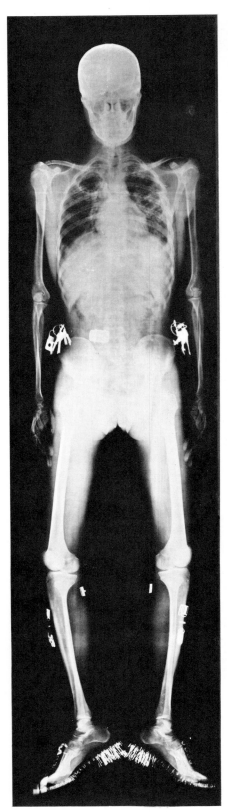

In an early demonstration Roentgen took an X ray of the entire body of a male subject. Note the buckle of his belt, the keys he had attached to the belt, and tacks in the soles and heels of his shoes. [Deutsches Museum, Munich.]

Toward a Twentieth-Century Frame of Mind

World War I is often regarded as the point of departure into the contemporary world. Although this view is possibly true for political and social developments, it is an incorrect assessment for intellectual history. The last quarter of the nineteenth century and the first decade of the twentieth century constitute the crucible of contemporary Western and European thought. During this period the kind of fundamental reassessment that Darwin's work had previously made necessary in biology and in understanding the place of human beings in nature was writ large in other areas of thinking. Philosophers, scientists, psychologists, and novelists began to portray physical reality, human nature, and human society in ways quite different from in the past. Their new concepts challenged the major presuppositions of mid-nineteenth-century science, rationalism, liberalism, and bourgeois morality.

Science: The Revolution in Physics

The modifications in the scientific world view originated within the scientific community itself. By the late 1870s considerable discontent existed over the excessive realism of mid-century science. It became felt that too many scientists believed that their mechanistic models, atoms, and absolute time and space actually described the real universe. In 1883 Ernst Mach (1838–1916) published *The Science of Mechanics,* in which he urged that the concepts of science be considered descriptive not of the physical world but of the sensations experienced by the scientific observer. Science could describe only the sensations, not the physical world that underlay the sensations. In line with Mach, the French scientist and mathematician Henri Poincaré (1854–1912) urged that the concepts and theories of scientists be regarded as hypothetical constructs of the human mind rather than as descriptions of the true state of nature. In 1911 Hans Vaihinger (1852–1933) suggested that the concepts of

The British scientist Ernest Rutherford was one of the first persons to explore the internal structure of the atom. The portrait is a 1932 painting by Oswald Birley. [Culver Pictures.]

Marie Curie (1867–1934), who was born in Poland but worked most of her life in France, was one of the leading figures in the turn-of-the-century advance of physics and chemistry. She is credited with the discovery of radium. [The Granger Collection.]

science be considered "as if" descriptions of the physical world. By World War I few scientists believed any longer that they could portray the "truth" about physical reality. Rather they saw themselves as recording the observations of instruments and as setting forth useful hypothetical or symbolic models of nature.

New discoveries in the laboratory paralleled the philosophical challenge to nineteenth-century science. With those discoveries the comfortable world of supposedly "complete" nineteenth-century physics vanished forever. In December 1895, Wilhelm Roentgen (1845–1923) published a paper on his discovery of X rays, a form of energy that penetrated various opaque materials. The publication of his paper was followed within a matter of months by major steps in the exploration of radioactivity. In 1896 Henri Becquerel (1852–1908), through a series of experiments following upon Roentgen's work, found that uranium emitted a similar form of energy. The next year J. J. Thomson (1856–1940), working in the Cavendish Laboratory of Cambridge University, formulated the theory of the electron. The interior world of the atom had become a new area for human exploration. In 1902 Ernest Rutherford (1871–1937), who had been Thomson's assistant, explained the cause of radiation through

the disintegration of the atoms of radioactive materials. Shortly thereafter he speculated upon the immense store of energy present in the atom.

The discovery of radioactivity and discontent with the existing mechanical models led to revolutionary theories in physics. In 1900 Max Planck (1858–1947) pioneered the articulation of the quantum theory of energy, according to which energy is a series of discrete quantities or packets rather than a continuous stream. In 1905 Albert Einstein (1879–1955) published his first epoch-making papers on relativity. He contended that time and space exist not separately but rather as a combined continuum. Moreover the measurement of space and time depend upon the observer as well as upon the entities being measured. In 1927 Werner Heisenberg (b. 1901) set forth the uncertainty principle, according to which the behavior of subatomic particles is a matter of statistical probability rather than of exactly determinable cause and effect. So much that only fifty years earlier had seemed certain and unquestionable about the physical universe had now once again become problematical.

Nineteen-century popularizers of science had urged its importance as a path to rational living and decision making. By the early twentieth century such optimistic hopes

The work of the German scientist Albert Einstein, who is seen here in a 1934 photograph made during an American lecture, set the fundamental theory of physics in a new direction just after the turn of the century. [Bettmann Archive.]

had been dashed by the developments in the scientific world itself. The mathematical complexity of twentieth-century physics meant that despite valiant efforts science would rarely again be successfully popularized. However, at the same time, through applied technology and further research in physics and medicine, science affected daily living more than ever before in human history. Consequently nonscientists in legal, business, and public life have been called upon to make decisions involving technological matters about which they rarely can or do understand in depth or detail. By the middle of this century some writers—such as the English essayist, novelist, and physicist, C. P. Snow (b. 1905)—spoke of the emergence of "two cultures," one of the scientists and one of literary persons. The problem was establishing ways in which they could communicate meaningfully with each other to address the major problems of human life.

Literature: Realism and Naturalism

Between 1850 and 1914 the moral certainties of learned and middle-class Europeans underwent modifications no less radical than their concepts of the physical universe. The realist movement in literature portrayed the hypocrisy, the physical and psychic brutality, and the dullness that underlay bourgeois life and society. By bringing scientific objectivity and observation to their work, the realist or naturalist writers used the mid-century cult of science so vital to the middle class to confront those same people with the harsh realities of life about them. Realism was a rejection of the romantic idealization of nature, the poor, love, and polite society. Realist novelists portrayed the dark, degraded, and dirty side of life almost, so some people thought, for its own sake.

An earlier generation of writers, including Charles Dickens (1812–1870) and Honoré de Balzac (1799–1850), had portrayed the cruelty of industrial life and of a society based wholly on money. Other authors, such as George Eliot (1819–1880), had paid close attention to the details of the scenes and the characters portrayed.

George Eliot was the pen name of Mary Ann Evans (1819–1880). She was an important English novelist who portrayed the life of the English countryside with much realistic detail. She was also a significant English religious and ethical thinker. [The Granger Collection.]

Émile Zola of France was the master of the realistic novel. Although his depiction of the harsh details of working class and peasant life shocked many of his readers, his novels sold well. Near the close of his life, he became one of the strongest supporters of Captain Alfred Dreyfus and demanded that the President of France seek justice for the military officer. His splendid portrait is by the photographer Nadar. [Bettmann Archive.]

However, there had always been room in their works for the play of the imagination, fancy, and self-conscious artistry. They had felt a better moral world possible. The major figures of late-century realism—Émile Zola (1840–1902), Gustave Flaubert (1821–1880), Ivan Turgenev (1818–1883), Anton Chekhov (1860–1904), Maksim Gorki (1868–1936), Henrik Ibsen (1828–1906), Arnold Bennett (1867–1931), and George Moore (1852–1933)—examined the dreary and unseemly side of life without being certain whether a better life was possible. In good Darwinian fashion they regarded and portrayed human beings as animals, subject to the passions, materialistic determinism, and the pressures of environment like any other animals. However, most of them also saw society itself as perpetuating evil.

Flaubert's *Madame Bovary* (1856), with its story of colorless provincial life and a woman's hapless search for love inside and out of marriage, is often considered the first genuinely realistic novel. It portrayed life without heroism, purpose, or even simple civility.

Nevertheless the author who turned realism into a movement was Émile Zola. As noted earlier, he saw himself as creating human experiments in his novels. He once declared, "I have simply done on living bodies the work of analysis which surgeons perform on corpses." [3] Between 1871 and 1893 Zola published twenty volumes of novels exploring subjects normally untouched by writers. In *L'Assommoir* (1877) he discussed the problem of alchoholism, and in *Nana* (1880) he followed the life of a prostitute. Others of his works considered the defeat of the French army and the social strife arising from attempts at labor organization. Zola refused to turn his pen or his readers' thoughts from the most ugly aspects of life. Nothing in his purview received the light of hope or the aura of romance. Although polite critics faulted his taste and middle-class moralists his subject matter, Zola enjoyed a wide following in France and elsewhere.

3 Quoted in George J. Becker, *Documents of Modern Literary Realism* (Princeton, N.J.: Princeton University Press, 1963), p. 159.

Henrik Ibsen (1828–1906) used his considerable skill as a playwright to probe the hypocrisy of middle class morality and its attitude toward women. [The Granger Collection.]

Virginia Woolf (1882–1941), shown here at age twenty-one, was one of the major voices urging the pursuit of literary and artistic modernism in Great Britain. Her novels constitute one of the monuments of twentieth-century British literature. [The Granger Collection.]

Realism in sculpture, as well as rising awareness of the condition of working people, is represented by the huge Belgian monument to labor by Constantin Émile Meunier (1831–1905). This is a portion of the work dedicated to miners. [Copyright by A. C. L., Brussels.]

Friedrich Nietzsche became the most influential German philosopher of the late nineteenth century. His books challenged existing morality and demanded a revaluation of values themselves. He has exerted a vast influence on twentieth-century literature and philosophy in both Europe and North America. [The Granger Collection.]

The Norwegian playwright Henrik Ibsen carried realism into the dramatic presentation of domestic life. He sought to achieve new modes of social awareness and to strip away the illusory mask of middle-class morality. His most famous play is *A Doll's House* (1879). Its chief character, Nora, is the spouse of a narrow-minded middle-class husband who cannot tolerate any independence of character or thought on her part. When for the first time she fully confronts this situation, the play ends as she leaves him, slamming the door behind her. In *Ghosts* (1881) a respectable middle-class woman must deal with a son suffering from syphilis inherited from her husband. In *The Master Builder* (1892) an aging architect kills himself while trying to impress a young woman who perhaps loves him. Ibsen's works were extremely controversial. He had dared to strike at sentimentality in life, the female angel of the house, and the cloak of respectability that hung so insecurely over the middle-class family.

One of Ibsen's greatest champions was the Irish writer George Bernard Shaw (1856–1950), who spent much of his life in England. During the late eighties he had vigorously defended Ibsen's work. He went on to make his own realistic onslaught against romanticism and false respectability. In *Mrs. Warren's Profession* (1893), a play long censored in England, he explored the matter of prostitution. In *Arms and the Man* (1894) and *Man and Superman* (1903) he heaped scorn on the romantic ideals of love and war, and in *Androcles and the Lion* (1913) he pilloried Christianity. Shaw added to the impact of his plays by writing long critical prefaces in which he drove home the point of his social criticism.

Realism struck the public ego in another fashion besides presenting unseemly social situations. The realists tended to see humankind as subject, and often helplessly so, to great physical or historical forces of determinism. Throughout *War and Peace* (1869) Leo Tolstoy (1828–1910) pictured his characters as being tossed upon the seas of historical change. The characters of Thomas Hardy's (1840–1928) novels are repeatedly challenged by curious turns of fate. Human beings in such settings could not control their lives and lacked the freedom to make conscious, meaningful moral choices. These characters possessed little or no nobility because the artists who created them had ceased to believe that human beings stood just a little lower than the angels or were creatures fully capable of rational behavior.

These writers and many others believed it the duty of the artist to portray reality and the commonplace. In dissecting what they considered the "real" world, they helped to change the moral perception of the good life. They refused to let existing public opinion dictate the subjects about which they wrote or the manner in which they treated them. By presenting their audiences with unmentionable subjects, they sought to remove the veneer of hypocrisy that had previously forbade such discussion. They hoped to destroy social and moral illusions and to compel the public to confront reality. That change in itself seemed good. However, few of the realist writers who raised the problems had solutions. They often left their readers unable to sustain old values and uncertain about the sources of new ones.

Philosophy: Revolt Against Reason

Within philosophical circles the adequacy of rational thinking to address the human situation was being questioned. No late nineteenth-century writer better exemplified this new attitude than the German philosopher Friedrich Nietzsche (1844–1900), who had been educated as a classicist rather than as an academic philosopher. His books remained unpopular until late in his life, when his brilliance had deteriorated into an almost totally silent insanity. He was a person wholly at odds with the predominant values of the age. At one time or another he attacked Christianity, democracy, nationalism, rationality, science, and progress. He sought less to change values than to probe the very sources of values in the human mind and character. He wanted not only to tear away the masks of respectable life but also to explore the ways in which human beings made such masks.

His first important work was *The Birth of Tragedy* (1872), in which he urged that the nonrational aspects of human nature were as important and noble as the rational characteristics. Here and elsewhere he insisted upon the positive function of instinct and ecstasy in human life. To limit human activity to strictly rational behavior was to impoverish human life and experience. In this work Nietzsche regarded Socrates as one of the major contributors to Western decadence because of the Greek philosopher's appeal for rationality in human affairs. In Nietzsche's view the strength for the heroic life and the highest artistic achievement arose from sources beyond rationality.

In later works, such as the prose poem *Thus Spake Zarathustra* (1883), Nietzsche criticized democracy and Christianity. Both would lead only to the mediocrity of sheepish masses. He announced the death of God and proclaimed the coming of the Overman (*Übermensch*), who would embody heroism and greatness. This latter term was frequently interpreted as some mode of superman or super race, but such was not Nietzsche's intention. He was highly critical of contemporary racism and anti-Semitism. What he sought was a return to the heroism that he associated with Greek life in the Homeric age. He thought that the values of Christianity and of bourgeois morality prevented humankind from achieving life on a heroic level. Those moralities forbade too much of human nature from fulfilling and expressing itself.

Two of Nietzsche's most profound works were *Beyond Good and Evil* (1886) and *The Genealogy of Morals* (1887). Both are difficult books. Much of the former was written in brief, ambiguous aphorisms. Nietzsche sought to discover not what is good and what is evil but rather the social and psychological sources of the judgment of good and evil. He declared, "There are no moral phenomena at all, but only a moral interpretation of phenomena." [4] He dared to raise the question of whether

morality itself was valuable: "We need a critique of moral values; the value of these values themselves must first be called in question." [5] In Nietzsche's view the basis of values was not rationality or religion but practicality. Morality was a human convention that had no independent existence apart from humankind. For Nietzsche this discovery did not condemn morality but liberated human beings to create life-affirming instead of life-denying values. Christianity, utilitarianism, and middle-class respectability could in good conscience be abandoned, and human beings could, if they so willed, create a new moral order for themselves.

What Nietzsche said about morality was indicative of what other philosophers were saying about similar subjects. There was a growing tendency to see all conceptual categories as being useful creations rather than exact descriptions.

The American philosopher William James (1842–1910) was one of the most influential figures to question the adequacy of nineteenth-century rationalism and science. He and his philosophy of pragmatism were very influential in Europe. James suggested that the truth of an idea or a description depended primarily upon how well it worked. Knowledge was less an instrument for knowing than for acting.

The most important European philosopher to pursue such lines of thought was the Frenchman Henri Bergson (1859–1941). His most significant works were *Time and Free Will* (1889), *Creative Evolution* (1907), and *Two Sources of Morality and Religion* (1932). Bergson glorified instinct, will, and subjectivism. He regarded human beings as dwelling in a world of becoming, where the only certain thing was their sense of themselves. The world was permeated with a great vital force in which all things to a greater or lesser degree participated. The evolutionary nature of the universe meant that both the knower and the object of knowledge were constantly changing. What Bergson did was to set down much of the thought

---

4 Walter Kaufman (Ed. and Trans.), *The Basic Writings of Nietzsche* (New York: The Modern Library, 1968), p. 275.

5 Ibid., p. 456.

Henri Bergson Criticizes Science and Philosophy

Bergson (1859–1941) was a French philosopher who argued that the knowledge provided by science could not include all of the experiences of life. He thought science could properly examine and explain those natural phenomena that were regular or repetitious in nature; these included molecular action, organic growth, and planetary motion. However, he thought philosophy was required to explain non-repetitious occurrences such as feelings, dreams, and other subjective experiences.

T HE *essential function of our intellect, as the evolution of life has fashioned it, is to be a light for our conduct, to make ready for our action on things, to foresee, for a given situation, the events, favorable or unfavorable, which may follow thereupon. Intellect therefore instinctively selects in a given situation whatever is like something already known; it seeks this out, in order that it may apply its principle that "like produces like." In just this does the prevision of the future by common sense consist. Science carries this faculty to the highest possible degree of exactitude and precision, but does not alter its essential character. Like ordinary knowledge, in dealing with things science is concerned only with the aspect of* repetition. *Though the whole be original, science will always manage to analyze it into elements or aspects which are approximately a reproduction of the past. Science can work only on what is supposed to repeat itself—that is to say, on what is withdrawn, by hypothesis, from the action of real time. Anything that is irreducible and irreversible in the successive moments of a history eludes science. To get a notion of this irreducibility and irreversibility, we must break with scientific habits which are adapted to the fundamental requirements of thought, we must do violence to the mind, go counter to the natural bent of the intellect. But that is just the function of philosophy.*

Henri Bergson, *Creative Evolution*, trans. by Arthur Mitchell (New York: The Modern Library, 1944), pp. 34–35. First published in 1907.

of earlier mystics in the language of evolutionary science.

In their appeal to the feelings and the emotions and in their questioning of the adequacy of rationalism, these writers drew upon the Romantic tradition. The kind of creative impulse earlier Romantics had considered the gift of artists, these latter writers saw as the burden of all human beings. The character of the human situation that these philosophers urged upon their contemporaries was that of an ever-changing flux in which little or nothing but change itself was permanent. Human beings from their own inner will and determination had to forge the truth and values that were to exist in the world. These philosophies in their impact upon twentieth-century developments threw into doubt not only the rigid domestic and religious morality of the nineteenth century but also the values of toleration, cosmopolitanism, and benevolence that had been championed during the Enlightenment.

The Birth of Psychoanalysis

A determination to probe beneath surface or public appearances united the major figures of late nineteenth-century science, literature, and philosophy. They sought to discern the various undercurrents, tensions, and complexities that lay beneath the smooth, calm surfaces of hard atoms, respectable families, rationality, and social relationships. Their theories and discoveries meant that articulate, educated Europeans could never again view the surface of life with smugness or complacency or even much confidence. No single intellectual development more clearly and stunningly exemplified this trend than the emergence of psychoanalysis through the work of Sigmund Freud.

Freud was born in 1856 into an Austrian Jewish family that shortly thereafter settled in Vienna. He originally planned to become a lawyer but soon moved to the study of physiology and then to medicine. In 1886 he opened his medical practice in Vienna, where he continued to live until driven out by the Nazis in 1938, a year before his death. All of Freud's research and writing was done from the base of his medical practice. His earliest medical interests had been psychic disorders, to which he sought to apply the critical method of science. In late 1885 he had studied for a few months in Paris with Jean-Martin Charcot, who used hypnosis to treat cases of hysteria. In

The Viennese physician Sigmund Freud (1856–1939) revolutionized the concept of human nature in the Western world. After his books, European thinkers have had to see rationality as only one aspect of human nature. [Bettmann Archive.]

Vienna he collaborated with another physician, Josef Breuer (1842–1925), and in 1895 they published *Studies in Hysteria.*

In the mid-nineties Freud changed the technique of his investigations. He abandoned hypnosis and allowed his patients to talk freely and spontaneously about themselves. Repeatedly he found that they associated their particular neurotic symptoms with experiences related to earlier experiences, going back to childhood. He also noticed that sexual matters were significant in his pa-

tients' problems. For a time he thought that perhaps some sexual incident during childhood accounted for the illness of his patients. However, by 1897 he had privately rejected this theory. In its place he formulated a theory of infantile sexuality, according to which sexual drives and energy exist in infants and do not simply emerge at puberty. In Freud's view human beings were creatures of sexuality from birth through adulthood. He thus questioned in the most radical manner the concept of childhood innocence. He also portrayed the little-discussed or -acknowledged matter of sex as one of the bases of mental order and disorder. In a classic example of the prejudices of everyday life holding back scientific inquiry, almost all of Freud's contemporaries heaped scorn and condemnation on his theory.

During the same decade Freud was also examining the psychic phenomena of dreams. Romantic writers had taken dreams very seriously, but most psychologists had not examined dreams scientifically. As a good rationalist Freud believed that there must exist a reasonable, scientific explanation for the irrational contents of dreams. That examination led him to a reconsideration of the general nature of the human mind. He came to the conclusion that during dreams unconscious wishes, desires, and drives that were excluded from everyday conscious life and experience enjoyed relatively free play in the mind. He argued, "The dream is the (disguised) fulfillment of a (suppressed, repressed) wish." [6] During the waking hours the mind repressed or censored those wishes, which were as important to our psychological makeup as conscious thought. In fact, those unconscious drives and desires contributed to conscious behavior. Freud developed these concepts and related them to his idea of infantile sexuality in *The Interpretation of Dreams,* published in 1900. It was his most important book.

In later books and essays Freud continued to urge the significance of the role played by the human unconscious.

6 *The Basic Writings of Sigmund Freud,* trans. by A. A. Brill (New York: The Modern Library, 1938), p. 235.

Freud Explains an Obstacle to Acceptance of Psychoanalysis

In addition to spawning numerous divergent views, the radical nature of Freud's theories caused them to be heard with misunderstanding, scorn, and opposition. Freud, in this 1915 passage, was at pains to give a rational explanation for the nonrational popular reaction to his work. He contended that civilization had been built largely through channeling sexual energies into nonsexual activity. For him, psychoanalysis revealed this important role of the sexual impulses. By so revealing them, psychoanalysis tended to make people uncomfortable. Consequently, public opinion played down the discoveries of psychoanalysis by claiming it was either dangerous or immoral.

WE BELIEVE *that civilization has been built up, under the pressure of the struggle for existence, by sacrifices in gratification of the primitive impulses, and that it is to a great extent for ever being recreated, as each individual, successively joining the community, repeats the sacrifice of his instinctive pleasures for the common good. The sexual are among the most important of the instinctive forces thus utilized: they are in this way sublimated, that is to say, their energy is turned aside from its sexual goal and diverted towards other ends, no longer sexual and socially more valuable. But the structure thus built up is insecure, for the sexual impulses are with difficulty controlled; in each individual who takes up his part in the work of civilization there is a danger that a rebellion of the sexual impulses may occur, against this diversion of their energy. Society can conceive of no more powerful menace to its culture than would arise from the liberation of the sexual impulses and a return of them to their original goal. Therefore society dislikes this sensitive place in its development being touched upon; that the power of the sexual instinct should be recognized, and the significance of the individual's sexual life revealed, is very far from its interests; with a view to discipline it has rather taken the course of diverting attention away from this whole field. For this reason, the revelations of psychoanalysis are not tolerated by it, and it would greatly prefer to brand them as aesthetically offensive, morally reprehensible, or dangerous. . . . It is characteristic of human nature to be inclined to regard anything which is disagreeable as untrue, and then without much difficulty to find arguments against it.*

Sigmund Freud, *A General Introduction to Psychoanalysis*, trans. by J. Riviere (Garden City, N.Y.: Garden City Publishing Company, 1943), pp. 23–24.

He portrayed a new internal organization of the mind. That inner realm was the arena for struggle and conflict among entities that he termed the *id*, the *ego*, and the *superego*. The first of these consisted of amoral, irrational, driving instincts for sexual gratification, aggression, and general physical and sensual pleasure. The superego constituted the external moral imperatives and expectations imposed upon the personality by its society and culture. The ego stood as the mediator between the impulses of the id and the asceticism of the superego. The ego allowed the personality to cope with the inner and outer demands of its existence. Consequently everyday behavior displayed the activity of the personality as its inner drives were partially repressed through the ego's coping with the external moral expectations as interpreted by the superego. It has been a grave misreading of Freud to see him as urging humankind to thrust off all repression. He believed that excessive repression could lead to mental disorder but that a certain degree of repression of sexuality and aggression was necessary for civilized living and the survival of humankind.

Freud's work led to nothing less than a revolution in the understanding of human nature. As his views gained adherents just before and after World War I, new dimensions of human life became widely recognized. Human beings were seen to be attaining rationality rather than merely exercising it. Civilization itself came to be regarded as a product of repressed or sublimated aggressions and sexual drive.

In Freud's appreciation of the role of instinct, will, dreams, and sexuality his thought pertained to the Romantic tradition of the nineteenth century. However, Freud must stand as a son of the Enlightenment. Like the *philosophes* he was a realist who wanted human beings to live free from fear and illusions by rationally understanding themselves and their world. He saw the personalities of human beings as being determined by finite physical and mental forces in a finite world. He was hostile to religion and spoke of it as an illusion. Freud, like the writers of the eighteenth century, wished to see civiliza-

Georges Sorel was the French author of *Reflections on Violence*, which portrayed the general strike as the strongest weapon for social change. [Photo Harlingue–Viollet.]

Max Weber was one of the most influential writers contributing to sociology and economics in the late nineteenth and twentieth centuries. [The Granger Collection.]

tion and humane behavior prevail. However, more fully than those predecessors, he understood the immense sacrifice of instinctual drives required for civilized behavior. He understood how many previously unsuspected obstacles lay in the way of rationality. Freud believed that the sacrifice and struggle were worthwhile, but he was pessimistic about the future of civilization in the West.

Freud's work marked the beginning of the psychoanalytic movement. By 1910 he had gathered around him a small but highly able group of disciples. Several of his early followers soon moved toward theories of which the master disapproved. The most important of these dissenters was Carl Jung (1875–1961). He was a Swiss whom for many years Freud regarded as his most distinguished and promising student. Before World War I the two men had, however, come to a parting of the ways. Jung had begun to question the primacy of sexual drives in forming human personality and in contributing to mental disorder. He also put much less faith in the guiding light of reason. Jung believed that the human subconscious contained inherited memories from previous generations of human beings. These collective memories as well as the personal experience of a person constituted his soul. Jung regarded human beings in the twentieth century as alienated from these useful collective memories. One of his more famous books was entitled *Modern Man in Search of a Soul* (1933). Here and elsewhere Jung's thought tended toward mysticism and toward ascribing positive values to religion. Freud was highly critical of most of Jung's work. If Freud's thought derived primarily from the Enlightenment, Jung's was more dependent upon Romanticism.

By the 1920s psychoanalysis had become even more fragmented as a movement. Nonetheless, in its several varieties the movement touched not only psychology but also sociology, anthropology, religious studies, and literary theory. It has been the single most important set of ideas whereby men and women in the twentieth century have come to understand themselves and their civilization.

Retreat from Rationalism in Politics

Both nineteenth-century liberals and socialists agreed that society and politics could be guided according to rational principles. Rational analysis could discern the problems of society and prepare solutions. They generally felt that once given the vote individuals would behave in their rational political self-interest. Improvement of society and the human condition was possible through education. By the close of the century these views were under attack in both theory and practice. Political scientists and sociologists painted politics as frequently irrational. Racial theorists questioned whether rationality and education could affect human society at all.

In the realm of political theory the major figures contributing to this questioning of rational liberal assumptions were Gustave LeBon, Émile Durkheim, and Georges Sorel in France; Vilfredo Pareto in Italy; Max Weber in Germany; and Graham Wallas in England. LeBon (1841–1931) was a psychologist who explored the activity of crowds and mobs. He believed that in crowd situations rational behavior was abandoned. Sorel (1847–1922) argued in *Reflections on Violence* (1908) that people did not pursue rationally perceived goals but were led to action by collectively shared ideals. Durkheim (1858–1917) and Wallas (1858–1932) became deeply interested in the necessity for shared values and activities in a society. These elements rather than a logical analysis of the social situation bound human beings together. Instinct, habit, and affections instead of reason directed human social behavior. Weber (1864–1920) in his famous essay on *The Protestant Ethic and the Spirit of Capitalism* (1905) traced much of the rational character of capitalist enterprise to the ascetic religious doctrines of Puritanism. Besides playing down the function of reason in society, all of these theorists emphasized the role of collective groups in politics rather than that of the individual formerly championed by liberals.

The same tendencies to question or even to deny the constructive activity of reason in human affairs and to

Karl Pearson Justifies Social Darwinism and Racism

Writers such as Karl Pearson, in this passage from a 1901 book, took the Darwinian idea of the survival of the fittest and applied it to human relationships. They argued that the strong and healthy had a better right to survive and prosper than did the weak. They also regarded the white races as naturally superior and more worthy of survival than other races.

CONSCIOUSLY *or unconsciously, one type of life is fighting against a second type, and all life is struggle with its physical environment. The safety of a gregarious animal—and man is essentially such—depends upon the intensity with which the social instinct has been developed. The stability of a race depends entirely on the extent to which the social feelings have got a real hold on it. The race which allows the physically or mentally stronger Tom to make the existence of the somewhat inferior Jack impossible will never succeed when it comes into contest with a second race. Jack has no interests in common with Tom; the oppressed will hardly get worse terms from a new master. That is why no strong and permanent civilization can be built upon slave labor, why an inferior race doing mental labour for a superior race can give no stable community; that is why we shall never have a healthy social state in South Africa until the white man replaces the dark in the fields and in the minds, and the Kaffir is pushed back towards the equator. The nation organized for the struggle must be a homogeneous whole, not a mixture of superior and inferior races. For this reason every new land we colonize with white men is a source of strength; every land of coloured men we simply rule may be needful as a source of food and mineral wealth, but it is not an element of stability in our community, and must ever be regarded with grave anxiety by our statesmen.*

Karl Pearson, *National Life from the Standpoint of Science* (Cambridge England: Cambridge University Press, 1901), pp. 47–48.

sacrifice the individual to the group manifested themselves in theories of race. Racial thinking had long existed in Europe. Renaissance explorers had displayed considerable prejudice against nonwhite peoples. Since at least the eighteenth century biologists and anthropologists had classified human beings according to color of skin, language, and stage of civilization. Late eighteenth-century linguistic scholars had observed similarities between European languages and Sanskrit. They then postulated the existence of an ancient race called the *Aryans*, who had spoken the original language from which the rest derived. During the Romantic period writers had called the different cultures of Europe races. The debates over slavery in European colonies and the United States had given further opportunity for the development of racial theory. However, in the late nineteenth century the concept of race emerged as a single dominant explanation for history and the character of large groups of people.

Arthur Gobineau (1816–1882), a reactionary French diplomat, enunciated the first important theory of race as the major determinant of human history. In his four-volume *Essay on the Inequality of the Human Races* (1853–1854) Gobineau portrayed the troubles of Western civilization as the result of the long degeneration of the original white Aryan race. It had unwisely intermarried with the inferior yellow and black races, thus diluting the qualities of greatness and ability that originally existed in its blood. Gobineau was deeply pessimistic because he saw no way to reverse the degeneration that had taken place.

Gobineau's essay remained relatively obscure for many years. In the meantime a growing literature of anthropologists and explorers helped to spread racial thinking. In the wake of Darwin's theory, the concept of survival of the fittest was applied to races and nations. The recognition of the animal nature of humankind made the racial idea all the more persuasive. At the close of the century Houston Stewart Chamberlain (1855–1927), a German writer, drew together these strands of racial thought into the two volumes of his *Foundations of the Nineteenth Century* (1899). He championed the concept of biological determinism through race, but he was somewhat more optimistic than Gobineau. Chamberlain believed that through genetics the human race could be improved and that even a superior race could be developed. Chamberlain added another element. He pointed to the Jews as the major enemy of European racial regeneration. Chamberlain's book and the lesser works upon which it drew aided the spread of anti-Semitism in European political life.

Political and racial anti-Semitism, which have cast such dark shadows across the twentieth century, emerged in part from this atmosphere of racial thought and the retreat from rationality in politics. Religious anti-Semitism dated from at least the Middle Ages. Since the French Revolution west European Jews had gradually gained entry into the civil life of Britain, France, and Germany. Popular anti-Semitism continued to exist as the Jewish community was identified with money and banking interests. During the last third of the century as finance capitalism changed the economic structure of Europe, people pressured by the changes became hostile toward the Jewish community. This was especially true of the socially and economically insecure middle class. In Vienna Mayor Karl Leugar (1844–1910) used such anti-Semitism as a major attraction to his successful Christian Socialist Party. In Germany the ultraconservative Lutheran chaplain Adolf Stoecker (1835–1909) revived anti-Semitism. The Dreyfus affair in France allowed a new flowering of hatred toward the Jews.

To this already ugly atmosphere, racial thought contributed the belief that no matter to what extent a Jew assimilated himself or his family to the culture of his country, his Jewishness would remain and thus his alleged danger to the society. The problem of race was not in the character but in the blood of the Jew. An important Jewish response to this new, rabid outbreak of anti-Semitism was the launching by the Austro-Hungarian Theodor Herzl (1860–1904) in 1896 of the Zionist movement to found a separate Jewish state.

Racial thinking and revived anti-Semitism were part of a wider late-century movement toward more aggressive nationalism. Previously nationalism had been a movement among European literary figures and liberals. From the seventies onward it became a movement with mass support, well-financed organizations, and political parties. Nationalists often defined nationality in terms of race. The new nationalism opposed the internationalism of both liberalism and socialism. The ideal of nationality was used to overcome the pluralism of class, religion, and geography. The nation and its duties replaced religion in the lives of many secularized people. It became a secular religion in the hands of state schoolteachers who were replacing clergymen as instructors of the youth. Nationalism would prove to be the most powerful ideology of the early twentieth century.

SUGGESTED READINGS

R. Aron, *Main Currents in Sociological Thought,* 2 vols. (1965, 1967). A useful introduction to the founders of the science.

F. L. Baumer, *Modern European Thought: Continuity and Change in Ideas, 1600–1950* (1977). The best work on the subject for this period.

F. L. Baumer, *Religion and the Rise of Scepticism* (1960). Traces the development of religious doubt from the seventeenth to the twentieth centuries.

M. D. Biddis, *Father of Racist Ideology: The Social and Political Thought of Count Gobineau* (1970). Sets the subject in the more general context of nineteenth-century thought.

J. W. Burrow, *Evolution and Society: A Study in Victorian Social Theory* (1966). An important study of evolutionary sociology.

D. G. Charlton, *Positivist Thought in France During the Second Empire, 1852–1870* (1959), and *Secular Religions in France, 1815–1870* (1963). Two clear introductions to important subjects.

C. M. Cipolla, *Literacy and Development in the West* (1969). Traces the explosion of literacy in the past two centuries.

C. C. Gillispie, *Genesis and Geology* (1951). An excellent discussion of the impact of modern geological theory during the early nineteenth century.

C. C. Gillispie, *The Edge of Objectivity* (1960). One of the best one-volume treatments of modern scientific ideas.

J. C. Greene, *The Death of Adam: Evolution and Its Impact on Western Thought* (1959). Emphasizes pre-Darwinian thought.

S. Hughes, *Consciousness and Society: The Reorientation of*

European Social Thought, 1890–1930 (1958). A wide-ranging discussion of the revolt against positivism.

W. Irvine, *Apes, Angels, and Victorians* (1955). A lively and sound account of Darwin and Huxley.

W. A. Kaufmann, *Nietzsche: Philosopher, Psychologist, Antichrist,* rev. ed. (1968). An exposition of Nietzsche's thought and its sources.

J. T. Merz, *A History of European Thought in the Nineteenth Century,* 4 vols. (1897–1914). Still a useful mine of information.

P. G. J. Pulzer, *The Rise of Political Anti-Semitism in Germany and Austria* (1964). A sound discussion of anti-Semitism in the world of central European politics.

P. Rief, *Freud: The Mind of the Moralist* (1959). Probably the best one-volume treatment.

L. Snyder, *Race: A History of Modern Ethnic Theories* (1939). A good introductory treatment.

A. Vidler, *The Church in an Age of Revolution* (1961). A sound account of the problems of Church and State in the nineteenth century.

R. Williams, *The Long Revolution* (1961). Explores the impact of literacy and popular publishing on English culture.

794

30
Imperialism, Alliances, and War

Expansion of European Power and the "New Imperialism"

DURING the second half of the nineteenth century, and especially after 1870, European influence and control over the rest of the world grew to an unprecedented degree. North and South America, as well as Australia and New Zealand, became almost integral parts of the European world as the great streams of European immigrants populated them. Until the nineteenth century Asia, (with the significant exception of India) and most of Africa had gone their own ways, having little contact with Europe. But the latter part of that century brought the partition of Africa among a number of European nations and the establishment of European economic and political power from the eastern to the western borders of Asia. By the next century this growth of European dominance had brought every part of the globe into a single world economy and had made events in any corner of the world significant thousands of miles away.

The explosive developments in nineteenth-century science, technology, industry, agriculture, transportation, communication, and military weapons provided the chief sources of European power. They made it possible for a small number of Europeans (or Americans) to impose their will on other peoples many times their number by force or by the threat of force. Institutional as well as material advantages allowed Westerners to have their

way. The growth of national states that commanded the loyalty, service, and resources of their inhabitants to a degree previously unknown was a Western phenomenon, and it permitted the European nations to deploy their resources in the most effective way. The Europeans also possessed another, less tangible weapon: a sense of the superiority of their civilization and way of life. This gave them a confidence that often took the form of an unpleasant arrogance but that fostered the expansionist mood.

The expansion of European influence was not anything new. Spain, Portugal, France, and Britain had controlled territories overseas for centuries, but by the mid-nineteenth century only Great Britain retained extensive holdings. The first half of the century was generally a period of hostility to colonial expansion. Even the British had been sobered by their loss of the American colonies. The French acquired Algeria and part of Indochina, and the British made some additional gains in territories adjacent to their holdings in Canada, India, Australia, and New Zealand. For the most part, however, the doctrine of free trade was dominant, and it opposed the idea of political interference in other lands.

Because Britain ruled the waves and had great commercial advantages as a result of being first in the Industrial Revolution, the British were usually content to let commerce go forward without annexations. Yet they were quite prepared to interfere forcefully if some "backward" country placed barriers in the way of their trade. Still at mid-century in Britain as elsewhere opinion stood predominantly against further political or military involvement overseas.

In the last third of the century, however, the European states swiftly spread their control over perhaps 10 million square miles and 150 million people, about a fifth of the world's land area and a tenth of its population. The movement has been called the *New Imperialism*.

The New Imperialism

Imperialism is a word that has come to be used so loosely as almost to be deprived of meaning. It may be

This scene of trench warfare on the western front in World War I characterizes the twentieth century's first great international conflict. The trenches were defended by barbed wire and machine guns, the devices that gave the defense the advantage in this war. The masks worn by the French soldiers in this picture were the response to the German attempts to break a deadlock by using poison gas. [Collection Viollet.]

useful to offer a definition that might be widely accepted: "The policy of extending a nation's authority by territorial acquisition or by the establishment of economic and political hegemony over other nations."[1] That definition seems to apply equally well to human actions as far back as ancient Egypt and Mesopotamia and to the performance of European nations in the late nineteenth century. But there were some new elements in the latter case. Previous imperialisms had either taken the form of seizing land and settling it with the conqueror's people or of establishing trading centers to exploit the resources of the dominated area. The New Imperialism did not completely abandon these devices, but it introduced new ones.

The usual pattern of the New Imperialism was for the European nation to invest capital in the "backward" country, to build productive enterprises and improved means of transportation, to employ great numbers of natives in the process, and thereby to transform the entire economy and culture of the dominated area. To guarantee their investments, the European states would make favorable arrangements with the local government either by enriching the rulers or by threatening them. If these arrangements proved inadequate, the dominant power established different degrees of political control, ranging from full annexation as a colony to protectorate status, whereby the local ruler was controlled by the dominant European state and maintained by its military power; to "spheres-of-influence" status, whereby the European state received special commercial and legal privileges without direct political involvement. Other novelties included the great speed with which European expansion went forward and the way in which participation in this expansion came to be regarded as necessary to retaining status as a great power.

MOTIVES FOR THE NEW IMPERIALISM. There has been considerable debate about the motives for the

1871	The end of the Franco–Prussian war; creation of the German Empire; German annexation of Alsace–Lorraine.
1873	The Three Emperors' League.
1875	The Russo–Turkish War.
1878	The Congress of Berlin.
1879	The Dual Alliance between Germany and Austria.
1881	The Three Emperors' League is renewed.
1882	Italy joins Germany and Austria in the Triple Alliance.
1888	William II becomes German Emperor.
1890	Bismarck is dismissed.
1894	The Franco–Russian alliance.
1898	Germany begins to build a battleship navy.
1902	The British alliance with Japan.
1904	The *Entente Cordiale* between Britain and France.
1904–1905	The Russo–Japanese War.
1905	The first Moroccan Crisis.
1907	The British agreement with Russia.
1908–1909	The Bosnian Crisis.
1911	The second Moroccan Crisis. Italy attacks Turkey.
1912–1913	The First and Second Balkan Wars.
1914	Outbreak of World War I.

New Imperialism. The most widespread interpretation has been economic, most typically in the form given by the English radical economist J. A. Hobson and later adapted by Lenin. As Lenin put it, "Imperialism is the monopoly stage of capitalism,"[2] the last stage of a dying capitalist system. According to this interpretation, competition inevitably led to the elimination of inefficient capitalists and, therefore, to monopoly. Powerful industrial and financial capitalists soon ran out of profitable areas of investment in their own countries and persuaded their governments to gain colonies in "backward" countries, where they could find higher profits from their investments, new markets for their products, and safe sources of the raw materials they needed.

The facts of the matter do not support this viewpoint. The European powers did export considerable amounts of capital in the form of investments abroad but not in such a manner as to fit the model of Hobson and Lenin.

1 *American Heritage Dictionary of the English Language* (New York: Houghton Mifflin Co., 1969), p. 660.

2 V. I. Lenin, *Imperialism, the Highest Stage of Capitalism,* (New York: International Publishers Co., Inc., 1939), p. 88.

This British advertisement of 1887 unconsciously makes the point that, in the minds of some, empire and colonies were closely connected with economic gain. The advertising copy below the picture read, "Pears' Soap in the Soudan. Even if our invasion of the Soudan has done nothing else it has at any rate left the Arab with something to puzzle his fuzzy head over, for the legend Pears' Soap Is the Best, [is] inscribed in huge white characters on the rock which marks the farthest point of our advance . . ." [Thames and Hudson Ltd.]

Britain, for example, made heavier investments abroad before 1875 than during the next two decades. Only a very small percentage of British and European investment overseas, moveover, went to the new colonial areas. Most went into Europe itself or into older, well-established areas like the United States, Canada, Australia, and New Zealand. Even when investments were made in the new areas, they were not necessarily put into colonies held by the investing country.

The facts are equally discouraging for those who emphasize the need for markets and raw materials. Colonies were not usually important markets for the great imperial nations, and all were forced to rely on areas that they did not control as sources of vital raw materials. It is not even clear that control of the new colonies was particularly profitable. As one of the leading students of the subject has said, "No one can determine whether the accounts of empire ultimately closed with a favorable cash balance."[3] That is true of the European imperial nations collectively, but it is certain that for some of them, like Italy and Germany, empire was a losing proposition. Some individuals and companies, of course, were able to make great profits from particular colonial ventures, but such people were able to influence national policy only occasionally. The motives for imperial policy must be sought elsewhere.

Advocates of imperialism put forth various justifications. Some argued that it was the responsibility of the advanced European nations to bring the benefits of their higher culture and superior civilization to the people of "backward" lands, but few people were influenced by such arrogant arguments, though many shared the intellectual assumptions. Religious groups argued for the responsibility of Western nations to bring the benefits of Christianity to the heathen with more extensive efforts and aid from their governments. Some politicians and diplomats argued for imperialism as a tool of social policy.

3 D. K. Fieldhouse, *The Colonial Empires* (New York: Delacorte Press, 1966), p. 393.

In Germany, for instance, a few conservatives suggested that imperial expansion might serve to deflect public interest away from domestic politics and social reform. But Germany acquired only a few colonies, and such considerations played little if any role.

In Britain such arguments were made, as was their opposite. The statesman Joseph Chamberlain (1836–1914) argued for the empire as a source of profit and economic security that would finance a great program of domestic reform and welfare. To the extent that they had any influence these arguments were not important as motives for imperialism because they were made well after the British had acquired most of their empire. Another common and apparently plausible justification was that colonies would provide a good place to settle surplus population. In fact, most European emigrants went to areas not controlled by their countries, chiefly to North and South America and Australia.

THE SCRAMBLE FOR AFRICA. Strategic and political considerations seem to have been more important in bringing on the New Imperialism. The scramble for Africa in the 1880s is one example. Britain was the only great power with extensive overseas holdings on the eve of the scramble. The completion of the Suez Canal in 1869 made Egypt an area of vital interest to the British

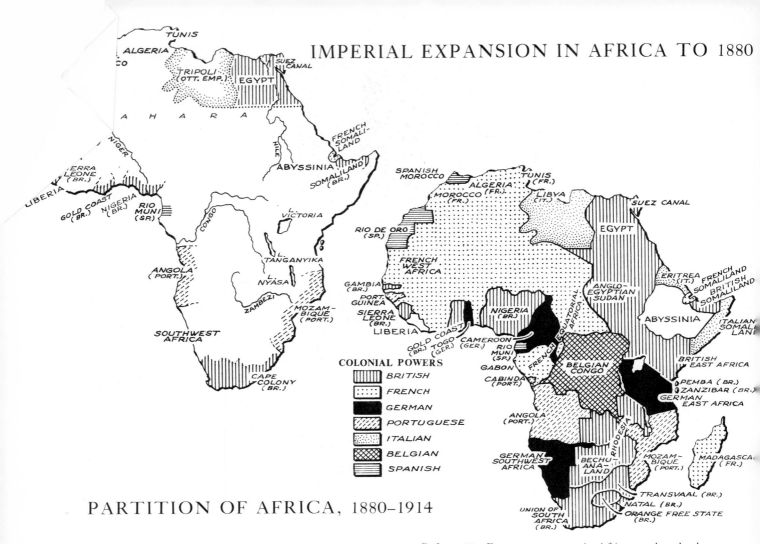

COLONIAL POWERS

- BRITISH
- FRENCH
- GERMAN
- PORTUGUESE
- ITALIAN
- BELGIAN
- SPANISH

PARTITION OF AFRICA, 1880–1914

Before 1880 European presence in Africa was largely the remains of early exploration by old imperialists and did not penetrate the heart of the continent. By 1914 the occupying powers included most large European states; only Liberia and Abyssinia remained independent.

because it sat astride the shortest route to India. Under Disraeli Britain purchased a major, but not a controlling, interest in the canal in 1875. When Egypt's stability was threatened by internal troubles in the 1880s, the British moved in and established a protectorate. Then to protect Egypt, they advanced into the Sudan.

France became involved in Africa in 1830 by sending a naval expedition to Algeria to attack the pirates based there. Before long French settlers arrived and established a colony but not because of economics or military security. By 1882 France was in full control of Algeria, and about the same time, to prevent Tunisia from falling into Italy's hand, France took over that area of North Africa also. Soon lesser states like Belgium, Portugal, Spain, and Italy were scrambling for African colonies. Their intervention had by the nineties compelled Britain to expand northward from the Cape of Good Hope into what is now Rhodesia. Britain may have had significant strategic reasons for protecting the Suez and Cape routes to India,

OPPOSITE, TOP: In this picture based on his own sketch, Henry M. Stanley (1841–1904), the explorer-adventurer sent in 1871 by the *New York Herald* to what was then called "darkest Africa" to find the supposedly lost missionary, David Livingston, arrives at an African village. The travels of these two men in Africa exemplify the diversity of motives that led westerners to explore the interior of the continent in the last half of the nineteenth century. [Radio Times Hulton Picture Library.]
OPPOSITE, BOTTOM: Christian missionaries were frequently part of the general pattern of European colonial penetration of Africa and Asia in the late nineteenth century. This print portrays a missionary in the West African German colony of Togoland, now part of the modern state of Ghana. [Culver Pictures.]

"Colonies for Germany, Too." This German cartoon of 1884 attacks Bismarck for neglecting imperial expansion overseas. He is shown attending to domestic social reform while the southern hemisphere is carved up by other nations. The caption to the cartoon read, "The Pacific Ocean is the Mediterranean of the future." [Thames and Hudson Ltd.]

but France and the smaller European nations did not have such reasons. Their motives were political, for they equated status as a great power (Britain stood as the chief model) with the possession of colonies. They therefore sought colonies as evidence of their own importance.

Bismarck appears to have pursued an imperial policy, however brief, from coldly political motives. In 1884 and 1885 Germany declared protectorates over Southwest Africa, Togoland, the Cameroons, and East Africa. None of these places was particularly valuable or of intrinsic strategic importance. Bismarck himself had no interest in overseas colonies and once compared them to fine furs worn by impoverished Polish noblemen who had no shirts underneath. His concern lay in Germany's exposed position in Europe. On one occasion he said, "My map of Africa lies in Europe. Here is Russia, and there is France, and here in the middle are we. That is my map of Africa." [4] He acquired colonies chiefly to improve Ger-

4 Quoted by J. Remak in *The Origins of World War I, 1871–1914,* (New York: Holt, Rhinehart and Winston, 1967), p. 5.

Bismarck Reminisces About His Foreign Policy

The following is Bismarck's own account of his foreign policy written during the years of his retirement, 1890–1898.

The triple alliance which I originally sought to conclude after the peace of Frankfurt, and about which I had already sounded Vienna and St. Petersburg, from Meaux, in September 1870, was an alliance of the three emperors with the further idea of bringing into it monarchical Italy. It was designed for the struggle which, as I feared, was before us; between the two European tendencies which Napoleon called Republican and Cossack, and which I, according to our present ideas, should designate on the one side as the system of order on a monarchical basis, and on the other as the social republic to the level of which the antimonarchical development is wont to sink, either slowly or by leaps and bounds, until the conditions thus created become intolerable, and the disappointed populace are ready for a violent return to monarchical institutions in a Cæsarean form. I consider that the task of escaping from this circulus vitiosus, or, if possible, of sparing the present generation and their children an entrance into it, ought to be more closely incumbent on the strong existing monarchies, those monarchies which still have a vigorous life, than any rivalry over the fragments of nations which people the Balkan peninsula. If the monarchical governments have no understanding of the necessity for holding together in the interests of political and social order, but make themselves subservient to the chauvinistic impulses of their subjects, I fear that the international revolutionary and social struggles which will have to be fought out will be all the more dangerous, and take such a form that the victory on the part of monarchical order will be more difficult. Since 1871 I have sought for the most certain assurance against those struggles in the alliance of the three emperors, and also in the effort to impart to the monarchical principle in Italy a firm support in that alliance.

Otto von Bismarck, *Reflections and Reminiscences,* ed. by Theodore S. Hamerow, (New York: Harper Torchbooks, 1968), pp. 236–237.

OPPOSITE: This is a satirical German cartoon of 1896 poking fun at German efficiency as applied to colonial adventures. In the upper picture is the deplorably idyllic jungle; in the bottom, the new and satisfactory tidiness brought about by German imperialism. [The Granger Collection.]

Expansion of European Power and the "New Imperialism" 801

many's diplomatic position in Europe. He tried to turn France from hostility against Germany by diverting the French toward colonial interests. At the same time German colonies in Africa could be used as a subtle weapon with which to persuade the British to be reasonable.

Germany's annexations started a wild scramble by the other European powers to establish claims on what was left of Africa. By 1890 almost all of the continent was parceled out. Great powers and small expanded into areas neither profitable nor strategic for reasons less calculating and rational than Bismarck's. "Empire in the modern period," D. K. Fieldhouse has observed, "was the product of European power: its reward was power or the sense of power."[5]

Such motives were not new. They had been well understood by the Athenian spokesman at Melos in 416 B.C., whose words are reported by Thucydides: "Of the gods we believe and of men we know clearly that by a necessity of their nature where they have the power they rule."[6]

IMPERIALISM IN THE PACIFIC. By the early years of the twentieth century the islands of the Pacific were also apportioned among the Western powers. Southeast Asia was divided among Britain in Burma, Malaya, and North Borneo, France in Indochina, and the Netherlands in the East Indies. China was able to maintain its territory and sovereignty in spite of European interference, in part because its central government continued to function, in part because of the antiforeign Boxer Rebellion of 1898–1900, but chiefly because of rivalry among the great powers. Still the powers established spheres of influence, opportunities for trade and investment immune from Chinese courts, and even military and naval bases. In addition to imperial nations of fairly long standing, China was of interest to two powers new on the international scene, Japan and the United States. Japan had been brought forcibly into contact with the Western world by

5 Fieldhouse, p. 393.
6 Thucydides, *The Peloponnesian War*, 5.105.2.

Kipling Advises the Americans: The Responsibility for Empire

THE WHITE MAN'S BURDEN
1899
(*The United States and the Philippine Islands*)

Take up the White Man's burden—
  Send forth the best ye breed—
Go bind your sons to exile
  To serve your captives' need;
To wait in heavy harness
  On fluttered folk and wild—
Your new-caught, sullen peoples,
  Half devil and half child.

Take up the White Man's Burden—
  In patience to abide,
To veil the threat of terror
  And check the show of pride;
By open speech and simple,
  An hundred times made plain,
To seek another's profit,
  And work another's gain.

Take up the White Man's burden—
  The savage wars of peace—
Fill full the mouth of Famine
  And bid the sickness cease;
And when your goal is nearest
  The end for others sought,
Watch Sloth and heathen Folly
  Bring all your hope to nought.

Take up the White Man's burden—
  No tawdry rule of kings,
But toil of serf and sweeper—
  The tale of common things.
The ports ye shall not enter,
  The roads ye shall not tread,
Go make them with your living,
  And mark them with your dead!

Take up the White Man's burden—
  And reap his old reward:
The blame of those ye better,
  The hate of those ye guard—
The cry of hosts ye humour
  (Ah, slowly!) toward the light:—
"Why brought ye us from bondage,
  "Our loved Egyptian night?"

The classical columns on the former British Viceroy's House in New Delhi, India, built in 1912, and now the residence of the President of India, illustrate the manner in which Western taste and design were imposed on much of the rest of the world during the age of imperialism. [Government of India Tourist Office, New York.]

the arrival in Tokyo Bay of an American naval force under Commodore Matthew Perry (1794–1858) in 1853. The constitutional and political reforms introduced in the Meiji era (1868–1912), as well as the rapid military and technological advance that accompanied it, swiftly made Japan a modern nation. Soon the Japanese adopted Western imperialism as well. In 1895 they defeated the Chinese in a one-sided war, took Formosa and the Liaotung Peninsula, and informally dominated the newly independent Korea.

The emergence of Japan frightened the other powers interested in China. The Russians were building a railroad across Siberia to Vladivostok and were afraid of any power that might threaten Manchuria. Together with France and Germany they applied diplomatic pressure that forced Japan out of the Liaotung Peninsula and its harbor, Port Arthur, and all pressed feverishly for concessions in China. Fearing that China, its markets, and its investment opportunities would soon be closed to its citizens, the United States in 1899 proposed the "Open Door Policy," which opposed foreign annexations in China and allowed businessmen of all nations to trade there on equal terms. The support of Britain helped win acceptance of the policy by all the powers except Russia.

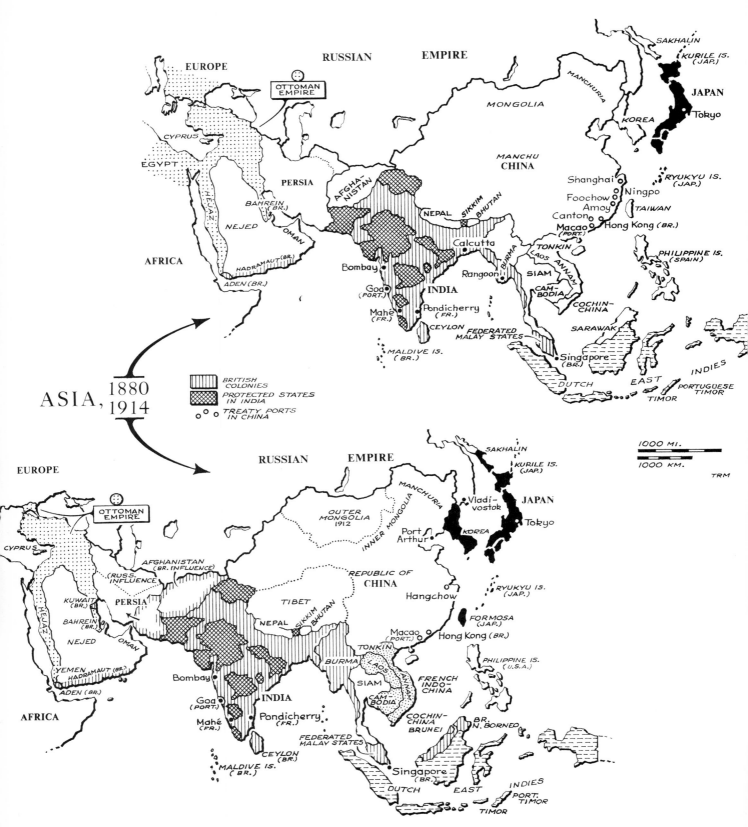

ASIA, $\begin{array}{c} 1880 \\ 1914 \end{array}$

BRITISH
COLONIES
PROTECTED STATES
IN INDIA
TREATY PORTS
IN CHINA

Top map labels:

EUROPE

RUSSIAN EMPIRE

OTTOMAN EMPIRE

CYPRUS

EGYPT

PERSIA

AFRICA

MONGOLIA

MANCHURIA

SAKHALIN

KURILE IS. (JAP.)

JAPAN

Tokyo

KOREA

MANCHU CHINA

Shanghai

Ningpo

Foochow

Amoy

Canton

Macao (PORT.)

Hong Kong (BR.)

RYUKYU IS. (JAP.)

TAIWAN

PHILIPPINE IS. (SPAIN)

AFGHA-NISTAN

NEPAL

SIKKIM

BHUTAN

BAHREIN (BR.)

NEJED

OMAN

HADRAMAUT (BR.)

ADEN (BR.)

Bombay

Goa (PORT.)

INDIA

Calcutta

Mahé (FR.)

Pondicherry (FR.)

CEYLON

MALDIVE IS. (BR.)

BURMA

Rangoon

SIAM

TONKIN

LAOS

ANNAM

CAM-BODIA

COCHIN-CHINA

FEDERATED MALAY STATES

SARAWAK

Singapore

DUTCH

EAST

INDIES

PORTUGUESE TIMOR

TIMOR

HEJAZ

Bottom map labels:

EUROPE

RUSSIAN EMPIRE

OTTOMAN EMPIRE

CYPRUS

HEJAZ

KUWAIT (BR.)

BAHREIN (BR.)

NEJED

OMAN

YEMEN

HADRAMAUT (BR.)

ADEN (BR.)

AFRICA

PERSIA

AFGHANISTAN (BR. INFLUENCE)

(RUSS. INFLUENCE)

OUTER MONGOLIA 1912

INNER MONGOLIA

MANCHURIA

SAKHALIN

KURILE IS. (JAP.)

Vladi-vostok

JAPAN

Port Arthur

KOREA

Tokyo

TIBET

REPUBLIC OF CHINA

Hangchow

RYUKYU IS. (JAP.)

FORMOSA (JAP.)

Macao (PORT.)

Hong Kong (BR.)

PHILIPPINE IS. (U.S.A.)

NEPAL

SIKKIM

BHUTAN

Bombay

Goa (PORT.)

INDIA

Mahé (FR.)

Pondicherry (FR.)

CEYLON (BR.)

MALDIVE IS. (BR.)

BURMA

TONKIN

LAOS

ANNAM

SIAM

CAM-BODIA

COCHIN-CHINA

FRENCH INDO-CHINA

BRUNEI

BR. N. BORNEO

FEDERATED MALAY STATES

Singapore (BR.)

DUTCH

EAST

INDIES

PORT. TIMOR

TIMOR

1000 MI.

1000 KM.

TRM

804 *Imperialism, Alliances, and War*

As in Africa, the decades before World War I saw imperialism spread widely and rapidly in Asia. Two new powers, Japan and the United States joined the British, French, and Dutch in extending control both to islands and to mainland and in exploiting an enfeebled China.

The United States had only recently emerged as a force in international affairs. After freeing itself from British rule and consolidating its independence during the Napoleonic Wars, the Americans had busied themselves with westward expansion on the North American continent until the end of the nineteenth century. The Monroe Doctrine of 1823, in effect, had made the entire Western Hemisphere an American protectorate. Cuba's attempt to gain independence from Spain was the spark for the new United States involvement in international affairs. Sympathy for the Cuban cause, American investments on the island, the desire for Cuban sugar, and concern over the island's strategic importance in the Carribean all helped win the Americans over to the idea of a war with Spain.

American victory in the Spanish–American War of 1898 brought an informal protectorate over Cuba and annexation of Puerto Rico and drove Spain completely out of the Western Hemisphere. The Americans also annexed the Philippine Islands and Guam, and Germany acquired the other Spanish islands in the Pacific. The Americans and the Germans also divided Samoa between them. What was left of the Pacific islands was soon taken by France and England. Hawaii had been under American influence for some time and had been asking for annexation, which was accomplished in 1898. This outburst of activity after the Spanish war made the United States an imperial and Pacific power. Soon after the turn of the century most of the world had come under the control of the advanced Western nations. The one remaining area of great vulnerability was the Ottoman Empire, but its fate was closely tied up with European developments and must be treated in that context.

Emergence of the German Empire and the Alliance Systems (1873–1890)

Prussia's victories over Austria and France and its creation of a large, powerful German Empire revolutionized European diplomacy. The sudden appearance of a vast new political unit that brought together the majority of the German people to form a nation of great and growing population, wealth, industrial capacity, and military power posed new problems. The balance of power created at the Congress of Vienna was altered radically. Britain retained its position and so did Russia, even though somewhat weakened by the Crimean War. Austria, however, had fallen quite a distance, and its position was destined to deteriorate further as the forces of nationalism threatened to disintegrate the Austro-Hungarian Empire. French power and prestige were badly damaged by the Franco-Prussian war and the German annexation of Alsace-Lorraine. The weakened French were both afraid of their powerful new neighbor and at the same time resentful of the defeat, the loss of territory and population, and the loss of their traditional position of dominance in Western Europe.

Until 1890 Bismarck continued to guide German policy. He insisted after 1871 that Germany was a satisfied power and wanted no further territorial gains, and he meant it. He only wanted to consolidate the new international situation by avoiding a new war that might undo his achievement. Aware of French resentment, he tried to assuage it by friendly relations and by supporting French colonial aspirations in order to turn French attention away from European discontents. At the same time he prepared for the worst. If France could not be conciliated, it must be isolated. The kernel of Bismarck's policy was to prevent an alliance between France and any other European power—especially Austria or Russia—that would threaten Germany with a war on two fronts.

WAR IN THE BALKANS. His first move was to establish the Three Emperors' League in 1873. It brought together the three great conservative empires of Germany, Austria, and Russia. The league soon collapsed as a result of the Russo-Turkish War, which broke out in 1875 because of an uprising in the Ottoman Balkan provinces of Bosnia and Herzegovina. The tottering Ottoman Empire was held together chiefly by the competing aims of those powers who awaited its demise. The

weakness of the Ottoman Empire encouraged Serbia and Montenegro to come to the aid of their fellow Slavs. Soon the rebellion spread to Bulgaria. Then Russia entered the fray and turned it into a major international crisis. The Russians hoped to pursue their traditional policy of expansion at Ottoman expense and especially hoped to achieve their most cherished goal: control of Constantinople and the Dardanelles. The Russian intervention also reflected the influence of the Pan-Slav movement, which sought to bring together all the Slavic peoples, even those under Austrian or Ottoman rule, under the protection of Holy Mother Russia.

The Ottoman Empire was weak, and before long it was forced to ask for peace. The Treaty of San Stefano of March 1878 was a Russian triumph. The Slavic states in the Balkans were freed of Ottoman rule, and Russia itself obtained territorial gains and a heavy monetary indemnity. But the Russian victory was not lasting. The other great powers were alarmed by the terms of the settlement. Austria feared that the great Slavic victory and the

powerful increase in Russian influence in the Balkans would cause dangerous shock waves in its own Balkan provinces. The British were alarmed by the damage the Russian victory would do to the European balance of power and especially by the thought of possible Russian control of the Dardanelles and access to the Mediterranean and Black Seas. Disraeli was determined to resist, and British public opinion supported him. A music hall song that became popular gave the language a new word for superpatriotism: *jingoism*.

> We don't want to fight,
> But by jingo if we do,
> We've got the men,
> We've got the ships,
> We've got the money too!

THE CONGRESS OF BERLIN. Even before the Treaty of San Stefano, Disraeli sent a fleet to Constantinople. After the magnitude of Russia's appetite was

OPPOSITE: William I and Bismarck, victors over France, at Versailles as the new German Empire is proclaimed, January 18, 1871. Anton von Werner's painting shows the same hall in which would be signed the Versailles Treaty of 1919 after World War I. [John R. Freeman.]

At the Congress of Berlin in 1878 Bismarck acted as the "honest broker" to settle various foreign policy disputes of the major European powers. Disraeli of England is standing toward the left, facing forward with his hand on his hip. The painter is again Anton von Werner. [The Granger Collection.]

known, Britain and Austria forced Russia to agree to an international conference at which the provisions of the treaty would be reviewed by the other great powers. The resulting Congress of Berlin met in June and July of 1878 under the presidency of Bismarck. The choice of site and presiding officer was a clear recognition of Germany's new importance and of its chancellor's claim that his policy called for no further territorial gains and aimed at preserving the peace. Bismarck referred to himself as an "honest broker," and the title seems justified. He agreed to the congress simply because he wanted to avoid a war between Russia and Austria into which he feared Germany would be drawn with nothing to gain and much to lose. From the collapsing Ottoman Empire he wanted nothing. "The Eastern Question," he said, "is not worth the healthy bones of a single Pomeranian musketeer."[7]

The decisions of the congress were a blow to Russian

7 Quoted by Hajo Holborn, A History of Modern Germany, 1840–1945, (New York: Alfred A. Knopf, 1969), p. 239.

ambitions. Bulgaria was reduced in size by two thirds and was deprived of access to the Aegean Sea. Austria–Hungary was given Bosnia and Herzegovina to "occupy and administer." Britain received Cyprus, and France gained permission to expand into Tunisia. These privileges were compensation for the gains that Russia was permitted to keep. Germany asked for nothing but got little credit from Russia for its restraint. The Russians believed that they had saved Prussia in 1807 from complete dismemberment by Napoleon and had expected a show of German gratitude. They were bitterly disappointed, and the Three Emperors' League was dead.

All of the Balkan states were also annoyed by the Berlin settlement. Romania wanted Bessarabia; Bulgaria wanted a return to the borders of the Treaty of San Stefano; and Greece wanted a part of the Ottoman spoils. The major trouble spot, however, was in the south Slavic states of Serbia and Montenegro. They deeply resented the Austrian occupation of Bosnia and Herzegovina, as did many of the natives of those provinces. The south

Slavic question no less than the estrangement between Russia and Germany was a threat to the peace of Europe.

GERMAN ALLIANCES WITH RUSSIA AND AUSTRIA. For the moment Bismarck could ignore the Balkans, but he could not ignore the breach in his eastern alliance system. With Russia alienated, he turned to Austria and concluded a secret treaty in 1879. The resulting Dual Alliance was defensive in character and was aimed at Russia. If the signatory countries were attacked by someone else, each promised at least to maintain neutrality. The treaty was for five years and was renewed regularly until 1918. As the central point in German policy, it was criticized at the time, and some have judged it mistaken in retrospect. It appeared to tie German fortunes to those of the troubled Austro-Hungarian Empire and in that way to borrow trouble. At the same time, by isolating the Russians, it pushed them in the direction of seeking alliances in the West.

Bismarck was fully aware of these dangers but discounted them with good reason. At no time did he allow his Austrian alliance to drag Germany into Austria's Balkan quarrels. As he put it himself, in any alliance there is a horse and a rider, and in this one Bismarck meant Germany to be the rider. He made it clear to the Austrians that the alliance was purely defensive and that Germany would never be a party to an attack on Russia. "For us," he said, "Balkan questions can never be a motive for war."[8]

Bismarck believed that monarchical, reactionary Russia would not seek an alliance either with republican, revolutionary France or with increasingly democratic Britain. In fact, he expected news of Austro-German negotiations to frighten Russia into seeking closer relations with Germany, and he was right. Russian diplomats soon approached him, and by 1881 he had concluded a renewal of the Three Emperor's League on a firmer basis. The three powers promised to maintain friendly neutrality in case either of the others was attacked by a fourth power. Other clauses included the right of Austria to annex Bosnia–Herzegovina whenever it wished and closed the Dardanelles to all nations in case of war. The agreement allayed German fears of a Russian–French alliance and Russian fears of a combination of Austria and Britain against it, of Britain's fleet sailing into the Black Sea, and of a hostile combination of Germany and Austria. Most important of all, the agreement aimed at a resolution of the conflicts in the Balkans between Austria and Russia. Though it did not put an end to such conflicts, it was a significant step toward peace.

THE TRIPLE ALLIANCE. In 1882 Italy, ambitious for colonial expansion and annoyed by French preemption of Tunisia, asked to join the Dual Alliance. The provisions of its entry were defensive and directed against France. At this point Bismarck's policy was a complete success. He was allied with three of the great powers and friendly with the other, Great Britain, which held aloof from all alliances. France was isolated and no threat. Bismarck's diplomacy was a great achievement, but an even greater challenge was to maintain this complicated system of secret alliances in the face of the continuing rivalries among Germany's allies. In spite of another Balkan war that broke out in 1885 and again estranged Austria and Russia, he succeeded. Although the Three Emperors' League lapsed, the Triple Alliance (Germany, Austria, and Italy) was renewed for another five years. To restore German relations with Russia, he negotiated the Reinsurance Treaty of 1887, in which both powers promised to remain neutral if either was attacked. All seemed smooth, but a change in the German monarchy soon overturned everything.

In 1888 William II (1888–1918) came to the German throne. He was twenty-nine years old, ambitious and impetuous. He was imperious by temperament and believed in monarchy by divine right. He had suffered an injury at birth that left him with a withered arm, and he compensated for this disability by means of vigorous exercise, by a military bearing and outlook, and some-

8 Quoted by J. Remak in *The Origins of World War I 1871–1914*, (New York: Holt, Rinehart and Winston, 1967), p. 14.

times by an embarrassingly loud and bombastic rhetoric.

Like many Germans of his generation, William II was filled with a sense of Germany's destiny as the leading power of Europe. He wanted to achieve recognition at least of equality from Britain, the land of his mother and of his grandmother, Queen Victoria. To achieve a "place in the sun," he and his contemporaries wanted a navy and colonies like Britain's. These aims, of course, ran counter to Bismarck's limited continental policy. When William argued for a navy as a defense against a British landing in north Germany, Bismarck replied, "If the British should land on our soil, I should have them arrested."[9] This was only one example of the great distance between the young emperor, or Kaiser, and his chancellor. In 1890 William used a disagreement over domestic policy to dismiss Bismarck.

So long as Bismarck held power, Germany was secure and there was peace among the great European powers. Although he made mistakes and was not always successful, there was much to admire in his understanding and management of international relations in the hard world of reality. He had a clear and limited idea of his nation's goals. He resisted pressures for further expansion with few and insignificant exceptions. He understood and used the full range of diplomatic weapons: appeasement and deterrence, threats and promises, secrecy and openness. He understood the needs and hopes of other countries and, where possible, tried to help to accomplish them or use them to his own advantage. His system of alliances created a stalemate in the Balkans at the same time that it ensured German security.

During Bismarck's time Germany was a force for European peace and was increasingly understood to be so. This would not, of course, have been possible without its great military power, but it also required the leadership of a statesman who was willing and able to exercise restraint and who could make a realistic estimate of what his country needed and what was possible.

9 See Document on p. 810.

Forging of the Triple Entente (1890–1907)

FRANCO-PRUSSIAN ALLIANCE. Almost immediately after Bismarck's retirement his system of alliances collapsed. His successor was General Leo von Caprivi (1831–1899), who had once asked, "What kind of jackass will dare to be Bismarck's successor?" Caprivi refused the Russian request to renew the Reinsurance Treaty, in part because he felt incompetent to continue Bismarck's complicated policy and in part because he wished to draw Germany closer to Britain. The results were unfortunate, as Britain remained aloof and Russia was alienated. Even Bismarck had assumed that ideological differences were too great to permit a Franco-Russian alliance, but political isolation and the need for foreign capital unexpectedly drove the Russians toward France. The French, who were even more isolated, were glad to encourage their investors to pour capital into Russia if it would help produce an alliance and security against Germany. In 1894 the Franco-Russian alliance against Germany was signed.

BRITAIN AND GERMANY.   Britain now became the key to the international situation. Colonial rivalries pitted the British against the Russians in Central Asia and against the French in Africa. Traditionally Britain had also opposed Russian control of Constantinople and the Dardanelles and French control of the Low Countries. There was no reason to think that Britain would soon become friendly with its traditional rivals or abandon its accustomed friendliness toward the Germans. Yet within a decade of William II's accession Germany had become the enemy in the minds of Englishmen. Before the turn of the century popular British thrillers about imaginary wars always portrayed the French as the invader; after the turn of the century the enemy was always German. This remarkable transformation has often been attributed to the economic rivalry, in which Germany made vast strides to challenge and even overtake British production in various materials and markets. There can be no doubt that Germany made such gains and that many Englishmen resented them, but the problem was not a serious cause of hostility and waned as the first decade of the century wore on. The real problem lay in the foreign and naval policies of the German emperor and his ministers.

William II's attitude toward Britain was respectful and admiring, especially with regard to its colonial empire and mighty fleet. At first Germany tried to win the British over to the Triple Alliance, but when Britain clung to its policy of "splendid isolation," German policy took a different tack. The idea was to demonstrate Germany's worthiness as an ally by withdrawing support and even making trouble for Britain. This odd manner of gaining

William II States His View of Germany's Future

Forced to abdicate in 1918, Emperor William II of Germany lived on quietly in the Netherlands until 1941. He was left with ample time to reflect on his life and on the background of World War I in which Germany was defeated. In his memoirs he contrasted his own and Bismarck's views on foreign policy during the short period between 1888 and 1890—that is, between William's accession to the throne and his dismissal of Bismarck.

I SPOKE *often with the Prince [Bismarck] about the colonial question and always found in him the intention to utilize the colonies as commercial objects, or objects for swapping purposes, other than to make them useful to the fatherland or utilize them as sources of raw materials. . . .*

I pointed out that steps must be taken for getting a fleet constructed in time, in order that German assets in foreign lands should not be without protection; that, since the Prince had unfurled the German flag in foreign parts, and the people stood behind it, there must also be a navy behind it. . . .

But the Prince turned a deaf ear to my statements and made use of his pet motto: "If the English should land on our soil I should have them arrested." His idea was that the colonies would be defended by us at home. . . .

The political interest of the Prince was, in fact, concentrated essentially upon continental Europe; England lay somewhat to one side among the cares that burdened him daily. . . .

Prince Bismarck did not realize that, through the acquisition of colonies for Germany, he would be obliged to look beyond Europe and be automatically forced to act, politically, on a large scale—with England especially. England, to be sure, was one of the five balls in his diplomatic-statesmanly game, but she was merely one of the five, and he did not grant her the special importance which was her due.

For this reason it was that the Foreign Office likewise was involved entirely in the continental interplay of politics, had not the requisite interest in colonies, navy, or England, and possessed no experience in world politics. The English psychology and mentality, as shown in the pursuit—constant, though concealed by all sorts of little cloaks—of world hegemony, was to the German Foreign Office a book sealed with seven seals.

William II, *The Kaiser's Memoirs*, trans. by Thomas R. Ybarra, (New York and London: Harper and Brothers, 1922), pp. 7–9.

King Edward VII of England and Emperor William II in Germany, August 1906. Edward was William's uncle, but the two men disliked each other. On learning of the outbreak of World War I, William wrote, "Edward VII dead is stronger after his death than I who am still alive!" [Bildarchiv Preussischer Kulturbesitz.]

an ally reflected the Kaiser's confused feelings toward Britain, which consisted of dislike and jealousy mixed with admiration. These feelings reflected those of many Germans, especially in the intellectual community, who like William were eager for Germany to pursue a "World Policy" rather than Bismarck's limited one that confined German interests to Europe. They too saw England as the barrier to German ambitions, and their influence in the schools, the universities, and the press guaranteed popular approval of actions and statements hostile to Britain.

The Germans began to exert pressure against Britain in Africa by barring British attempts to build a railroad from Capetown to Cairo. They also openly sympathized with the Boers of South Africa in their resistance to British expansion. In 1896 William insulted the British by sending a congratulatory telegram to Paul Kruger (1825–1904), president of the Transvaal, for repulsing a British raid "without having to appeal to friendly powers for assistance."

In 1898 William's dream of a German navy began to achieve reality with the passage of a naval law providing for nineteen battleships. In 1900 a second law doubled that figure. The architect of the new navy was Admiral

Alfred von Tirpitz (1849–1930), who openly proclaimed that Germany's naval policy was aimed at Britain. His "risk" theory argued that Germany could build a fleet strong enough not to defeat the British, but to do so much damage as to make the British navy inferior to other powers like France or the United States. The theory was, in fact, absurd because as Germany's fleet became menacing, the British would certainly build ships to maintain their advantage, and British resources were greater than Germany's. The naval policy, therefore, was doomed to failure. Over time its main achievements were to waste German resources and to begin a great naval race with Britain. It is not too much to say, moreover, that the threat posed by the German navy did more to antagonize British opinion than anything else. As the German navy grew and German policies seemed more threatening, the British became alarmed enough to abandon their traditional attitudes and policies.

At first, however, Britain was not unduly concerned. The British were embarrassed by the general hostility of world opinion during the Boer War (1899–1902) and suddenly alarmed that their isolation no longer seemed so splendid. The Germans, with the exception of the Kruger telegram, had acted with restraint during the war. Between 1898 and 1901 Joseph Chamberlain, the colonial secretary, made several attempts to conclude an alliance with Germany. The Germans, confident that a British alliance with France or Russia was impossible, refused and expected the British to make greater concessions in the future.

THE *ENTENTE CORDIALE*. The first breach in Britain's isolation came in 1902, when an alliance was concluded with Japan to relieve the pressure of defending British interests in the Far East against Russia. Next Britain abandoned its traditional antagonism toward France and in 1904 concluded a series of agreements with the French, collectively called the *Entente Cordiale*. It was not a formal treaty and had no military provisions, but it settled all outstanding colonial differences between the two nations. The Entente Cordiale was a long step toward aligning the British with Germany's great potential enemy.

Britain's new relationship with France was surprising, but in 1904 hardly anyone believed that the British whale and the Russian bear would ever come together. The Russo-Japanese war of 1904–1905 made such a development seem even less likely because Britain was allied with Russia's enemy. But Britain had behaved with restraint, and the Russians were chastened by their unexpected and humiliating defeat. The defeat had also led to the Russian Revolution of 1905. Although the revolution was put down, it left Russia weak and reduced British apprehensions in that direction. At the same time the British were concerned that Russia might again drift into the German orbit.

THE FIRST MOROCCAN CRISIS. At this point Germany decided to test the new understanding between Britain and Germany and to press for colonial gains. In March 1905 Emperor William II landed at Tangier, challenged the French protectorate there, and by implication asserted Germany's right to participate in Morocco's destiny. Germany's chancellor, Prince Bernhard von Bülow (1849–1929), intended to show France how weak it was and how little it could expect from Britain and at the same time to gain significant colonial concessions.

The Germans might well have achieved their aims, but they pushed too far and demanded an international conference of concerned states to make their point more dramatically. The conference met in 1906 at Algeciras in Spain. Austria sided with its German ally, but Spain, Italy, and the United States voted with Britain and France. The Germans had overplayed their hand, receiving trivial concessions, and the French were confirmed in their position in Morocco. German bullying had, moreover, driven Britain and France closer together. In the face of the threat of a German attack on France, Sir Edward Grey, the British foreign secretary, without making a firm commitment, authorized conversations between the British and the French general staffs. Their agreements became technically and morally binding as the years passed. By 1914 French and British military and naval plans were so mutually dependent that they were effectively, if not formally, allies.

BRITISH AGREEMENT WITH RUSSIA. Britain's fear of Germany's growing naval power, its concern over German ambitions in the Near East as represented by the German-sponsored plan to build a railroad from Berlin to Baghdad, and its closer relations with France made it desirable for Britain to become more friendly with France's ally, Russia. With French support the British made overtures to the Russians and in 1907 concluded an agreement with them much like the Entente Cordiale with France. It settled Russo-British quarrels in central Asia and opened the door for wider cooperation. The Triple Entente was now ranged against the Triple Alliance. Because Italy was unreliable, Germany and Austria–Hungary stood surrounded by two great land powers and Great Britain.

H.M.S. *Dreadnought* was completed by the British navy in 1906. It initiated a whole new class of battleships and gave rise to a new arms race in the decade before World War I. [The Granger Collection.]

William II and his ministers had turned Bismarck's nightmare of the prospect of a two-front war with France and Russia into a reality and had made it more horrible by adding Britain to the hostile coalition. The equilibrium that Bismarck had worked so hard to achieve was destroyed. Britain could no longer support Austria in restraining Russian ambitions in the Balkans. Germany, increasingly terrified by a sense of encirclement, was less willing to restrain the Austrians for fear of alienating them. In the Dual Alliance of Germany and Austria it had become less clear who was horse and who rider. Bismarck's alliance system had been intended to maintain peace, but the new one increased the risk of war and made the Balkans a likely spot for it to break out. Bismarck's diplomacy left France isolated and impotent; the new arrangement found France associated with the two greatest powers in Europe apart from Germany. The Germans could rely only on Austria, and such was the condition of that troubled empire that it was less likely to provide aid than to need it.

The Road to War
Growing Tensions (1908–1914)

The situation in the Balkans in the first decade of this century was exceedingly complicated. The weak Ottoman Empire controlled the central strip running west from Constantinople to the Adriatic. North and south of it were the independent states of Romania, Serbia, and Greece, as well as Bulgaria, technically still part of the empire but legally autonomous and practically independent. The Austro-Hungarian Empire included Croatia and Slovenia and since 1878 had "occupied and administered" Bosnia and Herzegovina.

With the exception of the Greeks and the Romanians most of the inhabitants of the Balkans spoke variants of the same Slavic language and felt a cultural and historical kinship with one another. For centuries they had been ruled by Austrians, Hungarians, or Turks, and the growing nationalism that characterized late nineteenth-century Europe made many of them eager for liberty. The more radical among them longed for a union of the south Slavic or Yugoslav peoples in a single nation. They looked to independent Serbia as the center of the new nation and hoped to detach all the Slavic provinces from Austria and

"The Mailed Fist of the Kaiser Strikes Agadir." This cartoon refers to the landing of the German gunboat *Panther* at Agadir in Morocco in 1911. William II's purpose was to press the French to make colonial concessions to Germany in Africa and, perhaps, to break up the Entente between the French and the British. The result, instead, was the second Moroccan crisis, which drew the Entente closer together and helped bring on World War I.

OPPOSITE: Two maps show the Balkans before and after the two Balkan wars; note the Ottoman retreat. In the center we see the geographical relationship of the Central Powers and their Bulgarian and Turkish allies. Tables give relative strength of World War I combatants.

especially Bosnia, which bordered on Serbia. In this regard Serbia was to unite the Slavs at the expense of Austria, as Piedmont had united the Italians and Prussia the Germans.

In 1908 a group of modernizing reformers called the Young Turks brought about a revolution in the Ottoman Empire. Their actions threatened to revive the life of the empire and to interfere with the plans of the European jackals preparing to pounce on the Ottoman corpse. These events brought on the first of a series of Balkan crises that would eventually lead to war.

THE BOSNIAN CRISIS. In 1908 the Austrian and Russian governments decided to act quickly before Turkey became strong enough to resist. They struck a bargain in which it was agreed that they would call an international conference where each of them would support the other's demands. Russia would agree to the Austrian annexation of Bosnia and Herzegovina, and Austria would support Russia's request to open the Dardanelles to Russian warships.

Austria, however, declared the annexation before any conference was called. The British, ever concerned about their own position in the Mediterranean, refused to agree to the Russian demand. The Russians felt betrayed, humiliated, and furious. Their "little brothers," the Serbs, were frustrated and angry at the loss of Bosnia, and the Russians were too weak to do anything but accept the new situation. The Germans had not been warned in advance of Austria's plans and were unhappy that the action threatened their relations with Russia. But Germany felt so dependent on the Dual Alliance that it assured Austria of its support. Austria had been given a free hand, and to an extent German policy was being made in Vienna. It was a dangerous precedent. At the same time, the failure of Britain and France to support Russia strained the Entente and made it harder for them to oppose Russian interests again in the future if they were to retain Russian friendship.

THE SECOND MOROCCAN CRISIS. The second Moroccan crisis in 1911 emphasized the French and British need for mutual support. When France sent in an army to put down a rebellion, Germany took the opportunity to assert its rights in Morocco as a means of extorting colonial concessions in the French Congo. To add force to their demands, they sent the gunboat *Panther* to the port of Agadir, allegedly to protect German citizens there. Once again, as in 1905, the Germans went too far. The *Panther*'s visit to Agadir provoked a strong reaction in Britain. For some time Anglo-German relations had been growing worse, chiefly because of the intensification of the naval race. In 1907 the Germans built the first new battleship of the dreadnought class, which Britain had developed in 1906. In 1908 Germany passed still another naval law, which accelerated the schedule of production to challenge British naval supremacy. These actions frightened and angered the British because of the clear threat to the security of the island kingdom and its empire. The German actions also forced Britain to increase taxes to pay for new armaments just when the Liberal government was launching its expensive program of social legislation. Negotiations failed to persuade William II and Tirpitz to slow down naval construction.

In this atmosphere the British heard of the *Panther*'s arrival in Morocco. They wrongly believed that the Germans meant to turn Agadir into a naval base on the Atlantic. The crisis passed when France yielded some insignificant bits of the Congo and Germany withdrew

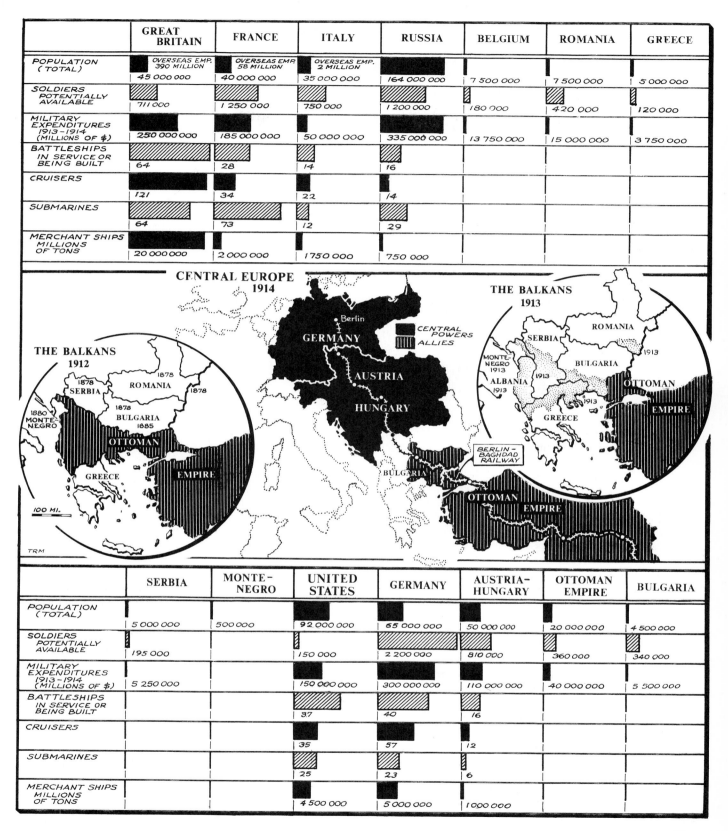

	GREAT BRITAIN	FRANCE	ITALY	RUSSIA	BELGIUM	ROMANIA	GREECE
POPULATION (TOTAL)	45 000 000 (OVERSEAS EMP. 390 MILLION)	40 000 000 (OVERSEAS EMP. 58 MILLION)	35 000 000 (OVERSEAS EMP. 2 MILLION)	164 000 000	7 500 000	7 500 000	5 000 000
SOLDIERS POTENTIALLY AVAILABLE	711 000	1 250 000	750 000	1 200 000	180 000	420 000	120 000
MILITARY EXPENDITURES 1913–1914 (MILLIONS OF $)	250 000 000	185 000 000	50 000 000	335 000 000	13 750 000	15 000 000	3 750 000
BATTLESHIPS IN SERVICE OR BEING BUILT	64	28	14	16			
CRUISERS	121	34	22	14			
SUBMARINES	64	73	12	29			
MERCHANT SHIPS MILLIONS OF TONS	20 000 000	2 000 000	1 750 000	750 000			

CENTRAL EUROPE 1914

Berlin

GERMANY

AUSTRIA

HUNGARY

CENTRAL POWERS

ALLIES

THE BALKANS 1913

ROMANIA

SERBIA

MONTE-NEGRO 1913

BULGARIA

ALBANIA 1913

1913

GREECE

OTTOMAN EMPIRE

BERLIN-BAGHDAD RAILWAY

BULGARIA

OTTOMAN EMPIRE

THE BALKANS 1912

ROMANIA

1878

SERBIA 1878

1878

1878

BULGARIA 1885

1880 MONTE-NEGRO

OTTOMAN EMPIRE

GREECE

100 MI.

TRM

	SERBIA	MONTE-NEGRO	UNITED STATES	GERMANY	AUSTRIA-HUNGARY	OTTOMAN EMPIRE	BULGARIA
POPULATION (TOTAL)	5 000 000	500 000	92 000 000	65 000 000	50 000 000	20 000 000	4 500 000
SOLDIERS POTENTIALLY AVAILABLE	195 000		150 000	2 200 000	810 000	360 000	340 000
MILITARY EXPENDITURES 1913–1914 (MILLIONS OF $)	5 250 000		150 000 000	300 000 000	110 000 000	40 000 000	5 500 000
BATTLESHIPS IN SERVICE OR BEING BUILT			37	40	16		
CRUISERS			35	57	12		
SUBMARINES			25	23	6		
MERCHANT SHIPS MILLIONS OF TONS			4 500 000	5 000 000	1 000 000		

from Morocco. The main result was to increase British fear and hostility and to draw them closer to France. Specific military plans were formulated for a British expeditionary force to defend France in case of German attack, and the British and French navies agreed to cooperate. Without any formal treaty the German naval construction and the Agadir crisis had turned the Entente Cordiale into an alliance that could not have been more binding. If France were attacked by Germany, Britain must defend the French, for its own security was inextricably tied up with that of France.

WAR IN THE BALKANS.   The second Moroccan crisis also provoked another crisis in the Balkans. Italy had long sought to gain colonies and to take its place among the great powers. It had long wanted Libya, which though worth little at the time was at least available. Italy feared that the recognition of the French protectorate in Morocco would encourage France to move into Libya. Consequently, in 1911 Italy attacked the Ottoman Empire to anticipate the French, defeated the faltering Turks, and obtained Libya and the Dodecanese Islands. The Italian victory encouraged the Balkan states to try their luck. In 1912 Bulgaria, Greece, Montenegro, and Serbia joined an attack on the Ottoman Empire and won easily. After this First Balkan War the victors fell out among themselves. The Serbs and the Bulgarians quarreled about the division of Macedonia, and in 1913 a Second Balkan War erupted. This time Turkey and Romania joined the other states against Bulgaria and stripped away much of what the Bulgarians had gained since 1878.

After the First Balkan War the alarmed Austrians became determined to limit Serbian gains and especially to prevent the Serbs from gaining a port on the Adriatic. This policy meant keeping Serbia out of Albania, but the Russians backed the Serbs and tensions mounted. An international conference sponsored by Britain in early 1913 resolved the matter in Austria's favor and called for an independent kingdom of Albania. But Austria felt humiliated by the public airing of Serbian demands. Then for some time the Serbs defied the powers and continued to occupy parts of Albania. Under Austrian pressure they withdrew, but in September 1913, after the Second Balkan War, the Serbs reoccupied sections of Albania. In mid-October Austria unilaterally issued an ultimatum to Serbia, and the latter country again withdrew its forces from Albania. During this crisis many people in Austria had wanted an all-out attack on Serbia to remove its threat once and for all from the empire. Those demands had been resisted by Emperor Francis Joseph and the heir to the throne, Archduke Francis Ferdinand. At the same time Pan-Slavic sentiment in Russia pressed Tsar Nicholas II to take a firm stand, but Russia once again let Austria have its way with Serbia. Throughout the crisis Britain, France, and Germany restrained their respective allies, although each worried about seeming too reluctant to help its friends.

The lessons learned from this crisis of 1913 profoundly influenced behavior in the final crisis, the crisis of 1914. The Russians had once again, as in 1908, been embarrassed by their passivity, and their allies were more reluctant to restrain them again. The Austrians were embarrassed by what had resulted from accepting an international conference and were determined not to repeat the experience. They had seen that better results might be obtained from a threat of direct force; they and their German allies did not miss the lesson.

Sarajevo and the Outbreak of War (June–August 1914)

THE ASSASSINATION.   On June 28, 1914, a young Bosnian nationalist shot and killed the Austrian Archduke Francis Ferdinand, heir to the throne, and his wife as they drove in an open car through the Bosnian capital of Sarajevo. The assassin was a member of a conspiracy hatched by a political terrorist society called Union or Death, better known as the Black Hand. A major participant in the planning and preparation of the crime was the chief of intelligence of the Serbian army's general staff.

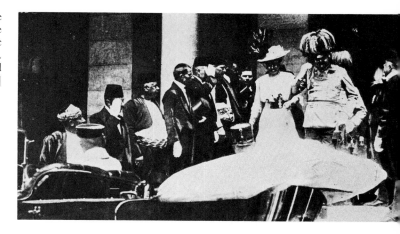

The Austrian Archduke Franz Ferdinand and his wife at Sarajevo, June 28, 1914. Later in the day the royal couple were assassinated by young Slavic revolutionaries trained and supplied in Serbia. The murders set off the crisis that led to World War I. [Popperfoto.]

Moments after the assassination of Archduke Ferdinand and his wife the Bosnian police captured one of the assassins in Sarajevo. [The Granger Collection.]

Even though his role was not actually known at the time, it was generally believed that Serbian officials were involved. The glee of the Serbian press lent support to that belief. The archduke was not a popular person in his own land, and his funeral evoked few signs of grief. He had been known to favor a form of federal government that would have given a higher status to the Slavs in the empire. This position alienated the conservatives and the Hungarians. It also alarmed radical Yugoslav nationalists, who feared that reform might end their dream of an independent south Slav state.

THE CENTRAL POWERS' RESPONSE. News of the assassination produced outrage and condemnation everywhere. To those Austrians who had long favored an attack on Serbia as a solution to the empire's Slavic problem, the opportunity seemed irresistible. But it was never easy for the Dual Monarchy to make a decision. Conrad von Hötzendorf, chief of the Austrian general

Count Leopold Berchtold (on the left), the Austro-Hungarian Foreign Minister, and Theodor von Bethmann-Hollweg, German Chancellor, meet in 1912. Both men played crucial roles in the war crisis of 1914.
[Ullstein Bilderdienst.]

staff, urged an attack as he had often done before. Count Tisza, speaking for Hungary, resisted. Berchtold, the Austro-Hungarian foreign minister, felt the need for strong action, but he knew that German support would be required in the likely event that Russia should decide to intervene to protect Serbia. He also knew that nothing could be done without Tisza's approval and that only German support could persuade the Hungarians to accept the policy of war. The question of peace or war, therefore, had to be answered in Berlin.

William II and Chancellor Theobald von Bethmann–Hollweg (1856–1921) readily promised German support for an attack on Serbia. It has often been said that they gave the Austrians a "blank check," but their message was firmer than that. They urged the Austrians to move swiftly while the other powers were still angry at Serbia, and they made the Austrians feel that a failure to act would be taken as evidence of Austria–Hungary's weakness and uselessness as an ally. Therefore, the Austrians never wavered in their determination to make war on Serbia. They hoped, with the protection of Germany, to fight a limited war that would not bring on a general European conflict, but they were prepared to risk even the latter. The Germans also knew that they risked a general war, but they hoped to "localize" the fight between Austria and Serbia.

Some scholars believe that Germany had long been plotting war, and some even think that a specific plan for war in 1914 was set in motion as early as 1912. The vast body of evidence on the crisis of 1914 gives no support to such notions. The German leaders plainly reacted to a crisis that they had not foreseen and just as plainly made decisions in response to events. The fundamental decision to support Austria, which made it very difficult if not impossible to avoid war, was made by the emperor and the chancellor without significant consultation with either military or diplomatic advisers.

William II appears to have reacted violently to the assassination. He was moved by his friendship for the archduke and by outrage at an attack on royalty. It is

The Austrian Ambassador Gets a "Blank Check" from the Kaiser

It was at a meeting at Potsdam on July 5, 1914 that the Austrian ambassador received from the Kaiser assurance that Germany would support Austria in the Balkans, even at the risk of war.

AFTER *lunch, when I again called attention to the seriousness of the situation, the Kaiser authorised me to inform our gracious Majesty that we might in this case, as in all others, rely upon Germany's full support. He must, as he said before, first hear what the Imperial Chancellor has to say, but he did not doubt in the least that Herr von Bethmann Hollweg would agree with him. Especially as far as our action against Serbia was concerned. But it was his (Kaiser Wilhelm's) opinion that this action must not be delayed. Russia's attitude will no doubt be hostile, but to this he had been for years prepared, and should a war between Austria–Hungary and Russia be unavoidable, we might be convinced that Germany, our old faithful ally, would stand at our side. Russia at the present time was in no way prepared for war, and would think twice before it appealed to arms. But it will certainly set other powers on to the Triple Alliance and add fuel to the fire in the Balkans. He understands perfectly well that His Apostolic Majesty in his well-known love of peace would be reluctant to march into Serbia; but if we had really recognised the necessity of warlike action against Serbia, he (Kaiser Wilhelm) would regret if we did not make use of the present moment, which is all in our favour.*

Outbreak of the World War: German Documents Collected by Karl Kautsky, Max Montgelas and Walther Schücking (eds.) (New York: Carnegie Endowment for International Peace, 1924), p. 76.

support. If Austria did not crush Serbia, the empire would soon collapse before the onslaught of Slavic nationalism defended by Russia. If Germany did not defend its ally, the Austrians might look elsewhere for help. His policy was one of "calculated risk."

The calculations proved to be incorrect. Bethmann-Hollweg hoped that the Austrians would strike swiftly and present the powers with a *fait accompli* while the outrage of the assassination was still fresh, and that German support would deter Russian involvement. Failing that, he was prepared for a continental war that would bring rapid victory over France and allow a full-scale attack on the Russians, who were always slow to bring their strength into action. All of this policy depended on British neutrality, and the German chancellor convinced himself that the British could be persuaded to stand aloof.

However, the Austrians were slow to act, as always, and did not even deliver their deliberately unacceqtable ultimatum to Serbia until July 24, when the general hostility toward Serbia had begun to subside. Serbia further embarrassed the Austrians by returning so soft and conciliatory an answer that the mercurial German emperor thought it removed all reason for war. But it was too late for Austria to turn back, and on July 28 the Austrians declared war on Serbia even though they could not put an army into the field until mid-August.

THE ENTENTE'S RESPONSE. The Russians, previously so often forced to back off, angrily responded to the Austrian demands on Serbia. The most conservative elements of the Russian government opposed war, fearing that it would bring on revolution as it had in 1905. But nationalists, Pan-Slavs, and most of the politically conscious classes in general demanded action. The government responded by ordering partial mobilization, against Austria only. This policy was militarily impossible, but its intention was the diplomatic one of putting pressure on Austria to hold back its attack on Serbia. Mobilization of any kind, however, was a dangerous political weapon because it was generally understood to be equivalent to an act of war. It was especially alarming to General Hel-

doubtful that a different provocation would have moved him so much. Bethmann-Hollweg was less emotional but under severe pressure. To resist the decision would have meant flatly to oppose the emperor. The chancellor, moreover, was suspected of being "soft" in the powerful military circles favored by his master. A conciliatory position would have been difficult. Beyond these considerations Bethmann-Hollweg, like many other Germans, viewed the future with apprehension. Russia was recovering its strength and would reach a military peak in 1917. The Entente was growing more powerful, and Germany's only reliable ally was Austria. The chancellor recognized the danger of support for Austria, but he believed it to be even more dangerous to withhold that

muth von Moltke (1848–1916), head of the German general staff. The possibility that the Russians might start mobilization before the Germans could move would upset the delicate timing of Germany's only battle plan, the Schlieffen Plan, and put Germany in great danger. From this point on, Moltke pressed for German mobilization and war, and the pressure of military necessity mounted until it became irresistible.

The Western powers were not eager for war. France's president and prime minister were on their way back from a visit to Russia when the crisis flared up again on July 24. The Austrians had, in fact, timed their ultimatum precisely so that these two men would be at sea at the crucial moment. Had they been at their desks, they might have attempted to restrain the Russians, but the French ambassador to Russia gave the Russians the same assurances that Germany had given its ally. The British worked hard to avoid trouble by traditional means, a conference of the powers. Austria, still smarting from its humiliation after the London Conference of 1913, would not hear of it. The Germans privately supported the Austrians but publicly took on a conciliatory tone in the hope of keeping the British neutral. Soon, however, Bethmann-Hollweg came to realize what he should have known from the first: if Germany attacked France, Britain must fight. Until July 30 his public appeals to Austria for restraint were a sham. Thereafter he sincerely tried to persuade the Austrians to negotiate and to avoid a general war, but it was too late. While Bethmann-Hollweg was urging restraint on the Austrians, Moltke was pressing them to act. The Austrians wondered who was in charge in Berlin, but they could not turn back.

On July 30 Austria ordered mobilization against Russia. Bethmann-Hollweg resisted the enormous pressure to mobilize, not because he had any further hope of avoiding war but because he wanted Russia to mobilize against Germany first and appear to be the aggressor. Only in that way could he win the support of the German nation for war, especially the pacifistic Social Democrats. His luck was good for a change. The news of Russian general mobilization came only minutes before Germany would have mobilized in any case. The Schlieffen Plan went into effect. The Germans invaded Luxembourg on August 1 and Belgium on August 3. The latter invasion violated the treaty of 1839 in which the British had guaranteed Belgian neutrality. This factor undermined the considerable sentiment in Britain for neutrality and united the nation against Germany. Germany then invaded France, and on August 4 Britain declared war on Germany. The Great War had begun. As Lord Grey put it, the lights were going out all over Europe. They would come on again, but Europe would never be the same.

World War I (1914–1918)

Throughout Europe jubilation greeted the outbreak of war. No general war had been fought since Napoleon, and the horrors of modern warfare were not yet understood. The dominant memory was of Bismarck's swift and decisive campaigns, in which costs and casualties were light and the rewards great. After the repeated crises of recent years and the fears and resentments they had created, war came as a release of tension. The popular press had increased public awareness of and interest in foreign affairs and had fanned the flames of patriotism. The prospect of war moved even a rational man of science like Sigmund Freud to say, "My whole libido goes out to Austria–Hungary."[10]

Strategies and Stalemate: 1914–1917

The strategies of both sides rested on Karl von Clausewitz's (1780–1831) interpretation of the Napoleonic mode of war, which constituted the dominant military theory of the day. Both sides expected to take the offensive, force a battle on favorable ground, and win a quick victory. The Entente powers—or the Allies, as they came to be called—held superiority in numbers and financial

10 Quoted in Joachim Remak, *The Origins of World War I* (New York. Holt, Rinehart and Winston, 1967), p. 134.

Germany's grand strategy for quickly winning the war against France in 1914 is shown by the wheeling arrows on the map. The crushing blows at France were, in the original plan, to be followed by the release of troops for use against Russia on Germany's Eastern front. But the plan was not adequately implemented, and the war on the Western front became a long contest in place.

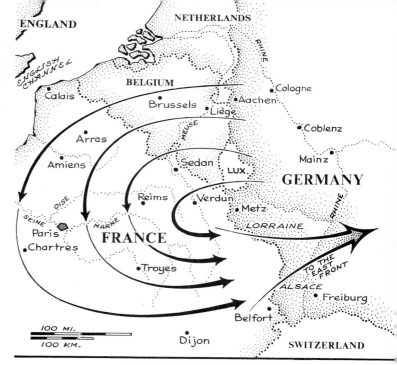

THE SCHLIEFFEN PLAN OF 1905

resources as well as command of the sea. Germany and Austria, the Central Powers, had the advantages of internal lines of communication and of having launched their attack first.

After 1905 Germany's only war plan was the one developed by Count Alfred von Schlieffen (1833–1913), chief of the German general staff from 1891 to 1906. It aimed at going around the French defenses by sweeping through Belgium to the channel, then wheeling to the south and east to envelop the French and to crush them against the German fortresses in Lorraine. The secret of success lay in making the German right wing immensely strong and deliberately weakening the left opposite the French frontier. The weakness of the left was meant to draw the French into the wrong place while the war was decided on the German right. As one keen military analyst has explained, "It would be like a revolving door—if a man pressed heavily on one side, the other side would spring round and strike him in the back. Here lay the real subtlety of the plan, not in the mere geographical detour."[11] In the east the Germans planned to stand on the defensive against Russia until France had been crushed, a task they thought would take only six weeks.

The apparent risk, besides the violation of Belgian neutrality and the consequent alienation of Britain, lay in weakening German defenses against a direct attack across the frontier. The strength of German fortresses and the superior firepower of German howitzers made that risk more apparent than real. The true danger was that the German striking force on the right through Belgium would not be powerful enough to make the swift progress vital to success. Schlieffen is said to have uttered the dying words: "It must come to a fight. Only make the right wing strong." The execution of his plan, however, was left to Helmuth von Moltke, the nephew of Bismarck's most effective general. The younger Moltke was a gloomy and nervous man who lacked the talent of his

11 B. H. Liddell Hart, *The Real War, 1914–1918* (Boston: Little, Brown and Co., 1964; first published in 1930), p. 47.

illustrious uncle and the theoretical daring of Schlieffen. He added divisions to the left wing and even weakened the Russian front for the same purpose. The consequence of this hesitant strategy was the failure of the Schlieffen Plan by a narrow margin.

THE WAR IN THE WEST. The French had also put their faith in the offensive, but with less reason than the Germans. They badly underestimated the numbers and effectiveness of the German reserves and set too much store by the importance of the courage and spirit of their troops. These proved insufficient against modern weapons, especially the machine gun. The French offensive on Germany's western frontier failed totally. In a sense this defeat was better than a partial success because it released troops for the use against the main German army. As a result the French and the British were able to stop the Germans at the Battle of the Marne in September 1914.

Thereafter the nature of the war in the west changed completely and became one of position instead of movement. Both sides dug in behind a wall of trenches protected by barbed wire that stretched from the North Sea to Switzerland. Strategically placed machine-gun nests made assaults difficult and dangerous. Both sides nonetheless attempted massive attacks prepared for by artillery barrages of unprecedented and horrible force and duration. Still the defense was always able to recover and bring up reserves fast enough to prevent a breakthrough. Sometimes assaults that cost hundreds of thousands of

WORLD WAR I IN EUROPE

T. R. MILLER

TRIPLE ENTENTE

ALLIES OF THE TRIPLE ENTENTE

CENTRAL POWERS

ALLIES OF THE CENTRAL POWERS

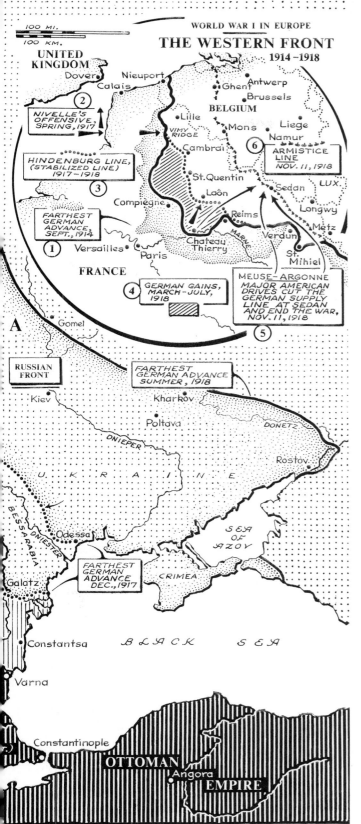

WORLD WAR I IN EUROPE
THE WESTERN FRONT
1914-1918

100 MI.
100 KM.

UNITED KINGDOM

Dover
Calais
Nieuport
Ghent
Antwerp
Brussels
BELGIUM
Lille
Mons
Liege
Namur

② NIVELLE'S OFFENSIVE, SPRING, 1917

VIMY RIDGE
Cambrai

⑥ ARMISTICE LINE NOV. 11, 1918

HINDENBURG LINE, (STABILIZED LINE) 1917-1918

③

St.Quentin
Laôn
LUX.
Sedan
Longwy
Metz

FARTHEST GERMAN ADVANCE, SEPT., 1914

Compiègne
Reims
Verdun

① Versailles
Paris
Chateau Thierry
St. Mihiel

FRANCE

④ GERMAN GAINS, MARCH-JULY, 1918

MEUSE-ARGONNE MAJOR AMERICAN DRIVES CUT THE GERMAN SUPPLY LINE AT SEDAN AND END THE WAR, NOV. 11, 1918

⑤

A
Gomel

RUSSIAN FRONT

FARTHEST GERMAN ADVANCE SUMMER, 1918

Kiev
Kharkov
Poltava
DONETZ
DNIEPER
Rostov

U · K · R · A · I · N · E

BESSARABIA
DNIESTER
Odessa
SEA OF AZOV

Galatz
FARTHEST GERMAN ADVANCE DEC., 1917
CRIMEA

Constantsa

B L A C K   S E A

Varna

Constantinople
OTTOMAN
Angora
EMPIRE

Despite the importance of military action in the Far East, in the Arab world, and at sea, the main theaters of activity in World War I were in the European areas shown here. The crucial Western front is seen in somewhat greater detail in the inset map.

lives produced advances that could be measured in hundreds of yards. The introduction of poison gas as a solution to the problem proved ineffective. Toward the end of the war the British introduced the tank, which proved to be the answer to the machine gun, but throughout the war defense was supreme. For three years after its establishment, the western front moved only a few miles in either direction.

THE WAR IN THE EAST. In the east the war began auspiciously for the Allies. The Russians advanced into Austrian territory and inflicted heavy casualties, but Russian incompetence and German energy soon reversed the situation. A young German officer, Erich Ludendorff (1865–1937), under the command of the elderly General Paul von Hindenburg (1847–1934), defeated the Russians at the Masurian Lakes and destroyed or captured an entire army at the Battle of Tannenberg. In 1915 the Central Powers pressed their advantage in the east and drove into the Baltic states and White Russia, inflicting over two million casualties in a single year. Russian confidence was badly shaken, but the Russian army stayed in the field.

As the battle lines hardened, both sides sought new allies. Turkey, because of its hostility to Russia, and Bulgaria, the enemy of Serbia, joined the Central Powers. Italy seemed an especially valuable prize, and both sides bid for Italian support with promises of a division of the spoils of victory. Because what the Italians wanted most was held by Austria, it was easier for the Allies to make the more attractive promises. In a secret treaty of 1915 the Allies agreed to deliver to Italy most of *Italia Irredenta* (i.e., the Trentino, the South Tyrol, Trieste, and some of the Dalmatian Islands) after victory. By the spring of 1915 Italy was engaging Austrian armies. Although the Italian campaign drained the strength of the Central Powers to a degree, the alliance with Italy generally proved a disappointment to the Allies and never produced significant results.

Romania joined the Allies in 1916 but was quickly defeated and driven from the war.

The military tank made its first appearance during World War I. It had the military advantages of giving its personnel armored protection, being able to cross many natural and manmade obstacles, and permitting a commander to advance fire power with some impunity closer to an enemy force than was possible by the traditional infantry charge. This photograph shows a light tank crossing an obstacle at a World War I British military experiment station. [Bettmann Archive.]

OPPOSITE: American soldiers in France. In 1918 the American army arrived in France in sufficient numbers to make a significant contribution. Here American forces take over a section in the Argonne forest, relieving tired Allied troops. [Radio Times Hulton Picture Library.]

In the Far East Japan honored its alliance with Britain and entered the war. The Japanese quickly overran the German colonies in China and the Pacific and used the opportunity to improve their own position against China.

Both sides also tried the tactic of subversion by appealing to nationalist sentiment in areas held by the enemy. The Germans supported nationalist movements among the Irish, the Flemings in Belgium, and the Poles and the Ukrainians under Russian rule. They even tried to persuade the Turks to lead a Moslem uprising against the British and the French in North Africa.

The Allies also used the device of subversion, with greater success. They sponsored movements of national autonomy for the Czechs, the Slovaks, the south Slavs, and the Poles that were under Austrian rule. They also favored a movement of Arab independence from Turkey. Led by Colonel T. E. Lawrence (1888–1935), this last scheme proved especially successful in the late years of the war.

In 1915 the Allies undertook to break the deadlock in the fighting by going around it. The idea came chiefly from Winston Churchill (1874–1965), first lord of the British Admiralty. He proposed an attack on the Dardanelles and the swift capture of Constantinople. This policy would knock Turkey from the war, bring help to the Balkan front, and ease communication with Russia. The plan was daring but promising and, in its original form, presented little risk. British naval superiority and the element of surprise would allow the forcing of the straits and the capture of Constantinople by purely naval action. Even if the scheme failed, the fleet could escape with little loss. Success depended on timing, speed, and daring leadership, but all of these were lacking. The execution of the attack was inept and overly cautious. Troops were landed, and as resistance continued, the

Allied commitment increased. Before the campaign was abandoned, the Allies lost almost 150,000 men and diverted three times that number from more useful occupation.

Both sides turned back to the west in 1916. General Erich von Falkenhayn (1861–1922), who had succeeded Moltke in September 1914, sought success by an attack on the French stronghold of Verdun. His plan was not to take the fortress or break through the line but rather to inflict enormously heavy casualties on the French, who must defend it against superior firepower coming from several directions. He, too, underestimated the superiority of the defense, and the French were able to hold Verdun with comparatively few men and to inflict almost as many casualties as they suffered. The commander of Verdun, Henri Pétain (1856–1951), became a national hero and "They shall not pass" a slogan of national defiance. The Allies tried to end the impasse by launching a major offensive along the River Somme in July. Aided by a Russian attack in the east that drew off some German strength and by an enormous artillery barrage, they hoped at last to break through. Once again the superiority of the defense was demonstrated. Enormous casualties on both sides brought no result. On all fronts losses were great and results meager. The war on land dragged on with no end in sight.

THE WAR AT SEA. As the war continued, control of the sea became more important. The British ignored the distinction between war supplies, which were contraband according to international law, and food or other peaceful cargo, which was not subject to seizure. They imposed a strict blockade meant to starve out the enemy, regardless of international law. The Germans responded with submarine warfare meant to destroy British shipping and starve the British. They declared the waters around

the British Isles a war zone, where even neutral ships would not be safe. Both policies were unwelcome to neutrals, and especially to the United States, which conducted extensive trade in the Atlantic, but the sinking of neutral ships by German submarines was both more dramatic and more offensive. In 1915 the British liner *Lusitania* was torpedoed by a German submarine. Among the 1,200 drowned were 118 Americans. President Woodrow Wilson (1856–1924) warned Germany that a repetition would not be accepted, and the Germans desisted rather than further anger the United States. This development gave the Allies a considerable advantage. The German fleet that had cost so much money and caused so much trouble played no significant part in the war. The only battle it fought was at Jutland in the spring of 1916. The battle resulted in a standoff and confirmed British domination of the surface of the sea.

AMERICA ENTERS THE WAR. In December 1916 President Woodrow Wilson of the United States intervened in an attempt to bring about a negotiated peace, but neither side was willing to renounce war aims that its opponent found unacceptable. The war seemed likely to continue until one or both sides reached exhaustian. Two events early in 1917 changed the situation radically. On February 1 the Germans announced the resumption of unrestricted submarine warfare, which led the United States to break off diplomatic relations. On April 6 the United States declared war on the Central Powers. One of the barriers to an earlier American intervention had been the presence of autocratic tsarist Russia among the Allies. Wilson could conceive of the war only as an idealistic crusade "to make the world safe for democracy." That problem was resolved in March of 1917 by a revolution in Russia that overthrew the tsarist government.

Field guns, under a red banner, in place in Petrograd (formerly St. Petersburg) during the Russian
Revolution in March 1917. [The Granger Collection.]

Revolutions in Russia
(March and November 1917)

The March Revolution in Russia was neither planned
nor led by any political faction. It was the result of the
collapse of the monarchy's ability to govern. Although
public opinion had strongly supported Russian entry into
the war, the conflict put far too great demands on the
resources of the country and the efficiency of the tsarist
government. Nicholas II was weak, incompetent, and
suspected of being under the domination of his German
wife and the insidious monk Rasputin, who was assassinated by noblemen in 1916. Military and domestic failures produced massive casualties, widespread hunger,
strikes by workers, and disorganization in the army. The
peasant discontent that had plagued the countryside before 1914 did not subside during the conflict. In 1916 the
tsar adjourned the Duma and proceeded to rule alone. All
political factions were in one way or another discontented.

In early March 1917 strikes and worker demonstrations erupted in Petrograd, as St. Petersburg had been
renamed. The ill-disciplined troops in the city refused to
fire on the demonstrators, and the tsar abdicated on
March 15. The government of Russia fell into the hands
of members of the Duma who soon constructed a provisional government composed chiefly of Constitutional
Democrats with Western sympathies. At the same time
the various socialists, including both Social Revolutionaries and Social Democrats of the Menshevik wing, began
to organize the workers into soviets. Initially they allowed
the provisional government to function without actually
supporting it. As relatively orthodox Marxists, they believed that a bourgeois stage of development must come
to Russia before the revolution of the proletariat could be
achieved.

In this climate the provisional government made the
important decision to remain loyal to the existing Russian
alliances and to continue the war against Germany. In
this regard, the provisional government was accepting the
tsarist foreign policy and was associating itself with the
source of much domestic suffering and discontent. The
fate of the provisional government was sealed by the
collapse of the new offensive in the summer of 1917.
Disillusionment with the war, shortages of food and other
necessities at home, and the growing demand by peasants
for land reform undermined the government, even after
its leadership had been taken over by the moderate socialist Alexander Kerenski (1881–1970). Moreover, discipline in the army had badly disintegrated.

Ever since April the Bolshevik wing of the Social

During the May Day parade of 1917 in Petrograd soldiers march under a banner reading, "Down with the old!" [The Granger Collection.]

Alexander Kerensky headed the shortlived provisional government in Russia after the Revolution of March 1917 and before the Bolshevik victory later that year. The photograph was made during his summer of authority. [The Granger Collection.]

Democratic Party had been working against the provisional government. The Germans, in their most successful attempt at subversion, had rushed the brilliant Bolshevik leader V. I. Lenin (1870–1924) in a sealed train from his exile in Switzerland across Germany to Petrograd in the hope that he would cause trouble for the revolutionary government.

Lenin saw the opportunity to achieve the political alliance of workers and peasants that he had discussed theoretically before the war. In speech after speech he hammered away on the theme of peace, bread, and land. The Bolsheviks soon gained control of the soviets, or councils of workers and soldiers. They demanded that all political power should go to the soviets. The failure of the summer offensive encouraged them to attempt a *coup*, but the effort was premature and a failure. Lenin fled to Finland, and his chief collaborator, Leon Trotsky (1877–1940), was imprisoned.

The failure of a right-wing counter *coup* led by General Kornilov gave the Bolsheviks another chance. Trotsky came out of prison to lead the powerful Petrograd Soviet. Lenin returned in October, insisted to his doubting colleagues that the time was ripe to take power, and by the extraordinary force of his personality persuaded them to act. Trotsky organized the coup that took place on November 6 and concluded with an armed assault upon the provisional government. The Bolsheviks, almost as much to their own astonishment as to that of the rest of the world, had come to rule Russia.

The victors moved to fulfill their promises and to assure their own security. The provisional government had decreed an election for late November to select a Constituent Assembly. The Social Revolutionaries won a large majority over the Bolsheviks. When the assembly gathered in January, it met for only a day before the Red Army dispersed it. All other political parties also ceased to

Lenin here addresses a meeting in Moscow. Leon Trotsky, his major collaborator, stands listening on the right. [Popperfoto.]

The Soviet Government Proclaims the Bolshevik Victory

On October 25 [November 7], 1917, through the agency of the Military-Revolutionary Committee of the Petrograd Soviet—headed by Trotsky—the Bolsheviks and their allies, the Left Socialist-Revolutionaries, forcibly overthrew Kerensky's government and assumed power in the name of the soviets. A new cabinet, designated the "Council of People's Commissars," was set up, with Lenin as chairman and Trotsky as Commissar of Foreign Affairs. Endorsement of the coup was secured from the Second All-Russian Congress of Soviets, which was concurrently in session. This was the "October Revolution."

To the *Citizens of Russia!*
The Provisional Government has been overthrown. The power of state has passed into the hands of the organ of the Petrograd Soviet of Workers' and Soldiers' Deputies, the Revolutionary Military Committee, which stands at the head of the Petrograd proletariat and garrison.

The cause for which the people have fought—the immediate proposal of a democratic peace, the abolition of landed proprietorship, workers' control over production and the creation of a Soviet government—is assured.

Long live the revolution of the soldiers, workers, and peasants!
    Revolutionary Military Committee
    of Petrograd
    Soviet of Workers' and Soldiers' Deputies.

R. V. Daniels, ed., *A Documentary History of Communism* (New York: Random House, 1960), Vol. 1, p. 117. The headnote in this instance consists of R. V. Daniels's introductory comment to the document.

function in any meaningful fashion. In November and January the Bolshevik government promulgated decrees that nationalized the land and turned it over to its peasant proprietors. Factory workers were put in charge of their plants. Banks were nationalized, and the debt of the tsarist government repudiated. Property of the church reverted to the state.

The Bolshevik government also took Russia out of the war, which they believed benefited only capitalism. They signed an armistice with Germany in December 1917. On March 3, 1918, they accepted the Treaty of Brest-Litovsk, by which Russia yielded Poland, the Baltic states, and the Ukraine. Some territory in the Transcaucasus region went to Turkey. In addition the Bolsheviks agreed to pay a heavy war indemnity. These terms were a terribly high price to pay for peace, but Lenin had no choice. Russia was incapable of renewing the war effort, and the Bolsheviks needed time to impose their rule on a devastated and chaotic Russia. Moreover Lenin seemed to believe that communist revolutions might soon sweep across other nations in Europe as a result of the war and the Russian example.

Until 1921 the new Bolshevik government confronted major domestic resistance. A civil war erupted between the "Red" Russians supporting the revolution and the "White" Russians, who opposed the Bolshevik triumph. In the summer of 1918 the tsar and his family were murdered. Loyal army officers continued to press against the revolution and eventually received aid from the Allied armies. However, under the leadership of Trotsky the Red Army eventually overcame the domestic opposition. By 1921 Lenin and his supporters were in firm control.

Lenin Establishes His Dictatorship

After the Bolshevik coup in October, elections for the Constituent Assembly were held in November. The results gave a majority to the Social Revolutionary Party and embarrassed the Bolsheviks. Using his control of the Red Army, Lenin closed the Constituent Assembly after only one day in January 1918 and established the rule of a revolutionary elite and his own dictatorship. Here is the crucial Bolshevik decree.

... *The Constituent Assembly, elected on the basis of lists drawn up prior to the October Revolution, was an expression of the old relation of political forces which existed when power was held by the compromisers and the Cadets. When the people at that time voted for the candidates of the Socialist-Revolutionary Party, they were not in a position to choose between the Right Socialist-Revolutionaries, the supporters of the bourgeoisie, and the Left Socialist-Revolutionaries, the supporters of Socialism. Thus the Constituent Assembly, which was to have been the crown of the bourgeois parliamentary republic, could not but become an obstacle in the path of the October Revolution and the Soviet power.*

The October Revolution, by giving the power to the Soviets, and through the Soviets to the toiling and exploited classes, aroused the desperate resistance of the exploiters, and in the crushing of this resistance it fully revealed itself as the beginning of the socialist revolution ... the majority in the Constituent Assembly which met on January 5 was secured by the party of the Right Socialist-Revolutionaries, the party of Kerensky, Avksentyev and Chernov. Naturally, this party refused to discuss the absolutely clear, precise and unambiguous proposal of the supreme organ of Soviet power, the Central Executive Committee of the Soviets, to recognize the program of the Soviet power, to recognize the "Declaration of Rights of the Toiling and Exploited People," to recognize the October Revolution and the Soviet power. ...

The Right Socialist-Revolutionary and Menshevik parties are in fact waging outside the walls of the Constituent Assembly a most desperate struggle against the Soviet power. ...

Accordingly, the Central Executive Committee resolves: The Constituent Assembly is hereby dissolved.

R. V. Daniels, ed., *A Documentary History of Communism* (New York: Random House, 1960), Vol. 1, pp. 133–135.

The End of World War I

The internal collapse of Russia and the later Treaty of Brest-Litovsk brought Germany to the peak of its success. The Germans controlled eastern Europe and its resources, especially food, and they were free to concentrate their forces on the western front. This turn of events would probably have been decisive had it not been balanced by American intervention. Still American troops would not arrive in significant numbers for about a year, and both sides tried to win the war in 1917. An Allied attempt to break through failed disastrously, bringing heavy losses to the British and the French and causing a mutiny in the French army. The Austrians, supported by the Germans, defeated the Italians at Caporetto and threatened to overrun Italy, but they were checked with the aid of Allied troops. The deadlock continued, but time was running out for the Central Powers.

In 1918 the Germans—persuaded chiefly by Ludendorff, who was by then a general—decided to gamble everything on one last offensive. The German army pushed forward and even reached the Marne again but got no farther. They had no more reserves, and the entire nation was exhausted. The Allies, on the other hand, were bolstered by the arrival of American troops in ever-increasing numbers. They were able to launch a counteroffensive that proved to be irresistible. As the Austrian fronts in the Balkans and Italy collapsed, the German high command knew that the end was imminent.

Ludendorff was determined that peace should be made before the German army could be thoroughly defeated in the field and that the responsibility should fall on civilians. For some time he had been the effective ruler of Germany under the aegis of the emperor. He now insisted that William II authorize a new government to be established on democratic principles and to seek peace immediately. The new government, under Prince Max of Baden, asked for peace on the basis of the Fourteen

The birth of the Weimar Republic. On November 9, 1918, William II abdicated and the decision was made to establish a German republic. In this picture the Social Democratic leader Philipp Scheidemann (1865–1939) proclaims the republic to the people of Berlin from a window in the Chancellory. [Bildarchiv Preussischer Kulturbesitz.]

Points that President Wilson had declared as American war aims. These were idealistic principles, including self-determination for nationalities, open diplomacy, freedom of the seas, disarmament, and establishment of a league of nations to keep the peace. Wilson insisted that he would deal only with a democratic German government because he wanted to be sure that he was dealing with the German people and not merely their rulers.

Thus encouraged, the Germans, led by the Social Democrats, forced William II to abdicate on November 9, 1918, and established a republic. Two days later this republican, socialist-led government signed the armistice that ended the war by accepting German defeat. At the time of the armistice the German people were, in general, unaware that their army had been defeated in the field and was crumbling. No foreign soldier stood on German soil. It appeared to many Germans that they could expect a negotiated and mild settlement. The real peace was quite different and embittered the German people, many of whom came to believe that Germany had not been defeated but had been tricked by the enemy and betrayed—even stabbed in the back—by republicans and socialists at home.

The victors rejoiced, but they also had much to mourn. The casualties on all sides came to about ten million dead and twice as many wounded. The economic and financial resources of the European states were badly strained. The victorious Allies, formerly creditors to the world, became debtors to the new American colossus, itself barely touched by the calamities of war.

The old international order, moreover, was dead. Russia was ruled by a Bolshevik dictatorship that preached world revolution and the overthrow of capitalism everywhere. Germany was in chaos, and Austria-Hungary had disintegrated into a swarm of small national states competing for the remains of the ancient empire. The kinds of change stirred the colonial territories ruled by the European powers, and overseas empires would never again be so secure as they had seemed before the war. Europe was no longer the center of the world, free to

In 1919 President Woodrow Wilson left the United States on board the *George Washington* to take part in the peace negotiations being held at Versailles in France. [Culver Pictures.]

interfere when it wished or to ignore the outer regions if it chose. Its easy confidence in material and moral progress was shattered by the brutal reality of four years of horrible war. The memory of that war lived on to shake the nerve of the victorious Western powers as they confronted the new conditions of the postwar world.

The Settlement at Versailles

The representatives of the victorious states gathered at Versailles and other Parisian suburbs in the first half of 1919. Wilson speaking for the United States, David Lloyd George (1863–1945) for Britain, Georges Clemenceau (1841–1929) for France, and Vittorio Emanuele Orlando (1860–1952) for Italy made up the Big Four. Japan, now recognized for the first time as a great power, also had an important part in the discussions. The diplomats who met in Paris had a far more difficult task than the one facing those who had sat at Vienna a century earlier. Both groups attempted to restore order to the world after long and costly wars, but Metternich and his associates could confine their thoughts to Europe. France acknowledged defeat and was willing, even eager, to take part in and uphold the Vienna settlement. The diplomats at Vienna were not much affected by public opinion, and they could draw the new map of Europe along practical lines determined by the realities of power softened by compromise.

The Peacemakers

The negotiators at Paris in 1919 were not so fortunate. They represented constitutional, generally democratic governments, and public opinion had become a mighty force. Though there were secret sessions, the conference often worked in the full glare of publicity. Nationalism had become almost a secular religion, and Europe's many ethnic groups could not be relied on to remain quiet while they were distributed on the map at the whim of the great powers. World War I, moreover, had been transformed by propaganda and especially by the intervention

of Woodrow Wilson into a moral crusade to achieve a peace that would be just as well as secure. The Fourteen Points set forth the right of nationalities to self-determination as an absolute value, in spite of the fact that there was no way to draw the map of Europe to match ethnic groups perfectly with their homelands. All these elements made compromise difficult.

Wilson's idealism, moreover, came into conflict with the more practical war aims of the victorious powers and with many of the secret treaties that had been made before and during the war. The British and French people had been told that Germany would be made to pay for the war, Russia had been promised control of Constantinople and the Dardanelles in return for recognition of the French claim to Alsace-Lorraine and British control of Egypt. Romania was promised Transylvania at the expense of Hungary. Some of the agreements contradicted others: Italy and Serbia had competing claims to the islands and shore of the Adriatic. During the war the British had encouraged Arab hopes of an independent Arab state carved out of the Ottoman Empire, but those plans conflicted with the Balfour Declaration (1917), in which the British seemed to accept Zionist ideology and to promise the Jews a national home in Palestine. Both of these plans stood in conflict with an Anglo-French agreement to divide the Near East between the two Western powers.

The continuing national goals of the victors presented further obstacles to an idealistic "peace without victors." France, keenly conscious of its numerical inferiority to Germany and of the low birth rate that would keep it inferior, was naturally eager to achieve a settlement that would permanently weaken Germany and preserve French superiority. Italy continued to seek the acquisition of *Italia Irredenta;* Britain continued to look to its imperial interests; Japan pursued its own advantage in Asia; and the United States insisted on freedom of the seas, which favored American commerce, while insisting on its right to maintain the Monroe Doctrine.

Finally, the peacemakers of 1919 faced a world still in turmoil. The greatest immediate threat appeared to be posed by the spread of Bolshevism. While Lenin and his colleagues were distracted by civil war, the Allies landed small armies at several places in Russia in the hope of overthrowing the Bolshevik regime. The revolution seemed likely to spread as Communist governments were established in Bavaria and Hungary, and Berlin experienced a dangerous Communist uprising led by the "Spartacus group." The Allies were sufficiently worried by these developments to allow and support suppression of these Communist movements by right-wing military forces, and they even allowed an army of German volunteers to operate against the Bolsheviks in the Baltic states. The fear of the spread of Communism played a part in the thinking of the diplomats at Versailles, but it was far from dominant. The Germans kept playing on such fears as a way of getting better terms, but the Allies, and especially the French, would not hear of it. Fear of Germany remained the chief concern for France, whereas attention to interests that were more traditional and more immediate governed the policies of the other Allies.

The Peace

The Versailles settlement consisted of five separate treaties between the victors and the defeated powers. Formal sessions began on January 18, 1919, and the last treaty was signed on August 10, 1920. Wilson arrived in Europe to unprecedented acclaim. Liberals and idealists expected a new kind of international order achieved in a new and better way, but they were soon disillusioned. "Open covenants openly arrived at" soon gave way to closed sessions in which Wilson, Clemenceau, and Lloyd George made arrangements that seemed cynical to outsiders. The notion of "a peace without victors" became a mockery when the Soviet Union (as Russia was now called) and Germany were excluded from the peace conference. The Germans were simply presented with a treaty and compelled to accept it in a manner that fully justified their complaint that the treaty had not been negotiated but dictated. The principle of national self-determination was violated many times, as was unavoidable, but the diplomats of the small nations were angered by their exclusion from decisions. The undeserved adulation accorded Wilson on his arrival gradually turned into equally undeserved scorn. He had not abandoned his ideals lightly but had merely given way to the irresistible force of reality.

THE LEAGUE OF NATIONS. Wilson was able to make unpalatable concessions without abandoning his ideals because he put great faith in a new instrument for peace and justice, the League of Nations. Its covenant was an essential part of the peace treaty. The League was not intended as an international government but as a body of sovereign states who agreed to pursue some common practices and to consult in the common interest, especially when war threatened. In that case the members promised to submit the matter to arbitration or to an international court or to the League Council. Refusal to abide by this agreement would justify League intervention in the form of economic and even military sanctions. But the League was unlikely to be effective because it had no armed forces at its disposal, and any action required the unanimous consent of its council, consisting of Britain, France, Italy, the United States, and Japan, as well as four other states who had temporary seats. The Covenant of the League bound its members to "respect and pre-

The Big Three at Versailles. Georges Clemenceau, French Prime Minister (left), American President Woodrow Wilson (center), and British Prime Minister David Lloyd George (right) tip their hats to the crowd after signing the Treaty of Versailles on June 28, 1919. [Culver Pictures.]

serve" the territorial integrity of all its members, and this was generally seen as a device to ensure the security of the victorious powers. The exclusion from the League Assembly of Germany and the Soviet Union further undermined the League's claim to evenhandedness.

COLONIES. Another provision of the covenant dealt with colonial areas. These were to be placed under the "tutelage" of one of the great powers under League supervision and encouraged to advance toward independence. Because there were no teeth in this provision, very little advance was made. Provisions for disarmament were doomed to be equally ineffective. Members of the League remained fully sovereign and continued to pursue their own national interests. Only Wilson seems to have put much faith in its future ability to produce peace and justice, and this belief allowed him to approve territorial settlements that violated his own principles.

GERMANY. In the west the main territorial issue was the fate of Germany. Although a united Germany was less than fifty years old, no one seems to have thought of undoing Bismarck's work and dividing it into its component parts. The French would have liked to detach the Rhineland and set it up as a separate buffer state, but Lloyd George and Wilson would not permit that. Still, they could not ignore France's need for protection against a resurgent Germany, France received Alsace-Lorraine and the right to work the coal mines of the Saar for fifteen years. Germany west of the Rhine and fifty kilometers east of it was to be a demilitarized zone, and Allied troops on the west bank could stay there for fifteen years. In addition to this physical barrier to a new German attack, the treaty provided that Britain and the United States would guarantee to aid France if it were attacked by Germany. Such an attack was made more unlikely by the permanent disarmament of Germany. Its army was limited to 100,000 men on long-term service; its fleet was all but eliminated; and it was forbidden to have war planes, submarines, tanks, heavy artillery, or poison gas. So long as these provisions were observed France would be safe.

THE EAST. The settlement in the east ratified the collapse of the great defeated empires that had ruled it for centuries. Germany's frontier was moved far to the west,

The Settlement at Versailles 833

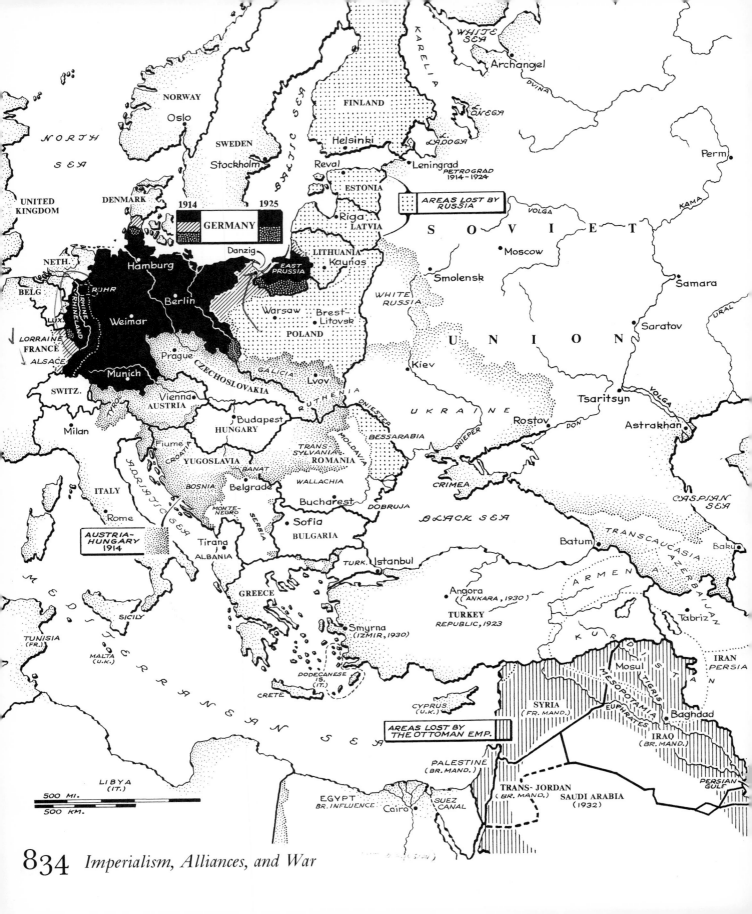

NORTH SEA

NORWAY
Oslo

SWEDEN
Stockholm

FINLAND
Helsinki

KARELIA

WHITE SEA
Archangel

DVINA
L. ONEGA
Perm

UNITED KINGDOM

DENMARK

GERMANY
1914   1925

Reval

Leningrad
PETROGRAD
1914-1924

VOLGA

KAMA

NETH.

Danzig

Hamburg

Berlin

Weimar

Munich

RHINE
RHINELAND
RUHR

LUX.

BELG.

LORRAINE
FRANCE
ALSACE

SWITZ.

ESTONIA

Riga
LATVIA

LITHUANIA
Kaunas

EAST PRUSSIA

Warsaw

Brest-Litovsk

POLAND

AREAS LOST BY RUSSIA

WHITE RUSSIA

Moscow

Smolensk

S O V I E T

U N I O N

Samara

Saratov

VOLGA

URAL

Prague

CZECHOSLOVAKIA

GALICIA

Lvov

RUTHENIA

Kiev

U K R A I N E

Rostov

DON

Tsaritsyn

Astrakhan

Milan

Vienna
AUSTRIA

TYROL

Budapest
HUNGARY

Fiume

CROATIA

YUGOSLAVIA

BOSNIA

Belgrade

BANAT

TRANS-SYLVANIA

ROMANIA

MOLDAVIA

BESSARABIA

WALLACHIA

DNIESTER

DNIEPER

CRIMEA

CASPIAN SEA

Baku

TRANSCAUCASIA

AZERBAIJAN

Batum

ITALY

Rome

ADRIATIC SEA

MONTE-NEGRO

SERBIA

Bucharest

DOBRUJA

Sofia

BULGARIA

Tirana
ALBANIA

AUSTRIA-HUNGARY 1914

BLACK SEA

ARMENIA

KURDISTAN

Tabriz

IRAN
PERSIA

GREECE

TURK. Istanbul

Angora
(ANKARA, 1930)

TURKEY
REPUBLIC, 1923

Mosul

MESOPOTAMIA

TIGRIS

Baghdad

TUNISIA
(FR.)

MALTA
(U.K.)

SICILY

MEDITERRANEAN SEA

Smyrna
(IZMIR, 1930)

DODECANESE IS.
(IT.)

CRETE

CYPRUS
(U.K.)

AREAS LOST BY THE OTTOMAN EMP.

SYRIA
(FR. MAND.)

EUPHRATES

IRAQ
(BR. MAND.)

PERSIAN GULF

LIBYA
(IT.)

500 MI.

500 KM.

EGYPT
BR. INFLUENCE

Cairo

SUEZ CANAL

PALESTINE
(BR. MAND.)

TRANS-JORDAN
(BR. MAND.)

SAUDI ARABIA
(1932)

WORLD WAR I PEACE SETTLEMENT IN EUROPE AND THE MIDDLE EAST

The map of central and Eastern Europe, as well as that of the Middle East, underwent drastic revision after World War I. The enormous geographical losses suffered by Germany, Austria-Hungary, the Ottoman Empire, Bulgaria, and Russia were the other side of the coin represented by gains for France, Italy, Greece, and Romania and the appearance, or reappearance, of at least eight new independent states from Finland in the north to Yugoslavia in the south. The mandate system for former Ottoman territories outside Turkey proper laid foundations for several new, mostly Arab, states in the Middle East.

excluding most of Silesia and much of East Prussia. What was left of East Prussia was cut off from the rest of Germany by a corridor carved out to give the revived state of Poland access to the sea. The Austro-Hungarian Empire disappeared entirely, giving way to many smaller successor states. Most of its German-speaking people were gathered in the small Republic of Austria, cut off from the Germans of Bohemia and forbidden to unite themselves with Germany. The Magyars occupied the Kingdom of Hungary. The Czechs of Bohemia and Moravia joined with the Slovaks and Ruthenians to the east to form Czechoslovakia, and this new state included several million unhappy Germans. The southern Slavs were united in the Kingdom of Serbs, Croats, and Slovenes, or Yugoslavia. Italy gained the Trentino and Trieste. Romania was enlarged by receiving Transylvania from Hungary and Bessarabia from Russia. Bulgaria was diminished by the loss of territory to Greece and Yugoslavia. Russia lost vast territories in the west. Finland, Estonia, Latvia, and Lithuania became independent states, and a good part of Poland was carved out of formerly Russian soil. The old Ottoman Empire disappeared. The new republic of Turkey was limited to little more than Constantinople and Asia Minor, while the former Ottoman territories of Palestine and Iraq came under British control and Syria and Lebanon under French control as mandates of the League. Germany's former colonies in Africa were divided among Britain, France, and South Africa, and her Pacific possessions went to Australia, New Zealand, and Japan.

REPARATIONS. Perhaps the most debated part of the peace settlement dealt with reparations for the damage done by Germany during the war. Before the armistice the Germans promised to pay compensation "for all damages done to the civilian population of the Allies and their property." The Americans judged that the amount would be between $15 billion and $25 billion and that Germany would be able to pay that amount. However, France and Britain, worried about repaying their war debts to the United States, were eager to have

Germany pay the full cost of the war, including pensions to survivors and dependents. There was general agreement that Germany could not afford to pay such a sum, whatever it might be, and no sum was fixed at the conference. In the meantime Germany was to pay $5 billion annually until 1921. At that time a final figure would be set, which Germany would have to pay in thirty years. The French did not regret the outcome. Either Germany would pay and be bled into impotence, or she would refuse to pay and justify French intervention.

To justify these huge reparations payments, the Allies inserted the notorious Clause 231 into the treaty:

> The Allied and Associated Governments affirm, and Germany accepts, the responsibility of Germany and her allies for causing all the loss and damage to which the Allied and Associated Governments and their nationals have been subjected as a consequence of the war imposed upon them by aggression of Germany and her allies.

The Germans, of course, did not believe that they were solely responsible for the war and bitterly resented the charge. They had suffered the loss of vast territories containing millions of Germans and great quantities of badly needed natural resources; they were presented with an astronomical and apparently unlimited reparations bill. To add insult to injury, they were required to admit to a war guilt that they did not feel. Finally, to heap insult upon insult, they were required to accept the entire treaty as it was written by the victors, without any opportunity for negotiation. Germany's Prime Minister Philipp Scheidemann (1865–1939) spoke of the treaty as the imprisonment of the German people and asked, "What hand would not wither that binds itself and us in these fetters?" But there was no choice. The Social Democrats and the Catholic Center Party formed a new government, and their representatives signed the treaty. These were the parties that formed the backbone of the Weimar government that ruled Germany until 1933, and they never overcame the stigma of accepting the Treaty of Versailles.

Evaluation of the Peace

Few peace settlements have undergone more severe attacks than the one negotiated in Paris in 1919. It is natural that the defeated powers should object to it, but the peace soon came under bitter criticism in the victorious countries as well. Many Frenchmen thought it failed to provide adequate security for France, because it tied that security to promises of aid from the unreliable Anglo-Saxon countries. In England and the United States a wave of bitter criticism arose in liberal quarters because the treaty seemed to violate the idealistic and liberal aims and principles that the Western leaders professed. It was not a peace without victors, did not put an end to imperialism, attempted to promote the national interests of the winning nations, and violated the principles of national self-determination by leaving significant pockets of minorities outside the borders of their national homelands.

The most influential critic was John Maynard Keynes (1883-1946), a brilliant British economist who took part in the peace conference. He resigned in disgust when he saw the direction it was taking and wrote a book called the *Economic Consequences of the Peace* (1919). It was a scathing attack, especially on reparations and the other economic aspects of the peace. It was also a skillful assault on the negotiators and particularly on Wilson, who was depicted as a fool and a hypocrite. Keynes argued that the Treaty of Versailles was both immoral and unworkable. It was a Carthaginian peace that would bring economic ruin and war to Europe unless it were repudiated. Keynes had a great effect on the British, who were already suspicious of France and glad of an excuse to withdraw from continental affairs. The decent and respectable position came to be one that aimed at revision of the treaty in favor of Germany. Even more important was the book's influence in the United States. It fed the traditional tendency toward isolationism and gave powerful weapons to Wilson's enemies. Wilson's own political mistakes helped

prevent American ratification of the treaty. Consequently America was out of the League and not bound to defend France. Britain, therefore, was also free from its obligation to France. France was left to protect itself without adequate means to do so for long.

Many of the attacks on the Treaty of Versailles are unjustified. It was not a Carthaginian peace. Germany was neither dismembered nor ruined. Reparations could be and were scaled down, and until the great world depression of the 1930s, the Germans recovered a high level of prosperity. Complaints agiinst the peace should also be measured against the peace that the victorious Germans imposed on Russia at Brest-Litovsk and the plans they made for a European settlement in case of victory. Both were far more severe than anything enacted at Versailles. The attempt at achieving self-determination for nationalities was less than perfect, but it was the best solution Europe had ever accomplished in that direction.

The peace, nevertheless, was unsatisfactory in important ways. The elimination of the Austro-Hungarian Empire, however inevitable that might seem, created a number of serious problems. Economically it was disastrous, for it separated raw materials from manufacturing areas and producers from their markets by new boundaries and tariff walls. In hard times this created friction and hostility that aggravated other quarrels also created by the peace treaties. Poland contained unhappy German minorities, and Czechoslovakia was a collection of nationalities who did not find it easy to live together as a nation. Disputes over territories in eastern Europe promoted further tension. The peace was inadequate on another level, as well. It rested on a victory that Germany did not admit. The Germans believed that they had been cheated rather than defeated. At the same time the high moral principles proclaimed by the Allies undercut the validity of the peace, for it plainly fell far short of those principles.

Finally, the great weakness of the peace was its failure to accept reality. Germany and Russia must inevitably play an important part in European affairs, yet they were excluded from the settlement and from the League of Nations. Given the many discontented parties, the peace was not self-enforcing; yet no satisfactory machinery for enforcing it was established. The league was never a serious force for this purpose. It was left to France, with no guarantee of support from Britain and no hope of help from the United States, to defend the new arrangements. Finland, the Baltic states, Poland, Romania, Czechoslovakia, and Yugoslavia were created as a barrier to the expansion westward of Russian Communism and as a threat in the rear to deter German revival. Most of these states, however, would have to rely on France in case of danger, and France was simply not strong enough for the task if Germany should rearm. The tragedy of Versailles was that it was neither conciliatory enough to remove the desire for change, even at the cost of war, nor harsh enough to make another war impossible. The only hope for a lasting peace required the enforcement of the disarmament of Germany while the more obnoxious clauses of the peace treaty were revised. Such a policy required continued attention to the problem, unity among the victors, and far-sighted leadership; but none of these was present in adequate supply during the next two decades.

SUGGESTED READINGS

L. ALBERTINI, *The Origins of the War of 1914,* 3 vols. (London, 1952, 1957). Discursive but invaluable.

M. BALFOUR, *The Kaiser and His Times* (New York, 1972). A fine biography of William II.

V. R. BERGHAHN, *Germany and the Approach of War in 1914* (New York, 1973). A work similar in spirit to Fischer's but stressing the importance of Germany's naval program.

V. DEDIJER, *The Road to Sarajevo* (London, 1967). A detailed study of the assassination of the Archduke Francis Ferdinand and its background.

S. B. FAY, *The Origins of the World War,* 2 vols. (New York, 1928). The best and most influential of the revisionist accounts.

D. K. FIELDHOUSE, *The Colonial Experience: A Compara-* *tive Study from the Eighteenth Century* (New York, 1966). An excellent recent study.

F. FISCHER, *Germany's Aims in the First World War* (New York, 1967). An influential interpretation that stirred a great controversy in Germany and around the world by emphasizing Germany's role in bringing on the war.

F. FISCHER, *War of Illusions* (New York, 1975). A long and diffuse book that tries to connect German responsibility for the war with internal social, economic, and political developments.

I. GEISS, *July 1914* (New York, 1967). A valuable collection of documents by a student of Fritz Fischer's. The emphasis is on German documents and responsibility.

O. J. HALE, *The Great Illusion 1900–1914* (New York, 1971). A fine survey of the period especially good on public opinion.

B. H. LIDDELL HART, *The Real War 1914–1918* (Boston, 1964). A fine short account by an outstanding military historian.

J. M. KEYNES, *The Economic Consequences of the Peace* (London, 1920). The famous and influential attack on the Versailles Treaty.

L. LAFORE, *The Long Fuse* (New York, 1965). A readable account of the origins of World War I that focuses on the problem of Austria–Hungary.

W. L. LANGER, *The Diplomacy of Imperialism* (New York, 1935). A continuation of the previous study for the years 1890–1902.

W. L. LANGER, *European Alliances and Allignments,* 2nd ed. (New York, 1966). A splendid diplomatic history of the years 1871–1890.

W. LAQUEUR AND G. L. MOSSE (Eds.), *1914; The Coming of the First World War* (New York, 1966). A collection of valuable esaays.

E. MANTOUX, *The Carthaginian Peace* (Pittsburgh, 1952). A vigorous attack on Keynes's view.

J. STEINBERG, *Yesterday's Deterrent* (London, 1965). An excellent study of Germany's naval policy and its consequences.

A. J. P. TAYLOR, *The Struggle for Mastery in Europe, 1848–1918* (Oxford, 1954). Clever but controversial.

L. C. F. TURNER, *Origins of the First World War* (New York, 1970). Especially good on the significance of Russia and its military plans.

838

31
Political Experiments of the 1920s

PURSUIT of experimentation in politics and of normality in economic life marked the decade following the conclusion of the Versailles Treaty. Many of the experiments failed, and the normality proved quite elusive. By the close of the decade the political path had been paved for the nightmares of brutally authoritarian governments and international aggression. Yet many of the people who had survived the Great War had hoped and worked for a better outcome. Totalitarianism and aggression were not the inexorable destiny of Europe. Their emergence was the result of failures in securing alternative modes of political life and international relations.

Political and Economic Factors After Versailles

New Governments

In 1919 experimental political regimes studded the map of Europe. From Ireland to Russia new governments were seeking to gain the active support of their citizens and to solve the grievous economic problems caused by the war. In the Soviet Union the Bolsheviks regarded themselves as forging nothing less than a new kind of civilization. They gave little significant consideration to anything but an authoritarian rule.

It was otherwise elsewhere on the Continent. Democratically elected parliamentary governments appeared where the autocratic, military empires of Germany and Austria–Hungary had previously held sway. Their goals

The signing of the Locarno Pacts in 1925 marked a high point in postwar international stability and cooperation for peace. The most prominent delegations are those of the Germans (left), the British (top), and the French (right). [United Press International Photo.]

were substantially more modest than those of the Bolsheviks. Yet to pursue parliamentary politics where it had never been meaningfully practiced proved no simple task. The Wilsonian vision of democratic, self-determined nations floundered on the harsh realities of economics, aggressive nationalism, and revived political conservatism. Too often the will for democratic, parliamentary government as well as experience in its exercise was absent from the nations on which it had been bestowed. Moreover, in many of the new democracies important sectors of the citizenry believed that parliamentary politics was by its very nature corrupt or unequal to great nationalistic enterprise.

Demands for Revision of Versailles

Several other Europe-wide problems haunted the early interwar period and directly affected the decisions and actions of individual nations. The Versailles settlement fostered both resentment and discontent in numerous countries. Germany had been humiliated. The arrangements for reparations led to seemingly endless haggling over payments. Various national groups in the successor states of eastern Europe felt that injustice had been done in their particular case of self-determination. There were demands for further border adjustments. On the other side, the victorious powers and especially France often believed that the provisions of the treaty were being inadequately enforced. Consequently, throughout the twenties calls both to revise or to enforce the Versailles Treaty contributed to domestic political turmoil across the Continent. All too many political figures were willing to fish in these troubled international waters for a large catch of domestic votes.

Post-War Economic Problems

Simultaneous with the move toward political experiment and demands for revision of the recently established international order was a widespread desire to return to the economic prosperity of the prewar years. However, after 1918 it was impossible to restore what American

President Warren Harding would shortly term "normalcy." During the conflict Europeans had turned against themselves and their civilization the vast physical power that they had created in the previous century. More than 750,000 British soldiers had perished. The combat deaths for France and Germany were 1,385,000 and 1,808,000, respectively. Russia had lost 1,700,000 troops. Scores of thousands more from other belligerent nations had also been killed. Still more millions had been wounded. These casualties meant not only the waste of human life and talent but also the loss of producers and consumers. There had also been widespread destruction of farmland, transport facilities, mines, and industry.

Another casualty of the conflict was the financial dominance and independence of Europe. At the opening of hostilities Europe had been the financial and credit center of the world. At the close of the fighting Europeans stood deeply in debt to each other and to the United States. The Bolsheviks had repudiated the debt of the tsarist government, much of which was owed to French creditors. Other nations could not pursue this revolutionary course. The Versailles settlement had imposed heavy financial obligations on Germany and its allies. The United States refused to ask reparations from Germany, but firmly demanded repayment of war debts from its own allies. On the one hand, the reparation and debt structure meant that no nation was fully in control of its own economic life. On the other hand, the absence of international economic cooperation meant that more than ever individual nations felt compelled to pursue or to attempt to pursue selfish, nationalistic economic aims. It was perhaps the worst of all possible international economic worlds.

The market and trade conditions that had prevailed before 1914 had also changed radically. Russia in large measure withdrew from the European economic order. The political reconstruction of eastern and central Europe into the multitude of small successor states broke up the trade region formerly encompassed by Germany and Austria–Hungary. Most of those new states had weak economies hardly capable of competing in modern economic life. The new boundaries separated raw materials from the factories using them. Railway systems on which finished and unfinished products traveled might now lie under the control of two or more nations. Political and economic nationalism went together. New customs barriers were raised.

International trade also followed new patterns. The United States became less dependent on European production and assumed the status of a major competitor. During the war the belligerents had been forced to sell many of their holdings on other continents to finance the conflict. As a consequence Europeans exercised less dominance over the world economy. Postwar economic growth within colonies or former colonies lowered the demand for European goods. The United States and Japan began to penetrate markets in Latin America and Asia previously dominated by European producers and traders.

New Roles for Government and Labor

The war effort in all countries occasioned new dimensions of state interference and direction in the economy. Large government bureaucracies had been organized to plan the course of production and distribution of goods. Prices had been controlled, raw materials stockpiled, consumer goods rationed, and economic priorities set by government technocrats. The mechanism of the freely operating market so dear to nineteenth-century liberals had been rejected as a vehicle for economic decision-making. The economic planning skills learned during the war could be transferred to peacetime operations. Moreover governments had learned about the immense productive and employment power of an economy placed under state control.

Labor had achieved new prominence within the wartime economic setting. The unions had actively supported the war effort of their nations. They had ensured labor peace for production. In turn, their members had received better wages, and their leaders had been admitted to high political councils. Although in peacetime wages might be lowered, they could not be reduced to prewar levels. European workers intended to receive their just share of the fruits of their labor. Collective bargaining and union recognition brought on by the war also could not be abandoned. This improvement in both the status and the effective influence of labor was one of the most significant social and political changes to flow from World War I. The social condition of the work force seemed to be improving while that of the middle class seemed to be stagnating or declining.

The war and peace settlement wrought one other major change that affected the course of political and economic life. The turn to liberal democracy and the extension of the franchise to women and previously disenfranchised males meant that for the first time in European history the governments handling economic matters were responsible to mass electorates. Economics and politics had become more intimately connected than ever before. The economic and social anxieties of the electorate could and eventually did overcome its political scruples. Whereas previously economic discontent had been articulated through riots and later through unions, it could now be voiced through the ballot box.

Joyless Victors

France and Great Britain, with the aid of the United States, had won the war. France became the strongest military power on the Continent. Britain had escaped with almost no physical damage. Both nations, however, had lost vast numbers of young men in the conflict. Their economies were weak, and their overseas wealth and power stood much diminished. Compared with contemporary events in Germany, Italy, and Russia, the interwar political development of the two major democracies seems rather tame. There was neither a revolution nor a shift to authoritarian government. Yet this surface calm was largely illusory. They were troubled democracies. To neither did victory in war bring the good life in peace.

France: The Search for Security

At the close of World War I, as after Waterloo, the revolution of 1848, and the defeat of 1871, the French voters elected a doggedly conservative Chamber of Deputies. The preponderance of military officers among its members led to the nickname of "the Horizon Blue Chamber." The overwelmingly conservative character of the chamber was registered in 1920 by its defeat of Georges Clemenceau's bid for the presidency. The crucial factor had been of all things the alleged leniency of the Versailles Treaty and the failure to establish a separate Rhineland state. The deputies wanted to achieve future security against Germany and Russian Communism. They intended to make as few concessions to domestic social reform as possible. The twenties were marked by fluctuations in ministries and a drift in domestic policy. The political turnstyle remained ever active. Between the end of the war and January 1933, France was governed by no fewer than twenty-seven different cabinets.

NEW ALLIANCES. During the first five years after the Treaty of Versailles France accepted its role as the leading European power. The French plan was to enforce strictly the clauses of the treaty that were meant to keep Germany weak and, at the same time, to build a system of eastern alliances to replace the lost prewar alliance with Russia. In 1920 and 1921 three eastern states who had much to lose from revision of the treaty—Czechoslovakia, Romania, and Yugoslavia—formed the Little Entente. Before long France made military alliances with these states as well as with Poland. A dispute with Czechoslovakia over the control of Teschen prevented the Poles from joining the Little Entente, but the very existence of Poland depended on the maintenance of the Versailles settlement. This new system of eastern alliances was the best France could do, but it was far weaker than the old Russian alliance. The new states combined were no match for the former power of imperial Russia, and they were neither united nor reliable. Poland and Romania

POINCARÉ
Notre vaillant président

Cliché BERT
23

JN
PARIS

Raymond Poincaré (1860–1934) became a leading French politician in the first decade of this century. He was president from 1913 to 1920 during World War I, and three times Prime Minister (1912–1913, 1922–1924, 1926–1929), therefore the leader of France for much of the decade after the War. He was exceedingly nationalistic—as is suggested by the inscription on this photographic postcard made probably in 1914 and certainly after the War had begun. [The Granger Collection.]

QUEST FOR REPARATIONS. In 1923 the Germans failed to meet the schedule of reparation payments. Raymond Poincaré (1860–1934), France's powerful nationalist prime minister, took the opportunity to teach the Germans a lesson and force them to comply. He sent the French army to occupy the Ruhr, and when the Germans adopted a policy of passive resistance, he sent French civilians to run the mines and railroads. France got its way. The Germans paid, but France paid a great price for its victory. The English were alienated by French heavy-handedness and took no part in the occupation. They became more suspicious of France and more sympathetic to Germany. The cost of the Ruhr occupation, moreover, increased French as well as German inflation and damaged the French economy. As one scholar has explained: the French "threatened to choke Germany to death; the Germans threatened to die. Neither side dared carry its threat to extremity." [1] From the French viewpoint, consequently, victory in the war and achievement of considerable military power seemed to have brought the nation little of the prestige and effective influence it sought.

In 1924 the conservative ministry gave way to a coalition of leftist parties, the so-called *Cartel des Gauches,* led by Edouard Herriot (1872–1957). The chief policy changes of the new Cabinet were recognition of the Soviet Union and a more conciliatory policy toward Germany. Leadership on this score came from Aristide Briand (1862–1932), who was foreign minister for the remainder of the decade. He championed the League of Nations and attempted to persuade his nation that its military power did not give it unlimited influence on the foreign affairs of Europe. Under the leftist coalition a mild inflation also occurred. It had begun under the conservatives but picked up intensity in 1925. When the value of the franc fell sharply on the international money market in 1926, Poincaré returned to office as head of a national

were more concerned about Russia than about Germany, and the main target of the Little Entente was Hungary. If one of the eastern states were threatened by a resurgent Germany, there was considerable doubt that the others would be eager to come to its aid.

The formation of this new alliance system heightened the sense of danger and isolation felt by the two excluded powers, Germany and the Soviet Union. In 1922, while the European states were holding an economic conference at Genoa, the Russians and the Germans met at Rapallo nearby and signed a treaty of their own. It established diplomatic and economic relations that proved useful to both sides. Although the treaty contained no secret political or military clauses, such arrangements were suspected. And it is now known that the Germans helped train the Russian army and gave their own army valuable experience in the use of tanks and planes in the Soviet Union. The news of Rapallo confirmed the French in their growing belief that Germany was unwilling to live up to the terms of the Versailles Treaty and helped move them to strong action.

[1] A. J. P. Taylor, *The Origins of the Second World War* (New York: Fawcett, 1961), p. 33.

Ramsay MacDonald was the first Labor Party Prime Minister of Great Britain. Although his first ministry lasted only a few months in 1924, he established Labor as the major alternative party to the Conservatives in Great Britain. He was again Prime Minister between 1929 and 1935. [Culver Pictures.]

government. The value of the franc recovered somewhat, and inflation cooled. For the rest of the twenties the conservatives remained in power. The country enjoyed a general prosperity that lasted until 1931, longer than in any other nation.

Great Britain

World War I profoundly changed British politics if not the political system. The electorate was expanded in 1918 to include all men aged twenty-one and women aged thirty. (In 1928 the age for women voters was also lowered to twenty-one.) The prewar structure of parties and leadership also shifted. A coalition Cabinet composed of Liberal, Conservative, and Labor ministers had directed the war effort. The wartime ministerial participation of the Labor Party did much to dispel its radical image. For the Liberal Party, however, the conflict brought unexpected division. Until 1916 Liberal Prime Minister Herbert Asquith had presided over the Cabinet. As disagreements over war management developed, he was ousted by fellow Liberal David Lloyd George. The party then became sharply split between followers of the two men. In 1918, against the wishes of both the Labor Party and the Asquith Liberals, Lloyd George decided to maintain the coalition through the tasks of the peace conference and the domestic reconstruction. The wartime coalition, now minus Labor members, won a stunning victory at the polls. However, Lloyd George could thereafter remain prime minister only so long as his dominant Conservative partners wished to keep him.

During the 1918 election campaign there had been much talk about creating "a land fit for heroes to live in." It did not happen. Except for the three years immediately after the war the British economy was depressed throughout the twenties. Genuine postwar recovery simply did not get under way. Unemployment never dipped below 10 per cent and often hovered near 11 per cent. There were never fewer than a million workers unemployed. Government insurance programs to cover unemployed workers, widows, and orphans were expanded.

But there was no similar meaningful expansion in the number of jobs available. From 1922 onward accepting the "dole" with little expectation of future employment became a wretched and degrading way of life for scores of thousands of poor British families.

THE FIRST LABOR GOVERNMENT. In October 1922 the Conservatives dropped Lloyd George and replaced him with Bonar Law (1858–1923), one of their own. A Liberal would never again be prime minister. Stanley Baldwin (1867–1947) soon replaced Law, who fell victim to throat cancer. Baldwin decided to attempt to cure Britain's economic plight by abandoning free trade and imposing protective tariffs. The voters rejected the proposed policy in 1923. At the election the Conservative Party lost its majority in the House of Commons, but only votes from both Liberal and Labor party members could provide an alternative majority. Labor had elected the second largest group of members to the Commons. Consequently, in December 1923, King George V (1910–1936) asked Ramsay MacDonald (1866–1937) to form the first Labor ministry in British history. The Liberal Party did not serve in the cabinet but provided the necessary votes in the House of Commons to give the Labor ministry a working majority.

The Labor Party was socialistic in its platform, but not revolutionary. The party had expanded beyond its early trade union base. MacDonald himself had opposed World War I and for a time had also broken with the party. His own version of socialism owed little, if anything, to Marx. His program consisted of plans for extensive social reform rather than for nationalization or public seizure of industry. A sensitive politician, if not a great leader, MacDonald understood that the most important task facing the ministry was proving to the nation that the Labor Party was both respectable and responsible. His nine months in office achieved just that goal if little else of major importance. The establishment of Labor as a viable governing party signaled the permanent demise of the Liberal Party. It has continued to exist, but the bulk of its voters have drifted into either the Conservative or the Labor ranks.

THE GENERAL STRIKE OF 1926. The Labor government fell in the autumn of 1924 over charges of inadequate prosecution of a communist writer. Stanley Baldwin returned to office, where he remained until 1929. The problem of the stagnant economy remained uppermost in the public mind. Business and political leaders continued to believe that all would be well if they could restore prewar conditions of trade. A major element in those conditions had been the gold standard as the basis for international trade. In 1925 the Conservative government returned to the gold standard in hopes of re-creating the former monetary stability. However, the government set the conversion rate for the pound against other currencies too high and thus in effect raised the price of British goods to foreign customers.

In order to make their products competitive on the world market, British management attempted to lower prices by cutting wages. The coal industry was the sector most directly effected by the wage cuts. It was inefficient and poorly managed and had been in trouble ever since the end of the war. Labor relations in the coal industry had been unruly for some time. In 1926, after cuts in wages and a breakdown in negotiations, the coal miners went out on strike. Soon thereafter, in May 1926, a general strike lasting nine days took place. There was much tension but little violence. In the end the miners and other unions capitulated. With such high levels of unemployment organized labor was in a relatively weak position. After the general strike the Baldwin government attempted to reconcile labor primarily through an expansion of housing and reforms in the poor laws. Despite the economic difficulties of these years the actual standard of living of most British workers, including those receiving government insurance payments, actually improved somewhat.

EMPIRE. World War I also modified Britain's imperial position. The aid given by the dominions, such as Canada and Australia, demonstrated a new independence on their part. Empire was a two-way proposition. The idea of self-determination as applied to Europe could not

Stanley Baldwin Reflects on the British General Strike

After halting much economic activity for more than a week in 1926, the British general strike came to a peaceful conclusion. Baldwin, who was the Conservative Prime Minister at the time, thought the outcome spoke well for British character and British freedom. In examining the impact of the strike, he was particularly concerned to present British institutions in a favorable light, as contrasted with the new social order then emerging in the Soviet Union. He hoped that communist doctrines would not come to influence the British labor movement.

IT MAY *have been a magnificent demonstration of the solidarity of labour, but it was at the same time a most pathetic evidence of the failure of all of us to live and work together for the good of all. . . . But if that strike showed solidarity, sympathy with the miners—whatever you like—it showed something else far greater. It proved the stability of the whole fabric of our own country, and to the amazement of the world not a shot was fired. We were saved by common sense and the good temper of our own people. We have been called a stupid people; but the moment the public grasped that what was at stake was not the solidarity of labour nor the fate of the miners, but the life of the State, then there was a response to the country's need deep and irresistible. And mark this: in my view there was that feeling in the country because the leaders of the strike and the men who were on strike felt it in their innermost hearts, too. They felt a conflict of loyalties. They knew that same conflict was raging in the breasts of thousands of men who had fought for their country ten years ago. Many of the strikers were uneasy in their minds and their consciences, because the British workman, as I know him, does not like breaking contracts, as so many of them did. I do not think many of them like stopping food supplies and shutting down the Press. I sometimes amuse myself with wondering what their language would have been like if these things had been done by the Government. And, after all, when all has been said about England, about the mistakes we make, and about our stupidity, and about how much better they do things in Russia, yet how many of those men or any of us, would prefer to have been born and brought up in any country in the world but this, or to send our children to be brought up there. In these post-war years, in spite of all the depression, in spite of all our troubles, never before has the wealth of this country, through the taxes and the rates, been so distributed to those less fortunate and for the provision of those thrown out of work. . . .*

RIGHT: Stanley Baldwin was the Conservative Party Prime Minister during the general strike of 1926. His solid, calm appearance seemed to many voters to suggest the qualities most needed in their government. [Bettmann Archive.]

BELOW: During the British general strike of May 1926, middle class workers devised various ways to continue about their business. Here they are using a truck as a bus to carry them to work. [The Granger Collection.]

I want to see our British Labour movement free from alien and foreign heresy. I want to see it pursued and developed on English lines, led by English men. The temptations that beset the growth of these vast organizations [the labor unions], in many respects as they are today outside the law, controlling multitudes of men and large sums of money—the temptation to set such a machine in motion and make people follow it is great indeed.

Stanley Baldwin, *Our Inheritance* (London: Hodder and Stoughton, 1928), pp. 222–224.

be prevented from filtering into imperial relationships. In India the Congress Party, led by Mohandas Gandhi (1869–1948), was beginning to attract widespread support. The British started to talk more about eventual self-government for the nation. Moreover, during the twenties the Indian government achieved the right to impose tariffs for the protection of its own industry rather than for the advantage of British manufacturers. The British textile producers no longer had totally free access to the vast Indian market.

IRELAND. A new chapter was written in the unhappy relations between Britain and Ireland during and after the war. In 1914 the Irish Home Rule Bill had passed Parliament, but its implementation was postponed for the duration of the conflict. As the war dragged on, Irish nationalists became determined to wait no longer. On Easter Monday 1916 a nationalist uprising occurred in Dublin. It was the only rebellion of a national group to occur against any government engaged in the war. The British suppressed it in less than a week but then made a grave tactical blunder. They executed the Irish nationalist leaders who had been responsible for the uprising. Overnight those rebels became national martyrs. Leadership of the nationalist cause quickly shifted from the Irish Party in Parliament to the extremist Sinn Fein ("Ourselves Alone") movement.

In the election of 1918 the Sinn Fein Party won all but four of the Irish parliamentary seats outside Ulster. They refused to go to the Parliament at Westminster. Instead they constituted themselves into a Dail Eireann, or Irish Parliament. On January 21, 1919, they declared Irish independence. The military wing of Sinn Fein became the Irish Republican Army (IRA). The first president was Eamon De Valera (1882–1975), who had been born in the United States. Very quickly what amounted to a guerrilla war broke out between the IRA and the British army supported by auxiliaries known as the Black and Tans. There was unusually intense bitterness and hatred on both sides.

In late 1921 secret negotiations commenced between the two governments. In the treaty concluded in December 1921 the Irish Free State took its place beside the earlier dominions in the British Commonwealth, Canada, Australia, New Zealand, and South Africa. The six counties of Ulster, or Northern Ireland, were permitted to remain part of what was now called the United Kingdom of Great Britain and Northern Ireland, with provisions for home rule. No sooner had the treaty been signed than a new Irish civil war broke out between Irish moderates and diehards. The moderates supported the treaty; the diehards wanted the oath to the British monarch abolished and a totally independent republic established. The second civil war continued until 1923. De Valera had supported the diehards, resigned the presidency, and organized resistance to the treaty. In 1932 he was again elected president. The next year the Dail Eireann abolished the oath of allegiance to the monarch.

During World War II Ireland remained neutral. In 1949 it declared itself the wholly independent republic of Eire.

Trials of the New Democracies

Both France and Great Britain had prewar experience in liberal democratic government. Their primary challenges lay in responding to economic pressures and allowing new groups, such as the Labor Party, to share political power. In Germany, Poland, Austria, Czechoslovakia, and the other successor states the issue for the twenties was to make new parliamentary governments function in a satisfactory and stable manner. Prior to the war both Germany and Austria–Hungary had possessed elected parliaments, but those bodies had not exercised genuine political power. The question after the war became whether those groups who had previously sat powerless in parliaments could assume both power and responsibility. Another question was how long conservative institutions, such as the armies and the conservative political groups, would tolerate or cooperate with the liberal experiments. At the same time all of these newly organized states confronted immense postwar economic difficulties.

Successor States in Eastern Europe

Only the barest outline can be given of the dreary political story of the successor states. It had been an article of faith among nineteenth-century liberals that only good could flow from the demise of Austria–Hungary. The new states in eastern Europe were to symbolize the principle of national self-determination and to provide a buffer against the westward spread of Bolshevism. However, they were in trouble from the beginning. They were poor, backward, and overwhelmingly rural nations dwelling in an industrialized world. Nationality problems continued to exist. The major social and political groups were generally unwilling to make compromises. With the exception of Czechoslovakia, all these states succumbed to some form of authoritarian government.

In Hungary during 1919 the Bolsheviks had erected a socialist government led by Béla Kun (1885–1937). The Allies quickly authorized an invasion by Romanian troops to remove the Communist danger. They then established Admiral Miklós Horty (1858–1957) as regent, a position he held until 1944. During the twenties the effective ruler of Hungary was Count Stephen Bethlen (1874–1947). He presided over a government that was parliamentary in form but aristocratic in character. In 1932 he was succeeded by General Julius Gömbös (1886–1936), who pursued policies of anti-Semitism and rigged elections. No matter how the popular vote turned out, the Gömbös party controlled the parliament. There was also deep resentment in Hungary over the territory it had lost to other nations at Versailles.

The situation in Austria was little better. The new Austria consisted of a capital city surrounded by some other territory. A quarter of the eight million Austrians lived in Vienna. Viable economic life was almost impossible, and union with Germany was forbidden by the Versailles Treaty. Throughout the twenties the leftist Social Democrats and the conservative Christian Socialists contended for power. Unwilling to use only normal political methods, both groups employed small armies to terrorize their opponents and to impress their followers. In 1933 the Christian Socialist Engelbert Dollfuss (1892–1934) became chancellor. He tried to steer a course between both the Communists and the German Nazis, who had begun to penetrate Austria. In 1934 he outlawed all political parties except those that composed his own Fatherland Front. He used government troops against the Social Democrats. During an unsuccessful Nazi *coup* in 1934, Dollfuss was shot. His successor, Kurt von Schuschnigg (b. 1897) presided over Austria until Hitler annexed it in 1938.

In southeastern Europe revision of the Versailles Treaty arrangements was somewhat less of an issue. Parliamentary government floundered nevertheless. In Yugoslavia (known as the Kingdom of the Serbs, Croats, and Slovenes until 1928), the clash of nationalities eventually led to the imposition of royal dictatorship in 1929 under King Alexander I (1921–1934). His dictatorship saw the outlawing of political parties and the jailing of popular politicians. Alexander I was assassinated in 1934, but the authoritarian government continued under the regency of his son. Other royal dictatorships were imposed in Romania by King Carol II (1930–1940) and in Bulgaria by King Boris III (1918–1943). They regarded their own illiberal regimes as countering even more extreme antiparliamentary movements and as quieting the discontent of nationalities within their borders. In Greece a parliamentary monarchy floundered amidst military coups and calls for a republic. In 1936 General John Metaxas (1871–1941) instituted a dictatorship that for the time being ended parliamentary life in Greece.

The nation whose postwar fortunes probably most disappointed liberal Europeans was Poland. For over a hundred years the country had been erased from the map. Restoration of an independent Poland had been one of Woodrow Wilson's Fourteen Points. When the country was finally reconstructed in 1919, nationalism proved

Thomas Masaryk (1850–1937) was the widely respected president of the democracy of Czechoslovakia after World War I. [The Granger Collection.]

an insufficient bond to overcome political disagreements stemming from class, diverse economic interests, and regionalism. The new parliament was plagued with a vast number of small political parties. The constitution assigned too little power to the executive. In 1926 General Josef Pilsudski (1857–1935) carried out a military *coup*. He ruled personally until the close of the decade, when the government passed into the hands of a group of military leaders.

Only one central European successor state escaped the fate of self-imposed authoritarian government. Czechoslovakia possessed a strong industrial base, a substantial middle class, and a tradition of liberal values. During the war Czechs and Slovaks had cooperated to aid the Allies. They had learned to work together and to trust each other. After the war the new government had carried out agrarian reform and had broken up large estates in favor of small peasant holdings. In the person of Thomas Masaryk (1850–1937) the nation possessed a gifted leader of immense integrity and fairness. The country had a real chance of constructing a viable modern nation state. However, it was plagued with discontent among its smaller national groups. The parliamentary regime might very well have been able to deal with this problem, but extreme German nationalists looked to Hitler for aid. For his part, the German dictator wished to expand into eastern Europe. In 1938 at Munich the great powers divided liberal Czechoslovakia to appease the aggressive instincts of Hitler.

The fate of the successor states proved most disappointing to those who had hoped for political liberty to result from the dissolution of the Hapsburg Empire and other border adjustments in eastern Europe. By the early thirties in most of those states the authoritarianism of the Hapsburgs had been replaced by that of other rulers. However, the most momentous democratic experiment between the wars was conducted in Germany. There, after a century of frustration and disappointment, a liberal state had been constructed. It was in Germany that parliamentary democracy and its future in Western civilization faced its major trial.

The Weimar Republic

The German Weimar Republic was born from the defeat of the imperial army, the revolution of 1918 against the Hohenzollerns, and the hopes of German Liberals and Social Democrats. Its name derived from the city in which its constitution was written and promulgated in August 1919. While the constitution was being debated, the republic, headed by the Social Democrats, accepted the humiliating terms of the Versailles Treaty. Although its officials had signed only under the threat of an Allied invasion, the republic was nevertheless permanently associated with the national disgrace and the economic burdens of the treaty. Throughout the twenties the government of the republic was required to fulfill the economic and military provisions imposed by the Versailles settlement. It became all too easy for nationalists and military figures whose policies had brought on the tragedy and defeat of the war to blame the young republic and the socialists for the results of the conflict. In Germany more than in other countries the desire to revise the treaty was closely related to a desire to change the mode of domestic government.

The Weimar Constitution was a highly enlightened document. It guaranteed the civil liberties and provided for direct election, by universal suffrage, of the *Reichstag* and the president. However, it also contained certain crucial structural flaws that allowed the eventual overthrow of its institutions. Within the *Reichstag* a complicated system of proportional representation was adopted. It resulted in shifting party combinations that led to considerable instability. Ministers were technically responsible to the *Reichstag*, but the president appointed and removed the chancellor. Perhaps most important, Article 48 allowed the president in times of emergency to rule by decree. In this manner the constitution permitted the possibility of presidential dictatorship.

Beyond the burden of the Versailles Treaty and the potential constitutional pitfalls, the Weimar Republic suffered from a lack of sympathy and a lack of loyalty on the part of many Germans. A social revolution had not accompanied the changes in political structure. Many important political figures actually favored a constitutional monarchy. The schoolteachers, civil servants, and judicial officials of the republic were generally the same people who had previously served the Kaiser and the empire. Prior to the war they had distrusted or even hated the Social Democratic Party, which figured so prominently in the politics of the republic. The officer corps was deeply suspicious of the government and profoundly resentful of the military provisions of the peace settlement. They and other nationalistic Germans perpetuated the myth that the German army had surrendered on foreign soil only because it had been stabbed in the back by civilians at home. In other words, large numbers of Germans in significant social and political positions wanted both to revise the peace treaty and to modify the system of government. The early years of the republic only solidified those sentiments.

A number of major and minor humiliations as well as considerable economic instability impinged on the new government. In March 1920 the right-wing Kapp *Putsch* erupted in Berlin. Led by a conservative civil servant and supported by army officers, the attempted *coup* failed. But the collapse occurred only after government officials had fled the city. The same month a series of strikes took place in the Ruhr mining district. The government sent in troops. Such extremism from both the left and the right would haunt the republic for all its days. In May 1921 the Allies presented a reparations bill for 132 billion gold marks. The German republican government accepted this preposterous demand only after new Allied threats of occupation. Throughout the early twenties there were numerous assassinations or attempted assassinations of important republican leaders. Violence was the hallmark of the first five years of the republic.

This is a characteristic drawing, made in 1921, by the German artist George Grosz (1893–1959). His art expressed hatred of the bourgeoisie, militarism, and capitalism; here he views the exploitation of the poor and the working class by overfed, callous property owners. [The Granger Collection.]

Lilo Linke Recalls the Mad Days of the German Inflation

In 1923 the presses that were printing paper currency in Germany could hardly keep up with the rising prices. This memoir recounts the difficulties of those days and the resentments that arose as money became worth less than the paper on which it was printed.

THE *whole population had suddenly turned into maniacs. Everyone was buying, selling, speculating, bargaining, and dollar, dollar, dollar was the magic word which dominated every conversation, every newspaper, every poster in Germany. Nobody understood what was happening. There seemed to be no sense, no rules in the mad game, but one had to take part in it if one did not want to be trampled underfoot at once. Only a few people were able to carry through to the end and gain by the inflation. The majority lost everything and broke down, impoverished and bewildered.*

The middle class was hurt more than any other, the savings of a lifetime and their small fortunes melted into a few coppers. They had to sell their most precious belongings for ten milliard inflated marks to buy a bit of food or an absolutely necessary coat, and their pride and dignity were bleeding out of many wounds. Bitterness remained for ever in their hearts. Full of hatred, they accused the international financiers, the Jews and Socialists—their old enemies—of having exploited their distress. They never forgot and never forgave and were the first to lend a willing ear to Hitler's fervent preaching.

In the shop, notices announced that we should receive our salaries in weekly parts, after a while we queued up at the cashier's desk every evening, and before long we were paid twice daily and ran out during the lunch hour to buy a few things, because as soon as the new rate of exchange became known in the early afternoon our money had again lost half its value.

Lilo Linke, *Restless Days* (New York: Alfred A. Knopf, 1935)\ pp. 131–132.

In 1923 German inflation became so extreme that eventually money was not worth the paper on which it was printed. In these photographs from that time, [ABOVE] a German housewife finds it cheaper to use the inflated currency to light her stove than to spend it on kindling wood, while [BELOW] poor citizens sell tin cans to raise money. [TOP: United Press International Photo; BOTTOM: The Granger Collection.]

In January 1923 French troops occupied the Ruhr region of Germany because of alleged defaults in the delivery of reparations to France. [The Granger Collection.]

The sensitive French-Belgian-German border area between the two world wars. In spite of efforts to restrain tension in the twenty-year period, there were persistent difficulties related to the Ruhr, Rhineland, Saar, and Eupen-Malmédy regions that necessitated strong defenses.

OCCUPIED BY THE ALLIES AND THE UNITED STATES TO 1923:
• ALL OF THE RHINELAND.
• THE RUHR.
• BRIDGEHEAD AREAS, EAST OF THE RHINE, EACH WITH A RADIUS OF 18 MILES, AND BORDERED BY A NEUTRAL ZONE, 6 MILES WIDE.
• OCCUPIED CITIES:
  – FOR 15 YEARS, COLOGNE, KOBLENZ AND MAINZ.
  – PUNITIVELY: RUHRORT, DÜSSELDORF, AND DUISBURG IN 1921, AND ESSEN IN 1923.

DEMILITARIZED AREAS:
• A 30-MILE-WIDE STRIP ALONG THE EAST BANK OF THE RHINE.

EUPEN AND MALMEDY, TO BELGIUM BY PLEBISCITE, 1920.

SAAR BASIN UNDER THE LEAGUE OF NATIONS, TO GERMANY BY PLEBISCITE, 1935.

FRENCH-GERMAN BOUNDARY, 1914.

MAGINOT LINE

50 MI.
50 KM.

GERMANY'S WESTERN FRONTIER

INVASION OF THE RUHR AND INFLATION. Inflation brought the major crisis of this period. The financing of the war and the continued postwar deficit spending generated an immense rise in prices. Consequently the value of German currency fell. By early 1921 the German mark traded against the American dollar at a ratio of 64 to 1, compared with a ratio of 4.2 to 1 in 1914. The German financial community contended that the value of the currency could not be stabilized until the reparations issue had been solved. In the meantime the printing presses kept pouring forth paper money, which was used to redeem government bonds as they fell due. In 1923 the Allies and France in particular declared Germany to be in technical default on its reparations payments. On January 11, to ensure receipt of the hard-won reparations, the French government ordered its troops to occupy the Ruhr mining and manufacturing district. The response of the Weimar Republic was to order passive resistance. This policy amounted to calling a general strike in the largest industrial region of the nation.

The invasion and the passive resistance produced cataclysmic inflation. The government paid subsidies to the Ruhr labor force, who had laid down their tools. Unemployment soon spread from the Ruhr to other parts of the country, creating a new drain on the treasury and also reducing tax revenues. The printing presses by this point had difficulty providing enough paper currency to keep up with the daily rise in prices. In November 1923 an American dollar was worth more than 800 million German marks. Money was literally not worth the paper it was printed on. Stores were unwilling to exchange goods for the worthless currency, and farmers withheld produce from the market. The moral and social values of thrift and prudence were thoroughly undermined. The security of middle-class savings, pensions, and insurance policies was wiped out. Simultaneously debts and mortgages could be paid off. Speculators in land, real estate, and industry made great fortunes. Union contracts generally allowed workers to keep up with rising prices. Inflation was not a disaster to everyone. However, to the middle class and the lower middle class the inflation was still one more traumatic experience coming hard on the heels of the military defeat and the peace treaty. Only when the social and economic upheaval of these months is grasped can the later German desire for order and security at almost any cost be comprehended.

HITLER'S EARLY CAREER. Late in 1923 Adolph Hitler (1889–1945) made his first major appearance on the German political scene. In 1889 he had been born the son of a minor Austrian customs official. By 1907 he had gone to Vienna, where his hopes of becoming an artist were soon dashed. He lived off money sent by his widowed mother and later off an Austrian orphan's allowance. He also painted postcards for further income and later found work as a day laborer. In Vienna he became acquainted with Mayor Karl Leugar's Christian Social Party which prospered on an ideology of anti-Semitism and from the social anxieties of the lower middle class. Hitler's own precarious situation and his observations taught him how desperately the lower middle class feared slipping into a proletarian condition. He also absorbed the rabid German nationalism and extreme anti-Semitism that flourished in Vienna. He came to hate socialism and Marxism, which he associated with Jews. During World War I Hitler fought with the German army, was wounded, was promoted to the rank of corporal, and was awarded the Iron Cross for bravery.

After the conflict Hitler settled in Munich. In the new surroundings he became associated with a small nationalistic, anti-Semitic political party that in 1920 adopted the name of National Socialist German Workers Party. The same year the group began to parade under a red banner with a black swastika. It issued a platform or program of

The National Socialist German Worker's Party Issues a Platform

These statements from the Nazi Party Twenty-five Points of 1920 illustrate the calls for nationalism, territorial expansion, anti-Semitic public policy, and aid for the poor and lower middle class that in time attracted broad support throughout Germany.

1. WE DEMAND *the union of all Germans to form a Great Germany on the basis of self-determination enjoyed by nations.*

2. *We demand equality of rights for the German people in its dealings with other nations, and abolition of the peace treaties of Versailles and Saint-Germain.*

3. *We demand land and territory (colonies) for the nourishment of our people and for settling our excess population.*

4. *None but members of the nation may be citizens of the state. None but those of German blood, whatever their creed, may be members of the nation. No Jew, therefore, may be a member of the nation.*

5. *Anyone who is not a citizen of the state may live in Germany only as a guest and must be regarded as being subject to foreign laws.*

. . . . .

7. *We demand that the state shall make it its first duty to promote the industry and livelihood of citizens of the state. If it is not possible to nourish the entire population of the state, foreign nationals (non-citizens of the state) must be excluded from the Reich.*

. . . . .

10. *It must be the first duty of each citizen of the state to work with his mind or with his body. The activities of the individual may not clash with the interests of the whole, but must proceed within the frame of the community and be for the general good.*

. . . . .

15. *We demand extensive development of provision for old age.*

16. *We demand creation and maintenance of a healthy middle class, immediate communalization of wholesale business premises, and their lease at a cheap rate to small traders, and that extreme considerations shall be shown to all small purveyors to the state, district authorities, and smaller localities.*

. . . . .

22. *We demand abolition of a paid army and formation of a national army.*

. . . . .

Raymond E. Murphy (Ed.), *National Socialism*, U.S. Department of State, Publication 1864 (Washington, 1943), pp. 222–224.

This picture of Adolf Hitler was made in May 1927. At the time he was not yet a major political figure, and the Nazi movement was relatively small. [United Press International Photo.]

Twenty-five Points. Among other things these called for the repudiation of the Versailles Treaty, the unification of Austria and Germany, the exclusion of Jews from German citizenship, agrarian reform, the prohibition of land speculation, the confiscation of war profits, the state administration of the giant cartels, and the replacement of department stores with small tradespeople. The "socialism" that Hitler and the Nazis had in mind was not state ownership of the means of production but the subordination of all economic enterprise to the welfare of the nation. It implied protection for very small economic enterprise. The social appeal of Nazism was to the lower middle class, which found itself squeezed between well-organized big business and socialist labor unions or political parties.

Soon after the promulgation of the Twenty-five Points, the Stormtroopers, or SA, were organized under the leadership of Captain Ernest Roehm. It was a paramilitary organization that initially provided members with food and uniforms and later in the decade with wages. In the mid-twenties the SA adopted its famous brown-shirted uniform. The Stormtroopers were the chief Nazi instrument for terror and intimidation before the party came into control of the government. They were a law unto themselves. The organization constituted a means of preserving military discipline and values outside the small army permitted by the Versailles settlement. The exist-

ence of such a private party army was a sign of the potential for violence in the Weimar Republic and the widespread contempt for the law and the institutions of the republic.

The economic turmoil following the Ruhr occupation provided the fledgling party, by now under Hitler's personal dominance, with an opportunity for direct action against the republic. On November 9, 1923, Hitler and a band of followers, accompanied by General Ludendorff, attempted an unsuccessful *Putsch* in Munich. When the local authorities crushed the rising, sixteen Naxis were killed. Hitler and Ludendorff were arrested and tried for treason. The general was acquitted. Hitler employed the trial to make himself into a national figure. In his defense he condemned the republic, the Versailles Treaty, the Jews, and the weakened condition of his adopted country. He was convicted and sentenced to five years in prison. He actually spent only a few months in jail, during which time he wrote *Mein Kampf* ("My Battle"). Another result of the brief imprisonment was a decision on Hitler's part that in the future he and his party must seek to seize political power by legal methods.

Trials of the New Democracies 853

Gustav Stresemann addressed the League of Nations in 1926 upon the admission of Germany to that international body. This event was one of the major outcomes of the Locarno agreements. [Bildarchiv Preussischer Kulturbesitz. Herbert Hoffmann.]

THE STRESEMANN YEARS. Elsewhere the officials of the republic were attempting to repair the damage from the inflation. Gustav Stresemann (1878–1929) was primarily responsible for the reconstruction of the republic and for its achievement of self-confidence. He served as chancellor only from August to November 1923, but he provided the nation with a new basis for stability. Stresemann abandoned the policy of passive resistance in the Ruhr. The country simply could not afford it. Then with the aid of banker Hjalmar Schacht, he introduced a new German currency. The rate of exchange was one trillion of the old German marks for one new *Rentenmark*. Stresemann also moved against challenges from both the left and the right. He supported the crushing of Hitler's abortive *Putsch* and smaller communist disturbances. In late November 1923 he resigned as chancellor and assumed the position of foreign minister, a post that he held until his death in 1929. In that office he exercised considerable influence over the affairs of the republic.

In 1924 the Weimar Republic and the Allies agreed to a new systematization of the reparation payments. The Dawes Plan, submitted by the American banker Charles Dawes, lowered the annual payments and allowed them to fluctuate according to the fortunes of the German economy. The Ruhr was to be evacuated, and the last French troops left that region in 1925. The same year Friedrich Ebert (1871–1925), the Social Democratic president of the republic, died. Field Marshal Paul von Hindenburg (1847–1934), a military hero and a conservative monarchist, was elected as his successor. He governed in strict accordance with the constitution, but his election suggested that a new conservative tenor had come to German politics. It looked as if conservative Germans had become reconciled to the republic. This conservatism was in line with the prosperity of the latter part of the decade. Foreign capital flowed into Germany, and employment, which had been poor throughout most of the postwar years, improved smartly. Giant industrial combines spread. The prosperity helped to establish broader acceptance and appreciation of the republic.

In foreign affairs Stresemann pursued a conciliatory course. He was committed to a policy of fulfilling the provisions of the Versailles Treaty, even as he attempted to revise it by diplomacy. He was willing to accept the settlement in the west but was a determined, if sometimes secret, revisionist in the east. He aimed to recover German territories lost to Poland and Czechoslovakia and possibly to unite with Austria, chiefly by diplomatic means. The first step, however, was to achieve respectability and economic recovery. That goal required a policy of accommodation and "Fulfillment," for the moment at least.

With the exception of the modernistic wing (toward the upper part of the picture), these buildings were the headquarters of the post-World War I League of Nations in Geneva, Switzerland. Today they house agencies of the United Nations. [United Nations.]

Germany sent troops into the demilitarized Rhineland. Significantly no such agreement was made about Germany's eastern frontier, but the Germans made treaties of arbitration with Poland and Czechoslovakia, and France strengthened its ties with the Little Entente. France supported German membership in the League of Nations and agreed to withdraw its troops from the Rhineland in 1930, five years earlier than specified at Versailles.

Germany was pleased to have achieved respectability and a guarantee against another Ruhr occupation, as well as the possibility of revision in the east. Britain was pleased to be allowed to play a more evenhanded role. Italy was glad to be recognized as a great power. The French were happy, too, because the Germans voluntarily accepted the permanence of their western frontier, which was also guaranteed by Britain and Italy, while France maintained its allies in the east. As A. J. P. Taylor has put it, "Any French statesman of 1914 could have been bewildered with delight by such an achievement."[2]

The Locarno Agreements brought a new spirit of hope to Europe. Germany's entry into the League of Nations was greeted with enthusiasm. Chamberlain, Briand, and Stresemann jointly received the Nobel Peace Prize in 1926. The spirit of Locarno was carried even further

LOCARNO.   These developments gave rise to the Locarno Agreements of October 1925. The spirit of conciliation led politicians Austen Chamberlain for Britain and Aristide Briand for France to accept Stresemann's proposal for a fresh start. France and Germany both accepted the western frontier established at Versailles as legitimate. Britain and Italy agreed to intervene against the aggressor if either side violated the frontier or if

2 Taylor, p. 58.

when the leading European states, Japan, and the United States signed the Kellogg–Briand Pact in 1928, renouncing "war as an instrument of national policy." The joy and optimism were not justified. France had merely recognized its inability to coerce Germany without help. Britain had shown its unwillingness to uphold the settlement in the east. Austen Chamberlain declared that no British government ever would "risk the bones of a British grenadier" for the Polish corridor. Germany was by no means reconciled to the eastern settlement. It continued its clandestine military connections with the Soviet Union, which had commenced with the Treaty of Rapallo, and planned to continue to press for revision.

In both France and Germany, moreover, the conciliatory politicians represented only a part of the nation. In Germany, especially, most people continued to reject Versailles and regarded Locarno as only an extension of it. When the Dawes Plan ran out in 1929, it was replaced by the Young Plan, which lowered the reparation payments, put a term on how long they must be made, and removed Germany entirely from outside supervision and control. The intensity of the outcry in Germany against the continuation of any reparations showed how far the Germans were from accepting their situation. In spite of these problems, major war was by no means inevitable. Europe, aided by American loans, was returning to prosperity. German leaders like Stresemann would certainly have continued to press for change, but there is little reason to think that they would have resorted to force, much less to a general war. Continued prosperity and diplomatic success might have won the loyalty of the German people for the Weimar Republic and moderate revisionism, but the Great Depression of the thirties brought new forces to power.

The Fascist Experiment in Italy

While its wartime allies continued to pursue parliamentary politics and its former enemies set out on the troubled path of democracy, Italy moved toward a new form of authoritarian government. From the Italian Fascist movement of Benito Mussolini (1883–1945) was derived the general term of *fascist*, which has frequently been used to describe the various right-wing dictatorships that arose between the wars.

The exact meaning of *fascism* as a political term remains much disputed among both historians and political scientists. However, a certain consensus does exist. The governments regarded as fascist were antidemocratic, anti-Marxist, antiparliamentary, and frequently anti-Semitic. They hoped to hold back the spread of Bolshevism, which seemed at the time a very real threat. They sought a world safe for the middle class, small businesses, owners of moderate amounts of property, and small farmers. The fascist regimes rejected the political inheritance of the French Revolution and of nineteenth-century liberalism. Their adherents believed that normal parliamentary politics and parties sacrificed national honor and greatness to petty party disputes. They wanted to overcome the class conflict of Marxism and the party conflict of liberalism by consolidating the various groups and classes within the nation for great national purposes. As Mussolini declared in 1931, "The fascist conception of the state is all-embracing, and outside of the state no human or spiritual values can exist, let alone be desirable."[3] Fascism was also highly elitist. The fascist governments were usually single-party dictatorships characterized by terrorism and police surveillance.

The Rise of Mussolini

The Italian *Fasci di Combattimento* ("Band of Combat") was founded in 1919 in Milan. Its members came largely from Italian war veterans who felt that the sacrifices of the conflict had been in vain. They resented the failure of Italy to gain the city of Fiume, toward the northern end of the Adriatic Sea, at the Paris conference. They feared socialism and inflation.

3 Quoted in Denis Mack Smith, *Italy: A Modern History* (Ann Arbor: University of Michigan Press, 1959), p. 412.

Their leader, Benito Mussolini, had been born the son of a blacksmith. For a time he had been a schoolteacher, then a day laborer. He became active in Italian socialist politics and by 1912 had become editor of the socialist newspaper *Avanti*. In 1914 Mussolini broke with the socialists and supported Italian entry into the war on the side of the Allies. His interventionist position lost him the editorship of *Avanti*. He then established his own paper, *Il Popolo d'Italia*. Later he served in the army and was wounded. In 1919, although of some prewar political stature, Mussolini was simply one of many Italian politicians. His *Fasci* organization was for its part simply one of numerous small political groups in a country characterized by such entities. As a politician Mussolini was an opportunist par excellence. He proved capable of changing his ideas and principles to suit every new occasion. Action for him was always more important than thought or rational justification. His one real rule was that of political survival.

Postwar Italian politics was a muddle. During the conflict the Italian Parliament had for all intents and purposes ceased to function. It had been quite willing to allow ministers to rule by decree. However, the parliamentary system as it then existed had begun to prove quite unsatisfactory to large sectors of the citizenry. Many Italians besides those in Mussolini's band of followers felt that Italy had emerged from the war as less than a victorious nation and had not been treated as a great power at the peace conference. The main spokesman for this discontent was the extreme nationalist poet and novelist Gabriele D'Annunzio (1863–1938). In 1919 he successfully led a force of patriotic Italians in an assault on Fiume. Troops of the Italian parliamentary government eventually drove him out. D'Annunzio had provided the example of the political use of a nongovernmental military force. The action of the government in removing him from Fiume gave the parliamentary ministry a somewhat less than patriotic appearance.

Between 1919 and 1921 Italy also experienced considerable internal social turmoil. Numerous industrial strikes

Gabriele D'Annunzio was an Italian poet and fervent nationalist. In 1919 he led a private military raid against Fiume, which he believed had wrongfully been denied to Italy by the Versailles Treaty. The painting is by Romaine Brooks. [The Granger Collection.]

OPPOSITE: Scenes from the
Fascist march on Rome in October 1922.
[ABOVE] When it was clear the king would not
authorize force against them, the marchers, in their
characteristic black shirts, posed for the friendly
photographer. [United Press International Photo.]
[BELOW] Benito Mussolini stands surrounded by his
followers after receiving his appointment as prime
minister from the king. [The Granger Collection.]

occurred, and workers occupied factories. Peasants seized uncultivated land from large estates. Parliamentary and constitutional government seemed incapable of dealing with this unrest. The Socialist Party had captured a plurality of seats in the Chamber of Deputies during the 1919 election. A new Catholic Popular Party had also done quite well. Both appealed to the working and agrarian classes. However, neither party would cooperate with the other, and parliamentary deadlock resulted. Under these conditions many Italians honestly and still others conveniently believed there existed the danger of a communist revolution.

Initially Mussolini was uncertain of the direction of the political winds. He first supported the factory occupations and land seizures. However, never one to be concerned with consistency, he soon reversed himself. He had discovered that large numbers of both upper-class and middle-class Italians who were pressured by inflation and who feared property loss had no sympathy for the workers or the peasants. They wanted order rather than some vague social justice that might harm their own interests. Consequently Mussolini and his Fascists took direct action in the face of the government inaction. They formed local squads of terrorists who disrupted Socialist meetings, mugged Socialist leaders, and terrorized Socialist supporters. They attacked strikers and farm workers and protected strikebreakers. Conservative land and factory owners were grateful. The officers and institutions of the law simply ignored the crimes of the Fascist squads. By early 1922 the Fascists had turned their intimidation against local officials in cities, such as Ferrara, Ravenna, and Milan. They controlled the local government in many parts of northern Italy.

In the election of 1921 Mussolini and thirty-four of his followers were sent to the Chamber of Deputies. Their importance grew as the local Fascists gained more direct power. The movement now had hundreds of thousands of supporters. In October 1922 the Fascists, dressed in their characteristic black shirts, began a march on Rome. King Victor Emmanuel III (1900–1946) refused to sign

a decree that would have authorized the use of the army against the marchers. Probably no other single decision so ensured a Fascist seizure of power. The cabinet resigned in protest. On October 29 the monarch telegraphed Mussolini in Milan and asked him to become prime minister. The next day Mussolini arrived in Rome by sleeping car and greeted his followers as head of the government when they entered the city.

Technically Mussolini had come into office by legal means. The monarch did possess the power to appoint the prime minister. However, Mussolini had no majority or even near majority in the Chamber of Deputies. Behind the legal façade of his assumption of power lay the months of terrorist disruption and intimidation and the threat of the Fascist march itself. The non-Fascist politicians, whose ineptitude had prepared the way for Mussolini, believed that his regime like others of previous months would be temporary. They failed to comprehend that he was not a traditional Italian politician.

The Fascists in Power

Mussolini had not really expected to be appointed prime minister. He moved cautiously to shore up his support and to consolidate his power. His success was the result of the impotence of his rivals, his own effective use of his office, his power over the masses, and his sheer ruthlessness. On November 23, 1922, the king and parliament granted Mussolini dictatorial authority for one year to bring order to the lower levels of the government. Wherever possible Mussolini appointed Fascists to office. Late in 1924, under Mussolini's guidance, the parliament changed the election law. Previously parties had been represented in the Chamber of Deputies in proportion to the popular vote cast for them. According to the new election law, the party that gained the largest popular vote (with a minimum of at least 25 per cent) received two thirds of the seats in the chamber. Coalition government, with all its compromises and hesitant policies, would no longer be necessary. In the election of 1924 the Fascists won a great victory and complete control of the

Mussolini was a powerful public orator. His gestures, which often appear comic in hindsight, were part of a carefully cultivated public image designed to make him appear at all times a leader. [Culver Pictures.]

Chamber of Deputies. They used that majority to end legitimate parliamentary life. A series of laws passed in 1925 and 1926 permitted Mussolini, in effect, to rule by decree. In 1926 all other political parties were dissolved. By the close of that year Italy had been transformed into a single-party, dictatorial state.

Their growing dominance over the government had not, however, diverted the Fascists from the course of violence and terror. They were put in charge of the police force, and the terrorist squads became institutionalized into government militia. In late 1924 their thugs murdered Giacomo Matteotti (1885-1924), a major non-Communist socialist leader. He had persistently criticized Mussolini and had exposed the criminality of the Fascist movement. In protest against the murder, a number of opposition deputies withdrew from the chamber. That tactic gave the prime minister an even freer hand. The deputies were refused readmission.

Support for the regime was sustained by the parallel organization of the party and the government. For every government institution there existed a corresponding party organization. In this manner the Fascist Party dominated the political structure at every level. As all other political parties were outlawed, citizens had to look to the Fascists in their community for political favors. They also knew the high price of opposition. By the late twenties the Grand Council of the party had become an organ of the state. It drew up and presented the list of persons who would stand for election to the Chamber of Deputies. Major policies to be approved by the chamber first passed the Grand Council. And Mussolini himself controlled the council.

The party used propaganda quite effectively. A cult of personality surrounded Mussolini. His skills in oratory and his general intelligence allowed him to hold his own with both large crowds and the leaders of the more respectable portions of the community. The latter tolerated and often admired him in the belief that he had saved them from Bolshevism. The persons who did have the courage to oppose Mussolini were usually driven into exile, and some were murdered.

The Italian Fascists Establish a New Set of Ten Commandments

These commandments of 1934 clearly illustrate the aggressive and authoritarian character of Italian Fascism. They also display the intense importance attached to Mussolini himself.

1. KNOW *that the Fascist, and in particular the soldier, must not believe in perpetual peace.*
2. *Days of imprisonment are always deserved.*
3. *The nation serves even as sentinel over a can of petrol.*
4. *A companion must be a brother, first, because he lives with you, and secondly because he thinks like you.*
5. *The rifle and cartridge belt, and the rest, are confided to you not to rust in leisure, but to be preserved in war.*
6. *Do not ever say "The Government will pay . . ." because it is you who pay; and the Government is that which you willed to have, and for which you put on a uniform.*
7. *Discipline is the soul of armies; without it there are no soldiers, only confusion and defeat.*
8. *Mussolini is always right.*
9. *For a volunteer there are no extenuating circumstances when he is disobedient.*
10. *One thing must be dear to you above all: the life of the Duce.*

Michael Oakeshott (Ed.), *The Social and Political Doctrines of Contemporary Europe* (Cambridge, England: Cambridge University Press, 1939), p. 180.

The Italian dictator made one important domestic departure that brought him significant political dividends. Through the Lateran Pact of February 1929, the Roman Catholic Church and the Italian state made peace with each other. Ever since the armies of Italian unification had seized papal lands in the 1860s, the church had been hostile to the state. The popes had remained virtual prisoners in the Vatican. The agreement of 1929 recognized the pope as the temporal ruler of Vatican City. The Italian government agreed to pay an indemnity to the papacy for confiscated land. The state also recognized Catholicism as the religion of the nation, exempted church property from taxes, and allowed church law to govern the institution of marriage. The Lateran Pact brought further respectability to Mussolini's authoritarian regime.

The Beginning of the Soviet Experiment

The political right had no monopoly on authoritarianism between the wars. The consolidation of the Bolshevik Revolution in Russia established the most extensive and durable of all twentieth-century authoritarian governments. However, the dictatorships of the left and the right did differ from each other. Unlike the Italian Fascists or the German National Socialists, the Bolsheviks had seized power illegally through revolution. For several years they confronted effective opposition, and their leaders long felt insecure about their hold on the country. The Communist Party was not a mass party nor a nationalistic one. Its early membership rarely exceeded more than 1 per cent of the Russian population. The Bolsheviks confronted a much less industrialized economy than existed in Italy or Germany. They believed in and practiced the collectivization of economic life attacked by the right-wing dictatorships. The Marxist–Leninist ideology was far more all-encompassing than the nationalism of the Fascists and the racism of the Nazis. Communism was an exportable commodity. The Communists regarded their government and their revolution not as local events in a national history but rather as an epoch-making event in the history of the world and the development of humanity.

The Third International

In a curious manner, however, certain policies of the early Russian Communist Revolution directly affected the rise of the Fascists and the Nazis in western Europe. The success of the revolution in Russia had the paradoxical effect of dividing socialist parties and socialist movements in the rest of Europe. In 1919 the Soviet Communists founded the Third International of the European socialist movement. It became better known as the Comintern. A year after its inception the Comintern imposed its Twenty-one Conditions upon any other socialist party that wished to become a member. The conditions included acknowledgement of leadership from Moscow, rejection of reformist or revisionist socialism, and repudiation of previous socialist leaders. The Comintern wished to make the Russian model of socialism as developed by Lenin the rule for all socialist parties outside the Soviet Union.

The decision whether to join or not to join the Comintern under these conditions split every major socialist party on the continent. As a result, separate communist parties and social democratic parties emerged. The former modeled themselves after the Soviet party and pursued policies dictated by Moscow. The social democratic parties attempted to pursue both social reform and liberal parliamentary politics. Throughout the twenties and early thirties the communists and the social democrats tended to fight each other more intensely than they fought either capitalism or conservative political parties. This division of the European political left meant that right-wing political movements rarely had to confront a united opposition on the political left.

War Communism

Within the Soviet Union the Red Armies under the organizational genius of Leon Trotsky had suppressed internal and foreign military opposition to the new government. Throughout the civil war Lenin had declared that the Bolshevik Party, as the vanguard of the revolution, was imposing the dictatorship of the proletariat. Political and economic administration became highly centralized. All major decisions flowed from the top in a nondemocratic manner. Under the economic policy of "War Communism" the revolutionary government confiscated and then operated the banks, the transport facilities, and heavy industry. The state also forcibly requisitioned grain produced by the peasants and shipped it from the countryside to feed the army and the workers in the cities. The fact of the civil war permitted suppression of possible resistance to this economic policy.

"War Communism" aided the victory of the Red Army over its opponents. The revolution had survived

The Third International Issues Conditions of Membership

After the Russian Revolution, the Russian Communist Party organized the Third Communist International. Any communist party outside the Soviet Union was required to accept these Twenty-one Conditions, adopted in 1919, in order to join the International. In effect, this program demanded that all such parties adopt a distinctly revolutionary program and cease operating as legal parties within their various countries. By this means, the Soviet Union sought to achieve leadership of the socialist movement throughout Europe. As non-Russian socialist parties debated whether to join the Third International, they quickly split into social democratic parties that remained independent of Moscow and communist parties that adopted the policy imposed by the Russian Communist Party.

1. *THE daily propaganda and agitation must bear a truly communist character and correspond to the program and all the decisions of the Third International. All the organs of the press that are in the hands of the party must be edited by reliable communists who have proved their loyalty to the cause of the proletarian revolution. . . .*

3. *The class struggle in almost all of the countries of Europe and America is entering the phase of civil war. Under such conditions the communists can have no confidence in bourgeois law. They must everywhere create a parallel illegal apparatus, which at the decisive moment could assist the party in performing its duty of revolution. . . .*

4. *The obligation to spread communist ideas includes the particular necessity of persistent, systematic propaganda in the army. . . .*

5. *It is necessary to carry on systematic and steady agitation in the rural districts. . . .*

7. *The parties desiring to belong to the Communist International must recognize the necessity of a complete and absolute rupture with reformism . . . , and they must carry on propaganda in favor of this rupture among the broadest circles of the party membership. . . .*

8. *. . . Every party desirous of belonging to the Third International must ruthlessly denounce the methods of "their own" imperialists in the colonies, supporting, not in words, but in deeds, every independence movement in the colonies. . . .*

14. *Every party that desires to belong to the Communist International must give every possible support to the*

Lenin addressing a May Day demonstration in Moscow in 1918. [Culver Pictures.]

Soviet Republics in their struggle against all counter-revolutionary forces. . . .

.   .   .   .

16. All decisions of the congresses of the Communist International . . . are binding on all parties affiliated to the Communist International. . . .

17. In connection with all this, all parties desiring to join the Communist International must change their names. Every party that wishes to join the Communist International must bear the name: Communist party of such-and-such country. This question as to name is not merely a formal one, but a political one of great importance. The Communist International has declared a decisive war against the entire bourgeois world and all the yellow, social democratic parties. Every rank-and-file worker must clearly understand the difference between the communist parties and the old official "social democratic" or "socialist" parties which have betrayed the cause of the working class.

18. Members of the party who reject the conditions and thesis of the Communist International, on principle, must be expelled from the party.

International Communism in the Era of Lenin: A Documentary History, ed. by Helmut Gruber (Garden City, N.Y.: Doubleday, 1972), pp. 241–246.

and triumphed. However, the policy generated domestic opposition to the Bolsheviks, who in 1920 numbered only about 600,000 members. The alliance of workers and peasants forged by the slogan of "Peace, Bread, and Land" had begun to come apart at the seams. Many Russians were no longer willing to make the sacrifices demanded by the central party bureaucrats. In 1920 and 1921 major strikes occurred in numerous factories. Peasants were discontented and resisted the requisition of grain. In March 1921 the navy mutinied at Kronstadt. Its rebellion was crushed by the Red Army with grave loss of life. Each of these incidents suggested that the proletariat itself was opposing the dictatorship of the proletariat. Also, by late 1920 it had become clear that further revolution would not sweep across the rest of Europe. For the time being the Soviet Union would constitute a vast island of revolutionary socialism in the larger sea of worldwide capitalism.

The New Economic Policy

Under these difficult conditions Lenin made a crucial strategic retreat. In March 1921, following the Kronstadt mutiny, he outlined the New Economic Policy, normally referred to as *NEP*. Apart from what he termed "the commanding heights" of banking, heavy industry, transportation, and international commerce, there was to be

The Beginning of the Soviet Experiment 863

considerable private economic enterprise. In particular, peasants were to be permitted to farm for a profit. They would pay taxes like other citizens, but they could sell their surplus grain on the open market. The NEP was in line with Lenin's earlier conviction that the Russian peasantry held the key to the success of revolution in the nation. After 1921 the countryside did become more stabilized, and a secure food supply seemed assured for the cities. Similar free enterprise flourished within light industry and domestic retail trade. By 1927 industrial production had reached its 1913 level. The revolution seemed to have transformed Russia into a land of small family farms and small privately owned shops and businesses.

An early tractor arrives on a Russian farm during the 1920s. [The Granger Collection.]

Stalin versus Trotsky

The New Economic Policy had caused sharp disputes within the Politburo, the highest governing committee of the Communist Party. The partial return to capitalism seemed to some members nothing less than a betrayal of sound Marxist principles. These frictions increased as Lenin's firm hand disappeared. In 1922 he suffered a stroke that broke his health. He returned to work but never again dominated party affairs. In 1924 Lenin died. As the power vacuum developed, an intense struggle for future leadership of the party commenced. Two factions emerged. One was led by Trotsky; the other by Josef Stalin (1879–1953), who had become General Secretary of the party in 1922. Shortly before his death Lenin had criticized both men. He was especially harsh toward Stalin. However, the General Secretary's base of power lay with the party membership and with the daily management of party affairs. Consequently he was able to withstand the posthumous strictures of Lenin.

The issue between the two factions was power within the party, but the struggle was fought out over the question of Russia's path toward industrialization and the future of the communist revolutionary movement. Trotsky, speaking for what became known as the left wing, urged rapid industrialization financed through the expropriation of farm production. Agriculture should be collectivised, and the peasants should be made to pay for industrialization. Trotsky further argued that the revolution in Russia could succeed only if new revolutions took place elsewhere in the world. Russia needed the skills and wealth of other nations to build its own economy. As Trotsky's influence within the party began to wane, he also demanded that party members be permitted to criticize the policies of the government and the party. However, Trotsky was very much a latecomer to the advocacy of open discussion. When in control of the Red Army, he had been known as an unflinching disciplinarian.

A right-wing faction opposed Trotsky. Its chief ideological voice was that of Nikolai Bukharin (1888–1938),

RIGHT: The youthful Stalin, possibly a tsarist police photo. As he worked his way up the Bolshevik political hierarchy he became a master of the details of its bureaucracy, experience that eventually helped him to oust and destroy his opponents, real and fancied, in the politburo. [The Granger Collection.]

BELOW: Leon Trotsky's brilliant organization of the Red Army secured the Bolshevik victory in the Russian Civil War. However, he later lost his power and influence when, following Lenin's death, Stalin outmaneuvered him in the party strife of the late 1920s. [Culver Pictures.]

the editor of *Pravda*. Stalin was the major political manipulator. In the mid-twenties this group pressed for the continuation of Lenin's NEP and a policy of relatively slow industrialization. Stalin emerged as the victor in these intraparty rivalries.

Stalin had been born in 1879 into a very poor family. Unlike the other early Bolshevik leaders, he had not spent a long period of exile in western Europe. He was much less of an intellectual and internationalist. He was also much more brutal. His handling of various recalcitrant national groups within Russia after the revolution had even shocked Lenin. Stalin's power lay in his command of bureaucratic and administrative methods. He was neither a brilliant writer nor an effective public speaker; however, he mastered the crucial, if dull, details of party structure, including admission and promotion. That mastery meant that he could draw upon the support of the lower levels of the party apparatus when he came into conflict with other leaders.

In the middle of the decade Stalin supported Bukharin's position on economic development. In 1924 he also enunciated in opposition to Trotsky the doctrine of "socialism in one country." He urged that socialism could be achieved in Russia alone. Russian success did not depend upon the fate of the revolution elsewhere. In this manner Stalin nationalized the previously international scope of the Marxist revolution. Stalin cunningly used the apparatus of the party and his control over the Central Com-

The Beginning of the Soviet Experiment 865

mittee of the Communist Party to edge out Trotsky and his supporters. By 1927 Trotsky had been removed from all his offices, expelled from the party, and exiled to Siberia. In 1929 he was sent out of Russia and eventually took up residence in Mexico, where he was murdered in 1940, presumably by one of Stalin's agents. With the removal of Trotsky from all positions of influence Stalin was firmly in control of the Soviet state. It remained to be seen where he would direct its course and what "socialism in one country" would mean in practice.

Results of the Decade of Experiment

At the close of the twenties it appeared that Europe had finally emerged from the difficulties of the World War I era. The initial resentments over the peace settlement seemed to have abated. The major powers were cooperating. Democracy was still functioning in Germany. The Labor Party was about to form its second ministry in Britain. France had settled into a less assertive international role. Mussolini's Fascism seemed to have little relevance to the rest of the continent. The successor states had not fulfilled the democratic hopes of the Versailles conference, but their troubles seemed their own. The Soviet Union, though still harboring a communist menace, stood largely withdrawn into its own internal development and power struggles.

The European economy seemed finally to be on an even keel. The frightening inflation was over, and unemployment had eased. American capital was flowing into the continent. The reparations payments had been systematized by the Young Plan. Yet both this economic and this political stability proved illusory and temporary. What brought them to an end was the deepest economic depression in the modern history of the West. As the governments and electorates responded to the economic collapse, the search for liberty gave way in more than one instance to a search for security. The political experiments of the twenties gave way to the political tragedies of the thirties.

SUGGESTED READINGS

K. D. BRACHER, *The German Dictatorship* (1970). A comprehensive treatment of both the origins and the functioning of the Nazi movement and government.

A. BULLOCK, *Hitler: A Study in Tyranny*, rev. ed. (1964). The best biography.

E. H. CARR, *A History of Soviet Russia*, 9 vols. (1950–19—). An extensive and important study.

G. D. H. COLE, *A History of the Labour Party from 1914* (1948). A straightforward account by a sympathetic supporter.

R. DAHRENDORF, *Society and Democracy in Germany* (1967). An important commentary by a leading sociologist.

I. DEUTSCHER, *The Prophet Armed* (1954), *The Prophet Unarmed* (1959), and *The Prophet Outcast* (1963). A major biography of Trotsky.

E. EYCK, *A History of the Weimar Republic*, 2 vols. (trans., 1963). The story as narrated by a liberal.

L. FISCHER, *The Life of Lenin* (1964). A sound biography by an American journalist.

P. GAY, *Weimar Culture: The Outsider as Insider* (1968). A sensitive analysis of the intellectual life of Weimar.

N. GREENE, *From Versailles to Vichy: The Third Republic, 1919–1940* (1970). A useful introduction to a difficult subject.

H. GRUBER, *International Communism in the Era of Lenin: A Documentary History* (1967). An excellent collection of otherwise difficult-to-find documents.

C. A. MACARTNEY AND A. W. PALMER, *Independent Eastern Europe: A History* (1962). The best one-volume survey.

A. MARWICK, *The Deluge: British Society and the First World War* (1965). Full of insights into both major and more subtle minor social changes.

E. NOLTE, *Three Faces of Fascism* (1963). An important, influential, and difficult work on France, Italy, and Germany.

R. PIPES, *The Formation of the Soviet Union*, 2nd ed. (1964). A study of internal policy with emphasis on Soviet minorities.

H. ROGGER AND E. WEBER (Eds.), *The European Right: A Historical Profile* (1965). An anthology of articles on right-wing political movements in various European countries.

H. Seton-Watson, *Eastern Europe Between the Wars, 1918–1941* (1946). Somewhat dated but still a useful work.

D. Mack Smith, *Italy: A Modern History*, rev. ed. (1969). Very good chapters on the Fascists and Mussolini.

R. J. Sontag, *A Broken World, 1919–1939* (1971). An exceptionally thoughtful and well-organized survey.

A. J. P. Taylor, *English History, 1914–1945* (1965). Lively and opinionated.

H. A. Turner, Jr. (Ed.), *Reappraisals of Fascism* (1975). A collection of very important recent articles on Fascist movements.

T. Wilson, *The Downfall of the Liberal Party, 1914–1935* (1966). A close examination of the surprising demise of a political party in Britain.

E. Wiskemann, *Fascism in Italy: Its Development and Influence* (1969). A comprehensive treatment.

For works on diplomatic developments, see Chapter 33.

868

32
Europe and the Depression of the 1930s

IN EUROPE, unlike the United States, the 1920s had not been "roaring." Economically they had been a decade of much insecurity, of a search for elusive stability, of a short-lived upswing, and then of collapse in finance and production. The depression that commenced in 1929 was the most severe downturn ever experienced by the capitalist economies. The unemployment, low production levels, financial instability, and contracted trade arrived and would not depart. Marxists thought that the final downfall of capitalism was at hand. Capitalist businessmen and political leaders despaired over the failure of the market mechanism to save them. Voters looked for new ways out of the doldrums, and statesmen sought escapes from the political pressures that the depression had brought upon them. One result of the fight for economic security was the establishment of the Nazi dictatorship in Germany. Another was the piecemeal construction of what has since become known as the *mixed economy;* that is, governments became directly involved in economic decisions. In both cases most of the political and economic guidelines of nineteenth-century liberalism were abandoned for good. Two other casualties of these years were decency and civility in political life.

Toward the Great Depression

Three factors combined to bring about the intense severity and the extended length of the depression. There was a financial crisis that stemmed directly from the war

An unemployed German in Berlin photographed about 1930 wearing a sign declaring "I seek work of any kind!" As his dress indicates, he was from either the upper working class or the lower middle class, and such people had rarely known unemployment during earlier periods of economic hardship in Europe. [Bildarchiv Preussischer Kulturbesitz. Herbert Hoffmann.]

and the peace settlement. To this was added a crisis in the production and distribution of goods in the world market. These two problems became intertwined in 1929, and so far as Europe was concerned they reached the breaking point in 1931. Finally, both of these difficulties became worse than might have been necessary because of the absence of strong economic leadership and responsibility on the part of any major west European country or the United States. Without cooperation or leadership in the Atlantic economic community, the economic collapse in finance and production simply lingered and deepened.

The Financial Tailspin

Most European nations emerged from World War I with inflated currencies. Immediately after the armistice the unleashed demand for consumer and industrial goods continued to drive up prices. The price and wage increases generally subsided after 1921, but the problem of maintaining the value of their currencies still haunted political leaders—and even more so after the German financial disaster of 1923. This frightening experience in part accounted for the refusal of most governments to run budget deficits when the depression struck. They feared inflation as a political danger in the same manner that European governments since World War II have feared unemployment.

The problems of reparation payments and international war-debt settlement further complicated the picture. France and the United States provided the stumbling blocks in these matters. France had paid reparations as a defeated nation after 1815 and 1871. As a victor it now intended to receive reparations and to finance its postwar recovery through them. The 1923 invasion of the Ruhr demonstrated French determination on this question.

The United States was no less determined that it receive repayments of the wartime loans extended to its allies. There were also various debts that the European Allies owed to each other. It soon became apparent that German reparations were to provide the means of repay-

This cartoon drawn in 1923 by Rollin Kirby pictures the attitude of the United States toward Europe. The Americans refused to join the League of Nations and demanded that their former European allies repay their war debts. [The Granger Collection.]

"I SYMPATHIZE DEEPLY WITH YOU, MADAME, BUT I CANNOT ASSOCIATE WITH YOU"

ment of the American and other Allied debts. Most of the money the Allies collected from each other also went to the United States.

In 1922 Great Britain announced that it would collect payment on its own debts only to the extent that the United States required payments from Britain. However, the American government would not relent. The reparations and the war debts made normal business, capital investment, and international trade very difficult and expensive for European nations. Various modes of government controls were exercised over credit, trade, and currency. Speculation in currency drew funds away from capital investment in productive enterprise. The monetary problems served to reinforce the general tendency toward high tariff policies. If a nation imported too many goods from abroad, it might have difficulty meeting those costs and the expenses of debt or reparations payments. The financial and money muddle thus discouraged trade and production and in turn harmed employment.

In 1924 the Dawes Plan brought more system to the administration and transfer of reparations. Those procedures in turn smoothed the debt repayments to the United States. Thereafter large amounts of private American capital flowed into Europe and especially into Germany. Much of this money, which provided the basis for Europe's brief prosperity after 1925, was in the form of short-term loans. In 1928 this lending began to contract as American money became diverted from European investments into the booming New York stock market. The crash of Wall Street in October 1929 saw the loss of large amounts of money. Within the United

States there occurred a major contraction of credit and numerous bank failures. Henceforth little American capital was available for investment in Europe. Loans already made to Europe were not renewed, as American banks used their funds to cover domestic shortages.

As the credit to Europe began to run out, a major financial crisis struck the continent. In May 1931 the Kreditanstalt, a major bank in Vienna, collapsed. It was a primary lending institution for much of central and eastern Europe. The German banking system came under severe pressure and was saved only through government guarantees. However, it became clear that under this crisis situation Germany would be unable to make its next reparation payment as stipulated in the 1929 Young Plan. As the German difficulties reached such large proportions, American President Herbert Hoover announced in June 1931 a one-year moratorium on all payments of international debts. The Hoover moratorium was a prelude to the end of reparations. Hoover's action was a sharp blow to the French economy, for which reparations had continued to be important. The Lausanne Conference of the summer of 1932 in effect brought the era of reparations to a close. The next year the debts owed to the United States were settled either through small token payments or simply through default. Nevertheless the financial politics of the twenties had done its damage.

Problems in Agricultural Commodities

In addition to the dramatic financial turmoil and collapse there was also a less dramatic, but equally fundamental downturn in production and trade. The twenties witnessed a contraction in the market demand for European goods relative to the continent's productive capacity. Part of this problem originated within Europe and part outside. In both instances the difficulty arose from agriculture. Better methods of farming, improved strains of wheat, expanded tillage, and more extensive transport facilities all over the globe vastly increased the quantity of grain produced. World wheat prices fell to record lows.

The League of Nations Reports the Collapse of European Agriculture

A crisis in agriculture was as much a cause of the Depression as was the turmoil in the financial community. The League of Nations reported in 1931 how, in part, the desperate situation in agriculture developed.

IT IS *the lowness of prices that constitutes the agricultural crisis. It is becoming difficult to sell products, and in many cases prices have reached a level at which they are scarcely, if at all, sufficient to cover the cost of production.*

The reason for the crisis and for its continuance is to be found in the fact that agricultural prices are low in comparision with the expenditure which the farmer must meet. . . . Agricultural products cost a lot to produce and then fetch very little in the market. In spite of the great technical progress achieved, operating costs remain implacably higher than selling prices, farmers obtain no longer a fair return on their labour or on their capital. Frequently the returns of agricultural undertakings are not enough to cover the necessary outlay for the purchase of the material or products necessary for continued operation or for the payment of wages and taxes and so forth.

This disproportion between the income and expenditure of agricultural undertakings . . . appears to constitute the dominant and decisive element of the prevailing agricultural depression.

Until 1929, prices were low as compared with prices of industrial products, but were above pre-war prices. The predominating tendency to a fall which was observed was not altogether general nor was it abnormally rapid. The general character of the price movement completely changed in 1930. A fall, sometimes catastrophic, spread with extreme violence to almost all agricultural produce. It was so rapid that at the end of the year, whilst some products reached the pre-war level of prices, others fell as low as one-quarter or one-half below the 1913 level. . . . Farmers throughout the world have suffered from it.

League of Nations, Economic Committee, *The Agricultural Crisis,* (1931), Vol. 1, pp. 7–8, reprinted in S. B. Clough, T. Moodie, and C. G. Moodie, *Economic History of Europe: The Twentieth Century* (New York: Harper and Row, 1968), pp. 216–217.

This development was, of course, initially good for consumers. However, it meant lower incomes for European farmers and especially for those of central and eastern Europe. At the same time higher industrial wages raised the cost of the industrial goods used by the farmer or peasant. The farmers could not purchase those products.

Moreover farmers began to have difficulty paying off their mortgages and normal annual operation debts. They borrowed money to plant their fields, expecting to pay the debt when the crops were sold. The fall in commodity prices raised problems of repayment.

The difficulties of agricultural finance became especially pressing in eastern Europe. Immediately after the war numerous land reform programs had been undertaken in this region. The democratic franchise in the successor states had opened the way for considerable redistribution of tillable soil. In Romania and Czechoslovakia large amounts of land changed hands. This occurred to a lesser extent in Hungary and Poland. However, the new relatively small farmers proved to be inefficient and were unable to earn sufficient incomes. Protective tariffs often prevented the export of grain among European countries. The credit and cost squeeze on east European farmers and on their counterparts in Germany played a major role in their disillusionment with liberal politics. For example, in Germany farmers provided the Nazis with a major source of political support.

Outside of Europe similar problems affected other producers of agricultural commodities. The prices they received for their products plummeted. Government-held reserves accumulated to record levels. This glut of major world commodities involved the supplies of wheat, sugar, coffee, rubber, wool, and lard. The people who produced these goods in underdeveloped nations could no longer make enough money to buy finished goods from industrial Europe. As world credit collapsed, the economic position of these commodity producers became all the worse. Commodity production had simply outstripped world demand.

The result of the collapse in the agricultural sector of the world economy and the financial turmoil was stagnation and depression for European industry. Coal, iron, and textiles had depended largely on international markets. Unemployment spread from these industries to those producing finished consumer goods. The persistent unemployment of Great Britain and to a lesser extent of Germany during the twenties already meant "soft" domestic markets. The policies of reduced government spending with which the governments confronted the depression further weakened domestic demand. By the early thirties the depression was growing on itself.

Areas of Growth Within the Depressed Economies

Despite the depression some economic growth did take place between the wars. Depression did not mean economic regression. The economic growth was spotty, unsteady, and concentrated in special areas. Three of these industries deserve brief mention. They were radio, automobiles, and synthetic goods. The technological basis for each of them had been developed prior to World War I but their major impact on the economy occurred afterwards.

RADIO. Radio and radio technology came of age in the twenties and thirties. The wartime requirements for communication had speeded up development and production of the wireless. In 1922 broadcasting facilities had been established in Britain. The nationalized British Broadcasting System was organized in 1926. Other radio broadcasting facilities spread across the continent during the same years. The radio was a consumer gadget of the first order. The expanding electric systems made its use possible. The radio itself was sold and then required other businesses to supply service and parts. The radio industry in turn expanded the scope and transformed the nature of advertising. By the end of the twenties millions of radios were in European homes. It was a product bought not by the wealthy, who had various other modes of leisure, but by the relatively poor and middle-class groups of the population. It was the first product of sophisticated electrical technology to capture the mass market. Radio—like its successor, television—transformed European life and tended to produce a more nearly uniform culture. Radio also helped to make the propaganda programs of the authoritarian states possible.

"All Germany listens to the Führer with the people's radio receiver," declares a sales poster in 1936 for a cheap radio. Instruments such as this were pushed by the Nazis because they quickly came to realize that the efficient exploitation of such a medium of mass electronic communication was of fundamental importance to an authoritarian regime and that the presence of these receivers in nearly every home allowed the Nazi propaganda to penetrate virtually the entire German nation at will. [Bildarchiv Preussischer Kulturbesitz.]

AUTOMOBILES. Automobiles were a second interwar growth industry. Only during those years did the motor car become a product of widespread consumption. In France Louis Renault and André Citroën built cars that the middle class wanted and could afford to buy. The automobile revolutionized European life rather less than it did American life. But the auto did bring new mobility and also possessed obvious military uses. Its production called forth new demand for steel, glass, rubber, petroleum, and highways. The automobile, like the radio, required a sales and service—as well as a production—industry.

SYNTHETICS. During these years the production of synthetic goods began to assume major economic significance. Rayon, invented before World War I, led the way in this area. Its production and consumption for hose and underwear grew rapidly. The product itself was soon much improved through the acetate process. Rayon began to replace cotton as the cheap textile for everyday use. The production of this synthetic fabric proved especially attractive to governments, such as those of Ger-

many and Italy, that sought economic self-sufficiency. The prospect of war in the late thirties led various governments to encourage chemical industries to search for other synthetic substances that might replace natural products if foreign sources for the latter were shut off.

Depression and Government Policy

It is important to remember these areas of industrial expansion between the wars. The depression did not mean absolute economic decline. Nor did it mean that everyone was out of a job. The numbers of employed always well exceeded those without work. What the economic downturn did mean was the spread of actual or potential insecurity. People in practically all walks of life feared that their own economic security and life style might be the next to go. The depression also brought on a frustration of social and economic expectations. People with jobs frequently improved their standard of living or received promotion much more slowly than they might have under sound economic conditions. Although they were employed, they seemed in their own eyes to be going nowhere. Their anxieties created a major source of social discontent.

The governments of the late twenties and early thirties were not particularly well fitted in either structure or ideology to confront these problems. The demand from the electorates was to do something. What the government did in large measure depended on the severity of the depression in a particular country and the self-confidence of the nation's political system. The Keynesian solution of governments' spending the economy out of depression was not yet available. John Maynard Keynes's *General Theory of Employment, Interest, and Money* was not published until 1936. The orthodox economic policy of the day called for cuts in government spending so as to avoid inflation. It was then expected that eventually the market mechanism would bring the economy back to prosperity. However, the length and severity of the depression, plus the possibility of direct democratic political pressure, led governments across Europe to interfere with the economy as never before.

Government participation in economic life was not new. One need only recall the policies of mercantilism or government encouragement of railway building. But from the early thirties onward government involvement increased rapidly. Private economic enterprise became subject to new trade, labor, and currency regulations. The political goals of restoration of employment and provision for defense established new state-related economic priorities. Generally speaking, as in the past, the extent of state intervention increased as one moved from west to east across the continent. These new economic policies in most cases also involved further political experimentation.

Confronting the Depression in the Democracies

The depression brought to an end the business-as-usual attitude that had marked the political life of Great Britain and France during the late twenties. In Britain the emergency led to a new coalition government and the abandonment of economic policies considered almost untouchable for a century. The economic stagnation in France proved the occasion for a bold political and economic program sponsored by the parties of the left. The relative success of the British venture gave the nation new confidence in the democratic processes; the new departures in France created social and political hostilities that undermined faith in republican institutions.

Great Britain: The National Government

In 1929 a second minority Labor government headed by Ramsay MacDonald assumed office. As the number of British unemployed rose to more than 2.5 million workers in 1931, the ministry became divided over the remedy for the problem. MacDonald believed that the budget should be slashed, government salaries reduced, and the benefits to people on government insurance lowered. This was a bleak program for a Labor government. MacDonald's strong desire to make the Labor Party respectable led him away from more radical programs. Many of the Cabinet ministers rejected MacDonald's proposals. They would not consent to taking income away from the poor and the unemployed. The prime minister requested the resignations of his cabinet and arranged for a meeting with King George V.

Everyone assumed that the Labor ministry was about to leave office. However, to the surprise of his party and the nation, MacDonald did not resign. At the urging of the king and probably of his own ambition, MacDonald formed a coalition ministry called the National Government composed of Labor, Conservative, and Liberal ministers. The bulk of the Labor Party believed that their leader had sold out. In the election of 1931 the National Government received a very comfortable majority. After the election, however, MacDonald, who remained prime minister until 1935, was little more than the tool of the Conservatives. They held a majority in their own right in the House of Commons, but the appearance of a coalition was useful for imposing unpleasant programs.

George Orwell Observes a
Woman in the Slums

Although Great Britain was beginning to emerge from the Great Depression by the late thirties, there remained much poverty and human degradation. This scene described in 1937 by the social critic George Orwell (1903–1950) captures a glimpse of the sadness and hopelessness that many British citizens experienced every day of their lives.

THE *train bore me away, through the monstrous scenery of slag-heaps, chimneys, piled scrap-iron, foul canals, paths of cindery mud criss-crossed by the prints of clogs. . . . As we moved slowly through the outskirts of the town we passed row after row of little grey slum houses running at right angles to the embankment. At the back of one of the houses a young woman was kneeling on the stones, poking a stick up the leaden waste-pipe which ran from the sink inside, and which I suppose was blocked. I had time to see everything about her—her sacking apron, her clumsy clogs, her arms reddened by the cold. . . . She had a round pale face, the usual exhausted face of the slum girl who is twenty-five and looks forty, thanks to miscarriages and drudgery; and it wore, for the second in which I saw it, the most desolate, hopeless expression I have ever seen. It struck me then that we are mistaken when we say that "It isn't the same for them as it would be for us," and that people bred in the slums can imagine nothing but the slums. For what I saw in her face was not the ignorant suffering of an animal. She knew well enough what was happening to her—understood as well as I did how dreadful a destiny it was to be kneeling there in the bitter cold, on the slimy stones of a slum backyard, poking a stick up a foul drain-pipe.*

George Orwell, *The Road to Wigan Pier* (New York: Berkeley Medallion Books, 1967, originally printed in 1937), p. 29.

The National Government took three decisive steps to attack the depression. To balance the budget, it raised taxes, cut insurance benefits to the unemployed and the elderly, and lowered government salaries. Its leaders argued that the fall in prices that had taken place meant that lowering those benefits and salaries did not appreciably cut real income. In September 1931 the National Government went off the gold standard. The value of the British pound on the international money market fell by about 30 per cent. Exports were somewhat stimulated by this move. In 1932 Parliament passed the Import Duties Bill, which placed a 10 per cent *ad valorum* tariff on all imports except those from the empire. In the context of previous British policy all of these steps were nothing less than extraordinary. Gold and free trade, the hallmarks of almost a century of British commercial policy, had been abandoned.

The policies of the National Government produced significant results. Great Britain avoided the banking crisis that hit other countries. By 1934 industrial production had expanded somewhat beyond the level for 1929. Britain was the first nation to achieve restoration of that level of production. Of course, the mediocre British industrial performance of the twenties made the British task easier. The government also encouraged lower interest rates. Those in turn led to the largest private housing boom in British history. Industries related to housing and the furnishing of homes prospered. Those people who were employed generally experienced an improvement in their standard of living. Nonetheless the hard core of unemployment remained. In 1937 the number of jobless had fallen to just below 1.5 million. That same year, when George Orwell described the laboring districts of the nation in *The Road to Wigan Pier*, his picture was dominated by the poverty and the workless days of the people whom he met.

Britain had entered the depression with a stagnant economy and left the era with a stagnant economy. Yet the political system itself was not fundamentally challenged. There were demonstrations of the unemployed, but social insurance, though hardly generous did support them. To the employed citizens of the country the National Government seemed to pursue a policy that avoided the extreme wings of both the Labor and the Conservative parties. When MacDonald retired in 1935, Stanley Baldwin again took office. He was succeeded in 1937 by Neville Chamberlain (1869–1940). The new prime minister is today known for the disaster of the Munich agreement. When he took office, he was known as one of the more progressive thinkers on social issues in the Conservative Party.

Oswald Mosley in May 1939 leads a demonstration in London of his British Union of Fascists and National Socialists. [United Press International Photo.]

Britain did see one movement that flirted with the extreme right-wing politics of the continent. In 1932 Sir Oswald Mosley (b. 1896) founded the British Union of Fascists. He had held a minor position in the second Labor government and was disappointed in its feeble attack on unemployment. Mosley urged a program of direct action through a new corporate structure for the economy. His group wore black shirts and attempted to hold mass meetings. He gained only a few thousand adherents. Mosley's popularity reached its height in 1934. Thereafter his anti-Semitism began to alienate supporters, and by the close of the decade he had become little more than a political oddity.

France: The Popular Front

The timing of the depression in France was the reverse of that in Britain. It came later and lasted much longer. Only in 1931 did the economic slide begin to affect the French economy. Even then unemployment did not become the major problem it did elsewhere. Rarely were more than a half million workers without jobs. However, in one industry after another wages were lowered. Tariffs were raised to protect French goods and especially French agriculture. Ever since that time French farmers have enjoyed unusual protection from the government. These measures helped maintain the home market but did little to overcome industrial stagnation. Relations between labor and management were tense.

The first political fallout of the depression was the election of another radical coalition government in 1932. Fearful of contributing to inflation as it had after 1924, the radical government pursued a generally deflationary

In February 1934 right-wing street riots broke out in Paris as a result of the political handling of the Stavisky Affair. Within a year these riots had given rise to new cooperation among French left-wing parties who feared the threat from the right. [The Granger Collection.]

policy. In the same year that the new ministry took office, reparation payments had stopped. As the economic crisis tightened, normal parliamentary and political life became a shambles.

Outside the Chamber of Deputies politics assumed a very ugly face. The old divisions between left and right hardened. Various right-wing groups with authoritarian tendencies became active. These leagues included the *Action Française*, founded prior to World War I in the wake of the Dreyfus Affair, and the *Croix de Feu*, composed of army veterans. The memberships of these and other similar groups numbered somewhat more than two million persons. Some wanted a monarchy; others favored what would have amounted to military rule. They were hostile to the idea of parliamentary government, socialism, and communism. They wanted what they regarded as the greater good and glory of the nation to be set above the petty machinations of political parties. In this regard they resembled the Fascists and the Nazis. Their activities and propaganda aided the dissolution of loyalty to republican government and injected bitterness and vindictiveness into French political life. The leagues also created one moment of extraordinary havoc that produced important long-range political consequences.

The incident grew out of the Stavisky affair, the last of those curious *causes célèbres* that punctuated the political fortunes of the Third Republic. Serge Stavisky was a small-time gangster who appears to have had good connections within the government. In 1933 he became involved in a fraudulent bond scheme. When finally tracked down by the police, he committed suicide in January 1934. The official handling of the matter suggested a political coverup. It was alleged that people in high places wished to halt the investigation. To the right wing in France the Stavisky incident symbolized all the seaminess, immorality, and corruption of republican politics. On February 6, 1934, a very large demonstration of the right-wing leagues took place in Paris. The exact purpose and circumstances of the rally remain uncertain, but the crowd did attempt to march on the Chamber of Deputies. Violence occurred. Fourteen demonstrators were killed; scores of others were injured. It was the largest disturbance in Paris since the Commune of 1871.

In the wake of the night of February 6, the radical ministry of Edouard Daladier (1884–1970) resigned and was replaced by a national coalition government composed of all living former premiers. The Chamber of Deputies permitted the ministry to deal with economic matters by decree. However, the major result of the right-wing demonstrations was a political self-reassessment by the parties of the left. Radicals, socialists, and communists began to realize that a right-wing *coup* might be possible in France. Consequently, between 1934 and 1936 the French left began to make peace within its own ranks. This was no easy task. French Socialists, led by Léon Blum (1872–1950), had been the major target of the French Communists since the split over joining the Comintern in 1920. Only Stalin's fear of fascism as a danger to the Soviet Union made this new cooperation possible. In spite of deep suspicions on all sides, the Popular Front had been established by Bastille Day in 1935. Its purpose was to preserve the republic and to press for social reform.

The election of 1936 gave the Popular Front a majority in the Chamber of Deputies. The Socialists were the largest single party for the first time in French history. Consequently they organized the cabinet as they had long promised they would do when they constituted the majority party of a coalition. Léon Blum assumed the premiership on June 5, 1936. From the early twenties this Jewish intellectual and humanitarian had opposed the communist version of socialism. Cast as the successor to

Jean Jaurès, who had been assassinated in 1914, Blum wanted socialism in the context of democratic, parliamentary government. He hoped to bring France a program akin to the New Deal that President Franklin Roosevelt had carried out in the United States.

During May 1936, before the Popular Front came to power, strikes had begun to spread throughout French industry. Immediately after assuming office on June 6, the Blum government faced further spontaneous work stoppages involving over a half million workers who had occupied factories in sit-down strikes. These were the most extensive labor disturbances in the history of the Third Republic. They aroused new fears in the conservative business community, which had already been frightened by the election of the Popular Front. Blum acted swiftly to bring together representatives of labor and management. On June 8 he announced the conclusion of the Matignon Accord, which reorganized labor–management relations in France. Wages were immediately raised from 7 to 15 per cent, depending on the job involved. Workers became free to join unions and to bargain collectively with employers. Annual paid two-week vacations for workers were adopted. The forty-hour week was established throughout French industry. Blum hoped to overcome labor hostility to French society, to establish a foundation for justice in labor–management relations, and to increase the domestic consumer demand of the nation.

Blum's labor policy was followed by other bold departures. He raised the salaries of civil servants and instituted a program of public works. Government loans were extended to small industry. Spending on armaments was increased, and some armament industries were nationalized. To aid agriculture, he set up a National Wheat Board to rationalize the production and sale of grain. Initially he had promised to resist devaluation of the franc. However, by the autumn of 1936 international monetary pressure forced him to devalue. He did so again in the spring of 1937. The devaluations brought little aid to French exports because they came too late. All of these

French Management and Labor Reach an Agreement

When the Popular Front government came to power in France in 1936, it immediately confronted widespread strikes. Premier Léon Blum called together the representatives of labor and management. The result of these negotiations was the Matignon Accord, which gave the unions more secure rights, raised wages, and brought the strikes to an end.

THE *delegates of the General Confederation of French Production (CGPF) and the General Confederation of Labour (CGT) have met under the chairmanship of the Premier (Léon Blum) and have concluded the following agreement, after arbitration by the Premier:*

1. The employer delegation agrees to the immediate conclusion of collective agreements.

2. These agreements must include, in particular, articles 3 and 5 below.

3. All citizens being required to abide by law, the employers recognize the freedom of opinion of workers and their right to freely join and belong to trade unions.

In their decisions on hiring, organization or assignment of work, disciplinary measures or dismissals, employers agree not to take into consideration the fact of membership or nonmembership in a union. . . .

The exercise of trade union rights must not give rise to acts contrary to law.

4. The wages actually paid to all workers as of 25 May 1936 will be raised, as of the resumption of work, by a decreasing percentage ranging from 15 per cent for the lowest rates down to 7 per cent for the highest rates. In no case must the total increase in any establishment exceed 12 per cent. . . .

The negotiations, which are to be launched at once, for the determination by collective agreement of minimum wages by regions and by occupations must take up, in particular, the necessary revision of abnormally low wages. . . .

. . . .

6. The employer delegation promises that there will be no sanctions for strike activities.

7. The CGT delegation will ask the workers on strike to return to work as soon as the managements of establishments have accepted this general agreement and as soon as negotiations for its application have begun between the managements and the personnel of the establishments.

V. R. Lorwin, *The French Labour Movement* (Cambridge, Mass.: Harvard University Press, 1954), pp. 313–315.

A display of unity by leaders of the French Popular
Front at a Bastille Day rally in Paris, July 14,
1937. Léon Blum of the Socialist Party is on the
left with Mme. Blum, and Maurice Thorez (1900–1964),
the Secretary of the French Communist Party, stands
beside him on the right. [Photo Trends.]

moves enraged the conservative banking and business
community. In March 1937 they brought sufficient influence to bear upon the ministry to cause Blum to halt
the program of reform. It was not taken up again. Blum's
Popular Front colleagues considered the pause in reform
an unnecessary compromise. In June 1937 Blum resigned. The Popular Front ministry itself held on until
April 1938, when it was replaced by a radical ministry
under Daladier.

The Popular Front had brought much hope to labor
and to socialists, but it did not lead France out of the
depression. Some of its programs actually harmed production. The business community, because of its apprehensions and hostility, became even less venturesome
after the Popular Front reforms. Not until 1939 did
French industrial production reach the level of 1929. In a
sense the Popular Front had come too late to give either
the economy or French political life new vitality. Internal
divisions and conservative opposition meant that the Popular Front had enjoyed less than a free hand. By the close
of the thirties citizens from all walks of life had begun to
wonder if the republic was worth preserving. The left
continued to remain divided. Businessmen found the
republic inefficient and in their opinion too much subject
to socialist pressures. The right wing hated the republic
in principle. When the time came in 1940 to defend the
republic, there were too many citizens who were less
than sure that it was worth defending.

Germany: The Nazi Seizure of Power

Depression and Political Deadlock

The outflow of foreign, and especially American, capital from Germany commencing in 1928 undermined the economic prosperity of the Weimar Republic. The resulting economic crisis brought parliamentary government to an end. In 1928 a coalition of center parties and the Social Democrats governed. All went reasonably well until the depression struck. Then the coalition partners differed sharply on economic policy. The Social Democrats wanted no reduction in social and unemployment insurance. The more conservative parties, remembering the inflation of 1923, insisted upon a balanced budget. The coalition dissolved in March 1930. To resolve the parliamentary deadlock in the *Reichstag*, President von Hindenburg appointed Heinrich Bruening (1885–1970) as chancellor. Lacking a majority in the *Reichstag*, the new chancellor governed through emergency presidential decrees as authorized by Article 48 of the constitution. The party divisions in the *Reichstag* prevented the overriding of the decrees. In this manner the Weimar Republic was transformed into a presidential dictatorship.

German unemployment rose from 2,258,000 in March 1930 to over 6,000,000 in March 1932. There had been persistent unemployment during the twenties, but nothing of such magnitude or duration. The economic downturn and the parliamentary deadlock worked to the advantage of the more extreme political parties. In the election of 1928 the Nazis had won only 12 seats in the *Reichstag*, and the Communists had won 54 seats. Two years later, after the election of 1930, the Nazis held 107 seats and the Communists 77.

The power of the Nazis in the streets was also on the rise. The unemployment fed thousands of men into the Stormtroopers, which had 100,000 members in 1930 and almost 1 million in 1933. The SA freely and viciously attacked Communists and Social Democrats. For the Nazis politics meant the capture of power through the instruments of terror and intimidation as well as by legal elections. Anything resembling decency and civility in political life vanished. The Nazis held rallies that resembled secular religious revivals. They paraded through the streets and the countryside. They gained powerful supporters and sympathizers in the business, military, and newspaper communities. Some intellectuals were also sympathetic. The Nazis were able to transform this discipline and enthusiasm born of economic despair and nationalistic frustration into impressive electoral results.

Hitler Comes to Power

For two years Bruening continued to govern through the confidence of Hindenburg. The economy did not improve, and the political situation deteriorated. In 1932 the eighty-three-year-old president stood for reelection. Hitler ran against him and forced a runoff. In the first election the Nazi leader garnered 30.1 per cent of the vote, and he later gained 36.8 per cent in the second. Although Hindenburg was returned to office, the results of the poll convinced him that Bruening no longer commanded sufficient confidence from conservative German voters. On May 30, 1932, he dismissed Bruening and appointed Franz von Papen (1879–1969) in his place. The new chancellor was one of a small group of extremely conservative advisers upon whom the aged Hindenburg had become increasingly dependent. Others included the president's son and several military figures. With the continued paralysis in the *Reichstag*, their influence over the president virtually amounted to control of the government. Consequently the crucial decisions of the next several months were made by only a handful of people.

Von Papen and the circle around the president wanted to find some way to draw the Nazis into cooperation with them without giving any effective power to Hitler. The government needed the mass popular support that only the Nazis seemed able to generate. The Hindenburg circle decided to convince Hitler that the Nazis could not come to power on their own. Von Papen removed the ban on Nazi meetings that Bruening had imposed and

Hitler and President von Hindenburg pictured riding together in an open carriage in 1933 shortly after the aged president had appointed Hitler chancellor. After von Hindenburg's death the next year, Hitler assumed the powers of the presidency as well as those of the chancellorship. [Culver Pictures.]

election for July 1932. The Nazis won 230 ...ed 37.2 per cent of the vote. As the price for ...to the cabinet, Hitler demanded appointment ...cellor. Hindenburg refused. Another election was ...d in November, partly as a means of wearing down ...ne Nazis' financial resources. It was successful in that regard. The number of Nazi seats fell to 196, and their percentage of the popular vote dipped to 33.1 per cent. The advisers around Hindenburg still refused to appoint Hitler to office.

In late December 1932 Von Papen resigned, and Kurt von Schleicher (1882–1934) became chancellor. There now existed much fear of civil war between groups on the left and right. Von Schleicher decided to attempt the construction of a broad-based coalition of conservative groups and trade unionists. The prospect of such a coalition, including groups from the political left, frightened the Hindenburg circle even more than the prospect of Hitler. They did not trust Von Schleicher's motives, which have never been very clear. Consequently they persuaded Hindenburg to appoint Hitler as chancellor. To control him and to see that he did little mischief, Von Papen was to be named vice-chancellor. On January 30, 1933, Adolph Hitler became the chancellor of Germany.

Hitler's Consolidation of Power

Hitler had come into office by legal means. All of the proper legal forms and procedures had been observed. This fact was very important, for it permitted the civil service, the courts, and the other agencies of the government to support him with good conscience. He had forged a rigidly disciplined party structure and had mastered the techniques of mass politics and propaganda. He understood how to touch the raw social and political nerves of the electorate. His major support came from the lower middle class, the farmers, and the young. Each of these groups had especially suffered from the insecurity of the twenties and the depression of the early thirties. Hitler promised them security against communists and socialists, effective government in place of the petty poli-

The Reichstag fire of February 27, 1933 created fear of a Communist revolution in Germany. In this political atmosphere the Nazis completed their seizure of power. [The Granger Collection.]

tics of the other parties, and an uncompromising nationalist vision of a strong, restored Germany.

Much credit was once given to German big business for the rise of Hitler. However, little evidence exists that business money financed the Nazis in a fashion that made any crucial difference to their success or failure. Hitler's supporters were frequently suspicious of business and giant capitalism. They wanted a simpler world and one in which small property would be safe from both socialism and large-scale capitalist consolidation. These people looked to Hitler and the Nazis rather than to the Social Democrats because the latter, though concerned with social issues, never appeared sufficiently nationalistic. The Nazis won out over other conservative nationalistic parties because, unlike the latter, they did address themselves to the problem of lower-middle-class social insecurity.

Once in office Hitler moved with almost lightning speed to consolidate his control. There were three facets to this process: the capture of full legal authority, the crushing of alternative political groups, and the purging of rivals within the Nazi Party itself.

On February 23, 1933, a mentally ill Dutch communist set fire to the *Reichstag* building in Berlin. The Nazis quickly turned the incident to their own advantage by claiming that the fire proved the existence of an immediate communist threat against the government. To the public it seemed plausible that the Communists might attempt some action against the state now that the Nazis

were in power. Under Article 48 Hitler suspended the civil liberties and proceeded to arrest Communists or alleged Communists. This decree was not revoked for as long as Hitler ruled Germany.

In early March another *Reichstag* election took place. The Nazis still received only 43.9 per cent of the vote. However, the arrest of the newly elected Communist deputies and the fear stemming from the fire meant that Hitler could control the *Reichstag* without a formal coalition. On March 23, 1933, the *Reichstag* passed an Enabling Act that permitted Hitler to rule by decree. Thereafter there were no legal limits on his exercise of power. The Weimar Constitution was never formally repealed or amended. It had simply been supplanted by the February Emergency Decree and the March Enabling Act.

Perhaps better than anyone else Hitler understood that he and his party had not inevitably come to power. All of his potential opponents had stood divided between 1929 and 1933. He intended to prevent them from regrouping. In a series of complex moves Hitler outlawed or undermined various German institutions that might have served as rallying points for opposition. In early May 1933 the offices, banks, and newspapers of the free trade unions were seized, and their leaders were arrested. This action was taken by the Nazi Party itself rather than by any government agency. In late June and early July all of the other German political parties were outlawed. By July 14, 1933, the National Socialists were the only legal party in Germany. During the same months the Nazis had moved against the governments of the individual federal states in Germany. By the close of 1933 all major institutions of potential opposition had been eliminated.

The final element in Hitler's consolidation of power involved the Nazi Party itself. By late 1933 the SA, or Stormtroopers, consisted of approximately one million active members and a larger number of reserves. The commander of this party army was Ernst Roehm, a possible rival to Hitler himself. The German army officer corps, upon whom Hitler depended to rebuild the national army, were jealous of the SA leadership. Conse-

The Nazi Party utilized massive rallies as one of
the major ways in which to show off its power. This
one took place in Nuremberg in 1938, and the
particular day shown in this photograph was devoted
to the Nazi youth movement. [Bildarchiv Preussischer
Kulturbesitz.]

quently, to protect his own position and to shore up support with the regular army, on June 30, 1934, Hitler personally ordered the murder of key SA officers, including Roehm. Others killed between June 30 and July 2 included the former chancellor General Kurt von Schleicher and his wife. The exact number of victims purged is unknown, but it has been estimated to have exceeded one hundred persons. The German army, which was the only institution in the nation that might have prevented the murders, did nothing. A month later, on August 2, 1934, President Von Hindenburg died. Thereafter the offices of chancellor and president were combined. Hitler was now the sole ruler of Germany and of the Nazi Party.

The Police State

Terror and intimidation had been a major factor in the Nazi march to office. As Hitler consolidated his power, he oversaw the organization of a police state. The chief vehicle of police surveillance was the SS, or security units, commanded by Heinrich Himmler (1900–1945). This group had originated in the mid-twenties as a bodyguard for Hitler and became a more elite paramilitary organization than the larger SA. In 1933 the SS was composed of approximately fifty-two thousand members. It was the instrument that carried out the blood purges of the party in 1934. By 1936 Himmler had become head of all police matters in Germany and stood second only to Hitler in power and influence.

The police character of the Nazi regime was all-pervasive, but the people who most consistently experienced the terror of the police state were German Jews. Anti-Semitism had been a key plank of the Nazi program. It was anti-Semitism based on biological racial theories stemming from late nineteenth-century thought rather than from religious discrimination. Prior to World War II the Nazi attack on the Jews went through three stages of increasing intensity. In 1933, shortly after assuming power, the Nazis excluded Jews from offices in the civil service. For a time they also attempted to enforce

The Nazis Pass Their Racial Legislation

Anti-Semitism had been a fundamental tenet of the Nazi Party and became a major policy of the Nazi government. This comprehensive legislation of September 15, 1935 carried anti-Semitism into all areas of public life and into some of the most personal areas of private life as well. It was characteristically titled the Law for the Protection of German Blood and Honor. Hardly any aspect of Nazi thought and action was as shocking to the non-German world as was their policy toward Jews.

IMBUED *with the knowledge that the purity of German blood is the necessary prerequisite for the existence of the German nation, and inspired by an inflexible will to maintain the existence of the German nation for all future times, the Reichstag has unanimously adopted the following law, which is now enacted:*

ARTICLE *I: (1) Any marriages between Jews and citizens of German or kindred blood are herewith forbidden. Marriages entered into despite this law are invalid, even if they are arranged abroad as a means of circumventing this law.*

(2) Annulment proceedings for marriages may be initiated only by the Public Prosecutor.

ARTICLE *II: Extramarital relations between Jews and citizens of German or kindred blood are herewith forbidden.*

ARTICLE *III: Jews are forbidden to employ as servants to their households female subjects of German or kindred blood who are under the age of forty-five years.*

ARTICLE *IV: (1) Jews are prohibited from displaying the Reich and national flag and from showing the national colors.*

(2) However, they may display the Jewish colors. The exercise of this right is under state protection.

ARTICLE *V: (1) Anyone who acts contrary to the prohibition noted in Article I renders himself liable to penal servitude.*

(2) The man who acts contrary to the prohibiton of Article II will be punished by sentence to either a jail or penitentiary.

(3) Anyone who acts contrary to the provisions of Articles III and IV will be punished with a jail sentence up to a year and with a fine, or with one of these penalties.

ARTICLE *VI: The Reich Minister of Interior, in conjunction with the Deputy to the Führer and the Reich Minister of Justice, will issue the required legal and administrative decrees for the implementation and amplification of this law.*

Two of Hitler's chief henchmen: [LEFT] Heinrich Himmler (1900-1945), who was head of the Nazi secret police; and [RIGHT] Joseph Goebbels (1897-1945), who headed the Nazi propaganda drive at home and abroad. [BOTH: The Granger Collection.]

ARTICLE *VII: This law shall go into effect on the day following its promulgation, with the exception of Article III, which shall go into effect on January 1, 1936.*

Louis L. Snyder (Ed. and Trans.), *Documents of German History* (New Brunswick, N.J.: Rutgers University Press, 1958), pp. 427-428.

During the night of November 9, 1938, all across Germany the windows of stores owned by Jewish businessmen were smashed in one of the major Nazi pre-war outbursts of anti-Semitism. This photograph was made in Berlin the following day. The Nazis then confiscated the insurance money and refused to allow the Jewish businesses to be compensated for their losses. [The Granger Collection.]

boycotts of Jewish shops and businesses. In 1935 a series of measures known as the Nuremberg Laws robbed German Jews of their citizenship. All persons with at least three Jewish grandparents were defined as Jews. The professions and the major occupations were closed to Jews. Marriage and sexual intercourse between Jews and non-Jews were prohibited. Legal exclusion and humiliation of Jews became the order of the day.

The persecution of the Jews increased again in 1938. Business careers were forbidden. In November 1938, under orders from the Nazi Party, thousands of Jewish stores and synagogues were burned or otherwise destroyed. The Jewish community itself was required to pay for the damage because the government confiscated the insurance money. In all manner of other ways, large and petty, the German Jews were harassed. This persecution allowed the Nazis to inculcate the rest of the population with the concept of a master race of pure German "Aryans" and also to display their own contempt for civil liberties. After the war broke out, Hitler decided in 1942 to destroy the Jews in Europe. It is thought that over six million Jews, mostly from east European nations, died as a result of that staggering decision, unprecedented in its scope and implementation.

Nazi Economic Policy

Besides consolidating power and persecuting allegedly inferior races, Hitler still had to confront the reality of the depression. German unemployment had been a major factor in his rise to power. The Nazis attacked this problem and achieved a degree of success that astonished and frightened the rest of Europe. By 1936, while the rest of the European economy continued to stagnate, the

specter of unemployment and other difficulties associated with the depression for all intents and purposes no longer haunted Germany. So far as the economic crisis was concerned, Hitler had become the most effective political leader in Europe. This fact was a most important element in accounting for the internal strength and support of his tyrannical regime. The Nazi success against the depression provided the regime with considerable contemporary credibility. As might be expected, the cost in terms of liberty and human dignity had been very high.

Hitler reversed the deflationary policy of the cabinets that had preceded him. He instituted what amounted to a massive program of public works and spending. Many of these projects related directly or indirectly to rearmament. Canals were built, and land was reclaimed. Construction of a large system of highways with clear military uses was begun. Some unemployed workers were sent back to farms if they had originally come from there. Other laborers were frozen in their jobs and were not permitted to change employment. Renunciation of the military provisions of the Versailles Treaty in 1935 led to open rearmament and expansion of the army with little opposition, as will be explained in Chapter 33. These measures essentially restored full employment. In 1936 Hitler instructed Hermann Goering (1893–1946), who had headed the air force since 1933, to undertake a Four-Year Plan to prepare the army and the economy for war. The state determined that Germany must be economically self-sufficient. Armaments received top priority. This economic program satisfied both the yearning for social and economic security and the desire for national fulfillment.

Nazi economic policies maintained private property and private capitalism. However, all significant economic enterprise and decisions became subordinated to the goals of the state. Prices were controlled and investments restricted. Currency regulation interfered with trade. Production that related to the military buildup received top priority and even redirected some industries. For example, in the late thirties, the German chemical producers diverted a large proportion of their resources toward the manufacture of various synthetics. With the crushing of the trade unions in 1933, strikes became illegal. There was no genuine collective bargaining. The government handled labor disputes through compulsory arbitration. Both workers and employers were required to participate in the Labor Front, the existence of which was intended to prove that class conflict had ended. It sponsored a "Strength Through Joy" program that provided vacations and other forms of recreation for the labor force. However, behind the direction of both business and labor stood the Nazi terror and police. The Nazi economic experiment proved that with the sacrifice of all political and civil liberty, of a free trade union movement, of private exercise of capital, and of consumer satisfaction, full employment for the purposes of war and aggression could be achieved.

The architect Albert Speer (born 1905) became a
favored member of Hitler's inner circle. He and
Hitler developed plans for an entire new design for
the city of Berlin. On the [LEFT] is a photograph of
the model designed by Speer for the new capital of
Hitler's Reich. In the center is the Brandenburg
Gate, the only major structure planned for preservation from Berlin's past. Beyond the gate is Unter
den Linden running up the picture to a vast domed
structure on the site of the former royal palace
and lined left and right with the massive offices
of the government.

On the [RIGHT] is one of the few structures
actually to be completed, the German Chancellory,
used by the Nazis until its destruction in World
War II.

[CHANCELLORY: Ullstein Bilderdienst. MODEL:
Courtesy Albert Speer. Photo Hermann Speer.]

Hermann Göring (1893-1946), Hitler's second in
command, is here photographed flanked by other
Nazi officers. [United Press International Photo.]

Fascist Economics in Italy

The Fascists had promised to bring order to the instability of Italian social and economic life. Discipline was a substitute for economic policy and creativity. During the twenties Mussolini undertook programs of public works, such as draining the Pontine Marshes for settlement. The shipping industry was subsidized, and protective tariffs were introduced. Mussolini desperately sought to make Italy self-sufficient. He embarked on the "battle of wheat" to prevent foreign grain from appearing in products on Italian tables. There was an extraordinary expansion of wheat farming in Italy. However, these policies did not keep the depression from affecting Italy. Production, exports, and wages fell. Even the increased wheat production backfired. So much poor marginal land that was expensive to cultivate came into production that the domestic price of wheat and thus of much food actually rose.

Both before and during the depression the Fascists sought to steer an economic course between socialism and a liberal *laissez-faire* system. Their policy was known as *Corporatism*. It constituted a planned economy linked to the private ownership of capital and to government arbitration of labor disputes. Major industries were first organized into syndicates representing labor and management. The two groups negotiated labor settlements within this framework and submitted differences to compulsory government arbitration. The Fascists contended that class conflict would be avoided if both labor and management looked to the greater goal of productivity for the nation. It is a matter of considerable dispute whether this arrangement favored workers or managers. What is certain is that from the mid-twenties Italian labor unions lost the right to strike and to pursue their own independent economic goals.

After 1930 these industrial syndicates were further organized into entities called *corporations*. These bodies included all industries relating to a major area of production, such as sugar beets or metallurgy, from raw materials through finished product and distribution. A total of twenty-two such corporations were established to encompass the whole economy. In 1938 Mussolini abolished the Italian Chamber of Deputies and replaced it with a Chamber of Corporations. This vast organization framework did not increase production; instead, it led to excessive bureaucracy and corruption. The corporate state allowed the government to direct much of the nation's economic life without a formal change in ownership. Consumers and owners simply no longer could determine what was to be produced. The Fascist government gained further direct economic power through the Institute for Industrial Reconstruction, which extended loans to businesses in financial difficulty. The loans, in effect, established partial state ownership.

How corporatism might have affected the Italian economy in the long run cannot really be calculated. In 1935 Italy invaded Ethiopia. Economic life was put on a formal wartime footing. The League of Nations imposed economic sanctions, urging member nations to refrain from purchasing Italian goods. Thereafter taxes rose. During 1935 the government imposed a forced loan on the citizenry by requiring property owners to purchase bonds. Wages continued to be depressed. As the international tensions increased during the late thirties, the Italian state assumed more and more direction over the economy. The order of Facism in Italy had not proved to be an order of prosperity. It had brought economic dislocation and a falling standard of living.

Stalin's Five-Year Plans and Purges

While the capitalist economies of western Europe floundered in the doldrums of the depression, the Soviet Union entered upon a period of tremendous industrial advance. Like similar eras of past Russian economic progress, the direction and impetus came from the top. Stalin far exceeded his tsarist predecessors in the intensity of state coercion and terror he brought to the task. Russia achieved its stunning economic growth during the thirties only at the cost of literally millions of human lives and the degradation of still other millions. Stalin's economic policy clearly proved that his earlier rivalry with Trotsky had been a matter of political power rather than one of substantial ideological difference.

The Decision for Rapid Industrialization

Through 1928 Lenin's New Economic Policy, as championed by Bukharin with Stalin's support, had charted the course of Soviet economic development. Private ownership and enterprise were permitted to flourish in the countryside as a means of ensuring an adequate food supply for workers in the cities. A few farmers, the *kulaks*, had become quite prosperous. They probably numbered less than 5 per cent of the rural population. During 1928 and 1929 these and other farmers withheld grain from the market because of dissatisfaction with prices. Food shortages occurred in the cities and provided a cause of potential unrest against the regime. The goals of NEP were no longer being fulfilled. Sometime during these troubled months Stalin came to a momentous decision. Russia must industrialize rapidly in order to match the economic and military power of the West. Agriculture must be collectivized to produce sufficient grain for food and export and to free peasant labor for factories. This program, which basically embraced Trotsky's earlier economic position, unleashed nothing less than a second Russian revolution. The costs and character of "Socialism in One Country" now became clear.

AGRICULTURAL POLICY. In 1929 Stalin ordered party agents into the countryside to confiscate any hoarded wheat. The *kulaks* were blamed for the grain shortages. As part of the general plan to erase the private ownership of land and to collectivize farming, a program was undertaken to eliminate the *kulaks* as a class. However, the definition of a *kulak* soon embraced anyone who opposed Stalin's policy. In the countryside there was extensive resistance from peasants and farmers at all levels of wealth. The stubborn peasants were determined to keep their land. They wreaked their own vengeance on

the policy of collectivization by slaughtering more than 100 million horses and cattle between 1929 and 1933. The situation in the countryside amounted to nothing less than open warfare. The peasant resistance caused Stalin to call a brief halt to the process in March 1930. He justified the slowdown on the grounds of "dizziness from success."

Soon thereafter the drive to collectivize the farms was renewed with vehemence, but the costs remained very high. As many as ten million peasants were killed, and millions of others were sent forcibly to collective farms or labor camps. Initially, because of the turmoil on the land, agricultural production fell. There was famine in 1932 and 1933. Milk and meat remained in short supply because of the livestock slaughter. Yet Stalin persevered. The uprooted peasants were moved to thousand-acre collective farms. The machinery for these units was provided by the state through machine-tractor stations. In this fashion the state retained control over major farm machines. That monopoly was a powerful weapon.

The upheaval of collectivization did change Russian farming in a very dramatic way. In 1928 approximately 98 per cent of Russian farmland consisted of small peasant holdings. Ten years later, despite all of the opposition, over 90 per cent of the land had been collectivized. During the same period agricultural production had increased approximately 15 per cent, but the quantity of farm produce directly handled by the government had risen by 40 per cent. Those shifts in control meant that the government now had primary direction over the food supply. The farmers and peasants could no longer determine whether there would be stability or unrest in the cities. Stalin and the Communist Party had won the battle of the wheat fields, but they had not solved the problem of producing sufficient quantities of grain. That difficulty has continued to plague the Soviet Union to the present day.

THE FIVE-YEAR PLANS. The revolution in agriculture had been undertaken for the sake of industrialization. The increased grain supply was to feed the labor force and provide exports to finance the imports required for industrial development. The scope of the industrial achievement of the Soviet Union between 1928 and World War II stands as one of the most striking accomplishments of the twentieth century. Russia made a more rapid advance toward economic growth than any other nation in the Western world has ever achieved during any similar period of time. By even the conservative estimates of Western observers, Soviet industrial production rose approximately 400 per cent between 1928 and 1940. Emphasis was placed on the production of iron, steel, coal, electrical power, tractors, combines, railway cars, and other heavy machinery. Few consumer goods were produced. The labor for this development was supplied internally. Capital was raised from the export of grain even at the cost of internal shortage. The technology was generally borrowed from already-industrialized nations.

The organizational vehicle for industrialization was a series of Five-Year Plans first begun in 1928. The State Planning Commission, or Gosplan, oversaw the program. It set goals of production and organized the economy to meet them. The task of coordinating all facets of production was immensely difficult and complicated. Deliveries of materials from mines or factories had to be assured before the next unit could carry out its part of the plan. There was many a slip between the cup and the lip. The troubles in the countryside were harmful. A vast program of propaganda was undertaken to sell the Five-Year Plans to the Russian people and to elicit cooperation. However, the industrial labor force soon became subject to regimentation similar to that being imposed on the peasants. By the close of the thirties the accomplishment of the three Five-Year Plans was truly impressive and probably allowed the Soviet Union to survive the German invasion. Industries that had never existed in Russia now challenged and in some cases, such as tractor production, surpassed their counterparts in the rest of the world. Large, new industrial cities had been built and populated by hundreds of thousands of people.

Stalin Explains the Problem of Agriculture

By the late 1920s Stalin had changed his earlier views and had decided that the Soviet Union must industrialize rapidly. That shift meant that the agricultural sector must also be modernized in order to feed industrial workers and to pay for needed imports. Stalin saw the means to improved farming in the large scale collectivization of agriculture and the introduction of farm machinery. When implemented, this policy led to widespread peasant resistance in the countryside.

THE *characteristic feature of the present state of our national economy is that we are faced by the fact of an excessive lag in the rate of development of grain farming behind the rate of development of industry, while at the same time the demand for marketable grain on the part of the growing towns and industrial areas is increasing by leaps and bounds. The task then is not to lower the rate of development of industry to the level of the development of grain farming . . . , but to bring the rate of development of grain farming into line with the rate of development of industry and to raise the rate of development of grain farming to a level that will guarantee rapid progress of the entire national economy, both industry and agriculture.*

Either we accomplish this task, and thereby solve the grain problem, or we do not accomplish it, and then a rupture between the socialist town and the small-peasant countryside will be inevitable.

.   .   .   .

What ways and means are necessary to accelerate the rate of development of agriculture in general, and of grain farming in particular?

There are three such ways, or channels:
(a) By increasing crop yields and enlarging the area sown by the individual poor and middle peasants.
(b) By further development of collective farms.
(c) By enlarging the old and establishing new state farms.

.   .   .   .

I should like to draw your attention to the collective farms, and especially to the states farms, as levers which facilitate the reconstruction of agriculture on a new technical basis, causing a revolution in the minds of the peasants and helping them to shake off conservatism, routine. The appearance of tractors, large agricultural machines and tractor columns in our grain regions cannot but have its effect on the surrounding peasant farms. Assistance rendered the surrounding peasants in the way of seed, machines and tractors will undoubtedly be appre-

By the late 1930s the cult of Stalin was an ever-present fact of Soviet life. Even at beach resorts his picture was always near. In this 1950 photograph swimmers in the Black Sea carry large pictures of him on small rafts. Notice the war ships in the background. [Sovfoto.]

ciated by the peasants and taken as a sign of the power and strength of the Soviet State, which is trying to lead them on to the high road of a substantial improvement of agriculture.

J. Stalin, *Collected Works* (Moscow: Foreign Language Publishing House, 1952–1956), Vol. 11 pp. 268–269, 272, 279. Originally written in 1928.

Many non-Russian contemporaries looked at the Soviet economic experiment quite uncritically. While the capitalist world lay in the throes of depression, the Soviet economy had grown at a pace never realized in the West. The American writer Lincoln Steffens reported after a trip to Russia, "I have seen the future and it works." Beatrice and Sydney Webb, the British Fabian socialists, spoke of "a new civilization" in the Soviet Union. These and other similar writers ignored the shortages in consumer goods and the poor housing. More important, they seem to have had little idea of the social cost of the Soviet achievement. Millions of human beings had been killed and millions more uprooted. The total picture of suffering

and human loss during those years will probably never be known; however, the deprivation and sacrifice of Soviet citizens far exceeded anything described by Marx and Engels in relation to nineteenth-century industrialization in western Europe.

The internal difficulties caused by collectivization and industrialization led Stalin to make an important shift in foreign policy. In 1934 he began to fear that the nation might be left isolated against future aggression by Nazi Germany. The Soviet Union was not yet strong enough to withstand such an attack. Consequently that year he ordered the Comintern to permit communist parties in other countries to cooperate with non-communist political parties against Nazism and fascism. This marked a reversal of the Comintern policy established by Lenin as part of the Twenty-one Conditions in 1919. The new Stalinist policy originating from Moscow allowed the formation of the Popular Front government in France.

After more than a decade of vicious rivalry between communists and democratic socialists, for a few years the two groups would attempt to cooperate against the common right-wing foe.

The Purges

Stalin's decisions to industrialize rapidly, to move against the peasants, and to reverse the Comintern policy did arouse internal political opposition. They were all departures from the policies of Lenin. In 1929 Stalin forced Bukharin, the fervent supporter of NEP and his own former ally, off the Politburo. Little detailed information is known about further opposition, but it does seem to have existed among lower-level party followers of Bukharin and other previous opponents of rapid industrialization. Sometime in 1933 Stalin began to fear loss of control over the party apparatus and the emergence of possibly effective rivals. These fears were probably produced as much by his own paranoia as by real plots. Nevertheless they resulted in the Great Purges, one of the most mysterious and horrendous political events of this century. The purges were not understood at the time and have not been fully comprehended either inside or outside the Soviet Union to the present day.

On December 1, 1934, Sergei Kirov (1888–1934), the popular party chief of Leningrad and a member of the Politburo, was assassinated. In the wake of the shooting thousands of people were arrested, and still larger numbers were expelled from the party and sent to labor camps. At the time it was believed that Kirov had been murdered by opponents of the regime. Direct or indirect complicity in the crime became the normal accusation against the persons whom Stalin attacked. It now seems practically certain that Stalin himself authorized Kirov's assassination in fear of eventual rivalry with the Leningrad leader.

The purges after Kirov's death were just the beginning of a larger process. Between 1936 and 1938 a series of spectacular show trials were held in Moscow. Previous high Soviet leaders, including former members of the Politburo, publicly confessed all manner of political crimes. They were convicted and executed. It is still not certain why they made their palpably false confessions. Still other leaders and lower-level party members were tried in private and shot. Thousands of people received no trial at all. The purges touched persons in all areas of party life. There was apparently little rhyme or reason as to why some were executed, others sent to labor camps, and still others left unmolested. After the civilian party members had been purged, the prosecutors turned against the army. Important officers, including heroes of the civil war, were sent to their deaths. Within the party itself hundreds of thousands of members were expelled, and applicants for membership were removed from the rolls. The exact figures for executions, imprisonments, and expulsions are unknown but certainly ran into the millions.

The trials and purges astonished Western observers. Nothing quite like this phenomenon had been seen before. Political murders and executions were not new, but the absurd confessions were novel. The scale of the political turmoil was also unprecedented. Russians themselves did not believe or comprehend what was occurring. There existed no national emergency or crisis. There were only accusations of sympathy for Trotsky or of complicity in Kirov's murder or of other nameless crimes. If a rational explanation is to be sought, it probably must be found in Stalin's concern over his own power. In effect, the purges created a new party structure absolutely loyal to him. The "old Bolsheviks" of the October Revolution were among his earliest targets. They and others active in the first years of the revolution knew how far Stalin had moved from Lenin's policies. New, younger members appeared to replace all of the party members executed or expelled. The newcomers had little knowledge of old Russia or of the ideals of the original Bolsheviks. They had not been loyal to Lenin, to Trotsky, or to any other Soviet leader except Stalin himself.

Scope of the Dictatorships

By the middle of the thirties dictators of the right and the left had established themselves across much of Europe. Political tyranny was hardly new to Europe, but several factors combined to give these rulers unique characteristics. They drew their immediate support from well-organized political parties. Except for the Bolsheviks, these were mass parties. The roots of the popularity of the dictators lay in nationalism, the social frustration of the depression, and political ideologies that promised to transform the social and political orders. So long as the new rulers seemed successful, they were not lacking in support. They had in the eyes of many citizens brought an end to the pettiness of everyday politics.

After coming to power, these dictators possessed a practical monopoly over mass communications. Through the armies, police forces, and party discipline they also held a monopoly on terror and coercive power. They could propagandize large populations and compel large groups of people to obey them and their followers. Finally, as a result of the Second Industrial Revolution, they commanded a vast amount of technology and a capacity for immense destruction. Earlier rulers in Europe may have shared the ruthless ambitions of Hitler, Mussolini, and Stalin, but they had not found at their disposal the ready implements of physical force to impose their wills. Mass political support, monopoly on police and military power, and technological capacity meant that the dictators of the thirties held more extensive sway over their nations than any other group of rulers who had ever governed on the continent. Soon the issue would become whether they would be able to maintain peace among themselves and with their democratic neighbors.

SUGGESTED READINGS

W. S. ALLEN, *The Nazi Seizure of Power: The Experience of a Single German Town, 1930–1935* (1965). A classic treatment of Nazism in a microcosmic setting.

J. COLTON, *Léon Blum: Humanist in Politics* (1966). One of the best biographies of any twentieth-century political figure.

R. CONQUEST, *The Great Terror: Stalin's Purges of the Thirties* (1968). The best treatment of the subject to this date.

G. CRAIG, *Germany, 1866–1945* (1978). An important new survey.

I. DEUTSCHER, *Stalin: A Political Biography,* 2nd ed. (1967). The best biography in English.

M. DOBB, *Soviet Economic Development Since 1917,* 6th ed. (1966). A basic introduction.

H. HOLBORN, *A History of Modern Germany: 1840–1945* (1969). A very comprehensive treatment.

C. KINDLEBERGER, *The World in Depression, 1929–1939* (1973). An account by a leading economist whose analysis is comprehensible to the layman.

D. LANDES, *The Unbound Prometheus: Technological Change and Industrial Development in Western Europe from 1750 to the Present* (1969). Includes an excellent analysis of both the Great Depression and the few areas of economic growth.

W. LAQUEUR AND G. L. MOSSE (Eds.), *The Great Depression* (1970). A useful collection of articles.

V. R. LORWIN, *The French Labor Movement* (1954). A good introduction.

D. SCHOENBAUM, *Hitler's Social Revolution: Class and Status in Nazi Germany* (1966). A fascinating analysis of Hitler's appeal to various social classes.

Reference should also be made to the works cited in Chapter 31.

894

33
World War II and the Cold War

Again the Road to War (1933–1939)

WORLD WAR I and the Versailles Treaty in and of themselves had only a marginal relationship to the world depression of the thirties. But in Germany, where the reparations settlement had contributed to the vast inflation of 1923, economic and social discontent focused on the Versailles settlement as the cause of all ills. Throughout the late twenties Adolf Hitler and the Nazi Party had never ceased denouncing Versailles as the source of all Germany's trouble, and the economic woes of the early thirties seemed to bear them out. Nationalism and attention to the social question, along with party discipline, had been the sources of Nazi success. They would continue to influence Hitler's foreign policy after he became chancellor in early 1933. Moreover the Nazi destruction of the Weimar Constitution and of political opposition meant that to an extraordinary degree German foreign policy lay in Hitler's own hands. Consequently it is important to know what his goals were and what plans he had for achieving them.

Hitler's Goals

For almost twenty years after the outbreak of World War II there was general agreement that the war was the outcome of Hitler's expansionist ambitions, which might have been unlimited but which certainly included vast conquests in eastern Europe and dominance of the European continent. A more recent view is that Hitler was not very much different from any other German statesman,

wanting only a revision of Germany's eastern boundaries, elimination of the restrictions of the Versailles Treaty, "and then to make Germany the greatest power in Europe by her natural weight."[1] The same view asserts that Hitler did not have a consistent plan in foreign policy but was an opportunist who went the way that events and opportunity took him, emphasizing his own statement: "I go the way that Providence dictates with the assurance of a sleepwalker."[2]

The truth appears to be a combination of these apparently contradictory views. From the first expression of his goals in *Mein Kampf* to his last days in the bunker where he died, Hitler's racial theories and goals held the central place in his thought. He meant to go far beyond Germany's 1914 boundaries, which were the limit of the vision of his predecessors. He meant to bring the entire German people (*Volk*), understood as a racial group, together into a single nation. The new Germany would include all the Germanic parts of the old Hapsburg Empire, including Austria. This virile and growing nation would need more space to live (*Lebensraum*), which would be taken from the Slavs, a lesser race, fit only for servitude. The new Germany would be purified by the removal of the Jews, another inferior race in Nazi theory. The plan always required the conquest of Poland and the Ukraine as the primary areas for the settlement of Germans and for the provision of badly needed food. Neither *Mein Kampf* nor later statements of policy were blueprints for action. Hitler was a brilliant improviser who sought after and made good use of opportunities as they arose, but he never lost sight of his goal, which would almost certainly require a major war.

THE DESTRUCTION OF VERSAILLES. When Hitler came to power, Germany was far too weak to

During the 1930s Mussolini of Italy and Hitler of Germany believed they could impose a new political order on Europe. In the end, however, they brought war to the world and destruction and defeat to their nations. [The Granger Collection.]

1 A. J. P. Taylor, *The Origins of the Second World War*, (New York: Atheneum, 1968), p. 70.
2 Quoted by Alan Bullock in "Hitler and the Origins of the Second World War," in E. M. Robertson, ed., *The Origins of the Second World War*, (London: Macmillan and Co., 1971), p. 192.

895

permit the direct approach. The first problem was to shake off the fetters of Versailles and to make Germany a formidable military power. In October of 1933 Germany withdrew from an international disarmament conference and also from the League of Nations. Hitler argued that because the other powers had not disarmed as they had promised, it was wrong to keep Germany helpless. These acts alarmed the French but were merely symbolic. In January of 1934 Germany made a nonaggression pact with Poland that was of greater concern, for it put into question France's chief means of containing the Germans. At last, in March 1935, Hitler formally renounced the disarmament provisions of the Versailles Treaty with the formation of a German Air Force, and soon he reinstated conscription, which aimed at an army of half a million men.

His path was made easier by growing evidence that the League of Nations was ineffective as a device for keeping the peace and that collective security was a myth. In September 1931 Japan occupied Manchuria, provoking an appeal to the League of Nations by China. The league responded by sending out a commission under the Earl of Lytton. The Lytton Report condemned the Japanese for resorting to force, but the powers were unwilling to impose sanctions. Japan withdrew from the league and kept control of Manchuria.

When Hitler announced his decision to rearm Germany, the league formally condemned that action, but it took no action to prevent Germany's rearming. The Allies' response was hostile, but they felt unable to object because they had not carried out their own promises to disarm. Instead, the Allies met with Mussolini in June to form the so-called Stresa Front, making an agreement even to use force to maintain the *status quo* in Europe. But Britain soon made a separate naval agreement with Hitler, allowing him to rebuild the German fleet to an acceptable size, and Italy's expansionist ambitions in Africa soon brought it into conflict with the Western powers. Hitler had taken a major step toward his goal without provoking serious opposition.

Hitler Describes His Goals in Foreign Policy

From his early career, Hitler had certain long-term general views and goals. They were set forth in his *Mein Kampf*, which appeared in 1925, and included consolidation of the German *Volk*, provision of more land for the Germans, contempt for such "races" as Slavs and Jews, and so on. Here are some views on land.

THE *National Socialist movement must strive to eliminate the disproportion between our population and our area—viewing this latter as a source of food as well as a basis for power politics—between our historical past and the hopelessness of our present impotence. . . .*

The demand for restoration of the frontiers of 1914 is a political absurdity of such proportions and consequences as to make it seem a crime. Quite aside from the fact that the Reich's frontiers in 1914 were anything but logical. For in reality they were neither complete in the sense of embracing the people of German nationality, nor sensible with regard to geo-military expediency. . . .

As opposed to this, we National Socialists must hold unflinchingly to our aim in foreign policy, namely, *to secure for the German people the land and soil to which they are entitled on this earth. . . .*

. . . The soil on which some day German generations of peasants can beget powerful sons will sanction the investment of the sons of today, and will some day acquit the responsible statesmen of blood-guilt and sacrifice of the people, even if they are persecuted by their contemporaries. . . .

Much as all of us today recognize the necessity of a reckoning with France, it would remain ineffectual in the long run if it represented the whole of our aim in foreign policy. It can and will achieve meaning only if it offers the rear cover for an enlargement of our people's living space in Europe. . . .

If we speak of soil in Europe today, we can primarily have in mind only Russia *and her vassal border states. . . .*

. . . See to it that the strength of our nation is founded, not on colonies, but on the soil of our European homeland. Never regard the Reich as secure unless for centuries to come it can give every scion of our people his own parcel of soil. Never forget that the most sacred right on this earth is a man's right to have earth to till with his own hands, and the most sacred sacrifice the blood that a man sheds for this earth.

Adolf Hitler, *Mein Kampf*, trans. by Ralph Manheim (Boston: Houghton, Mifflin, 1943), pp. 646, 649, 652, 653, 656.

In 1936, Haile Selassie (1891–1976), the Emperor of Ethiopia, addressed the League of Nations and asked for aid against Italian aggression in his nation. [The Granger Collection.]

Italy Attacks Ethiopia

The Italian attack on Ethiopia made the impotence of the League of Nations and the timidity of the Allies even clearer. Using a border incident as an excuse, Mussolini attacked Ethiopia in October 1935 to avenge the humiliating defeat at Adowa in 1896, to begin the restoration of Roman imperial glory, and, perhaps, to turn the thoughts of Italians away from the corruption of the Fascist regime and their economic misery. France and Britain were eager to appease Mussolini in order to offset the growing power of Germany. They were prepared to allow him the substance of conquest if he would only maintain Ethiopia's formal independence, but for Mussolini the form was more important than the substance. His attack outraged opinion in the West, and the French and British governments were forced at least to appear to resist. The League condemned Italian aggression and, for the first time, voted economic sanctions. It imposed an arms embargo that limited loans and credits to and imports from Italy. But Britain and France were afraid of alienating Mussolini, so they refused to place an embargo on oil, the one economic sanction that could have prevented Italian victory. Even more important, the British fleet did not prevent the movement of Italian troops and munitions through the Suez Canal. The results of this wavering policy were disastrous. The League and collective security were totally discredited, and Mussolini was alienated as well. He now turned to Germany, and by November 1, 1936, he could speak publicly of a Rome–Berlin "Axis."

Remilitarization of the Rhineland

No less important a result of the Ethiopian affair was its effect on Hitler's evaluation of the strength and determination of the Western powers. On March 7, 1936, he took his greatest risk yet, sending a small armed force into the demilitarized Rhineland. This was a breach not only of the Versailles Treaty but of the Locarno Agreements of 1925 as well, agreements that Germany had made voluntarily. It also removed one of the most impor-

Pablo Picasso's Guernica is the artist's vision of the terror-bombing in the Spanish Civil War of the Basque town of Guernica in northern Spain on April 26, 1937 by German airplanes aiding Franco—one of the first calculated aerial bombardments of civilians. It was painted by Picasso in May and June 1937. [Oil on canvas; 11′ 5$\frac{1}{2}$″ × 25′ 5$\frac{3}{4}$″. On extended loan to The Museum of Modern Art, New York, from the artist's estate.] (Another Picasso painting will be found in the color album.)

OPPOSITE: The dotted area on the map shows the large portion of Spain quickly overrun by Franco's insurgent armies during the first year of the war. In the following two years, progress came more slowly for the fascists as the war became a kind of international rehearsal for the coming World War II. Madrid's fall to Franco in the spring of 1939 had been preceded by that of Barcelona a few weeks earlier.

tant elements of French security. France and Britain had every right to resist, and the French especially had a claim to retain the only element of security left after the failure of the Allies to guarantee her defense, yet neither did anything but make a feeble protest with the League. British opinion would not permit any support for France. The French themselves were paralyzed by internal division and by military ideas that concentrated on defense and feared taking the offensive. Both countries were further weakened by a growing pacifism.

In retrospect it appears that the Allies lost a great opportunity to stop Hitler before he became a serious menace. The failure of his gamble, taken against the advice of his generals, might have led to his overthrow; at the least it would have made German expansion to the east dangerous if not impossible. Nor is there much reason to doubt that the French army could easily have routed the tiny German force in the Rhineland. As the German General Alfred Jodl said some years later, "The French covering army would have blown us to bits."[3]

A Germany that was rapidly rearming and had a defensible western frontier presented a completely new problem to the Western powers. Their response was the policy of "appeasement." It was based on the assumption that Germany had real grievances, that Hitler's goals were limited and ultimately acceptable, and that the correct policy was to bring about revision by negotiation and concession before a crisis could arise and lead to war. Behind this approach was the general horror at the thought of another war. Memories of the losses in the last war were still fresh, and the advent of aerial bombard-

ment made the thought of a new war terrifying. A firmer policy, moreover, would have required rapid rearmament, but British leaders especially were reluctant to pursue this path because of the expense and because of the widespread belief that the arms race had been a major cause of the last war. As Germany armed, the French huddled behind their newly constructed defensive wall, the Maginot Line, and the British hoped things would go well.

The Spanish Civil War

The new European alignment that found the Western democracies on one side and the fascist states on the other was made clearer by the Spanish Civil War, which broke out in July 1936. In 1931 the Spaniards had driven out their king and established a democratic republic. The

3 Quoted by W. L. Shirer in *The Collapse of the Third Republic*, (New York: Simon and Schuster, 1969), p. 281.

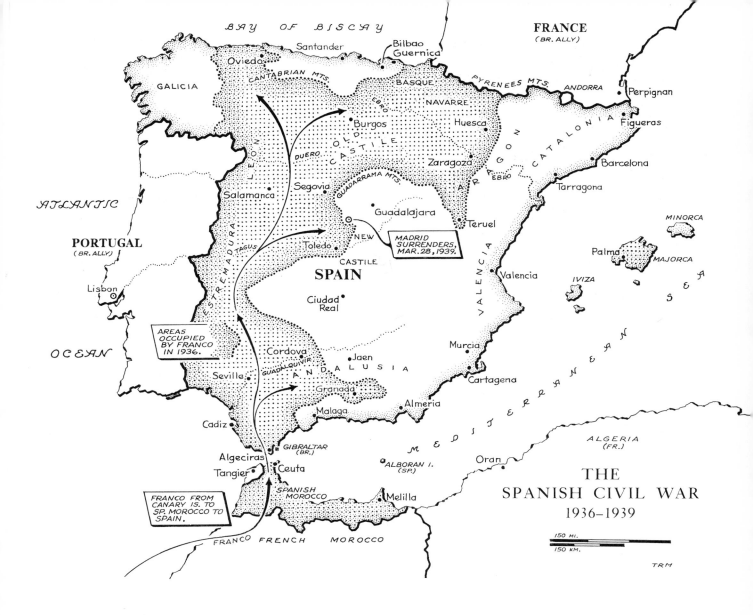

BAY OF BISCAY

FRANCE (BR. ALLY)

Santander
Bilbao
Guernica
Oviedo
GALICIA
CANTABRIAN MTS.
BASQUE
PYRENEES MTS.
ANDORRA
Perpignan
NAVARRE
EBRO
Burgos
Huesca
Figueras
OLD CASTILE
CATALONIA
DUERO
Barcelona
Zaragoza
ARAGON
EBRO
Tarragona
LEÓN
Segovia
GUADARRAMA MTS.
Salamanca
Teruel
ATLANTIC
Guadalajara
MINORCA
ESTREMADURA
NEW
MADRID SURRENDERS, MAR. 28, 1939.
PORTUGAL (BR. ALLY)
TAGUS
Toledo
CASTILE
Palma
MAJORCA
SPAIN
VALENCIA
Valencia
IVIZA
Lisbon
Ciudad Real
SEA
AREAS OCCUPIED BY FRANCO IN 1936.
OCEAN
Cordova
Murcia
GUADALQUIVIR
Jaen
ANDALUSIA
Seville
Cartagena
Granada
Almeria
ALGERIA (FR.)
Cadiz
Malaga
MEDITERRANEAN
GIBRALTAR (BR.)
ALBORAN I. (SP.)
Oran
THE SPANISH CIVIL WAR 1936–1939
Algeciras
Tangier
Ceuta
SPANISH MOROCCO
Melilla
FRANCO FROM CANARY IS. TO SP. MOROCCO TO SPAIN.
FRANCO FRENCH MOROCCO

150 MI.
150 KM.

TRM

new government followed a program of moderate reform that antagonized landowners, the Catholic Church, nationalists, and conservatives without satisfying the demands of peasants, workers, Catalan separatists, or radicals. Elections in February 1936 brought to power a Spanish Popular Front government ranging from republicans of the left to communists and anarchists. The defeated groups, especially the Falangists, the Spanish version of fascists, would not accept defeat at the polls. In July General Francisco Franco (1892–1975) led an army from Spanish Morocco in rebellion against the republic.

Thus began a civil war that lasted almost three years, cost hundreds of thousands of lives, and provided a training ground for World War II. Germany and Italy aided Franco with men, airplanes, and supplies. The Soviet Union sent airplanes, equipment, and advisers to the

republicans. Liberals and leftists from Europe and America volunteered to fight in the republican ranks against fascism.

This civil war, fought on blatantly ideological lines, had a profound effect on world politics. It brought Germany and Italy closer together, leading to the Rome–Berlin Axis Pact. The Axis powers were joined in the same year by Japan in the Anti-Comintern Pact, ostensibly against communism but really a new and powerful diplomatic alliance. The West, especially France, had a great interest in preventing Spain from falling into the hands of a fascist regime closely allied with Germany and Italy, but the appeasement mentality reigned. Although international law permitted the sale of weapons and munitions to the legitimate republican government, France and Britain forbade the export of war materials to either side, and the United States passed new neutrality legislation to the same end. When the city of Barcelona fell to Franco early in 1939, the fascists had won effective control of Spain.

Austria and Czechoslovakia

Hitler made good use of his new friendship with Mussolini. He had always planned to make his native Austria a part of the new Germany. In 1934 the Nazi Party in Austria assassinated the prime minister and tried to seize power, but Mussolini moved an army to the Brenner Pass in the Alps between Austria and Italy, preventing German intervention and causing the *coup* to fail. In 1938 the new diplomatic situation encouraged Hitler to try again. He seems to have hoped to achieve his goal by propaganda, bullying, and threats, but the Austrian Premier Schuschnigg refused to collapse. On March 9 the premier announced a plebiscite on the following Sunday, March 13, in which the Austrian people could decide the question of union with Germany for themselves. Hitler dared not let the plebiscite take place and sent his army into Austria on March 12. To his great relief Mussolini made no objection, and Hitler could march into Vienna to the cheers of his Austrian sympathizers. This peaceful outcome was fortunate for the Germans. Their army was far from ready for combat, and a high percentage of German tanks and trucks broke down along the roads of Austria.

The *Anschluss,* or union of Germany and Austria, was another clear violation of Versailles, but the treaty was now a dead letter; the latest violation produced no reaction from the West. It had great strategic significance, however, especially for the position of Czechoslovakia, one of the bulwarks of French security. The union with Austria left the Czechs surrounded by Germany on three sides.

The very existence of Czechoslovakia was an affront to Hitler. It was democratic and pro-Western; it had been created as a check on Germany and was allied both to France and to the Soviet Union. It also contained about 3.5 million Germans who lived in the Sudetenland near the German border. These Germans had been the dominant class in the old Austro-Hungarian Empire and resented their new minority position. Supported by Hitler and led by Konrad Henlein, they made ever increasing demands for privileges and autonomy within the Czech state. The Czechs made many concessions, but Hitler did not want to improve the lot of the Sudeten Germans. He wanted to destroy Czechoslovakia. He told Henlein "We must always demand so much that we can never be satisfied." [4]

As pressure mounted, the Czechs grew nervous. In May 1938 they received false rumors of an imminent attack by Germany and mobilized their army. The French, British, and Russians all issued warnings that they would support the Czechs. Hitler, who had not planned an attack at that time, was forced to make a public denial of any designs on Czechoslovakia. The public humiliation infuriated him, and from that moment he planned a military attack on the Czechs. The affair stiffened Czech resistance, but it appears to have frightened the French and the British. The French, as had become their custom, deferred to British leadership. The British prime minister was Neville Chamberlain, a man throughly committed to the policy of appeasement. He was determined not to allow Britain to come so close to war again. He put pressure on the Czechs to make further concessions to Germany, but no concession was enough.

On September 12, 1938, Hitler made a provocative speech at the Nuremberg Nazi Party rally. His assertions led to rioting in the Sudetenland and the declaration of martial law by the Czech government. German intervention seemed imminent. Chamberlain, aged sixty-nine, had never traveled before, but between September 15 and September 29 he made three flights to Germany in an attempt to appease Hitler at Czech expense and so

---

4 Quoted by Alan Bullock in *Hitler, A Study in Tyranny,* (New York: Harper and Row, 1962), p. 443.

Winston Churchill Warns on the Effects of the Munich Agreement

Churchill delivered his speech on the Munich agreement before the House of Commons on October 5, 1938. The following are excerpts from it.

The *Chancellor of the Exchequer [Sir John Simon] said it was the first time Herr Hitler had been made to retract—I think that was the word—in any degree. We really must not waste time after all this long Debate upon the difference between the positions reached at Berchtesgaden, at Godesberg and at Munich. They can be very simply epitomized, if the House will permit me to vary the metaphor. One pound was demanded at the pistol's point. When it was given, £2 were demanded at the pistol's point. Finally, the dictator consented to take £1 17s. 6d. and the rest in promises of good will for the future. . . .*

.   .   .   .

I do not grudge our loyal, brave people, who were ready to do their duty no matter what the cost, who never flinched under the strain of last week—I do not grudge them the natural, spontaneous outburst of joy and relief when they learned that the hard ordeal would no longer be required of them at the moment; but they should know the truth. They should know that there has been gross neglect and deficiency in our defenses; they should know that we have sustained a defeat without a war, the consequences of which will travel far with us along our road; they should know that we have passed an awful milestone in our history, when the whole equilibrium of Europe has been deranged, and that the terrible words have for the time being been pronounced against the Western democracies: "Thou art weighed in the balance and found wanting." And do not suppose that this is the end. This is only the beginning of the reckoning. This is only the first sip, the first foretaste of a bitter cup which will be proffered to us year by year unless, by a supreme recovery of moral health and martial vigor, we arise again and take our stand for freedom as in the olden time.

Winston S. Churchill, *Blood, Sweat, and Tears* (New York: G. P. Putnam's Sons, 1941), pp. 56, 66.

Hitler had raised his demands: he wanted cession of the Sudetenland in three days and immediate occupation by the German army.

Munich

Chamberlain returned to England thinking that he had failed, and France and Britain prepared for war. Almost at the last moment Mussolini proposed a conference of Germany, Italy, France, and Britain. It met on September 29 at Munich. Hitler received almost everything he had demanded. The Sudetenland, the key to Czech security, became part of Germany, thus depriving the Czechs of any chance of self-defense. In return the powers agreed to spare the rest of Czechoslovakia. Hitler promised: "I have no more territorial demands to make in Europe." Chamberlain returned to England and told a cheering crowd that he had brought "peace with honour. I believe it is peace for our time."

Even in the short run the appeasement of Hitler at Munich was a failure. Soon Poland and Hungary tore bits of territory from Czechoslovakia, and the Slovaks demanded autonomy. Finally, on March 15, 1939, Hitler broke his promise and occupied Prague, putting an end to Czechoslovakia and to illusions that his only goal was to restore Germans to the Reich. Defenders of the appeasers have argued that their policy was justified because it bought valuable time in which the West could prepare for war. But that argument was not made by the appeasers themselves, who thought that they were achieving peace, nor does the evidence appear to support it.

If the French and the British had been willing to attack Germany from the west while the Czechs fought in their own defense, there is reason to think that their efforts might have been successful. High officers in the German army were opposed to Hitler's risky policies and might have overthrown him. Even failing such developments, a war begun in October 1938 would have forced Hitler to fight without the friendly neutrality and material assistance of the Soviet Union and without the resources of eastern Europe that became available to him as a result of

avoid war. At Hitler's mountain retreat, Berchtesgaden, on September 15 Chamberlain accepted the separation of the Sudetenland from Czechoslovakia. And he and the French premier, Daladier, forced the Czechs to agree by threatening to desert them if they did not. A week later Chamberlain flew yet again to Germany only to find that

The Munich Conference, October 1938. The figures in front are, from left to right, Chamberlain of Great Britain, Daladier of France, Hitler of Germany, and Mussolini of Italy. [Imperial War Museum, London.]

appeasement. If, moreover, the West ever had a chance of alliance with the Soviet Union against Hitler, the exclusion of the Russians from Munich and the appeasement policy helped destroy it. Munich remains an example of short-sighted policy that helped bring on a war in disadvantageous circumstances because of the very fear of war and the failure to prepare for it.

Hitler's occupation of Prague discredited appeasement in the eyes of the British people. In the summer of 1939 a Gallup Poll showed that three quarters of the British public believed it worth a war to stop Hitler. Though Chamberlain himself had not lost all faith in his policy, he felt the need to respond to public opinion, and he responded to excess. It was apparent that Poland was the next target of German expansion. In the spring of 1939 the Germans put pressure on Poland to restore Danzig and to allow a railroad and a highway through the Polish Corridor to connect East Prussia with the rest of Germany. When the Poles would not yield, the usual propaganda campaign began, and the pressure mounted. On

March 31 Chamberlain announced a Franco-British guarantee of Polish independence. Hitler appears to have expected to fight a war with Poland but not with the Western allies, for he did not take their guarantee seriously. He had come to hold their leaders in contempt. He knew that both countries were unprepared for war and that large segments of their populations were opposed to fighting a war to save Poland.

Belief in the Polish guarantee was further undermined by the inability of the Allies to get effective help to the Poles. An attack on Germany's western front was out of the question for the French, still dominated by the defensive mentality of the Maginot Line. The only way to defend Poland was to bring Russia into the alliance

PARTITIONS OF CZECHOSLOVAKIA AND POLAND, 1938–1939

The immediate background of World War II is found in the complex international drama unfolding on Germany's eastern frontier in 1938 and 1939. Germany's expansion inevitably meant the victimization of Austria, Czechoslovakia, and Poland. With the failure of the Western powers' appeasement policy and the signing of a German-Soviet pact, the stage for the war was set.

against Hitler, but a Russian alliance posed many problems. Each side was profoundly suspicious of the other. The French and the British were hostile to Russia's communist ideology, and since Stalin's purge of the officer corps of the Red Army, they stood unconvinced of the military value of an alliance with Russia. Besides, the Russians could not help Poland without the right of transit through Romania and the right of entry into Poland. Both nations, suspicious of Russian intentions, and with good reason, refused to grant these rights. As a result Western negotiations with Russia moved forward slowly and cautiously.

Nazi-Soviet Pact

The Russians had at least equally good reason to hesitate. They resented being left out of the Munich agreement. They were annoyed by the low priority the West seemed to give to negotiations with Russia compared with the urgency with which they dealt with Hitler. They feared, quite rightly, that the Western powers meant them to bear the burden of the war against Germany. As a result they opened negotiations with Hitler, and on August 23, 1939, the world was shocked to learn of a Nazi-Soviet nonaggression pact. Its secret provisions, which were easily guessed and soon carried out, divided Poland between the two powers and allowed Russia to take over the Baltic states and to take Bessarabia from Romania. The most bitter ideological enemies had become allies. Communist parties in the West changed their line overnight from the ardent advocacy of resistance to Hitler to a policy of peace and quiet. Ideology gave way to political and military reality. The West offered the

On the eve of World War II, in August 1939, the Soviet Union and Nazi Germany shocked the rest of the world by signing a non-aggression pact. For years National Socialists and Communists had been the most bitter enemies and regularly hurled insults at each other, but now they came together in a marriage of convenience. This British cartoon by David Low (1891–1963) emphasizes the ironic character of the new relationship. [Cartoon by David Low. By arrangement with the Trustees and the London *Evening Standard*.]

Russians danger without much prospect of gain. Hitler offered Stalin gain without immediate danger. There could be little doubt as to the decision.

The Nazi–Soviet pact sealed the fate of Poland, and the Franco-British commitment guaranteed a general war. On September 1, 1939, the Germans invaded Poland. Two days later Britain and France declared war on Germany. World War II had begun.

World War II (1939–1945)

World War II has a better claim to its name than its predecessor, for it was truly global. Fighting took place in Europe and Asia, the Atlantic and the Pacific oceans, the Northern and Southern Hemispheres. The demand for the fullest exploitation of material and human resources for increased production, the use of blockades, and the intensive bombing of civilian targets made the war of 1939 even more "total," that is, comprehensive and intense, than that of 1914.

The German Conquest of Europe

The German attack on Poland produced swift success. The new style of "lightning warfare," or *Blitzkrieg*, employed fast-moving, massed armored columns supported by airpower. The Poles were inferior in tanks and planes, and their defense soon collapsed. The speed of the German victory astonished everyone, not least the Russians, who hastened to collect their share of the booty before Hitler could deprive them of it. On September 17 they invaded Poland from the east, dividing the country with the Germans. They then forced the encircled Baltic countries to sign treaties with them. By 1940 Estonia, Latvia, and Lithuania were absorbed as constituent republics into the USSR. In November 1940 the Russians invaded Finland, but the Finns put up a surprisingly effective resistance. Although they were finally worn down and compelled to yield territory and bases to Russia, they retained their independence. Russian difficulties in Finland may well have encouraged Hitler to invade the

Soviets just twenty-two months after the 1939 treaty.

Meanwhile the western front was quiet. The French huddled behind the Maginot Line while Hitler and Stalin swallowed Poland and the Baltic states. Britain hastily rearmed and organized the traditional naval blockade. Cynics in the West called it the phony war, or "*Sitzkrieg*," but Hitler shattered the stillness in the spring of 1940. In April, without warning and with swift success, the Germans invaded Denmark and Norway. Hitler's northern front was secure, and he now had both air and naval bases closer to Britain. A month later a combined land and air attack struck Belgium, the Netherlands, and Luxembourg. German airpower and armored divisions were irresistible. The Dutch surrendered in a few days, and the Belgians, though aided by the French and the British, surrendered less than two weeks later. The British and French armies were forced to flee to the English Channel to seek escape from the beaches of Dunkerque. By the heroic effort of hundreds of Britons manning small boats, over 200,000 British and 100,000 French soldiers were saved, but casualties were high and much valuable equipment was abandoned.

The Maginot Line ran from Switzerland to the Belgian frontier. The French had always expected the Belgians to

OPPOSITE: Dunkirk. Late in May 1940 the German army, having broken through the French defenses, reached the coast of the English Channel. The Germans might have destroyed the Allied armies, but their indecision allowed over 200,000 British troops and about two-thirds as many French to escape by sea to England. The British Navy, aided by countless civilian boats, rescued these men from the beach at Dunkirk, France. [Imperial War Museum, London.]

continue the fortifications along their German border. After Hitler remilitarized the Rhineland without opposition, the Belgians lost faith in their French alliance and returned to neutrality, leaving the Maginot Line exposed on the left flank. Hitler's swift advance through Belgium therefore circumvented France's main line of defense. The French army, poorly and hesitantly led by superannuated generals who lacked a proper understanding of the use of tanks and planes, quickly collapsed. Mussolini, eager to claim the spoils of victory when it was clearly safe to do so, sent an army across the French border on June 10, less than a week before the new French government, under the ancient hero of Verdun, Henri Philippe Pétain, asked for an armistice. In two months Hitler had accomplished what Germany had failed to achieve in four years of bitter fighting in the previous war.

The terms of the armistice, signed June 22, allowed the Germans to occupy more than half of France, including the Atlantic and English Channel coasts. In order to prevent many Frenchmen from fleeing to North Africa to continue the fight, and even more to prevent the French from turning their fleet over to Britain, Hitler left southern France unoccupied. Pétain set up a dictatorial regime at the resort city of Vichy and followed a policy

of collaboration with the Germans in order to preserve as much autonomy as possible. Most Frenchmen were too stunned to resist. Many thought that Hitler's victory was certain and saw no alternative to collaboration. A few, most notably General Charles de Gaulle (1890–1969), fled to Britain, where they organized the French National Committee of Liberation, or "Free French." Vichy controlled most of French North Africa and the navy, but the Free French began operating in central Africa and from London beamed messages of hope and defiance to their countrymen in France. As the passage of time dispelled expectations of a quick German victory, a French underground movement arose that organized many forms of resistance.

The Battle of Britain

The fall of France left Britain isolated, and Hitler expected the British to come to terms. He was prepared to allow Britain to retain its empire in return for a free hand for Germany on the continent. The British had never been willing to accept such an arrangement and had fought the long and difficult war against Napoleon to prevent it. If there was any chance that the British would consider such terms, that chance disappeared when Winston Churchill (1874–1965) replaced Chamberlain as prime minister in May of 1940.

Churchill had been an early and forceful critic of Hitler, the Nazis, and the policy of appeasement. A descendant and biographer of the Duke of Marlborough (1650–1722), who had fought to prevent the domination of Europe by Louis XIV in the seventeenth century, Churchill's sense of history, his feeling for British greatness, and his hatred of tyranny and love of freedom rejected any thought of compromise. His skill as a speaker and a writer allowed him to infuse the British people with his own courage and determination and to undertake what seemed almost a hopeless fight. Hitler and his allies, including the Soviet Union, controlled all of Europe. Japan was having its way in Asia. The United States was neutral, dominated by isolationist sentiment, and determined to avoid involvement outside the Western Hemisphere.

One of Churchill's greatest achievements was establishing a close relationship with the American President Franklin D. Roosevelt who found ways to help the British in spite of strong political opposition. In 1940 and 1941,

In May 1940 Winston Churchill replaced Neville Chamberlain as Prime Minister of Great Britain. The spirit of appeasement was dead, and David Low's cartoon celebrates the new spirit of determination and resistance Churchill inspired. The recognizable faces in the first three or four rows are those of the then leading British politicians of all parties; in the front row to the right of Churchill, who was a Conservative, are Clement Atlee and Ernest Bevin, the leaders of Labor. Chamberlain is behind Churchill. [Cartoon by David Low. By arrangement with the Trustees and the London *Evening Standard*.]

ALL BEHIND YOU, WINSTON

before the United States was at war, America sent military supplies, traded badly needed warships for leases on British naval bases, and even convoyed ships across the Atlantic to help the British survive.

As weeks passed and Britain remained defiant, Hitler was forced to contemplate an invasion, and that required control of the air. The first strikes by the German air force, directed against the airfields and fighter planes in southeastern England, began in August. There is reason to think that if these attacks had continued, Germany might soon have gained control of the air and with it the chance of a successful invasion. In early September, however, seeking revenge for some British bombing raids on German cities, the *Luftwaffe* made London its major target. For two months London was bombed every night. Much of the city was destroyed and about fifteen thousand people were killed, but the theories of victory through airpower alone proved vain. Casualties were many times fewer than expected and morale was not shattered. In fact, the bombings brought the British people together and made them more resolute. At the same time, the Royal Air Force inflicted heavy losses on the *Luftwaffe*. Aided by the newly developed radar and an excellent system of communications, the Spitfire and Hurricane fighter planes destroyed more than twice as many enemy planes than were lost by the RAF. Hitler had lost the Battle of Britain in the air and was forced to abandon his plans for invasion.

The German Attack on Russia

From the first, the defeat of Russia and the conquest of the Ukraine to provide *Lebensraum* for the German people had been a major goal for Hitler. Even before the assault on Britain, he had informed his staff of his intention to attack Russia as soon as conditions were favorable. In December of 1940, even while the bombing of England continued, he ordered his generals to prepare for an invasion of Russia by May 15, 1941. He appears to have thought that a *Blitzkrieg* victory in the east would destroy all hope and bring the British to their senses.

Operation Barbarossa, the code name for the invasion of Russia, aimed at knocking Russia out of the war before winter could set in. Success depended in part on an early start, but here Hitler's Italian alliance proved costly. Mussolini was jealous of Hitler's success and annoyed by the treatment he had received. Unable to make progress against the French army even while Hitler was crushing the part of it on his own frontier, Mussolini was not allowed any gain at the expense of France or even of French Africa. Instead he launched an attack against the British in Egypt and drove them back some sixty miles. Encouraged by this success, he invaded Greece from his base in Albania. His purpose was revealed by his remark to his son-in-law, Count Ciano: "Hitler always faces me with a *fait accompli*. This time I am going to pay him back in his own coin. He will find out in the newspapers that I have occupied Greece."[5] But in north Africa the British drove the Italians back into Libya, and the Greeks themselves pushed into Albania. In March 1941 the British sent help to the Greeks, and Hitler was forced to divert his attention to the Balkans and to Africa. General Erwin Rommel (1891–1944), later to earn the title "The Desert Fox," went to Africa and soon got the British out of Libya and back into Egypt. In the Balkans the German army swiftly occupied Yugoslavia and crushed Greek resistance, but the price was a delay of six weeks. The diversion caused by Mussolini's vanity proved to be costly the following winter.

Operation Barbarossa was launched against Russia on June 22, 1941, and it came very close to success. In spite of their deep suspicion of Germany and the allegation that the Nazi–Soviet Pact was meant to give Russia time to prepare, the Russians were taken quite by surprise. Stalin appears to have panicked. He had not fortified his frontier nor had he issued orders for his troops to withdraw when attacked. In the first two days some two thousand planes were destroyed on the ground. By No-

5 Quoted in Gordon Wright, *The Ordeal of Total War,* (New York: Harper and Row, 1968), pp. 35–36.

250 MI.
250 KM.

AXIS STATES
AND
ANNEXED AREAS

AXIS ALLIES

AXIS-
OCCUPIED

NORWAY

SWEDEN

FINLAND

Leningrad

NORTH
SEA

DENMARK

ESTONIA

LATVIA

Moscow

EIRE

UNITED
KINGDOM

London

NETH.

BELG.

EUPEN

LUX.

MEMEL-
LAND

Danzig

*EAST
PRUSSIA*

Vilna

LITHUANIA

*EASTERN
POLAND*

BIALYSTOK

SOVIET

Berlin

GREATER
GERMANY

POSEN

Warsaw

GOVERNMENT
GENERAL
OF
POLAND

UNION

Kiev

Paris

F R A N C E

LORRAINE

ALSACE

*SUDETEN-
LAND*

BOHEMIA

MORAVIA

Lemberg

*NORTHERN
BUKOVINA*

UKRAINE

Bordeaux

UNOCCUPIED

OCCUPIED

Vichy

VICHY
FRANCE

SWITZ.

AUSTRIA

SLOVAKIA

Budapest
HUNGARY

BESSARABIA

SPAIN

Milan

ITALY

Toulon

CROATIA

*YUGOSLAVIA
PARTITIONED
APR., 1941*

Belgrade

SERBIA

ROMANIA
Bucharest

DOBRUJA

*BLACK
SEA*

CORSICA
(VICHY)

Rome

ADRIATIC SEA

CATTARO
(IT.)

ALBANIA
(IT.)

Sofia
BULGARIA

(TURK.)

Istanbul

Ankara

SARDINIA
(IT.)

M E D I T E R R A N E A N

S E A

GREECE

TURKEY

ALGERIA
(FR.)

TUNISIA
(FR.)

SICILY

Athens

TRM

AXIS EUROPE, 1941

vember Hitler had gone further into Russia than Napoleon: the German army stood at the gates of Leningrad, on the outskirts of Moscow, and on the Don River. Of the 4.5 million troops with which the Russians had begun the fighting, they had lost 2.5 million; of their 15,000 tanks only 700 were left. Moscow was in panic, and a German victory seemed imminent.

But the Germans could not deliver the final blow. In August there was a delay in their advance to decide on a course of action. One plan was to drive directly for Moscow and take it before winter. There is some reason to think that such a plan might have worked and brought victory, for unlike the situation in Napoleon's time, Moscow was the hub of the Russian system of transportation. Hitler, however, imposed his own view on his generals, and diverted a significant part of his forces to the south. By the time he was ready to return to the offensive near Moscow, it was too late. Winter struck the German army, which was neither dressed nor equipped to face it. Given precious time, Stalin was able to restore order and build defenses for the city. Even more important, there was time for troops to come from Siberia, where they had

OPPOSITE: On the eve of the German invasion of the Soviet Union the Germany–Italy Axis bestrode most of Western Europe by annexation, occupation, or alliance—from Norway and Finland in the north to Greece in the south and from Poland to France. Britain, the Soviets, a number of insurgent groups, and, finally, America had before them the long struggle of conquering this Axis "fortress Europe."

Moscow or the Ukraine? Hitler and his generals study a map of the Russian front in August 1941. From left to right are Keitel, Brauchitsch, Warlimont, and Hitler. [Bibliothek für Zeitgeschichte, Stuttgart.]

been placed to check a possible Japanese attack. In November and December the Russians were able to counterattack. The *Blitzkrieg* had turned into a war of attrition, and the Germans began to have visions of Napoleon's retreat.

Hitler's Europe

Hitler often spoke of the "new order" that he meant to impose after he had established his Third Reich throughout Europe. The first two German empires (*Reichs*) were those of Charlemagne in the ninth century and William II in the nineteenth, and Hitler predicted that his own would last for a thousand years. If his organization of Germany before the war is a proper index, he had no single plan of government but relied frequently on intuition and pragmatism. His organization of conquered Europe had the same characteristics of spontaneity and patchwork. Some conquered territory was annexed to Germany; some was administered directly by German officials; some lands were nominally autonomous but were ruled by puppet governments.

The demands and distractions of war and the fact that Hitler's defeat prevented him from carrying out his plans fully make it hard to be sure what his intentions were, but the measures he took before his death provide indications. They give evidence of a regime probably unmatched in history for carefully planned terror and inhumanity. To accomplish his plan of giving *Lebensraum* to the Germans at the expense of people he deemed inferior, Hitler established colonies of Germans in parts of Poland, driving the local people from their land and employing them as cheap labor. He had similar plans on an even higher scale for Russia. The Russians would be driven eastward to central Asia and Siberia; they would be kept in check by frontier colonies of German war veterans, and the more desirable lands of European Russia would be settled by Germans.

Hitler's long-range plans included Germanization as well as colonization. In lands inhabited by people racially akin to the Germans, like the Scandinavian countries, the Netherlands, and Switzerland, the natives would be absorbed into the German nation. Such peoples would be reeducated and purged of dissenting elements, but there would be little or no colonization. He even had plans, only slightly realized, of adopting selected people from the lesser races into the master race. One of these plans involved bringing half a million Ukrainian girls into Germany as servants and finding German husbands for them; about fifteen thousand actually did reach Germany.

In the economic sphere Hitler regarded the conquered lands merely as a source of plunder. He removed everything useful, including entire industries. In Russia and Poland the Germans simply confiscated the land. In the west the conquered countries were forced to support the occupying army at a rate several times the real cost. The Germans used the profits to buy up everything useful and desirable, stripping the conquered peoples of most necessities. The Nazis were frank about their policies. One of Hitler's high officials said, "Whether nations live in prosperity or starve to death interests me only insofar as we need them as slaves for our culture." [6]

The most horrible aspect of the Nazi rule in Europe arose not from military or economic necessity but from the inhumanity and brutality inherent in Hitler's racial doctrines. He considered the Slavs *Untermenschen*, subhuman creatures like beasts who need not be thought of or treated like people. In parts of Poland the upper and professional classes were entirely removed, either jailed, deported, or killed. Schools and churches were closed; marriage was controlled by the Nazis to keep down the Polish birth rate; and harsh living conditions were imposed. In Russia things were even worse. Hitler spoke of his Russian campaign as a war of extermination. Heinrich Himmler (1900–1945), head of Hitler's elite SS guard, planned the elimination of thirty million Slavs to make room for the Germans, and he formed extermination

6 Quoted by Gordon Wright, *The Ordeal of Total War, 1939–1945*, (New York: Harper and Row, 1968), p. 117.

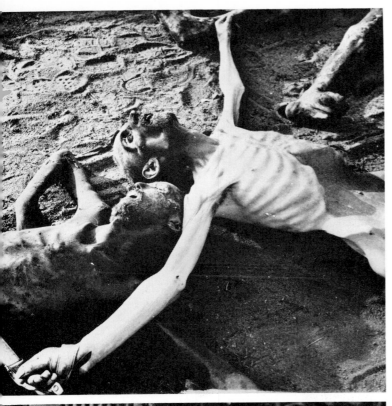

squads for the purpose. The number of Russian prisoners of war and deported civilian workers who died under Nazi rule may have reached six million.

Hitler had special plans for the Jews. He meant to make all Europe *Judenrein* ("free of Jews"). For a time he thought of sending them to the island of Madagascar, but later he arrived at the "final solution of the Jewish problem"—extermination. The Nazis built extermination camps in Germany and Poland and used the latest technology to achieve the most efficient means of killing millions of men, women, and children for no other reason than their birth into the designated group. Before the war was over, perhaps six million Jews had died in what has come to be called the Holocaust. Only about a million remained alive, those mostly in a pitiable condition.

World War II was unmatched in modern times in cruelty. When Stalin's armies conquered Poland and entered Germany, they raped, pillaged, and deported millions to the east. The British and American bombing of Germany killed thousands of civilians, and the dropping of atomic bombs on Japan inflicted terrible harm on civilian populations. The bombings, however, were thought of as acts of war that would help defeat the enemy. Stalin's atrocities were not widely known in the West at the time and are not even today. Little wonder,

German concentration camps—the dead and the dying as found by Western armies in 1945. The Nazis set up their first concentration camps in Germany to hold the German opponents of their regime, but later, after the war had begun and had moved east into non-German territory, the new camps established in Poland were deliberately planned as part of Hitler's "final solution," the extermination of the Jews, although Jews were not his only victims. Even in those camps not avowedly dedicated to extermination the conditions were brutal in the extreme, and the armies that liberated them in 1945 found in all of them scenes such as those in these photographs. [United Press International Photo.]

Hitler States His Plans for Russia

As was revealed in detail only after World War II, Hitler had definite, if vainglorious, views on Russians and positive plans for Germany's exploitation of Russia in the event of Germany's victory.

The German colonists ought to live on handsome, spacious farms. The German services will be lodged in marvelous buildings, the governors in palaces. Beneath the shelter of the administrative services, we shall gradually organize all that is indispensable to the maintenance of a certain standard of living. Around the city, to a depth of thirty to forty kilometers, we shall have a belt of handsome villages connected by the best roads. What exists beyond that will be another world, in which we mean to let the Russians live as they like. It is merely necessary that we should rule them. In the event of a revolution, we shall only have to drop a few bombs on their cities, and the affair will be liquidated. Once a year we shall lead a troop of Kirghizes through the capital of the Reich, in order to strike their imaginations with the size of our monuments.

What India was for England, the territories of Russia will be for us.

When one contemplates this primitive world, one is convinced that nothing will drag it out of its indolence unless one compels the people to work. The Slavs are a mass of born slaves, who feel the need of a master. . . . It's better not to teach them to read. They won't love us for tormenting them with schools. Even to give them a locomotive to drive would be a mistake. . . .

The Germans—this is essential—will have to constitute amongst themselves a closed society, like a fortress. The least of our stable-lads must be superior to any native.

For German youth, this will be a magnificent field of experiment. We'll attract to the Ukraine Danes, Dutch, Norwegians, Swedes. The army will find areas for maneuvers there, and our aviation will have the space it needs.

Hitler's Secret Conversations, 1941–1944, trans. by Norman Cameron and R. H. Stevens (New York: Farrar, Straus and Young, 1953) pp. 20, 28–29.

then, that the victorious Western Allies were shocked by what they saw when they came upon the Nazi extermination camps and their pitiful survivors, and little wonder that they were convinced that the effort of resistance to the Nazis and all the pain it cost were well worth it.

Japan and America's Entry into the War

The sympathies of the American government were very much on the British side, and the various forms of assistance that Roosevelt gave Britain would have justified a German declaration of war. Hitler, however, held back, and it is not clear that the United States government would have overcome isolationist sentiment and entered the war in the Atlantic if war had not been thrust on America in the Pacific. Since the Japanese conquest of Manchuria in 1931, American policy toward Japan had been suspicious and unfriendly. The outbreak of the war in Europe emboldened the Japanese to move forward more quickly in their drive to dominate Asia. They allied themselves with Germany and Italy, made a treaty of neutrality with the Soviet Union, and penetrated into Indochina at the expense of defeated France. At the same time they continued their war in China and made plans to gain control of Malaya and the East Indies at the expense of beleaguered Britain and the conquered Netherlands. The only barrier to Japanese expansion was the United States.

The Americans had temporized, unwilling to cut off vital supplies of oil and other materials for fear of provoking a Japanese attack on Southeast Asia and Indonesia. The Japanese seizure of Indochina in July 1941 changed that policy. The United States froze Japanese assets and cut off oil supplies; the British and Dutch did the same. Japanese plans for expansion could not continue without the conquest of the Indonesian oil fields and Malayan rubber and tin. In October a war faction led by General Tojo took power in Japan and decided to risk a war rather than yield. On Sunday morning, December 7, 1941, even while Japanese representatives were discussing negotiation in Washington, Japan launched an air attack on Pearl Harbor, Hawaii, the chief American naval base in the Pacific. The technique was similar to the one Japan had used against the Russian fleet at Port Arthur in 1904, and it caught the Americans equally by surprise. A large part of the American fleet and many airplanes were

Pearl Harbor, December 7, 1941. The successful
Japanese attack on the American base at Pearl Harbor
in Hawaii, together with simultaneous attacks on
other Pacific bases, brought the United States into
war against the Axis powers. This picture shows the
effects of the Japanese bombing upon the battleships *Arizona, Tennessee,* and *West Virginia.*
[Official United States Navy Photograph.]

Marshal Tito of Yugoslavia (born 1892, and whose original name was Josip Broz), on the right, led his country's partisan resistance against the Nazis during World War II. [The Granger Collection.]

destroyed, and the American capacity to wage war in the Pacific was destroyed for the time being. The next day the United States and Britain declared war on Japan, and three days later Germany and Italy declared war on the United States.

The Tide Turns

The potential power of the United States was enormous, but right after Pearl Harbor America was ill prepared for war. Though conscription had been introduced in 1940, the army was tiny, inexperienced, and ill supplied. American industry was not on a war footing. The Japanese swiftly captured Guam, Wake Island, and the Philippine Islands. At the same time they attacked Hong Kong, Malaya, Burma, and Indonesia. By the spring of 1942 they controlled these places and the Southwest Pacific as far as New Guinea. They were poised for an attack on Australia, and it seemed that nothing could stop them.

In the same year the Germans advanced deeper into Russia and almost reached the Caspian Sea in their drive for Russia's oil fields. In Africa, too, Axis fortunes were high. Rommel drove the British back into Egypt toward the Suez Canal and finally was stopped at El Alamein, only seventy miles from Alexandria. Relations between the democracies and their Soviet ally were still far from close; German submarine warfare was threatening British supplies; the Allies were being thrown back on every front; and the future looked bleak.

The first good news for the Allied cause in the Pacific came in the spring of 1942. A naval battle in the Coral Sea sent many Japanese ships to the bottom and gave security to Australia. A month later the United States defeated the Japanese in a fierce air and naval battle off Midway Island, blunting the chance of another assault on Hawaii and doing enough damage to halt the Japanese advance. Soon American Marines landed on Guadalcanal in the Solomon Islands and began in a small way to reverse the momentum of the war. The war in the Pacific was far from over, but Japan was checked sufficiently to allow the Allies to concentrate their efforts first in Europe.

The nations opposed to the Axis powers numbered more than twenty and were located all over the world, but the main combatants were Great Britain, the Soviet Union, and the United States. The two Western democracies cooperated in everything to an unprecedented degree, but suspicion between them and their Soviet ally continued. Although the Russians accepted all the aid they could get, they did not trust their allies, complained of inadequate help, and demanded that the democracies open a "second front" on the mainland of Europe. In 1942 American preparation and production were inadequate for an invasion of Europe, and control of the Atlantic by German submarines was such as to prevent safe crossing by the required number of troops. Not until 1944 were conditions right for the invasion, but in the meantime other developments forecast the doom of the Axis.

ALLIED LANDINGS IN AFRICA, SICILY, AND ITALY. In November 1942 an Allied force landed in French North Africa. Even before that landing the British General Bernard Montgomery (1887–1976), after stopping Rommel at El Alamein, had begun a drive to the west, and the American General Dwight D. Eisenhower (1890–1969) pushed eastward through Morocco and Algeria. The two armies caught the German army between them in Tunisia and crushed it. The Suez Canal and the Mediterranean were now under Allied control, and southern Europe was exposed. In July and August 1943 the Allies took Sicily. Mussolini was driven from power, and the new government tried to make peace, but

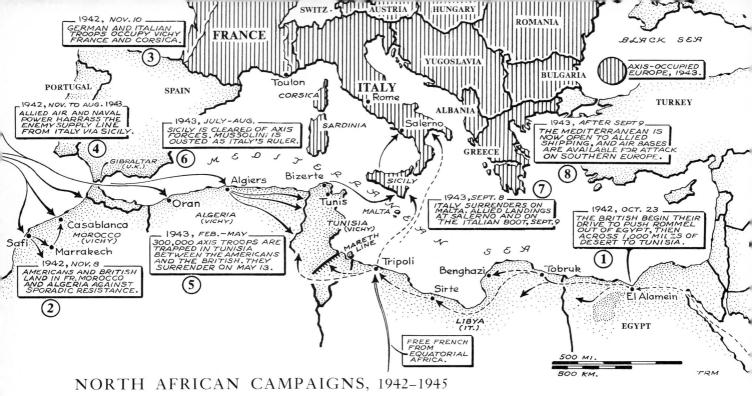

Map labels:

1942, NOV. 10
GERMAN AND ITALIAN TROOPS OCCUPY VICHY FRANCE AND CORSICA. — ③

1942, NOV. TO AUG. 1943
ALLIED AIR AND NAVAL POWER HARRASS THE ENEMY SUPPLY LINE FROM ITALY VIA SICILY. — ④

1943, JULY-AUG.
SICILY IS CLEARED OF AXIS FORCES. MUSSOLINI IS OUSTED AS ITALY'S RULER. — ⑥

1943, AFTER SEPT 9
THE MEDITERRANEAN IS NOW OPEN TO ALLIED SHIPPING, AND AIR BASES ARE AVAILABLE FOR ATTACK ON SOUTHERN EUROPE. — ⑧

1943, FEB.—MAY
300,000 AXIS TROOPS ARE TRAPPED IN TUNISIA BETWEEN THE AMERICANS AND THE BRITISH. THEY SURRENDER ON MAY 13. — ⑤

1943, SEPT. 8
ITALY SURRENDERS ON MALTA. ALLIED LANDINGS AT SALERNO AND ON THE ITALIAN BOOT, SEPT.9 — ⑦

1942, OCT. 23
THE BRITISH BEGIN THEIR DRIVE TO PUSH ROMMEL OUT OF EGYPT, THEN ACROSS 1,000 MILES OF DESERT TO TUNISIA. — ①

1942, NOV. 8
AMERICANS AND BRITISH LAND IN FR. MOROCCO AND ALGERIA AGAINST SPORADIC RESISTANCE. — ②

FREE FRENCH FROM EQUATORIAL AFRICA.

AXIS-OCCUPIED EUROPE, 1943.

500 MI.
500 KM.

TRM

NORTH AFRICAN CAMPAIGNS, 1942–1945

Control of North Africa was important to the Allies in order to have access to Europe from the south. The map diagrams this theater of the war from Morocco to Egypt and the Suez Canal.

Stalingrad after the battle: Russians returning to the ruined city in February 1943. In this crucial battle the Russians suffered terrible losses but stopped the German advance and cut off and destroyed an entire German army. This battle is generally regarded as the turning point of the war in the East. [Sovfoto.]

the Germans moved into Italy. The Allies landed in Italy and Marshal Badoglio, the leader of the new Italian government went over to their side, declaring war on Germany. Churchill had spoken of Italy as the "soft underbelly" of the Axis, but German resistance was tough and determined. Still the need to defend Italy put a strain on the Germans' manpower and resources and left them vulnerable on other fronts.

BATTLE OF STALINGRAD. The Russian campaign became especially demanding. In the summer of 1942 the Germans resumed the offensive on all fronts but were unable to get very far except in the south. The goal was the oil fields near the Caspian Sea, and they got as far as Stalingrad on the Volga, a key point for the protection of the flank of the German army in the south. Hitler was determined to take the city and Stalin to hold it. The battle raged for months with unexampled ferocity. The Russians lost more men than the Americans lost in combat during the entire war, but their heroic defense prevailed. Because Hitler again overruled his generals and would not allow a retreat, an entire German army was lost. Stalingrad marked the turning point of the Russian campaign. Thereafter Lend Lease help from America and, even more, increased production from their own industry, which had been built in or moved to the safety of central and eastern Russia, allowed the Russians to gain and keep the offensive. As German manpower and material resources dwindled, the Russians advanced westward inexorably.

STRATEGIC BOMBING. In 1943 the Allies began to gain ground in production and logistics as well. The industrial might of the United States began to come into full force, and at the same time new technology and tactics made great strides in eliminating the submarine menace. In the same year the American and British air forces began a series of massive bombardments of Germany by night and day. The Americans were more committed to the theory of "precision bombing" of military and industrial targets vital to the enemy war effort, so they flew the day missions. The British regarded precision bombing as impossible and therefore useless. They preferred indiscriminate "area bombing" aimed at destroying the morale of the German people, and this kind of mission could be done at night. It does not appear that either kind of bombing had much effect on the war until 1944. Then the Americans introduced long-range fighters that could protect the bombers and allow accurate missions by day. By 1945 the Allies had cleared the skies of German planes and could bomb at will. Concen-

Dresden in ruins. In February 1945, with the end of the war in sight, the Allies launched a series of air raids on Dresden in Germany, which was without defense. The raids destroyed the heart of the city and are thought to have caused twice as many casualties as those caused by the first atomic bomb dropped on Hiroshima, Japan, in August of the same year. [Bildarchiv Preussischer Kulturbesitz.]

trated attacks on industrial targets, especially communications centers and oil refineries, did very real damage and helped shorten the war. Terror bombing continued, too, but seems not to have had any useful result. The bombardment of Dresden in February 1945 was especially savage and destructive. It was much debated within the British government and has raised moral questions since, for it seems to have had no military value.

As this scene from Cologne, Germany, illustrates,
World War II witnessed unprecedented destruction.
Scores of bridges across major European rivers were
destroyed, including all of the bridges across the
Rhine, among them this one. [Bettmann Archive.]

D-Day, June 6, 1944. The Allied landing in France on the coast of Normandy. [Imperial War Museum, London.]

The Defeat of Nazi Germany

On June 6, 1944 ("D-Day"), American, British, and Canadian troops landed in force on the coast of Normandy. The "second front" was opened. General Dwight D. Eisenhower, the commander of the Allied armies, faced a difficult problem. The European coast was heavily fortified, and excellent communications systems allowed the Germans to move reserves swiftly to whatever point might be attacked. Amphibious assaults, moreover, are especially vulnerable to changes of wind and weather. Success depended on meticulous planning, advance preparation by heavy bombing, and successful feints to mask the point of attack. The German defense was strong, but the Allies were able to establish a beachhead and then to break out of it. In mid-August the Allies landed in southern France to put more pressure on the enemy. By the beginning of September France had been liberated.

All went smoothly until December, when the Germans launched a counterattack on the Belgian front through the Forest of Ardennes. Because the Germans were able to push forward into the Allied line, this was called the Battle of the Bulge, and it brought heavy losses and considerable alarm to the Allies. That effort, however, was the last gasp for the Germans. The Allies recovered the momentum and pushed eastward. They crossed the Rhine in March of 1945, and German resistance crumbled. This time there could be no doubt that the Germans had lost the war on the battlefield.

In the east the Russians swept forward no less swiftly. By March 1945 they were within reach of Berlin. Because the Allies insisted on unconditional surrender, the Germans fought on until May. Hitler and his intimates committed suicide in an underground hideaway in Berlin. The Russians occupied Berlin by agreement with their Western allies. The Third Reich had lasted a dozen years instead of the milennium predicted by Hitler.

[Text continued on page 921]

500 MI.

500 KM.

N. IRELAND

EIRE

UNITED KINGDOM

Liverpool • Hull

Coventry •

London •

NORTH SEA

NORWAY

Trondheim

Oslo

Stavanger •

SWEDEN

Stockholm •

DENMARK

Copenhagen

BALTIC SEA

FINLAND

L. ONEGA

L. LADOGA

Viborg •

Helsinki •

Leningrad

Reval •

Novgorod •

ESTONIA

Riga •

LATVIA

Rzhev •

Vitebsk •

Smolensk •

LITHUANIA

Memel

Kaunas •

Vilna •

BYELO-RUSSIA

KATYN FOREST

Bryansk

GERMAN SURRENDER IN REIMS, MAY 7, 1945 BERLIN, MAY 8, 1945

NETH.

Rotterdam •

BELG.

Dunkirk •

NORMANDY INV. JUNE 6, 1944

BATTLE OF THE BULGE DEC. 1944

St. Nazaire •

Paris •

Reims •

Orléans •

Tours •

FRANCE

Vichy •

Bordeaux •

Lyons •

AXIS TROOPS OCCUPY VICHY FRANCE, NOV. 10 AND 11, 1942

Hamburg •

Bremen •

Essen •

Cologne •

Remagen •

GREATER

RHINE CROSSING, MAR. 7, 1945

Nürnberg •

Strassburg •

Munich •

SWITZ.

Danzig •

Berlin •

Torgau •

Dresden •

GERMANY

Breslau •

BOHEMIA

MORAVIA

TYROL

Vienna •

AUSTRIA

EAST PRUSSIA

POSEN

POLAND

Warsaw •

Cracow •

Lemberg •

RUSSIAN FRONT JUNE 23, 1944

Kiev •

Kirov

BESSARABIA

DNIESTER

Jassi •

Odessa •

SLOVAKIA

HUNGARY

Budapest •

ROMANIA

Bucharest •

Varna •

SPAIN

Barcelona •

Valencia •

PROVENCE

Marseilles •

Toulon •

ALLIES LAND IN PROVENCE, AUG. 15, 1944

CORSICA (VICHY)

BALEARIC IS.

Milan •

Bologna •

Florence •

ITALY

Rome •

Anzio • Cassino •

Naples • Salerno •

SARDINIA (IT.)

ADRIATIC SEA

CROATIA

YUGOSLAVIA

SERBIA

MONTE-NEGRO

Tirana •

ALBANIA

Belgrade •

Skoplje •

BULGARIA

Sofia •

Salonika •

GREECE

Athens •

AEGEAN SEA

Izmir •

(TURK.)

Istanbul •

RHODES

Candia •

CRETE

ALLIES INVADE SICILY & ITALY, JULY-SEPT. 1943

CALABRIA

SICILY

ITALIAN SURRENDER, SEPT. 8, 1943

Algiers •

Bizerte •

AXIS TROOPS EVACUATED, MAY 1943

Tunis •

ALGERIA (VICHY)

TUNISIA (VICHY)

MALTA (U.K.)

MEDITERRANEAN SEA

918 *World War II and the Cold War*

DEFEAT OF THE AXIS IN EUROPE, 1942–1945

THE AXIS

ALLIED WITH THE AXIS

OCCUPIED BY THE AXIS

Jaroslavl

VOLGA

SOVIET

• Moscow

Kuibyshev (WARTIME CAPITAL)

Tula

..... DEC., 1941 FARTHEST AXIS ADVANCE

—— NOV. 1942

Orel

Voronezh

Kursk

Stalingrad

UNION

Kharkov

VOLGA

Astrakhan

'A I N E

DON

Rostov

Elista

C A S P I A N   S E A

DNIEPER

Kerch

Maikop

Grozny

CRIMEA

Yalta

T R A N S C A U C A S I A

Tiflis

B L A C K   S E A

Batum

Sinop

Kars

IRAN

Ankara

TURKEY

Mosul

TIGRIS

Adana

EUPHRATES

Antalya

Aleppo

IRAQ

CYPRUS (U.K.)

SYRIA

LEBANON

T R MILLER

This is the sequel to the map on page 908. Here we see some major steps in the progress toward Allied victory against Axis Europe. From the south through Italy, from the west through France, and from the east through Russia the Allies gradually conquered the continent to bring the war in Europe to a close.

The Red Flag flies over the Reichstag in Berlin. This picture shows a ceremony duplicating the scene of the Russian capture of Berlin on May 8, 1945, held on the twentieth anniversary of that event. The division of Germany for the purpose of military occupation hardened into a political division of Germany into two nations. [United Press International Photo.]

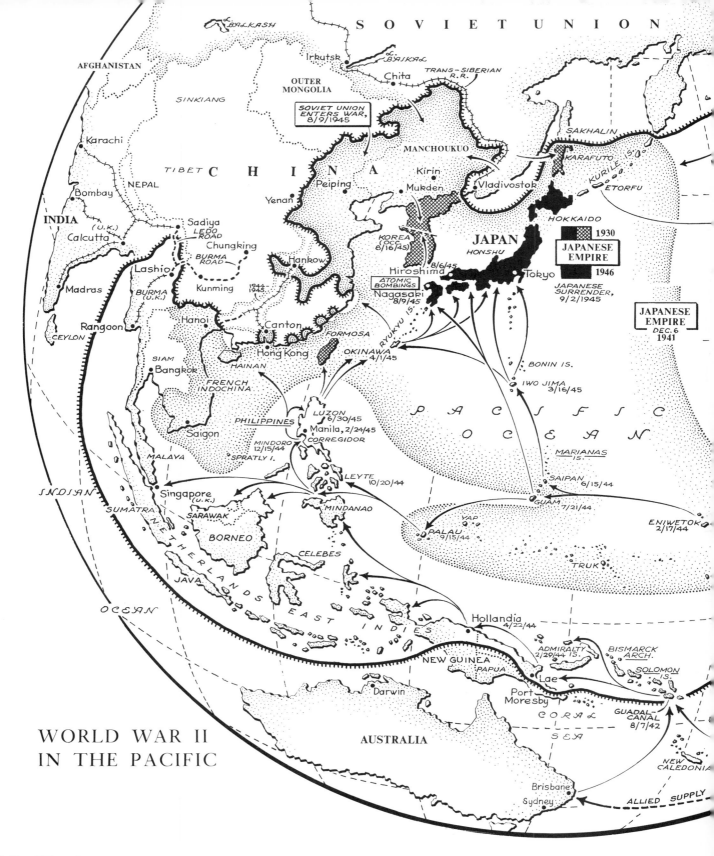

WORLD WAR II
IN THE PACIFIC

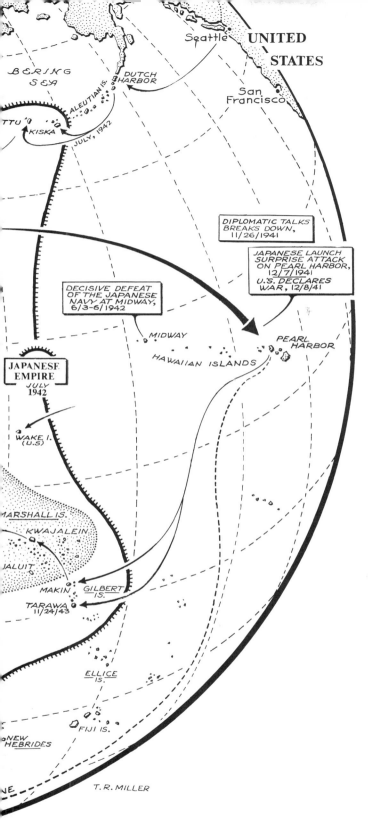

As in Europe, the Pacific war was a problem in Allied recapture of areas that had been quickly taken earlier by the enemy. The enormous area represented by the map shows the initial expansion of Japanese holdings to cover half the Pacific and its islands, as well as huge sections of eastern Asia, and the long struggle to push the Japanese back to their homeland and defeat them by the summer of 1945.

Fall of the Japanese Empire

The war in Europe ended on May 8, 1945, and by then victory over Japan was in sight. The original Japanese attack on the United States had been a calculated risk against the odds. The longer the war lasted, the greater the advantage to the American superiority in industrial production and manpower. Beginning in 1943 the American forces, still relatively small in number, began a campaign of "island hopping." They did not try to recapture every Pacific island held by the Japanese but selected major bases and places strategically located along the enemy supply line. Starting from the Solomons, they moved northeast toward the Japanese homeland. By June of 1944 they had reached the Mariana Islands, which they could use as bases for bombing the Japanese in the Philippines, in China, and in Japan itself. In October of the same year the Americans recaptured the Philippines and drove the Japanese fleet back into its home waters. In 1945 Iwo Jima and Okinawa fell, in spite of determined Japanese resistance that included "kamikaze" attacks, suicide missions in which specially trained pilots deliberately flew their explosive-filled planes into American warships. From these new bases, closer to Japan, the American bombers launched a terrible wave of bombings that destroyed Japanese industry and disabled the navy, but still the Japanese government, dominated by a military clique, refused to surrender.

Confronted with Japan's determination, the Americans made plans for a frontal assault on the Japanese homeland, which, they calculated, might cost a million American casualties and even greater losses for the Japanese. At this point science and technology presented the Americans with another choice. Since early in the war a secret program had been in progress. Its staff, made up in significant part by exiles from Hitler's Europe, was working to use atomic energy for military purposes. On August 6, 1945, an American plane dropped an atomic bomb on the city of Hiroshima. The city of 200,000 was destroyed and over 70,000 people were killed. Two days

The mushroom-shaped cloud of the atomic bomb has come to symbolize the possibility of total human destruction that has haunted the statesmen and peoples of the world since 1945. This photograph shows one of the post-war test explosions held on remote atolls in the Pacific. [Official United States Navy Photograph.]

later the Soviet Union declared war on Japan and invaded Manchuria. The next day a second atomic bomb fell, this time on Nagasaki. Even then the Japanese did not yield. The Japanese cabinet was prepared to resist further, to face an invasion rather than give up. It was only the unprecedented and unconstitutional intervention of Emperor Hirohito that convinced the government to surrender on August 14. Even then they made the condition that Japan could keep its emperor. Although the Allies had continued to insist on unconditional surrender, President Harry S. Truman who had come to office on April 12, 1945, on the death of Franklin D. Roosevelt, accepted the condition, and peace was formally signed aboard the *USS Missouri* in Tokyo Bay on September 2, 1945.

Revulsion and horror at the only use of atomic bombs, as well as hindsight arising from the Cold War have surrounded the decision to use the bomb against Japanese cities with debate. Some have suggested that the bombings were unnecessary to win the war and that their main purpose was to frighten the Russians into a more cooperative attitude after the war. Others have emphasized the bureaucratic, almost automatic nature of the decision, once it had been decided to develop the bomb. To the decision makers and their contemporaries, however, matters were simpler. The bomb was a way to end the war swiftly without the need of invasion or an extended period of bombardment, and it would save American lives. The decision to use it was conscious, not automatic, and required no ulterior motive.

The Cost of War

World War II was the most terrible war in history. Military deaths are estimated at some fifteen million, and at least as many civilians were killed. If deaths linked indirectly to the war are included, the figure of victims might reach as high as forty million. Most of Europe and significant parts of Asia were devastated. Yet the end of so terrible a war brought little opportunity for relaxation. The dawn of the Atomic Age and the dramatic end it brought to the war made men conscious that another major war might bring an end to humanity. Everything depended on the conclusion of a stable peace, but even as the fighting came to an end, conflicts among the victors made the prospects of a lasting peace doubtful.

Preparations for Peace and the Onset of the Cold War

The split between the Soviet Union and its wartime allies should cause no surprise. As the self-proclaimed center of world Communism, the Soviet Union was openly dedicated to the overthrow of the capitalist nations, though this message was muted when the occasion demanded. On the other side, the Western allies were no less open about their hostility to Communism and its chief purveyor, the Soviet Union. Though they had been friendly to the early stages of the Russian Revolution, they had sent troops in hopes of overthrowing the Bolshevik regime. The United States did not grant formal recognition to the USSR until 1933. The Western powers' exclusion of the Soviets from the Munich conference and Stalin's pact with Hitler did nothing to improve relations.

Though cooperation against a common enemy and strenuous propaganda efforts in the West helped improve western feeling toward the Soviet ally, Stalin remained suspicious and critical of the Western war effort, and Churchill never ceased planning to contain the Soviet

President Roosevelt and Prime Minister Churchill
meeting on a warship at Placentia Bay, Newfoundland,
in August 1941. There they signed the Atlantic
Charter, a vague and general statement of liberal
aims for the post-war world. [Imperial War Museum,
London.]

advance into Europe. For some time Roosevelt seems to
have been hopeful that the Allies could continue to work
together after the war, but even he was losing faith as the
war and his life drew to a close. Differences in historical
development and ideology, as well as traditional conflicts
over political power and influence, soon dashed whatever
hopes there were of a mutually satisfactory peace settlement and continued cooperation to uphold it.

The Atlantic Charter

In August 1941, even before the Americans were at
war, Roosevelt and Churchill had met on a ship off
Newfoundland and agreed to the Atlantic Charter, a
broad set of principles in the spirit of Wilson's Fourteen
Points, which provided a theoretical basis for the peace
they sought. When Russia and the United States joined
Britain in the war, the three powers entered a purely
military alliance in May 1942, leaving all political questions aside. The first political conference was the meeting
of foreign ministers in Moscow in October 1943. The
ministers reaffirmed earlier agreements to fight on until
the enemy surrendered without condition and to continue
cooperating after the war in a United Nations organization.

Teheran

The first meeting of the three leaders of state took
place at Teheran, the capital of Iran, in 1943. Western
promises to open a second front in France the next
summer and Stalin's agreement to join in the war against
Japan when Germany was defeated created an atmosphere of goodwill in which to discuss a postwar settlement. Stalin wanted to retain what he had gained in his
pact with Hitler and to dismember Germany. Roosevelt
and Churchill were conciliatory, but they made no firm
commitments. The most important decision was the one
that chose Europe's west coast as the point of attack
instead of southern Europe, by the way of the Mediterranean. That meant, in retrospect, that Soviet forces would
occupy eastern Europe and control its destiny. At Teheran in 1943 the Western allies did not foresee this clearly,
for the Russians were still fighting deep within their own

Preparations for Peace and the Onset of the Cold War

frontiers, and military considerations were paramount everywhere.

By 1944 the situation was different. In August Soviet armies were in sight of Warsaw, which had risen in expectation of liberation. But the Russians halted, allowing the Polish rebels to be annihilated while they turned south into the Balkans. They gained control of Romania and Hungary, advances of which centuries of expansionist tsars had only dreamed. Alarmed by these developments, Churchill went to Moscow and met with Stalin in October. They agreed to share power in the Balkans on the basis of Soviet predominance in Romania and Bulgaria, Western predominance in Greece, and equality of influence in Yugoslavia and Hungary. These agreements were not enforceable without American approval, and the Americans were known to be hostile to such un-Wilsonian devices as "spheres of influence."

Yalta

The next meeting of the "Big Three" was at Yalta in the Crimea in February 1945. The Western armies had not yet crossed the Rhine, and the Soviet army was within a hundred miles of Berlin. The war with Japan continued, and no atomic explosion had yet taken place. Roosevelt, faced with an invasion of Japan and heavy losses, was eager to bring the Russians into the Pacific war as soon as possible. As a true Wilsonian he also suspected Churchill's determination to maintain the British Empire and Britain's colonial advantages. The Americans thought that Churchill's plan to set up British spheres of influence in Europe would encourage the Russians to do the same and lead to friction and war. To encourage Russian participation in the war against Japan, Roosevelt and Churchill made extensive concessions to Russia in Sakhalin and the Kurile Islands, in Korea, and in Manchuria. Again in the tradition of Wilson, Roosevelt laid great stress on a United Nations organization: "Through the United Nations, he hoped to achieve a self-enforcing peace settlement that would not require American troops, as well as an open world without

spheres of influence in which American enterprise could work freely."[7] Soviet agreement on these points seemed well worth concessions elsewhere.

Agreement on European questions was more difficult. On Germany the three powers easily agreed on its disarmament and denazification and on its division into four zones of occupation by France and the Big Three. Churchill, however, began to balk at Stalin's plan to dismember Germany and objected to his demand for reparations in the amount of $20 billion as well as forced labor from all the zones and Russia to get half of everything. These matters were left undecided to fester and cause dissension in the future.

The settlement of Eastern Europe was no less a problem. Everyone agreed that the Soviet Union deserved neighboring governments that were friendly, but the West insisted that they also be independent, autonomous, and democratic. The Western leaders, and especially Churchill, were not eager to see Eastern Europe fall under Russian domination; they were also, especially Roosevelt, truly committed to democracy and self-determination. But Stalin knew that independent, freely elected governments in Poland and Romania would not be safely friendly to Russia. He had already established a subservient government in Poland at Lublin in competition with the Polish government-in-exile in London. Under pressure from the Western leaders, however, he agreed to reorganize the government and include some Poles friendly to the West. He also signed a Declaration on Liberated Europe promising self-determination and free democratic elections. Stalin may have been eager to avoid conflict before the war with Germany was over—he never was free of the fear that the Allies might still make an arrangement with Germany and betray him—and he probably thought it worth endorsing some meaningless principles as the price of continued harmony. In any case, he wasted little time in violating these agreements.

7 Robert O. Paxton, *Europe in the Twentieth Century*, (New York: Harcourt Brace, Jovanovich, Inc., 1975), p. 487.

The map pictures the shifts in territory following the defeat of the Axis. No treaty of peace has formally ended the war with Germany. (See also the map on page 930.)

At the Yalta Conference in February 1945 President Roosevelt and Stalin await the arrival of Churchill. Speaking to the President is Edward Stettinius, the American Secretary of State. [The Granger Collection.]

TERRITORIAL CHANGES
AFTER WORLD WAR II

President Harry Truman stands between Stalin and Churchill at the Potsdam Conference in July 1945. [The Granger Collection.]

Potsdam

The Big Three met for the last time in the Berlin suburb of Potsdam in July 1945. Much had changed since the last conference. Germany was defeated, and news of the successful explosion of an atomic weapon reached the American president during the meetings. The cast of characters was also different; Truman replaced Roosevelt, and Clement Attlee (1883–1967), leader of the Labour Party that had defeated Churchill's Conservatives in a general election, spoke for Britain. Previous agreements were reaffirmed but progress on undecided questions was slow.

Russia's western frontier was moved far into what had been Poland and included part of German East Prussia. In compensation Poland was allowed "temporary administration" over the rest of East Prussia and Germany east of the Oder–Neisse river line, a condition that became permanent. In effect Poland was moved about a hundred miles west, at the expense of Germany, to accommodate the Soviet Union. The Allies agreed that Germany would be divided into occupation zones until the final peace treaty was signed. As no such treaty has ever been made, Germany remains divided to this day.

A Council of Foreign Ministers was established to draft peace treaties for Germany's allies. Growing disagreements made the job difficult, and it was not until February 1946 that Italy, Romania, Hungary, Bulgaria, and Finland signed treaties. The Russians were dissatisfied with the treaty made with Japan in 1951 and signed their own agreements with the Japanese in 1956. These disagreements were foreshadowed at Potsdam.

Causes of the Cold War

Some scholars attribute the hardening of the atmosphere to the advent of Truman in place of the more sympathetic Roosevelt and to the American possession of an effective atomic bomb. The fact is that Truman was trying to carry Roosevelt's policies forward, and there is evidence that Roosevelt himself had become distressed by Soviet actions in Eastern Europe. Nor did Truman use the successful test of the atomic bomb to try to keep Russia out of the Pacific. On the contrary, he worked hard to ensure Russian intervention against Japan. In part the new coldness among the Allies arose from the mutual feeling that each had violated previous agreements. The Russians were plainly asserting permanent control of Poland and Romania under puppet Communist governments. The United States, on the other hand, was taking a harder line on the extent of German reparations to the Soviet Union.

In retrospect, however, it appears unlikely that friendlier styles on either side could have avoided a split that rested on basic differences of ideology and interest. The Soviet Union's attempt to extend its control westward into central Europe and the Balkans and southward into the Middle East was a continuation of the policy of tsarist Russia. It had been Britain's traditional role to try to restrain Russian expansion into these areas, and it was not surprising that the United States should inherit that task as Britain's power waned. The alternative was to permit a major change in the balance of power in the world in favor of a huge nation, traditionally hostile, dedicated in its official ideology to overthrow nations like the United States, governed by an absolute dictator who had already demonstrated many times his capacity for the most amazing deceptions and the most horrible cruelties. Few nations would be likely to take such risks.

Nevertheless the Americans made no attempt to roll back Soviet power where it existed, though American military forces were the greatest in their history, their industrial power was unmatched in the world, and atomic weapons were an American monopoly. In less than a year from the war's end American forces in Europe were reduced from 3.5 million to half a million men. The speed of the withdrawal was the result of pressure to "get the boys home" but was fully in accord with American plans and peacetime goals. These were the traditional ones of support for self-determination, autonomy and democracy in the political area, free trade, freedom of the seas, no barriers to investment, and the Open Door in the economic sphere. These goals agreed with American principles, and they also served American interests well. As the strongest, richest nation in the world, the one with the greatest industrial plant and the strongest currency, the United States would benefit handsomely if such an international order were established.

American hostility to colonial empires created tension with France and Britain, but these were minor. The main conflict came with the Soviet Union. From the Soviet perspective the extension of its frontiers and the domination of formerly independent states in Eastern Europe were necessary for the security of the USSR and a proper compensation for the fearful losses the Russians had suffered in the war. American resistance to the new state of things could be seen as a threat to Soviet security and legitimate aims. American objections about Poland and other states could be seen as attempts to undermine regimes friendly to Russia and to encircle the Soviet Union with hostile neighbors. Such behavior might be seen to justify attempts to overthrow regimes friendly to the United States in Western Europe and elsewhere.

The growth in France and Italy of large Communist parties plainly taking orders from Moscow led the Americans to believe that Stalin was engaged in a great worldwide plot to destroy capitalism and democracy by subversion. In the absence of reliable evidence about Stalin's intentions certainty is not possible, but most people in the West thought the suspicions plausible. Rivalry between the Soviet Union and the United States dominated inter-national relations for the next three decades, and in the flawed world of reality it is hard to see how things could have been otherwise. The important question was whether the conflict would take a diplomatic or a military form.

Cold War

Evidence of the new mood of hostility among the former allies was not long in coming. In February 1946 both Stalin and Molotov gave public speeches in which they spoke of the Western democracies as enemies. A month later Churchill gave a speech in Fulton, Missouri, in which he viewed Russian actions in eastern Europe with alarm. He spoke of an Iron Curtain that had descended upon Europe, dividing a free and democratic West from an East under totalitarian rule. He warned against Communist subversion and urged Western unity and strength as a response to the new menace. In this atmosphere difficulties grew.

The attempt to deal with the problem of atomic energy was an early victim of the Cold War. The Americans put forward a plan to place the manufacture and control of atomic weapons under international control, but the Russians balked at the proposed requirements for on-site inspection and for limits on the veto power in the United Nations. The plan fell through. The United States continued to develop its own atomic weapons in secrecy, and the Russians did the same. By 1949, with the help of information obtained by Soviet spies in Britain and the United States, the Soviet Union exploded its own atomic bomb, and the race to nuclear explosions was on.

Any hopes that the new United Nations organization, with its headquarters in New York as a symbol of firm American adherence to international responsibility, would resolve the world's conflicts were soon disappointed. Like the League of Nations, it is dependent on voluntary contributions of money and troops. The UN Charter, moreover, forbids interference in the internal affairs of nations, and many of the problems of the 1940s were internal in nature. Finally, the Security Council, which is responsible for maintaining world peace, gives a veto to each of the permanent members. Because the Soviet Union was generally in the minority, it used the veto repeatedly, making it clear that the United Nations was not adequate to resolve existing problems.

Western resistance to what the West increasingly perceived as Soviet intransigence and Communist plans for subversion and expansion took clearer form in 1947. Since 1944 civil war had been raging in Greece between the royalist government restored by Britain and insurgents supported by Communist countries, chiefly Yugoslavia. In 1947 Britain informed the United States that it was financially no longer able to support the Greeks. On March 12 President Truman asked Congress for legislation to support Greece and also Turkey, which was under Soviet pressure to yield control of the Dardanelles. Congress voted funds only to aid Greece and Turkey, but the Truman Doctrine, as enunciated in the speech of March 12 had a broader significance. The president advocated a policy of supporting "free people who are resisting attempted subjugation by armed minorities or by outside pressures," by implication anywhere in the world.

American aid to Greece and Turkey took the form of military equipment and advisers, but the threat in Western Europe was the growth of Communist parties fed by postwar poverty and hunger. To deal with this menace, the Americans devised the European Recovery Program, named the Marshall Plan after George C. Marshall, the secretary of state who introduced it. This was a plan for broad economic aid to European states on condition only that they work together for their mutual benefit. The invitation included the Soviet Union and its satellites. Finland and Czechoslovakia were willing to participate, and Poland and Hungary showed interest. The Soviets, fearing that American economic aid would attract many satellites out of their orbits, forbade them to take part. The Marshall Plan was a great success in restoring prosperity to Western Europe and setting the stage for its unprecedented economic growth since that time. It also

Churchill Invents the Iron Curtain; Cold War Declared

Winston Churchill chose an American audience (at Westminster College in Fulton, Missouri) for his March 5, 1946 speech that contributed "iron curtain" to the language and, more important, defined the existence of what came to be known as the "cold war" between the communist and the democratic camps.

A SHADOW *has fallen upon the scenes so lately lighted by the Allied victory. Nobody knows what Soviet Russia and its Communist international organization intends to do in the immediate future, or what are the limits, if any, to their expansive and proselytizing tendencies. . . .*

From Stettin in the Baltic to Trieste in the Adriatic, an iron curtain has descended across the Continent. Behind that line lie all the capitals of the ancient states of central and eastern Europe. Warsaw, Berlin, Prague, Vienna, Budapest, Belgrade, Bucharest and Sofia, all these famous cities and the populations around them lie in the Soviet sphere and all are subject in one form or another, not only to Soviet influence but to a very high and increasing measure of control from Moscow. Athens alone, with its immortal glories, is free to decide its future at an election under British, American and French observation. The Russian dominated Polish government has been encouraged to make enormous and wrongful inroads upon Germany, and mass expulsions of millions of Germans on a scale grievous and undreamed of are now taking place. The Communist parties, which were very small in all these eastern states of Europe, have been raised to pre-eminence and power far beyond their numbers and are seeking everywhere to obtain totalitarian control. Police governments are prevailing in nearly every case, and so far, except in Czechoslovakia, there is no true democracy. . . .

. . . I do not believe that Soviet Russia desires war. What they desire is the fruits of war and the indefinite expansion of their power and doctrines. . . .

. . . If the western democracies stand together in strict adherence to the principles of the United Nations Charter, their influence for furthering these principles will be immense and no one is likely to molest them. If, however, they become divided or falter in their duty, and if these all-important years are allowed to slip away, then indeed catastrophe may overwhelm us all.

"Winston Churchill's Speech at Fulton," in *Vital Speeches of the Day*, Vol. 12 (March 15, 1946) (New York: City News Publishing Co.), pp. 331–332.

The headquarters of the United Nations in New York City. [United Nations.]

Josef Cardinal Mindszenty was one of the major anti-communist heroes of the Cold War. As Roman Catholic primate of Hungary he was tried in 1949 by the Communists for treason, convicted, and imprisoned. This picture shows him at his trial flanked by two guards. During the 1956 uprising he escaped and took refuge in the American Embassy in Budapest, where he remained until 1971 when he was permitted to fly to Rome. [United Press International Photo.]

led to the waning of communist strength in the West and to the establishment of solid democratic regimes.

From the Western viewpoint this policy of "containment" was a new and successful response to the Soviet and communist challenge. To Stalin it may have seemed a renewal of the old Western attempt to isolate and encircle the USSR. His answer was to put an end to all multiparty governments behind the Iron Curtain and to replace them with thoroughly communist regimes completely under his control. He also called a meeting of all communist parties around the world at Warsaw in the autumn of 1947. There they organized the Communist Information Bureau (Cominform), a revival of the old Comintern, dedicated to spreading revolutionary communism throughout the world. The era of the popular front was officially over. Communist leaders in the West who favored friendship, collaboration, and reform were replaced by hard-liners who attempted to sabotage the new structures.

In February 1948 a more dramatic and brutal display of Stalin's new policy took place in Prague. The communists expelled the democratic members of what had been a coalition government and murdered Jan Masaryk, the foreign minister and son of the founder of Czechoslo-

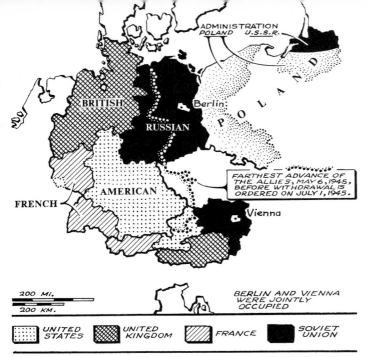

At the war's end, defeated Germany, including Austria, was occupied by the victorious Allies in the several zones shown here. Austria, by prompt agreement, was re-erected into an independent, neutral state and no longer occupied. But the German zones have hardened into an "East" Germany (the former Soviet zone) and a "West" Germany (the former British, French, and American zones). The city of Berlin, within the Soviet zone, was similarly divided.

OCCUPIED GERMANY AND AUSTRIA

vakia, Thomas Masaryk. President Beneš was also forced to resign, and Czechoslovakia was brought fully under Soviet rule.

These Soviet actions, especially those in Czechoslovakia, increased American determination to go ahead with its own arrangements in Germany. The wartime Allies had never agreed on the details of a German settlement and kept putting off decisions. At first they all agreed on the dismemberment of Germany but not on the form it should take. By the time of Yalta, Churchill had come to fear Russian control of Eastern and Central Europe and began to oppose dismemberment. There were differences in economic policy too. The Russians proceeded swiftly to dismantle German industry in the eastern zone, but the Americans acted differently. They concluded that such a policy would require the United States to support Germany for the foreseeable future. It would also cause political chaos and open the way for Communism. They preferred, therefore, to try to make Germany self-sufficient, and this meant restoring rather than destroying its industrial capacity. To the Soviets the restoration of a powerful industrial Germany, even in the western zones only, was frightening and unacceptable. The same difference of approach hampered agreement on reparations because the Soviets claimed the right to industrial equipment in all the zones, and the Americans resisted their demands.

Disagreement over Germany produced the most heated of postwar debates. When the Western powers agreed to go forward with a separate constitution for

Germany in the west in February 1948, the Soviets walked out of the joint Allied Control Commission. In the summer of that year the Western powers issued a new currency in their zone. Berlin, though well within the Soviet zone, was governed by all four powers. The Soviets feared the new currency circulating in Berlin at better rates than their own and chose to seal the city off by closing all railroads and highways to West Germany. The Western allies responded with an airlift of supplies to the city that lasted almost a year. In May 1949 the Russians were forced to back down and open access to Berlin, but the incident was decisive. It greatly increased tensions and suspicions between the opponents, and it hastened the lasting separation of Germany into two states. West Germany formally became the German Federated Republic in September 1949, and the eastern region became the German Democratic Republic a month later. Ironically Germany had been dismembered in a way no one had planned or expected.

NATO AND THE WARSAW PACT. Meanwhile the nations of Western Europe had been coming closer together. The Marshall Plan encouraged international cooperation, and in March 1948 Belgium, the Netherlands, Luxembourg, France, and Britain signed the Treaty of Brussels, providing for cooperation in economic and military matters. In April 1949 these nations joined with Italy, Denmark, Norway, Portugal, and Iceland to sign a treaty with Canada and the United States that formed the North Atlantic Treaty Organization (NATO). NATO committed its members to mutual assistance in case any was attacked. For the first time in history the United States was committed to defend allies outside the Western Hemisphere. The NATO treaty formed the West into a bloc. A few years later West Germany, Greece, and Turkey joined the alliance.

Soviet relations with the states of Eastern Europe were governed by a series of bilateral treaties providing for close ties and mutual assistance in case of attack. In 1949 the Council of Mutual Assistance (COMECON) was formed to integrate the economies of these states. Unlike

The North Atlantic Treaty Organization, which includes both Canada and the United States, stretches
as far east as Turkey. By contrast, the Warsaw Pact
nations are contiguous communist states of eastern
Europe, with the Soviet Union, of course, as the
dominant member.

- NON-EUROPEAN MEMBERS OF NATO:
  · UNITED STATES
  · CANADA
- SPECIAL TREATY BETWEEN THE UNITED STATES AND SPAIN.
- OTHER COMMUNIST NATIONS:
  · YUGOSLAVIA — NOT A MEMBER OF THE WARSAW PACT.
  · ALBANIA — WITHDREW FROM THE WARSAW PACT IN 1968.

MAJOR EUROPEAN ALLIANCE SYSTEMS

the NATO states the Eastern alliance system was under
direct Soviet domination through local communist parties
controlled from Moscow and overawed by the presence
of the Red Army. The Warsaw Pact of May 1955,
which included Albania, Bulgaria, Czechoslovakia, East
Germany, Hungary, Poland, Romania, and the Soviet
Union, merely gave formal recognition to a system that
already existed. Europe was divided into two unfriendly
blocs. The Cold War had taken firm shape in Europe.

SUGGESTED READINGS

A. BULLOCK, *Hitler: A Study in Tyranny*, rev. ed. (New
York, 1964). A brilliant biography.

W. S. CHURCHILL, *The Second World War*, 6 vols. (London, 1948–1954). The memoirs of the great British leader.

H. FEIS, *From Trust to Terror: The Onset of the Cold War,
1945–1950* (Princeton, 1970). The best general account.

H. W. GATZKE, *Stresemann and the Rearmament of Germany* (Baltimore, 1954). An important monograph.

H. W. GATZKE (Ed.), *European Diplomacy Between Two
Wars* (Chicago, 1972). A collection of important essays.

M. GILBERT, *The Roots of Appeasement* (New York, 1966).
A study of diplomacy and opinion in the 1920s.

M. GILBERT AND R. GOTT, *The Appeasers*, rev. ed.
(Boston, 1963). A revealing study of British policy in the
1930s.

B. H. LIDDELL HART, *History of the Second World War*,
2 vols. (New York, 1971). A good military history.

K. HILDEBRAND, *The Foreign Policy of the Third Reich*
(Berkeley, 1970).

G. KOLKO, *The Politics of War* (New York, 1968). An
interesting example of the new revisionist school that finds
the causes of the Cold War in economic considerations and
emphasizes American responsibility.

L. LAFORE, *The End of Glory* (Philadelphia and New York,
1970). A well-written interpretive essay on the origins of
World War II.

W. L. LANGER AND S. E. GLEASON, *The Challenge of
Isolation* (New York, 1952). American foreign policy in the
1930s.

E. M. ROBERTSON, *Hitler's Pre-War Policy and Military
Plans* (London, 1963).

E. M. ROBERTSON (Ed.), *The Origins of the Second World
War* (New York, 1971). A valuable collection of essays.

R. J. SONTAG, *A Broken World 1919–1939* (New York,
1971). An excellent survey.

A. J. P. TAYLOR, *The Origins of the Second World War*
(New York, 1966). A lively, controversial, even perverse
study.

C. THORNE, *The Approach of War 1938–1939* (London,
1967). A careful analysis of diplomacy.

J. W. WHEELER-BENNET, *Munich: Prologue to Tragedy* (London, 1966). A fine study of the crisis.

A. WOLFERS, *Britain and France Between Two Wars* (New
York, 1940). Still a valuable study of the policy of the
Western powers.

G. WRIGHT, *The Ordeal of Total War 1939–1945* (New York,
1968). An excellent survey.

932

34
Europe in the Era of the Superpowers

ABOUT thirty-five years have passed since the conclusion of World War II and the onset of the Cold War. In this period of considerably more than a human generation, Europe has remained divided between communist and non-communist states and between allies of the United States and those of the Soviet Union. Such division is hardly a new feature of European history. For centuries the continent was separated into Roman and barbarian areas, later into Christian and Islamic spheres, then into Protestant, Catholic, and Orthodox camps, and finally into liberal and conservative states. Each of these divisions left an imprint on the culture of Europe. This seems no less true of the Cold War separation, although the latter may prove less long-lived than the previous divisions.

The three decades of the Cold War have witnessed extraordinary changes in European political and economic life. These in turn have produced significant results for the rest of the world once dominated by Europeans. Leadership in the western part of the Continent shifted to the United States and in the eastern part to the Soviet Union. The successor states of the Austria–Hungarian Empire previously coveted by Hitler fell under Soviet domination. Britain, France, Belgium, the Netherlands, and Portugal have conducted what is no doubt a permanent retreat from world empire. They have thus concluded an era of European world dominance that had commenced during the Renaissance.

Many of those same nations began to cooperate economically and politically with each other as at no time in previous European experience. Peaceful economic integration and possible political unity became facts of everyday life. These same years also saw much of the Continent experience the most extensive material prosperity in its history. Even though the relative power of Europe has clearly declined since 1939, the Cold War rivalry, decolonization, the movement toward unity, and the economic growth have led to a continuing European influence elsewhere in the world.

Europe and the Soviet–American Rivalry

From approximately 1848 to 1948 the nation-state characterized European political life and rivalry. Generally these countries sought to expand their political influence and economic power at each other's expense. During the same century Europe's economic and technological supremacy allowed certain of its states to rule or administer a vast area of the globe inhabited by non-European peoples. These nation-states have obviously continued to exist, but the economic and political collapse occasioned by World War II led them to become more interrelated and interdependent. The loss of economic and military superiority coincided with and in some cases aided the rise of nationalism throughout the colonial world. The United States and the Soviet Union—with their extensive economic resources, military forces, and nuclear capacities—have filled the power vacuum created by the European collapse.

The new situation of Europe lying between two superpowers marked a genuine turning point in the history of the Continent. Prior to 1939 Great Britain, France, and Germany had been, in the context of the times, "world" powers. During the thirties even Italy through its ventures in Ethiopia had aspired to that position. By the onset of the 1960s it had become evident that all of these nations had become simply "European" powers and were no longer wholly independent states even in that

This vast statue, Worker and Peasant, by the Soviet sculptor V. Mukhina, stands in Moscow outside the Soviet Economics Achievement Exhibition. The sheer size of the monument is meant to suggest the subduing of physical nature by the workers and peasants and the productive power of the Soviet system. It may also symbolize the dominance of the Soviet Union over much of Europe since 1945. [Tass from Sovfoto.]

The "spirit of Geneva" is displayed in this picture of the four major leaders who met there in the summer of 1955 for a summit conference. From left to right they are Nikolai Bulganin of the Soviet Union, Dwight Eisenhower of the United States, Edgar Faure of France, and Anthony Eden of Great Britain. [United Press International Photo.]

position. The impact of the Marshall Plan and the nuclear deterrent power of America meant that the United States would exert a relatively permanent influence on Europe. There was to be no return to the isolationism that had characterized American policy after World War I. Europe as a whole, and more particularly Germany, became an arena for continuing confrontation and tension between the United States and the Soviet Union. The kind of direct and indirect power that European nations had once exerted elsewhere in the world was now being exercised over them.

The first round of Cold War confrontations culminated in the formation of NATO (1949) and the intervention of United States and United Nations forces in Korea (1950). In 1953 Stalin died, and later that year an armistice was concluded in Korea. Both events produced hope that international tensions might lessen. In early 1955 Austria agreed to become a neutral state, and Soviet occupation forces left. Later that year the leaders of France, Great Britain, the Soviet Union, and the United States held a summit conference at Geneva. Nuclear weapons and the future of divided Germany were the chief items on the agenda. Although there was much public display of friendliness among the participants, there were few substantial agreements on major problems. Nonetheless the fact that statesmen were discussing problems and issues produced the so-called "spirit of Geneva." This atmosphere proved short-lived, and the rivalry of power and polemics soon resumed.

The year 1956 was one of considerable significance for both the Cold War and the recognition of the realities of European power in the postwar era. In July President Gamal Nasser (1918–1970) of Egypt nationalized the Suez Canal. Great Britain and France feared that this action would close the canal to their supplies of oil in the Persian Gulf. In October 1956 war broke out between Egypt and the eight-year-old state of Israel. The British and the French seized the opportunity of this conflict to intervene. Publicly they spoke of acting to separate the combatants, but their real motive was to recapture the canal. The Anglo-French military operation was a fiasco of the first order and resulted in a humiliating diplomatic defeat. The United States refused to support their action. The Soviet Union protested in the most severe terms. The Anglo-French forces had to be withdrawn, and control of the canal remained with Egypt. The Suez intervention proved that without the support of the United States the nations of Western Europe could no longer undertake meaningful military operations. They could no longer impose their will on the rest of the world. At the same time, it appeared that the United States and the Soviet Union had acted to restrain allies from undertaking actions that might result in a wider conflict. The fact that neither of the superpowers wanted war put limitations on the actions of both Egypt and the Anglo-French forces.

The autumn of 1956 also saw important developments in Eastern Europe. These demonstrated in a similar fashion the limitations on independent action among the Soviet bloc nations. When the prime minister of Poland died, the Polish Communist Party leaders refused to choose as his successor the person selected by Moscow. Considerable tension developed. The Soviet leaders even visited Warsaw to make their opinions known. In the end Wladislav Gomulka (b. 1905) emerged as the new Communist leader of Poland. He was the choice of the Poles, and he proved acceptable to the Soviets because he promised continued economic and military cooperation. Within those limits he moved to halt collectivization of Polish agriculture and to improve the relationship between the Communist government and the Polish Roman Catholic Church.

Hungary provided the second trouble spot for the Soviet Union. In late October, as the Polish problem was approaching a solution, demonstrations and street fighting erupted in Budapest. A new government headed by former premier Imre Nagy (1896–1958) was installed. He was a communist who sought a more independent position for Hungary. He called for the removal of Soviet troops and the ultimate neutralization of Hungary. These

Budapest, October 1956. [ABOVE] Street battles raged for several days until Soviet tanks finally put down the Hungarian revolt. [LEFT] A woman carrying flowers and followed by a black flag leads a procession of mourners in an anti-Soviet demonstration in Marx Square. [BOTH: Raymond Darolle. Sygma.]

President Kennedy Defines the Cold War Arena

This passage is from President John F. Kennedy's speech at the time of the Berlin Wall crisis of 1961. He called for a democratic challenge to communism throughout the world. The commitment to Southeast Asia would later lead to the major war in Vietnam.

THE *immediate threat to free men is in West Berlin. But that isolated outpost is not an isolated problem. The threat is worldwide. Our effort must be equally wide and strong, and not be obsessed by any single manufactured crisis. We face a challenge in Berlin, but there is also a challenge in Southeast Asia, where the borders are less guarded, the enemy harder to find, and the dangers of Communism less apparent to those who have so little. We face a challenge in our own hemisphere, and indeed wherever else the freedom of human beings is at stake.*

Public Papers of the Presidents of the United States, John F. Kennedy. January 20 to December 31, 1961, ed. by Wayne C. Gover (Washington: U.S. Government Printing Office, 1962), pp. 533.

demands were wholly unacceptable to the Soviet Union. In early November Soviet troops invaded the country; deposed Nagy, who was later executed; and imposed Janos Kadar (b. 1912) as premier. The Suez intervention had provided an international diversion that helped to permit free action by the Soviet Union. The Polish and Hungarian disturbances had several results. They demonstrated the limitations of independence within the Soviet bloc, but they did not bring an end to independent action. They also demonstrated that the example of Austrian neutrality would not be imitated elsewhere in eastern Europe. Finally, the failure of the United States to take any action in the Hungarian uprising proved the hollowness of American political rhetoric about liberating the captive nations of eastern Europe.

The events of 1956 brought to a close the era of fully autonomous action by the European nation-states. In very different ways and to differing degrees the two superpowers had demonstrated the new political realities. After 1956 the Soviet Union began to talk about "peaceful coexistence" with the United States. In 1958 negotiations commenced between the two countries for limitations on the testing of nuclear weapons. However, that same year the Soviet Union announced that the status of West Berlin must be changed and the Allied occupation forces

withdrawn. The demand was refused. In 1959 tensions relaxed sufficiently for several Western leaders to visit Moscow and for Soviet Premier Nikita Khrushchev (1894–1971) to tour the United States. A summit meeting was scheduled for May 1960, and American President Eisenhower was to go to Moscow.

The Paris Summit Conference of 1960 proved anything but a repetition of the friendly days of 1955. Just before the gathering, the Soviet Union shot down an American U-2 aircraft that was flying reconnaissance over Soviet territory. Khrushchev demanded an apology from President Eisenhower and aborted the summit conference as the participants arrived in the French capital. Eisenhower's trip to the Soviet Union never took place.

The Soviets had long been aware of the American flights but chose to protest at this time for two reasons. Khrushchev had hoped that the leaders of Britain, France, and the United States would be sufficiently divided over the future of Germany so that a united Allied front would be impossible. The divisions did not come about as he had hoped. Consequently the conference would have been of little use to him. Second, by 1960 the communist world itself had become split between the Soviets and the Chinese. The latter were portraying the Russians as lacking sufficient revolutionary zeal. Khrushchev's action was in part a response to those charges and proof of the hard-line attitude of the Soviet Union toward the capitalist world.

The abortive Paris conference opened the most difficult period of the Cold War. In 1961 the new U.S. president, John F. Kennedy, and Premier Khrushchev met in Vienna. The conference was inconclusive, but the American president left wondering if the two nations could avoid war. Throughout 1961 thousands of refugees from East Germany were crossing the border into West Berlin. This outflow was a political embarrassment to East Germany and a detriment to its economic life. In August 1961 the East Germans erected a concrete wall along the border between East and West Berlin. Henceforth it was possible to cross only at designated checkpoints and with proper papers. The United States protested and sent Vice President Lyndon Johnson to Berlin to reassure its citizens, but the wall remained—and does so to the present day. The refugee stream was halted, and the United States commitment to West Germany was brought into doubt.

A year later the most dangerous days of the Cold War occurred during the Cuban missile crisis. The Soviet Union attempted to place missiles in Cuba, which was a nation friendly to Soviet aims lying less than a hundred miles from the United States. The United States blockaded Cuba, halted the shipment of new missiles, and demanded the removal of existing installations. After a very tense week, with numerous threats and messages between Moscow and Washington, the crisis ended and the Soviets backed down.

The Cuban missile crisis was the last major Cold War confrontation that would have involved Europe directly. Thereafter the American–Soviet rivalry shifted to the war in Vietnam and the Arab–Israeli conflict in the Near East. A "hotline" communications system was installed between Moscow and Washington for more rapid and direct exchange of diplomatic messages in times of crisis.

In 1963 the two powers concluded a Nuclear Test Ban treaty. This agreement marked the beginning of a lessening in the tensions between the United States and the Soviet Union. The German problem somewhat subsided in the late sixties as West Germany under Premier Willy Brandt (b. 1913) moved to improve its relations with the Soviet Union and eastern Europe. In 1968 the Soviet Union invaded Czechoslovakia to prevent its emergence into further independence. Although deplored by the United States, this action led to no renewal of tensions. During the presidency of Richard Nixon (1969–1974) the United States embarked on a policy of detente or reduction of tension with the Soviet Union. This policy involved trade agreements and mutual reduction of strategic armaments. In 1975 President Gerald Ford attended a conference in Helsinki, Finland, that in effect recognized the Soviet sphere of influence in eastern Eu-

rope. The Helsinki Treaty also committed its signatory powers, including the Soviet Union, to recognize and protect the human rights of their citizens. The foreign policy of President Jimmy Carter has stressed the observance of these human rights clauses.

The late sixties and early seventies saw other changes in postwar relations between Europe and the United States. The NATO alliance became somewhat weaker as France moved to oppose United States influence over Europeans. The unpopularity of United States involvement in Vietnam strained its relations with NATO allies. Moreover the genuine possibility of Communist governments in Portugal and Italy after 1974 raised new questions about the strength and unity of NATO. During the late seventies the influence of the United States over Western Europe remained, but it was clear that the desires of Europeans as well as of Americans would have to be taken into greater account as policy was formulated for the future.

Decolonization and the Cold War
Retreat from Empire

At the onset of World War II many of the nations of Europe were still imperial powers. Great Britain, France, the Netherlands, Belgium, Italy, and Portugal governed millions of non-European peoples. One of the most striking and significant postwar developments has been the decolonization of these imperial holdings and the consequent emergence of the so-called Third World political bloc. The process of retreat from empire involved the colonial powers in three major stages of difficulties. The first was the turmoil created by nationalist movements and revolts in the colonies. The second was the injection of Cold War diplomacy and rivalries into the power vacuums formed by the European withdrawals. Finally, in recent years the control of important natural resources and particularly of oil by the new nations of the Third World has put considerable economic pressure on both Western Europe and the United States. This last condi-

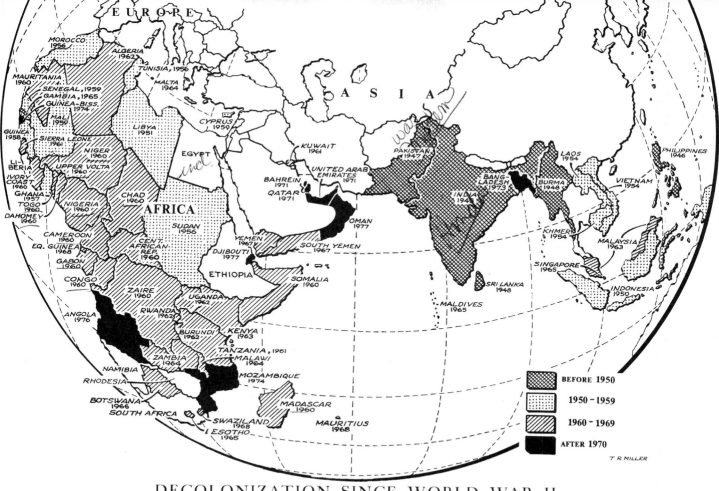

DECOLONIZATION SINCE WORLD WAR II

Legend:
- BEFORE 1950
- 1950-1959
- 1960-1969
- AFTER 1970

T R MILLER

tion may well prove the most important factor in world politics for the remainder of this century.

The decolonization that has occurred since 1945 has been a direct result of both the war itself and the rise of indigenous nationalist movements within the European colonial world. The conflict drew the military forces of the colonial powers back to Europe. The Japanese conquests of Asia helped to turn out the European powers in that area. After the military and political dislocations of the war came the postwar economic collapse. The latter meant that the colonial powers could no longer afford to maintain their positions abroad.

Finally, the war aims of the Allies undermined colonialism. It was difficult to fight against tyranny in Europe while maintaining colonial dominance abroad. Moreover the postwar policy of the United States generally opposed continuation of European empires. Within the colonies there had also arisen nationalist movements of varying strengths. These were often led by gifted persons who had been educated in Europe. The values and political ideologies they had learned in Europe itself helped them to present effective critiques of the colonial situation. Such leadership, as well as the frequently blatant injustice

imposed upon colonial peoples, paved the way for effective nationalist movements.

There was a wide variety in decolonization. Some cases were relatively systematic; in others the European powers simply beat a hasty retreat. In 1947 Britain left India. The result of internal disputes, including religious differences, was the creation of two states, India and Pakistan. In 1948 Burma became independent. During the fifties the British attempted to prepare colonies for self-government. Ghana (formerly the Gold Coast) and Nigeria—which became self-governing in 1957 and 1960, respectively—were the major examples of planned decolonization. In other areas, such as Malta and Cyprus, the British withdrawal occurred under the pressure of militant nationalist movements.

The smaller colonial powers had much less choice. The Dutch were forced from Indonesia in 1950. In 1960 the Belgian Congo, now Zaire, became independent in the midst of great turmoil. For a considerable time, as will be seen, France attempted to maintain its position in Southeast Asia but met defeat in 1954. It was similarly driven from North Africa. President De Gaulle carried out a policy of referendums within remaining French colonial possessions. By the late sixties only Portugal remained a traditional colonial power. In 1975 it finally abandoned its African colony of Angola.

The retreat from empire represents a major turning point in both European and world history. European and Western influences remain active in the former colonial world. Multinational corporations can and do exert considerable power over developing economies. The trade policies of the major Western industrial nations can do likewise. However, it now seems certain that in the future the command over natural resources possessed by these new nations will mean a considerable loss of independence by European and Western nations generally. At the end of the nineteenth century the technological power of Europe allowed certain nations to become colonial powers. At the close of the twentieth century the dependence of European industry and technology upon the resources of the underdeveloped world may very well mean that the former colonies will exert immense influence over the destiny of Europeans. The oil embargo of 1973 imposed on Europe by the oil-producing countries of the world demonstrated the potential for such powerful influence. The rest of this century will be largely devoted to the working out of this new economic balance. Although the political power of Europe will thus be lessened, the impact of its culture and of the technology originally developed in Europe will continue to expand as nations throughout the world continue to become westernized.

France, the United States, and Vietnam

So far as the general history of the West is concerned, the decolonization policies of France produced the major postwar upheavals. French decolonization became an integral part of the Cold War and led directly to the involvement of the United States in the Southeast Asian country of Vietnam. The problem of decolonization helped to transfer the Cold War rivalry that had developed in Europe to other continents. Nowhere did those rivalries become more intense than in Asia. Moreover,

there was a close relationship between events in Asia and in Europe.

KOREA. To elucidate how the United States became so deeply involved in the French attempt to maintain its position in Vietnam, brief attention must first be given to the Korean War.

Between 1910 and 1945 Japan as an Asian colonial power in its own right occupied and exploited Korea. By the close of World War II the Japanese had been driven out of the Korean peninsula. At home, under the direction of the United States, the Japanese nation was politically reconstructed into a democracy. The influence of the army and of large business combines was reduced. Women were allowed to vote, and representative institutions were imposed. General Douglas MacArthur was the representative of the United States during this crucial period. Maintenance of a democratic Japan was to be a cornerstone of postwar United States policy.

The Japanese empire still had to be dealt with. Consequently the United States and the Soviet Union presided over the division of Korea into two parts with the thirty-eighth parallel as the line of separation. It was anticipated that the country would eventually be reunited. However, by 1948 two separate states had been organized: the Democratic People's Republic of Korea under Kim Il-sung in the north and the Republic of Korea under Syngman Rhee in the south. The former was supported by the Soviet Union and the latter by the United States.

Numerous border clashes occurred between the two states. In late June 1950 forces from North Korea crossed the thirty-eighth parallel. The United States intervened and was soon supported by the mandate of the United Nations. Great Britain, Turkey, and Australia sent token forces. The troops were commanded by General MacArthur. The Korean police action was technically a United Nations venture to halt aggression. (It had been made possible by a boycott of the Soviet ambassador to the United Nations at the time of the key vote.) From the standpoint of the United States the point of the Korean conflict was to contain the spread and to halt the

The North Korean invasion of South Korea in 1950 and the bitter three-year war to repulse the invasion and stabilize a firm boundary near the thirty-eighth parallel are outlined here. The war was a dramatic application of the American policy of "containment" of communism.

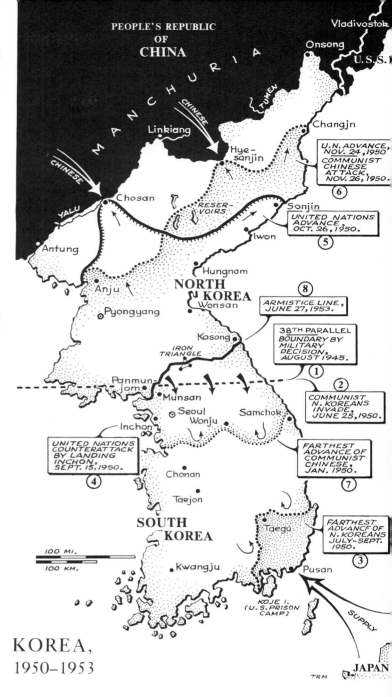

KOREA,
1950–1953

aggression of communism. The United States policy makers tended to conceive of the communist world as a single unit directed from Moscow. The movement of forces into South Korea was simply another example of communist pressure against a noncommunist state similar to that previously confronted in Europe.

General MacArthur's forces had initially repelled the North Koreans. He then pushed them almost to Manchuria. Late in 1950, however, the Chinese, responding to the pressure against their border, sent troops to support North Korea. The American forces had to retreat. The United States policymakers believed that the Chinese, who since 1949 had been under the communist government of Mao Tse-tung (1893–1976), were simply the puppets of Moscow. For over two years the war bogged down. Eventually a border near the thirty-eighth parallel was restored. The war lasted until June 26, 1953, when an armistice was signed. In Korea limited military action had halted and contained the military advance of a communist nation. The lessons of the Cold War learned in Europe had been successfully applied to Asia. The American government was confirmed in its faith in a policy of containment.

VIETNAM. During the years of the Korean conflict another war was being fought in Asia between France and the Viet Minh nationalist movement in Indochina. France, in its push for empire, had occupied this territory, including Laos, Cambodia, and Vietnam, between 1857 and 1883. It had administered the area and invested heavily in it, but the economy of Indochina remained overwhelmingly agrarian. During World War I tens of thousands of Indochinese troops supported France. The French also educated many people from the colony. However, neither the aid during the war nor the achievement of Western education allowed the Vietnamese to escape discrimination from their French colonial rulers. By the time of World War II, resistance to French government had developed in Vietnam.

By 1930 a movement against French colonial rule had been organized by Ho Chi Minh (1892–1969) into the Indochinese Communist Party. Ho had traveled throughout the world and had held jobs in several places in Europe prior to World War I. He and other Indochinese had lobbied at the Versailles Conference in 1919 to have the principle of self-determination applied to their country. In 1920 he was part of the wing of the French Socialist Party that formed the French Communist Party. In 1923 he was sent to Moscow. By 1925 he had formed the Vietnam Revolutionary Youth. After organizing the

Indochinese Communist Party, he traveled in Asia and spent considerable time in the Soviet Union. Throughout the thirties, however, the French succeeded in suppressing most activities by the Communist Party in their colony.

World War II provided new opportunities for Ho Chi Minh and other nationalists. When Japan invaded, it found the pro-Vichy French colonial administration ready to collaborate. Consequently action against the Japanese thereafter meshed quite neatly with action against the French. It was during these wartime circumstances that Ho Chi Minh established his position as a major nationalist leader. He was a Communist to be sure, but he was first and foremost a nationalist. Most important, he had achieved his position in Vietnam during the war independent of the support of the Chinese Communist movement.

In September 1945 Ho Chi Minh declared the independence of Vietnam under the Viet Minh. There was considerable internal Vietnamese resistance to this claim of political control. The opposition arose from religious groups and noncommunist nationalists. After the war the French immediately took advantage of these divisions to establish a government favorable to their own interests. The United States, in line with its wartime anticolonialist position, urged the French to make some kind of accommodation with Ho Chi Minh. In 1946 France and the Viet Minh reached an armistice. It proved quite temporary, and in 1947 full-fledged war broke out. The next year the French established a friendly Vietnamese government under Bao Dai. It was to be independent within a loose union with France. This arrangement would have meant very limited independence and was clearly unacceptable to both the Viet Minh and most other nationalists.

Until 1949 the United States had displayed only the most minimal concern in the Indochina War. However, the defeat in China of Chiang Kai-shek (1887–1975) in 1949 and the victors' establishment of the communist People's Republic of China changed that situation dra-

matically. This turn of events led the United States to regard the French colonial war against Ho Chi Minh as an integral part of the Cold War conflict. The French government, hoping for United States support, worked to maintain that point of view. Early in 1950 the United States recognized the Bao Dai government. At approximately the same time the Soviet Union and the People's Republic of China recognized the governement of Ho Chi Minh. Indochina was thus transformed from a colonial battleground into an area of Cold War confrontation.

In May 1950 the United States announced that it would supply financial aid to the French war effort. Between that time and 1954 more than $4 billion flowed from the United States to France. However, the war itself deteriorated for the French. In the spring of 1954 their army was overrun by the Viet Minh forces at the battle of Dien Bien Phu. Psychologically and militarily the French could not muster new energy for the war. Pierre Mendès-France (b. 1907) was elected premier in Paris on the promise of concluding the conflict. At this point the United States government was badly divided, but it decided against military intervention.

During the late spring and early summer of 1954 a conference was held at Geneva to settle the Indochina conflict. All in all it proved a most unsatisfactory gathering. To one degree or another, all of the major powers were involved in the proceedings, but they did not sign the agreements. Technically the agreements existed between the armed forces of France and those of the Viet Minh. The precedents for such arrangements were the surrender of the German army in 1945 and the Korean armistice of 1953. The Geneva conference provided for the division of Vietnam at the seventeenth parallel. This was to be a temporary border. By 1956 elections were to be held to reunify the country. North of the parallel, centered on the city of Hanoi, the Viet Minh were in charge; below it, the French were in charge, with Saigon the major city. The prospect of elections meant that theoretically both groups could function politically in the

VIETNAM AND ITS NEIGHBORS

The Southeast Asia scene of the long and complex struggle centered in Vietnam is shown by the map.

territory of the other. In effect, the conference attempted to transform a military conflict into a political one.

The United States was less than happy about the results of the Geneva discussions. Its first major response came in September 1954, with the formation of the Southeast Asia Treaty Organization (SEATO). It was a collective security agreement that in some respects paralleled the European NATO alliance. However, it did not involve the integration of forces achieved in NATO, nor did it include all the major states of the region. Its membership consisted of the United States, Great Britain, France, Australia, New Zealand, Thailand, Pakistan, and the Philippines.

By 1955 American policy makers had begun to think about the Indochina region, and more especially Vietnam, largely in terms of the Korean example. The United States government assumed that the government being established in North Vietnam was, like the government of North Korea, basically a communist puppet state. The same year French troops began to withdraw from the south. As they left, the various Vietnamese political groups began to fight for power. Into the turmoil of the power vacuum stepped the United States with military and economic aid. Among the Vietnamese politicians, it chose to support Ngo Dinh Diem. He was a strong noncommunist nationalist who had not collaborated with the French. The Americans hoped that he would become a leader around whom a noncommunist Vietnamese nationalist movement might rally. However, because the United States had publicly been deeply committed to the French, any government it supported would be and was viewed with suspicion by Vietnamese nationalists. In October 1955 Diem established a Republic of Vietnam in the territory for which the Geneva conference had made France responsible. By 1956 the United States was training troops and government officials, paying salaries, and providing military equipment.

In the meantime Diem announced that he and his newly established government were not bound by the Geneva agreements and that elections would not be held in 1956. The American government, which had not signed the Geneva documents, supported his position. Diem undertook an anticommunist campaign, attacking many citizens who had earlier resisted the French. This was the beginning of a program of political repression that characterized his regime and those that followed. There was a long series of ordinances that gave the government extraordinary power over its citizens. Diem alienated the peasants by restoring rents to landlords and generally strengthening large landowners. He abolished elected village councils and replaced them with his own officials, who had often come from the north. In fact, Diem's major base of political support lay with the more

Decolonization and the Cold War 943

Soldiers of the United States equipped with sophisticated weapons examine a Viet Cong guerilla booby trap in Vietnam. One of the great frustrations of the war for the Americans was the ability of relatively simple guerilla tactics of sabotage to slow or even halt altogether technologically advanced American operations. [Official United States Navy Photograph.]

than one million Vietnamese who had migrated to the south after 1954.

By 1960 Diem's policy had created considerable internal resistance in South Vietnam. In that year the National Liberation Front was founded, with the goals of overthrowing Diem, unifying the country, reforming the economy, and ousting the Americans. It was anticolonial, nationalist, and communist. Its military arm was called the Viet Cong. Sometime in the very late fifties the government of North Vietnam began to aid the insurgent forces of the south. The Viet Cong and their supporters carried out a program of widespread terrorism and political disruption. They imposed an informal government through much of the countryside. Many peasants voluntarily supported them; others supported them from fear of reprisals. In addition to the communist opposition, Diem confronted mounting criticism from noncommunist citizens. The Buddhists agitated against the Roman Catholic president. The army was less than satisfied with him. Diem's response to all of these pressures was further repression and dependence on an ever smaller group of advisers.

The Eisenhower and early Kennedy administrations in America continued to support Diem while demanding reforms. The American military presence grew from somewhat more than six hundred persons in early 1961 to over sixteen thousand troops in late 1963. The political situation in Vietnam became increasingly unstable. On November 1, 1963, Diem was overthrown and murdered in an army *coup*. The United States was deeply involved in this plot. Its officials hoped that if the Diem regime were eliminated, the path would be opened for the establishment of a new government in South Vietnam capable of generating popular support. Thereafter the political goal of the United States was to find a leader who could fill this need. It finally settled on Nguyen Van Thieu, who governed South Vietnam from 1966 to 1975.

President Kennedy was assassinated on November 22, 1963. His successor, Lyndon Johnson, continued and vastly expanded the commitment to South Vietnam. In

August 1964, after an attack on an American ship in the Gulf of Tonkin, the first bombing of North Vietnam was authorized. In February 1965 major bombing attacks began that continued with only brief pauses until the early weeks of 1973. The land war grew in extent, with over 500,000 Americans stationed in South Vietnam. In 1969 President Richard Nixon commenced a policy of gradual withdrawal of troops. The program was called *Vietnamization*. From the spring of 1968 onwards long-drawn-out peace negotiations were conducted in Paris. In January 1973 a cease-fire was finally arranged. The troops of the United States were pulled back, and prisoners of war held in North Vietnam were returned. Thereafter violations of the cease-fire occurred on both sides. In early 1975 an evacuation of South Vietnamese troops from the northern part of their country turned into a complete rout. On April 30, 1975 the city of Saigon fell to the troops of the Viet Cong and North Vietnam. The Second Indochina war had come to an end.

The Second Indochina War, which was in effect a continuation of the first war, which the French had lost, was an event of immense controversy and complexity. It was widely debated throughout the world at the time and will continue to be debated for many years. The United States saw the conflict as part of the Cold War and as a repetition of Korea. Aggression from the north had to be halted. There was also hope that the military power of the United States might buy time so that a strong nationalist, noncommunist regime could be established in South Vietnam. However, the United States misread the situation in Vietnam and especially its superficial resemblance to what had taken place in Korea. The United States ignored the basic colonial character of the Vietnamese political scene. It also overlooked the larger size of Vietnam, the different topography, the weakness of the South Vietnamese army, and the corruption of the government of South Vietnam.

The war grew out of a power vacuum left by decolonization. It produced a major impact on all the Western world. For a decade after the Cuban missile crisis the attention of the United States was largely diverted from Europe. American prestige suffered, and the American commitment to Western Europe came into question. Moreover the blundering of American policy in Southeast Asia made many Europeans wonder about the basic wisdom of the American government. Many young Europeans—and not a few Americans—born after World War II came to consider the United States not as a protector of liberty but as an ambitious, aggressive, and cruel power trying to keep colonialism alive after the end of the colonial era. The American involvement in Vietnam probably proved fundamental to the emergence of a new commitment to unity and economic integration in Europe. That involvement allowed Europeans still living in the shadow of American power and influence to reassert their own independence and to strike out in new directions.

Toward West-European Unification

Since 1945 the nations of Western Europe have taken unprecedented steps toward cooperation and potential unity. The idea of a single Europe is as old as Latin Christendom and as recent as the military exploits of Napoleon and Hitler. However, what has occurred since World War II fits into none of these patterns. The steps toward unification have related primarily to economic integration. These moves have arisen from American encouragement, in response to the Soviet domination of Eastern Europe, and from a sense of lack of effective political power by the states of Western Europe. The process of integration has not been steady, nor is it near completion, but it has provided a major factor in the domestic politics of the states involved.

The Marshall Plan of the United States created the Organization for European Economic Cooperation. It was a vehicle set up to require common planning and cooperation among the participating countries and to discourage a return to the prewar economic nationalism. The OEEC and later NATO gave the countries involved new experience working with each other and demonstrated the productivity, the efficiency, and the simple possibility of cooperative action. Although neither organization provided a means for political or economic integration, the experience was most important.

The movement toward unity could have occurred in at least three ways: politically, militarily, or economically. In 1949 ten European states organized the Council of Europe, which meets in Strasbourg, France. Its organization involved foreign ministers and a Consultative Assembly elected by the parliaments of the participants. The Council of Europe was and continues to be only an advisory body. It had been hoped by some persons that the council might become a parliament of Europe, but during the early fifties none of the major states was willing to surrender any of its sovereignty to the newly organized body. The initial failure of the council to bring about significant political cooperation meant that for the time being unity would not come about by political or parliamentary routes.

Between 1950 and 1954 there was some interest in a more thorough integration of the military forces of NATO. When the Korean War broke out, the United States began to urge the rearmament of Germany. The German forces would provide Western Europe with further protection against possible Soviet aggression while the United States was involved in Korea. France continued to fear a German army. In 1951 the French government suggested the creation of a European Defense Community that would constitute a supranational military organization. It would require a permanent British commitment of forces to the Continent to help France, in effect, counter any future German threat. The proposal continued to be considered for some time, but in 1954 the French Parliament itself vetoed the program. In 1955 Germany was permitted to rearm and to enter NATO. Supranational military organization had not been achieved.

Rather than in politics or the military the major moves toward European cooperation and potential unity came in the economic sphere. Unlike the other two possible paths of cooperation, economic activity involved little or no immediate loss of political sovereignty. Moreover the material benefits of combined economic activity would bring new popular support to all of the governments involved. Among European leaders and civil servants there existed a large body of opinion that only through the abandonment of economic nationalism could the newly organized democratic states avoid the economic turmoil that had proved such fertile ground for dictator-

The European Economic Community Is Established

The 1957 Treaty of Rome identified the major goals of the European Economic Community (Common Market) for the six (later nine) members.

Article 2: *It shall be the aim of the Community, by establishing a Common Market and progressively approximating the economic policies of Member States, to promote throughout the Community a harmonious development of economic activities, a continuous and balanced expansion, an increased stability, an accelerated raising of the standard of living and closer relations between its Member States.*

Article 3: *For the purposes set out in the preceding Article, the activities of the Community shall include, under the conditions and with the timing provided for in this Treaty:*

(a) the elimination, as between Member States, of customs duties and of quantitative restrictions in regard to the importation and exportation of goods, as well as of all other measures with equivalent effect;

(b) the establishment of a common customs tariff and a common commercial policy towards third countries;

(c) the abolition, as between Member States, of the obstacles to the free movement of persons, services and capital;

(d) the inauguration of a common agricultural policy;

(e) the inauguration of a common transport policy;

(f) the establishment of a system ensuring that competition shall not be distorted in the Common Market;

(g) the application of procedures which shall make it possible to co-ordinate the economic policies of Member States and to remedy disequilibria in their balances of payments;

(h) the approximation of their respective municipal law to the extent necessary for the functioning of the Common Market;

(i) the creation of a European Social Fund in order to improve the possibilities of employment for workers and to contribute to the raising of their standard of living;

(j) the establishment of a European Investment Bank intended to facilitate the economic expansion of the Community through the creation of new resources; and

(k) the association of overseas countries and territories with the Community with a view to increasing trade and to pursuing jointly their effort towards economic and social development.

Treaty Establishing the European Economic Community (Brussels: Secretariat of the Interim Committee for the Common Market and Euratom, 1957), pp. 17–18.

ship. Economic cooperation carried the possibility of greater efficiency, prosperity, and employment. The leading figures holding these opinions were Robert Schuman (1886–1963), the foreign minister of France; Konrad Adenauer (1876–1967), the chancellor of the Federal Republic of Germany; Alcide De Gasperi (1881–1954), the prime minister of Italy; and Paul-Henri Spaak (1899–1972), the prime minister of Belgium. Among major civil servants and bureaucrats, Jean Monnet (b. 1885) of France was the leading spokesman.

In 1950 Schuman proposed that the coal and steel production of Western Europe be undertaken on an integrated, cooperative basis. The next year France, West Germany, Italy, and the "Benelux" countries (Belgium, the Netherlands, and Luxembourg) organized the European Coal and Steel Community. Its activity was limited to a single part of the economy, but that was a sector that affected practically all other industrial production. An agency called the High Authority administered the plan. The authority was genuinely supranational, and its members could not be removed during their appointed terms. The Coal and Steel Community prospered. By 1955 coal production had grown by 23 per cent. Iron and steel production was up by almost 150 per cent. The community both benefited from and contributed to the immense growth of material production in Western Europe during this period. Its success reduced the suspicions of government and business groups about the concept of coordination and economic integration.

It took more than the prosperity of the European Coal and Steel Community to draw European leaders toward further unity. The unsuccessful Suez intervention and the resulting diplomatic isolation of France and Britain persuaded many Europeans that only through unified action could they exert any significant influence on the two superpowers or control their own destinies. Consequently, in 1957, through the Treaty of Rome, the six members of the Coal and Steel Community agreed to form a new organization. It was the European Economic Community. The *Common Market*, as the EEC soon

THE COMMON MARKET

The single most important development since World War II looking toward peaceful European cooperation and unity has been the Common Market, which by 1973 included the nine states shown here. Partly overlapping the Common Market is the European Free Trade Area. Greece is to become a Common Market member in 1981, and Spain and Portugal will probably be seeking membership thereafter.

Konrad Adenauer of West Germany and Charles De Gaulle of France were the two major West European statesmen of the late 1950s and early 1960s. They pursued policies of reconciliation between their two nations and a policy of a more nearly united Europe based on the Common Market. [United Press International Photo.]

came to be called, envisioned more than a free-trade union. Its members sought to achieve eventual elimination of tariffs, free flow of capital and labor, and similar wage and social benefits in all participating countries. Its chief institutions were a Council of Foreign Ministers and a High Commission composed of technocrats. The former came to be the dominant body.

The problems of the world-wide noncommunist economy are discussed by the participants in a summit conference in Bonn, West Germany, in July 1978. Here are (from left to right) Prime Minister Fukuda of Japan; President Carter of the United States; Prime Ministers Callaghan, Trudeau, and Andreotti of Great Britain, Canada, and Italy; President Giscard d'Estaing of France; and Chancellor Schmidt of West Germany. [United Press International Photo.]

The Common Market achieved a stunning degree of success during its early years. By 1968 all tariffs among the six members had been abolished well ahead of the planned schedule. Trade and labor migration among the members grew steadily. Moreover nonmember states began to copy the community and later to seek membership. In 1959 Britain, Denmark, Norway, Sweden, Switzerland, Austria, and Portugal formed the European Free Trade Area. However, by 1961 Great Britain had decided to seek Common Market membership. Twice, in 1963 and 1967, British membership was vetoed by President De Gaulle of France. The French president felt that Britain was too closely related to the United States and its policies to support the European Economic Community wholeheartedly.

The French veto of British membership demonstrated the major difficulty confronting the Common Market during the sixties. The Council of Ministers, representing the individual national interests of member states, came to have more influence than the High Commission. Political as well as economic factors increasingly entered into decision making. France particularly was unwilling to compromise on any matter that it regarded as pertaining to its sovereignty. On more than one occasion President De Gaulle demanded his own policies and refused French participation under any other conditions. This attitude caused major problems over agricultural policy.

Despite the French actions the Common Market survived and continued to prosper. In 1973 Great Britain, Ireland, and Denmark became members. Discussions continue on further steps toward integration, including a common currency. The future for the EEC may well be filled with difficulties, but there is little doubt that it will continue to be one of the major economic units of the world. The full ramifications of economic integration still remain to be seen, but the direction for the rest of this century will be almost certainly toward greater unity.

Internal Political Developments in Western Europe

After the war, with the exceptions of Portugal and Spain, which remained dictatorships until the mid-1970s, the nations of Western Europe continued to pursue the path of liberal democracy. But their leaders realized that the prewar democratic political structures alone had been insufficient to ensure peace, stability, material prosperity, and domestic liberty for their peoples. It had become clear that democracy required a social and economic base as well as a political structure. Economic prosperity and social security in the eyes of most Europeans became a duty of government as a way of staving off the kind of turmoil that had brought on tyranny and war. They also regarded such programs as a means of avoiding communism.

Except for the British Labor Party the vehicles of the new postwar politics were not, as might have been expected, the democratic socialist parties. On the whole those parties did not prosper after the onset of the Cold War. They stood opposed by both communists and groups more conservative than themselves. Rather the new departures were led by various Christian Democratic parties, usually leading coalition governments. These Christian Democratic political parties were a major new feature of postwar politics. They were largely Roman Catholic in leadership and membership. Catholic parties had previously existed in Europe. But from the late nineteenth century through the 1930s they had been very conservative and had tended to protect the social, political, and educational interests of the church. They had traditionally opposed communism but had few positive programs of their own. The postwar Christian Democratic parties of Germany, France, and Italy were progressive. They accepted democracy and advocated social reform. They welcomed non-Catholics to membership. Democracy, social reform, economic growth, and anticommunism were their hallmarks. Only in the late sixties were those goals seriously challenged or questioned.

The events of the war years in large measure determined the political leadership of the postwar decade. On the continent those groups and parties which had been active in the resistance against Nazis and fascism held an initial advantage. Until the Prague *coup* of 1948 those groups frequently included the Communist Party. Thereafter communists were quite systematically excluded from all Western European governments. This policy was quite naturally favored and encouraged by the United States. The immediate domestic problems after the war included not only those created by the physical damage of the conflict but often those that had existed in 1939. The war in most cases had not solved those prewar difficulties, but it had often opened new opportunities or possibilities for solution.

Great Britain: Power in Decline

In July 1945 the British electorate overwhelmingly voted for a Labor Party government. For the first time the Labor Party commanded in its own right a majority of the House of Commons. Clement Attlee (1883–1967) replaced Churchill as prime minister. The British had not so much rejected the great wartime leader as they had renounced the Conservative Party, which had in effect governed since 1931. In the public mind the Conservatives were associated with the economic problems of the thirties. For purposes of postwar reconstruction and redirection the Labor Party seemed to have a better program.

Attlee's ministry was socialist but clearly non-Marxist. It made a number of bold departures in both economic and social policy. The government nationalized major industries, including the Bank of England, the airlines, public transport, coal, electricity, and steel. The ministry also undertook a major housing program. Probably its most popular accomplishment was the establishment of a major program of welfare legislation. This involved further unemployment assistance, old-age pensions, school lunches, and, most important, free medical service to all citizens. All of these departures were expensive, and immediate postwar economic recovery was slow. By the

The British Labor Party Issues a Cautious Platform

The Labor Party was committed to a program of socialism in 1945. However, its platform of that year made clear that the party would move cautiously in carrying out its policy. Both the commitment to social change and the promise of caution proved attractive to the electorate, with the result that Labor came to power.

By the *test of war some industries have shown themselves capable of rising to new heights of efficiency and expansion. Others, including some of our older industries fundamental to our economic structure, have wholly or partly failed. . . .*

Each industry must have applied to it the test of national service. If it serves the nation, well and good; if it is inefficient and falls down on its job, the nation must see that things are put right.

These propositions seem indisputable, but for years before the war anti-Labour Governments set them aside, so that British industry over a large field fell into a state of depression, muddle and decay. Millions of working and middle-class people went through the horrors of unemployment and insecurity. It is not enough to sympathise with these victims: we must develop an acute feeling of national shame—and act.

The Labour Party is a Socialist Party, and proud of it. Its ultimate purpose at home is the establishment of the Socialist Commonwealth of Great Britain—free, democratic, efficient, progressive, public-spirited, its material resources organised in the service of the British people.

But Socialism cannot come overnight, as the product of a week-end revolution. The members of the Labour Party, like the British people, are practical-minded men and women.

There are basic industries ripe and over-ripe for public ownership and management in direct service of the nation. There are many smaller businesses rendering good service which can be left to go on with their useful work.

There are big industries not yet ripe for public ownership which must nevertheless be required by constructive supervision to further the nation's needs and not to prejudice national interests by restrictive anti-social monopoly or cartel agreements—caring for their own capital structures and profits at the cost of a lower standard of living for all.

Let Us Face the Future, cited in J. F. C. Harrison, *Society and Politics in England, 1780–1960* (New York: Harper and Row, 1965), pp. 450–451.

close of 1948 the drive toward further social reform had come to a halt. During the next several years the Labor Party itself became badly divided between one wing that advocated more socialism and government services and another that contended that the nation could for the time being afford few or no new programs.

The forward domestic policy of the Labor government was matched by a policy of gradual retreat on the world scene. In 1947 the enunciation of the Truman Doctrine in regard to Greece and Turkey marked the British admission that it could not afford to oversee the security of those areas. In the same year Britain recognized the independence of Pakistan and India. In the postwar era Britain would be repeatedly confronted by nationalist movements within the empire and would gradually and usually gracefully retreat from those outposts. In 1949 the government devalued the pound sterling from $4.03 to $2.80. The once-strong economy was clearly in trouble; the nation could earn insufficient foreign exchange from its exports to pay for its imports. The military, imperial, and economic power that had once made Britain the foremost of European nations had eroded and would continue to do so for the next three decades.

In 1951 the Conservative Party under Churchill returned to office and remained there until 1964. This was the longest period of continuous government by any party in modern British history. Internal Labor Party divisions contributed to this development, but so did the policies of the Conservatives. Under Churchill and then under his successors, Anthony Eden in 1955–1957, Harold Macmillan in 1957–1963, and Alec Douglas-Home in 1963–1964, the Conservatives attempted to draw a picture of major differences between themselves and the Labor Party. In reality, the differences were ones of degree rather than of kind. The Conservative government did denationalize steel, but it did not return to a free economy. The program of national welfare and health services continued, and the Conservatives actually undertook a building program larger than that of the Labor Party.

Wrecked ships were strewn throughout the Suez Canal
after the Franco-British attack of 1956. [United
Press International Photo.]

The problem of decline of power and prestige continued. From the mid-fifties onward one part of the empire
after another became independent. The Suez intervention
of 1956 brought an end to independent British military
intervention. Increasingly British policy was made subservient to that of the United States. However, the economy
constituted the most persistent difficulty. Throughout the
decade the slogan "Export or die" was heard. Exports did
grow rapidly, yet more slowly than imports. Productivity
remained discouragingly low. British unions were old-
fashioned and less forward-looking than those on the
Continent. Management was quite timid. Perhaps most
important, there was a low rate of capital investment in
both privately and nationally owned industries. The trade
unions were often more interested in carving up existing
wealth than in creating new wealth to be distributed. The
government too often favored economic programs that
were not aimed at long-term growth.

In 1964 the Labor Party returned to office under
Harold Wilson. It promised to right the economic situation, but the economy only worsened. The pound was
devalued further. Wilson renewed the attempt to join the
Common Market, which Macmillan had begun in 1963.
Labor, like the Conservatives, confronted the veto of
France. In 1970 the electorate again turned to the Conservative Party, then led by Edward Heath. His major
accomplishment was to take Britain into the Common
Market in 1973. However, domestically Heath floundered badly in his dealings with the trade unions. The
country suffered a crippling coal strike in the winter of
1973-1974.

In 1974 Wilson returned to office, primarily on the
grounds that the Labor Party might have better relations
with the unions. The Labor government was able to
reach some agreements on limitations for pay raises. Still
inflation raged and in 1976 the value of the pound sterling dipped below $1.60. The same year Wilson volun-
tarily resigned and was replaced by James Callaghan. In
1975 Margaret Thatcher had replaced Heath as leader of
the Conservative Party. The future political direction of

the nation remains unclear, as does its economic situation. The discovery of oil in the North Sea off Scotland may well give new strength to the economy.

In addition to the gravest economic situation in the Western world, Britain has also had to confront in recent years a major internal disturbance in Northern Ireland. By the treaty of 1921 the Ulster counties remained a part of the United Kingdom while retaining a large measure of self-government. The Protestant majority used its power to discriminate systematically against the Roman Catholic minority in the province. In 1968 a Catholic civil rights movement was launched. Demonstrations and counterdemonstrations resulted. Units of the Provisional Wing of the Irish Republican Army became active in seeking to unite Ulster with the Irish Republic. In turn militant Protestant organizations became mobilized. The British government sent in units of the army to restore order. Soon the army units became the target of both groups of militant Irish. Thus far the troops remain, and well over thirteen hundred people have been killed in terrorist activity. A peaceful solution has not yet proved forthcoming.

West Germany: The Economic Miracle

No country in Europe since the war has so contrasted with Britain as the Federal Republic of Germany. The nation was organized in 1949 from the three Western Allied occupation sectors. Its amazing material progress from the ruins of the conflict has become known as the economic miracle of postwar Europe. Between 1948 and 1964 West German industrial production grew by 600 per cent. Unemployment became practically unknown. All of this time the country remained the center of Cold War disputes and was occupied by thousands of foreign troops. In the midst of Cold War tensions the Germans prospered.

The economic growth of the nation stemmed from a number of favorable factors. The Marshall Plan provided an initial impetus to recovery. The government of the republic throughout the fifties and sixties pursued a policy of giving private industry a relatively free hand while providing sufficient planning to avoid economic crisis. The goods produced by Germany proved attractive to the customers of other nations. *Volkswagen* became a household word throughout the world. Moreover domestic demand was vigorous, and skilled labor and energetic management were available. The war had destroyed vast amounts of equipment. The replacements could employ the most advanced technology. Finally, Germany had very few foreign commitments or responsibilities. A relatively small portion of its national income had to be spent on defense. This situation aided capital formation.

In a very real sense postwar West Germany indulged in economic expansion rather than in politics or active international policy. Unlike the Weimar Constitution, the constitution of the Federal Republic did not permit the proliferation of splinter parties. Nor did the president possess extraordinary power. The Federal Republic returned to the arena of nations very slowly. In 1949 it participated in the Marshall Plan and two years later in the European Coal and Steel Community. In 1955 the nation joined NATO, and in 1957 it was one of the charter members of the European Economic Community. The Federal Republic has been perhaps the major champion of European cooperation.

Throughout this period political initiative lay with the Christian Democrats led by Konrad Adenauer. His policies were relatively simple and consistent. West Germany must become genuinely democratic and economically stable and prosperous. His foreign policy was profoundly anticommunist. Under what was known as the Hallstein Doctrine, the Federal Republic refused to have diplomatic ties with any nation, except the Soviet Union, that extended diplomatic recognition to East Germany. Adenauer's position on East Germany contributed to the Cold War climate, and it may have led the United States to overestimate the threat of communist aggression in Europe. The Hallstein Doctrine separated the Federal Republic from all the nations of Eastern Europe.

Few sights better illustrate the astounding economic recovery of Europe after 1945 than the contrast between these two views of Berlin. The ghostly picture [ABOVE] shows the heavy destruction caused by the intense wartime bombing of the city. The contrasting photograph [BELOW] shows the rebuilt center of West Berlin that emerged in the following decade. Only the ruins of the Emperor William I Memorial Church were left as they stood to serve as a permanent monument and a reminder of war's destruction. [ABOVE: United Press International Photo; BELOW: German Information Center, New York.]

Adenauer remained in office until 1963, when he retired at the age of eighty-seven. The Christian Democrats remained in power, led first by Ludwig Erhard and later by Kurt Kiesinger. In 1966, however, they were compelled to form a coalition with the Social Democrats (SDP). After the war this party had revived but had been unable to capture a parliamentary majority. By the early sixties the SDP had expanded their base beyond the working class and had become more a party of social and economic reform than a party of socialism. This shift reflected the growing prosperity of the German working class. The major leader of the SDP in the sixties was Willy Brandt, the mayor of West Berlin. In 1966 he became vice-chancellor in the coalition government. In 1969 Brandt and the SDP carried the election in their own right.

In one of the most moving events of Willy Brandt's effort to improve German relations with the states of eastern Europe, the German chancellor knelt at the memorial to Warsaw Jews killed by the Germans during World War II. He was in Poland in December 1970 to sign a treaty that would lead to regular diplomatic relations between the two countries. [United Press International Photo.]

The most significant departure of the SDP occurred in the area of foreign policy. While continuing to urge further Western unity through the Common Market, Brandt moved carefully but swiftly to establish better relations with eastern Europe (*Ostpolitik*). In 1970 he met with the leadership of East Germany. Later that year he went to Moscow to sign a treaty of cooperation. By November 1970 Brandt had completed a reconciliation treaty with Poland that recognized the Oder-Neisse River line as the Polish western border. A treaty with Czechoslovakia soon followed. In 1973 both the Federal Republic of Germany and the German Democratic Republic were admitted to the United Nations. Brandt's policy of *Ostpolitik* to a large extent regularized the German situation, but that regularity will probably remain only so long as the two superpowers desire it. Brandt's moves were in part a subdevelopment of the policy of detente on the part of the United States and the Soviet Union. In 1974 Brandt resigned. His successor was Helmut Schmidt.

France: Search for Stability and Glory

France experienced the most troubled postwar domestic political scene of any major European nation. The Third Republic had been in very deep difficulty in 1939. It had come to satisfy neither the left nor the right of the political world. More important, the republic had been incapable of staving off military defeat. To these inherited problems was added after the war the fact of wide-scale collaboration with the Nazi conquerors. A few trials, executions, and prison sentences superficially handled the problem of the Vichy collaborators, but much bitterness remained.

After the defeat of 1940 a little-known general named Charles De Gaulle (1890–1970) had organized a free French government in London. In 1944 De Gaulle presided over the provisional government in liberated France. He was an immensely proud, patriotic person who seemed to regard himself as personally embodying the spirit of France. He had a low regard for traditional liberal democratic politics and hated the machinations of political parties, which he thought unnecessarily divided the nation. In 1946 De Gaulle suddenly resigned from the government, believing that the newly organized Fourth Republic, like the Third, gave far too little power to the executive. The Fourth French Republic thus lost the single strong leader it had possessed. After De Gaulle's departure the republic returned to the rapid turnover of ministries that had characterized the Third Republic during the twenties and thirties. Between 1948 and 1958 there were no less than nineteen ministries. The faces of the ministers changed, but the problems remained.

A major source of domestic discontent related to colonial problems in North Africa and Indochina. Between 1947 and 1954 France fought the long, bitter war to retain some measure of control over Indochina. That conflict has been examined more closely earlier in this chapter. By 1954, however, Premier Mendès-France's government admitted defeat and began to preside over a withdrawal from the region. It marked a major defeat for a Western nation by a former colony. The Mendès-France government also granted independence to Tunisia. Morocco was soon moving toward independence. The Suez fiasco of 1956 marked another conspicuous loss of power and prestige for France.

Indochina, Tunisia, and Morocco were regarded as colonial problems by the French. However, in their eyes Algeria, conquered in 1830 and now possessing over a million French citizens, was not a colony but an integral part of France. In 1954 a revolt broke out in Algeria, led by the Algerian Liberation Movement (the FLN). The revolt deeply divided France. The army and right-wing political groups were determined to hold Algeria. Nevertheless the war, which was intensely bitter and brutal, became increasingly unpopular. There were demands for a negotiated settlement. When the civilian government began to make moves in that direction in 1958, an army mutiny occurred in Algeria and unrest soon spread to Corsica. France seemed on the brink of civil war.

At this point the politicians in Paris turned to General De Gaulle, whom the army trusted would uphold their cause. The general accepted office only on the conditions that he be given a free hand to govern and to submit a new constitution to the nation. De Gaulle created the Fifth French Republic, in which the president possessed extraordinary power. He could appoint and dismiss the premier and dissolve the Chamber of Deputies. De Gaulle submitted the constitution to a popular referendum, in which it was overwhelmingly approved. Having secured his own power, De Gaulle moved to attack the Algerian problem. He made large concessions to the FLN, and by 1962 Algeria was independent. There was much domestic opposition to De Gaulle's policy. Hundreds of thousands of French citizens in Algeria returned to France, putting new pressures on its economy and resources. However, the president of the republic held the nation behind him. He had become a symbol of stability and nationalism. There always existed the fear in the late fifties and early sixties that De Gaulle might again resign and leave the nation subject to possible disruptive forces.

De Gaulle combined the methods of Louis Napoleon with the patriotism of Clemenceau. Throughout the 1960s he pursued a policy of making France the leading nation in a united Europe. Often De Gaulle pursued

President De Gaulle Insists on Maintaining French Autonomy

De Gaulle was determined to maintain the national independence of France both in Europe and in the Atlantic community. In this 1966 speech he criticizes those who would compromise that independence by having France subordinate itself to various international organizations, such as NATO and the United Nations. He particularly resented the influence of the United States in European affairs.

IT IS *true that, among our contemporaries, there are many minds—and often some of the best—who have envisaged that our country renounce its independence under the cover of one or another international grouping. Having thus handed over to foreign bodies the responsibility for our destiny, our leaders would—according to the expression sanctioned by that school of thought—have nothing more to do than "plead France's case."*

". . . Thus some—exalting in the dream of the international—wanted to see our country itself, as they placed themselves, under the obedience of Moscow. Thus others—invoking either the supranational myth, or the danger from the East, or the advantage that the Atlantic West could derive from unifying its economy, or even the imposing utility of world arbitration—maintained that France should allow her policy to be dissolved in a tailor-made Europe, her defense in NATO, her monetary concepts in the Washington Fund, her personality in the United Nations, et cetera.

Certainly, it is a good thing that such institutions exist, and it is only in our interest to belong to them; but if we had listened to their extreme apostles, these organs in which, as everyone knows, the political protection, military protection, economic power and multiform aid of the United States predominate—these organs would have been for us only a cover for our submission to American hegemony. Thus, France would disappear swept away by illusion.

Cited in Ronald C. Monticone, *Charles De Gaulle* (Boston: Twayne Publishers, 1975), pp. 67–68.

strictly nationalist goals that frustrated those who favored united action. His nationalism was probably necessary as a means of healing the internal wounds to French pride and prestige brought about by the colonial and Algerian defeats. He pursued systematically good relations with Germany but was never friendly with Great Britain. He deeply resented the influence of the United States in Western Europe.

De Gaulle wanted Europe to become a third force in the world between the superpowers. For that reason he pushed for the development of a French nuclear capacity and refused to become a party to the 1963 Nuclear Test Ban Treaty. He took French forces out of NATO in 1967 and caused its headquarters to be moved from Paris to Brussels. He was highly critical of the American involvement in Vietnam. That American adventure served to convince him even further that Europe under French leadership must prepare to fend for itself.

It is not certain that the rest of the world ever understood De Gaulle or he them. He imposed a kind of presidential dictatorship on France but permitted the civil liberties to be observed and parliamentary politics to function. Yet what was important was what the president and his ministers decided. For ten years he succeeded. Then in 1968 he confronted a domestic unrest in France that was even more widespread than that confronted by Léon Blum in the spring of 1936. The troubles commenced among student groups in Paris, and then they spread to other major sectors of French life. Hundreds of thousands of workers went on strike. Having assured himself of the support of the army, De Gaulle made a brief television speech to rally his followers. Soon they too came into the streets to demonstrate for De Gaulle and stability. The strikes ended. Police often moved against the student groups. The government itself quickly moved to improve the wages and benefits to workers. May 1968 had revealed the fragile strength of the Fifth Republic. It had also revealed that the economic progress of France since the war had created a large body of citizens with sufficient stake in the *status quo* to fear and prevent its disruption.

In 1969 President De Gaulle resigned after some relatively minor constitutional changes were rejected in a referendum. The next election returned Georges Pompidou (1911–1974) to the presidency. He was a strong supporter of De Gaulle and his policies. He and his own successor, Valéry Giscard D'Estaing (b. 1926), set about to improve the economic conditions that had fostered discontent among factory workers in 1968. They have also continued to favor a strong policy favoring European unity. In 1973, three years after De Gaulle's death in political retirement, France permitted Great Britain to join the Common Market.

The center-right government of Valéry Giscard d'Estaing was elected in 1974 on a platform of social reform. The new president also spoke of an "opening" to the political left. It would seem that he might be willing to accept the support of the French Socialist Party for his programs. Giscard d'Estaing is essentially a technocrat who would like to see the traditionally harsh ideological split in France healed. He and others of his persuasion see such splits as preventing the serious handling of major economic problems. Yet to date his interest in some mode of alliance with the left has remained a matter of rhetoric. Indeed, during the parliamentary elections of 1978 he made major election-eve speeches deploring the possibility of a political victory for the left.

Such a victory had for a time seemed possible, on the one hand, because of disillusionment with Giscard d'Estaing's timid policies and, on the other, because of new cooperation between the French Socialist Party and the French Communist Party. Beginning in the late sixties François Mitterand led an impressive drive to reorganize the Socialist Party. Its membership increased, as did its performance at the polls. In 1972 the Socialist Party and the Communist Party led by Georges Marchais formed a Common Front and agreed on a social and economic program that they would enact if they were elected. The Socialists accepted the alliance because it seemed the only way that a left-wing majority could be achieved. The motives of the Communists were less clear, but it would seem they thought such an alliance would give them considerable political leverage within left-wing politics. They hoped to become the tail that wagged the dog.

However, after 1972 the strength of the Socialist Party

continued to grow while that of the Communist Party did not. It became clear by 1977 that if the proposed coalition won the election, the Communists would be able to exert relatively little pressure within the cabinet. Consequently in the middle of 1977 the Communist Party resumed its traditional stance of harshly criticizing the Socialists. In September 1977 the Common Front in effect came to an end. During the elections of 1978 the two left-wing parties failed to cooperate. Communists refused to vote for Socialists, and Socialists refused to vote for Communists. The result of the election was a victory for the right and the center. Since the election there have been pressures from French Communist intellectuals to reform and democratize the internal structures of the French Communist Party. These critics believe the Communist destruction of the alliance with the Socialists destroyed a major opportunity for a left-wing victory. Perhaps the major result of the election will be a continuation for some time of distrust between the Socialists and the Communists. Moreover, the possibility of a left-wing victory seems to have hardened the center and right-wing parties' resolve to prevent such victory in the future.

Instability in the Mediterranean World

For a quarter century after World War II the major Mediterranean states were stable, though for very different reasons. Spain and Portugal remained governed by General Francisco Franco (1892–1975) and Antonio Salazar (1889–1970), respectively. They had established themselves during the turmoil between the wars and continued to preside over illiberal regimes. Italy had attained a course of reasonably steady progress under the leadership of the Christian Democrats. Greece had become stabilized during the fifties, primarily thanks to American military and economic aid. By the middle of the sixties each of these nations had begun to experience internal tensions that have since led to considerable turmoil throughout the region. Moreover, at the far southeastern end of the Mediterranean the Arab-Israeli conflict has proved a continuing source of instability.

Salazar ruled Portugal with an iron hand until 1968, when a stroke removed him from the political scene. His successor, Marcelo Caetono, continued to pursue authoritarian policies. The government remained determined to hold its possessions in Africa long after other European states had abandoned traditional colonial policies. Both at home and abroad major opposition to the government developed within the army officer corps. In 1974 General Antonio de Spinola led an army revolt against Caetono.

Since that time Portugal has indulged itself in the kind of political activity that had been forbidden for almost half a century. There have been large numbers of popular demonstrations, intense political party activity, and broad discussion of economic, social, and political problems. The Portuguese Communist Party proved to be exceedingly well organized. It was able to contribute to the overthrow of the Spinola government. However, in the elections of 1975 the Communists did not do well. The government came under the control of the Socialists, led by Mario Soares. Whether they will remain in power for a substantial period remains to be seen. For the immediate future the two major problems confronting Portugal are the establishment of central political authority and the reviving of the economy, which has suffered from the turmoil since 1974.

Spain has also entered upon a period of considerable uncertainty. So long as he lived, Franco tolerated little or no political life outside that of his own supporters. The Spanish police were active against any political opposition. Many political activists remained either in exile or in jail. However, opposition continued to grow. A large number of illegal political parties had been organized. Franco died in 1976. As he had provided, his successor was Juan Carlos, from the old Bourbon royal family of Spain, who became king. The new monarch, though trained by Franco, has made it clear that he wishes Spain to be liberalized both politically and culturally. In December 1976 the Spanish voters approved a more liberal constitution. The question has now become whether Juan Carlos can obtain the cooperation and trust of the recently legalized political parties. If the monarch is successful, Spain might move to the path of some form of liberal democracy. Otherwise a period of great unrest and violence may commence. It is still too early to say in which direction Spain will go.

At the other end of the Mediterranean, Greece has also experienced a decade of upheaval. In 1965 King Constantine II (b. 1940) came into conflict with the officer corps of the army. During the next several months leftist and liberal Greek politicians hoped to exert new influence on the monarch. In the spring of 1967 conservative army officers deposed Constantine. They claimed to be acting to save the country from a communist takeover. The army junta imposed strongly authoritarian control over the entire population. Political opponents were imprisoned. In the summer of 1974, however, confrontation between Greece and Turkey over the future of Cyprus led to the collapse of the Greek military government. Turkey had invaded Cyprus under the pretext of protecting the Turkish part of the population. The Greek junta were incapable of dealing with the crisis. A civilian government took over. It was headed by Constantine Karamanlis (b. 1907), a former premier. In 1975 a referendum of the Greek people decided against restoration of the monarchy. The problem of the future of Cyprus remains a source of friction between Greece and Turkey.

Instability has threatened Italy from different sources. The transformation from a fascist to a nonfascist government commenced during the war. In 1943 the Grand Fascist Council had ousted Mussolini. He was later summarily executed by Italian partisans. A government friendly to the Allies was installed in southern Italy, and it expanded its control as the Allied armies moved northward. At the close of the conflict the prefascist political parties quickly reemerged. In 1946 the nation voted to abolish the monarchy.

The Christian Democrats governed under the leadership of Alcide de Gasperi. Until 1947 the Italian Communist Party served in the coalition, but it was excluded after the elections of that year. Thereafter Italy remained a nation with a single major large political party, the Christian Democrats, who formed coalitions with other smaller parties. Government by bargained coalition became the order of the day. Under this system, which resembled the system of *transformiso* that had prevailed before Mussolini, the Italian economy experienced a period of growth not unlike that of West Germany. Italy became a genuinely modern nation. It manufactured autos, refrigerators, and office equipment. The nation was very active in the drive for European unity.

However, by the late sixties and early seventies discontent was stirring against the Christian Democrats. Their methods of government had led to corruption, inefficiency, and political paralysis. Inflation became intense as economic growth stagnated. As a result, the Italian Communist Party, the largest and best organized in Western Europe, began to make significant inroads into political life. It won a considerable number of municipal elections. During 1976 the communists won over 35 per cent of the popular vote for the Chamber of Deputies. They were refused admission to the cabinet but were granted several important posts within the Chamber of Deputies.

The architect of the Communist advance within Italian politics was Enrico Berlinguer. He set forth a policy known as the "historic compromise." The policy represented a major break not only with the previous stand of the Italian Communist Party but also with a Moscow-dominated Communist movement. By the "historic compromise" Berlinguer announced the willingness of the Italian Communist Party to enter a coalition government with the Christian Democrats and other noncommunist parties. In other words, the Italian Communists have for the time being renounced revolution as the path to political power. They have also agreed to participate in a government that they would not dominate or control. The Italian Communist Party has also promised that as a partner in a coalition or as the governing party, should it be elected, it will govern constitutionally and will respect individuals' civil liberties. It has also urged continued Italian participation in NATO. To date these promises have not been put to the test. The compromises, however, represent an important example of the strains emerging among Communist Parties in Europe, just as a Communist electoral victory in Italy would be a major change from the postwar noncommunist solidarity of Western Europe.

The Italian Communist success stemming from its announced willingness to cooperate with middle class and Christian political parties has led to a further radicalization of the political left in Italy. The "historic compromise" has made the Italian Communist Party seem quite conservative to the unknown numbers of people who wish to see radical, but so far unclearly defined, political and social change in the nation. These groups have resorted to terrorism to make their power felt and to illustrate how the Communists have now become a pillar of the existing establishment. The best known of the terror-ist organizations is the Red Brigades. In the spring of 1978 while several members of the Red Brigades were on trial for earlier violence, other members kidnapped Aldo Moro, a former premier of Italy and a major leader of the Christian Democratic Party. The government refused to negotiate for his release. After several weeks of captivity Moro was assassinated, and his body was left in a car on a street in Rome. During the crisis both the Christian Democratic Party and the Italian Communist Party condemned terrorism.

The unrest in so much of Mediterranean Europe has been a cause of considerable concern for the United States and for many of its NATO allies. The conflict between Greece and Turkey over Cyprus constituted an intra-NATO dispute. The possibility of communist government in Italy has led to much rethinking about European defense arrangements. No matter what the political future of Spain may hold, there will be difficulties over agreements about the stationing of United States forces that would not have occurred under Franco. Taken as a whole, the Mediterranean turmoil is the most potent example of the disintegration of the framework of European alliances and political suppositions that have guided postwar Western European international relations. A period of considerable flux no doubt lies ahead.

A final source of instability in the Mediterranean world is the Arab-Israeli conflict. This dispute involves Europe because many of the citizens of Israel are immigrants from Europe and because Europe, like the United States, is highly dependent upon oil from Arab countries. Moreover, the Middle East also remains an arena for poten-

On May 9, 1978, the body of former Italian premier Aldo Moro was found in the rear of an automobile on a street in Rome. He had been kidnapped on March 16 by an Italian terrorist organization known as the Red Brigades and was murdered when the Italian government refused to negotiate for his release. [United Press International Photo.]

ISRAEL AND ITS NEIGHBORS

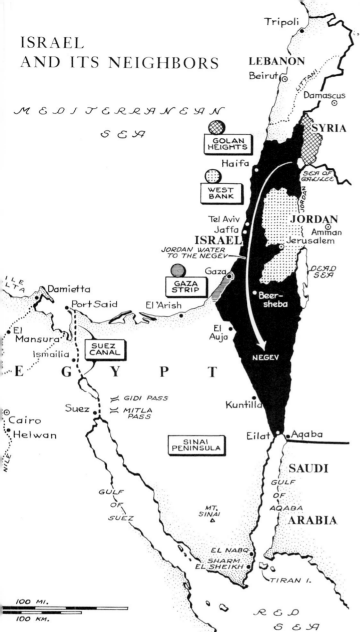

The map shows the geography of the difficult problem of Israel and its surrounding Arab neighbors. Syria, Jordan, and Egypt are the states with lands now occupied by Israel. The future of those lands and of earlier Palestinian refugees makes up the major set of problems still unresolved in the area.

cal parties, press, labor unions, and educational system. There were numerous conflicts with the Arabs already living in Palestine, for they considered the Jewish settlers as intruders. The British rather unsuccessfully attempted to mediate those clashes.

This situation might have prevailed longer in Palestine except for the outbreak of World War II and the attempt by Hitler to exterminate the Jewish population of central and eastern Europe. The Nazi persecution united Jews throughout the world behind the Zionist ideal of a Jewish state in Palestine. At the same time the knowledge of Nazi atrocities mobilized the conscience of the United States and the other Western powers. It seemed morally right that something be done for Jewish refugees from Nazi concentration camps. In 1947 the British turned over to the United Nations the whole problem of the relationship of Arabs and Jews in Palestine. That same year the United Nations passed a resolution calling for a division of the territory into a Jewish state and an Arab state.

The Arabs in Palestine and the surrounding area resisted the United Nations resolution. Not unnaturally, they resented the influx of new settlers. Large numbers of Palestinian Arabs were displaced and themselves became refugees. In May 1948 the Yishuv declared the independence of a new Jewish state called Israel. The United States through President Truman almost immediately recognized the new nation, whose first prime minister was David Ben Gurion. During 1948 and 1949 Israel fought its war of independence against the Arabs. In that war Israel expanded its borders beyond the limits originally set forth by the United Nations. By 1949 Israel had, through force of arms, secured its existence and peace, but it had not secured diplomatic recognition by its Arab neighbors—Egypt, Jordan, Syria, Saudi Arabia, to name the closest. The peace amounted to little more than an armed truce.

Then in 1952 a group of Egyptian army officers seized power in Egypt. Their leader was Gamal Abdel Nasser. He established himself as a dictator and, more important,

tial problems between the United States and the Soviet Union.

The modern state of Israel was the achievement of the world Zionist movement founded in 1897 by Theodore Herzl and later led by Chaim Weizmann. The British Balfour Declaration of 1917 had favored the establishment of a national home for the Jewish people in Palestine. Between the wars thousands of Jews, mainly from Europe, immigrated into the area, which was then governed by Great Britain under a mandate of the League of Nations. During the interwar period the Yishuv or Jewish community in Palestine developed its own politi-

President Carter was host to Prime Minister Begin of Israel and President Sadat of Egypt in September 1978 at a series of meetings that raised hopes for a peace treaty between the two eastern Mediterranean nations but left many unresolved difficulties between Israel and her neighbors. [United Press International Photo.]

as a spokesman for militant Arab nationalism. His policy was marked by a clear hatred of all the old imperial powers. In 1956 Nasser nationalized the Suez Canal. That same year, as noted previously, Great Britain and France responded to Nasser's action by attacking the canal. Israel joined with France and Britain. This alliance helped Israel fend off certain Arab guerilla attacks but associated Israel with the former imperial powers. After 1956 a United Nations peacekeeping force separated the armies of Israel and Egypt. The bases of the U.N. force were located in Egypt. Still there was no official Arab recognition of the existence of Israel.

An uneasy peace continued until 1967. Meanwhile, the Soviet Union increased its influence in Egypt, and the United States increased its influence in Israel. Both great powers supplied weapons to their friends in the area. In 1967 President Nasser made the calculation, which proved to be quite wrong, that the Arab nations could defeat Israel, which by then was nearly two decades old. He began to mass troops in the Sinai Peninsula, and he attempted to close the Gulf of Aqaba to Israeli shipping. He also demanded the withdrawal of the U.N. peacekeeping force. Diplomatic activity failed to stem the crisis and the Arab attempt to isolate Israel. On June 5, 1967 the armed forces of Israel, under the direction of Defense Minister Moshe Dayan, attacked Egyptian airfields rather than endure additional provocation by Egypt. Almost immediately Syria and Jordan entered the war on the side of Egypt. Yet by June 11 the Six Days' War was over, and Israel had won a stunning victory. The military forces of Egypt lay in shambles. Moreover, Israel occupied the entire Egyptian Sinai Peninsula, as well as the West Bank region along the Jordon River that had previously been part of the state of Jordan. This victory marked the height of Israeli power and prestige.

In 1970 President Nasser died. He was succeeded by Anwar el-Sadat. Sadat had first to shore up his support at home. The existing tensions between Israel and the defeated Egypt of course continued, and the Soviet Union still poured weapons into Egypt. However, Sadat deeply distrusted the Russians and in 1972 ordered them to leave the country. He and his advisors also felt that only another war with Israel could return to Egypt the lands lost in 1967. In October 1973, on the Jewish holy day of Yom Kippur, the military forces of Egypt launched an attack across the Suez Canal into Israeli-held territory. The invasion came as a complete surprise to the Israelis. Initially the Egyptian forces made considerable headway. Then the Israeli army thrust back the invasion. In November 1973 a truce was signed between the forces in the Sinai. Although Israel had been successful in repelling the Egyptians, the cost in troops and prestige was very high.

The Yom Kippur War added a major new element to the Middle East problem. In the fall of 1973 when the war broke out, the major Arab oil-producing states shut off the flow of oil to the United States and Europe. This dramatic move was an attempt to force the Western powers to use their influence to moderate the policy of Israel. The threat of the loss of oil was particularly frightening to Europeans, who possess almost no major sources of oil on which their industry depends. In the future this Arab oil can be expected to play an even more influential part in Middle East developments.

The most recent important development in the troubled area occurred in November 1977. President Sadat of Egypt, in a dramatic personal gesture, flew to Israel, addressed the Israeli parliament, and held discussions with Prime Minister Menahem Begin, although the two states were still technically at war. In effect, for the first time the head of a major Arab state recognized the existence of Israel. Previously all contacts had taken place either through the United Nations or other third parties. The Sadat initiative, roundly condemned in many Arab quarters, resulted in direct conversations, the most important of which occurred at Camp David in the United States under the direction of President Carter. Whether the Camp David accords of September 1978 will succeed in achieving peace remains to be seen. Tensions are still high. The Arab refugee problem is perhaps the major stumbling block, as the Palestine Liberation Organization demands the creation of a separate Palestinian state in the region. The Arab states to a greater or lesser degree have supported this position, but Israel believes such a state would inevitably become another major enemy rather than a "neighbor."

Eurocommunism in Western Europe

Within West European politics the past decade has witnessed the emergence of what may be a new version of Communism. Termed Eurocommunism, this development has characterized the policy and rhetoric of several Communist parties operating within the democracies of Western Europe. It has been particularly associated with the Communist parties of France, Italy, and Spain. Eurocommunism consists of two basic political policies. The first is the assertion of the independence of the parties involved from the influence of the Communist Party of the Soviet Union. Second, these parties have said publicly that they are willing to function within the existing parliamentary systems. The latter policy has been taken to mean a renunciation of revolution as a path to political power and the acceptance of existing constitutional arrangements. That is, these Communist parties have said that if they lose an election while in office, they will then surrender office to the victorious party. We have already noted these ideas in contemporary Italy.

Eurocommunism has developed primarily since 1968. The Soviet invasion of Czechoslovakia, the well-publicized persecution of Soviet dissidents, and the general absence of human rights in the Soviet Union made the Russian experience a rather unattractive model for young Europeans of the post-World War II generation. The West European Communist parties could hardly expect to win elections so long as they remained intimately aligned with the Soviet Union. Moreover, the postwar prosperity of Western Europe that has contrasted so markedly with the life of Eastern Europe also meant that western Communist parties felt the need to modify their tactics. The "historic compromise" of the Italian Communist Party and the cooperation of the French Communist Party with the French Socialists from 1972 to 1977 were examples of these new tactics. In Spain, under the leadership of Santiago Carillo the Communist Party has even attempted to introduce democratic procedures within the party itself. This latter policy has not been followed in France or Italy.

In 1977 the Soviet Union formally condemned Eurocommunism. The Soviet Union seems to have feared that too much independence on the part of West European Communist parties might lead to further unrest in Eastern Europe.

Although no European Communist Party advocating the policy of Eurocommunism has come to power, the phenomenon of Eurocommunism has made a large impression in the United States. European voters, on the other hand, and most particularly the large democratic socialist parties, have remained quite sceptical. There are several reasons for scepticism. First, Communist calls for independence from Moscow are not new. West European Communist parties have always displayed some independence of the Soviet Union and have insisted that the special conditions in their own nations must be taken into account in formulating policy. Second, from time to time in the past, most notably in the Popular Front governments of the 1930s and the immediate postwar cabinets of several countries, the Communists have participated. Neither of those previous developments changed the goal of the Communist parties from the pursuit of a monopoly of power in the state. On the whole European voters have not fully believed the Communist pledge to give up power upon the loss of future elections. Europeans of conservative, liberal, and democratic-socialist persuasion have seen the Communist parties change tactics and policies in the past. They remain uncertain about the sincerity and the permanence of the policies of Eurocommunism. They are not certain that once in power or in the cabinets the Communists would not revert to their former goals.

Finally, Europeans, unlike many American observers, have not equated the Eurocommunist call for independence from Moscow with democratic politics. With the exception of the Spanish Communist Party, the West European Communist parties have remained very centrally organized. They have not permitted any significant internal democracy or internal criticism. So long as this rigid organization is retained, European voters may remain wary of the democratic protestations of the Communists.

Nonetheless, Eurocommunism remains one of the most significant political phenomena of the present day in Europe. One major question is whether any of these parties will be able to enter a government. The Italian Communist Party is the one more likely to do so within the near future. But another question is whether the advance of Communist parties under the name of Eurocommunism will provoke a major conservative or right-wing political backlash. Such has often been the case with the political advance of the left in Europe, and it might again be the case in the future.

The Soviet Union and Eastern Europe
The Soviet Union Since the Death of Stalin (1953)

Many Russians had hoped that the end of the war would signal a lessening of Stalinism. No other nation had suffered greater losses or more deprivation than the Soviet Union. Its people anticipated some immediate reward for their sacrifice and heroism. They desired a reduction in the scope of the police state and a redirection of the economy away from heavy industry to consumer products. They were disappointed. Stalin did little or nothing to modify the character of the regime he had created. The police remained ever-present. The cult of personality expanded, and the central bureaucracy continued to grow. Heavy industry was still favored over production for consumers. Agriculture continued to be troubled. Stalin's personal authority over the party and the nation remained unchallenged. In foreign policy Stalin moved to solidify Soviet control over Eastern Europe for the purposes of both Communist expansion and Soviet national security. He attempted to impose the Soviet model on those nations. The Cold War stance of the United States simply served to confirm Stalin in his ways.

By late 1952 and early 1953 it appeared that Stalin might be ready to unloose a new series of purges. In January 1953 a group of Jewish physicians was arrested and charged with plotting the deaths of important leaders. Charges of extensive conspiracy appeared in the press. All of these developments were similar to the events that had preceded the purges of the thirties. Then quite suddenly in the midst of this new furor, on March 6, 1953, Stalin died. There have remained unconfirmed suspicions that his sudden death may have been related to the impending purges.

For a time no single leader replaced Stalin. Rather the Presidium (the renamed Politburo) pursued a policy of collective leadership. A considerable amount of reshuffling occurred among the top party leaders. Lavrenti Beria (1899–1953), the dreaded director of the secret police, was removed from his post and eventually executed. Georgi Malenkov (b. 1902) became premier, a position he held for about two years. Gradually, however, power and influence began to devolve on Nikita Khrushchev (1894–1971), who in 1953 had been named party secretary. By 1955 he had edged out Malenkov and had successfully urged the appointment of Nikolai Bulganin (1895–1975) in his place. Three years later Khrushchev himself became premier. His rise constituted the end of collective leadership, but at no time did he enjoy the extraordinary powers of Stalin.

The Khrushchev era, which lasted until the autumn of 1964, witnessed a marked retreat from Stalinism though not from extreme authoritarianism. Indeed, the political

Khrushchev Denounces the Crimes of Stalin: The Secret Speech

In 1956 Khrushchev denounced Stalin in a secret speech to the Party Congress. The *New York Times* published a text smuggled from Russia.

STALIN *acted not through persuasion, explanation, and patient cooperation with people, but by imposing his concepts and demanding absolute submission to his opinion. Whoever opposed this concept or tried to prove his viewpoint and the correctness of his position was doomed to removal from the leading collective [group] and to subsequent moral and physical annihilation. . . .*

Stalin originated the concept "enemy of the people." This term automatically rendered it unnecessary that the ideological errors of a man or men engaged in a controversy be proved; this term made possible the usage of the most cruel repression violating all norms of revolutionary legality, against anyone who in any way disagreed with Stalin, against those who were only suspected of hostile intent, against those who had bad reputations.

This concept "enemy of the people" actually eliminated the possibility of any kind of ideological fight or the making of one's views known on this or that issue, even those of a practical character. In the main, and in actuality, the only proof of guilt used, against all norms of current legal science, was the "confession" of the accused himself; and, as subsequent probing proved, "confessions" were acquired through physical pressures against the accused. . . .

Lenin used severe methods only in the most necessary cases, when the exploiting classes were still in existence and were vigorously opposing the revolution, when the struggle for survival was decidedly assuming the sharpest forms, even including civil war.

Stalin, on the other hand, used extreme methods and mass repressions at a time when the revolution was already victorious, when the Soviet State was strengthened, when the exploiting classes were already liquidated and Socialist relations were rooted solidly in all phases of national economy, when our party was politically consolidated and had strengthened itself both numerically and ideologically. It is clear that here Stalin showed in a whole series of cases his intolerance, his brutality and his abuse of power. Instead of proving his political correctness and mobilizing the masses, he often chose the path of repression and physical annihilation, not only against actual enemies, but also against individuals who had not committed any crimes against the party and the Soviet Government. . . .

The New York Times, June 5, 1956, pp. 13–16.

repression of Stalin had been so extensive that there was considerable room for relaxation of surveillance within the limits of tyranny. Politically the demise of Stalinism meant shifts in leadership and party structure by means other than purges. In 1956, at the Twentieth Congress of the Communist Party, Khrushchev made a secret speech (later published outside the Soviet Union) in which he denounced Stalin and his crimes against socialist justice during the purges of the thirties. The speech caused shock and consternation in party circles and opened the way for limited, but genuine, internal criticism of the Soviet government. Gradually the strongest supporters of Stalinist policies were removed from the Presidium. By 1958 all of Stalin's former supporters were gone, but none had been executed.

Soviet Premier Nikita Khrushchev attacked the policies of Stalin in a long secret speech before the 1956 Communist Party Congress in Moscow. Subsequently his own adventuresome foreign policy and unsuccessful agricultural policy led to his downfall in 1964. [United Press International Photo.]

Under Khrushchev, intellectuals were somewhat more able to express their opinions. This so-called thaw in the cultural life of the country was closely related to the premier's interest in the opinions of experts on problems of industry and agriculture. He often went outside the usual bureaucratic channels in search of information and new ideas. Novels such as Alexander Solzhenitsyn's (b. 1918) *One Day in the Life of Ivan Denisovich* (1963) could be published. However, Boris Pasternak (1890–1960), the author of *Dr. Zhivago,* was not permitted to accept the Nobel Prize for literature in 1958. The intellectual liberalization of Soviet life during this period should not be overestimated. It looked favorable only in comparison with what had preceded it and has continued to seem so because of the decline of such freedom of expression since Khrushchev's fall.

The economic policy also somewhat departed from the strict Stalinist mode. By 1953 the economy had recovered from the strains and destruction of the war. Consumer goods and housing still remained in very short supply. The problem of an adequate food supply also continued. Malenkov had favored improvements in meeting the demand for consumer goods; Khrushchev also favored such a departure. The latter also moved in a moderate fashion to decentralize economic planning and execution. During the late fifties Khrushchev often boasted that Soviet production of consumer goods would overtake that of the West. Steel, oil, and electric-power production continued to grow, but the consumer sector improved only marginally. The ever-growing defense budget and the space program that successfully launched the first man-made satellite of the earth, *Sputnik,* in 1957 made major demands on the nation's productive resources. Economically Khrushchev was attempting to move the country in too many directions at once.

Khrushchev strongly redirected Stalin's agricultural policy. He recognized that in spite of the collectivization of the thirties the Soviet Union had not produced an agricultural system capable of feeding its own people. Administratively Khrushchev removed many of the most restrictive regulations on private cultivation. The machine tractor stations were abandoned. Existing collective farms were further amalgamated. The government undertook an extensive "virgin lands" program to extend wheat cultivation by hundreds of thousands of acres. This policy initially increased grain production to new records. However, in a very few years the new lands became subject to erosion. The farming techniques applied had been inappropriate for the soil. The agricultural problem has simply continued to grow. Currently the Soviet Union imports vast quantities of grain from the United States and other countries. United States grain imports have constituted a major facet of the policy of detente.

Adventuresomeness also characterized Khrushchev's foreign policy. In 1956 the Soviet Union adopted the phrase "peaceful coexistence" in regard to its relationship to the United States. The policy implied no less competition with the capitalist world but suggested that war might not be the best way to pursue Communist expansion. The previous year Khrushchev had participated in the Geneva summit meeting alongside Bulganin. Thereafter followed visits around the world, culminating with one to the United States in 1959. By the early sixties it had become clear that Khrushchev had made few inroads on Western policy. He was under increasing domestic pressure and also pressure from the Chinese. The militancy of the denunciation of the U-2 flight, the aborting of the Paris summit meeting, the Berlin Wall, and the Cuban missile crisis were all responses to those pressures. The last of these adventures brought a clear Soviet retreat.

By 1964 numerous high Russian leaders and many people lower in the party had concluded that Khrushchev had tried to do too much too soon and had done it too poorly. On October 16, 1964, after defeat in the Central Committee of the Communist Party, Khrushchev resigned. He was replaced by Alexei Kosgygin (b. 1904) as Premier and Leonid Brezhnev (b. 1906) as party secretary. The latter eventually emerged as the dominant figure. In 1977 the constitution of the Soviet Union was

Anatoly Shcharansky represents the emergence of an open movement of dissent within the Soviet Union, just as his imprisonment shows the continuing official repression accompanying the movement. The fate of Shcharansky and others commanded international attention in 1978. [United Press International Photo.]

changed to combine the offices of president and party secretary. Brezhnev became president, and thus head of the state as well as of the party. He holds more personal power than any Soviet leader since Stalin.

Domestically the Soviet government has become markedly more repressive since 1964. All intellectuals have enjoyed less and less freedom and little direct access to the government leadership. In 1974 the government expelled Solzhenitsyn. Perhaps most important among recent developments, Jewish citizens of the Soviet Union have become subject to harassment. Major bureaucratic obstacles have been placed in the way of the emigration of Soviet Jews to Israel. These policies suggest a return to the limitations of the Stalinist period.

The internal repression has given rise to a dissident movement. Certain Soviet citizens have dared to criticize the regime in public and to carry out small demonstrations against the government. They have accused the Soviet government of violating the human rights provisions of the Helsinki agreements. The dissidents have included a number of prominent citizens such as the Nobel Prize physicist Andrei Sakharov. The response of the Soviet government to the dissident movement has been further repression. Prominent dissidents, such as Anatoly Shcharansky, Aleksandr Ginzburg, and Vladimir Slepak, have been arrested, tried on clearly trumped-up charges, and sentenced to long periods of imprisonment or internal exile in Siberia. The Soviet government obviously feels it cannot tolerate the dissident movement. The questions that now arise and cannot be answered have to do with how much internal opposition to the government exists in the Soviet Union and what, if any, possibility the opposition has of making its thought and will known.

In foreign policy the Brezhnev years have witnessed attempts to reach accommodation with the United States while continuing to press for expanded Soviet influence and further attempts to maintain Soviet leadership of the Communist movement. During the Vietnam war the Soviet Union pursued a policy of restrained support for North Vietnam. Under President Richard Nixon the United States pursued a policy of *détente* based on arms limitation and trade agreements. Nonetheless, Soviet spending on defense, and particularly on naval expansion, has continued to grow. During the Ford and Carter administrations in the United States, Soviet involvement in African affairs has been troubling. Soviet-African activities, as well as violation of the human rights of Russian dissidents, have brought a cooling of relations between the two superpowers. As with so many other aspects of contemporary Europe, the future direction of the Soviet Union remains unclear. Certainly in domestic policy authoritarianism will continue and may intensify. In foreign affairs divisions among the Communist nations and parties may determine the course of future policy.

Polycentrism in the Communist World

Throughout the Cold War observers in the West concentrated their attention on the tensions between the Soviet Union and the United States. But beyond its continuing confrontation of and rivalry with America, the Soviet government also had to deal with growing tension and division within the world communist movement. During most of the Stalin era the Soviet Union was the center of world communism. Stalin hoped to impose his model on other parties. Immediately after the war the Soviets attempted to construct governments in the people's democracies of Eastern Europe in the Stalinist mold. Since the late forties the unity of world communism, which was always more frail than Cold War rhetoric suggested, became strained and finally shattered. As early as 1948 Yugoslavia began to construct its own model for socialism independent of Moscow. From 1956 onward the governments of eastern Europe began to seek a freer hand in internal affairs. By the late fifties the monumental split between the Soviet Union and the People's Republic of China had developed. The communist world has come to have many centers—thus the descriptive term *polycentrism*—and the Soviet Union has had to compete for leadership.

There have been three stages in postwar relations

between the Soviet Union and eastern Europe. They were the years of Stalinism, then of revolt, and finally of socialist polycentrism. The stages closely paralleled internal developments in the Soviet Union itself.

Prior to the death of Stalin in 1953 the so-called peoples' democracies were brought steadily into line with Soviet policy. By 1948 single-party communist governments had been established in Bulgaria, Romania, Hungary, Yugoslavia, Albania, Czechoslovakia, Poland, and East Germany. Yugoslavia, headed by Marshal Tito (b. 1891), pursued an independent course of action and was bitterly denounced by Stalin. Elsewhere, however, Soviet troops and Stalinist party leaders prevailed. The economies of those states were made to conform to the requirements of Soviet economic recovery and growth. The Soviet Union paid low prices for its imports from Eastern Europe and demanded high prices for its exports. In this fashion and through outright reparations it drained the resources of the region for its own uses. The Soviet Union prevented the eastern European nations from participating in the Marshall Plan and responded with its own Council for Economic Mutual Assistance in 1949. In 1955 it organized the Warsaw Pact to confront NATO.

The Stalinist system of control was bound to generate discontent. This first manifested itself shortly after Stalin's death in 1953, when a brief revolt occurred in East Berlin. It was immediately crushed. Talk in the early Eisenhower administration in America about the "liberation" of eastern Europe may have contributed to this disturbance by raising hopes of some form of United States support. Khrushchev's speech of 1956 in which he denounced Stalin sent reverberations throughout eastern Europe as well as the Soviet Union. It was no accident that following the speech came the Polish October Revolution and the Hungarian Revolution of 1956. In the short run the bids for independence had the most limited kind of success; however, in retrospect they can be seen as marking the close of the Stalinist period and as paving the way for the emergence of polycentrism.

During the early years of the Cold War it was common in the West to regard the communist movement as a single monolithic structure. There was a failure to take into account the role of nationalism in eastern Europe and the potential for division between the Soviet Union and China. The events of 1956 delineated the limits of acceptable independence for the Soviet-dominated successor states. Those nations of eastern Europe must remain members of the Warsaw Pact, and their leaders had to be willing to consult and cooperate with the Soviet Union. They might trade with Western Europe and the United States and even establish cultural contacts, but their chief political and economic orientation must remain with the Soviet Union.

Since 1956, within these limits considerable diversity has appeared in eastern Europe. In Poland Wladyslaw Gomulka (b. 1905) and his successors have made peace with the Roman Catholic Church, halted land collectivization, established trade with the West, and participated in cultural exchange programs. However, Poland has experienced persistent shortages in food and consumer goods. Such discontent led to Gomulka's departure in 1970 and has remained a pervasive undercurrent in Polish affairs ever since. In Hungary the Janos Kadar (b. 1912) government, which was installed by Soviet troops, pursued a program of economic growth and consumer satisfaction. Hungary is now probably the most prosperous and stable country in the area. East Germany and Bulgaria retained the closest relationships to the Soviet Union. Only after the Berlin Wall crisis of 1961 and the subsequent halt in the outflow of refugees did the East German government begin to achieve anything resembling economic prosperity. Romania has witnessed a resurgence of limited nationalism. Under the leadership of President Nicolae Ceauşescu (b. 1918), it has maintained ties with both the Soviet Union and China. Moreover, it has cultivated friendly relations with the United States, as witnessed by President Nixon's visit in 1969 and President Ceauşescu's visit to America in 1977. However, in all of these countries the independence achieved still exists within the confines of one-party gov-

In the early summer of 1968, before the invasion of Czechoslovakia by the Soviet Union and others, the leaders of the Warsaw Pact nations met in Bratislava, Czechoslovakia. The front row of their striking group photograph is an all-star cast of East European Communist figures of the mid-1960s: (left to right) Janos Kadar, Hungary; Nikolai Podgorny and Alexei Kosygin, Soviet Union; Todor Zhivkov, Bulgaria; Ludvik Svoboda, Czechoslovakia; Leonid Brezhnev, Soviet Union; Wladyslav Gomulka, Poland; Walter Ulbricht, East Germany; Alexander Dubcek, Czechoslovakia; Mikhail Suslov, Soviet Union. [Camera Press.]

ernment, authoritarianism, and absence of the traditional civil liberties.

In 1968 the Soviet Union moved to crush an experiment in developing a socialist model independent of Soviet domination. In that year the nations of the Warsaw Pact invaded Czechoslovakia to halt the political experimentation of the Alexander Dubcek government. It was quite clear that the Soviet Union felt that it could

In the summer of 1968 troops of the Soviet Union and other Warsaw Pact nations invaded Czechoslovakia to bring to an end the Czech experiment in a more liberal version of communism. Unlike Budapest twelve years earlier, Prague offered little or no violent resistance by the Czechs to the invasion, as this scene reveals. [United Press International Photo.]

not tolerate so liberal a communist regime on its own borders. Dubcek was permitting in Czechoslovakia the very kind of intellectual freedom and discussion that was simultaneously being suppressed within Russia itself. At the time of the invasion Soviet Party Chairman Brezhnev declared the right of the Soviet Union to interfere in the domestic politics of other communist countries. Such interference has nevertheless not occurred since 1968. Moreover, at a conference of communist parties held in East Berlin in 1976 the Soviet Union accepted a declaration stating that there could be several paths to socialism. The main proponents of this policy were the communist parties of Western Europe. As the Communist Party of Italy in particular, as well as that of France, has seen election to full or shared power as a genuine possibility, it has attempted to put distance between itself and the Soviet Union. However, to date none of these declarations and acknowledgements of socialist independence from Soviet domination has been put to a meaningful test. A time of considerable trial and error probably lies ahead.

SUGGESTED READINGS

S. H. BEER, *British Politics in the Collectivist Age* (1965). The best discussion of twentieth-century political structures in Britain.

C. E. BLACK, *The Dynamics of Modernization: A Study in Comparative History* (1966). A useful study with implications for both European and non-European history.

Z. BRZEZINSKI, *The Soviet Block: Unity and Conflict* (1967). A discussion of Eastern Europe.

R. EMERSON, *From Empire to Nation: The Rise to Self-Assertion of Asian and African Peoples* (1960). An important discussion of the origins of decolonization.

B. B. FALL, *The Two Vietnams: A Political and Military Analysis,* rev. ed. (1967). A discussion by a journalist who spent many years on the scene.

R. HISCOCKS, *The Adenauer Era* (1966). A treatment of postwar German political development.

S. HOFFMAN (Ed.), *In Search of France* (1963). A useful collection of essays on the problems of postwar France.

W. W. KULSKI, *De Gaulle and the World: The Foreign Policy of the Fifth French Republic* (1968). A straightforward treatment of De Gaulle's drive toward French and European autonomy.

WALTER LAQUEUR, *Europe Since Hitler* (1970). A well-balanced and comprehensive account of postwar developments.

W. LEONHARD, *The Kremlin Since Stalin* (1962). A brief but informative discussion of the post-Stalin power struggles.

W. LEONHARD, *Three Faces of Communism* (1974). An analysis of the ideological divisions within the Communist world.

D. MACRAE, JR., *Parliament, Politics, and Society in France, 1946–1958* (1967). A close analysis of the turmoil of the Fourth Republic.

R. MAYNE, *The Recovery of Europe, 1945–1973* (1973). A sound treatment emphasizing the movement toward economic integration.

G. MYRDAL, *Asian Drama: An Inquiry into the Poverty of Nations,* 3 vols. (1968). A significant discussion of the economic and social problems of the postcolonial world by a thoughtful economist.

M. M. POSTAN, *An Economic History of Western Europe, 1945–1964* (1967). A basic survey.

A. SAMPSON, *The New Anatomy of Britain* (1973). A critical discussion of the British political and economic elite.

L. SCHAPIRO, *The Communist Party of the Soviet Union* (1960). An important analysis of the most important institution of Soviet Russia.

J. J. SERVAN-SCHREIBER, *The American Challenge* (trans., 1968). A French journalist's analysis of American economic influence in France.

R. SHAPLEN, *The Lost Revolution: The U.S. in Vietnam* (1965). A clear analysis of the problems that confronted the United States.

ADAM ULLAM, *Expansion and Coexistence: The History of Soviet Foreign Policy, 1917–1967* (1968). The best one-volume treatment.

H. C. WALLICH, *Mainsprings of the German Revival* (1955). A discussion of the origins of the German economic miracle.

35
Twentieth-Century States of Mind

THE PLURAL form of the word *state* in the title of this chapter is quite intentional. No single characteristic has so marked the thought of twentieth-century Europe as the absence of unity and shared values. As discussed in Chapter 29, many of the traditional religious and intellectual certainties dissolved during the fifty years prior to 1914. Already philosophers, theologians, writers, and social thinkers had found themselves compelled to look for new paths of thought and new intellectual signposts. The crises that flowed from the two world wars, the Great Depression, the conflict of political ideologies, and the shadow of atomic warfare have in turn created problems more rapidly, perhaps, than solutions can be formulated. The pressure of events, as well as the absence of intellectual certainty, has caused major thinkers to go in more different directions than ever before in the European experience. Anxiety, fear, and even desperation have been the chief features of that search for new values.

The intellectual life of this century has taken place amidst the most extreme social and political conditions. The world wars confirmed the power of human beings not simply to do great harm to each other but actually to destroy the species. From the opening months of World War I onward, Europeans have known that they could kill scores of thousands of each other between a single rising and setting of the sun. Since 1945 the entire world has been aware of the devastating potential of atomic weapons. Within individual nation-states, people have experienced the most extreme forms of political repres-

sion in the history of the West, and that repression has occurred under both right-wing and left-wing governments. In sheer magnitude the racial atrocities of the Nazis and the peasant slaughters under Stalin's agricultural policy were unprecedented. The economic unrest of the 1920s and 1930s brought uncertainty and in many cases extreme suffering to millions of people. Throughout the colonial world the onetime subject nations began to rebel and to condemn the major values of Western civilization. The attempts by Western nations to maintain colonial dominance and influence gave rise to widespread internal criticism. During all of these developments the technology that had brought Europe and the West to its pinnacle of world domination seemed to be turning against its creator, first in the destructiveness of war and then as a danger to the environment.

Such a time of turmoil was not entirely new to the Western experience. The third and fourth centuries saw a variety of differing attempts to come to grips with the social and political disintegration of the Roman Empire. The problems of the late empire brought about major political reorganization and the conversion to Christianity. Many twentieth-century intellectuals have regarded themselves as living in no less a tumultuous period.

Extreme social and political conditions have encouraged extreme intellectual solutions. Between the wars distinguished writers and philosophers in considerable numbers supported either fascism or communism. Other writers began to identify with the aspirations of the restive colonial peoples. These intellectuals condemned both colonialism and the civilization that fostered it. A major segment of the intellectual community rejected rationalism, reason, and science as the primary guides to a better and more humane life. Equally significant, most of the intellectual movements addressing themselves to modern problems have been very short-lived. Whereas one can see the Enlightenment as extending over most of the eighteenth century, the chief intellectual developments of this century have often sustained themselves for only a decade.

This picture of the earth, taken on May 20, 1969 from 100,000 miles in space during the first American flight to the moon, has come to illustrate both the technological accomplishment of the twentieth century and the sense that human beings must devote more care to the limited resources of their relatively small planet. [National Aeronautics and Space Administration.]

Head, by Amedeo Modigliani (1884–1920), an Italian painter and sculptor of the early twentieth century, displays the impact of nonwestern art on Europe. Its portrayal of a traditional subject of sculpture in a nontraditional manner illustrates the way in which various strains of European thought and art became transformed in the late nineteenth and early twentieth centuries. [The Tate Galley, London.]

Torso, by Antoine Pevsner (1886–1962), was completed in 1926. By depicting the traditional theme of the human form through use of new materials from the present, it illustrates a sense of disjunction between present and past cultures and of the artist's alienation from contemporary technology. The torso, with few recognizable features, has become what almost amounts to a plastic skeleton. To some, it suggests that technology has too radically reshaped human life. [Construction in plastic and copper: $29\frac{1}{2}''$ x $11\frac{5}{8}''$. Collection, The Museum of Modern Art, New York; Katherine S. Dreier Bequest.]

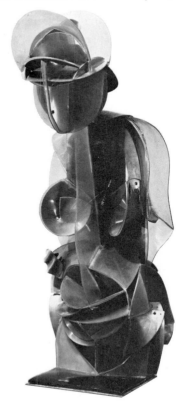

Twentieth-Century States of Mind

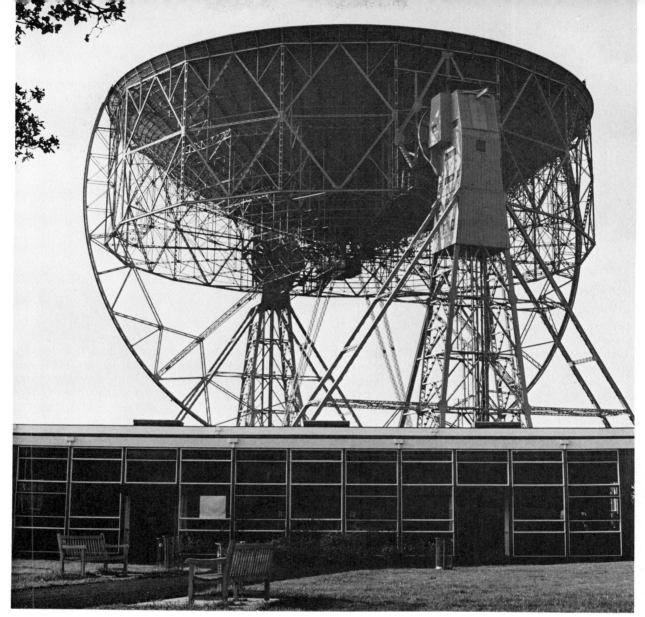

The Jodrell Bank radio telescope in Great Britain came into operation in 1957. It is an example of the vast new interest in space that commenced in the 1950s and of the many complex technologies, like that of radio astronomy, required to support that interest. [British Tourist Authority, New York.]

Although writers have been testing new solutions for the new problems of this century, there has also been considerable continuity with the past. New departures have not meant total separation. For example, although rationalism and the prestige of science have been challenged, science, medicine, and rational business and gov-ernment practices have touched the realities of everyday life as never before. Through World War II the most extreme modes of nationalism flourished in Europe, but since 1945 the kind of international cooperation that the *philosophes* of the eighteenth century desired has made unprecedented progress. This century has been one of ever-growing secularism, but Christian theologians and religious institutions have demonstrated considerable vitality. Finally, in its very self-criticism the civilization of twentieth-century Europe has displayed its links with the past. For it has been the capacity of the West to nurture internal criticism that has permitted it to adapt itself to new problems and conditions.

The Diffusion of Knowledge and Culture

The twentieth century has witnessed unparalleled changes in the pursuit and diffusion of knowledge. The invention and institutionalization of radio, television, and computers have created an informational revolution. The communications revolution has made the world smaller and has led to a wider uniformity of culture. The daily events of politics are reported instantaneously. Different nations can share the same programing, and the same products can be advertised. Through computer science more information of all kinds can be gathered and stored. There has also been a continuation of the vast explosion of printed matter that began about the middle of the nineteenth century. In the face of radio and television, Europeans have not ceased to read and write books. This century has seen more books of every kind printed than ever before; storage is now a problem for libraries. However, the printed word has become only one mode of public communication. The sheer quantity of information now available on practically every subject has in and of itself contributed to the fragmentation of public opinion and intellectual endeavor.

The increase in the quantity of information has been accompanied by a growing number of Europeans' receiving some form of university education. At the turn of the century in every major European country only a few thousand people were enrolled in the universities. By the 1970s that figure had risen to hundreds of thousands. More people from more different kinds of social and economic backgrounds were receiving higher education. Equally important, for the first time large numbers of women were receiving such training. This expansion in the student and educated populations has been closely related to the intense self-criticism of Europeans. Millions of citizens have become equipped with those critical intellectual skills that in previous centuries were usually the possession of very small literate elites.

The "student experience"—that is, leaving home and settling for several years in a community composed primarily of late adolescents—has come to be widely shared. Previously only a relatively few privileged persons had known this experience. Since World War II it has become one of the major features of European and Western society. One of its most striking results was the student rebellion of the late sixties. Students at the Sorbonne in Paris were the leading instigators of the events in France, which in May 1968 shook the foundations of the Gaullist government. About the same time German students forced the entire restructuring of the university system. Students were also in the forefront of the socialist experiment in Czechoslovakia, which was suppressed by the Soviet invasion in 1968. Student disturbances occurred in several of the British universities, and Italian students have been no less active. The growth in the number of students and their political activities in part accounted for the disunity of intellectual life. As more different kinds of people came to participate in university and intellectual life, there was bound to be less unity.

The expansion in the number of students has also meant a general increase in the numbers of university teachers. As a result, there have been more scientists, historians, economists, literary critics, and other professional intellectuals during the last seventy-five years than in all previous human history. Moreover, not since the early years of the Reformation have university intellectuals exerted such widespread influence. The major intellectual developments of the seventeenth, eighteenth, and nineteenth centuries took place primarily, though not entirely, outside the university. In the twentieth century the university has become the most likely home for the intellectual. And the symbol of success on the part of a writer in almost any field has been the inclusion of his work in the university curriculum.

All of these factors, in addition to the difficult political and social events of the century, have meant that the former unity of Western thought has become shattered. Some observers have considered this development as opening the possibility for new creativity. For one highly

significant group of twentieth-century writers the disruption of intellectual unity and the disappearance of former spiritual guideposts spawned a situation of extreme anxiety.

Existentialism

The single intellectual movement that perhaps best characterizes the predicament and mood of twentieth-century European culture is existentialism. It is symptomatic that most of the philosophers associated with this movement disagree with each other on major issues. Existentialism, which has been termed the philosophy of Europe in the twentieth century, like the modern Western mind in general, has been badly divided. The movement represents in part a continuation of the revolt against reason that commenced in the nineteenth century.

Friedrich Nietzsche, whose thought was considered in

Chapter 29, was one of the major forerunners of existentialism. Another was the Danish writer Sören Kierkegaard (1813–1855), who wrote during the second quarter of the nineteenth century but received little attention until after World War I. He was a rebel against Hegelian philosophy and Christianity as he found it in Denmark. In works such as *Fear and Trembling* (1843), *Either/Or* (1843), and *Concluding Unscientific Postscript* (1846), he urged that the truth of Christianity could not be contained in creeds, doctrines, and church organizations. It could be grasped only in the living experience of those who faced extreme human situations. This emphasis on lived experience as the true test of the validity of philosophy and religion has characterized most twentieth-century existential writers. Kierkegaard also criticized Hegelian philosophy and, by implication, all modes of academic rational philosophy. Its failure, he felt, was the attempt to contain all of life and human experience within abstract categories. Kierkegaard spurned this faith in the power of mere reason. "The conclusions of passion," he once declared, "are the only reliable ones." [1]

The intellectual and ethical crisis of World War I brought Kierkegaard's thought to the fore and also created new interest in Nietzsche's critique of reason. The human sacrifice and the destruction of property made many people doubt whether human beings were actually in control of their own destiny. The conflict stood as an affront to the concept of human improvement and the view of human beings as creatures of rationality. The war itself had been fought with the instruments developed through rational technology. The pride in rational human achievement that had characterized much nineteenth-century European civilization lay in ruins. The sunny faith in rational human development and advancement had not been able to withstand the extreme experiences of war.

Existential thought came to thrive in this climate and received further encouragement by the trauma of World War II. The major existential writers included the Germans Martin Heidegger (1889–1976) and Karl Jaspers (1883–1969) and the Frenchmen Jean-Paul Sartre (b. 1905) and Albert Camus (1913–1960). Their books were often very difficult and in some cases simply obscure, and the writers frequently disagreed with each other. Yet all of them in one way or another questioned the primacy of reason and scientific understanding as ways of coming to grips with the human situation. Heidegger went so far as to argue, "Thinking only begins at the point where we have come to know that Reason, glorified for centuries, is the most obstinate adversary of thinking." [2] The tradition of the Enlightenment suggested that analysis or the separation of human experience into its component parts was the proper path to understanding. Existential writers

1 Quoted in Walter Kaufmann (Ed.), *Existentialism from Dostoevsky to Sartre* (Cleveland: The World Publishing Company, 1962), p. 18.
2 Quoted in William Barrett, *Irrational Man* (Garden City, N.Y.: Doubleday, 1962), p. 20.

Sartre Discusses the Character of His Existentialism

Jean-Paul Sartre, dramatist and philosopher, is the most important French contemporary existentialist. He is widely read in European and American universities. In the first paragraph of this 1946 statement Sartre asserts that all human beings must experience a sense of anguish or the most extreme anxiety when undertaking a major commitment. That anguish arises because consciously or unconsciously they are deciding whether all human beings should make the same decision. In the second paragraph he argues that the existence or non-existence of God would make no difference for human affairs. What humankind must do is to discover the character of its own situation by itself.

THE *existentialist frankly states that man is in anguish. His meaning is as follows—When a man commits himself to anything, fully realizing that he is not only choosing what he will be, but is thereby at the same time a legislator deciding for the whole of mankind—in such a moment a man cannot escape from the sense of complete and profound responsibility. There are many, indeed, who show no such anxiety. But we affirm that they are merely disguising their anguish or are in flight from it. Certainly, many people think that in what they are doing they commit no one but themselves to anything: and if you ask them, "What would happen if everyone did so?" they shrug their shoulders and reply, "Everyone does not do so." But in truth, one ought always to ask oneself what would happen if everyone did as one is doing; nor can one escape from that disturbing thought except by a kind of self-deception. The man who lies in self-excuse, by saying "Everyone will not do it" must be ill at ease in his conscience, for the act of lying implies the universal value which it denies. By its very disguise his anguish reveals itself.*

.   .   .   .

Existentialism is nothing else but an attempt to draw the full conclusions from a consistently atheistic position. Its intention is not in the least that of plunging men into despair. And if by despair one means—as the Christians do—any attitude of unbelief, the despair of the existentialist is something different. Existentialism is not atheist in the sense that it would exhaust itself in demonstration of the non-existence of God. It declares, rather, that even if God existed that would make no difference from its point of view. Not that we believe God does exist, but we think that the real problem is not that of His existence; what man needs is to find himself again and to understand that nothing can save him from himself, not even a valid proof of the existence of God. In this sense existen-

Jean-Paul Sartre and Simone de Beauvoir (born 1908) have been two leading French intellectuals of the mid-century. His is a major voice of the existentialist movement, and she has written extensively on the social position, experience, and psychology of women, as well as on other social and philosophical issues. [United Press International Photo.]

tialism is optimistic. It is a doctrine of action, and it is only by self-deception, by confusing their own despair with ours that Christians can describe us as without hope.

Jean-Paul Sartre, *Existentialism and Humanism,* trans. by Philip Mairet (London: Methuen, 1960), in Walter Kaufman, ed., *Existentialism from Dostoevsky to Sartre* (New York: Meridian Books, Inc., 1956), pp. 292, 310–311.

rejected this approach. They argued that the human condition was greater than the sum of its parts and must be grasped as a whole.

The Romantic writers of the early nineteenth century had also questioned the primacy of reason, but they did so in a much less radical manner than the existentialists. The Romantics emphasized the imagination and intuition, but the existentialists tended to dwell primarily on the extremes of human experience. Death, dread, fear, and anxiety provided their themes. The titles of their works illustrate their sense of forboding and alienation: *Existence and Time* (1962) by Heidegger; *Nausea* (1938) and *Being and Nothingness* (1943) by Sartre; *The Plague* (1947) and *The Stranger* (1942) by Camus. The touchstone of philosophic truth became the experience of individual human beings under such extreme situations. The existentialists saw human beings as compelled to formulate their own ethical values rather than being able to find ethical guidance from traditional religion, rational philosophy, intuition, or social customs. This opportunity and necessity to lay down values for oneself became the dreadful freedom of existentialist philosophy.

In large measure the existentialists were protesting against a world in which reason, technology, and the rational policies of war and genocide had produced unreasonable results. Their thought reflected the uncertainty of social institutions and ethical values that existed during the era of the two world wars. However, since the

sixties their thought has become the subject of study in universities throughout the world. They will probably continue to be subjects of philosophy and literature classes, but it seems unlikely that they will again achieve their former popularity. In that respect their demise reflects the relative prosperity and material comfort achieved by a growing majority of Europeans during the last quarter century. The new generation of Europeans born after World War II has not known the experiences that gave rise to existential philosophy. Existentialism was the philosophy of the political and social crisis of Europe in the first half of the twentieth century. As the perceived crisis passed, so also has the immediate influence of existentialism.

Intellectuals and Politics

After World War I writers, philosophers, critics, and artists throughout Europe believed that a new course had to be set for their culture. Many of them thought that the political values and institutions of liberal democracy had failed. Liberalism had neither prevented the war nor achieved a minimum standard of decent living for the general population. Conservative intellectuals saw liberalism as fostering social and political unrest and undermining national greatness. Consequently considerable numbers of intellectuals during the twenties and the thirties felt that they must align themselves with either

The Unknown Political Prisoner, by the Italian sculptor Luciano Minguzzi, is an expressionist work that takes up the theme of hopeless entrapment. Its title identifies it socially with the experience of millions of Europeans under authoritarian regimes. [The Tate Gallery, London.]

fascism or communism. Political ideology had become the order of the day. Art, literature, and philosophy were subordinated to political ends.

Hitler and Mussolini attracted numerous intellectuals and university teachers to support their policies. Some of these writers were little more than paid literary hacks, but others were persons of considerable standing in the university community. However, the most important political movement to attract the allegiance of twentieth-century European intellectuals was communism. It seemed to provide a very direct manner of dealing with the social question and a vehicle for opposing the spread of fascism.

As the liberal democracies floundered in depression and as right-wing regimes spread across the continent, communism seemed to many people at the time a way to protect humane values. Throughout Europe students in the universities affiliated with the Communist Party. They and older intellectuals visited the Soviet Union and praised Stalin's achievements. Some of these writers did not know of Stalin's terror; others simply closed their eyes to it, somehow believing that humane ends might come from inhumane methods. During the late twenties and the thirties communism became little less than a substitute religion. One group of former Communists, writing after World War II, described their attraction and later disillusionment with communism in a book entitled *The God That Failed* (1949).

The Russian Revolution and its later developments led both to the attraction of intellectuals to communism and eventually to their later rejection of the ideology. In Russia the revolution had seemed to construct a new social order in the name and on the behalf of the proletariat. Under Lenin there had occurred a brief period of literary and artistic experimentation. Later the Soviet Union had also taken a lead in opposing fascism. However, the revolution had also split the ranks of socialists between communists and "democratic" socialists. Many writers and philosophers of left-wing orientation had chosen communism because of its discipline and because of its proved success in Russia. But as the brutal nature of Stalinism became known, numerous intellectuals attempted to set distance between themselves and the Soviet experiment.

Four events proved crucial to the disillusionment of the intellectuals. These were the great public purge trials of 1936 and later, the Spanish Civil War (1936–1939), the Nazi–Soviet Pact of 1939, and the Soviet invasion of Hungary in 1956. Arthur Koestler's *Darkness at Noon* (1940) recorded a former communist's view of the purges. George Orwell, who had never been a communist but who had sympathized, presented the disappointment with Stalin's policy in Spain in *Homage to Catalonia* (1938). The Nazi–Soviet Pact removed the image of Stalin as an opponent of fascism. Jean-Paul Sartre long put faith in the Soviet Union, but the Hungarian invasion cooled his ardor.

Yet disillusionment with the Soviet Union or with Stalin did not in all cases mean disillusionment with Marxism or with a radical socialist critique of European society. Some writers and social critics looked to the establishment of alternative communist governments based on non-Soviet modes. During the decade after World War II Yugoslavia provided such a different model. Since the late fifties radical students and intellectuals have looked for inspiration to the Chinese Revolution. Still other groups have hoped for the development of a European Marxist system. Among the more important

Karl Barth was the Swiss theologian whose books, appearing shortly after World War I, were part of a Protestant theological revival. [United Press International Photo.]

contributors to this non-Soviet tradition was the Italian communist Antonio Gramsci (1891–1937) and his work *Letters from Prison* (published posthumously in 1947). The thought of such non-Soviet communists has become very important to West European communist parties, such as that of Italy, which hope to gain office democratically.

Another mode of Marxist accommodation within mid-twentieth-century European thought has been a redefinition of the basic message of Marx himself. During the 1930s a considerable body of previously unprinted essays by Marx was published. These books and articles are quite abstract and philosophical and were written by Marx before *The Communist Manifesto* of 1848. They make the "young Marx" appear to belong more nearly to the humanist rather than to the revolutionary tradition of European thought. Since World War II these works, including *Philosophic Manuscripts of 1844* and *German Ideology*, have been widely read. Today many people are more familiar with them than with the *Manifesto* or *Capital*. The writings of young Marx have allowed many people to consider themselves sympathetic to Marxism without also seeing themselves as revolutionaries or supporters of the Soviet Union.

In effect, by the last quarter of this century Marxism and even communism have become fragmented. Politically their supporters stand divided in loyalty to the differing models of the Soviet Union, China, Yugoslavia, and others in the non-European world. Ideologically there are divisions among Soviet ideologues, Maoists, and the more independent thinkers of Western Europe. Yet in its various forms Marxism still remains probably the single most influential tradition of political thought in Europe today. Even for people who may not wish a communist state, Marxism has come to provide a vehicle for the criticism of contemporary European society. Moreover the impact of various modes of Marxist thought in the non-European world may now constitute the most important Western influence in the postcolonial age.

The Christian Heritage

In most ways Christianity has continued to be hard-pressed during the twentieth century. Material prosperity and political ideologies have replaced the faith as the dominant factors in many people's lives. However, despite their loss of much popular support and former legal privileges, the Christian churches still exercise considerable social and political influence. In Germany the Protestant churches were one of the few major institutions not wholly conquered by the Nazis. Lutheran clergymen, such as Martin Niemoller and Dietrich Bonhoffer, were leaders of the opposition to Hitler. After the war, in Poland and elsewhere in eastern Europe the Roman Catholic Church actively opposed the influence of communism. In western Europe religious affiliation provided much of the initial basis for the Christian Democratic parties. Across the continent the churches have raised critical questions about colonialism, nuclear weapons, human rights, and other moral issues. Consequently, in the most secular of all ages the Church has affected numerous issues of state.

A theological revival also took place during the first half of the century. Nineteenth-century theologians had frequently softened the concept of sin and had tended to portray human nature as not too far removed from the divine. The horror of World War I destroyed that optimistic faith. Many Europeans felt that evil had stalked the continent.

The most important Christian response to this experience was the theology of Karl Barth (1886–1968). In 1919 this Swiss pastor published *A Commentary on the Epistle to the Romans,* which reemphasized the transcendence of God and the dependence of humankind upon the divine. Barth portrayed God as wholly other than, and different from, humankind. In a sense Barth was returning to the Reformation theology of Luther, but the work of Kierkegaard had profoundly influenced his reading of the reformer. Barth, like the Danish writer,

[*Text continued on page 984*]

Two approaches to contemporary architecture are seen in these contrasting churches, where modern design is in service of age-old modes of Christian worship. [BELOW] The interior of the Church of Notre Dame at Le Raincy near Paris (1922) was designed by Auguste Perret (1874–1954). It is a high point in the new technology of architectural use of reinforced concrete. [OPPOSITE] The Church of the Holy Family in Barcelona is a major work of Spanish architect Antonio Gaudi (1852–1926). Rounded, growing forms characterize this structure, and it is still far from complete. [BELOW: French Cultural Services, New York. OPPOSITE: Spanish National Tourist Office, New York.]

regarded the lived experience of men and women as the best testimony to the truth of his theology. Those extreme moments of life described by Kierkegaard provided the basis for a real knowledge of humankind's need for God. This view totally challenged much nineteenth-century writing about human nature. Barth's theology, which became known as *neo-orthodoxy*, proved to be very influential throughout the West in the wake of new political disasters and human suffering.

Liberal theology, however, was not swept away by neo-orthodoxy. The German–American Paul Tillich (1886–1965) was the most important liberal theologian. He looked to a theology of culture and tended to regard religion as a human rather than a divine phenomenon. Whereas Barth saw God as dwelling outside humankind, Tillich believed that evidence of the divine had to be sought from within human nature and human culture. Other liberal theologians, such as Rudolf Bultmann (1884–1919), continued to work out the problems of naturalism and supernaturalism that had plagued earlier writers. His major writing took place prior to World War II but was popularized thereafter in Anglican Bishop John Robinson's *Honest to God* (1963). Another liberal Christian writer from Britain, C. S. Lewis (1878–1963), attracted millions of readers during and after World War II. He was a layman and his books were often in the form of letters or short stories. His most famous work is *The Screwtape Letters* (1942).

Perhaps the most significant postwar religious departures occurred within the Roman Catholic Church. Pope John XXIII (1958–1963) undertook the most extensive changes to occur in Catholicism for over a century and some would say since the Council of Trent in the sixteenth century. In 1959 Pope John summoned the twenty-first ecumenical council of the church to be called since the series started under the emperor Constantine in the fourth century. It was known as Vatican II. He died before it had completed its work; but his successor, Pope Paul VI, continued the council, which met between 1962 and 1965. Among the numerous changes in liturgy, the

Hans Küng Expresses His Hopes for Vatican II

Küng (born 1928) is one of the most important post-World War II liberal Roman Catholic theologians. In a book written in 1961, shortly before Vatican II, this Swiss theologian spoke of the opportunity for Christian renewal that the calling of the Council presented.

INSOFAR *as the Church is constantly, repeatedly deformed, she has to be constantly, repeatedly reformed. . . .*

But reform is necessary not only because of deformation. Fundamentally, it is not just a negative matter of house-cleaning and repairs, but a vast positive task of constructive building. It is not only because there are mistaken developments and mistaken attitudes in the Church that she has this task. Even if there were none (there always will be) the Church would still have the great task of renewal. For the mustard seed must grow. The Church . . . is in the stream of time: she has to keep adopting new forms, new embodiments. She has to keep giving herself a new form, a new shape in history; she is never simply finished and complete. She must go into all the world and preach the good news to every creature . . . , to all nations, to all cultures, to all ages, until Christ comes again. Such is her incomparably happy mission. Hence she is forever faced afresh with the task of renewing herself. Hence, again, this renewal is not just something which she stringently must *do, but which she joyously* may *do; a joyful service to the Kingdom of God, looking toward him who will make all things new, a new heaven and a new earth. The Pope's summons to renew the Church is, most solemnly and truly, a joyful summons.*

Hans Küng, *The Council, Reform, and Reunion,* trans. by Cecily Hastings (New York: Sheed and Ward, 1961), p. 36.

mass became celebrated in the vernacular. Free relations were established with other Christian denominations. More power was shared with bishops. Pope Paul also appointed a number of cardinals from nations of the former colonial world. For a brief time it seemed that Catholicism might experience a genuine revival. However, after having taken these very liberal moves, the pope firmly upheld the celibacy of priests and maintained the church's prohibition on contraception. The former position caused many men and women to leave the priesthood and religious orders. Many of the laity have deeply resented the policy on family planning. Today,

Pope Paul VI (1963–1978) at the altar of Saint Peter's in Rome presides over a session of the Second Vatican Council. The gathering initiated more changes in the Roman Catholic Church than had any development since the Council of Trent in the sixteenth century. [Archivio Fotografico, Musei Vaticani.]

John Paul II became pope October 17, 1978 after the brief thirty-four-day reign of John Paul I. In more than one way the choice of the new pope is epoch-making. At 58 he is the youngest pontiff since Pius IX. More important, he is the first non-Italian to hold the position since the sixteenth century; and, being Polish, he brings personal experience with the eastern, communist-dominated areas of Europe to the papacy for the first time. [United Press International Photo.]

after having made numerous important accommodations, the Roman Catholic Church still remains at odds with much of the spirit of modernity.

Toward the Twenty-first Century

A century ago a book like this one might have concluded with a statement of the superiority of Western over all other cultures. In that hundred years the position of Europe in power politics has changed. The century has seen vast destruction and inhumanity. Consequently this volume must conclude with a statement of the continuity of Western culture with its past, its potential for new creativity, and its capacity for new interaction with other cultures.

Europeans have not outgrown their history. Many of the formative influences traced in this volume continue to hold sway. For some observers technology may appear to be an enemy and a threat to the environment, but science touches in a positive manner the lives of more people than even fifty years ago might have been imagined. And it will be from scientific understanding that the problems of the environment and of resource shortages will be solved. Although many intellectuals have praised the irrational,

OPPOSITE: Chariot, by the Italian sculptor Alberto Giacometti (1901–1966), was completed in 1950 and displays the questioning spirit of the years immediately after World War II. It brings man and the machine together but suggests the idea of the diminution of humankind by forces larger than itself in the twentieth century. [Bronze, 57″ x 26⅛″. Collection, The Museum of Modern Art, New York.]

BELOW: Recumbent Figure, by the English sculptor Henry Moore (born 1898), uses basic shapes and materials in a traditional manner, but it exemplifies the twentieth-century search for new perspectives on human nature and on physical nature. Although the statue is clearly modern, its "eroded" form suggests less separation from past culture than do many contemporary works. [The Tate Gallery, London.]

rationalism in the processes of everyday life has never been more present, and the use of reason still promises the best hope of humankind. Since World War II the problems of constitutional order and human rights have continued to be major concerns of political life and discussion. Within both communist and noncommunist Europe the spirit of criticism still thrives, though in very different ways.

These persistent features of European life have not assured that its civilization, as well as the results flowing from it, will be morally good, but they have meant that it has possessed in itself the possibility of correcting itself and of raising the questions of what are the good life and the good society. The possibility of asking those questions is necessary before the desired improvement and reform can be attained. Perhaps the chief carriers of Western culture today are those within its midst who most criticize it and demand that it justify itself.

SUGGESTED READINGS

W. M. ABBOTT (Ed.), *The Documents of Vatican II* (1966). A useful way of looking at the changes in contemporary Catholicism.

R. ARON, *The Opium of the Intellectuals* (1957). A critical discussion of Communism and the intellectual community.

B. BARBER, *Science and the Social Order* (1952). A good introduction to the institutional impact of science in this century.

W. BARRETT, *Irrational Man* (1958). A sound treatment of existentialism in its broader intellectual context.

F. L. BAUMER, *Modern European Thought: Continuity and Change in Ideas, 1600–1950* (1977). Excellent chapters on this century.

R. CROSSMAN (Ed.), *The God That Failed* (1949). Essays from former Communist intellectuals.

W. P. DIZARD, *Television: A World Review* (1966). A useful discussion of an important topic.

D. FLEMING AND B. BAILYN (Eds.), *The Intellectual Migration: Europe and America, 1930–1960* (1969). An important collection of essays on the migration of European intellectuals to the United States largely due to the political situation in twentieth-century Europe.

E. FROMM (Ed.), *Socialist Humanism: An International Symposium* (1965). Essays dealing with humanistic approaches to Marxism.

H. S. HUGHES, *The Obstructed Path: French Social Thought in the Years of Desperation, 1930–1960* (1968). A book that well illustrates the fragmentation of twentieth-century thought.

M. JAY, *The Dialectical Imagination* (1973). An important work on the development of Marxist thought among German intellectuals.

W. KAUFMANN (Ed.), *Existentialism from Dostoevsky to Sartre* (1956). An excellent introduction to this movement of thought.

J. PASSMORE, *A Hundred Years of Philosophy* (1968). An exceptionally fine one-volume history.

S. P. SCHILLING, *Contemporary Continental Theologians* (1966). A basic survey of modern theology.

R. N. STROMBERG, *After Everything: Western Intellectual History Since 1945* (1975). A lively and thoughtful account of a very difficult subject.

W. WAGAR (Ed.), *European Intellectual History Since Darwin and Marx* (1966). A collection of high-quality essays.

W. WAGAR (Ed.), *Science, Faith, and Man: European Thought Since 1914* (1968). A collection of documents with good introductions.

Appendix
SOME PRINCIPAL EMPERORS, KINGS, AND POPES

ROMAN EMPIRE

Augustus	27 B.C.–A.D. 14
Tiberius	14– 37
Caligula	37– 41
Claudius	41– 54
Nero	54– 68
Vespasian	69– 79
Titus	79– 81
Domitian	81– 96
Trajan	98–117
Hadrian	117–138
Antoninus Pius	138–161
Marcus Aurelius	161–180
Commodus	180–193
Septimius Severus	193–211
Caracalla	211–217
Elagabalus	218–222
Severus Alexander	222–235
Philip the Arab	244–249
Decius	249–251
Valerian	253–260
Gallienus	260–268
Aurelian	270–275
Diocletian	284–286

WEST		EAST	
Maximian	286–305	Diocletian	284–305
Constantius	305–306	Galerius	305–311
		Maximius	308–313
		Licinius	308–324
Constantine	308–337	Constantine	324–337
Maxentius	307–312		
Constantine II	337–340		
Constans	337–350		
Constantius II	351–361	Constantius II	337–361
Julian	360–363	Julian	361–363
Jovian	363–364	Jovian	363–364
Valentinian	364–375	Valens	364–378
Gratian	375–383		
Valentinian II	383–392		
Theodosius	394–395	Theodosius	379–395

CAROLINGIAN KINGDOM

Pepin, Mayor of the Palace	680–714
Charles Martel, Mayor of the Palace	715–741
Pepin the Short, Mayor of the Palace	741–751
Pepin the Short, King	751–768
Charlemagne and Carloman, Joint Kings	768–771
Charlemagne, King	771–814
Charlemagne, Emperor	800–814
Louis the Pious, Emperor	814–840

WEST FRANKS	LOTHARINGIA	EAST FRANKS
Charles the Bald 840–877	Lothar 840–855	Louis the German 840–876
Louis II the Stammerer 877–879	Louis II 855–875	
	Charles 855–863	
	Lothar II 855–869	Carloman 876–880
Louis III 879–882		Louis 876–882
Carloman 879–884		Charles the Fat 884–887

WEST		EAST	
Honorius	395–423	Arcadius	393–408
		Theodosius II	408–450
Valentinian III	425–455	Marcian	450–457
		Leo	457–474
Romulus	475–476	Zeno	474–491
		Anastasius	491–518
		Justin	518–527
		Justinian	527–565

i

HOLY ROMAN EMPIRE

SAXONS

Henry the Fowler
              919– 936
Otto I   962– 973
Otto II   973– 983
Otto III   983–1002

SALIANS

Conrad II   1024–1039
Henry III   1039–1056
Henry IV   1056–1106
Henry V   1106–1125
Lothar II   1125–1137

HOHENSTAUFENS

Frederick I Barbarossa
           1152–1190
Henry VI   1190–1197
Philip of Swabia
           1198–1208
Otto IV (*Welf*)
           1198–1215
Frederick II 1215–1250
Conrad IV   1250–1254

LUXEMBURG, HAPSBURG, AND OTHER DYNASTIES

Rudolf of Hapsburg
           1273–1291
Adolph of Nassau
           1292–1298
Albert of Austria
           1298–1308
Henry VII of
   Luxemburg 1308–1313
Ludwig IV of Bavaria
           1314–1347
Charles IV   1347–1378

Wenceslas 1378–1400
Rupert   1400–1410
Sigismund 1410–1437

HAPSBURGS

Frederick III 1440–1493
Maximilian I 1493–1519
Charles V   1519–1556
Ferdinand I   1556–1564
Maximilian II 1564–1576
Rudolf II   1576–1612
Matthias   1612–1619
Ferdinand II 1619–1637
Ferdinand III 1637–1657
Leopold I   1658–1705
Joseph I   1705–1711
Charles VI   1711–1740
Charles VII 1742–1745
Francis I   1745–1765
Joseph II   1765–1790
Leopold II   1790–1792
Francis II   1792–1806

THE PAPACY

Leo I   440– 461
Gregory I   590– 604
Nicholas I   858– 867
Silvester II   999–1003
Leo IX   1049–1054
Nicholas II   1058–1061
Gregory VII 1073–1085
Urban II   1088–1099
Paschal II   1099–1118
Alexander III 1159–1181
Innocent III 1198–1216
Gregory IX   1227–1241
Boniface VIII 1294–1303
John XXII   1316–1334
Gregory XI   1370–1378
Martin V   1417–1431
Eugenius IV 1431–1447
Nicholas V   1447–1455
Pius II   1458–1464
Alexander VI 1492–1503
Julius II   1503–1513
Leo X   1513–1521
Adrian VI   1522–1523
Clement VII 1523–1534
Paul III   1534–1549
Paul IV   1555–1559
Pius V   1566–1572
Gregory XIII 1572–1585
Pius VII   1800–1823
Gregory XVI 1831–1846
Pius IX   1846–1878
Leo XIII   1878–1903
Pius X   1903–1914
Benedict XV 1914–1922
Pius XI   1922–1939
Pius XII   1939–1958
John XXIII 1958–1963
Paul VI   1963–1978
John Paul I   1978
John Paul II 1978–

Appendix: Some Principal Emperors, Kings, and Popes

ENGLAND

ANGLO-SAXONS

Alfred the Great	871– 900
Ethelred the Unready	978–1016
Canute (*Danish*)	1016–1035
Harold I	1035–1040
Hardicanute	1040–1042
Edward the Confessor	1042–1066
Harold II	1066

NORMANS

William the Conqueror	1066–1087
William II	1087–1100
Henry I	1100–1135
Stephen	1135–1154

ANGEVINS

Henry II	1154–1189
Richard I	1189–1199
John	1199–1216
Henry III	1216–1272
Edward I	1272–1307
Edward II	1307–1327
Edward III	1327–1377
Richard II	1377–1399

HOUSES OF LANCASTER AND YORK

Henry IV	1399–1413
Henry V	1413–1422
Henry VI	1422–1461
Edward IV	1461–1483
Edward V	1483
Richard III	1483–1485

TUDORS

Henry VII	1485–1509
Henry VIII	1509–1547
Edward VI	1547–1553
Mary I	1553–1558
Elizabeth I	1558–1603

STUARTS

James I	1603–1625
Charles I	1625–1649
Charles II	1660–1685
James II	1685–1688
William III and Mary II	1689–1694
William III alone	1694–1702
Anne	1702–1714

HANOVERIANS (from 1917, WINDSORS)

George I	1714–1727
George II	1727–1760
George III	1760–1820
George IV	1820–1830
William IV	1830–1837
Victoria	1837–1901
Edward VII	1901–1910
George V	1910–1936
Edward VIII	1936
George VI	1936–1952
Elizabeth II	1952–

FRANCE

CAPETIANS

Hugh Capet	987– 996
Robert II the Pious	996–1031
Henry I	1031–1060
Philip I	1060–1108
Louis VI	1108–1137
Louis VII	1137–1180
Philip II Augustus	1180–1223
Louis VIII	1223–1226
Louis IX	1226–1270
Philip III	1270–1285
Philip IV	1285–1314
Louis X	1314–1316
Philip V	1316–1322
Charles IV	1322–1328

VALOIS

Philip VI	1328–1350
John	1350–1364
Charles V	1364–1380
Charles VI	1380–1422
Charles VII	1422–1461
Louis XI	1461–1483
Charles VIII	1483–1498
Louis XII	1498–1515
Francis I	1515–1547
Henry II	1547–1559
Francis II	1559–1560
Charles IX	1560–1574
Henry III	1574–1589

BOURBONS

Henry IV	1589–1610
Louis XIII	1610–1643
Louis XIV	1643–1715
Louis XV	1715–1774
Louis XVI	1774–1792

POST 1792

Napoleon I, Emperor	1804–1814
Louis XVIII (*Bourbon*)	1814–1824
Charles X (*Bourbon*)	1824–1830
Louis Philippe (*Bourbon-Orléans*)	1830–1848
Napoleon III, Emperor	1851–1870

SPAIN

Ferdinand	1479–1516
and	
Isabella	1479–1504

HAPSBURGS

Philip I	1504–1506
Charles I (Holy Roman Emperor as Charles V)	1506–1556
Philip II	1556–1598
Philip III	1598–1621
Philip IV	1621–1665
Charles II	1665–1700

BOURBONS

Philip V	1700–1746
Ferdinand VI	1746–1759
Charles III	1759–1788
Charles IV	1788–1808
Ferdinand VII	1808
Joseph Bonaparte	1808–1813
Ferdinand VII (restored)	1814–1833
Isabella II	1833–1868
Amadeo	1870–1873
Alfonso XII	1874–1885
Alfonso XIII	1886–1931
Juan Carlos I	1975–

AUSTRIA AND AUSTRIA-HUNGARY

(Until 1806 all except Maria Theresa were also Holy Roman Emperors.)

Maximilian I, Archduke	1493–1519
Charles I (Emperor as Charles V)	1519–1556
Ferdinand I	1556–1564
Maximilian II	1564–1576
Rudolf II	1576–1612
Matthias	1612–1619
Ferdinand II	1619–1637
Ferdinand III	1637–1657
Leopold I	1658–1705
Joseph I	1705–1711
Charles VI	1711–1740
Maria Theresa	1740–1780
Joseph II	1780–1790
Leopold II	1790–1792
Francis II	1792–1835
Ferdinand I	1835–1848
Francis Joseph	1848–1916
Charles I	1916–1918

PRUSSIA AND GERMANY

HOHENZOLLERNS

Frederick William the Great Elector	1640–1688
Frederick I	1701–1713
Frederick William I	1713–1740
Frederick II the Great	1740–1786
Frederick William II	1786–1797
Frederick William III	1797–1840
Frederick William IV	1840–1861
William I	1861–1888
Frederick III	1888
William II	1888–1918

RUSSIA

Ivan III	1462–1505
Basil III	1505–1533
Ivan IV the Terrible	1533–1584
Theodore I	1584–1598
Boris Godunov	1598–1605
Theodore II	1605
Basil IV	1606–1610

ROMANOVS

Michael	1613–1645
Alexius	1645–1676
Theodore III	1676–1682
Ivan IV and Peter I	1682–1689
Peter I the Great alone	1689–1725
Catherine I	1725–1727
Peter II	1727–1730
Anna	1730–1740
Ivan VI	1740–1741
Elizabeth	1741–1762
Peter III	1762
Catherine II the Great	1762–1796
Paul	1796–1801
Alexander I	1801–1825
Nicholas I	1825–1855
Alexander II	1855–1881
Alexander III	1881–1894
Nicholas II	1894–1917

ITALY

Victor Emmanuel II	1861–1878
Humbert I	1878–1900
Victor Emmanuel III	1900–1946
Humbert II	1946

Appendix: Some Principal Emperors, Kings, and Popes

Index

Entries relating to the color album are preceded by the letter C.

I

Modena, 709
Modern Devotion, 287
See also Brothers of Common Life
Modern Man in Search of a Soul, 790
Modernism, 369
Modigliani, Amedeo, 974
Mohacs, battle of (1526), 375
Mohammed, 232–233
Molière (pseudonym of Jean Baptiste Poquelin), 479
Molotov, Vyacheslav Mikhailovich, 927
Moltke, General Helmut von, 820–821, 824
Monarchy
    effect of Black Death on, 322
    Egyptian, 16
    in fifteenth century, 332–336
    Greek, 41–42, 152
    Hellenistic, 113, 141–142, 160
    Hittite, 18
    Louis XIV of France, 448–461
    Macedonian, 106
    Mesopotamian, 6, 10
    Mycenaean, 38
    Roman, 127
Monasticism, 246, 260
    origins of, 236–237
    recruitment to, 285
    reform of, 260–261
Money and feudal dues, 292
Mongolia, 224
Monmouth, duke of (James Scott), 485
Monnet, Jean, 947
Monophysitism, 227, 234, 239
Monotheism, 24, 26
Monroe Doctrine, 659, 805, 832
Mont Saint-Michel, 256
Montaigne, Michel de, 367, 406–407, 473, 476
Montcalm, Marshall Louis Joseph, 556
Monte Cassino, 237
Montenegro, 806, 807, 816
Montesquieu, Charles Secondat, Baron de, 570, 579–580, 594
Montgomery, General Sir Bernard, 913
Montmorency, house of, 407, 408
Moore, George, 783
Moore, Henry, 986, C31
Moors, 334
More, Thomas, 367, 390, 391
Morel, Aubert, 318
Morning Chronicle, 679
Moro, Aldo, 960
Moro, Ludovico il, 340, 348, 354, 355
Morocco, 796, 797, 812, 814, 816, 835, 913, 955
    Spanish, 899
Morosini, Tommaso, 307
Morris, William, 755
Mosaics, Byzantine, 230–231
Moscow, 633, 828, 908, 909, 915, 923, 924, 927, 928, 931

Moses, 23–25, 29
Moslems, 232–235, 238, 251, 824
    and the crusades, 263–266
    in fifteenth-century Spain, 334
Mosley, Oswald, 876
Mountain, 608, 610–611
Moxon, Joseph, 538
Mrs. Warren's Profession, 785
Mukhina, Vera, 933
Munda, 158
Munich Conference, 897, 901–903, 922
Municipia, 114
Münster, 380, 432; town hall, 287
Müntzer, Thomas, 377, 380

N

Naevius, 169
Nagasaki, 922
Nagy, Imre, 935, 937
Nana, 783
Nantes, France, 549, 613
    Edict of (1598), 413–414, 415, 444, 448
    Revocation of Edict of (1685), 454, 455
Naples, 126, 287, 328, 334, 337, 343, 354, 355, 710
Napoleon I of France. *See* Bonaparte, Napoleon
Napoleon III of France, 695, 705–706, 708–710, 712–719, 753
Napoleonic Code, 622, 628
Naramsin, King of Akkad, 7
Narmer, 12
Narva, 500
Naseby, battle of (1645), 442
Nassau, 713
Nasser, Gamal Abdel, 935, 961–962
Nathan the Wise, 576
National Assembly, 598
National Constituent Assembly, 599–602, 604–607
National Guard, 600
National Insurance Act, 755
National Liberation Front, 944
National Socialist German Workers' Party, 852–853, 871, 880–887, 895, 896, 900, 904, 906, 909–911, 913
Nationalism, 319, 327–328, 343, 376
    in Bohemia, 370
    Czech, 724
    German, 628–630, 645–646, 652, 700–702
    and German Humanists, 366
    Italian, 706–710
    and liberalism, 661–662
    Magyar, 722–724
    in Reformation Germany, 371
    and Revolution of 1848, 693–702
Nationalist Society, 708
NATO. *See* North Atlantic Treaty Organization
Natural selection, 772
Natural Theology, 775

Naturalism in Literature, 782–785
Nausea, 979
Navarre, 334
Naxos, 66
Nazi-Soviet Pact, 897, 903, 904, 907
Nazis. *See* National Socialist German Workers' Party
Nearchus, 117
Nebuchadnezzar II, 23
Necker, Jacques, 594–596, 599
Nelson, Admiral Horatio Lord, 620, 624, 626
Nemea, 45, 59
Neolithic Age, 3–5, 125
Neo-orthodoxy, 984
Neoplatonism, 215, 219, 342, 367
Nepos, Cornelius, 168
Nero, 173, 176, 182, 186, 192
Netherlands, 315, 319, 369, 409, 491, 753, 802, 804, 904, 909, 911, 930
    revolt against Spain by, 418–421
Neumann, Balthasar, 574, 575, C18
Neuschwanstein, C25
Neustria, 240
New Carthage, 140, 141
New Delhi, 803
New Economic Policy, 863–864, 889
New Grub Street, 770
New Guinea, 913
New Harmony, Indiana, 687
New Lanark, 686–687
"New unionism," 755
New York, 927, 929
New York Herald, 799
New Zealand, 795, 797, 835
Newfoundland, 923
Newgate Prison, 542
Newport, Rhode Island, 549
Newton, Isaac, 470, 471–473, 485, 567–568
Nicaea, Council of, 216–217, 227, 239, 243
Nice, 709
Nicene-Constantinopolitan creed, 217, 239, 242
Nicholas I, Pope, 250
Nicholas I of Russia, 663, 699, 705, 722, 724
Nicholas II, Pope, 261
Nicholas II of Russia, 728, 764–765, 728, 816, 826
Nicholas V, Pope, 331, 343
Nicholas of Cusa, 330, 369
Nicias, 81, 82
Nicomedia, 203
Niemiess River, 626
Niemoller, Martin, 981
Nietzsche, Friedrich, 775, 785–786, 977
Nigeria, 939
Night of August 4, 600
Nightingale, Florence, 706
Nijmegen, Peace of (1676), 457; (1678–1679), 455
Nike, Temple of, 88–90
Nile River, 4, 11, 15, 16, 22, 29